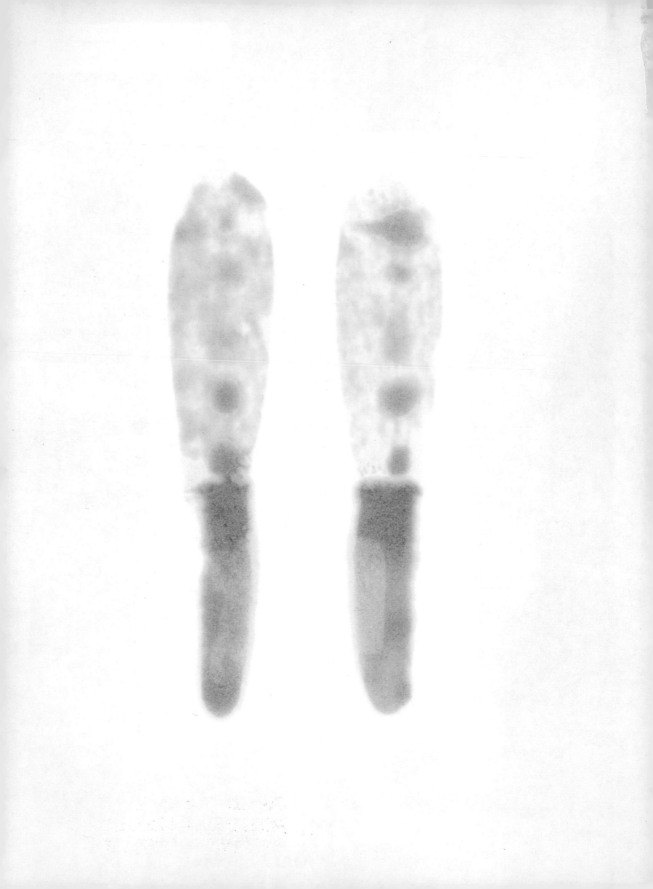

CONSTITUTIONAL LAW

CONSTITUTIONAL LAW
Cases and Comments

Peter Woll

Brandeis University

PRENTICE-HALL INC., Englewood Cliffs, New Jersey 07632

Library of Congress Cataloging in Publication Data

Woll, Peter (date)
    Constitutional law.

    1. United States—Constitutional law—Cases.
I. Title.
KF4549.W6   342.73   80-17872
ISBN 0-13-167957-0

*Editorial/production supervision and interior
  design by Linda Schuman*
Cover design by Edsal Enterprises
Manufacturing buyer: Edmund W. Leone

Printed in the United States of America

10 9 8 7 6 5 4 3 2 1

PRENTICE-HALL INTERNATIONAL, INC., *London*
PRENTICE-HALL OF AUSTRALIA PTY. LIMITED, *Sydney*
PRENTICE-HALL OF CANADA, LTD., *Toronto*
PRENTICE-HALL OF INDIA PRIVATE LIMITED, *New Delhi*
PRENTICE-HALL OF JAPAN, INC., *Tokyo*
PRENTICE-HALL OF SOUTHEAST ASIA PTE. LTD., *Singapore*
WHITEHALL BOOKS LIMITED, *Wellington, New Zealand*

For my brother,
Bob

Contents

NINE
Freedom of Expression
579

APPENDIX
The Constitution of the United States
911

Preface

The purpose of this book is to present the subject of constitutional law in a coherent and understandable manner to undergraduates through extensive comments, notes, and the incorporation of over 120 major cases. A special effort has been made not only to give the necessary factual background for each case, whether historical or contemporary, but also to provide students with an overall and specific analytical framework to help them understand the standards and tests applied by the Court. While undergraduates may find it relatively easy to grasp the importance of the political and social context within which the Supreme Court must function, it is usually far more difficult for students to discern the nature of the legal reasoning displayed in judicial opinions. Standards and tests embodied in such concepts as implied powers, direct and indirect effects upon commerce, fundamental and historical rights under due process, clear and present danger, secular purpose and effect in freedom of religion cases, and suspect classes in the area of equal protection of the laws are perfectly familiar to instructors but often remain mysterious to students even after they have delved extensively into relevant cases applying these criteria. A major purpose of this text is to lead students through the complex maze of judicial reasoning by the provision of explanatory comments and by raising relevant questions after the cases to extract the major components of the Court's reasoning.

The book is divided into roughly equal parts that respectively cover constitutional powers and civil liberties and rights. The discussion and cases of Chapter One covering judicial review are designed to launch students directly into constitutional law in a fundamental and interesting manner. The historical origins of judicial review are covered, and major cases, such as *Marbury* v. *Madison, Dred Scott* v. *Sanford, Luther* v. *Borden,* and *Baker* v. *Carr,* that have shaped judicial review are included. The political controversies that so frequently surround an active and interventionist Supreme Court are emphasized at the outset and throughout the book.

Constitutional powers are described and analyzed in separate chapters on the separation of powers, the constitutional powers of the President and Congress to make policy, federalism, the commerce power, national versus state power over commerce, and the national power to tax and spend. Civil liberties and rights are incorporated into chapters on due process of law, freedom of expression, freedom of religion, and equal protection of the laws.

Substantive and procedural due process are presented in one chapter to highlight the similarities and differences in the approach taken by the Court in these two important areas. It is emphasized that defining due process has always been a highly subjective process, whether or not it has been based upon the search for fundamental and historical rights or upon selective incorporation of the Bill of Rights. The controversies of the past and present raised by the use of a substantive due process formula are depicted and analyzed.

The chapter on freedom of expression includes the evolution of the clear and present danger doctrine, the conflict between a free press and the requirements of a fair trial, and First Amendment standards in the area of obscenity.

While the chapter on freedom of religion is divided into separate sections on the establishment clause and the free exercise clause, the tension that often exists between the requirements of the two clauses is discussed.

The chapter on equal protection covers the evolution of the separate but equal doctrine from its origin in *Plessy* v. *Ferguson* to its end in *Brown* v. *Board of Education*. Post-*Brown* cases that raise the issues of busing and reverse discrimination are examined. The chapter concludes with illustrations of equal protection scrutiny of suspect classifications and classifications affecting fundamental rights and a discussion of the right to equal political participation. At the outset of the chapter a separate section on equal protection standards and tests is included to give students an understanding of the formulas and standards the Court has applied.

Throughout the text the political and legal context of leading cases is illustrated by reference to contemporary accounts of the political environment at the time the cases were before the Court and from excerpts of the legal briefs of the litigants. Both politics and legal reasoning are important to the outcome of Supreme Court cases.

For instructors the text is accompanied by a manual that provides supplementary material as an aid in integrating the questions raised with the cases throughout the book.

The author is indebted to Nathan Goldman and Bernie Faigenbaum for their invaluable research assistance. Bruce A. Murphy read the entire manuscript with great care. His suggestions helped immeasurably in shaping the book. The consummate skill and professional dedication of Barbara Nagy made the preparation of the manuscript a happy experience. Linda Schuman skillfully turned a most unwieldly manuscript into a handsome book. Stan Wakefield was an indispensable beacon for the project from its inception to its completion.

Table of Cases

CONSTITUTIONAL LAW

ONE

Judicial Review

The judicial branch, with the Supreme Court standing at its pinnacle, occupies a unique position in the American political system, because of its power to declare the actions of Congress, the President, administrative agencies, and the states null and void for being, *in the view of the courts*, beyond the authority granted to those bodies by the Constitution. Although the ultimate authority of the Supreme Court to decide constitutional questions is now taken for granted, this was not always the case. And even after almost two centuries of development and refinement of the political system, the proper scope of the authority of the Supreme Court to exercise its prerogative of constitutional review is a subject of heated debate which on occasion leads to vehement opposition to the Court's decisions.

THE ORIGINS OF JUDICIAL REVIEW

As a generic concept the power of judicial review is the power of the courts to review the actions of other governmental bodies and to apply constitutional or *statutory* law to the decision of a case. A very significant area of judicial review today is over the actions of administrative agencies, and virtually all of this review is based upon statutory interpretation, not constitutional law. In Great Britain, where parliamentary law is supreme, judicial review is confined to executive and administrative actions, and the cases are decided on the basis of interpretations of the laws of Parliament. Because there is no recognized higher law than that of Parliament in Great Britain, the courts cannot declare parliamentary acts unconstitutional.

Whether judicial review is based upon constitutional or statutory interpretation, the implication of such review is the supremacy of the courts over the other branches of the government, and in the United States over the states as well. In the Anglo-American legal tradition the doctrine of the rule

1

of law has come to mean supremacy in the important sphere of interpretation of the law and in determining conformity to it by other parts of the government. Both the President and members of Congress take an oath to uphold the Constitution, but only the Supreme Court can say what the law is, even if that law has been passed by Congress. And only the Supreme Court has the ultimate authority to declare whether a congressional, presidential, administrative, or state action is constitutional. In Great Britain, while the courts cannot overrule parliamentary law, they can declare an official action to be beyond the authority granted by Parliament. Interpretation of legislative intent always gives courts a great deal of discretion in imposing their views on important issues of public policy, because legislatures rarely spell out the law in unequivocal terms. This is particularly true in the United States where Congress is not under the control of a cohesive political majority, which leads to a multitude of "intents" that can be found among those supporting a particular piece of legislation. This increases judicial discretion in interpretation of the law.

The principle of judicial review is essentially British and was transferred to the United States by the colonists who knew of British practice and found it in their interest to support it in colonial practice and in the governments created by the new state constitutions.

A broad power of judicial review was held to be a prerogative of the courts by Sir Edward Coke, the Lord Chief Justice of Great Britain in the early seventeenth century. At a time when the common law courts were struggling against the assertion of executive prerogatives by King James I, and before the establishment of parliamentary supremacy after the Glorious Revolution of 1688, Justice Coke asserted the following principle of judicial review in *Dr. Bonham's Case* in 1610:

> It appears in our books, that in many cases, the common law will control acts of Parliament, and sometimes adjudge them to be utterly void: for when an act of Parliament is against common right and reason, or repugnant, or impossible to be performed, the common law will control it, and adjudge such acts to be void.[1]

Although this dictum in *Dr. Bonham's Case* seems to imply a transcendent power in the common law courts to overrule decisions of Parliament which are found to be "unreasonable," in violation of the higher natural law that Coke felt should govern the realm, there is a certain amount of ambiguity as to Coke's real meaning. Clearly the actions of the King were to be controlled by the courts, but Parliament was on several occasions acknowledged by Coke to be the highest "court" of the land, supreme in its authority to declare what the law was.[2] At the same time it seems clear that Coke did not feel that Parliament could capriciously overrule fundamental law by simple legislative action. Parliament was to be bound by its own assertions of fun-

---

[1]Dr. Bonham's Case, 8 Co. 118a (1610), 77 English Reports 652.
[2]Edward S. Corwin, *The "Higher Law" Background of American Constitutional Law* (Ithaca, New York: Cornell University Press, 1955), pp. 56–57, 72–77. First published in the *Harvard Law Review*, 42 (1928–1929), 149–185, 365–409.

damental law, in such documents as Magna Charta and the Petition of Right that emerged from Parliament in 1628.

The evolution of the American legal system was profoundly influenced by Sir Edward Coke. Edward S. Corwin has eloquently summarized the contributions of Coke to American constitutional law.

> . . . First, in his dictum in *Bonham's Case* he furnished a form of words which, treated apart from his other ideas, as it was destined to be by a series of judges, commentators, and attorneys, became the most important single source of the notion of judicial review. This is true, even though we of the present day can see that, in view of the universal subordination of the common law as such to statute law, judicial review grounded simply on "common right and reason" could not have survived. But, as if in anticipation of this difficulty, Coke came forward with his second contribution, the doctrine of a law fundamental, binding Parliament and King alike, a law, moreover, embodied to great extent in a particular document and having verifiable content in the customary procedure of everyday institutions. From his version of Magna Carta, through the English Declaration and Bill of Rights of 1688 and 1689, to the Bill of Rights of our early American Constitution, the line of descent is direct; and if American constitutional law during the last half century has tended increasingly to minimize the importance of procedure niceties and to return to the vaguer test of "common right and reason," the intervening stage of strict law was nevertheless necessary. Lastly, Coke contributed to the notion of parliamentary supremacy *under* the law, which in time, with the differentiation of legislation and adjudication, became transmutable into the notion of *legislative* supremacy within a law subject to construction by the processes of adjudication.[3]

By the time the Constitution was framed in 1787, the principle of judicial review by courts independent of legislatures and executives had been recognized in the colonies and the newly created state constitutions. The famous *Writs of Assistance Case* that arose in Massachusetts in 1761 brought forth an unequivocal statement by James Otis, a young lawyer from Boston handling the case for the colonists, that the common law as applied by the Massachusetts courts should prevail over parliamentary law. Otis had read Coke and found his arguments much to his liking! The case involved "writs of assistance," which were broad search warrants issued to customs officials permitting them to search warehouses, ships, and any private building at any time for the purposes of carrying out their official responsibilities to enforce commercial regulations. Since the writs were issued by Parliament in the name of the King, when George II died in 1760, new writs had to be issued by Parliament in the name of George III, and customs officials in the colonies had to secure these writs from colonial courts. When the customs officials in Massachusetts applied for the writs from the superior court of the colony, local Boston merchants, using James Otis as their attorney, challenged their validity. Otis, citing *Dr. Bonham's Case* and other writings of Sir Edward Coke, asserted before the court that the writs were illegal because they violated fundamental principles of common law. Otis argued that "rea-

[3]Ibid., p. 57.

son and the Constitution are both against the writ . . . no act of Parliament can establish such a writ; though it should be made in the very words of the petition, it would be void. An act against the Constitution is void."[4]

James Otis's argument in the *Writs of Assistance Case* should not be taken as representative of a widespread view in the colonies supporting unequivocally the principle of judicial review over legislative acts. The principle was of course known, but its practice was not widespread and was generally limited to attacking the laws of Great Britain and not those of colonial or state legislatures. Clinton Rossiter, in pointing out that the principle of judicial review did not gain widespread acceptance until after 1776, notes that "James Otis's memorable harangue in the *Writs of Assistance Case* (1761), the action of a Virginia county court in declaring the Stamp Act unconstitutional, and the general popularity of an American rather than an English concept of unconstitutionality were heralds of a truly original contribution to constitutional government, but no one was yet so bold or irritated as to assert that the judiciary could refuse to enforce the unconstitutional acts of a representative legislature."[5]

It was between 1776 and 1787 that both the principle and practice of judicial review gained broad support in the states. Eight of the thirteen state constitutions adopted the principle, and before 1789 there were eight instances of state courts declaring state laws in violation of state constitutions.[6] Although judicial review was not explicitly spelled out in the Constitution, it was discussed at the Constitutional Convention of 1787 and supported by a number of the delegates. Article III of the Constitution, creating an independent judiciary with the authority to hear cases and controversies arising under the Constitution, laws, and treaties clearly implied, within the context of the time and of the historical Anglo-American tradition, the authority to declare what the law is and to refuse to uphold unconstitutional laws and actions of coordinate branches.

Alexander Hamilton, in Paper No. 78 of *The Federalist*, unequivocally proclaimed the principle of judicial review to the New York State ratifying convention and to any others who chose to read his article.

> Some perplexity respecting the right of the courts to pronounce legislative acts void, because contrary to the Constitution, has arisen from an imagination that the doctrine would imply a superiority of the judiciary to the legislative power. It is urged that the authority which can declare the acts of another void, must necessarily be superior to the one whose acts may be declared void. As this doctrine is of great importance in all the American constitutions, a brief discussion of the grounds on which it rests cannot be unacceptable.
>
> There is no position which depends on clearer principles than that every act of a delegated authority, contrary to the tenor of the commission under which it is exercised, is void. No legislative act, therefore, contrary to the Constitution, can be valid. To deny this would be to affirm that the deputy is greater than the prin-

---

[4]Reported by John Adams, as cited in Alfred H. Kelly and Winfred A. Harbison, *The American Constitution*, 4th ed. (New York: W. W. Norton & Co., 1970), p. 48.

[5]Clinton Rossiter, *Seedtime of the Republic* (New York: Harcourt Brace Jovanich, 1953), p. 420.

[6]Henry J. Abraham, *The Judicial Process*, 3rd ed. (New York: Oxford University Press, 1975), p. 306.

cipal; that the servant is above his master; that the representatives of the people are superior to the people themselves; that men, acting by virtue of powers, may do not only what their powers do not authorize, but what they forbid.

If it be said that the legislative bodies are themselves the constitutional judges of their own powers, and that the construction they put upon them is conclusive upon the other departments, it may be answered that this cannot be the natural presumption, where it is not to be collected from any particular provisions in the constitution. It is not otherwise to be supposed that the constitution could intend to enable the representatives of the people to substitute their *will* to that of their constituents. It is far more rational to suppose that the courts were designed to be an intermediate body between the people and the legislature, in order, among other things, to keep the latter within the limits assigned to their authority. The interpretation of the laws is the proper and peculiar province of the courts. A constitution is, in fact, and must be, regarded by the judges as a fundamental law. It must therefore belong to them to ascertain its meaning, as well as the meaning of any particular act proceeding from the legislative body. If there should happen to be an irreconcilable variance between the two, that which has the superior obligation and validity ought, of course, to be preferred; in other words, the constitution ought to be preferred to the statute, the intention of the people to the intention of their agents.

Nor does this conclusion by any means suppose a superiority of the judicial to the legislative power. It only supposes that the power of the people is superior to both; and that where the will of the legislature declared in its statutes, stands in opposition to that of the people declared in the constitution, the judges ought to be governed by the latter, rather than the former. . . .

Alexander Hamilton's arguments in *Federalist 78* found their way directly into Supreme Court dictum in Chief Justice John Marshall's opinion in *Marbury* v. *Madison* (1803).

THE NATURE OF JUDICIAL POWER
IN THE CONSTITUTION

Although Hamilton clearly stated that the Supreme Court would have the power to declare acts of Congress to be unconstitutional, and given the long history of judicial review in theory and practice in the Anglo-American legal tradition, it is a curious fact that nowhere in the Constitution is this power mentioned. By implication the Supreme Court's power would apply to the actions of the executive branch as well, although Hamilton, a firm supporter of strong executive power, might not have so readily granted the Court the power to veto executive actions. It seems doubtful that the states would have objected strongly to an explicit grant of authority to the Supreme Court to declare congressional laws unconstitutional. State politicians would not have wished, however, to have the Supreme Court given the authority to overturn *state* actions for being unconstitutional. If the power of judicial review had been explicitly granted to the Supreme Court, it would have been necessary to spell out its parameters. The Federalists would have demanded that it extend to state as well as federal laws, and this might have raised unnecessary complications in the ratification process. By leaving the issue for refinement at a later point, a clear path was opened towards extending judicial review to both federal and state laws and executive actions.

On their face the provisions of Article III of the Constitution appear to limit more than expand judicial authority. And, while Alexander Hamilton was proclaiming an expansive and independent judicial power in his papers of *The Federalist* dealing with the judiciary, James Madison's views in *Federalist 48* seem more consistent with what actually appeared in Article III. Madison stated that the judiciary is by its very nature the most limited branch of the government, while the legislature is superior. Madison pointed out in *Federalist 48*,

> The legislative department derives a superiority in our government from other circumstances. Its constitutional powers being at once more extensive, and less susceptible of precise limits, it can, with the greater facility, mask, under complicated and indirect measures, the encroachment which it makes on the coordinate departments. It is not infrequently a question of real nicety in legislative bodies, whether the operation of a particular measure will, or will not extend beyond the legislative sphere. On the other side, the executive power being restrained within a narrower compass, and being more simple in its nature; and the judiciary being described by landmarks, still less uncertain, projects of usurpation by either of these departments would immediately betray and defeat themselves.

Certainly Madison is not claiming a power of judicial review over acts of Congress for the Supreme Court, and in fact in *Federalist 51*, where he discusses the checks and balances system, he does not mention, as well he might have, judicial review as an appropriate check upon the legislature but states that Congress will be primarily checked through bicameralism and the executive veto.

The clear "landmarks" that Madison felt circumscribed judicial power are to be found in the "case and controversy" requirement of Article III, providing that the judicial power extends only to concrete cases and controversies arising under the Constitution, the laws of the United States, and treaties. Article III also strictly limits the original jurisdiction of the Supreme Court and gives Congress control over its appellate jurisdiction.

> In all cases affecting ambassadors, other public ministers and consuls, and those in which a state shall be a party, the Supreme Court shall have original jurisdiction. In all other cases beforementioned, the Supreme Court shall have appellate jurisdiction, both as to law and fact, with such exceptions, and under such regulations as the Congress shall make.

In addition to controlling the Supreme Court's appellate jurisdiction, it is Congress that determines the organization and, insofar as it wishes, the procedures of the entire federal judiciary below the Supreme Court.

While it is of course true that congressional control over the organization of the lower federal judiciary and the appellate jurisdiction of the Supreme Court is an important check upon judicial power, within the political context of the Constitutional Convention of 1787 congressional authority to establish inferior courts meant a more rather than a less powerful judiciary. "Inferior" courts could be used and have been instrumental in extending the operational scope of federal judicial power. And the provision for presidential appointment of Supreme Court and lower court justices was also viewed at the time of the Constitutional Convention as strengthening, not weakening, the judiciary. It was a check upon the courts, particularly the Supreme Court, but under a strong Federalist president, such as George Washington, for whom it has been said the Constitution was written, it could be used to appoint justices who would take a firm view in upholding the Constitution. The Federalist bench appointed by Presidents George Washington and John Adams, in addition to rendering decisions unequivocally strengthening the powers and flexibility of the national government over the states, established the principle of judicial review.

The Constitution, then, viewed from the perspective of its own period, represented a victory for judicial power, although it did not go as far in this direction as some of the framers wished. And those provisions of the original Constitution which were designed to strengthen the judiciary by allowing Congress to establish inferior courts, and giving the president the authority to appoint Supreme Court justices, have been used to curb as well as to fortify judicial power. The Supreme Court itself has used the "case and controversy" requirement to exercise judicial self-restraint by refusing to hear cases that do not meet its "case and controversy" criteria.

In the first Judiciary Act of 1789 the Federalists extended the power of the federal judiciary. In the act provision was made for a chief justice and five associate justices on the Supreme Court, thirteen federal district courts, and three circuit courts of appeal. In the early years of the Supreme Court it was the practice of justices to "ride the circuit," sitting as judges on the circuit courts of appeal. It was a practice for two Supreme Court justices to be assigned to the circuit courts along with one district judge. Supporters of this practice felt that it kept the Supreme Court close to the people and directly in tune with the realities of the cases over which they possessed ultimate jurisdiction. The practice of riding the circuit became extraordinarily burdensome, as the number of cases confronting the courts increased, along with the average age of the justices. Although the controversial Federalist-sponsored Judiciary Act of 1801 eliminated circuit court duty for Supreme Court justices, circuit court responsibilities were restored by the Republican Repeal Act of 1802. After 1802 Congress was reluctant to abandon the requirement for direct Supreme Court supervision over the circuit courts and specifically rejected judicial reform along such lines even though it was strongly urged by Presidents Madison and Monroe in the early nineteenth century.[7] The onerous task of riding the circuit continued well into the nineteenth century, and to this day Supreme Court justices are assigned formal responsibilities to oversee the activities of the circuit courts.

In addition to creating the core of a federal judiciary, a most controversial matter at the time because it symbolized potential power over the states, the Judiciary Act of 1789 also took direct steps to ensure the supremacy of

[7]Charles Warren, *The Supreme Court in United States History*, 3 vols. (Boston: Little, Brown & Co., 1922), 2:132–145.

the federal judiciary over the states in cases involving interpretations of the Constitution and federal law. The famous Section Twenty-five of the act provided that appeals could be taken from the highest state court to the Supreme Court when the state court had declared a federal law or treaty unconstitutional; upheld a state act against a claim that it violated the Constitution, or a federal law or treaty; or had ruled against a claim of right or privilege under the Constitution or federal law. The clear purpose of this section was to ensure the supremacy of the Constitution and federal law, under the protection of a strong national judiciary.

Debate in the First Congress was intense over Section Twenty-five, its opponents arguing that it was an excessive encroachment upon the sovereignty of the states, while its proponents claimed it was necessary to prevent the usurpation of jurisdiction over federal cases by state courts.[8] Section Twenty-five, in the view of the Federalists, remedied an important deficiency in the Constitution which had omitted any provision for appeals from state to federal courts. The Judiciary Act of 1789 in combination with a Federalist dominated Supreme Court, which became particularly active when John Marshall became Chief Justice in 1801, clearly established national supremacy.

EARLY ESTABLISHMENT OF JUDICIAL REVIEW

Although it was John Marshall's opinion in *Marbury* v. *Madison* in 1803 that unequivocally proclaimed the authority of the Supreme Court to declare acts of Congress unconstitutional, the issue had been raised before the Court in several previous cases. By the time of the *Marbury* decision Marshall's dictum was generally accepted by Supreme Court justices and federal judges, and a good part of the legal profession.

In *Hayburn's Case* in 1792 and related cases five of the six justices of the Supreme Court, acting as circuit court judges, agreed that they could not execute an act of Congress in their capacity as judges because the act delegated nonjudicial functions to the circuit courts. It delegated to the courts the power to pass upon pension claims for widows, orphans, and disabled veterans of the Revolutionary War and made the decisions of the circuit courts subject to review by the Secretary of War and ultimately the legislature. Essentially the act delegated to the circuit courts what today would be called administrative functions, subject to review not by higher courts but by the executive and legislative branches. The five Supreme Court justices (the sixth justice, Johnson, was not involved) sitting as circuit court judges, refused to carry out the act. Chief Justice John Jay and Justice William Cushing, sitting on the Circuit Court for the District of New York, issued a formal opinion in the case, while Justices John Blair, James Wilson, and James Iredell expressed their objection in letters written to the President.[9] Jay's opinion from the circuit court bench in the first case under the act empha-

---

[8]Warren, *The Supreme Court*, 1:10–11.
[9]Hayburn's Case, 2 Dallas 409, 410, fn. 2 (1792).

sized the importance of preserving the separation of powers among the legislative, executive, and judicial branches, which, he said, meant that no non-judicial functions can be given to the courts, nor can their opinions be subject to further review by coordinate branches.

IN RE HAYBURN'S CASE[10]

(Circuit Court for the District of New York, 1792,
cited in 2 Dallas 409, 410, fn. 2, 1792)

Chief Justice Jay, Justice Cushing, and District Judge Duane said in part:

That by the Constitution of the United States, the government thereof is divided into three distinct and independent branches, and that it is the duty of each to abstain from, and to oppose encroachments upon either.

That neither the Legislative nor the Executive branches, can constitutionally assign to the judicial any duties, but such as are properly judicial, and to be performed in a judicial manner.

That the duties assigned to the circuit courts, by this Act [passed on March 23, 1791, that assigned responsibilities for hearing certain Revolutionary pension claims to the circuit courts, subject to review by the Secretary of War and the Legislature] are not of that description, and that the Act itself does not appear to contemplate them, as such; inasmuch as it subjects the decisions of these courts, made pursuant to those duties, first to the consideration and suspension of the Secretary at War, and then to the revision of the Legislature; whereas, by the Constitution, neither the Secretary at War, nor any other executive officer, nor even the Legislature, are authorized to sit as a court of errors on judicial acts or opinions of this court.

As, therefore, the business assigned to this court, by the Act, is not judicial, nor directed to be performed judicially, the Act can only be considered as appointing commissioners for the purposes mentioned in it, by official, instead of personal, descriptions. . . .

That the judges of this court will, as usual, during the session thereof adjourn the court from day to day, or other short periods, as circumstances may render proper, and that they will, regularly, between the adjournments [when they are not sitting as a court], proceed as commissioners to execute the business of this Act in the same courtroom or chamber.

Chief Justice Jay's opinion as a circuit judge did not overrule the pension act but did refuse to comply with what the justices felt were unconstitutional provisions. They would agree to sit as commissioners, but not as judges, to hear the claims, and under such circumstances their role as judges would not be compromised. While Chief Justice Jay and Justice Cushing of the Supreme Court agreed to this adjustment to enable the pension act to be enforced, the Supreme Court justices on the Circuit Courts for the Districts of Pennsylvania and North Carolina were more emphatic in their refusal to exercise the jurisdiction Congress had granted them to hear the veterans' pension cases, refusing even to sit as "commissioners" in a nonjudicial capacity to rule upon the claims.

---

[10]Hayburn's Case arose in the circuit court in Pennsylvania in 1792. Chief Justice Jay's opinion is in a related case that arose in the New York circuit court.

Justices Blair and Wilson, writing for the Circuit Court of Pennsylvania, in which *Hayburn's Case* arose, and Justice Iredell, writing for the Circuit Court of the District of North Carolina, addressed letters to the President of the United States in which they held that the Constitution bound their actions to purely judicial matters, and Congress could not supersede the Constitution by delegating to the circuit courts nonjudicial functions. In particular the justices objected to the authority that was given to the Secretary of War to overrule their decisions. Even if they were to grant that passing upon pensioners' claims was a judicial function, which they were not about to do, they would never have been willing to allow an executive department to overrule them, for this was a clear violation of the constitutional separation of powers.[11] Supreme Court Justice Wilson wrote: "The Constitution is 'the supreme law of the land.' This supreme law 'all judicial officers of the United States are bound, by oath or affirmation to support.' "[12] Justice Iredell wrote that "The Legislative, Executive, and Judicial departments, are each formed in a separate and independent manner; and that the ultimate basis of each is the Constitution only within the limits of which each department can alone justify any act of authority."[13]

The refusal of the circuit court for Pennsylvania to carry out the terms of the congressional act led to a petition to the Supreme Court for a writ of mandamus to require the circuit court to hear the claim of William Hayburn, a pension applicant under the act whose claim the court had refused to hear on the basis of the reason stated in the justices' letter to the President. Attorney General Edmund Randolph first sought the mandamus ex officio, that is, out of his official authority as Attorney General, to see that the circuit courts enforced the act. After the Supreme Court rejected the ex officio motion for mandamus, the Attorney General then sought the mandamus in behalf of Hayburn. The same justices, now sitting as members of the Supreme Court and not justices on the circuit court, took the motion under advisement until the next Court term, but in the interim the issue became moot because Congress in 1793 passed another act that removed jurisdiction from the courts over determination of pension claims arising out of the Revolutionary War.

The views of the majority of the Supreme Court justices in *Hayburn's Case* were limited to overruling an act of Congress that directly involved the operation of the courts, but the direct action taken by the federal circuit court for Pennsylvania in refusing to hear Hayburn's claim was generally considered to be judicial review in the broader sense.[14] Although the authority claimed by Chief Justice John Marshall to exercise judicial review over acts of Congress was broader in *Marbury* v. *Madison* than in the statements of the justices in *Hayburn's Case,* the Court's views on judicial review were dictum in *Marbury* and the rule of law in *Hayburn's Case.*

The same year that the circuit courts, with the Supreme Court justices constituting a majority, declared the provisions of a congressional act ultra

---

[11]Hayburn's Case, 2 Dallas 409, 413–415 (1792).
[12]Ibid., p. 411.
[13]Ibid., p. 414.
[14]Warren, *The Supreme Court*, 1:70–81.

vires in *Hayburn's Case,* they overruled several state laws for violating constitutional provisions. In 1791, before *Hayburn's Case,* a federal circuit court overturned a Connecticut statute for being in conflict with the provisions of a treaty. Shortly after *Hayburn's Case* in 1792, Chief Justice Jay and Judge Cushing, both of the Supreme Court, sitting on the Circuit Court for the District of Rhode Island, overturned a Rhode Island statute for violating the provision of the Constitution in Article I, Section 10, forbidding states to impair the obligation of contracts.[15] These early decisions by the circuit courts overruling state action seem to have raised less opposition than surrounded *Hayburn's Case.* Certainly the peaceful reception of the circuit court's opinion enforcing national supremacy in the early 1790s did not suggest the violent opposition that would occur in southern and western states after the Supreme Court overturned a Maryland law as an unconstitutional impairment of national supremacy in *McCulloch* v. *Maryland* in 1819.

Before 1796 it was the circuit courts that had exercised the power of judicial review over an act of Congress and over state laws. In *Hayburn's Case* five out of six of the Supreme Court justices, sitting as circuit court judges, had essentially declared a congressional act unconstitutional. In the cases overruling state action as well, a majority of Supreme Court justices approved, but again they were sitting as circuit court judges. The first time the Supreme Court itself exercised the power of judicial review over a congressional action was in *Hylton* v. *United States* in 1796. Daniel Hylton, of Virginia, had challenged a congressional act imposing a tax on carriages as a violation of the Constitutional provision that direct taxes must be apportioned according to the census. He maintained that the tax in question was direct and not a duty, impost, or excise tax which does not have to be apportioned among the states according to the census but must only be uniform to meet constitutional requirements. The arguments for the plaintiff and the government before the Supreme Court attracted a great deal of attention, particularly because Alexander Hamilton was one of the attorneys for the government.

Only three Supreme Court justices participated in the *Hylton* case. Justice Wilson removed himself because he had sat on the circuit court that first considered the case, Justice Cushing was ill, and Chief Justice Ellsworth declined to take part in the decision because he had just been sworn in and had not heard all of the oral argument. In upholding the congressional act as a constitutional imposition of a duty and not a direct tax requiring apportionment, each participating justice rendered a long and complicated decision. There was no question that if the justices had found the law to be unconstitutional it would have been declared null and void. However, the constitutional authority of the Supreme Court to exercise judicial review over congressional actions was not made explicit in any of the three separate opinions. In particular, none of the justices declared the power of the Supreme Court to overrule Congress, a moot issue in this case because each of the justices found the congressional law to be within constitutional boundaries. Justice Samuel Chase, who had taken his seat on the Supreme Court a

---

[15]Warren, *The Supreme Court,* 1:66–67.

month before, explicitly stated the views implied in the decisions of Justices William Patterson and James Iredell.

> As I do not think the tax on carriages is a direct tax, it is unnecessary, at this time, for me to determine, whether this court constitutionally possesses the power to declare an act of Congress void, on the ground of its being made contrary to, and in violation of, the Constitution; but if the court has such power, I am free to declare, that I will never exercise it, but in a very clear case.[16]

This statement of Justice Chase is gratuitous within the context of the *Hylton* case. As dictum it contrasts sharply with Chief Justice Marshall's dictum in *Marbury* v. *Madison*. It can be argued that the Supreme Court was exercising a broader constitutional review in *Hylton* than in the *Marbury* case. In the latter, the Court was interpreting its own authority under Article III in refusing to exercise a mandamus power that it claimed was unconstitutionally granted to it by the Judiciary Act of 1789. In the *Hylton* case, however, the Court was reviewing the broad provisions of an act of Congress that in no way pertained to the judiciary. The power of judicial review implied in the *Hylton* case was broader than both that exercised in *Hayburn's Case* as well as in *Marbury* v. *Madison*.

The setting of *Marbury* v. *Madison* in 1801 was dramatic. On February 17, 1801, Jefferson had been chosen president by the House of Representatives, with Aaron Burr as his vice president, both men having received an equal number of electoral votes from the Republican majority in the Electoral College after the presidential election of 1800.[17] Feelings were running high between the Federalists and the Anti-Federalists (Republicans). The Federalists had lost control not only of the presidency in 1800 but of both branches of Congress. The lame duck Federalist Congress immediately proceeded to pass the Judiciary Act of 1801, adding six new circuit courts, sixteen circuit court judges, several district courts, and additional staff to service the new courts. This was a bold attempt to solidify and expand Federalist power in the judiciary, where it was already firmly entrenched both in personnel and in doctrine. Prior attempts had been made during the Adams administration to increase the number of courts, but strong opposition from the Anti-Federalists had delayed passage of legislation to this effect by the House of Representatives. Among other prominent Federalists, Alexander Hamilton had been involved in the drafting of legislation for judicial expansion.

The passage of the Judiciary Act of 1801 was seen by the Anti-Federalists as a purely political act to guarantee the continuation of Federalist power through the judiciary in spite of the fact that the party had been defeated

---

[16]Hylton v. United States, 3 Dallas 171, 175 (1796).

[17]The Constitution originally provided that the person receiving the highest number of electoral votes would be selected president, with the runner-up chosen as vice president. There was sufficient discipline in the Republican party in the election of 1800 to make each Republican elector cast his vote for both Jefferson and his running mate Burr. The inevitable deadlock threw the election into the House of Representatives. The Twelfth Amendment, which required separate voting in the Electoral College for president and vice president, remedied this failure of the original Electoral College scheme to take into account the possibility of disciplined political parties in the presidential selection process.

in the presidency and in Congress. The 1801 act was denounced as being wicked, shameful, arbitrary, and undemocratic.[18] Under the act, President Adams proceeded to appoint his "midnight judges," on the virtual eve of his leaving office on March 3, 1801.

Adding insult to injury, the Federalists, on February 27, 1801, passed the organic act for the District of Columbia that provided for the appointment of forty-two new justices of the peace for the counties of Alexandria and Washington. The commissions were prepared and given the seal of the Acting Secretary of State, Chief Justice John Marshall, who served in this capacity after his nomination to the Supreme Court, was confirmed by the Senate on January 27, 1801, and after he took his seat on the Court at the beginning of its 1801 term on February 4. A number of these commissions had not been delivered to the appointed justices of the peace by the time President Adams was forced to leave office at midnight on March 3, and incoming President Thomas Jefferson ordered the commissions to be withheld (although he later approved most of Adams's appointments). Jefferson strongly agreed with the Anti-Federalist views that the commissions, both of the judges and the justices of the peace, had been an "illegal" political act on the part of the Federalists. All of the appointees were strong Federalists.

The worst fears of the Republicans seemed to be materializing in actions by the Federalist courts during the first months of Jefferson's administration. Two Federalist judges on the newly created Circuit Court for the District of Columbia sought from the district attorney a libel action against an administration newspaper, the *National Intelligencer*, that had printed a letter containing a scurrilous attack upon the judiciary. As the district attorney was a Republican, no charges were made; however, the incident served to fuel the flames of Republican charges against the Federalist judiciary for being motivated more by politics than by justice.[19] In another circuit court case President Jefferson had attempted to intervene directly to change the order of the court that had directed that the proceeds from the sale of a captured French ship be paid to the United States Treasury. Jefferson held that treaty obligations required the funds to be paid to the owners of the French vessel. However, the Circuit Court for Connecticut defied the president, saying that his request violated both statutory and constitutional law.[20]

By the time the *Marbury* case was brought before the Court in December 1801, the battle lines had been drawn between Jefferson and the Federalists over the issue of judicial power. The issue was not, however, over whether or not the courts could exercise the power of judicial review over acts of Congress or of the executive, but whether the general jurisdiction and personnel of the federal courts would be extended under Federalist domination. When William Marbury, a justice of the peace appointed by President Adams before he left office, and three other appointees to the same office were denied their commissions by President Jefferson's Secretary of State, James Madison, they presented an original suit to the Supreme Court peti-

---

[18]Warren, *The Supreme Court*, 1:188–189.
[19]Warren, *The Supreme Court*, 1:194–198.
[20]Ibid., pp. 198–199.

tioning for a writ of mandamus to be directed to the Secretary of State to deliver their commissions. The Judiciary Act of 1789 had explicitly given the Supreme Court authority to issue writs of mandamus in pursuance of its original jurisdiction, which was defined in Article III of the Constitution. Even without such a statutory grant of authority, the Supreme Court clearly possessed the power to issue such a writ in any case properly within its jurisdiction.

Mandamus is a prerogative writ (originally derived from the prerogative of the King) that is an inherent power of the ordinary courts when the proper circumstances are presented. Mandamus is used by a superior court to compel the performance of ministerial or public duties by executive, administrative, or judicial officials or lower courts. The first reported case in which the writ was used in the modern sense was in 1573, although it was not until 1615 in *Bagg's Case* that a clear precedent for the modern writ was established.[21] The writ was used by the Court of King's Bench in England, which originally derived its authority from the King but which became essentially an independent common law court by the time of Chief Justice Coke in the beginning of the seventeenth century. Both colonial and state courts considered themselves the inheritors of the judicial prerogatives of the British courts, and the power to issue a writ of mandamus as a judicial prerogative (not based upon statutory or constitutional authority) was transferred from England to America.

The real question, then, presented by Marbury in his petition to the Supreme Court for a mandamus to compel Madison to deliver his commission should not have been the general authority of the Court to issue such a writ, but whether or not the case was properly brought in the original jurisdiction of the Court. Since that jurisdiction was explicitly limited to cases among the states, in which the states were parties, and cases affecting ambassadors, (foreign) public ministers, and consuls, it would have been reasonable to conclude that since the case affected Marbury and Madison, it was not properly within the original jurisdiction of the Court. But denying jurisdiction at the outset in *Marbury* v. *Madison* would not have enabled Chief Justice John Marshall both to reassert the already well-recognized authority of the Supreme Court to declare acts of Congress unconstitutional and to lecture President Jefferson on the proper performance of his duties. Marshall's opinion is a carefully couched political statement that conveys the message he wanted but avoids an open clash with Jefferson and the Republicans, for by denying the authority of the Supreme Court to issue a mandamus to public officers in original jurisdiction, the Court was denying its ability to force presidential action.

In effect, *Marbury* v. *Madison* changed nothing in American jurisprudence or practice. It did declare that section of the Judiciary Act of 1789 delegating the mandamus authority to the Supreme Court in original jurisdiction to be unconstitutional, but this insistence of the Court in defining its own powers under the Constitution was no different than in *Hayburn's Case*.

---

[21]S.A. de Smith, *Judicial Review of Administrative Action* (New York: Stevens/Oceana, 1959), p. 264.

From a political standpoint, had Marshall refused to hear the case he would have let the Federalist cause down, and had he issued a writ of mandamus it would very likely have been defied by President Jefferson, which would have undermined the authority of the Supreme Court. Marshall's decision satisfied the broad interests of both the Federalists and the Republicans in the case.

Preliminary Arguments of Plaintiffs and Respondents in *Marbury* v. *Madison* in 1801

The following account of the preliminary arguments and discussion before the Court in *Marbury* v. *Madison* is taken from a report of a Washington correspondent of the Republican newspaper, *Aurora,* who was on the scene on December 21, 1801, when the initial proceedings took place. Charles Lee, former Attorney General under President Adams, represented the plaintiff Marbury and asked the Court for a ruling that the respondents "show cause" why the mandamus should not issue.

> Mr. Lee entered very largely into a definition of the powers of the Court, and of the nature of Mandamus which he described as a species of appeal to a superior for redress of wrong done by an inferior authority. The chief justice . . . asked if the attorney general was in court, and had anything to offer. Mr. Lincoln (attorney general) replied that he had no instructions on the subject. The secretary of state had received notice on the preceding day, but he could not in the interval have turned his attention effectually to the subject. He would leave the proceedings under the discretion of the Court. The Chief Justice, after consultation, found none of the Bench ready but Judge Chase . . . who said if the attorney (Mr. Lee) would explain the extent of his evidence and lay it before the Court in form, he would give his opinion instantly. Some conversation took place on the etiquette of sealing and recording commissions, and Mr. Lee said the law spoke big words and that the act of recording, under his experience of the secretary's office, was esteemed done when a copy was delivered for entry, and that the copy remained sometimes six weeks unentered, but was still considered as recorded. The Court did not give any opinion, but Mr. Lee proposed to amend his affidavits by a statement that the Great Seal had been actually affixed to the commissions. The Tories talked of dragging the president before the Court and impeaching him and a wonderful deal of similar nothingness. But it is easy to perceive that it is all fume which can excite no more than a judicious irritation.[22]

The motion to show cause was granted, and a future day assigned for arguing the question whether or not the petitioners were entitled under the law to the writ of mandamus they sought. The preliminary action of the Court in granting the motion to show cause raised the ire of the Republicans, who considered it an unwarranted intrusion into the affairs of the executive branch.

The feelings of the Republicans against the Federalist judiciary were manifested in 1802 in the repeal of the Judiciary Act of 1801 under which the Federalists had expanded the courts under their control. After the pas-

---

[22]Warren, *The Supreme Court,* 1:202–203.

sage of the repeal bill in 1802 a major question became whether or not the
Federalist Supreme Court would hold the repeal unconstitutional. In the
heated debate that ensued more than one Republican declared that the Supreme Court did not have the authority to overturn acts of Congress. Such
views, however, arose out of the heat of the debate rather than from a recognition among the Republicans that the authority of the Supreme Court to
declare acts of Congress unconstitutional was in question. Fearing that the
Supreme Court would declare the repeal bill to be unconstitutional out of
the prevailing partisan controversy, Congress proceeded to pass legislation
that changed the term of the Court in such a way that it would not meet
again until 1803. The Court was thus forced to adjourn from December
1801 until February 1803 before it could take up the *Marbury* and repeal bill
(*Stuart* v. *Laird*) cases. This attempt to mitigate a potentially explosive political situation only served to heighten the political tension between the Federalists and the Republicans as the Court approached its 1803 term.

BRIEFS IN *MARBURY* v. *MADISON*

1 Cranch 138 (1803)

Charles Lee, former Attorney General, for the plaintiff Marbury:
   Mr. Lee then observed, that having proved the existence of the commissions,
he should confine such further remarks that he had to make in support of the
rule to three questions:
   1st. Whether the Supreme Court can award the writ of mandamus in any case?
   2d. Whether it will lie to a Secretary of State in any case whatever?
   3d. Whether, in the present case, the Court may award a mandamus to James
Madison, Secretary of State? . . .
   [In reference to the first question:] [T]his is the Supreme Court, and by reason
of its supremacy must have the superintendence of the inferior tribunal and officers, whether judicial or ministerial. In this respect there is no difference between a judicial and a ministerial officer. From this principle alone the Court of
King's Bench in England derives the power of issuing the writs of mandamus and
prohibition. 3 [Coke's] Inst. 70, 71. Shall it be said that the Court of King's Bench
has this power in consequence of its being the supreme court of judicature, and
shall we deny it to this court which the Constitution makes the supreme court? It
is a beneficial and a necessary power. . . .
   Congress, by a law passed at the very first session after the adoption of the Constitution . . . has expressly given the Supreme Court the power to issue writs of
mandamus. . . .
   Congress is not restrained from conferring original jurisdiction in other cases
than those mentioned in the Constitution. . . . This court has entertained jurisdiction on a mandamus in one case. . . . In this case the power of the court to issue
writs of mandamus was taken for granted in the arguments of counsel on both
sides and seems to have been so considered by the court. The mandamus was refused, because the case in which it was required was not a proper one to support
the motion. . . . [As to the second point] [m]any cases may be supposed, in which
a secretary of state ought to be compelled to perform his duty specifically. . . .
   . . . [A]fter the president has signed a commission for an office not held at his
will, and it comes to the secretary [of state] to be sealed, the president has done

with it, and nothing remains, but that the secretary perform those administerial acts which the law imposes upon him. It immediately becomes his duty to seal, record, and deliver it on command. In such a case the appointment becomes complete by the signing and sealing; and the secretary does wrong if he withholds the commission.

The third point is, whether, in the present case a writ of mandamus ought to be awarded to James Madison, Secretary of State. . . . [The mandamus should issue because the] requisites to be performed by the Secretary are ministerial, ascertained by law, and he has no discretion but must perform them. . . .[23]

The Attorney General, Mr. Lincoln, addressed himself to certain questions concerning the appearance of witnesses, particularly the secretary of state, and to the possession and disposition of the commissions in question, but did not argue as to the merits of the mandamus.[24]

Marbury v. *Madison*

1 Cranch 137; 2 L. Ed. 60 (1803)

CHIEF JUSTICE MARSHALL delivered the opinion of the Court:

. . . In the order in which the Court has viewed this subject, the following questions have been considered and decided.

1st. Has the applicant a right to the commission he demands? [Yes, and the President should have directed Madison to deliver the commission.]

2d. If he has a right, and that right has been violated, do the laws of his country afford him a remedy? [Yes, the laws must provide a remedy.]

3d. If they do afford him a remedy, is it a mandamus issuing from this Court? . . .

This, then, is a plain case for a mandamus, either to deliver the commission, or a copy of it from the record; and it only remains to be inquired,

Whether it can issue from this Court.

The act to establish the judicial courts of the United States authorizes the Supreme Court "to issue writs of mandamus in cases warranted by the principles and

usages of law, to any courts appointed, or persons holding office, under the authority of the United States."

The Secretary of State, being a person holding an office under the authority of the United States, is precisely within the letter of the description, and if this Court is not authorized to issue a writ of mandamus to such an officer, it must be because the law is unconstitutional, and therefore absolutely incapable of conferring the authority, and assigning the duties which its words purport to confer and assign.

The Constitution vests the whole judicial power of the United States in one Supreme Court, and such inferior courts as congress shall, from time to time, ordain and establish. . . .

In the distribution of this power it is declared that "the Supreme Court shall have original jurisdiction in all cases affecting ambassadors, other public ministers and consuls, and those in which a

[23]1 Cranch 137, 146, 146–151 (1803).
[24]Ibid., 143–145.

state shall be a party. In all other cases, the Supreme Court shall have appellate jurisdiction.". . .

If it had been intended to leave it in the discretion of the legislature to apportion the judicial power between the supreme and inferior courts according to the will of that body, it would certainly have been useless to have proceded [sic] further than to have defined the judicial power, and the tribunals in which it should be vested. The subsequent part of the section is mere surplusage, is entirely without meaning, . . . the distribution of jurisdiction, made in the Constitution, is form without substance. . . .

It cannot be presumed that any clause in the Constitution is intended to be without effect; and, therefore, such a construction is inadmissible, unless the words require it. . . .

To enable this Court, then, to issue a mandamus, it must be shown to be an exercise of appellate jurisdiction, or to be necessary to enable them to exercise appellate jurisdiction. . . .

It is the essential criterion of appellate jurisdiction, that it revises and corrects the proceedings in a cause already instituted, and does not create that cause. Although, therefore, a mandamus may be directed to courts, yet to issue such a writ to an officer for the delivery of a paper, is in effect the same as to sustain an original action for that paper, and, therefore, seems not to belong to appellate but to original jurisdiction. Neither is it necessary in such a case as this, to enable the court to exercise its appellate jurisdiction.

The authority, therefore, given to the Supreme Court, by the act establishing the judicial courts of the United States, to issue writs of mandamus to public officers, appears not to be warranted by the Constitution; and it becomes necessary to inquire whether a jurisdiction so conferred can be exercised.

The question, whether an act, repug-

nant to the Constitution, can become the law of the land, is a question deeply interesting to the United States; but, happily, not of an intricacy proportioned to its interest. It seems only necessary to recognize certain principles, supposed to have been long and well established, to decide it.

That the people have an original right to establish, for their future government, such principles, as, in their opinion, shall most conduce to their own happiness is the basis on which the whole American fabric has been erected. The exercise of this original right is a very great exertion; nor can it, nor ought it, to be frequently repeated. The principles, therefore, so established, are deemed fundamental. And as the authority from which they proceed is supreme, and can seldom act, they are designed to be permanent.

This original and supreme will organizes the government, and assigns to different departments their respective powers. It may either stop here, or establish certain limits not to be transcended by those departments.

The government of the United States is of the latter description. The powers of the legislature are defined and limited; and that those limits may not be mistaken, or forgotten, the Constitution is written. To what purpose are powers limited, and to what purpose is that limitation committed to writing, if these limits may, at any time, be passed by those intended to be restrained? The distinction between a government with limited and unlimited powers is abolished, if those limits do not confine the persons on whom they are imposed, and if acts prohibited and acts allowed, are of equal obligation. It is a proposition too plain to be contested, that the Constitution controls any legislative act repugnant to it; or, that the legislature may alter the Constitution by an ordinary act.

Between these alternatives there is no

middle ground. The Constitution is either a superior paramount law, unchangeable by ordinary means, or it is on a level with ordinary legislative acts, and, like other acts, is alterable when the legislature shall please to alter it.

If the former part of the alternative be true, then a legislative act contrary to the constitution is not law: if the latter part be true, then written constitutions are absurd attempts, on the part of the people, to limit a power in its own nature illimitable.

Certainly all those who have framed written constitutions contemplate them as forming the fundamental and paramount law of the nation, and, consequently, the theory of every such government must be, that an act of the legislature, repugnant to the constitution, is void.

This theory is essentially attached to a written constitution, and, is consequently, to be considered, by this court, as one of the fundamental principles of our society. It is not therefore to be lost sight of in the further consideration of this subject.

If an act of the legislature, repugnant to the Constitution, is void, does it, notwithstanding its invalidity, bind the courts, and oblige them to give it effect? Or, in other words, though it be not law, does it constitute a rule as operative as if it was a law? This would be to overthrow in fact what was established in theory; and would seem, at first view, an absurdity too gross to be insisted on. It shall, however, receive a more attentive consideration.

It is emphatically the province and duty of the judicial department to say what the law is. Those who apply the rule to particular cases, must of necessity expound and interpret that rule. If two laws conflict with each other, the courts must decide on the operation of each.

So if a law be in opposition to the Constitution; if both the law and the Constitution apply to a particular case, so that the court must either decide that case conformably to the law, disregarding the Con-

stitution; or conformably to the Constitution, disregarding the law; the court must determine which of these conflicting rules governs the case. This is of the very essence of judicial duty.

If, then, the courts are to regard the Constitution, and the Constitution is superior to any ordinary act of the legislature, the Constitution, and not such ordinary act, must govern the case to which they both apply.

Those, then, who controvert the principle that the Constitution is to be considered, in court, as a paramount law, are reduced to the necessity of maintaining that courts must close their eyes on the Constitution, and see only the law.

This doctrine would subvert the very foundation of all written constitutions. It would declare that an act which, according to the principles and theory of our government, is entirely void, is yet, in practice, completely obligatory. It would declare that if the legislature shall do what is expressly forbidden, such act, notwithstanding the express prohibition, is in reality effectual. It would be given to the legislature a practical and real omnipotence, with the same breath which professes to restrict their powers within narrow limits. It is prescribing limits, and declaring that those limits may be passed at pleasure.

That it thus reduces to nothing what we have deemed the greatest improvement on political institutions, a written constitution, would of itself be sufficient, in America, where written constitutions have been viewed with so much reverence, for rejecting the construction. But the peculiar expressions of the Constitution of the United States furnish additional arguments in favour of its rejection.

The judicial power of the United States is extended to all cases arising under the Constitution.

Could it be the intention of those who gave this power, to say that in using it the

Constitution should not be looked into? That a case arising under the Constitution should be decided without examining the instrument under which it arises?

This is too extravagant to be maintained.

In some cases, then, the Constitution must be looked into by the judges. And if they can open it at all, what part of it are they forbidden to read or to obey?

There are many other parts of the Constitution which serve to illustrate this subject.

It is declared that "no tax or duty shall be laid on articles exported from any state." Suppose a duty on the export of cotton, of tobacco, or of flour; and a suit instituted to recover it. Ought judgment to be rendered in such a case? Ought the judges to close their eyes on the Constitution, and only see the law?

The Constitution declares "that no bill of attainder or ex post facto law shall be passed."

If, however, such a bill should be passed, and a person should be prosecuted under it; must the court condemn to death those victims whom the Constitution endeavors to preserve?

"No person," says the Constitution, "shall be convicted of treason unless on the testimony of two witnesses to the same overt act, or on confession in open court."

Here the language of the Constitution is addressed especially to the courts. It prescribes, directly for them, a rule of evidence not to be departed from. If the legislature should change that rule, and declare one witness, or a confession out of court, sufficient for conviction, must the constitutional principle yield to the legislative act?

From these, and many other selections which might be made, it is apparent, that the framers of the Constitution contemplated that instrument as a rule for the government of courts, as well as of the legislature.

Why otherwise does it direct the judges to take an oath to support it? This oath certainly applies in an especial manner, to their conduct in their official character. How immoral to impose it on them, if they were to be used as the instruments, and the knowing instruments, for violating what they swear to support!

The oath of office, too, imposed by the legislature, is completely demonstrative of the legislative opinion on this subject. It is in these words: "I do solemnly swear that I will administer justice without respect to persons, and do equal right to the poor and to the rich; and that I will faithfully and impartially discharge all the duties incumbent on me as   , according to the best of my abilities and understanding agreeably to the constitution and laws of the United States."

Why does a judge swear to discharge his duties agreeably to the Constitution of the United States, if that Constitution forms no rule for his government? if it is closed upon him, and can not be inspected by him?

If such be the real state of things, this is worse than solemn mockery. To prescribe, or to take this oath, becomes equally a crime.

It is also not entirely unworthy of observation, that in declaring what shall be the supreme law of the land, the Constitution itself is first mentioned; and not the laws of the United States generally, but those only which shall be made in pursuance of the Constitution, have that rank.

Thus, the particular phraseology of the Constitution of the United States confirms and strengthens the principle, supposed to be essential to all written constitutions, that a law repugnant to the Constitution is void; and that courts, as well as other departments, are bound by that instrument.

The rule must be discharged.

Reaction to *Marbury* v. *Madison*

Chief Justice John Marshall's opinion in *Marbury* v. *Madison* contained lengthy dicta discoursing on the authority of the judiciary to say what the law is and to void unconstitutional statutes. The decision itself, in practical application, voided a section of the Judiciary Act of 1789 that delegated to the Supreme Court the authority to issue writs of mandamus in its original jurisdiction. But neither the obiter dictum announcing the power of judicial review, nor the overturning of a section of the 1789 Judiciary Act, caused any significant comment in the press after the decision was announced.

The doctrine of judicial review was well accepted and had been applied in a number of previous cases and, as pointed out above, was not really a matter of debate except as it was raised in reference to the Repeal Act of 1802. It was Marshall's lengthy, and in Jefferson's words, "gratuitous," discussion of the right of the defendants to their commissions, and the responsibility of the executive to deliver them, that raised a storm of criticism from Jefferson and the Republicans on the one hand, and praise from the Federalists on the other. Marshall's dicta in support of Marbury's legal right to the commission, and his direct statement that the President should carry out the laws of Congress and be "amenable to the laws for his conduct," was considered by the Republicans to be a gratuitous and unjustified intrusion upon the authority of the executive. Charles Warren reports Jefferson's reaction.

> . . . [Jefferson's] indignation over Marshall's opinion continued hot up to the day of his death. Writing four years later, at the time of the Burr trial, he stated that he had "long wished for a proper occasion to have the gratuitous opinion in *Marbury* v. *Madison* brought before the public and denounced as not law," and as late as 1823, he wrote to Judge William Johnson that "the practice of Judge Marshall in travelling out of his case to prescribe what law would be in a moot case not before the Court" was "very irregular and very censurable," and that in the *Marbury Case* "the Court determined at once that, being an original process, it had no cognizance of it; and therefore, the question before them was ended. But the Chief Justice went on to lay down what the law would be, had they jurisdiction of the case, to wit: that they should command the delivery [of the commissions]. The object was clearly to instruct any other Court having the jurisdiction what they should do if Marbury should apply to them. Besides the impropriety of this gratuitous interference [with the executive] could anything exceed the perversion of the law? . . . Yet this case of *Marbury* v. *Madison* is continually cited by Bench and Bar as if it were settled law, without any animadversion on its being merely an *obiter* dissertation of the Chief Justice. (Warren, *The Supreme Court*, 1:244–245)

Although Marshall's explicit elaboration of the authority of the Court to exercise judicial review went virtually unnoticed at the time, the case has historical importance because of the numerous occasions on which this dicta has been cited, not as an original justification of the power of judicial review, but as an affirmation of the authority of the Court to interpret and apply the Constitution to congressional *and executive* actions (see, for example, *United States* v. *Richard M. Nixon*, 418 U.S. 683, 1974), even though the part

of the *Marbury* v. *Madison* decision which discusses judicial review is limited
to an affirmation of the power in reference to congressional laws. Judicial
review of executive action, however, does come into the picture in *Marbury*
v. *Madison* because of Marshall's assertion that if the Court had the power to
issue a mandamus it would have done so, thus directly interfering in the internal affairs of the executive branch. President Jefferson had directed his
Secretary of State to withhold the commission. The inference of Marshall's
opinion was that if a proper action had been brought before the lower
court, a mandamus appropriately could have been issued to direct Madison
to deliver Marbury's commission. Marshall was not basing this part of his
decision upon the Constitution, but upon the District Act that had been
passed by Congress that authorized the President to appoint justices of the
peace. In refusing to deliver the commissions that had been executed under
the administration of President John Adams, President Jefferson had, although not mentioned by name in Marshall's opinion, violated statutory and
not constitutional law.

A week after Marshall's *Marbury* v. *Madison* opinion, Justice Paterson announced the Court's opinion in *Stuart* v. *Laird,* 1 Cranch 299 (1803), in
which a short four-paragraph opinion upheld the constitutionality of the
Circuit Court Act of 1802. This was the act that repealed the Federalist
backed 1801 Judiciary Act that had expanded the number of courts and
judges and had resulted in entrenching Federalists throughout the judiciary. The two issues that arose out of the Circuit Court Act of 1802 were,
first, the authority of Congress to repeal its previous legislation dealing with
the judiciary, which in its opinion the Court stated was an absolutely clear
constitutional power of the legislature[25] and, second, whether or not that
provision of the 1802 act that assigned Supreme Court justices circuit court
responsibilities was constitutional. This had been the practice from the very
beginning of the federal judiciary, but Chief Justice Marshall among others
questioned the validity of the practice which, having been abandoned in the
Judiciary Act of 1801, was now reinstated by the act of 1802.

From a political standpoint, overturning the 1802 repeal law would have
resulted in an explosive Republican reaction in opposition to the Court,
which would certainly have raised the possibility of impeachment of the justices even if the likelihood of removing the judges through this procedure
was remote. The real problem confronting the Federalist Supreme Court in

---

[25]Charles Lee, attorney for the plaintiff, argued extensively that the creation of new courts
by the Repeal Act, and the transfer of jurisdiction from courts established under the 1789 Judiciary Act, constituted unwarranted intrusion by the legislature into Article III courts. Congress, said Lee, has the power to create courts but not to destroy them, which amounts to improper dismissal of judges from constitutional courts where they are protected during good
behavior. "It is admitted that Congress has the power to modify, increase or diminish the power
of the courts and the judges. But that is a power totally different from the power to destroy the
courts and to deprive them of all power and jurisdiction. The one is permitted by the Constitution, the other is restrained by the regard which the Constitution pays to the independence
of judges . . . . This provision of the Constitution was intended to place the judges not only beyond the reach of executive power, of which the people were always jealous, but also to shield
them from the attack of that party spirit which always predominates in popular assemblies."
Stuart v. Laird, 1 Cranch 299, 303–304 (1803).

its consideration of the issue of assignment to circuit court duty was the fact that Supreme Court justices had acquiesced in this responsibility when it had been assigned to them by the Judiciary Act of 1789. Justice Marshall, although himself in opposition to the assignment of circuit court responsibilities, agreed to go along with the majority of the Court, which, largely on the basis of prior practice, accepted that section of the 1802 act that reinstated the circuit court assignments of Supreme Court justices.

Although parts of Marshall's opinion in *Marbury* v. *Madison* had irritated the Republicans, the fact was that the practical effect of *Marbury* v. *Madison* and *Stuart* v. *Laird* was in support of the policies and practices of the Republicans.

Years after the Supreme Court had settled the question of its power to overturn acts of Congress, the issue was brought up in the Pennsylvania Supreme Court in the case of *Eakin* v. *Raub.* Although an unimportant case, the dissenting opinion in *Eakin* v. *Raub* by Justice Gibson developed an important and elaborate argument to refute the idea that courts should exercise a general power of judicial review over legislative acts. Justice Gibson's argument was, of course, purely academic because as he himself well recognized, the right to judicial review was universally recognized as an inherent judicial power. In the course of his dissenting opinion he noted,

> But I may premise that it is not a little remarkable that although the right [to judicial review] in question has all along been claimed by the judiciary, no judge has ventured to discuss it except Chief Justice Marshall (in *Marbury* v. *Madison)* and if the argument of a jurist so distinguished for the strength of his ratiocinative powers be found inconclusive, it may fairly be set down to the weakness of the position which he attempts to defend.

What Gibson seems to imply in his opinion is not that Marshall was wrong in claiming that acts repugnant to the United States Constitution could not be overturned by the courts, but that there did not exist, as Marshall implied, a general judicial power of review over legislative acts under all circumstances. Justice Gibson disagreed with Marshall's unequivocal statement that "it is emphatically the province and duty of the judicial department to say what the law is. Those who apply the rule to particular cases, must of necessity expound and interpret that rule. If two laws conflict with each other, the Court must decide on the operation of each." Gibson argues that state courts do not have the inherent authority to overturn state laws on the basis of state constitutions, although they are bound to overturn state laws that contravene the federal Constitution. State constitutions are not "the supreme law of the land," whereas the federal Constitution is.

Although Gibson does not explicitly state it, one can infer from his opinion that if state courts are bound by the federal Constitution, so are federal courts. Therefore that part of Marshall's opinion that applies to the authority of the federal courts to exercise judicial review over congressional acts on the basis of the federal Constitution is warranted, although no inference can be made that this is an inherent judicial power under all circumstances.

While Judge Gibson may have been in only partial disagreement with

Marshall's opinion on judicial review, his opinion looked at in another way can support the conclusion that no courts should have the authority to overturn legislative acts. This can be done by transferring the arguments he presents within the context of the Pennsylvania political system to the context of the federal government. Within the Pennsylvania context he is arguing that each branch is equal, and that it is to be the judge of its own constitutional authority. If the legislature exceeds its constitutional mandate it is up to the people of the state to change the law, not for the courts to nullify it. Whereas the provisions of the federal Constitution make it clear that it is to be supreme over the states, there is nothing in the federal Constitution that gives the Supreme Court the power of judicial review. But, if it is the supremacy of the Constitution that gives to state courts the obligation to review and, where necessary, to declare state laws unconstitutional, by the same reasoning the federal judiciary could be argued to have the power of judical review because laws of Congress are inferior to the Constitution.

Although analytically it is possible to review Gibson's dissenting opinion in *Eakin* v. *Raub* as less than a full-fledged attack upon judicial review, to his contemporaries his opinion suggested strong opposition to judicial power to pass upon the constitutionality of legislation. In 1830, after the death of Justice Washington, Gibson was considered for the Supreme Court vacancy. He was strongly supported by John C. Calhoun and those in favor of states' rights and nullification, while he was opposed by others because of his strong views against judicial review. The controversy over Gibson denied him a possible seat on the Supreme Court, which is somewhat ironic in view of the fact that by 1845 he came out in support of judicial review in Pennsylvania in the case of *Norris* v. *Klymen*, 2 Pa. St. 281, stating that: "I have changed that opinion [on judicial review] for two reasons. The late [Pennsylvania constitutional] convention, by their silence, sanctioned the pretensions of the court to deal freely with the act of the legislature; and from experience of the necessity of the case."

Eakin v. *Raub*

12 Sergeant and Rawle (Pennsylvania Supreme Court) 330 (1825)

GIBSON, J. [dissenting] . . .

I am aware, that a right [in the judiciary] to declare all unconstitutional acts void . . . is generally held as a professional dogma; but, I apprehend, rather as a matter of faith than of reason. I admit that I once embraced the same doctrine, but without examination, and I shall therefore state the arguments that impelled me to abandon it, with great respect for those by whom it is still maintained. . . .

. . . I begin by observing that in this country, the powers of the judiciary are divisible into those that are POLITICAL, and those that are purely civil. Every power by which one organ of the government is enabled to control another, or to exert an influence over its acts, is a political power. . . .

The constitution and the right of the legislature to pass the act, may be in collision. But is that a legitimate subject for judicial determination? If it be, the judiciary must be a peculiar organ, to revise the proceedings of the legislature, and to correct its mistakes; and in what part of the constitution are we to look for this proud pre-eminence? Viewing the matter in the opposite direction, what would be thought of an act of assembly in which it should be declared that the Supreme Court had, in a particular case, put a wrong construction on the Constitution of the United States, and that the judgment should therefore be reversed? It would doubtless be thought a usurpation of judicial power. But it is by no means clear, that to declare a law void which has been enacted according to the forms prescribed in the constitution, is not a usurpation of legislative power. . . .

But it has been said to be emphatically the business of the judiciary, to ascertain and pronounce what the law is; and that this necessarily involves a consideration of the constitution. It does so: but how far? If the judiciary will inquire into anything besides the form of enactment, where shall it stop? There must be some point of limitation to such an inquiry; for no one will pretend that a judge would be justifiable in calling for the election returns, or scrutinizing the qualifications of those who composed the legislature. . . .

. . . In theory, all the organs of the government are of equal capacity; or, if not equal, each must be supposed to have superior capacity only for those things which peculiarly belong to it; and, as legislation peculiarly involves the consideration of those limitations which are put on the law-making power, and the interpretation of the laws when made, involves only the construction of the laws themselves, it follows that the construction of the constitution in this particular belongs to the legislature, which ought therefore to be taken to have superior capacity to judge of the constitutionality of its own acts. But suppose all to be of equal capacity in every respect, why should one exercise a controlling power over the rest? That the judiciary is of superior rank, has never been pretended, although it has been said to be co-ordinate. It is not easy, however, to comprehend how the power which gives law to all the rest, can be of no more than equal rank with one which receives it, and is answerable to the former for the observance of its statutes. Legislation is essentially an act of sovereign power; but the execution of the laws by instruments that are governed by prescribed rules and exercise no power of volition, is essentially otherwise. . . . It may be said, the power of the legislature, also, is limited by prescribed rules. It is so. But it is nevertheless, the power of the people, and sovereign as far as it extends. It cannot be said, that the judiciary is co-ordinate merely because it is established by the constitution. If that were sufficient, sheriffs, registers of wills, and recorders of deeds, would be so too. Within the pale of their authority, the acts of these officers will have the power of the people for their support; but no one will pretend, they are of equal dignity with the acts of the legislature. Inequality of rank arises not from the manner in which the organ has been constituted, but from its essence and the nature of its functions; and the legislative organ is superior to every other, inasmuch as the power to will and to command, is essentially superior to the power to act and to obey. . . .

Everyone knows how seldom men think exactly alike on ordinary subjects; and a government constructed on the principle of assent by all its parts, would be inadequate to the most simple operations. The notion of a complication of counter checks has been carried to an extent in theory, of which the framers of the constitution never dreamt. When the entire sovereignty was separated into its elementary parts, and distributed to the appropriate branches, all things incident to the exercise of its powers were committed to each branch exclusively. The negative which each part of the legislature may exercise, in regard to the acts of the other, was thought sufficient to prevent material infractions of the restraints which were put on the power of the whole; for, had it been intended to interpose the judiciary as an additional barrier, the matter would surely not have been left in doubt. The judges would not have been left to stand on the insecure and ever shifting ground of public opinion as to constructive powers; they would have been placed on the impregnable ground of an express grant. They would not have been compelled to resort to debates in the convention, or the opinion that was generally entertained at the time. A constitution, or a statute, is supposed to contain the whole will of the body from which it emanated; and I would just as soon resort to the debates in the legislature for the construction of an act of assembly, as to the debates in the convention for the construction of the constitution.

The power is said to be restricted to cases that are free from doubt or difficulty. But the abstract existence of a power cannot depend on the clearness or obscurity of the case in which it is to be exercised; for that is a consideration that cannot present itself, before the question of the existence of the power shall have been determined; and, if its existence be conceded, no considerations of policy arising from the obscurity of the particular case, ought to influence the exercise of it. . . .

To say, therefore, that the power is to be exercised but in perfectly clear cases, is to betray a doubt of the propriety of exercising it at all. Were the same caution used in judging of the existence of the power that is inculcated as to the exercise of it, the profession would perhaps arrive at a different conclusion. The grant of a power so extraordinary ought to appear so plain, that he who should run might read. . . .

What I have in view in this inquiry, is the supposed right of the judiciary to interfere, in cases where the constitution is to be carried into effect through the instrumentality of the legislature, and where that organ must necessarily first decide on the constitutionality of its own act. The oath to support the constitution is not peculiar to the judges, but is taken indiscriminately by every officer of the government, and is designed rather as a test of the political principles of the man, than to bind the officer in the discharge of his duty: otherwise it is difficult to determine what operation it is to have in the case of a recorder of deeds, for instance, who, in the execution of his office, has nothing to do with the constitution. But granting it to relate to the official conduct of the judge, as well as every other officer, and not to his political principles, still it must be understood in reference to supporting the constitution, *only as far as that may be involved in his official duty;* and, consequently, if his official duty does not comprehend an inquiry into the authority of the legislature, neither does his oath. . . .

But do not the judges do a positive act in violation of the constitution, when they give effect to an unconstitutional law? Not if the law has been passed according to the forms established in the constitution. The fallacy of the question is, in supposing that the judiciary adopts the acts of the legislature as its own; whereas the enactment of a law and the interpretation of it are not concurrent acts, and as the judiciary is not required to concur in the enactment, neither is it in the breach of the constitution which may be the consequence of the enactment. The fault is imputable to the legislature, and on it the responsibility exclusively rests. . . .

But it has been said, that this construction would deprive the citizen of the advantages which are peculiar to a written constitution, by at once declaring the power of the legislature in practice to be illimitable. . . . But there is no magic or inherent power in parchment and ink, to command respect and protect principles from violation. In the business of government a recurrence to first principles answers the end of an observation at sea with a view to correct the dead reckoning; and for this purpose, a written constitution is an instrument of inestimable value. It is of inestimable value, also, in rendering its first principles familiar to the mass of people; for, after all, there is no effectual guard against legislative usurpation but public opinion, the force of which, in this country is inconceivably great. . . . Once let public opinion be so corrupt as to sanction every misconstruction of the Constitution and abuse of power which the temptation of the moment may dictate, and the party which may happen to be predominant, will laugh at the puny efforts of a dependent power to arrest it in its course.

For these reasons, I am of [the] opinion that it rests with the people, in whom full and absolute sovereign power resides, to correct abuses in legislation, by instructing their representatives to repeal the obnoxious act. What is wanting to plenary power in the government, is reserved by the people for their own immediate use; and to redress an infringement of their rights in this respect, would seem to be an accessory of the power thus reserved. It might, perhaps, have been better to vest the power in the judiciary; as it might be expected that its habits of deliberation, and the aid derived from the arguments of counsel, would more frequently lead to accurate conclusions. On the other hand, the judiciary is not infallible; and an error by it would admit of no remedy but a more distinct expression of the public will, through the extraordinary medium of a convention; whereas, an error by the legislature admits of a remedy by an exertion of the same will, in the ordinary exercise of the right of suffrage,—a mode better calculated to attain the end, without popular excitement. It

may be said, the people would probably not notice an error of their representatives. But they would as probably do so, as notice an error of the judiciary; and, besides, it is a postulate in the theory of our government, and the very basis of the superstructure, that the people are wise, virtuous, and competent to manage their own affairs; and if they are not so, in fact, still every question of this sort must be determined according to the principles of the constitution, as it came from the hands of the framers, and the existence of a defect which was not foreseen, would not justify those who administer the government, in applying a corrective in practice, which can be provided only by convention. . . .

But in regard to an act of [a state] assembly, which is found to be in collision with the Constitution, laws, or treaties of the *United States,* I take the duty of the judiciary to be exactly the reverse. By becoming parties to the federal Constitution, the states have agreed to several limitations of their individual sovereignty, to enforce which, it was thought to be absolutely necessary to prevent them from giving effect to laws in violation of those limitations, through the instrumentality of their own judges. Accordingly, it is declared in the sixth article and second section of the federal Constitution, that "This Constitution, and the laws of the *United States* which shall be made in pursuance thereof, and all treaties made, or which shall be made under the authority of the *United States,* shall be the *supreme* law of the land; and the *judges* in every *state* shall be BOUND thereby: anything in the *laws* or *constitution* of any *state* to the contrary notwithstanding."

This is an express grant of a political power, and it is conclusive to show that no law of inferior obligation, as every state law must necessarily be, can be executed at the expense of the Constitution, laws, or treaties of the *United States.* It may be said, these are to furnish a rule only when there is no state provision on the subject. But, in that view, they could with no propriety be called supreme; for supremacy is a relative term, and cannot be predicted of a thing which exists separately and alone: and this law, which is called supreme, would change its character and become subordinate as soon as it should be found in conflict with a state law. But the judges are to be bound by the federal Constitution and laws, notwithstanding any thing in the constitution or laws of the particular state *to the contrary*. If, then, a state were to declare the laws of the *United States* not to be obligatory on her judges, such an act would unquestionably be void; for it will not be pretended that any member of the union can dispense with the obligation of the federal Constitution: and, if it cannot be done directly, and by a general declaratory law, neither can it indirectly, and by by-laws dispensing with it in particular cases. . . .

THE FIRST SUBSTANTIAL CASE OF JUDICIAL REVIEW OF A CONGRESSIONAL LAW

Chief Justice John Marshall's opinion in *Marbury* v. *Madison* set the stage for a government in which the Supreme Court would play a fundamental role in constitutional interpretation. Every case included in this book is an important link in the long chain of constitutional interpretation by the Supreme Court that has adapted the Constitution to the transitions that have taken place in the social, economic, and political fabric of the nation. The Court has not always acted positively to force its will upon Congress, the President, or the states. It has judiciously exercised self-restraint to avoid political controversies that would undermine its authority.

The principle of judicial review was obiter dictum in *Marbury* v. *Madison* and therefore was not applied to invalidate a congressional enactment. The first application of the power of judicial review over Congress was in *Dred Scott* v. *Sanford* in 1857. Perhaps no decision in the history of the Supreme Court was as important. Coming as it did at the height of the controversy over slavery, the fact that the Supreme Court voluntarily chose to enter a *real* political thicket by ruling on the question of whether or not Congress had the authority to limit slavery in the territories, and hence in practical terms in newly admitted states, was remarkable by any standards of judicial behavior. The decision was extremely controversial, more so than any case decided before or after 1857. The implications and controversies surrounding the *Dred Scott* case make the debates over the political activism of the Warren Court pale by comparison. The voices of the Republican party considered the decision to be a death blow to the possibility of political resolution of the issue of slavery. Moreover, the decision called into question the integrity of the Supreme Court, at least in the minds of the antislavery forces. A virulent Republican press helped to sway public opinion in the northern states against the Court. Among the terms used by the Republican press to characterize the Court after *Dred Scott* were "fanatical," "sinister," "usurpers," and "atrocious." Personal attacks were made upon the individual justices who supported the Court's opinion. And, after the Civil War, it was common for historians to blame the *Dred Scott* decision for causing the war.

While the decision in the *Dred Scott* case covered broad issues and had widespread impact, the facts of the case itself were limited, and the jurisdiction of the Court highly questionable. When the justices first heard the case in 1856, there was considerable doubt among themselves over whether or not jurisdiction should be accepted. If, as Justice Taney later wrote into his opinion in the *Dred Scott* case, a slave was not a citizen of the state in which he resided, nor of the United States, he could not sue in either a state or federal court for redress of grievances. Scott himself claimed that when his owners took him from the slave state of Missouri into the free state of Illinois, and into federal territory that was designated as free under the Missouri Compromise of 1820 passed by Congress, his status automatically changed from slave to free. After he was taken back to Missouri, he sued in the Missouri state court for his freedom and actually won a verdict in his favor in the lower court but lost on appeal to the Missouri Supreme Court. His attorney then brought suit in the Circuit Court for Missouri, where he lost again, and appealed to the Supreme Court on a writ of error.

While the Supreme Court justices were deliberating over whether or not to accept jurisdiction of the case, controversy was building in the country between slavery and antislavery forces over the question of the proper extent of the Court's authority to decide the slavery issue. Since the facts of the *Dred Scott* case did not dictate the scope of the Court's opinion, there was widespread fear before the decision that the Court, dominated by justices favoring or in sympathy with the cause of the South, would decide against congressional authority to curb the extension of slavery in the territories.[26]

When the *Dred Scott* case was finally placed before the Supreme Court three major issues emerged: First, can a black person be considered a citizen of the United States and therefore given the right to sue in federal courts (as opposed to being a state citizen with the right to sue in state courts, a matter that was within the jurisdiction of the states); second, did a slave obtain freedom when transported from a slave state to a free state or territory; and, third, does Congress have the right to prohibit slavery in the territories, as it did in the Missouri Compromise Act of 1820 which prohibited slavery north of a specified latitude?[27] These issues constituted the merits of the case which, once the Court accepted jurisdiction, had to be decided in whole or in part. The case could have been decided on any one of the issues, particularly the first two, as the constitutionality of the Missouri Compromise was not only a moot issue at the time because of its repeal by the Kansas-Nebraska Act of 1854, but also because a ruling on its constitutional validity was clearly not necessary to a determination of the immediate case.

The decision of the Court, postponed until after the election of 1856, ran to approximately one hundred pages, and each of the nine justices participating in the case (seven for the majority and two dissenting) wrote a separate opinion. Chief Justice Taney's opinion, although it differed in many

---

[26]The issue of the authority of Congress to prohibit slavery in the territories became temporarily moot with the passage of the Kansas-Nebraska Act on May 30, 1854, which specifically repealed the Missouri Compromise Act that had drawn a dividing line between the slave and free portions of the territory. The Kansas-Nebraska Act specifically declared that Congress was neutral on the issue of slavery in the territories.

[27]See footnote 26.

important respects from those of his brethren, was generally taken as representative of the opinion of the Court. The Chief Justice's long and complicated opinion reached all three of the major issues in the case, and his decision on them thrust the Court into the center of a political controversy from which it was not soon to recover.

Essentially Taney's opinion denied Congress the authority to ban slavery in the territories and further undermined the cause of the antislavery forces by holding that blacks, whether free or slave, were not citizens of the United States and competent to sue in federal courts. On the issue of black citizenship, Taney's reasoning was that blacks had come to the country as slaves before the Constitution was framed in 1787, and states had historically denied them citizenship. The Chief Justice overlooked the fact that political rights had been given to blacks by five original states which granted free native-born blacks citizenship (including North Carolina). In reasoning that was to be echoed in cases after the Civil War, Taney drew a distinction between state citizenship and citizenship of the United States. He held that the requirements for federal citizenship were entirely up to Congress, and states could in no way confer such citizenship. In order to sue in the federal courts, one had to be a citizen of the United States; therefore, blacks did not have standing to sue in federal jurisdiction.[28]

Taney illogically concluded from the doctrine of dual citizenship which he advanced that states could not grant blacks the same privileges and immunities required by the Constitution for citizens because it was the clear intent of the Constitution to extend federal citizenship only to white citizens, regardless of whether or not the states themselves granted blacks citizenship status.

Taney finally addressed himself to the question of whether or not Dred Scott's residence in a territory that had been designated as free by Congress automatically made him free. The Chief Justice concluded that Congress has no authority to regulate the property rights of persons residing in federal territories and therefore could not prohibit slavery since slaves were property. Moreover, Taney argued that the Bill of Rights applies to the territories, and changing a slave status to one of freedom would violate the due process clause of the Fifth Amendment by depriving the citizen who owned the slave of his property without due process of law.

Dred Scott v. Sanford

19 Howard 393; 15 L.Ed. 691 (1857)

MR. CHIEF JUSTICE TANEY delivered the opinion of the Court:

. . . The question is simply this: can a negro, whose ancestors were imported into this country and sold as slaves, become a member of the political commu-

[28]This raises the esoteric point of how the Court could justify ruling on the case if in fact it denied standing to Dred Scott to sue in federal courts. In fact, the Court did hold that the circuit court had improperly entertained the suit, but, the political imperatives of deciding the case made the Court overlook this important technicality in accepting jurisdiction on appeal from the circuit court rather than dismissing the case as seemed warranted by its own reasoning.

nity formed and brought into existence by the Constitution of the United States, and as such become entitled to all the rights, and privileges, and immunities, guaranteed by that instrument to the citizen. One of these rights is the privilege of suing in a court of the United States in the cases specified in the Constitution.

It will be observed, that the plea applies to that class of persons only whose ancestors were negroes of the African race, and imported into this country, and sold and held as slaves. The only matter in issue before the Court, therefore, is, whether the descendants of such slaves, when they shall be emancipated, or who are born of parents who had become free before their birth, are citizens of a state, in the sense in which the word "citizen" is used in the Constitution of the United States. And this being the only matter in dispute on the pleadings, the Court must be understood as speaking in this opinion of that class only; that is, of those persons who are the descendants of Africans who were . . . imported into this country and sold as slaves.

The words "people of the United States" and "citizens" are synonymous terms, and mean the same thing. They both describe the political body, who, according to our republican institutions, form the sovereignty, and who hold the power and conduct the government through their representatives. They are what we familiarly call the "sovereign people," and every citizen is one of this people, and a constituent member of this sovereignty. The question before us is, whether the class of persons described in the plea in abatement compose a portion of this people, and are constituent members of this sovereignty. We think they are not, and that they are not included, and were not intended to be included, under the word "citizens" in the Constitution, and can, therefore, claim none of the rights and privileges which that instrument provides for and secures to citizens of the United States. On the contrary, they were at that time considered as a subordinate and inferior class of beings, who had been subjugated by the dominant race, and whether emancipated or not, yet remained subject to their authority, and had no rights or privileges but such as those who held the power and the government might choose to grant them. . . .

In discussing this question, we must not confound the rights of citizenship which a state may confer within its own limits, and the rights of citizenship as a member of the Union. It does not by any means follow, because he has all the rights and privileges of a citizen of a State, that he must be a citizen of the United States. He may have all the rights and privileges of the citizen of a State, and yet not be entitled to the rights and privileges of a citizen in any other State. For, previous to the adoption of the Constitution of the United States, every State had the undoubted right to confer on whomsoever it pleased the character of a citizen, and to endow him with all its rights. But this character, of course, was confined to the boundaries of the State, and gave him no rights or privileges in other States beyond those secured to him by the laws of nations and the comity of States. Nor have the several States surrendered the power of conferring these rights and privileges by adopting the Constitution of the United States. Each State may still confer them upon an alien, or any one it thinks proper, or upon any class or description of persons; yet he would not be a citizen in the sense in which that word is used in the Constitution of the United States, nor entitled to sue as such in one of its courts, nor to the privileges and immunities of a citizen in the other States. The rights which he would acquire would be restricted to the State which gave them. The Constitution has conferred on Congress the right to establish an uniform rule of naturalization, and this right is evidently exclusive, and has always been held by this Court to be so. Consequently, no State, since the adoption of the Constitution, can, by naturalizing an alien, invest him with the rights and privileges secured to a citizen of a State under the federal government, although, so far as the State alone was concerned, he would undoubtedly be entitled to the rights of a citizen, and clothed with all the rights and immunities which the Constitution and laws of the State attached to that character.

It is very clear, therefore, that no State can, by any Act or law of its own, passed, since the adoption of the Constitution, introduce a new member into the political community created by the Constitution of the United States. It cannot make him a member of this community by making him a member of its own. And for the same reason it cannot introduce any person, or description of persons, who were not intended to be embraced in this new political family, which the Constitution brought into existence, but were intended to be excluded from it. . . .

It is true, every person, and every class and description of persons, who were at the time of the adoption of the Constitution recognized as citizens in the several States, became also citizens of this new political body; but none other; it was formed by them, and for them and their posterity, but for no one else. And the personal rights and privileges guaranteed to citizens of this new sovereignty were intended to embrace those only who were then members of the several state communities, or who should afterwards, by birthright or otherwise, become members, according to the provisions of the Constitution and the principles on which it was founded. . . .

It becomes necessary, therefore, to determine who were citizens of the several States when the Constitution was adopted. And in order to do this, we must recur to the governments and institutions of the thirteen Colonies, when they separated from Great Britain and formed new sovereignties, and took their places in the family of independent nations. We must inquire who, at that time, were recognized as the people or citizens of a State, whose rights and liberties had been outraged by the English Government; and who declared their independence, and assumed the powers of government to defend their rights by force of arms.

In the opinion of the Court, the legislation and histories of the times, and the language used in the Declaration of Independence, show, that neither the class of persons who had been imported as slaves, nor their descendants, whether they had become free or not, were then acknowledged as a part of the people, nor intended to be included in the general words used in that memorable instrument.

It is difficult at this day to realize the state of public opinion in relation to that unfortunate race, which prevailed in the civilized and enlightened portions of the world at the time of the Declaration of Independence, and when the Constitution of the United States was framed and adopted. But the public history of every European nation displays it, in a manner too plain to be mistaken.

They had far more than a century before been regarded as beings of an inferior order; and altogether unfit to associate with the white race, either in social or political relations; and so far inferior, that they had no rights which the white man was bound to respect; and that the negro might justly and lawfully be reduced to slavery for his benefit. He was bought and sold, and treated as an ordinary article of merchandise and traffic, whenever a profit could be made by it. This opinion was at that time fixed and universal in the civilized portion of the white race. It was regarded as an axiom in morals as well as in politics, which no one thought of disputing, or supposed to be open to dispute; and men in every grade and position in society daily and habitually acted upon it in their private pursuits, as well as in matters of public concern, without doubting for a moment the correctness of this opinion.

And in no nation was this opinion more firmly fixed or more uniformly acted upon than by the English government and English people. They not only seized them on the coast of Africa, and sold them or held them in slavery for their own use; but they took them as ordinary articles of merchandise to every country where they could make a profit on them, and were far more extensively engaged in this commerce than any other nation in the world.

The opinion thus entertained and acted upon in England was naturally impressed upon the colonies they founded on this side of the Atlantic. And, accordingly, a negro of the African race was regarded by them as an article of property, and held, and bought and sold as such, in every one of the thirteen Colonies which united in the Declaration of Independence, and afterwards formed the Constitution of the United States. The slaves were more or less numerous in the different Colonies, as slave labor was found more or less profitable. But no one seems to have doubted the correctness of the prevailing opinion of the time.

The legislation of the different Colonies furnishes positive and indisputable proof of the fact. . . .

We refer to these historical facts for the purpose of showing the fixed opinions concerning that race, upon which the statesmen of that day spoke and acted. It is necessary to do this, in order to determine whether the general terms used in the Constitution of the United States, as to the rights of man and the rights of the people, was intended to include them, or to give to them or their posterity the benefit of any of its provisions. . . .

No one, we presume, supposes that any change in public opinion or feeling in relation to this unfortunate race, in the civilized nations of Europe or in this country, should induce the court to give to the words of the Constitution a more liberal construction in their favor than they were intended to bear when the instrument was framed and adopted. Such an argument would be altogether inadmissible in any tribunal called on to interpret it. If any of its provisions are deemed unjust, there is a mode prescribed in the instrument itself by which it may be amended; but while it remains unaltered, it must be construed now as it was understood at the time of its adoption. It is not only the same in words, but the same in meaning, and delegates the same powers to the government, and reserves and secures the same rights and privileges to the citizen; and as long as it continues to exist in its present form, it speaks not only in the same words, but with the same meaning and intent with which it spoke when it came from the hands of its framers, and was voted on and adopted by the people of the United States. Any other rule of construction would abrogate the judicial character of this court, and make it the mere reflex of the popular opinion or passion of the day. This court was not created by the Constitution for such purposes. Higher and graver trusts have been confided to it, and it must not falter in the path of duty. . . .

And upon a full and careful consideration of the subject, the court is of opinion that, upon the facts stated in the plea in abatement, Dred Scott was not a citizen of Missouri within the meaning of the Constitution of the United States, and not entitled as such to sue in its courts; and, consequently, that the Circuit Court had no jurisdiction of the case, and that the judgment on the plea in abatement is erroneous. . . .

It is true that the result either way, by dismissal or by a judgment for the defendant, makes very little, if any difference in a pecuniary or personal point of view to either party. But the fact that the result would be very nearly the same to the parties in either form of judgment, would not justify this court in sanctioning an error in the judgment which is patent on the record, and which, if sanctioned, might be drawn into precedent, and lead to serious mischief and injustice in some future suit.

We proceed, therefore, to inquire whether the facts relied on by the plaintiff entitled him to his freedom. . . .

In considering this part of the controversy, two questions arise: 1st. Was he, together with his family, free in Missouri by reason of the stay in the territory of the United States hereinbefore mentioned? And 2d. If they were not, is Scott himself free by reason of his removal to Rock Island, in the State of Illinois, as stated in the above admissions?

We proceed to examine the first question.

The Act of Congress, upon which the plaintiff relies, declares that slavery and involuntary servitude, except as a punishment for crime, shall be forever prohibited in all that part of that territory ceded by France, under the name of Louisiana, which lies north of thirty-six degrees thirty minutes north latitude, and not included within the limits of Missouri. And the difficulty which meets us at the threshold of this part of the inquiry is, whether Congress was authorized to pass this law under any of the powers granted to it by the Constitution; for if the authority is not given by that instrument, it is the duty of this Court to declare it void and inoperative, and incapable of conferring freedom upon one who is held as a slave under the laws of any one of the States.

The counsel for the plaintiff has laid much stress upon that article in the Constitution which confers on Congress the power "to dispose of and make all needful rules and regulations respecting the territory or other property belonging to the United States;" but, in the judgment of the Court, that provision has no bearing

on the present controversy, and the power there given, whatever it may be, is confined, and was intended to be confined, to the territory which at that time belonged to, or was claimed by, the United States, and was within their boundaries as settled by the Treaty with Great Britain, and can have no influence upon a territory afterwards acquired from a foreign government. It was a special provision for a known and particular Territory, and to meet a present emergency, and nothing more.

A brief summary of the history of the times, as well as the careful and measured terms in which the article is framed, will show the correctness of this proposition. . . .

This brings us to examine by what provision of the Constitution the present Federal Government under its delegated and restricted powers, is authorized to acquire territory outside of the original limits of the United States, and what powers it may exercise therein over the person or property of a citizen of the United States, while it remains a territory, and until it shall be admitted as one of the States of the Union.

There is certainly no power given by the Constitution to the Federal Government to establish or maintain Colonies bordering on the United States or at a distance, to be ruled and governed at its own pleasure; nor to enlarge its territorial limits in any way, except by the admission of new States. . . .

We do not mean . . . to question the power of Congress [to admit new states]. The power to expand the territory of the United States by the admission of new States is plainly given; and in the construction of this power by all the departments of the government, it has been held to authorize the acquisition of territory, not fit for admission at the time, but to be admitted as soon as its population and situation would entitle it to admission. It is acquired to become a State, and not to be held as a colony and governed by Congress with absolute authority . . . through which they spoke and acted when the territory was obtained, it was not only within the scope of its powers, but it was its duty to pass such laws and establish such a government as would enable those by whose authority they acted to reap the advantages anticipated from its acquisition, and to gather there a population which would enable it to assume the position to which it was destined among the States of the Union. The power to acquire necessarily carries with it the power to preserve and apply to the purposes for which it was acquired. The form of government to be established necessarily rested in the discretion of Congress. It was their duty to establish the one that would be best suited for the protection and security of the citizens of the United States and other inhabitants who might be authorized to take up their abode there, and that must always depend upon the existing condition of the Territory, as to the number and character of its inhabitants, and the situation in the Territory. In some cases a government, consisting of persons appointed by the Federal Government, would best subserve the interests of the Territory, when the inhabitants were few and scattered, and new to one another. In other instances, it would be more advisable to commit the powers of self-government to the people who had settled in the territory, as being the most competent to determine what was best for their own interests. But some form of civil authority would be absolutely necessary to organize and preserve civilized society, and prepare it to become a state; and what is the best form must always depend on the condition of the territory at the time, and the choice of the mode must depend upon the exercise of a discretionary power by Congress acting within the scope of its constitutional authority, and not infringing upon the rights of person or rights of property of the citizen who might go there to reside or for

any other lawful purpose. It was acquired by the exercise of this discretion and it must be held and governed in like manner, until it is fitted to be a state.

But the power of Congress over the person or property of a citizen can never be a mere discretionary power under our Constitution and form of government. The powers of the government and the rights and privileges of the citizen are regulated and plainly defined by the Constitution itself. And when the territory becomes a part of the United States, the Federal Government enters into possession in the character impressed upon it by those who created it. It enters upon it with its powers over the citizen strictly defined, and limited by the Constitution, from which it derives its own existence, and by virtue of which alone it continues to exist and act as a government and sovereignty. It has no power of any kind beyond it; and it cannot, when it enters a territory of the United States, put off its character, and assume discretionary or despotic powers which the Constitution has denied to it. . . .

A reference to a few of the provisions of the Constitution will illustrate this proposition.

For example, no one, we presume, will contend that Congress can make any law in a territory respecting the establishment of religion or the free exercise thereof, or abridging the freedom of speech or of the press, or the right of the people of the territory peaceably to assemble and to petition the government for the redress of grievances.

Nor can Congress deny to the people the right to keep and bear arms, nor the right to trial by jury, nor compel anyone to be a witness against himself in a criminal proceeding.

These powers, and others in relation to rights of person, which it is not necessary here to enumerate, are, in express and positive terms, denied to the general government; and the rights of private property have been guarded with equal care. Thus the rights of property are united with the rights of person, and placed on the same ground by the Fifth Amendment to the Constitution, which provides that no person shall be deprived of life, liberty and property, without due process of law. And an Act of Congress which deprives a citizen of the United States of his liberty or property, merely because he came himself or brought his property into a particular Territory of the United States, and who had committed no offense against the laws, could hardly be dignified with the name of due process of law. . . .

Now, as we have already said in an earlier part of this opinion, upon a different point, the right of property in a slave is distinctly and expressly affirmed in the Constitution. The right to traffic in it, like an ordinary article of merchandise and property, was guaranteed to the citizens of the United States, in every State that might desire it, for twenty years. And the government in express terms is pledged to protect it in all future time, if the slave escapes from his owner. This is done in plain words—too plain to be misunderstood. And no word can be found in the Constitution which gives Congress a greater power over slave property, or which entitles property of that kind to less protection than property of any other description. The only power conferred is the power coupled with the duty of guarding and protecting the owner in his rights.

Upon these considerations, it is the opinion of the Court that the Act of Congress which prohibited a citizen from holding and owning property of this kind in the territory of the United States north of the line therein mentioned, is not warranted by the Constitution, and is therefore void; and that neither Dred Scott himself, nor any of his family, were made free by being carried there by the owner, with the intention of becoming a permanent resident.

We have so far examined the case, as it stands under the Constitution of the United States, and the powers thereby delegated to the Federal Government.

But there is another point in the case which depends on state power and state law. And it is contended, on the part of the plaintiff, that he is made free by being taken to Rock Island, in the State of Illinois, independently of his residence in the territory of the United States; and being so made free he was not again reduced to a state of slavery by being brought back to Missouri.

Our notice of this part of the case will be very brief; for the principle on which it depends was decided in this Court, upon much consideration, in the case of *Strader et al.* v. *Graham,* reported in 10 Howard, 82 [1850]. In that case, the slaves had been taken from Kentucky to Ohio, with the consent of the owner, and afterwards brought back to Kentucky. And this Court held that their status or condition, as free or slave, depended upon the laws of Kentucky, when they were brought back into that State, and not of Ohio; and that this Court had no jurisdiction to revise the judgment of a state court upon its own laws. This was the point directly before the Court, and the decision that this Court had no jurisdiction, turned upon it, as will be seen by the report of the case.

So in this case: as Scott was a slave when taken into the State of Illinois by his owner, and was there held as such, and brought back in that character, his status, as free or slave, depended on the laws of Missouri, and not of Illinois. . . .

Upon the whole, therefore, it is the judgment of this Court, that it appears by the record before us that the plaintiff in error is not a citizen of Missouri, in the sense in which that word is used in the Constitution; and that the Circuit Court of the United States, for that reason, had no jurisdiction in the case, and could give no judgment in it.

Its judgment for the defendant must, consequently, be reversed, and a mandate issued directing the suit to be dismissed for want of jurisdiction. . . .

JUSTICE CURTIS, dissenting:

To determine whether any free persons, descended from Africans held in slavery, were citizens of the United States under the Confederation, and consequently at the time of the adoption of the Constitution of the United States, it is only necessary to know whether any such persons were citizens of either of the States under the Confederation at the time of the adoption of the Constitution.

Of this there can be no doubt. At the time of the ratification of the Articles of Confederation, all free native-born inhabitants of the States of New Hampshire, Massachusetts, New York, New Jersey and North Carolina, though descended from African slaves, were not only citizens of those States, but such of them as had the other necessary qualifications possessed the franchise of electors on equal terms with other citizens. . . .

Did the Constitution of the United States deprive them or their descendants of citizenship?

That Constitution was ordained and established by the people of the United States through the action, in each State, of those persons who were qualified by its laws to act thereon, in behalf of themselves and all other citizens of that State. In some of the States, as we have seen, colored persons were among those qualified by law to act on this subject. These colored persons were not only included in the body of "the people of the United States by whom the Constitution was ordained and established," but in at least five of the States they had the power to act, and doubtless did act, by their suffrages, upon the question of its adoption. It would be strange, if we were to find in that instrument anything which deprived of their citizenship any part of the people of the United States who were among those by whom it was established.

I can find nothing in the Constitution which, proprio vigore [by its intrinsic meaning], deprives of their citizenship any class of persons who were citizens of the United States at the time of its adoption, or who should be native-born citizens of any State after its adoption; nor any power enabling Congress to disfranchise persons born on the soil of any State, and entitled to citizenship of such State by its constitution and laws. And my opinion is, that, under the Constitution of the United States, every free person born on the soil of a State, who is a citizen of that State by force of its Constitution or laws, is also a citizen of the United States. . . .

Aftermath of the *Dred Scott* Decision

The abolitionist press immediately began an attack upon the integrity of the Supreme Court after the *Dred Scott* decision, the flavor of which is partially indicated by the following selection from Horace Greeley's *New York Tribune:*

> The whole slavery agitation was reopened by the proceedings in the Supreme Court today, and that tribunal voluntarily introduced itself into the political arena. . . . Much feeling is excited by this decree, and the opinion is freely expressed that a new element of sectional strife has been wantonly imposed upon the country. (March 6, 1857)

> If the action of the Court in this case has been atrocious, the manner of it has been no better. The Court has rushed into politics, voluntarily and without other

purpose than to subserve the cause of slavery. They were not called upon, in the discharge of their duties to say a word about the subject . . . the vote stood 7 to 2—the 5 slaveholders and 2 doughfaces making up the 7. Their cunning chief had led the van, and plank by plank laid down a platform of historical falsehood and gross assumption, and thereon they all stood exultingly, thinking, or feigning to think, that their work would stand during the remainder of their lives at least. (March 7, 1857)[29]

The attacks upon the *Dred Scott* decision by the *New York Tribune* were especially virulent, and although they represented widespread feeling among the abolitionists, more conservative papers such as the *New York Times*, while criticizing the Court, did so in a moderate manner. As the *Tribune* and the abolitionist press raged on, the Democratic newspapers came to the defense of the Court. For example, *The Pennsylvanian* stated,

The Tribune may rave and fanaticism make earth hideous with its howlings, but all in vain. . . . There are certain points which are subtle and beyond the reach of the fanatics of the Nation. . . . The decision is a closing and clinching confirmation of the settlement of the issue. . . . Whoever now seeks to revive sectionalism arrays himself against the Constitution, and consequently against the Union. (March 10, 11, 12, 1857)[30]

THE CONDITIONS OF JUDICIAL REVIEW

The Supreme Court has made it clear from the very beginning of the Republic that it will not accept the delegation of nonjudicial responsibilities to the federal judiciary.[31] This is, of course, an important limitation upon the authority of the judiciary, because it cannot initiate cases. At the same time it gives to the courts flexibility in exercising judicial self-restraint because of the wide latitude judges have in refusing to hear cases on the grounds that they do not meet the case and controversy requirement of Article III.[32] The effect of the case and controversy requirement in limiting the judicial power is nicely summarized in the following passage from the late Justice Robert H. Jackson's book, *The Supreme Court as a Unit of Government*:

But perhaps the most significant and least comprehended limitation upon the judicial power is that this power extends only to cases and controversies. We know that this restriction was deliberate, for it was proposed in the convention that the Supreme Court be made part of a council of revision with a kind of veto power, and this was rejected.

The result of the limitation is that the Court's only power is to decide law suits between adversary litigants with real interests at stake, and its only method of proceeding is by the conventional judicial, as distinguished from legislative or administrative, process. This precludes the rendering of advisory opinions even at the request of the nation's President and every form of pronouncement on abstract,

[29]Warren, *The Supreme Court*, 3:26–27.
[30]Ibid., p. 33.
[31]See the discussion of Hayburn's Case, 2 Dallas 410 (1792), pp. 8–10.
[32]For an excellent discussion of this and other aspects of judicial self-restraint, see John P. Roche, "Judicial Self-Restraint," *The American Political Science Review*, 49 (September 1965), 762–772.

contingent, or hypothetical issues. It prevents acceptance for judicial settlement of issues in which the interests and questions involved are political in character. It also precludes imposition on federal constitutional courts of nonjudicial duties.[33]

While the case and controversy rule is seemingly unequivocal, in fact it requires broadly subjective interpretation by the judges applying it. For example, consider Justice Jackson's pronouncement of the content of the case and controversy rule. What is an "adversary litigant," a "real interest," an "abstract, contingent, or hypothetical issue," a "political question," a "nonjudicial duty?" All of these terms must be and have been on various occasions defined by the courts, frequently in conflicting fashion.

A case and controversy arises when adverse individual rights or interests are claimed or redress of a wrong is sought within the context of an adversary situation. A case and controversy becomes justiciable when it falls within the jurisdiction of the courts. Under Article III, a justiciable case and controversy is one in which adversary rights or interests are properly presented under the Constitution, laws, or treaties of the United States. It is possible to meet the generic conditions of a case and controversy without meeting the requirements for justiciability under Article III. By definition, a legal case and controversy automatically invokes jurisdiction of the courts.

An important doctrine ancillary to the case and controversy requirement is "standing to sue." Under this doctrine a private citizen complaining of the unlawful conduct of a government agency or officer must demonstrate that his or her individual substantive constitutional, statutory, or common law rights or interests have been invaded by the challenged action. Often statutes delegating authority to administrative officers will explicitly grant standing to private parties aggrieved by government action taken under the statute. Under such circumstances standing is relatively easy to demonstrate to the satisfaction of the courts. It is only where there is no statutory provision for judicial review to aggrieved parties that individuals must demonstrate an invasion of substantive constitutional, statutory, or common law rights. One can be an "aggrieved party" under a statutory judicial review provision even though there has been no invasion of substantive legal rights or interests. For example, there is no legal right in the Constitution or the common law to prevent honest competition. In the absence of a statutory provision for judicial review, or an explicit statutory right to limited competition, the courts will not allow standing on the basis that government action causes economic competition.[34] However, where there is a statutory provision stating that "a person aggrieved" by an agency action may secure judicial review of it, the courts have allowed standing to a party who has demonstrated possible economic injury due to competition from the challenged government action.[35]

[33]Robert H. Jackson, *The Supreme Court in the American System of Government* (Cambridge, Mass.: Harvard University Press, 1955), pp. 11–12.

[34]See Tennessee Electric Power Company v. TVA, 306 U.S. 118 (1939).

[35]Federal Communications Commission v. Sanders Radio Station, 309 U.S. 470 (1940), and Scripps-Howard Radio, Inc. v. Federal Communications Commission, 316 U.S. 4 (1942), Associated Industries of New York State, Inc. v. Ickes, 134 F. 2d 694 (1943). Cf. Hardin v. Kentucky Utilities Co., 390 U.S. 1 (1968).

A brief discussion of several critical Supreme Court cases concerning standing will serve to pinpoint the concerns and problems that arise. From the standpoint of the courts, the standing doctrine that is derivative from the case and controversy requirement is used both to limit the number of cases brought before the judiciary and to exercise judicial self-restraint. The standing doctrine therefore serves both a practical and political purpose. As a practical matter, the usefulness of the standing doctrine can be seen in reference to so-called taxpayers' suits. Does the mere payment of taxes give to each and every individual taxpayer the right to standing to challenge government action involving the expenditure of funds? Clearly if a taxpayer qua taxpayer could challenge such government action, the floodgates protecting the judiciary would be opened and an almost infinite number of suits could theoretically be thrust upon the courts for consideration. Such suits would arise where taxpayers claimed that their money was going to be spent for allegedly unconstitutional purposes. The Supreme Court came to grips with the problem of the taxpayers' suits in two cases, *Frothingham* v. *Mellon*, 262 U.S. 447 (1923), and *Flast* v. *Cohen*, 392 U.S. 83 (1968).

In *Frothingham* v. *Mellon* the Supreme Court denied to taxpayers the right to sue the government on the basis of their claim that revenues were going to be spent for unconstitutional purposes. The Maternity Act of 1921 had provided for grants-in-aid from the United States Treasury to the states for programs to help mothers and their infants. Mrs. Frothingham claimed that the act would result in taxation for illegal purposes and thereby take her property without due process of law. The Court disallowed the suit, declaring that there was insufficient personal interest demonstrated apart from the interests of taxpayers in general. The taxpayer's interest in the monies of the Treasury, said the Court, "is shared by millions of others, is comparatively minute and indeterminable, and the effect upon future taxation of any payment out of funds, so remote, fluctuating and uncertain, that no basis is afforded for an appeal to the preventive powers of a court of equity." Standing requires the demonstration of a personal interest that is sharp and distinct from the interests of taxpayers in general.

In *Flast* v. *Cohen* the Court modified the absolute bar upon taxpayers' suits that resulted from the *Frothingham* decision. In the course of its opinion in *Flast* the Court set forth the general conditions required for standing and noted that the *Frothingham* decision did not constitute an absolute bar to taxpayers' suits under all circumstances.

> The jurisdiction of federal courts is defined and limited by Article III of the Constitution. In terms relevant to the question for decision in this case, the judicial power of federal courts is constitutionally restricted to "cases" and "controversies." As is so often the question in constitutional adjudication, those two words have an iceberg quality, containing beneath their surface simplicity submerged complexities which go to the very heart of our constitutional form of government. Embodied in the words "cases" and "controversies" are two complementary but somehow different limitations. In part those words limit the business of federal courts to questions presented in an adversary context and in a form historically viewed as capable of resolution through the judicial process. And in part those words define the role assigned to the judiciary in a tripartite allocation of power to assure that the federal courts will not intrude into areas committed to the other

branches of the government. Justiciability is the term of art employed to give expression to this dual limitation placed upon federal courts by the case and controversy doctrine.

Justiciability is itself a concept of uncertain means and scope. Its reach is illustrated by the various grounds upon which questions sought to be adjudicated in federal courts have been held not to be justiciable. Thus, no justiciable controversy is presented when the parties seek adjudication of only a political question, when the parties are asking for an advisory opinion, when the question sought to be adjudicated has been mooted by subsequent developments, and when there is no standing to maintain the action. Yet it remains true that "[j]usticiability is . . . not a legal concept with a fixed content or suspectible of scientific verification. Its utilization is the resultant of many subtle pressures. . . ." *Poe* v. *Ullman* . . . As we understand it, the government's position is that the constitutional scheme of separation of powers, and the deference owed by the federal judiciary to the other two branches of government within that scheme, present an absolute bar to taxpayer suits challenging the validity of federal spending programs. The government views such suits as involving no more than the mere disagreement by the taxpayer "with the uses to which tax money is put." According to the government, the resolution of such disagreements is committed to other branches of the federal government and not to the judiciary. Consequently, the government contends that, under no circumstances should standing be conferred on federal taxpayers to challenge a federal taxing or spending program. An analysis of the function served by standing limitations compels a rejection of the government's position.

Standing is an aspect of justiciability and as such the problem of standing is surrounded by the same complexities and vagaries that inhere in justiciability. . . . The "gist of the question of standing" is whether the party seeking relief has "alleged such a personal stake in the outcome of the controversy as to assure that concrete adverseness which sharpens the presentation of issues upon which the Court so largely depends for illumination of difficult constitutional questions." *Baker* v. *Carr*. . . . In other words, when standing is placed in issue in a case, the question is whether the person whose standing is challenged is a proper party to request an adjudication of a particular issue and not whether the issue itself is justiciable. . . .

. . . A taxpayer may or may not have the requisite personal stake in the outcome, depending upon the circumstances of the particular case. Therefore, we find no absolute bar in Article III to suits by federal taxpayers challenging allegedly unconstitutional federal taxing and spending programs.[36]

Having established that taxpayers' suits were not absolutely barred, the Court in *Flast* went on to define the circumstances under which a suit could be brought. The Court held that there must be a "logical nexus" between the status of the taxpayer plaintiff and the character of the legislation being challenged. A taxpayer's suit can only be brought on that basis, said the Court, to challenge an exercise of congressional authority under the taxing and spending clause of Article I, Section 8 of the Constitution. Moreover, such an exercise of congressional authority cannot be challenged by a taxpayer qua taxpayer on the basis that the legislature has acted beyond its general constitutional authority but only on the grounds that it has exceeded its explicit taxing and spending power.

[36]Flast v. Cohen, 392 U.S. 83, 98–101 (1968).

Normally, in order to achieve standing, plaintiffs must demonstrate a unique personal interest in the government action that is being challenged, an interest that is distinguishable from the interests that the general citizenry might possess in the case. One of the reasons that the Court in the *Frothingham* case disallowed taxpayers' suits was the impossibility of proving such a unique personal involvement. Whatever interest is demonstrated by a taxpayer qua taxpayer is the same as every other taxpayer, because it is based upon the payment of taxes into the federal Treasury. *Flast* v. *Cohen* differs from other cases defining standing in that it allows federal taxpayers to demonstrate a personal stake in the outcome of government action without a showing of an interest distinguishable from other taxpayers. Once the logical nexus outlined by the Court is demonstrated, standing is granted.[37]

The easing of requirements to achieve standing in *Flast* v. *Cohen* was modified by the Supreme Court in a series of decisions beginning in 1974. In *U.S.* v. *Richardson*, 418 U.S. 166 (1974), the Court reverted in part to *Frothingham* v. *Mellon*, to support a decision that disallowed standing to sue as a taxpayer to challenge the government action that kept the budget of the Central Intelligence Agency secret. In citing the *Frothingham* decision, the Court stated that it prevented taxpayers from using the court as a forum to air general grievances about government policies and procedures. Nor, said the Court, does *Flast* v. *Cohen* provide a basis for a taxpayer's suit in the absence of the demonstration of a concrete injury suffered by the plaintiff.

In the *Richardson* case the original plaintiff had contended that the secrecy of the CIA budget violated Article I, Section 9 of the Constitution which provides that regular accounts of receipts and expenditures of all public money shall be published from time to time. While the *Richardson* decision modified *Flast* v. *Cohen* as to the requirement of demonstration of concrete injury in order to bring a taxpayer's suit, it supported the other parts of the *Flast* decision requiring the demonstration of a logical nexus between the asserted status and grievance of the taxpayer and the taxing and spending authority of the Constitution in order to achieve standing. The decision was a close one, 5–4, and the dissenting justices (Douglas, Brennan, Stuart, and Marshall) argued vigorously that standing should be granted to the plaintiff Richardson.

In *Schlesinger* v. *Reservists' Committee to Stop the War*, 418 U.S. 208 (1974), announced by the Court on the same day as the *Richardson* case, the majority of six justices again held that in order to bring a suit against the government a citizen must show an interest that is differentiated from the general interest of all citizens, a concrete injury, and a personal stake in the outcome of the case. The plaintiff was an association of present and former members of the Armed Forces Reserve who had organized to challenge the military involvement of the country in the Vietnam War. In this case they challenged the constitutional validity of the membership of congressmen in the military reserve, claiming that it violated the incompatibility clause of Article I, Sec-

---

[37]See Justice Harlan's dissent in Flast v. Cohen for a strong statement that the logical nexus test of the majority does not in any way measure the *personal* interest of the plaintiff in the case.

tion 6, which prohibits members of Congress from "holding any office under the United States." The group claimed that they were injured because congressmen holding positions in the reserve would be subject to undue executive influence and might not faithfully discharge their responsibilities to which all citizens and taxpayers are entitled. The Supreme Court, reversing the decision of the federal district court and court of appeals in the case, held that the plaintiffs did not have standing as taxpayers or citizens, having failed to demonstrate the required logical nexus between their asserted status and the claim which they sought to be adjudicated, nor, as citizens, having proven an interest in the case different from that of the general interest of the community at large. Again strong dissenting opinions were supported by the same justices that dissented in the *Richardson* case.

Continuing its tightening of restrictions on standing, in *Simon* v. *Eastern Kentucky Welfare Rights Organization*, 426 U.S. 26 (1976), the Court denied standing to welfare rights organizations and low income individuals to challenge an Internal Revenue Service policy granting tax exemption to hospitals regardless of whether or not they gave equal treatment to indigent and paying patients. In denying standing the Court asserted that the plaintiffs failed to show an injury to themselves *that would very likely be redressed by a favorable judicial decision.* The need to demonstrate that a decision in favor of the plaintiff would alleviate the grievance in order to achieve standing had been stated in *Warth* v. *Seldin*, 422 U.S. 490 (1975), in a suit attacking a town zoning ordinance.

The fact that the technicalities of the standing requirements have not been finally settled by the Supreme Court is more a reflection of differing political values and contrasting views on the proper role of the courts than of a lack of judicial expertise. The imposition of strict standing requirements gives the Court maximum discretion in the determination of which cases it will hear, and therefore justices favoring judicial self-restraint have advocated a strict approach to the doctrine of standing. Justices supporting a generous approach to the standing doctrine, on the other hand, have tended to see the courts as an important and necessary political power in the tripartite system of government. Powerful economic interests more often than not have little difficulty in achieving standing to sue. Liberalized rules of standing have given access to the courts to noneconomic groups, such as those representing environmental, conservation, and civil rights interests as well as to the powerful economic interests of society. It was the activation of these noneconomic interests in the 1960s and 1970s that generated sufficient political pressure to push the courts into granting concessions on the traditionally strict rules of standing under Article III.

LIMITS TO JUDICIAL REVIEW—POLITICAL CONTROL OVER THE JUDICIARY

Article III gives Congress important powers over the courts and their jurisdiction. Courts inferior to the Supreme Court must be created by Congress.

Moreover, while the Constitution defines the original jurisdiction of the Supreme Court, it leaves to Congress discretion over its appellate jurisdiction by providing that ". . . the Supreme Court shall have appellate jurisdiction both as to law and fact, with such acceptance, and under such regulation as the Congress shall make." The constitutional power of Congress to define the appellate jurisdiction of the Supreme Court by implication extends to the inferior courts as well.

Can Congress use its authority to determine the appellate jurisdiction of federal courts to remove cases involving constitutional issues from judicial review? The answer to this question depends entirely upon the courts and the times, which determine the degree to which judicial self-restraint will be exercised when the courts are confronted with congressional limitations upon their jurisdiction.

Ex Parte McCardle (1869) arose at a time when there were sharp political conflicts between a Congress dominated by radical Republicans and President Andrew Johnson who was about to be impeached. In *Mississippi* v. *Johnson* (1867) the Court had exercised self-restraint in refusing to enjoin the President from enforcing two Reconstruction Acts on the grounds that they were unconstitutional. The Court wanted to avoid a direct confrontation with Congress at all costs, and in this and other cases was easily able to find acceptable legal rationalizations for its position. (See pp. 152–154.) *Ex Parte McCardle* was also an example of judicial self-restraint, in which the Court acquiesced to a congressional limitation upon its jurisdiction that had the effect of denying it the opportunity to review the constitutionality of the Reconstruction Acts.

The events leading to *Ex Parte McCardle* began in 1867, when Congress authorized the federal courts to grant habeas corpus in "all cases where any person may be restrained of his or her liberty, in violation of the Constitution or of any treaty or law of the United States." Before the act the jurisdiction of the Supreme Court over habeas corpus cases was restricted, but the 1867 legislation extended its jurisdiction to any and all habeas corpus cases. A Mississippi newspaper editor, McCardle had been arrested and tried by a military commission in Mississippi under the authority of the first Reconstruction Act and unsuccessfully petitioned for a writ of habeas corpus in the federal circuit court. McCardle claimed that the Reconstruction Acts were unconstitutional, a claim that he intended to press upon the grant of habeas corpus. He appealed the circuit court action to the Supreme Court, and when jurisdiction was granted it was widely believed that the Court would declare the Reconstruction Acts to be unconstitutional. The Supreme Court heard arguments in the case and was proceeding to make its decision when Congress abruptly withdrew the Court's jurisdiction over the case by repealing the appellate jurisdiction over habeas corpus cases that had been granted in the 1867 law and prohibiting jurisdiction of appeals that had already been taken. Would the Court agree to this blatant and politically motivated limitation upon its jurisdiction over a case that it had already heard and was about to decide? The answer came in Chief Justice Chase's opinion in *Ex Parte McCardle*.

Ex Parte McCardle

7 Wallace 506; 19 L. Ed. 264 (1869)

THE CHIEF JUSTICE [CHASE] delivered the opinion of the Court:

. . . The first question necessarily is that of jurisdiction; for, if the Act of March, 1868, takes away the jurisdiction defined by the Act of February, 1867, it is useless, if not improper, to enter into any discussion of other questions.

It is quite true, as was argued by the counsel for the petitioner, that the appellate jurisdiction of this Court is not derived from Acts of Congress. It is, strictly speaking, conferred by the Constitution. But it is conferred "with such exceptions and under such regulations as Congress shall make."

It is unnecessary to consider whether, if Congress had made no exceptions and no regulations, this Court might not have exercised general appellate jurisdiction under rules prescribed by itself. From among the earliest Acts of the first Congress, at its first session, was the Act of September 24th, 1789, to establish the judicial courts of the United States. That Act provided for the organization of this court, and prescribed regulations for the exercise of its jurisdiction.

The source of that jurisdiction, and the limitations of it by the Constitution and by statute, have been on several occasions subjects of consideration here. In the case of *Durousseau* v. *U.S.* [1810]; *Wiscart* v. *Dauchy* [1796], particularly, the whole matter was carefully examined, and the Court held, that while "the appellate powers of this Court are not given by the Judicial Act, but are given by the Constitution," they are, nevertheless, "limited and regulated by that Act, and by such other Acts as have been passed on the subject." The Court said, further, that the Judicial Act was an exercise of the power given by the Constitution to Congress "of making exceptions to the appellate jurisdiction of the Supreme Court."

"They have described affirmatively," said the Court, "its jurisdiction, and this affirmative description has been understood to imply a negation of the exercise of such appellate power as is not comprehended within it."

The principle that the affirmation of appellate jurisdiction implies the negation of all such jurisdiction not affirmed having been thus established, it was an almost necessary consequence that Acts of Congress, providing for the exercise of jurisdiction, should come to be spoken of as Acts granting jurisdiction, and not as Acts making exceptions to the constitutional grant of it.

The exception to appellate jurisdiction in the case before us, however, is not an inference from the affirmation of other appellate jurisdiction. It is made in terms. The provision of the Act of 1867, affirming the appellate jurisdiction of this Court in cases of habeas corpus, is expressly repealed. It is hardly possible to imagine a plainer instance of positive exception.

We are not at liberty to inquire into the motives of the Legislature. We can only examine into its power under the Constitution; and the power to make exceptions to the appellate jurisdiction of this Court is given by express words.

What, then, is the effect of the repealing Act upon the case before us? We cannot doubt as to this. Without jurisdiction the Court cannot proceed at all in any cause. Jurisdiction is power to declare the law, and when it ceases to exist, the only function remaining to the Court is that of announcing the fact and dismissing the cause. And this is not less clear upon authority than upon principle.

Several cases were cited by the counsel for the petitioner in support of the position that jurisdiction of this case is not affected by the repealing Act. But none of them, in our judgment, afford any support to it. . . .

On the other hand, the general rule, supported by the best elementary writers . . . is, that "when an Act of the Legislature is repealed, it must be considered, except as to transactions past and closed, as if it never existed." And the effect of repealing Acts upon suits under Acts repealed, has been determined by the adjudications of this Court. The subject was fully considered in *Norris* v. *Crocker* [1852], and more recently in *Ins. Co.* v. *Ritchie* [1867]. In both of these cases it was held that no judgment could be rendered in a suit after the repeal of the Act under which it was brought and prosecuted.

It is quite clear, therefore, that this Court cannot proceed to pronounce judgment in this case, for it has no longer jurisdiction of the appeal; and judicial duty is not less fitly performed by declining ungranted jurisdiction than in exercising firmly that which the Constitution and the laws confer.

Counsel seem to have supposed, if effect be given to the repealing Act in question, that the whole appellate power of the Court, in cases of habeas corpus, is denied. But this is in error. The Act of 1868 does not except from that jurisdiction any cases but appeals from circuit courts under the Act of 1867. It does not affect the jurisdiction which was previously exercised. . . .

The appeal of the petitioner in this case must be dismissed for want of jurisdiction.

In the *McCardle* case the Court rather lamely did review one aspect of the constitutional authority of Congress to limit its jurisdiction and found that Article III justified the action that Congress had taken. But on theoretical grounds, the Court could have as easily refused to acquiesce in the restriction on its jurisdiction. In *United States* v. *Klein*, 13 Wall. 128 (1872), the Court refused to allow Congress to withdraw jurisdiction from the Court of Claims and the Supreme Court on appeal over certain cases concerning indemnification for property taxes during the Civil War. The Court had previously ruled that indemnification could result where amnesty had been granted by the President. The Supreme Court failed to follow the precedent of *Ex Parte McCardle* when it refused to apply the statute to Klein, whom the Court of Claims had awarded indemnification on the basis of a grant of amnesty. The Court held that the action of Congress was an unconstitutional invasion of its powers under Article III as it attempted to dictate a judicial decision in a pending case.

The judicial self-restraint exercised in such Civil War cases as *Ex Parte McCardle* and *Mississippi* v. *Johnson* can be presumed at least in part to be based upon the wariness of the Supreme Court to enter into a field in which it would be in unequal combat with Congress. Judicial self-restraint in reviewing congressional restrictions upon jurisdiction has also been due to a recognition by the courts of the need for administrative efficiency during times of crisis, as occurred during World War II.

For example, in *Yakus* v. *United States*, 321 U.S. 414 (1944), one of the issues confronting the Court was a section of the Emergency Price Control Act of 1942 that restricted the right of individuals to challenge price control regulations to actions before a special emergency court of appeals, subject to review by the Supreme Court. Persons charged with price violations and subjected to criminal prosecution could not challenge those regulations as part of their defense in their federal court trials. The full procedure required to challenge the regulations was first a protest before the administrator, whose determination would then be reviewed on complaints to the Emergency Court of Appeals and finally on certiorari by the Supreme Court. This general limitation upon equity jurisdiction was upheld in *Lockerty* v. *Phillips*, 319 U.S. 182 (1944).

Citing the *Lockerty* case in *Yakus*, the Court stated: "We held that these provisions conferred on the Emergency Court of Appeals, subject to review by this Court, exclusive equity jurisdiction to restrain enforcement of price regulations of the administrator, and that they withdrew such jurisdiction from all other courts. This was accomplished by the exercise of the constitutional power of Congress to prescribe the jurisdiction of inferior federal courts, and the jurisdiction of all state courts to determine federal questions, and to vest that jurisdiction in a single court, the Emergency Court of Appeals."[38] The Court continued: "The considerations which led us to that conclusion with respect to the equity jurisdiction of the district court, lead to the like conclusion as to its power to consider the validity of a price regulation as a defense to a criminal prosecution for its violation."[39] Against the claim that the procedure denied defendants in criminal prosecutions due process of law guaranteed by the Fifth Amendment, the Court held that Congress had not exceeded its constitutional authority in giving exclusive jurisdiction to the Emergency Court of Appeals and the Supreme Court. The procedures Congress had established to enable individuals to challenge price regulations were entirely adequate, said the Court. Moreover, the wartime crisis, the possibility of price inflation should the regulations be halted by constant court challenges, and administrative exigencies dictated a decision on balance in favor of Congress.

The crisis of World War II did not always produce judicial deference to restrictions upon court jurisdiction for purposes of administrative efficiency. The Selective Training and Service Act of 1940 provided that individuals could not challenge their classification in court before they were inducted. (They could challenge their classifications administratively before their Draft Boards and Presidential Appeal Boards.) The act thus precluded preinduction judicial review of the classification of registrants. Challenges to classification could only be raised as a defense in a criminal prosecution for failing to report for induction, or in a habeas corpus proceeding after induction. The classification actions of local boards were, by express statutory language, made final and were not subject to judicial review. The purpose of the statute was clear—to enable the Selective Service System to develop an efficient machine for inducting young men into the service. Constant

[38]Yakus v. United States, 321 U.S. 414, 429 (1944).
[39]Ibid.

challenges of classifications in the courts would presumably have impeded efficient administration of the Selective Service law.

The finality provision of the Selective Service Act was challenged in several cases. In *Falbo* v. *United States*, 320 U.S. 549 (1944), the Court upheld the statute with the statement that "Even if there were, as the petitioner argues, a constitutional requirement that judicial review must be available to test the validity of the decision of the local board, it is certain that Congress was not required to provide for judicial intervention before final acceptance of an individual for national service."[40] In *Estep* v. *United States*, 327 U.S. 114 (1946), Estep reported for induction but refused to enter the armed services. He was criminally indicted, and the question arose whether or not he could raise the defense of illegality of his classification in a criminal proceeding for refusal to submit to induction, given the fact that the law provided that only after induction could such a defense be made in a habeas corpus proceeding. The Court allowed the defense, stating: "We cannot believe that Congress intended that criminal sanctions were to be applied to orders issued by local boards no matter how flagrantly they violated the rules and regulations which define their jurisdiction. We are dealing here with a question of personal liberty."[41] Frankfurter, while voting with the majority for special reasons, nevertheless dissented from the opinion along with Justices Burton and Stone. Frankfurter argued that the language of the statute was clear, that Congress had the authority to prevent judicial review of draft board decisions regarding classification, that the decision of the majority "disrupts a whole scheme of legislation," and "Congress deemed it imperative to secure a vast citizen army with the utmost expedition."[42]

The majority in the *Estep* case was less concerned with the efficient gathering of a vast citizen army than with the protection of personal liberty. Where there is an overriding constitutional issue, the Court implied, statutory provisions for finality of administrative action will not be strictly upheld by the Court. As the Court explained,

> The provision making the decisions of local boards "final" means to us that Congress chose not to give administrative action under this Act the customary scope of judicial review which obtained under other statutes. It means that the courts are not to weigh the evidence to determine whether the classification made by the local boards was justified. The decisions of the local boards made in conformity with the regulations are final even though they may be erroneous. The question of jurisdiction of the local board is reached only if there is no basis in fact for the classification which it gave the registry.[43]

The implication of the *Estep* decision was that if a local board acted beyond its authority, its decision would be reviewable in court. But such action was defined very narrowly, as being action that has "no basis in fact." The majority opinion in the *Estep* case can be interpreted as giving great deference

[40]Falbo v. United States, 320 U.S. 549, 554 (1944).
[41]Estep v. United States, 327 U.S. 114, (1946).
[42]Ibid., pp. 137, 141.
[43]327, U.S. 114 at 122–123 (1946).

to both the authority of Congress to restrict the jurisdiction of the courts and the presumed expertise of administrative agencies.

Controversy over the finality clause in the Selective Service Act was raised once again during the Vietnam War. In *Wolff* v. *Selective Service Local Board No. 16* (1967), two New York Selective Service Boards, at the request of the New York City Director of Selective Service, reclassified two University of Michigan students for their demonstration to protest the Vietnam War at the offices of the Selective Service Local Board in Ann Arbor, Michigan, in October of 1965. The district court held that it did not have jurisdiction because of the legislative preclusion of judicial review, but on appeal the circuit court held that the action of the Selective Service System threatened constitutional rights. The court declared that "The threat to first amendment rights is of such immediate and irreparable consequence not simply to these students but to others as to require prompt action by the court to avoid an erosion of these precious constitutional rights."[44] Holding that the Selective Service Boards acted beyond their authority in reclassifying the students for their political demonstration, the circuit court in the *Wolff* case reversed the lower court's decision. The court found that although the Selective Service Act provided explicitly that the classification decisions of local boards shall be final, subject only to review within the Selective Service System, and challengeable only in criminal proceedings for failure to report to induction or in habeas corpus proceedings after induction, the finality clause applies only where the boards have acted within their legal jurisdiction. When boards act beyond their jurisdiction the courts can intervene even before administrative remedies have been exhausted. The exhaustion of administrative remedies is commonly required before the courts will exercise judicial review.

Congressional response to the *Wolff* case was swift and straightforward. Congress passed a new law that provided

> No judicial review shall be made of the classification or processing of any registrant by local boards, appeal boards, or the President, except as a defense to a criminal prosecution instituted under Section 12 of this title *after* the registrant has responded either affirmatively or negatively to an order to report for induction, or for civilian work in the case of a registrant determined to be opposed to participation in war in any form.[45]

The new statutory language made the intent of Congress clear. In recommending the amendment to the Selective Service Law, the Armed Services Committee of the House of Representatives stated that

> The committee was disturbed by the apparent inclination of some courts to review the classification action of local or appeal boards before the registrant had exhausted his administrative remedies. Existing law quite clearly precludes such a judicial review until after a registrant has been ordered to report for induction. . . . In view of this inclination of the courts to prematurely inquire into

---

[44] Wolff v. Selective Service Local Board No. 16, 372 F. 2d 817, 820 (1967).
[45] 50 U.S.C. Sect. 460 (B) (3). 81 Stat. 100, Sect. 10 (b) (C) (1967). Emphasis supplied.

the classification action of local boards, the committee has rewritten this provision of the law so as to more clearly enunciate this principle. The committee was prompted to take this action since continued disregard of this principle of the law by various courts could seriously affect the administration of the Selective Service System.[46]

How would the courts respond to this new law that so clearly precluded judicial review of Selective Service classifications before an order for induction? The issue was immediately raised in *Oestereich* v. *Selective Service System Local Board No. 11* (1968), which involved the reclassification of a theological school student from 4D, which granted exemption, to 1A, which made him immediately available for induction. Oestereich had returned his registration certificate to the government to express his dissent from its participation in the Vietnam War. It was in response to this action that his local board changed his classification from 4D to 1A. After his administrative appeal failed, he was ordered to report for induction and at that point he attempted to restrain his induction by a suit in a district court. The law clearly stated that there should be no judicial review of a registrant's classification at this stage but only as part of his defense in a criminal prosecution (which was not the case here). In reasoning similar to that used by the circuit court in the *Wolff* case, Justice Douglas, writing for the Supreme Court in *Oestereich*, held that the board's action was reviewable because it was fundamentally lawless. The board had acted ultra vires when it changed Oestereich's exempt classification (to which he was clearly entitled under the law as a student preparing for the ministry) to 1A because it considered his actions to constitute "delinquency" under the law. "Once a person registers and qualifies for a statutory exemption," wrote Douglas, "we find no legislative authority to deprive him of that exemption because of conduct or activities unrelated to the merits of granting or continuing that exemption."[47] Douglas continued: "We deal with conduct of a local board that is basically lawless. . . . To hold that a person deprived of his statutory exemption in such a blatantly lawless manner must either be inducted and raise his protest through habeas corpus or defy induction and defend his refusal in a criminal prosecution is to construe the act with unnecessary harshness."[48]

The *Wolff* and *Oestereich* cases illustrate that where there is a judicial will there is a way to overcome congressional limits on jurisdiction. But these cases indicated that the courts were not about to nullify congressional intent regarding judicial review except under the most extraordinary circumstances involving actions by local boards that were clearly beyond their statutory or constitutional authority. In *Clark* v. *Gabriel* (1968), decided the same day as the *Oestereich* case, the Court declined to allow judicial review of a local board classification that, while it might have been erroneous, did not violate any constitutional or statutory standard and was made after due deliberation by the board. In the *Clark* case the Court stated: "There is no doubt of

[46]H.R. Rept. No. 267, "Military Selective Service Act of 1967," 90th Congress, 1st session, pp. 30–31 (1967).
[47]Oestereich v. Selective Service System Local Board No. 11, 393 U.S. 233, 234 (1968).
[48]Ibid.

the board's statutory authority to take action which appellee challenges, and that action unmistakably involves a determination of facts and an exercise of judgment."[49] The Court continued: "A local board must make such a decision in respect of each of the many classifications and claims presented to it. To allow preinduction judicial review of such determinations would be to permit precisely the kind of 'litigious interruptions of procedures to provide necessary military manpower' . . . which Congress sought to prevent when it enacted Section 10 (B) (3) [precluding preinduction judicial review]."[50] Justice Douglas wrote a concurring opinion in the *Clark* case, noting that "in my view it takes the extreme case where the board can be said to flout the law as it did in *Oestereich* v. *Selective Service* to give preinduction review of its actions. . . ."[51]

The foregoing examples are not the only ones involving congressional restrictions of court jurisdiction, but they serve to illustrate the nature of judicial reaction to such congressional action. Where a case involves important constitutional questions on which a majority of the Court feels a ruling should be made, no congressional restrictions upon jurisdiction will prevent the Court from exercising judicial review.

THE DOCTRINE OF POLITICAL QUESTIONS

The Supreme Court has generally denied standing to parties involved in cases that are "political" in character. *Luther* v. *Borden* is a classic example of judicial self-restraint by the Supreme Court in the area of "political questions." But the political question involved in *Luther* v. *Borden* was no simple one, as it concerned broad and important issues of the right to self-government, methods of political change, standards of governmental legitimacy, and ultimately the question of which state and national bodies were the proper ones to resolve political conflict. The case of *Luther* v. *Borden* is a giant among the political question cases that have confronted the Supreme Court since the beginning of the Republic.

The events leading up to *Luther* v. *Borden* involved the State of Rhode Island in political turmoil and the rebellion of a faction headed by Thomas W. Dorr. This faction, as the result of political meetings and conventions in Newport and Providence, had written and adopted a new constitution for the state that had been submitted and approved by a majority of the voters over twenty-one who had resided in the state for one year and in the town where they voted for six months. These electoral requirements of the Dorr faction vastly enlarged the franchise in Rhode Island which had been severely restricted by the original charter government.

Confronted with a virtual insurrection led by Thomas Dorr, who was elected governor under the new constitution, the charter government declared martial law in the state, under which Borden, acting in the name of

---

[49]Clark v. Gabriel, 393 U.S. 256 (1968).
[50]Ibid.
[51]Ibid.

the state, broke into Luther's house and arrested him as an agent of the insurrectionists. Luther sued, claiming trespass. Some of the flavor of the actual event can be gotten from the record of the proceedings. The governor's proclamation of martial law warned

> . . . all persons against any intercourse or connection with the traitor, Thomas Wilson Dorr, or his deluded adherents, now assembled in arms and against the laws and authorities of this state, and admonish and command the said Thomas Wilson Dorr and his adherents immediately to throw down their arms and disperse, that peace and order may be restored to our suffering community, and as they will answer the contrary at their peril. Further, I exhort the good people of this state to aid and support by example, and by arms, the civil and military authorities thereof, in pursuing and bringing to condign punishment all engaged in said unholy and criminal enterprise against the peace and dignity of the state.[52]

The action taken against Martin Luther by Luther M. Borden under the governor's proclamation of martial law is described in the records submitted by the defendant Borden in a lively fashion.

> . . . [A]t the time when the trespasses mentioned and set forth in the plaintiff's said declaration are alleged to have been committed, and at divers[e] other times before that time, the plaintiff was aiding and abetting the aforesaid traitorous, malicious, and unlawful purposes and designs of overthrowing the government of said state by rebelling in a military force, and in making war upon said State, and upon the government and citizens thereof. . . .
> . . . John T. Child, on the 25th day of June, A.D. 1842, was duly commissioned and sworn as a quartermaster of the 4th Regiment of the 1st brigade of militia of Rhode Island, and continued to exercise such command until after the time when the trespasses mentioned in the plaintiff's declaration are alleged to have been committed; . . . on the 27th day of June, A.D. 1842, the said John T. Child received written orders from Thomas G. Turner, Esq., Lieutenant Colonel commanding said regiment, and duly commissioned and sworn, "To continue to keep a strong armed guard, night and day, in the said Warren, and to arrest every person, either citizens of Warren or otherwise, whose movements were in the least degree suspicious, or who expressed the least willingness to assist the insurgents who were in arms against the law and authorities of the state."
> . . . [T]hese defendants were ordered, by the said John T. Child, their commander as aforesaid, to arrest and take the said Martin Luther, and, if necessary for the purpose of arresting said Luther, these defendants were ordered to break into the dwelling house of said Luther.
> . . . [T]hese defendants, in compliance with said orders, and for the purpose of arresting and taking said Luther, proceeded to his house and knocked at the door, and, not being able to obtain admission therein, forced the latch of the door of said house, and entered the same for the purpose of making said arrest, doing as little damage as possible.
> . . . [A]t the time these defendants were ordered to arrest the said Martin Luther, as before stated, the town of Warren was in danger of attack from the said Martin Luther and his confederates, and the inhabitants of said town were in great alarm on account thereof.[53]

[52]7 Howard 1, 9 (1849).
[53]Ibid., p. 10

In 1844 Thomas Dorr was convicted and imprisoned for treason. Dorr's rebellion had received considerable support from state Democratic, or, as they were called, Locofoco, parties outside of Rhode Island, and the issue of the legitimacy of his cause became a party issue.[54] The original action for trespass was filed by Martin Luther in the Federal Circuit Court for the District of Rhode Island, which acted as the trial court of original jurisdiction. The case was heard before a jury, and the circuit court guaranteed a verdict in favor of the defendant Borden by refusing to admit before the court the evidence submitted by the plaintiff concerning the legitimacy of the Dorr government, and further instructed the jury that, on the basis of the facts presented, the actions of the defendants were legally justified.

A verdict in favor of the defendants before the circuit court was appealed on a writ of error to the Supreme Court, before which Daniel Webster and John Whipple of Rhode Island argued the case for the defendants, the plaintiffs being represented by Robert J. Walker of Mississippi and Benjamin F. Hallett of Massachusetts.

Robert J. Walker and Benjamin F. Hallett for the plaintiff:
... [B]y the fundamental principles of government and of sovereignty of the people acknowledged and acted upon in the United States, and the federal states thereof, at least ever since the Declaration of Independence in 1776, the Constitution and frame of government prepared, adopted, and established [by Thomas Dorr in Rhode Island] ... was, and became thereby, the supreme fundamental law of the State of Rhode Island, and was in full force and effect, as such, when the trespass alleged in the plaintiff's writ was committed by the defendants.
... [T]his conclusion also follows from one of the foregoing fundamental principles of the American system of government, which is, that government is instituted by the people, and for the benefit, protection, and security of the people, nation or community, and that when any government shall be found inadequate or contrary to these purposes, a majority of the community hath an indubitable, inalienable, and indefeasible right to reform, alter, or abolish the same, in such manner as shall be judged most conducive to the public weal ...

1st the [original Rhode Island] charter government was, ipso facto, dissolved by the adoption of the People's Constitution, and by the organization and proceedings of the new government under the same.

2d. Consequently, the Act of March 1842, "in relation to offences against the sovereign power of the state," and the act "declaring martial law" passed June 24, 1842, were both void.

3d. The act of June 1842, being void, affords no justification of the acts complained of in the plaintiff's declaration.

4th. Those acts by the common law, amount to trespass, the facts being admitted by the defendant.[55]

Mr. Daniel Webster for the defendants:
... The Constitution recognizes the existence of states, and guarantees to each the republican form of government, and to protect them against domestic violence. The thing which is to be protected is the existing state government. This is clear by referring to the act of Congress of 1795. In case of an insurrection

---

[54]Warren, *The Supreme Court*, 2:460–469.
[55]7 Howard 1, 19–21.

against a state, or the government thereof, the President is to interfere. The Constitution proceeds upon the idea that each state will take care to establish its own government upon proper principles, and does not contemplate these extraneous and irregular alterations of existing government. . . .

. . . Can this Court, or could the court below, take cognizance of the questions which are raised in the record [by the plaintiff]? If not, the proof [offered by the plaintiff] was properly rejected.

The question which the Court was called upon to decide was one of sovereignty. Two legislatures were in existence at the same time. Both could not be legitimate. If legal power had not passed away from the [original Rhode Island] charter government, it could not have gotten to Dorr's. The position taken on the other side is that it had so passed away, and it is attempted to be proved by votes and proceedings of meetings, etc., out of Dorr's. This Court must look elsewhere—to the Constitution and laws, and acts of the government of the United States. How did the President of the United States treat this question? Acting under the Constitution and laws of 1795, he decided that the existing government was the one which he was bound to protect. He took his stand accordingly, and we say that this is obligatory upon this Court, which always follows an executive recognition of a foreign government. The proof offered below, and rejected by the Court, would have led to a different result. Its object was to show that the Dorr constitution was adopted by a majority of the people. But how could a court judge of this? How can it know how many persons were present, how many of them qualified voters, and all this to be proved by testimony? . . .

[Even] [i]f the court below had admitted the evidence offered by the other side, and the facts which they alleged had been established by proof, still they would not have afforded any ground of justification. . . .

It has been before stated that the government of Mr. Dorr, if it ever existed at all, only lasted for two days. Even the French Revolution, rapid as it was, required three. . . . The government was nothing but a shadow. It was all paper and patriotism; and went out on the 4th of May, admitting itself to be, what everyone must now consider it, nothing but a contemptible sham.[56]

Luther v. Borden

7 Howard 1; 12 L. Ed. 581 (1849)

MR. CHIEF JUSTICE TANEY delivered the opinion of the Court:

. . . Certainly, the question which the plaintiff proposed to raise by the testimony he offered has not heretofore been recognized as a judicial one in any of the State courts. . . .

Moreover, the Constitution of the United States, as far as it has provided for an emergency of this kind, and authorized the general government to interfere in the domestic concerns of a State, has treated the subject as political in its nature, and placed the power in the hands of that department.

The fourth section of the fourth article of the Constitution of the United States provides that the United States shall guarantee to every State in the Union a republican form of government, and shall protect each of them against invasion; and on the application of the Legislature or of

[56]Ibid., pp. 32–34.

the executive (when the Legislature cannot be convened) against domestic violence.

Under this article of the Constitution it rests with Congress to decide what government is the established one in a State. For as the United States guarantee to each State a republican government, Congress must necessarily decide what government is established in the State before it can determine whether it is republican or not. And when the senators and representatives of a State are admitted into the councils of the Union, the authority of the government under which they are appointed, as well as its republican character, is recognized by the proper constitutional authority. And its decision is binding on every other department of the government, and could not be questioned in a judicial tribunal. It is true that the contest in this case did not last long enough to bring the matter to this issue; and as no senators or representatives were elected under the authority of the government of which Mr. Dorr was the head, Congress was not called upon to decide the controversy. Yet the right to decide is placed there, and not in the courts.

So, too, as relates to the clause in the above mentioned article of the Constitution providing for cases of domestic violence.

It rested with Congress, too, to determine upon the means proper to be adopted to fulfill this guarantee. They might, if they had deemed it most advisable to do so, have placed it in the power of a court to decide when a contingency had happened which required the federal government to interfere. But Congress thought otherwise, and no doubt wisely; and by the Act of February 28, 1795, provided, that, "in case of an insurrection in any State against the government thereof it shall be lawful for the President of the United States, on application of the Legislature of such State or of the executive (when the Legislature cannot be convened), to call forth such number of the militia of any other State or States, as may be applied for, as he may judge sufficient to suppress such insurrection."

By this act, the power of deciding whether the exigency had arisen upon which the government of the United States is bound to interfere, is given to the President. He is to act upon the application of the Legislature or of the executive, and consequently he must determine what body of men constitute the Legislature, and who is the governor, before he can act. The fact that both parties claim the right to the government cannot alter the case, for both cannot be entitled to it. If there is an armed conflict, like the one of which we are speaking, it is a case of domestic violence, and one of the parties must be in insurrection against the lawful government. And the President must, of necessity, decide which is the government, and which party is unlawfully arrayed against it, before he can perform the duty imposed upon him by the act of Congress.

After the President has acted and called out the militia, is a circuit court of the United States authorized to inquire whether his decision was right? Could the court, while the parties were actually contending in arms for the possession of the government, call witnesses before it and inquire which party represented a majority of the people? If it could, then it would become the duty of the court (provided it came to the conclusion that the President had decided incorrectly) to discharge those who were arrested or detained by the troops in the service of the United States or the government, which the President was endeavoring to maintain. If the judicial power extends so far, the guarantee contained in the Constitution of the United States is a guarantee of anarchy, and not of order. Yet if this right does not reside in the courts when the conflict is raging, if the judicial power is at that time bound to follow the decision of the political, it must be equally bound when the contest is over. It cannot, when peace is restored, punish as offenses and crimes the acts which it before recognized, and was bound to recognize, as lawful.

It is true that in this case the militia were not called out by the President. But upon the application of the governor under the charter government, the President recognized him as the executive power of the State, and took measures to call out the milita to support his authority if it should be found necessary for the general government to intefere; and it is admitted in the argument, that it was the knowledge of this decision that put an end to the armed opposition to the charter government, and prevented any further efforts to establish by force the proposed constitution. The interference of the President, therefore, by announcing his determination, was as effectual as if the militia had been assembled under his orders. And it should be equally authoritative. For certainly no court of the United States, with a knowledge of this decision, would have been justified in recognizing the opposing party as the lawful government; or in treating as wrong-doers or insurgents the officers of the government which the President had recognized, and was prepared to support by an armed force. In the case of foreign nations, the government acknowledged by the President is always recognized in the courts of justice. And this principle has been applied by the act of Congress to the sovereign States of the Union.

It is said that this power in the President is dangerous to liberty, and may be abused. All power may be abused if placed in unworthy hands. But it would be difficult, we think, to point out any other hands in which this power would be more safe, and at the same time equally effectual. When citizens of the same state are in arms against each other, and the constitued authorities unable to execute the laws, the interposition of the United States must be prompt, or it is of little value. The ordinary course of proceedings in courts of justice would be utterly unfit for the crisis. And the elevated office of the President, chosen as he is by the people of the United States, and the high responsibility he could not fail to feel when acting in a case of so much moment, appear to furnish as strong safeguards against a willful abuse of power as human prudence and foresight could well provide. At all events, it is conferred upon him by the Constitution and laws of the United States, and must therefore be respected and enforced in its judicial tribunals. . . .

Undoubtedly, if the President in exercising this power shall fall into error, or invade the rights of the people of the State, it would be in the power of Congress to apply the proper remedy. But the courts must administer the law as they find it. . . .

Much of the argument on the part of the plaintiff turned upon political rights and political questions, upon which the Court has been urged to express an opinion. We decline doing so. The high power has been conferred on this Court of passing judgment upon the acts of the State sovereignties, and of the legislative and executive branches of the federal government, and of determining whether they are beyond the limits of power marked out for them respectively by the Constitution of the United States. This tribunal, therefore, should be the last to overstep the boundaries which limit its own jurisdiction. And while it should always be ready to meet any questions confided to it by the Constitution, it is equally its duty not to pass beyond its appropriate sphere of action, and to take care not to involve itself in discussions which properly belong to other forums. No one, we believe, has ever doubted the proposition, that, according to the institutions of this country, the sovereignty in every State resides in the people of the State, and that they may alter and change their form of government at their own pleasure. But whether they have changed it or not by abolishing an old government, and establishing a new one in its place, is a question to be settled by the political power. And when that power has decided, the courts are bound to take notice of its decision, and to follow it.

The judgment of the Circuit Court must therefore be affirmed.

Aftermath of *Luther* v. *Borden*

Taney's decision in *Luther* v. *Borden* was masterful, an exercise of judicial self-restraint that appeared to both sides in the case to remove the High Court from partisan battle, particularly because a majority of the Court had been appointed from the Locofoco (Democratic) party, and therefore there was a widespread presumption of sympathy on the part of those judges with the Dorr faction in Rhode Island. In commenting upon Taney's decision, Charles Warren says that "The Court removed itself from the realm of purely political subjects, and proved its determination to withstand appeals to any partisan views which it might be supposed to hold. The fact that both political parties professed to be satisfied with the decision was a singular feature of this disposition of the case."[57] The issues involved in *Luther* v. *Borden* were not necessarily more political on the surface than those involved in later cases in which the Court refused jurisdiction on the basis of the doctrine of political questions. They were more sharply *partisan*, however, in terms of the division among political parties than such political issues as electoral reapportionment faced by the Supreme Court more than a hundred years after *Luther* v. *Borden*.

The guaranty clause of Article IV, Section 4 of the Constitution provides that "the United States shall guarantee to every state in this union a republican form of government, and shall protect each of them against invasion; and on application of the legislature, or of the executive (when the legislature cannot be convened) against domestic violence." This constitutional provision was used in the decision of Chief Justice Taney to justify judicial self-restraint in the case. Taney found that under the guaranty clause it was the responsibility of Congress to determine conflicting claims to legitimate representation of the people in individual states, both in state governments and in representation in Congress. And, Taney argued, it is up to Congress to determine the means to guarantee republican governments and protection against domestic violence in the states. By the Act of 1795 Congress had provided that the President would have the authority, on application of the legislature or executive of a standing state government, to call up the militia

---

[57]Warren, *The Supreme Court*, 2:467.

of the state to protect against domestic violence. It is not the proper responsibility of the courts to review congressional or executive actions under the guaranty clause.

POLITICAL QUESTIONS REDEFINED

Until 1962 the Court had adopted a posture of self-restraint concerning the important political question of electoral reapportionment. In the historic case of *Baker* v. *Carr* the Supreme Court for the first time required the federal district courts to accept jurisdiction over the matter of electoral reapportionment in the states. In doing this the Court implemented what in effect had been the opinion, but not the actual decision, of a majority of the justices in the 1946 case of *Colegrove* v. *Green.* In the *Colegrove* case Justice Frankfurter wrote a *minority* opinion in support of a decision that was concurred in by Justice Rutledge on other grounds. Of the eight justices sitting at the time, Justice Jackson did not participate in the case, which ended up as a 4–3 decision in favor of refusal of acceptance of jurisdiction over a suit challenging the apportionment of *congressional* districts in Illinois. Because the suit had come at a time directly preceding the Illinois congressional elections of 1946, Justice Rutledge felt that the Court should exercise judicial self-restraint on practical grounds, namely that if there was judicial intervention the elections would be thrown into chaos because in effect their legitimacy would be questioned if they were undertaken under the conditions challenged in the suit. Moreover, the short time period remaining before the elections would not enable judicial relief to be fashioned effectively for the plaintiffs in *Colegrove* should the Court decide in their favor. But Justice Rutledge did feel that the constitutional claims under the equal protection clause of the Fourteenth Amendment and Article I, Section 2, requiring Congress to apportion representatives among the states according to population, were justiciable.

Thus a majority of the Court in *Colegrove* v. *Green* essentially held the matter of electoral reapportionment in reference to congressional districts to be within the jurisdiction of federal courts. The constitutional challenge in *Colegrove* v. *Green* and *Baker* v. *Carr* was not based upon the guaranty clause, and hence (Justice Frankfurter to the contrary notwithstanding) *Luther* v. *Borden* could not properly be used as a precedent to decline judicial intervention. Clearly, in the generic sense, the issue of electoral reapportionment was of course political, as are so many other issues that come before the courts. It was not, however, a nonjusticiable political issue as was that in *Luther* v. *Borden.*

It is interesting that sixteen years elapsed between the *Colegrove* decision in 1946 and *Baker* v. *Carr* in 1962. If the *Colegrove* decision had been properly understood it would seem likely that a subsequent challenge both to the apportionment of congressional and state electoral districts by the state legislatures would have ensued. However, it was clear that the *Colegrove* decision was in fact widely interpreted as supporting judicial self-restraint in the matter of electoral reapportionment.[58] Nowhere was this more clearly revealed than in the immediate dismissal of the suit in *Baker* v. *Carr* by the federal district court, on the basis of Justice Frankfurter's minority opinion in *Colegrove*. In that opinion Frankfurter noted,

> We are of opinion that the petitioners ask of this Court what is beyond its competence to grant. This is one of those demands on judicial power which cannot be met by verbal fencing about "jurisdiction." It must be resolved by considerations on the basis of which this Court, from time to time, has refused to intervene in controversies. It has refused to do so because due regard for the effective working of our government revealed this issue to be of a particularly political nature and therefore not meet for judicial determination. . . .
>
> The appellants urge with great zeal that the conditions of which they complain are grave evils and offend public power to provide against these evils. But due regard for the Constitution as a viable system precludes judicial correction. Authority for dealing with such problems resides elsewhere. . . . The short of it is that the Constitution has conferred upon Congress [in Article I, Section 4] exclusive authority to secure fair representation by the states in the popular house and left to that house determination whether states have fulfilled their responsibility. . . .
>
> To sustain this action would cut very deep into the very being of Congress. Courts ought not to enter this political thicket. The remedy for unfairness in districting is to secure state legislatures that will apportion properly, or to invoke the ample powers of Congress. The Constitution has many commands that are ample powers of Congress. The Constitution has many commands that are not enforceable by courts because they clearly fall outside the conditions and purposes that circumscribe judicial action. . . .[59]

The plaintiffs in *Baker* v. *Carr* were qualified voters for members of the Tennessee legislature who brought a class action to restrain state officials from conducting further elections under the Tennessee Apportionment Act of 1901, the provisions of which had resulted in gross malapportionment of state legislative districts due to population shifts over the years. After the three-judge district court (required for the consideration of constitutional issues) turned down their plea, direct appeal was taken to the United States Supreme Court, which is authorized by statute to accept appeals from the decisions of three-judge district courts. The opinion of Justice Brennan, representing six members of the Court, held that the district court erred in refusing jurisdiction of the subject matter of the case, that the issue was justiciable, and that the plaintiffs had standing as voters of Tennessee to sue the government of the state. Although the majority of the Court did not in fact claim that the equal protection clause had been violated by the Tennessee Apportionment Act, its granting of jurisdiction to the district courts made this determination a foregone conclusion. As a result, the landmark decision of *Baker* v. *Carr* resulted, very gradually, in a reapportionment revolution throughout the fifty states. By the middle 1970s there was equal ap-

[58]See, for example Anthony Lewis, "Legislative Apportionment in the Federal Courts," *Harvard Law Review*, 71 (1958), 1057–1098.

[59]Colegrove v. Green, 328 U.S. 549, 554–556 (1946).

portionment of state legislative districts, and as a result of the post–*Baker* v. *Carr* decisions of *Reynolds* v. *Sims* (1964), and *Wesberry* v. *Sanders* (1964), state senatorial and congressional districts were also reapportioned in accordance with the one person–one vote principle.

BAKER v. CARR

Brief for the Appellants by Hobart Atkins, et al.:

The "political" nature of the right to vote in equality is no bar to its judicial vindication under the precedents of this Court . . . [T]his is not a case in which it can be argued that political judgment or discretion has been conferred upon the legislature to order its conception of balance between representation and voting rights. In this case, the violation of appellants' federal rights to equal protection of the laws is unmistakable and measurable by approximate mathematical standards provided by law.

In this case . . . there is no alternative to judicial assistance if the doors to relief are to be unlocked. . . .

This Court is appellant's last and only hope if appellants' federally assured rights are to be vindicated.

Jurisdiction exists. . . . The Court is not called upon to "remap" the state, or to hurriedly provide relief in the face of an impending election. . . .

Notwithstanding its "political" nature, the measurable right to equality in voting denied in this case is protected by the Fourteenth Amendment.[60]

George F. McCantess, Attorney General of Tennessee, et al., for the Appellees:

The rule is elementary that there must be parties before the court with opposing legal interests. In their absence, the suit must fail for want of justiciability. Here, the appellants, as voters, have interests which are the same as all other Tennessee voters. Special injury is not alleged. . . .

Since the case involves only peculiarly political issues, the district court was without jurisdiction to entertain the action. . . . The issues are wholly political. . . .

The appellants, in the guise of citizens denied the right to vote, asked the court to enforce the republican form of government in the state of Tennessee.

This Court has always held that the enforcement of the guaranty of a republican form of government is not a question properly falling within its jurisdiction [cf. *Luther* v. *Borden*].

Under the constitution of Tennessee, reapportionment is a question solely for the legislature.[61]

Archibald Cox, Solicitor General, et al., Brief for the United States as Amicus Curiae:

Appellants have "standing" to bring this action in the sense of having sufficient personal interest in the relief sought. . . .

The constitutional issue is not a "political question" beyond the power of the federal court to decide.

Appellants assert a gross violation of important rights protected by the Fourteenth Amendment. The constitutional and legal questions arising out of such Fourteenth Amendment rights are not "political" in the sense of being nonjusticiable, merely because elections are involved.[62]

---

[60]Philip P. Kurland and Gerhard Casper (eds.), *Landmark Briefs and Arguments of the Supreme Court of the United States* (Arlington, Va.: University Publications of America, Inc., 1975), Vol. 56, pp. 113–114, 125. The *Landmark Briefs* will hereafter be referred to as LB.

[61]Ibid., pp. 157, 170,172.

[62]Ibid., pp. 298, 301.

Baker v. Carr

369 U.S. 186; 82 S. Ct. 691; 7 L. Ed. 2d 663 (1962)

MR. JUSTICE BRENNAN delivered the opinion of the Court:

This civil action was brought . . . to redress the alleged deprivation of federal constitutional rights. The complaint, alleging that by means of a 1901 statute of Tennessee apportioning the members of the General Assembly among the State's 95 counties, "these plaintiffs and others similarly situated, are denied the equal protection of the laws accorded them by the Fourteenth Amendment to the Constitution of the United States by virtue of the debasement of their votes," was dismissed by a three-judge court. . . . We hold that the dismissal was error, and remand the cause to the District Court for trial and further proceedings consistent with this opinion.

The General Assembly of Tennessee consists of the Senate with 33 members and the House of Representatives with 99 members. . . .

. . . Tennessee's standard for allocating legislative representation among her counties is the total number of qualified voters resident in the respective counties, subject only to minor qualifications. . . . In 1901 the General Assembly abandoned separate enumeration in favor of reliance upon the Federal Census and passed the Apportionment Act here in controversy. In the more than 60 years since that action, all proposals in both Houses of the General Assembly for reapportionment have failed to pass.

Between 1901 and 1961, Tennessee has experienced substantial growth and redistribution of her population. In 1901 the population was 2,020,616, of whom 487,380 were eligible to vote. The 1960 Federal Census reports the State's population at 3,567,089, of whom 2,092,891 are eligible to vote. The relative standings of the counties in terms of qualified voters have changed significantly. It is primarily the continued application of the 1901 Apportionment Act to this shifted and enlarged voting population which gives rise to the present controversy.

Indeed, the complaint alleges that the 1901 statute, even as of the time of its passage, "made no apportionment of Representatives and Senators in accordance with the constitutional formula . . . , but instead arbitrarily and capriciously apportioned representatives in the Senate and House without reference . . . to any logical or reasonable formula whatever." It is further alleged that "because of the population changes since 1900, and the failure of the Legislature to reapportion itself since 1901," the 1901 statute became "unconstitutional and obsolete." Appellants also argue that, because of the composition of the legislature effected by the 1901 Apportionment Act, redress in the form of a state constitutional amendment to change the entire mechanism for reapportioning, or any other change short of that, is difficult or impossible. The complaint concludes that "these plaintiffs and others similarly situated, are denied the equal protection of the laws accorded them by the Fourteenth Amendment to the Constitution of the United States by virtue of the debasement of their votes." They seek a declaration that the 1901 statute is unconstitutional and an injunction restraining the appellees from acting to conduct any further elections under it. They also pray that unless and until the General Assembly enacts a valid reapportionment, the District Court should either decree a reapportionment by mathematical application of the Tennessee constitutional formulae to the most recent Federal Census figures, or direct the appellees to conduct legislative elections, primary and general, at large. They also pray for such other and further relief as may be appropriate.

<h1 style="text-align:center">I
THE DISTRICT COURT'S OPINION
AND ORDER OF DISMISSAL</h1>

In light of the District Court's treatment of the case, we hold today only (a) that the court possessed jurisdiction of the subject matter; (b) that a justiciable cause of action is stated upon which appellants would be entitled to appropriate relief; and (c) because appellees raise the issue before this Court, that the appellants have standing to challenge the Tennessee apportionment statutes. Beyond noting that we have no cause at this stage to doubt the District Court will be able to fashion relief if violations of constitutional rights are found, it is improper now to consider what remedy would be most appropriate if appellants prevail at the trial.

<h1 style="text-align:center">II
JURISDICTION
OF THE SUBJECT MATTER</h1>

The District Court was uncertain whether our cases withholding federal judicial relief rested upon a lack of federal jurisdiction or upon the inappropriateness of the subject matter for judicial consideration— what we have designated "nonjusticiability." The distinction between the two grounds is significant. In the instance of nonjusticiability, consideration of the cause is not wholly and immediately foreclosed; rather, the Court's inquiry necessarily proceeds to the point of deciding whether the duty asserted can be judicially identified and its breach judicially determined, and whether protection for the right asserted can be judicially molded. In the instance of lack of jurisdiction the cause either does not "arise under" the Federal Constitution, laws or treaties (or fall within one of the other enumerated categories of Art. III, § 2), or is not a "case or controversy" within the meaning of that section; or the cause is not one described by any jurisdictional statute. Our conclusion, *infra*, that this cause presents no nonjusticiable "political question" settles the only possible doubt that it is a case or controversy. Under the present heading of "Jurisdiction of the Subject Matter" we hold only that the matter set forth in the complaint does arise under the Constitution . . . .

Article III, § 2, of the Federal Constitution provides that "The judicial Power shall extend to all Cases, in Law and Equity, arising under this Constitution, the Laws of the United States, and Treaties made, or which shall be made, under their Authority . . . ." It is clear that the cause of action is one which "arises under" the Federal Constitution. The complaint alleges that the 1901 statute effects an apportionment that deprives the appellants of the equal protection of the laws in violation of the Fourteenth Amendment. Dismissal of the complaint upon the ground of lack of jurisdiction of the subject matter would, therefore, be justified only if that claim were "so attenuated and unsubstantial as to be absolutely devoid of merit." . . . Since the District Court obviously and correctly did not deem the asserted federal constitutional claim unsubstantial and frivolous, it should not have dismissed the complaint for want of jurisdiction of the subject matter. And of course no further consideration of the merits of the claim is relevant to a determination of the court's jurisdiction of the subject matter. . . .

An unbroken line of our precedents sustains the federal courts' jurisdiction of the subject matter of federal constitutional claims of this nature. The first cases involved the redistricting of States for the purpose of electing Representatives to the

Federal Congress. When the Ohio Supreme Court sustained Ohio legislation against an attack for repugnancy to Art. I, § 4, of the Federal Constitution, we affirmed on the merits and expressly refused to dismiss for want of jurisdiction "In view . . . of the subject-matter of the controversy and the Federal characteristics which inhere in it . . . ." . . . When the Minnesota Supreme Court affirmed the dismissal of a suit to enjoin the Secretary of State of Minnesota from acting under Minnesota redistricting legislation, we reviewed the constitutional merits of the legislation and reversed the State Supreme Court. . . .

The appellees refer to *Colegrove* v. *Green* as authority that the District Court lacked jurisdiction of the subject matter. Appellees misconceive the holding of that case. The holding was precisely contrary to their reading of it. Seven members of the Court participated in the decision. Unlike many other cases in this field which have assumed without discussion that there was jurisdiction, all three opinions filed in *Colegrove* discussed the question. Two of the opinions expressing the views of four of the Justices, a majority, flatly held that there was jurisdiction of the subject matter. Mr. Justice Black joined by Mr. Justice Douglas and Mr. Justice Murphy stated: "It is my judgment that the District Court had jurisdiction . . . ." Mr. Justice Rutledge, writing separately, expressed agreement with this conclusion. . . .

We hold that the District Court has jurisdiction of the subject matter of the federal constitutional claim asserted in the complaint.

III
STANDING

A federal court cannot "pronounce any statute, either of a State or of the United States, void, because irreconcilable with the Constitution, except as it is called upon to adjudge the legal rights of litigants in actual controversies." . . . Have the appellants alleged such a personal stake in the outcome of the controversy as to assure that concrete adverseness which sharpens the presentation of issues upon which the court so largely depends for illumination of difficult constitutional questions? This is the gist of the question of standing. It is, of course, a question of federal law . . . .

We hold that the appellants do have standing to maintain this suit. Our decisions plainly support this conclusion. Many of the cases have assumed rather than articulated the premise in deciding the merits of similar claims. And *Colegrove* v. *Green* squarely held that voters who allege facts showing disadvantage to themselves as individuals have standing to sue. . . .

These appellants seek relief in order to protect or vindicate an interest of their own, and of those similarly situated. Their constitutional claim is, in substance, that the 1901 statute constitutes arbitrary and capricious state action, offensive to the Fourteenth Amendment in its irrational disregard of the standard of apportionment prescribed by the State's Constitution or of any standard, effecting a gross disproportion of representation to voting population. The injury which appellants assert is that this classification disfavors the voters in the counties in which they reside, placing them in a position of constitutionally unjustifiable inequality *vis-à-vis* voters in irrationally favored counties. A citizen's right to a vote free of arbitrary impairment by state action has been judicially recognized as a right secured by the Constitution, when such impairment resulted from dilution by a false tally, . . . or by a refusal to count votes from arbitrarily selected precincts . . . or by a stuffing of the ballot box. . . .

It would not be necessary to decide whether appellants' allegations of impairment of their votes by the 1901 apportionment will, ultimately, entitle them to any relief, in order to hold that they have standing to seek it. If such impairment does produce a legally cognizable injury, they are among those who have sustained it. They are asserting "a plain, direct and adequate interest in maintaining the effectiveness of their votes," . . . not merely a claim of "the right, possessed by every citizen, to require that the Government be administered according to law. . . ." . . . They are entitled to a hearing and to the District Court's decision on their claims. "The very essence of civil liberty certainly consists in the right of every individual to claim the protection of the laws, whenever he receives an injury." . . .

IV
JUSTICIABILITY

In holding that the subject matter of this suit was not justiciable, the District Court relied on *Colegrove* v. *Green* and subsequent *per curiam* cases. The court stated: "From a review of these decisions there can be no doubt that the federal rule . . . is that the federal courts . . . will not intervene in cases of this type to compel legislative reapportionment." We understand the District Court to have read the cited cases as compelling the conclusion that since the appellants sought to have a legislative apportionment held unconstitutional, their suit presented a "political question" and was therefore nonjusticiable. We hold that this challenge to an apportionment presents no nonjusticiable "political question." The cited cases do not hold the contrary.

Of course the mere fact that the suit seeks protection of a political right does not mean it presents a political question. Such an objection "is little more than a play upon words." . . . Rather, it is argued that apportionment cases, whatever the actual wording of the complaint, can involve no federal constitutional right except one resting on the guaranty of a republican form of government, and that complaints based on that clause have been held to present political questions which are nonjusticiable.

We hold that the claim pleaded here neither rests upon nor implicates the Guaranty Clause and that its justiciability is therefore not foreclosed by our decisions of cases involving that clause. The District Court misinterpreted *Colegrove* v. *Green* and other decisions of this Court on which it relied. Appellants' claim that they are being denied equal protection is justiciable, and if "discrimination is sufficiently shown, the right to relief under the equal protection clause is not diminished by the fact that the discrimination relates to political rights." . . . To show why we reject the argument based on the Guaranty Clause, we must examine the authorities under it. But because there appears to be some uncertainty as to why those cases did present political questions, and specifically as to whether this apportionment case is like those cases, we deem it necessary first to consider the contours of the "political question" doctrine.

Our discussion, even at the price of extending this opinion, requires review of a number of political question cases, in order to expose the attributes of the doctrine—attributes which, in various settings, diverge, combine, appear, and disappear in seeming disorderliness. Since that review is undertaken solely to demonstrate that neither singly nor collectively do these cases support a conclusion that this apportionment case is nonjusticiable, we of course do not explore their implications in other contexts. That review reveals that in the Guaranty Clause cases and in the other "political question" cases, it is the relationship between the judiciary and the coordinate branches of the Federal Government, and not the federal judiciary's relationship to the States, which gives rise to the "political question."

We have said that "In determining whether a question falls within [the political question] category, the appropriateness under our system of government of attributing finality to the action of the political departments and also the lack of satisfactory criteria for a judicial determination are dominant considerations." . . . The nonjusticiability of a political question is primarily a function of the separation of powers. Much confusion results from the capacity of the "political question" label to obscure the need for case-by-case inquiry. Deciding whether a matter has in any measure been committed by the Constitution to another branch of government, or whether the action of that branch exceeds whatever authority has been committed, is itself a delicate exercise in constitutional interpretation, and is a responsibility of this Court as ultimate interpreter of the Constitution. To demonstrate this requires no less than to analyze representative cases and to infer from them the analytical threads that make up the political question doctrine. We shall then show that none of those threads catches this case. . . .

We come, finally, to the ultimate inquiry whether our precedents as to what constitutes a nonjusticiable "political question" bring the case before us under the umbrella of that doctrine. A natural beginning is to note whether any of the common characteristics which we have been able to identify and label descriptively are present. We find none: The question here is the consistency of state action with the Federal Constitution. We have no question decided, or to be decided, by a political branch of government coequal with this Court. Nor do we risk embarrassment of our government abroad, or grave disturbance at home if we take

issue with Tennessee as to the constitutionality of her action here challenged. Nor need the appellants, in order to succeed in this action, ask the Court to enter upon policy determinations for which judicially manageable standards are lacking. Judicial standards under the Equal Protection Clause are well developed and familiar, and it has been open to courts since the enactment of the Fourteenth Amendment to determine, if on the particular facts they must, that a discrimination reflects *no* policy, but simply arbitrary and capricious action. . . .

We conclude that the complaint's allegations of a denial of equal protection present a justiciable constitutional cause of action upon which appellants are entitled to a trial and a decision. The right asserted is within the reach of judicial protection under the Fourteenth Amendment.

The judgment of the District Court is reversed and the cause is remanded for further proceedings consistent with this opinion.

Reversed and remanded.

MR. JUSTICE WHITTAKER did not participate in the decision of this case.

MR. JUSTICE DOUGLAS, concurring:
While I join the opinion of the Court and, like the Court, do not reach the merits, a word of explanation is necessary. I put to one side the problems of "political" questions involving the distribution of power between this Court, the Congress, and the Chief Executive. We have here a phase of the recurring problem of the relation of the federal courts to state agencies. More particularly, the question is the extent to which a State may weight one person's vote more heavily than it does another's. . . .

I agree with my Brother Clark that if the allegations in the complaint can be sustained a case for relief is established. We are told that a single vote in Moore County, Tennessee, is worth 19 votes in Hamilton County, that one vote in Stewart or in Chester County is worth nearly eight times a single vote in Shelby or Knox County. The opportunity to prove that an "invidious discrimination" exists should therefore be given the appellants. . . .

With the exceptions of *Colgrove* v. *Green* [1946], *MacDougall* v. *Green* [1948], *South* v. *Peters* [1950], and the decisions they spawned, the Court has never thought that protection of voting rights was beyond judicial cognizance. Today's treatment of those cases removes the only impediment to judicial cognizance of the claims stated in the present complaint. . . .

MR. JUSTICE CLARK, concurring:

One emerging from the rash of opinions with their accompanying clashing of views may well find himself suffering a mental blindness. The Court holds that the appellants have alleged a cause of action. However, it refuses to award relief here—although the facts are undisputed—and fails to give the District Court any guidance whatever. One dissenting opinion, bursting with words that go through so much and conclude with so little, contemns the majority action as "a massive repudiation of the experience of our whole past." Another describes the complaint as merely asserting conclusory allegations that Tennessee's apportionment is "incorrect," "arbitrary," "obsolete," and "unconstitutional." I believe it can be shown that this case is distinguishable from earlier cases dealing with the distribution of political power by a State, that a patent violation of the Equal Protection Clause of the United States Constitution has been shown, and that an appropriate remedy may be formulated.

I

. . . The widely heralded case of *Colegrove* v. *Green* was one not only in which the Court was bobtailed but in which there was no majority opinion. Indeed, even the "political question" point in Mr. Justice Frankfurter's opinion was no more than an alternative ground. Moreover, the appellants did not present an equal protection argument. While it has served as a Mother Hubbard to most of the subsequent cases, I feel it was in that respect ill-cast and for all of these reasons put it to one side. . . .

II

The controlling facts cannot be disputed. . . . The frequency and magnitude of the inequalities in the present districting admit of no policy whatever . . . it leaves but one conclusion, namely that Tennessee's apportionment is a crazy quilt without rational basis. . . .

The truth is that—although this case has been here for two years and has had over six hours' argument (three times the ordinary case) and has been most carefully considered over and over again by us in Conference and individually—no one, not even the State nor the dissenters, has come up with any rational basis for Tennessee's apportionment statute. . . . Like the District Court, I conclude that appellants have met the burden of showing "Tennessee is guilty of a clear violation of the state constitution and of the [federal] rights of the plaintiffs. . . ."

III

Although I find the Tennessee apportionment statute offends the Equal Protection Clause, I would not consider intervention by this Court into so delicate a field if there were any other relief available to the people of Tennessee. But the majority of the people of Tennessee have no "practical opportunities for exerting their political weight at the polls" to correct the existing "invidious discrimination." Tennessee has no initiative and referendum. I have searched diligently for other "practical opportunities" present under the law. I find none other than through the federal courts. . . .

IV

As John Rutledge (later Chief Justice) said 175 years ago in the course of the Constitutional Convention, a chief function of the Court is to secure the national rights. Its decision today supports the proposition for which our forebears fought and many died, namely, that to be fully conformable to the principle of right, the form of government must be representative. That is the keystone upon which our government was founded and lacking which no republic can survive. It is well for this Court to practice self-restraint and discipline in constitutional adjudication, but never in its history have those principles received sanction where the national rights of so many have been so clearly infringed for so long a time. National respect for the courts is more enhanced through the forthright enforcement of those rights rather than by rendering them nugatory through the interposition of subterfuges. In my view the ultimate decision today is in the greatest tradition of this Court.

MR. JUSTICE STEWART wrote a brief concurring opinion.

MR. JUSTICE FRANKFURTER, whom MR. JUSTICE HARLAN joins, dissenting:

The Court today reverses a uniform course of decision established by a dozen cases, including one by which the very claim now sustained was unanimously rejected only five years ago. The impressive body of rulings thus cast aside reflected the equally uniform course of our political history regarding the relationship between population and legislative representation—a wholly different matter from denial of the franchise to individuals because of race, color, religion or sex. Such a massive repudiation of the experience of our whole past in asserting destructively novel judicial power demands a detailed analysis of the role of this Court in our constitutional scheme. Disregard of inherent limits in the effective exercise of the Court's "judicial Power" not only presages the futility of judicial intervention in the essentially political conflict of forces by which the relation between population and representation has time out of mind been and now is determined. It may well impair the Court's position as the ultimate organ of "the supreme Law of the Land" in that vast range of legal problems, often strongly entangled in popular feeling, on which this Court must pronounce. The Court's authority—possessed of neither the purse nor the sword—ultimately rests on sustained public confidence in its moral sanction. Such feeling must be nourished by the Court's complete detachment, in fact and in appearance, from political entanglements and by abstention from injecting itself into the clash of political forces in political settlements. . . .

The Framers carefully and with deliberate forethought refused so to enthrone the judiciary. In this situation, as in others of like nature, appeal for relief does not belong here. Appeal must be to an informed, civically militant electorate. In a democratic society like ours, relief must come through an aroused popular conscience that sears the conscience of the people's representatives. In any event there is nothing judicially more unseemly nor more self-defeating than for this Court to make *in terrorem* pronouncements, to indulge in merely empty rhetoric, sounding a word of promise to the ear, sure to be disappointing to the hope. . . .

MR. JUSTICE HARLAN wrote a dissenting opinion in which MR. JUSTICE FRANKFURTER joined.

Aftermath of *Baker* v. *Carr*

The decision of the Supreme Court in *Baker* v. *Carr* literally wrought a reapportionment revolution, to be brought about by the district courts that now were mandated to accept jurisdiction over the issue of electoral apportionment. The process was a slow one, however, because, as in the *Brown* case, the Supreme Court in *Baker* v. *Carr* did not give to the district courts specific guidelines to be used in fashioning their orders in reapportionment cases. Moreover, the necessary limitations of the judicial process meant that the decision of the Supreme Court required further adjudication in order to effect an overall judicial policy of reapportionment. Suits had to be brought in each state in the district courts challenging reapportionment statutes of those states before they could be changed. As a result of the *Brown* decision in 1954, the district courts were given discretion as to the timing of desegregation orders in de jure segregation states. In *Baker* v. *Carr* the Court offered less guidance, and the formulas bringing about equal apportionment (one person–one vote) were up to each district court. The result was a great deal of confusion and delays in implementation of reapportionment plans, which in some cases forced at-large elections because of the inability of states to conform to court orders before elections subsequent to them were to take place.

Baker v. *Carr* applied only to the popular bodies of state assemblies. This left hanging the question of whether or not the "upper" bodies of state legislatures could be challenged on the basis of denial of equal protection and the issue of apportionment of congressional districts which at the time of *Baker* v. *Carr* were grossly malapportioned in the plans that had been adopted by state legislatures throughout the country. In *Reynolds* v. *Sims,* 377 U.S. 533 (1964), the Supreme Court ruled that both houses of bicameral state legislatures had to be apportioned on the basis of population and that the one person–one vote rule within certain permissible variations had to be applied. In *Wesberry* v. *Sanders,* 376 U.S. 1 (1964), the Court settled the issue of congressional apportionment that had first been raised in *Colegrove* v. *Green* in 1946. It held that Article I, Section 2 of the Constitution, which requires that representatives be chosen "by the people of the several states," required as far as practicable that one person's vote in a congressional election be equal to another's. The one person–one vote rule was thus extended to congressional elections, and this decision coupled with *Baker* v. *Carr* extended the reapportionment revolution to a vast additional array of electoral districts. Not until a decade after the *Wesberry* and *Reynolds* decisions in

1964 was it possible to say that the states had adopted plans for state and congressional districts that conformed to the one person–one vote rule.

LEGISLATIVE IMMUNITY FROM THE JUDICIAL PROCESS—A POLITICAL QUESTION?

Powell v. *McCormack* (1969) raised the issue of the proper scope of court jurisdiction over the internal affairs of Congress. Article I, Section 5 provides that "Each House shall be the judge of the elections, returns and qualifications of its own members . . . [and] each House may . . . punish its members for disorderly behavior, and, with the concurrence of two-thirds, expel a member." This seems to be a clear constitutional commitment to Congress to determine the qualifications of its members and to expel them by a two-thirds vote.

Powell v. *McCormack* arose from the action taken by the House on March 1, 1967, refusing to seat Adam Clayton Powell, Jr., a black representative who had for many years represented the Harlem section of New York City. The action of the House was not without precedent, as Congress had on several occasions refused to seat members in the past. There had been no court challenges to these congressional actions, and it was generally assumed at the time of the *Powell* case that the courts did not have jurisdiction to limit congressional control of its own members.

Powell v. *McCormack*

395 U.S. 486; 81 S. Ct. 1944; 23 L. Ed. 2d 491 (1969)

MR. CHIEF JUSTICE WARREN delivered the opinion of the Court:

In November 1966, petitioner Adam Clayton Powell, Jr., was duly elected from the 18th Congressional District of New York to serve in the United States House of Representatives for the 90th Congress. However, pursuant to a House resolution, he was not permitted to take his seat. Powell (and some of the voters of his district) then filed suit in Federal District Court, claiming that the House could exclude him only if it found he failed to meet the standing requirements of age, citizenship, and residence contained in Art. I, § 2, of the Constitution—requirements the House specifically found Powell met—and thus had excluded him unconstitutionally. The District Court dismissed petitioners' complaint "for want of jurisdiction of the subject matter." A panel of the Court of Appeals affirmed the dismissal, although on somewhat different grounds, each judge filing a separate opinion. We have determined that it was error to dismiss the complaint and that petitioner Powell is entitled to a declaratory judgment that he was unlawfully excluded from the 90th Congress.

I

FACTS

During the 89th Congress, a Special Subcommittee on Contracts of the Committee on House Administration conducted an investigation into the expenditures of the Committee on Education and Labor, of which petitioner Adam Clayton Powell, Jr., was chairman. The Special Subcommittee issued a report concluding that Powell and certain staff employees had deceived the House authorities as to travel expenses. The report also indicated there was strong evidence that certain illegal salary payments had been made to Powell's wife at his direction. . . . No formal action was taken during the 89th Congress. However, prior to the organization of the 90th Congress, the Democratic members-elect met in caucus and voted to remove Powell as chairman of the Committee on Education and Labor. . . . When the 90th Congress met to organize in January 1967, Powell was asked to step aside while the oath was administered to the other members-elect. Following the administration of the oath to the remaining members, the House discussed the procedure to be followed in determining whether Powell was eligible to take his seat. After some debate, by a vote of 363 to 65 the House adopted House Resolution No. 1, which provided that the Speaker appoint a Select Committee to determine Powell's eligibility. . . . Although the resolution prohibited Powell from taking his seat until the House acted on the Select Committee's report, it did provide that he should receive all the pay and allowances due a member during the period.

The Select Committee, composed of nine lawyer-members, issued an invitation to Powell to testify before the Committee. The invitation letter stated that the scope of the testimony and investigation would include Powell's qualifications as to age, citizenship, and residency; his involvement in a civil suit (in which he had been held in contempt); and "[m]atters of . . . alleged official misconduct since January 3, 1961." See Hearings on HR Res No. 1 before Select Committee Pursuant to HR Res No. 1, 90th Cong, 1st Sess, 5 (1967)

(hereinafter Hearings). Powell appeared at the Committee hearing held on February 8, 1967. After the Committee denied in part Powell's request that certain adversary-type procedures be followed, Powell testified. He would, however, give information relating only to his age, citizenship, and residency; upon the advice of counsel, he refused to answer other questions.

On February 10, 1967, the Select Committee issued another invitation to Powell. In the letter, the Select Committee informed Powell that its responsibility under the House Resolution extended to determining not only whether he met the standing qualifications of Art. I, § 2, but also to "inquir[ing] into the question of whether you should be punished or expelled pursuant to the powers granted . . . the House under Article I, Section 5, . . . of the Constitution. In other words, the Select Committee is of the opinion that at the conclusion of the present inquiry, it has authority to report back to the House recommendations with respect to . . . seating, expulsion or other punishment," See Hearings 110. Powell did not appear at the next hearing, held February 14, 1967. However, his attorneys were present, and they informed the Committee that Powell would not testify about matters other than his eligibility under the standing qualifications of Art. 2, § 2. Powell's attorneys reasserted Powell's contention that the standing qualifications were the exclusive requirements for membership, and they further urged that punishment or expulsion was not possible until a member had been seated. . . .

The Committee held one further hearing at which neither Powell nor his attorneys were present. Then, on February 23, 1967, the Committee issued its report, finding that Powell met the standing qualifications of Art. I, § 2. . . . However, the Committee further reported that Powell had asserted an unwarranted privilege and immunity from the processes of the courts of New York; that he had wrongfully diverted House funds for the use of others and himself; and that he had made false reports on expenditures of foreign currency to the Committee on House Administration. . . . The Committee recommended that Powell be sworn and seated as a member of the 90th Congress but that he be censured by the House, fined $40,000 and be deprived of his seniority. . . .

The report was presented to the House on March 1, 1967, and the House debated the Select Committee's proposed resolution. At the conclusion of the debate, by a vote of 222 to 202 the House rejected a motion to bring the resolution to a vote. An amendment to the resolution was then offered; it called for the exclusion of Powell and a declaration that his seat was vacant. The Speaker ruled that a majority vote of the House would be sufficient to pass the resolution if it were so amended. . . . After further debate, the amendment was adopted by a vote of 248 to 176. Then the House adopted by a vote of 307 to 116 House Resolution No. 278 in its amended form, thereby excluding Powell and directing that the Speaker notify the Governor of New York that the seat was vacant.

Powell and 13 voters of the 18th Congressional District of New York subsequently instituted this suit in the United States District Court for the District of Columbia. Five members of the House of Representatives were named as defendants individually and "as representatives of a class of citizens who are presently serving . . . as members of the House of Representatives." John W. McCormack was named in his official capacity as Speaker, and the Clerk of the House of Representatives, the Sergeant at Arms and the Doorkeeper were named individually and in their official capacities. The complaint alleged that House Resolution No. 278 violated the Constitution, specifically Art. I, § 2, cl 1, because the resolution was inconsistent with the mandate that the members of the House shall be elected by the people of each State, and Art. I, § 2, cl 2, which, petitioners alleged, sets forth the exclusive qualifications for membership. The complaint further alleged that the Clerk of the House threatened to refuse to perform the service for Powell to which a duly elected Congressman is entitled, that the Sergeant at Arms refused to pay Powell his salary, and that the Doorkeeper threatened to deny Powell admission to the House chamber.

Petitioners asked that a three-judge court be convened. Further, they requested that the District Court grant a permanent injunction restraining respondents from executing the House Resolution, and enjoining the Speaker from refusing to administer the oath, the Clerk from refusing to perform the duties due a Representative, the Sergeant at Arms from refusing to pay Powell his salary, and the Doorkeeper from refusing to admit Powell to the Chamber. The complaint also requested a declaratory judgment that Powell's exclusion was unconstitutional. . . .

Respondents press upon us a variety of arguments to support the court below; they will be considered in the following order. (1) Events occurring subsequent to the grant of certiorari have rendered this litigation moot. (2) The Speech or Debate Clause of the Constitution, Art. I, § 6, insulates respondents' action from judicial review. (3) The decision to exclude petitioner Powell is supported by the power granted to the House of Representatives to expel a member. (4) This Court lacks subject matter jurisdiction over petitioners' action. (5) Even if subject matter jurisdiction is present, this litigation is not justiciable either under the general criteria established by this Court or because a political question is involved.

II
MOOTNESS

After certiorari was granted, respondents filed a memorandum suggesting that two events which occurred subsequent to our grant of certiorari require that the case be dismissed as moot. On January 3, 1969, the House of Representatives of the 90th Congress officially terminated, and petitioner Powell was seated as a member of the 91st Congress. . . . Respondents insist that the gravamen of petitioners' complaint was the failure of the 90th Congress to seat Petitioner Powell and that, since the House of Representatives is not a continuing body and Powell has now been seated, his claims are moot. Petitioners counter that three issues remain unresolved and thus this litigation presents a "case or controversy" within the meaning of Art. III: (1) whether Powell was unconstitutionally deprived of his seniority by his exclusion from the 90th Congress; (2) whether the resolution of the 91st Congress imposing as "punishment" a $25,000 fine is a continuation of respondents' allegedly unconstitutional exclusion . . . and (3) whether Powell is entitled to salary withheld after his exclusion from the 90th Congress. We conclude that Powell's claim for back salary remains viable even though he has been seated in the 91st Congress and thus find it unnecessary to determine whether the other issues have become moot. . . .

III
SPEECH OR DEBATE CLAUSE

Respondents assert that the Speech or Debate Clause of the Constitution, Art. I, § 6, is an absolute bar to petitioners' action. This Court has on four prior occasions—*Dombrowski* v. *Eastland* [1967], *United States* v. *Johnson* [1966], *Tenney* v. *Brandhove* [1951], and *Kilbourn* v. *Thompson* [1881]—been called upon to determine if allegedly unconstitutional action taken by legislators or legislative employees is insulated from judicial review by the Speech or Debate Clause. Both parties insist that their respective positions find support in these cases and tender for decision three distinct issues: (1) whether respondents in participating in the exclusion of petitioner Powell were "acting in the sphere of legitimate legislative activity," . . . (2) assuming that respondents were so acting, whether the fact that petitioners seek neither damages from any of the respondents nor a criminal prosecution lifts the bar of the clause; and (3) even if this action may not be maintained against a Congressman, whether those respondents who are merely employees of the House may plead the bar of the clause. We find it necessary to treat only the last of these issues.

The Speech or Debate Clause, adopted by the Constitutional Convention without debate or opposition, finds its roots in the conflict between Parliament and the Crown culminating in the Glorious Revolution of 1688 and the English Bill of Rights of 1689. Drawing upon this history, we concluded in *United States* v. *Johnson*, that the purpose of this clause was "to prevent intimidation [of legislators] by the executive and accountability before a possibly hostile judiciary." Although the clause sprang from a fear of seditious libel actions instituted by the Crown to punish unfavorable speeches made in Parliament, we have held that it would be a "narrow view" to confine the protection of the Speech or Debate Clause to words spoken in debate. Committee reports, resolutions, and the act of voting are equally covered, as are "things generally done in a session of the House by one of its members in relation to the business before it." *Kilbourn* v. *Thompson.* Furthermore, the clause not only provides a defense on the merits but also protects a legislator from the burden of defending himself. *Dombrowski* v. *Eastland*. . . .

Our cases make it clear that the legislative immunity created by the Speech or Debate Clause performs an important function in representative government. It insures that legislators are free to represent the interests of their constituents without fear that they will be later called to task in the courts for that representation. Thus, in *Tenney* v. *Brandhove,* the Court quoted the writings of James Wilson as illuminating the reason for legislative immunity: "In order to enable and encourage a representative of the publick to discharge his publick trust with firmness and success, it is indispensably necessary, that he should enjoy the fullest liberty of speech, and that he should be protected from the resentment of every one, however powerful, to whom the exercise of that liberty may occasion offence."

Legislative immunity does not, of course, bar all judicial review of legislative acts. That issue was settled by implication as early as 1803, see *Marbury* v. *Madison,* and expressly in *Kilbourn* v. *Thompson,* the first of this Court's cases interpreting the reach of the Speech or Debate Clause. Challenged in *Kilbourn* was the constitutionality of a House Resolution ordering the arrest and imprisonment of a recalcitrant witness who had refused to respond to a subpoena issued by a House investigating committee. While holding that the Speech or Debate Clause barred Kilbourn's action for false imprisonment brought against several members of the House, the Court nevertheless reached the merits of Kilbourn's attack and decided that, since the House had no power to punish for contempt, Kilbourn's imprisonment pursuant to the resolution was unconstitutional. It therefore allowed Kilbourn to bring his false imprisonment action against Thompson, the House's Sergeant at Arms,

who had executed the warrant for Kilbourn's arrest.

The Court first articulated in *Kilbourn* and followed in *Dombrowski* v. *Eastland* the doctrine that, although an action against a Congressman may be barred by the Speech or Debate Clause, legislative employees who participated in the unconstitutional activity are responsible for their acts. Despite the fact that petitioners brought this suit against several House employees—the Sergeant at Arms, the Doorkeeper and the Clerk—as well as several Congressmen, respondents argue that Kilbourn and Dombrowski are distinguishable. Conceding that in *Kilbourn* the presence of the Sergeant at Arms and in *Dombrowski* the presence of a congressional subcommittee counsel as defendants in the litigation allowed judicial review of the challenged congressional action, respondents urge that both cases concerned an affirmative act performed by the employee outside the House having a direct effect upon a private citizen. Here, they continue, the relief sought relates to actions taken by House agents solely within the House. Alternatively, respondents insist that Kilbourn and Dombrowski payed for damages while petitioner Powell asks that the Sergeant at Arms disburse funds, an assertedly greater interference with the legislative process. We reject the proffered distinctions.

That House employees are acting pursuant to express orders of the House does not bar judicial review of the constitutionality of the underlying legislative decision. Kilbourn decisively settles this question, since the Sergeant at Arms was held liable for false imprisonment even though he did nothing more than execute the House Resolution that Kilbourn be arrested and imprisoned. Respondents' suggestions thus ask us to distinguish between affirmative acts of House employees and situations in which the House orders its employees not to act or between actions for damages and claims for salary. We can find no basis in either the history of the Speech or Debate Clause or our cases for either distinction. The purpose of the protection afforded legislators is not to forestall judicial review of legislative action but to insure that legislators are not distracted from or hindered in the performance of their legislative tasks by being called into court to defend their actions. A legislator is no more or no less hindered or distracted by litigation against a legislative employee calling into question the employee's affirmative action than he would be by a lawsuit questioning the employee's failure to act. Nor is the distraction or hindrance increased because the claim is for salary rather than damages, or because the litigation questions action taken by the employee within rather than without the House. Freedom of legislative activity and the purposes of the Speech or Debate Clause are fully protected if legislators are relieved of the burden of defending themselves. In *Kilbourn* and *Dombrowski* we thus dismissed the action against members of Congress but did not regard the Speech or Debate Clause as a bar to reviewing the merits of the challenged congressional action since congressional employees were also sued. Similarly, though this action may be dismissed against the Congressmen petitioners are entitled to maintain their action against House employees and to judicial review of the propriety of the decision to exclude petitioner Powell. As was said in *Kilbourn,* in language which time has not dimmed:

Especially is it competent and proper for this Court to consider whether its [the legislature's] proceedings are in conformity with the Constitution and laws, because, living under a written constitution, no branch or department of the government is supreme; and it is the province and duty of the judicial department to determine in cases regularly brought before them, whether the powers of any branch of the government, and even those of the legislature in the enactment of laws, have been exercised in conformity to the Constitution; and if they have not, to treat their acts as null and void. . . .

IV
EXCLUSION OR EXPULSION

The resolution excluding petitioner Powell was adopted by a vote in excess of two-thirds of the 434 Members of Congress—307 to 116 . . . Article I, § 5, grants the House authority to expel a member "with the concurrence of two thirds." Respondents assert that the House may expel a member for any reason whatsoever and that, since a two-thirds vote was obtained, the procedure by which Powell was denied his seat in the 90th Congress should be regarded as an expulsion not an exclusion. Cautioning us not to exalt form over substance, respondents quote from the concurring opinion of Judge McGowan in the court below:

Appellant Powell's cause of action for a judicially compelled seating thus boils down, in my view, to the narrow issue of whether a member found by his colleagues . . . to have engaged in official misconduct must, because of the accidents of timing, be formally admitted before he can be either investigated or expelled. The sponsor of the motion to exclude stated on the floor that he was proceeding on the theory that the power to expel included the power to exclude, provided a two-thirds vote was forthcoming. It was. Therefore, success for Mr. Powell on the merits would mean that the District Court must admonish the House that it is form, not substance, that should govern in great affairs, and accordingly command the House members to act out a charade. . . .

Although respondents repeatedly urge this Court not to speculate as to the reasons for Powell's exclusion, their attempt to equate exclusion with expulsion would require a similar speculation that the House would have voted to expel Powell had it been faced with that question. Powell had not been seated at the time House Resolution No. 278 was debated and passed. After a motion to bring the Select Committee's proposed resolution to an immediate vote had been defeated, an amendment was offered which mandated Powell's exclusion. Mr. Celler, chairman of the Select Committee, then posed a parliamentary inquiry to determine whether a two-thirds vote was necessary to pass the resolution if so amended "in the sense that it might amount to an expulsion." . . . The Speaker replied that "action by a majority vote would be in accordance with the rules." . . . Had the amendment been regarded as an attempt to expel Powell, a two-thirds vote would have been constitutionally required. The Speaker ruled that the House was voting to exclude Powell, and we will not speculate what the result might have been if Powell had been seated and expulsion proceedings subsequently instituted.

Nor is the distinction between exclusion and expulsion merely one of form. The misconduct for which Powell was charged occurred prior to the convening of the 90th Congress. On several occasions the House has debated whether a member can be expelled for actions taken during a prior Congress and the House's own manual of procedure applicable in the 90th Congress states that "both Houses have distrusted their power to punish in such cases." . . . The House rules manual reflects positions taken by prior Congresses. For example, the report of the Select Committee appointed to consider the expulsion of John W. Langley states unequivocally that the House will not expel a member for misconduct committed during an earlier Congress:

[I]t must be said that with practical uniformity the precedents in such cases are to the effect that the House will not expel a Member for reprehensible action prior to his election as a Member, not even for conviction for an offense. On May 23, 1884, Speaker Carlisle de-

cided that the House had no right to punish a Member for any offense alleged to have been committed previous to the time when he was elected a Member, and added, "That has been so frequently decided in the House that it is no longer a matter of dispute.

Members of the House having expressed a belief that such strictures apply to its own power to expel, we will not assume that two-thirds of its members would have expelled Powell for his prior conduct had the Speaker announced that House Resolution No. 278 was for expulsion rather than exclusion.

Finally, the proceedings which culminated in Powell's exclusion cast considerable doubt upon respondents' assumption that the two-thirds vote necessary to expel would have been mustered. These proceedings have been succinctly described by Congressman Eckhardt:

The House voted 202 votes for the previous question leading toward the adoption of the [Select] Committee report. It voted 222 votes against the previous question, opening the floor for the Curtis Amendment which ultimately excluded Powell.

Upon adoption of the Curtis Amendment, the vote again fell short of two-thirds, being 248 yeas to 176 nays. Only on the final vote, adopting the Resolution as amended, was more than a two-thirds vote obtained, the vote being 307 yeas to 116 nays. On this last vote, as a practical matter, members who would not have denied Powell a seat if they were given the choice to punish him had to cast an aye vote or else record themselves as opposed to the only punishment that was likely to come before the House. Had the matter come up through the processes of expulsion, it appears that the two-thirds vote would have failed, and then members would have been able to apply a lesser penalty.

We need express no opinion as to the accuracy of Congressman Eckhardt's prediction that expulsion proceedings would have produced a different result. However, the House's own views of the extent of its power to expel combined with the

Congressman's analysis counsel that exclusion and expulsion are not fungible proceedings. The Speaker ruled that House Resolution No. 278 contemplated an exclusion proceeding. We must reject respondents' suggestion that we overrule the Speaker and hold that, although the House manifested an intent to exclude Powell, its action should be tested by whatever standards may govern an expulsion.

V
SUBJECT MATTER JURISDICTION

As we pointed out in *Baker* v. *Carr* ... there is a significant difference between determining whether a federal court has "jurisdiction of the subject matter" and determining whether a cause over which a court has subject matter jurisdiction is "justiciable." The District Court determined that "to decide this case on the merits ... would constitute a clear violation of the doctrine of separation of powers" and then dismissed the complaint "for want of jurisdiction of the subject matter." ... However, as the Court of Appeals correctly recognized, the doctrine of separation of powers is more properly considered in determining whether the case is "justiciable." We agree with the unanimous conclusion of the Court of Appeals that the District Court had jurisdiction over the subject matter of this case. However, for reasons set forth in Part VI, infra, we disagree with the Court of Appeals' conclusion that this case is not justiciable.

In *Baker* v. *Carr* we noted that a federal district court lacks jurisdiction over the subject matter (1) if the cause does not "arise under" the Federal Constitution, laws, or treaties (or fall within one of the other enumerated categories of Art. III); or (2) if it is not a "case or controversy" within the meaning of that phrase in Art. III; or (3) if the cause is not one described

by any jurisdictional statute. And, as in *Baker* v. *Carr,* our determination that this case presents no nonjusticiable "political question" disposes of respondents' contentions that this cause is not a "case or controversy."

Respondents first contend that this is not a case "arising under" the Constitution within the meaning of Art. III. They emphasize that Art. I, § 5, assigns to each House of Congress the power to judge the elections and qualifications of its own members and to punish its members for disorderly behavior. Respondents also note that under Art. I, § 3, the Senate has the "sole power" to try all impeachments. Respondents argue that these delegations (to "judge," to "punish," and to "try") to the Legislative Branch are explicit grants of "judicial power" to the Congress and constitute specific exceptions to the general mandate of Art. III that the "judicial power" shall be vested in the federal courts. Thus, respondents maintain, the "power conferred on the courts by article III does not authorize this Court to do anything more than declare its lack of jurisdiction to proceed."

We reject this contention. Article III, § 1, provides that the "judicial Power ... shall be vested in one supreme Court, and in such inferior Courts as the Congress may ... establish." Further, § 2 mandates that the "judicial Power shall extend to all Cases ... arising under this Constitution. ..." It has long been held that a suit "arises under" the Constitution if a petitioner's claim "will be sustained if the Constitution ... [is] given one construction and will be defeated if [it is] given another." Thus, this case clearly is one "arising under" the Constitution as the Court has interpreted that phrase. Any bar to federal courts reviewing the judgments made by the House or Senate in excluding a member arises from the allocation of powers between the two branches of the Federal Government (a question of justiciability), and not from the petitioners' failure to state a claim based on federal law. . . .

VI
JUSTICIABILITY

Having concluded that the Court of Appeals correctly ruled that the District Court had jurisdiction over the subject matter, we turn to the question whether the case is justiciable. Two determinations must be made in this regard. First, we must decide whether the claim presented and the relief sought are of the type which admit of judicial resolution. Second, we must determine whether the structure of the Federal Government renders the issue presented a "political question"—that is, a question which is not justiciable in federal court because of the separation of powers provided by the Constitution.

A. General Considerations

In deciding generally whether a claim is justiciable, a court must determine whether "the duty asserted can be judicially identified and its breach judicially determined, and whether protection for the right asserted can be judicially molded." . . . Respondents do not seriously contend that the duty asserted and its alleged breach cannot be judicially determined. If petitioners are correct, the House had a duty to seat Powell once it determined he met the standing requirements set forth in the Constitution. It is undisputed that he met those requirements and that he was nevertheless excluded.

Respondents do maintain, however, that this case is not justiciable because, they assert, it is impossible for a federal court to "mold effective relief for resolving this case." Respondents emphasize that petitioners asked for coercive relief against the officers of the House, and,

they contend, federal courts cannot issue mandamus or injunctions compelling officers or employees of the House to perform specific official acts. Respondents rely primarily on the Speech or Debate Clause to support this contention.

We need express no opinion about the appropriateness of coercive relief in this case, for petitioners sought a declaratory judgment, a form of relief the District Court could have issued. The Declaratory Judgment Act, 28 USC § 2201, provides that a district court may "declare the rights . . . of any interested party . . . whether or not further relief is or could be sought." The availability of declaratory relief depends on whether there is a live dispute between the parties . . . and a request for declaratory relief may be considered independently of whether other forms of relief are appropriate. . . . We thus conclude that in terms of the general criteria of justiciability, this case is justiciable.

B. Political Question Doctrine

1. Textually Demonstrable Constitutional Commitment

Respondents maintain that even if this case is otherwise justiciable, it presents only a political question. It is well established that the federal courts will not adjudicate political questions. See, e.g., *Coleman* v. *Miller,* [1939]. . . . In *Baker* v. *Carr* we noted that political questions are not justiciable primarily because of the separation of powers within the Federal Government. After reviewing our decisions in this area, we concluded that on the surface of any case held to involve a political question was at least one of the following formulations: "a textually demonstrable constitutional commitment of the issue to a coordinate political department; or a lack of judicially discoverable and manageable standards for resolving it; or the impossibility of deciding without an initial policy determination of a kind clearly for nonjudicial discretion; or the impossibility of a court's undertaking independent resolution without expressing lack of the respect due coordinate branches of government; or an unusual need for unquestioning adherence to a political decision already made; or the potentiality of embarrassment from multifarious pronouncements by various departments on one question.". . .

Respondent's first contention is that this case presents a political question because under Art. I, § 5, there has been a "textually demonstrable constitutional commitment" to the House of the "adjudicatory power" to determine Powell's qualifications. Thus it is argued that the House, and the House alone, has power to determine who is qualified to be a member.

In order to determine whether there has been a textual commitment to a coordinate department of the Government, we must interpret the Constitution. In other words, we must first determine what power the Constitution confers upon the House through Art. I, § 5, before we can determine to what extent, if any, the exercise of that power is subject to judicial review. Respondents maintain that the House has broad power under § 5, and, they argue, the House may determine which are the qualifications necessary for membership. On the other hand, petitioners allege that the Constitution provides that an elected representative may be denied his seat only if the House finds he does not meet one of the standing qualifications expressly prescribed by the Constitution.

If examination of § 5 disclosed that the Constitution gives the House judicially unreviewable power to set qualifications for membership and to judge whether prospective members meet those qualifications, further review of the House de-

termination might well be barred by the political question doctrine. On the other hand, if the Constitution gives the House power to judge only whether elected members possess the three standing qualifications set forth in the Constitution, further consideration would be necessary to determine whether any of the other formulations of the political question doctrine are "inextricable from the case at the bar.". . .

In other words, whether there is a "textually demonstrable constitutional commitment of the issue to a coordinate political department" of government and what is the scope of such commitment are questions we must resolve for the first time in this case. For, as we pointed out in *Baker v. Carr,* "[d]eciding whether a matter has in any measure been committed by the Constitution to another branch of government, or whether the action of that branch exceeds whatever authority has been committed, is itself a delicate exercise in constitutional interpretation, and is a responsibility of this Court as ultimate interpreter of the Constitution.". . .

In order to determine the scope of any "textual commitment" under Art. I, § 5, we necessarily must determine the meaning of the phrase to "be the Judge of the Qualifications of its own Members." Petitioners argue that the records of the debates during the Constitutional Convention; available commentary from the post-Convention, pre-ratification period; and early congressional applications of Art. I, § 5, support their construction of the section. Respondents insist, however, that a careful examination of the pre-Convention practices of the English Parliament and American colonial assemblies demonstrates that by 1787, a legislature's power to judge the qualifications of its members was generally understood to encompass exclusion or expulsion on the ground that an individual's character or past conduct rendered him unfit to serve. When the Constitution and the debates over its adoption are thus viewed in historical perspective, argue respondents, it becomes clear that the "qualifications" expressly set forth in the Constitution were not meant to limit the long-recognized legislative power to exclude or expel at will, but merely to establish "standing incapacities," which could be altered only by a constitutional amendment. Our examination of the relevant historical materials leads us to the conclusion that petitioners are correct and that the Constitution leaves the House without authority to *exclude* any person, duly elected by his constituents, who meets all the requirements for membership expressly prescribed in the Constitution.

a. The pre-convention precedents

Since our rejection of respondents' interpretation of § 5 results in significant measure from a disagreement with their historical analysis, we must consider the relevant historical antecedents in considerable detail. As do respondents, we begin with the English and colonial precedents.

The earliest English exclusion precedent appears to be a declaration by the House of Commons in 1553 "that Alex. Nowell, being Prebendary [i.e., a clergyman] in Westminster, and thereby having voice in the Convocation House, cannot be a member of this House. . . ." . . . This decision, however, was consistent with a long-established tradition that clergy who participated in their own representative assemblies or convocations were ineligible for membership in the House of Commons. . . . The traditional ineligibility of clergymen was recognized as a standing incapacity. . . . Nowell's exclusion, therefore, is irrelevant to the present case, for petitioners concede—and we agree—that if Powell had not met one of the standing

qualifications set forth in the Constitution, he could have been excluded under Art. I, § 5. The earliest colonial exclusions also fail to support respondents' theory.

Respondents' remaining 16th and 17th century English precedents all are cases of expulsion, although some were for misdeeds not encompassed within recognized standing incapacities existing either at the time of the expulsions or at the time the Constitution was drafted in 1787. Although these early expulsion orders occasionally contained statements suggesting that the individual expelled was thereafter ineligible for re-election, at least for the duration of the Parliament from which he was expelled, there is no indication that any were re-elected and thereafter excluded. Respondents' colonial precedents during this period follow a similar pattern.

Apparently the re-election of an expelled member first occurred in 1712. The House of Commons had expelled Robert Walpole for receiving kickbacks for contracts relating to "foraging the Troops," . . . and committed him to the Tower. Nevertheless, two months later he was re-elected. The House thereupon resolved "[t]hat Robert Walpole, Esquire, having been, this Session of Parliament, committed a Prisoner to the *Tower* of *London*, and expelled [from] this House, . . . is, incapable of being elected a Member to serve *in this present Parliament. . . .*" . . . (Second emphasis added.) A new election was ordered, and Walpole was not re-elected. At least two similar exclusions after an initial expulsion were effected in the American colonies during the first half of the 18th century. Respondents urge that the Walpole case provides strong support for their conclusion that the pre-Convention English and colonial practice was that members-elect could be excluded for their prior misdeeds at the sole discretion of the legislative body to which they had been elected. However, this conclusion overlooks an important limiting characteristic of the Walpole case and of both the colonial exclusion cases on which respondents rely: the excluded member had been previously expelled. Moreover, Walpole was excluded only for the remainder of the Parliament from which he had been expelled. "The theory seems to have been that expulsion lasted as long as the Parliament. . . ." . . . Thus, Walpole's exclusion justifies only the proposition that an expulsion lasted for the remainder of the particular Parliament, and the expelled member was therefore subject to subsequent exclusion if re-elected prior to the next general election. The two colonial cases arguably support a somewhat broader principle, i.e., that the assembly could permanently expel. Apparently the colonies did not consistently adhere to the theory that an expulsion lasted only until the election of a new assembly. . . . Clearly, however, none of these cases supports respondents' contention that by the 18th century the English Parliament and colonial assemblies had assumed absolute discretion to exclude any member-elect they deemed unfit to serve. Rather, they seem to demonstrate that a member could be excluded only if he had first been expelled.

Even if these cases could be construed to support respondents' contention, their precedential value was nullified prior to the Constitutional Convention. By 1782, after a long struggle, the arbitrary exercise of the power to exclude was unequivocally repudiated by a House of Commons resolution which ended the most notorious English election dispute of the 18th Century—the John Wilkes case. While serving as a member of Parliament in 1763, Wilkes published an attack on a recent peace treaty with France, calling it a product of bribery and condemning the Crown's ministers as " 'the tools of despotism and corruption.' " . . . Wilkes and

others who were involved with the publication in which the attack appeared were arrested. Prior to Wilkes' trial, the House of Commons expelled him for publishing "a false, scandalous, and seditious libel." . . . Wilkes then fled to France and was subsequently sentenced to exile. . . .

Wilkes returned to England in 1768, the same year in which the Parliament from which he had been expelled was dissolved. He was elected to the next Parliament, and he then surrendered himself to the Court of King's Bench. Wilkes was convicted of seditious libel and sentenced to 22 months' imprisonment. The new Parliament declared him ineligible for membership and ordered that he be "expelled this House." . . . Although Wilkes was reelected to fill the vacant seat three times, each time the same Parliament declared him ineligible and refused to seat him. . . .

Wilkes was released from prison in 1770 and was again elected to Parliament in 1774. For the next several years, he unsuccessfully campaigned to have the resolutions expelling him and declaring him incapable of re-election expunged from the record. Finally, in 1782, the House of Commons voted to expunge them, resolving that the prior House actions were "subversive of the rights of the whole body of electors of this kingdom." . . .

With the successful resolution of Wilkes' long and bitter struggle for the right of the British electorate to be represented by men of their own choice, it is evident that, on the eve of the Constitutional Convention, English precedent stood for the proposition that "the law of the land had regulated the qualifications of members to serve in Parliament" and those qualifications were "not occasional but fixed." . . . Certainly English practice did not support, nor had it ever supported, respondents' assertion that the power to judge qualifications was generally understood to encompass the right to exclude members-elect for general misconduct not within standing qualifications. With the repudiation in 1782 of the only two precedents for excluding a member-elect who had been previously expelled, it appears that the House of Commons also repudiated any "control over the eligibility of candidates, except in the administration of the laws which define their [standing] qualifications." . . .

The resolution of the Wilkes case similarly undermined the precedential value of the earlier colonial exclusions, for the principles upon which they had been based were repudiated by the very body the colonial assemblies sought to imitate and whose precedents they generally followed. . . . Thus, in 1784 the Council of Censors of the Pennsylvania Assembly denounced the prior expulsion of an unnamed assemblyman, ruling that his expulsion had not been effected in conformity with the recently enacted Pennsylvania Constitution. In the course of its report, the Council denounced by name the Parliamentary exclusions of both Walpole and Wilkes, stating that they "reflected dishonor on none but the authors of these violences." . . .

Wilkes' struggle and his ultimate victory had a significant impact in the American colonies. His advocacy of libertarian causes and his pursuit of the right to be seated in Parliament became a cause célèbre for the colonists. "[T]he cry of 'Wilkes and Liberty' echoed loudly across the Atlantic Ocean as wide publicity was given to every step of Wilkes's public career in the colonial press. . . . The reaction in America took on significant proportions. Colonials tended to identify their cause with that of Wilkes. They saw him as a popular hero and a martyr to the struggle for liberty. . . . They named towns, counties, and even children in his honour." . . . It is within this historical context that we must examine the Convention debates in 1787, just five years after Wilkes' final victory.

b. Convention debates

Relying heavily on Charles Warren's analysis of the Convention debates, petitioners argue that the proceedings manifest the Framers' unequivocal intention to deny either branch of Congress the authority to add to or otherwise vary the membership qualifications expressly set forth in the Constitution. We do not completely agree, for the debates are subject to other interpretations. However, we have concluded that the records of the debates, viewed in the context of the bitter struggle for the right to freely choose representatives which had recently concluded in England and in light of the distinction the Framers made between the power to expel and the power to exclude, indicate that petitioners' ultimate conclusion is correct.

The Convention opened in late May 1787. By the end of July, the delegates adopted, with a minimum of debate, age requirements for membership in both the Senate and the House. The Convention then appointed a Committee of Detail to draft a constitution incorporating these and other resolutions adopted during the preceding months. Two days after the Committee was appointed, George Mason, of Virginia, moved that the Committee consider a clause " 'requiring certain qualifications of landed property & citizenship' " and disqualifying from membership in Congress persons who had unsettled accounts or who were indebted to the United States. . . . A vigorous debate ensued. Charles Pinckney and General Charles C. Pinckney, both of South Carolina, moved to extend these incapacities to both the judicial and executive branches of the new government. But John Dickinson, of Delaware, opposed the inclusion of any statement of qualifications in the Constitution. He argued that it would be "impossible to make a compleat one, and a partial one would by implication tie up the hands of the Legislature from supplying the omissions." . . . Dickinson's argument was rejected; and, after eliminating the disqualification of debtors and the limitation to "landed" property, the Convention adopted Mason's proposal to instruct the Committee of Detail to draft a property qualification. . . .

The Committee reported in early August, proposing no change in the age requirement; however, it did recommend adding citizenship and residency requirements for membership. After first debating what the precise requirements should be, on August 8, 1787, the delegates unanimously adopted the three qualifications embodied in Art. I, § 2. . . .

On August 10, the Convention considered the Committee of Detail's proposal that the "Legislature of the United States shall have authority to establish such uniform qualifications of the members of each House, with regard to property, as to the said Legislature shall seem expedient." . . . The debate on this proposal discloses much about the views of the Framers on the issue of qualifications. For example, James Madison urged its rejection, stating that the proposal would vest "an improper & dangerous power in the Legislature. The qualifications of electors and elected were fundamental articles in a Republican Govt. and ought to be fixed by the Constitution. If the Legislature could regulate those of either, it can by degrees subvert the Constitution. A Republic may be converted into an aristocracy or oligarchy as well by limiting the number capable of being elected, as the number authorised to elect. . . . It was a power also, which might be made subservient to the views of one faction agst. another. Qualifications founded on artificial distinctions may be devised, by the stronger

in order to keep out partizans of [a weaker] faction." . . . Significantly, Madison's argument was not aimed at the imposition of a property qualification as such, but rather at the delegation to the Congress of the discretionary power to establish any qualifications. The parallel between Madison's arguments and those made in Wilkes' behalf is striking.

In view of what followed Madison's speech, it appears that on this critical day the Framers were facing and then rejecting the possibility that the legislature would have power to usurp the "indisputable right [of the people] to return whom they thought proper" to the legislature. Oliver Ellsworth, of Connecticut, noted that a legislative power to establish property qualifications was exceptional and "dangerous because it would be much more liable to abuse." . . . Gouverneur Morris then moved to strike "with regard to property" from the Committee's proposal. His intention was "to leave the Legislature entirely at large." . . . Hugh Williamson, of North Carolina, expressed concern that if a majority of the legislature should happen to be "composed of any particular description of men, of lawyers for example, . . . the future elections might be secured to their own body." . . . Madison then referred to the British Parliament's assumption of the power to regulate the qualifications of both electors and the elected and noted that "the abuse they had made of it was a lesson worthy of our attention. They had made the changes in both cases subservient to their own views, or to the views of political or Religious parties." . . . Shortly thereafter, the Convention rejected both Gouverneur Morris' motion and the Committee's proposal. Later the same day, the Convention adopted without debate the provision authorizing each House to be "the judge of the . . . qualifications of its own members." . . .

One other decision made the same day

is very important to determining the meaning of Art. I, § 5. When the delegates reached the Committee of Detail's proposal to empower each House to expel its members, Madison "observed that the right of expulsion . . . was too important to be exercised by a bare majority of a quorum: and in emergencies [one] faction might be dangerously abused." . . . He therefore moved that "with the concurrence of two-thirds" be inserted. With the exception of one State, whose delegation was divided, the motion was unanimously approved without debate, although Gouverneur Morris noted his opposition. The importance of this decision cannot be over-emphasized. None of the parties to this suit disputes that prior to 1787 the legislative powers to judge qualifications and to expel were exercised by a majority vote. Indeed, without exception, the English and colonial antecedents to Art. I, § 5, cls. 1 and 2, support this conclusion. Thus, the Convention's decision to increase the vote required to expel, because that power was "too important to be exercised by a bare majority," while at the same time not similarly restricting the power to judge qualifications, is compelling evidence that they considered the latter already limited by the standing qualifications previously adopted.

Respondents urge, however, that these events must be considered in light of what they regard as a very significant change made in Art. I, § 2, cl. 2, by the Committee of Style. When the Committee of Detail reported the provision to the Convention, it read:

Every member of the House of Representatives shall be of the age of twenty five years at least; shall have been a citizen of [in] the United States for at least three years before his election; and shall be, at the time of his election, a resident of the State in which he shall be chosen. . . .

However, as finally drafted by the Committee of Style, these qualifications were stated in their present negative form. Respondents note that there are no records of the "deliberations" of the Committee of Style. Nevertheless, they speculate that this particular change was designed to make the provision correspond to the form used by Blackstone in listing the "standing incapacities" for membership in the House of Commons. . . . Blackstone, who was an apologist for the anti-Wilkes forces in Parliament, had added to his Commentaries after Wilkes' exclusion the assertion that individuals who were not ineligible for the Commons under the standing incapacities could still be denied their seat if the Commons deemed them unfit for other reasons. Since Blackstone's Commentaries was widely circulated in the Colonies, respondents further speculate that the Committee of Style rephrased the qualifications provision in the negative to clarify the delegates' intention "only to prescribe the standing incapacities without imposing any other limit on the historic power of each house to judge qualifications on a case by case basis."

Respondents' argument is inherently weak, however, because it assumes that legislative bodies historically possessed the power to judge qualifications on a case-by-case basis. As noted above, the basis for that conclusion was the Walpole and Wilkes cases, which, by the time of the Convention, had been denounced by the House of Commons and repudiated by at least one State government. Moreover, respondents' argument misrepresents the function of the Committee of Style. It was appointed only "to revise the stile of and arrange the articles which had been agreed to. . . ." . . .[T]he Committee . . . had no authority from the Convention to make alterations of substance in the Constitution as voted by the Convention, nor did it purport to do so; and certainly the Convention had no belief . . . that any important change was, in fact, made in the provisions as to qualifications adopted by it on August 10."

Petitioners also argue that the post-Convention debates over the Constitution's ratification support their interpretation of § 5. For example, they emphasize Hamilton's reply to the antifederalist charge that the new Constitution favored the wealthy and well-born:

The truth is that there is no method of securing to the rich the preference apprehended but by prescribing qualifications of property either for those who may elect or be elected. But this forms no part of the power to be conferred upon the national government. Its authority would be expressly restricted to the regulation of the *times*, the *places*, the *manner* of elections. *The qualifications of the persons who may choose or be chosen, as has been remarked upon other occasions, are defined and fixed in the Constitution, and are unalterable by the legislature. . . .*

Madison had expressed similar views in an earlier essay, and his arguments at the Convention leave no doubt about his agreement with Hamilton on this issue.

Respondents counter that Hamilton was actually addressing himself to criticism of Art. I, § 4, which authorizes Congress to regulate the times, places, and manner of electing members of Congress. They note that prominent antifederalists had argued that this power could be used to "confer on the rich and *well-born,* all honours." . . . Respondents' contention, however, ignores Hamilton's express reliance on the immutability of the qualifications set forth in the Constitution.

The debates at the state conventions also demonstrate the Framers' understanding that the qualifications for members of Congress had been fixed in the Constitution. . . .

c. Post-ratification

As clear as these statements appear, respondents dismiss them as "general statements . . . directed to other issues." They suggest that far more relevant is Congress' own understanding of its power to judge qualifications as manifested in post-ratification exclusion cases. Unquestionably, both the House and the Senate have excluded members-elect for reasons other than their failure to meet the Constitution's standing qualifications. For almost the first 100 years of its existence, however, Congress strictly limited its power to judge the qualifications of its members to those enumerated in the Constitution.

Congress was first confronted with the issue in 1807, when the eligibility of William McCreery was challenged because he did not meet additional residency requirements imposed by the State of Maryland. In recommending that he be seated, the House Committee of Elections reasoned:

The committee proceeded to examine the Constitution, with relation to the case submitted to them, and find that qualifications of members are therein determined, without reserving any authority to the State Legislatures to change, add to, or diminish those qualifications; and that, by that instrument, Congress is constituted the sole judge of the qualifications prescribed by it, and are obliged to decide agreeably to the Constitutional rules. . . .

Lest there be any misunderstanding of the basis for the committee's recommendation, during the ensuing debate the chairman explained the principles by which the committee was governed:

The Committee of Elections considered the qualifications of members to have been unalterably determined by the Federal Convention, unless changed by an authority equal to that which framed the Constitution at first; that neither the State nor the Federal Legislatures are vested with authority to add to those qualifications, so as to change them. . . . Congress, by the Federal Constitution, are not authorized to prescribe the qualifications of their own members, but they are authorized to judge of their qualifications; in doing so, however, they must be governed by the rules prescribed by the Federal Constitution, and by them only. These are the principles on which the Election Committee have made up their reports, and upon which their resolution is founded. . . .

There was no significant challenge to these principles for the next several decades. They came under heavy attack, however, "during the stress of civil war [but initially] the House of Representatives declined to exercise the power [to exclude], even under circumstances of great provocation." . . . The abandonment of such restraint, however, was among the casualties of the general upheaval produced in war's wake. In 1868, the House voted for the first time in its history to exclude a member-elect. It refused to seat two duly elected representatives for giving aid and comfort to the Confederacy. . . . "This change was produced by the North's bitter enmity toward those who failed to support the Union cause during the war, and was effected by the Radical Republican domination of Congress. It was a shift brought about by the naked urgency of power and was given little doctrinal support." . . .

From that time until the present, congressional practice has been erratic; and on the few occasions when a member-elect was excluded although he met all the qualifications set forth in the Constitution, there were frequently vigorous dissents. Even the annotations to the official manual of procedure for the 90th Congress manifest doubt as to the House's power to exclude a member-elect who has met the constitutionally prescribed qualifications. . . .

Had these congressional exclusion precedents been more consistent, their precedential value still would be quite limited. . . . That an unconstitutional action has been taken before surely does not render that same action any less unconstitutional at a later date. Particularly in view of the Congress' own doubts in those few cases where it did exclude members-

elect, we are not inclined to give its precedents controlling weight. The relevancy of prior exclusion cases is limited largely to the insight they afford in correctly ascertaining the draftsmen's intent. Obviously, therefore, the precedential value of these cases tends to increase in proportion to their proximity to the Convention in 1787. . . . And, what evidence we have of Congress' early understanding confirms our conclusion that the House is without power to exclude any member-elect who meets the Constitution's requirements for membership.

d. Conclusion

Had the intent of the Framers emerged from these materials with less clarity, we would nevertheless have been compelled to resolve any ambiguity in favor of a narrow construction of the scope of Congress' power to exclude members-elect. A fundamental principle of our representative democracy is, in Hamilton's words, "that the people should choose whom they please to govern them." . . . As Madison pointed out at the Convention, this principle is undermined as much by limiting whom the people can select as by limiting the franchise itself. In apparent agreement with this basic philosophy, the Convention adopted his suggestion limiting the power to expel. To allow essentially that same power to be exercised under the guise of judging qualifications, would be to ignore Madison's warning, borne out in the Wilkes case and some of Congress' own post-Civil War exclusion cases, against "vesting an improper & dangerous power in the Legislature." . . . Moreover, it would effectively nullify the Convention's decision to require a two-thirds vote for expulsion. Unquestionably, Congress has an interest in preserving its institutional integrity, but in most cases that interest can be sufficiently safeguarded by the exercise of its power to punish its members for disorderly behavior and, in extreme cases, to expel a member with the concurrence of two-thirds. In short, both the intention of the Framers, to the extent it can be determined, and an examination of the basic principles of our democratic system persuade us that the Constitution does not vest in the Congress a discretionary power to deny membership by a majority vote.

For these reasons, we have concluded that Art. I, § 5, is at most a "textually demonstrable commitment" to Congress to judge only the qualifications expressly set forth in the Constitution. Therefore, the "textual commitment" formulation of the political question doctrine does not bar federal courts from adjudicating petitioners' claims.

2. *Other Considerations*

Respondents' alternate contention is that the case presents a political question because judicial resolution of petitioners' claim would produce a "potentially embarrassing confrontation between coordinate branches" of the Federal Government. But, as our interpretation of Art. I, § 5, discloses, a determination of petitioner Powell's right to sit would require no more than an interpretation of the Constitution. Such a determination falls within the traditional role accorded courts to interpret the law, and does not involve a "lack of the respect due [a] coordinate [branch] of government," nor does it involve an "initial policy determination of a kind clearly for nonjudicial discretion." *Baker* v. *Carr* . . . Our system of government requires that federal courts on occasion interpret the Constitution in a manner at variance with the construction given the document by another branch. The alleged conflict that such an adjudication may cause cannot justify the courts' avoiding their constitutional responsibility. . . .

Nor are any of the other formulations

of a political question "inextricable from the case at bar." . . . Petitioners seek a determination that the House was without power to exclude Powell from the 90th Congress, which, we have seen, requires an interpretation of the Constitution—a determination for which clearly there are "judicially . . . manageable standards." Finally, a judicial resolution of petitioners' claim will not result in "multifarious pronouncements by various departments on one question." For, as we noted in *Baker* v. *Carr* . . . it is the responsibility of this Court to act as the ultimate interpreter of the Constitution. *Marbury* v. *Madison* [1803]. Thus, we conclude that petitioners' claim is not barred by the political question doctrine, and, having determined that the claim is otherwise generally justiciable, we hold that the case is justiciable.

VII
CONCLUSION

To summarize, we have determined the following: (1) This case has not been mooted by Powell's seating in the 91st Congress. (2) Although this action should be dismissed against respondent Congressmen, it may be sustained against their agents. (3) The 90th Congress' denial of membership to Powell cannot be treated as an expulsion. (4) We have jurisdiction over the subject matter of this controversy. (5) The case is justiciable.

Further, analysis of the "textual commitment" under Art. I, § 5 has demonstrated that in judging the qualifications of its members Congress is limited to the standing qualifications prescribed in the Constitution. Respondents concede that Powell met these. Thus, there is no need to remand this case to determine whether he was entitled to be seated in the 90th Congress. Therefore, we hold that, since Adam Clayton Powell, Jr., was duly elected by the voters of the 18th Congressional District of New York and was not ineligible to serve under any provision of the Constitution, the House was without power to exclude him from its membership.

Petitioners seek additional forms of equitable relief, including mandamus for the release of petitioner Powell's back pay. The propriety of such remedies, however, is more appropriately considered in the first instance by the courts below. Therefore, as to respondents McCormack, Albert, Ford, Celler, and Moore, the judgment of the Court of Appeals for the District of Columbia Circuit is affirmed. As to respondents Jennings, Johnson, and Miller, the judgment of the Court of Appeals for the District of Columbia Circuit is reversed and the case is remanded to the United States District Court for the District of Columbia with instructions to enter a declaratory judgment and for further proceedings consistent with this opinion.

It is so ordered.

MR. JUSTICE DOUGLAS wrote a concurring opinion.

MR. JUSTICE STEWART, dissenting:

I believe that events which have taken place since certiorari was granted in this case on November 18, 1968, have rendered it moot, and that the Court should therefore refrain from deciding the novel, difficult, and delicate constitutional questions which the case presented at its inception.

I

The essential purpose of this lawsuit by Congressman Powell and members of his constituency was to regain the seat from which he was barred by the 90th Congress. That purpose, however, became impossible of attainment on January 3, 1969, when the 90th Congress passed into history and the 91st Congress came into being. On that date, the petitioners' prayer for a judicial decree restraining enforcement of House Resolution No. 278 and commanding the respondents to admit Congressman Powell to membership in the 90th Congress became incontestably moot.

In the *Powell* case the Court cited *Marbury* v. *Madison* to support its position that it alone is the interpreter of the Constitution and that in effect there is no absolute commitment of power by the Constitution to Congress or the President. The Court claimed that the House of Representatives is without power to exclude a duly elected member who meets the age, citizenship, and residence requirements stated in Article I, Section 2 of the Constitution. Do you agree that on the basis of the language of that section of the Constitution, Congress must seat elected members who meet those constitutional requirements? Does the Court's distinction between expulsion and exclusion of members, and the consequences that flow from that distinction, seem reasonable? On the basis of the *Powell* decision, are there any limits upon judicial control of coordinate branches? For example, could the Court review an impeachment by the House or a decision to convict by the Senate? Article III, Section 4 of the Constitution provides that ". . . the President, Vice President and all civil officers of the United States shall be removed from office on impeachment for, and conviction of, treason, bribery, or other high crimes and misdemeanors. . . ."

The Constitution commands in Article I, Section 10 that "No state shall . . . pass any . . . law impairing the obligation of contracts. . . ." This provision, in combination with the constitutional prohibition upon state authority to emit bills of credit, was included because of the state practice before the adoption of the Constitution of passing debtor relief laws that stayed the payment of debts and made paper money legal tender. The framers of the Constitution were concerned lest vested property rights be overturned by popularly elected majorities in the state legislatures.

The narrow intent of the contract clause did not prevent its being raised in cases where the issues of "contract" were far broader than the impairment of contracts between creditors and debtors. In *Fletcher* v. *Peck,* 6 Cranch. 87 (1810), Chief Justice Marshall held that the Georgia legislature could not rescind a previous act that had granted land titles. Such an act, he wrote, would constitute an impairment of contract forbidden by the Constitution.[63] In holding that the contract clause covered public as well as private contracts, Marshall considerably broadened the intent of the framers of the Constitution.

The following case arose out of an attempt by the New Hampshire legislature to remove control over Dartmouth College from the private trustees appointed under a charter granted to the college by George III in 1769. The Republican governor and the legislature of New Hampshire saw in the Federalist trustees of the college an obstacle to their political power which they wanted removed. The New Hampshire Superior Court upheld the legislative act, claiming that the college was a public corporation that operated for public purposes and therefore could be subjected to public control. The trustees appealed to the Supreme Court by a writ of error.

Dartmouth College v. *Woodward*

4 Wheaton 518, 4 L. Ed. 629 (1819)

CHIEF JUSTICE MARSHALL delivered the opinion of the Court:

. . . This Court can be insensible neither to the magnitude nor delicacy of this question. The validity of a legislative act is to be examined; and the opinion of the highest law tribunal of a state is to be revised: an opinion which carries with it intrinsic evidence of the diligence, of the ability, and the integrity, with which it was formed. On more than one occasion this court has expressed the cautious circumspection with which it approaches the consideration of such questions; and has declared that, in no doubtful case would it pronounce a legislative act to be contrary to the Constitution. But the American people have said, in the Constitution of the United States, that "no state shall pass any bill of attainder, ex post facto

---

[63]The rescinding act arose out of charges that the legislators who made the original land grant had been bribed. Marshall held that the alleged corruption of the legislature was beyond judicial review.

law, or law impairing the obligation of contracts." In the same instrument they have also said, "that the judicial power shall extend to all cases in law and equity arising under the Constitution." On the judges of this Court, then, is imposed the high and solemn duty of protecting, from even legislative violation, those contracts which the Constitution of our country has placed beyond legislative control; and, however irksome the task may be, this is a duty from which we dare not shrink. . . .

It can require no argument to prove that the circumstances of this case constitute a contract. An application is made to the crown for a charter to incorporate a religious and literary institution. In the application, it is stated that large contributions have been made for the object, which will be conferred on the corporation as soon as it shall be created. The charter is granted, and on its faith the property is conveyed. Surely in this transaction every ingredient of a complete and legitimate contract is to be found.

The points for consideration are:

1. Is this contract protected by the constitution of the United States?

2. Is it impaired by the acts under which the defendant holds?

1. On the first point it has been argued, that the word "contract," in its broadest sense, would comprehend the political relations between the government and its citizens, would extend to offices held within a state for state purposes, and to many of those laws concerning civil institutions, which must change with circumstances, and be modified by ordinary legislation; which deeply concern the public, and which, to preserve good government, the public judgment must control. That even marriage is a contract, and its obligations are affected by the laws respecting divorces. That the clause in the Constitution, if construed in its greatest latitude, would prohibit these laws. Taken in its broad unlimited sense, the clause would

be an unprofitable and vexatious interference with the internal concerns of a state, would unnecessarily and unwisely embarrass its legislation, and render immutable those civil institutions which are established for purposes of internal government, and which, to subserve those purposes, ought to vary with varying circumstances. That as the framers of the Constitution could never have intended to insert in that instrument a provision so unnecessary, so mischievous, and so repugnant to its general spirit, the term "contract" must be understood in a more limited sense. That it must be understood as intended to guard against a power of at least doubtful utility, the abuse of which had been extensively felt; and to restrain the legislature in future from violating the right to property. That anterior to the formation of the Constitution, a course of legislation had prevailed in many, if not in all, of the states, which weakened the confidence of man in man, and embarrassed all transactions between individuals, by dispensing with a faithful performance of engagements. To correct this mischief, by restraining the power which produced it, the state legislatures were forbidden "to pass any law impairing the obligation of contracts," that is, of contracts respecting property, under which some individual could claim a right to something beneficial to himself; and that since the clause in the Constitution must in construction receive some limitation, it may be confined, and ought to be confined, to cases of this description; to cases within the mischief it was intended to remedy.

The general correctness of these observations cannot be controverted. That the framers of the Constitution did not intend to restrain the states in the regulation of their civil institutions, adopted for internal government, and that the instrument they have given us is not to be so construed, may be admitted. The provision of the Constitution never has been under-stood to embrace other contracts than those which respect property, or some object of value, and confer rights which may be asserted in a court of justice. It never has been understood to restrict the general right of the legislature to legislate on the subject of divorces. Those acts enable some tribunal, not to impair a marriage contract, but to liberate one of the parties because it has been broken by the other. When any state legislature shall pass an act annulling all marriage contracts, or allowing either party to annul it without the consent of the other, it will be time enough to inquire whether such an act be constitutional.

The parties in this case differ less on general principles, less on the true construction of the Constitution in the abstract, than on the application of those principles to this case, and on the true construction of the charter of 1769. This is the point on which the cause essentially depends. If the act of incorporation be a grant of political power, if it create a civil institution to be employed in the administration of the government, or if the funds of the college be public property, or if the state of New Hampshire, as a government, be alone interested in its transactions, the subject is one in which the legislature of the state may act according to its own judgment, unrestrained by any limitation of its power imposed by the Constitution of the United States.

But if this be a private eleemosynary institution, endowed with a capacity to take property for objects unconnected with government, whose funds are bestowed by individuals on the faith of the charter; if the donors have stipulated for the future disposition and management of those funds in the manner prescribed by themselves, there may be more difficulty in the case, although neither the persons who have made these stipulations nor those for whose benefit they are made, should be parties to the cause. Those who are no longer interested in the property, may yet retain such an interest in the preservation of their own arrangements as to have a right to insist that those arrangements shall be held sacred. Or, if they have themselves disappeared, it becomes a subject of serious and anxious inquiry, whether those whom they have legally empowered to represent them forever may not assert all the rights which they possessed, while in being; whether, if they be without personal representatives who may feel injured by a violation of the compact, the trustees be not so completely their representatives, in the eye of the law, as to stand in their place, not only as respects the government of the college, but also as respects the maintenances of the college charter.

It becomes, then, the duty of the court most seriously to examine this charter and to ascertain its true character. . . .

A corporation is an artificial being, invisible, intangible, and existing only in contemplation of law. Being the mere creature of law, it possesses only those properties which the charter of its creation confers upon it, either expressly or as incidental to its very existence. These are such as are supposed best calculated to effect the object for which it was created. Among the most important are immortality, and, if the expression may be allowed, individuality; properties by which a perpetual succession of many persons are considered as the same, and may act as a single individual. They enable a corporation to manage its own affairs, and to hold property without the perplexing intricacies, the hazardous and endless necessity, of perpetual conveyances for the purpose of transmitting it from hand to hand. It is chiefly for the purpose of clothing bodies of men, in succession, with these qualities and capacities, that corporations were invented, and are in use. By these means, a perpetual succession of individuals are capable of acting for the promotion of the particular object, like one immortal being. . . . It is no more a state instrument than a natural person exercising the same powers would be. If, then, a natural person, employed by individuals in the education of youth, or for the government of a seminary in which youth is educated, would not become a public officer, or be considered as a member of the civil government, how is it that this artificial being, created by law, for the purpose of being employed by the same individuals for the same purposes, should become a part of the civil government of the country? Is it because its existence, its capacities, its powers, are given by law? Because the government has given it the power to take and to hold property in a particular form, and for particular purposes, has the government a consequent right substantially to change that form, or to vary the purposes to which the property is to be applied? This principle has never been asserted or recognized, and is supported by no authority. Can it derive aid from reason?

The objects for which a corporation is created are universally such as the government wishes to promote. . . . The benefit to the public is considered as an ample compensation for the faculty it confers, and the corporation is created. If the advantages to the public constitute a full compensation for the faculty it gives, there can be no reason for exacting a further compensation, by claiming a right to exercise over this artificial being a power which changes its nature, and touches the fund, for the security and application of which it was created. There can be no reason for implying in a charter, given for a valuable consideration, a power which is not only not expressed, but is in direct contradiction to its express stipulations.

From the fact, then, that a charter of incorporation has been granted, nothing can be inferred which changes the char-

acter of the institution, or transfers to the government any new power over it. The character of civil institutions does not grow out of their incorporation, but out of the manner in which they are formed, and the objects for which they are created. The right to change them is not founded on their being incorporated, but on their being the instruments of government, created for its purposes. The same institutions, created for the same objects, though not incorporated, would be public institutions, and, of course, be controllable by the legislature. The incorporating act neither gives nor prevents this control. Neither, in reason, can the incorporating act change the character of a private eleemosynary institution. . . .

From this review of the charter, it appears that Dartmouth College is an eleemosynary institution, incorporated for the purpose of perpetuating the application of the bounty of the donors, to the specified objects of that bounty; that its trustees or governors were originally named by the founder, and invested with the power of perpetuating themselves; that they are not public officers, nor is it a civil institution, participating in the administration of government; but a charity school, or a seminary of education, incorporated for the preservation of its property, and the perpetual application of that property to the objects of its creation.

Yet a question remains to be considered, of more real difficulty, on which more doubt has been entertained than on all that have been discussed. The founders of the college, at least those whose contributions were in money, have parted with the property bestowed upon it, and their representatives have no interest in that property. The donors of land are equally without interest, so long as the corporation shall exist. Could they be found, they are unaffected by any alteration in its constitution, and probably regardless of its form, or even of its existence. The students are fluctuating, and no individual among our youth has a vested interest in the institution, which can be asserted in a court of justice. Neither the founders of the college nor the youth for whose benefit it was founded, complain of the alteration made in its charter, or think themselves injured by it. The trustees alone complain, and the trustees have no beneficial interest to be protected. Can this be such a contract as the Constitution intended to withdraw from the power of state legislation? Contracts, the parties to which have a vested beneficial interest, and those only, it has been said, are the objects about which the Constitution is solicitous, and to which its protection is extended.

The Court has bestowed on this argument the most deliberate consideration, and the result will be stated. Dr. Wheelock, acting for himself, and for those who, at his solicitation, had made contributions to his school, applied for this charter, as the instrument which should enable him, and them, to perpetuate their beneficent intention. It was granted. An artificial, immortal being, was created by the crown, capable of receiving and distributing forever, according to the will of the donors, the donations which should be made to it. On this being, the contributions which had been collected were immediately bestowed. These gifts were made, not, indeed, to make a profit for the donors, or their posterity, but for something in their opinion of inestimable value; for something which they deemed a full equivalent for the money with which it was purchased. The consideration for which they stipulated, is the perpetual application of the fund to its object, in the mode prescribed by themselves. Their descendants may take no interest in the preservation of this consideration. But in this respect their descendants are not their representatives. They are rep-

resented by the corporation. The corporation is the assignee of their rights, stands in their place, and distributes their bounty, as they would themselves have distributed it, had they been immortal. So with respect to the students who are to derive learning from this source. The corporation is a trustee for them also. Their potential rights, which, taken distributively, are imperceptible, amount collectively to a most important interest. These are, in the aggregate, to be exercised, asserted and protected, by the corporation. They were as completely out of the donors, at the instant of their being vested in the corporation, and as incapable of being asserted by the students, as at present.

According to the theory of the British constitution, their parliament is omnipotent. To annul corporate rights might give a shock to public opinion, which that government has chosen to avoid; but its power is not questioned. Had parliament, immediately after the emanation of this charter, and the execution of those conveyances which followed it, annulled the instrument, so that the living donors would have witnessed the disappointment of their hopes, the perfidy of the transaction would have been universally acknowledged. Yet then, as now, the donors would have had no interest in the property; then, as now, those who might be students would have had no rights to be violated; then, as now, it might be said, that the trustees, in whom the rights of all were combined, possessed no private, individual, beneficial interest in the property confided to their protection. Yet the contract would at that time have been deemed sacred by all. What has since occurred to strip it of its inviolability? Circumstances have not changed it. In reason, in justice, and in law, it is now what it was in 1769.

This is plainly a contract to which the

donors, the trustees, and the crown (to whose rights and obligations New Hampshire succeeds), were the original parties. It is a contract made on a valuable consideration. It is a contract for the security and disposition of property. It is a contract, on the faith of which real and personal estate has been conveyed to the corporation. It is then a contract within the letter of the Constitution, and within its spirit also, unless the fact that the property is invested by the donors in trustees for the promotion of religion and education, for the benefit of persons who are perpetually changing, though the objects remain the same, shall create a particular exception, taking this case out of the prohibition contained in the Constitution.

It is more than possible that the preservation of rights of this description was not particularly in the view of the framers of the Constitution when the clause under consideration was introduced into that instrument. It is probable that interferences of more frequent recurrence, to which the temptation was stronger, and of which the mischief was more extensive, constituted the great motive for imposing this restriction on the state legislatures. But although a particular and a rare case may not, in itself, be of sufficient magnitude to induce a rule, yet it must be governed by the rule when established, unless some plain and strong reason for excluding it can be given. It is not enough to say that this particular case was not in the mind of the convention when the article was framed, nor of the American people when it was adopted. It is necessary to go farther, and to say that, had this particular case been suggested, the language would have been so varied as to exclude it, or it would have been made a special exception. The case being within the words of the rule, must be within its operation likewise, unless there be something in the literal construction so ob-

viously absurd, or mischievous, or repugnant to the general spirit of the instrument, as to justify those who expound the constitution in making it an exception.

On what safe and intelligible ground can this exception stand. There is no exception in the Constitution, no sentiment delivered by its contemporaneous expounders, which would justify us in making it. In the absence of all authority of this kind, is there, in the nature and reason of the case itself, that which would sustain a construction of the Constitution, not warranted by its words? Are contracts of this description of a character to excite so little interest that we must exclude them from the provisions of the Constitution, as being unworthy of the attention of those who framed the instrument? Or does public policy so imperiously demand their remaining exposed to legislative alteration, as to compel us, or rather permit us to say that these words, which were introduced to give stability to contracts, and which in their plain import comprehend this contract, must yet be so construed as to exclude it?

Almost all eleemosynary corporations, those which are created for the promotion of religion, of charity, or of education, are of the same character. The law of this case is the law of all. . . .

If the insignificance of the object does not require that we should exclude contracts respecting it from the protection of the Constitution, neither, as we conceive, is the policy of leaving them subject to legislative alteration so apparent as to require a forced construction of that instrument in order to effect it. These eleemosynary institutions do not fill the place, which would otherwise be occupied by government, but that which would otherwise remain vacant. They are complete acquisitions to literature. They are donations to education; donations which any government must be disposed rather to encourage than to discountenance. It requires no very critical examination of the human mind to enable us to determine that one great inducement to these gifts is the conviction felt by the giver, that the disposition he makes of them is immutable. It is probable that no man ever was, and that no man ever will be, the founder of a college, believing at the time that an act of incorporation constitutes no security for the institution; believing that it is immediately to be deemed a public institution, whose funds are to be governed and applied, not by the will of the donor, but by the will of the legislature. All such gifts are made in the pleasing, perhaps delusive hope, that the charity will flow forever in the channel which the givers have marked out for it. If every man finds in his own bosom strong evidence of the universality of this sentiment, there can be but little reason to imagine that the framers of our Constitution were strangers to it, and that, feeling the necessity and policy of giving permanence and security to contracts, of withdrawing them from the influence of legislative bodies, whose fluctuating policy, and repeated interferences, produced the most perplexing and injurious embarrassments, they still deemed it necessary to leave these contracts subject to those interferences. The motives for such an exception must be very powerful, to justify the construction which makes it. . . .

The opinion of the Court, after mature deliberation, is, that this is a contract, the obligation of which cannot be impaired without violating the Constitution of the United States. This opinion appears to us to be equally supported by reason, and by the former decisions of this Court.

2. We next proceed to the inquiry whether its obligation has been impaired by those acts of the legislature of New Hampshire to which the special verdict refers.

From the review of this charter, which has been taken, it appears that the whole power of governing the college, of appointing and removing tutors, of fixing their salaries, of directing the course of study to be pursued by the students, and of filling up vacancies created in their own body, was vested in the trustees. On the part of the crown it was expressly stipulated that this corporation, thus constituted, should continue forever; and that the number of trustees should forever consist of twelve, and no more. By this contract the crown was bound, and could have made no violent alteration in its essential terms, without impairing its obligation.

By the revolution, the duties, as well as the powers, of government devolved on the people of New Hampshire. It is admitted, that among the latter was comprehended the transcendent power of parliament, as well as that of the executive department. It is too clear to require the support of argument, that all contracts, and rights, respecting property, remained unchanged by the revolution. The obligations, then, which were created by the charter to Dartmouth College, were the same in the new that they had been in the old government. The power of the government was also the same. A repeal of this charter at any time prior to the adoption of the present Constitution of the United States, would have been an extraordinary and unprecedented act of power, but one which could have been contested only by the restrictions upon the legislature, to be found in the constitution of the state. But the Constitution of the United States has imposed this additional limitation, that the legislature of a state shall pass no act "impairing the obligation of contracts."

It has been already stated that the act "to amend the charter, and enlarge and improve the corporation of Dartmouth

College," increases the number of trustees to twenty-one, gives the appointment of the additional members to the executive of the state, and creates a board of overseers, to consist of twenty-five persons, of whom twenty-one are also appointed by the executive of New Hampshire, who have power to inspect and control the most important acts of the trustees.

On the effect of this law, two opinions cannot be entertained. Between acting directly, and acting through the agency of trustees and overseers, no essential difference is perceived. The whole power of governing the college is transferred from trustees appointed according to the will of the founder, expressed in the charter, to the executive of New Hampshire. The management and application of the funds of this eleemosynary institution, which are placed by the donors in the hands of trustees named in the charter, and empowered to perpetuate themselves, are placed by this act under the control of the government of the state. The will of the state is substituted for the will of the donors in every essential operation of the college. This is not an immaterial change. The founders of the college contracted, not merely for the perpetual application of the funds which they gave, to the objects for which those funds were given; they contracted also to secure that application by the constitution of the corporation. They contracted for a system which should, as far as human foresight can provide, retain forever the government of the literary institution they had formed, in the hands of persons approved by themselves. This system is totally changed. The charter of 1769 exists no longer. It is re-organized; and re-organized in such a manner as to convert a literary institution, moulded according to the will of its founders, and placed under the control of private literary men, into a machine entirely subservient to the will of government.

This may be for the advantage of this college in particular, and may be for the advantage of literature in general, but it is not according to the will of the donors, and is subversive of that contract, on the faith of which their property was given.

In the view which has been taken of this interesting case, the Court has confined itself to the right possessed by the trustees, as the assignees and representatives of the donors and founders, for the benefit of religion and literature. Yet it is not clear that the trustees ought to be considered as destitute of such beneficial interest in themselves as the law may respect. In addition to their being the legal owners of the property, and to their having a freehold right in the powers confided to them, the charter itself countenances the idea that trustees may also be tutors with salaries. The first president was one of the original trustees; and the charter provides, that in case of vacancy in that office, "the senior professor or tutor, being one of the trustees, shall exercise the office of president, until the trustees shall make choice of, and appoint a president." According to the tenor of the charter, then, the trustees might, without impropriety, appoint a president and other professors from their own body. This is a power not entirely unconnected with an interest. Even if the proposition of the counsel for the defendant were sustained; if it were admitted that those contracts only are protected by the Constitution, a beneficial interest in which is vested in the party, who appears in court to assert that interest; yet it is by no means clear that the trustees of Dartmouth College have no beneficial interest in themselves.

But the Court has deemed it unnecessary to investigate this particular point, being of opinion, on general principles, that in these private eleemosynary institutions, the body corporate, as possessing the whole legal and equitable interest, and completely representing the donors, for the purpose of executing the trust, has rights which are protected by the Constitution.

It results from this opinion, that the acts of the legislature of New Hampshire, which are stated in the special verdict found in this cause, are repugnant to the Constitution of the United States; and that the judgment on this special verdict ought to have been for the plaintiffs. The judgment of the State Court must therefore be reversed.

Assuming that the intent of the framers was to limit the contract clause to private contracts and essentially to the impairment of contracts between creditors and debtors through legislative enactments, how does Chief Justice Marshall expand the substantive definition of the clause? How does Marshall support his position while admitting that "the framers of the Constitution did not intend to restrain the states in the regulation of their civil institutions?"

The *Dartmouth College* decision broadened the reach of the contract clause. However, the Court's later decisions on the effect of the clause were by no means unambiguous. In *Sturges* v. *Crowninshield,* 4 Wheat. 122 (1819), a New York law discharging debtors of their contractural obligations upon the surrender of their property was held unconstitutional. In *Ogden* v. *Saunders,* 12 Wheat. 213 (1827), a state bankruptcy law that permitted persons, upon the surrender of their property, to be discharged of their debts and of claims upon property acquired in the future, was upheld. The four majority justices arrived at their conclusions by different reasoning. One argued that bankruptcy laws in existence at the time a contract was made became part of the contract itself; therefore, at any given time a bankruptcy law governed future contracts. Two justices held that it was up to the states to determine the obligation of contracts within them. The remaining majority justice deferred to the judgment of the state because considerations of federalism required that the states have broad latitude in governing contracts. Chief Justice Marshall, in his only dissent during his tenure on the Court, reaffirmed his view that contractual obligations are based upon principles of natural law that cannot be altered by state legislation.

Modern Interpretation of the Contract Clause

The leading modern case on contract impairment is *Home Building and Loan Association* v. *Blaisdell* (1934). The Court's decision upheld the Minnesota Mortgage Moratorium Law of 1933, which was enacted to meet the extreme hardships caused by the Depression for those who had mortgaged their property, particularly farmers. Under the terms of the law state courts were authorized to prevent mortgage foreclosure sales for a time period that they deemed "just and equitable," but not beyond May 1, 1935. While the law did not retroactively impair the formal terms of mortgage contracts, it did permit a temporary suspension of the means of legal enforcement. In upholding the law, the Court stressed that it was enacted in pursuance of legitimate state interests in protecting the community during an emergency.

Its terms were reasonable, resulting in only a temporary suspension and not a permanent impairment of contracts. Chief Justice Hughes's opinion for the Court emphasized that states possess the authority to safeguard vital community interests, and legislation to that end is appropriate even if it results in the modification or abrogation of contracts already in existence. The Court stated that not only "are existing laws read into contracts in order to fix obligations as between the parties, but the reservation of essential attributes of sovereign power is also read into contracts as a postulate of the legal order. The policy of protecting contracts against impairment presupposes the maintenance of a government by virtue of which contractual relations are worthwhile—a government which retains adequate authority to secure the peace and good order of society."[64] This statement implied that state legislatures can retroactively change the terms of contracts when they reasonably conclude that it is in the public interest.

Interpretation of the Contract Clause after *Blaisdell*

Both the early decision of the Court in *Ogden* v. *Saunders* (1827) and its opinion in *Blaisdell* stressed that private contracts are not sacrosanct but may be subject to retroactive or future alteration by state legislation. The *Ogden* v. *Saunders* decision was based upon the premise that private contracts may be altered by legislation that predates their origination. The Court in *Blaisdell* allowed the state to impose a retroactive moratorium on mortgage contracts.

Whether retroactive or future alteration of contracts is involved, the authority of the state is not absolute and must be determined on the basis of a balancing of the public interest with private rights. Retroactive impairment of contractual obligations is in particular closely scrutinized by the Court, which has tended to apply stricter standards to the demonstration of a requisite public interest to sustain such action than has been adopted for legislation affecting future contracts.[65] However, in *El Paso* v. *Simmons* (1965) the Court upheld against an impairment of contract challenge a 1941 Texas law that amended the terms of an 1895 statute under which public land was sold in 1910. The Court stated that "It is not every modification of a contractual promise that impairs the obligation of contract under federal law, any more than it is every alteration of existing remedies that violates the contract clause."[66] The Court concluded that the state had a clear interest in modifying the original contract, which was not outweighed by the interests of the individual purchasers of the land.

[64]Home Building and Loan Association v. Blaisdell, 290 U.S. 398, 435 (1934).

[65]See Wood v. Lovett, 313 U.S. 362 (1941) and Worthen Co. v. Cavanaugh, 295 U.S. 56 (1936), for examples of court invalidation of state attempts to change retroactively contractual obligations. An example of court invalidation under the contract clause of a state law affecting future contracts is Worthen Co. v. Thomas, 292 U.S. 426 (1934). The Court overturned an Arkansas law that exempted life insurance benefits from garnishment on the grounds that it was too broad because it had set no time limit and was not based upon the circumstances of the individual cases.

[66]El Paso v. Simmons, 379 U.S. 497, 506–507 (1965).

Although Justice Black, dissenting in the *El Paso* case, accused the Court of balancing away the "plain guarantee" of the contract clause, Justice White's majority opinion noted that the "power of a state to modify or affect the obligation of contract is not without limit."[67] In *United States Trust Co. of New York* v. *New Jersey* (1977), the Court invalidated 1974 legislation passed by the states of New York and New Jersey that repealed the provisions of a 1962 statutory convenant between the states under which bonds were issued by the Port Authority. The states had taken the action in order to divert funds pledged as security for the bonds to subsidize rail passenger transportation. The states wanted to encourage the users of private automobiles to shift to public transportation. Justice Blackmun, writing for the Court, stated,

> Mass transportation, energy conservation, and environmental protection are goals that are important and of legitimate public concern. Appellees contend that these goals are so important that any harm to bondholders from repeal of the 1962 convenant is greatly outweighed by the public benefit. We do not accept this invitation to engage in a utilitarian comparison of public benefit and private laws. Contrary to Mr. Justice Black's fear, expressed on sole dissent in *El Paso* v. *Simmons* . . . the Court has not "balanced away" the limitation on state action imposed by the contract clause. Thus a state cannot refuse to meet its legitimate financial obligations simply because it would prefer to spend the money to promote the public good rather than the private welfare of its creditors. We can only sustain the repeal of the 1962 covenant if that impairment was both reasonable and necessary to serve the admittedly important purposes claimed by the state.[68]

The Court held that the states could accomplish in other ways the goals they sought without modifying the covenant. Moreover, the concern that led to the alteration of the original contractual agreement were "not unknown" in 1962 when the covenant originated; therefore the retroactive alteration of the contract was not warranted by changed circumstances. In short, the impairment was neither reasonable nor necessary.

JUDICIAL REVIEW IN PERSPECTIVE

Throughout history there have been serious challenges to the power of the Supreme Court to nullify the acts of coordinate branches of the federal government and of state governments. In the twentieth century the most serious challenge to the Court came during the 1930s, when Chief Justice Charles Evans Hughes and a majority of conservative colleagues on the Court declared important early New Deal legislation to be unconstitutional. This thwarted the efforts of President Franklin D. Roosevelt to carry out what he felt was a popular mandate to exercise economic initiatives to solve the problems of the depression. Roosevelt's "court-packing" scheme, which would have allowed the President to appoint one new Supreme Court justice for each justice over the age of seventy (a total of six during Roosevelt's first

---

[67]Ibid, p. 509.
[68]United States Trust Co. of New York v. New Jersey, 431 U.S. 1, 28–29 (1977).

term), would have given the New Deal White House the ability to appoint a Supreme Court majority favorable to its views. Roosevelt's bold attack upon the Court never had a serious chance of passage in Congress. By the time the plan was presented in 1937 the initial congressional honeymoon with the President had ended. Congress was asserting its prerogatives under the separation of powers system by exercising careful scrutiny over presidential programs and opposing those that would upset the vested interest within Congress, as well as those without clearcut popular mandates. From Capitol Hill Roosevelt's court-packing plan was seen as an aggrandizement of the presidency, from which Congress would suffer, not as an attempt to ease judicial approval of its legislation.

While the New Deal period witnessed the most serious challenge to the authority of the Supreme Court in the twentieth century, the extraordinary actions of the Warren Court in the expansion of national standards governing state action raised the issue of the proper scope of the Court's authority in a different context than it had been presented during the New Deal. During the 1930s the issue was primarily, although not exclusively, the extent to which the Supreme Court should overrule acts of Congress that were presumably based upon the will of the majority. During the era of the Warren Court the issue was the proper balance between national and state spheres of authority and the extent to which the Supreme Court should enunciate constitutional standards that would control the states. The era of the Warren Court was characterized by the nationalization of the Bill of Rights vis-à-vis the states in a variety of critical policy areas—school desegregation, electoral reapportionment, school prayer, and the rights of those accused of crime. The states considered each of these areas of public policy to be within their reserved powers. Therefore strong opposition inevitably developed to judicial attempts to impose standards that were agreed upon in many cases by only five men who constituted a majority of the Supreme Court.

As the activism of the Warren Court began to wane due to the conservative appointments of President Richard M. Nixon, controversy over the extent of the Court's power diminished but did not die. Inevitably the Supreme Court is thrust into the arena of political controversy because it cannot avoid deciding cases that bear upon sensitive issues of public policy. A liberal court will be attacked by conservatives, and vice versa. The Supreme Court and lower federal courts were attacked in the post–Warren era for highly controversial decisions requiring the busing of school children to achieve integration and denying states the absolute right to prohibit abortion. Liberals as well as conservatives joined in opposition to decisions requiring busing. As the Burger Court tried to resolve constitutional questions in policy areas such as sex discrimination, the death penalty, and obscenity, to mention only a few, it inevitably found its position uncomfortable regardless of what decisions were made.

Under certain circumstances the Supreme Court can and will avoid controversial cases by exercising *judicial self-restraint*.[69] Since the passage of the Judiciary Act of 1925 the discretion of the Supreme Court to pick and

---

[69]See footnote 32 *supra*.

choose what cases it will hear has been greatly expanded, and the right to appeal a case to the Supreme Court that existed in a wide variety of cases before 1925 was limited. Today a vote of four justices is required to grant a writ of certiorari, the most common review writ after 1925 that is used to review the decisions of lower courts by calling up the record of the proceeding to the higher court. Appeal to the Supreme Court as a matter of right is strictly limited to those cases from the highest state court, or from federal courts where there is a conflict of federal and state law, or where federal or state laws have been held unconstitutional. While the Supreme Court has used its discretionary authority to refuse the issuance of writs of certiorari to avoid a multitude of questions raised in lower court decisions, the mix of ideological viewpoints on the Court has usually meant that the necessary four votes are there to grant certiorari in cases where important constitutional or statutory issues are involved. Moreover, whether they like it or not, Supreme Court justices operate within a political milieu, and attempts to avoid consistently controversial cases, even if they could be technically successful, would cause a political maelstrom comparable to any that would be created by ruling on the issues in conflict. And, perhaps most important of all, the Court by its very power and prestige does not encourage passivity within the institutional context in which it functions. An institution with such power more often than not encourages its members to exercise it, not to abdicate their opportunities and responsibilities.

The constitutional prerogatives of the Supreme Court are buttressed by a governmental system in which pluralistic stagnation is more common than rule by a cohesive political majority. The Madisonian model of government, contained in the Constitution, and described in *The Federalist,* papers 47, 48, and 51 (see Chapter 2), has by aiding in the fragmentation of the national government created a power vacuum into which the Supreme Court has frequently stepped to rule on major issues of public policy and thereby to create policy. Federalism too has fortified the power of the Supreme Court by creating a multitude of separate and conflicting jurisdictions, which not only require the Supreme Court to act in certain cases but also in effect make it possible for the Court to divide and conquer when it announces national standards in controversial intergovernmental cases.

It is doubtful, for example, that the Court's decision in 1954 in *Brown* v. *Board of Education* would have been sustained if its effect had fallen equally upon all of the states. Even so, powerful opposition from the South prevented meaningful integration of public education there until the end of the 1960s. In another area, that of nationalization of the Bill of Rights under the due process clause of the Fourteenth Amendment, the gradual incorporation of most of the Bill of Rights by the Supreme Court was facilitated by the fact that a variety of states already had protections similar to those of the Bill of Rights in their own constitutions and laws. This prevented a united front of opposition to the Supreme Court as it proceeded to apply the Bill of Rights to the states. By the time *Gideon* v. *Wainwright* was decided in 1962, incorporating the right to counsel under the due process clause of the Fourteenth Amendment, thirty-seven states provided a right to counsel in all felony cases. Moreover, of the remaining thirteen states, eight provided counsel as a matter of practice. This in effect meant that the *Gideon* decision would directly affect only five states.[70] This is a dramatic illustration of how the federal system, with contrasting state interests and practices, can enable the Supreme Court to set national standards that will receive more support than opposition from the states.

The Supreme Court has been far more active in exercising its prerogative of constitutional review over state actions than at the national level. Henry J. Abraham has estimated that through the fall of 1979 while the Supreme Court declared "122 or 123 provisions of *federal* laws unconstitutional in whole or in part out of a total of over 85,000 public and private laws passed, some 950 *state* laws and provisions of *state* constitutions have run wholly or partly afoul of that judicial checkmate since 1789—some 850 of these coming after 1870."[71] It is not surprising that the most serious opposition to the Supreme Court, with the exception of the New Deal, has resulted from its decisions overruling state, not national, actions.

[70]Anthony Lewis, *Gideon's Trumpet* (New York: Random House, Vintage Edition, 1966), p. 132.

[71]Henry J. Abraham, *The Judicial Process*, 4th ed. (New York: Oxford University Press, 1980), pp. 296–297.

TWO

The Separation of Powers

The terms *separation of powers* and *checks and balances* are commonly used descriptions of American government. These phrases do not, however, have a precise and unambiguous meaning. From the very beginning the separation of powers concept has been shrouded in ambiguity. The idea of the importance of a division of governmental powers to prevent tyranny and guarantee political stability dates back to Plato's *Laws.* From Plato onward numerous political theorists have seen some kind of mixed government as essential for the ideal polity. But ancient political theory did not concentrate upon the importance of a constitutional division of authority among the branches of government as the essential ingredient in a mixed government. Theorists before the eighteenth century concentrated upon the idea of balancing social, economic, and class interests to prevent centralization and create a sound government. The nature of the "mixture" of interests and how they were to be represented in government was never clearly articulated by any theorist, nor was it a subject of agreement among them.

The confusion in political theory about the proper form mixed governments should take reflected the divergent political practices and experiences that theorists drew upon. In England, the struggles of the seventeenth century that culminated in the Glorious Revolution of 1688 reflected in part the struggle to establish a separation of powers between the King and the common law courts. At the same time that a judicial-executive separation of powers was developing, the Glorious Revolution established in practice the principle of parliamentary supremacy. As England embarked upon the eighteenth century its government had a separation of powers only in the sense that the common law courts exercised a judicial power independently of Parliament and the cabinet. There was no separation of powers between the executive and legislative branches, for the executive authority of the king had been taken over by the cabinet, which was elected by a majority of Parliament.

The origins of the modern theory of separation of powers are customarily traced to Montesquieu's *Esprit des Lois* published in 1748. Montesquieu's theory of the separation of powers was widely read and quoted by literate colonists and found its way into Madison's exegesis on the subject in *The Federalist*. While Madison went along with the tenor of the times by citing Montesquieu, in fact the American practice of the separation of powers both in colonial charters and in state constitutions went beyond the British constitution by establishing the principle of separation between legislative and executive branches.

Although Montesquieu misunderstood the British constitution, proclaiming that it in fact created a separation of powers among legislative, executive, and judicial branches, his theory was an important milestone. He was the first to emphasize the importance of legal divisions of authority among the branches of government. Each branch would have its own preserve of power, delegated to it by the Constitution, and at the same time would be given sufficient powers to check coordinate branches.

Montesquieu's theory provided a basis for James Madison's discussion of the separation of powers in *The Federalist*. A constitutional system of the separation of powers has come to be known as the *Madisonian model* of government. An underlying premise of the model is that there is a natural division of governmental power into the legislative, executive, and judicial categories. These functions are separate and distinct and are appropriately exercised by separate branches of government. The functions of government should be comingled through the checks and balances system only insofar as is necessary to preserve the integrity of each branch. The primary thrust of the assumption of a natural division of governmental authority is that the separation of powers is necessary for efficient governmental performance.

In *The Federalist*, however, James Madison did not emphasize the efficiency of government that would be created by the new Constitution but concentrated upon how the separation of powers would prevent arbitrary and capricious government. Madison stated the premise of this negative aspect of the separation of powers in *Federalist 47*, that "the accumulation of all powers, legislation, executive, and judiciary, in the same hands, whether of one, a few, or many, and whether hereditary, self-appointed, or elected, may justly be pronounced the very definition of tyranny." Madison's presentation of the separation of powers in this light has always resulted in identifying the Madisonian model with a system that emphasizes the need to control and inhibit government action, rather than the importance of insuring effective performance of legislative, executive, and judicial functions.[1]

Alexander Hamilton's views of the separation of powers in *The Federalist*

[1]See, for example, James MacGregor Burns, *The Deadlock of Democracy* (Englewood Cliffs, N.J.: Prentice-Hall, Inc., 1963) for the development of the view that the Madisonian model has been an important contributing factor toward paralysis of government. It is of historical interest to note that at the Constitutional Convention Madison at first argued for a more unitary form of government that would have merged the legislative and executive branches, a plan that came to be known as the Randolph or Virginia Plan. For a discussion of the Convention see John P. Roche, "The Founding Fathers: A Reform Caucus in Action," *American Political Science Review*, 61 (December 1961), 799–816.

are in sharp contrast to those of Madison. In *Federalist 70,* Hamilton proclaimed that "Energy in the executive is a leading character in the definition of good government. It is essential to the protection of a community against foreign attacks; it is not less essential to the steady administration of the laws, to the protection of property against those irregular and high-handed combinations, which sometimes interrupt the ordinary course of justice, to the security of liberty against the enterprises and assaults of ambition, of faction, and of anarchy." Effective, not limited, government was Hamilton's goal. "A feeble executive implies a feeble execution of the government," said Hamilton. And, "a feeble execution is but another phrase for a bad execution; and a government ill executed, whatever it may be in theory, must be, in practice, a bad government." The *Hamiltonian model* conflicts with the Madisonian model in its premises that efficiency and effectiveness are the desired ends of government and that the separation of powers through its creation of an independent executive makes a major contribution to this end.

The Madisonian and Hamiltonian models contrasted not only in their approaches to the goals of the separation of legislative and executive power but in their explanations of the role of the judiciary. Madison was more inclined towards the Jeffersonian view that although the judiciary should be independent, its powers should be limited. Hamilton, by contrast, boldly proclaimed in *Federalist 78* that an independent judiciary with the authority to overturn unconstitutional acts of Congress was essential to effective constitutional government.

The fact that Madison and Hamilton could view the same Constitution in contrasting ways reflected inherent constitutional ambiguities that, under the doctrine of *Marbury* v. *Madison,* would ultimately have to be resolved by the Court. "It is emphatically the province and duty of the judicial department to say what the law is," said John Marshall in the *Marbury* opinion. It would be up to the Court to resolve any constitutional ambiguities over the legal boundaries of the separation of powers. In resolving these constitutional questions judges supporting the Madisonian model would tend to declare unconstitutional bold exercises of executive discretion, such as those which occurred in *Youngstown Sheet and Tube* v. *Sawyer* in 1952. Madison would have looked favorably upon the majority's decision, whereas Hamilton would have endorsed the vigorous dissent of Chief Justice Vinson who supported the constitutionality of independent executive action to meet national emergencies. In each of the cases in this chapter dealing with the separation of powers a question is presented as to the relative power that one branch should be able to exercise in relation to another.

CONSTITUTIONAL BACKGROUND

The Madisonian model of the separation of powers is set forth in the *Federalist* papers 47, 48, and 51. Madison was careful to point out that although liberty requires the separation of the three branches, neither the theory nor the practice of the separation of powers requires an absolute separation among the branches. Citing Montesquieu, Madison notes that "his meaning ... can amount to no more than this, that where the *whole* power of one department is exercised by the same hands which possessed the *whole* power of another department, the fundamental principles of a free constitution are subverted. . . ." Moreover, Madison said, "If we look into the constitutions of the several states, we find that notwithstanding the emphatical and, in some instances, the unqualified terms in which this axiom has been laid down, there is not a single instance in which the several departments of power have been kept absolutely separate and distinct. . . " *(Federalist 47)*. Madison cites theory and practice to support his conclusion that the separation of powers can only be maintained if there is a blend of power among the branches, so that each has a constitutional check upon the other, and each has the means to defend itself against encroachments by coordinate branches.

The separation of powers is to be maintained not only through checks and balances but also by the creation of contrasting motivations for each branch of the government. This was accomplished by giving each branch a separate constituency—Congress being responsible to the people and the states respectively in the House and the Senate, and the President accountable to the Electoral College. The Supreme Court and the judiciary, although selected by the President by and with the advice and consent of the Senate, were to be independent of the other branches. Each branch "should have a will of its own," wrote Madison in *Federalist 51*. He continued: "The great security against a gradual concentration of the several powers in the same department [branch] consists in giving to those who administer each department, the necessary constitutional means, and *personal motives* to resist encroachments of the others." The personal motives to resist encroachments were supplied by the separate constituencies.

Regardless of how elaborate the constitutional system to prevent the arbitrary exercise of political power was, Madison warned against the possibility of a dominant legislative branch. The future development of the Republic was to see the rise of the "imperial presidency," at least in part due to liberal Supreme Court interpretations of the scope of executive authority under the Constitution. But executive power was the least of the expressed concerns of Madison in *The Federalist*. It is not possible, he wrote, "to give to each department an equal power of self-defense. In republican government, the legislative authority [branch] necessarily predominates. The remedy for this inconvenience is to divide the government into different branches; and to render them by different modes of election and different principles of action, as little connected with each other, as the nature of their common functions, and their common dependence on the society will admit" *(Federalist 51)*. By contrast, the inherent weakness of the executive requires that it be fortified, by giving it such powers as the veto over legislative actions. Madison found the source of legislative superiority in the connection between the legislative branch and the people, which inspires the legislative branch "with an intrepid confidence in its own strength." The legislature is "sufficiently numerous to feel all the passions which actuate a multitude; yet not so numerous as to be incapable of pursuing the objects of its passions, by means which reason prescribes; it is against the enterprising ambition of this department, that the people ought to indulge all their jealousy and exhaust all their precautions."

Madison wrote that another reason for the superiority of the legislature was that "its constitutional powers being at once more extensive, and less susceptible of precise limits, it can, with the greater facility [than other branches] mask, under complicated and indirect measures, the encroachment which it makes on the coordinate departments. It is not infrequently a question of real nicety in legislative bodies, whether the operation of a particular measure will, or will not extend beyond the legislative sphere" *(Federalist 48)*.

There are many implications of the Madisonian model to the interpretation of the separation of powers. Acceptance of Madison's premises would lead to a wary view of the motivations and powers of Congress that would strike down legislative action that appeared to intrude upon the executive or judiciary. On the other hand, since Madison's assumption was that executive power is "restrained within a narrower compass, and . . . [is] more simple in its nature [than legislative power]," a more lenient view would be taken to executive prerogative actions that would allow an expansion of presidential discretion. The relatively simple and constricted nature of both executive and judicial power led Madison to the conclusion that "projects of usurpation by either of these departments would immediately betray and defeat themselves" *(Federalist 48)*.

Neither the theory of the constitutional separation of powers as stated by Madison in the *Federalist* papers 47, 48, and 51 nor the provisions of the Constitution that implement the separation of powers create clear and unequivocal divisions of power that are to prevail among the three branches. Articles I, II, and III of the Constitution, called the *distributing clauses*, respectively delegate legislative, executive, and judicial powers to Congress, the President, and the Supreme Court. Article I provides that "All legislative powers herein granted shall be vested in a Congress of the United States, which shall consist of a Senate and House of Representatives." Article II states: "The executive power shall be vested in a President of the United States of America." And Article III provides: "The Judicial power of the United States, shall be vested in one Supreme Court, and in such inferior courts as the Congress may from time to time ordain and establish." On their face, these articles would seem to imply that no branch can exercise the general powers of coordinate branches. However, the distributing clauses do not themselves segregate governmental powers but delegate to each branch some of the powers of coordinate branches in the form of checks and balances. Thus, while "all legislative power" is to reside in Congress, the President is explicitly given the veto power over Congress, which is a clear grant of legislative authority to the President. Under the doctrine of *Marbury* v. *Madison*, the Supreme Court can nullify executive and legislative acts. Since congressional action can be vetoed by the President and nullified by the Supreme Court, "all legislative power" does not reside in Congress. Other constitutional checks and balances, although they do not give any branch the authority to exercise directly the powers of coordinate branches, may impede branches in the exercise of their primary constitutional powers.

The language of the Constitution in combination with Madison's statement of constitutional premises and principles in *The Federalist* make it clear that there is not to be a complete separation of powers among the three branches. The principle of separation of powers is violated only where *all* legislative, executive, and judicial powers reside in the same hands. Each branch must maintain control over the exercise of its primary constitutional function and at the same time can exercise powers that intrude upon the spheres of other branches if provided for by the constitutional system of checks and balances or if necessary and incidental to the exercise of its primary responsibility. The President can exercise a legislative veto because it is provided by the Constitution. The President can also be given the responsibility by Congress to exercise legislative functions (although not primary legislative power) that are incidental to executive power.

The need for judicial resolution of questions concerning the separation of powers arises under several circumstances. Usually questions arise when Congress has passed a statute that delegates to itself, to the President, or to the judiciary nonlegislative, nonexecutive, or nonjudicial functions respectively. Sometimes the President by prerogative action invades the spheres of coordinate branches.

The question of separation of powers in *Springer* v. *Philippine Islands* arose out of actions by the Philippine legislature that delegated to itself executive powers. Congress, in the organic act of the Philippine Islands, had provided for a separation of powers in the island government analogous to that which prevailed in the Constitution. The Philippine legislature had amended legislation creating government corporations to deny the governor-general the exclusive authority he had possessed under the original statute to vote the stock in these corporations. The amended laws provided that the voting power of the stock of various government corporations would henceforth reside in a committee consisting of the governor-general, the president of the Senate, and Speaker of the House of Representatives. As Justice Sutherland noted in his majority opinion in the *Springer* case, "The suggestion of the Solicitor-General [of the United States] that this indicates a systematic plan on the part of the legislature [of the Philippines] to take over through its presiding officers, the direct control generally of nationally organized or controlled stock corporations would seem to be warranted." The governor-general immediately challenged the action of the legislature and refused to participate in voting for the directors of the government corporations involved. Directors were subsequently chosen by the president of the Senate and the Speaker of the House, and the governor-general successfully challenged, in a *quo warranto* action in the Supreme Court of the Philippines, their right to hold office.[2] Springer and other directors elected by the legislative officers successfully sought a writ of certiorari from the Supreme

---

[2]As early as the twelfth century, the King challenged barons and others who were holding offices and franchises that the crown wished to control by demanding that they show by what right—quo warranto—they were exercising the powers of the office. In the twentieth century a quo warranto proceeding is a civil action testing the right of a government official to hold office.

Court to review the decision of the Supreme Court of the Philippine Islands that ousted them.

The majority opinion in the *Springer* case, written by Justice Sutherland, made it clear that the Court considered the actions of the Philippine legislature to be a violation of the separation of powers contained in the island's organic act. Legislative power, said the majority, is the authority to make the laws, not to enforce them nor to appoint agents charged with the responsibility of enforcement. The latter are executive functions. Even though the legislation in question did not give legislative officers the direct responsibility to enforce laws or to appoint officials, this was done by indirection in giving the presiding officers of the legislature the power to vote the stock of government corporations, hence giving them the authority to name the directors of the corporations.

Justice Holmes, joined by Justice Brandeis, dissented in the *Springer* case. He pointed out that there are many ambiguous provisions in the Constitution, including the separation of powers. The dissenting opinion cited numerous instances in which Congress took action that violated a strict separation of powers among the branches by giving both the executive and the courts lawmaking functions and in which it assumed for itself executive responsibilities. And, said the dissenting justices, the Supreme Court did not overturn these seeming transgressions of the separation of powers.

Springer v. *Philippine Islands*

277 U.S. 189; 48 S. Ct. 122; 72 L. Ed. 845 (1928)

Mr. Justice Sutherland gave the opinion of the Court:

... Not having the power of appointment, unless expressly granted or incidental to its powers, the legislature cannot engraft executive duties upon a legislative office, since that would be to usurp the power of appointment by indirection; ... Here the members of the legislature who constitute a majority of the "board" ... are not charged with the performance of any legislative functions ... by the legislature. ... It is clear that they are not legislative in character, and still more clear that they are not judicial. The fact that they do not fall within the authority of either of these two constitutes logical ground for concluding that they do fall within that of the remaining one of the three among which the powers of government are divided. ...

Mr. Justice Holmes, dissenting:

The great ordinances of the Constitution do not establish and divide fields of black and white. Even the more specific of them are found to terminate in a penumbra shading gradually from one extreme to the other. Property must not be taken without compensation, but with the help of a phrase (the police power) some property may be taken or destroyed for public use without paying for it, if you do not take too much. When we come to the fundamental distinctions it is still more obvious that they must be received with a certain latitude or our government could not go on.

To make a rule of conduct applicable to an individual who but for such action would be free from it is to legislate—yet it is what the judges do whenever they determine which of two competing principles of policy shall prevail. At an early date it was held that Congress could delegate to the courts the power to regulate process, which certainly is lawmaking so far as it goes. . . . With regard to the Executive, Congress has delegated to it or to some branch of it the power to impose penalties, . . . to make regulations as to forest reserves, . . . and other powers not needing to be stated in further detail. . . . Congress has authorized the President to suspend the operation of a statute, even one suspending commercial intercourse with another country, . . . and very recently it has been decided that the President might be given power to change the tariff. *J. W. Hampton, Jr. & Co.* v. *United States* [1928] . . . It is said that the powers of Congress cannot be delegated, yet Congress has established the Interstate Commerce Commission, which does legislative, judicial and executive acts, only softened by a quasi; makes regulations, . . . issues reparation orders, and per-

forms executive functions in connection with Safety Appliance Acts, Boiler Inspection Acts, etc. Congress also has made effective excursions in the other direction. It has withdrawn jurisdiction of a case after it has been argued. *Ex parte McCardle*, 7 Wall 506 [1869]. . . . It has granted an amnesty, notwithstanding the grant to the President of the power to pardon. . . .

. . . It is said that the functions of the Board of Control are not legislative or judicial and therefore they must be executive. I should say rather that they plainly are no part of the executive functions of the government but rather fall into the indiscriminate residue of matters within legislative control. I think it would be lamentable even to hint a doubt as to the legitimacy of the action of Congress in establishing the Smithsonian as it did, and I see no sufficient reason for denying the Philippine legislature a similar power.

MR. JUSTICE BRANDEIS agrees with this opinion.

MR. JUSTICE McREYNOLDS dissented in part.

THE DELEGATION OF LEGISLATIVE POWER

The *Institutes of Justinian*, published A.D. 533, established the rule that *delegata potestas non potest delegari*—a delegated power cannot be delegated. Although we are not governed by the corpus juris civilis of Justinian, there is a nondelegation doctrine in American law. In its purest form it states that power once delegated by the Constitution cannot be redelegated. This implies that the legislative power delegated to Congress in Article I cannot be redelegated to the President or administrative agencies. Justice Harlan stated in *Field* v. *Clark* (1892): "That Congress cannot delegate legislative power to the President is a principle universally recognized as vital to the integrity and maintenance of the system of government ordained by the Constitution." The principle of nondelegation is based upon the conclusion that once the sovereign delegates authority its delegatee has no further authority to act without the sovereign's consent. The Constitution was ordained and ratified by the people, and its fundamental principles cannot be altered without going through the formal amendment process. If the people have ordained in their Constitution that all legislative authority is to reside in Congress, then Congress does not have the right to overturn the wishes of the sovereign by further delegation to the executive of the authority it has received from the Constitution.

While the nondelegation doctrine has not been altered in theory, in practice by skillfull exegesis the courts have permitted vast delegations of legislative authority without altering the rhetoric of the nondelegation doctrine. This has been accomplished by permitting Congress to delegate legislative authority, provided it does not delegate the "primary" legislative power, the "whole" power of Congress under the Constitution. What constitutes "primary" legislative power, however, is a matter of subjective interpretation of the Constitution by the courts.

In allowing delegations of legislative authority the judiciary has essentially turned the delegation doctrine on its head by permitting Congress to delegate legislative authority if it meets the criteria set by the courts. The major judicial principle of delegation is that Congress must state its intent clearly enough so that the boundaries of the power it delegates can be ascertained. In this way Congress retains primary control over its legislative function, and its agents act in accordance with the wishes of the legislature. The courts become the guardians of legislative intent. The agents of Congress— the President or administrative agencies—must act within defined boundaries and in accordance with standards established by the legislature. Questions of delegation before the courts do not involve what substantive policy has been approved by Congress but whether that policy has been stated clearly enough to ascertain legislative intent.

Regardless of the good intentions of the judiciary to adhere to the non-delegation model, and thereby to preserve the purity of our constitutional system, meaningful delegations of real legislative authority have occurred from the early days of the Republic. Whether or not the "primary" authority of Congress has been delegated, however, is a matter of debate. But certainly lawmaking in the generic sense is performed outside of Congress, particularly by the federal bureaucracy. Legislating, or lawmaking, involves the formulation of general rules applicable to the community as a whole. It is prospective and does not become applicable against individuals until further proceedings are undertaken by administrative agents.

When performed by the bureaucracy legislating is usually called *rule making*. Administrative authority to make rules is delegated to agencies by Congress. For example, the Environmental Protection Agency has been given the authority to set standards through rule making for auto emissions and permissible levels of air and water pollution. The Federal Communications Commission has been delegated the authority, which it has so far not used, to make rules governing mergers in the broadcasting industry. The Internal Revenue Service makes voluminous rules interpreting tax legislation. Sometimes the IRS seems to go beyond its authority under tax legislation in rule making. At the end of 1978 the IRS conducted hearings on a proposed rule to deny tax-exempt status to private schools that had not demonstrated that they had undertaken a conscious and positive effort to provide racial balance. More than one member of Congress appeared before the IRS to protest that it was usurping the authority of Congress, which had not given the IRS this power.

Congressional intent governing the rule-making activities of administrative agencies is usually expressed in very vague terms. The agencies are mandated to carry out the public interest, convenience, and necessity and to establish "just and reasonable" rates. But the Supreme Court has only overturned two congressional delegations in its history, in *Panama Refining Company* v. *Ryan* (1935) and in *Schechter Poultry Corp.* v. *United States* (1935). In those cases the conservative New Deal Court, led by Chief Justice Charles Evans Hughes who wrote the opinions in each case, almost gleefully used the doctrine of nondelegation exclusively in the *Panama* case and as part of its opinion in *Schechter* to overturn the National Industrial Recovery Act, a key component of Roosevelt's early New Deal program.

Prior to the New Deal, congressional legislation was attacked on various occasions for being an unconstitutional delegation of legislative authority. Tariff legislation was particularly vulnerable to this charge. Congress customarily delegated the authority to raise or lower tariffs to the President, and in some cases to administrative officials, provided they found that certain conditions existed. The Tariff Act of 1890 gave the President the power to suspend the free introduction of "sugar, molasses, coffee, tea and hides" into the United States if he found that countries producing and exporting these commodities were levying "reciprocally unequal and unreasonable" duties on agricultural or other products from the United States. Upon presidential suspension of free trade in these commodities, certain duties specified by Congress were to go into effect automatically. In 1892 the Supreme Court upheld this delegation of power, stating that the "legislative power was exercised when Congress declared that the suspension should take effect upon a named *contingency*. What the President was required to do was simply in execution of the Act of Congress. *It was not the making of law.* He was the mere agent of the law-making department to ascertain and declare the event upon which its expressed will was to take effect."[3] The discretion of the President under the Tariff Act of 1890 was relatively narrow, in light of what was to happen in later delegations.

In the Tariff Act of 1922 the President was given broad discretion to adjust tariffs whenever he found differences in production costs between the United States and competing foreign countries. The Supreme Court upheld this delegation, stating: "If Congress shall lay down by legislative act an intelligible principle to which the person or body authorized to fix such rates is directed to conform, such legislative action is not a forbidden delegation of legislative power."[4] *Intelligible principle* was now added to contingency as standards justifying congressional delegations to the executive. Do these standards, however, permit the courts to determine when the executive acts

---

[3]Field v. Clark, 143 U.S. 649, 693 (1892). (Emphasis supplied.)
[4]J.W. Hampton, Jr. and Co. v. United States, 276 U.S. 394, 409 (1928).

beyond the delegated authority? Does anything in the legislation limit the President's discretion? Has Congress in fact retained the primary lawmaking power for itself or has this been transferred to the executive?

Unconstitutional Delegations of Power

The New Deal Court seemed to mark an abrupt change in judicial policy concerning the way in which the nondelegation doctrine was to be applied. Before the New Deal the Court was fond of stating the doctrine, upholding it in principle but not in practice. Principle and practice merged in the *Panama* decision. Section 9 of the National Industrial Recovery Act authorized the President to prohibit the shipment in interstate commerce of "hot oil"— oil produced in excess of state quotas established by such agencies as the Texas Railroad Commission. Under the act the President had issued an executive order prohibiting such oil shipments. Writing for all members of the Court but Justice Cardozo, who dissented, Chief Justice Hughes declared the congressional delegation to be unconstitutional. The Chief Justice stated that the question of whether or not oil should be interdicted in interstate commerce was one of legislative policy. Congress, he said, had established no standard to guide the President, and indeed Section 9 (c) gives to the President "an unlimited authority to determine the policy and to lay down the prohibition, or not to lay it down, as he may see fit."[5]

The *Schechter* decision followed *Panama* and has become the beacon for those supporting the nondelegation doctrine. The "Schechter rule" proclaimed unequivocally that Congress cannot delegate legislative power to the executive. The decision declared the entire National Industrial Recovery Act to be unconstitutional, not only on the basis of the delegation doctrine, but because Congress did not have the requisite authority under the commerce clause to justify the legislation.[6] Section 1 of the act declared a national emergency to exist and stated that it was the intention of Congress to eliminate obstructions to commerce, provide for the general welfare by aiding cooperative action among firms within particular industries, facilitate management-labor unity, erase unfair competitive practices, fully utilize existing productive capacity, reduce unemployment, improve labor standards, and "otherwise to rehabilitate industry and to conserve natural resources." Section 3 of the NRA authorized the President to establish codes of fair competition for trades and industries upon application from industrial associations or groups or on his own initiative. Violations of such codes could be prosecuted in the courts and constituted a misdemeanor subject to a $500 fine for each offense, each day a violation continued being regarded as a separate offense.

Not surprisingly, Chief Justice Hughes's decision in the *Schechter* case found that Congress had delegated legislative authority without providing adequate standards, making the act unconstitutional. Even Justice Cardozo, who had strongly dissented in the *Panama* decision, agreed with the Chief

[5]Panama Refining Company v. Ryan, 293 U.S. 388, 415 (1935).
[6]For the portion of the Schechter decision dealing with the commerce clause, see pp. 334–339.

Justice, making the decision of the Court unanimous. Cardozo wrote in a concurring opinion: "The delegated power of legislation which has found expression in this code [under consideration in the *Schechter* case] is not canalized within banks that keep it from overflowing. It is unconfined and vagrant. . . ."

Schechter Poultry Corporation v. United States

295 U.S. 495, 55 S. Ct. 837, 79 L. Ed. 1570 (1935)

Mr. Chief Justice Hughes delivered the opinion of the Court:

Petitioners . . . were convicted in the District Court of the United States for the Eastern District of New York on eighteen counts of an indictment charging violations of what is known as the "Live Poultry Code." . . . [T]he defendants contended (1) that the Code had been adopted pursuant to an unconstitutional delegation by Congress of legislative power. . . .

The "Live Poultry Code" was promulgated under § 3 of the National Industrial Recovery Act. That section . . . authorizes the President to approve "codes of fair competition." Such a code may be approved for a trade or industry, upon application by one or more trade or industrial associations or groups, if the President finds (1) that such associations or groups "impose no inequitable restrictions on admission to membership therein and are truly representative," and (2) that such codes are not designed "to promote monopolies or to eliminate or oppress small enterprises and will not operate to discriminate against them, and will tend to effectuate the policy" of Title I of the Act. Such codes "shall not permit monopolies or monopolistic practices." As a condition of his approval, the President may "impose such conditions (including requirements for the making of reports and the keeping of accounts) for the protection of consumers, competitors, employees, and others, and in furtherance of the public interest, and may provide such exceptions to and exemptions from the provisions of such code as the President in his discretion deems necessary to effectuate the policy herein declared." Where such a code has not been approved, the President may prescribe one, either on his own motion or on complaint. . . .

First. Two preliminary points are stressed by the Government with respect to the appropriate approach to the important questions presented. We are told that the provision of the statute authorizing the adoption of codes must be viewed in the light of the grave national crisis with which Congress was confronted. Undoubtedly, the conditions to which power is addressed are always to be considered when the exercise of power is challenged. Extraordinary conditions may call for extraordinary remedies. But the argument necessarily stops short of an attempt to justify action which lies outside the sphere of constitutional authority. Extraordinary conditions do not create or enlarge constitutional power. The Constitution established a national government with powers deemed to be adequate, as they have proved to be both in war and peace, but these powers of the national government are limited by the constitutional grants. Those who act under these grants are not at liberty to transcend the imposed limits because they believe that more or different power is necessary. Such assertions of extra-constitutional authority were anticipated and precluded by the explicit terms of the Tenth Amendment,—"The powers not delegated to the United States by the Constitution, nor prohibited by it to the States, are reserved to the States respectively, or to the people."

The further point is urged that the national crisis demanded a broad and intensive coöperative effort by those engaged in trade and industry, and that this necessary coöperation was sought to be fostered by permitting them to initiate the adoption of codes. But the statutory plan is not simply one for voluntary effort. It does not seek merely to endow voluntary trade or industrial associations or groups with privileges or immunities. It involves the coercive exercise of the law-making power. The codes of fair competition which the statute attempts to authorize are codes of laws. If valid, they place all persons within their reach under the obligation of positive law, binding equally those who assent and those who do not assent. Violations of the provisions of the codes are punishable as crimes.

Second. The question of the delegation of legislative power. We recently had occasion to review the pertinent decisions and the general principles which govern the determination of this question. *Panama Refining Co. v. Ryan* [1935]. The Constitution provides that "All legislative powers herein granted shall be vested in a Congress of the United States, which shall consist of a Senate and House of Representatives." Art I, § 1. And the Congress is authorized "To make all laws which shall be necessary and proper for carrying into execution" its general powers. Art. I, § 8, par. 18. The Congress is not permitted to abdicate or to transfer to others the essential legislative functions with which it is thus vested. We have repeatedly recognized the necessity of adapting legislation to complex conditions involving a host of details with which the national legislature cannot deal directly. We pointed out in the *Panama Company* case that the Constitution has never been regarded as deny-

ing to Congress the necessary resources of flexibility and practicality, which will enable it to perform its function in laying down policies and establishing standards, while leaving to selected instrumentalities the making of subordinate rules within prescribed limits and the determination of facts to which the policy as declared by the legislature is to apply. But we said that the constant recognition of the necessity and validity of such provisions, and the wide range of administrative authority which has been developed by means of them, cannot be allowed to obscure the limitations of the authority to delegate, if our constitutional system is to be maintained.

Accordingly, we look to the statute to see whether Congress has overstepped these limitations,—whether Congress in authorizing "codes of fair competition" has itself established the standards of legal obligation, thus performing its essential legislative function, or, by the failure to enact such standards, has attempted to transfer that function to others.

The aspect in which the question is now presented is distinct from that which was before us in the case of the *Panama Company*. There, the subject of the statutory prohibition was defined. National Industrial Recovery Act, § 9 (c). That subject was the transportation in interstate and foreign commerce of petroleum and petroleum products which are produced or withdrawn from storage in excess of the amount permitted by state authority. The question was with respect to the range of discretion given to the President in prohibiting that transportation. As to the "codes of fair competition," under § 3 of the Act, the question is more fundamental. It is whether there is any adequate definition of the subject to which the codes are to be addressed.

What is meant by "fair competition" as the term is used in the Act? Does it refer to a category established in the law, and is the authority to make codes limited accordingly? Or is it used as a convenient designation for whatever set of laws the formulators of a code for a particular trade or industry may propose and the President may approve (subject to certain restrictions), or the President may himself prescribe, as being wise and beneficent provisions for the government of the trade or industry in order to accomplish the broad purposes of rehabilitation, correction and expansion which are stated in the first section of Title I?

The Act does not define "fair competition." "Unfair competition," as known to the common law, is a limited concept. . . . [I]t is evident that in its widest range, "unfair competition," as it has been understood in the law, does not reach the objectives of the codes which are authorized by the National Industrial Recovery Act. The codes may, indeed, cover conduct which existing law condemns, but they are not limited to conduct of that sort. The Government does not contend that the Act contemplates such a limitation. It would be opposed both to the declared purposes of the Act and to its administrative construction.

The Federal Trade Commission Act (§ 5) introduced the expression "unfair methods of competition," which were declared to be unlawful. That was an expression new in the law. Debate apparently convinced the sponsors of the legislation that the words "unfair competition," in the light of their meaning at common law, were too narrow. We have said that the substituted phrase has a broader meaning, that it does not admit of precise definition, its scope being left to judicial determination as controversies arise. . . . What are "unfair methods of competition" are thus to be determined in particular instances, upon evidence, in the light of particular competitive conditions and of what is found to be a specific and substantial public interest. . . . To make

this possible, Congress set up a special procedure. A Commission, a quasi-judicial body, was created. Provision was made for formal complaint, for notice and hearing, for appropriate findings of fact supported by adequate evidence, and for judicial review to give assurance that the action of the Commission is taken within its statutory authority. . . .

In providing for codes, the National Industrial Recovery Act dispenses with this administrative procedure and with any administrative procedure of an analogous character. But the difference between the code plan of the Recovery Act and the scheme of the Federal Trade Commission Act lies not only in procedure but in subject matter. We cannot regard the "fair competition" of the codes as antithetical to the "unfair methods of competition" of the Federal Trade Commission Act. The "fair competition" of the codes has a much broader range and a new significance. The Recovery Act provides that it shall not be construed to impair the powers of the Federal Trade Commission, but, when a code is approved, its provisions are to be the "standards of fair competition" for the trade or industry concerned, and any violation of such standards in any transaction in or affecting interstate or foreign commerce is to be deemed "an unfair method of competition" within the meaning of the Federal Trade Commission Act. § 3 (b).

For a statement of the authorized objectives and content of the "codes of fair competition" we are referred repeatedly to the "Declaration of Policy" in section one of Title I of the Recovery Act. Thus, the approval of a code by the President is conditioned on his finding that it "will tend to effectuate the policy of this title." § 3 (a). The President is authorized to impose such conditions "for the protection of consumers, competitors, employees, and others, and in furtherance of the public interest, and may provide such exceptions to and exemptions from the provisions of such code as the President in his discretion deems necessary to effectuate the policy herein declared." The "policy herein declared" is manifestly that set forth in section one. That declaration embraces a broad range of objectives. Among them we find the elimination of "unfair competitive practices." But even if this clause were to be taken to relate to practices which fall under the ban of existing law, either common law or statute, it is still only one of the authorized aims described in section one. It is there declared to be "the policy of Congress" "to remove obstructions to the free flow of interstate and foreign commerce which tend to diminish the amount thereof; and to provide for the general welfare by promoting the organization of industry for the purpose of coöperative action among trade groups, to induce and maintain united action of labor and management under adequate governmental sanctions and supervision, to eliminate unfair competitive practices, to promote the fullest possible utilization of the present productive capacity of industries, to avoid undue restriction of production (except as may be temporarily required), to increase the consumption of industrial and agricultural products by increasing purchasing power, to reduce and relieve unemployment, to improve standards of labor, and otherwise to rehabilitate industry and to conserve natural resources."

Under § 3, whatever "may tend to effectuate" these general purposes may be included in the "codes of fair competition." We think the conclusion is inescapable that the authority sought to be conferred by § 3 was not merely to deal with "unfair competitive practices" which offend against existing law, and could be the subject of judicial condemnation without further legislation, or to create administrative machinery for the application

of established principles of law to particular instances of violation. Rather, the purpose is clearly disclosed to authorize new and controlling prohibitions through codes of laws which would embrace what the formulators would propose, and what the President would approve, or prescribe, as wise and beneficient measures for the government of trades and industries in order to bring about their rehabilitation, correction and development, according to the general declaration of policy in section one. Codes of laws of this sort are styled "codes of fair competition."

We find no real controversy upon this point and we must determine the validity of the Code in question in this aspect. As the Government candidly says in its brief: "The words 'policy of this title' clearly refer to the 'policy' which Congress declared in the section entitled 'Declaration of Policy'—§ 1. All of the policies there set forth point toward a single goal—the rehabilitation of industry and the industrial recovery which unquestionably was the major policy of Congress in adopting the National Industrial Recovery Act." And that this is the controlling purpose of the Code now before us appears both from its repeated declarations to that effect and from the scope of its requirements. It will be observed that its provisions as to the hours and wages of employees and its "general labor provisions" were placed in separate articles, and these were not included in the article on "trade practice provisions" declaring what should be deemed to constitute "unfair methods of competition." The Secretary of Agriculture thus stated the objectives of the Live Poultry Code in his report to the President, which was recited in the executive order of approval:

"That said code will tend to effectuate the declared policy of Title I of the National Industrial Recovery Act as set forth in section 1 of said Act in that the terms and provisions of such code tend (a) To remove obstructions to the free flow of interstate and foreign commerce which tend to diminish the amount thereof; (b) to provide for the general welfare by promoting the organization of industry for the purpose of coöperative action among trade groups; (c) to eliminate unfair competitive practices; (d) to promote the fullest possible utilization of the present productive capacity of industries; (e) to avoid undue restriction of production (except as may be temporarily required); (f) to increase the consumption of industrial and agricultural products by increasing purchasing power; and (g) otherwise to rehabilitate industry and to conserve natural resources."

The Government urges that the codes will "consist of rules of competition deemed fair for each industry by representative members of that industry—by the persons most vitally concerned and most familiar with its problems." Instances are cited in which Congress has availed itself of such assistance; as *e.g.*, in the exercise of its authority over the public domain, with respect to the recognition of local customs or rules of miners as to mining claims, or, in matters of a more or less technical nature, as in designating the standard height of drawbars. But would it be seriously contended that Congress could delegate its legislative authority to trade or industrial associations or groups so as to empower them to enact the laws they deem to be wise and beneficent for the rehabilitation and expansion of their trade or industries? Could trade or industrial associations or groups be constituted legislative bodies for that purpose because such associations or groups are familiar with the problems of their enterprises? And, could an effort of that sort be made valid by such a preface of generalities as to permissible aims as we find in section 1 of Title I? The answer is obvious. Such a delegation of legislative power is unknown to our law and is utterly inconsistent with the constitutional prerogatives and duties of Congress.

The question, then, turns upon the authority which § 3 of the Recovery Act vests in the President to approve or prescribe. If the codes have standing as penal statutes, this must be due to the effect of the executive action. But Congress cannot delegate legislative power to the President to exercise an unfettered discretion to make whatever laws he thinks may be needed or advisable for the rehabilitation and expansion of trade or industry. . . .

Accordingly we turn to the Recovery Act to ascertain what limits have been set to the exercise of the President's discretion. *First*, the President, as a condition of approval, is required to find that the trade or industrial associations or groups which propose a code, "impose no inequitable restrictions on admission to membership" and are "truly representative." That condition, however, relates only to the status of the initiators of the new laws and not to the permissible scope of such laws. *Second*, the President is required to find that the code is not "designed to promote monopolies or to eliminate or oppress small enterprises and will not operate to discriminate against them." And, to this is added a proviso that the code "shall not permit monopolies or monopolistic practices." But these restrictions leave virtually untouched the field of policy envisaged by section one, and, in that wide field of legislative possibilities, the proponents of a code, refraining from monopolistic designs, may roam at will and the President may approve or disapprove their proposals as he may see fit. That is the precise effect of the further finding that the President is to make— that the code "will tend to effectuate the policy of this title." While this is called a finding, it is really but a statement of an opinion as to the general effect upon the promotion of trade or industry of a scheme of laws. These are the only findings which Congress has made essential in order to put into operation a legislative code having the aims described in the "Declaration of Policy."

Nor is the breadth of the President's discretion left to the necessary implications of this limited requirement as to his findings. As already noted, the President in approving a code may impose his own conditions, adding to or taking from what is proposed, as "in his discretion" he thinks necessary "to effectuate the policy" declared by the Act. Of course, he has no less liberty when he prescribes a code on his own motion or on complaint, and he is free to prescribe one if a code has not been approved. The Act provides for the creation by the President of administrative agencies to assist him, but the action or reports of such agencies, or of his other assistants,—their recommendations and findings in relation to the making of codes—have no sanction beyond the will of the President, who may accept, modify or reject them as he pleases. Such recommendations or findings in no way limit the authority which § 3 undertakes to vest in the President with no other conditions than those there specified. And this authority relates to a host of different trades and industries, thus extending the President's discretion to all the varieties of laws which he may deem to be beneficial in dealing with the vast array of commercial and industrial activities throughout the country.

Such a sweeping delegation of legislative power finds no support in the decisions upon which the Government especially relies. By the Interstate Commerce Act, Congress has itself provided a code of laws regulating the activities of the common carriers subject to the Act, in order to assure the performance of their services upon just and reasonable terms, with adequate facilities and without unjust discrimination. Congress from time to time has elaborated its requirements, as needs have been disclosed. To facilitate the application of the standards prescribed by the Act, Congress has provided an expert body. That administrative agency, in dealing with particular cases, is required to act upon notice and hearing, and its orders must be supported by findings of fact which in turn are sustained by evidence. . . . When the Commission is authorized to issue, for the construction, extension or abandonment of lines, a certificate of "public convenience and necessity," or to permit the acquisition by one carrier of the control of another, if that is found to be "in the public interest," we have pointed out that these provisions are not left without standards to guide determination. The authority conferred has direct relation to the standards prescribed for the service of common carriers and can be exercised only upon findings, based upon evidence, with respect to particular conditions of transportation. . . .

Similarly, we have held that the Radio Act of 1927 established standards to govern radio communications and, in view of the limited number of available broadcasting frequencies, Congress authorized allocation and licenses. The Federal Radio Commission was created as the licensing authority, in order to secure a reasonable equality of opportunity in radio transmission and reception. The authority of the Commission to grant licenses "as public convenience, interest or necessity requires" was limited by the nature of radio communications, and by the scope, character and quality of the services to be rendered and the relative advantages to be derived through distribution of facilities. These standards established by Congress were to be enforced upon hearing, and evidence, by an administrative body acting under statutory restrictions adapted to the particular activity. . . .

In *Hampton & Co.* v. *United States* [1928], the question related to the "flexible tariff provision" of the Tariff Act of 1922. We held that Congress had described its plan "to secure by law the imposition of customs duties on articles of imported merchandise which should equal the difference between the cost of producing in a foreign country the articles in question and laying them down for sale in the United States, and the cost of producing and selling like or similar articles in the United States." As the differences in cost might vary from time to time, provision was made for the investigation and determination of these differences by the executive branch so as to make "the adjustments necessary to conform the duties to the standard underlying that policy and plan." The Court found the same principle to be applicable in fixing customs duties as that which permitted Congress to exercise its rate-making power in interstate commerce, "by declaring the rule which shall prevail in the legislative fixing of rates" and then remitting "the fixing of such rates" in accordance with its provisions "to a rate-making body." The Court

fully recognized the limitations upon the delegation of legislative power.

To summarize and conclude upon this point: Section 3 of the Recovery Act is without precedent. It supplies no standards for any trade, industry or activity. It does not undertake to prescribe rules of conduct to be applied to particular states of fact determined by appropriate administrative procedure. Instead of prescribing rules of conduct, it authorizes the making of codes to prescribe them. For that legislative undertaking, § 3 sets up no standards, aside from the statement of the general aims of rehabilitation, correction and expansion described in section one. In view of the scope of that broad declaration, and of the nature of the few restrictions that are imposed, the discretion of the President in approving or prescribing codes, and thus enacting laws for the government of trade and industry throughout the country is virtually unfettered. We think that the code-making authority thus conferred is an unconstitutional delegation of legislative power. . . .

MR. JUSTICE CARDOZO wrote a concurring opinion. (See pp. 337–339.)

The Scope of Delegated Power since the *Schechter* Decision

Cardozo's statement in his concurring opinion in the *Schechter* case that "this is delegation running riot" summed up the feelings of the Court. The *Panama* and *Schechter* decisions, as well as the act they overturned, remain unique in the history of American constitutional law. Under the act the jurisdiction of the President was limitless, all business being subjected to his discretionary control in the broadest sense. The *Panama* and *Schechter* decisions remain the only ones overturning congressional action because of too broad delegation of legislative authority.

If the *Schechter* rule is interpreted to mean that Congress must establish definite, unequivocal, and reasonable standards to guide executive or administrative agents in carrying out legislative responsibilities, that rule has never prevailed before or since *Schechter*. Extraordinary delegations have occurred since the *Schechter* ruling. Where Congress has failed to establish clearcut standards in its legislation the courts have justified the legislation on other grounds. Particularly important is the fact that the courts have allowed broad legislative delegations where the agencies themselves prescribe standards that are self-limiting. Agency action violating its own standards then is illegal and upon judicial review will be invalidated or remanded to the agency for further action.

The importance of administrative standards as a replacement for a comprehensive statement of legislative intent was demonstrated shortly after the *Schechter* decision in the case of *Yakus* v. *United States* (1944). World War II saw the virtual abdication of congressional power to the President and the administrative branch on many occasions. Extraordinary delegations were made and upheld by the courts, and it was during this period that the substitution of administrative for congressional standards was permitted. The *Yakus* case involved the Emergency Price Control Act of 1942, which authorized a price administrator, who was the head of the Office of Price Administration (OPA), to fix prices for commodities, rents, and the services which "in his judgment will be generally fair and equitable and will effectuate the purposes of this Act." The purposes of the Act were "to stabilize prices and to prevent speculative, unwarranted and abnormal increases in prices and rents." The administrator was "so far as practicable" to consult with representatives of the industries and to "give due consideration to the prices prevailing between October 1 and October 15, 1941," in making his determinations. The power to set price ceilings is clearly legislative in nature. However, regardless of the relatively vague congressional guidelines in the 1942 act, the Supreme Court upheld the delegation with the statement that

> It is for Congress to say whether the data on the basis of which prices are to be fixed are to be confined within a narrow or broad range. In either case the only concern of courts is to ascertain whether the will of Congress has been obeyed. This depends not upon the breadth of the definition of the facts or conditions which the administrative officer is to find, but upon the determination whether the definition sufficiently *marks the field* within which the administrator is to act so that it may be known whether he has kept within it in compliance with the legislative will.[7]

The Court then went on to point out the importance of administrative standards with the statement that

> The standards prescribed by the present Act, *with the aid of* the "statement of considerations" required to be made by the administrator, are sufficiently definite and precise to enable Congress, the courts and the public to ascertain whether the administrator, in fixing the designated prices, has conformed to those standards.[8]

The *Yakus* decision seemed to be reaching for a justification of congressional delegation that went well beyond the *Schechter* rule. Justice Roberts

---

[7]Yakus v. United States, 321 U.S. 414, 425 (1944). (Emphasis supplied.)
[8]Ibid., p. 426. (Emphasis supplied.)

dissented in *Yakus*, claiming that the decision of the majority clearly over-ruled *Schechter* and that in fact there was little difference in the extent of delegation that took place under the statutes involved in the two cases.

In addition to the Emergency Price Control Act of 1942, other World War II statutes were challenged as being unconstitutional delegations of leg-islative authority, but in every instance they were upheld by the Supreme Court.[9]

It was not the exigencies of World War II, however, that suggested the *Schechter* rule was unique. The Court had upheld all delegations of legisla-tive authority before the *Panama* and *Schechter* decisions, and after World War II seeming blanket delegations of legislative authority were upheld. For example, in *Arizona* v. *California* (1963) a statute was challenged which del-egated to the Secretary of the Interior virtually total discretion in allocating the waters of the Colorado River among seven western states. Under the Boulder Canyon Project Act of 1928 the Secretary was authorized to con-struct a dam to create a storage reservoir. In allocating waters from the dam he was to follow an order of legislative priorities "first, for river regu-lation, improvement of navigation, and flood control; second, for irrigation and domestic uses and satisfaction of present perfected rights [to use the waters of the Colorado River] . . . ; and third, for power."[10] On the basis of these standards could you determine whether the Secretary was acting be-yond the delegated authority? The majority of the Court found the stand-ards adequate in conjunction with other guidelines and limits stated in the act. "We are satisfied," said the majority opinion, "that the Secretary's power must be construed to permit him, within the boundaries set down in the Act, to allocate and distribute the waters of the main stream of the Colorado River."[11]

The *Arizona* case produced a vigorous dissent by Justice Harlan, joined by Justices Douglas and Stewart. Harlan agreed with the majority that there were limits upon the Secretary under the "present perfected rights" stand-ard, which guaranteed California a certain share of the Colorado River waters. Moreover the act provided a ceiling for water that could be allocated to California. Beyond these limits, however, Harlan found no adequate guidelines in the statute to control the actions of the Secretary of the Inte-rior. "Under the Court's construction of the Act," he wrote, "Congress has made a gift to the Secretary of almost one million five hundred thousand

[9]Perhaps the most uncontrolled delegation in history was that involved in Lichter v. United States, 334 U.S. 742 (1948). The Renegotiation Act of 1942 was challenged as an unconstitu-tional delegation of legislative power. The act had authorized administrative officials to recover excessive profits made by corporations supplying goods to the government. No standard at all was provided in the original act, but several months after its passage Congress defined the term *excessive profits* to mean "any amount of a contract or subcontract price which is found as a result of renegotiation to represent excessive profits." In other words, an excessive profit was defined as an excessive profit. Was this an unconstitutional delegation of legislative power? The Su-preme Court upheld the delegation in the Lichter case because the executive branch had taken the care to create its own formula for excessive profits, a formula that later was put into the act itself by Congress. This, said the Court, indicated that the act all along was being administered in accordance with congressional intent!

[10]45 Stat. 1057, sect. 6 (1928).

[11]Arizona v. California, 373 U.S. 546, 590 (1963).

acre feet of water a year, to allocate virtually as he pleases in the event of any shortage preventing the fulfillment of all of his delivery commitments."[12] Harlan then went on to state that the Court should adhere to the *Schechter* rule.

> The delegation of such unrestrained authority to an executive official raises, to say the least, the gravest constitutional doubts. See . . . *Schechter Poultry Corp.* v. *United States,* . . . *Panama Refining Co.* v. *Ryan* . . . *Youngstown Sheet and Tube Co.* v. *Sawyer.* . . . The principle that authority granted by the legislature must be limited by adequate standards serves two primary functions vital to preserving the separation of powers required by the Constitution. *First,* it ensures that the fundamental policy decisions in our society will be made not by an appointed official but by the body immediately responsible to the people. *Second,* it prevents judicial review from becoming merely an exercise-at-large by providing the courts with some measure against which to judge the official action that has been challenged.[13]

Reference to the *Schechter* rule surfaced again in *Zemel* v. *Rusk* (1965). The State Department had denied a citizen's request to have his passport validated to travel to Cuba as a tourist. The citizen then sued the Secretary of State and the Attorney General, seeking a judgment that he was entitled under the Constitution and the laws of the country to travel to Cuba and, *inter alia,* that the 1926 Passport Act unconstitutionally delegated legislative authority to the President and the Secretary of State. The act provided that "the Secretary of State may grant and issue passports, and cause passports to be granted, issued, and verified in foreign countries . . . under such rules as the President shall designate and prescribe."[14] On its face, this legislation seemed to delegate unbridled discretion to the President to engage in lawmaking. Chief Justice Earl Warren wrote the opinion for the Court's majority of six that upheld the Secretary's action and the statute against the charge of an overbroad delegation of legislative power. Warren agreed that the delegation was indeed very broad but dismissed the argument that it was unconstitutional on the basis that the executive must have more discretionary authority in foreign than in domestic affairs. A key case cited by Warren for precedent was *United States* v. *Curtiss Wright Corp.* (1936).

Justice Black wrote a strong dissenting opinion on the issue of delegation in the *Zemel* case stating,

> . . . quite obviously, the government does not exaggerate in saying that this Act "does not provide any specific standards for the Secretary" and "delegates to the President and Secretary a general discretionary power over passports"—a power so broad, in fact, as to be marked by no bounds except an unlimited discretion. It is plain therefore that Congress had not itself passed a law regulating passports; it has merely referred the matter to the Secretary of State and the President in words that say in effect, "We delegate to you our constitutional power to make

[12]Ibid., p. 625.
[13]Ibid., pp. 625–626.
[14]44 Stat. 887, 22 U.S.C., sec. 211a (1958 ed.).

such laws regulating passports as you see fit." . . . For Congress to attempt to delegate such an undefined law-making power to the Secretary, the President or both, makes applicable to this 1926 Act what Mr. Justice Cardozo said about the National Industrial Recovery Act: "This is delegation running riot. No such plenitude of power is susceptible of transfer." . . . *Schechter Poultry Corp.* v. *United States,* . . . *Panama Refining Co.* v. *Ryan.* . . .

Our Constitution has ordained that laws restricting the liberty of our people can be enacted by the Congress and by the Congress only. I do not think our Constitution intended that this vital legislative function could be farmed out in large blocs to any governmental official, whoever he might be, or to any governmental department and/or bureau, whatever administrative expertise it might be thought to have.[15]

There is an inference in Black's dissent that the *Schechter* rule should particularly be applied when Congress is legislating in the area of civil liberties and civil rights.

The *Schechter* rule was resurrected again by Justice Brennan in his concurring opinion in *United States* v. *Robel* (1967). At issue was a section of the Subversive Activities Control Act of 1950, which provided that a member of a group that the Board had designated to be a "Communist action organization" could not engage in employment in a defense facility. The majority of the Court found this section to be an abridgement of the First Amendment right of association. Justice Brennan, however, held that the law should be voided because of congressional vagueness in delegating authority to the executive. In general, wrote Justice Brennan, broad delegations are permissible, but where fundamental liberties are at stake as in this case stringent congressional control of administrative action is required by the Constitution. He wrote that "the numerous deficiencies connected with vague legislative directives . . . are far more serious when liberty and the exercise of *fundamental* rights are at stake."[16] Implying that the *Schechter* rule should be strictly enforced only in the area of civil liberties and civil rights, Brennan stated that "Congress *ordinarily* may delegate power under broad standards. . . . No other general rule would be feasible or desirable. Delegation of power under general directives is an inevitable consequence of our complex society, with its myriad, ever-changing, highly technical problems."[17]

Regardless of whether the congressional delegation of authority involves civil liberties or civil rights or economic powers, the *Schechter* rule has become an anachronism. In the economic sphere a *Schechter* plea occurred before a three-judge District Court in the District of Columbia in 1971.[18] The Economic Stabilization Act of 1970 was challenged as an unconstitutional delegation of legislative authority because of lack of guiding standards for the executive. The act authorized the President to issue orders and regula-

[15]Zemel v. Rusk, 381 U.S. 1, 21–22 (1965).
[16]United States v. Robel, 389 U.S. 258, 275 (1967).
[17]Ibid., p. 274.
[18]Amalgamated Meat Cutters and Butcher Workmen v. Connally, 337 F. Supp. 737 (D.D.C. 1971).

tions that he deemed "appropriate to stabilize prices, rents, wages, and salaries at levels not less than those prevailing on May 25, 1970. Such orders and regulations may provide for the making of such adjustments as may be necessary to prevent gross inequities." President Nixon in August of 1971 issued an executive order stabilizing prices, rents, wages, and salaries for a ninety-day period at levels that were not to exceed those prevailing during the thirty-day period ending August 14, 1971. The Cost of Living Council was established to administer the stabilization program. Challenged as a grant of "unbridled legislative power" to the President the act was sustained, with the three-judge court choosing to use the *Yakus* precedent rather than to apply the *Schechter* rule. The court was particularly impressed with the act's requirement for administrative standards to be developed if wage and price controls were to be continued by the President. Such administrative standards, the court held, were an adequate substitute for the lack of explicit congressional guidelines. Administrative action would be controlled by judicial review that would take into account explicit administrative standards and the general guidelines of the statute.

Delegation in Foreign Affairs

With the exception of *Zemel* v. *Rusk* the debate over the degree to which the *Schechter* rule should prevail has concerned delegations of legislative authority affecting only the domestic sphere. These delegations admittedly have been just as broad as the legislative grants to the President to make foreign policy. However, the Court has developed a different doctrine of delegation of legislative authority in the foreign policy sphere than it has applied to domestic affairs.

In the *Curtiss-Wright* case a joint resolution of Congress delegating legislative authority to the President in the foreign policy sphere was challenged. The resolution provided that the President should prohibit the sale of arms and munitions in the United States to countries engaged in armed conflict in the Chaco (Bolivia and Paraguay) if he found that it would "contribute to the reestablishment of peace between those countries." The President was authorized to embargo the sale of arms by proclamation "after consultation with the governments of other American republics, and with their cooperation." Violators of the President's proclamation were subject to fine and imprisonment.

The appellees in the *Curtiss-Wright* case argued that the Joint Resolution granted the President total discretion to make or not to make law. As was the case with the NIRA previously overturned by the Court in the *Schechter* case, the President was *authorized* but not required to take action. Whether or not to issue the proclamation banning the sale of arms was entirely within the President's discretion. The Court's opinion stated that even if the resolution would be an unconstitutional delegation of legislative authority in the domestic sphere, the fact that it pertained to foreign affairs required the application of a different set of constitutional standards. The Court held that the President must be allowed more discretion to formulate and implement policy in foreign than in domestic affairs. It implied that delegations that would be unconstitutional in the domestic sphere may be justified in foreign policy making.

United States v. Curtiss-Wright

299 U.S. 304; 57 S. Ct. 216; 81 L. Ed. 255 (1936)

MR. JUSTICE SUTHERLAND delivered the opinion of the Court:

On January 27, 1936, an indictment was returned in the court below, the first count of which charges that appellees, beginning with the 29th day of May, 1934, conspired to sell in the United States certain arms of war, namely fifteen machine guns, to Bolivia, a country then engaged in armed conflict in the Chaco, in violation of the Joint Resolution of Congress approved May 28, 1934, and the provisions of a proclamation issued on the same day by the President of the United States pursuant to authority conferred by § 1 of the resolution. In pursuance of the conspiracy, the commission of certain overt acts was alleged, details of which need not be stated. The Joint Resolution . . . follows:

Resolved by the Senate and House of Representatives of the United States of America in Congress assembled, That if the President finds that the prohibition of the sale of arms and munitions of war in the United States to those countries now engaged in armed conflict in the Chaco may contribute to the reëstablishment of peace between those countries, and if after consultation with the governments of other American Republics and with their coöperation, as well as that of such other governments as he may deem necessary, he makes proclamation to that effect, it shall be unlawful to sell, except under such limitations and exceptions as the President prescribes, any arms or munitions of war in any place in the United States to the countries now engaged in that armed conflict, or to any person, company, or association acting in the interest of either country, until otherwise ordered by the President or by Congress.

Sec. 2. Whoever sells any arms or munitions of war in violation of section 1 shall, on conviction, be punished by a fine not exceeding $10,000 or by imprisonment not exceeding two years, or both. . . .

Appellees severally demurred to the first count of the indictment on the grounds (1) that it did not charge facts sufficient to show the commission by appellees of any offense against any law of the United States; . . . The points urged in support of the demurrers were, first, that the joint resolution effects an invalid delegation of legislative power to the executive; second, that the joint resolution never became effective because of the failure of the President to find essential jurisdictional facts. . . .

The court below sustained the demurrers upon the first point, but overruled them on the second and third points. . . . The government appealed to this Court under the provisions of the Criminal Appeals Act of March 2, 1907. . . . That act authorizes the United States to appeal from a district court direct to this Court in criminal cases where, among other things, the decision sustaining a demurrer to the indictment or any count thereof is based upon the invalidity or construction of the statute upon which the indictment is founded.

First. It is contended that by the Joint Resolution, the going into effect and continued operation of the resolution was conditioned (a) upon the President's judgment as to its beneficial effect upon the reëstablishment of peace between the countries engaged in armed conflict in the Chaco; (b) upon the making of a proclamation, which was left to his unfettered discretion, thus constituting an attempted substitution of the President's will for that of Congress; (c) upon the making of a proclamation putting an end to the operation of the resolution, which again was left to the President's unfettered discretion; and (d) further, that the extent of its operation in particular cases was subject to limitation and exception by the President, controlled by no standard. In each of these particulars, appellees urge that Congress abdicated its essential functions and delegated them to the Executive.

Whether, if the Joint Resolution had related solely to internal affairs it would be open to the challenge that it constituted an unlawful delegation of legislative power to the Executive, we find it unnecessary to determine. The whole aim of the resolution is to affect a situation entirely external to the United States, and falling within the category of foreign affairs. The determination which we are called to make, therefore, is whether the Joint Resolution, as applied to that situation, is vulnerable to attack under the rule that forbids a delegation of the law-making power. In other words, assuming (but not deciding) that the challenged delegation, if it were confined to internal affairs, would be invalid, may it nevertheless be sustained on the ground that its exclusive aim is to afford a remedy for a hurtful condition within a foreign territory?

It will contribute to the elucidation of the question if we first consider the differences between the powers of the federal government in respect of foreign or external affairs and those in respect of domestic or internal affairs. That there are differences between them, and that these differences are fundamental, may not be doubted.

The two classes of powers are different, both in respect of their origin and their nature. The broad statement that the federal government can exercise no powers except those specifically enumerated in the Constitution, and such implied powers as are necessary and proper to carry into effect the enumerated powers, is categorically true only in respect of our internal affairs. In that field, the primary purpose of the Constitution was to carve from the general mass of legislative powers *then possessed by the states* such portions as it was thought desirable to vest in the federal government, leaving those not included in the enumeration still in the states. . . . That this doctrine applies only to powers which the states had, is self evident. And since the states severally never possessed international powers, such powers could not have been carved from the mass of state powers but obviously were transmitted to the United States from some other source. During the colonial period, those powers were possessed exclusively by and were entirely under the control of the Crown. By the Declaration of Independence, "the Representatives of the United States of America" declared the United [not the several] Colonies to be free and independent states, and as such to have "full Power to levy War, conclude Peace, contract Alliances, establish Commerce and to do all other Acts and Things which Independent States may of right do."

As a result of the separation from Great Britain by the colonies acting as a unit, the powers of external sovereignty passed from the Crown not to the colonies severally, but to the colonies in their collective and corporate capacity as the United States of America. Even before the Declaration, the colonies were a unit in foreign affairs, acting through a common agency—namely the Continental Congress, composed of delegates from the thirteen colonies. That agency exercised the powers of war and peace, raised an army, created a navy, and finally adopted the Declaration of Independence. Rulers come and go; governments end and forms of government change; but sovereignty survives. A political society cannot endure without a supreme will somewhere. Sovereignty is never held in suspense. When, therefore, the external sovereignty of Great Britain in respect of the colonies ceased, it immediately passed to the Union. . . . That fact was given practical application almost at once. The treaty of peace, made on September 23, 1783, was concluded between his Britannic Majesty and the "United States of America." . . .

The Union existed before the Constitution, which was ordained and established among other things to form "a more perfect Union." Prior to that event, it is clear that the Union, declared by the Articles of Confederation to be "perpetual," was the sole possessor of external sovereignty and in the Union it remained without change save in so far as the Constitution in express terms qualified its exercise. . . .

It results that the investment of the federal government with the powers of external sovereignty did not depend upon the affirmative grants of the Constitution. The powers to declare and wage war, to conclude peace, to make treaties, to maintain diplomatic relations with other sovereignties, if they had never been mentioned in the Constitution, would have vested in the federal government as necessary concomitants of nationality. Neither the Constitution nor the laws passed in pursuance of it have any force in foreign territory unless in respect of our own citizens . . .; and operations of the nation in such territory must be governed by treaties, international understandings and compacts, and the principles of international law. As a member of the family of nations, the right and power of the United States in that field are equal to the right and power of the other members of the international family. Otherwise, the United States is not completely sovereign. The power to acquire territory by discovery and occupation . . . , the power to expel undesirable aliens . . . , the power to make such international agreements as do not constitute treaties in the constitutional sense . . . , none of which is expressly affirmed by the Constitution, nevertheless exist as inherently inseparable from the conception of nationality. This the court recognized, and in each of the cases cited found the warrant for its conclusions not in the provisions of the Constitution, but in the law of nations. . . .

Not only, as we have shown, is the federal power over external affairs in origin and essential character different from that over internal affairs, but participation in the exercise of the power is significantly limited. In this vast external realm, with its important, complicated, delicate and manifold problems, the President alone has the power to speak or listen as a representative of the nation. He *makes* treaties with the advice and consent of the Senate; but he alone negotiates. Into the field of negotiation the Senate cannot intrude; and Congress itself is powerless to invade it. . . .

It is important to bear in mind that we are here dealing not alone with an authority vested in the President by an exertion of legislative power, but with such an authority plus the very delicate, plenary and exclusive power of the President as the sole organ of the federal government in the field of international relations—a power which does not require as a basis for its exercise an act of Congress, but which, of course, like every other governmental power, must be exercised in subordination to the applicable provisions of the Constitution. It is quite apparent that if, in the maintenance of our international relations, embarrassment—perhaps serious embarrassment—is to be avoided and success for our aims achieved, congressional legislation which is to be made effective through negotiation and inquiry within the international field must often accord to the President a degree of discretion and freedom from statutory restriction which would not be admissible were domestic affairs alone involved. Moreover, he, not Congress, has the better opportunity of knowing the conditions which prevail in foreign countries, and especially is this true in time of war. He has his confidential sources of information. He has his agents in the form of diplomatic, consular and other officials. Secrecy in respect of information gathered by them may be highly necessary, and the premature disclosure of it productive of harmful results. . . .

In the light of the foregoing observations, it is evident that this Court should not be in haste to apply a general rule which will have the effect of condemning legislation like that under review as constituting an unlawful delegation of legislative power. The principles which justify such legislation find overwhelming support in the unbroken legislative practice which has prevailed almost from the inception of the national government to the present day. . . .

Practically every volume of the United States Statutes contains one or more acts or joint resolutions of Congress authorizing action by the President in respect of subjects affecting foreign relations, which either leave the exercise of the power to his unrestricted judgment, or provide a standard far more general than that which has always been considered requisite with regard to domestic affairs. . . .

A legislative practice such as we have here, evidenced not by only occasional instances, but marked by the movement of a steady stream for a century and a half of time, goes a long way in the direction

of proving the presence of unassailable ground for the constitutionality of the practice, to be found in the origin and history of the power involved, or in its nature, or in both combined. . . .

We deem it unnecessary to consider, *seriatim*, the several clauses which are said to evidence the unconstitutionality of the Joint Resolution as involving an unlawful delegation of legislative power. It is enough to summarize by saying that, both upon principle and in accordance with precedent, we conclude there is sufficient warrant for the broad discretion vested in the President to determine whether the enforcement of the statute will have a beneficial effect upon the reëstablishment of peace in the affected countries; whether he shall make proclamation to bring the resolution into operation; whether and when the resolution shall cease to operate and to make proclamation accordingly; and to prescribe limitations and exceptions to which the enforcement of the resolution shall be subject.

Second. The second point raised by the demurrer was that the Joint Resolution never became effective because the President failed to find essential jurisdictional facts. . . .

1. The Executive proclamation recites, "I have found that the prohibition of the sale of arms and munitions of war in the United States to those countries now engaged in armed conflict in the Chaco may contribute to the reëstablishment of peace between those countries, and that I have consulted with the governments of other American Republics *and have been assured of the coöperation of such governments as I have deemed necessary as contemplated by the said joint resolution.*" This finding satisfies every requirement of the Joint Resolution. There is no suggestion that the resolution is fatally uncertain or indefinite; and a finding which follows its language, as this finding does, cannot well be challenged as insufficient. . . .

The judgment of the court below must be reversed and the cause remanded for further proceedings in accordance with the foregoing opinion.

Reversed.

Mr. Justice McReynolds does not agree. He is of opinion that the court below reached the right conclusion and its judgment ought to be affirmed.

Mr. Justice Stone took no part in the consideration or decision of this case.

Does the Court in the *Curtiss-Wright* case adequately answer the contention of the appellees that

> The Congress cannot, under the Constitution, delegate to the executive its function of making laws which may affect our foreign relations. . . . The government contends in effect that Congress can delegate to the executive, without restriction, its legislative function with respect to laws which may affect our relations with foreign nations; the government's contention necessarily goes to this length since it relies upon certain early statutes purporting to grant to the President the power, *in his sole discretion,* to put into effect or suspend the operation of laws prohibiting commercial intercourse with the then warring nations of Europe [the latest law being dated April 22, 1808]. . . . All of them were enacted in times of great national stress, when Congress and the executive alike are prone to disregard the limitations which the Constitution imposed upon them.[19]

Justice Sutherland's opinion in *Curtiss-Wright* held that the President's "plenary and exclusive power" in international relations "does not require as a basis for its exercise an Act of Congress."

The major thrust of the *Curtiss-Wright* case was to recognize the prerogative power of the President under Article II to conduct foreign relations without congressional consent. Because of the scope of presidential discretion in foreign affairs under Article II, broad delegations of authority from Congress to the executive are justified. The "imperial presidency" is in large part based upon the extraordinary powers of the President in foreign affairs, which range from his ability to negotiate executive agreements without the consent of Congress (see *United States* v. *Belmont,* p. 191) to his power to engage United States military forces in foreign operations.

The prerogative power of the President to conduct foreign relations was seriously challenged for the first time during the Vietnam War. In numerous cases suits were instituted to challenge the authority of the government to conduct the war, based upon the contention that Congress had never formally declared war. In *Mora* v. *McNamara* (1967) draftees ordered to go to Vietnam brought suit to overturn the orders, and requested a declaratory judgment that the United States military activity in Vietnam was "illegal." The district court dismissed the suit, the court of appeals affirmed, and the Supreme Court denied the draftees' petition for a writ of certiorari. Justice Stewart, joined by Justice Douglas, wrote a rare dissenting opinion to the

[19]LB Vol. 32, p. 982.

motion to deny certiorari. The dissenters felt that the case involved "questions of great magnitude," among them:

    I. Is the present United States military activity in Vietnam a "war" within the meaning of Article I, Sect. 8, clause II of the Constitution?

   II. If so, may the executive constitutionally order the petitioners to participate in that military activity, when no war has been declared by the Congress?

  III. Of what relevance to question II are the present treaty obligations of the United States?

  IV. Of what relevance to question II is the joint congressional (Tonkin Gulf) resolution of August 10, 1964?

       (a) Do present United States military operations fall within the terms of the joint resolution?

       (b) If the joint resolution purports to give the Chief Executive authority to commit United States forces to armed conflict limited in scope only by his own absolute discretion, is the resolution a constitutionally impermissible delegation of all or part of Congress's power to declare war?

These are large and deeply troubling questions. Whether the Court would ultimately reach them depends, of course, upon the resolution of serious preliminary issues of justiciability. We cannot make these problems go away simply by refusing to hear the case of three obscure Army privates. I intimate not even tentative views upon any of these matters, but I think the Court should squarely face them by granting certiorari and setting this case for oral argument.[20]

The Court's reluctance to accept cases challenging the Vietnam War did not deter the Massachusetts legislature from voting in 1970 to mandate its Attorney General to file a suit in the Supreme Court challenging the validity of the Vietnam War. The suit was brought in the original jurisdiction of the Court by naming the Secretary of Defense, Melvin Laird, the citizen of another state as the defendant. The Supreme Court rejected the suit, but Justice Douglas filed a long and vigorous dissenting opinion, claiming that conditions of standing and justiciability were met by the plaintiff. Massachusetts sought to enjoin the Secretary of Defense "from carrying out, issuing or causing to be issued any further orders which would increase the present level of United States troops in Indochina." Moreover, it sought, in the absence of a congressional declaration of war within ninety days, an injunction against the Secretary of Defense from any further orders "directing any inhabitant of the Commonwealth of Massachusetts to Indochina for the purpose of participating in combat or supporting combat troops in the Vietnam War." In his dissenting opinion from the Court's decision to deny certiorari, Justice Douglas stated that the courts do have the authority and responsibility to confront issues concerning the proper exercise of powers by coordinate branches. The Court has the authority, said Douglas, to determine that the Vietnam War is unconstitutional because it lacks a congressional declaration of war.

[20]Mora v. McNamara, 389 U.S. 934, 934–935 (1967).

The failure of the Court to curb presidential discretion to make war did not satisfy those who felt that presidential actions in Indochina had clearly exceeded his constitutional authority. The continuation of the Indochina war, particularly President Nixon's escalation of the war to Cambodia by using both ground forces and bombing, finally led Congress to take unprecedented action in its passage of the War Powers Resolution of 1973. On its face, the resolution seemed to set a severe curb upon presidential discretion to make war. It provided that the President could not commit United States troops abroad beyond sixty days without a specific congressional authorization. The commitment could be extended to ninety days if it was found to be necessary for the safe withdrawal of the troops. The President was directed to consult with Congress at all stages before taking action. At any time Congress could terminate the commitment of United States forces by a concurrent resolution, which does not require the President's signature to take effect. President Nixon predictably vetoed the measure, but on November 7, 1973, Congress voted the required two-thirds majority to override by a narrow four-vote margin in the House (284–135) and a comfortable thirteen-vote margin in the Senate (75–18). The President's press secretary, Ronald L. Ziegler, reported that the President felt that "The action seriously undermines this nation's ability to act decisively and convincingly in times of international crisis."[21] Nixon's October 24 veto message called the resolution both dangerous and unconstitutional.

While Nixon and most members of Congress viewed the War Powers Resolution as an important curb upon presidential discretion, Senator Thomas Eagleton suggested that the resolution was unconstitutional because it was based upon the premise that the President had the authority to commit troops.[22] Indeed, the resolution itself authorized the President to commit troops for a period up to ninety days.

Among the questions raised by the resolution are whether or not Congress has the authority to redefine constitutional relationships with regard to the power to make war. Since the authority to declare war is an exclusive congressional power, can Congress delegate this power even in a limited way to the President as was provided in the War Powers Resolution?

CONSTITUTIONAL DIVISION OF PRESIDENTIAL AND CONGRESSIONAL AUTHORITY OVER THE EXECUTIVE AND ADMINISTRATIVE BRANCHES

The Constitution says very little about the executive branch of government and nothing about the administrative branch. American bureaucracy has developed into a hybrid form. Administrative agencies have been delegated by Congress the authority to perform not only executive functions but legislative and judicial functions as well. In the exercise of legislative functions,

---

[21]Congressional Quarterly Weekly Report, November 10, 1973, p. 2985.
[22]Thomas Eagleton, *War and Presidential Power* (New York: Liveright, 1974).

administrative agencies are clearly to be agents of Congress. In their performance of judicial and quasi-judicial functions, the agencies are agents of Congress because of their responsibility to adhere to congressional policies in the adjudication of individual cases.

The growth of the bureaucracy and its expansion into legislative and judicial areas are not easily accommodated by the Constitution. The existence of an executive branch is implied in Article II, but the control the President is to exercise over executive officials is not set forth in detail. Obvious executive functions, such as those of appointment of ambassadors, public ministers and consuls, and officers of the United States are explicitly put into the hands of the President. Also the authority to grant reprieves and pardons was a traditional executive power given to the President. But even the appointment power of the President was not unambiguous. Article II, Section 2 limited the President's appointment power by requiring him to share with the Senate his authority to appoint ambassadors, public ministers, consuls, judges of the Supreme Court, and "all other officers of the United States, whose appointments are not here and otherwise provided for, and which shall be established by law: *but* the Congress may by law vest to the appointment of such inferior officers, as they think proper, in the President alone, in the court of law, or in the heads of departments." (Emphasis supplied.)

Article II also provides that the President "shall take care that the laws be faithfully executed" and that "he may require the opinion in writing of the principal officer in each of the executive departments, upon any subject relating to the duties of their respective offices."

The seemingly simple delegation of executive power to the President in Article II, including his authority to appoint public ministers and officers of the United States, does not clarify explicitly how far these presidential powers are to extend. The implied authority to create the executive branch is given to Congress by the Constitution, and it is the legislature that establishes the conditions under which the executive branch is to function. While the appointment power of the President clearly extends to "public ministers" and "officers of the United States," the Constitution does not define these terms. What is the difference between an "officer of the United States" and an "inferior officer"? Congress has without any constitutional difficulty removed a large portion of the executive branch from the appointment power of the President by creating a vast civil service system. And Congress has limited the President's appointment power of "officers of the United States" in a wide array of regulatory commissions, boards, and agencies. This has been done by providing for limited terms of office of appointees and limiting the appointments that can be made from any one political party to multiheaded agencies.

Limiting the President's appointment power by creating fixed terms for appointees also limits the President's removal power. In many cases Congress defines the conditions that must be met before the President can remove officials involved in exercising regulatory functions. The question of the President's removal power arose first in a nonregulatory context in the case of *Myers* v. *United States,* 272 U.S. 52 (1926). The *Myers* case involved an

1876 law that limited the President's removal power over postmasters. The law in question stated that

> Postmasters of the first, second, and third classes shall be appointed and may be removed by the President by and with the advice and consent of the Senate and shall hold their offices for four years unless sooner removed or suspended according to law.

President Woodrow Wilson appointed Myers to be a first-class postmaster in Portland, Oregon, in 1917 and subsequently removed him from this position in 1920 without consulting the Senate, as the law required. Myers sued for his salary in the Court of Claims, and when he received an adverse judgment he appealed to the Supreme Court. Chief Justice Taft, a former President, strongly asserted in his majority opinion denying Myers's claim that the President has a constitutional right to appoint and remove subordinate officials for political and other reasons, regardless of the functions they perform. Such power, said Taft, was implied in the provision of Article II giving the President the responsibility to see that the laws are faithfully executed, as well as in the other general executive powers stated in Article II. The President cannot carry out his constitutional responsibilities, argued Taft, if Congress interferes with his ability to control the executive branch. The almost belligerent tone of the *Myers* opinion made it seem as if Taft were still speaking from the White House rather than taking an appropriately dispassionate view of a Supreme Court justice. Neither history nor common sense, wrote Taft, would dictate that the Constitution should be interpreted to limit the President's removal power.

Taft confined his decision to officers appointed by the President by and with the advice of the Senate. These were, he said, "officers of the United States" under Article II. He rejected the argument that his decision would help to reintroduce the spoils system by curbing congressional power to create a civil service system based upon merit. "The extension of the merit system rests with Congress," wrote Taft, and may be enlarged by legislation. But as long as postmasters remain political appointments requiring the consent of the Senate, Congress cannot place limits upon the President's removal power over them. As long as the President continues to enjoy the power of appointment, Congress cannot place restrictions upon it beyond those which are already stipulated in the Constitution.

The Taft opinion in the *Myers* case implied that where the President exercised the power of appointment Congress could not curb it beyond requiring the consent of the Senate. Taft held that the power of appointment implied the power of removal and that any restrictions upon removal would constitute an unconstitutional usurpation of power on the part of Congress. However, Congress on numerous occasions had placed conditions upon presidential removal of officers of many agencies, including the Interstate Commerce Commission, the Federal Trade Commission, the Tariff Commission, the Controller General, and the Postmaster General. The enabling statutes for these agencies and for virtually all of the regulatory agencies that had been created by the time of the *Myers* case seemed to violate the broad implications of Chief Justice Taft's decision if not its specific terms. Taft did not go into the question of congressional restraints upon presidential removal power beyond those that existed in the specific statute in question in the *Myers* case, which required senatorial consent to removal. This was a highly unusual restriction, the more common one being simple statutory statements that the President could not remove administrative officers except for specified causes, such as malfeasance, dereliction of duty, or moral turpitude.

Justice McReynolds's dissent in the *Myers* case argued that Taft's opinion would allow the President to override congressional intent to limit the President's removal power under any circumstances. Challenging what he considered to be the alarming implication of Taft's opinion, which McReynolds felt unconstitutionally exalted the powers of the President relative to those of Congress in controlling the power to appoint and remove executive officials, he wrote,

> May the President oust at will all postmasters appointed with the Senate's consent for definite terms under an act which inhibits removal without consent of that body? May he approve a statute which creates an inferior office and prescribes restrictions on removal, appoint an incumbent, and then remove without regard to the restrictions? Has he power to appoint to an inferior office for a definite term under an act which prohibits removal except as therein specified, and then arbitrarily dismiss the incumbent and deprive him of the emoluments? I think there is no such power. Certainly it is not given by any plain words of the Constitution; and the argument advanced to establish it seems to me forced and unsubstantial.

The *Myers* decision was clarified and limited in *Humphrey's Executor* v. *United States*, 295 U. S. 602 (1935). William E. Humphrey had been nominated by President Hoover for a second term as a member of the Federal Trade Commission, and his appointment was confirmed by the Senate as required by the Federal Trade Commission Act of 1914. That act also provided: "Any Commissioner may be removed by the President for inefficiency, neglect of duty, or malfeasance in office." On its face, this statutory provision did not limit the President's removal power to the causes stated. With an eye on the broad presidential prerogative of removal implied in the *Myers* decision, President Roosevelt requested Humphrey's resignation in 1933, writing the commission that "The aims and purposes of the administration with respect to the work of the Commission can be carried out most effectively with personnel of my own selection." Roosevelt was removing Humphrey for political reasons and not because of inadequate performance on the job as defined by the statute or by Roosevelt.

The scope of the executive prerogative of appointment and removal stated by Taft in the *Myers* decision supported Roosevelt's action. In his brief for the United States, the Solicitor General argued: "It is a settled rule of construction that the mere statutory enumeration of causes for which an appointee may be removed does not confine the exercise of the President's power to remove for one or more of those causes."[23] Citing the *Myers* deci-

---

[23]LB Vol. 30, pp. 100–101.

sion throughout his brief, the Solicitor General stated, inter alia: "A statute limiting the President's power to remove for certain causes is an unwarranted interference with the executive power as is a statute requiring participation by the Senate in a removal manifestly unsound."[24] Nor can the President's removal power over the Federal Trade Commission be limited because the agency is quasi-legislative or quasi-judicial, said the Solicitor General. Executive departments perform the same function, and under the *Myers* rule the President's removal power over these departments cannot be restricted.

The attorneys for Humphrey's executor (Rathbun) attempted to refute the arguments of the Solicitor General by stating that the Federal Trade Commission was not intended by Congress to be an integral part of the executive branch. "We submit," they argued, "that Section 1 of the Federal Trade Commission Act showed that Congress intended to create the Federal Trade Commission as an independent, nonpartisan, administrative agent, free from the domination of the President through the exercise of an unlimited power of removal."[25] They continued: "The provision of Section 1 of the Federal Trade Commission Act that 'any commissioner may be removed by the President for inefficiency, neglect of duty or malfeasance in office' restricts the power of the President to remove except upon one or more of the causes stated. . . ."[26]

Justice Sutherland, who delivered the Court's opinion in the *Humphrey* case, supported the view that Congress can indeed limit presidential removal power over quasi-legislative and quasi-judicial officers. "The *Myers* case cannot be accepted as controlling our decision here," wrote Sutherland, for it concerns only "a postmaster [who] is an executive officer restricted to the performance of executive functions." The *Myers* decision, said Sutherland, reaches only the question of presidential removal authority over executive departments and officers. Administrative agencies, such as the Federal Trade Commission, that perform quasi-legislative and quasi-judicial functions are not controlled by the *Myers* decision. The Court concluded that Congress, in the Federal Trade Commission Act, intended to limit the removal power of the President over FTC Commissioners and that Roosevelt could not remove a commissioner for a reason that was not stated in the statute.

The decision in the *Humphrey* case occurred at a time when the Supreme Court was systematically striking down New Deal legislation. It was decided on the same day as the *Schechter* ruling overturning the National Industrial Recovery Act. The *Schechter* and *Humphrey* cases respectively expressed the unanimous opinion of the Court that the powers granted to and exercised by the President overstepped the constitutional boundaries dictated by the separation of powers doctrine.

While the Court and many members of Congress considered the *Humphrey* decision as a vindication of congressional independence of the executive in exercising control over the administrative branch, Roosevelt and his advisers were little perturbed. At a cabinet meeting shortly after the deci-

[24]Ibid., p. 103.
[25]Ibid., p. 27.
[26]Ibid., p. 16.

sion, Vice President John Nance Garner told the group that in light of the *Humphrey* case greater care should be taken in making appointments to administrative agencies because of difficulties that would be faced in the future if the President wanted to remove unsatisfactory officials. He felt that in the past appointment to such commissions "was altogether too slipshod."[27] Garner said that Humphrey should never have been named to the Federal Trade Commission in the first place, and Roosevelt replied that "he had made a mistake in not preferring charges. He had actual proof of malfeasance in office, but he didn't want to file such charges against Humphrey, believing as he did that he could get rid of him by milder methods."[28]

The *Humphrey* case was again brought up when difficulties occurred in the relationship between Roosevelt and the Chairman of the Board of the Tennessee Valley Authority, Dr. A. E. Morgan. At a meeting with the President on March 17, 1938, Interior Secretary Harold L. Ickes, a close confidant and adviser of the President, told him that "Chairman Morgan had been openly impertinent and insubordinate."[29] He continued: "I told the President that Burlew [Assistant Secretary of the Interior] had looked up the law Saturday afternoon and had brought in to me the decision of the Supreme Court in the *Humphrey* case. We both believe that the President has the right to fire Morgan."[30] The President then followed Ickes's advice and fired Morgan. Upon challenge, the decision was upheld by the circuit court of appeals on the grounds that the TVA was an executive agency which Congress had intended to be directly under the President's control. The 1940 Circuit Court opinion was appealed to the Supreme Court in 1941, which declined to review the lower court's decision.

The fact that the *Myers* and *Humphrey* cases together did not finally solve the issue of the constitutional scope of presidential authority over the executive branch was evident as yet another case arose over the question in *Wiener* v. *United States* in 1958. Wiener had been appointed to the War Claims Commission, an adjudicative body, by President Truman in 1950, and Senate confirmation followed. The commission was composed of three members and was to continue in existence not later than three years after the statutory limit for the filing of war claims. When President Eisenhower entered the White House he requested Wiener's resignation and, when he did not receive it, removed him with the statement that "I regard it as in the national interest to complete the administration of the War Claims Act of 1948, as amended, with personnel of my own selection." The War Claims Act said nothing about the removal power of the President over commission members. What, if any, decision was dictated by the precedents of the *Myers* and *Humphrey* cases? Would the fact that the War Claims Commission was a quasi-judicial body by itself justify limitation of the President's removal power over its members?

The brief for the petitioner (Wiener) argued that the *Humphrey* decision

[27]Harold L. Ickes, *The Secret Diary of Harold L. Ickes: The First Thousand Days, 1933–1936* (New York: Simon and Schuster, 1953), p. 374.

[28]Ibid.

[29]Ibid., Vol. 2: *The Inside Struggle*, p. 337.

[30]Ibid.

had decided that the President's removal power over quasi-legislative and quasi-judicial statutory officers is not illimitable. Where Congress has fixed a term of office for officials engaged in either quasi-legislative or quasi-judicial functions, or both, the President cannot remove them for political reasons. "The President does not possess under the Constitution power to remove at his pleasure quasi-legislative or quasi-judicial officers," argued Wiener.[31] Attempting to refute Wiener's position, the Solicitor General argued that the "petitioner was an executive officer and that hence the President's removal power was illimitable. . . ."[32] On the basis of these arguments the major determination to be made by the Court was whether or not Wiener was in fact a quasi-legislative or quasi-judicial official. Would such a determination indicate per se whether or not it was the intent of Congress to limit the President's removal power? These and other considerations formed an important part of Justice Frankfurter's opinion for the Court.

Wiener v. United States

357 U.S. 349; 78 S. Ct. 1275 2 L. Ed. 2d 1377 (1958)

Mr. Justice Frankfurter delivered the opinion of the Court:

. . . In the present case, Congress provided for a tenure defined by the relatively short period of time during which the War Claims Commission was to operate—that is, it was to wind up not later than three years after the expiration of the time for filing of claims. But nothing was said in the Act about removal.

This is another instance in which the most appropriate legal significance must be drawn from congressional failure of explicitness. Necessarily this is a problem in probabilities. We start with one certainty. The problem of the President's power to remove members of the agencies entrusted with duties of the kind with which the War Claims Commission was charged was within the lively knowledge of Congress. Few contests between Congress and the President have so recurringly had the attention of Congress as that pertaining to the power of removal. Not the least significant aspect of the Myers Case is that on the Court's special

invitation Senator George Wharton Pepper, of Pennsylvania, presented the position of Congress at the bar of this Court.

Humphrey's case was a cause célèbre—and not least in the halls of Congress. And what is the essence of the decision in Humphrey's case? It drew a sharp line of cleavage between officials who were part of the Executive establishment and were thus removable by virtue of the President's constitutional powers, and those who are members of a body "to exercise its judgment without the leave or hindrance of any other official or any department of the government," . . . as to whom a power of removal exists only if Congress may fairly be said to have conferred it. This sharp differentiation derives from the difference in functions between those who are part of the Executive establishment and those whose tasks require absolute freedom from Executive interference. "For it is quite evident," again to quote Humphrey's Executor, "that one who holds his office only during the pleasure of another, cannot be depended

[31]LB, Vol. 41, p. 21.
[32]Ibid., p. 43.

upon to maintain an attitude of independence against the latter's will." . . .

Thus, the most reliable factor for drawing an inference regarding the President's power of removal in our case is the nature of the function that Congress vested in the War Claims Commission. What were the duties that Congress confided to this Commission? And can the inference fairly be drawn from the failure of Congress to provide for removal that these Commissioners were to remain in office at the will of the President? For such is the assertion of power on which petitioner's removal must rest. The ground of President Eisenhower's removal of petitioner was precisely the same as President Roosevelt's removal of Humphrey. Both Presidents desired to have Commissioners, one on the Federal Trade Commission, the other on the War Claims Commission, "of my own selection." They wanted these Commissioners to be their men. The terms of removal in the two cases are identical and express the assumption that the agencies of which the two Commissioners were members were subject in the discharge of their duties to the control of the Executive. An analysis of the Federal Trade Commission Act left this Court in no doubt that such was not the conception of Congress in creating the Federal Trade Commission. The terms of the War Claims Act of 1948 leave no doubt that such was not the conception of Congress regarding the War Claims Commission.

The history of this legislation emphatically underlines this fact. The short of it is that the origin of the Act was a bill, . . . passed by the House that placed the administration of a very limited class of claims by Americans against Japan in the hands of the Federal Security Administrator and provided for a Commission to inquire into and report upon other types of claims. . . . The Federal Security Administrator was indubitably an arm of the President. When the House bill reached the Senate, it struck out all but the enacting clause, rewrote the bill, and established a Commission with "jurisdiction to receive and adjudicate according to law" three classes of claims, as defined by §§ 5, 6 and 7. The Commission was established as adjudicating body with all the paraphernalia by which legal claims are put to the test of proof, with finality of determination "not subject to review by any other official of the United States or by any court, by mandamus or otherwise," § 11. Awards were to be paid out of a War Claims Fund in the hands of the Secretary of the Treasury, whereby such claims were given even more assured collectability than adheres to judgments rendered in the Court of Claims. . . . Congress could, of course, have given jurisdiction over these claims to the District Courts or to the Court of Claims. The fact that it chose to establish a Commission to "adjudicate according to law" the classes of claims defined in the statute did not alter the intrinsic judicial character of the task with which the Commission was charged. The claims were to be "adjudicated according to law," that is, on the merits of each claim, supported by evidence and governing legal considerations, by a body that was "entirely free from the control or coercive influence, direct or indirect," of either the Executive or the Congress. If, as one must take for granted, the War Claims Act precluded the President from influencing the Commission in passing on a particular claim, a fortiori must it be inferred that Congress did not wish to have hang over the Commission the Damocles' sword of removal by the President for no reason other than that he preferred to have on that Commission men of his own choosing.

For such is this case. We have not a removal for cause involving the rectitude of a member of an adjudicatory body, nor even a suspensory removal until the Senate could act upon it by confirming the appointment of a new Commissioner or otherwise dealing with the matter. Judging the matter in all the nakedness in which it is presented, namely, the claim that the President could remove a member of an adjudicatory body like the War Claims Commission merely because he wanted his own appointees on such a Commission, we are compelled to conclude that no such power is given to the President directly by the Constitution, and none is impliedly conferred upon him by statute simply because Congress said nothing about it. The philosophy of Humphrey's Executor, in its explicit language as well as its implications, precludes such a claim.

The judgment is reversed.

After the *Wiener* case it seemed to be settled doctrine that the President has constitutional authority to remove purely executive officials but he may not, absent explicit congressional authorization, remove quasi-legislative or quasi-judicial officers. Frankfurter's opinion in the *Wiener* case implied congressional intent to restrain presidential removal power over officers exercising quasi-legislative or quasi-judicial functions even though there were no explicit boundaries placed on the removal power of the President in statutory language.

The *Myers, Humphrey,* and *Wiener* decisions did not, however, finally settle the constitutional boundaries between the President and Congress over the power to remove administrative officials. A new circumstance was presented to the Court when President Nixon summarily fired Watergate Special Prosecutor Archibald Cox on October 20, 1973. Cox was exercising the prosecutorial functions, placing him in a different category than Humphrey and Wiener, who were members of agencies exercising quasi-legislative and quasi-judicial functions. Since prosecutorial functions are clearly executive in character, it is reasonable to assume that they should be under the control of the chief executive officer, which in the Cox case was the President. For example, in the absence of statutory limitations, the President can remove the Attorney General and other prosecutors within the Justice Department for political reasons. Customarily new Presidents remove United States Attorneys (who are the prosecutors of the Justice Department) of the opposition party from office when they assume power. There is no judicial presumption of congressional intent to protect such officials.

Archibald Cox, however, was not an ordinary United States Attorney. He was not appointed by the President but by the Attorney General under congressional statutes that authorized the creation of an Office of Special Prosecutor. When Attorney General Elliot Richardson hired Mr. Cox, he specifically promulgated a regulation that limited the Attorney General's authority to fire him. The formal Department of Justice regulation provided that "The Special Prosecutor will not be removed from his duties except for extraordinary impropriety on his part." Ignoring the implication of this regulation, which on its face would seem to protect the Special Prosecutor from summary dismissal, President Nixon ordered Acting Attorney General Robert Bork (Richardson had resigned, refusing to carry out the President's order of dismissal) to fire Cox, which he did in a deed that was commonly referred to as the Saturday Night Massacre. Challenging the President's action, Ralph Nader and three members of Congress sued for a declaration that the dismissal was illegal and for an injunction against Bork. Cox himself was not involved in the suit. Judge Gesell of the District Court of the District of Columbia dismissed Nader as a plaintiff on the grounds that he had no standing to sue. However, Judge Gesell granted standing to the three members of Congress, claiming that as representatives of the legislature and of special committees dealing with matters concerning the role of the Special Prosecutor, their interests were substantial enough to justify a judicial determination regarding the legality of firing Cox. On the merits, the district court held that the President had no authority to fire Cox because he was an agent of Congress, appointed by the Attorney General, who had issued a special regulation limiting the conditions of his removal. He could not be removed except for "extraordinary impropriety," and this had not been demonstrated by the President nor by the Acting Attorney General. If no condition had been stated limiting the Attorney General's power to remove Cox, the Special Prosecutor could have been summarily dismissed. Once the administrative regulations were promulgated, however, they had the full force of law.[33]

The doctrine of separation of powers permits some constraints upon the authority of the President to remove quasi-legislative and quasi-judicial officials. To what extent does the separation of powers doctrine allow Congress to involve itself in the process of appointment of executive officials? Does the appointments clause of Article II, Section 2 give exclusive authority to the President to control executive appointments subject only to constitutional and statutory prescriptions requiring the advice and consent of the Senate? This issue confronted the Supreme Court in the 1976 case of *Buckley v. Valeo,* in which the Court ruled on the constitutionality of the Federal Election Campaign Act of 1971, as amended in 1974. The 1971 law was designed to tighten the reporting requirements for political contributions and to control expenditures for political candidates. Limits were placed upon the amounts contributors and candidates alike could spend for political campaigns. Public financing of presidential primary and general election campaigns was established. The act was to be administered by a Federal Election Commission of six members, two of which were to be appointed by the president pro tempore of the Senate, and two to be appointed by the Speaker of the House. The remaining two were appointed by the President, and all six members were subject to confirmation by a majority of both branches of Congress. To administer the act the commission was given rule-making, adjudicative, and enforcement powers.

The law was challenged as a violation of the First Amendment rights of candidates and contributors and as a breach of the separation of powers because of the provisions for direct congressional appointment of a majority

[33]Nader v. Bork, 366 F. Supp. 104 (1973). Although Ralph Nader was not granted standing, his disqualification came from the bench and the case remained in the books in his name. Archibald Cox was not a party to the suit because he had no interest in returning to his job, and when the Court finally ruled in his favor he did not resume his duties.

of the members of the Federal Election Commission. With respect to the First Amendment challenge, the Court upheld provisions of the law that (1) set limits on how much individuals and political committees might contribute to candidates; (2) provided for the public financing of presidential primary and general election campaigns; and (3) required disclosure of campaign contributions of more than $100 and expenditures of more than $10. The spending limits on individuals and groups under the 1974 amendments, including limits on the use of personal funds by political candidates, were ruled an unconstitutional infraction of the First Amendment rights of free expression and association.

In the following portion of the opinion the Court considers the constitutionality of the structure of the Federal Election Commission under the standards of the separation of powers.

Buckley v. Valeo

424 U.S. 1; 96 S. Ct. 612; 46 L. Ed. 2d 659 (1976)

The Court, per curiam:

IV
THE FEDERAL ELECTION
COMMISSION

The 1974 Amendments to the Act created an eight-member Federal Election Commission, and [vested] in it primary and substantial responsibility for administering and enforcing the Act. The question that we address in this portion of the opinion is whether, in view of the manner in which a majority of its members are appointed, the Commission may under the Constitution exercise the powers conferred upon it. We find it unnecessary to parse the complex statutory provisions in order to sketch the full sweep of the Commission's authority. It will suffice for present purposes to describe what appear to be representative examples of its various powers. . . .

The Commission's enforcement power is both direct and wide-ranging. . . .

The body in which this authority is reposed consists of eight members. The Secretary of the Senate and the Clerk of the House of Representatives are ex officio members of the Commission without the right to vote. Two members are appointed by the President pro tempore of the Senate "upon the recommendations of the majority leader of the Senate and the minority leader of the Senate." Two more are to be appointed by the Speaker of the House of Representatives, likewise upon the recommendations of its respective majority and minority leaders. The remaining two members are appointed by the President. Each of the six voting members of the Commission must be confirmed by the majority of both Houses of Congress, and each of the three appointing authorities is forbidden to choose both of their appointees from the same political party. . . .

The Merits

Appellants urge that since Congress has given the Commission wide-ranging rule-making and enforcement powers with respect to the substantive provisions of the

Act, Congress is precluded under the principle of separation of powers from vesting in itself the authority to appoint those who will exercise such authority. Their argument is based on the language of Art II, § 2, cl 2, of the Constitution, which provides in pertinent part as follows:

[The President] shall nominate, and by and with the Advice and Consent of the Senate, shall appoint . . . all other Officers of the United States, whose Appointments are not herein otherwise provided for, and which shall be established by Law: but the Congress may by Law vest the Appointment of such inferior Officers, as they think proper, in the President alone, in the Courts of Law, or in the Heads of Departments.

Appellants' argument is that this provision is the exclusive method by which those charged with executing the laws of the United States may be chosen. Congress, they assert, cannot have it both ways. If the legislature wishes the Commission to exercise all of the conferred powers, then its members are in fact "Officers of the United States" and must be appointed under the Appointments Clause. But if Congress insists upon retaining the power to appoint, then the members of the Commission may not discharge those many functions of the Commission which can be performed only by "Officers of the United States," as that term must be construed within the doctrine of separation of powers.

Appellee Federal Election Commission and amici in support of the Commission urge that the Framers of the Constitution, while mindful of the need for checks and balances among the three branches of the National Government, had no intention of denying to the Legislative Branch authority to appoint its own officers. Congress, either under the Appointments Clause or under its grants of substantive legislative authority and the Necessary and Proper Clause in Art I, is in their

view empowered to provide for the appointment to the Commission in the manner which it did because the Commission is performing "appropriate legislative functions."

The majority of the Court of Appeals recognized the importance of the doctrine of separation of powers which is at the heart of our Constitution, and also recognized the principle enunciated in *Springer* v. *Philippine Islands* [1928] . . . that the Legislative Branch may not exercise executive authority by retaining the power to appoint those who will execute its laws. But it described appellants' argument based upon Art II, § 2, cl 2, as "strikingly syllogistic," and concluded that Congress had sufficient authority under the Necessary and Proper Clause of Art I of the Constitution not only to establish but appoint the Commission's members. As we have earlier noted, it upheld the constitutional validity of congressional vesting of certain authority in the Commission, and concluded that the question of the constitutional validity of the vesting of its remaining functions was not yet ripe for review. The three dissenting judges in the Court of Appeals concluded that the method of appointment for the Commission did violate the separation of powers.

1. Separation of Powers

We do not think appellants' arguments based upon Art II, § 2, cl 2, of the Constitution may be so easily dismissed as did the majority of the Court of Appeals. Our inquiry of necessity touches upon the fundamental principles of the Government established by the Framers of the Constitution, and all litigants and all of the courts which have addressed themselves to the matter start on common ground in the recognition of the intent of the Framers that the powers of the three great branches of the National Government be largely separate from one another.

James Madison, writing in the Federalist No. 47, defended the work of the Framers against the charge that these three governmental powers were not *entirely* separate from one another in the proposed Constitution. He asserted that while there was some admixture, the Constitution was nonetheless true to Montesquieu's well-known maxim that the legislative, executive, and judicial departments ought to be separate and distinct:

The reasons on which Montesquieu grounds his maxim are a further demonstration of his meaning. "When the legislative and executive powers are united in the same person or body," says he, "there can be no liberty, because apprehensions may arise lest *the same* monarch or senate should *enact* tyrannical laws to execute them in a tyrannical manner." Again: "Were the power of judging joined with the legislative, the life and liberty of the subject would be exposed to arbitrary control, for *the judge* would then be *the legislator*. Were it joined to the executive power, *the judge* might behave with all the violence of *an oppressor*." Some of these reasons are more fully explained in other passages; but briefly stated as they are here, they sufficiently establish the meaning which we have put on this celebrated maxim of this celebrated author.

Yet it is also clear from the provisions of the Constitution itself, and from the Federalist Papers, that the Constitution by no means contemplates total separation of each of these three essential branches of Government. The President is a participant in the law-making process by virtue of his authority to veto bills enacted by Congress. The Senate is a participant in the appointive process by virtue of its authority to refuse to confirm persons nominated to office by the President. The men who met in Philadelphia in the summer of 1787 were practical statesmen, experienced in politics, who viewed the principle of separation of powers as a vital check against tyranny. But they likewise saw that a hermetic sealing off of the three branches of Government from one another would preclude the establishment of a Nation capable of governing itself effectively.

Chief Justice Taft, writing for the Court in *Hampton and Co.* v. *United States*, [1928] . . . after stating the general principle of separation of powers found in the United States Constitution, went on to observe:

[T]he rule is that in the actual administration of the government Congress or the Legislature should exercise the legislative power, the President or the State executive, the Governor, the executive power, and the Courts or the judiciary the judicial power, and in carrying out that constitutional division into three branches it is a breach of the National fundamental law if Congress gives up its legislative power and transfers it to the President, or to the Judicial branch, or if by law it attempts to invest itself or its members with either executive power or judicial power. This is not to say that the three branches are not co-ordinate parts of one government and that each in the field of its duties may not invoke the action of the two other branches in so far as the action invoked shall not be an assumption of the constitutional field of action of another branch. In determining what it may do in seeking assistance from another branch, the extent and character of that assistance must be fixed according to common sense and the inherent necessities of the governmental co-ordination. . . .

More recently, Mr. Justice Jackson, concurring in the opinion and the judgment of the Court in *Youngstown Co.* v. *Sawyer*, [1952], . . . succinctly characterized this understanding:

While the Constitution diffuses power the better to secure liberty, it also contemplates that practice will integrate the dispersed powers into a workable government. It enjoins upon its branches separateness but interdependence, autonomy but reciprocity.

The Framers regarded the checks and balances that they had built into the tripartite Federal Government as a self-executing safeguard against the encroachment or aggrandizement of one branch at the expense of the other. As Madison put it in Federalist No. 51:

This policy of supplying, by opposite and rival interests, the defect of better motives, might be traced through the whole system of human affairs, private as well as public. We see it particularly displayed in all the subordinate distributions of power, where the constant aim is to divide and arrange the several offices in such a manner as that each day may be a check on the other—that the private interest of every individual may be a sentinel over the public rights. These inventions of prudence cannot be less requisite in the distribution of the supreme powers of the State.

This Court has not hesitated to enforce the principles of separation of powers embodied in the Constitution when their application has proved necessary for the decision of cases and controversies properly before it. The Court has held that executive or administrative duties of a nonjudicial nature may not be imposed on judges holding office under Art III of the Constitution. *United States* v. *Ferreira* [1852] ... *Hayburn's Case* [1792] ... The Court has held that the President may not execute and exercise legislative authority belonging only to Congress. *Youngstown Co.* v. *Sawyer.* In the course of its opinion in that case, the Court said:

In the framework of our Constitution, the President's power to see that the laws are faithfully executed refutes the idea that he is to be a lawmaker. The Constitution limits his functions in the lawmaking process to the recommending of laws he thinks ·wise and the vetoing of laws he thinks bad. And the Constitution is neither silent nor equivocal about who shall make laws which the President is to execute. The first section of the first article says that "All legislative Powers herein granted shall be vested in a Congress of the United States. . . ."

More closely in point to the facts of the present case is this Court's decision in *Springer* v. *Philippine Islands, supra,* where the Court held that the legislature of the Philippine Islands could not provide for legislative appointment to executive agencies.

2. *The Appointments Clause*

The principle of separation of powers was not simply an abstract generalization in the minds of the Framers: it was woven into the document that they drafted in Philadelphia in the summer of 1787. Article I declares: "All legislative Powers herein granted shall be vested in a Congress of the United States." Article II vests the executive power "in a President of the United States of America," and Art III declares that "the judicial Power of the United States, shall be vested in one supreme Court, and in such inferior Courts as the Congress may from time to time ordain and establish." The further concern of the Framers of the Constitution with maintenance of the separation of powers is found in the so-called "ineligibility" and "Incompatibility" Clauses contained in § 6 of Art I:

No Senator or Representative shall, during the Time for which he was elected, be appointed to any civil Office under the Authority of the United States, which shall have been created, or the Emoluments whereof shall have been increased during such time; and no Person holding any Office under the United States, shall be a Member of either House during his Continuance in Office.

It is in the context of these cognate provisions of the document that we must examine the language of Art II, § 2, cl 2, which appellants contend provides the only authorization for appointment of those to whom substantial executive or administrative authority is given by statute. Because of the importance of its language, we again set out the provision:

[The President] shall nominate, and by and with the Advice and Consent of the Senate, shall appoint Ambassadors, other public Ministers and Consuls, Judges of the Supreme Court, and all other Officers of the United States, whose Appointments are not herein otherwise provided for, and which shall be established by Law: but the Congress may by Law vest the Appointment of such inferior Officers, as they think proper, in the President alone, in the Courts of Law, or in the Heads of Departments.

The Appointments Clause could, of course, be read as merely dealing with etiquette or protocol in describing "Officers of the United States," but the drafters had a less frivolous purpose in mind. This conclusion is supported by language from *United States* v. *Germaine,* 99 U.S. 508, 509–510 [1879] . . .

The Constitution for purposes of appointment very clearly divides all its officers into two classes. The primary class requires a nomination by the President and confirmation by the Senate. But foreseeing that when offices became numerous, and sudden removals necessary, this mode might be inconvenient, it was provided that, in regard to officers inferior to those specially mentioned, Congress might by law vest their appointment in the President alone, in the courts of law, or in the heads of departments. *That all persons who can be said to hold an office under the government about to be established under the Constitution were intended to be included within one or the other of these modes of appointment there can be little doubt.* (Emphasis supplied.)

We think that the term "Officers of the United States" as used in Art II, defined to include "all persons who can be said to hold an office under the government" in *United States* v. *Germaine,* is a term intended to have substantive meaning. We think its fair import is that any appointee exercising significant authority pursuant to the laws of the United States is an Officer of the United States, and must, therefore, be appointed in the manner prescribed by § 2, cl 2 of that Article.

If "all persons who can be said to hold an office under the government about to be established under the Constitution were intended to be included within one or the other of these modes of appointment," *United States* v. *Germaine,* it is difficult to see how the members of the Commission may escape inclusion. If a Postmaster first class, *Myers* v. *United States,* [1926] . . . and the Clerk of a District Court, *Matter of Hennen,* 13 Pet 230 [1839] . . . are inferior officers of the United States within the meaning of the Appointments Clause, as they are, surely the Commissioners before us are at the very least such "inferior Officers" within the meaning of that Clause.

Although two members of the Commission are initially selected by the President, his nominations are subject to confirmation not merely by the Senate, but by the House of Representatives as well. The remaining four voting members of the Commission were appointed by the President pro tempore of the Senate and by the Speaker of the House. While the second part of the Clause authorizes Congress to vest the appointment of the officers described in that part in "the Courts of Law, or in the Heads of Departments," neither the Speaker of the House nor the President pro tempore of the Senate comes within this language.

The phrase "Heads of Departments," used as it is in conjunction with the phrase "Courts of Law," suggests that the Departments referred to are themselves in the Executive Branch or at least have some connection with that branch. While the Clause expressly authorizes Congress to vest the appointment of certain officers in the "Courts of Law," the absence of similar language to include Congress must mean that neither Congress nor its officers were included within the language "Heads of Departments" in this part of cl 2.

Thus with respect to four of the six voting members of the Commission, neither the President, the head of any department, nor the judiciary has any voice in their selection.

The Appointments Clause specifies the method of appointment only for "Officers of the United States" whose appointment is not "otherwise provided for" in the Constitution. But there is no provision of the Constitution remotely providing any alternative means for the selection of the members of the Commission or for anybody like them. Appellee Commission has argued, and the Court of Appeals agreed, that the Appointments Clause of Art II should not be read to exclude the "inherent power of Congress" to appoint its own officers to perform functions necessary to that body as an institution. But there is no need to read the Appointments Clause contrary to its plain language in order to reach the result sought by the Court of Appeals. Article I, § 3, cl 5, expressly authorizes the selection of the President pro tempore of the Senate, and § 2, cl 5, of that Article provides for the selection of the Speaker of the House. Ranking nonmembers, such as the Clerk of the House of Representatives, are elected under the internal rules of each House and are designated by statute as "officers of the Congress." There is no occasion for us to decide whether any of these member officers are "Officers of the United States" whose "appointment" is otherwise provided for within the meaning of the Appointments Clause, since even if they were such officers their appointees would not be. Contrary to the fears expressed by the majority of the Court of Appeals, nothing in our holding with respect to Art II, § 2, cl 2, will deny to Congress "all power to appoint its own inferior officers to carry out appropriate legislative functions."

Appellee Commission and amici contend somewhat obliquely that because the Framers had no intention of relegating Congress to a position below that of the coequal Judicial and Executive Branches of the National Government, the Appointments Clause must somehow be read to include Congress or its officers as among those in whom the appointment power may be vested. But the debates of the Constitutional Convention, and the Federalist Papers, are replete with expressions of fear that the Legislative Branch of the National Government will aggrandize itself at the expense of the other two branches. The debates during the Convention, and the evolution of the draft version of the Constitution, seem to us to lend considerable support to our reading of the language of the Appointments Clause itself.

An interim version of the draft Constitution had vested in the Senate the authority to appoint Ambassadors, public Ministers, and Judges of the Supreme Court, and the language of Art II as finally adopted is a distinct change in this regard. We believe that it was a deliberate change made by the Framers with the intent to deny Congress any authority itself to appoint those who were "Officers of the United States." The debates on the floor of the Convention reflect at least in part the way the change came about.

On Monday, August 6, 1787, the Committee on Detail to which had been referred the entire draft of the Constitution reported its draft to the Convention, including the following two articles that bear on the question before us:

Article IX, Section 1 "The Senate of the United States shall have power . . . to appoint Ambassadors, and Judges of the Supreme Court."

Article X, Section 2 "[The President] shall commission all the officers of the United States; and shall appoint officers in all cases not otherwise provided for by this Constitution."

It will be seen from a comparison of these two articles that the appointment of Ambassadors and Judges was confided to the

Senate, and that the authority to *appoint*—not merely nominate, but to actually appoint—all other officers was reposed in the President. During a discussion of a provision in the same draft from the Committee on Detail which provided that the "Treasurer" of the United States should be chosen by both Houses of Congress, Mr. Read moved to strike out that clause, "leaving the appointment of the Treasurer *as of other officers* to the Executive." Opposition to Read's motion was based, not on objection to the principle of executive appointment, but on the particular nature of the office of the "Treasurer."

On Thursday, August 23, the Convention voted to insert after the word "Ambassadors" in the text of draft Art IX the words "and other public Ministers." Immediately afterwards, the section as amended was referred to the "Committee of Five." The following day the Convention took up Art X. Roger Sherman objected to the draft language of § 2 because it conferred too much power on the President, and proposed to insert after the words "not otherwise provided for by this Constitution" the words "or by law." This motion was defeated by a vote of nine States to one. On September 3 the Convention debated the Ineligibility and Incompatibility Clauses which now appear in Art I, and made the Ineligibility Clause somewhat less stringent.

Meanwhile, on Friday, August 30, a motion had been carried without opposition to refer such parts of the Constitution as had been postponed or not acted upon to a Committee of Eleven. Such reference carried with it both Arts IX and X. The following week the Committee of Eleven made its report to the Convention, in which the present language of Art II, § 2, cl 2, dealing with the authority of the President to nominate is found, virtually word for word, as § 4 of Art X. The same Committee also reported a revised Article concerning the Legislative Branch to the Convention. The changes are obvious. In the final version, the Senate is shorn of its power to appoint Ambassadors and Judges of the Supreme Court. The President is given, not the power to *appoint* public officers of the United States, but only the right to *nominate* them, and a provision is inserted by virtue of which Congress may require Senate confirmation of his nominees.

It would seem a fair surmise that a compromise had been made. But no change was made in the concept of the term "Officers of the United States," which since it had first appeared in Art X had been taken by all concerned to embrace all appointed officials exercising responsibility under the public laws of the Nation.

Appellee Commission and amici urge that because of what they conceive to be the extraordinary authority reposed in Congress to regulate elections, this case stands on a different footing than if Congress had exercised its legislative authority in another field. There is of course no doubt that Congress has express authority to regulate congressional elections, by virtue of the power conferred in Art I, § 4. This Court has also held that it has very broad authority to prevent corruption in national Presidential elections. *Burroughs* v. *United States* [1934] . . . . But Congress has plenary authority in all areas in which it has substantive legislative jurisdiction, *McCulloch* v. *Maryland* [1819] . . . so long as the exercise of that authority does not offend some other constitutional restriction. We see no reason to believe that the authority of Congress over federal election practices is of such a wholly different nature from the other grants of authority to Congress that it may be employed in such a manner as to offend well established constitutional restrictions stemming from the separation of powers.

The position that because Congress has been given explicit and plenary authority to regulate a field of activity, it must therefore have the power to appoint those who are to administer the regulatory statute is both novel and contrary to the language of the Appointments Clause. Unless their selection is elsewhere provided for, all officers of the United States are to be appointed in accordance with the Clause. Principal officers are selected by the President with the advice and consent of the Senate. Inferior officers Congress may allow to be appointed by the President alone, by the heads of departments, or by the judiciary. No class or type of officer is excluded because of its special functions. The President appoints judicial as well as executive officers. Neither has it been disputed—and apparently it is not now disputed—that the Clause controls the appointment of the members of a typical administrative agency even though its functions, as this Court recognized in *Humphrey's Executor* v. *United States* [1935] . . . , may be "predominantly quasi-judicial and quasi-legislative" rather than executive. The Court in that case carefully emphasized that although the members of such agencies were to be independent of the executive in their day-to-day operations, the executive was not excluded from selecting them. . . .

Appellees argue that the legislative authority conferred upon the Congress in Art I, § 4, to regulate "the Times, Places and Manner of holding Elections for Senators and Representatives" is augmented by the provision in § 5 that "Each House shall be the Judge of the Elections, Returns, and Qualifications of its own Members." Section 5 confers, however, not a general legislative power upon the Congress, but rather a power "judicial in character" upon each House of the Congress. *Barry* v. *United States ex rel. Cunningham* [1929] . . . The power of each House to judge whether one claiming election as Senator or Representative has met the requisite qualifications, *Powell* v. *McCormack* [1969] . . . cannot reasonably be translated into a power granted to the Congress itself to impose substantive qualifications on the right to so hold such office. Whatever power Congress may have to legislate such qualifications must derive from § 4, rather than § 5, of Art I.

Appellees also rely on the Twelfth Amendment to the Constitution insofar as the authority of the Commission to regulate practices in connection with the Presidential election is concerned. This amendment provides that certificates of the votes of the electors be "sealed [and] directed to the President of the Senate," and that the "President of the Senate shall, in the presence of the Senate and House of Representatives, open all the certificates and the votes shall then be counted." The method by which Congress resolved the celebrated disputed Hayes-Tilden election of 1876, reflected in 19 Stat 227, supports the conclusion that Congress viewed this Amendment as conferring upon its two Houses the same sort of power "judicial in character," . . . as was conferred upon each House by Art I, § 5, with respect to elections of its own members.

We are also told by appellees and amici that Congress had good reason for not vesting in a Commission composed wholly of Presidential appointees the authority to administer the Act, since the administration of the Act would undoubtedly have a bearing on any incumbent President's campaign for re-election. While one cannot dispute the basis for this sentiment as a practical matter, it would seem that those who sought to challenge incumbent Congressmen might have equally good reason to fear a Commission which was unduly responsive to Members of Congress whom they are seeking to unseat.

But such fears, however rational, do not by themselves warrant a distortion of the Framer's work.

Appellee Commission and amici finally contend, and the majority of the Court of Appeals agreed with them, that whatever shortcomings the provisions for the appointment of members of the Commission might have under Art II, Congress had ample authority under the Necessary and Proper Clause of Art I to effectuate this result. We do not agree. The proper inquiry when considering the Necessary and Proper Clause is not the authority of Congress to create an office or a commission, which is broad indeed, but rather its authority to provide that its own officers may appoint to such office or commission.

So framed, the claim that Congress may provide for this manner of appointment under the Necessary and Proper Clause of Art I stands on no better footing than the claim that it may provide for such manner of appointment because of its substantive authority to regulate federal elections. Congress could not, merely because it concluded that such a measure was "necessary and proper" to the discharge of its substantive legislative authority, pass a bill of attainder or ex post facto law contrary to the prohibitions contained in § 9 of Art I. No more may it vest in itself, or in its officers, the authority to appoint officers of the United States when the Appointments Clause by clear implication prohibits it from doing so.

The trilogy of cases from this Court dealing with the constitutional authority of Congress to circumscribe the President's power to *remove* Officers of the United States is entirely consistent with this conclusion. In *Myers* v. *United States* [1926] . . . the Court held that Congress could not by statute divest the President of the power to remove an officer in the Executive Branch whom he was initially authorized to appoint. In explaining its

reasoning in that case, the Court said:

The vesting of the executive power in the President was essentially a grant of the power to execute the laws. But the President alone and unaided could not execute the laws. He must execute them by the system of subordinates. . . . As he is charged specifically to take care that they be faithfully executed, the reasonable implication, even in the absence of express words, was that as part of his executive power he should select those who were to act for him under his direction in the execution of the laws.

Our conclusion on the merits, sustained by the arguments before stated, is that Article II grants to the President the executive power of the Government, i. e., the general administrative control of those executing the laws, including the power of appointment and removal of executive officers—a conclusion confirmed by his obligation to take care that the laws be faithfully executed. . . . 272 U.S., at 117, 163–164 . . .

In the later case of *Humphrey's Executor,* where it was held that Congress could circumscribe the President's power to remove members of independent regulatory agencies, the Court was careful to note that it was dealing with an agency intended to be independent of executive authority *"except in its selection." Wiener* v. *United States* [1958] . . . which applied the holding in *Humphrey's Executor* to a member of the War Crimes Commission, did not question in any respect that members of independent agencies are not independent of the executive with respect to their appointments.

This conclusion is buttressed by the fact that Mr. Justice Sutherland, the author of the Court's opinion in Humphrey's Executor, likewise wrote the opinion for the Court in *Springer* v. *Philippine Islands,* in which it was said:

Not having the power of appointment, unless expressly granted or incidental to its powers, the legislature cannot engraft executive duties upon a legislative office, since that would be to usurp the power of appointment by indirection; though the case might be different if the additional duties devolved upon an appointee of the executive. 277 U.S., at 202 . . .

3. The Commission's Powers

Thus, on the assumption that all of the powers granted in the statute may be exercised by an agency whose members *have been* appointed in accordance with the Appointments Clause, the ultimate question is which, if any, of those powers may be exercised by the present Commissioners, none of whom *was* appointed as provided by that Clause. Our previous description of the statutory provisions . . . disclosed that the Commission's powers fall generally into three categories: functions relating to the flow of necessary information—receipt, dissemination, and investigation; functions with respect to the Commission's task of fleshing out the statute—rule-making and advisory opinions; and functions necessary to ensure compliance with the statute and rules—informal procedures, administrative determinations and hearings, and civil suits.

Insofar as the powers confided in the Commission are essentially of an investigative and informative nature, falling in the same general category as those powers which Congress might delegate to one of its own committees, there can be no question that the Commission as presently constituted may exercise them. *Kilbourn* v. *Thompson* [1881] . . . *McGrain* v. *Daugherty* [1927] . . . As this Court stated in *McGrain,*

A legislative body cannot legislate wisely or effectively in the absence of information respecting the conditions which the legislation is intended to affect or change; and where the legislative body does not itself possess the requisite information—which not infrequently is true—recourse must be had to others who do possess it. Experience has taught that mere requests for such information are often unavailing, and also that information which is volunteered is not always accurate or complete; so some means of compulsion are essential to attain what is needed. All this was true before and when the Constitution was framed and adopted. In that period the power of inquiry—with enforcing process—was regarded and employed as a necessary and appropriate attribute of the power to legislate—indeed, was treated as inhering in it.

But when we go beyond this type of authority to the more substantial powers exercised by the Commission, we reach a different result. The Commission's enforcement power, exemplified by its discretionary power to seek judicial relief, is authority that cannot possibly be regarded as merely in aid of the legislative function of Congress. A law suit is the ultimate remedy for a breach of the law, and it is to the President, and not to the Congress, that the Constitution entrusts the responsibility to "take Care that the Laws be faithfully executed." Art II, § 3.

Congress may undoubtedly under the Necessary and Proper Clause create "offices" in the generic sense and provide such method of appointment to those "offices" as it chooses. But Congress' power under that Clause is inevitably bounded by the express language of Art II, § 2, cl 2, and unless the method it provides comports with the latter, the holders of those offices will not be "Officers of the United States." They may, therefore, properly perform duties only in aid of those functions that Congress may carry out by itself, or in an area sufficiently removed from the administration and enforcement of the public law as to permit them being performed by persons not "Officers of the United States."

This Court observed more than a century ago with respect to litigation conducted in the courts of the United States:

Whether tested, therefore, by the requirements of the Judiciary Act, or by the usage of the government, or by the decisions of this

Court, it is clear that all such suits, so far as the interests of the United States are concerned, are subject to the direction, and within the control of, the Attorney-General. Confiscation Cases, 7 Wall 454 [1869] . . .

The Court echoed similar sentiments 60 years later in *Springer* v. *Philippine Islands,* . . . saying:

Legislative power, as distinguished from executive power, is the authority to make laws, but not to enforce them or appoint the agents charged with the duty of such enforcement. The latter are executive functions. It is unnecessary to enlarge further upon the general subject, since it has so recently received the full consideration of this Court . . . in *Myers* v. *United States* . . .

Not having the power of appointment, unless expressly granted or incidental to its powers, the legislature cannot engraft executive duties upon a legislative office, since that would be to usurp the power of appointment by indirection; though the case might be different if the additional duties were devolved upon an appointee of the executive.

We hold that these provisions of the Act, vesting in the Commission primary responsibility for conducting civil litigation in the courts of the United States for vindicating public rights, violate Art II, cl 2, § 2, of the Constitution. Such functions may be discharged only by persons who are "Officers of the United States" within the language of that section.

All aspects of the Act are brought within the Commission's broad administrative powers: rule-making, advisory opinions, and determinations of eligibility for funds and even for federal elective office itself. These functions, exercised free from day-to-day supervision of either Congress or the Executive Branch, are more legislative and judicial in nature than are the Commission's enforcement powers, and are of kinds usually performed by independent regulatory agencies or by some department in the Executive Branch under the direction of an Act of Congress. Congress viewed these broad powers as essential to effective and impartial administration of the entire substantive framework of the Act. Yet each of these functions also represents the performance of a significant governmental duty exercised pursuant to a public law. While the President may not insist that such functions be delegated to an appointee of his removable at will, *Humphrey's Executor* v. *United States,* none of them operates merely in aid of congressional authority to legislate or is sufficiently removed from the administration and enforcement of public law to allow it to be performed by the present Commission. These administrative functions may therefore be exercised only by persons who are "Officers of the United States."

It is also our view that the Commission's inability to exercise certain powers because of the method by which its members have been selected should not affect the validity of the Commission's administrative actions and determinations to this date, including its administration of those provisions, upheld today, authorizing the public financing of federal elections. The past acts of the Commission are therefore accorded de facto validity, just as we have recognized should be the case with respect to legislative acts performed by legislators held to have been elected in accordance with an unconstitutional apportionment plan. . . . We also draw on the Court's practice in the apportionment and voting rights cases and stay, for a period not to exceed 30 days, the Court's judgment insofar as it affects the authority of the Commission to exercise the duties and powers granted it under the Act. This limited stay will afford Congress an opportunity to reconstitute the Commission by law or to adopt other valid enforcement mechanisms without interrupting enforcement of the provisions the Court sustains, allowing the present Commission in the interim to function de facto in accordance with the substantive provisions of the Act. . . .

CONCLUSION

. . . [W]e hold that most of the powers conferred by the Act upon the Federal Election Commission can be exercised only by "Officers of the United States," appointed in conformity with Art II, § 2, cl 2, of the Constitution, and therefore cannot be exercised by the Commission as presently constituted. . . .

So ordered.

Mr. Justice Stevens took no part in the consideration or decision of these cases.

The holding of the Court that the Federal Election Commission was unconstitutional on the eve of the 1976 presidential primary campaigns produced a quandary which Congress resolved by passing a revised law on May 3, 1976, to meet the Court's objections. Funds continued to be held up, however, until President Ford finally agreed to sign the new campaign finance law on May 11, 1976. The 1976 campaign finance law amended the 1974 statute by making the Federal Election Commission a six-member body appointed by the President and confirmed by the Senate. The new law also removed the spending limits that had been placed upon House, Senate, and presidential campaigns, as well as on party nominating conventions, although it did retain spending limits for presidential candidates who accepted public funds.

EXECUTIVE IMMUNITY FROM THE JUDICIAL PROCESS

The courts have the authority to review presidential as well as congressional acts and to judge whether or not the President has conformed with the Constitution or statutory law. Usually judicial review of executive action involves authority that has been delegated to administrative agencies, either directly by Congress or subdelegated by the President and does not involve the President himself. At only a few times in history has the President been a named defendant in a court suit or been personally the subject of a judicial writ. The first major Supreme Court case involving the issue of executive immunity from the judicial process was *Mississippi* v. *Johnson* (1867). The government of Mississippi, composed of loyalists who had accepted presidential amnesty under Johnson's plan for the reconstruction of the southern states, was about to be replaced by a military tribunal created by the Reconstruction Acts. The reconstruction government of Mississippi sought to enjoin the President from enforcing those acts, on the grounds that they were unconstitutional. The Court was caught in the middle between a radical Republican Congress and President Andrew Johnson, who had futilely vetoed the Reconstruction Acts. Article II commits to the President the power to see that the laws are faithfully executed. Could the Court enjoin the President from executing the law?

Mississippi v. Johnson

4 Wallace 475; 18 L. Ed. 437 (1867)

MR. CHIEF JUSTICE CHASE delivered the opinion of the Court:

... The single point which requires consideration is this: Can the President be restrained by injunction from carrying into effect an act of Congress alleged to be unconstitutional?

It is assumed by the counsel for the state of Mississippi, that the President, in the execution of the Reconstruction Acts, is required to perform a mere ministerial duty. In this assumption there is, we think, a confounding of the terms "ministerial" and "executive," which are by no means equivalent in import.

A ministerial duty, the performance of which may, in proper cases, be required of the head of a department, by judicial process, is one in respect to which nothing is left to discretion. It is a simple definite duty, arising under conditions admitted or proved to exist, and imposed by law. . . .

Very different is the duty of the President in the exercise of the power to see that the laws are faithfully executed, and among these laws the acts named in the bill. By the first of these acts he is required to assign generals to command in the several military districts, and to detail sufficient military force to enable such officers to discharge their duties under the law. By the supplementary act, other duties are imposed on the several commanding generals, and these duties must necessarily be performed under the supervision of the President as Commander-in-Chief. The duty thus imposed on the President is in no just sense ministerial. It is purely executive and political.

An attempt on the part of the Judicial Department of the government to enforce the performance of such duties by the President might be justly characterized, in the language of Chief Justice Marshall, as "an absurd and excessive extravagance."

It is true that in the instance before us the interposition of the Court is not sought to enforce action by the Executive under constitutional legislation, but to restrain such action under legislation alleged to be unconstitutional. But we are unable to perceive that this circumstance takes the case out of the general principles which forbid judicial interference with the exercise of executive discretion.

It was admitted on the argument that the application now made to us is without a precedent; and this is of much weight against it.

Had it been supposed at the bar that this Court would, in any case, interpose, by injunction, to prevent the execution of an unconstitutional act of Congress, it can hardly be doubted that applications with that object would have been heretofore addressed to it.

Occasions have not been wanting.

The constitutionality of the act for the annexation of Texas was vehemently denied. It made important and permanent changes in the relative importance of states and sections, and was by many supposed to be pregnant with disastrous results to large interests in particular states. But no one seems to have thought of an application for an injunction against the execution of the act by the President.

And yet it is difficult to perceive upon what principle the application now before us can be allowed and similar applications in that and other cases would be denied.

The fact that no such application was ever before made in any case indicates the general judgment of the profession that no such application should be entertained.

It will hardly be contended that Congress can interpose in any case, to restrain the enactment of an unconstitutional law, and yet how can the right to judicial inter-position to prevent such an enactment, when the purpose is evident and the execution of that purpose certain, be distinguished, in principle, from the right to such interposition against the execution of such a law by the President?

The Congress is the Legislative Department of the government; the President is the Executive Department. Neither can be restrained in its action by the Judicial Department; though the acts of both, when performed, are, in proper cases, subject to its cognizance.

The impropriety of such interference will be clearly seen upon consideration of its possible consequences.

Suppose the bill filed and the injunction prayed for allowed. If the President refuse obedience, it is needless to observe that the Court is without power to enforce its process. If, on the other hand, the President complies with the order of the Court and refuses to execute the acts of Congress, is it not clear that a collision may occur between the Executive and Legislative Departments of the Government? May not the House of Representatives impeach the President for such refusal? And in that case could this court interfere in behalf of the President, thus endangered by compliance with its mandate, and restrain by injunction the Sen-ate of the United States from sitting as a court of impeachment? Would the strange spectacle be offered to the public wonder of an attempt by this Court to arrest proceedings in that court?

These questions answer themselves.

It is true that a state may file an original bill in this Court. And it may be true, in some cases, that such a bill may be filed against the United States. But we are fully satisfied that this Court has no jurisdiction of a bill to enjoin the President in the performance of his official duties; and that no such bill ought to be received by us.

It has been suggested that the bill contains a prayer that, if the relief sought cannot be had against Andrew Johnson, as President, it may be granted against Andrew Johnson as a citizen of Tennessee. But it is plain that relief as against the execution of an act of Congress by Andrew Johnson, is relief against its execution by the President. A bill praying an injunction against the execution of an act of Congress by the incumbent of the presidential office cannot be received, whether it describes him as President or as a citizen of a state.

The motion for leave to file the bill is, therefore,

Denied.

The Court's opinion in *Mississippi* v. *Johnson* noted both political and practical dilemmas that would be faced if it sought to enjoin presidential enforcement of a congressional law. "If the President refuse obedience [to the injunction]," said the Court, "it is needless to observe that the Court is without power to enforce its process. If, on the other hand, the President complies with the order of the Court and refuses to execute the acts of Congress, is it not clear that a collision may occur between the executive and legislative departments of the government? May not the House of Representatives impeach the President for such refusal?" Aside from these considerations, the Court found the intent of the Constitution precluded judicial interference in initial legislative or executive performance: "The Congress is the legislative department of the government; the President is the executive department. Neither can be restrained in its action by the judicial department; though the acts of both, *when performed,* are, in proper cases, subject to its cognizance." (Emphasis supplied.)

Mississippi v. *Johnson* was one precedent cited by President Richard M. Nixon's attorneys to defend him against a judicial subpoena in *United States* v. *Nixon* in 1974. The case arose out of the trial in the District Court for the District of Columbia under Judge John Sirica of six former aides to President Nixon who were accused of conspiring to conceal the break-in and burglary of the Democratic National Headquarters in the Watergate complex in 1972. In pursuance of the trial Special Watergate Prosecutor Leon Jaworski had successfully sought from Judge Sirica a subpoena directing the President to produce tapes and documents in his possession that contained evidence pertinent to the charge of a Watergate coverup on the part of the defendants.

The President appealed the district court's subpoena to the circuit court of appeals, but upon petition by both the government and the President the Supreme Court took the case from the court of appeals before judgment. The President's decision to acquiesce in appealing directly to the Supreme Court in the hope of a favorable judgment was a gamble that he lost. The argument of the President was based upon the concept of executive privilege, which allows the President to withhold information from coordinate branches of the government when the release of such information would clearly undermine the ability of the President to carry out his responsibilities. Executive privilege is usually based upon arguments that military necessity and national security require it, and in such cases the assertion of the privilege has not been overturned by the courts nor seriously challenged in Congress. President Nixon did not invoke the argument that military and national security demanded withholding the information but stated only that the subpoenaed material involved "confidential conversations between a President and his close advisers that it would be inconsistent with the public interest to produce." This was essentially a claim of absolute privilege on the part of the President to withhold whatever information he chose, at any time, and for any reason.

In their arguments in support of the President's position, Nixon's attorneys cited the cases of *United States* v. *Burr* and *Mississippi* v. *Johnson*.[34] The Supreme Court's refusal to enjoin President Andrew Johnson from enforcing the Reconstruction Acts was observed by counsel for the President but was not mentioned directly by the Court in its decision. However, *United States* v. *Burr* was used extensively by the Court to make the point, as did President Nixon's attorneys, that the President was indeed no ordinary individual. But the Court emphasized that the President was not above the law, which was implied by the arguments of Nixon's attorneys.[35]

From a technical point of view, the subpoena issue in *United States* v. *Burr*

[34]United States v. Burr, 25 Fed. Cas. 187 (1807); Mississippi v. Johnson, 4 Wall. 475 (1867).

[35]In 1977 former President Nixon flatly stated to television interviewer David Frost that under some circumstances the President is indeed above the law. He can, said the former President, violate the Constitution in order to preserve it. In reply to a question by Frost, Nixon said: "When the President does it, that means that it is not illegal." Frost replied, "By definition?" "Exactly," said Nixon. See *Newsweek,* May 30, 1977, p. 19.

in 1807 was quite similar to that in the *Nixon* case. Aaron Burr had traveled west to the Mississippi and south to Louisiana after his disgrace following what many contemporaries considered to be his coldblooded killing of Alexander Hamilton in a duel. Burr had engaged in meetings in which, Jefferson suspected, plans were being made to commit treason by organizing forces to attack the United States.

Burr and his alleged accomplices were arrested, and Burr himself was charged with treason and tried in the federal circuit court in Richmond, Virginia, with Chief Justice John Marshall, who was riding circuit, presiding. The trial was preceded for several years by constant Republican attacks upon the Federalist judiciary and by moves for impeachment by Jefferson against judges whom he considered unsympathetic to himself and the Republican cause. Jefferson's contempt for the judiciary, as well as the antagonistic feelings of the Republicans, was also illustrated by his recommendation for the authority to suspend the writ of habeas corpus after a federal district court had issued the writ to show cause why several men arrested for the Burr conspiracy should be held in prison. Jefferson ignored several writs of habeas corpus issued by the federal courts for the Burr conspirators and secured the passage of a bill suspending the writ in the Senate, which later was overwhelmingly defeated in the House.

The atmosphere surrounding the Burr conspiracy trial was one of extreme hostility between the Federalist judiciary and the Republican President. In the *Nixon* case, although the President was no friend of the judiciary, nor of Judge Sirica, Nixon did not consider himself to be engaged in mortal combat with the Supreme Court and most of the judiciary as was the case with Jefferson. Like Jefferson, however, Nixon did feel that he had the right as President to defy the judiciary, and he apparently seriously considered refusal to obey the judgment of the Supreme Court upholding the subpoena that had been issued by Judge Sirica's federal district court. Only the fact that such an act would almost automatically lead to impeachment, conviction, and desertion of the President by all who had supported him, including his attorneys, caused Nixon to change his mind.

The subpoena issue in the *Burr* trial arose out of Burr's discovery that letters had been written to President Jefferson by General Wilkinson (the general who had declared martial law in New Orleans) upon discovery of the Burr conspiracy and the arrest of Burr's accomplices. Burr thought the letters contained evidence that would help to clear him of the treason charge. Burr, who assisted his attorneys in his own defense, requested the production of the letters, which immediately raised an issue over the responsibilities of the President to obey a judicial subpoena. United States Attorney George Hay, in response to Burr's request, said he had the letters, "and would produce [them]. . . . But there were some matters in the letters of General Wilkinson which ought not to be made public. It would be extremely improper to submit the whole of his letters to public inspection. He [Hay] was willing to put them in the hands of the clerk [of the court] confidentially, and . . . [the clerk] could copy all those parts which had relation to the cause."[36]

[36]United States v. Burr, 25 Fed. Cas. 187, 190 (1807).

Burr was not satisfied with Hay's response, and as the case proceeded the question became whether or not the letters had to be produced in aid of the trial and, if produced, whether parts of them could be withheld by the President or his agent, attorney Hay. In a long opinion on this preliminary issue, Chief Justice Marshall held that the President could not refuse to produce letters requested by the defendant Burr which were necessary to the evidence of the case. But, continued Marshall, the President and only the President could, on the general grounds of public interest, indicate to the court those parts of the letters which should be withheld from the defense. Marshall declared that the President cannot withhold information from a judicial trial without stating the cause, nor can he withhold subpoenaed material from the court, but only from the defense and the jury if the court accedes. The court should give the benefit of the doubt to the wishes of the President to keep material secret. In Marshall's words, "the President is not to be treated as an ordinary individual" before the courts. But, just as clearly, the President is not above the law nor above the judicial process, and the ultimate decision over the determination of the scope of executive privilege lies with the court and not the President. The full information requested of the President must be presented first to the court, with a statement of what should be expunged and the reasons for withholding the information. The court then makes its judgment to withhold or divulge the material.

Although *United States* v. *Burr* recognized executive privilege, Marshall's opinion was not an assertion of an absolute privilege, especially when evidence in a criminal trial was involved. While President Nixon's attorneys could and did cite the *Burr* opinion to support executive privilege, it was an entirely inappropriate case to sustain the President's action of withholding *from the court* information contained in the subpoenaed material. Moreover, Marshall's opinion implied that even though the public interest could be cited by the President as a reason for withholding information from the defense and the jury and hence from the public, the nature of the public interest requiring such secrecy would have to be explained to the satisfaction of the court if it was to uphold the President's request. President Nixon and his attorneys were on shaky ground indeed in their arguments in support of an absolute executive privilege.[37]

UNITED STATES v. NIXON

Leon Jaworski, Special Prosecutor, et al., for the plaintiff, the United States:
The narrow issue presented to this Court is whether the President, in a pending prosecution against his former aides and associates being conducted in the name of the United States by a Special Prosecutor not subject to presidential directions, may withhold material evidence from the court merely on his assertion that the evidence involves confidential governmental deliberations. . . .

The Executive's legitimate interests in secrecy are more than adequately protected by the qualified privilege defined and applied by the courts. . . .

[37]Chief Justice Marshall supported President Jefferson's deletions from the letters of General Wilkinson in the Burr trial. The trial itself resulted in Burr's acquittal, much to the dismay of Jefferson and the Republicans who for months afterwards berated the court for undermining justice and letting a "traitor" escape.

But as this Court has recognized, an absolute privilege which permitted the Executive to make a binding determination would lead to intolerable abuse. . . . The President cannot be a proper judge of whether the greater public interest lies in disclosing evidence subpoenaed for trial, when that evidence may have a material bearing on whether he is impeached and will bear heavily on the 'guilt or innocence of close aides and trusted advisers.[38]

James B. St. Clair, et al., for President Richard M. Nixon:

Under the doctrine of separation of powers, the judiciary is without jurisdiction to intervene in the intra-branch dispute between the President and the Special Prosecutor. . . .

Inherent in the Executive power vested in the President under Article 2 of the Constitution is executive privilege. . . .

The President is not subject to the criminal process whether that process is invoked directly or indirectly. . . .

Under the Constitution, the President, as the highest executive officer, was expressly delegated all prosecutorial authority when he alone was vested with the responsibility "to take care that the laws be faithfully executed." . . .

Because the President in all criminal proceedings has the right to determine what confidential or sensitive material should not be used to assist a federal prosecutor, as this right was not delegated to the Special Prosecutor, the Court remains without jurisdiction to intervene in his prosecutorial discretion by the Chief Executive. . . .

A presidential assertion of privilege is not reviewable by the Court. . . .

The separation of powers doctrine precludes judicial review of the use of executive privilege by a president. . . .

The President's sole discretion to decide what presidential communications he will disclose, and to control the circumstances of disclosure, is independently grounded in the right of privacy and the constitutionally protected freedom of expression possessed by the President, his advisers and others with whom he confers in the course of carrying out his official responsibilities. . . .[39]

Reply brief for the petitioner, the United States:

Principles of "separation of powers," frequently quoted in the President's brief, show why on the fact of the present case there are *no* obstacles to the Court's authority to entertain and decide this controversy. The Court's jurisdiction to consider and resolve this dispute on the merits stems from the fundamental role of the courts in our tripartite constitutional system. . . .

The First Amendment erects no absolute privileges for the President to withhold relevant evidence. . . .[40]

Reply brief for the President:

This dispute raises a question of justiciability because it involves a political dispute solely between two officials of the executive branch. . . . Under Article 3, Section 2 of the Constitution, the judicial branch does not have the constitutional power to resolve such a political question. . . .

The President, as we have noted, *is* the Executive Department. If he could be enjoined, restrained, indicted, arrested, or ordered by judges, grand juries, or marshals, these individuals would have the power to control the executive branch. This would nullify the separation of powers and the co-equality of the Executive.[41]

[38]LB, vol. 79, pp. 339, 341–342.
[39]Ibid., pp. 493–495, 516, 521, 525, 546.
[40]Ibid., pp. 656–657, 677.
[41]Ibid., pp. 521–522, 729.

United States v. Nixon

418 U.S. 683; 94 S. Ct. 3090; 41 L. Ed. 2d 1039 (1974)

MR. CHIEF JUSTICE BURGER delivered the opinion of the Court:

. . . [W]e turn to the claim that the subpoena should be quashed because it demands "confidential conversations between a President and his close advisers that it would be inconsistent with the public interest to produce." The first contention is a broad claim that the separation of powers doctrine precludes judicial review of a President's claim of privilege. The second contention is that if he does not prevail on the claim of absolute privilege, the court should hold as a matter of constitutional law that the privilege prevails over the subpoena duces tecum.

In the performance of assigned constitutional duties each branch of the Government must initially interpret the Constitution, and the interpretation of its powers by any branch is due great respect from the others. The President's counsel . . . reads the Constitution as providing an absolute privilege of confidentiality for all Presidential communications. Many decisions of this Court, however, have unequivocally reaffirmed the holding of *Marbury* v. *Madison* [1803] . . . that "[i]t is emphatically the province and duty of the judicial department to say what the law is." . . .

No holding of the Court has defined the scope of judicial power specifically relating to the enforcement of a subpoena for confidential Presidential communications for use in a criminal prosecution, but other exercises of power by the Executive Branch and the Legislative Branch have been found invalid as in conflict with the Constitution. . . . Since this Court has consistently exercised the power to construe and delineate claims arising under express powers, it must follow that the Court has authority to interpret claims with respect to powers alleged to derive from enumerated powers. . . .

B

In support of his claim of absolute privilege, the President's counsel urges two grounds, one of which is common to all governments and one of which is peculiar to our system of separation of powers. The first ground is the valid need for protection of communications between high Government officials and those who advise and assist them in the performance of their manifold duties; the importance of this confidentiality is too plain to require further discussion. . . . Whatever the nature of the privilege of confidentiality of Presidential communications in the exercise of Art II powers, the privilege can be said to derive from the supremacy of each branch within its own assigned area of constitutional duties. Certain powers and privileges flow from the nature of enumerated powers; the protection of the confidentiality of Presidential communications has similar constitutional underpinnings.

The second ground asserted by the President's counsel in support of the claim of absolute privilege rests on the doctrine of separation of powers. Here it is argued that the independence of the Executive Branch within its own sphere . . . insulates a President from a judicial subpoena in an ongoing criminal prosecution, and thereby protects confidential Presidential communications.

However, neither the doctrine of separation of powers, nor the need for confidentiality of high-level communications, without more, can sustain an absolute, unqualified Presidential privilege of immunity from judicial process under all circumstances. The President's need for complete candor and objectivity from advisers calls for great deference from the courts. However, when the privilege depends solely on the broad, undifferentiated claim of public interest in the confidentiality of such conversations, a confrontation with other values arises. Absent a claim of need to protect military, diplomatic, or sensitive national security secrets, we find it difficult to accept the argument that even the very important interest in confidentiality of Presidential communications is significantly diminished by production of such material for in camera inspection with all the protection that a district court will be obliged to provide.

The impediment that an absolute, unqualified privilege would place in the way of the primary constitutional duty of the Judicial Branch to do justice in criminal prosecutions would plainly conflict with the function of the courts under Art III. In designing the structure of our Government and dividing and allocating the sovereign power among three co-equal branches, the Framers of the Constitution sought to provide a comprehensive system, but the separate powers were not intended to operate with absolute independence.

While the Constitution diffuses power the better to secure liberty, it also contemplates that practice will integrate the dispersed powers into a workable government. It enjoins upon its branches separateness but interdependence, autonomy but reciprocity. *Youngstown Sheet & Tube Co.* v. *Sawyer* [1952] . . . (Jackson, J., concurring.)

C

Since we conclude that the legitimate needs of the judicial process may outweigh Presidential privilege, it is necessary to resolve those competing interests in a manner that preserves the essential functions of each branch. The right and indeed the duty to resolve that question does not free the judiciary from according high respect to the representations made on behalf of the President. *United States* v. *Burr* [1807]. . . .

The expectation of a President to the confidentiality of his conversations and correspondence, like the claim of confidentiality of judicial deliberations, for example, has all the values to which we accord deference for the privacy of all citizens and added to those values the necessity for protection of the public interest in candid, objective, and even blunt or harsh opinions in Presidential decision making. . . . These are the considerations justifying a presumptive privilege for Presidential communications. The privilege is fundamental to the operation of government and inextricably rooted in the separation of powers under the Constitution. In *Nixon* v. *Sirica* [1973] . . . the Court of Appeals held that such Presidential communications are "presumptively privileged," . . . and this position is accepted by both parties in the present litigation. We agree with Mr. Chief Justice Marshall's observation, therefore, that "[i]n no case of this kind would a court be required to proceed against the President as against an ordinary individual." *United States* v. *Burr.* . . .

But this presumptive privilege must be considered in light of our historic commitment to the rule of law. This is nowhere more profoundly manifest than in our view that "the twofold aim [of criminal justice] is that guilt shall not escape or innocence suffer." *Berger* v. *United States* [1935]. . . . We have elected to employ an adversary system of criminal justice in which the parties contest all issues before a court of law. The need to develop all relevant facts in the adversary system is both fundamental and comprehensive. The ends of criminal justice would be defeated if judgments were to be founded on a partial or speculative presentation of the facts. The very integrity of the judicial system and public confidence in the system depend on full disclosure of all the facts, within the framework of the rules of evidence. To ensure that justice is done, it is imperative to the function of courts that compulsory process be available for the production of evidence needed either by the prosecution or by the defense. . . .

In this case the President challenges a subpoena served on him as a third party requiring the production of materials for use in a criminal prosecution; he does so on the claim that he has a privilege against disclosure of confidential communications. He does not place his claim of privilege on the ground they are military or diplomatic secrets. As to these areas of Art II duties the courts have traditionally shown the utmost deference to Presidential responsibilities. . . .

No case of the Court . . . has extended this high degree of deference to a President's generalized interest in confidentiality. Nowhere in the Constitution . . . is there any explicit reference to a privilege of confidentiality, yet to the extent this interest relates to the effective discharge of a President's powers, it is constitutionally based.

The right to the production of all evidence at a criminal trial similarly has constitutional dimensions. The Sixth Amendment explicitly confers upon every defendant in a criminal trial the right "to be confronted with the witnesses against him" and "to have compulsory process for obtaining witnesses in his favor." Moreover, the Fifth Amendment also guarantees that no person shall be deprived of liberty without due process of law. It is the manifest duty of the courts to vindicate those guarantees, and to accomplish that it is essential that all relevant and admissible evidence be produced.

In this case we must weigh the importance of the general privilege of confidentiality of Presidential communications in performance of his responsibilities against the inroads of such a privilege on the fair administration of criminal justice. The interest in preserving confidentiality is weighty indeed and entitled to great respect. However, we cannot conclude that advisers will be moved to temper the candor of their remarks by the infrequent occasions of disclosure because of the possibility that such conversations will be called for in the context of a criminal prosecution.

On the other hand, the allowance of the privilege to withhold evidence that is demonstrably relevant in a criminal trial would cut deeply into the guarantee of due process of law and gravely impair the basic function of the courts. A President's acknowledged need for confidentiality in the communications of his office is general in nature, whereas the constitutional need for production of relevant evidence in a criminal proceeding is specific and central to the fair adjudication of a particular criminal case in the administration of justice. Without access to specific facts a criminal prosecution may be totally frustrated. . . .

We conclude that when the ground for asserting privilege as to subpoenaed materials sought for use in a criminal trial is based only on the generalized interest in confidentiality, it cannot prevail over the fundamental demands of due process of law in the fair administration of criminal justice. The generalized assertion of privilege must yield to the demonstrated, specific need for evidence in a pending criminal trial. . . .

Affirmed.

MR. JUSTICE REHNQUIST took no part in the consideration of this case.

While both the *Burr* and *Nixon* cases recognized executive privilege, it was more broadly defined in the *Nixon* case than in the *Burr* case. In fact, the

Nixon decision expands the concept of executive privilege and gives it legitimacy.

> . . . The President's need for complete candor and objectivity from advisers calls for great deference from the Court. However, when the privilege depends *solely* on the broad, undifferentiated claim of public interest in the confidentiality of such conversations, a confrontation with other values arises. Absent a claim of need to protect military, diplomatic or sensitive national security secrets, we find it difficult to accept the argument that even the very important interest in confidentiality of presidential communications is significantly diminished by production of such material for in camera inspection with all the protection that a district court will be obliged to provide.[42]

This statement which seemingly limits executive privilege actually expands it, requiring only a presidential reference to the need to protect military, diplomatic, or sensitive national security secrets in order to justify using executive privilege to shield the President from outside inquiry. This expanded view of executive privilege is supported by the Court's conclusion of its *Nixon* opinion.

> . . . Moreover, a President's communications and activities encompass a vastly wider range of sensitive material than would be true of any "ordinary individual." It is therefore necessary in the public interest to afford presidential confidentiality the greatest protection consistent with the fair administration of justice. The need for confidentiality even as to idle conversations with associates in which casual reference might be made concerning political leaders within the country or foreign statesmen is too obvious to call for further treatment.[43]

It was only because the evidence subpoenaed from the President was considered necessary for the fair administration of justice in a criminal trial that the Supreme Court upheld the subpoena directed to the President in *United States* v. *Nixon*.

The essential constitutional issue in the *Nixon* case was whether the separation of powers doctrine precluded the judiciary from intervening in the internal affairs of the executive branch. But what are the internal affairs of the executive branch? Are these to be defined by the President alone, thus giving him absolute discretion to determine his own immunity from the judicial process where matters such as executive privilege are concerned? The information requested by the Court in the *Nixon* case was as vital to the administration of justice as to faithful executive execution of the laws under Article II. The case did not establish a precedent for capricious judicial intervention in the affairs of the President but recognized that under the proper circumstances broad executive privilege would be upheld.

---

[42]United States v. Nixon, 418 U.S. 683, 706 (1974). (Emphasis added.)
[43]Ibid., p. 715.

THREE

The Constitutional Powers
of the President and Congress
to Make Policy

The separation of powers does not clearly and unambiguously define the balance of power that is to exist between the President and Congress to make national policy. The Madisonian model presumed the dominance of Congress, while the Hamiltonian model was based upon an active and energetic presidency.

Articles I and II of the Constitution do not provide much help in delineating the boundaries between presidential and congressional authority to make law. Strictly construed, Article I would seem to provide for exclusive congressional authority in the lawmaking process by delegating to Congress "all legislative power." But legislation and lawmaking are not one and the same thing. The President, in effect, makes law through executive actions and by interpreting congressional statutes or the Constitution. The President regulates private conduct by his actions just as Congress does through passing legislation. To what degree must the President have explicit congressional or constitutional authorization for his acts? The imperial presidency has been built upon numerous presidential actions taken independently of Congress that have established precedents for the inherent or prerogative powers of the President. The scope of presidential and congressional power has been as much defined by historical events and political realities as by the words of the Constitution. Domestic and international crises, particularly wartime emergencies, have pushed the Court into allowing the expansion of congressional and presidential powers generally and particularly have expanded the prerogatives of the President.

THE IMPLIED POWERS DOCTRINE

Article I, Section 8 of the Constitution enumerates the powers of Congress. It also grants Congress the authority "to make all laws which shall be necessary and proper for carrying into execution the foregoing [enumerated] powers, and all powers vested by this Constitution in the government of the United States, or in any department or officer thereof." In the first decades of the Republic the Supreme Court faced the question of the constitutional scope of congressional powers. Was Congress to be limited to the exercise of those powers explicitly enumerated, with the necessary and proper clause being narrowly interpreted to encompass only the means of execution of the enumerated powers? Or was Congress to be granted wide latitude in exercising powers that could be broadly implied from the enumerated provisions of Article I?

The early debate over what constituted legitimate congressional authority arose within the context of federalism, reflecting the underlying political controversy over the boundaries of national power in relation to the states. It was Alexander Hamilton's successful attempt to establish a national bank in 1791 that focused the debate between the Federalists (now a political party) and the anti-Federalists (now the Republican Party) over the proper scope of national power in relation to the states. Hamilton's arguments in favor of the bank essentially repeated those he had made in *The Federalist* that supported expanded national powers that went far beyond the expressly enumerated powers of Article I.[1] After Congress passed its first legislation creating a national bank in 1791, Washington requested the views of Hamilton and Jefferson regarding the bank's constitutionality. Hamilton wrote to the President,

> ... It is conceded that *implied powers* are to be considered as delegated equally with *expressed ones*. Then it follows, that as a power of erecting a corporation may as well be *implied* as any other thing, it may as well be employed as an *instrument* or *means* of carrying into execution any of the specified powers, as any other *instrument* or *means* whatever. The only question must be in this, as in every other case, whether the means to be employed, or, in this instance the corporation to be erected, has a natural relation to any of the acknowledged objects or lawful ends of the government. Thus a corporation may not be directed by Congress for superintending the police of the city of Philadelphia, because they are not authorized to *regulate* the *police* of that city. But one may be erected in relation to the collection of taxes, or to the trade with foreign nations, or to the trade between the states, or with the Indian tribes; because it is the province of the federal government to *regulate* those objects, and because it is incident to a general *sovereign* or *legislative* power to *regulate* a thing, to employ all the means which relate to its regulation to the best and greatest advantage.[2]

Jefferson countered Hamilton's views with the statement that

> I considered the foundation of the Constitution as laid on this ground: That "all powers not delegated to the United States, by the Constitution, nor prohibited by it to the states, are reserved to the states or to the people.". . . To take a single step beyond the boundaries thus specially drawn around the powers of Congress, is to take possession of a boundless field of power, no longer susceptible of any definition.

[1] See pp. 255–259 for Hamilton's statements in *The Federalist*.
[2] Gerald Gunther, *Cases and Materials on Constitutional Law,* 9th ed. (Mineola, N. Y.: The Foundation Press, Inc., 1975), p. 101.

> The incorporation of a bank, and the powers assumed by this bill, have not, in my opinion, been delegated to the United States by the Constitution.[3]

Jefferson went on to point out that the power to incorporate a bank is not specifically enumerated, nor can it be implied from the enumerated powers. A bank, therefore, is not a means for carrying into execution any of the enumerated powers, nor added Jefferson, is it necessary for the execution of such powers.[4]

The Hamiltonian opinion won the day in 1791 when Washington signed the bill creating the first bank of the United States. By 1811, however, the Republican party with a Jeffersonian cast controlled Congress and refused to grant a new charter to the bank, which then was dissolved. The subsequent financial chaos caused by the burgeoning of state banks issuing paper money, compounded by the financial crisis created by the War of 1812, convinced a Republican Congress and President Madison to reestablish the bank in 1816. Madison and many of his Republican colleagues in Congress, including the great states-rights advocate, John C. Calhoun, of South Carolina, now agreed that a national bank was both constitutional and necessary. Opponents of the bank repeated the strict constructionist arguments that had been advanced by Jefferson in 1790 against the first bank act.

The question of the constitutional validity of the bank faced the Supreme Court in *McCulloch* v. *Maryland* in 1819. The Maryland legislature had passed a law that in effect levied a tax upon a branch of the national bank operating in the state. In contravention of the state law the bank had issued notes without paying the requisite fee under state legislation. The state sued McCulloch, a cashier of the Baltimore branch of the national bank, in the Baltimore County Court, and McCulloch lost. The judgment, affirmed by the Maryland Court of Appeals, was appealed to the United States Supreme Court by a writ of error.

McCulloch v. *Maryland*

4 Wheaton 316; 4 L. Ed. 579 (1819)

MR. CHIEF JUSTICE MARSHALL delivered the opinion of the Court:

In the case now to be determined, the defendant, a sovereign state, denies the obligation of a law enacted by the legislature of the Union, and the plaintiff, on his part, contests the validity of an act which has been passed by the legislature of that state. The Constitution of our country, in its most interesting and vital parts, is to be considered; the conflicting powers of the government of the Union and of its members, as marked in that Constitution, are to be discussed; and an opinion given, which may essentially influence the great operations of the government. No tribunal can approach such a question without a deep sense of its importance, and of the awful responsibility involved in its decision. But it must be decided peacefully, or remain a source of hostile legislation, perhaps of hostility of a still more serious nature; and if it is to be so decided, by this tribunal alone can

[3]Ibid., p. 100.
[4]Ibid., pp. 100–101.

the decision be made. On the Supreme Court of the United States has the Constitution of our country devolved this important duty.

The first question made in the cause is, has Congress power to incorporate a bank? . . .

In discussing this question, the counsel for the state of Maryland have deemed it of some importance, in the construction of the Constitution, to consider that instrument not as emanating from the people, but as the act of sovereign and independent states. The powers of the general government, it has been said, are delegated by the states, who alone are truly sovereign; and must be exercised in subordination to the states, who alone possess supreme dominion.

It would be difficult to sustain this proposition. The convention which framed the Constitution was indeed elected by the state legislatures. But the instrument, when it came from their hands, was a mere proposal, without obligation, or pretensions to it. It was reported to the then existing Congress of the United States, with a request that it might "be submitted to a convention of delegates, chosen in each state by the people thereof, under the recommendation of its legislature, for their assent and ratification." This mode of proceeding was adopted; and by the convention, by Congress, and by the state legislatures, the instrument was submitted to the people. They acted upon it in the only manner in which they can act safely, effectively, and wisely, on such a subject, by assembling in convention. It is true, they assembled in their several states— and where else should they have assembled? No political dreamer was ever wild enough to think of breaking down the lines which separate the states, and of compounding the American people into one common mass. Of consequence, when they act, they act in their states. But the measures they adopt do not, on that account, cease to be the measures of the people themselves, or become the measures of the state governments.

From these conventions the Constitution derives its whole authority. The government proceeds directly from the people; as "ordained and established" in the name of the people; and is declared to be ordained, "in order to form a more perfect union, establish justice, insure domestic tranquillity, and secure the blessings of liberty to themselves and to their posterity." The assent of the states, in their sovereign capacity, is implied in calling a convention, and thus submitting that instrument to the people. But the people were at perfect liberty to accept or reject it; and their act was final. It required not the affirmance, and could not be negatived, by the state governments. The Constitution, when thus adopted, was a complete obligation, and bound the state sovereignties.

It has been said that the people had already surrendered all their powers to the state sovereignties, and had nothing more to give. But, surely, the question whether they may resume and modify the powers granted to government does not remain to be settled in this country. Much more might the legitimacy of the general government be doubted, had it been created by the states. The powers delegated to the state sovereignties were to be exercised by themselves, not by a distinct and independent sovereignty, created by themselves. To the formation of a league, such as was the confederation, the state sovereignties were certainly competent. But when "in order to form a more perfect union," it was deemed necessary to change this alliance into an effective government, possessing great and sovereign powers, and acting directly on the people, the necessity of referring it to the people, and of deriving its powers directly from them, was felt and acknowledged by all.

The government of the Union, then (whatever may be the influence of this fact on the case), is, emphatically, and truly, a government of the people. In form and in substance it emanates from them. Its powers are granted by them, and are to be exercised directly on them, and for their benefit.

This government is acknowledged by all to be one of enumerated powers. The principle, that it can exercise only the powers granted to it, would seem too apparent to have required to be enforced by all those arguments which its enlightened friends, while it was depending before the people, found it necessary to urge, That principle is now universally admitted. But the question respecting the extent of the powers actually granted, is perpetually arising, and will probably continue to arise, as long as our system shall exist.

In discussing these questions, the conflicting powers of the general and state governments must be brought into view, and the supremacy of their respective laws, when they are in opposition, must be settled.

If any one proposition could command the universal assent of mankind, we might expect it would be this—that the government of the Union, though limited in its powers, is supreme within its sphere of action. This would seem to result necessarily from its nature. It is the government of all; its powers are delegated by all; it represents all, and acts for all. Though any one state may be willing to control its operations, no state is willing to allow others to control them. The nation, on those subjects on which it can act, must necessarily bind its component parts. But this question is not left to mere reason; the people have, in express terms, decided it by saying, "this Constitution, and the laws of the United States, which shall be made in pursuance thereof," "shall be the supreme law of the land," and by requiring that the members of the state legislatures, and the officers of the executive and judicial departments of the states shall take the oath of fidelity to it.

The government of the United States,

then, though limited in its powers, is supreme; and its laws, when made in pursuance of the Constitution, form the supreme law of the land, "anything in the Constitution or laws of any state to the contrary notwithstanding."

Among the enumerated powers, we do not find that of establishing a bank or creating a corporation. But there is no phrase in the instrument which, like the articles of confederation, excludes incidental or implied powers; and which requires that everything granted shall be expressly and minutely described. Even the Tenth Amendment, which was framed for the purpose of quieting the excessive jealousies which had been excited, omits the word "expressly," and declares only that the powers "not delegated to the United States, nor prohibited to the states, are reserved to the states or to the people;" thus leaving the question, whether the particular power which may become the subject of contest has been delegated to the one government, or prohibited to the other, to depend on a fair construction of the whole instrument. The men who drew and adopted this amendment had experienced the embarrassments resulting from the insertion of this word in the articles of confederation, and probably omitted it to avoid those embarrassments. A constitution, to contain an accurate detail of all the subdivisions of which its great powers will admit, and of all the means by which they may be carried into execution, would partake of a prolixity of a legal code, and could scarcely be embraced by the human mind. It would probably never be understood by the public. Its nature, therefore, requires, that only its great outlines should be marked, its important objects designated, and the minor ingredients which compose those objects be deduced from the nature of the objects themselves. That this idea was entertained by the framers of the American Constitution, is not only to be inferred from the nature of the instrument, but from the language. Why else were some of the limitations, found in the ninth section of the 1st article, introduced? It is also, in some degree, warranted by their having omitted to use any restrictive term which might prevent its receiving a fair and just interpretation. In considering this question, then, we must never forget that it is a Constitution we are expounding.

Although, among the enumerated powers of government, we do not find the word "bank" or "incorporation," we find the great powers to lay and collect taxes; to borrow money; to regulate commerce; to declare and conduct a war; and to raise and support armies and navies. The sword and the purse, all the external relations, and no inconsiderable portion of the industry of the nation, are entrusted to its government. It can never be pretended that these vast powers draw after them others of inferior importance, merely because they are inferior. Such an idea can never be advanced. But it may with great reason be contended, that a government, entrusted with such ample powers, on the due execution of which the happiness and prosperity of the nation so vitally depends, must also be entrusted with ample means for their execution. The power being given, it is the interest of the nation to facilitate its execution. It can never be their interest, and cannot be presumed to have been their intention, to clog and embarrass its execution by withholding the most appropriate means. Throughout this vast republic, from the St. Croix to the Gulf of Mexico, from the Atlantic to the Pacific, revenue is to be collected and expended, armies are to be marched and supported. The exigencies of the nation may require that the treasure raised in the north should be transported to the south, that raised in the east conveyed to the west, or that this order should be reversed. Is that construction of the Constitution to be preferred which would render these opera-

tions difficult, hazardous, and expensive? Can we adopt that construction (unless the words imperiously require it) which would impute to the framers of that instrument, when granting these powers for the public good, the intention of impeding their exercise by withholding a choice of means? If, indeed, such be the mandate of the Constitution, we have only to obey; but that instrument does not profess to enumerate the means by which the powers it confers may be executed; nor does it prohibit the creation of a corporation, if the existence of such a being be essential to the beneficial exercise of those powers. It is, then, the subject of fair inquiry, how far such means may be employed. It is not denied that the powers given to the government imply the ordinary means of execution. That, for example, of raising revenue, and applying it to national purposes, is admitted to imply the power of conveying money from place to place, as the exigencies of the nation may require, and of employing the usual means of conveyance. But it is denied that the government has its choice of means; or, that it may employ the most convenient means, if, to employ them, it be necessary to erect a corporation. . . .

The power of creating a corporation, though appertaining to sovereignty, is not, like the power of making war, or levying taxes, or of regulating commerce, a great substantive and independent power, which cannot be implied as incidental to other powers, or used as a means of executing them. It is never the end for which other powers are exercised, but a means by which other objects are accomplished. No contributions are made to charity for the sake of an incorporation, but a corporation is created to administer the charity; no seminary of learning is instituted in order to be incorporated, but the corporate character is conferred to subserve the purposes of education. No city was ever built with the sole object of being incorporated, but is incorporated as affording the best means of being well governed. The power of creating a corporation is never used for its own sake, but for the purpose of effecting something else. No sufficient reason is, therefore, perceived, why it may not pass as incidental to those powers which are expressly given, if it be a direct mode of executing them.

But the Constitution of the United States has not left the right of Congress to employ the necessary means for the execution of the powers conferred on the government to general reasoning. To its enumeration of powers is added that of making "all laws which shall be necessary and proper, for carrying into execution the foregoing powers, and all other powers vested by this Constitution, in the government of the United States, or in any department thereof."

The counsel for the State of Maryland have urged various arguments, to prove that this clause, though in terms a grant of power, is not so in effect; but is really restrictive of the general right, which might otherwise be implied, of selecting means for executing the enumerated powers.

In support of this proposition, they have found it necessary to contend, that this clause was inserted for the purpose of conferring on Congress the power of making laws. That, without it, doubts might be entertained whether Congress could exercise its powers in the form of legislation.

But could this be the object for which it was inserted? . . . That a legislature, endowed with legislative powers, can legislate, is a proposition too self-evident to have been questioned.

But the argument on which most reliance is placed, is drawn from the peculiar language of this clause. Congress is not empowered by it to make all laws, which may have relation to the powers conferred on the government, but such only

as may be "necessary and proper" for carrying them into execution. The word "necessary" is considered as controlling the whole sentence, and as limiting the right to pass laws for the execution of the granted powers, to such as are indispensable, and without which the power would be nugatory. That it excludes the choice of means, and leaves to Congress, in each case, that only which is most direct and simple.

Is it true that this is the sense in which the word "necessary" is always used? Does it always import an absolute physical necessity, so strong that one thing, to which another may be termed necessary, cannot exist without that other? We think it does not. If reference be had to its use, in the common affairs of the world, or in approved authors, we find that it frequently imports no more than that one thing is convenient, or useful, or essential to another. To employ the means necessary to an end, is generally understood as employing any means calculated to produce the end, and not as being confined to those single means, without which the end would be entirely unattainable. Such is the character of human language, that no word conveys to the mind, in all situations, one single definite idea; and nothing is more common than to use words in a figurative sense. Almost all compositions contain words, which, taken in their rigorous sense, would convey a meaning different from that which is obviously intended. It is essential to just construction, that many words which import something excessive should be understood in a more mitigated sense—in that sense which common usage justifies. The word "necessary" is of this description. It has not a fixed character peculiar to itself. It admits of all degrees of comparison; and is often connected with other words, which increase or diminish the impression the mind receives of the urgency it imports. A thing may be necessary, very necessary, absolutely or indispensably necessary. To no mind would the same idea be conveyed by these several phrases. . . . This word, then, like others, is used in various senses; and, in its construction, the subject, the context, the intention of the person using them, are all to be taken into view.

Let this be done in the case under consideration. The subject is the execution of those great powers on which the welfare of a nation essentially depends. It must have been the intention of those who gave these powers, to insure, as far as human prudence could insure, their beneficial execution. This could not be done by confining the choice of means to such narrow limits as not to leave it in the power of Congress to adopt any which might be appropriate, and which were conducive to the end. This provision is made to a Constitution intended to endure for ages to come, and, consequently, to be adapted to the various crises of human affairs. To have prescribed the means by which government should, in all future time, execute its powers, would have been to change, entirely, the character of the instrument, and give it the properties of a legal code. It would have been an unwise attempt to provide, by immutable rules, for exigencies which, if foreseen at all, must have been seen dimly, and which can be best provided for as they occur. To have declared that the best means shall not be used, but those alone without which the power given would be nugatory, would have been to deprive the legislature of the capacity to avail itself of experience, to exercise its reason, and to accommodate its legislation to circumstances. . . .

But the argument which most conclusively demonstrates the error of the construction contended for by the counsel for the state of Maryland, is founded on the intention of the Convention, as manifested in the whole clause. To waste time and argument in proving that without it

Congress might carry its powers into execution, would be not much less idle than to hold a lighted taper to the sun. As little can it be required to prove, that in the absence of this clause, Congress would have some choice of means. That it might employ those which, in its judgment, would most advantageously effect the object to be accomplished. That any means adapted to the end, any means which tended directly to the execution of the constitutional powers of the government, were in themselves constitutional. This clause, as construed by the state of Maryland, would abridge, and almost annihilate this useful and necessary right of the legislature to select its means. That this could not be intended, is, we should think, had it not been already controverted, too apparent for controversy. We think so for the following reasons:

1st. This clause is placed among the powers of Congress, not among the limitations on those powers.

2d. Its terms purport to enlarge, not to diminish the powers vested in the government. It purports to be an additional power, not a restriction on those already granted. No reason has been, or can be assigned for thus concealing an intention to narrow the discretion of the national legislature under words which purport to enlarge it. The framers of the Constitution wished its adoption, and well knew that it would be endangered by its strength, not by its weakness. Had they been capable of using language which would convey to the eye one idea, and, after deep reflection, impress on the mind another, they would rather have disguised the grant of power than its limitation. If, then, their intention had been, by this clause, to restrain the free use of means which might otherwise have been implied, that intention would have been inserted in another place, and would have been expressed in terms resembling these. "In carrying into execution the foregoing powers, and all others," etc., "no laws shall be passed but such as are necessary and proper." Had the intention been to make this clause restrictive, it would unquestionably have been so in form as well as in effect.

The result of the most careful and attentive consideration bestowed upon this clause is, that if it does not enlarge, it cannot be construed to restrain the powers of Congress, or to impair the right of the legislature to exercise its best judgment in the selection of measures to carry into execution the constitutional powers of the government. If no other motive for its insertion can be suggested, a sufficient one is found in the desire to remove all doubts respecting the right to legislate on that vast mass of incidental powers which must be involved in the Constitution, if that instrument be not a splendid bauble.

We admit, as all must admit, that the powers of the government are limited, and that its limits are not to be transcended. But we think the sound construction of the Constitution must allow to the national legislature that discretion, with respect to the means by which the powers it confers are to be carried into execution, which will enable that body to perform the high duties assigned to it, in the manner most beneficial to the people. Let the end be legitimate, let it be within the scope of the Constitution, and all means which are appropriate, which are plainly adapted to that end, which are not prohibited, but consist with the letter and spirit of the Constitution, are constitutional. . . .

If a corporation may be employed indiscriminately with other means to carry into execution the powers of the government, no particular reason can be assigned for excluding the use of a bank, if required for its fiscal operations. To use one, must be within the discretion of Congress, if it be an appropriate mode of executing the powers of government. That it is a convenient, a useful, and essential instrument in the prosecution of its fiscal operations, is not now a subject of controversy. All those who have been concerned in the administration of our finances, have concurred in representing the importance and necessity; and so strongly have they been felt, that statesmen of the first class, whose previous opinions against it had been confirmed by every circumstance which can fix the human judgment, have yielded those opinions to the exigencies of the nation. . . .

But, were its necessity less apparent, none can deny its being an appropriate measure; and if it is, the degree of its necessity, as has been very justly observed, is to be discussed in another place. Should Congress, in the execution of its powers, adopt measures which are prohibited by the Constitution; or should Congress, under the pretext of executing its powers, pass laws for the accomplishment of objects not entrusted to the government, it would become the painful duty of this tribunal, should a case requiring such a decision come before it to say that such an act was not the law of the land. But where the law is not prohibited, and is really calculated to effect any of the objects entrusted to the government, to undertake here to inquire into the degree of its necessity, would be to pass the line which circumscribes the judicial department, and to tread on legislative ground. This Court disclaims all pretensions to such a power. . . .

After the most deliberate consideration, it is the unanimous and decided opinion of this Court that the act to incorporate the bank of the United States is a law made in pursuance of the Constitution, and is a part of the supreme law of the land. . . .

It being the opinion of the Court that the act incorporating the bank is constitutional, and that the power of establishing a branch in the state of Maryland might be properly exercised by the bank itself, we proceed to inquire:

2. Whether the state of Maryland may, without violating the Constitution, tax that branch?

That the power of taxation is one of vital importance; that it is retained by the states; that it is not abridged by the grant of a similar power to the government of the Union; that it is to be concurrently exercised by the two governments; are truths which have never been denied. But, such is the paramount character of the Constitution that its capacity to withdraw any subject from the action of even this power, is admitted. The states are expressly forbidden to lay any duties on imports or exports, except what may be absolutely necessary for executing their inspection laws. If the obligation of this prohibition must be conceded—if it may restrain a state from the exercise of its taxing power on imports and exports—the same paramount character would seem to restrain, as it certainly may restrain, a state from such other exercise of this power, as is in its nature incompatible with, and repugnant to, the constitutional laws of the Union. A law, absolutely repugnant to another, as entirely repeals that other as if express terms of repeal were used.

On this ground the counsel for the bank place its claim to be exempted from the power of a state to tax its operations. There is no express provision for the case, but the claim has been sustained on a principle which so entirely pervades the Constitution, is so intermixed with the materials which compose it, so interwoven with its web, so blended with its texture, as to be incapable of being separated from it without rendering it into shreds.

This great principle is, that the Constitution and the laws made in pursuance thereof are supreme; that they control the constitutions and laws of the respective states, and cannot be controlled by them. From this, which may be almost termed

an axiom, other propositions are deduced as corollaries, on the truth or error of which, and on their application to this case, the cause has been supposed to depend. These are, 1st. that a power to create implies a power to preserve. 2d. That a power to destroy, if wielded by a different hand, is hostile to, and incompatible with these powers to create and to preserve. 3d. That where this repugnancy exists, that authority which is supreme must control, not yield to that over which it is supreme. . . .

The power of Congress to create, and of course to continue, the bank, was the subject of the preceding part of this opinion; and is no longer to be considered as questionable.

That the power of taxing it by the states may be exercised so as to destroy it, is too obvious to be denied. But taxation is said to be an absolute power, which acknowledges no other limits than those expressly prescribed in the Constitution, and like sovereign power of every other description, is trusted to the discretion of those who use it.

That the power to tax involves the power to destroy; that the power to destroy may defeat and render useless the power to create; that there is a plain repugnance, in conferring on one government a power to control the constitutional measures of another, which other, with respect to those very measures, is declared to be supreme over that which exerts the control, are propositions not to be denied. But all inconsistencies are to be reconciled by the magic of the word confidence. Taxation, it is said, does not necessarily and unavoidably destroy. To carry it to the excess of destruction would be an abuse, to presume which, would banish that confidence which is essential to all government.

But is this a case of confidence? Would the people of any one state trust those of another with a power to control the most insignificant operations of their state government? We know they would not. Why, then, should we suppose that the people of any one state should be willing to trust those of another with a power to control the operations of a government to which they have confided the most important and most valuable interests? In the legislature of the Union alone, are all represented. The legislature of the Union alone, therefore, can be trusted by the people with the power of controlling measures which concern all, in the confidence that it will not be abused. This, then, is not a case of confidence, and we must consider it as it really is.

If we apply the principle for which the state of Maryland contends, to the Constitution generally, we shall find it capable of changing totally the character of that instrument. We shall find it capable of arresting all the measures of the government, and of prostrating it at the foot of the states. The American people have declared their Constitution, and the laws made in pursuance thereof, to be supreme; but this principle would transfer the supremacy, in fact, to the states.

If the states may tax one instrument, employed by the government in the execution of its powers, they may tax any and every other instrument. They may tax the mail; they may tax the mint; they may tax patent-rights; they may tax the papers of the custom-house; they may tax judicial process; they may tax all the means employed by the government, to an excess which would defeat all the ends of government. This was not intended by the American people. This did not design to make their government dependent on the states. . . .

It has also been insisted, that, as the power of taxation in the general and state governments is acknowledged to be concurrent, every argument which would sustain the right of the general government to tax banks chartered by the states, will equally sustain the right of the states to tax banks chartered by the general government.

But the two cases are not on the same reason. The people of all the states have created the general government, and have conferred upon it the general power of taxation. The people of all the states, and the states themselves, are represented in Congress, and, by their representatives, exercise this power. When they tax the chartered institutions of the states, they tax their Constituents; and these taxes must be uniform. But, when a state taxes the operations of the government of the United States, it acts upon institutions created, not by their own constituents, but by people over whom they claim no control. It acts upon the measures of a government created by others as well as themselves, for the benefit of others in common with themselves. The difference is that which always exists, and always must exist, between the action of the whole on a part, and the action of a part on the whole—between the laws of a government declared to be supreme, and those of a government which, when in opposition to those laws, is not supreme.

But if the full application of this argument could be admitted, it might bring into question the right of Congress to tax the state banks, and could not prove the right of the states to tax the Bank of the United States.

The Court has bestowed on this subject its most deliberate consideration. The result is a conviction that the states have no power, by taxation or otherwise, to retard, impede, burden, or in any manner control the operations of the constitutional laws enacted by Congress to carry into execution the powers vested in the general government. This is, we think, the unavoidable consequence of that supremacy which the Constitution has declared.

We are unanimously of opinion that the law passed by the legislature of Maryland, imposing a tax on the Bank of the United States, is unconstitutional and void.

This opinion does not deprive the states of any resources which they originally possessed. It does not extend to a tax paid by the real property of the bank, in common with the other real property within the state, nor to a tax imposed on the interest which the citizens of Mary-land may hold in this institution, in common with other property of the same description throughout the state. But this is a tax on the operations of the bank, and is, consequently, a tax on the operation of an instrument employed by the government of the Union to carry its powers into execution. Such a tax must be unconstitutional. . . .

Aftermath of *McCulloch* v. *Maryland*

The far-reaching decision of Chief Justice John Marshall in the *McCulloch* case inspired strong reactions throughout the country. Generally praised in the North, the decision was denounced by most political leaders and editorial writers in the South and West. Thomas Ritchie, editor of the *Richmond Enquirer*, wrote,

> If such a spirit as breathes in this opinion is forever to preside over the judiciary, then indeed it is high time for the states to tremble . . . all their great rights may be swept away one by one. If Congress can select any means which they consider "convenient," "useful," "conducive to" the execution of the specified and granted powers; if the word "necessary" is thus to be frittered away, then we may bid adieu to the sovereignty of the states; they sink into contemptible corporations; the gulf of consolidation yawns to receive them. This doctrine is as alarming, if not more so, than any which ever came from Mr. A. Hamilton on this question of a bank or any other question under the Constitution. . . . The people should not pass it over in silence; otherwise this opinion might prove the knell of our most important state rights. This opinion must be controverted and exposed.[5]

James Madison, who as President in 1815 and 1816 had strongly supported a bill for a national bank (he vetoed the 1815 bill only because he thought it to be insufficient), criticized Marshall's opinion in *McCulloch* v. *Maryland* because it went too far in supporting broad national powers over the states. Madison wrote to the Virginia Judge Spencer Roane, in a letter dated September 2, 1819,

> The occasion [*McCulloch* v. *Maryland*] did not call for the general and abstract doctrine interwoven with the decision of the particular case. I have always supposed that the meaning of a law, and for a like reason, of a constitution, so far as it depends on judicial interpretation, was to result from a course of particular decisions, and not these from a previous and abstract comment on the subject. The example in this instance tends to reverse the rule. . . . [The] latitude in expounding the Constitution . . . seems to break down the landmarks intended by a specification of the powers of Congress, and to substitute for a definite connection between means and ends a legislative discretion as to the former to which no practical limit can be assigned. . . . It was anticipated, I believe, by few if any of the framers of the Constitution, that a rule of construction would be introduced

[5]Charles Warren, *The Supreme Court*, I, p. 516.

as broad and pliant as what has occurred. And those who shared in what passed in the state conventions through which the people ratified the Constitution, with respect to the extent of the powers vested in Congress, cannot easily be persuaded that the avowal of such a rule would not have prevented its ratification.[6]

THE WAR POWER AND THE NECESSARY AND PROPER CLAUSE

McCulloch v. *Maryland* (1819) interpreted the necessary and proper clause not, as the State of Maryland wished, to limit the government but to permit the expansion of the enumerated powers of Congress through the doctrine of implied powers. "A government," said Chief Justice John Marshall in that opinion, "entrusted with such ample powers [as the powers to lay and collect taxes, to borrow money, to regulate commerce, to declare and conduct a war, and to raise and support armies and navies], on the due execution of which the happiness and prosperity of the nation so vitally depends, must also be entrusted with ample means for their execution. The power being given, it is the interest of the nation to facilitate its execution. It can never be their interest, and cannot be presumed to have been their intention, to clog and embarrass its execution by withholding the most appropriate means."

While the *McCulloch* decision mentions the war power, the case involves only domestic affairs. In the *McCulloch* case the state of Maryland argued that federalism—the division of authority between national and state governments—required Congress to adhere strictly to its enumerated powers in making public policy. Considerations of federalism have on many occasions limited the powers Congress exercises under the necessary and proper clause. But such limitations are more historical than an important component of modern constitutional doctrine.

The war power may be used to support national controls in areas traditionally reserved to state and local governments. In *Woods* v. *Miller* the Court had to decide the question of whether or not Congress could extend rent controls in peacetime on the basis of its war powers.

Woods v. *Miller*

333 U.S. 138; 92 L. Ed. 596 (1948)

Mr. Justice Douglas delivered the opinion of the Court:

The case is here on a direct appeal . . . from a judgment of the District Court holding unconstitutional Title II of the Housing and Rent Act of 1947.

The Act became effective on July 1, 1947, and the following day the appellee demanded of its tenants increases of 40% and 60% for rental accommodations in the Cleveland Defense-Rental Area, an admitted violation of the Act and regulations adopted pursuant thereto. . . .

The District Court was of the view that the authority of Congress to regulate rents by virtue of the war power . . .

[6]Ibid., pp. 517–518.

ended with the Presidential Proclamation terminating hostilities on December 31, 1946, since that proclamation inaugurated "peace-in-fact" though it did not mark termination of the war. It also concluded that, even if the war power continues, Congress did not act under it because it did not say so, and only if Congress says so, or enacts provisions so implying, can it be held that Congress intended to exercise such power. That Congress did not so intend, said the District Court, follows from the provision that the Housing Expediter can end controls in any area without regard to the official termination of the war, and from the fact that the preceding federal rent control laws (which were concededly exercises of the war power) were neither amended nor extended. The District Court expressed the further view that rent control is not within the war power because "the emergency created by housing shortage came into existence long before the war." . . .

We conclude, in the first place, that the war power sustains this legislation. The Court said in *Hamilton* v. *Kentucky Distilleries Co.* [1919] . . . that the war power includes the power "to remedy the evils which have arisen from its rise and progress" and continues for the duration of that emergency. Whatever may be the consequences when war is officially terminated, the war power does not necessarily end with the cessation of hostilities. We recently held that it is adequate to support the preservation of rights created by wartime legislation, *Fleming* v. *Mohawk Wrecking & Lumber Co.* [1947] . . . But it has a broader sweep. In *Hamilton* v. *Kentucky Distilleries Co.* and *Ruppert* v. *Caffey* [1920]. . . , prohibition laws which were enacted after the Armistice in World War I were sustained as exercises of the war power because they conserved manpower and increased efficiency of production in the critical days during the period of demobilization, and helped to husband the

supply of grains and cereals depleted by the war effort. . . .

The constitutional validity of the present legislation follows a *fortiori* from those cases. The legislative history of the present Act makes abundantly clear that there has not yet been eliminated the deficit in housing which in considerable measure was caused by the heavy demobilization of veterans and by the cessation or reduction in residential construction during the period of hostilities due to the allocation of building materials to military projects. Since the war effort contributed heavily to that deficit, Congress has the power even after the cessation of hostilities to act to control the forces that a short supply of the needed article created. If that were not true, the Necessary and Proper Clause, Art. I, § 8, cl. 18, would be drastically limited in its application to the several war powers. The Court has declined to follow that course in the past. . . . We decline to take it today. The result would be paralyzing. It would render Congress powerless to remedy conditions the creation of which necessarily followed from the mobilization of men and materials for successful prosecution of the war. So to read the Constitution would be to make it self-defeating.

We recognize the force of the argument that the effects of war under modern conditions may be felt in the economy for years and years, and that if the war power can be used in days of peace to treat all the wounds which war inflicts on our society, it may not only swallow up all other powers of Congress but largely obliterate the Ninth and the Tenth Amendments as well. There are no such implications in today's decision. We deal here with the consequences of a housing deficit greatly intensified during the period of hostilities by the war effort. Any power, of course, can be abused. But we cannot assume that Congress is not alert to its constitutional responsibilities. And the question whether the war power has been properly employed in cases such as this is open to judicial inquiry. . . .

The question of the constitutionality of action taken by Congress does not depend on recitals of the power which it undertakes to exercise. Here it is plain from the legislative history that Congress was invoking its war power to cope with a current condition of which the war was a direct and immediate cause. Its judgment on that score is entitled to the respect granted like legislation enacted pursuant to the police power. . . .

Reversed.

MR. JUSTICE JACKSON, concurring:

I agree with the result in this case, but the arguments that have been addressed to us lead me to utter more explicit misgivings about war powers than the Court has done. The Government asserts no constitutional basis for this legislation other than this vague, undefined and undefinable "war power."

No one will question that this power is the most dangerous one to free government in the whole catalogue of powers. It usually is invoked in haste and excitement when calm legislative consideration of constitutional limitation is difficult. It is executed in a time of patriotic fervor that makes moderation unpopular. And, worst of all, it is interpreted by judges under the influence of the same passions and pressures. Always, as in this case, the Government urges hasty decision to forestall some emergency or serve some purpose and pleads that paralysis will result if its claims to power are denied or their confirmation delayed.

Particularly when the war power is invoked to do things to the liberties of people, or to their property or economy that only indirectly affect conduct of the war and do not relate to the management of the war itself, the constitutional basis should be scrutinized with care.

I think we can hardly deny that the war power is as valid a ground for federal rent control now as it has been at any time. We still are technically in a state of war. I would not be willing to hold that war powers may be indefinitely prolonged merely by keeping legally alive a state of war that had in fact ended. I cannot accept the argument that war powers last as long as the effects and consequences of war, for if so they are permanent—as permanent as the war debts. But I find no reason to conclude that we could find fairly that the present state of war is merely technical. We have armies abroad exercising our war power and have made no peace terms with our allies, not to mention our principal enemies. I think the conclusion that the war power has been applicable during the lifetime of this legislation is unavoidable.

As you read cases that deal directly with or touch upon the scope of the war power of Congress, keep in mind Justice Jackson's statement in his concurring opinion in the *Woods* case that the war power is "the most dangerous one to free government in the whole catalog of powers." Under what circumstances does Jackson feel that the constitutional basis of the war power should be scrutinized with special care?

The majority in the *Woods* case held that the war power continues for the duration of the war emergency. The war power "does not necessarily end with the cessation of hostilities." The war contributed heavily to the housing deficit, said the Court, and under the necessary and proper clause, in combination with its war powers, Congress can act after the cessation of hostilities to deal with the short supply of housing. Contrast this view of the majority with Jackson's statement that he "cannot accept the argument that war powers last as long as the effects and consequences of war, for if so they are permanent—as permanent as the war debts."

The War Power and Individual Rights

The war powers of Congress in combination with the necessary and proper clause are potentially an important constitutional basis for the expansion of legislative authority in many spheres. For example, clause 14 of Article I delegates to Congress the authority "to make rules for the government and regulation of the land and naval forces." On the basis of this clause Congress passed the uniform code of military justice that placed within military jurisdiction "all persons serving with, employed by, or accompanying the armed forces without the continental limits of the United States." In *Reid* v. *Covert,* 354 U.S. 1 (1957), the Court faced the issue of the constitutionality of this section of the uniform code. Could the provision for the extension of military jurisdiction to civilian employees and dependents of armed services personnel be justified on the basis of clause 14 in combination with the necessary and proper clause?

Mrs. Smith and Mrs. Covert, charged with murdering their soldier-husbands on foreign military bases, were tried and convicted by military tribunals that had taken jurisdiction under the uniform code. The government contended that clause 14 plus the necessary and proper clause constituted "a broad grant of power 'without limitation' authorizing Congress to subject all persons, civilian and soldiers alike, to military trial if 'necessary and proper' to govern and regulate the land and naval forces."[7] But, wrote Justice Black for a plurality of the Court, "The necessary and proper clause cannot operate to extend military jurisdiction to any group of persons beyond that class described in clause 14—'the land and the naval forces.' "[8] The Bill of Rights, said Black, applies to United States citizens living abroad.

Having rejected the necessary and proper clause as a basis for extending military jurisdiction to civilians, Justice Black next turned to the question of whether or not the NATO status of forces agreement between the United States and Great Britain, which provided for the type of military trial under challenge, could supersede basic constitutional requirements. Treaties are the supreme law of the land, and in *Missouri* v. *Holland* (1920) the Court held that under certain circumstances congressional legislation based upon treaties could be upheld even if it would be unconstitutional in the absence of a treaty.[9] Moreover, *In Re Ross,* 140 U.S. 453 (1891), had decided that Americans living abroad did not have the same constitutional rights as citizens residing within the United States. And a series of cases, called the *Insular Cases,* decided from 1901 to 1905, denied the protection of the Bill of Rights to areas Congress had not incorporated into the United States. Black

[7]Reid v. Covert, 354 U.S. 1, 20 (1957).
[8]Ibid., pp. 20–21.
[9]For a discussion of Missouri v. Holland see pp. 187–189.

rejected the precedents of these cases, holding that they did not apply under the present circumstances. Congress could make no law based upon an executive agreement nor a treaty, said Black, that would deprive American citizens living abroad of fundamental constitutional rights.

The *Reid* case applied to dependents of servicemen overseas charged with *capital* crimes. Would the Court extend the Bill of Rights to civilian dependents charged with *noncapital* offenses? Or would the Court hold that the necessary and proper clause in combination with the war powers of Congress, specifically clause 14, permitted the extension of military jurisdiction to civilian dependents involved in noncapital cases? The issue confronted the Court three years after the *Reid* decision in *Kinsella* v. *United States*.

Kinsella v. United States Ex Rel. Singleton

361 U.S. 234; 80 S. Ct. 297; L. Ed. 2d 268 (1960)

MR. JUSTICE CLARK delivered the opinion of the Court:

This direct appeal tests the constitutional validity of peacetime court-martial trials of civilian persons "accompanying the armed forces outside the United States" and charged with noncapital offenses under the Uniform Code of Military Justice, 10 U.S.C § 802, 70A Stat. 37. Appellee contends that the dependent wife of a soldier can be tried only in a court that affords her the safeguards of Article III and of the Fifth and Sixth Amendments of the Constitution. The trial court held Article 2 (11) of the Code unconstitutional as applied to civilian dependents accompanying the armed forces overseas and charged with noncapital offenses, 164 F. Supp. 707, and the Government appealed. We noted probable jurisdiction and permitted appellee to proceed *in forma pauperis*. 359 U.S. 903.

The appellee is the mother of Mrs. Joanna S. Dial, the wife of a soldier who was assigned to a tank battalion of the United States Army. The Dials and their three children lived in government housing quarters at Baumholder, Germany. In consequence of the death of one of their children, both of the Dials were charged with unpremeditated murder, under Ar-

ticle 118 (2) of the Uniform Code of Military Justice. Upon the Dials' offer to plead guilty to involuntary manslaughter under Article 119 of the Code, both charges were withdrawn and new ones charging them separately with the lesser offense were returned. They were then tried together before a general court-martial at Baumholder. Mrs. Dial challenged the jurisdiction of the court-martial over her but, upon denial of her motion, pleaded guilty, as did her husband. Each was sentenced to the maximum penalty permitted under the Code. Their convictions were upheld by the Court of Military Appeals, and Mrs. Dial was returned to the United States and placed in the Federal Reformatory for Women at Alderson, West Virginia. Thereafter the appellee filed this petition for habeas corpus and obtained Mrs. Dial's discharge from custody. From this judgment the warden has appealed.

As has been noted, the jurisdiction of the court-martial was based upon the provisions of Article 2 (11) of the Code. The Congress enacted that article in an effort to extend, for disciplinary reasons, the coverage of the Uniform Code of Military Justice to the classes of persons therein enumerated. The jurisdiction of the Code only attached, however, when and if its applicability in a given foreign territory was sanctioned under "any treaty or agreement to which the United States is or may be a party" with the foreign sovereignty, or under "any accepted rule of international law." The existence of such an agreement here is admitted. The constitutionality of Article 2 (11), as it applies in time of peace to civilian dependents charged with noncapital offenses under the Code, is the sole issue to be decided. . . . *Reid* v. *Covert* . . . held that the power over "Territories," as applied by the *In Re Ross* doctrine, was neither applicable nor controlling. It found that trial by court-martial was the exercise of an exceptional jurisdiction springing from the power granted the Congress in Art. I. § 8, cl. 14, "To make Rules for the Government and Regulation of the land and naval Forces," as supplemented by the Necessary and Proper Clause of Art. I. § 8, cl. 18. But as applied to the civilian dependents there involved it must be considered, the Court said, in relation to Article III and the Fifth and Sixth Amendments. The majority concluded that, in those capital cases, trial by court-martial as provided could not constitutionally be justified.

The appellee contends that this result, declaring civilian dependents charged with capital offenses not to be subject to the provisions of the Code, bears directly on its applicability to the same class charged with non-capital crimes. She says that the test of whether civilian dependents come within the power of Congress as granted in Clause 14's limitation to the "land and naval Forces" is the status of the person involved. Her conclusion is that if civilian dependents charged with capital offenses are not within that language, *a fortiori*, persons in the same class charged with noncapital offenses cannot be included, since the clause draws no distinction as to offenses. The Government fully accepts the holding in the [*Reid* v.] *Covert* case. It

contends that the case is controlling only where civilian dependents are charged with capital offenses, and that in fact the concurrences indicate that considerations of a compelling necessity for prosecution by courts-martial of civilian dependents charged with noncapital offenses might permit with reason the inclusion of that limited category within court-martial jurisdiction. It submits that such necessities are controlling in the case of civilian dependents charged with noncapital crimes. It points out that such dependents affect the military community as a whole; that they have, in fact, been permitted to enjoy their residence in such communities on the representation that they are subject to military control; and that realistically they are a part of the military establishment. It argues that, from a morale standpoint, the present need for dependents to accompany American forces maintained abroad is a pressing one; that their special status as integral parts of the military community requires disciplinary control over them by the military commander; that the effectiveness of this control depends upon a readily available machinery affording a prompt sanction and resulting deterrent present only in court-martial jurisdiction; and that not only is court-martial procedure inherently fair but there are no alternatives to it. The Government further contends that it has entered into international agreements with a large number of foreign governments permitting the exercise of military jurisdiction in the territory of the signatories, and pursuant to the same it has been utilizing court-martial procedures at various American installations abroad. Its legal theory is based on historical materials which it asserts indicate a well-established practice of court-martial jurisdiction over civilians accompanying the armed forces, during Colonial days as well as the formative period of our Constitution. From this it concludes that civilian dependents may be included as a necessary and proper incident to the congressional power "To make Rules for the Government and Regulation of the land and naval Forces," as granted in Clause 14.

In this field, *Toth* v. *Quarles*, 350 U.S. 11 (1955), cited with approval by a majority in the [*Reid* v.] *Covert* case, is a landmark. Likewise, of course, we must consider the effect of the latter case on our problem. We therefore turn to their teachings. The *Toth* case involved a discharged soldier who was tried by court-martial after his discharge from the Army, for an offense committed before his discharge. It was said there that the Clause 14 "provision itself does not empower Congress to deprive people of trials under Bill of Rights safeguards," and that military tribunals must be restricted "to the narrowest jurisdiction deemed absolutely essential to maintaining discipline among troops in active service." . . . We brushed aside the thought that "considerations of discipline" could provide an excuse for "*new expansion* of court-martial jurisdiction at the expense of the normal and constitutionally preferable system of trial by jury." . . . (Italics supplied.) We were therefore "not willing to hold that power to circumvent those safeguards should be inferred through the Necessary and Proper Clause." . . . The holding of the case may be summed up in its own words, namely, that "the power granted Congress 'To make Rules' to regulate 'the land and naval Forces' would seem to restrict court-martial jurisdiction to persons who are actually members or part of the armed forces."

It was with this gloss on Clause 14 that the Court reached the [*Reid* v.] *Covert* case. There, as we have noted, the person involved was the civilian dependent of a soldier, who was accompanying him outside the United States when the capital offense complained of was committed. The majority concluded that "Trial by court-martial is constitutionally permissible *only* for persons who can, *on a fair appraisal*, be regarded as falling within the authority given to Congress under Article I to regulate the 'land and naval Forces' . . . ." Concurring opinion. (Italics supplied.) The test for jurisdiction, it follows, is one of *status*, namely, whether the accused in the court-martial proceeding is a person who can be regarded as falling within the term "land and naval Forces." The Court concluded that civilian dependents charged with capital offenses were not included within such authority, the concurring Justices expressing the view that they did not think "that the proximity, physical and social, of these women to the 'land and naval Forces' is, with due regard to all that has been put before us, so clearly demanded by the effective 'Government and Regulation' of those forces as reasonably to demonstrate a justification for court-martial jurisdiction over capital offenses." . . .

In the [*Reid* v.] *Covert* case, each opinion supporting the judgment struck down the article as it was applied to civilian dependents charged with capital crimes. The separate concurrences supported the judgment on the theory that the crime being "in fact punishable by death," . . . the question to be decided is "analogous, ultimately, to issues of due process." . . . The Justices joining in the opinion announcing the judgment, however, did not join in this view, but held that the constitutional safeguards claimed applied in "*all* criminal trials" in Article III courts and applied "outside of the States," pointing out that both the Fifth and Sixth Amendments were "all inclusive with their sweeping references to 'no person' and to 'all criminal prosecutions.' " . . . The two dissenters found "no distinction in the Constitution between capital and other cases," . . . but said that the constitutional safeguards claimed were not required under the power granted Congress in Art.

IV, § 3, and the cases heretofore mentioned. The briefs and argument in *Covert* reveal that it was argued and submitted by the parties on the theory that no constitutional distinction could be drawn between capital and noncapital offenses for the purposes of Clause 14.

We have given careful study to the contentions of the government. They add up to a reverse of form from the broad presentation in *Covert*, where it asserted that no distinction could be drawn between capital and noncapital offenses. But the same fittings are used here with only adaptation to noncapital crimes. The Government asserts that the [*Reid* v.] *Covert* case, rather than foreclosing the issue here, indicates that military tribunals would have jurisdiction over civilian dependents charged with offenses less than capital. It says that the trial of such a person for a noncapital crime is "significantly different" from his trial for a capital one, that the maintaining of different standards or considerations in capital cases is not a new concept, and that, therefore, there must be a fresh evaluation of the necessities for court-martial jurisdiction and a new balancing of the rights involved. . . .

We now reach the Government's suggestion that, in the light of the noncapital nature of the offense here, as opposed to the capital one in the *Covert* case, we should make a "fresh evaluation and a new balancing." But the power to "make Rules for the Government and Regulation of the land and naval Forces" bears no limitation as to offenses. The power there granted includes not only the creation of offenses but the fixing of the punishment therefor. If civilian dependents are included in the term "land and naval Forces" at all, they are subject to the full power granted the Congress therein to create capital as well as noncapital offenses. This Court cannot diminish and expand that power, either on a case-by-case basis or on a balancing of the power there granted

Congress against the safeguards of Article III and the Fifth and Sixth Amendments. Due process cannot create or enlarge power. . . . Nor do we believe that due process considerations bring about an expansion of Clause 14 through the operation of the Necessary and Proper Clause. If the exercise of the power is valid it is because it is granted in Clause 14, not because of the Necessary and Proper Clause. The latter clause is not itself a grant of power, but a *caveat* that the Congress possesses all the means necessary to carry out the specifically granted "foregoing" powers of § 8 "and all other Powers vested by this Constitution. . . ." As James Madison explained, the Necessary and Proper Clause is "but merely a declaration, for the removal of all uncertainty, that the means of carrying into execution those [powers] otherwise granted are included in the grant." VI Writings of James Madison, edited by Gaillard Hunt, 383. There can be no question but that Clause 14 grants the Congress power to adopt the Uniform Code of Military Justice. Our initial inquiry is whether Congress can include civilian dependents within the term "land and naval Forces" as a proper incident to this power and necessary to its execution. If answered in the affirmative then civilian dependents are amenable to the Code. In the [*Reid* v.] *Covert* case, it was held they were not so amenable as to capital offenses. Our final inquiry, therefore, is narrowed to whether Clause 14, which under the [*Reid* v.] *Covert* case has been held not to include civilian dependents charged with capital offenses, may now be expanded to include civilian dependents who are charged with noncapital offenses. We again refer to James Madison:

When the Constitution was under the discussions which preceded its ratification, it is well known that great apprehensions were expressed by many, lest the omission of some positive exception, from the powers delegated, of certain rights, . . . might expose them to the danger of being drawn, by construction, within some of the powers vested in Congress, more especially of the power to make all laws necessary and proper for carrying their other powers into execution. In reply to this objection, it was invariably urged to be a fundamental and characteristic principle of the Constitution, that all powers not given by it were reserved; that no powers were given beyond those enumerated in the Constitution, and such as were fairly incident to them. . . .

We are therefore constrained to say that since this Court has said that the Necessary and Proper Clause cannot expand Clause 14 so as to include prosecution of civilian dependents for capital crimes, it cannot expand Clause 14 to include prosecution of them for noncapital offenses.

Neither our history nor our decisions furnish a foothold for the application of such due process concept as the Government projects. Its application today in the light of the irreversibility of the death penalty would free from military prosecution a civilian accompanying or employed by the armed services who committed a capital offense, while the same civilian could be prosecuted by the military for a noncapital crime. It is illogical to say that "the power respecting the land and naval forces encompasses . . . all that Congress may appropriately deem 'necessary' for their good order" and still deny to Congress the means to exercise such power through the infliction of the death penalty. But that is proposed here. In our view this would militate against our whole concept of power and jurisdiction. It would likewise be contrary to the entire history of the Articles of War. Even prior to the Constitutional Convention, the Articles of War included 17 capital offenses applicable to all persons whose status brought them within the term "land and naval Forces." There were not then and never have been any exceptions as to per-

sons in the applicability of these capital offenses. In 1806 when the Articles of War were first revised, Congress retained therein 16 offenses that carried the death penalty, although there was complaint that "almost every article in the bill was stained with blood." 15 Annals of Cong. 326.

Nor do we believe that the exclusion of noncapital offenses along with capital ones will cause any additional disturbance in our "delicate arrangements with many foreign countries." The Government has pointed to no disruption in such relations by reason of the [*Reid* v.] *Covert* decision. Certainly this case involves no more "important national concerns into which we should be reluctant to enter" than did *Covert*. In truth the problems are identical and are so intertwined that equal treatment of capital and noncapital cases would be a palliative to a troubled world.

We therefore hold that Mrs. Dial is protected by the specific provisions of Article III and the Fifth and Sixth Amendments and that her prosecution and conviction by court-martial are not constitutionally permissible. The judgment must therefore be

Affirmed.

MR. JUSTICE HARLAN, whom MR. JUSTICE FRANKFURTER joins, dissenting . . . :

. . . Article I, § 8, cl. 14, speaks not in narrow terms of soldiers and sailors, but broadly gives Congress power to prescribe "Rules for the Government and Regulation of the land and naval Forces." This power must be read in connection with Clause 18 of the same Article, authorizing Congress

To make all Laws which shall be necessary and proper for carrying into Execution the foregoing Powers, and all other Powers vested by this Constitution in the Government of the United States, or in any Department or Officer thereof.

Thus read, the power respecting the land and naval forces encompasses, in my opinion, all that Congress may appropriately deem "necessary" for their good order. It does not automatically exclude the regulation of non-military personnel.

I think it impermissible to conclude, as some of my brethren have indicated on an earlier occasion [in *Reid* v. *Covert*], and as the Court now holds, . . . that the Necessary and Proper Clause may not be resorted to in judging constitutionality in cases of this type. The clause, itself a part of Art. I, § 8, in which the power to regulate the armed forces is also found, applies no less to that power than it does to the other § 8 congressional powers, and indeed is to be read "as an integral part of each" such power. . . . As Mr. Justice Brandeis put it . . .

Whether it be for purposes of national defense, or for the purpose of establishing post offices and post roads or for the purpose of regulating commerce among the several States Congress has the power "to make all laws which shall be necessary and proper for carrying into execution" the duty so reposed in the Federal Government. While this is a Government of enumerated powers it has full attributes of sovereignty within the limits of those powers. . . . Some confusion of thought might perhaps have been avoided, if, instead of distinguishing between powers by the terms express and implied, the terms specific and general had been used. For the power conferred by clause 18 of § 8 "to make all laws which shall be necessary and proper for carrying into execution" powers specifically enumerated is also an express power. . . .

Of course, the Necessary and Proper Clause cannot be used to "expand" powers which are otherwise constitutionally limited, but that is only to say that when an asserted power is not appropriate to the exercise of an express power, to which all "necessary and proper" powers must relate, the asserted power is not a "proper" one. But to say, as the Court does now,

that the Necessary and Proper Clause "is not itself a grant of power" is to disregard Clause 18 as one of the enumerated powers of § 8 of Art. I.

Viewing Congress' power to provide for the governing of the armed forces in connection with the Necessary and Proper Clause, it becomes apparent, I believe, that a person's "status" with reference to the military establishment is but one, and not alone the determinative, factor in judging the constitutionality of a particular exercise of that power. By the same token, the major premise on which the Court ascribes to *Covert* a controlling effect in these noncapital cases disappears. . . .

It is one thing to hold that nonmilitary personnel situated at our foreign bases may be tried abroad by courts-martial in times of peace for noncapital offenses, but quite another to say that they may be so tried where life is at stake. In the latter situation I do not believe that the Necessary and Proper Clause, which alone in cases like this brings the exceptional Article I jurisdiction into play, can properly be taken as justifying the trial of nonmilitary personnel without the full protections of an Article III court. . . . Before the constitutional existence of such a power can be found, for me a much more persuasive showing would be required that Congress had good reason for concluding that such a course is necessary to the proper maintenance of our military establishment abroad than has been made in any of the cases of this kind which have thus far come before the Court. . . .

Nothing in the supplemental historical data respecting courts-martial which have been presented in these cases persuades me that we would be justified in holding that Congress' exercise of its constitutional powers in this area was without a rational and appropriate basis, so far as noncapital cases are concerned. . . . I submit that once it is shown that Congress' choice was not excluded by a rational judgment concerned with the problem it is beyond our competence to find constitutional command for other procedures.

MR. JUSTICE WHITTAKER, joined by JUSTICE STEWART, dissented.

What does the majority of the Court in the *Kinsella* case mean by the statement that "Due process cannot create or enlarge power"? Does the Court's opinion narrow congressional power based upon the necessary and proper clause? Is this not implied by the Court's statement that since "the necessary and proper clause cannot expand clause 14 so as to include prosecution of civilian dependents for capital crimes, it cannot expand clause 14 to include prosecution of them for noncapital offenses?"

Do you feel that the Court's opinion adequately answers Justice Harlan's argument in his dissenting opinion that clause 14 "speaks not in narrow terms of soldiers and sailors, but broadly gives Congress power to prescribe 'rules for the government and regulation of the land and naval forces.' This power must be read in connection with clause 18 of the same article [the necessary and proper clause], . . . [and] thus read, the power respecting the land and naval forces encompasses . . . all that Congress may appropriately deem 'necessary' for their good order. It does not automatically exclude the regulation of non-military personnel." Considering the power of Congress to govern the armed forces in connection with the necessary and proper clause, Harlan argued that "status" should not be the only determining factor in judging whether or not the power exercised is constitutional.

Harlan's dissent rejects the conclusions of the majority regarding the nonseparability of capital and noncapital offenses in determining the permissible scope of the jurisdiction of military tribunals. What arguments and evidence does he use to support his view that the differences between capital and noncapital offenses are constitutionally significant?

GOVERNMENTAL POWERS BASED ON TREATIES AND EXECUTIVE AGREEMENTS

The necessary and proper clause does not only expand the powers of Congress based upon the enumerated provisions of Article I but also authorizes Congress "to make all laws which shall be necessary and proper for carrying into execution . . . all other powers vested by this Constitution in the government of the United States, or in any department or officer thereof." The treaty-making power is an example of one of these "other powers" vested in "any department or officer" of the government. The President makes treaties by and with the consent of the Senate. Moreover, constitutional doctrine has placed the unilateral authority in the hands of the President to make executive agreements, which are accorded the same legal status as treaties. Can Congress, in pursuance of a treaty or an executive agreement, pass legislation that would otherwise be held unconstitutional as an unnecessary and improper exercise of its powers? This question becomes even more significant because of the provision in Article VI: "This Constitution, and the laws of the United States which shall be made in pursuance thereof; *and* all treaties made, or which shall be made, under the authority of the United States, shall be the supreme law of the land; and the judges in every state shall be bound thereby, anything in the Constitution or the laws of any state to the contrary notwithstanding." (Emphasis supplied.) The necessary and proper clause in combination with Article VI raises the possibility of a law being made in pursuance of a treaty that might supersede an explicit constitutional standard such as a provision of the Bill of Rights. *Reid* v. *Covert* and *Kinsella* v. *United States,* however, held that the Bill of Rights could never be abrogated for American citizens through executive agreements or treaties.[10]

Congressional reliance upon the necessary and proper clause in pursuit of a treaty to pass legislation that otherwise would be unconstitutional was the issue in *Missouri* v. *Holland* (1920). The United States and Great Britain had entered into a treaty for the protection of migratory birds, under the terms of which several species of migratory birds flying between Canada and the United States were to be protected. In 1918 Congress passed the legislation delegating to the Secretary of Agriculture the authority to issue regulations to implement the treaty's provisions. The State of Missouri claimed that the statute was unconstitutional and a violation of its reserve powers because Congress had no express or implied authority to regulate migratory birds. In fact, prior to the treaty, Congress in 1913 had passed a migratory bird act which had been declared unconstitutional in the lower federal courts because, they said, there was no way the power to regulate migratory birds could be implied from the enumerated powers of Article I. Missouri claimed that a treaty could not convey powers to Congress that it did not otherwise possess in the Constitution. In its brief, Missouri stated,

> The fact that the present act of Congress purports to give effect to a treaty between the United States and Great Britain cannot validate such act of Congress when its effect is not only to accomplish that which under the Constitution Congress has no power to do, but also to do that which is forbidden to the entire Federal Government in all or any of its departments under the terms of the Constitution. Any and every treaty must be presumed to be made subject to the rightful powers of the governments concerned, and neither the treaty-making power alone, nor the treaty-making power in conjunction with [the powers of] any or all other departments of the government can bind the government to do that which the Constitution forbids.[11]

The government contended in *Missouri* v. *Holland* that a treaty made by the President and ratified by the Senate "becomes a part of the supreme law of the land, and, being so, Congress has the power to enact legislation necessary to carry into effect its provisions."[12] Missouri countered that "in its ultimate analysis the adoption of the treaty-supremacy theory means that the federal government, through the treaty-making department of the gov-

[10]See pp. 178–185.
[11]LB, Vol. 16, p. 43.
[12]Ibid., p. 10.

ernment, has a general negative upon all state laws passed by the states in the exercise of their reserved powers."[13]

Of particular significance in the *Missouri* case was the issue of federalism as it involved the reserved powers of the states. Missouri argued that the federal government cannot under any circumstances invade the domain of reserved powers and that "without exception wild game has been held to be a part of this mass which is within the exclusive and absolute power of the state. When the power of the states over purely internal affairs is destroyed, the system of government devised by the Constitution is destroyed.[14] The government responded that "whatever may be said of this proposition when applied to the ordinary legislative powers of Congress and the legislative powers of the several states, it has no application to the treaty-making power, for the reason that . . . the reserved powers of the states are those powers which remain after deducting from the full powers of sovereignty those which were committed to Congress to be exercised in purely domestic affairs, and also those powers included in the treaty-making power . . . which are necessary for the regulation of our relations with foreign countries."[15]

Missouri v. Holland

252 U.S. 416; 40 S. Ct. 382; 64 L. Ed. 641 (1920)

MR. JUSTICE HOLMES delivered the opinion of the Court:

. . . [A]s we have said, the question raised is the general one whether the treaty and statute are void as an interference with the rights reserved to the states.

To answer this question it is not enough to refer to the Tenth Amendment, reserving the powers not delegated to the United States, because by Article 2, § 2, the power to make treaties is delegated expressly, and by Article 6, treaties made under the authority of the United States, along with the Constitution and laws of the United States, made in pursuance thereof, are declared the supreme law of the land. If the treaty is valid, there can be no dispute about the validity of the statute under Article 1, § 8, as a necessary and proper means to execute the powers

of the government. The language of the Constitution as to the supremacy of treaties being general, the question before us is narrowed to an inquiry into the ground upon which the present supposed exception is placed.

It is said that a treaty cannot be valid if it infringes the Constitution; that there are limits, therefore, to the treaty-making power; and that one such limit is that what an act of Congress could not do unaided, in derogation of the powers reserved to the states, a treaty cannot do. An earlier act of Congress that attempted by itself, and not in pursuance of a treaty, to regulate the killing of migratory birds within the states, had been held bad in the district court. *United States* v. *Shauver*, 214 Fed. 154 [1914]; *United States* v. *McCullagh*, 221 Fed. 288 [1915]. Those deci-

[13]Ibid., p. 92.
[14]Ibid., p. 64.
[15]Ibid., p. 35.

sions were supported by arguments that migratory birds were owned by the states in their sovereign capacity, for the benefit of their people, and that under cases like *Geer* v. *Connecticut,* 161 U.S. 519 [1896], . . . this control was one that Congress had no power to displace. The same argument is supposed to apply now with equal force.

Whether the two cases cited were decided rightly or not, they cannot be accepted as a test of the treaty power. Acts of Congress are the supreme law of the land only when made in pursuance of the Constitution, while treaties are declared to be so when made under the authority of the United States. It is open to question whether the authority of the United States means more than the formal acts prescribed to make the convention. We do not mean to imply that there are no qualifications to the treaty-making power; but they must be ascertained in a different way. It is obvious that there may be matters of the sharpest exigency for the national well-being that an act of Congress could not deal with, but that a treaty followed by such an act could, and it is not lightly to be assumed that, in matters requiring national action, "a power which must belong to and somewhere reside in every civilized government" is not to be found. . . . We are not yet discussing the particular case before us, but only are considering the validity of the test proposed. With regard to that, we may add that when we are dealing with words that also are a constituent act, like the Constitution of the United States, we must realize that they have called into life a being the development of which could not have been foreseen completely by the most gifted of its begetters. It was enough for them to realize or to hope that they had created an organism; it has taken a century and has cost their successors much sweat and blood to prove that they cre-

ated a nation. The case before us must be considered in the light of our whole experience, and not merely in that of what was said a hundred years ago. The treaty in question does not contravene any prohibitory words to be found in the Constitution. The only question is whether it is forbidden by some invisible radiation from the general terms of the Tenth Amendment. We must consider what this country has become in deciding what that amendment has reserved.

The state, as we have intimated, founds its claim of exclusive authority upon an assertion of title to migratory birds,—an assertion that is embodied in statute. No doubt it is true that, as between a state and its inhabitants, the state may regulate the killing and sale of such birds, but it does not follow that its authority is exclusive of paramount powers. To put the claim of the state upon title is to lean upon a slender reed. Wild birds are not in the possession of anyone; and possession is the beginning of ownership. The whole foundation of the state's rights is the presence within their jurisdiction of birds that yesterday had not arrived, to-morrow may be in another state, and in a week a thousand miles away. If we are to be accurate, we cannot put the case of the state upon higher ground than that the treaty deals with creatures that for the moment are within the state borders, that it must be carried out by officers of the United States within the same territory, and that, but for the treaty, the state would be free to regulate this subject itself.

As most of the laws of the United States are carried out within the states, and as many of them deal with matters which, in the silence of such laws, the state might regulate, such general grounds are not enough to support Missouri's claim. Valid treaties, of course, "are as binding within the territorial limits of the states as they are effective throughout the dominion of the United States." . . . No doubt the great body of private relations usually falls within the control of the state, but a treaty may override its power. . . .

Here a national interest of very nearly the first magnitude is involved. It can be protected only by national action in concert with that of another power. The subject-matter is only transitorily within the state, and has no permanent habitat therein. But for the treaty and the statute, there soon might be no birds for any powers to deal with. We see nothing in the Constitution that compels the government to sit by while a food supply is cut off and the protectors of our forests and of our crops are destroyed. It is not sufficient to rely upon the states. The reliance is vain, and were it otherwise, the question is whether the United States is forbidden to act. We are of opinion that the treaty and statute must be upheld. . . .

Decree affirmed.

MR. JUSTICE VAN DEVANTER and MR. JUSTICE PITNEY dissent.

Ware v. *Hylton*, 3 Dall. 199 (1796), overruled a Virginia statute that permitted confiscation of alien property in violation of the terms of a treaty. A similar Virginia statute was overruled as a violation of a treaty in *Hauenstein* v. *Lynham*, 100 U.S. 483 (1880). These and other cases have supported treaties as "the supreme law of the land" that take precedence over contrary state laws. Considerations of federalism, then, have been held inadequate to override treaties. In 1890 Justice Field wrote, in *Geofroy* v. *Riggs*,

> The treaty power, as expressed in the Constitution, is in terms unlimited except by those restraints which are found in that instrument against the action of the government or of its departments, and those arising from the nature of the government itself and of that of the states. It would not be contended that it extends so far as to authorize what the Constitution forbids, or a change in the character of the government or in that of one of the states, or a cession of any portion of the territory of the latter without its consent . . . but with these exceptions, it is not perceived that there is any limit to the questions which can be adjusted touching any matter which is properly the subject of negotiation with a foreign country.[16]

The potential authority of Congress to expand its power beyond explicit or implied constitutional provisions, and particularly the implications of *Missouri* v. *Holland* that states' rights and the reserved powers of the states were insufficient to prevent a federal invasion of the spheres of the states based upon treaties, led some conservatives to support the "Bricker amendment" in the early 1950s, sponsored by Senator John Bricker of Ohio. There had been some grass roots agitation for such an amendment, including petitions from state legislatures and recommendations of the American Bar Association for an amendment to provide that "a provision of a treaty that conflicts with any provision of this Constitution shall not be of any force and effect." The amendment was not only aimed at protecting states' rights but at curb-

---

[16]Geofroy v. Riggs, 133 U.S. 258, 267 (1890).

ing the discretion of the President to make executive agreements. It provided the following:

Section 1. A provision of a treaty which conflicts with this Constitution shall not be of any force and effect.

Section 2. A treaty shall become effective as internal law only through legislation which would be valid in the absence of a treaty.

Section 3. Congress shall have the power to regulate all executive and other agreements with any foreign power or international organization. All such agreements shall be subject to the limitations imposed on treaties by this article.

The Bricker amendment stirred intense controversy. Its proponents, however, had little chance of securing congressional approval of such a drastic constitutional change, and the amendment eventually vanished from the political scene. Justice Black's majority opinion in *Reid* v. *Covert* in 1957 at least partially assuaged the fears of those who were concerned that Congress in combination with the executive could exceed constitutional limits by exercising power based on treaties or executive agreements.

Missouri v. *Holland* held that states could not rely upon their reserved powers to overturn congressional legislation based upon a treaty. Unlike treaties, executive agreements are negotiated and approved unilaterally by the President, although they may be submitted to Congress for approval by a majority of the House and the Senate. Would the Court accord the same constitutional status to executive agreements as it did to treaties in the *Missouri* case, when confronted with a state challenge? The issue arose in *United States* v. *Belmont* (1937). As part of the agreement with the Soviet Union leading to recognition in 1933, President Roosevelt secured from Maxim Litvinov, the representative of the Soviet Union, the assignment to the United States of all funds held by Americans in Russian corporations that were claimed by the Soviet Union. The purpose of the "Litvinov assignment" was to protect the property of American citizens, guaranteeing them payment before assets in which they had an interest were distributed either to the Soviet government as a result of its nationalization decrees or to foreign creditors of Russian corporations. The Court noted in the *Belmont* case that the "recognition [of the Soviet Union], establishment of diplomatic relations, the [Litvinov] assignment, and agreements with respect thereto, were all parts of one transaction, resulting in an international compact between the two governments." The terms of this international compact conflicted with the laws of New York State, which had established standards for the distribution of the assets of corporations doing business in the state to both American citizens and foreign creditors. The *Belmont* case involved a suit by the United States to recover the funds that a Russian corporation had deposited in a New York bank, in violation of the terms of the international compact negotiated by President Roosevelt.

United States v. Belmont

301 U.S. 324; 57 S. Ct. 758; 81 L. Ed. 1134 (1937)

MR. JUSTICE SUTHERLAND delivered the opinion of the Court:

First. We do not pause to inquire whether in fact there was any policy of the State of New York to be infringed, since we are of opinion that no state policy can prevail against the international compact here involved.

This Court has held that every sovereign state must recognize the independence of every other sovereign state; and that the courts of one will not sit in judgment upon the acts of the government of another, done within its own territory. . . . This Court held that the conduct of foreign relations was committed by the Constitution to the political departments of the government, and the propriety of what may be done in the exercise of this political power was not subject to judicial inquiry or decision; that who is the sovereign of a territory is not a judicial question, but one the determination of which by the political departments conclusively binds the courts; and that recognition by these departments is retroactive and validates all actions and conduct of the government so recognized from the commencement of its existence. . . .

We take judicial notice of the fact that coincident with the assignment set forth in the complaint, the President recognized the Soviet Government, and normal diplomatic relations were established between that government and the Government of the United States, followed by an exchange of ambassadors. The effect of this was to validate, so far as this country is concerned, all acts of the Soviet Government here involved from the commencement of its existence. The recognition, establishment of diplomatic relations, the assignment, and agreements with respect thereto, were all parts of one transaction, resulting in an international compact between the two governments. That the negotiations, acceptance of the assignment and agreements and understandings in respect thereof were within the competence of the President may not be doubted. Governmental power over internal affairs is distributed between the national government and the several states. Governmental power over external affairs is not distributed, but is vested exclusively in the national government. And in respect of what was done here, the Executive had authority to speak as the sole organ of that government. The assignment and the agreements in connection therewith did not, as in the case of treaties, as that term is used in the treaty making clause of the Constitution (Art. II, § 2), require the advice and consent of the Senate.

A treaty signifies "a compact made between two or more independent nations with a view to the public welfare." . . . But an international compact, as this was, is not always a treaty which requires the participation of the Senate. There are many such compacts, of which a protocol, a modus vivendi, a postal convention, and agreements like that now under consideration are illustrations. . . . The distinction was pointed out by this Court in the *Altman* case [1912], which arose under § 3 of the Tariff Act of 1897, authorizing the President to conclude commercial agreements with foreign countries in certain specified matters. We held that although this might not be a treaty requiring ratification by the Senate, it was a compact negotiated and proclaimed under the authority of the President, and as such was a "treaty" within the meaning of the Circuit Court of Appeals Act, the construction of which might be reviewed upon direct appeal to this Court.

Plainly, the external powers of the United States are to be exercised without regard to state laws or policies. The supremacy of a treaty in this respect has been recognized from the beginning. Mr. Madison, in the Virginia Convention, said that if a treaty does not supersede existing state laws, as far as they contravene its operation, the treaty would be ineffective. "To counteract it by the supremacy of the state laws, would bring on the Union the just charge of national perfidy, and involve us in war." . . . And while this rule in respect of treaties is established by the express language of cl. 2, Art. VI, of the Constitution, the same rule would result in the case of all international compacts and agreements from the very fact that complete power over international affairs is in the national government and is not and cannot be subject to any curtailment or interference on the part of the several states. . . . In respect of all international negotiations and compacts, and in respect of our foreign relations generally, state lines disappear. As to such purposes the State of New York does not exist. Within the field of its powers, whatever the United States rightfully undertakes, it necessarily has warrant to consummate. And when judicial authority is invoked in aid of such consummation, state constitutions, state laws, and state policies are irrelevant to the inquiry and decision. It is inconceivable that any of them can be in-terposed as an obstacle to the effective operation of a federal constitutional power. . . .

Second. The public policy of the United States relied upon as a bar to the action is that declared by the Constitution, namely, that private property shall not be taken without just compensation. But the answer is that our Constitution, laws and policies have no extraterritorial operation, unless in respect of our own citizens. . . . What another country has done in the way of taking over property of its nationals, and especially of its corporations, is not a matter for judicial consideration here. Such nationals must look to their own government for any redress to which they may be entitled. So far as the record shows, only the rights of the Russian corporation have been affected by what has been done; and it will be time enough to consider the rights of our nationals when, if ever, by proper judicial proceeding, it shall be made to appear that they are so affected as to entitle them to judicial relief. The substantive right to the moneys, as now disclosed, became vested in the Soviet Government as the successor to the corporation; and this right that government has passed to the United States. It does not appear that respondents have any interest in the matter beyond that of a custodian. Thus far no question under the Fifth Amendment is involved. . . .

Judgment Reversed

JUSTICES STONE, BRANDEIS, and CARDOZO concurred.

The question in the *Belmont* case was not whether the Constitution could overrule an executive agreement or treaty but whether state laws or policies could supersede international agreements. The Court stated that the conduct of foreign relations is within the discretion of the political departments of government and that the question of who is the sovereign of a territory is not subject to judicial review. What would the Courts have done if under the terms of the international compact with the Soviet Union the assets of Americans in Russian corporations had been made subject to Soviet confiscation?

United States v. *Pink,* 315 U.S. 203 (1942), buttressed the *Belmont* decision. There the issue was also one of conflict between New York State law and the international agreement that was part of the United States recognition of the Soviet Union. The State of New York wanted to distribute the assets of a Russian corporation to its foreign creditors. The majority opinion written by Justice Douglas stated that the power of the President "includes the power to determine the policy which is to govern the question of recognition."[17] Douglas continued: "We would usurp the executive function if we held that that decision [the international agreement and the Litvinov assignment] was not final and conclusive in the courts."[18] The *Pink* decision was an unequivocal statement of the doctrine of national supremacy and of the broad scope of presidential prerogatives in international affairs. However, Douglas implied that treaties and executive agreements were not entirely outside of the scrutiny of the courts, and considerations of federalism would be taken into account upon judicial review. Douglas stated that "It is, of course, true that even treaties with foreign nations will be carefully construed so as not to derogate from the authority and jurisdiction of the states of this nation unless clearly necessary to effectuate the national policy."[19] The major import of the *Pink* decision, however, was stated by Douglas in his conclusion.

> We repeat that there are limitations on the sovereignty of the states. No state can rewrite our foreign policy to conform to its own domestic policies. Power over external affairs is not shared by the states; it is vested in the national government exclusively. It need not be so exercised as to conform to state laws or state policies, whether they be expressed in constitutions, statutes, or judicial decrees. And the policies of the states become wholly irrelevant to judicial inquiry when the United States, acting within its constitutional sphere, seeks enforcement of its foreign policy in the courts.[20]

CONGRESSIONAL POWERS INCIDENTAL TO LAWMAKING

Just as the Constitution governs the scope of the substantive powers exercised by Congress, it controls certain aspects of the procedures Congress may employ in lawmaking.[21] Congress from its beginning has claimed and used the power to conduct investigations and require testimony from wit-

[17]United States v. Pink, 315 U.S. 203, 229 (1942).
[18]Ibid., p. 230.
[19]Ibid., p. 230.
[20]Ibid., pp. 233–234.
[21]Similarly, of course, the Constitution controls the procedures that may be used by the President and the administrative branch.

nesses. Congress has the power to cite recalcitrant witnesses for contempt by a simple resolution of the House or the Senate and to punish such persons by imprisonment for the duration of the session of the Congress that cited for contempt. The Compulsory Testimony Act of 1857 provided an alternative contempt procedure for Congress, by making it a crime for persons subpoenaed by Congress or one of its committees to refuse to testify or answer questions, with a maximum penalty of a $1000 fine or imprisonment for one year. When the House or Senate wishes to invoke the statute it passes a resolution recommending to the United States Attorney in the District of Columbia that an indictment be made in the Federal District Court for contempt of Congress.

The Court has defined the scope of the investigatory and contempt power of Congress in several cases. *Anderson* v. *Dunn,* 6 Wheat. 204 (1821), upheld the direct contempt authority of Congress without resort to the courts. In *Kilbourn* v. *Thompson,* 103 U.S. 168 (1881), the conviction of a person for refusing to testify in a congressional investigation of the financial dealings of Jay Cook and Company was overturned. The Court held that Congress does not have a "general power of making inquiry into the private affairs of the citizen" and that the investigative authority of Congress is limited to matters over which it has jurisdiction. Writing for the Court in the *Kilbourn* case, Justice Miller was particularly concerned that the resolution authorizing the investigation contained no mention of possible legislation that would result from the inquiry.

The scope of congressional authority to conduct investigations was again challenged in *McGrain* v. *Daugherty,* 273 U.S. 135 (1927). The Senate had undertaken an investigation of Attorney General Daugherty's administration of the Justice Department under President Warren G. Harding. Daugherty was accused of dereliction of duty for failing to prosecute Harding administration officials involved in the Teapot Dome and other scandals, as well as for failure to enforce the antitrust laws. During the course of its investigation the Senate committee subpoenaed Mally S. Daugherty, the brother of the Attorney General, to testify on the Attorney General's conduct. When the brother failed to appear, the Senate voted to issue a warrant directing its sergeant-at-arms to arrest him and bring him before the committee to testify. McGrain was the deputy sergeant-at-arms who made the arrest. Daugherty's brother then successfully sought a writ of habeas corpus in the federal district court, which ordered his release because, it said, "The Senate's action is invalid and absolutely void in that, in ordering and conducting the investigation it is exercising the judicial function, and power to exercise that function, in such a case as we have here, has not been conferred upon it expressly or by fair implication."[22] The Senate has put the Attorney General on trial, said the district court, and its investigation was not for legitimate purposes of legislation.

On appeal to the Supreme Court the district court was overruled and the action of the Senate upheld. The Court found that while it was true that the Senate resolution directing the investigation "does not in terms avow that it

---

[22]McGrain v. Daugherty, 273 U.S. 135, 177 (1927).

is intended to be in aid of legislation," the subject of the investigation—the administration of the Justice Department—is a legitimate concern of Congress. "Plainly," the Court said,

> the subject was one on which legislation could be had and would be materially aided by the information which the investigation was calculated to elicit. This becomes manifest when it is reflected that the functions of the Department of Justice, the powers and duties of the Attorney General, and the duties of his assistants are all subject to regulation by congressional legislation and that the department is maintained and its activities are carried on under such appropriations as in the judgment of Congress are needed from year to year. [Therefore, the] only legitimate object the Senate could have in ordering the investigation was to aid it in legislating; and we think the subject matter was such that the presumption should be indulged that this was the real object.[23]

The creation of a Committee on Un-American Activities in 1938 by the House of Representatives eventually raised new problems concerning the powers of Congress to investigate.[24] The mandate of the committee was both broad and vague, authorizing it to investigate all aspects of subversive activities and "all other questions in relation thereto that would aid the Congress in any necessary remedial legislation." While the committee was controversial from the very beginning, used more to conduct inquisitorial trials than serious investigations for legislative purposes, it was during the 1950s that the committee came under particularly strong attacks by those who felt that it was conducting "witch hunts" that violated individual rights.

The *Watkins* case involved an appeal from a contempt conviction of a labor union official who had been called to testify before the Un-American Activities Committee. He agreed to testify about his political activities and those of current members of the party. However, he told the committee, "I am not going to plead the Fifth Amendment, but I refuse to answer certain questions that I believe are outside the proper scope of your committee's activities." He then declined to testify about former party members. Could the Court adequately deal with the issue on the basis of the former cases that had defined the scope of congressional investigative power? Or were there new considerations involved requiring the Court to develop a fresh approach in deciding the case?

Watkins v. *United States*

354 U.S. 178; 77 S. Ct. 1173; 1 L. Ed. 2d 1273 (1957)

Mr. Chief Justice Warren delivered the opinion of the Court:

. . . We start with several basic premises on which there is general agreement. The power of the Congress to conduct investigations is inherent in the legislative process. That power is broad. It encompasses inquiries concerning the administration of

---

[23]Ibid., pp. 177–178.

[24]The committee became a permanent standing committee in 1945. In 1969 its name was changed to the Committee on Internal Security, which was abolished in 1975.

existing laws as well as proposed or possibly needed statutes. It includes surveys of defects in our social, economic or political system for the purpose of enabling the Congress to remedy them. It comprehends probes into departments of the Federal Government to expose corruption, inefficiency or waste. But broad as is this power of inquiry, it is not unlimited. There is no general authority to expose the private affairs of individuals without justification in terms of the functions of the Congress. This was freely conceded by the Solicitor General in his argument of this case. Nor is the Congress a law enforcement or trial agency. These are functions of the executive and judicial departments of government. No inquiry is an end in itself; it must be related to and in furtherance of a legitimate task of the Congress. Investigations conducted solely for the personal aggrandizement of the investigators or to "punish" those investigated are indefensible.

It is unquestionably the duty of all citizens to cooperate with the Congress in its efforts to obtain the facts needed for intelligent legislative action. It is their unremitting obligation to respond to subpoenas, to respect the dignity of the Congress and its committees and to testify fully with respect to matters within the province of proper investigation. This, of course, assumes that the constitutional rights of witnesses will be respected by the Congress as they are in a court of justice.

The Bill of Rights is applicable to investigations as to all forms of governmental action. Witnesses cannot be compelled to give evidence against themselves. They cannot be subjected to unreasonable search and seizure. Nor can the First Amendment freedoms of speech, press, religion, or political belief and association be abridged. . . .

In the decade following World War II, there appeared a new kind of congressional inquiry unknown in prior periods of American history. Principally this was

the result of the various investigations into the threat of subversion of the United States Government, but other subjects of congressional interest also contributed to the changed scene. This new phase of legislative inquiry involved a broad-scale intrusion into the lives and affairs of private citizens. It brought before the courts novel questions of the appropriate limits of congressional inquiry. . . . In the more recent cases, the emphasis shifted to problems of accommodating the interest of the Government with the rights and privileges of individuals. The central theme was the application of the Bill of Rights as a restraint upon the assertion of governmental power in this form.

It was during this period that the Fifth Amendment privilege against self-incrimination was frequently invoked and recognized as a legal limit upon the authority of a committee to require that a witness answer its questions. Some early doubts as to the applicability of that privilege before a legislative committee never matured. When the matter reached this Court, the Government did not challenge in any way that the Fifth Amendment protection was available to the witness, and such a challenge could not have prevailed. It confined its argument to the character of the answers sought and to the adequacy of the claim of privilege. . . .

A far more difficult task evolved from the claim by witnesses that the committees' interrogations were infringements upon the freedoms of the First Amendment. Clearly, an investigation is subject to the command that the Congress shall make no law abridging freedom of speech or press or assembly. While it is true that there is no statute to be reviewed, and that an investigation is not a law, nevertheless an investigation is part of lawmaking. It is justified solely as an adjunct to the legislative process. The First Amendment may be invoked against infringement of the protected freedoms by law or by law-making.

Abuses of the investigative process may imperceptibly lead to abridgment of protected freedoms. The mere summoning of a witness and compelling him to testify, against his will, about his beliefs, expressions or associations is a measure of governmental interference. And when those forced revelations concern matters that are unorthodox, unpopular, or even hateful to the general public, the reaction in the life of the witness may be disastrous. This effect is even more harsh when it is past beliefs, expressions or associations that are disclosed and judged by current standards rather than those contemporary with the matters exposed. Nor does the witness alone suffer the consequences. Those who are identified by witnesses and thereby placed in the same glare of publicity are equally subject to public stigma, scorn and obloquy. Beyond that, there is the more subtle and immeasurable effect upon those who tend to adhere to the most orthodox and uncontroversial views and associations in order to avoid a similar fate at some future time. That this impact is partly the result of non-governmental activity by private persons cannot relieve the investigators of their responsibility for initiating the reaction. . . .

Accommodation of the congressional need for particular information with the individual and personal interest in privacy is an arduous and delicate task for any court. We do not underestimate the difficulties that would attend such an undertaking. It is manifest that despite the adverse effects which follow upon compelled disclosure of private matters, not all such inquiries are barred. . . . The critical element is the existence of, and the weight to be ascribed to, the interest of the Congress in demanding disclosures from an unwilling witness. We cannot simply assume, however, that every congressional investigation is justified by a public need that overbalances any private rights affected. To do so would be to abdicate the responsibility placed by the

Constitution upon the judiciary to insure that the Congress does not unjustifiably encroach upon an individual's right to privacy nor abridge his liberty of speech, press, religion or assembly.

Petitioner has earnestly suggested that the difficult questions of protecting these rights from infringement by legislative inquiries can be surmounted in this case because there was no public purpose served in his interrogation. His conclusion is based upon the thesis that the Subcommittee was engaged in a program of exposure for the sake of exposure. . . .

We have no doubt that there is no congressional power to expose for the sake of exposure. The public is, of course, entitled to be informed concerning the workings of its government. That cannot be inflated into a general power to expose where the predominant result can only be an invasion of the private rights of individuals. But a solution to our problem is not to be found in testing the motives of committee members for this purpose. Such is not our function. Their motives alone would not vitiate an investigation which had been instituted by a House of Congress if that assembly's legislative purpose is being served.

. . . The theory of a committee inquiry is that the committee members are serving as the representatives of the parent assembly in collecting information for a legislative purpose. Their function is to act as the eyes and ears of the Congress in obtaining facts upon which the full legislature can act. . . .

An essential premise in this situation is that the House or Senate shall have instructed the committee members on what they are to do with the power delegated to them. It is the responsibility of the Congress, in the first instance, to insure that compulsory process is used only in furtherance of a legislative purpose. That requires that the instructions to an investigating committee spell out that group's jurisdiction and purpose with sufficient particularity. Those instructions are embodied in the authorizing resolution. That document is the committee's character. Broadly drafted and loosely worded, however, such resolutions can leave tremendous latitude to the discretion of the investigators. The more vague the committee's charter is, the greater becomes the possibility that the committee's specific actions are not in conformity with the will of the parent House of Congress.

The authorizing resolution of the Un-American Activities Committee was adopted in 1938 when a select committee, under the chairmanship of Representative Dies, was created. Several years later, the Committee was made a standing organ of the House with the same mandate. It defines the Committee's authority as follows:

"The Committee on Un-American Activities, as a whole or by subcommittee, is authorized to make from time to time investigations of (i) the extent, character, and objects of un-American propaganda activities in the United States, (ii) the diffusion within the United States of subversive and un-American propaganda that is instigated from foreign countries or of a domestic origin and attacks the principle of the form of government as guaranteed by our Constitution, and (iii) all other questions in relation thereto that would aid Congress in any necessary remedial legislation."

It would be difficult to imagine a less explicit authorizing resolution. Who can define the meaning of "un-American"? What is that single, solitary "principle of the form of government as guaranteed by our Constitution"? There is no need to dwell upon the language, however. At one time, perhaps, the resolution might have been read narrowly to confine the Committee to the subject of propaganda. The events that have transpired in the fifteen years before the interrogation of petitioner make such a construction impossible at this date.

The members of the Committee have clearly demonstrated that they did not feel themselves restricted in any way to propaganda in the narrow sense of the word. Unquestionably the Committee conceived of its task in the grand view of its name. Un-American activities were its target, no matter how or where manifested. Notwithstanding the broad purview of the Committee's experience, the House of Representatives repeatedly approved its continuation. . . .

Combining the language of the resolution with the construction it has been given, it is evident that the preliminary control of the Committee exercised by the House of Representatives is slight or nonexistent. No one could reasonably deduce from the charter the kind of investigation that the Committee was directed to make. As a result, we are asked to engage in a process of retroactive rationalization. Looking backward from the events that transpired, we are asked to uphold the Committee's actions unless it appears that they were clearly not authorized by the charter. As a corollary to this inverse approach, the Government urges that we must view the matter hospitably to the power of the Congress—that if there is any legislative purpose which might have been furthered by the kind of disclosure sought, the witness must be punished for withholding it. No doubt every reasonable indulgence of legality must be accorded to the actions of a coordinate branch of our Government. But such deference cannot yield to an unnecessary and unreasonable dissipation of precious constitutional freedoms.

The Government contends that the public interest at the core of the investigations of the Un-American Activities Committee is the need by the Congress to be informed of efforts to overthrow the Government by force and violence so that adequate legislative safeguards can be erected. From this core, however, the Committee can radiate outward infinitely to any topic thought to be related in some way to armed insurrection. The outer reaches of this domain are known only by the content of "un-American activities." . . .

The consequences that flow from this situation are manifold. In the first place, a reviewing court is unable to make the kind of judgment made by the Court in *United States* v. *Rumely* [1953]. . . . The Committee is allowed, in essence, to define its own authority, to choose the direction and focus of its activities. In deciding what to do with the power that has been conferred upon them, members of the Committee may act pursuant to motives that seem to them to be the highest. Their decisions, nevertheless, can lead to ruthless exposure of private lives in order to gather data that is neither desired by the Congress nor useful to it. Yet it is impossible in this circumstance, with constitutional freedoms in jeopardy, to declare that the Committee has ranged beyond the area committed to it by its parent assembly because the boundaries are so nebulous.

More important and more fundamental than that, however, it insulates the House that has authorized the investigation from the witnesses who are subjected to the sanctions of compulsory process. There is a wide gulf between the responsibility for the use of investigative power and the actual exercise of that power. This is an especially vital consideration in assuring respect for constitutional liberties. Protected freedoms should not be placed in danger in the absence of a clear determination by the House or the Senate that a particular inquiry is justified by a specific legislative need.

. . . An excessively broad charter, like that of the House Un-American Activities Committee, places the courts in an untenable position if they are to strike a balance between the public need for a particular interrogation and the right of citizens to carry on their affairs free from unnecessary governmental interference. It is im-

possible in such a situation to ascertain whether any legislative purpose justifies the disclosures sought and, if so, the importance of that information to the Congress in furtherance of its legislative function. The reason no court can make this critical judgment is that the House of Representatives itself has never made it. Only the legislative assembly initiating an investigation can assay the relative necessity of specific disclosures.

Absence of the qualitative consideration of petitioner's questioning by the House of Representatives aggravates a serious problem, revealed in this case, in the relationship of congressional investigating committees and the witnesses who appear before them. Plainly these committees are restricted to the missions delegated to them, i.e., to acquire certain data to be used by the House or the Senate in coping with a problem that falls within its legislative sphere. No witness can be compelled to make disclosures on matters outside that area. This is a jurisdictional concept of pertinency drawn from the nature of a congressional committee's source of authority. It is not wholly different from nor unrelated to the element of pertinency embodied in the criminal statute under which petitioner was prosecuted. When the definition of jurisdictional pertinency is as uncertain and wavering as in the case of the Un-American Activities Committee, it becomes extremely difficult for the Committee to limit its inquiries to statutory pertinency.

Since World War II, the Congress has practically abandoned its original practice of utilizing the coercive sanction of contempt proceedings at the bar of the House. The sanction there imposed is imprisonment by the House until the recalcitrant witness agrees to testify or disclose the matters sought, provided that the incarceration does not extend beyond adjournment. The Congress has instead invoked the aid of the federal judicial system in protecting itself against contumacious conduct. It has become customary to refer these matters to the United States Attorneys for prosecution under criminal law.

The appropriate statute is found in 2 U.S.C. § 192. It provides:

"Every person who having been summoned as a witness by the authority of either House of Congress to give testimony or to produce papers upon any matter under inquiry before either House, or any joint committee established by a joint or concurrent resolution of the two Houses of Congress, or any committee of either House of Congress, willfully makes default, or who, having appeared, refuses to answer any question pertinent to the question under inquiry, shall be deemed guilty of a misdemeanor, punishable by a fine of not more than $1,000 nor less than $100 and imprisonment in a common jail for not less than one month nor more than twelve months."

In fulfillment of their obligation under this statute, the courts must accord to the defendants every right which is guaranteed to defendants in all other criminal cases. Among these is the right to have available, through a sufficiently precise statute, information revealing the standard of criminality before the commission of the alleged offense. Applied to persons prosecuted under § 192, this raises a special problem in that the statute defines the crime as refusal to answer "any question pertinent to the question under inquiry." Part of the standard of criminality, therefore, is the pertinency of the questions propounded to the witness.

The problem attains proportion when viewed from the standpoint of the witness who appears before a congressional committee. He must decide at the time the questions are propounded whether or not to answer. As the Court said in *Sinclair* v. *United States* [1929] . . . the witness acts at his peril. He is ". . . bound rightly to construe the statute." . . . An erroneous determination on his part, even if made in the utmost good faith, does not exculpate him if the court should later rule that the questions were pertinent to the question under inquiry.

It is obvious that a person compelled to make this choice is entitled to have knowledge of the subject to which the interrogation is deemed pertinent. That knowledge must be available with the same degree of explicitness and clarity that the Due Process Clause requires in the expression of any element of a criminal offense. The "vice of vagueness" must be avoided here as in all other crimes. There are several sources that can outline the "question under inquiry" in such a way that the rules against vagueness are satisfied. The authorizing resolution, the remarks of the chairman or members of the committee, or even the nature of the proceedings themselves might sometimes make the topic clear. This case demonstrates, however, that these sources often leave the matter in grave doubt.

The first possibility is that the authorizing resolution itself will so clearly declare the "question under inquiry" that a witness can understand the pertinency of questions asked him. The Government does not contend that the authorizing resolution of the Un-American Activities Committee could serve such a purpose. Its confusing breadth is amply illustrated by the innumerable and diverse questions into which the Committee has inquired under this charter since 1938. If the "question under inquiry" were stated with such sweeping and uncertain scope, we doubt that it would withstand an attack on the ground of vagueness. . . .

No aid is given as to the "question under inquiry" in the action of the full Committee that authorized the creation of the Subcommittee before which petitioner appeared. The Committee adopted a formal resolution giving the Chairman the power to appoint subcommittees ". . . for the purpose of performing any and all acts which the Committee as a whole is authorized to do." In effect, this was a device to enable the investigations to proceed with a quorum of one or two members and sheds no light on the relevancy of the questions asked of petitioner.

The Government believes that the topic of inquiry before the Subcommittee concerned Communist infiltration in labor. In his introductory remarks, the Chairman made reference to a bill, then pending before the Committee, which would have penalized labor unions controlled or dominated by persons who were, or had been, members of a "Communist-action" organization, as defined in the Internal Security Act of 1950. The Subcommittee, it is contended, might have been endeavoring to determine the extent of such a problem. . . .

Having exhausted the several possible indicia of the "question under inquiry," we remain unenlightened as to the subject to which the questions asked petitioner were pertinent. Certainly, if the point is that obscure after trial and appeal, it was not adequately revealed to petitioner when he had to decide at his peril whether or not to answer. Fundamental fairness demands that no witness be compelled to make such a determination with so little guidance. Unless the subject matter has been made to appear with undisputable clarity, it is the duty of the investigative body, upon objection of the witness on grounds of pertinency, to state for the record the subject under inquiry at that time and the manner in which the propounded questions are pertinent thereto. To be meaningful, the explanation must describe what the topic under inquiry is and the connective reasoning whereby the precise questions asked relate to it.

The statement of the Committee Chairman in this case, in response to petitioner's protest, was woefully inadequate to convey sufficient information as to the pertinency of the questions to the subject under inquiry. Petitioner was thus not accorded a fair opportunity to determine whether he was within his rights in refusing to answer, and his conviction is necessarily invalid under the Due Process Clause of the Fifth Amendment.

. . . The conclusions we have reached in this case will not prevent the Congress, through its committees, from obtaining any information it needs for the proper fulfillment of its role in our scheme of government. The legislature is free to determine the kinds of data that should be collected. It is only those investigations that are conducted by use of compulsory process that give rise to a need to protect the rights of individuals against illegal encroachment. That protection can be readily achieved through procedures which prevent the separation of power from responsibility and which provide the constitutional requisites of fairness for witnesses. A measure of added care on the part of the House and the Senate in authorizing the use of compulsory process and by their committees in exercising that power would suffice. That is a small price to pay if it serves to uphold the principles of limited, constitutional government without constricting the power of the Congress to inform itself.

The judgment of the Court of Appeals is reversed, and the case is remanded to the District Court with instructions to dismiss the indictment.

It is so ordered.

MR. JUSTICE BURTON and MR. JUSTICE WHITTAKER took no part in the consideration or decision of this case.

MR. JUSTICE FRANKFURTER concurred in a separate opinion.

MR. JUSTICE CLARK wrote a strong dissenting opinion.

What were Chief Justice Warren's main reasons for overturning Watkins's contempt conviction? How did he apply the due process clause of the Fifth Amendment? What limits did Warren suggest exist upon congressional investigative powers?

In light of the facts of the *Watkins* case, do you agree with the dissenting opinion of Justice Clark that

> It may be that at times the House Committee on Un-American Activities has, as the Court says, "conceived of its task in the grand view of its name." And, perhaps, as the Court indicates, the rules of conduct placed upon the committee by the House admit of individual abuse and unfairness. But that is none of our affair. So long as the object of a legislative inquiry is legitimate, and the questions propounded are pertinent thereto, it is not for the courts to interfere with the committee system of inquiry. To hold otherwise would be an infringement on the power given the Congress to inform itself, and thus a trespass upon the fundamental American principle of separation of powers. The majority has substituted the judiciary as the grand inquisitor and supervisor of congressional investigations. It has never been so. . . .[25]

A companion case to *Watkins* v. *United States* was *Sweezy* v. *New Hampshire*, 354 U.S. 234 (1957). Decided on the same day as the *Watkins* decision, the Court overturned a New Hampshire contempt conviction of a state university professor for failing to answer questions from the attorney general covering a wide range of matters including Socialist party affiliations and the content of his lectures. The state legislature had authorized the attorney general to act as a one-man committee to conduct investigations into subversive activities. Warren held that the legislative charge was too vague and that there was no clear intent that the legislature had authorized the attorney general to ask the questions he did. Warren wrote: "The lack of any indications that the legislature wanted the information the Attorney General attempted to elicit from petitioner must be treated as the absence of authority. It follows that the use of the contempt power, notwithstanding the interference with constitutional rights, was not in accordance with the due process requirements of the Fourteenth Amendment."[26]

The scope of the investigative authority of Congress again arose in *Barenblatt* v. *United States* (1959). Barenblatt was called as a witness before the House Un-American Activities Committee which was investigating Communism in higher education. Claiming First Amendment protection, Barenblatt refused to answer the committee's questions and was convicted for contempt under 2 U.S.C. sect. 192, the Compulsory Testimony Act of 1857. The Supreme Court granted certiorari to review a unanimous opinion of the court of appeals upholding Barenblatt's contempt conviction. Relying upon the *Watkins* precedent, Barenblatt pleaded before the Supreme Court that "because of the vagueness of the [House Un-American Activities] committee's mandate, it is . . . clear that the use of compulsory process and the contempt conviction based thereon violates petitioner's constitutional rights. Under

[25]Watkins v. United States, 354 U.S. 178, 218 (1957).
[26]Sweezy v. New Hampshire, 354 U.S. 234, 254–255 (1957).

due process of law no one can be required to respond to governmental authority delegated in language as vague and meaningless as that of the House resolution and the statute."[27] Barenblatt claimed that Congress "did not authorize the committee to conduct by compulsory process an investigation in the field of education."[28] The committee's interference with First Amendment rights, said Barenblatt, "was not justified by a legislative purpose."[29]

Replying to Barenblatt's argument, the Solicitor General, in support of the authority of Congress to conduct broad investigations into Communism, stated: "That Congress itself has the power to inquire into, and to legislate with respect to, the subjects of Communism and the Communist party, in areas in which they may have an impact, is, we submit, well settled. . . ."[30] While the Supreme Court in the *Watkins* case had criticized the resolution creating the committee, argued the Solicitor General, this did not invalidate the committee's mandate. That mandate "clearly authorizes the committee to inquire into the subject of Communism and Communist activities. To that extent, at the least, it cannot be said that there was 'an absence of authority for any legislation.' "[31] The Solicitor General concluded that "The committee had a valid legislative purpose in interrogating petitioner which outweighed his interest in nondisclosure."[32]

On the basis of the *Watkins* decision, and taking into account the arguments of Barenblatt and the United States, how would you have decided the case?

Barenblatt v. United States

360 U.S. 109; 79 S. Ct. 1081; 3 L. Ed. 2d 1115 (1959)

MR. JUSTICE HARLAN delivered the opinion of the Court:

Once more the Court is required to resolve the conflicting constitutional claims of congressional power and of an individual's right to resist its exercise. The congressional power in question concerns the internal process of Congress in moving within its legislative domain; it involves the utilization of its committees to secure "testimony needed to enable it efficiently to exercise a legislative function belonging to it under the Constitution." *McGrain* v. *Daugherty* [1927]. . . . The power

of inquiry has been employed by Congress throughout our history, over the whole range of the national interests concerning which Congress might legislate or decide upon due investigation not to legislate; it has similarly been utilized in determining what to appropriate from the national purse, or whether to appropriate. The scope of the power of inquiry, in short, is as penetrating and far-reaching as the potential power to enact and appropriate under the Constitution.

Broad as it is, the power is not, however, without limitations. Since Congress

[27]LB, Vol. 5, pp. 20–21.
[28]Ibid., p. 25.
[29]Ibid., p. 50.
[30]Ibid., p. 22.
[31]Ibid., p. 38.
[32]Ibid., p. 61.

may only investigate into those areas in which it may potentially legislate or appropriate, it cannot inquire into matters which are within the exclusive province of one of the other branches of the Government. Lacking the judicial power given to the Judiciary, it cannot inquire into matters that are exclusively the concern of the Judiciary. Neither can it supplant the Executive in what exclusively belongs to the Executive. And the Congress, in common with all branches of the Government, must exercise its powers subject to the limitations placed by the Constitution on governmental action, more particularly in the context of this case the relevant limitations of the Bill of Rights.

The congressional power of inquiry, its range and scope, and an individual's duty in relation to it, must be viewed in proper perspective. . . . The power and the right of resistance to it are to be judged in the concrete, not on the basis of abstractions. In the present case congressional efforts to learn the extent of a nationwide, indeed world wide, problem have brought one of its investigating committees into the field of education. Of course, broadly viewed, inquiries cannot be made into the teaching that is pursued in any of our educational institutions. When academic teaching-freedom and its corollary learning-freedom, so essential to the well-being of the Nation, are claimed, this Court will always be on the alert against intrusion by Congress into this constitutionally protected domain. But this does not mean that the Congress is precluded from interrogating a witness merely because he is a teacher. An educational institution is not a constitutional sanctuary from inquiry into matters that may otherwise be within the constitutional legislative domain merely for the reason that inquiry is made of someone within its walls.

In the setting of this framework of constitutional history, practice and legal precedents, we turn to the particularities of this case.

We here review petitioner's conviction under 2 U.S.C. § 192 for contempt of Congress, arising from his refusal to answer certain questions put to him by a Subcommittee of the House Committee on Un-American Activities during the course of an inquiry concerning alleged Communist infiltration into the field of education. . . .

Petitioner's various contentions resolve themselves into three propositions: First, the compelling of testimony by the Subcommittee was neither legislatively authorized nor constitutionally permissible because of the vagueness of Rule XI of the House of Representatives, Eighty-third Congress, the charter of authority of the parent Committee. Second, petitioner was not adequately apprised of the pertinency of the Subcommittee's questions to the subject matter of the inquiry. Third, the questions petitioner refused to answer infringed rights protected by the First Amendment.

SUBCOMMITTEE'S AUTHORITY TO COMPEL TESTIMONY

At the outset it should be noted that Rule XI authorized this Subcommittee to compel testimony within the framework of the investigative authority conferred on the Un-American Activities Committee. Petitioner contends that *Watkins* v. *United States* nevertheless held the grant of this power in all circumstances ineffective because of the vagueness of Rule XI in delineating the Committee jurisdiction to which its exercise was to be appurtenant. This view of *Watkins* was accepted by two of the dissenting judges below.

The *Watkins* case cannot properly be read as standing for such a proposition. A principal contention in *Watkins* was that the refusals to answer were justified because the requirement of 2 U.S.C. § 192 that the questions asked be "pertinent to the question under inquiry" had not been satisfied. . . . This Court reversed the conviction solely on that ground, holding that Watkins had not been adequately apprised of the subject matter of the Subcommittee's investigation or the pertinency thereto of the questions he refused to answer. . . . In so deciding the Court drew upon Rule XI only as one of the facets in the total mise en scène in its search for the "question under inquiry" in that particular investigation. . . . The Court, in other words, was not dealing with Rule XI at large, and indeed in effect stated that no such issue was before it. . . . That the vagueness of Rule XI was not alone determinative is also shown by the Court's further statement that aside from the Rule "the remarks of the chairman or members of the committee, or even the nature of the proceedings themselves, might sometimes make the topic [under inquiry] clear." In short, while *Watkins* was critical of Rule XI, it did not involve the broad and inflexible holding petitioner now attributes to it.

Petitioner also contends, independently of *Watkins*, that the vagueness of Rule XI deprived the Subcommittee of the right to compel testimony in this investigation into Communist activity. We cannot agree with this contention, which in its furthest reach would mean that the House Un-American Activities Committee under its existing authority has no right to compel testimony in any circumstances. Granting the vagueness of the Rule, we may not read it in isolation from its long history in the House of Representatives. Just as legislation is often given meaning by the gloss of legislative reports, administrative interpretation, and long usage, so the proper meaning of an authorization to a congressional committee is not to be derived alone from its abstract terms unrelated to the definite content furnished them by the course of congressional actions. The Rule comes to us with a "persuasive gloss of legislative history," . . . which shows beyond doubt that in pursuance of its legislative concerns in the domain of "national

security" the House has clothed the Un-American Activities Committee with pervasive authority to investigate Communist activities in this country. . . .

In the context of these unremitting pursuits, the House has steadily continued the life of the Committee at the commencement of each new Congress; it has never narrowed the powers of the Committee, whose authority has remained throughout identical with that contained in Rule XI; and it has continuingly supported the Committee's activities with substantial appropriations. Beyond this, the Committee was raised to the level of a standing committee of the House in 1945, it having been but a special committee prior to that time.

In light of this long and illuminating history it can hardly be seriously argued that the investigation of Communist activities generally, and the attendant use of compulsory process, was beyond the purview of the Committee's intended authority under Rule XI.

We are urged, however, to construe Rule XI so as at least to exclude the field of education from the Committee's compulsory authority. . . .

In this framework of the Committee's history we must conclude that its legislative authority to conduct the inquiry presently under consideration is unassailable, and that independently of whatever bearing the broad scope of Rule XI may have on the issue of "pertinency" in a given investigation into Communist activities, as in *Watkins*, the Rule cannot be said to be constitutionally infirm on the score of vagueness. The constitutional permissibility of that authority otherwise is a matter to be discussed later.

PERTINENCY CLAIM

Undeniably a conviction for contempt under 2 U.S.C. § 192 cannot stand unless the questions asked are pertinent to the subject matter of the investigation. *Wat-*

kins v. *United States.* But the factors which led us to rest decision on this ground in *Watkins* were very different from those involved here.

In *Watkins* the petitioner had made specific objection to the Subcommittee's questions on the ground of pertinency; the question under inquiry had not been disclosed in any illuminating manner; and the questions asked the petitioner were not only amorphous on their face, but in some instances clearly foreign to the alleged subject matter of the investigation—"Communism in labor." . . .

In contrast, petitioner in the case before us raised no objections on the ground of pertinency at the time any of the questions were put to him. . . .

We need not, however, rest decision on petitioner's failure to object on this score, for here "pertinency" was made to appear "with undisputable clarity." . . .

First of all, it goes without saying that the scope of the Committee's authority was for the House, not a witness, to determine, subject to the ultimate reviewing responsibility of this Court. What we deal with here is whether petitioner was sufficiently apprised of "the topic under inquiry" thus authorized "and the connective reasoning whereby the precise questions asked relate[d] to it." . . .

In light of his prepared memorandum of constitutional objections there can be no doubt that this petitioner was well aware of the Subcommittee's authority and purpose to question him as it did. . . . In addition the other sources of this information which we recognized in *Watkins* . . . leave no room for a "pertinency" objection on this record. The subject matter of the inquiry had been identified at the commencement of the investigation as Communist infiltration into the field of education. Just prior to petitioner's appearance before the Subcommittee, the scope of the day's hearings had been announced as "in the main Communism in education and the experiences and background in the party by Francis X. T. Crowley. It will deal with activities in Michigan, Boston, and in some small degree, New York." Petitioner had heard the Subcommittee interrogate the witness Crowley along the same lines as he, petitioner, was evidently to be questioned, and had listened to Crowley's testimony identifying him as a former member of an alleged Communist student organization at the University of Michigan while they both were in attendance there. Further, petitioner had stood mute in the face of the Chairman's statement as to why he had been called as a witness by the Subcommittee. And, lastly, unlike *Watkins,* . . . petitioner refused to answer questions as to his own Communist Party affiliations, whose pertinency of course was clear beyond doubt.

Petitioner's contentions on this aspect of the case cannot be sustained.

CONSTITUTIONAL CONTENTIONS

Our function, at this point, is purely one of constitutional adjudication in the particular case and upon the particular record before us, not to pass judgment upon the general wisdom or efficacy of the activities of this Committee in a vexing and complicated field.

The precise constitutional issue confronting us is whether the Subcommittee's inquiry into petitioner's past or present membership in the Communist Party transgressed the provisions of the First Amendment, which of course reach and limit congressional investigations. *Watkins.* . . .

The Court's past cases establish sure guides to decision. Undeniably, the First Amendment in some circumstances protects an individual from being compelled to disclose his associational relationships. However, the protections of the First Amendment, unlike a proper claim of the privilege against self-incrimination under the Fifth Amendment, do not afford a witness the right to resist inquiry in all circumstances. Where First Amendment rights are asserted to bar governmental interrogation resolution of the issue always involves a balancing by the courts of the competing private and public interests at stake in the particular circumstances shown. These principles were recognized in the *Watkins Case*. . . .

The first question is whether this investigation was related to a valid legislative purpose, for Congress may not constitutionally require an individual to disclose his political relationships or other private affairs except in relation to such a purpose. See *Watkins* v. *United States*. . . .

That Congress has wide power to legislate in the field of Communist activity in this Country, and to conduct appropriate investigations in aid thereof, is hardly debatable. The existence of such power has never been questioned by this Court, and it is sufficient to say, without particularization, that Congress has enacted or considered in this field a wide range of legislative measures, not a few of which have stemmed from recommendations of the very Committee whose actions have been drawn in question here. In the last analysis this power rests on the right of self-preservation, "the ultimate value of any society," *Dennis* v. *United States*. . . . Justification for its exercise in turn rests on the long and widely accepted view that the tenets of the Communist Party include the ultimate overthrow of the Government of the United States by force and violence, a view which has been given formal expression by the Congress. . . .

. . . To suggest that because the Communist Party may also sponsor peaceable political reforms the constitutional issues before us should now be judged as if that Party were just an ordinary political party from the standpoint of national security, is to ask this Court to blind itself to world affairs which have determined the whole course of our national policy since the close of World War II, . . . and to the vast burdens which these conditions have entailed for the entire Nation.

We think that investigatory power in this domain is not to be denied Congress solely because the field of education is involved. Nothing in the prevailing opinions in *Sweezy* v. *New Hampshire* . . . stands for a contrary view. The vice existing there was that the questioning of Sweezy, who had not been shown ever to have been connected with the Communist Party, as to the contents of a lecture he had given at the University of New Hampshire, and as to his connections with the Progressive Party, then on the ballot as a normal political party in some 26 States, was too far removed from the premises on which the constitutionality of the State's investigation had to depend to withstand attack under the Fourteenth Amendment. . . . This is a very different thing from inquiring into the extent to which the Communist Party has succeeded in infiltrating into our universities, or elsewhere, persons and groups committed to furthering the objective of overthrow. Indeed we do not understand petitioner here to suggest that Congress in no circumstances may inquire into Communist activity in the field of education.

Rather, his position is in effect that this particular investigation was aimed not at the revolutionary aspects but at the theoretical classroom discussion of communism.

In our opinion this position rests on a too constricted view of the nature of the investigatory process, and is not supported by a fair assessment of the record before us. An investigation of advocacy of or preparation for overthrow certainly embraces the right to identify a witness as a member of the Communist Party . . . and to inquire into the various manifestations of the Party's tenets. The strict requirements of a prosecution under the

Smith Act, see *Dennis* v. *United States* . . . and *Yates* v. *United States,* . . . are not the measure of the permissible scope of a congressional investigation into "overthrow," for of necessity the investigatory process must proceed step by step. Nor can it fairly be concluded that this investigation was directed at controlling what is being taught at our universities rather than at overthrow. The statement of the Subcommittee Chairman at the opening of the investigation evinces no such intention, and so far as this record reveals nothing thereafter transpired which would justify our holding that the thrust of the investigation later changed. The record discloses considerable testimony concerning the foreign domination and revolutionary purposes and efforts of the Communist Party. That there was also testimony on the abstract philosophical level does not detract from the dominant theme of this investigation—Communist infiltration furthering the alleged ultimate purpose of overthrow. And certainly the conclusion would not be justified that the questioning of petitioner would have exceeded permissible bounds had he not shut off the Subcommittee at the threshold.

Nor can we accept the further contention that this investigation should not be deemed to have been in furtherance of a legislative purpose because the true objective of the Committee and of the Congress was purely "exposure." So long as Congress acts in pursuance of its constitutional power, the Judiciary lacks authority to intervene on the basis of the motives which spurred the exercise of that power. . . . "It is, of course, true," as was said in *McCray* v. *United States* [1904] "that if there be no authority in the judiciary to restrain a lawful exercise of power by another department of the government, where a wrong motive or purpose has impelled to the exertion of the power, that abuses of a power conferred may be temporarily effectual. The remedy for this,

however, lies, not in the abuse by the judicial authority of its functions, but in the people, upon whom, after all, under our institutions, reliance must be placed for the correction of abuses committed in the exercise of a lawful power." These principles of course apply as well to committee investigations into the need for legislation as to the enactments which such investigations may produce. . . . Thus, in stating in the *Watkins* case that "there is no congressional power to expose for the sake of exposure," we at the same time declined to inquire into the "motives of committee members," and recognized that their "motives alone would not vitiate an investigation which had been instituted by a House of Congress if that assembly's legislative purpose is being served." Having scrutinized this record we cannot say that the unanimous panel of the Court of Appeals which first considered this case was wrong in concluding that "the primary purposes of the inquiry were in aid of legislative processes." 240 F2d, at 881. Certainly this is not a case like *Kilbourn* v. *Thompson* . . . where "the House of Representatives not only exceeded the limit of its own authority, but assumed a power which could only be properly exercised by another branch of the government, because it was in its nature clearly judicial." . . . The constitutional legislative power of Congress in this instance is beyond question.

Finally, the record is barren of other factors which in themselves might sometimes lead to the conclusion that the individual interests at stake were not subordinate to those of the state. There is no indication in this record that the Subcommittee was attempting to pillory witnesses. Nor did petitioner's appearance as a witness follow from indiscriminate dragnet procedures, lacking in probable cause for belief that he possessed information which might be helpful to the Subcommittee. And the relevancy of the questions put to him by the Subcommittee is not open to doubt.

We conclude that the balance between the individual and the governmental interests here at stake must be struck in favor of the latter, and that therefore the provisions of the First Amendment have not been offended.

We hold that petitioner's conviction for contempt of Congress discloses no infirmity, and that the judgment of the Court of Appeals must be

Affirmed.

Mr. Justice Black, with whom The Chief Justice and Mr. Justice Douglas concur, dissenting:

. . . The Court today affirms, and thereby sanctions the use of the contempt power to enforce questioning by congressional committees in the realm of speech and association. I cannot agree with this disposition of the case for I believe that the resolution establishing the House Un-American Activities Committee and the questions that Committee asked Barenblatt violate the Constitution in several respects. (1) Rule XI creating the Committee authorizes such a sweeping, unlimited, all-inclusive and undiscriminating compulsory examination of witnesses in the field of speech, press, petition and assembly that it violates the procedural requirements of the Due Process Clause of the Fifth Amendment. (2) Compelling an answer to the questions asked Barenblatt abridges freedom of speech and association in contravention of the First Amendment. (3) The Committee proceedings were part of a legislative program to stigmatize and punish by public identification and exposure all witnesses considered by the Committee to be guilty of Communist affiliations, as well as all witnesses who refused to answer Committee questions on constitutional grounds; the Committee was thus improperly seeking to try, con-

vict, and punish suspects, a task which the Constitution expressly denies to Congress and grants exclusively to the courts, to be exercised by them only after indictment and in full compliance with all safeguards provided by the Bill of Rights. . . .

The First Amendment says in no equivocal language that Congress shall pass no law abridging freedom of speech, press, assembly or petition. The activities of this Committee, authorized by Congress, do precisely that, through exposure, obloquy and public scorn. . . . The Court does not really deny this fact but relies on a combination of three reasons for permitting the infringement: (A) The notion that despite the First Amendment's command Congress can abridge speech and association if this Court decides that the governmental interest in abridging speech is greater than an individual's interest in exercising that freedom, (B) the Government's right to "preserve itself," (C) the fact that the Committee is only after Communists or suspected Communists in this investigation. . . .

To apply the Court's balancing test under such circumstances is to read the First Amendment to say "Congress shall pass no law abridging freedom of speech, press, assembly and petition, unless Congress and the Supreme Court reach the joint conclusion that on balance the interest of the Government in stifling these freedoms is greater than the interest of the people in having them exercised." This is closely akin to the notion that neither the First Amendment nor any other provision of the Bill of Rights should be enforced unless the Court believes it is *reasonable* to do so. Not only does this violate the genius of our *written* Constitution, but it runs expressly counter to the injunction to Court and Congress made by Madison when he introduced the Bill of Rights. "If they [the first ten amendments] are incorporated into the Constitution, independent tribunals of justice will consider themselves in a peculiar manner the guardians of those rights; they will be an impenetrable bulwark against *every* assumption of power in the Legislative or Executive; they will be naturally led to resist *every* encroachment upon rights expressly stipulated for in the Constitution by the declaration of rights." Unless we return to this view of our judicial function, unless we once again accept the notion that the Bill of Rights means what it says and that this Court must enforce that meaning, I am of the opinion that our great charter of liberty will be more honored in the breach than in the observance.

But even assuming what I cannot assume, that some balancing is proper in this case, I feel that the Court after stating the test ignores it completely. At most it balances the right of the Government to preserve itself, against Barenblatt's right to refrain from revealing Communist affiliations. Such a balance, however, mistakes the factors to be weighed. In the first place, it completely leaves out the real interest in Barenblatt's silence, the interest of the people as a whole in being able to join organizations, advocate causes and make political "mistakes" without later being subjected to governmental penalties for having dared to think for themselves. It is this right, the right to err politically, which keeps us strong as a Nation. For no number of laws against communism can have as much effect as the personal conviction which comes from having heard its arguments and rejected them, or from having once accepted its tenets and later recognized their worthlessness. Instead, the obloquy which results from investigations such as this not only stifles "mistakes" but prevents all but the most courageous from hazarding any views which might at some later time become disfavored. This result, whose importance cannot be overestimated, is dou-

bly crucial when it affects the universities, on which we must largely rely for the experimentation and development of new ideas essential to our country's welfare. It is these interests of society, rather than Barenblatt's own right to silence, which I think the Court should put on the balance against the demands of the Government, if any balancing process is to be tolerated. Instead they are not mentioned, while on the other side the demands of the Government are vastly overstated and called "self-preservation." It is admitted that this Committee can only seek information for the purpose of suggesting laws, and that Congress' power to make laws in the realm of speech and association is quite limited, even on the Court's test. Its interest in making such laws in the field of education, primarily a state function, is clearly narrower still. Yet the Court styles this attenuated interest self-preservation and allows it to overcome the need our country has to let us all think, speak, and associate politically as we like and without fear of reprisal. Such a result reduces "balancing" to a mere play on words and is completely inconsistent with the rules this Court has previously given for applying a "balancing test," where it is proper. . . .

III

Finally, I think Barenblatt's conviction violates the Constitution because the chief aim, purpose and practice of the House Un-American Activities Committee, as disclosed by its many reports, is to try witnesses and punish them because they are or have been Communists or because they refuse to admit or deny Communist affiliations. The punishment imposed is generally punishment by humiliation and public shame. There is nothing strange or novel about this kind of punishment. It is in fact one of the oldest forms of governmental punishment known to mankind;

branding, the pillory, ostracism and subjection to public hatred being but a few examples of it. Nor is there anything strange about a court's reviewing the power of a congressional committee to inflict punishment. In 1880 this Court nullified the action of the House of Representatives in sentencing a witness to jail for failing to answer questions of a congressional committee. *Kilbourn* v. *Thompson*. The Court held that the Committee in its investigation of the Jay Cooke bankruptcy was seeking to exercise judicial power, and this, it emphatically said, no committee could do. It seems to me that the proof that the Un-American Activities Committee is here undertaking a purely judicial function is overwhelming, far stronger, in fact, than it was in the Jay Cooke investigation which, moreover,

concerned only business transactions, not freedom of association. . . .

MR. JUSTICE BRENNAN, dissenting:
I would reverse this conviction. It is sufficient that I state my complete agreement with my Brother Black that no purpose for the investigation of Barenblatt is revealed by the record except exposure purely for the sake of exposure. This is not a purpose to which Barenblatt's rights under the First Amendment can validly be subordinated. An investigation in which the processes of law-making and law-evaluating are submerged entirely in exposure of individual behavior—in adjudication, of a sort, through the exposure process—is outside the constitutional pale of congressional inquiry. *Watkins* v. *United States*. . . .

Does Justice Harlan's decision in *Barenblatt* overrule the Court's opinion in *Watkins* v. *United States*? In the *Watkins* decision the Court found that the vagueness in the committee's mandate did not guarantee to the witness the necessary "standard of specificity" required by the due process clause of the Fifth Amendment. On what basis did Justice Harlan, in the *Barenblatt* opinion, uphold the resolution creating the committee? How did Harlan use the "balancing test" to support the authority of the committee to conduct investigations concerning Communist affiliation in higher education? What were Justice Black's criticisms of the application of the balancing test to the case by Justice Harlan?

A companion decision to *Barenblatt* was *Uphaus* v. *Wyman*, 360 U.S. 72 (1959), which upheld the authority of the New Hampshire attorney general to compel the executive director of World Fellowship Inc. to supply him with a list of guests at his organization's summer camp in 1954 and 1955. The attorney general was acting as a one-man investigating committee of the state legislature under authority it had delegated to him. The Court upheld the contempt conviction of Uphaus, the executive director of World Fellowship, for refusing to supply the requested guest list. Justice Clark, writing for the majority, used the balancing test to justify the Court's position. He stated that "the governmental interest in self-preservation is sufficiently compelling to subordinate the interest in associational privacy of persons who, at least to the extent of the [New Hampshire] guest registration statute [which required guests of hotels and camps to register] made public at the inception the association they now wish to keep private."[33] Justice Brennan, joined by Chief Justice Warren and Justices Black and Douglas, dissented, saying in part,

> I think I have indicated that there has been no valid legislative interest of the state actually defined and shown in the investigation as it operated, so that there is really nothing against which the appellants' rights of association and expression can be balanced. But if some proper legislative end of the inquiry can be surmised, through what must be a process of speculation, I think it is patent that there is really no subordinating interest in it demonstrated on the part of the state. . . . Here we must demand some initial showing by the state sufficient to counterbalance the interest in privacy as it relates to freedom of speech and assembly.[34]

After the *Barenblatt* decision the Court continued to affirm contempt convictions for refusal to answer questions before congressional committees. In *Wilkinson* v. *United States*, 365 U.S. 399 (1961), and *Braden* v. *United States*, 365 U.S. 431 (1961), the majority opinions of Justice Stewart upheld the contempt convictions of two journalists who had refused to answer questions before a subcommittee of the House Un-American Activities Committee. The journalists were covering the hearings of the subcommittee on Communism in southern industry that were being conducted in Atlanta, only to find themselves suddenly subpoenaed to testify on their own Communist party affiliations. The journalists invoked their rights under the Fifth Amendment and challenged the legality of the committee as well. Justice Stewart, however, found that the rights of the witnesses had not been violated, that the questions asked of them were pertinent to the inquiry, and that the investigation was pursuant to a valid legislative purpose. Justice Black, joined by Justices Douglas and Brennan, dissented, claiming that the House Un-American Activities Committee was using the contempt power to silence its critics.

Deutch v. *United States*, 367 U.S. 456 (1961), signaled the successful application of new grounds for challenging congressional inquiries. Under 2 U.S.C. Sect. 192 a person can be cited for contempt only for failing to answer questions "pertinent" to a legislative investigation. In the *Deutch* case the Court held that this *statutory* requirement was not met because "the government at the trial failed to carry its burden of proving the pertinence of the questions."[35] In *Russell* v. *United States*, 369 U.S. 749 (1962), six convictions for contempt of Congress for failure to answer questions were overturned on the basis that "the indictment returned by the grand jury failed to identify the subject under congressional subcommittee inquiry at the time the witness was interrogated."[36]

The Supreme Court limited the scope of investigations at the state level

---

[33]Uphaus v. Wyman, 360 U.S. 72, 81 (1959).
[34]Ibid., pp. 106–107.
[35]Deutch v. United States, 367 U.S. 456, 469 (1961).
[36]Russell v. United States, 369 U.S. 749, 752 (1962).

in *Gibson* v. *Florida Legislative Investigation Committee,* 372 U.S. 539 (1963). The president of the Miami branch of the NAACP was ordered to appear before the legislative committee and to bring records of the association pertaining to the identity of members and contributors. The president, Gibson, refused to bring the records but agreed to testify on the basis of his own personal knowledge of the organization. He claimed that the request of the legislative committee to produce the records of the organization violated the associational rights that had been incorporated under the due process clause of the Fourteenth Amendment. Gibson was brought before a state court and, after hearing, was held to be in contempt and was sentenced to six months in prison and fined $1200. The Supreme Court overturned the contempt conviction in a 5–4 decision. Justice Goldberg delivered the opinion of the Court, writing that

... significantly, the parties are in substantial agreement as to the proper test to be applied to reconcile the competing claims of government and individual and to determine the propriety of the committee's demands. As declared by the respondent committee in its brief to this Court, "Basically, this case hinges entirely on the question of whether the evidence before the committee [was] sufficient to show probable cause or nexus between the NAACP Miami Branch and Communist activities." We understand this to mean—regardless of the label applied, be it "nexus," "foundation," or whatever—that it is an essential prerequisite to the validity of an investigation which intrudes into the area of constitutionally protected rights of speech, press, association and petition that the state convincingly show a substantial relation between the information sought and a subject of overriding and compelling state interest. . . .

Applying these principles to the facts of this case, the respondent committee contends that the prior decisions of this Court [in *Uphouse, Barenblatt, Wilkinson,* and *Braden*] compel a result here upholding the legislative right of inquiry. In *Barenblatt, Wilkinson,* and *Braden,* however, it was a refusal to answer a question or questions concerning the witness' *own* past or present membership *in the Communist Party* which supported his conviction. It is apparent that the necessary preponderating governmental interest and, in fact, the very result in those cases were founded on the holding that the Communist Party is not an ordinary or legitimate political party, as known in this country, and that, because of its particular nature, membership therein is *itself* a permissible subject of regulation and legislative scrutiny. . . .

Here, however, it is not alleged Communists who are the witnesses before the committee, and it is not discovery of their membership in that party which is the object of the challenged inquiries. Rather, it is the NAACP itself which is the subject of the investigation. . . . Nor is there any indication that the activities or policies of the NAACP were either Communist dominated or influenced. In fact, this very record indicates that the association was and is against Communism and has voluntarily taken steps to keep Communists from being members. . . .

[Here the Court summarizes the differences between the present case and previous cases upholding the right of legislative inquiry, and points out in particular that there is no evidence in the record to support the existence of a relationship between the NAACP and subversive or Communist activities.]

... The strong associational interest in maintaining the privacy of membership lists of groups engaged in the constitutionally protected free trade in ideas and beliefs may not be substantially infringed upon such a slender showing as here made by the respondent. . . .

To permit legislative inquiry to proceed on less than an adequate foundation would be to sanction unjustified and unwarranted intrusions into the very heart of the constitutional privilege to be secure in association in legitimate organizations engaged in the exercise of First and Fourteenth Amendment rights; to impose a lesser standard than we here do would be inconsistent with the maintenance of those essential conditions basic to the preservation of our democracy. . . .[37]

Justice Harlan wrote a strong dissenting opinion, joined by Justices Clark, Stewart, and White (who also wrote a separate dissenting opinion). Harlan found ample evidence to uphold the interest of the government in investigating Communist activity in the NAACP, against the claim that such an investigation violated the right to freedom of association. In his separate dissenting opinion Justice White argued that the *Gibson* decision overruled previous cases, such as *Barenblatt*, that had properly permitted broad powers of legislative investigation into Communist activities.

PRESIDENTIAL POWERS IN FOREIGN AND MILITARY AFFAIRS

While the Court has waivered in its definition of the boundaries of inherent presidential powers in domestic affairs, in foreign and military affairs it has permitted the exercise of broad executive power based upon the Commander-in-Chief and Chief Executive clauses of Article II. *United States* v. *Curtiss-Wright Corp.* traced the historical basis for the constitutional doctrine that grants wide discretion to the President in the conduct of foreign affairs. That case, however, did not directly involve the prerogative powers of the President, but the permissible scope of congressional delegation of legislative authority to the executive to conduct foreign affairs. Justice Jackson cited *Curtiss-Wright* as an example of his category 1: "When the President acts pursuant to an express or implied authorization of Congress, his authority is at its maximum, for it includes all that he possesses in his own right plus all that Congress can delegate."

International crises and more particularly military emergencies have dictated the prerogative power of the President under Article II. For example, in April 1861, President Lincoln ordered the blockade of southern ports without congressional authorization and before Congress had declared war. Lincoln's action was tantamount to a declaration of war; however, the Constitution delegated the war-making power to Congress. The blockade was challenged in *The Prize Cases* (1863). The majority opinion of the Court admitted that "by the Constitution, Congress alone has the power to declare a national or foreign war." The President, said the Court, "has no power to initiate or declare a war either against a foreign nation or a domestic state." Such a constitutional interpretation would seem to be a formidable obstacle to upholding President Lincoln's unilateral action that ordered the blockade and a confiscation of any ships violating it.

[37]Gibson v. Florida, 372 U.S. 539, 546–558 (1963).

The Prize Cases

2 Black 635, 17 L. Ed. 459 (1863)

MR. JUSTICE GRIER delivered the opinion of the Court:

. . . There are certain propositions of law which must, necessarily, affect the ultimate decision of these cases and many others, which it will be proper to discuss and decide before we notice the special facts peculiar to each.

They are, 1st. Had the President a right to institute a blockade of ports in possession of persons in armed rebellion against the government, on the principles of international law, as known and acknowledged among civilized States?

2d. Was the property of persons domiciled or residing within those States a proper subject of capture on the seas as "enemies' property"? . . .

That a blockade de facto actually existed, and was formally declared and notified by the President on the 27th and 30th of April, 1861, is an admitted fact in these cases.

That the President, as the Executive Chief of the Government and Commander-in-Chief of the Army and Navy, was the proper person to make such notification, has not been, and cannot be disputed.

The right of prize and capture has its origin in the "jus belli," and is governed and adjudged under the laws of nations. To legitimate the capture of a neutral vessel or property on the high seas, a war must exist de facto, and the neutral must have a knowledge or notice of the intention of one of the parties belligerent to use this mode of coercion against a port, city or territory, in possession of the other.

Let us inquire whether, at this time this blockade was instituted, a state of war existed which would justify a resort to these means of subduing the hostile force.

War has been well defined to be, "That state in which a nation prosecutes its right by force."

The parties belligerent in a public war are independent nations. But it is not necessary to constitute war, that both parties should be acknowledged as independent nations or sovereign States. A war may exist where one of the belligerents claims sovereign rights as against the other.

Insurrection against a government may or may not culminate in an organized rebellion, but a civil war always begins by insurrection against the lawful authority of the government. A civil war is never solemnly declared; it becomes such by its accidents—the number, power, and organization of the persons who originate and carry it on. . . .

As a civil war is never publicly proclaimed, eo nomine against insurgents, its actual existence is a fact in our domestic history which the Court is bound to notice and to know.

The true test of its existence, as found in the writing of the sages of the common law, may be thus summarily stated: "When the regular course of justice is interrupted by revolt, rebellion or insurrection, so that the courts of justice cannot be kept open, civil war exists and hostilities may be prosecuted on the same footing as if those opposing the government were foreign enemies invading the land.

By the Constitution, Congress alone has the power to declare a national or foreign war. It cannot declare war against a State or any number of States, by virtue of any clause in the Constitution. The Constitution confers on the President the whole executive power. He is bound to take care that the laws be faithfully executed. He is Commander-in-Chief of the Army and Navy of the United States, and of the militia of the several States, when called into the actual service of the United States. He has no power to initiate or declare a war either against a foreign nation or a domestic State. But by the Acts of Congress of Feb. 28th, 1795, ch. 36 (1 Stat. at L., 424), and 3d of March, 1807, ch. 39 (2 Stat. at L., 443), he is authorized to call out the militia and use the military and naval forces of the United States in case of invasion by foreign nations, and to suppress insurrection against the government of a State or of the United States.

If a war be made by invasion of a foreign nation, the President is not only authorized but bound to resist force, by force. He does not initiate the war, but is bound to accept the challenge without waiting for any special legislative authority. And whether the hostile party be a foreign invader, or States organized in rebellion, it is none the less a war, although the declaration of it be "*unilateral.*" Lord Stowell (*The Eliza Ann,* 1 Dod., 247) observes, "It is not the less a war on that account, for war may exist without declaration on either side. It is so laid down by the best writers on the law of nations. A declaration of war by one country only, is not a mere challenge to be accepted or refused at pleasure by the other." . . .

As soon as the news of the attack on Fort Sumter, and the organization of a government by the seceding States, assuming to act as belligerents, could become known in Europe, to wit: on the 13th of May, 1861, the Queen of England issued her proclamation of neutrality, "recognizing hostilities as existing between the Government of the United States of America and certain States styling themselves the Confederate States of America." This was immediately followed by similar declarations or silent acquiescence by other nations.

After such an official recognition by the sovereign, a citizen of a foreign State is estopped to deny the existence of a war, with all its consequences, as regards neutrals. They cannot ask a court to affect a technical ignorance of the existence of a war, which all the world acknowledges to be the greatest civil war known in the history of the human race, and thus cripple the arm of the government and paralyze its power by subtle definitions and ingenious sophisms. . . .

Whether the President in fulfilling his duties, as Commander-in-Chief, in suppressing an insurrection, has met with such armed hostile resistance, and a civil war of such alarming proportions as will compel him to accord to them the character of belligerents, is a question to be decided by him, and this Court must be governed by the decisions and acts of the Political Department of the government to which this power was intrusted. "He must determine what degree of force the crisis demands." The proclamation of blockade is, itself, official and conclusive evidence to the Court that a state of war existed which demanded and authorized a recourse to such a measure, under the circumstances peculiar to the case. . . .

If it were necessary to the technical existence of a war, that it should have a legislative sanction, we find it in almost every Act passed at the extraordinary session of the Legislature of 1861, which was wholly employed in enacting laws to enable the government to prosecute the war with vigor and efficiency. And finally, in 1861 we find Congress "*cx majore cautela*" and in anticipation of such astute objections, passing an Act "approving, legalizing and making valid all the acts, proclamations, and orders of the President, &c., as if they had been issued and done under the previous express authority and direction of the Congress of the United States."

Without admitting that such an Act was necessary under the circumstances, it is plain that if the President had in any manner assumed powers which it was necessary should have the authority or sanction of Congress, . . . this ratification has operated to perfectly cure the defect. . . .

On this first question, therefore, we are of the opinion that the President had a right, *jure belli*, to institute a blockade of ports in possession of the States in rebellion which neutrals are bound to regard.

II. We come now to the consideration of the second question. What is included in the term "enemies' property"? . . .

Whether the property be liable to capture as "enemies' property" does not in any manner depend on the personal allegiance of the owner. "It is the illegal traffic that stamps it as "enemies' property." It is of no consequence whether it belongs to an ally or a citizen. . . .

MR. JUSTICE NELSON, joined by JUSTICES CATRON, CLIFFORD, and CHIEF JUSTICE TANEY, dissenting:

This great and pervading change in the existing condition of a country, and in the relations of all her citizens or subjects, external and internal, from a state of peace, is the immediate effect and result of a state of war: and hence the same code which has annexed to the existence of a war all these disturbing consequences has declared that the right of making war belongs exclusively to the supreme or sovereign power of the State.

This power in all civilized nations is regulated by the fundamental laws or municipal constitutions of the country.

By our Constitution this power is lodged in Congress. Congress shall have power "to declare war, grant letters of marque and reprisal, and make rules concerning captures on land and water." . . .

In the case of a rebellion or resistance of a portion of the people of a country against the established government, there is no doubt, if in its progress and enlargement the government thus sought to be overthrown sees fit, it may by the competent power recognize or declare the existence of a state of civil war, which will draw after it all the consequences and rights of war between the contending parties as in the case of a public war. . . . It is not to be denied, therefore, that if a civil war existed between that portion of the people in organized insurrection to overthrow this government at the time this vessel and cargo were seized, and if she was guilty of a violation of the blockade, she would be lawful prize of war. But before this insurrection against the established government can be dealt with on the footing of a civil war, within the meaning of the law of nations and the Constitution of the United States, and which will draw after it belligerent rights, it must be recognized or declared by the war-making power of the government. No power short of this can change the legal *status* of the government or the relations of its citizens from that of peace to a state of war, or bring into existence all those duties and obligations of neutral third parties growing out of a state of war. The war power of the government must be exercised before this changed condition of the government and people and of neutral third parties can be admitted. There is no difference in this respect between a civil and a public war. . . .

An idea seemed to be entertained that all that was necessary to constitute a war was organized hostility in the district or country in a state of rebellion—that conflicts on land and on sea—and taking of towns and capture of fleets—in fine, the magnitude and dimensions of the resistance against the government—constituted war with all the belligerent rights belonging to civil war. . . .

Now, in one sense, no doubt this is war, and may be a war of the most extensive and threatening dimensions and effects, but it is a statement simply of its existence in a material sense, and has no relevancy or weight when the question is what constitutes war in a legal sense, in the sense of the law of nations, and of the Constitution of the United States? For it must be a war in this sense to attach to it all the consequences that belong to belligerent rights. Instead, therefore, of inquiring after armies and navies, and victories lost and won, or organized rebellion against the General Government, the inquiry should be into the law of nations and into the municipal fundamental laws of the government. For we find there that to constitute a civil war in the sense in which we are speaking, before it can exist, in contemplation of law, it must be recognized or declared by the sovereign power of the State, and which sovereign power by our Constitution is lodged in the Congress of the United States—civil war, therefore, under our system of government, can exist only by an Act of Congress, which requires the assent of two of the great departments of the government, the Executive and Legislative. . . .

So the war carried on by the President against the insurrectionary districts in the Southern States, as in the case of the King of Great Britain in the American Revolution, was a personal war against those in rebellion, and with encouragement and support of loyal citizens with a view to their co-operation and aid in suppressing the insurgents, with this difference, as the war-making power belonged to the King, he might have recognized or declared the war at the beginning to be a civil war which would draw after it all the rights of a belligerent, but in the case of the President no such power existed; the war, therefore, from necessity, was a personal war, until Congress assembled and acted upon this state of things. . . .

Upon the whole, after the most careful consideration of this case which the pressure of other duties has admitted, I am compelled to the conclusion that no civil war existed between this Government and the States in insurrection till recognized by the Act of Congress 13th July, 1861; that the President does not possess the power under the Constitution to declare war or recognize its existence within the meaning of the law of nations, which carries with it belligerent rights, and thus change the country and all its citizens from a state of peace to a state of war; that this power belongs exclusively to the Congress of the United States and, consequently, that the President had no power to set on foot a blockade under the law of nations, and the capture of the vessel and cargo in this case, and in all cases before us in which the capture occurred before the 13th July, 1861, for breach of blockade, or as enemies' property, are illegal and void, and that the decrees of condemnation should be reversed and the vessel and cargo restored.

The Court's decision in *The Prize Cases* stated that President Lincoln had the authority to order the blockade as Commander-in-Chief of the Armed Forces, an Article II power. If the nation is invaded the President "does not initiate the war, but is bound to accept the challenge without waiting for any special legislative authority. And whether the hostile party be a foreign invader, or states organized in rebellion, it is nonetheless a war, although the declaration of it be '*unilateral.*'" The President alone, as Commander-in-Chief, must make the decision whether or not a state of war exists and take appropriate action. In this regard the Court held: "Whether the President in fulfilling his duties, as Commander-in-Chief, in suppressing an insurrection, has met with such armed hostile resistance, and a civil war of such alarming proportions as will compel him to accord to them the character of belligerence, is a question to be decided by him, and this Court must be governed by the decisions and acts of the political department of the government to which this power was entrusted."

While the Court is careful to point out in *The Prize Cases* that in fact the President had on several occasions been authorized by Congress to take necessary action to repel foreign invasions, the majority implied that such an authorization was unnecessary to support President Lincoln's blockade order.

The willingness of the Supreme Court to uphold presidential prerogative powers in *The Prize Cases* was at first evident in other cases arising in the Civil War period. The creation of military tribunals had caused sharp controversy among those subject to their jurisdiction. Such tribunals operated not only in war zones but often in places where there was no direct military conflict. In *Ex Parte Vallandigham,* 1 Wallace 243 (1864), a former Democratic congressman from Ohio was arrested by military authority for public speeches he made bitterly denouncing the Lincoln administration. He was found guilty by a military tribunal and sentenced to confinement. His application for a writ of habeas corpus to the federal circuit court was turned down, and his motion for a writ of certiorari to review his sentence was rejected by the Supreme Court. The Court's decision in *Ex Parte Vallandigham* refused jurisdiction on the basis that a military commission was not a court, and therefore its decisions were not subject to judicial review.

The issue of the reviewability of the decisions of military tribunals arose again in *Ex Parte Milligan* in 1866. The question before the Court was whether or not the President had the power to order trials by military tribunals during wartime in localities where the civil courts were open. Milligan had been arrested by the commanding general of the military district of Indiana and tried by a military commission on charges ranging from conspiracy against the government to disloyalty and giving aid and comfort to the rebel cause. He was found guilty and sentenced to be hanged on May 19, 1865. He petitioned to the circuit court on May 10 for a writ of habeas corpus, and the circuit court, disagreeing with the application of the law, certified the case to the Supreme Court.

Ex Parte Milligan

4 Wallace 2; 18 L. Ed. 281 (1866)

Mr. Justice Davis delivered the opinion of the Court:

. . . The importance of the main question presented by this record cannot be overstated, for it involves the very framework of the government and the fundamental principles of American liberty.

During the late wicked Rebellion the temper of the times did not allow that calmness in deliberation and discussion so necessary to a correct conclusion of a purely judicial question. Then, considerations of safety were mingled with the exercise of power, and feelings and interests prevailed which are happily terminated. Now that the public safety is assured, this question, as well as all others, can be discussed and decided without passion or the admixture of any element not required to form a legal judgment. We approach the investigation of this case fully sensible of the magnitude of the inquiry and the necessity of full and cautious deliberation. . . .

The controlling question in the case is this: Upon the facts stated in Milligan's petition, and the exhibits filed, had the Military Commission mentioned in it jurisdiction, legally, to try and sentence him? Milligan, not a resident of one of the rebellious states, or a prisoner of war, but a citizen of Indiana for twenty years past, and never in the military or naval service, is, while at his home, arrested by the military power of the United States, imprisoned and, on certain criminal charges preferred against him, tried, convicted, and sentenced to be hanged by a military commission, organized under the direction of the military commander of the military district of Indiana. Had this tribunal the legal power and authority to try and punish this man?

No graver question was ever considered by this Court, nor one which more nearly concerns the rights of the whole people; for it is the birthright of every American citizen when charged with crime, to be tried and punished according to law. The power of punishment is alone through the means which the laws have provided for that purpose, and if they are ineffectual, there is an immunity from punishment, no matter how great an offender the individual may be, or how much his crimes may have shocked the sense of justice of the country, or endangered its safety. By the protection of the law human rights are secured; withdraw that protection, and they are at the mercy of wicked rulers, or the clamor of an excited people. If there was law to justify this military trial, it is not our province to interfere; if there was not, it is our duty to declare the nullity of the whole proceedings. The decision of this question does not de-

pend on argument or judicial precedents, numerous and highly illustrative as they are. These precedents inform us of the extent of the struggle to preserve liberty and to relieve those in civil life from military trials. The founders of our government were familiar with the history of that struggle; and secured in a written Constitution every right which the people had wrested from power during a contest of ages. By that Constitution and the laws authorized by it, this question must be determined. The provisions of that instrument on the administration of criminal justice are too plain and direct to leave room for misconstruction or doubt of their true meaning. Those applicable to this case are found in that clause of the original Constitution which says "that the trial of all crimes, except in case of impeachment, shall be by jury"; and in the fourth, fifth, and sixth articles of the amendments. . . .

Time has proven the discernment of our ancestors; for even these provisions, expressed in such plain English words, that it would seem the ingenuity of man could not evade them, are now, after the lapse of more than seventy years, sought to be avoided. Those great and good men foresaw that troublous times would arise, when rulers and people would become restive under restraint, and seek by sharp and decisive measures to accomplish ends deemed just and proper; and that the principles of constitutional liberty would be in peril, unless established by irrepealable law. The history of the world had taught them that what was done in the past might be attempted in the future. The Constitution of the United States is a law for rulers and people, equally in war and in peace, and covers with the shield of its protection all classes of men, at all times, and under all circumstances. No doctrine, involving more pernicious consequences, was ever invented by the wit of man than that any of its provisions can be suspended during any of the great exigencies of government. Such a doctrine leads directly to anarchy or despotism, but the theory of necessity on which it is based is false: for the government, within the Constitution, has all the powers granted to it which are necessary to preserve its existence, as has been happily proved by the result of the great effort to throw off its just authority.

Have any of the rights guaranteed by the Constitution been violated in the case of Milligan? and if so, what are they?

Every trial involves the exercise of judicial power: and from what source did the Military Commission that tried him derive their authority? Certainly no part of the judicial power of the country was conferred on them; because the Constitution expressly vests it "in one Supreme Court and such inferior courts as the Congress may from time to time ordain and establish." and it is not pretended that the commission was a court ordained and established by Congress. They cannot justify on the mandate of the President; because he is controlled by law, and has his appropriate sphere of duty, which is to execute, not to make, the laws: and there is "no unwritten criminal code to which resort can be had as a source of jurisdiction."

But it is said that the jurisdiction is complete under the "laws and usages of war."

It can serve no useful purpose to inquire what those laws and usages are, whence they originated, where found, and on whom they operate; they can never be applied to citizens in states which have upheld the authority of the government, and where the courts are open and their process unobstructed. This Court has judicial knowledge that in Indiana the Federal authority was always unopposed, and its courts always open to hear criminal accusations and redress grievances; and no usage of war could sanction a military trial there for any offense whatever of a citizen in civil life, in nowise connected with the military service. Congress could grant no such power; and to the honor of our national legislature be it said, it has never been provoked by the state of the country even to attempt its exercise. One of the plainest constitutional provisions was, therefore, infringed when Milligan was tried by a court not ordained and established by Congress, and not composed of judges appointed during good behavior.

Why was he not delivered to the circuit court of Indiana to be proceeded against according to law?[38] No reason of necessity could be urged against it; because Congress had declared penalties against the offenses charged, provided for their punishment, and directed that court to hear and determine them. And soon after this military tribunal was ended, the circuit court met, peacefully transacted its business, and adjourned. It needed no bayonets to protect it, and required no military aid to execute its judgments. It was held in a state, eminently distinguished for patriotism, by judges commissioned during the Rebellion, who were provided with juries, upright, intelligent, and selected by a marshal appointed by the President. The government had no right to conclude that Milligan, if guilty, would not receive in that court merited punishment; for its records disclose that it was constantly engaged in the trial of similar offenses, and

[38]The law referred to here is the Habeas Corpus Act of 1863. That law attempted to guarantee political prisoners the right to habeas corpus without at the same time unduly interfering with executive and military authority. The President was authorized to defend the writ of habeas corpus and military officers were not required to respond to the writ. However, the Secretaries of War and State were required to furnish lists of political prisoners to the court, and indictments against them were to be made only by grand juries. If the grand juries did not issue the indictments prisoners were to be released upon taking an oath of allegiance. [Editor's Note.]

was never interrupted in its administration of criminal justice. If it was dangerous, in the distracted condition of affairs, to leave Milligan unrestrained of his liberty, because he "conspired against the government, afforded aid and comfort to rebels, and incited the people to insurrection," the law said arrest him, confine him closely, render him powerless to do further mischief; and then present his case to the grand jury of the district, with proofs of his guilt and, if indicted, try him according to the course of the common law. If this had been done, the Constitution would have been vindicated, the law of 1863 enforced, and the securities for personal liberty preserved and defended.

Another guarantee of freedom was broken when Milligan was denied a trial by jury. The great minds of the country have differed on the correct interpretation to be given to various provisions of the Federal Constitution; and judicial decision has been often invoked to settle their true meaning; but until recently no one ever doubted that the right of trial by jury was fortified in the organic law against the power of attack. It is now assailed; but if ideas can be expressed in words, and language has any meaning, this right—one of the most valuable in a free country—is preserved to every one accused of crime who is not attached to the Army or Navy or Militia in actual service. The Sixth Amendment affirms that "in all criminal prosecutions the accused shall enjoy the right to a speedy and public trial by an impartial jury," language broad enough to embrace all persons and cases; but the Fifth, recognizing the necessity of an indictment, or presentment, before anyone can be held to answer for high crimes, "excepts cases arising in the land or naval forces, or in the militia, when in actual service, in time of war or public danger"; and the framers of the Constitution, doubtless, meant to limit

the right to trial by jury, in the Sixth Amendment, to those persons who were subject to indictment or presentment in the Fifth.

The discipline necessary to the efficiency of the Army and Navy, required other and swifter modes of trial than are furnished by the common law courts; and, in pursuance of the power conferred by the Constitution, Congress has declared the kinds of trial and the manner in which they shall be conducted, for offenses committed while the party is in the military or naval service. Every one connected with these branches of public service is amenable to the jurisdiction which Congress has created for their government, and, while thus serving, surrenders his right to be tried by the civil courts. All other persons, citizens of states where the courts are open, if charged with crime, are guaranteed the inestimable privilege of trial by jury. . . .

It is claimed that martial law covers with its broad mantle the proceedings of this Military Commission. The proposition is this: That in a time of war the commander of an armed force (if in his opinion the exigencies of the country demand it, and of which he is to judge), has the power, within the lines of his military district, to suspend all civil rights and their remedies, and subject citizens as well as soldiers to the rule of his will; and in the exercise of his lawful authority cannot be restrained, except by his superior officer or the President of the United States.

If this position is sound to the extent claimed, then when war exists, foreign or domestic, and the country is subdivided into military departments for mere convenience, the commander of one of them can, if he chooses, within the limits, on the plea of necessity, with the approval of the Executive, substitute military force for and the exclusion of the laws, and punish all persons, as he thinks right and proper, without fixed or certain rules.

The statement of this proposition shows its importance; for, if true, republican government is a failure, and there is an end of liberty regulated by law. Martial law, established on such a basis, destroys every guaranty of the Constitution, and effectually renders the "military independent of and superior to the civil power"—the attempt to do which by the King of Great Britain was deemed by our fathers such an offense, that they assigned it to the world as one of the causes which impelled them to declare their independence. Civil liberty and this kind of martial law cannot endure together; the antagonism is irreconcilable and, in the conflict, one or the other must perish.

This nation, as experience has proved, cannot always remain at peace, and has no right to expect that it will always have wise and humane rulers, sincerely attached to the principles of the Constitution. Wicked men, ambitious of power, with hatred of liberty and contempt of law, may fill the place once occupied by Washington and Lincoln; and if this right is conceded, and the calamities of war again befall us, the dangers to human liberty are frightful to contemplate. If our fathers had failed to provide for just such a contingency, they would have been false to the trust reposed in them. They knew— the history of the world told them—the nation they were founding, be its existence short or long, would be involved in war; how often or how long continued, human foresight could not tell; and that unlimited power, wherever lodged at such a time, was especially hazardous to freemen. For this, and other equally weighty reasons, they secured the inheritance they had fought to maintain, by incorporating in a written Constitution the safeguards which time had proved were essential to its preservation. Not one of these safeguards can the President or Congress or the Judiciary disturb, except the one concerning the writ of habeas corpus.

It is essential to the safety of every government that, in a great crisis, like the one we have just passed through, there should be a power somewhere of suspending the writ of habeas corpus. In every war, there are men of previously good character, wicked enough to counsel their fellow citizens to resist the measures deemed necessary by a good government to sustain its just authority and overthrow its enemies; and their influence may lead to dangerous combinations. In the emergency of the times, an immediate public investigation according to law may not be possible; and yet, the peril to the country may be too imminent to suffer such persons to go at large. Unquestionably, there is then an exigency which demands that the government, if it should see fit, in the exercise of a proper discretion, to make arrests, should not be required to produce the person arrested in answer to a writ of habeas corpus. The Constitution goes no further. It does not say after a writ of habeas corpus is denied a citizen, that he shall be tried otherwise than by the course of common law. If it had intended this result, it was easy by the use of direct words to have accomplished it. The illustrious men who framed that instrument were guarding the foundations of civil liberty against the abuses of unlimited power; they were full of wisdom, and the lessons of history informed them that a trial by an established court, assisted by an impartial jury, was the only sure way of protecting the citizen against oppression and wrong. Knowing this, they limited the suspension to one great right, and left the rest to remain forever inviolable. But it is insisted that the safety of the country in time of war demands that this broad claim for martial law shall be sustained. If this were true, it could be well said that a country, preserved at the sacrifice of all the cardinal principles of liberty, is not worth the cost of preservation. Happily, it is not so.

It will be borne in mind that this is not

a question of the power to proclaim martial law, when war exists in a community and the courts and civil authorities are overthrown. Nor is it a question what rule a military commander, at the head of his army, can impose on States in rebellion to cripple their resources and quell the insurrection. The jurisdiction claimed is much more extensive. The necessities of the service, during the late Rebellion, required that the loyal states should be placed within the limits of certain military districts and commanders appointed in them; and, it is urged, that this, in a military sense, constituted them the theater of military operations: and, as in this case, Indiana had been and was again threatened with invasion by the enemy, the occasion was furnished to establish martial law. The conclusion does not follow from the premises. If armies were collected in Indiana, they were to be employed in another locality, where the laws were obstructed and the national authority disputed. On her soil there was no hostile foot; if once invaded, that invasion was at an end, and with it all pretext for martial law. Martial law cannot arise from a threatened invasion. The necessity must be actual and present; the invasion real, such as effectually closes the courts and deposes the civil administration.

It is difficult to see how the safety of the country required martial law in Indiana. If any of her citizens were plotting treason, the power of arrest could secure them, until the government was prepared for their trial, when the courts were open and ready to try them. It was as easy to protect witnesses before a civil as a military tribunal; and as there could be no wish to convict, except on sufficient legal evidence, surely an ordained and established court were better able to judge of this than a military tribunal composed of gentlemen not trained to the profession of the law.

It follows, from what has been said on this subject, that there are occasions when martial rule can be properly applied. If, in foreign invasion or civil war, the courts are actually closed, and it is impossible to administer criminal justice according to law, then, on the theater of actual military operations, where war really prevails, there is a necessity to furnish a substitute for the civil authority, thus overthrown, to preserve the safety of the army and society; and as no power is left but the military, it is allowed to govern by martial rule until the laws can have their free course. A necessity creates the rule, so it limits its duration; for, if this government is continued after the courts are reinstated, it is a gross usurpation of power. Martial rule can never exist where the courts are open, and in the proper and unobstructed exercise of their jurisdiction. It is also confined to the locality of actual war. Because, during the late Rebellion it could have been enforced in Virginia, where the national authority was overturned and the courts driven out, it does not follow that it should obtain in Indiana, where that authority was never disputed, and justice was always administered. And so in the case of a foreign invasion, martial rule may become a necessity, in one state, when, in another, it would be "mere lawless violence." . . .

The two remaining questions in this case must be answered in the affirmative. The suspension of the privilege of the writ of habeas corpus does not suspend the writ itself. The writ issues as a matter of course; and on the return made to it the court decides whether the party applying is denied the right of proceeding any further with it.

If the military trial of Milligan was contrary to law, then he was entitled, on the facts stated in his petition, to be discharged from custody by the terms of the act of Congress of March 3d, 1863. The provisions of this law having been considered in a previous part of this opinion, we will not restate the views there presented. Milligan avers he was a citizen of Indiana, not in the military or naval service, and was detained in close confinement, by order of the President, from the 5th day of October, 1864, until the 2d day of January, 1865, when the circuit court for the district of Indiana, with a grand jury, convened in session at Indianapolis; and afterwards, on the 27th day of the same month, adjourned without finding an indictment or presentment against him. If these averments were true (and their truth is conceded for the purposes of this case), the court was required to liberate him on taking certain oaths prescribed by the law, and entering into recognizance for his good behavior.

But it is insisted that Milligan was a prisoner of war, and, therefore, excluded from the privileges of the statute. It is not easy to see how he can be treated as a prisoner of war, when he lived in Indiana for the past twenty years, was arrested there, and had not been, during the late troubles, a resident of any of the states in rebellion. If in Indiana he conspired with bad men to assist the enemy, he is punishable for it in the courts of Indiana; but, when tried for the offense, he cannot plead the rights of war; for he was not engaged in legal acts of hostility against the government, and only such persons, when captured, are prisoners of war. If he cannot enjoy the immunities attaching to the character of a prisoner of war, how can he be subject to their pains and penalties? . . .

MR. CHIEF JUSTICE CHASE delivered the following opinion:

. . . We agree in the proposition that no department of the government of the United States—neither President, nor Congress, nor the courts—possesses any power not given by the Constitution. . . .

The Constitution itself provides for military government as well as for civil government. And we do not understand it to be claimed that the civil safeguards of the Constitution have application in cases within the proper sphere of the former.

What, then, is that proper sphere? Congress has power to raise and support armies; to provide and maintain a navy; to make rules for the government and regulation of the land and naval forces; and to provide for governing such part of the militia as may be in the service of the United States.

It is not denied that the power to make rules for the government of the army and navy is a power to provide for trial and punishment by military courts without a jury. It has been so understood and exercised from the adoption of the Constitution to the present time. . . .

We think, therefore, that the power of Congress in the government of the land and naval forces and of the militia, is not at all affected by the Fifth or any other amendment. It is not necessary to attempt any precise definition of the boundaries of this power. But may it not be said that government includes protection and defense as well as the regulation of internal administration? And is it impossible to imagine cases in which citizens conspiring or attempting the destruction or great injury of the national forces may be subjected by Congress to military trial and punishment in the just exercise of this undoubted constitutional power? Congress is but the agent of the nation, and does not the security of individuals against the abuse of this, as of every other power, depend on the intelligence and virtue of the people, on their zeal for public and private liberty, upon official responsibility secured by law, and upon the frequency of elections, rather than upon doubtful constructions of legislative powers? . . .

In Indiana, for example, at the time of the arrest of Milligan and his co-conspirators, it is established by the papers in the record, that the state was a military district, was the theater of military operations, had been actually invaded, and was constantly threatened with invasion. It appears, also, that a powerful secret association, composed of citizens and others, existed within the state, under military organization, conspiring against the draft, and plotting insurrection, the liberation of the prisoners of war at various depots, the seizure of the state and national arsenals, armed co-operation with the enemy, and war against the national government.

We cannot doubt that, in such a time of public danger, Congress had power, under the Constitution, to provide for the organization of a military commission, and for trial by that commission of persons engaged in this conspiracy. The fact that the Federal courts were open was regarded by Congress as a sufficient reason for not exercising the power; but that fact could not deprive Congress of the right to exercise it. Those courts might be open and undisturbed in the execution of their functions, and yet wholly incompetent to avert threatened danger, or to punish, with adequate promptitude and certainty, the guilty conspirators.

In Indiana, the judges and officers of the courts were loyal to the government. But it might have been otherwise. In times of rebellion and civil war it may often happen, indeed, that judges and marshals will be in active sympathy with the rebels, and courts their most efficient allies.

We have confined ourselves to the question of power. It was for Congress to determine the question of expediency. And Congress did determine it. That body did not see fit to authorize trials by military commission in Indiana, but by the strongest implication prohibited them.

With that prohibition we are satisfied, and should have remained silent if the answers to the questions certified had been put on that ground, without denial of the existence of a power which we believe to be constitutional and important to the public safety—a denial which, as we have already suggested, seems to draw in question the power of Congress to protect from prosecution the members of military commissions who acted in obedience to their superior officers, and whose action, whether warranted by law or not, was approved by that upright and patriotic President under whose administration the Republic was rescued from threatened destruction. . . .

We think that the power of Congress, in such times and in such localities, to authorize trials for crimes against the security and safety of the national forces, may be derived from its constitutional authority to raise and support armies and to declare war, if not from its constitutional authority to provide for governing the national forces.

We have no apprehension that this power, under our American system of government, in which all official authority is derived from the people, and exercised under direct responsibility to the people, is more likely to be abused than the power to regulate commerce or the power to borrow money. And we are unwilling to give our assent by silence to expressions of opinion which seem to us calculated, though not intended to cripple the constitutional powers of the government, and to augment the public dangers in times of invasion and rebellion.

Mr. Justice Wayne, Mr. Justice Swayne, and Mr. Justice Miller concur with me in these views.

The Court states in the *Milligan* decision that the appropriate sphere of the duty of the President "is to execute, not to make the laws." How does the Court apply this principle to the *Milligan* case? Would the Court's decision have been the same if fundamental personal liberties were not at stake? Under what circumstances would the Court approve of a military commander, under presidential authority, substituting military force for procedures authorized by Congress or the Constitution? What limits does the Court place upon the President's authority to proclaim martial law?

During the Civil War President Lincoln took various unilateral actions, establishing censorship, authorizing the Secretary of War to make military arrests, and suspending the writ of habeas corpus, all of which denied citizens fundamental constitutional rights. At the outset of the war Chief Justice Taney defied Lincoln's authorization of the suspension of the writ of habeas corpus in the case of *Ex Parte Merryman*, 17 Fed. Cases 9487 (1861), only to find the President in defiance and insistent upon his authority under Article II to suspend civil liberties where it was necessary for the public safety. In justification of his position, Lincoln wrote in a letter to Erastus Corning, dated June 12, 1863,

> Thoroughly imbued with a reverence for the guaranteed rights of individuals, I was slow to adopt the strong measures by which degrees I have been forced to regard as being within the exceptions of the Constitution and as indispensable to the public safety. . . . I concede that the class of arrests complained of can be constitutional only when in cases of rebellion or invasion of public safety may require them; and I insist that in such cases they are constitutional wherever the public safety does require them, as well as in places where they may prevent the rebellion extending as in those where it may already be prevailing.[39]

Does Lincoln's reasoning justify his position in support of expanded presidential prerogative powers during wartime?

Although the decision in the *Milligan* case was principally aimed at the President, the Court also decided to take the opportunity to discourse on the extent of the war power of Congress *should* the legislature ever decide to replace civilian courts with military tribunals. "Congress could grant no such power [to establish military tribunals]," said the Court, "and to the honor of national legislature be it said, it has never been provoked by the state of the country even to attempt its exercise."[40] It was the majority statement that *Congress* had no authority to establish military tribunals that would assume the functions of civilian courts during wartime that Chief Justice Chase and three of his brethren attacked in their dissenting opinion in the *Milligan* case.

Wartime crises subsequent to the Civil War made the constitutional doctrine developed by the Court during the administrations of Presidents Lincoln and Andrew Johnson into an important precedent. On February 19, 1942, President Franklin D. Roosevelt issued an executive order that was to have far-reaching consequences in constitutional law.

---

[39]Charles Warren, *The Supreme Court*, III, p. 95.

[40]Although Congress did not provide expressly for military tribunals, it did, in a series of acts beginning in 1863, support presidential authority to suspend the writ of habeas corpus and presidential orders for military arrests and detention. See Beard v. Burts, 95 U.S. 434 (1877), and Bean v. Beckwith, 98 U.S. 266 (1878).

EXECUTIVE ORDER 9066

Authorizing the Secretary of War
to Prescribe Military Areas

Whereas the successful prosecution of the war requires every possible protection against espionage and against sabotage to national defense materiel, national defense premises, and national defense utilities . . . :

NOW, THEREFORE, by virtue of the authority vested in me as President of the United States, and Commander-in-Chief of the Army, and Navy, I hereby authorize and direct the Secretary of War, and the military commanders whom he may from time to time designate, whenever he or any designated commander deems such action necessary or desirable, to prescribe military areas in such places and of such extent as he or the appropriate military commander may determine, from which any and all persons may be excluded, and with respect to which, the right of any person to enter, remain in, or leave shall be subject to whatever restrictions the Secretary of War or the appropriate military commander may impose in his discretion. The Secretary of War is hereby authorized to provide for residents of any such area who are excluded therefrom, such transportation, food, shelter, and other accommodations as may be necessary, in the judgment of the Secretary of War or the said military commander, and until other arrangements are made, to accomplish the purpose of this order. . . .

I hereby further authorize and direct the Secretary of War and the said military commanders to take such other steps as he or the appropriate military commander may deem advisable to enforce compliance with the restrictions applicable to each military area herein above authorized to be designated, including the use of federal troops and other federal agencies, with authority to accept assistance of state and local agencies.

I hereby further authorize and direct all executive departments, independent establishments and other federal agencies, to assist the Secretary of War or the said military commanders in carrying out this executive order, including the furnishing of medical aid, hospitalization, food, clothing, transportation, use of land, shelter, and other supplies, equipment, utilities, facilities, and services. . . .

Using the decisions of the Court you have already read regarding the prerogative powers of the President during wartime, would the Court uphold Executive Order 9066 in the absence of any explicit congressional authorization for it? That decision never confronted the Court, for Congress on March 21, 1942, passed legislation that substantially embodied the provisions of the President's sweeping executive order. On May 3, 1942, Lieutenant General J. L. DeWitt issued civilian exclusion order No. 34 which provided that "All persons of Japanese ancestry, both alien and non-alien, be excluded from . . . military area No. 1," which was described as containing the coastal area of Northern California around San Francisco. A subsequent order established a military zone in the Pacific Coast area of Southern California, but this was not at issue in the *Korematsu* case.

Prior to the *Korematsu* case the Supreme Court had dealt with the constitutional implications of the March 21, 1942, congressional statute that had embodied the provisions of Executive Order 9066. The act provided for a fine not to exceed $5000 or imprisonment up to one year for any person who "shall enter, remain in, leave, or commit any act in any military area or military zone prescribed under the authority of an executive order of the President, by the Secretary of War, or by any military commander designated by the Secretary of War, contrary to the restrictions applicable to any such area or zone or contrary to the order of the Secretary of War or any such military commander. . . ."[41]

In *Hirabayashi* v. *United States*, 320 U.S. 81 (1943), a Japanese-American had been convicted of violating a military curfew and failing to report to a designated civilian control station. Hirabayashi contended that "Congress unconstitutionally delegated its legislative power to the military commander by authorizing him to impose the challenged regulation, and that, even if the regulation were in other respects lawfully authorized, the Fifth Amendment prohibits the discrimination made between citizens of Japanese descent and those of other ancestry."[42] The Court confined itself to the validity of the curfew order. The majority opinion of Chief Justice Stone found that "Executive Order No. 9066 promulgated in time of war for the declared purpose of prosecuting the war by protecting national defense resources from sabotage and espionage, *and* the Act of March 21, 1942, ratifying and confirming the executive order, were *each* an exercise of the power to wage war conferred on the Congress *and* on the President, as Commander-in-Chief of the Armed Forces, by Articles I and II of the Constitution. . . ."[43] Did Stone's opinion imply that the executive order would have been valid in the absence of the subsequent congressional statute? Justice Stone continued: "Since the Constitution committed to the executive *and* the Congress the exercise of the war power in all the vicissitudes and conditions of warfare, it has necessarily given them wide scope in determining the nature and extent of the threatened injury and in the selection of the means for resisting it."[44]

After affirming the vast sweep of the war powers of Congress and the prerogatives of the President as Commander-in-Chief, the Court dismissed the charge that the curfew order involved an unlawful delegation of legislative power. Congress is not precluded, said Justice Stone, "from resorting to the aid of executive and administrative officers in determining by findings whether the facts are such as to call for the application of previously adopted legislative standards or definitions of congressional policy."[45] Could the claim of unconstitutional legislative authority have been dismissed as well on the basis that the President had the prerogative power as Commander-in-Chief to authorize the creation of war zones and the exclusion of persons from them on the grounds of military necessity?

Not only did the *Hirabayashi* case buttress the constitutional powers of Congress and the President during wartime but held that the obvious racial discrimination in the curfew order aimed only at persons of Japanese ancestry did not violate constitutional standards. The exigencies of war overrode

[41]Public Law 503, March 21, 1942.
[42]Hirabayashi v. United States, 320 U.S. 81, 89 (1943).
[43]Ibid., p. 92.
[44]Ibid., p. 93. (Emphasis supplied.)
[45]Ibid., p. 102.

individual rights. "We cannot say," said the Court, "that the war-making branches of the government did not have grounds for believing that in a critical hour such persons [citizens of Japanese ancestry] could not readily be isolated and separately dealt with, and constituted a menace to the national defense and safety, which demanded that prompt and adequate measures be taken. . . ."[46] Stone agreed that "Distinctions between citizens solely because of their ancestry are by their very nature odious to a free people whose institutions are founded upon the doctrine of equality."[47] Racial discrimination is usually held to be unconstitutional, wrote Stone, but "it by no means follows that in dealing with the perils of war, Congress and the executive are wholly precluded from taking into account those facts and circumstances which are relevant to measures for our national defense and for the successful prosecution of the war, and which may in fact place citizens of one ancestry in a different category from others. . . ."[48] Justice Murphy, in a concurring opinion, found that the "critical military situation" justified upholding the constitutionality of the curfew, although distinctions based on color and ancestry "are utterly inconsistent with our traditions and our ideals." Murphy felt that the curfew order bore "a melancholy resemblance to the treatment accorded to members of the Jewish race in Germany and in other parts of Europe."[49]

The *Hirabayashi* decision gave little hope to Korematsu as he sought to overturn his conviction under Public Law 503 for violating the civilian exclusion order No. 34 that had been issued by military authorities. Korematsu's conviction in the Federal District Court had been upheld by the Circuit Court of Appeals, and he successfully petitioned the Supreme Court for a writ of certiorari.

Korematsu's plea to the Supreme Court was stated in bold and provocative terms.

> Can a loyal American citizen be branded a criminal under the provisions of Public Law No. 503 of the Act of March 21, 1942, for resisting military *lettres de cachet,* issued in an area free from martial rule, which commanded his seizure, removal from his home, detention in a stockade, banishment from a state-embracing military department, and final imprisonment in a concentration camp, all without trial and without accusation of crime being brought against him?[50]

Korematsu claimed that the issues of exclusion and detention were inseparable and that the Court should consider the constitutionality of each in reviewing his case. He contended that neither the executive order of the President nor the subsequent law passed by Congress expressly authorized the exclusion from military zones of citizens of Japanese ancestry. He reiterated

---

[46]Ibid., p. 100.
[47]Ibid.
[48]Ibid., p. 101.
[49]Ibid., p. 111.
[50]LB, Volume 42, pp. 1–2. *Lettres de cachet* were letters issued and signed by the Kings of France that authorized the imprisonment up to life of persons out of favor with the king, displeasing to him, or otherwise aggravating to the king and his friends. They were abolished with the Revolution of 1789.

the claim previously made by Hirabayashi that the statute in any event was unconstitutional because of overbroad delegation of legislative authority. The statute did not contain specific standards as required by *Schechter* v. *United States*. (See pp. 109–124 for an analysis of this aspect of the *Schechter* decision.) One other contention made by Korematsu was that military necessity did not require exclusion and detention.

The reply brief by the government in the *Korematsu* case declared that the war powers of Congress and the Commander-in-Chief clause of Article II clearly gave the legislative and executive branches the authority to exclude citizens from war zones. The military order was clearly authorized by the executive order and legislation preceding it. The exclusion was based upon the same dangers that the Court had taken notice of in the *Hirabayashi* case. The danger was real, and considerations of due process were overridden by the wartime emergency. Finally, the government argued that the issues of exclusion and detention were separable, that detention was not at issue in this case because Korematsu himself had not been placed in a detention center; therefore, he had no standing to challenge this aspect of military policy.

On the basis of the cases you have read dealing with the scope of the war powers of the President and the Congress, and taking into consideration the decision in the *Hirabayashi* case, did the Court properly decide *Korematsu* v. *United States*?

Korematsu v. *United States*

323 U.S. 214, 65 S. Ct. 193, 89 L. Ed. 194 (1944)

MR. JUSTICE BLACK delivered the opinion of the Court:

In the light of the principles we announced in the *Hirabayashi* case, we are unable to conclude that it was beyond the war power of Congress and the Executive to exclude those of Japanese ancestry from the West Coast war area at the time they did. True, exclusion from the area in which one's home is located is a far greater deprivation than constant confinement to the home from 8 p. m. to 6 a. m. Nothing short of apprehension by the proper military authorities of the gravest imminent danger to the public safety can constitutionally justify either. But exclusion from a threatened area, no less than curfew, has a definite and close relationship to the prevention of espionage and sabotage. The military authorities, charged with the primary responsibility of defending our shores, concluded that curfew provided inadequate protection and ordered exclusion. They did so, as pointed out in our *Hirabayashi* opinion, in accordance with Congressional authority to the military to say who should, and who should not, remain in the threatened areas.

In this case the petitioner challenges the assumptions upon which we rested our conclusions in the *Hirabayashi* case. He also urges that by May 1942, when Order No. 34 was promulgated, all danger of Japanese invasion of the West Coast had disappeared. After careful consideration of these contentions we are compelled to reject them.

Here, as in the *Hirabayashi* case, . . . ". . . we cannot reject as unfounded the judgment of the military authorities and of Congress that there were disloyal members of that population, whose number and strength could not be precisely and quickly ascertained. We cannot say that the war-making branches of the Government did not have ground for believing that in a critical hour such persons could not readily be isolated and separately dealt with, and constituted a menace to the national defense and safety, which demanded that prompt and adequate measures be taken to guard against it."

Like curfew, exclusion of those of Japanese origin was deemed necessary because of the presence of an unascertained number of disloyal members of the group, most of whom we have no doubt were loyal to this country. It was because we could not reject the finding of the military authorities that it was impossible to bring about an immediate segregation of the disloyal from the loyal that we sustained the validity of the curfew order as applying to the whole group. In the instant case, temporary exclusion of the entire group was rested by the military on the same ground. The judgment that exclusion of the whole group was for the same reason a military imperative answers the contention that the exclusion was in the nature of group punishment based on antagonism to those of Japanese origin. That there were members of the group who retained loyalties to Japan has been confirmed by investigations made subsequent to the exclusion. Approximately five thousand American citizens of Japanese ancestry refused to swear unqualified allegiance to the United States and to renounce allegiance to the Japanese Emperor, and several thousand evacuees requested repatriation to Japan.

We uphold the exclusion order as of the time it was made and when the petitioner violated it. . . . In doing so, we are not unmindful of the hardships imposed by it upon a large group of American citizens. . . . But hardships are part of war, and war is an aggregation of hardships. All citizens alike, both in and out of uniform, feel the impact of war in greater or lesser measure. Citizenship has its responsibilities as well as its privileges, and in time of war the burden is always heavier. Compulsory exclusion of large groups of citizens from their homes, except under circumstances of direst emergency and peril, is inconsistent with our basic governmental institutions. But when under conditions of modern warfare our shores are threatened by hostile forces, the power to protect must be commensurate with the threatened danger. . . .

We are . . . being asked to pass at this time upon the whole subsequent detention program in both assembly and relocation centers, although the only issues framed at the trial related to petitioner's remaining in the prohibited area in violation of the exclusion order. Had petitioner here left the prohibited area and gone to an assembly center we cannot say either as a matter of fact or law that his presence in that center would have resulted in his detention in a relocation center. Some who did report to the assembly center were not sent to relocation centers, but were released upon condition that they remain outside the prohibited zone until the military orders were modified or lifted. This illustrates that they pose different problems and may be governed by different principles. The lawfulness of one does not necessarily determine the lawfulness of the others. This is made clear when we analyze the requirements of the separate provisions of the separate orders. These separate requirements were that those of Japanese ancestry (1) depart from the area; (2) report to and temporarily remain in an assembly center; (3) go under military control to a relocation center there to remain for an indeterminate period until released conditionally or unconditionally by the military authorities.

Each of these requirements, it will be noted, imposed distinct duties in connection with the separate steps in a complete evacuation program. Had Congress directly incorporated into one Act the language of these separate orders, and provided sanctions for their violations, disobedience of any one would have constituted a separate offense. There is no reason why violations of these orders, insofar as they were promulgated pursuant to Congressional enactment, should not be treated as separate offenses. . . .

It is said that we are dealing here with the case of imprisonment of a citizen in a concentration camp solely because of his ancestry, without evidence or inquiry concerning his loyalty and good disposition towards the United States. Our task would be simple, our duty clear, were this a case involving the imprisonment of a loyal citizen in a concentration camp because of racial prejudice. Regardless of the true nature of the assembly and relocation centers—and we deem it unjustifiable to call them concentration camps with all the ugly connotations that term implies—we are dealing specifically with nothing but an exclusion order. To cast this case into outlines of racial prejudice, without reference to the real military dangers which were presented, merely confuses the issue. Korematsu was not excluded from the Military Area because of hostility to him or his race. He *was* excluded because we are at war with the Japanese Empire, because the properly constituted military authorities feared an invasion of our West Coast and felt constrained to take proper security measures, because they decided that the military urgency of the situation demanded that all citizens of Japanese ancestry be segregated from the West Coast temporarily, and finally, because Congress, reposing its confidence in this time of war in our military leaders—as inevitably it must—determined that they should

have the power to do just this. . . . We cannot—by availing ourselves of the calm perspective of hindsight—now say that at that time these actions were unjustified.

MR. JUSTICE FRANKFURTER concurred.

MR. JUSTICE ROBERTS, dissenting:
I dissent, because I think the indisputable facts exhibit a clear violation of Constitutional rights.

This is not a case of keeping people off the streets at night as was *Hirabayashi* v. *United States*, . . . nor a case of temporary exclusion of a citizen from an area for his own safety or that of the community, nor a case of offering him an opportunity to go temporarily out of an area where his presence might cause danger to himself or to his fellows. On the contrary, it is the case of convicting a citizen as a punishment for not submitting to imprisonment in a concentration camp, based on his ancestry, and solely because of his ancestry, without evidence or inquiry concerning his loyalty and good disposition towards the United States. If this be a correct statement of the facts disclosed by this record, and facts of which we take judicial notice, I need hardly labor the conclusion that Constitutional rights have been violated. . . .

MR. JUSTICE MURPHY, dissenting:
This exclusion of "all persons of Japanese ancestry, both alien and non-alien," from the Pacific Coast area on a plea of military necessity in the absence of martial law ought not to be approved. Such exclusion goes over "the very brink of constitutional power" and falls into the ugly abyss of racism.

In dealing with matters relating to the prosecution and progress of a war, we must accord great respect and consideration to the judgments of the military authorities who are on the scene and who have full knowledge of the military facts. The scope of their discretion must, as a matter of necessity and common sense, be wide. And their judgments ought not to be overruled lightly by those whose training and duties ill-equip them to deal intelligently with matters so vital to the physical security of the nation.

At the same time, however, it is essential that there be definite limits to military discretion, especially where martial law has not been declared. Individuals must not be left impoverished of their constitutional rights on a plea of military necessity that has neither substance nor support. Thus, like other claims conflicting with the asserted constitutional rights of the individual, the military claim must subject itself to the judicial process of having its reasonableness determined and its conflicts with other interests reconciled.

. . . Being an obvious racial discrimination, the order deprives all those within its scope of the equal protection of the laws as guaranteed by the Fifth Amendment. It further deprives these individuals of their constitutional rights to live and work where they will, to establish a home where they choose and to move about freely. In excommunicating them without benefit of hearings, this order also deprives them of all their constitutional rights to procedural due process. Yet no reasonable relation to an "immediate, imminent, and impending" public danger is evident to support this racial restriction which is one of the most sweeping and complete deprivations of constitutional rights in the history of this nation in the absence of martial law.

It must be conceded that the military and naval situation in the spring of 1942 was such as to generate a very real fear of invasion of the Pacific Coast, accompanied by fears of sabotage and espionage in that area. The military command was therefore justified in adopting all reasonable means necessary to combat these dangers. In adjudging the military action taken in light of the then apparent dangers, we must not erect too high or too meticulous standards; it is necessary only that the action have some reasonable relation to the removal of the dangers of invasion, sabotage and espionage. But the exclusion, either temporarily or permanently, of all persons with Japanese blood in their veins has no such reasonable relation. And that relation is lacking because the exclusion order necessarily must rely for its reasonableness upon the assumption that *all* persons of Japanese ancestry may have a dangerous tendency to commit sabotage and espionage and to aid our Japanese enemy in other ways. It is difficult to believe that reason, logic or experience could be marshalled in support of such an assumption.

That this forced exclusion was the result in good measure of this erroneous assumption of racial guilt rather than bona fide military necessity is evidenced by the Commanding General's Final Report on the evacuation from the Pacific Coast area. In it he refers to all individuals of Japanese descent as "subversive," as belonging to "an enemy race" whose "racial strains are undiluted," and as constituting "over 112,000 potential enemies . . . at large today" along the Pacific Coast. In support of this blanket condemnation of all persons of Japanese descent, however, no reliable evidence is cited to show that such individuals were generally disloyal, or had generally so conducted themselves in this area as to constitute a special menace to defense installations or war industries, or had otherwise by their behavior furnished reasonable ground for their exclusion as a group.

Justification for the exclusion is sought, instead, mainly upon questionable racial and sociological grounds not ordinarily within the realm of expert military judgment. . . .

The main reasons relied upon by those

responsible for the forced evacuation, therefore, do not prove a reasonable relation between the group characteristics of Japanese Americans and the dangers of invasion, sabotage and espionage. The reasons appear, instead, to be largely an accumulation of much of the misinformation, half-truths and insinuations that for years have been directed against Japanese Americans by people with racial and economic prejudices—the same people who have been among the foremost advocates of the evacuation. A military judgment based upon such racial and sociological considerations is not entitled to the great weight ordinarily given the judgments based upon strictly military considerations. Especially is this so when every charge relative to race, religion, culture, geographical location, and legal and economic status has been substantially discredited by independent studies made by experts in these matters.

The military necessity which is essential to the validity of the evacuation order thus resolves itself into a few intimations that certain individuals actively aided the enemy, from which it is inferred that the entire group of Japanese Americans could not be trusted to be or remain loyal to the United States. No one denies, of course, that there were some disloyal persons of Japanese descent on the Pacific Coast who did all in their power to aid their ancestral land. Similar disloyal activities have been engaged in by many persons of German, Italian and even more pioneer stock in our country. But to infer that examples of individual disloyalty prove group disloyalty and justify discriminatory action against the entire group is to deny that under our system of law individual guilt is the sole basis for deprivation of rights. Moreover, this inference, which is at the very heart of the evacuation orders, has been used in support of the abhorrent and despicable treatment of minority groups by the dictatorial tyrannies which

this nation is now pledged to destroy. To give constitutional sanction to that inference in this case, however well-intentioned may have been the military command on the Pacific Coast, is to adopt one of the cruelest of the rationales used by our enemies to destroy the dignity of the individual and to encourage and open the door to discriminatory actions against other minority groups in the passions of tomorrow.

No adequate reason is given for the failure to treat these Japanese Americans on an individual basis by holding investigations and hearings to separate the loyal from the disloyal, as was done in the case of persons of German and Italian ancestry. . . . It is asserted merely that the loyalties of this group "were unknown and time was of the essence." Yet nearly four months elapsed after Pearl Harbor before the first exclusion order was issued; nearly eight months went by until the last order was issued; and the last of these "subversive" persons was not actually removed until almost eleven months had elapsed. Leisure and deliberation seem to have been more of the essence than speed. And the fact that conditions were not such as to warrant a declaration of martial law adds strength to the belief that the factors of time and military necessity were not as urgent as they have been represented to be. . . .

The limitation under which courts always will labor in examining the necessity for a military order are illustrated by this case. How does the Court know that these orders have a reasonable basis in necessity? No evidence whatever on that subject has been taken by this or any other court. There is sharp controversy as to the credibility of the DeWitt report. So the Court, having no real evidence before it, has no choice but to accept General DeWitt's own unsworn, self-serving statement, untested by any cross-examination, that what he did was reasonable. And thus it will always be when courts try to look into the reasonableness of a military order.

In the very nature of things, military decisions are not susceptible of intelligent judicial appraisal. They do not pretend to rest on evidence, but are made on information that often would not be admissible and on assumptions that could not be proved. Information in support of an order could not be disclosed to courts without danger that it would reach the enemy. Neither can courts act on communications made in confidence. Hence courts can never have any real alternative to accepting the mere declaration of the authority that issued the order that it was reasonably necessary from a military viewpoint.

Much is said of the danger to liberty from the Army program for deporting and detaining these citizens of Japanese extraction. But a judicial construction of the due process clause that will sustain this order is a far more subtle blow to liberty than the promulgation of the order itself. A military order, however unconstitutional, is not apt to last longer than the military emergency. Even during that period a succeeding commander may revoke it all. But once a judicial opinion rationalizes such an order to show that it conforms to the Constitution, or rather rationalizes the Constitution to show that the Constitution sanctions such an order, the Court for all time has validated the principle of racial discrimination in criminal procedure and of transplanting American citizens. The principle then lies about like a loaded weapon ready for the hand of any authority that can bring forward a plausible claim of an urgent need. Every repetition imbeds that principle more deeply in our law and thinking and expands it to new purposes. All who observe the work of courts are familiar with what Judge Cardozo described as "the tendency of a principle to expand itself to the limit of its logic." A military commander may overstep the bounds of con-

stitutionality, and it is an incident. But if we review and approve, that passing incident becomes the doctrine of the Constitution. There it has a generative power of its own, and all that it creates will be in its own image. Nothing better illustrates this danger than does the Court's opinion in this case.

It argues that we are bound to uphold the conviction of Korematsu because we upheld one in *Hirabayashi* v. *United States,* . . . when we sustained these orders in so far as they applied a curfew requirement to a citizen of Japanese ancestry. I think we should learn something from that experience.

In that case we were urged to consider only the curfew feature, that being all that technically was involved, because it was the only count necessary to sustain Hirabayashi's conviction and sentence. We yielded, and the Chief Justice guarded the opinion as carefully as language will do. He said: "Our investigation here does not go beyond the inquiry whether, in the light of all the relevant circumstances preceding and attending their promulgation, the challenged orders and statute *afforded a reasonable basis for the action taken in imposing the curfew.*" . . . "We decide only the issue as we have defined it—we decide only that the *curfew order* as applied, and at the time it was applied, was within the boundaries of the war power." . . . And again: "It is unnecessary to consider whether or to what extent *such findings would support orders differing from the curfew order.*" . . . (Italics supplied.) However, in spite of our limiting words we did validate a discrimination on the basis of ancestry for mild and temporary deprivation of liberty. Now the principle of racial discrimination is pushed from support of mild measures to very harsh ones, and from temporary deprivations to indeterminate ones. And the precedent which it is said requires us to do so is *Hirabayashi.* The Court is now saying that in *Hirabay-*

ashi we did decide the very things we there said we were not deciding. Because we said that these citizens could be made to stay in their homes during the hours of dark, it is said we must require them to leave home entirely; and if that, we are told they may also be taken into custody for deportation; and if that, it is argued they may also be held for some undetermined time in detention camps. How far the principle of this case would be extended before plausible reasons would play out, I do not know.

I should hold that a civil court cannot be made to enforce an order which violates constitutional limitations even if it is a reasonable exercise of military authority. The courts can exercise only the judicial power, can apply only law, and must abide by the Constitution, or they cease to be civil courts and become instruments of military policy.

Of course the existence of a military power resting on force, so vagrant, so centralized, so necessarily heedless of the individual, is an inherent threat to liberty.

But I would not lead people to rely on this Court for a review that seems to me wholly delusive. The military reasonableness of these orders can only be determined by military superiors. If the people ever let command of the war power fall into irresponsible and unscrupulous hands, the courts wield no power equal to its restraint. The chief restraint upon those who command the physical forces of the country, in the future as in the past, must be their responsibility to the political judgments of their contemporaries and to the moral judgments of history.

My duties as a justice as I see them do not require me to make a military judgment as to whether General DeWitt's evacuation and detention program was a reasonable military necessity. I do not suggest that the courts should have attempted to interfere with the Army in carrying out its task. But I do not think they may be asked to execute a military expedient that has no place in law under the Constitution. I would reverse the judgment and discharge the prisoner.

Do you agree with Justice Douglas's comment on the *Hirabayashi* and *Korematsu* cases made thirty years later in *Defunis* v. *Odegaard*, 416 U.S. 312 (1974): "The decisions were extreme and went to the verge of wartime power; and they have been severely criticized. It is, however, easy in retrospect to denounce what was done, as there actually was no attempted Japanese invasion of our country.... But those making plans for defense of the nation had no such knowledge and were planning for the worst"?

PRESIDENTIAL POWERS IN DOMESTIC AFFAIRS

Article II provides that the President has the duty to "take care that the laws be faithfully executed." On its face this phrase would seem to limit the President to executing the laws of Congress and acting within the boundaries of congressional statutes. But on several occasions the President has been granted independent lawmaking power by the courts in the domestic sphere.

The Court held in *In Re Neagle*, 135 U.S. 1 (1890), that an order of the Attorney General to Deputy Marshal Neagle to act as a bodyguard for a judge of the Supreme Court whose life had been threatened by a disappointed litigant was a law of the United States under Section 753 of the revised statutes. Neagle had killed the litigant in the course of an attack upon the justice and was arrested by state authorities for murder. He was able to obtain a writ of habeas corpus to have his case transferred to the federal circuit court on the basis that he was illegally being held in custody for "an act done in pursuance of a law of the United States." To obtain habeas corpus under Section 753 it had to be shown that the defendant was "in custody for an act done or omitted in pursuance of a law of the United States." In countering the argument that habeas corpus should not be issued because there was no law explicitly authorizing the Attorney General to provide protection for a Supreme Court justice, the majority of the Court held that

> . . . it is not supposed that any special act of Congress exists which authorizes the marshals or deputy marshals of the United States in express terms to accompany the judges of the Supreme Court through their circuits and act as a bodyguard to them, to defend them against malicious assaults against their persons. But we are of opinion that this view of the statute [Sect. 753] is an unwarranted restriction of the meaning of a law designed to extend in a liberal manner the benefit of the writ of habeas corpus to persons imprisoned for the performance of their duty. . . .
>
> In the view we take of the Constitution of the United States, any obligation fairly and properly inferrable from that instrument, or any duty of the marshal to be derived from the general scope of his duties under the laws of the United States, is "a law" within the meaning of this phrase. . . .[51]

The Attorney General's instructions to the marshals were tantamount to instructions from the President and a proper exercise of presidential power, said the Court. The President has the prerogative to make such "laws" under the general provisions of Article II. Is the President's duty, asked the Court, limited to the enforcement of acts of Congress or of treaties of the United States according to their expressed terms or does it include the "rights, duties and obligations growing out of the Constitution itself, our international relations, and all the protections implied by the nature of the government under the Constitution"?[52] The question was rhetorical. The Court held that the authority of the President to make law extended far beyond expressed statutory provisions or the explicit terms of Article II. And, declared the Court, "We cannot doubt the power of the President to take measures for the protection of a judge of one of the courts of the United States who, while in the discharge of the duties of his office, is threatened with a personal attack which may probably result in his death, and we think it clear that where his protection is to be afforded through the civil power, the Department of Justice is the proper one to set in motion the necessary means of protection."[53]

Several years after the *Neagle* case, the Court again relied on the doctrine

[51]In Re Neagle, 135 U.S. 1, 59 (1890).
[52]Ibid., p. 64.
[53]Ibid., p. 67.

of inherent presidential authority to make law in the case of *In Re Debs*, 158 U.S. 564 (1895). The Court found that the President possessed inherent powers to seek an injunction from the United States circuit court to prevent strikes encumbering interstate commerce and preventing the free flow of the mail. President Cleveland had instructed a United States attorney in Chicago to obtain an injunction against the Pullman strike of 1895. The leader of the Pullman union, Eugene V. Debs, defied the injunction, and the violence and disorder surrounding the strike continued. Debs was cited for contempt, sentenced to imprisonment, and appealed to the Supreme Court for a writ of habeas corpus. The Court upheld the presidential action on the basis of national sovereignty and supremacy over commerce. While granting that there was no statutory basis for the injunction, the strike adversely affected the public, and the President had inherent powers to seek an injunction to prevent it.

The inherent powers of the President to act as a guardian of the public interest were challenged in *Youngstown Sheet and Tube Company* v. *Sawyer* (1952). Claiming a national emergency, and invoking his inherent constitutional authority under Article II as Chief Executive and the Commander-in-Chief, President Truman, on April 8, 1952, issued an order directing his Secretary of Commerce, Sawyer, to seize the steel mills to prevent a strike by the steelworkers. The events leading up to the seizure were long and complicated, and in the end the President felt he had no choice but to act unilaterally to prevent the strike.[54] Recalling his action in his memoirs, Truman wrote that "A little reading of history would have shown that there was nothing unusual about this action—that strike-threatened plants had been seized before by the government, even before the nation was engaged in any shooting conflicts."[55] The President based his executive order seizing the mills on "the authority vested in me by the Constitution and the laws of the United States, and as President of the United States and Commander-in-Chief of the Armed Forces of the United States." The companies immediately sought a court injunction against the implementation of the order. The president of Inland Steel, Clarence Randall, claimed in a radio and television address to the nation, that the President "has seized the steel plants of the nation, the private property of one million people, most of whom now hear the sound of my voice. This he has done without the slightest shadow of legal right. No law passed by the Congress gave him this power. He knows this, and speaks of general authority conferred upon him by the Constitution. But I say, my friends, that the Constitution was adopted by our forefathers to prevent tyranny, not to create it. . . ."[56]

Congress had in 1947 passed the Taft-Hartley Act authorizing the President to seek a court injunction against any strike threatening the national health and safety. During the eighty-day "cooling-off period" a board of inquiry was to be established to attempt to resolve the dispute. Truman had

---

[54]For a description of the events surrounding the case and documents pertaining to it see Alan F. Weston, *The Anatomy of a Constitutional Law Case* (New York: Macmillan, 1958).

[55]Harry S. Truman, *Memoirs: Years of Trial and Hope*, II, 475 (New York: Doubleday, 1956).

[56]Weston, *The Anatomy*, p. 18.

avoided the use of the Taft-Hartley provisions largely for political reasons, as the act was repugnant to the Democratic party. Truman himself had promised to repeal it in his 1948 campaign.

On April 9, 1952, the Federal District Court for the District of Columbia heard arguments for and against the motion by the steel companies for a temporary restraining order. The Assistant Attorney General of the United States, citing Article II, argued: "These provisions of the Constitution are sufficiently broad that the executive powers vested in the President of the United States is, in itself, a grant to the President of all executive power, not specifically divested by other provisions of the Constitution."[57] The Court asked: "What is meant by 'executive powers' . . . ? Isn't it the power to execute statutes?"[58] The attorney for the government replied: "Well, among other things it is the power to protect the country in times of national emergency by whatever means seem appropriate to achieve the end."[59]

The district court refused to issue the injunction, claiming that it would in effect lie against the President and under the doctrine of *Mississippi* v. *Johnson* (see p. 153) such judicial interference in the exercise of executive functions would be questionable. Moreover, the Court held that the steel companies had an adequate remedy through a suit for damages against the government.[60]

Following the district court's denial of a temporary restraining order, the steel companies filed suits in the district court in Washington for a permanent injunction. The government argued that "[t]here is not one single instance in which the courts have enjoined executive power where it was based upon the Constitution and not upon statute."[61] The Court held,

> There is no express grant of power in the Constitution authorizing the President to direct this seizure. There is no grant of power from which it reasonably can be implied. There is no enactment of Congress authorizing it. On what, then, does defendant rely to sustain his act? According to his brief, reiterated in oral argument, he relies upon the President's "broad residuum of power" sometimes referred to as "inherent" power under the Constitution which, as I understand his counsel, is not to be confused with "implied" powers as that term is generally understood, namely, those which are reasonably appropriate to the exercise of a granted power.
>
> . . . The government of the United States . . . derives its authority wholly from the powers granted to it by the Constitution, which is the only source of power authorizing action by any branch of government. It is a government of limited, enumerated, and delegated powers. The office of President of the United States is a branch of the government, namely, that branch where the executive power is vested, and his powers are limited along with the powers of the two other great

[57]Ibid., p. 38.

[58]Ibid.

[59]Ibid.

[60]Normally, under the doctrine of sovereign immunity it is difficult or impossible to sustain suits for damages against the government. However, the doctrine has been diluted through legislation that allows the government to pay damages for torts committed by government officers. In the initial argument in the Youngstown case the government counsel conceded that under the Federal Tort Claims Act the steel companies could sue for compensation in the court of claims.

[61]Weston, *The Anatomy*, p. 65.

branches or departments of government, namely, the legislative and judicial.

The President therefore must derive this broad "residuum of power" or "inherent" power from the Constitution itself, more particularly Article 2 thereof. . . .

The nonexistence of this "inherent" power in the President has been recognized by eminent writers, and I cite in this connection the unequivocal language of the late Chief Justice Taft in his treatise entitled "Our Chief Magistrate and His Powers" (1916), wherein he says: "The true view of the executive function is, as I conceive it, that the President can exercise no power which cannot be fairly and reasonably traced to some specific grant of power or justly implied and included within such express grant as proper and necessary to its exercise." . . .

Enough has been said to show the utter and complete lack of authoritative support for the defendant's position. . . .[62]

The government appealed the district court's ruling to the Federal Court of Appeals for the District of Columbia, requesting a stay of its order that returned the steel mills to private management. The government sought the stay in order to allow the presidential order to remain in effect while government attorneys petitioned the Supreme Court to allow them to bypass the court of appeals and have the Supreme Court directly review the district court's decision on the merits. The court of appeals granted the government's request, at which point the steel companies asked the Supreme Court for a writ of certiorari to review the circuit court's temporary stay. At the same time the government requested certiorari to have the Supreme Court review the permanent injunction that had been issued by the district court. The Supreme Court granted the steel companies' request for certiorari, and they became the plaintiffs.

In *Youngstown Sheet and Tube* v. *Sawyer,* the Supreme Court had to rule on the question of the extent of the inherent prerogative power of the President derived from Article II to take unilateral action by seizing the steel mills in order to prevent a national emergency. The steel companies declared that if the government contentions regarding the prerogative powers of the President were accepted, "The President may exercise virtually unlimited powers in any field where he chooses to say that an emergency exists."[63] The President, contended the plaintiffs, should follow the procedures established by Congress in the Taft-Hartley Act to resolve the dispute. The President, they stated, is not required by law to invoke the act, "but it does follow that by failing to use the procedure provided by Congress the executive can thereby create for itself a right to invoke unwarranted emergency procedures altogether contrary both to the Constitution and the plain intent of Congress."[64]

The government brief in the *Youngstown* case argued that "Under Article 2 of the Constitution the President possessed power to seize the steel mills in order to avoid a cessation of steel production which would gravely endanger the national interests which it is his duty to protect."[65] Each of the granting clauses of Article II, namely the authority given to the President as

[62]Cited in Weston, *The Anatomy,* pp. 69–70.
[63]LB, Vol. 48, p. 446.
[64]Ibid., p. 443.
[65]Ibid., p. 634.

Chief Executive and as Commander-in-Chief, "is sufficiently broadly drawn and wide in purpose to support emergency executive action."[66] The President, "without specific statutory authority, may seize property to avert crises in time of war or national emergency. . . ."[67] The government told the Court that a review of a variety of congressional statutes, not simply the Taft-Hartley Act, makes it clear that congressional intent is to preserve the national security and that the President's seizure was in accordance with this intent.

The *Youngstown* decision was written by Justice Black. Justice Jackson concurred in an important and lengthy opinion. Justices Frankfurter, Douglas, Burton, and Clark also wrote concurring opinions. Chief Justice Vinson, joined by Justices Reed and Minton, wrote a vigorous dissent. The division of opinion in the Court reflected not only the difficulty of the constitutional issue it faced but also a delicate political situation caused by the intense and vociferous opposition to the President's decision that had been expressed in Congress and in the press.

Youngstown Sheet and Tube Company v. *Sawyer*

343 U.S. 579; 72 S. Ct. 863; 96 L. Ed. 1153 (1952)

Mr. Justice Black delivered the opinion of the Court:

We are asked to decide whether the President was acting within his constitutional power when he issued an order directing the Secretary of Commerce to take possession of and operate most of the Nation's steel mills. The mill owners argue that the President's order amounts to lawmaking, a legislative function which the Constitution has expressly confided to the Congress and not to the President. The Government's position is that the order was made on findings of the President that his action was necessary to avert a national catastrophe which would inevitably result from a stoppage of steel production, and that in meeting this grave emergency the President was acting within the aggregate of his constitutional powers as the Nation's Chief Executive and the Commander in Chief of the Armed Forces of the United States. . . .

II

The President's power, if any, to issue the order must stem either from an act of Congress or from the Constitution itself. There is no statute that expressly authorizes the President to take possession of property as he did here. Nor is there any act of Congress to which our attention has been directed from which such a power can fairly be implied. Indeed, we do not understand the Government to rely on statutory authorization for this seizure. There are two statutes which do authorize the President to take both personal and real property under certain conditions. However, the Government admits that these conditions were not met and that the President's order was not rooted in either of the statutes. The Government refers to the seizure provisions of one of these statutes (§ 201 (b) of the Defense Production Act) as "much too cumber-

[66]Ibid., p. 703.
[67]Ibid., p. 709.

some, involved, and time-consuming for the crisis which was at hand."

Moreover, the use of the seizure technique to solve labor disputes in order to prevent work stoppages was not only unauthorized by any congressional enactment; prior to this controversy, Congress had refused to adopt that method of settling labor disputes. When the Taft-Hartley Act was under consideration in 1947, Congress rejected an amendment which would have authorized such governmental seizures in cases of emergency. Apparently it was thought that the technique of seizure, like that of compulsory arbitration, would interfere with the process of collective bargaining. Consequently, the plan Congress adopted in that Act did not provide for seizure under any circumstances. Instead, the plan sought to bring about settlements by use of the customary devices of mediation, conciliation, investigation by boards of inquiry, and public reports. In some instances temporary injunctions were authorized to provide cooling-off periods. All this failing, unions were left free to strike after a secret vote by employees as to whether they wished to accept their employers' final settlement offer.

It is clear that if the President had authority to issue the order he did, it must be found in some provision of the Constitution. And it is not claimed that express constitutional language grants this power to the President. The contention is that presidential power should be implied from the aggregate of his powers under the Constitution. Particular reliance is placed on provisions in Article II which say that "The executive Power shall be vested in a President . . ."; that "he shall take Care that the Laws be faithfully executed"; and that he "shall be Commander in Chief of the Army and Navy of the United States."

The order cannot properly be sustained as an exercise of the President's military power as Commander in Chief of the Armed Forces. The Government attempts to do so by citing a number of cases upholding broad powers in military commanders engaged in day-to-day fighting in a theater of war. Such cases need not concern us here. Even though "theater of war" be an expanding concept, we cannot with faithfulness to our constitutional system hold that the Commander in Chief of the Armed Forces has the ultimate power as such to take possession of private property in order to keep labor disputes from stopping production. This is a job for the Nation's lawmakers, not for its military authorities.

Nor can the seizure order be sustained because of the several constitutional provisions that grant executive power to the President. In the framework of our Constitution, the President's power to see that the laws are faithfully executed refutes the idea that he is to be a lawmaker. The Constitution limits his functions in the lawmaking process to the recommending of laws he thinks wise and the vetoing of laws he thinks bad. And the Constitution is neither silent nor equivocal about who shall make laws which the President is to execute. The first section of the first article says that "All legislative Powers herein granted shall be vested in a Congress of the United States. . . ." . . .

The President's order does not direct that a congressional policy be executed in a manner prescribed by Congress—it directs that a presidential policy be executed in a manner prescribed by the President. The preamble of the order itself, like that of many statutes, sets out reasons why the President believes certain policies should be adopted, proclaims these policies as rules of conduct to be followed, and again, like a statute, authorizes a government official to promulgate additional rules and regulations consistent with the policy proclaimed and needed to carry that policy into execution. The power of Congress to adopt such public policies as those proclaimed by the order is beyond question. It can authorize the taking of private property for public use. It can make laws regulating the relationships between employers and employees, prescribing rules designed to settle labor disputes, and fixing wages and working conditions in certain fields of our economy. The Constitution does not subject this lawmaking power of Congress to presidential or military supervision or control.

It is said that other Presidents without congressional authority have taken possession of private business enterprises in order to settle labor disputes. But even if this be true, Congress has not thereby lost its exclusive constitutional authority to make laws necessary and proper to carry out the powers vested by the Constitution "in the Government of the United States, or any Department or Officer thereof."

The Founders of this Nation entrusted the lawmaking power to the Congress alone in both good and bad times. It would do no good to recall the historical events, the fears of power and the hopes for freedom that lay behind their choice. Such a review would but confirm our holding that this seizure order cannot stand.

The judgment of the District Court is

Affirmed.

MR. JUSTICE FRANKFURTER, concurring: . . . Apart from his vast share of responsibility for the conduct of our foreign relations, the embracing function of the President is that "he shall take Care that the Laws be faithfully executed. . . ." Art. II, § 3. The nature of that authority has for me been comprehensively indicated by Mr. Justice Holmes. "The duty of the President to see that the laws be executed is a duty that does not go beyond the laws or require him to achieve more than Congress sees fit to leave within his power." *Myers* v. *United States* [1926]. The powers

of the President are not as particularized as are those of Congress. But unenumerated powers do not mean undefined powers. The separation of powers built into our Constitution gives essential content to undefined provisions in the frame of our government. . . .

A scheme of government like ours no doubt at times feels the lack of power to act with complete, all-embracing, swiftly moving authority. No doubt a government with distributed authority, subject to be challenged in the courts of law, at least long enough to consider and adjudicate the challenge, labors under restrictions from which other governments are free. It has not been our tradition to envy such governments. In any event our government was designed to have such restrictions. The price was deemed not too high in view of the safeguards which these restrictions afford. . . .

MR. JUSTICE DOUGLAS, concurring:
There can be no doubt that the emergency which caused the President to seize these steel plants was one that bore heavily on the country. But the emergency did not create power; it merely marked an occasion when power should be exercised. And the fact that it was necessary that measures be taken to keep steel in production does not mean that the President, rather than the Congress, had the constitutional authority to act. The Congress, as well as the President, is trustee of the national welfare. The President can act more quickly than the Congress. The President with the armed services at his disposal can move with force as well as with speed. All executive power—from the reign of ancient kings to the rule of modern dictators—has the outward appearance of efficiency.

Legislative power, by contrast, is slower to exercise. There must be delay while the ponderous machinery of committees, hearings, and debates is put into motion. That takes time; and while the Congress slowly moves into action, the emergency may take its toll in wages, consumer goods, war production, the standard of living of the people, and perhaps even lives. Legislative action may indeed often be cumbersome, time-consuming, and apparently inefficient. But as Mr. Justice Brandeis stated in his dissent in *Myers* v. *United States,*

The doctrine of the separation of powers was adopted by the Convention of 1787, not to promote efficiency but to preclude the exercise of arbitrary power. The purpose was, not to avoid friction, but, by means of the inevitable friction incident to the distribution of the governmental powers among three departments, to save the people from autocracy.

We therefore cannot decide this case by determining which branch of government can deal most expeditiously with the present crisis. The answer must depend on the allocation of powers under the Constitution. That in turn requires an analysis of the conditions giving rise to the seizure and of the seizure itself.... .

The great office of President is not a weak and powerless one. The President represents the people and is their spokesman in domestic and foreign affairs. The office is respected more than any other in the land. It gives a position of leadership that is unique. The power to formulate policies and mould opinion inheres in the Presidency and conditions our national life. The impact of the man and the philosophy he represents may at times be thwarted by the Congress. Stalemates may occur when emergencies mount and the Nation suffers for lack of harmonious, reciprocal action between the White House and Capitol Hill. That is a risk inherent in our system of separation of powers. The tragedy of such stalemates might be avoided by allowing the President the use of some legislative authority. The Framers with memories of the tyrannies produced by a blending of executive and legislative power rejected that political

arrangement. Some future generation may, however, deem it so urgent that the President have legislative authority that the Constitution will be amended. We could not sanction the seizures and condemnations of the steel plants in this case without reading Article II as giving the President not only the power to execute the laws but to make some. Such a step would most assuredly alter the pattern of the Constitution.

We pay a price for our system of checks and balances, for the distribution of power among the three branches of government. It is a price that today may seem exorbitant to many. Today a kindly President uses the seizure power to effect a wage increase and to keep the steel furnaces in production. Yet tomorrow another President might use the same power to prevent a wage increase, to curb trade-unionists, to regiment labor as oppressively as industry thinks it has been regimented by this seizure.

MR. JUSTICE JACKSON, concurring in the judgment and opinion of the Court:

... A judge, like an executive adviser, may be surprised at the poverty of really useful and unambiguous authority applicable to concrete problems of executive power as they actually present themselves. Just what our forefathers did envision, or would have envisioned had they foreseen modern conditions, must be divined from materials almost as enigmatic as the dreams Joseph was called upon to interpret for Pharaoh. A century and a half of partisan debate and scholarly speculation yields no net result but only supplies more or less apt quotations from respected sources on each side of any question. They largely cancel each other. And court decisions are indecisive because of the judicial practice of dealing with the largest questions in the most narrow way.

The actual art of governing under our Constitution does not and cannot conform to judicial definitions of the power of any of its branches based on isolated clauses or even single Articles torn from context. While the Constitution diffuses power the better to secure liberty, it also contemplates that practice will integrate the dispersed powers into a workable government. It enjoins upon its branches separateness but interdependence, autonomy but reciprocity. Presidential powers are not fixed but fluctuate, depending upon their disjunction or conjunction with those of Congress. We may well begin by a somewhat over-simplified grouping of practical situations in which a President may doubt, or others may challenge, his powers, and by distinguishing roughly the legal consequences of this factor of relativity.

1. When the President acts pursuant to an express or implied authorization of Congress, his authority is at its maximum, for it includes all that he possesses in his own right plus all that Congress can delegate. In these circumstances, and in these only, may he be said (for what it may be worth) to personify the federal sovereignty. If his act is held unconstitutional under these circumstances, it usually means that the Federal Government as an undivided whole lacks power. A seizure executed by the President pursuant to an Act of Congress would be supported by the strongest of presumptions and the widest latitude of judicial interpretation, and the burden of persuasion would rest heavily upon any who might attack it.

2. When the President acts in absence of either a congressional grant or denial of authority, he can only rely upon his own independent powers, but there is a zone of twilight in which he and Congress may have concurrent authority, or in which its distribution is uncertain. Therefore, congressional inertia, indifference or quiescence may sometimes, at least as a practical matter, enable, if not invite, measures on independent presidential responsibility. In this area, any actual test of power is likely to depend on the imperatives of events and contemporary imponderables rather than on abstract theories of law.

3. When the President takes measures incompatible with the expressed or implied will of Congress, his power is at its lowest ebb, for then he can rely only upon his own constitutional powers minus any constitutional powers of Congress over the matter. Courts can sustain exclusive presidential control in such a case only by disabling the Congress from acting upon the subject. Presidential claim to a power at once so conclusive and preclusive must be scrutinized with caution, for what is at stake is the equilibrium established by our constitutional system.

Into which of these classifications does this executive seizure of the steel industry fit? It is eliminated from the first by admission, for it is conceded that no congressional authorization exists for this seizure. That takes away also the support of the many precedents and declarations which were made in relation, and must be confined, to this category.

Can it then be defended under flexible tests available to the second category? It seems clearly eliminated from that class because Congress has not left seizure of private property an open field but has covered it by three statutory policies inconsistent with this seizure. . . .

This leaves the current seizure to be justified only by the severe tests under the third grouping, where it can be supported only by any remainder of executive power after subtraction of such powers as Congress may have over the subject. In short, we can sustain the President only by holding that seizure of such strike-bound industries is within his domain and beyond control by Congress. . . .

I did not suppose, and I am not persuaded, that history leaves it open to question, at least in the courts, that the executive branch, like the Federal Government as a whole, possesses only delegated powers. . . . However, because the President does not enjoy unmentioned powers does not mean that the mentioned ones should be narrowed by a niggardly construction. . . . I . . . give to the enumerated powers the scope and elasticity afforded by what seem to be reasonable, practical implications instead of the rigidity dictated by a doctrinaire textualism.

The Solicitor General seeks the power of seizure in three clauses of the Executive Article, the first reading, "The executive Power shall be vested in a President of the United States of America." Lest I be thought to exaggerate, I quote the interpretation which his brief puts upon it: "In our view, this clause constitutes a grant of all the executive powers of which the Government is capable." If that be true, it is difficult to see why the forefathers bothered to add several specific items, including some trifling ones. . . .

I cannot accept the view that this clause is a grant in bulk of all conceivable executive power but regard it as an allocation to the presidential office of the generic powers thereafter stated.

The clause on which the Government next relies is that "The President shall be Commander in Chief of the Army and Navy of the United States. . . ." These cryptic words have given rise to some of the most persistent controversies in our constitutional history. Of course, they imply something more than an empty title. But just what authority goes with the name has plagued presidential advisers who would not waive or narrow it by nonassertion yet cannot say where it begins or ends. It undoubtedly puts the Nation's armed forces under presidential command. Hence, this loose appellation is sometimes advanced as support for any presidential action, internal or external, involving use of force, the idea being that it vests power to do anything, anywhere, that can be done with an army or navy.

That seems to be the logic of an argument tendered at our bar—that the President having, on his own responsibility, sent American troops abroad derives from that act "affirmative power" to seize the means of producing a supply of steel for them. . . .

. . . No doctrine that the Court could promulgate would seem to me more sinister and alarming than that a President whose conduct of foreign affairs is so largely uncontrolled, and often even is unknown, can vastly enlarge his mastery over the internal affairs of the country by his own commitment of the Nation's armed forces to some foreign venture. I do not, however, find it necessary or appropriate to consider the legal status of the Korean enterprise to discountenance argument based on it.

Assuming that we are in a war *de facto*, whether it is or is not a war *de jure*, does that empower the Commander in Chief to seize industries he thinks necessary to supply our army? The Constitution expressly places in Congress power "to raise and *support* Armies" and "to *provide* and *maintain* a Navy." (Emphasis supplied.) This certainly lays upon Congress primary responsibility for supplying the armed forces. Congress alone controls the raising of revenues and their appropriation and may determine in what manner and by what means they shall be spent for military and naval procurement. I suppose no one would doubt that Congress can take over war supply as a Government enterprise. . . .

There are indications that the Constitution did not contemplate that the title Commander in Chief *of the Army and Navy* will constitute him also Commander in Chief of the country, its industries and its inhabitants. He has no monopoly of "war powers," whatever they are. While Congress cannot deprive the President of the command of the army and navy, only Congress can provide him an army or navy to command. It is also empowered to make rules for the "Government and Regulation of land and naval Forces," by which it may to some unknown extent impinge upon even command functions.

That military powers of the Commander in Chief were not to supersede representative government of internal affairs seems obvious from the Constitution and from elementary American history. . . .

We should not use this occasion to circumscribe, much less to contract, the lawful role of the President as Commander in Chief. I should indulge the widest latitude of interpretation to sustain his exclusive function to command the instruments of national force, at least when turned against the outside world for the security of our society. But, when it is turned inward, not because of rebellion but because of a lawful economic struggle between industry and labor, it should have no such indulgence. . . .

The third clause in which the Solicitor General finds seizure powers is that "he shall take Care that the Laws be faithfully executed. . . ." That authority must be matched against words of the Fifth Amendment that "No person shall be . . . deprived of life, liberty or property, without due process of law. . . ." One gives a governmental authority that reaches so far as there is law, the other gives a private right that authority shall go no farther. These signify about all there is of the principle that ours is a government of laws, not of men, and that we submit ourselves to rulers only if under rules.

The Solicitor General lastly grounds support of the seizure upon nebulous, inherent powers never expressly granted but said to have accrued to the office from the customs and claims of preceding administrations. The plea is for a resulting power to deal with a crisis or an emergency according to the necessities of the case, the unarticulated assumption being that necessity knows no law.

Loose and irresponsible use of adjectives colors all nonlegal and much legal discussion of presidential powers. "Inherent" powers, "implied" powers, "incidental" powers, "plenary" powers, "war" powers and "emergency" powers are used, often interchangeably and without fixed or ascertainable meanings.

The vagueness and generality of the clauses that set forth presidential powers afford a plausible basis for pressures within and without an administration for presidential action beyond that supported by those whose responsibility it is to defend his actions in court. The claim of inherent and unrestricted presidential powers has long been a persuasive dialectical weapon in political controversy. While it is not surprising that counsel should grasp support from such unadjudicated claims of power, a judge cannot accept self-serving press statements of the attorney for one of the interested parties as authority in answering a constitutional question, even if the advocate was himself. But prudence has counseled that actual reliance on such nebulous claims stops short of provoking a judicial test. . . .

In view of the ease, expedition and safety with which Congress can grant and has granted large emergency powers, certainly ample to embrace this crisis, I am quite unimpressed with the argument that we should affirm possession of them without statute. Such power either has no beginning or it has no end. If it exists, it need submit to no legal restraint. I am not alarmed that it would plunge us straightway into dictatorship, but it is at least a step in that wrong direction. . . .

Executive power has the advantage of concentration in a single head in whose choice the whole Nation has a part, making him the focus of public hopes and expectations. . . .

Moreover, rise of the party system has made a significant extraconstitutional supplement to real executive power. . . .

But I have no illusion that any decision by this Court can keep power in the hands of Congress if it is not wise and timely in meeting its problems. A crisis that challenges the President equally, or perhaps primarily, challenges Congress. If not good law, there was worldly wisdom in the maxim attributed to Napoleon that "The tools belong to the man who can use them." We may say that power to legislate for emergencies belongs in the hands of Congress, but only Congress itself can prevent power from slipping through its fingers.

The essence of our free Government is "leave to live by no man's leave, underneath the law"—to be governed by those impersonal forces which we call law. Our Government is fashioned to fulfill this concept so far as humanly possible. The Executive, except for recommendation and veto, has no legislative power. The executive action we have here originates in the individual will of the President and represents an exercise of authority without law. No one, perhaps not even the President, knows the limits of the power he may seek to exert in this instance and the parties affected cannot learn the limit of their rights. We do not know today what powers over labor or property would be claimed to flow from Government possession if we should legalize it, what rights to compensation would be claimed or recognized, or on what contingency it would end. With all its defects, delays and inconveniences, men have discovered no technique for long preserving free government except that the Executive be under the law, and that the law be made by parliamentary deliberations.

Such institutions may be destined to pass away. But it is the duty of the Court to be last, not first, to give them up.

MR. JUSTICE BURTON, concurring in both the opinion and judgment of the Court:

. . . In the case before us, Congress authorized a procedure which the President declined to follow. Instead, he followed another procedure which he hoped might eliminate the need for the first. Upon its failure, he issued an executive order to seize the steel properties in the face of the reserved right of Congress to adopt or reject that course as a matter of legislative policy.

This brings us to a further crucial question. Does the President, in such a situation, have inherent constitutional power to seize private property which makes congressional action in relation thereto unnecessary? We find no such power available to him under the present circumstances. The present situation is not comparable to that of an imminent invasion or threatened attack. We do not face the issue of what might be the President's constitutional power to meet such catastrophic situations. Nor is it claimed that the current seizure is in the nature of a military command addressed by the President, as Commander-in-Chief, to a mobilized nation waging, or imminently threatened with, total war.

The controlling fact here is that Congress, within its constitutionally delegated power, has prescribed for the President specific procedures, exclusive of seizure, for his use in meeting the present type of emergency. Congress has reserved to itself the right to determine where and when to authorize the seizure of property in meeting such an emergency. Under these circumstances, the President's order of April 8 invaded the jurisdiction of Congress. It violated the essence of the principle of the separation of governmental powers. Accordingly, the injunction against its effectiveness should be sustained.

MR. JUSTICE CLARK, concurring in the judgment of the Court:

... In my view ... the Constitution does grant to the President extensive authority in times of grave and imperative national emergency. In fact, to my thinking, such a grant may well be necessary to the very existence of the Constitution itself. As Lincoln aptly said, "[is] it possible to lose the nation and yet preserve the Constitution?" In describing this authority I care not whether one calls it "residual," "inherent," "moral," "implied," "aggregate," "emergency," or otherwise. ...

I conclude that where Congress has laid down specific procedures to deal with the type of crisis confronting the President, he must follow those procedures in meeting the crisis; but that in the absence of such action by Congress, the President's independent power to act depends upon the gravity of the situation confronting the nation. I cannot sustain the seizure in question because here Congress had prescribed methods to be followed by the President in meeting the emergency at hand. ...

... The Government made no effort to comply with the procedures established by the Selective Service Act of 1948, a statute which expressly authorizes seizures when producers fail to supply necessary defense matériel. ...

MR. CHIEF JUSTICE VINSON, with whom MR. JUSTICE REED and MR. JUSTICE MINTON join, dissenting:

... One is not here called upon even to consider the possibility of executive seizure of a farm, a corner grocery store or even a single industrial plant. Such considerations arise only when one ignores the central fact of this case—that the Nation's entire basic steel production would have shut down completely if there had been no Government seizure. ...

Accordingly, if the President has any power under the Constitution to meet a critical situation in the absence of express statutory authorization, there is no basis whatever for criticizing the exercise of such power in this case. ...

... We are not called upon today to expand the Constitution to meet a new situation. For, in this case, we need only look to history and time-honored principles of constitutional law—principles that have been applied consistently by all branches of the Government throughout our history. It is those who assert the invalidity of the Executive Order who seek to amend the Constitution in this case.

III

A review of executive action demonstrates that our Presidents have on many occasions exhibited the leadership contemplated by the Framers when they made the President Commander in Chief, and imposed upon him the trust to "take Care that the Laws be faithfully executed." With or without explicit statutory authorization, Presidents have at such times dealt with national emergencies by acting promptly and resolutely to enforce legislative programs, at least to save those programs until Congress could act. Congress and the courts have responded to such executive initiative with consistent approval.

Our first President displayed at once the leadership contemplated by the Framers. When the national revenue laws were openly flouted in some sections of Pennsylvania, President Washington, without waiting for a call from the state government, summoned the militia and took decisive steps to secure the faithful execution of the laws. When international disputes engendered by the French revolution threatened to involve this country in war, and while congressional policy remained uncertain, Washington issued his Proclamation of Neutrality. ...

Jefferson's initiative in the Louisiana

Purchase, the Monroe Doctrine, and Jackson's removal of Government deposits from the Bank of the United States further serve to demonstrate by deed what the Framers described by word when they vested the whole of the executive power in the President.

Without declaration of war, President Lincoln took energetic action with the outbreak of the War Between the States. He summoned troops and paid them out of the Treasury without appropriation therefor. He proclaimed a naval blockade of the Confederacy and seized ships violating that blockade. Congress, far from denying the validity of these acts, gave them express approval. The most striking action of President Lincoln was the Emancipation Proclamation, issued in aid of the successful prosecution of the War Between the States, but wholly without statutory authority.

In an action furnishing a most apt precedent for this case, President Lincoln without statutory authority directed the seizure of rail and telegraph lines leading to Washington. Many months later, Congress recognized and confirmed the power of the President to seize railroads and telegraph lines and provided criminal penalties for interference with Government operation. . . .

In *In Re Neagle* [1890] this Court held that a federal officer had acted in line of duty when he was guarding a Justice of this Court riding circuit. It was conceded that there was no specific statute authorizing the President to assign such a guard. In holding that such a statute was not necessary, the Court broadly stated the question as follows:

[The President] is enabled to fulfil the duty of his great department, expressed in the phrase that "he shall take care that the laws be faithfully executed."

Is this duty limited to the enforcement of acts of Congress or of treaties of the United States according to their *express terms*, or does it include the rights, duties and obligations growing out of the Constitution itself, our international relations, and all the protection implied by the nature of the government under the Constitution?

The latter approach was emphatically adopted by the Court.

President Hayes authorized the widespread use of federal troops during the Railroad Strike of 1877. President Cleveland also used the troops in the Pullman Strike of 1895 and his action is of special significance. No statute authorized this action. No call for help had issued from the Governor of Illinois; indeed Governor Altgeld disclaimed the need for supplemental forces. But the President's concern was that federal laws relating to the free flow of interstate commerce and the mails be continuously and faithfully executed without interruption. To further this aim his agents sought and obtained the injunction upheld by this Court in *In Re Debs* [1895].

During World War I, President Wilson established a War Labor Board without awaiting specific direction by Congress. With William Howard Taft and Frank P. Walsh as co-chairmen, the Board had as its purpose the prevention of strikes and lockouts interfering with the production of goods needed to meet the emergency. Effectiveness of War Labor Board decision was accomplished by Presidential action, including seizure of industrial plants. Seizure of the Nation's railroads was also ordered by President Wilson.

Beginning with the Bank Holiday Proclamation and continuing through World War II, executive leadership and initiative were characteristic of President Franklin D. Roosevelt's administration. . . .

Some six months before Pearl Harbor, a dispute at a single aviation plant at Inglewood, California, interrupted a segment of the production of military aircraft. . . . President Roosevelt ordered the seizure of the plant "pursuant to the powers vested in [him] by the Constitution and laws of the United States, as President of the United States of America and Commander in Chief of the Army and Navy of the United States." The Attorney General (Jackson) vigorously proclaimed that the President had the moral duty to keep this Nation's defense effort a "going concern." His ringing moral justification was coupled with a legal justification equally well stated:

The Presidential proclamation rests upon the aggregate of the Presidential powers derived from the Constitution itself and from statutes enacted by the Congress. . . .

[Before and after Pearl Harbor] . . . industrial concerns were seized to avert interruption of needed production. During the same period, the President directed seizure of the Nation's coal mines to remove an obstruction to the effective prosecution of the war. . . .

At the time of the seizure of the coal mines . . . [a] bill to provide a statutory basis for seizures . . . [was] before Congress. As stated by its sponsor, the purpose of the bill was not to augment Presidential power, but to "let the country know that the Congress is squarely behind the President." . . .

This is but a cursory summary of executive leadership. But it amply demonstrates that Presidents have taken prompt action to enforce the laws and protect the country whether or not Congress happened to provide in advance for the particular method of execution. . . . The fact that Congress and the courts have consistently recognized and given their support to such executive action indicates that such a power of seizure has been accepted throughout our history. . . .

Much of the argument in this case has been directed at straw men. We do not now have before us the case of a President acting solely on the basis of his own notions of the public welfare. Nor is there

any question of unlimited executive power in this case. The President himself closed the door to any such claim when he sent his Message to Congress stating his purpose to abide by any action of Congress, whether approving or disapproving his seizure action. Here, the President immediately made sure that Congress was fully informed of the temporary action he had taken only to preserve the legislative programs from destruction until Congress could act.

The absence of a specific statute authorizing seizure of the steel mills as a mode of executing the laws—both the military procurement program and the anti-inflation program—has not until today been thought to prevent the President from executing the laws. Unlike an administrative commission confined to the enforcement of the statute under which it was created, or the head of a department when administering a particular statute, the President is a constitutional officer charged with taking care that a "mass of legislation" be executed. Flexibility as to mode of execution to meet critical situations is a matter of practical necessity. . . .

. . . In this case, there is no statute prohibiting the action taken by the President in a matter not merely important but threatening the very safety of the Nation. Executive inaction in such a situation, courting national disaster, is foreign to the concept of energy and initiative in the Executive as created by the Founding Fathers. . . .

The broad executive power granted by Article II to an officer on duty 365 days a year cannot, it is said, be invoked to avert disaster. Instead, the President must confine himself to sending a message to Congress recommending action. Under this messenger-boy concept of the Office, the President cannot even act to preserve legislative programs from destruction so that Congress will have something left to act upon. . . .

Justice Black's opinion for the Court is a broad negation of inherent presidential powers in the domestic sphere. Under what circumstances, if any, would the majority of the Court allow the President to exercise prerogative powers in cases of national emergency? Refer to the previous discussion of the delegation of legislative authority, pp. 109–124, and contrast the statement of Black that the Constitution limits the President's functions in the lawmaking process "to the recommending of laws he thinks wise and the vetoing of laws he thinks bad. And the Constitution is neither silent nor equivocal about who shall make laws which the President is to execute. The first section of the first article says that 'All legislative powers herein granted shall be vested in a Congress of the United States. . . .' " Is not this statement somewhat inaccurate in light of historical precedent before the *Youngstown* decision? Did the President in fact act contrary to the intent of Congress in his seizure of the steel mills?

Justice Jackson deals with the issue by creating three categories of presidential action—actions pursuant to congressional authority, actions taken where Congress is silent, and "when the President takes measures incompatible with the expressed or implied will of Congress." Jackson holds that the President's seizure is in the third category where "his power is at its lowest ebb, for then he can rely only upon his own constitutional powers minus any constitutional powers of Congress over the matter." Jackson would uphold presidential decisions based upon inherent powers in the second category. There, he writes, the actual test of powers "is likely to depend on the imperatives of events and contemporary imponderables rather than on abstract theories of law." Jackson cites Lincoln's suspension of the writ of habeas corpus as an example of a proper exercise of presidential prerogative power. Can you think of other independent presidential actions that Jackson would uphold? Apply Jackson's categories to the cases of independent presidential action cited in Vinson's dissenting opinion. Vinson states that "if the President has any power under the Constitution to meet a critical situation in the absence of express statutory authorization, there is no basis whatever for criticizing the exercise of such power in this case. . . ." Jackson clearly disagrees. Which justice has most accurately interpreted the application of the Constitution to the facts of the case?

FOUR

Federalism

While the proper relationship between the national government and the states remains an important question in contemporary politics, the *constitutional* division of authority between nation and states has been settled for a long time. But, before, during, and after the inception of the Republic in 1789 the question of the proper scope of national power in relation to the states was *the* question of the day. The federal form of government was adopted by the framers of the Constitution to accommodate state interests while assuring that the national government would be able to exercise sufficient power to deal with the common concerns of the nation. Those supporting federalism in the eighteenth century were the nationalists of their time, advancing federalism as a form of government that would permit the exercise of national power over the states.

The supporters of the Constitution were called Federalists, not to be confused with the Federalist or Federal party which was formed later. In the generic sense Federalists were those who supported the federal form of government, while their opponents were called the anti-Federalists. The Federalists and the anti-Federalists were not parties in the sense in which that term was later used to identify political organizations created to put their members into elected offices. Although the Federalists of 1787 were not a party, many, such as Alexander Hamilton, became prominent members of the Federalist party that was formed in the 1790s and early 1800s. Both at the Convention and later in the party, Federalist leaders such as Alexander Hamilton and Chief Justice John Marshall shaped both the Constitution and its early interpretation to allow the expansion of national power over the states.

At the time of the framing of the Constitution and during the ratification campaign, the anti-Federalists were deeply concerned about the possibility that the new government would destroy the sovereignty of the states. They pointed to both the "necessary and proper" clause of Article I, Section 8 and the "supremacy" clause of Article VI as the major constitutional provisions that would sanction the exercise of virtually unlimited national power over the states. The exposition of Alexander Hamilton and James Madison in *The Federalist,* designed to assuage the fears of the states' rights advocates, did not succeed. The authors of *The Federalist* admitted that the authority of the national government would extend beyond its explicitly enumerated powers. Moreover, *The Federalist* made it clear that, in the words of Hamilton in *Federalist 27,* "the laws of the Confederacy [the national government under the Constitution of 1787] as to the *enumerated* and *legitimate* objects of its jurisdiction will become the *supreme law* of the land; to the observance of which all officers, legislative, executive, and judicial in each state will be bound by the sanctity of an oath."

Hamilton recognized in *Federalist 33* that the necessary and proper clause and the supremacy clause

> have been the source of much virulent invective and petulant declamation against the proposed Constitution. They have been held up to the people in all the exaggerated colors of misrepresentation as the pernicious engines by which their local governments were to be destroyed and their liberties exterminated; as the hideous monster whose devouring jaws would spare neither sex nor age, nor high nor low, nor sacred nor profane; and yet, strange as it may appear, after all this clamor, to those who may not have happened to contemplate them in the same light, it may be affirmed with perfect confidence that the constitutional operation of the intended government would be precisely the same if these clauses were entirely obliterated as if they were repeated in every article.

The enumerated powers of Congress imply the power to carry them into execution. Why was the necessary and proper clause put into the Constitution if it is redundant? "The answer," wrote Hamilton, "is that it could only have been done for greater caution, and to guard against all cavilling refinements in those who might hereafter feel a disposition to curtail and evade the legitimate authorities of the Union." Hamilton continued,

> Who is to judge of the necessity and propriety of the laws to be passed for executing the powers of the Union? I answer first that this question arises as well and as fully upon the simple grant of those powers as upon the declaratory clause; and I answer in the second place that the national government, like every other, must judge in the first instance, of the proper exercise of its powers, and its constituents in the last. If the federal government should overpass the just bounds of its authority and make a tyrannical use of its powers, the people, whose creature it is, must appeal to the standards they have formed, and take such measures to redress the injury done to the Constitution as the exigency may suggest and prudence justify.

Turning to the supremacy clause, Hamilton pointed out in *Federalist 34* that it too was nothing more than an explicit statement of what would otherwise be implied, for a "law, by the very meaning of the term, includes supremacy." But the supremacy clause will not result in the subordination of state interests, because only laws made pursuant to the Constitution are supreme.

The views of Hamilton and Madison on the scope of constitutional authority granted to the national government, the necessary and proper clause, and the supremacy clause are presented in the following *Federalist* papers. Note, in particular, Hamilton's declaration in *Federalist 23* of the implied powers of the national government without reference to the necessary and proper clause.

The Federalist

No. 23: Hamilton

THE necessity of a Constitution, at least equally energetic with the one proposed, to the preservation of the Union is the point at the examination of which we are now arrived.

This inquiry will naturally divide itself into three branches—the objects to be provided for by a federal government, the quantity of power necessary to the accomplishment of those objects, the persons upon whom that power ought to operate. Its distribution and organization will more properly claim our attention under the succeeding head.

The principal purposes to be answered by union are these—the common defense of the members; the preservation of the public peace, as well against internal convulsions as external attacks; the regulation of commerce with other nations and between the States; the superintendence of our intercourse, political and commercial, with foreign countries.

The authorities essential to the common defense are these: to raise armies, to build and equip fleets; to prescribe rules for the government of both; to direct their operations; to provide for their support. These powers ought to exist without limitation, *because it is impossible to foresee or to define the extent and variety of national exigencies, and the correspondent extent and variety of the means which may be necessary to satisfy them.* The circumstances that endanger the safety of nations are infinite, and for this reason no constitutional shackles can wisely be imposed on the power to which the care of it is committed. This power ought to be coextensive with all the possible combinations of such circumstances; and ought to be under the direction of the same councils which are appointed to preside over the common defense.

This is one of those truths which to a correct and unprejudiced mind carries its own evidence along with it, and may be obscured, but cannot be made plainer by argument or reasoning. It rests upon axioms as simple as they are universal; the *means* ought to be proportioned to the *end;* the persons from whose agency the attainment of any *end* is expected ought to possess the *means* by which it is to be attained.

Whether there ought to be a federal government intrusted with the care of the common defense is a question in the first instance open to discussion; but the moment it is decided in the affirmative, it will follow that that government ought to be clothed with all the powers requisite to complete execution of its trust. And unless it can be shown that the circumstances which may affect the public safety are reducible within certain determinate limits; unless the contrary of this position can be fairly and rationally disputed, it must be admitted as a necessary consequence that there can be no limitation of that authority which is to provide for the defense and protection of the community in any matter essential to its efficacy—that is, in any matter essential to the *formation, direction,* or *support* of the NATIONAL FORCES.

Defective as the present Confederation has been proved to be, this principle appears to have been fully recognized by the framers of it; though they have not made proper or adequate provision for its exercise. Congress have an unlimited discretion to make requisitions of men and money; to govern the army and navy; to direct their operations. As their requisitions are made constitutionally binding upon the States, who are in fact under the most solemn obligations to furnish the supplies required of them, the intention evidently was that the United States should command whatever resources were by them judged requisite to the "common defense and general welfare." It was presumed that a sense of their true interests, and a regard to the dictates of good faith, would be found sufficient pledges for the punctual performance of the duty of the members to the federal head.

The experiment has, however, demonstrated that this expectation was ill-founded and illusory; and the observations made under the last head will, I imagine, have sufficed to convince the impartial and discerning that there is an absolute necessity for an entire change in the first principles of the system; that if we are in earnest about giving the Union energy and duration we must abandon the vain project of legislating upon the States in their collective capacities; we must extend the laws of the federal government to the individual citizens of America; we must discard the fallacious scheme of quotas and requisitions as equally impracticable and unjust. The result from all this is that the Union ought to be invested with full power to levy troops; to build and equip fleets; and to raise the revenues which will be required for the formation and support of an army and navy in the customary and ordinary modes practiced in other governments.

If the circumstances of our country are such as to demand a compound instead of a simple, a confederate instead of a sole, government, the essential point which will remain to be adjusted will be to discriminate the OBJECTS, as far as it can be done, which shall appertain to the different provinces or departments of power; allowing to each the most ample authority for fulfilling the objects committed to its charge. Shall the Union be constituted the guardian of the common safety? Are fleets and armies and revenues necessary to this purpose? The government of the Union must be empowered to pass all laws, and to make all regulations which have relation to them. The same must be the case in respect to commerce, and to every other matter to which its jurisdiction is permitted to extend. Is the administration of justice between the citizens of the same State the proper department of the local governments? These must possess all the authorities which are connected with this object, and with every other that may be allotted to their particular cognizance and direction. Not to confer in each case a degree of power commensurate to the end would be to violate the most obvious rules of prudence and propriety, and improvidently to trust the great interests of the nation to hands which are disabled from managing them with vigor and success.

Who so likely to make suitable provisions for the public defense as that body to which the guardianship of the public safety is confided; which, as the center of information, will best understand the extent and urgency of the dangers that threaten; as the representative of the WHOLE, will feel itself most deeply interested in the preservation of every part;

which, from the responsibility implied in the duty assigned to it, will be most sensibly impressed with the necessity of proper exertions; and which, by the extension of its authority throughout the States, can alone establish uniformity and concert in the plans and measures by which the common safety is to be secured? Is there not a manifest inconsistency in devolving upon the federal government the care of the general defense and leaving in the State governments the *effective* powers by which it is to be provided for? Is not a want of co-operation the infallible consequence of such a system? And will not weakness, disorder, an undue distribution of the burdens and calamities of war, an unnecessary and intolerable increase of expense, be its natural and inevitable concomitants? Have we not had unequivocal experience of its effects in the course of the revolution which we have just achieved?

Every view we may take of the subject, as candid inquirers after truth will serve to convince us that it is both unwise and dangerous to deny the federal government an unconfined authority in respect to all those objects which are intrusted to its management. It will indeed deserve the most vigilant and careful attention of the people to see that it be modeled in such a manner as to admit of its being safely vested with the requisite powers. If any plan which has been, or may be, offered to our consideration should not, upon a dispassionate inspection, be found to answer this description, it ought to be rejected. A government, the constitution of which renders it unfit to be trusted with all the powers which a free people *ought to delegate to any government,* would be an unsafe and improper depositary of the NATIONAL INTERESTS. Wherever THESE can with propriety be confided, the co-incident powers may safely accompany them. This is the true result of all just reasoning upon the subject. And the adversaries of the plan promulgated by the Convention

would have given a better impression of their candor if they had confined themselves to showing that the internal structure of the proposed government was such as to render it unworthy of the confidence of the people. They ought not to have wandered into inflammatory declamations and unmeaning cavils about the extent of the powers. The POWERS are not too extensive for the OBJECTS of federal administration, or, in other words, for the management of our NATIONAL INTERESTS; nor can any satisfactory argument be framed to show that they are chargeable with such an excess. If it be true, as has been insinuated by some of the writers on the other side, that the difficulty arises from the nature of the thing, and that the extent of the country will not permit us to form a government in which such ample powers can safely be reposed, it would prove that we ought to contract our views, and resort to the expedient of separate confederacies, which will move within more practicable spheres. For the absurdity must continually stare us in the face of confiding to a government the direction of the most essential national interests, without daring to trust it to the authorities which are indispensable to their proper and efficient management. Let us not attempt to reconcile contradictions, but firmly embrace a rational alternative.

I trust, however, that the impracticability of one general system cannot be shown. I am greatly mistaken if anything of weight has yet been advanced of this tendency; and I flatter myself that the observations which have been made in the course of these papers have served to place the reverse of that position in as clear a light as any matter still in the womb of time and experience is susceptible of. This, at all events, must be evident, that the very difficulty itself, drawn from the extent of the country, is the strongest argument in favor of an energetic government; for any other can certainly never preserve the Union of so large an empire. If we embrace the tenets of those who oppose the adoption of the proposed Constitution as the standard of our political creed we cannot fail to verify the gloomy doctrines which predict the impracticability of a national system pervading the entire limits of the present Confederacy.

Publius

No. 44: Madison

A *fifth* class of provisions in favor of the federal authority consists of the following restrictions on the authority of the several States.

1. "No State shall enter into any treaty, alliance, or confederation; grant letters of marque and reprisal; coin money; emit bills of credit; make anything but gold and silver a legal tender in payment of debts; pass any bill of attainder, *ex post facto* law, or law impairing the obligation of contracts; or grant any title of nobility."

The prohibition against treaties, alliances, and confederations makes a part of the existing articles of Union; and for reasons which need no explanation, is copied into the new Constitution. The prohibition of letters of marque is another part of the old system, but is somewhat extended in the new. According to the former, letters of marque could be granted by the States after a declaration of war; according to the latter, these licenses must be obtained as well during war as previous to its declaration, from the government of the United States. This alteration is fully justified by the advantage of uniformity in all points which relate to foreign powers; and of immediate responsibility to the nation in all those for whose conduct the nation itself is to be responsible.

The right of coining money, which is here taken from the States, was left in their hands by the Confederation as a concurrent right with that of Congress, under an exception in favor of the exclusive right of Congress to regulate the alloy and value. In this instance, also, the new provision is an improvement on the old. Whilst the alloy and value depended on the general authority, a right of coinage in the particular States could have no other effect than to multiply expensive mints and diversify the forms and weights of the circulating pieces. The latter inconveniency defeats one purpose for which the power was originally submitted to the federal head; and as far as the former might prevent an inconvenient remittance of gold and silver to the central mint for recoinage, the end can be as well attained by local mints established under the general authority.

The extension of the prohibition to bills of credit must give pleasure to every citizen in proportion to his love of justice and his knowledge of the true springs of public prosperity. The loss which America has sustained since the peace, from the pestilent effects of paper money on the necessary confidence between man and man, on the necessary confidence in the public councils, on the industry and morals of the people, and on the character of republican government, constitutes an enormous debt against the States chargeable with this unadvised measure, which must long remain unsatisfied; or rather an accumulation of guilt, which can be expiated no otherwise than by a voluntary sacrifice on the altar of justice of the power which has been the instrument of it. In addition to these persuasive considerations, it may be observed that the same reasons which show the necessity of denying to the States the power of regulating coin prove with equal force that they ought not to be at liberty to substitute a paper medium in the place of coin. Had every State a right to regulate the value of its coin, there might be as many different currencies as States, and thus the intercourse among them would be impeded; retrospective alterations in its value might be made, and thus the citizens of other States be injured, and animosities be kindled among the States themselves. The subjects of foreign powers might suffer from the same cause, and hence the Union be discredited and embroiled by the indiscretion of a single member. No one of these mischiefs is less incident to a power in the States to emit paper money than to coin gold or silver. The power to make anything but gold and silver a tender in payment of debts is withdrawn from the States on the same principle with that of issuing a paper currency.

Bills of attainder, *ex post facto* laws, and laws impairing the obligation of contracts, are contrary to the first principles of the social compact and to every principle of sound legislation. The two former are expressly prohibited by the declarations prefixed to some of the State constitutions, and all of them are prohibited by the spirit and scope of these fundamental charters. Our own experience has taught us, nevertheless, that additional fences against these dangers ought not to be omitted. Very properly, therefore, have the convention added this constitutional bulwark in favor of personal security and private rights; and I am much deceived if they have not, in so doing, as faithfully consulted the genuine sentiments as the undoubted interests of their constituents. The sober people of America are weary of the fluctuating policy which has directed the public councils. They have seen with regret and indignation that sudden changes and legislative interferences, in cases affecting personal rights, become jobs in the hands of enterprising and influential speculators, and snares to the

more industrious and less informed part of the community. They have seen, too, that one legislative interference is but the first link of a long chain of repetitions, every subsequent interference being naturally produced by the effects of the preceding. They very rightly infer, therefore, that some thorough reform is wanting, which will banish speculations on public measures, inspire a general prudence and industry, and give a regular course to the business of society. The prohibition with respect to titles of nobility is copied from the Articles of Confederation and needs no comment.

2. "No State shall, without the consent of the Congress, lay any imposts or duties on imports or exports, except what may be absolutely necessary for executing its inspection laws, and the net produce of all duties and imposts laid by any State on imports or exports shall be for the use of the treasury of the United States; and all such laws shall be subject to the revision and control of the Congress. No State shall, without the consent of Congress, lay any duty on tonnage, keep troops or ships of war in time of peace, enter into any agreement or compact with another State, or with a foreign power, or engage in war unless actually invaded, or in such imminent danger as will not admit of delay."

The restraint on the power of the States over imports and exports is enforced by all the arguments which prove the necessity of submitting the regulation of trade to the federal councils. It is needless, therefore, to remark further on this head, than that the manner in which the restraint is qualified seems well calculated at once to secure to the States a reasonable discretion in providing for the conveniency of their imports and exports, and to the United States a reasonable check against the abuse of this discretion. The remaining particulars of this clause fall within reasonings which are either so obvious, or have been so fully developed, that they may be passed over without remark.

The *sixth* and last class consists of the several powers and provisions by which efficacy is given to all the rest.

1. Of these the first is the "power to make all laws which shall be necessary and proper for carrying into execution the foregoing powers, and all other powers vested by this Constitution in the government of the United States, or in any department or office thereof."

Few parts of the Constitution have been assailed with more intemperance than this; yet on a fair investigation of it, as has been elsewhere shown, no part can appear more completely invulnerable. Without the *substance* of this power, the whole Constitution would be a dead letter. Those who object to the article, therefore, as a part of the Constitution, can only mean that the *form* of the provision is improper. But have they considered whether a better form could have been substituted?

There are four other possible methods which the Convention might have taken on this subject. They might have copied the second article of the existing Confederation, which would have prohibited the exercise of any power not *expressly* delegated; they might have attempted a positive enumeration of the powers comprehended under the general terms "necessary and proper"; they might have attempted a negative enumeration of them by specifying the powers excepted from the general definition; they might have been altogether silent on the subject, leaving these necessary and proper powers to construction and inference.

Had the Convention taken the first method of adopting the second article of Confederation, it is evident that the new Congress would be continually exposed, as their predecessors have been, to the alternative of construing the term *"expressly"* with so much rigor as to disarm the government of all real authority whatever, or with so much latitude as to destroy altogether the force of the restriction. It would be easy to show, if it were necessary, that no important power delegated by the Articles of Confederation has been or can be executed by Congress, without recurring more or less to the doctrine of *construction* or *implication*. As the powers delegated under the new system are more extensive, the government which is to administer it would find itself still more distressed with the alternative of betraying the public interests by doing nothing, or of violating the Constitution by exercising powers indispensably necessary and proper, but, at the same time, not *expressly* granted.

Had the Convention attempted a positive enumeration of the powers necessary and proper for carrying their other powers into effect, the attempt would have involved a complete digest of laws on every subject to which the Constitution relates; accommodated too not only to the existing state of things, but to all the possible changes which futurity may produce; for in every new application of a general power, the *particular powers*, which are the means of attaining the *object* of the general power, must always necessarily vary with that object, and be often properly varied whilst the object remains the same.

Had they attempted to enumerate the particular powers or means not necessary or proper for carrying the general powers into execution, the task would have been no less chimerical; and would have been liable to this further objection, that every defect in the enumeration would have been equivalent to a positive grant of authority. If, to avoid this consequence, they had attempted a partial enumeration of the exceptions, and described the residue by the general terms *not necessary or proper,* it must have happened that the enumeration would comprehend a few of the excepted powers only; that these would be

such as would be least likely to be assumed or tolerated, because the enumeration would of course select such as would
be least necessary or proper; and that the
unnecessary and improper powers included in the residuum would be less forcibly excepted than if no partial enumeration had been made.

Had the Constitution been silent on
this head, there can be no doubt that all
the particular powers requisite as means
of executing the general powers would
have resulted to the government by unavoidable implication. No axiom is more
clearly established in law, or in reason,
than that wherever the end is required,
the means are authorized; wherever a
general power to do a thing is given,
every particular power necessary for doing
it is included. Had this last method, therefore, been pursued by the Convention,
every objection now urged against their
plan would remain in all its plausibility;
and the real inconveniency would be incurred of not removing a pretext which
may be seized on critical occasions for
drawing into question the essential powers of the Union.

If it be asked what is to be the consequence, in case the Congress shall misconstrue this part of the Constitution and exercise powers not warranted by its true
meaning, I answer the same as if they
should misconstrue or enlarge any other
power vested in them; as if the general
power had been reduced to particulars,
and any one of these were to be violated;
the same, in short, as if the State legislatures should violate their respective constitutional authorities. In the first instance, the success of the usurpation will
depend on the executive and judiciary departments, which are to expound and
give effect to the legislative acts; and in
the last resort a remedy must be obtained
from the people, who can, by the election
of more faithful representatives, annul
the acts of the usurpers. The truth is that

this ultimate redress may be more confided in against unconstitutional acts of
the federal than of the State legislatures,
for this plain reason that as every such act
of the former will be an invasion of the
rights of the latter, these will be ever
ready to mark the innovation, to sound
the alarm to the people, and to exert their
local influence in effecting a change of
federal representatives. There being no
such intermediate body between the State
legislatures and the people interested in
watching the conduct of the former, violations of the State constitutions are more
likely to remain unnoticed and unredressed.

2. "This Constitution and the laws of
the United States which shall be made in
pursuance thereof, and all treaties made,
or which shall be made, under the authority of the United States, shall be the supreme law of the land, and the judges in
every State shall be bound thereby, anything in the constitution or laws of any
State to the contrary notwithstanding."

The indiscreet zeal of the adversaries
to the Constitution has betrayed them
into an attack on this part of it also, without which it would have been evidently
and radically defective. To be fully sensible of this, we need only suppose for a
moment that the supremacy of the State
constitutions had been left complete by a
saving clause in their favor.

In the first place, as these constitutions
invest the State legislatures with absolute
sovereignty in all cases not excepted by
the existing Articles of Confederation, all
the authorities contained in the proposed
Constitution, so far as they exceed those
enumerated in the Confederation, would
have been annulled, and the new Congress would have been reduced to the
same impotent condition with their predecessors.

In the next place, as the constitutions
of some of the States do not even expressly and fully recognize the existing

powers of the Confederacy, an express saving of the supremacy of the former would, in such States, have brought into question every power contained in the proposed Constitution.

In the third place, as the constitutions of the States differ much from each other, it might happen that a treaty or national law of great and equal importance to the States would interfere with some and not with other constitutions, and would consequently be valid in some of the States at the same time that it would have no effect in others.

In fine, the world would have seen, for the first time, a system of government founded on an inversion of the fundamental principles of all government; it would have seen the authority of the whole society everywhere subordinate to the authority of the parts; it would have seen a monster, in which the head was under the direction of the members.

3. "The senators and representatives, and the members of the several State legislatures, and all executive and judicial officers, both of the United States and the several States, shall be bound by oath or affirmation to support this Constitution."

It has been asked why it was thought necessary that the State magistracy should be bound to support the federal Constitution, and unnecessary that a like oath should be imposed on the officers of the United States in favor of the State constitutions.

Several reasons might be assigned for the distinction. I content myself with one, which is obvious and conclusive. The members of the federal government will have no agency in carrying the State constitutions into effect. The members and officers of the State governments, on the contrary, will have an essential agency in giving effect to the federal Constitution. The election of the President and Senate will depend, in all cases, on the legislatures, of the several States. And the election of the House of Representatives will equally depend on the same authority in the first instance; and will, probably, forever be conducted by the officers and according to the laws of the States.

4. Among the provisions for giving efficacy to the federal powers might be added those which belong to the executive and judiciary departments: but as these are reserved for particular examination in another place, I pass them over in this.

We have now reviewed, in detail, all the articles composing the sum or quantity of power delegated by the proposed Constitution to the federal government, and are brought to this undeniable conclusion that no part of the power is unnecessary or improper for accomplishing the necessary objects of the Union. The question, therefore, whether this amount of power shall be granted or not resolves itself into another question, whether or not a government commensurate to the exigencies of the Union shall be established; or, in other words, whether the Union itself shall be preserved.

Publius

No. 45: Madison

HAVING shown that no one of the powers transferred to the federal government is unnecessary or improper, the next question to be considered is whether the whole mass of them will be dangerous to the portion of authority left in the several States.

The adversaries to the plan of the Convention, instead of considering in the first place what degree of power was absolutely necessary for the purposes of the federal government, have exhausted themselves in a secondary inquiry into the possible consequences of the proposed degree of power to the governments of the particular States. But if the Union, as has been shown, be essential to the security of the people of America against foreign danger; if it be essential to their security against contentions and wars among the different States; if it be essential to guard them against those violent and oppressive factions which embitter the blessings of liberty and against those military establishments which must gradually poison its very fountain; if, in a word, the Union be essential to the happiness of the people of America, is it not preposterous to urge as an objection to a government, without which the objects of the Union cannot be attained, that such a government may derogate from the importance of the governments of the individual States? Was, then, the American Revolution effected, was the American Confederacy formed, was the precious blood of thousands spilt, and the hard-earned substance of millions lavished, not that the people of America should enjoy peace, liberty, and safety, but that the governments of the individual States, that particular municipal establishments, might enjoy a certain extent of power and be arrayed with certain dignities and attributes of sovereignty? We have heard of the impious doctrine in the old world, that the people were made for kings, not kings for the people. Is the same doctrine to be revived in the new, in another shape—that the solid happiness of the people is to be sacrificed to the views of political institutions of a different form? It is too early for politicians to presume on our forgetting that the public good, the real welfare of the great body of the people, is the supreme object to be pursued; and that no form of government whatever has any other value than as it

may be fitted for the attainment of this object. Were the plan of the Convention adverse to the public happiness, my voice would be, Reject the plan. Were the Union itself inconsistent with the public happiness, it would be, Abolish the Union. In like manner, as far as the sovereignty of the States cannot be reconciled to the happiness of the people, the voice of every good citizen must be, Let the former be sacrificed to the latter. How far the sacrifice is necessary has been shown. How far the unsacrificed residue will be endangered is the question before us.

Several important considerations have been touched in the course of these papers, which discountenance the supposition that the operation of the federal government will by degrees prove fatal to the State governments. The more I revolve the subject, the more fully I am persuaded that the balance is much more likely to be disturbed by the preponderancy of the last than of the first scale.

We have seen, in all the examples of ancient and modern confederacies, the strongest tendency continually betraying itself in the members to despoil the general government of its authorities, with a very ineffectual capacity in the latter to defend itself against the encroachments. Although, in most of these examples, the system has been so dissimilar from that under consideration as greatly to weaken any inference concerning the latter from the fate of the former, yet, as the States will retain under the proposed Constitution a very extensive portion of active sovereignty, the inference ought not to be wholly disregarded. In the Achæan league it is probable that the federal head had a degree and species of power which gave it a considerable likeness to the government framed by the Convention. The Lycian Confederacy, as far as its principles and form are transmitted, must have borne a still greater analogy to it. Yet history does not inform us that either of them ever degenerated, or tended to degenerate, into one consolidated government. On the contrary, we know that the ruin of one of them proceeded from the incapacity of the federal authority to prevent the dissensions, and finally the disunion, of the subordinate authorities. These cases are the more worthy of our attention as the external causes by which the component parts were pressed together were much more numerous and powerful than in our case; and consequently less powerful ligaments within would be sufficient to bind the members to the head and to each other.

In the feudal system, we have seen a similar propensity exemplified. Notwithstanding the want of proper sympathy in every instance between the local sovereigns and the people, and the sympathy in some instances between the general sovereign and the latter, it usually happened that the local sovereigns prevailed in the rivalship for encroachments. Had no external dangers enforced internal harmony and subordination, and particularly, had the local sovereigns possessed the affections of the people, the great kingdoms in Europe would at this time consist of as many independent princes as there were formerly feudatory barons.

The State governments will have the advantage of the federal government, whether we compare them in respect to the immediate dependence of the one on the other; to the weight of personal influence which each side will possess; to the powers respectively vested in them; to the predilection and probable support of the people; to the disposition and faculty of resisting and frustrating the measures of each other.

The State governments may be regarded as constituent and essential parts of the federal government; whilst the latter is nowise essential to the operation or organization of the former. Without the intervention of the State legislatures, the President of the United States cannot be elected at all. They must in all cases have a great share in his appointment, and will, perhaps, in most cases, of themselves determine it. The Senate will be elected absolutely and exclusively by the State legislatures. Even the House of Representatives, though drawn immediately from the people, will be chosen very much under the influence of that class of men whose influence over the people obtains for themselves an election into the State legislatures. Thus, each of the principal branches of the federal government will owe its existence more or less to the favor of the State governments, and must consequently feel a dependence, which is much more likely to beget a disposition too obsequious than too overbearing towards them. On the other side, the component parts of the State governments will in no instance be indebted for their appointment to the direct agency of the federal government, and very little, if at all, to the local influence of its members.

The number of individuals employed under the Constitution of the United States will be much smaller than the number employed under the particular States. There will consequently be less of personal influence on the side of the former than of the latter. The members of the legislative, executive, and judiciary departments of thirteen and more States, the justices of peace, officers of militia, ministerial officers of justice, with all the county, corporation, and town officers, for three millions and more of people, intermixed and having particular acquaintance with every class and circle of people must exceed, beyond all proportion, both in number and influence, those of every description who will be employed in the administration of the federal system. Compare the members of the three great departments of the thirteen States, excluding from the judiciary department the justices of peace, with the members of the corresponding departments of the single government of the Union; compare the militia officers of three millions of people with the military and marine officers of any establishment which is within the compass of probability, or, I may add, of possibility, and in this view alone, we may pronounce the advantage of the States to be decisive. If the federal government is to have collectors of revenue, the State governments will have theirs also. And as those of the former will be principally on the seacoast, and not very numerous, whilst those of the latter will be spread over the face of the country, and will be very numerous, the advantage in this view also lies on the same side. It is true that the Confederacy is to possess, and may exercise, the power of collecting internal as well as external taxes throughout the States; but it is probable that this power will not be resorted to, except for supplemental purposes of revenue; that an option will then be given to the States to supply their quotas by previous collections of their own; and that the eventual collection, under the immediate authority of the Union, will generally be made by the officers, and according to the rules, appointed by the several States. Indeed it is extremely probable that in other instances, particularly in the organization of the judicial power, the officers of the States will be clothed with the correspondent authority of the Union. Should it happen, however, that separate collectors of internal revenue should be appointed under the federal government, the influence of the whole number would not bear a comparison with that of the multitude of State officers in the opposite scale. Within every district to which a federal collector would be allotted, there would not be less than thirty or forty, or even more, officers of different descriptions, and many of them persons of character and weight whose influence would lie on the side of the State.

The powers delegated by the proposed Constitution to the federal government are few and defined. Those which are to remain in the State governments are numerous and indefinite. The former will be exercised principally on external objects, as war, peace, negotiation, and foreign commerce; with which last the power of taxation will, for the most part, be connected. The powers reserved to the several States will extend to all the objects which, in the ordinary course of affairs, concern the lives, liberties, and properties of the people, and the internal order, improvement, and prosperity of the State.

The operations of the federal government will be most extensive and important in times of war and danger; those of the State governments in times of peace and security. As the former periods will probably bear a small proportion to the latter, the State governments will here enjoy another advantage over the federal government. The more adequate, indeed, the federal powers may be rendered to the national defense, the less frequent will be those scenes of danger which might favor their ascendancy over the governments of the particular States.

If the new Constitution be examined with accuracy and candor, it will be found that the change which it proposes consists much less in the addition of NEW POWERS to the Union than in the invigoration of its ORIGINAL POWERS. The regulation of commerce, it is true, is a new power; but that seems to be an addition which few oppose and from which no apprehensions are entertained. The powers relating to war and peace, armies and fleets, treaties and finance, with the other more considerable powers, are all vested in the existing Congress by the Articles of Confederation. The proposed change does not enlarge these powers; it only substitutes a more effectual mode of administering them. The change relating to taxation may be regarded as the most important; and yet the present Congress have as complete authority to REQUIRE of the

States indefinite supplies of money for the common defense and general welfare as the future Congress will have to require them of individual citizens; and the latter will be no more bound than the States themselves have been to pay the quotas respectively taxed on them. Had the States complied punctually with the Articles of Confederation, or could their compliance have been enforced by as peaceable means as may be used with success towards single persons, our past experience is very far from countenancing an opinion that the State governments would have lost their constitutional powers, and have gradually undergone an entire consolidation. To maintain that such an event would have ensued would be to say at once that the existence of the State governments is incompatible with any system whatever that accomplishes the essential purposes of the Union.

Publius

Does the explication of federalism by Hamilton and Madison clearly delineate the constitutional divisions of authority between national and state governments? Would their arguments in *The Federalist* have satisfied the concern of proponents of states' rights that the Constitution sanctioned broad encroachments by the national government upon the domain of state power?

The lack of a clear constitutional definition of the division of authority between national and state governments inevitably put the Supreme Court at the center of a continuing controversy between supporters of states' rights and those who favored a strong national government. Chief Justice John Marshall, a leading Federalist, was to write the doctrine of national supremacy and implied powers explicitly into the Constitution in *McCulloch v. Maryland* (1819), giving form and substance to the discourse of *The Federalist,* particularly the papers written by Alexander Hamilton, that favored a strong central government with broad powers.

NATIONAL JUDICIAL POWER OVER THE STATES

The decision of Chief Justice John Marshall in *McCulloch* v. *Maryland* was one of many made by the Marshall Court in support of expansive national power and supremacy over the states. In proclaiming the primacy of national sovereignty over the states, the Marshall Court was firmly continuing a trend of Supreme Court decisions that began as early as 1793 in the case of *Chisholm* v. *Georgia.* There the issue was not one of the scope of congressional power over the states but of the extent of national judicial power over a case claimed by Georgia to be exclusively within its sovereign jurisdiction.

The *Chisholm* case concerned a fundamental principle of sovereignty in the common law, and one deeply rooted in Anglo-American jurisprudence, the *doctrine of sovereign immunity.* The doctrine is that a sovereign cannot be sued without its consent. Specifically, the principle of sovereign immunity prohibits suits for the money or property of the sovereign unless the sovereign has passed a law explicitly permitting such suits.[1] If the states

[1]Sovereign immunity also precludes suits that would burden the "effective public administration" of the state.

retained this aspect of sovereignty after the Constitution, suits could not lie against them without their permission. Article III gave to the Supreme Court original jurisdiction over "controversies between a state and citizens of another state." This clause raised the possibility, because of state indebtedness and insolvency, that states might be sued for the collection of debts by citizens outside their borders. However, the framers of the Constitution never intended this clause to permit suits against the states for the collection of debts.

During the ratification campaign even the most ardent Federalists agreed that the Constitution did not change the application of the doctrine of sovereign immunity to the states. Alexander Hamilton, in *Federalist 81*, sought to allay the fears of proponents of states' rights on this point.

> ... Let us now examine in what manner the judicial authority is to be distributed between the supreme and the inferior courts of the Union.
>
> The Supreme Court is to be invested with original jurisdiction only "in cases affecting ambassadors, other public ministers, and consuls, and those in which a state shall be a party." ... In cases in which a state might happen to be a party, it would ill suit its dignity to be turned over to an inferior tribunal.
>
> Though it may rather be a digression from the immediate subject of this paper, I shall take occasion here to mention here a supposition which has excited some alarm upon very mistaken grounds. It has been suggested that an assignment of the public securities of one state to the citizens of another would enable them to prosecute that state in the federal courts for the amount of those securities; a suggestion which the following considerations prove to be without foundation.
>
> It is inherent in the nature of sovereignty not to be amenable to the suit of an individual *without its consent*. This is the general sense and the general practice of mankind; and the exemption, as one of the attributes of sovereignty, is now enjoyed by the government of every state in the Union. Unless, therefore, there is a surrender of this immunity in the plan of the Convention, it will remain with the states and the danger intimated must be merely ideal. ... [T]here is no color to pretend the state governments would, by the adoption of that plan [the Constitution], be divested of the privilege of paying their own debts in their own way, free from every constraint but that which flows from the obligations of good faith. ... To what purpose would it be to authorize suits against states for the debts they owe? How could recoveries be enforced? It is evident that it could not be done without waging war against the contracting state; and to ascribe to the federal courts, by mere implication, and in destruction of a preexisting right of the state governments, a power which would involve such a consequence, would be altogether forced and unwarrantable.

In *Chisholm* case, Georgia was sued by Alexander Chisholm, a Charleston, South Carolina, merchant, for the payment of a debt owed by the state to the estate of Robert Farquhar, a Charleston merchant for whose estate Chisholm was the executor. Chisholm unsuccessfully sought to obtain payment from the state, then sued Georgia in the United States circuit court. Georgia claimed that the federal court did not have jurisdiction, and this position was sustained by Supreme Court Justice James Iredell, who was riding circuit at the time, and by the circuit court judge. Chisholm then filed a separate original suit in the Supreme Court for the collection of the debt, claiming that Article III of the Constitution permitted such suits in the Court's original jurisdiction.

As the Supreme Court confronted the *Chisholm* case the justices were well aware of the assurances made by Hamilton, Madison, and other proponents of the Constitution that the federal courts would not have jurisdiction over suits against states for the collection of debts. Justice James Iredell had supported this position in his opinion when the case was at the circuit court level, stating that the Constitution in no way changed the applicability of the doctrine of sovereign immunity to the states. Now it was up to the Supreme Court to decide if it had jurisdiction of the case, which if decided affirmatively would mean that the states could not claim sovereign immunity against suits brought in the original jurisdiction of the Supreme Court by citizens of other states. The Court did not hear the arguments of Georgia, for the state refused to appear, denying that the Supreme Court had jurisdiction.

Chisholm v. *Georgia*

2 Dallas 419, 1 L. Ed. 440 (1793)

JUSTICE WILSON delivered the opinion of the Court:

... This is a case of uncommon magnitude. One of the parties to it is a state; certainly respectable, claiming to be sovereign. The question to be determined, is, whether this state, so respectable, and whose claim soars so high, is amenable to the jurisdiction of the Supreme Court of the United States? This question, important in itself, will depend on others, more important still; and, may, perhaps, be ultimately resolved into one, no less radical than this—"do the people of the United States form a nation?" ...

To the Constitution of the United States the term sovereign, is totally unknown. There is but one place where it could have been used with propriety. But, even in that place it would not, perhaps, have comported with the delicacy of those, who ordained and established that Constitution. They might have announced themselves "sovereign" people of the United States: But serenely conscious of the fact, they avoided the ostentatious declaration. . . .

... In one sense, the term sovereign, has for its correlative, subject. In this sense, the term can receive no application; for it has no object in the Constitution of the United States. Under that constitution there are citizens, but no subjects. "Citizens of the United States." "Citizens of another state," "Citizens of different states." "A state or citizen thereof." The term, subject, occurs, indeed, once in the instrument; but to mark the contrast strongly, the epithet "foreign" is prefixed. In this sense, I presume the state of Georgia has no claim upon her own citizens: In this sense, I am certain, she can have no claim upon the citizens of another state. . . .

... As a judge of this Court, I know, and can decide upon the knowledge, that the citizens of Georgia, when they acted upon the large scale of the union, as a part of the "People of the United States," did not surrender the supreme or sovereign power to that state; but, as to the purposes of the union, retained it to themselves. As to the purposes of the union, therefore, Georgia is not a sovereign state. . . .

. . . Under this view the question is naturally subdivided into two others. 1. Could the Constitution of the United States vest a jurisdiction over the state of Georgia? 2. Has that Constitution vested such jurisdiction in this Court? I have already remarked, that in the practice, and even in the science of politics, there has been frequently a strong current against the natural order of things; and an inconsiderate or an interested disposition to sacrifice the end to the means. This remark deserves a more particular illustration. Even in almost every nation, which has been denominated free, the state has assumed a supercilious pre-eminence above the people who have formed it: Hence the haughty notions of state independence, state sovereignty, and state supremacy. In despotic governments, the Government has usurped, in a similar manner, both upon the state and the people: Hence all arbitrary doctrines and pretensions concerning the supreme, absolute, and incontrollable, power of government. In each, man is degraded from the prime rank, which he ought to hold in human affairs: In the latter, the state as well as the man is degraded. Of both degradations, striking instances occur in history, in politics, and in common life. . . .

In the United States, and in the several states which compose the union, we go not so far: but still we go one step farther than we ought to go in this unnatural and inverted order of things. The states, rather than the people, for whose sakes the states exist, are frequently the objects which attract and arrest our principal attention. This, I believe, has produced much of the confusion and perplexity, which have appeared in several proceedings and several publications on state politics, and on the politics too, of the United States. Sentiments and expressions of this inaccurate kind prevail in our common, even in our convivial, language. Is a toast asked? "The United States" instead of the "People of the United States," is the toast given. This is not politically correct. The toast is meant to present to view the first great object in the union: It presents only the second: It presents only the artificial person, instead of the natural persons, who spoke it into existence. A state I cheerfully admit, is the noblest work of man: But man himself, free and honest, is, I speak as to this world, the noblest work of God. . . .

. . . With the strictest propriety, therefore, classical and political, our national scene opens with the most magnificent object which the nation could present. "The people of the United States" are the first personages introduced. Who were those people? They were the citizens of thirteen states, each of which had a separate constitution and government, and all of which were connected together by articles of confederation. To the purposes of public strength and felicity, that confederacy was totally inadequate. A requisition on the several states terminated its legislative authority: Executive or judicial authority it had none. In order, therefore, to form a more perfect union, to establish justice, to ensure domestic tranquillity, to provide for common defense, and to secure the blessings of liberty, those people among whom were the people of Georgia, ordained and established the present constitution. By that constitution legislative power is vested, executive power is vested, judicial power is vested.

The question now opens fairly to our view; could the people of those states, among whom were those of Georgia, bind those states, and Georgia among the others, by the legislative, executive, and judicial power so vested? If the principles, on which I have founded myself, are just and true, this question must unavoidably receive an affirmative answer. If those states were the work of those people; those people, and, that, I may apply the case closely, the people of Georgia, in particular, could alter, as they pleased, their former work: To any given degree, they could diminish as well as enlarge it. Any or all of the former state powers they could extinguish or transfer. The inference, which necessarily results, is, that the Constitution ordained and established by those people; and, still closely to apply the case, in particular by the people of Georgia, could vest jurisdiction or judicial power over those states and over the state of Georgia in particular.

The next question under this head, is—Has the Constitution done so? Did those people mean to exercise this, their undoubted power? These questions may be resolved, either by fair and conclusive deductions, or by direct and explicit declarations. In order, ultimately, to discover, whether the people of the United States intended to bind those states by the judicial power vested by the national Constitution, a previous enquiry will naturally be: Did those people intend to bind those states by the legislative power vested by that Constitution? The articles of confederation, it is well known, did not operate upon individual citizens; but operated only upon states. This defect was remedied by the national Constitution, which, as all allow, has an operation on individual citizens. But if an opinion, which some seem to entertain, be just; the defect remedied, on one side, was balanced by a defect introduced on the other. For they seem to think, that the present Constitution operates only on individual citizens, and not on states. This opinion, however, appears to be altogether unfounded. When certain laws of the states are declared to be "subject to the revision and control of the Congress," it cannot surely, be contended that the legislative power of the national government was meant to have no operation on the several states. The

fact, uncontrovertibly established in one instance, proves the principle in all other instances, to which the facts will be found to apply. We may then infer, that the people of the United States intended to bind the several states, by the legislative power of the national government. . . .

Whoever considers, in a combined and comprehensive view, the general texture of the Constitution, will be satisfied, that the people of the United States intended to form themselves into a nation for national purposes. They instituted for such purposes, a national government, complete in all its parts, with powers legislative, executive, and judiciary; and in all those powers extending over the whole nation. Is it congruous, that, with regard to such purposes, any man, or body of men, any person, natural or artificial, should be permitted to claim successfully an entire exemption from the jurisdiction of the national government? Would not such claims, crowned with success, be repugnant to our very existence as a nation? When so many trains of deduction coming from different quarters, converge and unite, at last, in the same point; we may safely conclude, as the legitimate result of this Constitution, that the state of Georgia is amenable to the jurisdiction of this Court.

But, in my opinion, this doctrine rests not upon the legitimate result of fair and conclusive deduction from the Constitution: It is confirmed beyond all doubt, by the direct and explicit declaration of the Constitution itself. "The judicial power of the United States shall extend, to controversies between two states." Two states are supposed to have a controversy between them: This controversy is supposed to be brought before those vested with the judicial power of the United States: Can the most consummate degree of professional ingenuity devise a mode by which this "controversy between two states" can be brought before a court of law; and yet neither of those states be a defendant? "The judicial power of the United States shall extend to controversies, between a state and citizens of another state." Could the strictest legal language; could even that language, which is peculiarly appropriated to an art, deemed, by a great master, to be one of the most honorable, laudable, and profitable things in our law; could this strict and appropriated language, describe, with more precise accuracy, the cause now pending before the tribunal? Causes and not parties to causes, are weighed by justice in her equal scales: On the former solely, her attention is fixed: To the latter, she is as she is painted, blind. . . .

CHIEF JUSTICE JAY delivered the following opinion:

The question we are now to decide has been accurately stated, [namely:] Is a state suable by individual citizens of another state? . . .

The revolution or rather the Declaration of Independence, found the people already united for general purposes, and at the same time providing for their more domestic concerns by state conventions, and other temporary arrangements. From the crown of Great Britain, the sovereignty of their country passed to the people of it; and it was then not an uncommon opinion, that the unappropriated lands, which belonged to that crown, passed not to the people of the colony or states within whose limits they were situated, but to the whole people; on whatever principles this opinion rested, it did not give way to the other, and thirteen sovereignties were considered as emerged from the principles of the revolution, combined with local convenience and considerations; the people nevertheless continued to consider themselves, in a national point of view, as one people; and they continued without interruption to manage their national concerns accordingly; afterwards, in the hurry of the war, and in the warmth of mutual confidence, they made a confederation of the states, the basis of a general government. Experience disappointed the expectations they had formed from it; and then the people, in their collective and national capacity established the present Constitution. It is remarkable that in establishing it, the people exercised their own rights, and their own proper sovereignty, and conscious of the plentitude of it, they declared with becoming dignity, "We the people of the United States, do ordain and establish this Constitution." Here we see the people acting as sovereigns of the whole country; and in the language of sovereignty, establishing a Constitution by which it was their will, that the state governments should be bound, and to which the state constitutions should be made to conform. Every state constitution is a compact made by and between the citizens of a state to govern themselves in a certain manner; and the Constitution of the United States is likewise a compact made by the people of the United States to govern themselves as to general objects, in a certain manner. By this great compact however, many prerogatives were transferred to the national government, such as those of making war and peace, contracting alliances, coining money, etc. etc. . . .

It may be asked, what is the precise sense and latitude in which the words "to establish justice," as here used, are to be understood? The answer to this question will result from the provisions made in the Constitution on this head. They are specified in the 2d section of the 3d article, where is ordained, that the judicial power of the United States shall extend to . . . controversies between two or more states; because domestic tranquillity requires, that the contentions of states should be peaceably terminated by a common judicatory; and, because, in a free country justice ought not to depend on the will of either of the litigants. . . .

. . . It is politic, wise, and good, that, not only the controversies, in which a state is plaintiff, but also those in which a state is defendant, should be settled, both cases, therefore, are within the reason of the remedy; and ought to be so adjudged, unless the obvious, plain, and literal sense of the words forbid it. If we attend to the words, we find them to be express, positive, free from ambiguity, and without room for such implied expressions: "The judicial power of the United States shall extend to controversies between a state and citizens of another state." If the Constitution really meant to extend these powers only to those controversies in which a state might be plaintiff, to the exclusion of those in which citizens had demands against a state, it is inconceivable that it should have attempted to convey that meaning in words, not only so incompetent, but also repugnant to it; if it meant to exclude a certain class of these controversies, why were they not expressly excepted; on the contrary, not even an intimation of such intention appears in any part of the Constitution. It cannot be pretended that where citizens urge and insist upon demands against a state, which the state refuses to admit and comply with, that there is no controversy between them. If it is a controversy between them, then it clearly falls not only within the spirit, but the very words of the Constitution. What is it to the cause of justice, and how can it affect the definition of the word, controversy, whether the demands which cause the dispute, are made by a state against citizens of another state, or by the latter against the former? When power is thus extended to a controversy, it necessarily, as to all judicial purposes, is also extended to those, between whom it subsists. . . .

I perceive, and therefore candor urges me to mention, a circumstance, which seems to favor the opposite side of the question. It is this: the same section of the Constitution which extends the judicial power to controversies "between a state and the citizens of another state," does also extend that power to controversies to which the United States are a party. Now, it may be said, that if the word, party comprehends both plaintiff and defendant, it follows, that the United States may be sued by any citizen, between whom and them there may be a controversy. This appears to me to be fair reasoning; but the same principles of candor which urge me to mention this objection, also urge me to suggest an important difference between the two cases. It is this: in all cases of actions against states or individual citizens, the national courts are supported in all their legal and constitutional proceedings and judgments, by the arm of the executive power of the United States; but in cases of actions against the United States, there is no power which the courts can call to their aid. From this distinction important conclusions are deducible, and they place the case of a state and the case of the United States, in very different points of view. . . .

JUSTICE IREDELL dissented.

The Georgia House of Representatives in November of 1793 responded to the *Chisholm* decision by passing a law stating that "Any federal marshall or any other person" who executed the mandate of *Chisholm* v. *Georgia* shall be declared "guilty of felony, and shall suffer death, without the benefit of clergy, by being hanged."[2] The bill never became law but reflected senti-

[2]Warren, *The Supreme Court*, I, 100.

ment throughout the country by political leaders of all persuasions that the Court had overstepped its bounds. Calls immediately were heard from state legislatures and in Congress for a constitutional amendment to overturn *Chisholm* v. *Georgia* that resulted in congressional submission of the Eleventh Amendment to the states in 1794, which provided: "The judicial power of the United States shall not be construed to extend to any suit in law or equity, commenced or prosecuted against one of the United States by citizens of another state, or by citizens or subjects of any foreign state." The amendment was adopted in 1798.

In *Federalist 81* Hamilton argued that it would be foolhardy for the federal courts to assume jurisdiction over a matter that was essentially unenforceable by national authority. Does the *Chisholm* decision and the reaction to it support Hamilton's viewpoint? Should the Court have exercised judicial self-restraint by refusing jurisdiction of the case?

In *Chisholm* v. *Georgia* the Supreme Court overrode state objections to an expansion of its original jurisdiction to include matters that the states considered to be exclusively within the boundaries of their sovereign authority. Even the nationalists at the time of the *Chisholm* case agreed that it had not been the intent of the framers of the Constitution to have the Supreme Court entertain suits for the recovery of debts owed by the states. Conflict over states' rights emerged again in the case of *Martin* v. *Hunter's Lessee* in 1816. At issue was the scope of the Supreme Court's authority to review the decisions of the highest state courts under Section 25 of the Judiciary Act of 1789. Section 25 provided that when the highest state court rejected a claim based on the Constitution, treaties, or the laws of the United States, the claim "may be reexamined and reversed or affirmed in the Supreme Court of the United States upon a writ of error."

The *Martin* case arose from a Supreme Court ruling in the case of *Fairfax's Devisee* v. *Hunter's Lessee,* 7 Cranch 603 (1813). The decision, written by Justice Story, upheld the claim of the heir of Lord Fairfax, a Virginia Loyalist and landowner, to the lands of Fairfax that had been confiscated under Virginia law during the revolution. Virginia had also passed an inheritance act which denied aliens the right to inherit real property. Under a treaty with Great Britain, however, Fairfax's heir did have the right to the property. The litigation over the matter was long and complicated and involved future Chief Justice John Marshall in its early stages in the 1790s, which led Marshall to recuse himself from the decision when it reached the Supreme Court.

After the Court's initial ruling on the matter in the *Fairfax* case, the judges of the Virginia Court of Appeals (the highest state court), led by Spencer Roane, declared Section 25 of the Judiciary Act unconstitutional and refused to comply with the mandate of the Supreme Court. This resulted in the case being raised once again before the Supreme Court, which now confronted direct state defiance in an atmosphere of extreme agitation over states' rights. The Virginia judges argued that the sovereignty of the states was as inviolate as the sovereignty of the national government and that there was nothing in the Constitution that granted authority to the national government to invade state sovereignty by reviewing the decisions of state courts. They proclaimed that just as the state governments cannot operate on the federal government, even where it has encroached upon state authority, the federal government cannot act upon the states where they have allegedly infringed upon federal authority. The Virginia judges stated that their duty was to their state constitution and laws because they were state and not federal judges. State sovereignty and federal sovereignty are equal, and, argued the judges, the decision of the Supreme Court essentially turned them into inferior federal judges. The Virginia judges recognized the supremacy of federal laws under Article VI and their obligation to uphold these laws in state court adjudication. In the *Martin* case, however, the Virginia court claimed that the Fairfax property had been seized prior to the treaties of 1783 and 1794 with Great Britain which protected alien property rights.

As Justice Story embarked upon the writing of the Court's opinion in *Martin* v. *Hunter's Lessee,* he was compelled to answer the arguments of the Virginia judges. The questions involved in the case, said Justice Story, "are of great importance and delicacy. Perhaps it is not too much to affirm, that, upon their right decision, rests some of the most solid principles that have hitherto been supposed to sustain and protect the Constitution itself."

Martin v. *Hunter's Lessee*

1 Wheaton 304, 4 L. Ed. 97 (1816)

MR. JUSTICE STORY delivered the opinion of the Court, saying in part:

This is a writ of error from the Court of Appeals of Virginia, founded upon the refusal of that court to obey the mandate of this Court, requiring the judgment rendered in this very cause, at February term, 1813, to be carried into due execution. The following is the judgment of the Court of Appeals rendered on the mandate: "The court is unanimously of opinion that the appellate power of the Supreme Court of the United States does not extend to this court, under a sound construction of the Constitution of the United States; that so much of the 25th section of the act of Congress to establish the judicial courts of the United States, as extends the appellate jurisdiction of the Supreme Court to this court, is not in pursuance of the Constitution of the United States; that the writ of error, in this cause, was improvidently allowed un-

der the authority of that act; that the proceedings thereon in the Supreme Court were, coram non judice, in relation to this court, and that obedience to its mandate be declined by the court."

The questions involved in this judgment are of great importance and delicacy. Perhaps it is not too much to affirm that, upon their right decision, rest some of the most solid principles which have hitherto been supposed to sustain and protect the Constitution itself. . . .

Before proceeding to the principal questions, it may not be unfit to dispose of some preliminary considerations which have grown out of the arguments at the bar.

The Constitution of the United States was ordained and established, not by the states in their sovereign capacities, but emphatically, as the preamble of the Constitution declares, by "the people of the United States." There can be no doubt that it was competent to the people to invest the general government with all the powers which they might deem proper and necessary; to extend or restrain these powers according to their own good pleasure, and to give them a paramount and supreme authority. As little doubt can there be that the people had a right to prohibit to the states the exercise of any powers which were, in their judgment, incompatible with the objects of the general compact; to make the powers of the state governments, in given cases, subordinate to those of the nation, or to reserve to themselves those sovereign authorities which they might not choose to delegate to either. The Constitution was not, therefore, necessarily carved out of existing state sovereignties, nor a surrender of powers already existing in state institutions, for the powers of the states depend upon their own constitutions; and the people of every state had the right to modify and restrain them, according to their own views of policy or principle. On the other hand, it is perfectly clear that the sovereign powers vested in the state governments, by their respective constitutions, remained unaltered and unimpaired, except so far as they were granted to the government of the United States.

These deductions do not rest upon general reasoning, plain and obvious as they seem to be. They have been positively recognized by one of the articles in amendment of the Constitution, which declares, that "the powers not delegated to the United States by the Constitution, nor prohibited by it to the states, are reserved to the states respectively, or to the people."

The government, then, of the United States, can claim no powers which are not granted to it by the Constitution, and the powers actually granted, must be such as are expressly given, or given by necessary implication. On the other hand, this instrument, like every other grant, is to have a reasonable construction, according to the import of its terms; and where a power is expressly given in general terms, it is not to be restrained to particular cases, unless that construction grow out of the context expressly, or by necessary implication. The words are to be taken in their natural and obvious sense, and not in a sense unreasonably restricted or enlarged.

The Constitution unavoidably deals in general language. It did not suit the purposes of the people, in framing this great charter of our liberties, to provide for minute specifications of its powers, or to declare the means by which those powers should be carried into execution. It was foreseen that this would be a perilous and difficult, if not an impracticable, task. The instrument was not intended to provide merely for the exigencies of a few years, but was to endure through a long lapse of ages, the events of which were locked up in the inscrutable purposes of Providence. It could not be foreseen what new changes and modifications of power might be indispensable to effectuate the general objects of the charter; and restrictions and specifications which, at the present, might seem salutary, might, in the end, prove the overthrow of the system itself. Hence its powers are expressed in general terms, leaving to the legislature, from time to time, to adopt its own means to effectuate legitimate objects, and to mold and model the exercise of its powers, as its own wisdom and the public interests should require.

With these principles in view—principles in respect to which no difference of opinion ought to be indulged—let us now proceed to the interpretation of the Constitution, so far as regards the great points in controversy.

The third article of the Constitution is that which must principally attract our attention. . . .

This leads us to the consideration of the great question as to the nature and extent of the appellate jurisdiction of the

United States. We have already seen that appellate jurisdiction is given by the Constitution to the Supreme Court in all cases, where it has not original jurisdiction; subject, however, to such exceptions and regulations as Congress may prescribe. It is, therefore, capable of embracing every case enumerated in the Constitution, which is not exclusively to be decided by way of original jurisdiction. But the exercise of appellate jurisdiction is far from being limited by the terms of the Constitution to the Supreme Court. There can be no doubt that Congress may create a succession of inferior tribunals, in each of which it may vest appellate as well as original jurisdiction. . . .

As, then, by the terms of the Constitution, the appellate jurisdiction is not limited as to the Supreme Court, and as to this Court it may be exercised in all other cases than those of which it has original cognizance, what is there to restrain its exercise over state tribunals in the enumerated cases? The appellate power is not limited by the terms of the third article to any particular courts. The words are, "the judicial power (which includes apppellate power) shall extend to all cases," etc., and "in all other cases before mentioned the Supreme Court shall have appellate jurisdiction." It is the case, then, and not the court, that gives the jurisdiction. If the judicial power extends to the case, it will be in vain to search in the letter of the Constitution for any qualification as to the tribunal where it depends. It is incumbent, then, upon those who assert such a qualification to show its existence by necessary implication. If the text be clear and distinct, no restriction upon its plain and obvious import ought to be admitted, unless the inference be irresistible. . . .

But it is plain that the framers of the Constitution did contemplate that cases within the judicial cognizance of the United States not only might but would arise in the state courts, in the exercise of their ordinary jurisdiction. With this view the sixth article declares, that "this Constitution, and the laws of the United States which shall be made in pursuance thereof, and all treaties made, or which shall be made, under the authority of the United States, shall be the supreme law of the land, and the judges in every state shall be bound thereby, anything in the Constitution or laws of any state to the contrary notwithstanding." It is obvious that this obligation is imperative upon the state judges in their official, and not merely in their private, capacities. From the very nature of their judicial duties they would be called upon to pronounce the law applicable to the case in judgment. They were not to decide merely according to the laws or constitution of the state, but according to the Constitution, laws and treaties of the United States—"the supreme law of the land.". . .

It must, therefore, be conceded that the Constitution not only contemplated, but meant to provide for cases within the scope of the judicial power of the United States, which might yet depend before state tribunals. It was foreseen that in the exercise of their ordinary jurisdiction, state courts would incidentally take cognizance of cases arising under the Constitution, the laws and treaties of the United States. Yet to all these cases the judicial power, by the very terms of the Constitution, is to extend. It cannot extend by original jurisdiction if that was already rightfully and exclusively attached in the state courts, which (as has been already shown) may occur; it must, therefore, extend by appellate jurisdiction, or not at all. It would seem to follow that the appellate power of the United States must, in such cases, extend to state tribunals; and if in such cases, there is no reason why it should not equally attach upon all others within the purview of the constitution.

It has been argued that such an appellate jurisdiction over state courts is inconsistent with the genius of our governments, and the spirit of the Constitution. That the latter was never designed to act upon state sovereignties, but only upon the people, and that if the power exists, it will materially impair the sovereignty of the states, and the independence of their courts. We cannot yield to the force of this reasoning; it assumes principles which we cannot admit, and draws conclusions to which we do not yield our assent.

It is a mistake that the Constitution was not designed to operate upon states, in their corporate capacities. It is crowded with provisions which restrain or annul the sovereignty of the states in some of the highest branches of their prerogatives. The tenth section of the first article contains a long list of disabilities and prohibitions imposed upon the states. Surely, when such essential portions of state sovereignty are taken away, or prohibited to be exercised, it cannot be correctly asserted that the Constitution does not act upon the states. The language of the Constitution is also imperative upon the states as to the performance of many duties. It is imperative upon the sate legislatures to make laws prescribing the time, places, and manner of holding elections for senators and representatives, and for electors of President and Vice-President. And in these, as well as some other cases, Congress have a right to revise, amend, or supersede the laws which may be passed by state legislatures. When, therefore, the states are stripped of some of the highest attributes of sovereignty, and the same are given to the United States; when the legislatures of the states are, in some respects, under the control of Congress, and in every case are, under the Constitution, bound by the paramount authority of the United States; it is certainly difficult to support the argument that the appellate power over the decisions of state courts is contrary to the genius of our institutions. The courts of the United States can, without question, revise the proceed-ings of the executive and legislative authorities of the states, and if they are found to be contrary to the Constitution, may declare them to be of no legal validity. Surely the exercise of the same right over judicial tribunals is not a higher or more dangerous act of sovereign power.

Nor can such a right be deemed to impair the independence of state judges. It is assuming the very ground in controversy to assert that they possess an absolute independence of the United States. In respect to the powers granted to the United States, they are not independent; they are expressly bound to obedience by the letter of the Constitution; and if they should unintentionally transcend their authority, or misconstrue the Constitution, there is no more reason for giving their judgments an absolute and irresistible force than for giving it to the acts of the other co-ordinate departments of state sovereignty.

The argument urged from the possibility of the abuse of the revising power is equally unsatisfactory. It is always a doubtful course to argue against the use or existence of a power, from the possibility of its abuse. It is still more difficult, by such an argument, to ingraft upon a general power a restriction which is not to be found in the terms in which it is given. From the very nature of things, the absolute right of decision, in the last resort, must rest somewhere—wherever it may be vested it is susceptible of abuse. In all questions of jurisdiction the inferior, or appellate court, must pronounce the final judgment; and common sense, as well as legal reasoning, has conferred it upon the latter. . . .

This is not all. A motive of another kind, perfectly compatible with the most sincere respect for state tribunals, might induce the grant of appellate power over their decisions. That motive is the importance, and even necessity of uniformity of decisions throughout the whole United

States, upon all subjects within the purview of the Constitution. Judges of equal learning and integrity, in different states, might differently interpret a statute, or a treaty of the United States, or even the Constitution itself. If there were no revising authority to control these jarring and discordant judgments, and harmonize them into uniformity, the laws, the treaties, and the Constitution of the United States would be different in different states, and might, perhaps, never have precisely the same construction, obligation, or efficacy, in any two states. The public mischiefs that would attend such a state of things would be truly deplorable; and it cannot be believed that they could

have escaped the enlightened Convention which formed the Constitution. What, indeed, might then have been only prophecy, has now become fact; and the appellate jurisdiction must continue to be the only adequate remedy for such evils. . . .

It is the opinion of the whole Court that the judgment of the Court of Appeals of Virginia, rendered on the mandate in this cause, be reversed, and the judgment of the District Court, held at Winchester, be, and the same is hereby affirmed.

MR. JUSTICE JOHNSON delivered a concurring opinion.

What arguments does Justice Story present in the *Martin* case to support the appellate jurisdiction of the Supreme Court in cases where both state and federal courts have concurrent jurisdiction? Did Justice Story agree with the Virginia judges that the implications of Supreme Court review of the decisions of the highest state courts where both federal and state courts had jurisdiction essentially incorporated the state courts into the federal system? On what basis did Justice Story claim that Section 25 of the Judiciary Act, in addition to being constitutional, was also necessary to maintain the supremacy of national law?

The attacks by proponents of states' rights on the constitutionality of Section 25 of the Judiciary Act of 1789 continued unabated and even increased after the Court's 1816 decision in *Martin* v. *Hunter's Lessee.* The Court's decision in *McCulloch* v. *Maryland* (1819) only served to fuel the opposition to the Court by the advocates of states' rights.

In 1821, in the case of *Cohens* v. *Virginia,* the Court was once again confronted with the question of the extent of its appellate jurisdiction over the states under Section 25. A Virginia court had convicted the Cohens of violating a state statute by selling in the state lottery tickets for the District of Columbia, the lottery having been authorized by an act of Congress. The Cohens, claiming that their rights under a federal law had been violated, appealed for a writ of error to the Virginia court under Section 25. Chief Justice John Marshall, who had recused himself from the *Martin* decision, now had a chance to express his views on the scope of the Court's appellate jurisdiction over state courts under Section 25. Counsel for Virginia, recognizing that the Court would not overturn its decision in *Martin* v. *Hunter's Lessee,* argued that the present case was distinguished from *Martin* because it was a criminal prosecution, whereas the *Martin* case was a civil action. Moreover, argued the state, Congress had no authority to authorize the sale of lottery tickets in Virginia.

At the close of his argument in the *Cohens* case, the counsel for Virginia told the Court that it was desirable to prevent the "clashing of federal and state powers." He continued: "Let each operate within their respective spheres, and let each be confined to their assigned limits. We are all bound to support the Constitution. How will that be best effected? Not by claiming and exercising unacknowledged power. The strength thus obtained will prove pernicious. The confidence of the people constitutes the real strength of this government. Nothing can so much endanger it as exciting the hostility of the state governments. With them it is, to determine how long this government shall endure."[3]

The counsel for the Cohens told the Court: "The particular portion of the judicial power of the Union is indispensably necessary to the existence of the Union. The judicial control of the Union over state encroachments and usurpations was indispensable to the sovereignty of the Constitution—to its integrity—to its very existence. Take it away, and the Union becomes again a false and foolish confidence—a delusion and a mockery!"[4] Countering the argument of Virginia that state criminal cases were outside of the appellate jurisdiction of the Supreme Court under Section 25, the Cohens' counsel argued that it was precisely in criminal cases that the Supreme Court should have appellate jurisdiction because in such cases "the sovereignty of the state—state pride—state interests—are here in paramount vigor, as inducements to error; and judicial usurpation is countenanced by legislative support and popular prejudice."[5]

Two weeks after hearing these arguments, Chief Justice John Marshall delivered the opinion of the Court on March 3, 1821.

Cohens v. *Virginia*

6 Wheaton 264, 5 L. Ed. 257 (1821)

MR. CHIEF JUSTICE MARSHALL delivered the opinion of the Court:

This is a writ of error to a judgment rendered in the Court of Hustings for the borough of Norfolk, on an information for selling lottery tickets, contrary to an act of the legislature of Virginia. In the state court, the defendant claimed the protection of an act of Congress. A case was agreed between the parties, which states the act of Assembly on which the prosecution was founded, and the act of Congress on which the defendant relied, and concludes in these words: "If upon this case the court shall be of opinion that the acts of Congress before mentioned were valid, and on the true construction of those acts, the lottery tickets sold by the defendants as aforesaid, might lawfully be sold within the state of Virginia, notwithstanding the act or statute of the General Assembly of Virginia prohibiting such sale, then judgment to be entered for the defendants. And if the court should be of opinion that the statute or act of the General Assembly of the state of Virginia, prohibiting such sale, is valid, notwithstanding the said acts of Congress, then

[3]Warren, *The Supreme Court,* II, 9.
[4]Ibid.
[5]Ibid.

judgment to be entered that the defendants are guilty, and that the commonwealth recover against them one hundred dollars and costs."

Judgment was rendered against the defendants; and the court in which it was rendered being the highest court of the state in which the cause was cognizable, the record has been brought into this Court by a writ of error.

The defendant in error moves to dismiss this writ, for want of jurisdiction.

In support of this motion, three points have been made, and argued with the ability which the importance of the question merits. These points are:

1st. That a state is a defendant.

2d. That no writ of error lies from this Court to a state court.

3d. The third point has been presented in different forms by the gentlemen who have argued it. The counsel who opened the cause said, that the want of jurisdiction was shown by the subject-matter of the case. The counsel who followed him said, that jurisdiction was not given by the judiciary act. The Court has bestowed all its attention on the arguments of both gentlemen, and supposes that their tendency is to show that this Court has no jurisdiction of the case, or, in other words, has no right to review the judgment of the state court, because neither the constitution nor any law of the United States has been violated by that judgment.

The questions presented to the Court by the two first points made at the bar are of great magnitude, and may be truly said vitally to affect the Union. They exclude the inquiry whether the Constitution and laws of the United States have been violated by the judgment which the plaintiffs in error seek to review; and maintain that, admitting such violation, it is not in the power of the government to apply a corrective. They maintain that the nation does not possess a department capable of restraining peaceably, and by authority of law, any attempts which may be made, by a part, against the legitimate powers of the whole; and that the government is reduced to the alternative of submitting to such attempts, or of resisting them by force. They maintain that the Constitution of the United States has provided no tribunal for the final construction of itself, or of the laws or treaties of the nation; but that this power may be exercised in the last resort by the courts of every state of the Union. That the Constitution laws, and treaties, may receive as many constructions as there are states; and that this is not a mischief, or, if a mischief, is irremediable. . . .

1st. The first question to be considered is, whether the jurisdiction of this Court is excluded by the character of the parties, one of them being a state, and the other a citizen of that state?

The second section of the third article of the Constitution defines the extent of the judicial power of the United States. Jurisdiction is given to the courts of the Union in two classes of cases. In the first, their jurisdiction depends on the character of the cause, whoever may be the parties. This class comprehends "all cases in law and equity arising under this Constitution, the laws of the United States, and treaties made, or which shall be made, under their authority." This clause extends the jurisdiction of the Court to all the cases described, without making in its terms any exception whatever, and without any regard to the condition of the party. If there be any exception, it is to be implied against the express words of the article.

In the second class, the jurisdiction depends entirely on the character of the parties. In this are comprehended "controversies between two or more states, between a state and citizens of another state," "and between a state and foreign states, citizens or subjects." If these be the parties, it is entirely unimportant what may be the subject of controversy. Be it what it may, these parties have a constitutional right to come into the courts of the Union. . . .

If . . . a case arising under the Constitution, or a law, must be one in which a party comes into court to demand something conferred on him by the Constitution or a law, we think the construction too narrow. A case in law or equity consists of the right of the one party, as well as of the other, and may truly be said to arise under the Constitution or a law of the United States, whenever its correct decision depends on the construction of either. . . .

The jurisdiction of the Court, then, being extended by the letter of the Constitution to all cases arising under it, or under the laws of the United States, it follows that those who would withdraw any case of this description from the jurisdiction, must sustain the exemption they claim on the spirit and true meaning of the Constitution, which spirit and true meaning must be so apparent as to overrule the words which its framers have employed.

The counsel for the defendant in error have undertaken to do this; and have laid down the general proposition, that a sovereign independent state is not suable except by its own consent.

This general proposition will not be controverted. But its consent is not requisite in each particular case. It may be given in a general law. And if a state has surrendered any portion of its sovereignty, the question whether a liability to suit be a part of this portion, depends on the instrument by which the surrender is made. If, upon a just construction of that instrument, it shall appear that the state has submitted to be sued, then it has parted with this sovereign right of judging in every case on the justice of its own pretensions, and has entrusted that power to a tribunal in whose impartiality it confides.

The American States, as well as the American people, have believed a close and firm Union to be essential to their liberty and to their happiness. They have been taught by experience, that this Union cannot exist without a government for the whole; and they have been taught by the same experience that this government would be a mere shadow, that must disappoint all their hopes, unless invested with large portions of that sovereignty which belongs to independent states. Under the influence of this opinion, and thus instructed by experience, the American people, in the conventions of their respective states, adopted the present Constitution.

If it could be doubted, whether from its nature, it were not supreme in all cases where it is empowered to act, that doubt would be removed by the declaration, that "this Constitution, and the laws of the United States, which shall be made in pursuance thereof, and all treaties made, or which shall be made, under the authority of the United States, shall be the supreme law of the land; and the judges in every state shall be bound thereby; anything in the Constitution or laws of any state to the contrary notwithstanding."

This is the authoritative language of the American people; and, if gentlemen please, of the American States. It marks, with lines too strong to be mistaken, the characteristic distinction between the government of the Union and those of the states. The general government, though limited as to its objects, is supreme with respect to those objects. This principle is a part of the Constitution; and if there be any who deny its necessity, none can deny its authority.

To this supreme government ample powers are confided; and if it were possible to doubt the great purposes for which they were so confided, the people of the United States have declared, that they are given "in order to form a more perfect union, establish justice, ensure domestic tranquility, provide for the common defense, promote the general welfare, and secure the blessings of liberty to themselves and their posterity."

With the ample powers confided to this supreme government, for these interesting purposes, are connected many express and important limitations on the sovereignty of the states, which are made for the same purposes. The powers of the Union, on the great subjects of war, peace, and commerce, and on many others, are in themselves limitations of the sovereignty of the states; but in additon to these, the sovereignty of the states is surrendered in many instances where the surrender can only operate to the benefit of the people, and where, perhaps, no other power is conferred on Congress than a conservative power to maintain the principles established in the Constitution. The maintenance of these principles in their purity, is certainly among the great duties of the government. One of the instruments by which this duty may be peaceably performed, is the judicial department. It is authorized to decide all cases of every description, arising under the Constitution or laws of the United States. From this general grant of jurisdiction, no exception is made of those cases in which a state may be a party. When we consider the situation of the government of the Union and of a state, in relation to each other; the nature of our Constitution; the subordination of the state governments to that Constitution; the great purpose for which jurisdiction over all cases arising under the Constitution and laws of the United States is confided to the judicial department, are we at liberty to insert in this general grant, an exception of those cases in which a state may be a party? Will the spirit of the Constitution justify this attempt to control its words? We think it will not. We think a case arising under the Constitution or laws of the United States, is cognizable in the courts of the Union, whoever

may be the parties to that case. . . .

One of the express objects, then, for which the judicial department was established, is the decision of controversies between states, and between a state and individuals. The mere circumstance, that a state is a party, gives jurisdiction to the Court. How, then, can it be contended, that the very same instrument, in the very same section, should be so construed as that this same circumstance should withdraw a case from the jurisdiction of the Court, where the Constitution or laws of the United States are supposed to have been violated? The Constitution gave to every person having a claim upon a state, a right to submit his case to the Court of the nation. However unimportant his claim might be, however little the community might be interested in its decision, the framers of our Constitution thought it necessary, for the purposes of justice, to provide a tribunal as superior to influence as possible, in which that claim might be decided. . . .

The mischievous consequences of the construction contended for on the part of Virginia, are also entitled to great consideration. It would prostrate, it has been said, the government and its laws at the feet of every state in the Union. And would not this be its effect? What power of the government could be executed by its own means, in any state disposed to resist its execution by a course of legislation? The laws must be executed by individuals acting within the several states. If these individuals may be exposed to penalties, and if the courts of the Union cannot correct the judgments by which these penalties may be enforced, the course of the government may be, at any time, arrested by the will of one of its members. Each member will possess a veto on the will of the whole. . . .

These collisions may take place in times of no extraordinary commotion. But a constitution is framed for ages to come, and is designed to approach immortality as nearly as human institutions can approach it. Its course cannot always be tranquil. It is exposed to storms and tempests, and its framers must be unwise statesmen indeed, if they have not provided it, as far as its nature will permit, with the means of self-preservation from the perils it may be destined to encounter. No government ought to be so defective in its organization as not to contain within itself the means of securing the execution of its own laws against other dangers than those which occur every day. Courts of justice are the means most usually employed; and it is reasonable to expect that a government should repose on its own courts, rather than on others. There is certainly nothing in the circumstances under which our Constitution was formed; nothing in the history of the times, which would justify the opinion that the confidence reposed in the states was so implicit as to leave in them and their tribunals the power of resisting or defeating, in the form of law, the legitimate measures of the Union. . . .

If jurisdiction depended entirely on the character of the parties, and was not given where the parties have not an original right to come into court, that part of the 2d section of the 3d article which extends the judicial power to all cases arising under the Constitution and laws of the United States, would be mere surplusage. It is to give jurisdiction where the character of the parties would not give it, that this very important part of the clause was inserted. It may be true, that the partiality of the state tribunals, in ordinary controversies between a state and its citizens, was not apprehended, and therefore the judicial power of the Union was not extended to such cases; but this was not the sole nor the greatest object for which this department was created. A more important, a much more interesting object, was the preservation of the Constitution and laws of the United States, so far as they can be preserved by judicial authority;

and therefore the jurisdiction of the courts of the Union was expressly extended to all cases arising under that Constitution and those laws. If the Constitution or laws may be violated by proceedings instituted by a state against its own citizens, and if that violation may be such as essentially to affect the Constitution and the laws such as to arrest the progress of government in its constitutional course, why should these cases be excepted from that provision which expressly extends the judicial power of the Union to all cases arising under the Constitution and laws? . . .

It is most true that this Court will not take jurisdiction if it should not; but it is equally true, that it must take jurisdiction if it should. The judiciary cannot, as the legislature may, avoid a measure because it approaches the confines of the Constitution. We cannot pass it by because it is doubtful. With whatever doubts, with whatever difficulties, a case may be attended, we must decide it if it be brought before us. We have no more right to decline the exercise of jurisdiction which is given, than to usurp that which is not given. The one or the other would be treason to the Constitution. Questions may occur which we would gladly avoid, but we cannot avoid them. All we can do, is to exercise our best judgment, and conscientiously to perform our duty. In doing this, on the present occasion, we find this tribunal invested with appellate jurisdiction in all cases arising under the Constitution and laws of the United States. We find no exception to this grant, and we cannot insert one. . . .

This leads to a consideration of the Eleventh Amendment.

It is in these words: "The judicial power of the United States shall not be construed to extend to any suit in law or equity commenced or prosecuted against one of the United States, by citizens of another state, or by citizens or subjects of any foreign state."

It is a part of our history, that, at the

adoption of the Constitution, all the states were greatly indebted; and the apprehension that these debts might be prosecuted in the federal courts, formed a very serious objection to that instrument. Suits were instituted; and the Court maintained its jurisdiction. The alarm was general; and, to quiet the apprehensions that were so extensively entertained, this amendment was proposed in Congress, and adopted by the state legislatures. That its motive was not to maintain the sovereignty of a state from the degradation supposed to attend a compulsory appearance before the tribunal of the nation, may be inferred from the terms of the amendment. It does not comprehend controversies between two or more states, or between a state and a foreign state. The jurisdiction of the Court still extends to these cases; and in these a state may still be sued. We must ascribe the amendment, then, to some other cause than the dignity of a state. There is no difficulty in finding this cause. Those who were inhibited from commencing a suit against a state, or from prosecuting one which might be commenced before the adoption of the amendment, were persons who might probably be its creditors. There was not much reason to fear that foreign or sister states would be creditors to any considerable amount, and there was reason to retain the jurisdiction of the Court in those cases, because it might be essential to the preservation of peace. The amendment, therefore, extended to suits commenced or prosecuted by individuals, but not to those brought by states. . . .

A general interest might well be felt in leaving to a state the full power of consulting its convenience in the adjustment of its debts, or of other claims upon it; but no interest could be felt in so changing the relations between the whole and its parts, as to strip the government of the means of protecting, by the instrumentality of its courts, the Constitution and laws from active violation. . . .

Under the judiciary act, the effect of a writ of error is simply to bring the record into court, and submit the judgment of the inferior tribunal to re-examination. It does not in any manner act upon the parties; it acts only on the record. It removes the record into the supervising tribunal. Where, then, a state obtains a judgment against an individual, and the court, rendering such judgment, overrules a defense set up under the Constitution or laws of the United States, the transfer of this record into the Supreme Court, for the sole purpose of inquiring whether the judgment violates the Constitution or laws of the United States, can with no propriety, we think, be denominated a suit commenced or prosecuted against the state whose judgment is so far re-examined. Nothing is demanded from the state. No claim against it of any description is asserted or prosecuted. The party is not to be restored to the possession of anything. Essentially, it is an appeal on a single point; and the defendant who appeals from a judgment rendered against him, is never said to commence or prosecute a suit against the plaintiff who has obtained the judgment. . . .

It is, then, the opinion of the Court, that the defendant who removes a judgment rendered against him by a state court into this Court, for the purpose of re-examining the question, whether that judgment be in violation of the Constitution or laws of the United States, does not commence or prosecute a suit against the state, . . .

2d. The second objection to the jurisdiction of the Court is, that its appellate power cannot be exercised, in any case, over the judgment of a state court.

This objection is sustained chiefly by arguments drawn from the supposed total separation of the judiciary of a state from that of the Union, and their entire independence of each other. The argument considers the federal judiciary as completely foreign to that of a state; and as being no more connected with it, in any respect whatever, than the court of a foreign state. If this hypothesis be just, the argument founded on it is equally so; but if the hypothesis be not supported by the Constitution, the argument fails with it.

This hypothesis is not founded on any words in the Constitution, which might seem to countenance it, but on the unreasonableness of giving a contrary construction to words which seem to require it; and on the incompatibility of the application of the appellate jurisdiction to the judgments of state courts, with that constitutional relation which subsists between the government of the Union and the governments of those states which compose it.

Let this unreasonableness, this total incompatibility, be examined.

That the United States form, for many, and for most important purposes, a single nation, has not yet been denied. In war, we are one people. In making peace, we are one people. In all commercial regulations, we are one and the same people. In many other respects, the American people are one; and the government which is alone capable of controlling and managing their interests in all these respects, is the government of the Union. It is their government, and in that character they have no other. America has chosen to be, in many respects, and to many purposes, a nation; and for all these purposes, her government is complete; to all these objects, it is competent. The people have declared, that in the exercise of all powers given for these objects it is supreme. It can, then, in effecting these objects, legitimately control all individuals or governments within the American territory. The constitution and laws of a state, so far as they are repugnant to the Constitution and laws of the United States, are absolutely void. These states are constituent parts of the United States. They are members of one great empire—for some purposes sovereign, for some purposes subordinate.

In a government so constituted, is it unreasonable that the judicial power should be competent to give efficacy to the constitutional laws of the legislature? That department can decide on the validity of the constitution or law of a state, if it be repugnant to the Constitution or to a law of the United States. Is it unreasonable that it should also be empowered to decide on the judgment of a state tribunal enforcing such unconstitutional law? Is it so very unreasonable as to furnish a justification for controlling the words of the Constitution?

We think it is not. We think that in a government acknowledgedly supreme, with respect to objects of vital interest to the nation, there is nothing inconsistent with sound reason, nothing incompatible with the nature of government, in making all its departments supreme, so far as respects those objects, and so far as is necessary to their attainment. The exercise of the appellate power over those judgments of the state tribunals which may contravene the Constitution or laws of the United States, is, we believe, essential to the attainment of those objects.

The propriety of entrusting the construction of the Constitution, and laws made in pursuance thereof, to the judiciary of the Union, has not, we believe, as yet, been drawn into question. It seems to be a corollary from this political axiom, that the federal courts should either possess exclusive jurisdiction in such cases, or a power to revise the judgment rendered in them, by the state tribunals. If the federal and state courts have concurrent jurisdiction in all cases arising under the Constitution, laws, and treaties of the United States; and if a case of this description brought in a state court cannot be removed before judgment, nor revised after judgment, then the construction of the Constitution, laws, and treaties of the

United States, is not confided particularly to their judicial department, but is confided equally to that department and to the state courts, however they may be constituted. "Thirteen independent courts," says a very celebrated statesman (and we have now more than twenty such courts), "of final jurisdiction over the same causes, arising upon the same laws, is a hydra in government, from which nothing but contradiction and confusion can proceed."

Dismissing the unpleasant suggestion, that any motives which may not be fairly avowed, or which ought not to exist, can ever influence a state or its courts, the necessity of uniformity, as well as correctness in expounding the Constitution and laws of the United States, would itself suggest the propriety of vesting in some single tribunal the power of deciding, in the last resort, all cases in which they are involved.

We are not restrained, then, by the political relations between the general and state governments, from construing the words of the Constitution, defining the judicial power, in their true sense. We are not bound to construe them more restrictively than they naturally import.

They give to the Supreme Court appellate jurisdiction in all cases arising under the Constitution, laws, and treaties of the United States. The words are broad enough to comprehend all cases of this description, in whatever court they may be decided. . . .

The framers of the Constitution would naturally examine the state of things existing at the time; and their work suffi-

ciently attests that they did so. All acknowledge that they were convened for the purpose of strengthening the confederation by enlarging the powers of the government, and by giving efficacy to those which it before possessed, but could not exercise. They inform us themselves, in the instrument they presented to the American public, that one of its objects was to form a more perfect union. . . .

This opinion has been already drawn out to too great a length to admit of entering into a particular consideration of the various forms in which the counsel who made this point has, with much ingenuity, presented his argument to the Court. The argument in all its forms is essentially the same. It is founded, not on the words of the Constitution, but on its spirit, a spirit extracted, not from the words of the instrument, but from his view of the nature of our Union, and of the great fundamental principles on which the fabric stands.

To this argument, in all its forms, the same answer may be given. Let the nature and objects of our Union be considered; let the great fundamental principles, on which the fabric stands, be examined; and we think the result must be, that there is nothing so extravagantly absurd in giving to the Court of the nation the power of revising the decisions of local tribunals on questions which affect the nation, as to require that words which import this power should be restricted by a forced construction. . . .

Judgment affirmed.

Contrast Marshall's opinion in the *Cohens* case with Justice Story's decision in the *Martin* case. What similarities and differences do you observe? Is the *Cohens* opinion a stronger statement of federal judicial power than the *Martin* decision? Contrast the arguments of counsel for Virginia and for the Cohens with regard to the question of the reviewability of criminal prosecutions under Section 25. How does Marshall's opinion handle the argument that the action taken by the Cohens was essentially a suit against the state of Virginia and therefore precluded by the Eleventh Amendment?[6]

While Marshall's decision of the *Cohens* case in effect upheld the Virginia court, Justice Roane and other backers of the states' rights position continued their criticism of the Supreme Court's decision. The real issue in the *Cohens* as in the *Martin* case was that of the scope of the appellate jurisdiction of the Supreme Court over state courts under Section 25.

The controversy over the scope of state sovereignty in relation to the national government that arose in the early decades of the Supreme Court was not settled by the far-reaching decisions of the Marshall Court in support of broad national powers and national supremacy. Over two million men died on the battlefields of the Civil War to preserve the Union. The triumph of the legal doctrines of national supremacy and the decisions of the Marshall Court aggravated the underlying conflict between the nationalists and the champions of states' rights. These decisions also raised questions about the proper role of the Supreme Court in the political system. Many proponents of states' rights argued that the Court was usurping the authority of Congress as well as of the states by unilaterally changing the Constitution through its opinions.

The charge that the Supreme Court was acting unconstitutionally as a superlegislature became a recurrent theme in attacks upon the Court by states' rights advocates. This criticism emerged with particular sharpness after the decision of the Court in *Brown* v. *Board of Education* (1954) and after its later decisions in such cases as *Swann* v. *Charlotte Mecklenburg County Board of Education* (1971), that upheld busing as a means to achieve the integration of public schools.

The political response to the Marshall Court's decisions also were precedents of later attempts to curb the Court's power. In the wake of the *Martin* and *Cohens* cases, the backers of states' rights in Congress attempted to repeal Section 25. Other efforts to curb the Court's authority included, for example, a proposal to require the concurrence of seven judges to declare a state law invalid.[7] Numerous variations of these proposals to curb the Court were introduced in Congress during the 1820s, but their proponents were unable to muster the necessary political support for their enactment. At the state level efforts were made in the legislatures to pass laws limiting the authority of the Supreme Court, and the courts of at least seven states independently challenged the authority of the Supreme Court under Section 25.

The doctrine that a state may reject the mandate of the Supreme Court or another branch of the federal government is called *interposition*. The doctrine of interposition was first applied after *Chisholm* v. *Georgia* when the

[6]The doctrine of sovereign immunity does not automatically protect the sovereign against *all* suits but only against those that in effect "lie against the sovereign," that is, "stop the sovereign in its tracks." Suits against which the defense of sovereign immunity may be used are generally those seeking money or property from the sovereign, or which would impede the effective operation of the government of the sovereign. See, for example, State of Hawaii v. Gordon, 373 U.S. 57 (1963); Malone v. Bowdoin, 369 U.S. 643 (1962); Larson v. Domestic and Foreign Commerce Corporation, 337 U.S. 682 (1949).

[7]Warren, *The Supreme Court,* II, 124.

state refused to honor the Court's mandate. Interposition may be implemented by the legislatures, courts, or executives of states. It was an accepted doctrine by proponents of states' rights before the Civil War and was resurrected after *Brown* v. *Board of Education* in 1954 in legislative resolutions of Alabama, Georgia, Mississippi, South Carolina, and Virginia. See *Cooper* v. *Aaron*, 358 U.S. 1 (1958), and *Bush* v. *Orleans Parish School Board*, 364 U.S. 500 (1960).

STATE SOVEREIGNTY AS A LIMIT ON CONGRESSIONAL POWER

In the early decades of the Republic, the Supreme Court, in such cases as *McCulloch* v. *Maryland,* firmly established the principle that national sovereignty limits the states in a variety of ways. All of the cases that have been considered in this chapter were part of the early trend toward nationalism. While the Constitution, in the supremacy clause, explicitly provides for national sovereignty over the states, the Constitution says little about state sovereignty as a limit upon the national government. The Tenth Amendment provides: "The powers not delegated to the United States by the Constitution, nor prohibited by it to the states, are reserved to the states respectively, or to the people." This would seem to imply a sphere of state sovereignty into which the national government cannot intrude. Moreover, the original Constitution does contain a few constraints upon the authority of the national government to invade state sovereignty. For example, Article I, Section 8, clause 16 reserves for the states the authority to appoint officers in the militia and the authority to train the militia "according to the discipline prescribed by Congress." Article I, Section 9, clause 1 prohibits the Congress from interfering in the slave trade authorized by any state until the year 1808. Article I, Section 9, clause 5 forbids Congress from taxing articles exported from any state, and Article I, section 9, clause 6 bars Congress from giving preference to the ports of one state over those of another, "nor shall vessels bound to, or from, one state, be obliged to enter, clear, or pay duties in another." Article IV, Section 3 prohibits Congress from invading state sovereignty in the creation of new states, and Article V provides that "No state, without its consent, shall be deprived of its equal suffrage in the Senate."

The paucity of constitutional provisions that explicitly limit congressional authority to act upon the states reflects the fact that at the time of the framing of the Constitution the states were sovereign units considered perfectly capable of defending themselves against national encroachments. Politically and economically the states were the dominant bodies in 1787 and for most of the nineteenth century. Early Federalists and later nationalists recognized that if the national government was to survive it was important to expand its power through constitutional interpretation. Even Republican Supreme Court justices did not always find that state sovereignty had to be defended from the bench.

State Immunity from Federal Taxation

In *McCulloch* v. *Maryland,* Chief Justice John Marshall held that the exercise of national sovereignty—the creation of a national bank—could not be burdened by a state tax. The power to tax is the power to destroy, said Marshall, and allowing states to exercise the taxing power over the legitimate instruments of the federal government would threaten national sovereignty. The power of the *state* governments to tax, said Marshall, cannot extend beyond their sovereignty. Would Marshall apply the same principle to the national government, that is, limiting its authority to tax people and property to its sphere of sovereignty? If the national government cannot be impeded in the execution of its sovereign powers by state taxation, does the converse principle apply, that is, that the national government cannot burden through taxation the exercise by the states of powers within their sovereignty?

The issue of state immunity from federal taxation was involved in *Collector* v. *Day* (1871). The question was whether Congress could impose a tax upon the salary of a state judge. The Court had previously held in *Dobbins* v. *Erie County*, 16 Pet. 435 (1842), that the states could not tax the salary of a federal officer. The majority opinion of Justice Nelson in *Collector* v. *Day* stood *McCulloch* v. *Maryland* on its head and held that the states cannot be impaired by a federal tax in carrying out their sovereign responsibilities. Justice Nelson wrote,

> Two of the great departments of the government, the executive and legislative, depend upon the exercise of the powers, or upon the people of the states. The Constitution guarantees to the states a republican form of government, and protects each against invasion or domestic violence. Such being the separate and independent condition of the states in our complex system, as recognized by the Constitution, and the existence of which is so indispensable, that, without them, the general government itself would disappear from the family of nations, it would seem to follow, as a reasonable, if not a necessary consequence, that the means and instrumentalities employed for carrying on the operations of their governments, for preserving their existence, and fulfilling the high and responsible duties assigned to them in the Constitution, should be left free and unimpaired; should not be liable to be crippled, much less defeated by the taxing power of another government, which power acknowledges no limits but the will of the legislative body imposing the tax. And, more especially, those means and instrumentalities which are the creation of their sovereign and reserved rights, one of which is the establishment of the judicial department, and the appointment of officers to administer their laws. Without this power, and the exercise of it, we risk nothing in saying that no one of the states, under the form of government guaranteed by the Constitution, could long preserve its existence.[8]

In *Helvering* v. *Gerhardt* (1938) the employees of the Port Authority of New York claimed that the federal income tax on their salaries was an unconstitutional burden on New York and New Jersey, the states that had es-

[8]Collector v. Day, 11 Wall. 113, 126 (1871).

tablished the Authority. The court of appeals held that the salaries were exempt from the federal tax, and the Supreme Court granted certiorari. Was it reasonable to assume on the basis of the precedent of *Collector* v. *Day* that the Court would uphold state immunity from federal taxation of the Port Authority's employees?

Helvering v. Gerhardt

304 U.S. 405, 58 S. Ct. 969, 82 L. Ed. 1427 (1938)

MR. JUSTICE STONE delivered the opinion of the Court:

The question for decision is whether the imposition of a federal income tax for the calendar years 1932 and 1933 on salaries received by respondents, as employees of the Port of New York Authority, places an unconstitutional burden on the States of New York and New Jersey.

The Port Authority is a bi-state corporation, created by compact between New York and New Jersey.... The compact authorized the Authority to acquire and operate "any terminal or transportation facility" within a specified district embracing the Port of New York and lying partially within each state....

The Board of Tax Appeals found that the Port Authority was engaged in the performance of a public function for the States of New York and New Jersey, and ruled that the compensation received by the Authority's employees was exempt from federal income tax. The Court of Appeals ... affirmed....

The Constitution contains no express limitation on the power of either a state or the national government to tax the other, or its instrumentalities. The doctrine that there is an implied limitation stems from *McCulloch* v. *Maryland*, ... in which it was held that a state tax laid specifically upon the privilege of issuing bank notes, and in fact applicable alone to the notes of national banks, was invalid since it impeded the national government in

the exercise of its power to establish and maintain a bank. ... It was held that Congress, having power to establish a bank by laws which ... are supreme, also had power to protect the bank by striking down state action impeding its operations; and it was thought that the state tax in question was so inconsistent with Congress's constitutional action in establishing the bank as to compel the conclusion that Congress intended to forbid application of the tax to the federal bank notes....

We need not stop to inquire how far, as indicated in *McCulloch* v. *Maryland*, ... the immunity of federal instrumentalities from state taxation rests on a different basis from that of state instrumentalities; or whether or to what degree it is more extensive. As to those questions, other considerations may be controlling which are not pertinent here. It is enough for present purposes that the state immunity from the national taxing power, when recognized in *Collector* v. *Day*, ... was narrowly limited to a state judicial officer engaged in the performance of a function which pertained to state governments at the time the Constitution was adopted, without which no state "could long preserve its existence."

There are cogent reasons why any constitutional restriction upon the taxing power granted to Congress, so far as it can be properly raised by implication, should be narrowly limited. One, as was pointed out by Chief Justice Marshall ... is that the people of all the states have created the national government and are represented in Congress. Through that representation they exercise the national taxing power. The very fact that when they are exercising it they are taxing themselves, serves to guard against its abuse through the possibility of resort to the usual processes of political action which provides a readier and more adaptable means than any which courts can afford, for securing accommodation of the competing demands for national revenue, on the one hand, and for reasonable scope for the independence of state action, on the other.

Another reason rests upon the fact that any allowance of a tax immunity for the protection of state sovereignty is at the expense of the sovereign power of the nation to tax. Enlargement of the one involves diminution of the other. When enlargement proceeds beyond the necessity of protecting the state, the burden of the immunity is thrown upon the national government with benefit only to a privileged class of taxpayers. . . . Once impaired by the recognition of a state immunity found to be excessive, restoration of that power is not likely to be secured through the action of state legislatures; for they are without the inducements to act which have often persuaded Congress to waive immunities thought to be excessive. . . .

In a period marked by a constant expansion of government activities and the steady multiplication of the complexities of taxing systems, it is perhaps too much to expect that the judicial pronouncements marking the boundaries of state immunity should present a completely logical pattern. But they disclose no purposeful departure from, and indeed definitely establish, two guiding principles of limitation for holding the tax immunity of state instrumentalities to its proper function. The one, dependent upon the nature of the function being performed by the state or in its behalf, excludes from the immunity activities thought not to be essential to the preservation of state governments even though the tax be collected from the state treasury. The state itself was taxed for the privilege of carrying on the liquor business in *South Carolina* v. *United States* [1905] . . .; and a tax on the income of a state officer engaged in the management of a state-owned corporation operating a street railroad was sustained in *Helvering* v. *Powers* [1934] . . . , because it was thought that the functions discouraged by these taxes were not indispensable to the maintenance of a state government. The other principle, exemplified by those cases where the tax laid upon individuals affects the state only as the burden is passed on to it by the taxpayer, forbids recognition of the immunity when the burden on the state is so speculative and uncertain that if allowed it would restrict the federal taxing power without affording any corresponding tangible protection to the state government. . . .

With these controlling principles in mind we turn to their application in the circumstances of the present case. The challenged taxes . . . are upon the net income of respondents, derived from their employment in common occupations not shown to be different in their methods or duties from those of similar employees in private industry. . . . Even though, to some unascertainable extent, the tax deprives the states of the advantage of paying less than the standard rate for the services which they engage, it does not curtail any of those functions which have been thought hitherto to be essential to their continued existence as states. . . . The effect of the immunity if allowed would be to relieve respondents of their duty of financial support to the national government, in order to secure to the state a theoretical advantage so speculative in its character and measurement as to be unsubstantial. A tax immunity devised for protection of the states as governmental entities cannot be pressed so far. . . .

MR. JUSTICE BLACK concurred.

MR. JUSTICE BUTLER, joined by MR. JUSTICE McREYNOLDS, dissented.

Reversed.

On what basis did Justice Stone uphold the federal income tax on the employees of the Port Authority of New York? Under what circumstances does his decision suggest that the states could claim immunity from federal taxation? How does Justice Stone distinguish the facts of *Helvering* from those of *Collector* v. *Day*?

In *Graves* v. *New York ex rel. O'Keefe*, 306 U.S. 466 (1939), Justice Stone wrote the Court's opinion that rejected the claim of an employee of the Federal Homeowner's Loan Corporation for exemption from the New York State income tax. Justice Stone wrote: "Assuming, as we do, that the Homeowner's Loan Corporation is clothed with the same immunity from state taxation as the [national] government itself, we cannot say that the present tax on the income of its employees lays any unconstitutional burden upon it. All the reasons for refusing to imply a constitutional prohibition of federal income taxation of salaries of state employees, stated at length in the *Gerhardt* case, are of equal force when immunity is claimed from state income tax on salaries paid by the national government or its agencies. . . . *Collector* v. *Day* and *New York ex rel. Rogers* v. *Graves*, [which held that New York could not tax the salary of an employee of the Panama Railroad Company, a national government corporation] are overruled so far as they recognize an implied constitutional immunity from income taxation of the salaries of officers or employees of the national or a state government or their instrumentalities."[9]

Federal taxation of the states again was the issue in the 1946 case *New York* v. *United States*, in which the state sought to overturn the United States Revenue Act of 1932 that taxed the sale of bottled mineral water. The state was engaged in the business of bottling for resale mineral water from Saratoga Springs, New York. On what basis could the state claim immunity from federal taxation? As you read Justice Frankfurter's opinion, under what circumstances does he consider federal taxation of the state to be unconstitutional?

New York v. United States

326 U.S. 572; 66 S. Ct. 310; 90 L. Ed. 326 (1946)

MR. JUSTICE FRANKFURTER announced the judgment of the Court and delivered an opinion in which MR. JUSTICE RUTLEDGE joined:

[9] *Graves* v. *New York ex rel. O'Keefe*, 306 U.S. 466, 486 (1939).

... [T]he 1932 Revenue Act ... imposed a tax on mineral waters. The United States brought this suit to recover taxes assessed against the State of New York on the sale of mineral waters taken from Saratoga Springs, New York. The State claims immunity from this tax on the ground that "in the bottling and sale of the said waters the defendant State of New York was engaged in the exercise of a usual, traditional and essential governmental function." The claim was rejected by the District Court and judgment went for the United States.... The judgment was affirmed by the Circuit Court of Appeals for the Second Circuit.... The strong urging of New York for further clarification of the amenability of States to the taxing power of the United States led us to grant certiorari....

On the basis of authority the case is quickly disposed of. When States sought to control the liquor traffic by going into the liquor business, they were denied immunity from federal taxes upon the liquor business. *South Carolina* v. *United States* [1905]; *Ohio* v. *Helvering* [1934]. And in rejecting a claim of immunity from federal taxation when Massachusetts took over the street railways of Boston, this Court a decade ago said: "We see no reason for putting the operation of a street railway [by a State] in a different category from the sale of liquors." *Helvering* v. *Powers* [1934]. We certainly see no reason for putting soft drinks in a different constitutional category from hard drinks....

One of the greatest sources of strength of our law is that it adjudicates concrete cases and does not pronounce principles in the abstract. But there comes a time when even the process of empiric adjudication calls for a more rational disposition than that the immediate case is not different from preceding cases. The argument pressed by New York and the forty-five other States who, as *amici curiae*, have joined her deserves an answer.

Enactments levying taxes made in pursuance of the Constitution are, as other laws are, "the supreme Law of the Land.".... The first of the powers conferred upon Congress is the power "To lay and collect Taxes, Duties, Imposts and Excises ..." Art. I, § 8. By its terms the Constitution has placed only one limitation upon this power, other than limitations upon methods of laying taxes not here relevant: Congress can lay no tax "on Articles exported from any State." Art. I, § 9. Barring only exports, the power of Congress to tax "reaches every subject." ... But the fact that ours is a federal constitutional system, as expressly recognized in the Tenth Amendment, carries with it implications regarding the taxing power as in other aspects of government.... Thus, for Congress to tax State activities while leaving untaxed the same activities pursued by private persons would do violence to the presuppositions derived from the fact that we are a Nation composed of States.

But the fear that one government may cripple or obstruct the operations of the other early led to the assumption that there was a reciprocal immunity of the instrumentalities of each from taxation by the other. It was assumed that there was an equivalence in the implications of taxation by a State of the governmental activities of the National Government and the taxation by the National Government of State instrumentalities. This assumed equivalence was nourished by the phrase of Chief Justice Marshall that "the power to tax involves the power to destroy." *McCulloch* v. *Maryland* ... To be sure, it was uttered in connection with a tax of Maryland which plainly discriminated against the use by the United States of the Bank of the United States as one of its instruments. What he said may not have been irrelevant in its setting. But Chief Justice Marshall spoke at a time when social complexities did not so clearly reveal as now the practical limitations of a rhetorical absolute. . . . The phrase was seized upon as the basis of a broad doctrine of intergovernmental immunity, while at the same time an expansive scope was given to what were deemed to be "instrumentalities of government" for purposes of tax immunity. As a result, immunity was until recently accorded to all officers of one government from taxation by the other, and it was further assumed that the economic burden of a tax on any interest derived from a government imposes a burden on that government so as to involve an interference by the taxing government with the functioning of the other government. . . .

In the older cases, the emphasis was on immunity from taxation. The whole tendency of recent cases reveals a shift in emphasis to that of limitation upon immunity. They also indicate an awareness of the limited rôle of courts in assessing the relative weight of the factors upon which immunity is based. Any implied limitation upon the supremacy of the federal power to levy a tax like that now before us, in the absence of discrimination against State activities, brings fiscal and political factors into play. The problem cannot escape issues that do not lend themselves to judgment by criteria and methods of reasoning that are within the professional training and special competence of judges. . . .

We have already held that by engaging in the railroad business a State cannot withdraw the railroad from the power of the federal government to regulate commerce. . . . Surely the power of Congress to lay taxes has impliedly no less a reach than the power of Congress to regulate commerce. There are, of course, State activities and State-owned property that partake of uniqueness from the point of view of intergovernmental relations. These inherently constitute a class by themselves. Only a State can own a Statehouse; only a State can get income by taxing. These could not be included for purposes of federal taxation in any abstract category of taxpayers without taxing the State as a State. But so long as Congress generally taps a source of revenue by whomsoever earned and not uniquely capable of being earned only by a State, the Constitution of the United States does not forbid it merely because its incidence falls also on a State. . . .

The process of Constitutional adjudication does not thrive on conjuring up horrible possibilities that never happen in the real world and devising doctrines sufficiently comprehensive in detail to cover the remotest contingency. . . . So we decide enough when we reject limitations upon the taxing power of Congress derived from such untenable criteria as "proprietary" against "governmental" activities of the States, or historically sanctioned activities of government, or activities conducted merely for profit, and find no restriction upon Congress to include the States in levying a tax exacted equally from private persons upon the same subject matter.

Judgment affirmed.

MR. JUSTICE JACKSON took no part in the consideration or decision of this case.

MR. JUSTICE RUTLEDGE, concurring:
I join in the opinion of Mr. Justice Frankfurter and in the result. I have no doubt upon the question of power. The shift from immunity to taxability has gone too far, and with too much reason to sustain it, as respects both state functionaries and state functions, for backtracking to doctrines founded in philosophies of sovereignty more current and perhaps more

realistic in an earlier day. Too much is, or may be, at stake for the nation to permit relieving the states of their duty to support it, financially as otherwise, when they take over increasingly the things men have been accustomed to carry on as private, and therefore taxable, enterprise. Competitive considerations unite with the necessity for securing the federal revenue, in a time when the federal burden grows heavier proportionately than that of the states, to forbid that they be free to undermine rather than obligated to sustain the nation's financial requirements.

All agree that not all of the former immunity is gone. For the present I assent to the limitation against discrimination, which I take to mean that state functions may not be singled out for taxation when others performing them are not taxed or for special burdens when they are. What would happen if the state should take over a monopoly of traditionally private, income-producing business may be left for the future, in so far as this has not been settled by *South Carolina* v. *United States.* . . . Perhaps there are other limitations also, apart from the practical one imposed by the state's representation in Congress. If the way were open, I would add a further restricting factor, not of constitutional import, but of construction.

With the passing of the former broad immunity, I should think two considerations well might be taken to require that, before a federal tax can be applied to activities carried on directly by the states, the intention of Congress to tax them should be stated expressly and not drawn merely from general wording of the statute applicable ordinarily to private sources of revenue. One of these is simply a reflection of the old immunity, in the presence of which, of course, it would be inconceivable that general wording, such as the statute now in question contains, could be taken as intended to apply to the states. The other is that, quite apart from reflections of that immunity, I should expect that Congress would say so explicitly, were its purpose actually to include state functions, where the legal incidence of the tax falls upon the state. . . .

Nevertheless, since *South Carolina* v. *United States,* . . . such a rule of construction seems not to have been thought required. Accordingly, although I gravely doubt that when Congress taxed every "person" it intended also to tax every state, the ruling has been made and I therefore acquiesce in this case.

Mr. Chief Justice Stone, concurring:

Mr. Justice Reed, Mr. Justice Murphy, Mr. Justice Burton and I concur in the result. We are of the opinion that the tax here involved should be sustained and the judgment below affirmed.

In view of our [past] decisions . . . we would find it difficult not to sustain the tax in this case, even though we regard as untenable the distinction between "governmental" and "proprietary" interests on which those cases rest to some extent. But we are not prepared to say that the national government may constitutionally lay a non-discriminatory tax on every class of property and activities of States and individuals alike.

Concededly a federal tax discriminating against a State would be an unconstitutional exertion of power over a coexisting sovereignty within the same framework of government. But our difficulty with the formula, now first suggested as offering a new solution for an old problem, is that a federal tax which is not discriminatory as to the subject matter may nevertheless so affect the State, merely because it is a State that is being taxed, as to interfere unduly with the State's performance of its sovereign functions of government. The counterpart of such undue interference has been recognized since Marshall's day as the implied immunity of each of the dual sovereignties of our constitutional system from taxation by the other. *McCulloch* v. *Maryland*. . . . We add nothing to this formula by saying, in a new form of words, that a tax which Congress applies generally to the property and activities of private citizens may not be in some instances constitutionally extended to the States, merely because the States are included among those who pay taxes on a like subject of taxation.

If the phrase "non-discriminatory tax" is to be taken in its long accepted meaning as referring to a tax laid on a like subject matter, without regard to the personality of the taxpayer, whether a State, a corporation or a private individual, it is plain that there may be non-discriminatory taxes which, when laid on a State, would nevertheless impair the sovereign status of the State quite as much as a like tax imposed by a State on property or activities of the national government. . . . This is not because the tax can be regarded as discriminatory but because a sovereign government is the taxpayer, and the tax, even though non-discriminatory, may be regarded as infringing its sovereignty.

A State may, like a private individual, own real property and receive income. But in view of our former decisions we could hardly say that a general non-discriminatory real estate tax (apportioned), or an income tax laid upon citizens and States alike could be constitutionally applied to the State's capitol, its State-house, its public school houses, public parks, or its revenues from taxes or school lands, even though all real property and all income of the citizen is taxed. . . .

It is enough for present purposes that the immunity of the State from federal taxation would, in this case, accomplish a withdrawal from the taxing power of the nation a subject of taxation of a nature which has been traditionally within that

power from the beginning. Its exercise now, by a non-discriminatory tax, does not curtail the business of the state government more than it does the like business of the citizen. It gives merely an accustomed and reasonable scope to the federal taxing power. . . . [This] taxation does not unduly impair the State's functions of government. . . .

The problem is not one to be solved by a formula, but we may look to the structure of the Constitution as our guide to decision. "In a broad sense, the taxing power of either government, even when exercised in a manner admittedly necessary and proper, unavoidably has some effect upon the other. . . . Taxation by either the state or the federal government affects in some measure the cost of operation of the other.

"But neither government may destroy the other nor curtail in any substantial manner the exercise of its powers. Hence the limitation upon the taxing power of each, so far as it affects the other, must receive a practical construction which permits both to function with the minimum of interference each with the other; and that limitation cannot be so varied or extended as seriously to impair either the taxing power of the government imposing the tax . . . or the appropriate exercise of the functions of the government affected by it.". . .

Since all taxes must be laid by general, that is, workable, rules, the effect of the immunity on the national taxing power is to be determined not quantitatively but by its operation and tendency in withdrawing taxable property or activities from the reach of federal taxation. Not the extent to which a particular State engages in the activity, but the nature and extent of the activity by whomsoever performed is the relevant consideration.

Regarded in this light we cannot say that the Constitution either requires immunity of the State's mineral water business from federal taxation, or denies to the federal government power to lay the tax.

Mr. Justice Douglas, with whom Mr. Justice Black concurs, dissenting:

If *South Carolina* v. *United States* . . . is to stand, the present judgment would have to be affirmed. For I agree that there is no essential difference between a federal tax on South Carolina's liquor business and a federal tax on New York's mineral water business. Whether *South Carolina* v. *United States* reaches the right result is another matter. . . .

I do not believe *South Carolina* v. *United States* states the correct rule. A State's project is as much a legitimate governmental activity whether it is traditional, or akin to private enterprise, or conducted for profit. . . . What might have been viewed in an earlier day as an improvident or even dangerous extension of state activities may today be deemed indispensable. . . . any activity in which a State engages within the limits of its police power is a legitimate governmental activity. . . . Must it pay the federal government for the privilege of exercising that inherent power? . . .

II

The notion that the sovereign position of the States must find its protection in the will of a transient majority of Congress is foreign to and a negation of our constitutional system. . . .

The immunity of the States from federal taxation is no less clear because it is implied. . . . The Constitution is a compact between sovereigns. The power of one sovereign to tax another is an innovation so startling as to require explicit authority if it is to be allowed. If the power of the federal government to tax the States is conceded, the reserved power of the States guaranteed by the Tenth Amendment does not give them the independence which they have always been assumed to have. They are relegated to a more servile status. They become subject to interference and control both in the functions which they exercise and the methods which they employ. They must pay the federal government for the privilege of exercising the powers of sovereignty guaranteed them by the Constitution, whether, as here, they are disposing of their natural resources, or tomorrow they issue securities or perform any other acts within the scope of their police power. . . .

The crux of Frankfurter's opinion, which upheld the federal tax, is contained in his statement that "so long as Congress generally taps a source of revenue by whomsoever earned and not uniquely capable of being earned only by a state, the Constitution of the United States does not forbid it merely because its incidence falls also on a state." There are unique state activities, said Frankfurter, which constitute a *class* against which a federal tax cannot discriminate. Does Chief Justice Stone's concurring opinion agree fully with the nondiscrimination rule implied in Frankfurter's opinion?

South Carolina v. *United States*, 199 U.S. 437 (1905), is mentioned in both the opinions of the Court and in the dissenting opinion of Justice Douglas. That case reaffirmed the rule that had been established in a long line of cases which separated the "governmental" from the "proprietary" functions of a state or local government and which permitted federal taxation of the latter but not the former. *Ohio* v. *Helvering*, 292 U.S. 360 (1934), cited by Frankfurter, reaffirmed this rule. What does the Court state is the basis for the rule, and why does Justice Douglas argue that the doctrine of *South Carolina* v. *United States* should not prevail?

THE DOCTRINE OF NATIONAL PREEMPTION

Under the Constitution the national government and the states exercise concurrent jurisdiction in many areas, most notably in their authority to regulate commerce. Concurrent jurisdiction exists because the delegation of powers to the national government does not automatically preclude their exercise by the states. Article VI provides: "This Constitution, and the laws of the United States which shall be made in pursuance thereof; and all treaties made, or which shall be made, under the authority of the United States, shall be the supreme law of the land; and the judges in every state shall be bound thereby, anything in the Constitution or laws of any state to the contrary notwithstanding." This "supremacy clause" clearly prohibits state enactment of laws that conflict directly with federal statutes. However, there is a vast area of law in which such conflict is not explicit and unambiguous. Where the conflict between a federal and state law is not clear, and when the state law is challenged on the basis that it conflicts with a federal statute, the Supreme Court faces the difficult task of defining the permissible scope of state authority. Most cases in which the doctrine of federal preemption has been applied are in the field of commerce. Preemption decisions do not usually involve constitutional criteria per se, but the Court's reading of the Constitution may indirectly influence its application of the preemption doctrine. It may use that doctrine to preclude state action that it would declare unconstitutional in the absence of a congressional statute that can be used to declare congressional preemption of the field.

While Congress may clearly express its intent to preempt a field, this is not usually the case. The Court must often base its judgment in preemption cases on an indirect assessment of congressional intent and interpretation of congressional law that goes beyond explicit or implied provisions in the statute itself and beyond the language of the committee report on the bill as well. The Court often will interpret the intent of Congress to preempt a field if it finds as a matter of fact that the state law conflicts with a federal statute. Such "conflict" may result from a state law that interferes with the administration of a federal statute or one that subordinates the national interest to local concerns.

In *Pennsylvania* v. *Nelson* (1956), a member of the Communist party was convicted of a violation of the Pennsylvania sedition act, which made it a crime not only to conspire against the government of Pennsylvania but also against the government of the United States. The defendant, Steve Nelson, was indicted and convicted under the Pennsylvania statute for conspiring to overthrow the government of the United States by force and violence. In 1940 Congress had passed the Smith Act, which made it a crime to conspire to overthrow the government of the United States by force and violence.

The Pennsylvania Supreme Court reversed Nelson's conviction, ruling that the Smith Act preempted state legislation governing sedition against the United States. There was no evidence, said the Pennsylvania court, that the defendant had conspired against the state. The Supreme Court granted Pennsylvania's appeal for a writ of certiorari.

Pennsylvania v. Nelson

350 U.S. 497; 76 S. Ct. 477; 100 L. Ed. 640 (1956)

MR. CHIEF JUSTICE WARREN delivered the opinion of the Court:

The respondent Steve Nelson, an acknowledged member of the Communist Party, was convicted . . . of a violation of the Pennsylvania Sedition Act and sentenced to imprisonment for twenty years and to a fine of $10,000. . . . The Superior Court affirmed the conviction. . . . The Supreme Court of Pennsylvania, recognizing but not reaching many alleged serious trial errors and conduct of the trial court infringing upon the respondent's right to due process of law, decided the case on the narrow issue of supersession of the state law by the Federal Smith Act. In its opinion, the court stated:

And, while the Pennsylvania statute proscribes sedition against either the Government of the United States or the Government of Pennsylvania, it is only alleged sedition against the United States with which the instant case is concerned. Out of all the voluminous testimony, we have not found, nor has anyone pointed to, a single word indicating a seditious act or even utterance directed against the Government of Pennsylvania.

The precise holding of the court, and all that is before us for review, is that the Smith Act of 1940, as amended in 1948, which prohibits the knowing advocacy of the overthrow of the Government of the United States by force and violence, supersedes the enforceability of the Pennsylvania Sedition Act which proscribes the same conduct. . . .

It should be said at the outset that the decision in this case does not affect the right of States to enforce their sedition laws at times when the Federal Government has not occupied the field and is not protecting the entire country from seditious conduct. The distinction between the two situations was clearly recognized by the court below. Nor does it limit the jurisdiction of the States where the Constitution and Congress have specifically given them concurrent jurisdiction, as was done under the Eighteenth Amendment and the Volstead Act. . . . Neither does it limit the right of the State to protect itself at any time against sabotage or attempted violence of all kinds. Nor does it prevent the State from prosecuting where the same act constitutes both a federal offense and a state offense under the police power. . . .

Where, as in the instant case, Congress has not stated specifically whether a federal statute has occupied a field in which the States are otherwise free to legislate, different criteria have furnished touchstones for decision. Thus,

[T]his Court, in considering the validity of state laws in the light of . . . federal laws touching the same subject, has made use of the following expressions: conflicting; contrary to; occupying the field; repugnance; difference; irreconcilability; inconsistency; violation; curtailment; and interference. But none of these expressions provides an infallible constitutional test or an exclusive constitutional yardstick. In the final analysis, there can be no one crystal clear distinctly marked formula. *Hines v. Davidowitz* [1941]. . . .

... In this case, we think that each of several tests of supersession is met.

First, "[t]he scheme of federal regulation [is] so pervasive as to make reasonable the inference that Congress left no room for the States to supplement it." ... The Congress determined in 1940 that it was necessary for it to re-enter the field of antisubversive legislation, which had been abandoned by it in 1921. In that year, it enacted the Smith Act which proscribes advocacy of the overthrow of any government—federal, state or local—by force and violence and organization of and knowing membership in a group which so advocates. Conspiracy to commit any of these acts is punishable under the general criminal conspiracy provisions in 18 U. S. C. § 371. . . .

We examine these Acts only to determine the congressional plan. Looking to all of them in the aggregate, the conclusion is inescapable that Congress has intended to occupy the field of sedition. Taken as a whole, they evince a congressional plan which makes it reasonable to determine that no room has been left for the States to supplement it. Therefore, a state sedition statute is superseded regardless of whether it purports to supplement the federal law. . . .

Second, the federal statutes "touch a field in which the federal interest is so dominant that the federal system [must] be assumed to preclude enforcement of state laws on the same subject." . . . Congress has devised an all-embracing program for resistance to the various forms of totalitarian aggression. Our external defenses have been strengthened, and a plan to protect against internal subversion has been made by it. It has appropriated vast sums, not only for our own protection, but also to strengthen freedom throughout the world. It has charged the Federal Bureau of Investigation and the Central Intelligence Agency with responsibility for intelligence concerning Communist seditious activities against our Government, and has denominated such activities as part of a world conspiracy. It accordingly proscribed sedition against all government in the nation—national, state and local. Congress declared that these steps were taken "to provide for the common defense, to preserve the sovereignty of the United States as an independent nation, and to guarantee to each State a republican form of government. . . . " Congress having thus treated seditious conduct as a matter of vital national concern, it is in no sense a local enforcement problem. . . .

Third, enforcement of state sedition acts presents a serious danger of conflict with the administration of the federal program. Since 1939, in order to avoid a hampering of uniform enforcement of its program by sporadic local prosecutions, the Federal Government has urged local authorities not to intervene in such matters, but to turn over to the federal authorities immediately and unevaluated all information concerning subversive activities. The President made such a request on September 6, 1939, when he placed the Federal Bureau of Investigation in charge of investigation in this field:

The Attorney General has been requested by me to instruct the Federal Bureau of Investigation of the Department of Justice to take charge of investigative work in matters relating to espionage, sabotage, and violations of the neutrality regulations. . . .

And in addressing the Federal-State Conference on Law Enforcement Problems of National Defense, held on August 5 and 6, 1940, only a few weeks after the passage of the Smith Act, the Director of the Federal Bureau of Investigation said:

The fact must not be overlooked that meeting the spy, the saboteur and the subverter is a problem that must be handled on a nationwide basis. An isolated incident in the middle west may be of little significance, but when fitted into a national pattern of similar incidents, it may lead to an important revelation of subversive activity. It is for this reason that the President requested all of our citizens and law enforcing agencies to report directly to the Federal Bureau of Investigation any complaints or information dealing with espionage, sabotage or subversive activities. In such matters, time is of the essence. It is unfortunate that in a few States efforts have been made by individuals not fully acquainted with the far-flung ramifications of this problem to interject superstructures of agencies between local law enforcement and the FBI to sift what might be vital information, thus delaying its immediate reference to the FBI. This cannot be, if our internal security is to be best served. This is no time for red tape or amateur handling of such vital matters. There must be a direct and free flow of contact between the local law enforcement agencies and the FBI. The job of meeting the spy or saboteur is one for experienced men of law enforcement.

Moreover, the Pennsylvania Statute presents a peculiar danger of interference with the federal program. For, as the court below observed:

Unlike the Smith Act, which can be administered only by federal officers acting in their official capacities, indictment for sedition under the Pennsylvania statute can be initiated upon an information made by a private individual. The opportunity thus present for the indulgence of personal spite and hatred or for furthering some selfish advantage or ambition need only be mentioned to be appreciated. Defense of the Nation by law, no less than by arms, should be a public and not a private undertaking. It is important that punitive sanctions for sedition *against the United States* be such as have been promulgated by the central governmental authority and administered under the supervision and review of that authority's judiciary. If that be done, sedition will be detected and punished, no less, wherever it may be found, and the right of the individual to speak freely and without fear, even in criticism of the government, will at the same time be protected.

In his brief, the Solicitor General states that forty-two States plus Alaska and Ha-

waii have statutes which in some form prohibit advocacy of the violent overthrow of established government. These statutes are entitled anti-sedition statutes, criminal anarchy laws, criminal syndicalist laws, etc. Although all of them are primarily directed against the overthrow of the United States Government, they are in no sense uniform. And our attention has not been called to any case where the prosecution has been successfully directed against an attempt to destroy state or local government. Some of these Acts are studiously drawn and purport to protect fundamental rights by appropriate definitions, standards of proof and orderly procedures in keeping with the avowed congressional purpose "to protect freedom from those who would destroy it, without infringing upon the freedom of all our people." Others are vague and are almost wholly without such safeguards. Some even purport to punish mere membership in subversive organizations which the federal statutes do not punish where federal registration requirements have been fulfilled.

When we were confronted with a like situation in the field of labor-management relations, Mr. Justice Jackson wrote:

A multiplicity of tribunals and a diversity of procedures are quite as apt to produce incompatible or conflicting adjudications as are different rules of substantive law.

Should the States be permitted to exercise a concurrent jurisdiction in this area, federal enforcement would encounter not only the difficulties mentioned by Mr. Justice Jackson, but the added conflict engendered by different criteria of substantive offenses.

Since we find that Congress has occupied the field to the exclusion of parallel state legislation, that the dominant interest of the Federal Government precludes state intervention, and that administration of state Acts would conflict with the operation of the federal plan, we are convinced that the decision of the Supreme Court of Pennsylvania is unassailable.

We are not unmindful of the risk of compounding punishments which would be created by finding concurrent state power. In our view of the case, we do not reach the question whether double or multiple punishment for the same overt acts directed against the United States has constitutional sanction. Without compelling indication to the contrary, we will not assume that Congress intended to permit the possibility of double punishment. . . .

The judgment of the Supreme Court of Pennsylvania is

Affirmed.

MR. JUSTICE REED, with whom MR. JUSTICE BURTON and MR. JUSTICE MINTON join, dissenting:

. . . Congress has not, in any of its statutes relating to sedition, specifically barred the exercise of state power to punish the same Acts under state law. And, we read the majority opinion to assume for this case that, absent federal legislation, there is no constitutional bar to punishment of sedition against the United States by both a State and the Nation. The majority limits to the federal courts the power to try charges of sedition against the Federal Government. . . .

. . . [I]t is quite apparent that since 1940 Congress has been keenly aware of the magnitude of existing state legislation proscribing sedition. It may be validly assumed that in these circumstances this Court should not void state legislation without a clear mandate from Congress.

We cannot agree that the federal criminal sanctions against sedition directed at the United States are of such a pervasive character as to indicate an intention to void state action.

Secondly, the Court states that the federal sedition statutes touch a field "in which the federal interest is so dominant" they must preclude state laws on the same subject. This concept is suggested in a comment on *Hines* v. *Davidowitz*. . . . The Court in *Davidowitz* ruled that federal statutes compelling alien registration preclude enforcement of state statutes requiring alien registration. We read *Davidowitz* to teach nothing more than that, when the Congress provided a single nation-wide integrated system of regulation so complete as that for aliens' registration (with fingerprinting, a scheduling of activities, and continuous information as to their residence), the Act bore so directly on our foreign relations as to make it evident that Congress intended only one uniform national alien registration system. . . .

Thirdly, the Court finds ground for abrogating Pennsylvania's antisedition statute because, in the Court's view, the State's administration of the Act may hamper the enforcement of the federal law. Quotations are inserted from statements of President Roosevelt and Mr. Hoover, the Director of the Federal Bureau of Investigation, to support the Court's position. But a reading of the quotations leads us to conclude that their purpose was to gain prompt knowledge of evidence of subversive activities so that the federal agency could be fully advised. We find no suggestion from any official source that state officials should be less alert to ferret out or punish subversion. The Court's attitude as to interference seems to us quite contrary to that of the Legislative and Executive Departments. Congress was advised of the existing state sedition legislation when the Smith Act was enacted and has been kept current with its spread. No declaration of exclusiveness followed. . . .

Finally, and this one point seems in and of itself decisive, there is an independent reason for reversing the Pennsylvania Supreme Court. The Smith Act appears in Title 18 of the United States Code, which Title codifies the federal criminal laws. Section 3231 of that Title provides:

Nothing in this title shall be held to take away or impair the jurisdiction of the courts of the several States under the laws thereof.

That declaration springs from the federal character of our Nation. It recognizes the fact that maintenance of order and fair-ness rests primarily with the States. The section was first enacted in 1825 and has appeared successively in the federal criminal laws since that time. This Court has interpreted the section to mean that States may provide concurrent legislation in the absence of explicit congressional intent to the contrary. . . . The majority's position in this case cannot be reconciled with that clear authorization of Congress. . . .

Although Warren used the preemption doctrine to overrule the Pennsylvania statute, is there any reason to believe that in fact he reached this conclusion because he believed the statute to be unconstitutional? Does the opinion support the view that Congress *intended* to preempt the field of sedition legislation? What evidence does Warren cite in defining congressional intent to preempt the field? Does the opinion support Warren's statement that a dominant federal interest precludes the enforcement of state laws in the area of sedition? If Congress withdrew from the field, could the states then enact sedition statutes that would make it a crime to conspire against the United States?

Adverse reaction to the *Nelson* case was particularly sharp among conservative groups throughout the country. One of the most conservative congressmen on Capitol Hill, "Judge" Smith of Virginia, the principal sponsor of the Smith Act, introduced H.R. 3 in the second session of the 85th Congress (1958), which declared that "No act of Congress shall be construed as indicating an intent on the part of Congress to occupy the field in which such act operates, to the exclusion of any state laws on the same subject matter, unless such act contains an express provision to the effect or unless there is a direct and positive conflict between such act and the state law, so that the two cannot be reconciled or consistently stand together." H.R. 3, introduced in January 1957, passed the House in July of 1958 and in June of 1959. The Smith resolution did not become law, however, because the Senate failed to act. The opposition of the Eisenhower administration to H.R. 3 was an important factor in the Senate's refusal to act on it.

The Court did not reach a constitutional question in *Pennsylvania* v. *Nelson,* perhaps because the doctrine of preemption could be so readily and easily applied to strike down that part of the Pennsylvania statute that permitted the state to prosecute individuals for subversive activities against the United States. While the *Nelson* decision left standing state sedition laws insofar as they were limited to sedition against the states, in *Dombrowski* v. *Pfister,* 380 U.S. 479 (1965), the Court did strike down such a subversive activities control law in Louisiana on the grounds of unconstitutional vagueness. The Court, of course, could not apply the preemption doctrine because there was no federal statute involved.

FIVE

The Commerce Power

Article I, Section 8 gives to Congress the authority to "regulate commerce . . . among the several states." To provide national authority to regulate commerce was a principal purpose of the Constitution. The lack of national power to regulate commerce, wrote Hamilton in *Federalist 22*, rendered the government under the Articles of Confederation "altogether unfit for the administration of the affairs of the Union." He added, "[i]t is indeed evident, on the most superficial view, that there is no object, either as it respects the interest of trade or finance that more strongly demands a federal superintendence." The regulation of commerce, said Hamilton, requires a consistency of policy that cannot emerge from the divergent group of states. Hamilton stated that the lack of a national authority to regulate commerce "has already operated as a bar to the formation of beneficial treaties with foreign powers, and has given occasions of dissatisfactions between the states." The commerce power, wrote James Madison in *Federalist 42*, is one of those powers "which provide for the harmony and proper intercourse among the states. . . . The defect of power in the existing confederacy to regulate the commerce between its several members [has] . . . been clearly pointed out by experience." In *Federalist 45*, Madison wrote: "If the new Constitution be examined with accuracy and candor, it will be found that the change which it proposes consists much less in the addition of NEW POWERS to the Union than in the invigoration of its ORIGINAL POWERS. The regulation of commerce, it is true, is a new power; but that seems to be an addition which few oppose and from which no apprehensions are entertained."

The early regulation of commerce by Congress produced little, if any, conflict with the states. Congress passed various laws regulating foreign commerce but saw no need to regulate commerce among the states because the states had eliminated restrictions on interstate commerce. In 1793, Congress passed a law that provided for the licensing of "vessels employed in the coasting trade."[1] In the early nineteenth century the steamboat, developed by Robert Fulton and Robert Livingston, became the most important means of transportation in the coastal trade and on inland rivers and lakes. Members of the Livingston family comprised an important part of the leadership of the Republican party of New York State, which controlled its legislature. Political influence helped Robert Livingston obtain in 1798 the exclusive privilege to navigate by steam the rivers and waters of the state, provided he could build a boat that would travel at four miles an hour against the current of the Hudson River. A two-year time limitation was imposed, and the conditions were not met; however, New York renewed its grant for two years in 1803 and again in 1807.

In 1807 Robert Fulton, who now held the exclusive license with Livingston, completed and put into operation a steamboat which met the legislative conditions. The New York legislature now provided that a five-year extension of their monopoly would be given to Livingston and Fulton for each new steamboat they placed into operation on New York waters. The monopoly could not exceed thirty years, but during that period anyone wishing to navigate New York water by steam had first to obtain a license from Livingston and Fulton, who were given the authority to confiscate unlicensed boats. New Jersey and Connecticut passed retaliatory laws, the former authorizing confiscation of any New York ship for each ship confiscated by Livingston and Fulton and the latter prohibiting boats licensed in New York from entering Connecticut waters. Ohio also passed retaliatory legislation that denied boats licensed by the Livingston-Fulton monopoly from entering its waters. In 1811, Louisiana granted exclusive rights to the Livingston-Fulton company, and other states, including Georgia, Massachusetts, New Hampshire, and Vermont passed laws providing for different individuals to have the exclusive right to license steamboats. Open commercial warfare seemed a possibility among the states of the Union, prompting William Wirt, one of the attorneys for Gibbons, to tell the Court in his final argument that New York, New Jersey, Connecticut, and Ohio, "were almost on the eve of a civil war.[2]

The Livingston-Fulton monopoly was challenged in *Gibbons* v. *Ogden* (1824). Aaron Ogden and Thomas Gibbons joined in a partnership to operate a steamboat line between New York and New Jersey. John Livingston obtained an injunction against them for violating the Livingston-Fulton monopoly. Ogden agreed to continue under a license from Livingston, while Gibbons refused and continued to operate a steamboat line competitive with Ogden under a coasting license granted by the federal government under the 1793 Coasting Act. Ogden obtained an injunction against Gibbons from the New York state courts which upheld the Livingston-Fulton monopoly. Gibbons appealed to the Supreme Court; the case was docketed and became the first major case to deal with the authority of Congress under the commerce clause.

[1]Stat. 305 (1793).
[2]Charles Warren, *The Supreme Court*, II, 58.

Was the commerce clause to be interpreted strictly or loosely? To what degree could Congress imply authority from the commerce clause? In dealing with these questions Chief Justice Marshall confronted the argument of Thomas J. Oakley, the counsel for Ogden, who argued that

> The Constitution of the United States is one of limited and expressly delegated powers, which can only be exercised as granted, or in the cases enumerated. This principle, which distinguishes a national from the state governments, is derived from the nature of the Constitution itself, as being a delegation of power, and not a restriction of power previously possessed; and from the express stipulation in the Tenth Amendment, that "the powers not delegated to the United States by the Constitution, nor prohibited by it to the states, are reserved to the states respectively, or to the people." The national Constitution must therefore be construed strictly, as regards the powers expressly granted, and the objects to which those powers are to be applied.[3]

Daniel Webster, one of the counsel representing Gibbons, told the Court that

> The power of Congress to regulate commerce was complete and entire. . . . Nothing was more complex than commerce; and in such an age as this, no words embraced a wider field than commercial regulation. Almost all the business and intercourse of life may be connected, incidentally, more or less, with commercial regulations. . . . It was in vain to look for a precise and exact definition of the powers of Congress, on several subjects. The Constitution did not undertake the task of making such exact definitions. In conferring powers, it proceeded in the way of enumeration, stating the powers conferred, one after another, in few words; and where the power was general, or complex in its nature, the extent of the grant must necessarily be judged of, and limited by, its object, and by the nature of the power.[4]

Nothing was clearer, continued Webster, than that the prevailing motive for the adoption of the Constitution was to regulate commerce. The following portion of Marshall's opinion in *Gibbons* v. *Ogden* addresses itself to the general authority of Congress under the commerce clause and whether or not the clause is to be interpreted strictly or flexibly. (That part of the decision which concerns the exclusive nature of the authority of Congress under the commerce clause, and the extent of the concurrent power of the states, is reprinted in Chapter 6.)

Gibbons v. *Ogden*

9 Wheat 1; 6 L. Ed. 23 (1824)

Mr. Chief Justice Marshall delivered the opinion of the Court:

The appellant contends that this decree is erroneous, because the laws which

[3]Gibbons v. Ogden, 9 Wheat. 1, 33–34 (1824).
[4]Ibid., pp. 9–11.

purport to give the exclusive privilege it sustains, are repugnant to the Constitution and laws of the United States.

They are said to be repugnant:

1st. To that clause in the Constitution which authorizes Congress to regulate commerce. . . .

This instrument [Constitution] contains an enumeration of powers expressly granted by the people to their government. It has been said that these powers ought to be construed strictly. But why ought they to be so construed? Is there one sentence in the Constitution which gives countenance to this rule? In the last of the enumerated powers, that which grants, expressly, the means of carrying all others into execution, Congress is authorized "to make all laws which shall be necessary and proper" for the purpose. But this limitation on the means which may be used, is not extended to the powers which are conferred; nor is there one sentence in the Constitution which has been pointed out by the gentlemen of the bar, or which we have been able to discern, that prescribes this rule. We do not, therefore, think ourselves justified in adopting it. What do gentlemen mean by a strict construction? If they contend only against that enlarged construction which would extend words beyond their natural and obvious import, we might question the application of the term, but should not controvert the principle. If they contend for that narrow construction which, in support of some theory not to be found in the Constitution, would deny to the government those powers which the words of the grant, as usually understood, import, and which are consistent with the general views and objects of the instrument; for that narrow construction, which would cripple the government and render it unequal to the objects for which it is declared to be instituted, and to which the powers given, as fairly understood, render it competent; then we cannot perceive

the propriety of this strict construction, nor adopt it as the rule by which the constitution is to be expounded. As men, whose intentions require no concealment, generally employ the words which most directly and aptly express the ideas they intend to convey, the enlightened patriots who framed our Constitution, and the people who adopted it, must be understood to have employed words in their natural sense, and to have intended what they have said. If, from the imperfection of human language, there should be serious doubts respecting the extent of any given power, it is a well-settled rule, that the objects for which it was given, especially when those objects are expressed in the instrument itself, should have great influence in the construction. We know of no reason for excluding this rule from the present case. The grant does not convey power which might be beneficial to the grantor, if retained by himself, or which can enure solely to the benefit of the grantee, but is an investment of power for the general advantage, in the hands of agents selected for that purpose; which power can never be exercised by the people themselves, but must be placed in the hands of agents or lie dormant. We know of no rule for construing the extent of such powers, other than is given by the language of the instrument which confers them, taken in connection with the purposes for which they were conferred.

The words are: "Congress shall have power to regulate commerce with foreign nations, and among the several states, and with the Indian tribes."

The subject to be regulated is commerce; and our Constitution being, as was aptly said at the bar, one of enumeration, and not of definition, to ascertain the extent of the power it becomes necessary to settle the meaning of the word. The counsel for the appellee would limit it to traffic, to buying and selling, or the interchange of commodities, and do not admit that it comprehends navigation. This would restrict a general term, applicable to many objects, to one of its significations. Commerce, undoubtedly, is traffic, but it is something more; it is intercourse. It describes the commercial intercourse between nations, and parts of nations, in all its branches, and is regulated by prescribing rules for carrying on that intercourse. The mind can scarcely conceive a system for regulating commerce between nations, which shall exclude all laws concerning navigation, which shall be silent on the admission of the vessels of the one nation into the ports of the other, and be confined to prescribing rules for the conduct of individuals, in the actual employment of buying and selling, or of barter.

If commerce does not include navigation, the government of the Union has no direct power over that subject, and can make no law prescribing what shall constitute American vessels, or requiring that they shall be navigated by American seamen. Yet this power has been exercised from the commencement of the government, has been exercised with the consent of all, and has been understood by all to be a commercial regulation. All America understands, and has uniformly understood, the word "commerce" to comprehand navigation. It was so understood, and must have been so understood, when the Constitution was framed. The power over commerce, including navigation, was one of the primary objects for which the people of America adopted their government, and must have been contemplated in forming it. The Convention must have used the word in that sense; because all have understood it in that sense, and the attempt to restrict it comes too late.

If the opinion that "commerce" as the word is used in the Constitution, comprehends navigation also, requires any additional confirmation, that additional confirmation is, we think, furnished by the words of the instrument itself.

It is a rule of construction, acknowledged by all, that the exceptions from a power mark its extent; for it would be absurd, as well as useless, to except from a granted power, that which was not granted—that which the words of the grant could not comprehend. If, then, there are in the Constitution plain exceptions from the power over navigation, plain inhibitions to the exercise of that power in a particular way, it is a proof that those who made these exceptions, and prescribed these inhibitions, understood the power to which they applied as being granted.

The 9th section of the 1st article declares that "no preference shall be given, by any regulation of commerce or revenue, to the ports of one state over those of another." This clause cannot be understood as applicable to those laws only which are passed for the purposes of revenue, because it is expressly applied to commercial regulations; and the most obvious preference which can be given to one port over another, in regulating commerce, relates to navigation. But the subsequent part of the sentence is still more explicit. It is, "nor shall vessels bound to or from one state, be obliged to enter, clear, or pay duties, in another." These words have a direct reference to navigation. . . .

The word used in the Constitution, then, comprehends, and has been always understood to comprehend, navigation within its meaning; and a power to regulate navigation is as expressly granted as if that term had been added to the word "commerce."

To what commerce does this power extend? The Constitution informs us, to commerce "with foreign nations, and among the several states, and with the Indian tribes."

It has, we believe, been universally admitted that these words comprehend every species of commercial intercourse between the United States and foreign nations. No sort of trade can be carried on between this country and any other, to which this power does not extend. It has been truly said, that commerce, as the word is used in the Constitution, is a unit, every part of which is indicated by the term.

If this be the admitted meaning of the word, in its application to foreign nations, it must carry the same meaning throughout the sentence, and remain a unit, unless there be some plain intelligible cause which alters it.

The subject to which the power is next applied, is to commerce "among the several states." The word "among" means intermingled with. A thing which is among others, is intermingled with them. Commerce among the states cannot stop at the external boundary line of each state, but may be introduced into the interior.

It is not intended to say that these words comprehend that commerce which is completely internal, which is carried on between man and man in a state, or between different parts of the same state, and which does not extend to or affect other states. Such a power would be inconvenient, and is certainly unneccessary.

Comprehensive as the word "among" is, it may very properly be restricted to that commerce which concerns more states than one. The phrase is not one which would probably have been selected to indicate the completely interior traffic of a state, because it is not an apt phrase for that purpose; and the enumeration of the particular classes of commerce to which the power was to be extended, would not have been made had the intention been to extend the power to every description. The enumeration presupposes something not enumerated; and that something, if we regard the language or the subject of the sentence, must be the exclusively internal commerce of a state. The genius and character of the whole government

seem to be, that its action is to be applied to all the external concerns of the nation, and to those internal concerns which affect the states generally; but not to those which are completely within a particular state, which do not affect other states, and with which it is not necessary to interfere, for the purpose of executing some of the general powers of the government. The completely internal commerce of a state, then, may be considered as reserved for the state itself.

But, in regulating commerce with foreign nations, the power of Congress does not stop at the jurisdictional lines of the several states. It would be a very useless power if it could not pass those lines. The commerce of the United States with foreign nations, is that of the whole United States. Every district has a right to participate in it. The deep streams which penetrate our country in every direction, pass through the interior of almost every state in the Union, and furnish the means of exercising this right. If Congress has the power to regulate it, that power must be exercised whenever the subject exists. If it exists within the states, if a foreign voyage may commence or terminate at a port within a state, then the power of Congress may be exercised within a state.

This principle is, if possible, still more clear, when applied to commerce "among the several states." They either join each other, in which case they are separated by a mathematical line, or they are remote from each other, in which case other states lie between them. What is commerce "among" them; and how is it to be conducted? Can a trading expedition between two adjoining states commence and terminate outside of each? And if the trading intercourse be between two states remote from each other, must it not commence in one, terminate in the other, and probably pass through a third? Commerce among the states must, of necessity, be commerce with the states. In the regulation of trade with the Indian tribes, the action of the law, especially when the Constitution was made, was chiefly within a state. The power of Congress, then, whatever it may be, must be exercised within the territorial jurisdiction of the several states. The sense of the nation, on this subject, is unequivocally manifested by the provisions made in the laws for transporting goods, by land, between Baltimore and Providence, between New York and Philadelphia, and between Philadelphia and Baltimore.

We are now arrived at the inquiry, What is this power?

It is the power to regulate; that is, to prescribe the rule by which commerce is to be governed. This power, like all others vested in Congress, is complete in itself, may be exercised to its utmost extent, and acknowledges no limitations, other than are prescribed in the Constitution. These are expressed in plain terms, and do not affect the questions which arise in this case, or which have been discussed at the bar. If, as has always been understood, the sovereignty of Congress, though limited to specified objects, is plenary as to those objects, the power over commerce with foreign nations, and among the several States, is vested in Congress as absolutely as it would be in a single government, having in its constitution the same restrictions on the exercise of the power as are found in the Constitution of the United States. The wisdom and the discretion of Congress, their identity with the people, and the influence which their constituents possess at election, are, in this, as in many other instances, as that, for example, of declaring war, the sole restraints on which they have relied, to secure them from its abuse. They are the restraints on which the people must often rely solely, in all representative governments.

The power of Congress, then, comprehends navigation within the limits of every state in the Union; so far as that navigation may be, in any manner, connected with "commerce with foreign nations, or among the several states, or with the Indian tribes." It may, of consequence, pass the jurisdictional line of New York, and act upon the very waters to which the prohibition now under consideration applies. . . .

How did Chief Justice Marshall respond to the plea of Ogden's counsel that the authority of Congress under the commerce clause should be construed narrowly? What was Marshall's reasoning to support his statement that commerce was more than merely "traffic"? What did Marshall mean when he stated that the Constitution was "one of enumeration, and not of definition"? Is there any evidence in Marshall's opinion rejecting the strict constructionist view of the Constitution that he was taking into account political considerations? On what grounds does Marshall assert that the commerce power does not stop at the jurisdictional lines of the states? Does Marshall suggest that there are any limits upon the authority of Congress to regulate commerce?

THE COMMERCE POWER REDEFINED: THE ERA OF ECONOMIC REGULATION FROM 1887–1914

The passage of the Interstate Commerce Act of 1887, and the Sherman Antitrust Act of 1890, marked the beginning of an era that would see a vast expansion in the national regulation of the economy. Inevitably, powerful private interests who failed to get their way in national and state legislatures resorted to the courts to challenge the authority of Congress under laws they considered to be detrimental to their interests. Most congressional legislation was explicitly based upon the commerce power. As challenges to such legislation mounted, the courts were confronted with the task of defining the scope of the commerce power. An acceptance of the simple empirical test of Justice Marshall in *Gibbons* v. *Ogden*, which upheld congressional legislation regulating activities that affected interstate commerce, would support a vast and virtually unlimited network of federal regulation.

United States v. *E.C. Knight Co.* (1895) involved a challenge to government action taken under the Sherman Antitrust Act. Section 1 of the act provided that

> Every contract, combination in the form of trust or otherwise, or conspiracy, in restraint of trade or commerce among the several states, or with foreign nations, is hereby declared to be illegal. . . .

Section 2 provided that

> Every person who shall monopolize, or attempt to monopolize, or combine or conspire with any other person or persons, to monopolize any part of the trade or commerce among the several states, or with foreign nations, shall be deemed guilty of a misdemeanor. . . .

In the *Knight*, or as it is called the *Sugar Trust Case*, the government claimed that the acquisition of the E.C. Knight Co. and four other companies by the American Sugar Refining Company was a violation of the antitrust law. As a result of the acquisition the American Sugar Refining Company would control over 90 percent of the companies manufacturing refined sugar in the United States. This, said the government, would constitute a restraint of trade among the states in violation of the Sherman Act. The lower federal courts had dismissed the government's suit, claiming that the "manufacturing" activities of the American Sugar Refining Company were not part of interstate commerce and therefore not subject to the Sherman Act.

United States v. *E.C. Knight Co.*

156 U.S. 1; 15 S. Ct. 249; 39 L. Ed. 325 (1895)

MR. CHIEF JUSTICE FULLER delivered the opinion of the Court:

By the purchase of the stock of the four Philadelphia refineries, with shares of its own stock, the American Sugar Refining Company acquired nearly complete control of the manufacture of refined sugar within the United States. The bill charged that the contracts under which these purchases were made constituted combinations in restraint of trade, and that in entering into them the defendants combined and conspired to restrain the trade and commerce in refined sugar among the several states and with foreign nations, contrary to the Act of Congress of July 2, 1890. . . .

The fundamental question is whether conceding that the existence of a monopoly in manufacture is established by the evidence, that monopoly can be directly suppressed under the Act of Congress in the mode attempted by this bill.

It cannot be denied that the power of a state to protect the lives, health, and property of its citizens, and to preserve good order and the public morals, "the power to govern men and things within the limits of its dominion," is a power originally and always belonging to the states, not surrendered by them to the general government, nor directly restrained by the Constitution of the United States, and essentially exclusive. The relief of the citizens of each state from the burden of monopoly and the evils resulting from the restraint of trade among such citizens was left with the states to deal with, and this Court has recognized their possession of that power even to the extent of holding that an employment or business carried on by private individuals, when it becomes a matter of such public interest and importance as to create a common charge or burden upon the citizen; in other words, when it becomes a practical monopoly, to which the citizen is compelled to resort and by means of which a tribute can be exacted from the community, is subject to regulation by state legislative power. On the other hand, the power of Congress to regulate commerce among the several states is also exclusive. The Constitution does not provide that interstate commerce shall be free, but, by the grant of this exclusive power to regulate it, it was left free except as Congress might impose restraints. Therefore it has been determined that the failure of Congress to exercise this exclusive power in any case is an expression of its will that the subject shall be free

from restrictions or impositions upon it by several states, and if a law passed by a state in the exercise of its acknowledged powers comes into conflict with that will, the Congress and the state cannot occupy the position of equal opposing sovereignties, because the Constitution declares its supremacy and that of the laws passed in pursuance thereof; and that which is not supreme must yield to that which is supreme. "Commerce, undoubtedly, is traffic," said Chief Justice Marshall, "but it is something more; it is intercourse. It describes the commercial intercourse between nations and parts of nations in all its branches, and is regulated by prescribing rules for carrying on that intercourse." That which belongs to commerce is within the jurisdiction of the United States, but that which does not belong to commerce is within the jurisdiction of the police power of the state. . . .

The argument is that the power to control the manufacture of refined sugar is a monopoly over a necessary of life, to the enjoyment of which by a large population of the United States interstate commerce is indispensable, and that, therefore, the general government in the exercise of the power to regulate commerce may repress such monopoly directly and set aside the instruments which have created it. But this argument cannot be confined to necessaries of life merely, and must include all articles of general consumption. Doubtless the power to control the manufacture of a given thing involves in a certain sense the control of its disposition, but this is a secondary and not the primary sense; and although the exercise of that power may result in bringing the operation of commerce into play, it does not control it, and affects it only incidentally and indirectly. Commerce succeeds to manufacture, and is not a part of it. The power to regulate commerce is the power to prescribe the rule by which commerce shall be governed, and is a power independent of the power to suppress monopoly. But it may operate in repression of monopoly whenever that comes within the rules by which commerce is governed or whenever the transaction is itself a monopoly of commerce. . . .

It is vital that the independence of the commercial power and of the police power, and the delimitation between them, however sometimes perplexing, should always be recognized and observed, for while the one furnishes the strongest bond of union, the other is essential to the preservation of the autonomy of the states as required by our dual form of government; and acknowledged evils, however grave and urgent they may appear to be, had better be borne, than the risk be run, in the effort to suppress them, of more serious consequences by resort to the expedients of even doubtful constitutionality. . . .

Contracts, combinations, or conspiracies to control domestic enterprise in manufacture, agriculture, mining, production in all its forms, or to raise or lower prices or wages, might unquestionably tend to restrain external as well as domestic trade, but the restraint would be an indirect result, however inevitable and whatever its extent, and such result would not necessarily determine the object of the contract, combination, or conspiracy.

Again, all the authorities agree that in order to vitiate a contract or combination it is not essential that its result should be a complete monopoly; it is sufficient if it really tends to that end and to deprive the public of the advantages which flow from free competition. Slight reflection will show that if the national power extends to all contracts and combinations in manufacture, agriculture, mining, and other productive industries, whose ultimate result may affect external commerce, comparatively little of business operations and affairs would be left for state control.

It was in the light of well settled principles that the Act of July 2, 1890, was framed. Congress did not attempt thereby to assert the power to deal with monopoly directly as such; or to limit and restrict the rights of corporations created by the states or the citizens of the states in the acquisition, control, or disposition of property; or to regulate or prescribe the price or prices at which such property or the products thereof should be sold; or to make criminal the acts of persons in the acquisition and control of property which the states of their residence or creation sanctioned or permitted. Aside from the provisions applicable where Congress might exercise municipal power, what the law struck at was combinations, contracts, and conspiracies to monopolize trade and commerce among the several states or with foreign nations; but the contracts and acts of the defendants related exclusively to the acquisition of the Philadelphia refineries and the business of sugar refining in Pennsylvania, and bore no direct relation to commerce between the states or with foreign nations. The object was manifestly private gain in the manufacture of the commodity, but not through the control of interstate or foreign commerce. It is true that the bill alleged that the products of these refineries were sold and distributed among the several states, and that all the companies were engaged in trade or commerce with the several states and with foreign nations; but this was no more than to say that trade and commerce served manufacture to fulfill its function. Sugar was refined for sale, and sales were probably made at Philadelphia for consumption, and undoubtedly for resale by the first purchasers throughout Pennsylvania and other states, and refined sugar was also forwarded by the companies to other states for sale. Nevertheless it does not follow that an attempt to monopolize, or the actual monopoly of, the manufacture was an attempt, whether executory or consummated, to monopolize commerce, even though, in order to dispose of the product, the instrumentality of commerce was necessarily invoked. There was nothing in the proofs to indicate any intention to put a restraint upon trade or commerce, and the fact, as we have seen, that trade or commerce might be indirectly affected was not enough to entitle complainants to a decree. . . .

Decree affirmed.

MR. JUSTICE HARLAN, dissenting:

. . . In its consideration of the important constitutional question presented, this Court assumes on the record before us that the result of the transactions disclosed by the pleadings and proof was the creation of a monopoly in the manufacture of a necessary of life. If this combination, so far as its operations necessarily or directly affect interstate commerce, cannot be restrained or suppressed under some power granted to Congress, it will be cause for regret that the patriotic statesmen who framed the Constitution did not foresee the necessity of investing the national government with power to deal with gigantic monopolies holding in their grasp, and injuriously controlling in their own interest, the entire trade *among the states* in food products that are essential to the comfort of every household in the land. . . .

It would seem to be indisputable that no *combination* of corporations or individuals can, *of right,* impose unlawful restraints upon *interstate* trade, whether upon transportation or upon such interstate intercourse and traffic as precede transportation, any more than it can, *of right,* impose unreasonable restraints upon the completely internal traffic of a state. The supposition cannot be indulged that this general proposition will be disputed. If it be true that a *combination* of corporations or individuals may, so far as the power of Congress is concerned, subject interstate trade, in any of its stages, to unlawful re-

straints, the conclusion is inevitable that the Constitution has failed to accomplish one primary object of the Union, which was to place commerce *among the states* under the control of the common government of all the people, and thereby relieve or protect it against burdens or restrictions imposed, by whatever authority, for the benefit of particular localities or special interests. . . .

The power of Congress covers and protects the absolute freedom of such intercourse and trade among the states as may or must succeed manufacture and precede transportation from the place of purchase. This would seem to be conceded; for, the Court in the present case expressly declares that "contracts to buy, sell, or exchange goods to be transported among the several states, the transportation and its instrumentalities, and articles, bought, sold, or exchanged for the purpose of such transit among the states, or put in the way of transit, may be regulated, but this is because they form part of interstate trade or commerce." Here is a direct admission—one which the settled doctrines of this Court justify—that contracts to buy and the purchasing of goods to be transported from one state to another, and transportation, with its instrumentalities, are all parts of interstate trade or commerce. Each part of such trade is then under the protection of Congress. And yet, by the opinion and judgment in this case, if I do not misapprehend them, Congress is without power to protect the commercial intercourse that such purchasing necessarily involves against the restraints and burdens arising from the existence of combinations that meet purchasers from whatever state they come, with the threat—for it is nothing more nor less than a threat—that they shall not purchase what they desire to purchase, except at the prices fixed by such combinations. . . .

In my judgment, the citizens of the several states composing the Union are entitled, of right, to buy goods in the state where they are manufactured, or in any other state, without being confronted by an illegal combination whose business extends throughout the whole country, which by the law everywhere is an enemy to the public interests, and which prevents such buying, except at prices arbitrarily fixed by it. I insist that the free course of trade among the states cannot coexist with such combinations. When I speak of trade I mean the buying and selling of articles of every kind that are recognized articles of interstate commerce. Whatever improperly obstructs the free course of interstate intercourse and trade, as involved in the buying and selling of articles to be carried from one state to another, may be reached by Congress, under its authority to regulate commerce among the states. The exercise of that authority so as to make trade among the states, in all recognized articles of commerce, absolutely free from unreasonable or illegal restrictions imposed by combinations, is justified by an express grant of power to Congress and would redound to the welfare of the whole country. I am unable to perceive that any such result would imperil the autonomy of the states, especially as that result cannot be attained through the action of any one state. . . .

To the general government has been committed the control of commercial intercourse among the states, to the end that it may be free at all times from any restraints except such as Congress may impose or permit for the benefit of the whole country. The common government of all the people is the only one that can adequately deal with a matter which directly and injuriously affects the entire commerce of the country, which concerns equally all the people of the Union, and which, it must be confessed, cannot be adequately controlled by any one state. Its authority should not be so weakened by construction that it cannot reach and eradicate evils that, beyond all question, tend to defeat an object which that government is entitled, by the Constitution, to accomplish. "Powerful and ingenious minds," this Court has said, "taking, as postulates, that the powers expressly granted to the government of the Union, are to be contracted by construction into the narrowest possible compass, and that the original powers of the states are retained if any possible construction will retain them, may, by a course of well digested, but refined and metaphysical reasoning, founded on these premises, explain away the Constitution of our country, and leave it, a magnificent structure, indeed, to look at, but totally unfit for use. They may so entangle and perplex the understanding as to obscure principles which were before thought quite plain, and induce doubts where, if the mind were to pursue its own course, none would be perceived." *Gibbons* v. *Ogden.* . . .

Chief Justice Fuller does not hold the Sherman Act to be unconstitutional in the *E.C. Knight* case but *construes* the act, on the basis of constitutional standards, not to reach manufacturing activities. By excluding "manufacturing" from "commerce" the chief justice was placing an important limit upon congressional power under the commerce clause. By contrast, Chief Justice Marshall's broad definition of commerce in *Gibbons* v. *Ogden* expanded the scope of congressional authority to regulate commerce.

To what extent is Fuller's opinion based upon considerations of federalism? In his development of a distinction between manufacturing and commerce, he relied upon *Kidd* v. *Pearson*, 128 U.S. 1 (1888), which upheld the authority of Iowa to prohibit the manufacture of liquor that was to be exported to other states. Would Fuller have upheld a *state* law regulating the manufacturing activities of the American Sugar Refining Company?

Chief Justice John Marshall, in *Gibbons v. Ogden,* uses an empirical test to determine the relationship between intrastate and interstate commerce. What test does Fuller employ to determine this relationship in the *E.C. Knight* case?

What rights does Justice Harlan discuss in his dissenting opinion, and what conclusions does he reach from his analysis? What is Harlan's definition of the commerce power?

Justice Fuller in the *E.C. Knight* opinion distinguished between activities that have an *indirect* effect from those having a *direct* effect upon commerce and confined the reach of the commerce power of Congress to the latter category. The Fuller opinion went a long way toward vitiating the Sherman Antitrust Act, although it by no means precluded successful government suits under the act.[5]

While the direct and indirect test to determine activities affecting interstate commerce was not explictly overruled, in the area of railroad regulation the Court developed the "substantial economic effect" test to determine when intrastate commerce could be considered an integral part of interstate commerce properly subject to federal regulation. This new approach to defining the commerce power is illustrated in the *Shreveport Rate Case* (1914). The Interstate Commerce Commission established railway rates between Shreveport, Louisiana, and locations in Texas. This was clearly a regulation of *interstate* commerce. However, at the same time the commission ordered the railroads to charge proportionately the same rates between points within Texas as were required between Louisiana and Texas. Shreveport was in competition with cities in East Texas for shipments, and the ICC wanted to prevent lower rates for hauls within Texas that were equal to the distance between Shreveport and Texas cities. Challenging the ICC order, the railroads argued that "Congress is impotent to control the intrastate charges of an interstate carrier even to the extent necessary to prevent injurious discrimination against interstate traffic."

The Shreveport Case

Houston, East and West Texas Ry. Co. v. United States

234 U.S. 342; 34 S. Ct. 833; 58 L. Ed. 1341 (1914)

MR. JUSTICE HUGHES delivered the opinion of the Court:

These suits were brought in the commerce court by the Houston, East & West

---

[5]See, for example, United States v. Trans-Missouri Freight Association, 166 U.S. 290 (1897), holding that an association of western railroads to fix rail rates was monopolistic and in violation of the Sherman Act; Addison Pipe and Steel Company v. United States, 175 U.S. 211 (1899), holding that agreements made among six companies manufacturing iron pipe constituted a "direct restraint upon interstate commerce" in violation of the Sherman Act. See also, Northern Securities Company v. United States, 193 U.S. 197 (1904); Swift and Co. v. United States, 196 U.S. 375 (1905).

Texas Railway Company and the Houston & Shreveport Railroad Company, and by the Texas & Pacific Railway Company, respectively, to set aside an order of the Interstate Commerce Commission, dated March 11, 1912, upon the ground that it exceeded the Commission's authority. . . .

The order of the Interstate Commerce Commission was made in a proceeding initiated in March, 1911, by the Railroad Commission of Louisiana. The complaint was that the appellants, and other interstate carriers, maintained unreasonable rates from Shreveport, Louisiana, to various points in Texas, and, further, that these carriers, in the adjustment of rates over their respective lines, unjustly discriminated in favor of traffic within the state of Texas, and against similar traffic between Louisiana and Texas. The carriers filed answers; numerous pleas of intervention by shippers and commercial bodies were allowed; testimony was taken and arguments were heard.

The gravamen of the complaint, said the Interstate Commerce Commission, was that the carriers made rates out of Dallas and other Texas points into eastern Texas which were much lower than those which they extended into Texas from Shreveport. The situation may be briefly described: Shreveport, Louisiana, is about 40 miles from the Texas state line, and 231 miles from Houston, Texas, on the line of the Houston, East & West Texas and Houston & Shreveport Companies (which are affiliated in interest); it is 189 miles from Dallas, Texas, on the line of the Texas & Pacific. Shreveport competes with both cities for the trade of the intervening territory. The rates on these lines from Dallas and Houston, respectively, eastward to intermediate points in Texas, were much less, according to distance, than from Shreveport westward to the same points. It is undisputed that the difference was substantial, and injuriously affected the commerce of Shreveport. It appeared, for example, that a rate of 60

cents carried first-class traffic a distance of 160 miles to the eastward from Dallas, while the same rate would carry the same class of traffic only 55 miles into Texas from Shreveport. . . . The rate on wagons from Dallas to Marshall, Texas, 147.7 miles, was 36.8 cents, and from Shreveport to Marshall, 42 miles, 56 cents. . . . These instances of differences in rates are merely illustrative; they serve to indicate the character of the rate adjustment.

. . . The Interstate Commerce Commission found that the carriers maintained "higher rates from Shreveport to points in Texas" than were in force "from cities in Texas to such points under substantially similar conditions and circumstances," and that thereby "an unlawful and undue preference and advantage" was given to the Texas cities, and a "discrimination" that was "undue and unlawful" was effected against Shreveport. In order to correct this discrimination, the carriers were directed to desist from charging higher rates for the transportation of any commodity from Shreveport to Dallas and Houston, respectively, and intermediate points, than were contemporaneously charged for the carriage of such commodity from Dallas and Houston toward Shreveport for equal distances, as the Commission found that relation of rates to be reasonable. . . .

. . . There are, it appears, commodity rates fixed by the Railroad Commission of Texas for intrastate hauls, which are substantially less than the class, or standard, rates prescribed by the Commission; and thus the commodity rates charged by the carriers from Dallas and Houston eastward to Texas points are less than the rates which they demand for the transportation of the same articles for like distances from Shreveport into Texas. The present controversy relates to these commodity rates.

The point of the objection to the order is that, as the discrimination found by the Commission to be unjust arises out of the relation of intrastate rates, maintained under state authority, to interstate rates that have been upheld as reasonable, its correction was beyond the Commission's power. Manifestly the order might be complied with, and the discrimination avoided, either by reducing the interstate rates from Shreveport to the level of the competing intrastate rates, or by raising these intrastate rates to the level of the interstate rates, or by such reduction in the one case and increase in the other as would result in equality. But it is urged that, so far as the interstate rates were sustained by the Commission as reasonable, the Commission was without authority to compel their reduction in order to equalize them with the lower intrastate rates. The holding of the commerce court was that the order relieved the appellants from further obligation to observe the intrastate rates, and that they were at liberty to comply with the Commission's requirements by increasing these rates sufficiently to remove the forbidden discrimination. The invalidity of the order in this aspect is challenged upon two grounds:

(1) That Congress is impotent to control the intrastate charges of an interstate carrier even to the extent necessary to prevent injurious discrimination against interstate traffic; and

(2) That, if it be assumed that Congress has this power, still it has not been exercised, and hence the action of the Commission exceeded the limits of the authority which has been conferred upon it.

First. It is unnecessary to repeat what has frequently been said by this Court with respect to the complete and paramount character of the power confided to Congress to regulate commerce among the several states. It is of the essence of this power that, where it exists, it dominates. Interstate trade was not left to be destroyed or impeded by the rivalries of local government. The purpose was to make impossible the recurrence of the evils which had overwhelmed the Confed-

eration, and to provide the necessary basis of national unity by insuring "uniformity of regulation against conflicting and discriminating state legislation." By virtue of the comprehensive terms of the grant, the authority of Congress is at all times adequate to meet the varying exigencies that arise, and to protect the national interest by securing the freedom of interstate commercial intercourse from local control. . . .

Congress is empowered to regulate,—that is, to provide the law for the government of interstate commerce; to enact "all appropriate legislation" for its "protection and advancement" . . . to adopt measures "to promote its growth and insure its safety" . . . "to foster, protect, control, and restrain". . . . Its authority, extending to these interstate carriers as instruments of interstate commerce, necessarily embraces the right to control their operations in all matters having such a close and substantial relation to interstate traffic that the control is essential or appropriate to the security of that traffic, to the efficiency of the interstate service, and to the maintenance of conditions under which interstate commerce may be conducted upon fair terms and without molestation or hindrance. As it is competent for Congress to legislate to these ends, unquestionably it may seek their attainment by requiring that the agencies of interstate commerce shall not be used in such manner as to cripple, retard, or destroy it. The fact that carriers are instruments of intrastate commerce, as well as of interstate commerce, does not derogate from the complete and paramount authority of Congress over the latter, or preclude the Federal power from being exerted to prevent the intrastate operations of such carriers from being made a means of injury to that which has been confided to Federal care. Wherever the interstate and intrastate transactions of carriers are so related that the government of the one involves the control of the other, it is Congress, and not the state, that is entitled to prescribe the final and dominant rule, for otherwise Congress would be denied the exercise of its constitutional authority, and the state, and not the nation, would be supreme within the national field. . . .

. . . This is not to say that Congress possesses the authority to regulate the internal commerce of a state, as such, but that it does possess the power to foster and protect interstate commerce, and to take all measures necessary or appropriate to that end, although intrastate transactions of interstate carriers may thereby be controlled.

This principle is applicable here. We find no reason to doubt that Congress is entitled to keep the highways of interstate communications open to interstate traffic upon fair and equal terms. That an unjust discrimination in the rates of a common carrier, by which one person or locality is unduly favored as against another under substantially similar conditions of traffic, constitutes an evil, is undeniable; and where this evil consists in the action of an interstate carrier in unreasonably discriminating against interstate traffic over its line, the authority of Congress to prevent it is equally clear. It is immaterial, so far as the protecting power of Congress is concerned, that the discrimination arises from intrastate rates as compared with interstate rates. The use of the instrument of interstate commerce in a discriminatory manner so as to inflict injury upon that commerce, or some part thereof, furnishes abundant ground for Federal intervention. Nor can the attempted exercise of state authority alter the matter, where Congress has acted, for a state may not authorize the carrier to do that which Congress is entitled to forbid and has forbidden. . . .

It is also clear that, in removing the injurious discriminations against interstate traffic arising from the relation of intrastate to interstate rates, Congress is not bound to reduce the latter below what it may deem to be a proper standard, fair to the carrier and to the public. Otherwise, it could prevent the injury to interstate commerce only by the sacrifice of its judgment as to interstate rates. Congress is entitled to maintain its own standards as to these rates, and to forbid any discriminatory action by interstate carriers which will obstruct the freedom of movement of interstate traffic over their lines in accordance with the terms it establishes.

Having this power, Congress could provide for its execution through the aid of a subordinate body; and we conclude that the order of the Commission now in question cannot be held invalid upon the ground that it exceeded the authority which Congress could lawfully confer. . . .

In conclusion: Reading the order in the light of the report of the Commission, it does not appear that the Commission attempted to require the carriers to reduce their interstate rates out of Shreveport below what was found to be a reasonable charge for that service. So far as these interstate rates conformed to what was found to be reasonable by the Commission, the carriers are entitled to maintain them, and they are free to comply with the order by so adjusting the other rates, to which the order relates, as to remove the forbidden discrimination. But this result they are required to accomplish.

The decree of the Commerce Court is affirmed in each case.

Affirmed.

MR. JUSTICE LURTON and MR. JUSTICE PITNEY dissent.

Would the Court's opinion in the *Shreveport* case necessarily have been different if it had applied the criteria of the *E.C. Knight* case? The opinion of Justice Hughes stated that Congress had the authority to control intra-state activities that have a "close and substantial relation to interstate traffic." How does this test differ from the direct and indirect criteria of Justice Fuller in the *E.C. Knight* case? Did Justice Hughes bring the Court back to the constitutional standards of Chief Justice Marshall in *Gibbons* v. *Ogden* for determining the scope of the commerce power?

Contrast the *Shreveport Rate Case* decision with that of the Court in *Southern Railway Company* v. *United States*, 222 U.S. 20 (1911). There the Court upheld a penalty imposed by the ICC under the Federal Safety Appliance Act against the railroad for failing to equip the cars it used in intrastate traffic in compliance with the safety regulations of the commission. The statute covered railroad cars "used on any railroad engaged in interstate commerce." The Court sustained the commission's application of the statute to intrastate traffic because the cars were used "on a railroad which is a highway of interstate commerce." The Court added that the act did not require that the cars be used "in moving interstate traffic."[6] Does this decision constitute an expansion of congressional authority under the commerce clause?

THE DEVELOPMENT OF A FEDERAL POLICE POWER
UNDER THE COMMERCE CLAUSE

There is no mention of a *police power* in the Constitution. Historically, police power was defined as the power to protect the health, morals, and safety of the community. *Black's Law Dictionary* states that whatever "affects the peace, good order, morals, and health of the community comes within . . . [the police power's] scope."[7] Traditionally the police power was a function of state and local governments, and by implication under the Constitution it is one of the reserved powers of the states.

The Federal Lottery Act of 1895 was clearly aimed at protecting the morals of states and local communities. It prohibited the shipment by any means including the mails of lottery tickets in interstate commerce. The Wells Fargo Express Company was indicted for violating the law by shipping a container of Paraguayan lottery tickets from Texas to California. The defendants appealed their conviction in the lower federal courts to the Supreme Court.

Champion v. *Ames*

188 U.S. 321; 23 S. Ct. 321; 47 L. Ed. 492 (1903)

MR. JUSTICE HARLAN delivered the opinion of the Court:

The general question arising upon this appeal involves the constitutionality of the 1st section of the act of Congress of March 2d, 1895, chap. 191, entitled "An

---

[6]222 U.S. 20, 25, 26 (1911).

[7]Henry Campbell Black, M.A., *Black's Law Dictionary*, 4th ed. (St. Paul, Minnesota: West Publishing Co., 1968), p. 1317.

Act for the Suppression of Lottery Traffic through National and Interstate Commerce and the Postal Service, Subject to the Jurisdiction and Laws of the United States." . . .

The appellant insists that the carrying of lottery tickets from one state to another state by an express company engaged in carrying freight and packages from state to state, although such tickets may be contained in a box or package, does not constitute, and cannot by any act of Congress be legally made to constitute, *commerce* among the states within the meaning of the clause of the Constitution of the United States providing that Congress shall have power "to regulate commerce with foreign nations, and among the several states, and with the Indian Tribes"; consequently, that Congress cannot make it an offense to cause such tickets to be carried from one state to another. . . .

We are of opinion that lottery tickets are subjects of traffic, and therefore are subjects of commerce, and the regulation of the carriage of such tickets from state to state, at least by independent carriers, is a regulation of commerce among the several states.

But it is said that the statute in question does not regulate the carrying of lottery tickets from state to state, but by punishing those who cause them to be so carried Congress in effect prohibits such carrying; that in respect of the carrying from one state to another of articles or things that are, in fact, or according to usage in business, the subjects of commerce, the authority given Congress was not to *prohibit*, but only to *regulate*. . . .

It is to be remarked that the Constitution does not define what is to be deemed a legitimate regulation of interstate commerce. In *Gibbons* v. *Ogden* it was said that the power to regulate such commerce is the power to prescribe the rule by which it is to be governed. But this general observation leaves it to be determined, when

the question comes before the Court, whether Congress, in prescribing a particular rule, has exceeded its power under the Constitution. While our government must be acknowledged by all to be one of enumerated powers (*McCulloch* v. *Maryland*) . . . the Constitution does not attempt to set forth all the means by which such powers may be carried into execution. It leaves to Congress a large discretion as to the means that may be employed in executing a given power. The sound construction of the Constitution, this Court has said, "must allow to the national legislature that discretion with respect to the means by which the powers it confers are to be carried into execution, which will enable that body to perform the high duties assigned to it, in the manner most beneficial to the people. Let the end be legitimate, let it be within the scope of the Constitution, and all means which are appropriate, which are plainly adapted to that end, which are not prohibited, but consist with the letter and spirit of the Constitution, are constitutional." . . .

We have said that the carrying from state to state of lottery tickets constitutes interstate commerce, and that the regulation of such commerce is within the power of Congress under the Constitution. Are we prepared to say that a provision which is, in effect, a *prohibition* of the carriage of such articles from state to state is not a fit or appropriate mode for the *regulation* of that particular kind of commerce? If lottery traffic, *carried on through interstate commerce*, is a matter of which Congress may take cognizance and over which its power may be exerted, can it be possible that it must tolerate the traffic, and simply regulate the manner in which it may be carried on? Or may not Congress, for the protection of the people of all the states, and under the power to regulate interstate commerce, devise such means, within the scope of the Constitution, and not prohibited by it, as will drive that traffic out of commerce among the states?

In determining whether regulation may not under some circumstances properly take the form or have the effect of prohibition, the nature of the interstate traffic which it was sought by the act of May 2d, 1895, to suppress cannot be overlooked. When enacting that statute Congress no doubt shared the views upon the subject of lotteries heretofore expressed by this Court. In *Phalen* v. *Virginia* [1850] . . . after observing that the suppression of nuisances injurious to public health or morality is among the most important duties of government, this Court said: "Experience has shown that the common forms of gambling are comparatively innocuous when placed in contrast with the widespread pestilence of lotteries. The former are confined to a few persons and places, but the latter infests the whole community; it enters every dwelling; it reaches every class; it preys upon the hard earnings of the poor; it plunders the ignorant and simple." . . .

If a state, when considering legislation for the suppression of lotteries within its own limits, may properly take into view the evils that inhere in the raising of money, in that mode, why may not Congress, invested with power to regulate commerce among the several states, provide that such commerce shall not be polluted by the carrying of lottery tickets from one state to another? In this connection it must not be forgotten that the power of Congress to regulate commerce among the states is plenary, is complete in itself, and is subject to no limitations except such as may be found in the Constitution. What provision in that instrument can be regarded as limiting the exercise of the power granted? . . .

If it be said that the act of 1895 is inconsistent with the Tenth Amendment, reserving to the states respectively, or to the people, the powers not delegated to the United States, the answer is that the power to regulate commerce among the states has been expressly delegated to Congress.

Besides, Congress, by that act, does not assume to interfere with traffic or commerce in lottery tickets carried on exclusively within the limits of any state, but has in view only commerce of that kind among the several states. It has not assumed to interfere with the completely internal affairs of any state, and has only legislated in respect of a matter which concerns the people of the United States. As a state may, for the purpose of guarding the morals of its own people, forbid all sales of lottery tickets within its limits, so Congress, for the purpose of guarding the people of the United States against the "widespread pestilence of lotteries" and to protect the commerce which concerns all the states, may prohibit the carrying of lottery tickets from one state to another. In legislating upon the subject of the traffic in lottery tickets, as carried on through interstate commerce, Congress only supplemented the action of those states—perhaps all of them—which, for the protection of the public morals, prohibit the drawing of lotteries, as well as the sale or circulation of lottery tickets, within their respective limits. It said, in effect, that it would not permit the declared policy of the states, which sought to protect their people against the mischiefs of the lottery business, to be overthrown or disregarded by the agency of interstate commerce. We should hesitate long before adjudging that an evil of such appalling character, carried on through interstate commerce, cannot be met and crushed by the only power competent to that end. . . .

It is said, however, that in order to suppress lotteries carried on through interstate commerce, Congress may exclude lottery tickets from such commerce. That principle leads necessarily to the conclusion that Congress may arbitrarily exclude from commerce among the states any article, commodity, or thing, of whatever kind or nature, or however useful or valuable, which it may choose, no matter with what motive, to declare shall not be carried from one state to another. It will be time enough to consider the constitutionality of such legislation when we must do so. The present case does not require the court to declare the full extent of the power that Congress may exercise in the regulation of commerce among the states. We may, however, repeat, in this connection, what the Court has heretofore said, that the power of Congress to regulate commerce among the states, although plenary, cannot be deemed arbitrary, since it is subject to such limitations or restrictions as are prescribed by the Constitution. This power, therefore, may not be exercised so as to infringe rights secured or protected by that instrument. It would not be difficult to imagine legislation that would be justly liable to such an objection as that stated, and be hostile to the objects for the accomplishment of which Congress was invested with the general power to regulate commerce among the several states. But, as often said, the possible abuse of a power is not an argument against its existence. There is probably no governmental power that may not be exerted to the injury of the public. If what is done by Congress is manifestly in excess of the powers granted to it, then upon the courts will rest the duty of adjudging that its action is neither legal nor binding upon the people. But if what Congress does is within the limits of its power, and is simply unwise or injurious, the remedy is that suggested by Chief Justice Marshall in *Gibbons* v. *Ogden,* when he said: "The wisdom and the discretion of Congress, their identity with the people, and the influence which their constituents possess at elections, are, in this, as in many other instances, as that, for example, of declaring war, the sole restraints on which they have relied, to secure them from its abuse. They are the restraints on which the people must often rely solely, in all representative governments." . . .

Affirmed.

Mr. Chief Justice Fuller, with whom concur Mr. Justice Brewer, Mr. Justice Shiras, and Mr. Justice Peckham, dissenting:

. . . The power of the state to impose restraints and burdens on persons and property in conservation and promotion of the public health, good order, and prosperity is a power originally and always belonging to the states, not surrendered by them to the general government, nor directly restrained by the Constitution of the United States, and essentially exclusive, and the suppression of lotteries as a harmful business falls within this power, commonly called of police. . . .

It is urged, however, that because Congress is empowered to regulate commerce between the several states, it, therefore, may suppress lotteries by prohibiting the carriage of lottery matter. Congress may, indeed, make all laws necessary and proper for carrying the powers granted to it into execution, and doubtless an act prohibiting the carriage of lottery matter would be necessary and proper to the execution of a power to suppress lotteries; but that power belongs to the states, and not to Congress. To hold that Congress has general police power would be to hold that it may accomplish objects not intrusted to the general government, and to defeat the operation of the Tenth Amendment, declaring that "the powers not delegated to the United States by the Constitution, nor prohibited by it to the states, are reserved to the states respectively, or to the people." . . .

. . . To say that the mere carrying of an article which is not an article of commerce in and of itself nevertheless becomes such the moment it is to be transported from one state to another, is to transform a non-commercial article into a commercial one simply because it is transported. I cannot conceive that any such result can properly follow.

It would be to say that everything is an article of commerce the moment it is taken to be transported from place to place, and of interstate commerce if from state to state.

An invitation to dine, or to take a drive, or a note of introduction, all become articles of commerce under the ruling in this case, by being deposited with an express company for transportation. This in effect breaks down all the differences between that which is, and that which is not, an article of commerce, and the necessary consequence is to take from the states all jurisdiction over the subject so far as interstate communication is concerned. It is a long step in the direction of wiping out all traces of state lines, and the creation of a centralized government.

Does the grant to Congress of the power to regulate interstate commerce impart the absolute power to prohibit it? . . .

It will not do to say—a suggestion which has heretofore been made in this case—that state laws have been found to be ineffective for the suppression of lotteries, and therefore Congress should interfere. The scope of the commerce clause of the Constitution cannot be enlarged because of present views of public interest. . . .

"To what purpose are powers limited, and to what purpose is that limitation committed to writing, if these limits may, at any time, be passed by those intended to be restrained?" asked Marshall, in *Marbury* v. *Madison*. . . .

"Should Congress," said the same great magistrate in *McCulloch* v. *Maryland*, "under the pretext of executing its powers, pass laws for the accomplishment of objects not intrusted to the government, it would become the painful duty of this tribunal, should a case requiring such a decision come before it, to say that such an act was not the law of the land." . . .

. . . The power to prohibit the transportation of diseased animals and infected goods over railroads or on steamboats is an entirely different thing, for they would be in themselves injurious to the transaction of interstate commerce, and, moreover, are essentially commercial in their nature. And the exclusion of diseased persons rests on different ground, for nobody would pretend that persons could be kept off the trains because they were going from one state to another to engage in the lottery business. However enticing that business may be, we do not understand these pieces of paper themselves can communicate bad principles by contact. . . .

I regard this decision as inconsistent with the views of the framers of the Constitution, and of Marshall, its great expounder. Our form of government may remain notwithstanding legislation or decision, but, as long ago observed, it is with governments, as with religions: the form may survive the substance of the faith.

In my opinion the act in question in the particular under consideration is invalid, and the judgments below ought to be reversed, and my brothers Brewer, Shiras, and Peckham concur in this dissent.

Justice Harlan cites Marshall's opinions in *Gibbons* v. *Ogden* and *McCulloch* v. *Maryland* to support his view that the commerce power is complete and absolute and includes the authority to prohibit the transportation of lottery tickets in interstate commerce. Justice Fuller's dissenting opinion also quotes Marshall's opinion in the *McCulloch* case. Which use of Marshall do you feel would most accurately represent his views of the present case? What does Harlan suggest are the implications of the principle he announces that Congress may exclude lottery tickets from interstate commerce? Does he suggest that the plenary authority of Congress to regulate commerce may be exercised in an arbitrary manner? Are there any aspects of Justice Fuller's majority opinion in the *E.C. Knight* case that emerge in his dissenting opinion in *Champion* v. *Ames*? In what way does Fuller consider the intent of Congress to be an important consideration in determining the constitutionality of the law? What does Fuller consider to be the proper exercise of the police power? How did Fuller challenge Harlan's assumptions that the power to regulate commerce included the right to prohibit it and that the authority of Congress over commerce among the states was as broad as its power over foreign commerce?

The decision in *Champion* v. *Ames* provided the legal basis for the expansion of national regulation of activities that did not necessarily have a substantial effect upon interstate commerce. The Pure Food and Drug Act of 1906, sustained in *Hipolite Egg Company* v. *United States*, 220 U.S. 45 (1911), and the Mann Act, which prohibited the transportation of women for immoral purposes in interstate commerce, upheld in *Hoke* v. *United States*, 227 U.S. 308 (1913), are examples of many laws that were passed to proscribe the shipment of "harmful" products (and in the case of the Mann Act, harmful persons) in interstate commerce. These decisions seemed to leave no doubt that the Court would sustain congressional prohibitions upon "illegitimate articles" in interstate commerce. The opinion in the *Hoke* case explicitly recognized the existence of a national police power, stating that

> We are one people; and the powers reserved to the states and those conferred on the nation are adapted to be exercised, whether independently or concurrently, to promote the general welfare, material and moral. This is the effect of [many of] the decisions [of the Court], and surely if the facility of interstate transportation can be taken away from the demoralization of lotteries [*Champion* v. *Ames*] the debasement of obscene literature [*United States* v. *Popper*, 98 Fed. 423 (N.D. Cal. 1899)], the contagion of diseased cattle or persons, the impurity of food and drugs, the like facility can be taken away from the systematic enticement to and the enslavement in prostitution and debauchery of women, and, more insistently, of girls. . . . The principle established by the cases is the simple one . . . that Congress has power over transportation "among the states"; that the power is complete in itself, and that Congress, as an incident to it, may adopt not only means necessary but convenient to its exercise, and the means may have the quality of police regulations.[8]

The question of the extent of a national police power under the commerce clause arose again in *Hammer* v. *Dagenhart* (1918). Congress had passed the Child Labor Act in 1916, which attempted to regulate the conditions of child labor by prohibiting the transportation in interstate com-

---

[8]Hoke v. United States, 227 U.S. 308, 322–323 (1913).

merce of goods produced by children under fourteen and by children between fourteen and sixteen if their employers required them to work more than eight hours a day six days a week or at night. The act was challenged by a father of two children who were employed in a textile mill in North Carolina. The district court issued an injunction against the enforcement of the law on the basis that it was beyond the authority of Congress under the commerce clause and a violation of the reserved powers of the states. In its appeal, the government argued that the law "is a legitimate exercise of the legislative power for the protection of the public health."[9] The appellees (who had challenged the act) argued,

> . . . though Congress has no police power, it may, nevertheless, accomplish what may be called a police result in the exercise of any of its delegated powers, [but] we confidently contend that any valid statute passed by Congress, under its power to regulate commerce, that restricts or prohibits commerce, must be predicated on a real evil or injury involved in, or attendant upon, the commerce itself. . . .
>
> The view that Congress may, by the form of the statute, thus impose its will on processes of manufacture, of other local affairs, in the various states, for what it conceives to be the good of the people of the state of manufacture, when there is no real evil accomplished by the commerce itself, is unsound. . . .
>
> This statute is not one of ordinary regulation of commerce or its instrumentalities, but is a use of the power to regulate in order to prohibit, and the Court should be astute to see that such prohibition invades none of the rights of the state under its reserved power. . . .[10]

Hammer v. Dagenhart

247 U.S. 251; 38 S. Ct. 529; 62 L. Ed. 1101 (1918)

MR. JUSTICE DAY delivered the opinion of the Court:

A bill was filed in the United States district court for the western district of North Carolina by a father in his own behalf and as next friend of his two minor sons, one under the age of fourteen years and the other between the ages of fourteen and sixteen years, employees in a cotton mill at Charlotte, North Carolina, to enjoin the enforcement of the act of Congress intended to prevent interstate commerce in the products of child labor. . . .

The district court held the act unconstitutional and entered a decree enjoining its enforcement. This appeal brings the case here. . . .

The attack upon the act rests upon three propositions: First. It is not a regulation of interstate and foreign commerce. Second. It contravenes the Tenth Amendment to the Constitution. Third. It conflicts with the Fifth Amendment to the Constitution. . . .

The power essential to the passage of this act, the government contends, is found in the commerce clause of the Constitution, which authorizes Congress to regulate commerce with foreign nations and among the states.

In *Gibbons* v. *Ogden* [1824], Chief Jus-

[9]LB, Vol. 62, p. 1102.
[10]Ibid., pp. 1103–1104.

tice Marshall, speaking for this Court, and defining the extent and nature of the commerce power, said: "It is the power to regulate,—that is, to prescribe the rule by which commerce is to be governed." In other words, the power is one to control the means by which commerce is carried on, which is directly the contrary of the assumed right to forbid commerce from moving and thus destroy it as to particular commodities. But it is insisted that adjudged cases in this Court establish the doctrine that the power to regulate given to Congress incidentally includes the authority to prohibit the movement of ordinary commodities, and therefore that the subject is not open for discussion. The cases demonstrate the contrary. They rest upon the character of the particular subjects dealt with and the fact that the scope of governmental authority, state or national, possessed over them, is such that the authority to prohibit is, as to them, but the exertion of the power to regulate.

The first of these cases is *Champion* v. *Ames* [1903] . . . the so-called *Lottery Case*, in which it was held that Congress might pass a law having the effect to keep the channels of commerce free from use in the transportation of tickets used in the promotion of lottery schemes. In *Hipolite Egg Co.* v. *United States* [1911] . . . this Court sustained the power of Congress to pass the Pure Food and Drug Act, which prohibited the introduction into the states by means of interstate commerce of impure foods and drugs. In *Hoke* v. *United States* [1913] . . . this Court sustained the constitutionality of the so-called "White Slave Traffic Act," whereby transportation of a woman in interstate commerce for the purpose of prostitution was forbidden. In that case we said, having reference to the authority of Congress, under the regulatory power, to protect the channels of interstate commerce:

"If the facility of interstate transportation can be taken away from the demoralization of lotteries, the debasement of

obscene literature, the contagion of diseased cattle or persons, the impurity of food and drugs, the like facility can be taken away from the systematic enticement to and the enslavement in prostitution and debauchery of women, and, more insistently, of girls."

In *Caminetti* v. *United States* [1917] . . . we held that Congress might prohibit the transportation of women in interstate commerce for the purposes of debauchery and kindred purposes. In *Clark Distilling Co.* v. *Western Maryland R. Co.* [1917] . . . the power of Congress over the transportation of intoxicating liquors was sustained. In the course of the opinion it was said:

"The power conferred is to regulate, and the very terms of the grant would seem to repel the contention that only prohibition of movement in interstate commerce was embraced. And the cogency of this is manifest since, if the doctrine were applied to those manifold and important subjects of interstate commerce as to which Congress from the beginning has regulated, not prohibited, the existence of government under the Constitution would be no longer possible."

And concluding the discussion which sustained the authority of the government to prohibit the transportation of liquor in interstate commerce, the Court said:

"The exceptional nature of the subject here regulated is the basis upon which the exceptional power exerted must rest, and affords no ground for any fear that such power may be constitutionally extended to things which it may not, consistently with the guaranties of the Constitution, embrace."

In each of these instances the use of interstate transportation was necessary to the accomplishment of harmful results. In other words, although the power over interstate transportation was to regulate, that could only be accomplished by prohibiting the use of the facilities of interstate commerce to effect the evil intended.

This element is wanting in the present case. The thing intended to be accomplished by this statute is the denial of the facilities of interstate commerce to those manufacturers in the states who employ children within the prohibited ages. The act in its effect does not regulate transportation among the states, but aims to standardize the ages at which children may be employed in mining and manufacturing within the states. The goods shipped are of themselves harmless. The act permits them to be freely shipped after thirty days from the time of their removal from the factory. When offered for shipment, and before transportation begins, the labor of their production is over, and the mere fact that they were intended for interstate commerce transportation does not make their production subject to Federal control under the commerce power.

Commerce "consists of intercourse and traffic . . . and includes the transportation of persons and property, as well as the purchase, sale and exchange of commodities." The making of goods and the mining of coal are not commerce, nor does the fact that these things are to be afterwards shipped, or used in interstate commerce, make their production a part thereof. . . .

Over interstate transportation, or its incidents, the regulatory power of Congress is ample, but the production of articles intended for interstate commerce is a matter of local regulation. "When the commerce begins is determined not by the character of the commodity, nor by the intention of the owner to transfer it to another state for sale, nor by his preparation of it for transportation, but by its actual delivery to a common carrier for transportation, or the actual commencement of its transfer to another state." . . . This principle has been recognized often in this court. . . . If it were otherwise, all manufacture intended for interstate shipment would be brought under Federal

control to the practical exclusion of the authority of the states,—a result certainly not contemplated by the framers of the Constitution when they vested in Congress the authority to regulate commerce among the states. . . .

It is further contended that the authority of Congress may be exerted to control interstate commerce in the shipment of child-made goods because of the effect of the circulation of such goods in other states where the evil of this class of labor has been recognized by local legislation, and the right to thus employ child labor has been more rigorously restrained than in the state of production. In other words, that the unfair competition thus engendered may be controlled by closing the channels of interstate commerce to manufacturers in those states where the local laws do not meet what Congress deems to be the more just standard of other states.

There is no power vested in Congress to require the states to exercise their police power so as to prevent possible unfair competition. Many causes may co-operate to give one state, by reason of local laws or conditions, an economic advantage over others. The commerce clause was not intended to give to Congress a general authority to equalize such conditions. In some of the states laws have been passed fixing minimum wages for women; in others the local law regulates the hours of labor of women in various employments. Business done in such states may be at an economic disadvantage when compared with states which have no such regulations; surely, this fact does not give Congress the power to deny transportation in interstate commerce to those who carry on business where the hours of labor and the rate of compensation for women have not been fixed by a standard in the use in other states and approved by Congress.

The grant of power to Congress over the subject of interstate commerce was to enable it to regulate such commerce, and not to give it authority to control the states in their exercise of the police power over local trade and manufacture.

The grant of authority over a purely Federal matter was not intended to destroy the local power always existing and carefully reserved to the states in the Tenth Amendment to the Constitution.

Police regulations relating to the internal trade and affairs of the states have been uniformly recognized as within such control. "This," said this Court in *United States* v. *Dewitt* [1870], . . . "has been so frequently declared by this Court, results so obviously from the terms of the Constitution, and has been so fully explained and supported on former occasions, that we think it unnecessary to enter again upon the discussion." . . .

That there should be limitations upon the right to employ children in mines and factories in the interest of their own and the public welfare, all will admit. That such employment is generally deemed to require regulation is shown by the fact that the brief of counsel states that every state in the Union has a law upon the subject, limiting the right to thus employ children. In North Carolina, the state wherein is located the factory in which the employment was had in the present case, no child under twelve years of age is permitted to work.

It may be desirable that such laws be uniform, but our Federal government is one of enumerated powers: "this principle," declared Chief Justice Marshall in *McCulloch* v. *Maryland* . . . "is universally admitted." . . .

In interpreting the Constitution it must never be forgotten that the nation is made up of states, to which are intrusted the powers of local government. And to them and to the people the powers not expressly delegated to the national government are reserved. . . . The power of the states to regulate their purely internal affairs by such laws as seem wise to the local authority is inherent, and has never been surrendered to the general government. . . . To sustain this statute would not be, in our judgment, a recognition of the lawful exertion of congressional authority over interstate commerce, but would sanction an invasion by the Federal power of the control of a matter purely local in its character, and over which no authority has been delegated to Congress in conferring the power to regulate commerce among the states.

We have neither authority nor disposition to question the motives of Congress in enacting this legislation. The purposes intended must be attained consistently with constitutional limitations, and not by an invasion of the powers of the states. This court has no more important function than that which devolves upon it the obligation to preserve inviolate the constitutional limitations upon the exercise of authority, Federal and state, to the end that each may continue to discharge, harmoniously with the other, the duties intrusted to it by the Constitution.

In our view the necessary effect of this act is, by means of a prohibition against the movement in interstate commerce of ordinary commercial commodities, to regulate the hours of labor of children in factories and mines within the states,—a purely state authority. Thus the act in a twofold sense is repugnant to the Constitution. It not only transcends the authority delegated to Congress over commerce, but also exerts a power as to a purely local matter to which the Federal authority does not extend. The far-reaching result of upholding the act cannot be more plainly indicated than by pointing out that if Congress can thus regulate matters intrusted to local authority by prohibition of the movement of commodities in interstate commerce, all freedom of commerce will be at an end, and the power of the states over local matters may be eliminated, and thus our system of government be practically destroyed.

For these reasons we hold that this law

exceeds the constitutional authority of Congress. It follows that the decree of the district court must be affirmed.

MR. JUSTICE HOLMES, dissenting:

The single question in this case is whether Congress has power to prohibit the shipment in interstate or foreign commerce of any product of cotton mill situated in the United States, in which, within thirty days before the removal of the product, children under fourteen have been employed, or children between fourteen and sixteen have been employed more than eight hours in a day, or more than six days in any week, or between 7 in the evening and 6 in the morning. The objection urged against the power is that the states have exclusive control over their methods of production and that Congress cannot meddle with them; and taking the proposition in the sense of direct intermeddling I agree to it and suppose that no one denies it. But if an act is within the powers specifically conferred upon Congress, it seems to me that it is not made any less constitutional because of the indirect effects that it may have, however obvious it may be that it will have those effects; and that we are not at liberty upon such grounds to hold it void.

The first step in my argument is to make plain what no one is likely to dispute,—that the statute in question is within the power expressly given to Congress if considered only as to its immediate effects, and that if invalid it is so only upon some collateral ground. The statute confines itself to prohibiting the carriage of certain goods in interstate or foreign commerce. Congress is given power to regulate such commerce in unqualified terms. It would not be argued today that the power to regulate does not include the power to prohibit. Regulation means the prohibition of something, and when interstate commerce is the matter to be regulated I cannot doubt that the regulations may prohibit any part of such com-

merce that Congress sees fit to forbid. At all events it is established by the *Lottery Case* and others that have followed it that a law is not beyond the regulative power of Congress merely because it prohibits certain transportation out and out. *Champion* v. *Ames*. . . . So I repeat that this statute in its immediate operation is clearly within the Congress's constitutional power.

The question, then, is narrowed to whether the exercise of its otherwise constitutional power by Congress can be pronounced unconstitutional because of its possible reaction upon the conduct of the states in a matter upon which I have admitted that they are free from direct control. I should have thought that that matter had been disposed of so fully as to leave no room for doubt. I should have thought that the most conspicuous decisions of this Court had made it clear that the power to regulate commerce and other constitutional powers could not be cut down or qualified by the fact that it might interfere with the carrying out of the domestic policy of any state.

The manufacture of oleomargarine is as much a matter of state regulation as the manufacture of cotton cloth. Congress levied a tax upon the compound when colored so as to resemble butter that was so great as obviously to prohibit the manufacture and sale. In a very elaborate discussion the present Chief Justice excluded any inquiry into the purpose of an act which, apart from that purpose, was within the power of Congress. *McCray* v. *United States* [1904]. . . . Fifty years ago a tax on state banks, the obvious purpose and actual effect of which was to drive them, or at least their circulation, out of existence, was sustained, although the result was one that Congress had no constitutional power to require. The court made short work of the argument as to the purpose of the act. "The judicial cannot prescribe to the legislative departments of the government limitations upon the exercise of its acknowledged powers."

Veazie Bank v. *Fenno* [1869]. . . . And to come to cases upon interstate commerce, notwithstanding *United States* v. *E.C. Knight Co.* . . . the Sherman Act has been made an instrument for the breaking up of combinations in restraint of trade and monopolies, using the power to regulate commerce as a foothold, but not proceeding because that commerce was the end actually in mind. The objection that the control of the states over production was interfered with was urged again and again, but always in vain. . . .

The Pure Food and Drug Act was sustained in *Hipolite Egg Co.* v. *United States* [1911] . . . with the intimation that "no trade can be carried on between the states to which it [the power of Congress to regulate commerce] does not extend," applies not merely to articles that the changing opinions of the time condemn as intrinsically harmful, but to others innocent in themselves, simply on the ground that the order for them was induced by a preliminary fraud. . . . It does not matter whether the supposed evil precedes or follows the transportation. It is enough that, in the opinion of Congress, the transportation encourages the evil. . . .

The notion that prohibition is any less prohibition when applied to things now thought evil I do not understand. But if there is any matter upon which civilized countries have agreed,—far more unanimously than they have with regard to intoxicants and some other matters over which this country is now emotionally aroused,—it is the evil of premature and excessive child labor. I should have thought that if we were to introduce our own moral conceptions where, in my opinion, they do not belong, this was pre-eminently a case for upholding the exercise of all its powers by the United States.

But I had thought that the propriety of the exercise of a power admitted to exist in some cases was for the consideration of Congress alone, and that this Court always had disavowed the right to intrude its judgment upon questions of policy or morals. It is not for this court to pronounce when prohibition is necessary to regulation if it ever may be necessary,—to say that it is permissible as against strong drink, but not as against the product of ruined lives.

The act does not meddle with anything belonging to the states. They may regulate their internal affairs and their domestic commerce as they like. But when they seek to send their products across the state line they are no longer within their rights. If there were no Constitution and no Congress their power to cross the line would depend upon their neighbors. Under the Constitution such commerce belongs not to the states, but to Congress to regulate. It may carry out its views of public policy whatever indirect effect they may have upon the activities of the states. Instead of being encountered by a prohibitive tariff at her boundaries, the state encounters the public policy of the United States which it is for Congress to express. The public policy of the United States is shaped with a view to the benefit of the nation as a whole. If, as has been the case within the memory of men still living, a state should take a different view of the propriety of sustaining a lottery from that which generally prevails, I cannot believe that the fact would require a different decision from that reached in *Champion* v. *Ames.* Yet in that case it would be said with quite as much force as in this that Congress was attempting to intermeddle with the state's domestic affairs. The national welfare as understood by Congress may require a different attitude within its sphere from that of some self-seeking state. It seems to me entirely constitutional for Congress to enforce its understanding by all the means at its command.

Mr. Justice McKenna, Mr. Justice Brandeis, and Mr. Justice Clarke concur in this opinion.

Does Justice Day's opinion in *Hammer* v. *Dagenhart* follow the reasoning of previous Court precedents dealing with the scope of the commerce power and the national police power under the commerce clause? Compare Day's opinion with that of the Court in *Champion* v. *Ames*.[11] Contrast Justice Harlan's use of *Gibbons* v. *Ogden* in *Champion* v. *Ames* with Day's reference to the *Gibbons* case. Compare the ways in which considerations of federalism are taken into account in Day's opinion and in the dissenting opinion of Justice Holmes.

The rejection of the Child Labor Law by the Court in *Hammer* v. *Dagenhart* did not put the matter to rest. Congress passed the Child Labor Tax Law in 1919, which attempted to proscribe child labor through the imposition of a federal excise tax. This was declared unconstitutional in *Bailey* v. *Drexel Furniture Company*, 259 U.S. 20 (1922).[12] *Hammer* v. *Dagenhart* was overruled in *United States* v. *Darby*, 312 U.S. 100 (1941).[13]

THE RESTRICTION AND EXPANSION
OF THE COMMERCE POWER
DURING THE NEW DEAL 1933–1945

The political turbulence of the New Deal did not spare the Supreme Court. During Roosevelt's first term a highly conservative Supreme Court, led by Chief Justice Charles Evans Hughes, took an active stance in applying what it considered to be constitutional principles to strike down much of Roosevelt's New Deal legislation. A central component of the early New Deal program was the National Industrial Recovery Act passed in 1933. It delegated far-reaching powers to the President to deal with economic problems through the imposition of "codes of fair competition" and through prohibitions in interstate commerce of "hot oil," which was oil produced in excess of state quotas. In *Panama Refining Company* v. *Ryan*, 293 U.S. 388 (1935), the Court struck down the section of the act authorizing the President to prohibit interstate shipments of hot oil on the grounds that it was an unconstitutional delegation of legislative authority.[14]

The entire NIRA was challenged in *Schechter Poultry Corporation* v. *United States* (1935). The act was based upon the authority of Congress to regulate commerce and promote the general welfare. Section 1 of the legislation declared that it was the policy of Congress "to remove obstructions to the free flow of interstate and foreign commerce." The President was authorized to approve of codes of fair competition upon the application by "representative" trade associations.

Under the terms of the act a "live poultry code" was promulgated for the New York area, and the Schechter Poultry Corporation, operating a kosher slaughterhouse, was convicted of various violations of the code, including wage and hour provisions, the "straight killing" requirement that prohibited

[11]See pp. 321–325.
[12]For a discussion of the Bailey case see, pp. 432–436.
[13]See pp. 353–357.
[14]See pp. 111–112.

the selected sale of chickens to retailers, and for selling "unfit" chickens. The circuit court of appeals sustained the conviction for the violation of the "straight killing" requirement and the Supreme Court granted review on a writ of certiorari requested by both Schechter and the government (seeking constitutional clarification of its authority under the statute).

On the basis of the contentions of the government and the challenges of the plaintiffs, Chief Justice Hughes considered three questions. First, was the legislation justified "in the light of the grave national crisis with which Congress was confronted"? The Court answered in the negative. Second, was the law an unconstitutional delegation of legislative authority?[15] Third, did those sections of the act that authorized the promulgation of the live poultry code exceed the authority of Congress under the commerce power? Chief Justice Hughes's majority opinion (the decision of the Court was unanimous, but Justice Cardozo wrote a concurring opinion joined by Justice Stone) on the third question follows.

Schechter Poultry Corp. v. United States

295 U.S. 495; 55 S. Ct. 837; 79 L. Ed. 1570 (1935)

MR. CHIEF JUSTICE HUGHES delivered the opinion of the Court:

. . . Third. The question of the application of the provisions of the Live Poultry Code to intrastate transactions. Although the validity of the codes (apart from the question of delegation) rests upon the commerce clause of the Constitution, § 3 (a) is not in terms limited to interstate and foreign commerce. From the generality of its terms, and from the argument of the Government at the bar, it would appear that § 3 (a) was designed to authorize codes without that limitation. But under § 3 (f) penalties are confined to violations of a code provision "in any transaction in or affecting interstate or foreign commerce." This aspect of the case presents the question whether the particular provisions of the Live Poultry Code, which the defendants were convicted for violating and for having conspired to violate, were within the regulating power of Congress.

These provisions relate to the hours and wages of those employed by defendants in their slaughterhouses in Brooklyn and to the sales there made to retail dealers and butchers.

(1) Were these transactions *"in"* interstate commerce? Much is made of the fact that almost all the poultry coming to New York is sent there from other States. But the code provisions, as here applied, do not concern the transportation of the poultry from other States to New York, or the transactions of the commission men or others to whom it is consigned, or the sales made by such consignees to defendants. When defendants had made their purchases, whether at the West Washington Market in New York City or at the railroad terminals serving the City, or elsewhere, the poultry was trucked to their slaughterhouses in Brooklyn for local disposition. The interstate transactions in relation to that poultry then ended. Defendants held the poultry at their slaughterhouse markets for slaughter and local sale to retail dealers and butchers who in turn sold directly to consumers. Neither

---

[15]This portion of the opinion is reprinted at pp. 113–119.

the slaughtering nor the sales by defendants were transactions in interstate commerce. . . .

The undisputed facts thus afford no warrant for the argument that the poultry handled by defendants at their slaughterhouse markets was in a *"current"* or *"flow"* of interstate commerce and was thus subject to congressional regulation. The mere fact that there may be a constant flow of commodities into a State does not mean that the flow continues after the property has arrived and has become commingled with the mass of property within the State and is there held solely for local disposition and use. So far as the poultry here in question is concerned, the flow in interstate commerce had ceased. The poultry had come to a permanent rest within the State. It was not held, used, or sold by defendants in relation to any further transactions in interstate commerce and was not destined for transportation to other States. Hence, decisions which deal with a stream of interstate commerce—where goods come to rest within a State temporarily and are later to go forward in interstate commerce—and with the regulations of transactions involved in that practical continuity of movement, are not applicable here. . . .

(2) Did the defendants' transactions directly *"affect"* interstate commerce so as to be subject to federal regulation? The power of Congress extends not only to the regulation of transactions which are part of interstate commerce, but to the protection of that commerce from injury. It matters not that the injury may be due to the conduct of those engaged in intrastate operations. Thus, Congress may protect the safety of those employed in interstate transportation "no matter what may be the source of the dangers which threaten it." . . . We said in *Second Employers' Liability Cases* [1912], that it is the "effect upon interstate commerce," not "the source of the injury," which is "the crite-

rion of congressional power." We have held that, in dealing with common carriers engaged in both interstate and intrastate commerce, the dominant authority of Congress necessarily embraces the right to control their intrastate operations in all matters having such a close and substantial relation to interstate traffic that the control is essential or appropriate to secure the freedom of that traffic from interference or unjust discrimination and to promote the efficiency of the interstate service. *The Shreveport Case* [1914]. . . . And combinations and conspiracies to restrain interstate commerce, or to monopolize any part of it, are none the less within the reach of the Anti-Trust Act because the conspirators seek to attain their end by means of intrastate activities. . . .

. . . This is not a prosecution for a conspiracy to restrain or monopolize interstate commerce in violation of the Anti-Trust Act. Defendants have been convicted, not upon direct charges of injury to interstate commerce or of interference with persons engaged in that commerce, but of violations of certain provisions of the Live Poultry Code and of conspiracy to commit these violations. Interstate commerce is brought in only upon the charge that violations of these provisions—as to hours and wages of employees and local sales—*"affected"* interstate commerce.

In determining how far the federal government may go in controlling intrastate transactions upon the ground that they "affect" interstate commerce, there is a necessary and well-established distinction between direct and indirect effects. The precise line can be drawn only as individual cases arise, but the distinction is clear in principle. Direct effects are illustrated by the railroad cases we have cited, as *e.g.*, the effect of failure to use prescribed safety appliances on railroads which are the highways of both interstate and intrastate commerce, injury to an employee engaged in interstate transportation by the negligence of an employee engaged in an intrastate movement, the fixing of rates for intrastate transportation which unjustly discriminate against interstate commerce. But where the effect of intrastate transactions upon interstate commerce is merely indirect, such transactions remain with the domain of state power. If the commerce clause were construed to reach all enterprises and transactions which could be said to have an indirect effect upon interstate commerce, the federal authority would embrace practically all the activities of the people and the authority of the State over its domestic concerns would exist only by sufferance of the federal government. Indeed, on such a theory, even the development of the State's commercial facilities would be subject to federal control. . . .

The question of chief importance relates to the provisions of the Code as to the hours and wages of those employed in defendants' slaughterhouse markets. It is plain that these requirements are imposed in order to govern the details of defendants' management of their local business. The persons employed in slaughtering and selling in local trade are not employed in interstate commerce. Their hours and wages have no direct relation to interstate commerce. The question of how many hours these employees should work and what they should be paid differs in no essential respect from similar questions in other local businesses which handle commodities brought into a State and there dealt in as a part of its internal commerce. This appears from an examination of the considerations urged by the Government with respect to conditions in the poultry trade. Thus, the Government argues that hours and wages affect prices; that slaughterhouse men sell at a small margin above operating costs; that labor represents 50 to 60 per cent. of these costs; that a slaughterhouse opera-

tor paying lower wages or reducing his cost by exacting long hours of work, translates his saving into lower prices; that this results in demands for a cheaper grade of goods; and that the cutting of prices brings about a demoralization of the price structure. Similar conditions may be adduced in relation to other businesses. The argument of the Government proves too much. If the federal government may determine the wages and hours of employees in the internal commerce of a State, because of their relation to cost and prices and their indirect effect upon interstate commerce, it would seem that a similar control might be exerted over other elements of cost, also affecting prices, such as the number of employees, rents, advertising, methods of doing business, etc. All the processes of production and distribution that enter into cost could likewise be controlled. If the cost of doing an intrastate business is in itself the permitted object of federal control, the extent of the regulation of cost would be a question of discretion and not of power.

The Government also makes the point that efforts to enact state legislation establishing high labor standards have been impeded by the belief that unless similar action is taken generally, commerce will be diverted from the States adopting such standards, and that this fear of diversion has led to demands for federal legislation on the subject of wages and hours. The apparent implication is that the federal authority under the commerce clause should be deemed to extend to the establishment of rules to govern wages and hours in intrastate trade and industry generally throughout the country, thus overriding the authority of the States to deal with domestic problems arising from labor conditions in their internal commerce.

It is not the province of the Court to consider the economic advantages or disadvantages of such a centralized system. It is sufficient to say that the Federal Constitution does not provide for it. Our growth and development have called for wide use of the commerce power of the federal government in its control over the expanded activities of interstate commerce, and in protecting that commerce from burdens, interferences, and conspiracies to restrain and monopolize it. But the authority of the federal government may not be pushed to such an extreme as to destroy the distinction, which the commerce clause itself establishes, between commerce "among the several States" and the internal concerns of a State. The same answer must be made to the contention that is based upon the serious economic situation which led to the passage of the Recovery Act,—the fall in prices, the decline in wages and employment, and the curtailment of the market for commodities. Stress is laid upon the great importance of maintaining wage distributions which would provide the necessary stimulus in starting "the cumulative forces making for expanding commercial activity." Without in any way disparaging this motive, it is enough to say that the recuperative efforts of the federal government must be made in a manner consistent with the authority granted by the Constitution.

We are of the opinion that the attempt through the provisions of the Code to fix the hours and wages of employees of defendants in their intrastate business was not a valid exercise of federal power. . . .

On both the grounds we have discussed, the attempted delegation of legislative power, and the attempted regulation of intrastate transactions which affect interstate commerce only indirectly, we hold the code provisions here in question to be invalid and that the judgment of conviction must be reversed.

MR. JUSTICE CARDOZO, concurring:
The delegated power of legislation which has found expression in this code is not canalized within banks that keep it

from overflowing. It is unconfined and vagrant, if I may borrow my own words in an earlier opinion. *Panama Refining Co.* v. *Ryan* [1935]. . . .

This Court has held that delegation may be unlawful though the act to be performed is definite and single, if the necessity, time and occasion of performance have been left in the end to the discretion of the delegate. *Panama Refining Co.* v. *Ryan* . . . I thought that ruling went too far. I pointed out in an opinion that there had been "no grant to the Executive of any roving commission to inquire into evils and then, upon discovering them, do anything he pleases." Choice, though within limits, had been given him "as to the occasion, but none whatever as to the means." Here, in the case before us, is an attempted delegation not confined to any single act nor to any class or group of acts identified or described by reference to a standard. Here in effect is a roving commission to inquire into evils and upon discovery correct them.

I have said that there is no standard, definite or even approximate, to which legislation must conform. Let me make my meaning more precise. If codes of fair competition are codes eliminating "unfair" methods of competition ascertained upon inquiry to prevail in one industry or another, there is no unlawful delegation of legislative functions when the President is directed to inquire into such practices and denounce them when discovered. For many years a like power has been committed to the Federal Trade Commission with the approval of this court in a long series of decisions. . . . Delegation in such circumstances is born of the necessities of the occasion. The industries of the country are too many and diverse to make it possible for Congress, in respect of matters such as these, to legislate directly with adequate appreciation of varying conditions. Nor is the substance of the power changed because the President may act at the instance of trade or industrial associations having special knowledge of the facts. Their function is strictly advisory; it is the *imprimatur* of the President that begets the quality of law. ... When the task that is set before one is that of cleaning house, it is prudent as well as usual to take counsel of the dwellers.

But there is another conception of codes of fair competition, their significance and function, which leads to very different consequences, though it is one that is struggling now for recognition and acceptance. By this other conception a code is not to be restricted to the elimination of business practices that would be characterized by general acceptation as oppressive or unfair. It is to include whatever ordinances may be desirable or helpful for the well-being or prosperity of the industry affected. In that view, the function of its adoption is not merely negative, but positive; the planning of improvements as well as the extirpation of abuses. What is fair, as thus conceived, is not something to be contrasted with what is unfair or fraudulent or tricky. The extension becomes as wide as the field of industrial regulation. If that conception shall prevail, anything that Congress may do within the limits of the commerce clause for the betterment of business may be done by the President upon the recommendation of a trade association by calling it a code. This is delegation running riot. No such plenitude of power is susceptible of transfer. The statute, however, aims at nothing less, as one can learn both from its terms and from the administrative practice under it. Nothing less is aimed at by the code now submitted to our scrutiny.

The code does not confine itself to the suppression of methods of competition that would be classified as unfair according to accepted business standards or accepted norms of ethics. It sets up a comprehensive body of rules to promote the welfare of the industry, if not the welfare

of the nation, without reference to standards, ethical or commercial, that could be known or predicted in advance of its adoption. One of the new rules, the source of ten counts in the indictment, is aimed at an established practice, not unethical or oppressive, the practice of selective buying. Many others could be instanced as open to the same objection if the sections of the code were to be examined one by one. The process of dissection will not be traced in all its details. Enough at this time to state what it reveals. Even if the statute itself had fixed the meaning of fair competition by way of contrast with practices that are oppressive or unfair, the code outruns the bounds of the authority conferred. What is excessive is not sporadic or superficial. It is deep-seated and pervasive. The licit and illicit sections are so combined and welded as to be incapable of severance without destructive mutilation.

But there is another objection, far-reaching and incurable, aside from any defect of unlawful delegation.

If this code had been adopted by Congress itself, and not by the President on the advice of an industrial association, it would even then be void unless authority to adopt it is included in the grant of power "to regulate commerce with foreign nations and among the several states." United States Constitution, Art. I, § 8, Clause 3.

I find no authority in that grant for the regulation of wages and hours of labor in the intrastate transactions that make up the defendants' business. As to this feature of the case little can be added to the opinion of the Court. There is a view of causation that would obliterate the distinction between what is national and what is local in the activities of commerce. Motion at the outer rim is communicated perceptibly, though minutely, to recording instruments at the center. A society such as ours "is an elastic medium which transmits all tremors throughout its territory; the only question is of their size." Per Learned Hand, J., in the court below. The law is not indifferent to considerations of degree. Activities local in their immediacy do not become interstate and national because of distant repercussions. What is near and what is distant may at times be uncertain. . . . There is no penumbra of uncertainty obscuring judgment here. To find immediacy or directness here is to find it almost everywhere. If centripetal forces are to be isolated to the exclusion of the forces that oppose and counteract them, there will be an end to our federal system.

To take from this code the provisions as to wages and the hours of labor is to destroy it altogether. If a trade or an industry is so predominantly local as to be exempt from regulation by the Congress in respect of matters such as these, there can be no "code" for it at all. This is clear from the provisions of § 7a of the Act with its explicit disclosure of the statutory scheme. Wages and the hours of labor are essential features of the plan, its very bone and sinew. There is no opportunity in such circumstances for the severance of the infected parts in the hope of saving the remainder. A code collapses utterly with bone and sinew gone.

I am authorized to state that Mr. Justice Stone joins in this opinion.

Although Chief Justice Hughes does not resurrect the *E.C. Knight* case in his opinion, what similarities exist between his definition of the scope of the commerce power and that of Justice Fuller in the *Knight* case? The cases cited by the government in defense of the NIRA were *Swift and Company* v. *United States*, 196 U.S. 375 (1905), *Stafford* v. *Wallace*, 258 U.S. 495 (1922), and the *Shreveport Case* (1914). The first two of these cases supported congressional regulation of activities that were "in" commerce, or part of the "current of commerce," regardless of whether or not the activities had a substantial effect upon interstate commerce, which was the criteria of the *Shreveport Case*. Does Hughes's opinion properly interpret and apply these precedents to the facts of the *Schechter* case? What considerations of federalism are taken into account in the opinions of Hughes and Cardozo?

A year after its momentous decision in the *Schechter* case, the Court faced another challenge to New Deal legislation enacted under the authority of the commerce clause in the case of *Carter* v. *Carter Coal Company*. The Bituminous Coal Act of 1935 declared that the coal industry was "affected with a national public interest," and that "control of such production and regulation of the prices . . . are necessary to promote its interstate commerce. . . ." The law created a National Bituminous Coal Commission that, with the aid of district boards elected by producers, had the authority to promulgate codes setting wages and hours for the industry, and prices, for different regions of the country. A 15 percent tax was to be levied on all coal sold at the mine, with a 90 percent rebate going to those producers who agreed to accept a code formulated under the act. Carter, a stockholder of the Carter Coal Company, sued to enjoin the company from paying the tax, or complying with the code. The Commissioner of Internal Revenue was joined as a defendant with the company. The district court sustained the act, and the Supreme Court, citing the importance of the question, immediately granted certiorari before the court of appeals heard the case.

Against the argument of the government that the purpose of the act was to promote interstate commerce in coal through the regulation of conditions surrounding its production and distribution, the plaintiff (Carter) contended,

> The object and purpose of this statute is . . . not to regulate interstate commerce in coal, but to stabilize the industry by the regulation of wages, by the prevention of free competition, and by the allocation of production among the states, to the end that the producers as a whole may obtain larger returns from their operations, and the miners higher wages than in the past. Otherwise expressed, the purpose is to insure to those engaged in the industry, whether operators or miners, a larger share of the national income than they have heretofore enjoyed. . . .
>
> None of the powers stated [in the act] is within the enumerated powers specifically delegated to the Congress. To read them into the commerce clause is in effect to convert that clause into a general welfare clause, under which the Congress would be empowered to enact any statute, affecting the economic life of the nation, deemed by it to be wise or expedient for the purpose of promoting the national welfare.[16]

Carter v. *Carter Coal Co.*

298 U.S. 238; 56 S. Ct. 855; 80 L. Ed. 1160 (1936)

MR. JUSTICE SUTHERLAND delivered the opinion of the Court:

. . . Certain recitals contained in the act plainly suggest that its makers were of opinion that its constitutionality could be sustained under some general federal power, thought to exist, apart from the specific grants of the Constitution. . . . The recitals are to the effect that the distribution of bituminous coal is of national interest, affecting the health and comfort of the people and the general welfare of the nation. . . . These affirmations—and the further ones that the production and distribution of such coal "directly affect interstate commerce," because of which and of the waste of the national coal resources and other circumstances, the regulation is necessary for the protection of such commerce—do not constitute an exertion of the *will* of Congress which is legislation, but a recital of considerations which in the *opinion* of that body existed and justified the expression of its will in the present act. Nevertheless, this preamble may not be disregarded. On the contrary it is important, because it makes clear, except for the pure assumption that the conditions described "directly" affect interstate commerce, that the powers which Congress undertook to exercise are not specific but of the most general character. . . .

The proposition, often advanced and as often discredited, that the power of the federal government inherently extends to purposes affecting the nation as a whole with which the states severally cannot deal or cannot adequately deal, and the related notion that Congress, entirely apart from those powers delegated by the Constitution, may enact laws to promote the general welfare, have never been accepted but always definitely rejected by this court. . . .

. . . [T]he general purposes which the act recites . . . are beyond the power of Congress except so far, and only so far, as they may be realized by an exercise of some specific power granted by the Constitution. . . . [W]e shall find no grant of power which authorizes Congress to leg-

[16]LB, Vol. 32, pp. 149–150.

islate in respect of these general purposes unless it be found in the commerce clause—and this we now consider. . . .

. . . [T]he word "commerce" is the equivalent of the phrase "intercourse for the purposes of trade." Plainly, the incidents leading up to and culminating in the mining of coal do not constitute such intercourse. The employment of men, the fixing of their wages, hours of labor and working conditions, the bargaining in respect of these things—whether carried on separately or collectively—each and all constitute intercourse for the purposes of production, not of trade. The latter is a thing apart from the relation of employer and employee, which in all producing occupations is purely local in character. Extraction of coal from the mine is the aim and the completed result of local activities. Commerce in the coal mined is not brought into being by force of these activities, but by negotiations, agreements, and circumstances entirely apart from production. Mining brings the subject matter of commerce into existence. Commerce disposes of it.

. . . [T]he effect of the labor provisions of the act, including those in respect of minimum wages, wage agreements, collective bargaining, and the Labor Board and its powers, primarily falls upon production and not upon commerce; and confirms the further resulting conclusion that production is a purely local activity. It follows that none of these essential antecedents of production constitutes a transaction in or forms any part of interstate commerce. *Schechter Corp.* v. *United States.* . . . Everything which moves in interstate commerce has had a local origin. Without local production somewhere, interstate commerce, as now carried on, would practically disappear. Nevertheless, the local character of mining, of manufacturing and of crop growing is a fact, and remains a fact, whatever may be done with the products. . . .

That the production of every commodity intended for interstate sale and transportation has some effect upon interstate commerce may be, if it has not already been, freely granted; and we are brought to the final and decisive inquiry, whether here that effect is direct, as the "preamble" recites, or indirect. The distinction is not formal, but substantial in the highest degree, as we pointed out in the *Schechter* case. . . .

Whether the effect of a given activity or condition is direct or indirect is not always easy to determine. The word "direct" implies that the activity or condition invoked or blamed shall operate proximately—not mediately, remotely, or collaterally—to produce the effect. It connotes the absence of an efficient intervening agency or condition. And the extent of the effect bears no logical relation to its character. The distinction between a direct and an indirect effect turns, not upon the magnitude of either the cause or the effect, but entirely upon the manner in which the effect has been brought about. If the production by one man of a single ton of coal intended for interstate sale and shipment, and actually so sold and shipped, affects interstate commerce indirectly, the effect does not become direct by multiplying the tonnage, or increasing the number of men employed, or adding to the expense or complexities of the business, or by all combined. It is quite true that rules of law are sometimes qualified by considerations of degree, as the government argues. But the matter of degree has no bearing upon the question here, since the question is not—What is the *extent* of the local activity or condition, or the *extent* of the effect produced upon interstate commerce? but—What is the *relation* between the activity or condition and the effect?

Much stress is put upon the evils which come from the struggle between employers and employees over the matter of wages, working conditions, the right of collective bargaining, etc., and the resulting strikes, curtailment and irregularity of production and effect on prices; and it is insisted that interstate commerce is *greatly* affected thereby. But, in addition to what has just been said, the conclusive answer is that the evils are all local evils over which the federal government has no legislative control. The relation of employer and employee is a local relation. . . . And the controversies and evils, which it is the object of the act to regulate and minimize, are local controversies and evils affecting local work undertaken to accomplish that local result. Such effect as they may have upon commerce, however extensive it may be, is secondary and indirect. An increase in the greatness of the effect adds to its importance. It does not alter its character. . . .

. . . A reading of the entire opinion makes clear, what we now declare, that the want of power on the part of the federal government is the same whether the wages, hours of service, and working conditions, and the bargaining about them, are related to production before interstate commerce has begun, or to sale and distribution after it has ended. . . .

Separate opinion of MR. CHIEF JUSTICE HUGHES:

The power to regulate interstate commerce embraces the power to protect that commerce from injury, whatever may be the source of the dangers which threaten it, and to adopt any appropriate means to that end. . . . Congress thus has adequate authority to maintain the orderly conduct of interstate commerce and to provide for the peaceful settlement of disputes which threaten it. . . . But Congress may not use this protective authority as a pretext for the exertion of power to regulate activities and relations within the States which affect interstate commerce only indirectly. . . .

But . . . [t]he Act also provides for the regulation of the prices of bituminous coal sold in interstate commerce and pro-

hibits unfair methods of competition in interstate commerce. Undoubtedly transactions in carrying on interstate commerce are subject to the federal power to regulate that commerce and the control of charges and the protection of fair competition in that commerce are familiar illustrations of the exercise of the power, as the Interstate Commerce Act, the Packers and Stockyards Act, and the Anti-Trust Acts abundantly show. . . .

. . . The marketing provisions in relation to interstate commerce can be carried out as provided in Part II without regard to the labor provisions contained in Part III. That fact, in the light of the congressional declaration of separability, should be considered of controlling importance.

In this view, the Act, and the Code for which it provides, may be sustained in relation to the provisions for marketing in interstate commerce, and the decisions of the courts below, so far as they accomplish that result, should be affirmed.

MR. JUSTICE CARDOZO . . . [Dissenting]: . . . I am satisfied that the Act is within the power of the central government in so far as it provides for minimum and maximum prices upon sales of bituminous coal in the transactions of interstate commerce and in those of intrastate commerce where interstate commerce is directly or intimately affected. Whether it is valid also in other provisions that have been considered and condemned in the opinion of the Court, I do not find it necessary to determine at this time. Silence must not be taken as importing acquiescence. . . .

Regulation of prices being an exercise of the commerce power in respect of interstate transactions, the question remains whether it comes within that power as applied to intrastate sales where interstate prices are directly or intimately affected. Mining and agriculture and manufacture are not interstate commerce considered by themselves, yet their relation to that commerce may be such that for the protection of the one there is need to regulate the other. *Schechter Poultry Corp.* v. *United States.* . . . Sometimes it is said that the relation must be "direct" to bring that power into play. In many circumstances such a description will be sufficiently precise to meet the needs of the occasion. But a great principle of constitutional law is not susceptible of comprehensive statement in an adjective. The underlying thought is merely this, that "the law is not indifferent to considerations of degree." *Schechter* . . . concurring opinion. . . . It cannot be indifferent to them without an expansion of the commerce clause that would absorb or imperil the reserved powers of the states. At times, as in the case cited, the waves of causation will have radiated so far that their undulatory motion, if discernible at all, will be too faint or obscure, too broken by crosscurrents, to be heeded by the law. In such circumstances the holding is not directed at prices or wages considered in the abstract, but at prices or wages in particular conditions. The relation may be tenuous or the opposite according to the facts. Always the setting of the facts is to be viewed if one would know the closeness of the tie. Perhaps, if one group of adjectives is to be chosen in preference to another, "intimate" and "remote" will be found to be as good as any. At all events, "direct" and "indirect," even if accepted as sufficient, must not be read narrowly. . . . A survey of the cases shows that the words have been interpreted with suppleness of adaptation and flexibility of meaning. The power is as broad as the need that evokes it.

One of the most common and typical instances of relation characterized as direct has been that between interstate and intrastate rates for carriers by rail where the local rates are so low as to divert business unreasonably from interstate competitors. In such circumstances Congress has the power to protect the business of its carriers against disintegrating encroachments. To be sure, the relation even then may be characterized as indirect if one is nice or over-literal in the choice of words. Strictly speaking, the intrastate rates have a primary effect upon the intrastate traffic and not upon any other, though the repercussions of the competitive system may lead to secondary consequences affecting interstate traffic also. . . . What the cases really mean is that the causal relation in such circumstances is so close and intimate and obvious as to permit it to be called direct without subjecting the word to an unfair or excessive strain. There is a like immediacy here. Within rulings the most orthodox, the prices for intrastate sales of coal have so inescapable a relation to those for interstate sales that a system of regulation for transactions of the one class is necessary to give adequate protection to the system of regulation adopted for the other. The argument is strongly pressed by intervening counsel that this may not be true in all communities or in exceptional conditions. If so, the operators unlawfully affected may show that the Act to that extent is invalid as to them. . . .

I am authorized to state that Mr. Justice Brandeis and Mr. Justice Stone join in this opinion.

To what extent did Justice Sutherland return to the precedent of the *E.C. Knight* case in his opinion? Why did Sutherland hold that the "stream of commerce" doctrine was inapplicable to the *Carter Coal Company* case? Contrast the separate opinion of Chief Justice Hughes with the majority opinion. To what extent are considerations of federalism raised in both opinions? Why did Hughes hold that the labor provisions of the act were unconstitutional, but the pricing provisions were within the scope of the commerce power? Contrast Hughes's opinion in the *Schechter* case with his opinion in the *Carter Coal Company* case. Would there have been any reason to predict on the basis of his *Schechter* opinion that he might have agreed with the majority in the *Carter Coal Company* case that the entire act should be declared unconstitutional because it was beyond the scope of the commerce power? Justice Cardozo, dissenting, agreed with the separate opinion of Chief Justice Hughes that the pricing provisions of the act were constitutional. What did Cardozo mean when he stated that a survey of the cases dealing with the scope of the national commerce power "shows that the words [*direct* and *indirect*] have been interpreted with subtleness of adaptation and flexibility of meaning. The power is as broad as the need that evokes it"?

The decisions of the Court in the *Schechter* and *Carter* v. *Carter Coal Company* cases, and in other cases as well, were interpreted by President Roosevelt and his followers as an indication that a hostile and conservative Supreme Court would continue to strike down liberal New Deal legislation.[17] Roosevelt had not been able to appoint a single justice to the Supreme Court during his first term, and the Court remained a conservative stronghold. The President and his aides discussed the possibility of proposing a constitutional amendment to support New Deal legislation but rejected this course of action because they felt such an amendment could be too easily defeated. At the beginning of Roosevelt's second term, with no possible relief from the trend of Supreme Court decisions in sight, the President proposed a plan to "reform" the judiciary, which in fact was nothing more than a thinly veiled court-packing scheme. Under the plan the President would be given the authority to appoint a new federal judge for each judge over seventy years of age who did not retire within six months of his seventieth birthday. The proposal limited to fifty the number of judges that could be appointed on this basis and provided that there could be no more than fifteen members of the Supreme Court. At that time, six Supreme Court justices were over seventy.[18] If the plan had been enacted Roosevelt would have been able to appoint a majority of the Court. However, widespread opposition to this scheme both among conservatives and even among many members of the President's own party doomed the plan from the start. Those in opposition considered the plan a blatant and unwarranted presidential intrusion upon the traditional constitutional powers of the Court. The bill was proposed by the President on February 5, 1937, and the Senate Judiciary Committee issued an unfavorable report on it on June 14, 1937. The committee report concluded that the proposal undermined the independence of the courts "in direct violation of the spirit of the American Constitution." The Senate voted 70–20 to kill the bill by recommitting it to the committee on July 22, 1937.

[17]Another key 1936 case overturning the Agricultural Adjustment Act as outside of the scope of the congressional spending power was United States v. Butler, 297 U.S. 1, discussed at pp. 441–448.

[18]Brandeis (81), Van Devanter (78), McReynolds (75), Sutherland (75), Hughes (75), Butler (71).

During the debate over Roosevelt's court-packing scheme in 1937, the Supreme Court once again confronted challenges to the constitutionality of New Deal legislation. Would the delicate political situation in which the Court found itself in any way affect the outcome of these new challenges? In this highly charged political atmosphere the Supreme Court confronted the question of the constitutionality of the National Labor Relations Act of 1935 in the case of *National Labor Relations Board* v. *Jones and Laughlin Steel Corp.* (1937). The act broadly regulated labor-management relations in industry. Its constitutional justification was that labor strife, which the act sought to prevent, affected interstate commerce even when it arose in "local" companies. The National Labor Relations Board was empowered to take action to prevent unfair labor practices, enumerated in the act, "affecting commerce." Clearly, the labor practices being regulated were not themselves "commerce" within the meaning of any previous definition of the term. The act regulated conditions of production. In the *Jones and Laughlin* case the NLRB had found that the company had engaged in "unfair labor practices" as defined by the act in discharging employees for union activity. When the company refused to comply with a board order to cease and desist from such practices, the NLRB under the terms of the statute unsuccessfully sought judicial enforcement of the order in the court of appeals, which held that the order was outside of the scope of federal power.

On appeal to the Supreme Court, the government argued that the National Labor Relations Act "constitutes an exercise of the power of Congress to protect interstate commerce from the burden and injury caused by industrial strife. . . ."[19] The farflung activities of the Jones and Laughlin Steel Corp., declared the government, affect interstate commerce and therefore come within the scope of the act. "It is well settled," stated the government, "that an industrial dispute involving an intent to restrain commerce is within the control power of Congress, even though arising out of local activity. . . . Consequently, where the situation in a particular enterprise presents a reasonable likelihood that a dispute, if it occurred, would involve an intent to restrain commerce, then the Board can apply the statute to that enterprise." The respondent corporation countered that limiting the act to transactions "affecting commerce" does not make it constitutional. The act is a regulation of labor, not of commerce, contended the respondent, and "the use of a word or phrase in the statute, limiting its provisions to activities 'affecting commerce' however dramatic or effective, cannot alter the provinces of the state or federal governments one whit, nor change that which is not interstate commerce into that which is."[20] The brief for the respondents concluded that the power of Congress under the commerce clause "is limited to the bonafide regulation of interstate commerce."[21]

Chief Justice Hughes wrote the opinion of the Court in the *Jones and Laughlin* case. Can you guess from his opinion in the *Schechter* case and his separate opinion in *Carter* v. *Carter Coal Company* how he decided the case?

---

[19]LB, Vol. 33, p. 222.
[20]Ibid., p. 366.
[21]Ibid., p. 351.

National Labor Relations Board v. Jones and Laughlin Steel Corporation

301 U.S. 1; 57 S. Ct. 615; 81 L. Ed. 893 (1937)

Mr. Chief Justice Hughes delivered the opinion of the Court:

First. The scope of the Act.—The Act is challenged in its entirety as an attempt to regulate all industry, thus invading the reserved powers of the States over their local concerns. It is asserted that the references in the Act to interstate and foreign commerce are colorable at best; that the Act is not a true regulation of such commerce or of matters which directly affect it but on the contrary has the fundamental object of placing under the compulsory supervision of the federal government all industrial labor relations within the nation. The argument seeks support in the broad words of the preamble (section one) and in the sweep of the provisions of the Act, and it is further insisted that its legislative history shows an essential universal purpose in the light of which its scope cannot be limited by either construction or by the application of the separability clause.

If this conception of terms, intent and consequent inseparability were sound, the Act would necessarily fall by reason of the limitation upon the federal power which inheres in the constitutional grant, as well as because of the explicit reservation of the Tenth Amendment. . . . The authority of the federal government may not be pushed to such an extreme as to destroy the distinction, which the commerce clause itself establishes, between commerce "among the several States" and the internal concerns of a State. That distinction between what is national and what is local in the activities of commerce is vital to the maintenance of our federal system.

But we are not at liberty to deny effect to specific provisions, which Congress has constitutional powers to enact, by super- imposing upon them inferences from general legislative declarations of an ambiguous character, even if found in the same statute. The cardinal principle of statutory construction is to save and not to destroy. We have repeatedly held that as between two possible interpretations of a statute, by one of which it would be unconstitutional and by the other valid, our plain duty is to adopt that which will save the act. . . .

We think it clear that the National Labor Relations Act may be construed so as to operate within the sphere of constitutional authority. The jurisdiction conferred upon the Board, and invoked in this instance, is found in § 10 (a), which provides:

"Sec. 10 (a). The Board is empowered, as hereinafter provided, to prevent any person from engaging in any unfair labor practice (listed in section 8) affecting commerce."

The critical words of this provision, prescribing the limits of the Board's authority in dealing with the labor practices, are "affecting commerce." The Act specifically defines the "commerce" to which it refers (§ 2[6]):

"The term 'commerce' means trade, traffic, commerce, transportation, or communication among the several States, or between the District of Columbia or any Territory of the United States and any State or other Territory, or between any foreign country and any State, Territory, or the District of Columbia, or within the District of Columbia or any Territory, or between points in the same State but through any other State or any Territory or the District of Columbia or any foreign country."

There can be no question that the commerce thus contemplated by the Act (aside from that within a Territory or the District of Columbia) is interstate and foreign commerce in the constitutional sense. The Act also defines the term "affecting commerce" (§2 [7]):

"The term 'affecting commerce' means in commerce, or burdening or obstructing commerce or the free flow of commerce, or having led or tending to lead to a labor dispute burdening or obstructing commerce or the free flow of commerce."

This definition is one of exclusion as well as inclusion. The grant of authority to the Board does not purport to extend to the relationship between all industrial employees and employers. Its terms do not impose collective bargaining upon all industry regardless of effects upon interstate or foreign commerce. It purports to reach only what may be deemed to burden or obstruct that commerce and, thus qualified, it must be construed as contemplating the exercise of control within constitutional bounds. It is a familiar principle that acts which directly burden or obstruct interstate or foreign commerce, or its free flow, are within the reach of the congressional power. Acts having that effect are not rendered immune because they grow out of labor disputes. . . . It is the effect upon commerce, not the source of the injury, which is the criterion. . . . Whether or not particular action does affect commerce in such a close and intimate fashion as to be subject to federal control, and hence to lie within the authority conferred upon the Board, is left by the statute to be determined as individual cases arise. We are thus to inquire whether in the instant case the constitutional boundary has been passed. . . .

Third. The application of the Act to employees engaged in production.—The principle involved.—Respondent says that whatever may be said of employees engaged in interstate commerce, the industrial relations and activities in the manufacturing department of respondent's enterprise are not subject to federal regulation. The argument rests upon the proposition that manufacturing in itself is not commerce. *Kidd* v. *Pearson* [1888] . . . *Schechter Corp.* v. *United States* [1935] . . . *Carter* v. *Carter Coal Co.* [1936]. . . .

The Government distinguishes these cases. The various parts of respondent's enterprise are described as interdependent and as thus involving "a great movement of iron ore, coal and limestone along well-defined paths to the steel mills, thence through them, and thence in the form of steel products into the consuming centers of the country—a definite and well-understood course of business." It is urged that these activities constitute a "stream" or "flow" of commerce, of which the Aliquippa manufacturing plant is the focal point, and that industrial strife at that point would cripple the entire movement. Reference is made to our decision sustaining the Packers and Stockyards Act. *Stafford* v. *Wallace* [1922]. . . . The Court found that the stockyards were but a "throat" through which the current of commerce flowed and the transactions which there occurred could not be separated from that movement. Hence the sales at the stockyards were not regarded as merely local transactions, for while they created "a local change of title" they did not "stop the flow," but merely changed the private interests in the subject of the current. . . . Applying the doctrine of *Stafford* v. *Wallace*, . . . the Court sustained the Grain Futures Act of 1922 with respect to transactions on the Chicago Board of Trade, although these transactions were "not in and of themselves interstate commerce." Congress had found that they had become "a constantly recurring burden and obstruction to that commerce." *Chicago Board of Trade* v. *Olsen* [1923]. . . .

Respondent contends that the instant case presents material distinctions. Respondent says that the Aliquippa plant is extensive in size and represents a large investment in buildings, machinery and equipment. The raw materials which are brought to the plant are delayed for long periods and, after being subjected to manufacturing processes, "are changed substantially as to character, utility and value." The finished products which emerge "are to a large extent manufactured without reference to pre-existing orders and contracts and are entirely different from the raw materials which enter at the other end." Hence respondent argues that "If importation and exportation in interstate commerce do not singly transfer purely local activities into the field of congressional regulation, it should follow that their combination would not alter the local situation." . . .

We do not find it necessary to determine whether these features of defendant's business dispose of the asserted analogy to the "stream of commerce" cases. The instances in which that metaphor has been used are but particular, and not exclusive, illustrations of the protective power which the Government invokes in support of the present Act. The congressional authority to protect interstate commerce from burdens and obstructions is not limited to transactions which can be deemed to be an essential part of a "flow" of interstate or foreign commerce. Burdens and obstructions may be due to injurious action springing from other sources. The fundamental principle is that the power to regulate commerce is the power to enact "all appropriate legislation" for "its protection and advancement" . . . to adopt measures "to promote its growth and insure its safety" . . . "to foster, protect, control and restrain." . . . That power is plenary and may be exerted to protect interstate commerce "no matter what the source of the dangers which threaten it." . . . Although activities may be intrastate in character when separately considered, if they have such a close and substantial relation to interstate commerce that their control is essential or appropriate to pro-

tect that commerce from burdens and obstructions, Congress cannot be denied the power to exercise that control. . . . Undoubtedly the scope of this power must be considered in the light of our dual system of government and may not be extended so as to embrace effects upon interstate commerce so indirect and remote that to embrace them, in view of our complex society, would effectually obliterate the distinction between what is national and what is local and create a completely centralized government. The question is necessarily one of degree. . . .

That intrastate activities, by reason of close and intimate relation to interstate commerce, may fall within federal control is demonstrated in the case of carriers who are engaged in both interstate and intrastate transportation. There federal control has been found essential to secure the freedom of interstate traffic from interference or unjust discrimination and to promote the efficiency of the interstate service. *Shreveport Case* [1914]. . . . It is manifest that intrastate rates deal *primarily* with local activity. But in rate-making they bear such a close relation to interstate rates that effective control of the one must embrace some control over the other. Under the Transportation Act, 1920, Congress went so far as to authorize the Interstate Commerce Commission to establish a state-wide level of intrastate rates in order to prevent an unjust discrimination against interstate commerce. . . .

The close and intimate effect which brings the subject within the reach of federal power may be due to activities in relation to productive industry although the industry when separately viewed is local. This has been abundantly illustrated in the application of the federal Anti-Trust Act. In the *Standard Oil* [1911] and *American Tobacco* [1911] cases . . . that statute was applied to combinations of employers engaged in productive industry.

Upon the same principle, the Anti-

Trust Act has been applied to the conduct of employees engaged in production. *Loewe v. Lawlor* [1908]. . . .

It is thus apparent that the fact that the employees here concerned were engaged in production is not determinative. The question remains as to the effect upon interstate commerce of the labor practice involved. In the *Schechter* case . . . we found that the effect there was so remote as to be beyond the federal power. To find "immediacy or directness" there was to find it "almost everywhere," a result inconsistent with the maintenance of our federal system. In the *Carter* case . . . the Court was of the opinion that the provisions of the statute relating to production were invalid upon several grounds,—that there was improper delegation of legislative power, and that the requirements not only went beyond any sustainable measure of protection of interstate commerce but were also inconsistent with due process. These cases were not controlling here.

Fourth. Effects of the unfair labor practice in respondent's enterprise.—Giving full weight to respondent's contention with respect to a break in the complete continuity of the "stream of commerce" by reason of respondent's manufacturing operations, the fact remains that the stoppage of those operations by industrial strife would have a most serious effect upon interstate commerce. In view of respondent's far-flung activities, it is idle to say that the effect would be indirect or remote. It is obvious that it would be immediate and might be catastrophic. We are asked to shut our eyes to the plainest facts of our national life and to deal with the question of direct and indirect effects in an intellectual vacuum. Because there may be but indirect and remote effects upon interstate commerce in connection with a host of local enterprises throughout the country, it does not follow that other industrial activities do not have such a close and intimate relation to interstate commerce as to

make the presence of industrial strife a matter of the most urgent national concern. When industries organize themselves on a national scale, making their relation to interstate commerce the dominant factor in their activities, how can it be maintained that their industrial labor relations constitute a forbidden field into which Congress may not enter when it is necessary to protect interstate commerce from the paralyzing consequences of industrial war? We have often said that interstate commerce itself is a practical conception. It is equally true that interferences with that commerce must be appraised by a judgment that does not ignore actual experience.

Experience has abundantly demonstrated that the recognition of the right of employees to self-organization and to have representatives of their own choosing for the purpose of collective bargaining is often an essential condition of industrial peace. Refusal to confer and negotiate has been one of the most prolific causes of strife. This is such an outstanding fact in the history of labor disturbances that it is a proper subject of judicial notice and requires no citation of instances. The opinion in the case of *Virginian Railway Co. v. System Federation, No. 40* [1937] . . . points out that, in the case of carriers, experience has shown that before the amendment, of 1934, of the Railway Labor Act "when there was no dispute as to the organizations authorized to represent the employees and when there was a willingness of the employer to meet such representative for a discussion of their grievances, amicable adjustment of differences had generally followed and strikes had been avoided." That, on the other hand, "a prolific source of dispute had been the maintenance by the railroad of company unions and the denial by railway management of the authority of representatives chosen by their employees." The opinion in that case also points to the large measure of success of the labor policy embodied in the Railway Labor Act. But with respect to the appropriateness of the recognition of self-organization and representation in the promotion of peace, the question is not essentially different in the case of employees in industries of such a character that interstate commerce is put in jeopardy from the case of employees of transportation companies. And of what avail is it to protect the facility of transportation, if interstate commerce is throttled with respect to the commodities to be transported!

These questions have frequently engaged the attention of Congress and have been the subject of many inquiries. The steel industry is one of the great basic industries of the United States, with ramifying activities affecting interstate commerce at every point. The Government aptly refers to the steel strike of 1919–1920 with its far-reaching consequences. The fact that there appears to have been no major disturbance in that industry in the more recent period did not dispose of the possibilities of future and like dangers to interstate commerce which Congress was entitled to foresee and to exercise its protective power to forestall. It is not necessary again to detail the facts as to respondent's enterprise. Instead of being beyond the pale, we think that it presents in a most striking way the close and intimate relation which a manufacturing industry may have to interstate commerce and we have no doubt that Congress had constitutional authority to safeguard the right of respondent's employees to self-organization and freedom in the choice of representatives for collective bargaining.

Fifth. The means which the Act employs.— Questions under the due process clause and other constitutional restrictions.—Respondent asserts its right to conduct its business in an orderly manner without being subjected to arbitrary restraints. What we have said points to the fallacy in the argument. Employees have their correlative right to organize for the purpose of securing the redress of grievances and to promote agreements with employers relating to rates of pay and conditions of work.... Restraint for the purpose of preventing an unjust interference with that right cannot be considered arbitrary or capricious....

The Act does not compel agreements between employers and employees. It does not compel any agreement whatever. It does not prevent the employer "from refusing to make a collective contract and hiring individuals on whatever terms" the employer "may by unilateral action determine." The Act expressly provides in § 9 (a) that any individual employee or a group of employees shall have the right at any time to present grievances to their employer. The theory of the Act is that free opportunity for negotiation with accredited representatives of employees is likely to promote industrial peace and may bring about the adjustments and agreements which the Act in itself does not attempt to compel. ... The Act does not interfere with the normal exercise of the right of the employer to select its employees or to discharge them. The employer may not, under cover of that right, intimidate or coerce its employees with respect to their self-organization and representation, and, on the other hand, the Board is not entitled to make its authority a pretext for interference with the right of discharge when that right is exercised for other reasons than such intimidation and coercion. The true purpose is the subject of investigation with full opportunity to show the facts. It would seem that when employers freely recognize the right of their employees to their own organizations and their unrestricted right of representation there will be much less occasion for controversy in respect to the free and appropriate exercise of the right of selection and discharge.

The Act has been criticised as one-sided in its application; that it subjects the employer to supervision and restraint and leaves untouched the abuses for which employees may be responsible; that it fails to provide a more comprehensive plan,—with better assurances of fairness to both sides and with increased chances of success in bringing about, if not compelling, equitable solutions of industrial disputes affecting interstate commerce. But we are dealing with the power of Congress, not with a particular policy or with the extent to which policy should go. We have frequently said that the legislative authority, exerted within its proper field, need not embrace all the evils within its reach. The Constitution does not forbid "cautious advance, step by step," in dealing with the evils which are exhibited in activities within the range of legislative power. . . . The question in such cases is whether the legislature, in what it does prescribe, has gone beyond constitutional limits. . . .

Our conclusion is that the order of the Board was within its competency and that the Act is valid as here applied. . . .

Reversed.

MR. JUSTICE McREYNOLDS delivered the following dissenting opinion in the cases preceding:

Mr. Justice Van Devanter, Mr. Justice Sutherland, Mr. Justice Butler, and I are unable to agree with the decisions just announced. . . .

The Court, as we think, departs from well-established principles followed in *Schechter Corp.* v. *United States,* . . . and *Carter* v. *Carter Coal Co.* . . . Upon the authority of those decisions . . . the power of Congress under the commerce clause does not extend to relations between employers and their employees engaged in manufacture, and therefore the Act conferred upon the National Labor Relations Board no authority in respect of matters covered by the questioned orders. . . . No decision or judicial opinion to the contrary has been cited, and we find none. Every consideration brought forward to uphold the Act before us was applicable to support the Acts held unconstitutional in causes decided within two years. And the lower courts rightly deemed them controlling.

By its terms the Labor Act extends to employers—large and small—unless excluded by definition, and declares that if one of these interferes with, restrains, or coerces any employee regarding his labor affiliations, etc., this shall be regarded as unfair labor practice. . . .

The three respondents happen to be manufacturing concerns—one large, two relatively small. The Act is now applied to each upon grounds common to all. Obviously what is determined as to these concerns may gravely affect a multitude of employers who engage in a great variety of private enterprises—mercantile, manufacturing, publishing, stock-raising, mining, etc. It puts into the hands of a Board power of control over purely local industry beyond anything heretofore deemed permissible.

Any effect on interstate commerce by the discharge of employees shown here, would be indirect and remote in the highest degree, as consideration of the facts will show. In No. 419 ten men out of ten thousand were discharged; in the other cases only a few. The immediate effect in the factory may be to create discontent among all those employed and a strike may follow, which, in turn, may result in reducing production, which ultimately may reduce the volume of goods moving in interstate commerce. By this chain of indirect and progressively remote events we finally reach the evil with which it is said the legislation under consideration undertakes to deal. A more remote and indirect interference with interstate commerce or a more definite invasion of the powers reserved to the states is difficult, if not impossible, to imagine.

The Constitution still recognizes the existence of states with indestructible powers; the Tenth Amendment was supposed to put them beyond controversy. . . .

How did Hughes apply the "stream of commerce" doctrine to the *Jones and Laughlin* case? What did the Chief Justice have to say about the importance of the distinction between direct and indirect effects upon commerce? Under what circumstances does Hughes suggest that considerations of federalism limit the commerce power? Are you satisfied with the distinctions made in the opinion between the *Schechter* and *Carter* cases and the present decision? Does the *Jones and Laughlin* decision in any way overrule the *Schechter* and *Carter* decisions? Did the Hughes decision in the *Jones and Laughlin* case return to the empirical test of Marshall in *Gibbons* v. *Ogden* to determine the scope of the commerce power?

The *Jones and Laughlin* decision seemed to open the way for a vast expansion of national regulatory power under the commerce clause. Under the empirical test announced by the Court, any activities having a "most serious effect upon interstate commerce" could be regulated by Congress. The "substantial" economic effect test of the *Shreveport Case* was restored. Under the test, manufacturing and production facilities could be regulated, even if of a purely local nature, provided there was evidence that the activities regulated had a substantial economic effect upon interstate commerce.

The *Jones and Laughlin* decision did not stop challenges to New Deal legislation based upon the commerce clause. In *United States* v. *Darby* (1941) the Fair Labor Standards Act of 1938 was challenged. The act prohibited the shipment in interstate commerce of goods manufactured by employees whose wages and hours did not conform to the standards of the act. The prohibitory device of the statute was similar to that approved by the Court in *Champion* v. *Ames* in 1903.[22] Legislation similar to the Fair Labor Standards Act had been declared unconstitutional in *Hammer* v. *Dagenhart* in 1918.[23]

The stated purpose of the Fair Labor Standards Act was not only to regulate the conditions of labor but through such regulation to remove burdens on commerce and guarantee the free flow of goods. Substandard labor conditions, the act declared, "burdens commerce and the free flow of goods in commerce; constitutes an unfair method of competition in commerce; leads to labor disputes burdening and obstructing commerce; and interferes with the orderly and fair marketing of goods in commerce."

The government sought an indictment against the Darby Lumber Company for violating the wage and hour provisions of the act. The company demurred to the indictment, which meant that it admitted the facts of the case but challenged the government's right to proceed. The district court sustained the demurrer and quashed the indictment. The government ap-

[22]See pp. 321–325.
[24]See pp. 327–332.

pealed directly to the Supreme Court under a provision of the judicial code permitting such appeals where the district court had invalidated a federal statute.

The appellee (Darby) contended that the act "is an unconstitutional attempt to regulate conditions in production of goods and commodities, and it cannot be sustained as a regulation of interstate commerce. . . ." The Darby Company's attorneys argued that the real purpose of the statute was to regulate labor conditions, and not commercial activity, and therefore the statute could not be sustained under the commerce power. Manufacture and production, they said, are not within the regulatory authority of Congress. The government responded that the purpose of the statute was explicitly to regulate commerce, but "even if the act were concerned simply with humanitarian ends, it would nonetheless be within the commerce power."[24]

United States v. *Darby*

312 U.S. 100; 61 S. Ct. 451; 85 L. Ed. 609 (1941)

MR. JUSTICE STONE delivered the opinion of the Court:

The two principal questions raised by the record in this case are, *first,* whether Congress has constitutional power to prohibit the shipment in interstate commerce of lumber manufactured by employees whose wages are less than a prescribed minimum or whose weekly hours of labor at that wage are greater than a prescribed maximum, and, *second,* whether it has the power to prohibit the employment of workmen in the production of goods "for interstate commerce" at other than prescribed wages and hours. A subsidiary question is whether in connection with such prohibitions Congress can require the employer subject to them to keep records showing the hours worked each day and week by each of his employees including those engaged "in the production and manufacture of goods to-wit, lumber, for 'interstate commerce.' " . . .

The Fair Labor Standards Act set up a comprehensive legislative scheme for preventing the shipment in interstate commerce of certain products and commodities produced in the United States under labor conditions as respects wages and hours which fail to conform to standards set up by the Act. Its purpose, as we judicially know from the declaration of policy in § 2 (a) of the Act, and the reports of Congressional committees proposing the legislation . . . is to exclude from interstate commerce goods produced for the commerce and to prevent their production for interstate commerce, under conditions detrimental to the maintenance of the minimum standards of living necessary for health and general well-being; and to prevent the use of interstate commerce as the means of competition in the distribution of goods so produced, and as the means of spreading and perpetuating such substandard labor conditions among the workers of the several states. The Act also sets up an administrative procedure whereby those standards may from time to time be modified generally as to industries subject to the Act or within an industry in accordance with

[24]Ibid., pp. 541–542.

specified standards, by an administrator acting in collaboration with "Industry Committees" appointed by him. . . .

The indictment charges that appellee is engaged, in the State of Georgia, in the business of acquiring raw materials, which he manufactures into finished lumber with the intent, when manufactured, to ship it in interstate commerce to customers outside the state, and that he does in fact so ship a large part of the lumber so produced. . . .

The prohibition of shipment of the proscribed goods in interstate commerce. Section 15 (a) (1) prohibits, and the indictment charges, the shipment in interstate commerce, of goods produced for interstate commerce by employees whose wages and hours of employment do not conform to the requirements of the Act. Since this section is not violated unless the commodity shipped has been produced under labor conditions prohibited by § 6 and § 7, the only question arising under the commerce clause with respect to such shipments is whether Congress has the constitutional power to prohibit them.

While manufacture is not of itself interstate commerce, the shipment of manufactured goods interstate is such commerce and the prohibition of such shipment by Congress is indubitably a regulation of the commerce. The power to regulate commerce is the power "to prescribe the rule by which commerce is governed." *Gibbons* v. *Ogden.* It extends not only to those regulations which aid, foster and protect the commerce, but embraces those which prohibit it. . . . It is conceded that the power of Congress to prohibit transportation in interstate commerce includes noxious articles, . . . stolen articles, . . . kidnapped persons, . . . and articles such as intoxicating liquor or convict made goods, traffic in which is forbidden or restricted by the laws of the state of destination. . . .

But it is said that the present prohibition falls within the scope of none of these categories; that while the prohibition is nominally a regulation of the commerce its motive or purpose is regulation of wages and hours of persons engaged in manufacture, the control of which has been reserved to the states and upon which Georgia and some of the states of destination have placed no restriction; that the effect of the present statute is not to exclude the proscribed articles from interstate commerce in aid of state regulation as in *Kentucky Whip & Collar Co.* v. *Illinois Central R. Co.* [1937] . . . but instead, under the guise of a regulation of interstate commerce, it undertakes to regulate wages and hours within the state contrary to the policy of the state which has elected to leave them unregulated.

The power of Congress over interstate commerce "is complete in itself, may be exercised to its utmost extent, and acknowledges no limitations other than are prescribed in the Constitution." *Gibbons* v. *Ogden.* . . . That power can neither be enlarged nor diminished by the exercise or non-exercise of state power. . . . Congress, following its own conception of public policy concerning the restrictions which may appropriately be imposed on interstate commerce, is free to exclude from the commerce articles whose use in the states for which they are destined it may conceive to be injurious to the public health, morals or welfare, even though the state has not sought to regulate their use. . . .

Such regulation is not a forbidden invasion of state power merely because either its motive or its consequence is to restrict the use of articles of commerce within the states of destination; and is not prohibited unless by other Constitutional provisions. It is no objection to the assertion of the power to regulate interstate commerce that its exercise is attended by the same incidents which attend the exercise of the police power of the states. . . .

The motive and purpose of the present regulation are plainly to make effective the Congressional conception of public policy that interstate commerce should not be made the instrument of competition in the distribution of goods produced under substandard labor conditions, which competition is injurious to the commerce and to the states from and to which the commerce flows. The motive and purpose of a regulation of interstate commerce are matters for the legislative judgment upon the exercise of which the Constitution places no restriction and over which the courts are given no control. . . . "The judicial cannot prescribe to the legislative department of the government limitations upon the exercise of its ackknowledged power." *Veazie Bank* v. *Fenno* [1869]. . . . Whatever their motive and purpose, regulations of commerce which do not infringe some constitutional prohibition are within the plenary power conferred on Congress by the Commerce Clause. Subject only to that limitation, presently to be considered, we conclude that the prohibition of the interstate shipment of goods produced under the forbidden substandard labor conditions is within the constitutional authority of Congress.

In the more than a century which has elapsed since the decision of *Gibbons* v. *Ogden,* these principles of constitutional interpretation have been so long and repeatedly recognized by this Court as applicable to the Commerce Clause, that there would be little occasion for repeating them now were it not for the decision of this Court twenty-two years ago in *Hammer* v. *Dagenhart* [1918]. In that case it was held by a bare majority of the Court over the powerful and now classic dissent of Mr. Justice Holmes setting forth the fundamental issues involved, that Con-

gress was without power to exclude the products of child labor from interstate commerce. The reasoning and conclusion of the Court's opinion there cannot be reconciled with the conclusion which we have reached, that the power of Congress under the Commerce Clause is plenary to exclude any article from interstate commerce subject only to the specific prohibitions of the Constitution.

Hammer v. *Dagenhart* has not been followed. The distinction on which the decision was rested that Congressional power to prohibit interstate commerce is limited to articles which in themselves have some harmful or deleterious property—a distinction which was novel when made and unsupported by any provision of the Constitution—has long since been abandoned. . . . The thesis of the opinion that the motive of the prohibition or its effect to control in some measure the use or production within the states of the article thus excluded from the commerce can operate to deprive the regulation of its constitutional authority has long since ceased to have force. . . . And finally we have declared "The authority of the federal government over interstate commerce does not differ in extent or character from that retained by the states over intrastate commerce." *United States* v. *Rock Royal Co-operative* [1939].

The conclusion is inescapable that *Hammer* v. *Dagenhart,* was a departure from the principles which have prevailed in the interpretation of the Commerce Clause both before and since the decision and that such vitality, as a precedent, as it then had has long since been exhausted. It should be and now is overruled.

Validity of the wage and hour requirements. Section 15 (a) (2) and §§ 6 and 7 require employers to conform to the wage and hour provisions with respect to all employees engaged in the production of goods for interstate commerce. As appellee's employees are not alleged to be "engaged in interstate commerce" the validity of the prohibition turns on the question whether the employment, under other than the prescribed labor standards, of employees engaged in the production of goods for interstate commerce is so related to the commerce and so affects it as to be within the reach of the power of Congress to regulate it. . . .

. . . The power of Congress over interstate commerce is not confined to the regulation of commerce among the states. It extends to those activities intrastate which so affect interstate commerce or the exercise of the power of Congress over it as to make regulation of them appropriate means to the attainment of a legitimate end, the exercise of the granted power of Congress to regulate interstate commerce. . . .

A recent example is the National Labor Relations Act for the regulation of employer and employee relations in industries in which strikes, induced by unfair labor practices named in the Act, tend to disturb or obstruct interstate commerce. See *National Labor Relations Board* v. *Jones & Laughlin Steel Corp.* [1937] . . . But long before the adoption of the National Labor Relations Act this Court had many times held that the power of Congress to regulate interstate commerce extends to the regulation through legislative action of activities intrastate which have a substantial effect on the commerce or the exercise of the Congressional power over it.

In such legislation Congress has sometimes left it to the courts to determine whether the intrastate activities have the prohibited effect on the commerce, as in the Sherman Act. It has sometimes left it to an administrative board or agency to determine whether the activities sought to be regulated or prohibited have such effect, as in the case of the Interstate Commerce Act, and the National Labor Relations Act, or whether they come within the statutory definition of the prohibited Act, as in the Federal Trade Commission Act. And sometimes Congress itself has said that a particular activity affects the commerce, as it did in the present Act, the Safety Appliance Act and the Railway Labor Act. In passing on the validity of legislation of the class last mentioned the only function of courts is to determine whether the particular activity regulated or prohibited is within the reach of the federal power. . . .

Congress, having by the present Act adopted the policy of excluding from interstate commerce all goods produced for the commerce which do not conform to the specified labor standards, it may choose the means reasonably adapted to the attainment of the permitted end, even though they involve control of intrastate activities. . . . A familiar like exercise of power is the regulation of intrastate transactions which are so commingled with or related to interstate commerce that all must be regulated if the interstate commerce is to be effectively controlled. *Shreveport Case* [1914]. . . . Similarly Congress may require inspection and preventive treatment of all cattle in a disease infected area in order to prevent shipment in interstate commerce of some of the cattle without the treatment. . . . It may prohibit the removal, at destination, of labels required by the Pure Food & Drugs Act to be affixed to articles transported in interstate commerce. . . . And we have recently held that Congress in the exercise of its power to require inspection and grading of tobacco shipped in interstate commerce may compel such inspection and grading of all tobacco sold at local auction rooms from which a substantial part but not all of the tobacco sold is shipped in interstate commerce. . . .

We think also that § 15 (a) (2), now under consideration, is sustainable independently of § 15 (a) (1), which prohibits shipment or transportation of the proscribed goods. As we have said the evils aimed at by the Act are the spread of substandard labor conditions through the use of the facilities of interstate commerce for competition by the goods so produced with those produced under the prescribed or better labor conditions; and the consequent dislocation of the commerce itself caused by the impairment or destruction of local businesses by competition made effective through interstate commerce. The Act is thus directed at the suppression of a method or kind of competition in interstate commerce which it has in effect condemned as "unfair," as the Clayton Act has condemned other "unfair methods of competition" made effective through interstate commerce. . . .

The Sherman Act and the National Labor Relations Act are familiar examples of the exertion of the commerce power to prohibit or control activities wholly intrastate because of their effect on interstate commerce. . . .

The means adopted by § 15 (a) (2) for the protection of interstate commerce by the suppression of the production of the condemned goods for interstate commerce is so related to the commerce and so affects it as to be within the reach of the commerce power. . . . Congress, to attain its objective in the suppression of nationwide competition in interstate commerce by goods produced under substandard labor conditions, has made no distinction as to the volume or amount of shipments in the commerce or of production for commerce by any particular shipper or producer. It recognized that in present day industry, competition by a small part may affect the whole and that the total effect of the competition of many small producers may be great. . . . The legislation aimed at a whole embraces all its parts. . . .

So far as *Carter* v. *Carter Coal Co.* . . . is inconsistent with this conclusion, its doctrine is limited in principle by the decisions under the Sherman Act and the National Labor Relations Act, which we have cited and which we follow. . . .

Our conclusion is unaffected by the Tenth Amendment which provides: "The powers not delegated to the United States by the Constitution, nor prohibited by it to the States, are reserved to the States respectively, or to the people." The amendment states but a truism that all is retained which has not been surrendered. There is nothing in the history of its adoption to suggest that it was more than declaratory of the relationship between the national and state governments as it had been established by the Constitution before the amendment or that its purpose was other than to allay fears that the new national government might seek to exercise powers not granted, and that the states might not be able to exercise fully their reserved powers. . . .

From the beginning and for many years the amendment has been construed as not depriving the national government of authority to resort to all means for the exercise of a granted power which are appropriate and plainly adapted to the permitted end. . . . Whatever doubts may have arisen of the soundness of that conclusion, they have been put at rest by the decisions under the Sherman Act and National Labor Relations Act which we have cited. . . .

Reversed.

Does the *Darby* decision suggest that there are any limits upon the authority of Congress to prohibit the transportation of goods in interstate commerce? Do considerations of federalism limit the scope of this congressional power? Would Justice Stone have sustained the statute if its stated purpose was to achieve humanitarian ends rather than the regulation of commerce? What test does Stone employ to determine congressional authority over intrastate commerce? Does Stone hold that the intent of Congress is important in determining the scope of its authority to regulate commerce? In what ways does the Court's opinion make reference to congressional intent?

The *Jones and Laughlin* and *Darby* decisions seemed to mark a major changing point in Supreme Court doctrine interpreting the commerce power. While each of these decisions required an empirical test to determine if in fact the activities regulated affected interstate commerce, activities "affecting commerce" were broadly interpreted. The conditions of manufacturing and production were brought within the sweep of the commerce power if the goods produced were destined in any way to reach interstate commerce. The companies involved in the *Jones and Laughlin* and *Darby* cases, particularly in the former, were clearly connected with interstate commerce.

In *Wickard* v. *Filburn* (1942) the Court confronted the question of whether or not Congress could extend its regulatory authority under the commerce power to individual acts that did not by themselves affect interstate commerce. The Agricultural Adjustment Act of 1938 authorized the Secretary of Agriculture to establish a national acreage allotment to be apportioned among the states, resulting in quotas for individual farmers.[25] The act provided for penalties to farmers who produced wheat in excess of their quotas. Filburn, an Ohio farmer, produced wheat in excess of the quota, and the Department of Agriculture imposed a penalty. Filburn refused to pay and successfully sued to enjoin the Secretary of Agriculture from enforcing the penalty against him. The district court did not hold that the act was beyond the commerce power of Congress but declared the Secretary's action illegal on other grounds. Wickard appealed directly to the Supreme Court.[26]

In presenting his case, Filburn argued that he did not produce wheat for sale in interstate commerce. His brief stated that the "wheat on the farm grown for feed, seed and food is still under the control of the farmer and has not yet moved into any channel of trade. It is still private property until the farmer disposes of it in some manner."[27] Filburn claimed that there was not a close and substantial relation between his activities and interstate commerce, which is required if the federal government is to extend regulation to his activities. There has been no shipment of goods in interstate commerce, declared Filburn, and while the decisions of the Court in the *Darby* and *Jones and Laughlin* cases grant a wide scope to the commerce power, they require an empirical finding that the regulated activities are connected with the flow of goods in interstate commerce.

The government granted the fact that the regulated wheat did not flow in interstate commerce. Nevertheless, it contended that under the necessary and proper clause Congress can adopt any reasonable means to execute its enumerated powers. Congress was seeking to control the price of wheat

[25]A two-thirds vote of the wheat farmers was necessary to approve of the national quota.

[26]Under the Judicial Code appeals from three-judge district courts are taken directly to the Supreme Court.

[27]LB, Vol. 39, pp. 832–833.

moving in interstate commerce, and the adoption of a *general* quota system for *all* wheat production was a proper means to this end. "In the present case," stated the government, "there can be no doubt that the method adopted by Congress is reasonably calculated to attain the end of restricting the flow of wheat in interstate commerce and preventing a large surplus from forcing prices down to ruinous levels."[28] Indeed, declared the government, there is no other effective way to control the amount of wheat marketed and its price.

On the basis of the facts of this case, and all of the precedents, especially the *Darby* and *Jones and Laughlin* cases, how would you decide *Wickard* v. *Filburn?*

Wickard v. Filburn

317 U.S. 111; 63 S. Ct. 82; 87 L. Ed. 122 (1942)

Mr. Justice Jackson delivered the opinion of the Court:

It is urged that under the Commerce Clause of the Constitution, Article I, § 8, clause 3, Congress does not possess the power it has in this instance sought to exercise. The question would merit little consideration since our decision in *United States* v. *Darby* [1941] . . . sustaining the federal power to regulate production of goods for commerce, except for the fact that this Act extends federal regulation to production not intended in any part for commerce but wholly for consumption on the farm. The Act includes a definition of "market" and its derivatives, so that as related to wheat, in addition to its conventional meaning, it also means to dispose of "by feeding (in any form) to poultry or livestock which, or the products of which, are sold, bartered, or exchanged, or to be so disposed of." Hence, marketing quotas not only embrace all that may be sold without penalty but also what may be consumed on the premises. Wheat produced on excess acreage is designated as "available for marketing" as so defined, and the penalty is imposed thereon. Penalties do not depend upon whether any part of the wheat, either within or without the quota, is sold or intended to be sold. The sum of this is that the Federal Government fixes a quota including all that the farmer may harvest for sale or for his own farm needs, and declares that wheat produced on excess acreage may neither be disposed of nor used except upon payment of the penalty, or except it is stored as required by the Act or delivered to the Secretary of Agriculture.

Appellee says that this is a regulation of production and consumption of wheat. Such activities are, he urges, beyond the reach of Congressional power under the Commerce Clause, since they are local in character, and their effects upon interstate commerce are at most "indirect." In answer the Government argues that the statute regulates neither production nor consumption, but only marketing; and, in the alternative, that if the Act does go beyond the regulation of marketing it is sustainable as a "necessary and proper" implementation of the power of Congress over interstate commerce.

The Government's concern lest the Act be held to be a regulation of production or consumption, rather than of market-

[28]Ibid., p. 814.

ing, is attributable to a few dicta and decisions of this Court which might be understood to lay it down that activities such as "production," "manufacturing," and "mining" are strictly "local" and, except in special circumstances which are not present here, cannot be regulated under the commerce power because their effects upon interstate commerce are, as matter of law, only "indirect." Even today, when this power has been held to have great latitude, there is no decision of this Court that such activities may be regulated where no part of the product is intended for interstate commerce or intermingled with the subjects thereof. We believe that a review of the course of decision under the Commerce Clause will make plain, however, that questions of the power of Congress are not to be decided by reference to any formula which would give controlling force to nomenclature such as "production" and "indirect" and foreclose consideration of the actual effects of the activity in question upon interstate commerce. . . .

The Court's recognition of the relevance of the economic effects in the application of the Commerce Clause . . . has made the mechanical application of legal formulas no longer feasible. Once an economic measure of the reach of the power granted to Congress in the Commerce Clause is accepted, questions of federal power cannot be decided simply by finding the activity in question to be "production," nor can consideration of its economic effects be foreclosed by calling them "indirect." The present Chief Justice has said in summary of the present state of the law: "The commerce power is not confined in its exercise to the regulation of commerce among the states. It extends to those activities intrastate which so affect interstate commerce, or the exertion of the power of Congress over it, as to make regulation of them appropriate means to the attainment of a legitimate end, the effective execution of the granted

power to regulate interstate commerce. . . . The power of Congress over interstate commerce is plenary and complete in itself, may be exercised to its utmost extent, and acknowledges no limitations other than are prescribed in the Constitution. . . . It follows that no form of state activity can constitutionally thwart the regulatory power granted by the commerce clause to Congress. Hence the reach of that power extends to those intrastate activities which in a substantial way interfere with or obstruct the exercise of the granted power." . . .

Whether the subject of the regulation in question was "production," "consumption," or "marketing" is, therefore, not material for purposes of deciding the question of federal power before us. That an activity is of local character may help in a doubtful case to determine whether Congress intended to reach it. The same consideration might help in determining whether in the absence of Congressional action it would be permissible for the state to exert its power on the subject matter, even though in so doing it to some degree affected interstate commerce. But even if appellee's activity be local and though it may not be regarded as commerce, it may still, whatever its nature, be reached by Congress if it exerts a substantial economic effect on interstate commerce, and this irrespective of whether such effect is what might at some earlier time have been defined as "direct" or "indirect." . . .

The effect of consumption of home-grown wheat on interstate commerce is due to the fact that it constitutes the most variable factor in the disappearance of wheat crop. Consumption on the farm where grown appears to vary in an amount greater than 20 per cent of average production. The total amount of wheat consumed as food varies but relatively little, and use as seed is relatively constant. . . .

It is well established by decisions of this Court that the power to regulate commerce includes the power to regulate the prices at which commodities in that commerce are dealt in and practices affecting such prices. One of the primary purposes of the Act in question was to increase the market price of wheat, and to that end to limit the volume thereof that could affect the market. It can hardly be denied that a factor of such volume and variability as home-consumed wheat would have a substantial influence on price and market conditions. This may arise because being in marketable condition such wheat overhangs the market and, if induced by rising prices, tends to flow into the market and check price increases. But if we assume that it is never marketed, it supplies a need of the man who grew it which would otherwise be reflected by purchases in the open market. Home-grown wheat in this sense competes with wheat in commerce. The stimulation of commerce is a use of the regulatory function quite as definitely as prohibitions or restrictions thereon. This record leaves us in no doubt that Congress may properly have considered that wheat consumed on the farm where grown, if wholly outside the scheme of regulation, would have a substantial effect in defeating and obstructing its purpose to stimulate trade therein at increased prices.

It is said, however, that this Act, forcing some farmers into the market to buy what they could provide for themselves is an unfair promotion of the markets and prices of specializing wheat growers. It is of the essence of regulation that it lays a restraining hand on the self-interest of the regulated and that advantages from the regulation commonly fall to others. The conflicts of economic interest between the regulated and those who advantage by it are wisely left under our system to resolution by the Congress under its more flexible and responsible legislative process. Such conflicts rarely lend themselves to judicial determination. And with the wisdom, workability, or fairness, of the plan of regulation we have nothing to do.

Reversed.

Justice Jackson uses the "substantial economic effect" doctrine in upholding the statute. How does he show, in this case, that the regulated activity has a "substantial economic effect" on interstate commerce? Do the *Darby* and *Jones and Laughlin* opinions support the conclusions of the Court in the *Wickard* case? Does Jackson agree with the position of the government that the establishment of general production quotas for all wheat farmers is the only effective means for accomplishing the purposes of the statute?

THE USE OF THE COMMERCE POWER TO PROTECT CIVIL RIGHTS

The commerce power has not only been used to regulate commercial activity and to prohibit the transportation of "harmful" items and goods in interstate commerce, but also to protect individuals against discrimination. Title II of the Civil Rights Act of 1964 prohibited discrimination in public accommodations and provided that all persons had the right to "the full and equal enjoyment" of "any place of public accommodation."[29] In a preface to the listing of the establishments covered, the act stated that "each of the follow-

[29]78 Stat. 241, Sec. 201 (1964).

ing establishments which serves the public is a place of public accommodation in the meaning of this title if its operations affect commerce, or if discrimination or segregation by it is supported by state action."[30] The act then lists the covered establishments, including inns, hotels, motels, restaurants, and motion picture houses and theaters. The law declared that the "operations of an establishment affect commerce . . . if . . . it serves or offers to serve interstate travelers or a substantial portion of the food which it serves, or gasoline or other products which it sells, has moved in commerce; . . . it customarily presents films, performances, athletic teams, exhibitions, or other sources of entertainment which move in commerce."[31] The statute further provided that any establishment operating within the premises of an establishment whose operations affected or were in interstate commerce was covered by the act. Commerce was defined as "travel, trade, traffic, commerce, transportation, or communication among the several states, or between the District of Columbia and any state, or between any foreign country or any territory or possession and any state or the District of Columbia, or between points in the same state but through any other state or the District of Columbia or a foreign country."

By using its authority under the commerce power in addition to the Fourteenth Amendment as a basis for the public accommodations section, the number of covered establishments was greatly expanded by Congress. But could such a regulation of public accommodations be based upon the commerce power? The purpose of the act was not to regulate commercial activity, nor did it use the prohibitory device to close the channels of interstate commerce to the transportation of goods.

The law was immediately challenged after its passage in 1964 in *Heart of Atlanta Motel* v. *United States*. The plaintiff contended that the Civil Rights Act of 1964 "seeks to extend the power of Congress to regulate interstate commerce. We submit that all motels are not part of interstate commerce and do not affect interstate commerce. . . ."[32] The plaintiff continued,

> . . . In adopting the Civil Rights Act of 1964 Congress has simply said that commerce between the states includes the movement of people, and that since people use motels for sleeping purposes, all motels are therefore engaged in interstate commerce. But passing a law and stating that green is red does not necessarily make green red. The Civil Rights Act of 1964 can find no source of authority in the Constitution. . . .
>
> The theory advanced in the trial court by the government . . . was that Congress in passing the Civil Rights Act of 1964 was simply exercising its full power under the commerce clause. If that is the theory of our government now, then Congress can do no wrong and can legislate on any and all matters affecting people on the grounds that they are part of interstate commerce. . . . The next act of Congress . . . would include your home—and then we shall have arrived at the full and complete socialistic state that framers of the Constitution despised, dreaded and detested. . . .[33]

[30]Ibid.
[31]Ibid.
[32]LB, Vol. 60, p. 319.
[33]Ibid., pp. 326–327, 330.

The argument of the plaintiff was essentially that "persons and people are not part of trade or commerce. Persons and people are not the objects, the means or the end of trade or commerce. People conduct commerce and engage in trade, but people are not part of commerce and trade."[34]

Solicitor General Archibald Cox led the government team supporting the use of the commerce clause to sustain Title II. "In arguing that the commerce power is broad enough to sustain both the general plan of Title II and also its specific application to the petitioner," stated Cox, "we invoke no novel constitutional doctrine and seek no extension of existing principles."[35] The government asserted that the "factual connection between racial discrimination and interstate commerce . . . adopted by Congress for fostering and promoting interstate commerce is reasonably adapted to that objective. Appellant has no 'right' contrary to its contention, to select its guests as it sees fit, free from governmental regulation."

The government had successfully sought an injunction from a three-judge district court against the refusal of the Heart of Atlanta Motel to accept black lodgers.

Heart of Atlanta Motel, Inc. v. United States

379 U.S. 241; 85 S. Ct. 348; 13 L. Ed. 2d 258 (1964)

MR. JUSTICE CLARK delivered the opinion of the Court:

This is a declaratory judgment action . . . attacking the constitutionality of Title II of the Civil Rights Act of 1964. . . . Appellees counterclaimed for enforcement under § 206 (a) of the Act and asked for a three-judge district court under § 206 (b). A three-judge court, . . . sustained the validity of the Act and issued a permanent injunction on appellees' counterclaim restraining appellant from continuing to violate the Act. . . . We affirm the judgment.

1. The Factual Background and Contentions of the Parties.

The case comes here on admissions and stipulated facts. Appellant owns and operates the Heart of Atlanta Motel which has 216 rooms available to transient guests. The motel is located on Courtland Street, two blocks from downtown Peachtree Street. It is readily accessible to interstate highways 75 and 85 and state highways 23 and 41. Appellant solicits patronage from outside the State of Georgia through various national advertising media, including magazines of national circulation; it maintains over 50 billboards and highway signs within the State, soliciting patronage for the motel; it accepts convention trade from outside Georgia and approximately 75% of its registered guests are from out of State. Prior to passage of the Act the motel had followed a practice of refusing to rent rooms to Negroes, and it alleged that it intended to continue to do so. In an effort to perpetuate that policy this suit was filed.

The appellant contends that Congress in passing this Act exceeded its power to regulate commerce under Art. I, § 8, cl. 3, of the Constitution of the United States; that the Act violates the Fifth Amendment because appellant is deprived of the

[34]Ibid., p. 362.
[35]Ibid., p. 371.

right to choose its customers and operate its business as it wishes, resulting in a taking of its liberty and property without due process of law and a taking of its property without just compensation; and, finally, that by requiring appellant to rent available rooms to Negroes against its will, Congress is subjecting it to involuntary servitude in contravention of the Thirteenth Amendment. . . .

2. *The History of the Act.*

. . . The Act as finally adopted was most comprehensive, undertaking to prevent through peaceful and voluntary settlement discrimination in voting, as well as in places of accommodation and public facilities, federally secured programs and in employment. Since Title II is the only portion under attack here, we confine our consideration to those public accommodation provisions.

3. *Title II of the Act.*

This Title is divided into seven sections beginning with § 201 (a) which provides that:

All persons shall be entitled to the full and equal enjoyment of the goods, services, facilities, privileges, advantages, and accommodations of any place of public accommodation, as defined in this section, without discrimination or segregation on the ground of race, color, religion, or national origin.

There are listed in § 201 (b) four classes of business establishments, each of which "serves the public" and "is a place of public accommodation" within the meaning of § 201 (a) "if its operations affect commerce, or if discrimination or segregation by it is supported by State action." The covered establishments are:

(1) any inn, hotel, motel, or other establishment which provides lodging to transient guests, other than an establishment located within a building which contains not more than five rooms for rent or hire and which is actually occupied by the proprietor of such establishment as his residence;

(2) any restaurant, cafeteria . . . [not here involved];
(3) any motion picture house . . . [not here involved];
(4) any establishment . . . which is physically located within the premises of any establishment otherwise covered by this subsection, or . . . within the premises of which is physically located any such covered establishment . . . [not here involved].

Section 201 (c) defines the phrase "affect commerce" as applied to the above establishments. It first declares that "any inn, hotel, motel, or other establishment which provides lodging to transient guests" affects commerce *per se.* . . .

Finally, § 203 prohibits the withholding or denial, etc., of any right or privilege secured by § 201 . . . or the intimidation, threatening or coercion of any person with the purpose of interfering with any such right or the punishing, etc., of any person for exercising or attempting to exercise any such right.

The remaining sections of the Title are remedial ones for violations of any of the previous sections. Remedies are limited to civil actions for preventive relief. The Attorney General may bring suit where he has "reasonable cause to believe that any person or group of persons is engaged in a pattern or practice of resistance to the full enjoyment of any of the rights secured by this title, and that the pattern or practice is of such a nature and is intended to deny the full exercise of the rights herein described. . . ."

4. *Application of Title II to Heart of Atlanta Motel.*

It is admitted that the operation of the motel brings it within the provisions of § 201 (a) of the Act and that appellant refused to provide lodging for transient Negroes because of their race or color and that it intends to continue that policy unless restrained.

The sole question posed is, therefore, the constitutionality of the Civil Rights

Act of 1964 as applied to these facts. The legislative history of the Act indicates that Congress based the Act on § 5 and the Equal Protection Clause of the Fourteenth Amendment as well as its power to regulate interstate commerce under Art. I, § 8, cl. 3, of the Constitution.

The Senate Commerce Committee made it quite clear that the fundamental object of Title II was to vindicate "the deprivation of personal dignity that surely accompanies denials of equal access to public establishments." At the same time, however, it noted that such an objective has been and could be readily achieved "by congressional action based on the commerce power of the Constitution." . . . Our study of the legislative record, made in the light of prior cases, has brought us to the conclusion that Congress possessed ample power in this regard, and we have therefore not considered the other grounds relied upon. This is not to say that the remaining authority upon which it acted was not adequate, a question upon which we do not pass, but merely that since the commerce power is sufficient for our decision here we have considered it alone. . . .

5. *The Civil Rights Cases, 109 U.S. 3 (1883), and their Application.*

In light of our ground for decision, it might be well at the outset to discuss the *Civil Rights Cases,* . . . which declared provisions of the Civil Rights Act of 1875 unconstitutional. . . . We think that decision inapposite, and without precedential value in determining the constitutionality of the present Act. Unlike Title II of the present legislation, the 1875 Act broadly proscribed discrimination in "inns, public conveyances on land or water, theaters, and other places of public amusement," without limiting the categories of affected businesses to those impinging upon interstate commerce. In contrast, the applicability of Title II is carefully limited to enterprises having a direct and substantial relation to the interstate flow of goods and people, except where state action is involved. Further, the fact that certain kinds of businesses may not in 1875 have been sufficiently involved in interstate commerce to warrant bringing them within the ambit of the commerce power is not necessarily dispositive of the same question today. Our populace had not reached its present mobility, nor were facilities, goods and services circulating as readily in interstate commerce as they are today. Although the principles which we apply today are those first formulated by Chief Justice Marshall in *Gibbons* v. *Ogden* . . . , the conditions of transportation and commerce have changed dramatically, and we must apply those principles to the present state of commerce. The sheer increase in volume of interstate traffic alone would give discriminatory practices which inhibit travel a far larger impact upon the Nation's commerce than such practices had on the economy of another day. . . .

6. *The Basis of Congressional Action.*

While the Act as adopted carried no congressional findings the record of its passage through each house is replete with evidence of the burdens that discrimination by race or color places upon interstate commerce. . . . This testimony included the fact that our people have become increasingly mobile with millions of people of all races traveling from State to State; that Negroes in particular have been the subject of discrimination in transient accommodations, having to travel great distances to secure the same; that often they have been unable to obtain accommodations and have had to call upon friends to put them up overnight, . . . and that these conditions had become so acute as to require the listing of available lodging for Negroes in a special guidebook which was itself "dramatic testimony to the difficulties" Negroes encounter in travel. . . . These exclusionary practices were found to be nationwide, the Under Secretary of Commerce testifying that there is "no question that the discrimination in the North still exists to a large degree" and in the West and Midwest as well. . . . This testimony indicated a qualitative as well as quantitative effect on interstate travel by Negroes. The former was the obvious impairment of the Negro traveler's pleasure and convenience that resulted when he continually was uncertain of finding lodging. As for the latter, there was evidence that this uncertainty stemming from racial discrimination had the effect of discouraging travel on the part of a substantial portion of the Negro community. . . . This was the conclusion not only of the Under Secretary of Commerce but also of the Administrator of the Federal Aviation Agency who wrote the Chairman of the Senate Commerce Committee that it was his "belief that air commerce is adversely affected by the denial to a substantial segment of the traveling public of adequate and desegregated public accommodations." . . . We shall not burden this opinion with further details since the voluminous testimony presents overwhelming evidence that discrimination by hotels and motels impedes interstate travel.

7. The Power of Congress over Interstate Travel.

The power of Congress to deal with these obstructions depends on the meaning of the Commerce Clause. Its meaning was first enunciated 140 years ago by the great Chief Justice John Marshall in *Gibbons* v. *Ogden*. . . .

. . . In short, the determinative test of the exercise of power by Congress under the Commerce Clause is simply whether the activity sought to be regulated is "commerce which concerns more States than one" and has a real and substantial relation to the national interest. Let us now turn to this facet of the problem.

That the "intercourse" of which the Chief Justice spoke included the move-ment of persons through more States than one was settled as early as 1849, in the *Passenger Cases* [1849] . . . where Mr. Justice McLean stated: "That the transportation of passengers is a part of commerce is not now an open question." Again in 1913 Mr. Justice McKenna, speaking for the Court, said: "Commerce among the States, we have said, consists of intercourse and traffic between their citizens, and includes the transportation of persons and property." *Hoke* v. *United States*. . . . And only four years later in 1917 in *Caminetti* v. *United States* . . . Mr. Justice Day held for the Court:

The transportation of passengers in interstate commerce, it has long been settled, is within the regulatory power of Congress, under the commerce clause of the Constitution, and the authority of Congress to keep the channels of interstate commerce free from immoral and injurious uses has been frequently sustained, and is no longer open to question.

Nor does it make any difference whether the transportation is commercial in character. In *Morgan* v. *Virginia* [1946] . . . Mr. Justice Reed observed as to the modern movement of persons among the States:

The recent changes in transportation brought about by the coming of automobiles [do] not seem of great significance in the problem. People of all races travel today more extensively than in 1878 when this Court first passed upon state regulation of racial segregation in commerce. [It but] emphasizes the soundness of this Court's early conclusion in *Hall* v. *DeCuir* [1878] . . .

The same interest in protecting interstate commerce which led Congress to deal with segregation in interstate carriers and the white-slave traffic has prompted it to extend the exercise of its power to gambling . . . ; to criminal enterprises . . . ; to deceptive practices in the sale of products . . . ; to fraudulent security transactions . . . ; to misbranding of drugs . . . ; to wages and hours . . . ; to members of labor unions . . . ; to crop control . . . ;

to discrimination against shippers . . . ; to the protection of small business from injurious price cutting . . . ; to resale price maintenance . . . ; to professional football . . . ; and to racial discrimination by owners and managers of terminal restaurants. . . .

That Congress was legislating against moral wrongs in many of these areas rendered its enactments no less valid. In framing Title II of this Act Congress was also dealing with what it considered a moral problem. But that fact does not detract from the overwhelming evidence of the disruptive effect that racial discrimination has had on commercial intercourse. It was this burden which empowered Congress to enact appropriate legislation, and, given this basis for the exercise of its power, Congress was not restricted by the fact that the particular obstruction to interstate commerce with which it was dealing was also deemed a moral and social wrong.

It is said that the operation of the motel here is of a purely local character. But, assuming this to be true, "[i]f it is interstate commerce that feels the pinch, it does not matter how local the operation which applies the squeeze." . . . As Chief Justice Stone put it in *United States* v. *Darby:*

The power of Congress over interstate commerce is not confined to the regulation of commerce among the states. It extends to those activities intrastate which so affect interstate commerce or the exercise of the power of Congress over it as to make regulation of them appropriate means to the attainment of a legitimate end, the exercise of the granted power of Congress to regulate interstate commerce. . . .

Thus the power of Congress to promote interstate commerce also includes the power to regulate the local incidents thereof, including local activities in both the States of origin and destination, which might have a substantial and harmful effect upon that commerce. One need only examine the evidence which we have discussed above to see that Congress may—as it has—prohibit racial discrimination by motels serving travelers, however "local" their operations may appear.

Nor does the Act deprive appellant of liberty or property under the Fifth Amendment. The commerce power invoked here by the Congress is a specific and plenary one authorized by the Constitution itself. The only questions are: (1) whether Congress had a rational basis for finding that racial discrimination by motels affected commerce, and (2) if it had such a basis, whether the means it selected to eliminate that evil are reasonable and appropriate. If they are, appellant has no "right" to select its guests as it sees fit, free from governmental regulation.

There is nothing novel about such legislation. Thirty-two States now have it on their books either by statute or executive order and many cities provide such regulation. Some of these Acts go back fourscore years. It has been repeatedly held by this Court that such laws do not violate the Due Process Clause of the Fourteenth Amendment. . . .

. . . As a result the constitutionality of such state statutes stands unquestioned. "The authority of the Federal Government over interstate commerce does not differ . . . in extent or character from that retained by the states over intrastate commerce." . . .

It is doubtful if in the long run appellant will suffer economic loss as a result of the Act. Experience is to the contrary where discrimination is completely obliterated as to all public accommodations. But whether this be true or not is of no consequence since this Court has specifically held that the fact that a "member of the class which is regulated may suffer economic losses not shared by others . . . has never been a barrier" to such legislation. . . . Likewise in a long line of cases this Court has rejected the claim that the prohibition of racial discrimination in public accommodations interferes with personal liberty. . . .

We find no merit in the remainder of appellant's contentions, including that of "involuntary servitude." . . .

We, therefore, conclude that the action of the Congress in the adoption of the Act as applied here to a motel which concededly serves interstate travelers is within the power granted it by the Commerce Clause of the Constitution, as interpreted by this Court for 140 years. It may be argued that Congress would have pursued other methods to eliminate the obstructions it found in interstate commerce caused by racial discrimination. But this is a matter of policy that rests entirely with the Congress not with the courts. How obstructions in commerce may be removed—what means are to be employed—is within the sound and exclusive discretion of the Congress. It is subject only to one caveat—that the means chosen by it must be reasonably adapted to the end permitted by the Constitution. We cannot say that its choice here was not so adapted. The Constitution requires no more.

Affirmed.

MR. JUSTICE BLACK, concurring:
. . . Long ago this Court, speaking through Mr. Chief Justice Marshall, said:

Let the end be legitimate, let it be within the scope of the Constitution, and all means which are appropriate, which are plainly adapted to that end, which are not prohibited, but consist with the letter and spirit of the Constitution, are constitutional. *McCulloch* v. *Maryland* . . .

By this standard Congress acted within its power here. In view of the Commerce Clause it is not possible to deny that the aim of protecting interstate commerce from undue burdens is a legitimate end. In view of the Thirteenth, Fourteenth and Fifteenth Amendments, it is not possible to deny that the aim of protecting Negroes from discrimination is also a le-

gitimate end. The means adopted to achieve these ends are also appropriate, plainly adopted to achieve them and not prohibited by the Constitution but consistent with both its letter and spirit. . . .

MR. JUSTICE DOUGLAS, concurring:
Though I join the Court's opinions, I am somewhat reluctant here, as I was in *Edwards* v. *California* [1941] . . . to rest solely on the Commerce Clause. My reluctance is not due to any conviction that Congress lacks power to regulate commerce in the interests of human rights. It is rather my belief that the right of people to be free of state action that discriminates against them because of race, like the "right of persons to move freely from State to State" . . . "occupies a more protected position in our constitutional system than does the movement of cattle, fruit, steel and coal across state lines." Moreover, when we come to the problem of abatement in *Hamm* v. *City of Rock Hill* [1964] . . . the result reached by the Court is for me much more obvious as a protective measure under the Fourteenth Amendment than under the Commerce Clause. For the former deals with the constitutional status of the individual not with the impact on commerce of local activities or vice versa.

A decision based on the Fourteenth Amendment would have a more settling effect, making unnecessary litigation over whether a particular restaurant or inn is within the commerce definitions of the Act or whether a particular customer is an interstate traveler. Under my construction, the Act would apply to all customers in all the enumerated places of public accommodation. And that construction would put an end to all obstructionist strategies and finally close one door on a bitter chapter in American history. . . .

MR. JUSTICE GOLDBERG, concurring:
I join in the opinions and judgments of the Court, since I agree "that the action of

the Congress in the adoption of the Act as applied here ... is within the power granted it by the Commerce Clause of the Constitution, as interpreted by this Court for 140 years" ...

In my concurring opinion in *Bell* v. *Maryland* [1964], ... I expressed my conviction that § 1 of the Fourteenth Amendment guarantees to all Americans the constitutional right "to be treated as equal members of the community with respect to public accommodations," and that "Congress [has] authority under § 5 of the Fourteenth Amendment, or under the Commerce Clause, Art. I, § 8, to implement the rights protected by § 1 of the Fourteenth Amendment. In the give-and-take of the legislative process, Congress can fashion a law drawing the guidelines necessary and appropriate to facilitate practical administration and to distinguish between genuinely public and private accommodations." The challenged Act is just such a law and, in my view, Congress clearly had authority under both § 5 of the Fourteenth Amendment and the Commerce Clause to enact the Civil Rights Act of 1964.

The case of *Katzenbach* v. *McClung* was joined with the *Heart of Atlanta Motel* case. In the *McClung* case a three-judge district court had ruled that the act could not apply to Ollie's Barbeque, which was McClung's restaurant in Birmingham, Alabama. While the restaurant provided a take-out service for blacks, it refused to serve them in its dining room. Katzenbach, the Attorney General, appealed the ruling to the Supreme Court.

Katzenbach v. *McClung*

379 U.S. 294; 85 S. Ct. 377; 13 L. Ed. 2d (1964)

MR. JUSTICE CLARK delivered the opinion of the Court:

This case was argued with *Heart of Atlanta Motel* v. *United States* ... in which we upheld the constitutional validity of Title II of the Civil Rights Act of 1964 against an attack by hotels, motels, and like establishments. This complaint for injunctive relief against appellants attacks the constitutionality of the Act as applied to a restaurant. . . .

2. The Facts.

Ollie's Barbecue is a family-owned restaurant in Birmingham, Alabama, specializing in barbecued meats and homemade pies, with a seating capacity of 220 customers. It is located on a state highway 11 blocks from an interstate one and a somewhat greater distance from railroad and bus stations. The restaurant caters to a family and white-collar trade with a take-out service for Negroes. It employs 36 persons, two thirds of whom are Negroes.

In the 12 months preceding the passage of the Act, the restaurant purchased locally approximately $150,000 worth of food, $69,683 or 46% of which was meat that it bought from a local supplier who had procured it from outside the State. The District Court expressly found that a substantial portion of the food served in the restaurant had moved in interstate commerce. The restaurant has refused to serve Negroes in its dining accommodation since its original opening in 1927, and since July 2, 1964, it has been operating in violation of the Act. The court below concluded that if it were required to serve Negroes it would lose a substantial amount of business.

On the merits, the District Court held

that the Act could not be applied under the Fourteenth Amendment because it was conceded that the State of Alabama was not involved in the refusal of the restaurant to serve Negroes. . . . As to the Commerce Clause, the court found . . . that the clause was also a grant of power "to regulate intrastate activities, but only to the extent that action on its part is necessary or appropriate to the effective execution of its expressly granted power to regulate interstate commerce." There must be, it said, a close and substantial relation between local activities and interstate commerce which requires control of the former in the protection of the latter. The court concluded, however, that the Congress, rather than finding facts sufficient to meet this rule, had legislated a conclusive presumption that a restaurant affects interstate commerce if it serves or offers to serve interstate travelers or if a substantial portion of the food which it serves has moved in commerce. This, the court held, it could not do because there was no demonstrable connection between food purchased in interstate commerce and sold in a restaurant and the conclusion of Congress that discrimination in the restaurant would affect that commerce. . . .

3. The Act As Applied.

Section 201 (a) of Title II commands that all persons shall be entitled to the full and equal enjoyment of the goods and services of any place of public accommodation without discrimination or segregation on the ground of race, color, religion or national origin; and § 201 (b) defines establishments as places of public accommodation if their operations affect commerce or segregation by them is supported by state action. Sections 201 (b) (2) and (c) place any "restaurant . . . principally engaged in selling food for consumption on the premises" under the Act "if . . . it serves or offers to serve interstate travelers or a substantial portion of the food

which it serves . . . has moved in commerce."

Ollie's Barbecue admits that it is covered by these provisions of the Act. The Government makes no contention that the discrimination at the restaurant was supported by the State of Alabama. There is no claim that interstate travelers frequented the restaurant. The sole question, therefore, narrows down to whether Title II, as applied to a restaurant annually receiving about $70,000 worth of food which has moved in commerce, is a valid exercise of the power of Congress. The Government has contended that Congress had ample basis upon which to find that racial discrimination at restaurants which receive from out of state a substantial portion of the food served does, in fact, impose commercial burdens of national magnitude upon interstate commerce. The appellees' major argument is directed to this premise. They urge that no such basis existed. It is to that question that we now turn.

4. The Congressional Hearings.

As we noted in *Heart of Atlanta Motel* both Houses of Congress conducted prolonged hearings on the Act. And, as we said there, while no formal findings were made, which of course are not necessary, it is well that we make mention of the testimony at these hearings the better to understand the problem before Congress and determine whether the Act is a reasonable and appropriate means toward its solution. The record is replete with testimony of the burdens placed on interstate commerce by racial discrimination in restaurants. A comparison of per capita spending by Negroes in restaurants, theaters, and like establishments indicated less spending, after discounting income differences, in areas where discrimination is widely practiced. This condition, which was especially aggravated in the South, was attributed in the testimony of the Under Secretary of Commerce to racial segregation. . . . This diminutive spending springing from a refusal to serve Negroes and their total loss as customers has, regardless of the absence of direct evidence, a close connection to interstate commerce. The fewer customers a restaurant enjoys the less food it sells and consequently the less it buys. . . . In addition, the Attorney General testified that this type of discrimination imposed "an artificial restriction on the market" and interfered . . . with the flow of merchandise. . . . In addition, there were many references to discriminatory situations causing wide unrest and having a depressant effect on general business conditions in the respective communities. . . .

Moreover there was an impressive array of testimony that discrimination in restaurants had a direct and highly restrictive effect upon interstate travel by Negroes. This resulted, it was said, because discriminatory practices prevent Negroes from buying prepared food served on the premises while on a trip, except in isolated and unkempt restaurants and under most unsatisfactory and often unpleasant conditions. This obviously discourages travel and obstructs interstate commerce for one can hardly travel without eating. Likewise, it was said, that discrimination deterred professional, as well as skilled, people from moving into areas where such practices occurred and thereby caused industry to be reluctant to establish there. . . .

We believe that this testimony afforded ample basis for the conclusion that established restaurants in such areas sold less interstate goods because of the discrimination, that interstate travel was obstructed directly by it, that business in general suffered and that many new businesses refrained from establishing there as a result of it. Hence the District Court was in error in concluding that there was no connection between discrimination and

the movement of interstate commerce. The court's conclusion that such a connection is outside "common experience" flies in the face of stubborn fact.

It goes without saying that, viewed in isolation, the volume of food purchased by Ollie's Barbecue from sources supplied from out of state was insignificant when compared with the total foodstuffs moving in commerce. But, as our late Brother Jackson said for the Court in *Wickard* v. *Filburn* [1942] . . .

That appellee's own contribution to the demand for wheat may be trivial by itself is not enough to remove him from the scope of federal regulation where, as here, his contribution, taken together with that of many others similarly situated, is far from trivial.

We noted in *Heart of Atlanta Motel* that a number of witnesses attested to the fact that racial discrimination was not merely a state or regional problem but was one of nationwide scope. Against this background, we must conclude that while the focus of the legislation was on the individual restaurant's relation to interstate commerce, Congress appropriately considered the importance of that connection with the knowledge that the discrimination was but "representative of many others throughout the country, the total incidence of which if left unchecked may well become far-reaching in its harm to commerce." . . .

With this situation spreading as the record shows, Congress was not required to await the total dislocation of commerce. . . .

5. The Power of Congress to Regulate Local Activities.

Article I. § 8, cl. 3, confers upon Congress the power "[t]o regulate Commerce . . . among the several States" and Clause 18 of the same Article grants it the power "[t]o make all Laws which shall be necessary and proper for carrying into Execution the foregoing Powers. . . ." This grant, as we have pointed out in *Heart of Atlanta Motel* "extends to those activities intrastate which so affect interstate commerce, or the exertion of the power of Congress over it, as to make regulation of them appropriate means to the attainment of a legitimate end, the effective execution of the granted power to regulate interstate commerce." . . . Much is said about a restaurant business being local but "even if appellee's activity be local and though it may not be regarded as commerce, it may still, whatever its nature, be reached by Congress if it exerts a substantial economic effect on interstate commerce. . . ." *Wickard* v. *Filburn* . . . The activities that are beyond the reach of Congress are "those which are completely within a particular State, which do not affect other States, and with which it is not necessary to interfere, for the purpose of executing some of the general powers of the government." . . . This rule is as good today as it was when Chief Justice Marshall laid it down almost a century and a half ago. . . .

Nor are the cases holding that interstate commerce ends when goods come to rest in the State of destination apposite here. That line of cases has been applied with reference to state taxation or regulation but not in the field of federal regulation.

The appellees contend that Congress has arbitrarily created a conclusive presumption that all restaurants meeting the criteria set out in the Act "affect commerce." Stated another way, they object to the omission of a provision for a case-by-case determination—judicial or administrative—that racial discrimination in a particular restaurant affects commerce.

But Congress' action in framing this Act was not unprecedented. In *United States* v. *Darby,* [1941] . . . this Court held constitutional the Fair Labor Standards Act of 1938. There Congress determined that the payment of substandard wages to employees engaged in the production of goods for commerce, while not itself commerce, so inhibited it as to be subject to federal regulation. The appellees in that case argued, as do the appellees here, that the Act was invalid because it included no provision for an independent inquiry regarding the effect on commerce of substandard wages in a particular business. . . . But the Court rejected the argument, observing that:

[S]ometimes Congress itself has said that a particular activity affects the commerce, as it did in the present Act, the Safety Appliance Act and the Railway Labor Act. In passing on the validity of legislation of the class last mentioned the only function of courts is to determine whether the particular activity regulated or prohibited is within the reach of the federal power.

Here, as there, Congress has determined for itself that refusals of service to Negroes have imposed burdens both upon the interstate flow of food and upon the movement of products generally. Of course, the mere fact that Congress has said when particular activity shall be deemed to affect commerce does not preclude further examination by this Court. But where we find that the legislators, in light of the facts and testimony before them, have a rational basis for finding a chosen regulatory scheme necessary to the protection of commerce, our investigation is at an end. The only remaining question—one answered in the affirmative by the court below—is whether the particular restaurant either serves or offers to serve interstate travelers or serves food a substantial portion of which has moved in interstate commerce. . . .

Confronted as we are with the facts laid before Congress, we must conclude that it has a rational basis for finding that racial discrimination in restaurants had a direct and adverse effect on the free flow of interstate commerce. Insofar as the sections of the Act here relevant are concerned, §§ 201 (b) (2) and (c), Congress prohibited discrimination only in those establishments having a close tie to interstate commerce, *i.e.,* those, like the McClungs', serving food that has come from out of the State. We think in so doing that Congress acted well within its power to protect and foster commerce in extending the coverage of Title II only to those restaurants offering to serve interstate travelers or serving food, a substantial portion of which has moved in interstate commerce.

The absence of direct evidence connecting discriminatory restaurant service with the flow of interstate food, a factor on which the appellees place much reliance, is not, given the evidence as to the effect of such practices on other aspects of commerce, a crucial matter.

The power of Congress in this field is broad and sweeping; where it keeps within its sphere and violates no express constitutional limitation it has been the rule of this Court, going back almost to the founding days of the Republic, not to interfere. The Civil Rights Act of 1964, as here applied, we find to be plainly appropriate in the resolution of what the Congress found to be a national commercial problem of the first magnitude. We find it in no violation of any express limitations of the Constitution and we therefore declare it valid.

The judgment is therefore

Reversed.

Justices Black, Goldberg, and Douglas wrote concurring opinions.

Would the Court have extended the reach of the commerce power as it did in the *Heart of Atlanta* case if individual rights had not been involved? Does the *McClung* case differ in this respect from *Heart of Atlanta?* Is Justice Clark's comparison, in *Heart of Atlanta,* between the use of the commerce power to prohibit "moral wrongs" and to support Title II reasonable and valid? Does Clark's opinion in either case suggest that there are any limits remaining on the commerce power? What principle does Clark use in the *McClung* case to extend the commerce power to an admittedly intrastate establishment? Contrast the test for determining the scope of the commerce power that the Court uses in *Katzenbach* v. *McClung* with its opinion in *Wickard* v. *Filburn.*

STATE IMMUNITY FROM FEDERAL REGULATION

The distinction between *governmental* and *proprietary* functions of state and local governments has generally been used only as a basis for determining immunity from federal taxation.[36] Federal regulation of the states is usually based upon the commerce clause, and the authority of the national government has been declared virtually total in this sphere. In *National League of Cities* v. *Usery* (1976) the Court confronted what on its face seemed to be a simple case involving the authority of Congress under the commerce clause

[36]See New York v. United States, 326 U.S. 572 (1946); Helvering v. Gerhardt, 304 U.S. 405 (1938); South Carolina v. United States, 199 U.S. 437 (1905). These cases are covered in Chapter 4.

to regulate state and local activities. In 1974 Congress amended the Fair Labor Standards Act to extend the minimum wage and maximum hour provisions to the public employees of state and local governments. The National League of Cities challenged the amendment as an unconstitutional infringement on state sovereignty.

In 1966 Congress extended the coverage of the Fair Labor Standards Act to state hospitals and schools, and this was upheld as a proper exercise of congressional authority under the commerce clause in *Maryland* v. *Wirtz*, 392 U.S. 183 (1968). In *Fry* v. *United States*, 421 U.S. 542 (1975), the Court reaffirmed the wide powers of Congress under the commerce clause. Two Ohio state employees had challenged the provisions of the Economic Stabilization Act of 1970 that extended wage and salary controls to state employees. The employees contended that the act interfered with sovereign state functions. Citing *Maryland* v. *Wirtz*, the Court upheld the Stabilization Act under the commerce power. However, in a footnote to the opinion, the Court added,

> Petitioners have stated their argument not in terms of the commerce power, but in terms of the limitations on that power imposed by the Tenth Amendment. While the Tenth Amendment has been characterized as a "truism," stating merely that "all is retained which has not been surrendered," . . . it is not without significance. The Amendment expressly declares the constitutional policy that Congress may not exercise power in a fashion that impairs the states' integrity or their ability to function effectively in a federal system. Despite the extravagant claims on this score made by some amici, we are convinced that the wage restriction regulations constituted no such drastic invasion of state sovereignty.[37]

Justice Rehnquist dissented in the *Fry* case. "The state," declared Rehnquist, "is not simply asserting an absence of congressional legislative authority, but rather is asserting an affirmative constitutional right, inherent in its capacity as a state, to be free from such congressionally asserted authority."[38] Rehnquist asserted that a state may have at least an equal claim to immunity from federal regulations as from federal taxation. He wrote: "Immunity from the plenary authority of the national government to tax . . . should [not] . . . be any higher on the scale of constitutional values than is a state's claim to be free from the imposition of Congress's plenary authority under the commerce clause." Rehnquist then went on to cite Chief Justice Stone's concurring opinion in *New York* v. *United States*, to the effect that *any* form of federal taxation, discriminatory or nondiscriminatory, that interferes with the proper functioning of state government is unconstitutional. (The majority in the *New York* case held that only taxes which discriminated against the proprietary functions of states were unconstitutional.) Justice Stone's decision implied that in tax immunity cases the primary issue should not be whether or not the tax is discriminatory but whether or not it intrudes upon legitimate state functions. Similarly, Rehnquist wanted the Court to consider the commerce clause not as an absolute sanction for federal regulation of

[37]Fry v. United States, 421 U.S. 542, 547 n. 7 (1975).
[38]Ibid., p. 550.

the states but as limited by state sovereignty. In his dissent in the *Fry* case, Rehnquist stated that *Maryland* v. *Wirtz* should be overruled. He wrote: "The operation of schools, hospitals, and like facilities involved in *Maryland* v. *Wirtz* is an activity sufficiently closely allied with traditional state functions that the wages paid by the state to employees of such facilities should be beyond Congress's commerce authority."[39] And, referring to the *Fry* case, Rehnquist concluded: "I do not believe that the commerce clause alone is sufficient to sustain the broad and sweeping federal regulation of the maximum salaries which Ohio may pay its employees, nor do I believe that the showing of national emergency made here is sufficient to make this case one in which congressional authority may be derived from sources other than the commerce clause."

The *Wirtz* and *Fry* cases were important precedents as the Court took under consideration *National League of Cities* v. *Usery*. Justice Rehnquist wrote the plurality opinion in the *Usery* case. Would he apply the precedents, or would he, with the consent of his brethren, take the opportunity to upgrade his dissent in the *Fry* case?

National League of Cities v. *Usery*

426 U.S. 833; 96 S. Ct. 2465; 49 L. Ed. 2d 245 (1976)

MR. JUSTICE REHNQUIST delivered the opinion of the Court:

. . . In 1974, Congress again broadened the coverage of the [Fair Labor Standards] Act. . . . The Act . . . imposes upon almost all public employment the minimum wage and maximum hour requirements previously restricted to employees engaged in interstate commerce. These requirements are essentially identical to those imposed upon private employers. . . .

. . . [T]he District Court granted appellee Secretary of Labor's motion to dismiss the complaint for failure to state a claim upon which relief might be granted. The District Court stated it was "troubled" by appellants' contentions that the amendments would intrude upon the States' performance of essential governmental functions. The court went on to say that it considered their contentions

substantial and that it may well be that the Supreme Court will feel it appropriate to draw

back from the far-reaching implications of [*Maryland* v. *Wirtz*]; but that is a decision that only the Supreme Court can make, and as a Federal district court we feel obliged to apply the *Wirtz* opinion as it stands. *National League of Cities* v. *Brennan* [1974]. . . .

We noted probable jurisdiction in order to consider the important questions recognized by the District Court. . . . We agree with the District Court that the appellants' contentions are substantial. Indeed upon full consideration of the question we have decided that the "far-reaching implications" of *Wirtz* should be overruled, and that the judgment of the District Court must be reversed.

II

It is established beyond peradventure that the Commerce Clause of Art. I of the Constitution is a grant of plenary authority to Congress. That authority is, in the

[39]Ibid., p. 558

words of Mr. Chief Justice Marshall in *Gibbons* v. *Ogden,* ... "the power to regulate; that is, to prescribe the rule by which commerce is to be governed." ...

Congressional power over areas of private endeavor, even when its exercise may pre-empt express state-law determinations contrary to the result which has commended itself to the collective wisdom of Congress, has been held to be limited only by the requirement that "the means chosen by [Congress] must be reasonably adapted to the end permitted by the Constitution." *Heart of Atlanta Motel* v. *United States* [1964] ...

Appellants in no way challenge these decisions establishing the breadth of authority granted Congress under the commerce power. Their contention, on the contrary, is that when Congress seeks to regulate directly the activities of States as public employers, it transgresses an affirmative limitation on the exercise of its power akin to other commerce power affirmative limitations contained in the Constitution. Congressional enactments which may be fully within the grant of legislative authority contained in the Commerce Clause may nonetheless be invalid because found to offend against the Sixth [and] ... Fifth Amendment[s] ... Appellants' essential contention is that the 1974 amendments to the Act, while undoubtedly within the scope of the Commerce Clause, encounter a similar constitutional barrier because they are to be applied directly to the States and subdivisions of States as employers.

This Court has never doubted that there are limits upon the power of Congress to override state sovereignty, even when exercising its otherwise plenary powers to tax or to regulate commerce which are conferred by Art. I of the Constitution. In *Wirtz,* for example, the Court took care to assure the appellants that it had "ample power to prevent ... 'the utter destruction of the State as a sovereign political entity,'" which they feared.

... Appellee Secretary in this case, both in his brief and upon oral argument, has agreed that our federal system of government imposes definite limits upon the authority of Congress to regulate the activities of the States as States by means of the commerce power. ... In *Fry,* the Court recognized that an express declaration of this limitation is found in the Tenth Amendment:

While the Tenth Amendment has been characterized as a 'truism,' stating merely that 'all is retained which has not been surrendered,' *United States* v. *Darby* [1941] ..., it is not without significance. The Amendment expressly declares the constitutional policy that Congress may not exercise power in a fashion that impairs the States' integrity or their ability to function effectively in a federal system. ...

In *New York* v. *United States* [1946], Mr. Chief Justice Stone, speaking for four Members of an eight-Member Court in rejecting the proposition that Congress could impose taxes on the States so long as it did so in a nondiscriminatory manner, observed:

A State may, like a private individual, own real property and receive income. But in view of our former decisions we could hardly say that a general non-discriminatory real estate tax (apportioned), or an income tax laid upon citizens and States alike could be constitutionally applied to the State's capitol, its State-house, its public school houses, public parks, or its revenues from taxes or school lands, even though all real property and all income of the citizen is taxed. ...

The expressions in these more recent cases trace back to earlier decisions of this Court recognizing the essential role of the States in our federal system of government. Mr. Chief Justice Chase, perhaps because of the particular time at which he occupied that office, had occasion more than once to speak for the Court on this point. In *Texas* v. *White,* [1869], he declared that "[t]he Constitution, in all its provisions, looks to an indestructible Union, composed of indestructible States."

In *Lane County* v. *Oregon* [1869], his opinion for the Court said: . . .

[I]n many articles of the Constitution the necessary existence of the States, and, within their proper spheres, the independent authority of the States, is distinctly recognized. . . .

In *Metcalf & Eddy* v. *Mitchell* [1926], the Court likewise observed that "neither government may destroy the other nor curtail in any substantial manner the exercise of its powers." . . .

Appellee Secretary argues that the cases in which this Court has upheld sweeping exercises of authority by Congress, even though those exercises pre-empted state regulation of the private sector, have already curtailed the sovereignty of the States quite as much as the 1974 amendments to the Fair Labor Standards Act. We do not agree. It is one thing to recognize the authority of Congress to enact laws regulating individual businesses necessarily subject to the dual sovereignty of the government of the Nation and of the State in which they reside. It is quite another to uphold a similar exercise of congressional authority directed, not to private citizens, but to the States as States. We have repeatedly recognized that there are attributes of sovereignty attaching to every state government which may not be impaired by Congress, not because Congress may lack an affirmative grant of legislative authority to reach the matter, but because the Constitution prohibits it from exercising the authority in that manner. In *Coyle* v. *Oklahoma* [1911], the Court gave this example of such an attribute:

The power to locate its own seat of government and to determine when and how it shall be changed from one place to another, and to appropriate its own public funds for that purpose, are essentially and peculiarly state powers. . . .

One undoubted attribute of state sovereignty is the States' power to determine the wages which shall be paid to those whom they employ in order to carry out

their governmental functions, what hours those persons will work, and what compensation will be provided where these employees may be called upon to work overtime. The question we must resolve here, then, is whether these determinations are " 'functions essential to separate and independent existence,' " quoting from *Lane County* v. *Oregon* . . . so that Congress may not abrogate the States' otherwise plenary authority to make them.

In their complaint appellants advanced estimates of substantial costs which will be imposed upon them by the 1974 amendments. . . .

Judged solely in terms of increased costs in dollars, these allegations show a significant impact on the functioning of the governmental bodies involved. . . .

Quite apart from the substantial costs imposed upon the States and their political subdivisions, the Act displaces state policies regarding the manner in which they will structure delivery of those governmental services which their citizens require. The Act, speaking directly to the States *qua* States, requires that they shall pay all but an extremely limited minority of their employees the minimum wage rates currently chosen by Congress. It may well be that as a matter of economic policy it would be desirable that States, just as private employers, comply with these minimum wage requirements. But it cannot be gainsaid that the federal requirement directly supplants the considered policy choices of the States' elected officials and administrators as to how they wish to structure pay scales in state employment. The State might wish to employ persons with little or no training, or those who wish to work on a casual basis, or those who for some other reason do not possess minimum employment requirements, and pay them less than the federally prescribed minimum wage. It may wish to offer part-time or summer employment to teenagers at a figure less than the minimum wage, and if unable to do so may decline to offer such employment at all. But the Act would forbid such choices by the States. The only "discretion" left to them under the Act is either to attempt to increase their revenue to meet the additional financial burden imposed upon them by paying congressionally prescribed wages to their existing complement of employees, or to reduce that complement to a number which can be paid the federal minimum wage without increasing revenue.

This dilemma presented by the minimum wage restrictions may seem not immediately different from that faced by private employers, who have long been covered by the Act and who must find ways to increase their gross income if they are to pay higher wages while maintaining current earnings. The difference, however, is that a State is not merely a factor in the "shifting economic arrangements" of the private sector of the economy . . . but is itself a coordinate element in the system established by the Framers for governing our Federal Union. . . .

Our examination of the effect of the 1974 amendments, as sought to be extended to the States and their political subdivisions, satisfies us that both the minimum wage and the maximum hour provisions will impermissibly interfere with the integral governmental functions of these bodies. . . .

III

One final matter requires our attention. Appellee has vigorously urged that we cannot, consistently with the Court's decisions in *Maryland* v. *Wirtz* . . . , rule against him here. It is important to examine this contention so that it will be clear what we hold today, and what we do not.

With regard to *Fry*, we disagree with appellee. There the Court held that the Economic Stabilization Act of 1970 was constitutional as applied to temporarily freeze the wages of state and local government employees. The Court expressly noted that the degree of intrusion upon the protected area of state sovereignty was in that case even less than that worked by the amendments to the FLSA which were before the Court in *Wirtz*. The Court recognized that the Economic Stabilization Act was "an emergency measure to counter severe inflation that threatened the national economy." . . .

We think our holding today quite consistent with *Fry*. The enactment at issue there was occasioned by an extremely serious problem which endangered the well-being of all the component parts of our federal system and which only collective action by the National Government might forestall. The means selected were carefully drafted so as not to interfere with the States' freedom beyond a very limited, specific period of time. The effect of the across-the-board freeze authorized by that Act, moreover, displaced no state choices as to how governmental operations should be structured, nor did it force the States to remake such choices themselves. Instead, it merely required that the wage scales and employment relationships which the States themselves had chosen be maintained during the period of the emergency. Finally, the Economic Stabilization Act operated to reduce the pressures upon state budgets rather than increase them. These factors distinguish the statute in *Fry* from the provisions at issue here. The limits imposed upon the commerce power when Congress seeks to apply it to the States are not so inflexible as to preclude temporary enactments tailored to combat a national emergency. "[A]lthough an emergency may not call into life a power which has never lived, nevertheless emergency may afford a reason for the exertion of a living power already enjoyed." *Wilson* v. *New* [1917]. . . .

With respect to the Court's decision in *Wirtz*, we reach a different conclusion.

... There are undoubtedly factual distinctions between the two situations, but in view of the conclusions expressed earlier in this opinion we do not believe the reasoning in *Wirtz* may any longer be regarded as authoritative.

Wirtz relied heavily on the Court's decision in *United States* v. *California* [1936]. The opinion quotes the following language from that case:

> [We] look to the activities in which the states have traditionally engaged as marking the boundary of the restriction upon the federal taxing power. But there is no such limitation upon the plenary power to regulate commerce. The state can no more deny the power if its exercise has been authorized by Congress than can an individual. . . .

But we have reaffirmed today that the States as States stand on a quite different footing from an individual or a corporation when challenging the exercise of Congress' power to regulate commerce. We think the dicta from *United States* v. *California,* simply wrong. Congress may not exercise that power so as to force directly upon the States its choices as to how essential decisions regarding the conduct of integral governmental functions are to be made. We agree that such assertions of power, if unchecked, would indeed, as Mr. Justice Douglas cautioned in his dissent in *Wirtz,* allow "the National Government [to] devour the essentials of state sovereignty," and would therefore transgress the bounds of the authority granted Congress under the Commerce Clause. While there are obvious differences between the schools and hospitals involved in *Wirtz,* and the fire and police departments affected here, each provides an integral portion of those governmental services which the States and their political subdivisions have traditionally afforded their citizens. We are therefore persuaded that *Wirtz* must be overruled.

The judgment of the District Court is accordingly reversed, and the cases are remanded for further proceedings consistent with this opinion.

So ordered.

MR. JUSTICE BLACKMUN, concurring:

... Although I am not untroubled by certain possible implications of the Court's opinion—some of them suggested by the dissents—I do not read the opinion so despairingly as does my Brother Brennan. In my view, the result with respect to the statute under challenge here is necessarily correct. I may misinterpret the Court's opinion, but it seems to me that it adopts a balancing approach, and does not outlaw federal power in areas such as environmental protection, where the federal interest is demonstrably greater and where state facility compliance with imposed federal standards would be essential. . . . With this understanding on my part of the Court's opinion, I join it.

MR. JUSTICE BRENNAN, with whom MR. JUSTICE WHITE and MR. JUSTICE MARSHALL join, dissenting:

The Court concedes, as of course it must, that Congress enacted the 1974 amendments pursuant to its exclusive power under Art. I, § 8, cl. 3, of the Constitution "[t]o regulate Commerce . . . among the several States." It must therefore be surprising that my Brethren should choose this bicentennial year of our independence to repudiate principles governing judicial interpretation of our Constitution settled since the time of Mr. Chief Justice John Marshall, discarding his postulate that the Constitution contemplates that restraints upon exercise by Congress of its plenary commerce power lie in the political process and not in the judicial process. For 152 years ago Mr. Chief Justice Marshall enunciated that principle to which, until today, his successors on this Court have been faithful. . . .

[T]he power over commerce . . . is vested in Congress as absolutely as it would be in a single government, having in its constitution the same restrictions on the exercise of the power as are found in the constitution of the United States. *The wisdom and the discretion of Congress, their identity with the people, and the influence which their constituents possess at elections, are . . . the sole restraints on which they have relied, to secure them from its abuse. They are the restraints on which the people must often rely solely, in all representative governments. Gibbons* v. *Ogden . . .* (emphasis added).

Only 34 years ago, *Wickard* v. *Filburn* [1942] . . . reaffirmed that "[a]t the beginning Chief Justice Marshall . . . made emphatic the embracing and penetrating nature of [Congress' commerce] power by warning that effective restraints on its exercise must proceed from political rather than from judicial processes."

My Brethren do not successfully obscure today's patent usurpation of the role reserved for the political process by their purported discovery in the Constitution of a restraint derived from sovereignty of the States on Congress' exercise of the commerce power. Mr. Chief Justice Marshall recognized that limitations "prescribed in the Constitution," *Gibbons* v. *Ogden . . .* , restrain Congress' exercise of the power. . . . Thus laws within the commerce power may not infringe individual liberties protected by the First Amendment . . . the Fifth Amendment . . . or the Sixth Amendment. . . . But there is no restraint based on state sovereignty requiring or permitting judicial enforcement anywhere expressed in the Constitution; our decisions over the last century and a half have explicitly rejected the existence of any such restraint on the commerce power.

We said in *United States* v. *California* [1936] . . . for example: "The sovereign power of the states is necessarily diminished to the extent of the grants of power to the federal government in the Consti-

tution. . . . [T]he power of the state is subordinate to the constitutional exercise of the granted federal power." This but echoed another principle emphasized by Mr. Chief Justice Marshall:

If any one proposition could command the universal assent of mankind, we might expect it would be this—that the government of the Union, though limited in its powers, is supreme within its sphere of action. . . . *McCulloch* v. *Maryland*. . . .

The commerce power "is an affirmative power commensurate with the national needs." *North American Co.* v. *SEC.* [1946]. . . . "There is no room in our scheme of government for the assertion of state power in hostility to the authorized exercise of Federal power." *The Minnesota Rate Cases* [1913]. . . .

My Brethren thus have today manufactured an abstraction without substance, founded neither in the words of the Constitution nor on precedent. An abstraction having such profoundly pernicious consequences is not made less so by characterizing the 1974 amendments as legislation directed against the "States *qua* States." . . . Of course, regulations that this Court can say are not regulations of "commerce" cannot stand, *Santa Cruz Fruit Packing Co.* v. *NLRB* [1938] . . . , and in this sense "[t]he Court has ample power to prevent . . . 'the utter destruction of the State as a sovereign political entity.'" *Maryland* v. *Wirtz* [1968]. . . . But my Brethren make no claim that the 1974 amendments are not regulations of "commerce"; rather they overrule *Wirtz* in disagreement with historic principles. . . . Clearly, therefore, my Brethren are also repudiating the long line of our precedents holding that a judicial finding that Congress has not unreasonably regulated a subject matter of "commerce" brings to an end the judicial role. . . .

The reliance of my Brethren upon the Tenth Amendment as "an express declaration of [a state sovereignty] limitation," ... not only suggests that they overrule governing decisions of this Court that address this question but must astound scholars of the Constitution. For not only early decisions, *Gibbons* v. *Ogden* ... *McCulloch* v. *Maryland* ... and *Martin* v. *Hunter's Lessee* ..., hold that nothing in the Tenth Amendment constitutes a limitation on congressional exercise of powers delegated by the Constitution to Congress.... Rather, as the Tenth Amendment's significance was more recently summarized:

The amendment states but a truism that all is retained which has not been surrendered. ... *United States* v. *Darby* [1941]. ...

My Brethren purport to find support for their novel state-sovereignty doctrine in the concurring opinion of Mr. Chief Justice Stone in *New York* v. *United States*. ... That reliance is plainly misplaced.... [T]he Chief Justice was addressing not the question of a state-sovereignty restraint upon the exercise of the commerce power, but rather the principle of implied immunity of the States and Federal Government from taxation by the other: "The counterpart of such undue interference has been recognized since Marshall's day as the implied immunity of each of the dual sovereignties of our constitutional system from taxation by the other." ...

Today's repudiation of this unbroken line of precedents that firmly reject my Brethren's ill-conceived abstraction can only be regarded as a transparent cover for invalidating a congressional judgment with which they disagree. The only analysis even remotely resembling that adopted today is found in a line of opinions dealing with the Commerce Clause and the Tenth Amendment that ultimately provoked a constitutional crisis for the Court in the 1930s. *E.g.*, *Carter* v. *Carter Coal Co.* [1936], ... *United States* v. *Butler* [1936], ... *Hammer* v. *Dagenhart* [1918]. ... We

tend to forget that the Court invalidated legislation during the Great Depression, not solely under the Due Process Clause, but also and primarily under the Commerce Clause and the Tenth Amendment. It may have been the eventual abandonment of that overly restrictive construction of the commerce power that spelled defeat for the Court-packing plan, and preserved the integrity of this institution, *id.*, at 682, see, *e.g.*, *United States* v. *Darby* [1941], ... *Mulford* v. *Smith* [1939], ... *NLRB* v. *Jones & Laughlin Steel Corp.* [1937], ... but my Brethren today are transparently trying to cut back on that recognition of the scope of the commerce power. My Brethren's approach to this case is not far different from the dissenting opinions in the cases that averted the crisis. See, *e.g.*, *Mulford* v. *Smith* ... (Butler, J., dissenting); *NLRB* v. *Jones & Laughlin Steel Corp.* ... (McReynolds, J., dissenting).

That no precedent justifies today's result is particularly clear from the awkward extension of the doctrine of state immunity from federal taxation—an immunity conclusively distinguished by Mr. Justice Stone in *California,* and an immunity that is "narrowly limited" because "the people of all the states have created the national government and are represented in Congress," *Helvering* v. *Gerhardt* [1938]—to fashion a judicially enforceable restraint on Congress' exercise of the commerce power that the Court has time and again rejected as having no place in our constitutional jurisprudence. ...

Certainly the paradigm of sovereign action—action *qua* State—is in the enactment and enforcement of state laws. Is it possible that my Brethren are signaling abandonment of the heretofore unchallenged principle that Congress "can, if it chooses, entirely displace the States to the full extent of the far-reaching Commerce Clause"? ... Indeed, that principle sometimes invalidates state laws regulating subject matter of national importance even when Congress has been silent. *Gibbons* v. *Ogden*. . . . In either case the ouster of state laws obviously curtails or prohibits the States' prerogatives to make policy choices respecting subjects clearly of greater significance to the "State *qua* State" than the minimum wage paid to state employees. The Supremacy Clause dictates this result under "the federal system of government embodied in the Constitution." . . .

My Brethren do more than turn aside longstanding constitutional jurisprudence that emphatically rejects today's conclusion. More alarming is the startling restructuring of our federal system, and the role they create therein for the federal judiciary. This Court is simply not at liberty to erect a mirror of its own conception of desirable governmental structure. If the 1974 amendments have any "vice," . . . my Brother Stevens is surely right that it represents "merely . . . a policy issue which has been firmly resolved by the branches of government having power to decide such questions." *Post*, at 881. It bears repeating "that effective restraints on . . . exercise [of the commerce power] must proceed from political rather than from judicial processes." *Wickard* v. *Filburn*. . . .

It is unacceptable that the judicial process should be thought superior to the political process in this area. Under the Constitution the Judiciary has no role to play beyond finding that Congress has not made an unreasonable legislative judgment respecting what is "commerce." My Brother Blackmun suggests that controlling judicial supervision of the relationship between the States and our National Government by use of a balancing approach diminishes the ominous implications of today's decision. Such an approach, however, is a thinly veiled rationalization for judicial supervision of a policy judgment that our system of government reserves to Congress.

Judicial restraint in this area merely recognizes that the political branches of our Government are structured to protect the interests of the States, as well as the Nation as a whole, and that the States are fully able to protect their own interests in the premises. Congress is constituted of representatives in both the Senate and House *elected from the States*. . . . Decisions upon the extent of federal intervention under the Commerce Clause into the affairs of the States are in that sense decisions of the States themselves. Judicial redistribution of powers granted the National Government by the terms of the Constitution violates the fundamental tenet of our federalism that the extent of federal intervention into the States' affairs in the exercise of delegated powers shall be determined by the States' exercise of political power through their representatives in Congress. . . .

We are left then with a catastrophic judicial body blow at Congress' power under the Commerce Clause. Even if Congress may nevertheless accomplish its objectives—for example, by conditioning grants of federal funds upon compliance with federal minimum wage and overtime standards, cf. *Oklahoma* v. *CSC* [1947]—there is an ominous portent of disruption of our constitutional structure implicit in today's mischievous decision. I dissent.

MR. JUSTICE STEVENS, dissenting:

The Court holds that the Federal Government may not interfere with a sovereign State's inherent right to pay a substandard wage to the janitor at the state capitol. The principle on which the holding rests is difficult to perceive.

The Federal Government may, I believe, require the State to act impartially when it hires or fires the janitor, to withhold taxes from his paycheck, to observe safety regulations when he is performing his job, to forbid him from burning too much soft coal in the capitol furnace, from dumping untreated refuse in an adjacent waterway, from overloading a state-owned garbage truck, or from driving either the truck or the Governor's limousine over 55 miles an hour. Even though these and many other activities of the capitol janitor are activities of the State *qua* State, I have no doubt that they are subject to federal regulation.

I agree that it is unwise for the Federal Government to exercise its power in the ways described in the Court's opinion. For the proposition that regulation of the minimum price of a commodity—even labor—will increase the quantity consumed is not one that I can readily understand. That concern, however, applies with even greater force to the private sector of the economy where the exclusion of the marginally employable does the greatest harm and, in all events, merely reflects my views on a policy issue which has been firmly resolved by the branches of government having power to decide such

questions. As far as the complexities of adjusting police and fire departments to this sort of federal control are concerned, I presume that appropriate tailor-made regulations would soon solve their most pressing problems. After all, the interests adversely affected by this legislation are not without political power.

My disagreement with the wisdom of this legislation may not, of course, affect my judgment with respect to its validity. On this issue there is no dissent from the proposition that the Federal Government's power over the labor market is adequate to embrace these employees. Since I am unable to identify a limitation on that federal power that would not also invalidate federal regulation of state activities that I consider unquestionably permissible, I am persuaded that this statute is valid. Accordingly, with respect and a great deal of sympathy for the views expressed by the Court, I dissent from its constitutional holding.

How did the Court distinguish federal regulation of private persons and businesses from regulation "directed not to private citizens, but to the states as states"? Can you explain the Court's sharp departure from previous decisions interpreting the commerce clause? Note the Rehnquist dissent in *Fry* v. *United States*. The states have always had a constitutional right to survive. Did the Court feel that states' survival was at stake in the *Usery* case? Rehnquist, in his dissent in the *Fry* case, referred to the constitutional right of a state to be free from congressional authority. Does the *Usery* opinion define the rights of states against the national government? Is the Court placing the rights of states on the same footing with the rights of individuals? Is it in any way linking individual rights with the rights of state governments? For example, do individuals have a right to the *services* of their state and local governments?

The decisions of the Court in the cases dealing with state and local governmental tax immunities, and the *Usery* decision limiting the scope of the national commerce power, suggest that the extent of state sovereignty is not a dormant constitutional issue. The historical trend of constitutional cases dealing with federalism has been to expand national power and reaffirm national supremacy over the states, and while this trend remains intact, the tax immunity and *Usery* decisions place limits on the constitutional scope of national power over the states.

SIX

National versus State Power
over Commerce

The commerce clause does not give Congress exclusive authority over the regulation of commerce. There are no explicit constitutional provisions limiting state regulation of interstate commerce as there are controlling state interference in foreign commerce.[1] The boundaries of state authority to regulate commerce were determined on a case-by-case basis as state laws were challenged in the courts. Constitutional proscriptions upon state interference in commerce resulted from judicial interpretation of constitutional requirements under the commerce clause and of congressional intent to preclude or permit concurrent state regulation of commerce. Justice Robert H. Jackson, in his opinion for the Court in *H. P. Hood and Sons* v. *Dumond* (1949), noted the importance of judicial interpretation of the commerce clause.

> The commerce clause is one of the most prolific sources of national power and an equally prolific source of conflict with legislation of the states. While the Constitution vests in Congress the power to regulate commerce among the states, it does not say what the states may or may not do in the absence of congressional action, nor how to draw a line between what is and what is not commerce among the states. Perhaps even more than by interpretation of its written word, this Court has advanced the solidarity and prosperity of this nation by the meaning it has given to these great silences of the Constitution.[2]

Gibbons v. *Ogden* (1824) was the first major case not only to raise the issue of the scope of the commerce power but the question of the impact of the commerce clause upon state authority. (The facts of *Gibbons* v. *Ogden* and

[1]Article I, Section 10 states: "No state shall, without the consent of the Congress, lay any imposts or duties on imports or exports, except what may be absolutely necessary for executing its inspection laws."
[2]H.P. Hood and Sons v. Dumond, 336 U.S. 525, 535 (1949).

384

that portion of the opinion which concerned congressional authority under the commerce clause are on pp. 305–311. In presenting his arguments before the Court on the question of the impact of the national commerce power upon states, Daniel Webster (for the appellant Gibbons) cited the need to control "this extreme belligerent legislation of the states [which had permitted state-authorized monopolies for steamboats]."[3] Webster contended that "[t]he power of Congress to regulate commerce was complete and entire, and to a certain extent necessarily exclusive; that the act [state laws] in question were regulations of commerce, in a most important particular; and affecting it in those respects in which it was under the exclusive authority of Congress."[4] Webster stated that he did not "mean to say that all regulations which might, in their operation, affect commerce, were exclusively in the power of Congress; but that such power as had been exercised in this case did not remain with the states."[5] He told the Court that nothing was clearer

than that the prevailing motive [which led to the adoption of the Constitution] was to regulate commerce; to rescue it from the embarrassing and destructive consequences resulting from the legislation of so many different states, and to place it under the protection of a uniform law. . . . We do not find, in the history of the formation and adoption of the Constitution, that any man speaks of a general concurrent power, in the regulation of foreign and domestic trade, as still residing in the states. The very object intended, more than any other, was to take away such power. If it had not so provided, the Constitution would not have been worth accepting.[6]

Although at one point in his argument Webster conceded that in some cases the states possessed concurrent jurisdiction to regulate commerce, as he continued to present his case to the Court he seemed to disclaim concurrent state power over commerce. In establishing the Constitution, he said, the people intended "to transfer from the several states to a general government, those high and important powers over commerce, which, in their exercise, were to maintain a uniform and general system. From the very nature of the case, these powers must be exclusive."[7] Referring to "this supposed concurrent power [to regulate commerce] in the states," Webster

found great difficulty in understanding what was meant by it. It was generally qualified by saying that it was a power by which the states could pass laws on the subjects of commercial regulation, which would be valid, until Congress should pass other laws controlling them, or inconsistent with them, and that then the state laws must yield. What sort of concurrent powers were these, which could not exist together? Indeed, the very reading of the clause in the Constitution must put to flight this notion of a general concurrent power. The Constitution was formed for all the states; and Congress was to have power to regulate commerce.[8]

[3] 9 Wheat. 1, 5 (1824).
[4] Ibid., p. 9.
[5] Ibid.
[6] Ibid., pp. 11, 13.
[7] Ibid., p. 13.
[8] Ibid., p. 15.

Webster continued that "[t]his doctrine of a general concurrent power in the states is insidious and dangerous. If it be admitted, no one can say where it will stop."[9] If the states could exercise concurrent jurisdiction over commerce, which could be annulled by Congress at any time, Webster told the Court: "What is there to recommend a construction which leads to a result like this? Here would be a perpetual hostility; one legislature enacting laws, till another legislature should repeal them; one sovereign power giving the rule, till another sovereign power should abrogate it; and all this under the idea of concurrent legislation."[10] The New York law, said Webster, should be declared void as an unconstitutional state regulation of commerce, regardless of whether or not it conflicted directly with a congressional enactment.[11] If the Court did not accept his argument that the commerce power was exclusive, Webster told the Court that in the present case it should declare the New York State law void because in fact it did conflict with a law of Congress.

Thomas J. Oakley, counsel for Ogden, countered Webster's claims with the statement that "[i]t is perfectly settled that an affirmative grant of power to the United States does not, of itself, divest the states of a like power."[12] He declared that the commerce power is shared between the national government and the states. "As to concurrent powers," he said, "it is highly important to hold all powers concurrent, where it can be done without violating the plain letter of the Constitution. All these powers are essential to state sovereignty, and are constantly exercised for the good of the state. These powers [such as the regulation of commerce] can be best exercised by the state, in relation to all its internal concerns, connected with the objects of the power. All powers, therefore, not *expressly* exclusive, or clearly exclusive in their nature, ought to be deemed concurrent,"[13] Oakley argued that the commerce power is a concurrent power.

> . . . It [the commerce power] was fully possessed by the states, after the Declaration of Independence, and constantly exercised. It is one of the attributes of sovereignty, especially designated in that instrument, "to establish commerce." It is not granted [by the Constitution], in exclusive terms, to Congress. It is not prohibited, generally, to the states. The only express restraints upon the power of the states, in this respect, are against laying any impost or duty upon imports or exports (except for the execution of their own inspection laws), or of tonnage; against making any agreement or compact with a foreign power; and against entering into any treaty. All of these prohibitions, being partial, are founded on the supposition that the whole power resided in the states. They are, accordingly, all in restraint of state power. It is a clear principle of interpretation that where a general power is given, but not in exclusive terms, and the states are restrained, in express terms, from exercising that power in particular cases, that in all other cases the power remains in the states as a concurrent power.[14]

[9]Ibid., p. 17.
[10]Ibid., pp. 24–25.
[11]Ibid., pp. 26–27.
[12]Ibid., p. 35.
[13]Ibid., p. 36–37. (Emphasis supplied.)
[14]Ibid., pp. 60–61.

Oakley concluded by telling the Court that the New York State law establishing the steamboat monopoly "is only a regulation of the internal trade and right of navigation, within the territorial limits of the state; . . . the power to regulate this is exclusively in the state; . . . the state has exercised it in the same manner, both by land and water; . . . the law is valid, although incidentally it may affect the right of intercourse between the states."[15]

Gibbons v. Ogden

9 Wheat. 1; 61 L. Ed. 23 (1824)

MR. CHIEF JUSTICE MARSHALL delivered the opinion of the Court:

. . . But it has been urged with great earnestness, that although the power of Congress to regulate commerce with foreign nations, and among the several states, be co-extensive with the subject itself, and have no other limits than are prescribed in the Constitution, yet the states may severally exercise the same power within their respective jurisdictions. In support of this argument, it is said that they possessed it as an inseparable attribute of sovereignty, before the formation of the Constitution, and still retain it, except so far as they have surrendered it by that instrument; that this principle results from the nature of the government, and is secured by the Tenth Amendment; that an affirmative grant of power is not exclusive, unless in its own nature it be such that the continued exercise of it by the former possessor is inconsistent with the grant, and that this is not of that description.

The appellant, conceding these postulates, except the last, contends that full power to regulate a particular subject, implies the whole power, and leaves no residuum; that a grant of the whole is incompatible with the existence of a right in another to any part of it.

Both parties have appealed to the Constitution, to legislative acts, and judicial decisions; and have drawn arguments from all these sources to support and illustrate the propositions they respectively maintain.

The grant of the power to lay and collect taxes is, like the power to regulate commerce, made in general terms, and has never been understood to interfere with the exercise of the same power by the states; and hence has been drawn an argument which has been applied to the question under consideration. But the two grants are not, it is conceived, similar in their terms or their nature. Although many of the powers formerly exercised by the states are transferred to the government of the Union, yet the state governments remain, and constitute a most important part of our system. The power of taxation is indispensable to their existence, and is a power which, in its own nature, is capable of residing in, and being exercised by, different authorities at the same time. We are accustomed to see it placed, for different purposes, in different hands. Taxation is the simple operation of taking small portions from a perpetually accumulating mass, susceptible of almost infinite division; and a power in one to take what is necessary for certain purposes, is not, in its nature, incompatible with a power in another to take what

---

[15] Ibid., p. 78.

is necessary for other purposes. Congress is authorized to lay and collect taxes, etc., to pay the debts, and provide for the common defense and general welfare of the United States. This does not interfere with the power of the states to tax for the support of their own governments; nor is the exercise of that power by the states an exercise of any portion of the power that is granted to the United States. In imposing taxes for state purposes, they are not doing what Congress is empowered to do. Congress is not empowered to tax for those purposes which are within the exclusive province of the states. When, then, each government exercises the power of taxation, neither is exercising the power of the other. But, when a state proceeds to regulate commerce with foreign nations, or among the several states, it is exercising the very power that is granted to Congress, and is doing the very thing which Congress is authorized to do. There is no analogy, then, between the power of taxation and the power of regulating commerce.

In discussing the question, whether this power is still in the states, in the case under consideration, we may dismiss from it the inquiry, whether it is surrendered by the mere grant to Congress, or is retained until Congress shall exercise the power. We may dismiss that inquiry, because it has been exercised, and the regulations which Congress deemed it proper to make, are now in full operation. The sole question is, can a state regulate commerce with foreign nations and among the states, while Congress is regulating it? . . .

. . . The idea that the same measure might, according to circumstances, be arranged with different classes of power, was no novelty to the framers of our Constitution. Those illustrious statesmen and patriots had been, many of them, deeply engaged in the discussion which preceded the war of our Revolution, and all of them were well read in those discussions.

The right to regulate commerce, even by the imposition of duties, was not controverted; but the right to impose a duty for the purpose of revenue, produced a war as important, perhaps, in its consequences to the human race, as any the world has ever witnessed.

These restrictions, then, are on the taxing power, not on that to regulate commerce; and presuppose the existence of that which they restrain, not of that which they do not purport to restrain.

But, the inspection laws are said to be regulations of commerce, and are certainly recognized in the Constitution, as being passed in the exercise of a power remaining with the states.

That inspection laws may have a remote and considerable influence on commerce, will not be denied; but that a power to regulate commerce is the source from which the right to pass them is derived, cannot be admitted. The objects of inspection laws are to improve the quality of articles produced by the labor of the country; to fit them for exportation; or it may be, for domestic use. They act upon the subject before it becomes an article of foreign commerce, or of commerce among the states and prepared it for that purpose. They form a portion of that immense mass of legislation which embraces everything within the territory of a state not surrendered to the general government; all which can be most advantageously exercised by the states themselves. Inspection laws, quarantine laws, health laws of every description, as well as laws for regulating the internal commerce of a state, and those which respect turnpike-roads, ferries, etc., are component parts of this mass.

No direct general power over these objects is granted to Congress; and, consequently, they remain subject to state legislation. If the legislative power of the Union can reach them, it must be for national purposes; it must be where the power is expressly given for a special purpose, or is clearly incidental to some power which is expressly given. It is obvious, that the government of the Union, in the exercise of its express powers, that, for example, of regulating commerce with foreign nations and among the states, may use means that may also be employed by a state, in the exercise of its acknowledged power; that, for example, of regulating commerce within the state. If Congress license vessels to sail from one port to another, in the same state, the act is supposed to be, necessarily, incidental to the power expressly granted to Congress, and implies no claim of a direct power to regulate the purely internal commerce of a state, or to act directly on its system of police. So, if a state, in passing laws on subjects acknowledged to be within its control, and with a view to those subjects, shall adopt a measure of the same character with one which Congress may adopt, it does not derive its authority from the particular power which has been granted, but from some other, which remains with the state, and may be executed by the same means. All experience shows that the same measures, or measures scarcely distinguishable from each other, may flow from distinct powers; but this does not prove that the powers themselves are identical. Although the means used in their execution may sometimes approach each other so nearly as to be confounded, there are other situations in which they are sufficiently distinct to establish their individuality.

In our complex system, presenting the rare and difficult scheme of one general government, whose action extends over the whole, but which possesses only certain enumerated powers, and of numerous state governments, which retain and exercise all powers not delegated to the Union, contests respecting power must arise. Were it even otherwise, the measures taken by the respective governments to execute their acknowledged powers, would often be of the same description, and might, sometimes, interfere. This, however, does not prove that the one is exercising, or has a right to exercise, the powers of the other. . . .

The act passed in 1803, prohibiting the importation of slaves into any state which shall itself prohibit their importation, implies, it is said, an admission that the states possessed the power to exclude or admit them; from which it is inferred that they possess the same power with respect to other articles.

If this inference were correct; if this power was exercised, not under any particular clause in the Constitution, but in virtue of a general right over the subject of commerce, to exist as long as the Constitution itself, it might now be exercised. Any state might now import African slaves into its own territory. But it is obvious that the power of the states over this subject, previous to the year 1808, constitutes an exception to the power of Congress to regulate commerce, and the exception is expressed in such words as to manifest clearly the intention to continue the pre-existing right of the states to admit or exclude, for a limited period. The words are: "The migration or importation of such persons as any of the states, now existing, shall think proper to admit, shall not be prohibited by the Congress prior to the year 1808." The whole object of the exception is to preserve the power to those states which might be disposed to exercise it; and its language seems to the Court to convey this idea unequivocally. The possession of this particular power, then, during the time limited in the Constitution, cannot be admitted to prove the possession of any other similar power.

It has been said that the act of August 7th, 1789, acknowledges a concurrent power in the states to regulate the conduct of pilots, and hence is inferred an admission of their concurrent right with

Congress to regulate commerce with foreign nations, and amongst the states. But this inference is not, we think, justified by the fact.

Although Congress cannot enable a state to legislate, Congress may adopt the provisions of a state on any subject. When the government of the Union was brought into existence, it found a system for the regulation of its pilots in full force in every state. The act which has been mentioned, adopts this system, and gives it the same validity as if its provisions had been specially made by Congress. But the act, it may be said, is prospective also, and the adoption of laws to be made in future, presupposes the right in the maker to legislate on the subject.

The act unquestionably manifests an intention to leave this subject entirely to the states, until Congress should think proper to interpose; but the very enactment of such a law indicates an opinion that it was necessary; that the existing system would not be applicable to the new state of things, unless expressly applied to it by Congress. . . .

These acts were cited at the bar for the purpose of showing an opinion in Congress that the states possess, concurrently with the legislature of the Union, the power to regulate commerce with foreign nations and among the states. Upon reviewing them, we think they do not establish the proposition they were intended to prove. They show the opinion that the states retain powers enabling them to pass the laws to which allusion has been made, not that those laws proceed from the particular power which has been delegated to Congress.

It has been contended by the counsel for the appellant, that, as the word "to regulate" implies in its nature, full power over the thing to be regulated, it excludes, necessarily, the action of all others that would perfrom the same operation of the same thing. That regulation is designed for the entire result, applying to those parts which remain as they were, as well as to those which are altered. It produces a uniform whole, which is as much disturbed and deranged by changing what the regulating power designs to leave untouched, as that on which it has operated.

There is great force in this argument, and the Court is not satisfied that it has been refuted.

Since, however, in exercising the power of regulating their own purely internal affairs, whether of trading or police, the states may sometimes enact laws, the validity of which depends on their interfering with, and being contrary to, an act of Congress passed in pursuance of the Constitution, the Court will enter upon the inquiry, whether the laws of New York, as expounded by the highest tribunal of that state, have, in their application to this case, come into collision with an act of Congress, and deprived a citizen of a right to which that act entitles him. Should this collision exist, it will be immaterial whether those laws were passed in virtue of a concurrent power "to regulate commerce with foreign nations and among the several states," or in virtue of a power to regulate their domestic trade and police. In one case and the other, the acts of New York must yield to the law of Congress; and the decision sustaining the privilege they confer, against a right given by a law of the Union, must be erroneous.

This opinion has been frequently expressed in this Court, and is founded as well on the nature of the government as on the words of the Constitution. In argument, however, it has been contended that if a law, passed by a state in the exercise of its acknowledged sovereignty, comes into conflict with a law passed by Congress in pursuance of the Constitution, they affect the subject, and each other, like equal opposing powers.

But the framers of our Constitution foresaw this state of things, and provided for it, by declaring the supremacy not only of itself, but of the laws made in pursuance of it. The nullity of any act, inconsistent with the Constitution, is produced by the declaration that the Constitution is the supreme law. The appropriate application of that part of the clause which confers the same supremacy on laws and treaties, is to such acts of the state legislatures as do not transcend their powers, but, though enacted in the execution of acknowledged state powers, interfere with, or are contrary to the laws of Congress, made in pursuance of the Constitution, or some treaty made under the authority of the United States. In every such case, the act of Congress, or the treaty, is supreme; and the law of the state, though enacted in the exercise of powers not controverted, must yield to it. . . .

The questions, then, whether the conveyance of passengers be a part of the coasting trade, and whether a vessel can be protected in that occupation by a coasting license, are not, and cannot be, raised in this case. The real and sole question seems to be, whether a steam machine, in actual use, deprives a vessel of the privileges conferred by a license.

In considering this question, the first idea which presents itself, is that the laws of Congress, for the regulation of commerce, do not look to the principle by which vessels are moved. That subject is left entirely to individual discretion; and, in that vast and complex system of legislative enactment concerning it, which embraces everything that the legislature thought it necessary to notice, there is not, we believe, one word respecting the peculiar principle by which vessels are propelled through the water, except what may be found in a single act, granting a particular privilege to steamboats. With this exception, every act, either prescribing duties, or granting privileges, applies to every vessel, whether navigated by the instrumentality of wind or fire, of sails or machinery. The whole weight of proof, then, is thrown upon him who would introduce a distinction to which the words of the law give no countenance.

If a real difference could be admitted to exist between vessels carrying passengers and others, it has already been observed that there is no fact in this case which can bring up that question. And, if the occupation of steamboats be a matter of such general notoriety that the Court may be presumed to know it, although not specially informed by the record, then we deny that the transportation of passengers is their exclusive occupation. It is a matter of general history, that, in our western waters, their principal employment is the transportation of merchandise; and all know, that in the waters of the Atlantic they are frequently so employed.

But all inquiry into this subject seems to the Court to be put *completely* at rest by the act already mentioned, entitled, "An act for the enrolling and licensing of steamboats."

This act authorizes a steamboat employed, or intended to be employed, only in a river or bay of the United States, owned wholly or in part by an alien, resident within the United States, to be enrolled and licensed as if the same belonged to a citizen of the United States.

This act demonstrates the opinion of Congress, that steamboats may be enrolled and licensed, in common with vessels using sails. They are, of course, entitled to the same privileges, and can no more be restrained from navigating waters, and entering ports which are free to such vessels, than if they were wafted on their voyage by the winds, instead of being propelled by the agency of fire. The one element may be as legitimately used as the other, for every commercial purpose authorized by the laws of the Union; and the act of a state inhibiting the use of either to any vessel having a license under the act of Congress, comes, we think, in direct collision with that act.

As this decides the cause, it is unnecessary to enter in an examination of that part of the Constitution which empowers Congress to promote the progress of science and the useful arts. . . .

JUSTICE JOHNSON, concurring:

. . . The history of the times will . . . sustain the opinion that the grant of power over commerce, if intended to be commensurate with the evils existing, and the purpose of remedying those evils, could be only commensurate with the power of the states over the subject. . . .

The "power to regulate commerce," here meant to be granted, was that power to regulate commerce which previously existed in the states. But what was that power? The states were, unquestionably, supreme, and each possessed that power over commerce which is acknowledged to reside in every sovereign state. The definition and limits of that power are to be sought among the features of international law; and, as it was not only admitted, but insisted on by both parties, in argument, that, "unaffected by a state of war, by treaties, or by municipal regulations, all commerce among independent states was legitimate," there is no necessity to appeal to the oracles of the jus commune for the correctness of that doctrine. The law of nations, regarding man as a social animal, pronounces all commerce legitimate in a state of peace, until prohibited by positive law. The power of a sovereign state over commerce, therefore, amounts to nothing more than a power to limit and restrain it at pleasure. And since the power to prescribe the limits to its freedom necessarily implies the power to determine what shall remain unrestrained, it follows that the power must be exclusive; it can reside but in one potentate; and hence, the grant of this power

carries with it the whole subject, leaving nothing for the state to act upon. . . .

. . . Power to regulate foreign commerce is given in the same words, and in the same breath, as it were, with that over the commerce of the states and with the Indian tribes. But the power to regulate foreign commerce is necessarily exclusive. The states are unknown to foreign nations; their sovereignty exists only with relation to each other and the general government. Whatever regulations foreign commerce should be subjected to in the ports of the Union, the general government would be held responsible for them; and all other regulations, but those which Congress had imposed, would be regarded by foreign nations as trespasses and violations of national faith and comity.

But the language which grants the power as to one description of commerce, grants it as to all; and, in fact, if ever the exercise of a right, or acquiescence in a construction, could be inferred from contemporaneous and continued assent, it is that of the exclusive effect of this grant.

A right over the subject has never been pretended to in any instance, except as incidental to the exercise of some other unquestionable power. . . .

When speaking of the power of Congress over navigation, I do not regard it as a power incidental to that of regulating commerce; I consider it as the thing itself; inseparable from it as vital motion is from vital existence.

Commerce, in its simplest signification, means an exchange of goods; but in the advancement of society, labor, transportation, intelligence, care and various mediums of exchange, become commodities, and enter into commerce; the subject, the vehicle, the agent, and their various operations, become the objects of commercial regulation. Shipbuilding, the carrying trade, and propagation of seamen, are such vital agents of commercial prosperity, that the nation which could not legislate over these subjects would not possess power to regulate commerce. . . .

It is impossible, with the views which I entertained of the principle on which the commercial privileges of the people of the United States, among themselves, rest, to concur in the view which this Court takes of the effect of the coasting license in this cause. I do not regard it as the foundation of the right set up in behalf of the appellant. If there was any one object riding over every other in the adoption of the Constitution, it was to keep the commercial intercourse among the states free from all invidious and partial restraints. And I cannot overcome the conviction, that if the licensing act was repealed tomorrow, the rights of the appellant to a reversal of the decision complained of, would be as strong as it is under this license. . . .

Does Marshall consider the national commerce power to be exclusive? In what way does he distinguish the commerce power from the objects upon which the power operates? Does Marshall suggest under what circumstances the states may regulate commerce? What limits exist upon state power over commerce?

Marshall's opinion in *Gibbons* v. *Ogden* did not clearly delineate the boundaries of national and state power over commerce. As a result, the Supreme Court was forced to become the arbiter of suits challenging the authority of national and state governments over commerce. In *Brown* v. *Maryland* (1827) the Court was confronted with the question of whether Maryland's statute requiring importers and sellers of foreign goods to obtain a special license infringed upon the national commerce power or could be sustained under the state taxing power.

Brown v. *Maryland*

12 Wheat 419; 6 L. Ed. 678 (1827)

Mr. Chief Justice Marshall delivered the opinion of the Court:

This is a writ of error to a judgment rendered in the Court of Appeals of Maryland, affirming a judgment of the City Court of Baltimore, on an indictment found in that court against the plaintiffs in error, for violating an act of the legislature of Maryland. . . . The indictment charges the plaintiffs in error with having imported and sold one package of foreign dry goods without having license to do so. A judgment was rendered against them on demurrer for the penalty which the act prescribes for the offense; and that judgment is now before this Court.

The cause depends entirely on the question, whether the legislature of a state can constitutionally require the importer of foreign articles to take out a license from the state, before he shall be permitted to sell a bale or package so imported.

It has been truly said, that the presumption is in favor of every legislative act, and that the whole burden of proof lies on him who denies its constitutionality. The plaintiffs in error take the burden upon themselves, and insist that the act under consideration is repugnant to two provisions in the Constitution of the United States:

1. To that which declares that "no state shall, without the consent of Congress, lay any imposts, or duties on imports or exports, except what may be absolutely necessary for executing its inspection laws."

2. To that which declares that Congress shall have power "to regulate commerce with foreign nations, and among the several states, and with the Indian tribes."

1. The first inquiry is into the extent of the prohibition upon states "to lay any imposts or duties on imports or exports." The counsel for the state of Maryland would confine this prohibition to the laws imposing duties on the act of importation or exportation. The counsel for the plaintiffs in error give them a much wider scope.

In performing the delicate and important duty of constructing clauses in the Constitution of our country, which involve conflicting powers of the government of the Union, and of the respective states, it is proper to take a view of the literal meaning of the words to be expounded, of their connection with other words, and of the general objects to be accomplished by the prohibitory clause, or by the grant of power.

What, then, is the meaning of the words, "imposts, or duties on imports or exports"?

An impost, or duty on imports, is a custom or a tax levied on articles brought into a country, and is most usually secured before the importer is allowed to exercise his rights of ownership over them, because evasions of the law can be prevented more certainly by executing it while the articles are in its custody. It would not, however, be less an impost or duty on the articles, if it were to be levied on them after they were landed. The policy and consequent practice of levying or securing the duty before, or on entering the port, does not limit the power to that state of things, nor consequently, the prohibition, unless the true meaning of the clause so confines it. What, then, are "imports"? The lexicons inform us, they are "things imported." If we appeal to usage for the meaning of the word, we shall receive the same answer. They are the articles themselves which are brought into the country. "A duty on imports," then, is not merely a duty on the act of importation, but is a duty on the thing imported. It is not, taken in its literal sense, confined to a duty levied while the article is entering the country, but extends to a duty levied after it has entered the country. The succeeding words of the sentence which limit the prohibition show the extent in which it was understood. The limitation is, "except what may be absolutely necessary for executing its inspection laws." Now, the inspection laws, so far as they act upon articles for exportation, are generally executed on land, before the article is put on board the vessel; so far as they act upon importations, they are generally executed upon articles which are landed. The tax or duty of inspection, then, is a tax which is frequently, if not always, paid for service performed on land, while the article is in the bosom of the country. Yet this tax is an exception to the prohibition on the states to lay duties on imports or exports. The exception was made because the tax would otherwise have been within the prohibition.

If it be a rule of interpretation to which all assent, that the exception of a particular thing from general words, proves that, in the opinion of the law-giver, the thing excepted would be within the general clause had the exception not been made, we know no reason why this general rule should not be as applicable to the Constitution as to other instruments. If it be applicable, then this exception in favor of duties for the support of inspection laws, goes far in proving that the framers of the Constitution classed taxes of a similar character with those imposed for the purposes of inspection, with duties on imports and exports, and supposed them to be prohibited.

If we quit this narrow view of the subject, and passing from the literal interpretation of the words, look to the objects of the prohibition, we find no reason for withdrawing the act under consideration from its operation.

From the vast inequality between the different states of the confederacy, as to commercial advantages, few subjects were viewed with deeper interest, or excited more irritation, than the manner in which the several states exercised, or seemed disposed to exercise, the power of laying duties on imports. From motives which were deemed sufficient by the statesmen of that day, the general power of taxation, indispensably necessary as it was, and jealous as the states were of any encroachment on it, was so far abridged as to forbid them to touch imports or exports, with the single exception which has been noticed. Why are they restrained from imposing these duties? Plainly because, in the general opinion, the interest of all would be best promoted by placing that whole subject under the control of Congress. Whether the prohibition to "lay imposts, or duties on imports or exports," proceeded from an apprehension that the power might be so exercised as to disturb that equality among the states which was generally advantageous, or that harmony between them which it was desirable to preserve, or to maintain unimpaired our commercial connections with foreign nations, or to confer this source of revenue on the government of the Union, or whatever other motive might have induced the prohibition, it is plain that the object would be as completely defeated by a power to tax the article in the hands of the importer the instant it was landed as by a power to tax it while entering the port. There is no difference, in effect, between a power to prohibit the sale of an article and a power to prohibit its introduction into the country. The one would be a necessary consequence of the other. No goods would be imported if none could be sold. No object of any description can be accomplished by laying a duty on importation, which may not be accomplished with equal certainty by laying a duty on the thing imported in the hands of the importer. It is obvious that the same power which imposes a light duty can impose a very heavy one, one which amounts to a prohibition. Questions of power do not depend on the degree to which it may be exercised. If it may be exercised at all, it must be exercised at the will of those in whose hands it is placed. If the tax may be levied in this form by a state, it may be levied to an extent which will defeat the revenue by impost, so far as it is drawn from importations into the particular state. We are told, that such wild and irrational abuse of power is not to be apprehended, and is not to be taken into view when discussing its existence. All power may be abused; and if the fear of its abuse is to constitute an argument against its existence, it might be urged against the existence of that which is universally acknowledged, and which is indispensable to the general safety. The states will never be so mad as to destroy their own commerce, or even to lessen it. . . .

The counsel for the state of Maryland insist, with great reason, that if the words of the prohibition be taken in their utmost latitude, they will abridge the power of taxation, which all admit to be essential to the states, to an extent which has never yet been suspected, and will deprive them of resources which are necessary to supply revenue, and which they have heretofore been admitted to possess. These words must therefore be construed with some limitation; and, if this be admitted, they insist, that entering the country is the point of time when the prohibition ceases, and the power of the state to tax commences.

It may be conceded that the words of the prohibition ought not to be pressed to their utmost extent; that in our complex system, the object of the powers conferred on the government of the Union, and the nature of the often conflicting powers which remain in the states, must always be taken into view, and may aid in expounding the words of any particular clause. But, while we admit that sound principles of construction ought to restrain all courts from carrying the words of the prohibition beyond the object the Constitution is intended to secure, that there must be a point of time when the prohibition ceases, and the power of the state to tax commences; we cannot admit that this point of time is the instant that the articles enter the country. It is, we think, obvious, that this construction would defeat the prohibition.

The constitutional prohibition on the states to lay a duty on imports—a prohibition which a vast majority of them must feel an interest in preserving—may certainly come in conflict with their acknowledged power to tax persons and property within their territory. The power, and the restriction on it, though quite distinguishable when they do not approach each other, may yet, like the intervening colors between white and black, approach so nearly as to perplex the understanding, as colors perplex the vision in marking the distinction between them. Yet the distinction exists, and must be marked as the cases arise. Till they do arise, it might be premature to state any rule as being universal in its application. It is sufficient for the present to say, generally, that when the importer has so acted upon the thing imported that it has become incorporated and mixed up with the mass of property in the country, it has, perhaps, lost its distinctive character as an import, and has become subject to the taxing power of the state; but while remaining the property of the importer, in his warehouse, in the original form or package in which it was imported, a tax upon it is too plainly a duty on imports to escape the prohibition in the Constitution.

The counsel for the plaintiffs in error contend that the importer purchases, by payment of the duty to the United States, a right to dispose of his merchandise, as well as to bring it into the country; and certainly the argument is supported by strong reason, as well as by the practice of nations, including our own. The object of importation is sale; it constitutes the motive for paying the duties; and if the United States possess the power of conferring the right to sell, as the consideration for which the duty is paid, every principle of fair dealing requires that they should be understood to confer it. . . .

The counsel for the defendant in error have endeavored to illustrate their proposition, that the constitutional prohibition ceases the instant the goods enter the country, by an array of the consequences which they suppose must follow the denial of it. If the importer acquires the right to sell by the payment of duties, he may, they say, exert that right when, where, and as he pleases, and the state cannot regulate it. He may sell by retail, at auction, or as an itinerant peddler. He may introduce articles, as gunpowder, which endanger a city, into the midst of its population; he may introduce articles which endanger the public health, and the power of self-preservation is denied. An importer may bring in goods, as plate, for his own use, and thus retain much valuable property exempt from taxation.

These objections to the principle, if

well founded, would certainly be entitled to serious consideration. But we think they will be found, on examination, not to belong necessarily to the principle, and consequently, not to prove that it may not be resorted to with safety, as a criterion by which to measure the extent of the prohibition.

This indictment is against the importer, for selling a package of dry goods in the form in which it was imported, without a license. This state of things is changed if he sells them, or otherwise mixes them with the general property of the state, by breaking up his packages, and traveling with them as an itinerant peddler. In the first case, the tax intercepts the import, as an import, in its way to become incorporated with the general mass of property, and denies it the privilege of becoming so incorporated until it shall have contributed to the revenue of the state. It denies to the importer the right of using the privilege which he has purchased from the United States, until he shall have also purchased it from the state. In the last cases, the tax finds the article already incorporated with the mass of property by the act of the importer. He has used the privilege he had purchased, and has himself mixed them up with the common mass, and the law may treat them as it finds them. The same observations apply to plate, or other furniture used by the importer. . . .

The power to direct the removal of gunpowder is a branch of the police power, which unquestionably remains, and ought to remain, with the states. If the possessor stores it himself out of town, the removal cannot be a duty on imports, because it contributes nothing to the revenue. If he prefers placing it in a public magazine it is because he stores it there, in his own opinion, more advantageously than elsewhere. We are not sure that this may not be classed among inspection laws.

The removal or destruction of infectious or unsound articles is, undoubtedly, an exercise of that power, and forms an express exception to the prohibition we are considering. Indeed, the laws of the United States expressly sanction the health laws of a state. . . .

But if it should be proved that a duty on the article itself would be repugnant to the Constitution, it is still argued that this is not a tax upon the article, but on the person. The state, it is said, may tax occupations, and this is nothing more.

It is impossible to conceal from ourselves that this is varying the form, without varying the substance. It is treating a prohibition which is general, as if it were confined to a particular mode of doing the forbidden thing. All must perceive that a tax on the sale of an article, imported only for sale, is a tax on the article itself. It is true, the state may tax occupations generally, but this tax must be paid by those who employ the individual, or is a tax on his business. The lawyer, the physician, or the mechanic, must either charge more on the article in which he deals, or the thing itself is taxed through his person. This the state has a right to do, because no constitutional prohibition extends to it. So, a tax on the occupation of an importer is, in like manner, a tax on importation. It must add to the price of the article, and be paid by the consumer, or by the importer himself, in like manner as a direct duty on the article itself would be made. This the state has not a right to do, because it is prohibited by the Constitution. . . .

Is it also repugnant to that clause in the Constitution which empowers "Congress to regulate commerce with foreign nations, and among the several states, and with the Indian tribes?"

The oppressed and degraded state of commerce previous to the adoption of the Constitution can scarcely be forgotten. It was regulated by foreign nations with a single view to their own interests; and our disunited efforts to counteract their restrictions were rendered impotent by want of combination. Congress, indeed, possessed the power of making treaties, but the inability of the federal government to enforce them had become so apparent as to render that power in a great degree useless. Those who felt the injury arising from this state of things, and those who were capable of estimating the influence of commerce on the prosperity of nations, perceived the necessity of giving the control over this important subject to a single government. It may be doubted whether any of the evils proceeding from the feebleness of the federal government contributed more to that great revolution which introduced the present system, than the deep and general conviction that commerce ought to be regulated by Congress. It is not, therefore, matter of surprise, that the grant should be as extensive as the mischief, and should comprehend all foreign commerce and all commerce among the states. To construe the power so as to impair its efficacy, would tend to defeat an object, in the attainment of which the American public took, and justly took, that strong interest which arose from a full conviction of its necessity. . . .

If this power reaches the interior of a state, and may be there exercised, it must be capable of authorizing the sale of those articles which it introduces. Commerce is intercourse; one of its most ordinary ingredients is traffic. It is inconceivable that the power to authorize this traffic, when given in the most comprehensive terms, with the intent that its efficacy should be complete, should cease at the point when its continuance is indispensable to its value.

It has been contended, that this construction of the power to regulate commerce, as was contended in construing the prohibition to lay duties on imports, would abridge the acknowledged power of a state to tax its own citizens, or their property within its territory.

We admit this power to be sacred; but cannot admit that it may be used so as to obstruct the free course of a power given to Congress. We cannot admit that it may be used so as to obstruct or defeat the power to regulate commerce. It has been observed, that the powers remaining with the states may be so exercised as to come in conflict with those vested in Congress. When this happens, that which is not supreme must yield to that which is supreme. This great and universal truth is inseparable from the nature of things, and the Constitution has applied it to the often interfering powers of the general and state governments, as a vital principle of perpetual operation. It results, necessarily, from this principle, that the taxing power of the states must have some limits. It cannot reach and restrain the action of the national government within its proper sphere. It cannot reach the administration of justice in the courts of the Union, or the collection of the taxes of the United States, or restrain the operation of any law which Congress may constitutionally pass. It cannot interfere with any regulation of commerce. If the states may tax all persons and property found on their territory, what shall restrain them from taxing goods in their transit through the state from one port to another, for the purpose of re-exportation? The laws of trade authorize this operation, and general convenience requires it. . . .

It may be proper to add, that we suppose the principles laid down in this case, to apply equally to importations from a sister state. We do not mean to give any opinion on a tax discriminating between foreign and domestic articles.

We think there is error in the judgment of the Court of Appeals of the State of Maryland, in affirming the judgment of the Baltimore City Court. . . . The judgment is to be reversed, and the cause remanded to that court, with instructions to enter judgment in favor of the appellants.

In applying the commerce clause to the *Brown* case, does Marshall distinguish between the authority of Congress to regulate foreign commerce and its power over commerce among the states? Does he suggest the exclusivity of the national commerce power? Under what circumstances could the states tax commerce?

Two years after *Brown* v. *Maryland,* in *Willson* v. *Blackbird Creek Marsh Company* (1829), Marshall wrote the Court's opinion upholding a Delaware statute that authorized the state to drain a marshy creek which was an interstate waterway upon which federally licensed boats occasionally operated. In upholding the statute, Marshall emphasized the fact that Congress had passed no law that directly conflicted with the state legislation. Moreover, his opinion implied that one of the purposes of the state law was to protect the health of its inhabitants, a purpose that fell within the police power of the state. William Wirt, one of the counsel representing the company which claimed that the state law was constitutional, argued that the primary purpose of the law was to protect the public health. Marshall concluded that the "value of the property on its banks must be enhanced by excluding the water from the marsh, and the health of the inhabitants probably improved. Measures calculated to produce these objects, provided they do not come into collision with the powers of the general government, are undoubtedly within those which are reserved to the states."[16] The recognition of a state police power had been parenthetically noted in *Brown* v. *Maryland* when Marshall stated: "The power to direct the removal of gunpowder is a branch of the police power, which unquestionably remains, and ought to remain, with the states."[17] The implication of these Marshall statements was that state laws affecting commerce that were in the nature of the exercise of the state police power would be held constitutional in the absence of a direct conflict with a federal statute.[18]

John Marshall died in 1835, and President Andrew Jackson appointed one of his ardent supporters, Roger B. Taney, as Chief Justice. Once a Federalist, Taney had become a strong Jacksonian Democrat after the demise of his old party. The passing of John Marshall and the appointment of Taney marked the end of an era in Supreme Court history, one in which the Court had been dominated by the Federalist viewpoint. Would the

---

[16]Willson v. Blackbird Creek Marsh Company, 2 Pet. 245, 249 (1829).

[17]Brown v. Maryland, 12 Wheat. 419, 443 (1827).

[18]See also, Mayor of the City of New York v. Miln, 11 Pet. 102 (1837), upholding a New York State statute requiring the masters of vessels arriving in the Port of New York to register the names and addresses of their passengers. The Court held the statute to be an exercise of the state police power, not a regulation of commerce.

Court, now controlled by the Democrats, support the expansive view of national authority that had been taken by the Marshall Court?

The first major test of the Taney Court's approach to defining the boundaries of national and state power to regulate commerce came in three cases decided together as the *License Cases*. Massachusetts, New Hampshire, and Rhode Island had passed laws regulating and taxing the sale of liquor, including liquor imported from other states. Marshall's opinion in *Brown* v. *Maryland* implied that such laws would be an unconstitutional state infringement upon the national commerce power, especially where the tax was levied upon the "original package" containing the goods. The New Hampshire case involved the resale in its original cask of gin purchased in Boston. The Court unanimously upheld the state laws but without a majority concurring in any of the six separate opinions written by the six justices participating in the case. Taney's opinion announcing the judgment of the Court declared,

> It appears to me to be very clear that the mere grant of power to the general government cannot . . . be construed to be an absolute prohibition to the exercise of any power over the same subject by the states. The controlling and supreme power over commerce with foreign nations and the several states is undoubtedly conferred upon Congress. Yet, in my judgment the state may nevertheless, for the safety or convenience of trade, or for the protection of the health of its citizens, make regulations of commerce for its own ports and harbours, and for its own territory; and such regulations are valid unless they come in conflict with a law of Congress.[19]

Taney's opinion reflected general agreement on the Court that insofar as the state legislation was aimed at protecting the public health, it constituted a proper exercise of the police power that could not be declared unconstitutional merely because it incidentally affected interstate commerce.

In the *Passenger Cases,* 7 How. 283 (1849), the Court reviewed challenges to New York and Massachusetts laws that taxed the masters of ships coming from any out of state port for each passenger (applicable only to alien passengers in Massachusetts). The New York law stated that the purpose of the tax was to defray the costs of examining passengers for contagious diseases and to maintain hospitals to treat those found to be diseased. The Massachusetts statute was aimed at the prevention of pauperism, requiring in addition to the tax a $1,000 bond to be posted by masters for each alien passenger found likely to become a public charge. In a 5–4 decision, with Chief Justice Taney on the dissenting side, the Court held the state laws void because they directly regulated interstate commerce. Taney's dissenting opinion was that the laws constituted a valid exercise of the state police power because they were aimed at the prevention of disease and pauperism.[20]

The Taney Court again confronted the issue of permissible state regulation of commerce in *Cooley* v. *Board of Wardens of the Port of Philadelphia* (1851). In 1803 Pennsylvania passed legislation requiring ships entering or

[19]License Cases, 5 How. 504, 578 (1847).
[20]Henderson v. Mayor of New York, 92 U.S. 259 (1876).

leaving the port of Philadelphia to employ local pilots. If the ships failed to comply, they were required to pay one-half of the pilotage fee to the Board of Wardens. This fee would go into a fund for retired pilots and dependents. Cooley, a consignee of two vessels leaving Philadelphia, refused to pay the fee, and he appealed to the Supreme Court from judgments against him in the state courts. In considering whether the Pennsylvania law was a valid regulation of commerce, the Court had to take into account the fact that Congress had passed legislation in 1789 that provided for the continuance of state pilotage laws.

Cooley v. Board of Wardens

12 Howard 299; 13 L. Ed. 996 (1851)

MR. JUSTICE CURTIS delivered the opinion of the Court:

It remains to consider the objection, that it [the state pilotage law] is repugnant to the third clause of the eighth section of the first article. "The Congress shall have power to regulate commerce with foreign nations and among the several States, and with the Indian tribes."

That the power to regulate commerce includes the regulation of navigation, we consider settled. And when we look to the nature of the service performed by pilots, to the relations which that service and its compensations bear to navigation between the several States, and between the ports of the United States, and foreign countries, we are brought to the conclusion, that the regulation of the qualifications of pilots, of the modes and times of offering and rendering their services, of the responsibilities which shall rest upon them, of the powers they shall possess, of the compensation they may demand, and of the penalties by which their rights and duties may be enforced, do constitute regulations of navigation, and consequently of commerce, within the just meaning of this clause of the Constitution.

The power to regulate navigation is the power to prescribe rules in conformity with which navigation must be carried on. It extends to the persons who conduct it, as well as to the instruments used. Accordingly, the first Congress assembled under the Constitution passed laws, requiring the masters of ships and vessels of the United States to be citizens of the United States, and established many rules for the government and regulation of officers and seamen. These have been from time to time added to and changed, and we are not aware that their validity has been questioned.

Now, a pilot, so far as respects the navigation of the vessel in that part of the voyage which is his pilotage ground, is the temporary master charged with the safety of the vessel and cargo, and of the lives of those on board, and intrusted with the command of the crew. He is not only one of the persons engaged in navigation, but he occupies a most important and responsible place among those thus engaged. And if Congress has power to regulate the seamen who assist the pilot in the management of the vessel, a power never denied, we can perceive no valid reason why the pilot should be beyond the reach of the same power. It is true that, according to the usages of modern commerce on the ocean, the pilot is on board only during a part of the voyage between ports of different states, or between ports of the United States and foreign countries; but if he is on board for such a purpose and during so much of the voyage as to be engaged in navigation, the power to regulate navigation extends to him while thus engaged, as clearly as it would if he were to remain on board throughout the whole passage, from port to port. For it is a power which extends to every part of the voyage, and may regulate those who conduct or assist in conducting navigation in one part of a voyage as much as in another part, or during the whole voyage.

Nor should it be lost sight of, that this subject of the regulation of pilots and pilotage has an intimate connection with, and an important relation to, the general subject of commerce with foreign nations and among the several States, over which it was one main object of the Constitution to create a national control. . . .

. . . The Act of 1789, already referred to, contains a clear legislative exposition of the Constitution by the first Congress, to the effect that the power to regulate pilots was conferred on Congress by the Constitution; as does also the Act of March the 2d, 1837, the terms of which have just been given. The weight to be allowed to this contemporaneous construction, and the practice of Congress under it, has, in another connection, been adverted to. And a majority of the Court are of opinion that a regulation of pilots is a regulation of commerce, within the grant to Congress of the commercial power, contained in the third clause of the eighth section of the first article of the Constitution.

It becomes necessary, therefore, to consider whether this law of Pennsylvania, being a regulation of commerce, is valid.

The Act of Congress of the 7th of August, 1789, sec. 4, is as follows:

"That all pilots in the bays, inlets, rivers, harbors, and ports of the United States, shall continue to be regulated in conformity with the existing laws of the States, respectively, wherein such pilots may be, or with such laws as the States may respectively hereafter enact for the purpose, until further legislative provision shall be made by Congress."

If the law of Pennsylvania, now in question, had been in existence at the date of this Act of Congress, we might hold it to have been adopted by Congress, and thus made a law of the United States, and so valid. Because this Act does, in effect, give the force of an Act of Congress, to the then existing state laws on this subject, so long as they should continue unrepealed by the State which enacted them.

But the law on which these actions are founded was not enacted till 1803. What effect, then, can be attributed to so much of the Act of 1789 as declares that pilots shall continue to be regulated in conformity "with such laws as the States may respectively hereafter enact for the purpose, until further legislative provision shall be made by Congress?"

If the States were divested of the power to legislate on this subject by the grant of the commercial power to Congress, it is plain this Act could not confer upon them power thus to legislate. If the Constitution excluded the States from making any law regulating commerce, certainly Congress cannot regrant, or in any manner reconvey to the States that power. And yet this Act of 1789 gives its sanction only to laws enacted by the States. This necessarily implies a constitutional power to legislate; for only a rule created by the sovereign power of a state acting in its legislative capacity, can be deemed a law, enacted by a state; and if the State has so limited its sovereign power that it no longer extends to a particular subject, manifestly it cannot, in any proper sense, be said to enact laws thereon. Entertaining these views we are brought directly and unavoidably to the consideration of the question, whether the grant of the commercial power to Congress, did per se deprive the States of all power to regulate pilots. This question has never been decided by this Court, nor, in our judgment, has any case depending upon all the considerations which must govern this one, come before this Court. The grant of commercial power to Congress does not contain any terms which expressly exclude the States from exercising an authority over its subject matter. If they are excluded it must be because the nature of the power, thus granted to Congress, requires that a similar authority should not exist in the States. If it were conceded on the one side, that the nature of this power, like that to legislate for the District of Columbia, is absolutely and totally repugnant to the existence of similar power in the States, probably no one would deny that the grant of the power to Congress, as effectually and perfectly excludes the States from all future legislation on the subject, as if express words had been used to exclude them. And on the other hand, if it were admitted that the existence of this power in Congress, like the power of taxation, is compatible with the existence of a similar power in the States, then it would be in conformity with the contemporary exposition of the Constitution (Federalist, No. 32) and with the judicial construction, given from time to time by this Court, after the most deliberate consideration, to hold that the mere grant of such a power to Congress, did not imply a prohibition on the States to exercise the same power; that it is not the mere existence of such a power, but its exercise by Congress, which may be incompatible with the exercise of the same power by the States, and that the States may legislate in the absence of congressional regulations. . . .

The diversities of opinion, therefore, which have existed on this subject, have arisen from the different views taken of the nature of this power. But when the nature of a power like this is spoken of, when it is said that the nature of the power requires that it should be exercised exclusively by Congress, it must be intended to refer to the subjects of that power, and to say they are of such a nature as to require exclusive legislation by Congress. Now, the power to regulate commerce, embraces a vast field, containing not only many, but exceedingly various subjects, quite unlike in their nature; some imperatively demanding a single uniform rule, operating equally on the commerce of the United States in every port; and some, like the subject now in question, as imperatively demanding that diversity, which alone can meet the local necessities of navigation.

Either absolutely to affirm, or deny, that the nature of this power requires exclusive legislation by Congress, is to lose sight of the nature of the subjects of this power, and to assert concerning all of them, what is really applicable but to a part. Whatever subjects of this power are in their nature national, or admit only of one uniform system, or plan of regulation, may justly be said to be of such a nature as to require exclusive legislation by Congress. That this cannot be affirmed of laws for the regulation of pilots and pilotage is plain. The Act of 1789 contains a clear and authoritative declaration by the first Congress, that the nature of this subject is such, that until Congress should find it necessary to exert its power, it should be left to the legislation of the States; that it is local and not national; that it is likely to be the best provided for, not by one system, or plan of regulations, but by as many as the legislative discretion of the several States should deem applicable to the local peculiarities of the ports within their limits.

Viewed in this light, so much of this Act of 1789 as declares that pilots shall continue to be regulated "by such laws as the States may respectively hereafter enact for that purpose," instead of being held to be inoperative, as an attempt to confer on the States a power to legislate, of which the Constitution had deprived them, is allowed an appropriate and important signification. It manifests the understanding of Congress, at the outset of the government, that the nature of this subject is not such as to require its exclusive legislation. The practice of the States, and of the national government, has been in conformity with this declaration, from the origin of the national government to this time; and the nature of the subject, when examined, is such as to leave no doubt of the superior fitness and propriety, not to say the absolute necessity, of different systems of regulation, drawn from local knowledge and experience, and conformed to local wants. How, then, can we say, that by the mere grant of power to regulate commerce, the States are deprived of all the power to legislate on this subject, because from the nature of the power the legislation of Congress must be exclusive. This would be to affirm that the nature of the power is, in any case, something different from the nature of the subject to which, in such case, the power extends, and that the nature of the power necessarily demands, in all cases, exclusive legislation by Congress, while the nature of one of the subjects of that power, not only does not require such exclusive legislation, but may be best provided for by many different systems enacted by the States, in conformity with the circumstances of the ports within their limits. In construing an instrument designed for the formation of a government, and in determining the extent of one of its important grants of power to legislate, we can make no such distinction between the nature of the power and the nature of the subject on which that power

was intended practically to operate, nor consider the grant more extensive by affirming of the power, what is not true of its subject now in question.

It is the opinion of a majority of the Court that the mere grant to Congress of the power to regulate commerce, did not deprive the States of power to regulate pilots, and that although Congress has legislated on this subject, its legislation manifests an intention, with a single exception, not to regulate this subject, but to leave its regulation to the several States. To these precise questions, which are all we are called on to decide, this opinion must be understood to be confined. It does not extend to the question what other subjects, under the commercial power, are within the exclusive control of Congress, or may be regulated by the States in the absence of all congressional legislation; nor to the general question how far any regulation of a subject by Congress may be deemed to operate as an exclusion of all legislation by the States upon the same subject. We decide the precise questions before us, upon what we deem sound principles, applicable to this particular subject in the state in which the legislation of Congress has left it. We go no farther. . . .

We are of opinion that this state law was enacted by virtue of a power, residing in the State to legislate; that it is not in conflict with any law of Congress; that it does not interfere with any system which Congress has established by making regulations, or by intentionally leaving individuals to their own unrestricted action; that this law is therefore valid, and the judgment of the Supreme Court of Pennsylvania in each case must be affirmed.

MESSRS. JUSTICES MCLEAN and WAYNE dissented. MR. JUSTICE DANIEL, although he concurred in the judgment of the Court, yet dissented from its reasoning.

The *Cooley* doctrine was that state regulation of interstate and foreign commerce should be permitted if the regulated activities are local in character, requiring local treatment. Conversely, the Court held that Congress has exclusive power under the commerce clause to regulate commercial activity that is national in character. How does the Court distinguish between "local" and "national" activities in commerce? Are the boundaries clear? What reasons does the Court give for supporting the *exclusive* national regulation of the "national" aspects of commerce? To what extent under the *Cooley* doctrine are states to be given exclusive authority to regulate the subjects of commerce that are local in character?

Cooley v. *Board of Wardens of the Port of Philadelphia* was a landmark decision in the interpretation of the commerce clause. Under the Cooley doctrine states were permitted to exercise a concurrent commerce power where the subjects of regulation were local, but where the subject matter was national, exclusive authority to regulate commerce was granted to the federal government. In 1886 the Court applied the Cooley doctrine in one of its most historic cases, *Wabash, St. Louis and Pacific Ry. Co.* v. *Illinois*. At the time the case was before the Court, Congress had not yet enacted the Interstate Commerce Act of 1886, creating national regulation of the railroads through the Interstate Commerce Commission. But many states had passed legislation creating regulatory commissions that regulated railroad rates and practices. Many of the provisions of the Interstate Commerce Act of 1887, including its creation of a commission form of regulation, were patterned upon state legislation.

After the Civil War agrarian interests intensified their efforts to curb what they considered to be railroad abuses by appealing to state legislatures for strong regulatory legislation. Strong agrarian support from the Granger movement in states such as Illinois and Wisconsin provided the impetus for strict state control of railroads and subsidiary operations. So strong was the feeling against the railroads in Illinois that elaborate provisions for their regulation were written into the state constitution, adopted in 1870. In 1871 the legislature created the powerful Illinois Board of Railroad and Warehouse Commissioners with regulatory authority over the railroads. Since most railroads, by their nature, were interstate carriers, a serious constitutional doubt was raised as to the validity of state regulation over those portions of an industry engaged in interstate commerce. The issue arose in *Peik* v. *Chicago and Northwestern Railway Co.*, (1877), in which the authority of the state of Wisconsin to regulate an interstate carrier was challenged. The Court held that "Until Congress acts in reference to the relations of this company to interstate commerce, it is certainly within the power of Wisconsin to regulate its fares, etc., so far as they are of domestic concern. With the people of Wisconsin this company has domestic relations. Incidentally, these may reach beyond the state. But certainly, until the Congress undertakes to legislate for those who are without the state, Wisconsin may provide for those within, even though it may indirectly affect those without."[21]

---

[21]Peik v. Chicago and Northwestern Railway Co., 94 U.S. 164, 178 (1887).

In the *Wabash* case an Illinois ban on long-haul, short-haul rate discrimination in interstate shipments to and from Illinois customers was challenged.

Wabash, Saint Louis and Pacific Ry. Co. v. Illinois

118 U.S. 557; 7 S. Ct. 4; 30 L. Ed 244 (1886)

JUSTICE MILLER delivered the opinion of the Court:

This is a writ of error to the supreme court of Illinois. . . .

. . . The supreme court of Illinois does not place its judgment [upholding the State statute against the claim that it unconstitutionally burdens interstate commerce] in the present case on the ground that the transportation and the charge are exclusively state commerce, but, conceding that it may be a case of commerce among the states, or interstate commerce, which Congress would have the right to regulate if it had attempted to do so, argues that this statute of Illinois belongs to that class of commercial regulations which may be established by the laws of a state until Congress shall have exercised its power on that subject. . . . In support of its view of the subject the supreme court of Illinois cites the cases of *Munn* v. *Illinois* . . . and *Peik* v. *Chicago & N. W. R. Co.* . . . It cannot be denied that the general language of the Court in these cases, upon the power of Congress to regulate commerce, may be susceptible of the meaning which the Illinois court places upon it.

In *Munn* v. *Illinois* [1877], the language of this Court upon that subject is as follows: "We come now to consider the effect upon this statute [of Illinois, requiring grain elevators to be licensed and regulating grain storage prices] of the power of Congress to regulate commerce. '[I]t is not everything that affects commerce that amounts to a regulation of it, within the meaning of the Constitution.' The warehouses of these plaintiffs in error are situated, and their business car-

ried on, exclusively within the limits of the state of Illinois. They are used as instruments by those engaged in state as well as those engaged in interstate commerce, but they are no more necessarily a part of commerce itself than the dray or cart by which, but for them, grain would be transferred from one railroad station to another. Incidentally they may become connected with interstate commerce, but not necessarily so. Their regulation is a thing of domestic concern, and, certainly, until Congress acts in reference to their interstate relations, the state may exercise all the powers of government over them, even though in so doing it may indirectly operate upon commerce outside its immediate jurisdiction. We do not say that a case may not arise in which it will be found that a state, under the form of regulating its own affairs, has encroached upon the exclusive domain of Congress in respect to interstate commerce; but we do say that upon the facts as they are represented to us in this record, that has not been done." . . .

. . . [T]he strongest language used by this Court . . . is to be found in *Peik* v. *Chicago & N. W. R. Co.* [1887] . . ., as follows: "As to the effect of the [state] statute as a regulation of interstate commerce. The law is confined to state commerce, or such interstate commerce as directly affects the people of Wisconsin. Until Congress acts in reference to the relations of this company to interstate commerce, it is certainly within the power of Wisconsin to regulate its fares, etc., so far as they are of domestic concern. With the people of Wisconsin this company has domestic relations. Incidentally these may reach beyond the state. But certainly, until Congress undertakes to legislate for those who are without the state, Wisconsin may provide for those within, even though it may indirectly affect those without."

These extracts show that the question of the right of the state to regulate the rates of fares and tolls on railroads, and how far that right was affected by the commerce clause of the Constitution of the United States, was presented to the Court in those cases. And it must be admitted that, in a general way, the Court treated the cases then before it as belonging to that class of regulations of commerce which, like pilotage, bridging navigable rivers, and many others, could be acted upon by the states, in the absence of any legislation by Congress on the same subject. By the slightest attention to the matter, it will be readily seen that the circumstances under which a bridge may be authorized across a navigable stream within the limits of a state for the use of a public highway, and the local rules which shall govern the conduct of the pilots of each of the varying harbors of the coasts of the United States, depend upon principles far more limited in their application and importance than those which should regulate the transportation of persons and property across the half or the whole of the continent, over the territories of half a dozen states, through which they are carried without change of car or breaking bulk. . . .

. . . [In] the case now under consideration, . . . [w]hatever may be the instrumentalities by which this transportation from the one point to the other is effected, it is but one voyage,—as much so as that of the steam-boat on the Mississippi river. It is not the railroads themselves that are regulated by this act of the Illinois legislature so much as the charge for transportation; and, . . . if each one of the states through whose territories these

goods are transported can fix its own rules for prices, for modes of transit, for times and modes of delivery, and all the other incidents of transportation to which the word "regulation" can be applied, it is readily seen that the embarrassments upon interstate transportation, as an element of interstate commerce, might be too oppressive to be submitted to. "It was," in the language of the Court cited above [*Hall* v. *DeCuir*, 95 U.S. 485 (1878)], "to meet just such a case that the commerce clause of the Constitution was adopted." It cannot be too strongly insisted upon that the right of continuous transportation, from one end of the country to the other, is essential, in modern times, to that freedom of commerce, from the restraints which the states might choose to impose upon it, that the commerce clause was intended to secure. This clause, giving to Congress the power to regulate commerce among the states, and with foreign nations, as this Court has said before, was among the most important of the subjects which prompted the formation of the Constitution. . . . And it would be a very feeble and almost useless provision, but poorly adapted to secure the entire freedom of commerce among the states which was deemed essential to a more perfect union by the framers of the Constitution, if, at every stage of the transportation of goods and chattels through the country, the state within whose limits a part of this transportation must be done could impose regulations concerning the price, compensation, or taxation, or any other restrictive regulation interfering with and seriously embarrassing this commerce.

The argument on this subject can never be better stated than it is by Chief Justice Marshall in *Gibbons* v. *Ogden.* . . . He there demonstrates that commerce among the states, like commerce with foreign nations, is necessarily a commerce which crosses state lines, and extends into the states, and the power of Congress to regulate it exists wherever that commerce is found. Speaking of navigation as an element of commerce, which it is only as a means of transportation, now largely superseded by railroads, he says: "The power of Congress, then, comprehends navigation within the limits of every state in the Union, so far as that navigation may be, in any manner, connected with 'commerce with foreign nations, or among the several states, or with the Indian tribes.' It may, of consequence, pass the jurisdictional line of New York, and act upon the very waters [the Hudson river] to which the prohibition now under consideration applies." So the same power may pass the line of the state of Illinois, and act upon its restriction upon the right of transportation extending over several states, including that one. . . .

We must therefore hold that it is not, and never has been, the deliberate opinion of a majority of this Court that a statute of a state which attempts to regulate the fares and charges by railroad companies within its limits, for a transportation which constitutes a part of commerce among the states, is a valid law. . . .

The judgment of the supreme court of Illinois is therefore reversed, and . . . the case is remanded to the court for further consideration.

What was the reasoning of the Court in coming to the conclusion that the Illinois regulation impeded the flow of interstate commerce? Did the regulation, *by itself,* disrupt interstate commerce? Was the *Cooley* doctrine helpful to the Court in coming to its factual conclusion that the regulated activity was national and therefore the exclusive province of Congress? Was the subject of regulation in the *Wabash* case national or local? Was the Court more concerned with classifying the subject matter of regulation or focusing upon the implications of the method of state regulation?

After the *Wabash* decision the Court began to modify the *Cooley* test to determine the permissible scope of state regulation of interstate commerce. At first an attempt was made to devise a test to measure more broadly the impact of state regulation upon the flow of interstate commerce than was possible through the strict use of the *Cooley* doctrine. The *Wabash* decision itself seemed to go beyond the *Cooley* criteria by taking into account the impact of state regulatory procedures upon interstate commerce, rather than by focusing upon whether or not the *subjects* regulated were local or national. In post-*Wabash* cases the Court modified the *Cooley* doctrine by applying the test of whether or not state action had a direct or indirect effect upon interstate commerce, upholding state regulation when it fell into the latter category. For example, in *Fort Richmond and Bergen Point Ferry Company v. Board* (1914), the Court added to the *Cooley* formula the direct versus indirect test. In upholding the authority of New Jersey to regulate interstate ferry rates, the Court stated: "A state may not impose direct burdens upon interstate commerce, for this is to say that the states may not regulate or restrain that which from its nature should be under the control of one authority [the national government] and be free from restriction save as it is governed by a valid federal rule."[22]

Did the addition of the direct versus indirect test to the *Cooley* formula

[22]Fort Richmond and Bergen Point Ferry Company v. Board, 234 U.S. 317, 330 (1914).

aid the Court in determining what were in fact justifiable state burdens upon interstate commerce? In *South Carolina State Highway Department* v. *Barnwell Bros., Inc.* (1938), the Court found the modified *Cooley* formula inadequate to deal with the question of how far states should be permitted to establish safety standards for trucks using their highways. Such regulations would necessarily cover trucks engaged in interstate commerce. A three-judge district court had overruled a South Carolina law providing for such regulation on the basis that "an appropriate state regulation when applied to intrastate traffic may be prohibited because of its effect on interstate commerce, although the conditions attending the two classes of traffic with respect to safety and protection of the highways are the same."[23] The Supreme Court reversed the district court decision.

In upholding the South Carolina legislation the Court referred to the *Cooley* doctrine, under which "it has been recognized that there are matters of local concern, the regulation of which unavoidably involves some regulation of interstate commerce but which, because of their local character and their number and diversity, may never be fully dealt with by Congress. Notwithstanding the commerce clause, such regulation in the absence of congressional action has for the most part been left to the states."[24] The state regulation affected but did not discriminate against interstate commerce, and its subject matter—state highways—was local in character. So far the Court was following the reasoning of the *Cooley* case. However, Justice Stone, who wrote the opinion in the *Barnwell* case, added an additional consideration to be taken into account in defining state power over interstate commerce. The courts must exercise judicial self-restraint, wrote Stone, in reviewing state laws regulating interstate commerce. As long as state action does not discriminate against interstate commerce, judicial review under the commerce clause "stops with the inquiry whether the state legislature in adopting regulations [such as the present South Carolina law] has acted within its province, and whether the means of regulation chosen are reasonably adapted to the end sought."[25] Stone continued,

> . . . [C]ourts do not sit as legislatures, either state or national. They cannot act as Congress does when after weighing all the conflicting interests, state and national, it determines when and how much the state regulatory power shall yield to the larger interests of a national commerce. . . . When the action of a legislature is within the scope of its power, fairly debateable questions as to its reasonableness, wisdom and propriety are not for the determination of courts, but for the legislative body. . . . It is not any the less a legislative power committed to the states because it affects interstate commerce, and courts are not any the more entitled, because interstate commerce is affected, to substitute their own for the legislative judgment.[26]

The clear implication of Stone's opinion was that the courts should not generally substitute their judgment for that of Congress or state legislatures

[23]South Carolina State Highway Dept. v. Barnwell Bros., Inc., 303 U.S. 177, 184 (1938).
[24]Ibid., p. 185.
[25]Ibid., p. 190.
[26]Ibid., pp. 190–191.

in determining what is an appropriate local or national subject of regulation by the states or the national government. In the absence of congressional action or a discriminatory effect, reasonable state burdens upon interstate commerce should be upheld by the courts.

Justice Stone again wrote the opinion of the Court in *Southern Pacific Company v. Arizona* (1945), which involved a challenge to the Arizona train limit law of 1912 that prohibited the operation of a railroad train of more than fourteen passenger or seventy freight cars within the state. When the state sued the Southern Pacific Company for the recovery of penalties under the law for violation of the statute, the Arizona trial court held that the law was an unconstitutional burden on interstate commerce. The Arizona Supreme Court reversed, holding that the law was a reasonable exercise by the state of its police power to protect the health and safety of the community. Would you expect Justice Stone to uphold the law if he followed his reasoning in the *Barnwell* case?

Southern Pacific v. Arizona

325 U.S. 761, 65 S. Ct. 1515, 89 L. Ed. 1915 (1945)

MR. CHIEF JUSTICE STONE delivered the opinion of the Court:

The contention, faintly urged, that the provisions of the Safety Appliance Act, 45 U.S.C. §§ 1 and 9, providing for brakes on trains, and of § 25 of Part I of the Interstate Commerce Act, 49 U.S.C. § 26 (b), permitting the Commission to order the installation of train stop and control devices, operate of their own force to exclude state regulation of train lengths, has even less support. Congress, although asked to do so, has declined to pass legislation specifically limiting trains to seventy cars. We are therefore brought to appellant's principal contention, that the state statute contravenes the commerce clause of the Federal Constitution.

Although the commerce clause conferred on the national government power to regulate commerce, its possession of the power does not exclude all state power of regulation. Ever since *Willson v. Black-Bird Creek Marsh Co.* [1829] . . . and *Cooley v. Board of Wardens* [1851] . . . it has been recognized that, in the absence of conflicting legislation by Congress, there

is a residuum of power in the state to make laws governing matters of local concern which nevertheless in some measure affect interstate commerce or even, to some extent, regulate it. . . . Thus the states may regulate matters which, because of their number and diversity, may never be adequately dealt with by Congress. . . . When the regulation of matters of local concern is local in character and effect, and its impact on the national commerce does not seriously interfere with its operation, and the consequent incentive to deal with them nationally is slight, such regulation has been generally held to be within state authority. . . .

But ever since *Gibbons* v. *Ogden* . . . the states have not been deemed to have authority to impede substantially the free flow of commerce from state to state, or to regulate those phases of the national commerce which, because of the need of national uniformity, demand that their regulation, if any, be prescribed by a single authority. . . .

In the application of these principles some enactments may be found to be plainly within and others plainly without state power. But between these extremes lies the infinite variety of cases, in which regulation of local matters may also operate as a regulation of commerce, in which reconciliation of the conflicting claims of state and national power is to be attained only by some appraisal and accommodation of the competing demands of the state and national interests involved. . . .

For a hundred years it has been accepted constitutional doctrine that the commerce clause, without the aid of Congressional legislation, thus affords some protection from state legislation inimical to the national commerce, and that in such cases, where Congress has not acted, this Court, and not the state legislature, is under the commerce clause the final arbiter of the competing demands of state and national interests. . . .

Congress has undoubted power to redefine the distribution of power over interstate commerce. It may either permit the states to regulate the commerce in a manner which would otherwise not be permissible. . . , or exclude state regulation even of matters of peculiarly local concern which nevertheless affect interstate commerce. . . .

But in general Congress has left it to the courts to formulate the rules thus interpreting the commerce clause in its application, doubtless because it has appreciated the destructive consequences to the commerce of the nation if their protection were withdrawn, . . . and has been aware that in their application state laws will not be invalidated without the support of relevant factual material which will "afford a sure basis" for an informed judgment. . . . Meanwhile, Congress has accommodated its legislation, as have the states, to these rules as an established feature of our constitutional system. There has thus been left to the states wide scope for the regulation of matters of local state concern, even though it in some measure affects

the commerce, provided it does not materially restrict the free flow of commerce across state lines, or interfere with it in matters with respect to which uniformity of regulation is of predominant national concern.

Hence the matters for ultimate determination here are the nature and extent of the burden which the state regulation of interstate trains, adopted as a safety measure, imposes on interstate commerce, and whether the relative weights of the state and national interests involved are such as to make inapplicable the rule, generally observed, that the free flow of interstate commerce and its freedom from local restraints in matters requiring uniformity of regulation are interests safeguarded by the commerce clause from state interference. . . .

The findings show that the operation of long trains, that is trains of more than fourteen passenger and more than seventy freight cars, is standard practice over the main lines of the railroads of the United States, and that, if the length of trains is to be regulated at all, national uniformity in the regulation adopted, such as only Congress can prescribe, is practically indispensable to the operation of an efficient and economical national railway system. . . .

The unchallenged findings leave no doubt that the Arizona Train Limit Law imposes a serious burden on the interstate commerce conducted by appellant. It materially impedes the movement of appellant's interstate trains through the state and interposes a substantial obstruction to the national policy proclaimed by Congress, to promote adequate, economical and efficient railway transportation service. . . . Enforcement of the law in Arizona, while train lengths remain unregulated or are regulated by varying standards in other states, must inevitably result in an impairment of uniformity of efficient railroad operation because the railroads are subjected to regulation which is not uniform in its application. Compliance with a state statute limiting train lengths requires interstate trains of a length lawful in other states to be broken up and reconstituted as they enter each state according as it may impose varying limitations upon train lengths. The alternative is for the carrier to conform to the lowest train limit restriction of any of the states through which its trains pass, whose laws thus control the carriers' operations both within and without the regulating state. . . .

If one state may regulate train lengths, so may all the others, and they need not prescribe the same maximum limitation. The practical effect of such regulation is to control train operations beyond the boundaries of the state exacting it because of the necessity of breaking up and reassembling long trains at the nearest terminal points before entering and after leaving the regulating state. The serious impediment to the free flow of commerce by the local regulation of train lengths and the practical necessity that such regulation, if any, must be prescribed by a single body having a nation-wide authority are apparent.

The trial court found that the Arizona law had no reasonable relation to safety, and made train operation more dangerous. Examination of the evidence and the detailed findings makes it clear that this conclusion was rested on facts found which indicate that such increased danger of accident and personal injury as may result from the greater length of trains is more than offset by the increase in the number of accidents resulting from the larger number of trains when train lengths are reduced. In considering the effect of the statute as a safety measure, therefore, the factor of controlling significance for present purposes is not whether there is basis for the conclusion of the Arizona

Supreme Court that the increase in length of trains beyond the statutory maximum has an adverse effect upon safety of operation. The decisive question is whether in the circumstances the total effect of the law as a safety measure in reducing accidents and casualties is so slight or problematical as not to outweigh the national interest in keeping interstate commerce free from interferences which seriously impede it and subject it to local regulation which does not have a uniform effect on the interstate train journey which it interrupts. . . .

We think, as the trial court found, that the Arizona Train Limit Law, viewed as a safety measure, affords at most slight and dubious advantage, if any, over unregulated train lengths, because it results in an increase in the number of trains and train operations and the consequent increase in train accidents of a character generally more severe than those due to slack action. Its undoubted effect on the commerce is the regulation, without securing uniformity, of the length of trains operated in interstate commerce, which lack is itself a primary cause of preventing the free flow of commerce by delaying it and by substantially increasing its cost and impairing its efficiency. In these respects the case differs from those where a state, by regulatory measures affecting the commerce, has removed or reduced safety hazards without substantial interference with the interstate movement of trains. . . .

The principle that, without controlling Congressional action, a state may not regulate interstate commerce so as substantially to affect its flow or deprive it of needed uniformity in its regulation is not to be avoided by "simply invoking the convenient apologetics of the police power." . . .

Appellees especially rely on the full train crew cases, [e.g. *Missouri Pacific R. Co.* v. *Norwood*, 283 U.S. 249 (1931)], and also on *South Carolina Highway Dept.* v. *Barnwell Bros.* [1938] ... as supporting the state's authority to regulate the length of interstate trains. While the full train crew laws undoubtedly placed an added financial burden on the railroads in order to serve a local interest, they did not obstruct interstate transportation or seriously impede it. ...

... *South Carolina Highway Dept.* v. *Barnwell Bros.*, was concerned with the power of the state to regulate the weight and width of motor cars passing interstate over its highways, a legislative field over which the state has a far more extensive control than over interstate railroads. In that case, ... we were at pains to point out that there are few subjects of state regulation affecting interstate commerce which are so peculiarly of local concern as is the use of the state's highways. Unlike the railroads local highways are built, owned and maintained by the state or its municipal subdivisions. The state is responsible for their safe and economical administration. Regulations affecting the safety of their use must be applied alike to intrastate and interstate traffic. The fact that they affect alike shippers in interstate and intrastate commerce in great numbers, within as well as without the state, is a safeguard against regulatory abuses. Their regulation is akin to quarantine measures, game laws, and like local regulations of rivers, harbors, piers, and docks, with respect to which the state has exceptional scope for the exercise of its regulatory power, and which, Congress not acting, have been sustained even though they materially interfere with interstate commerce. ...

The contrast between the present regulation and the full train crew laws in point of their effects on the commerce, and the like contrast with the highway safety regulations, in point of the nature of the subject of regulation and the state's interest in it, illustrate and emphasize the considerations which enter into a determination of the relative weights of state and national interests where state regulation affecting interstate commerce is attempted. Here examination of all the relevant factors makes it plain that the state interest is outweighed by the interest of the nation in an adequate, economical and efficient railway transportation service, which must prevail.

Reversed.

MR. JUSTICE RUTLEDGE concurs in the result.

MR. JUSTICE BLACK, dissenting:

... [T]he determination of whether it is in the interest of society for the length of trains to be governmentally regulated is a matter of public policy. Someone must fix that policy—either the Congress, or the state, or the courts. A century and a half of constitutional history and government admonishes this Court to leave that choice to the elected legislative representatives of the people themselves, where it properly belongs both on democratic principles and the requirements of efficient government.

I think that legislatures, to the exclusion of courts, have the constitutional power to enact laws limiting train lengths, for the purpose of reducing injuries brought about by "slack movements." Their power is not less because a requirement of short trains might increase grade crossing accidents. This latter fact raises an entirely different element of danger which is itself subject to legislative regulation. For legislatures may, if necessary, require railroads to take appropriate steps to reduce the likelihood of injuries at grade crossings. ... And the fact that grade-crossing improvements may be expensive is no sufficient reason to say that an unconstitutional "burden" is put upon a railroad even though it be an interstate road. . . .

There have been many sharp divisions of this Court concerning its authority, in the absence of congressional enactment, to invalidate state laws as violating the Commerce Clause. . . . That discussion need not be renewed here, because even the broadest exponents of judicial power in this field have not heretofore expressed doubt as to a state's power, absent a paramount congressional declaration, to regulate interstate trains in the interest of safety. . . .

This record in its entirety leaves me with no doubt whatever that many employees have been seriously injured and killed in the past, and that many more are likely to be so in the future, because of "slack movement" in trains. Everyday knowledge as well as direct evidence presented at the various hearings, substantiates the report of the Senate Committee that the danger from slack movement is greater in long trains than in short trains. It may be that offsetting dangers are possible in the operation of short trains. The balancing of these probabilities, however, is not in my judgment a matter for judicial determination, but one which calls for legislative consideration. Representatives elected by the people to make their laws, rather than judges appointed to interpret those laws, can best determine the policies which govern the people. That at least is the basic principle on which our democratic society rests. I would affirm the judgment of the Supreme Court of Arizona.

MR. JUSTICE DOUGLAS, dissenting:

I have expressed my doubts whether the courts should intervene in situations like the present and strike down state legislation on the grounds that it burdens interstate commerce. *McCarroll* v. *Dixie Greyhound Lines,* 309 U.S. 176, 183–189 [1940]. . . . My view has been that the courts should intervene only where the state legislation discriminated against interstate commerce or was out of harmony with laws which Congress had enacted. . . . It seems to me particularly appropriate that that course be followed here. For Congress has given the Interstate Commerce Commission broad powers of regulation over interstate carriers. . . .

. . . [W]e are dealing here with state legislation in the field of safety where the propriety of local regulation has long been recognized. . . . Whether the question arises under the Commerce Clause or the Fourteenth Amendment, I think the legislation is entitled to a presumption of validity. . . . I am not persuaded that the evidence adduced by the railroads overcomes the presumption of validity to which this train limit law is entitled. . . .

Is Justice Stone's view of the proper role of the courts in cases concerning state burdens on interstate commerce consistent in the *Barnwell* and *Southern Pacific Company* cases? What standard does Stone apply to overrule state action in *Southern Pacific*? Is this standard consistent with the general criteria announced in *Southern Pacific* for judicial review of such cases? Contrast the dissenting opinions of Black and Douglas with Stone's opinion in the prior *Barnwell* case. Are these dissenting opinions more consistent with the reasoning of the Court and its opinion in *Barnwell* than Stone's majority opinion in *Southern Pacific*?

The *Barnwell* and *Southern Pacific* opinions recognized that in addition to the *Cooley* criteria a balancing test should be applied to cases involving state regulation of interstate commerce. This test weighed the state interest in the regulation of interstate commerce against the national interest in preventing burdens upon commerce. The implication of Stone's opinion in *Barnwell* was that this test should be applied by Congress and state legislatures, not by the courts. Stone seemed to reverse himself in *Southern Pacific* when he noted that the decisive question *before the Court* "is whether in the circumstances the total effect of the law as a safety measure in reducing accidents and casualties is so slight or problematical as not to outweigh the national interest in keeping interstate commerce free from interferences which seriously impede it and subject it to local regulation which does not have a uniform effect on the interstate train journey which it interrupts." The thrust of the *Barnwell* decision seemed to support Douglas's dissenting view in *Southern Pacific* that "the courts should intervene only where the state legislation *discriminated* against interstate commerce or was out of harmony with the laws which *Congress* had enacted." But in *Bibb* v. *Navajo Freight Lines, Inc.* (1959), Douglas wrote the majority opinion that overturned an Illinois statute regulating mudguards on trucks that Douglas admitted did not discriminate against interstate commerce. Douglas wrote: "This is one of those cases—few in number—where local safety measures that are nondiscriminatory place an unconstitutional burden on interstate commerce."[27] Douglas's decision in *Bibb* was closer to Stone's opinion in *Southern Pacific* than in *Barnwell*.

STATE RESTRICTIONS ON ACCESS
BY OUT-OF-STATE SELLERS AND BUYERS

State laws affecting interstate commerce extend beyond the regulation of transportation which has been the primary focus of the cases considered above. States have also placed burdens upon interstate commerce by placing restrictions on the access of out-of-state sellers and buyers to local markets. In reviewing challenges to such restrictions on the free flow of trade among states, the Supreme Court has looked closely at the intent of state legislatures in passing restrictive laws. Where the legislation is directed at a legitimate state goal, such as protection of state citizens against fraud,[28] protection of the health of the community,[29] or protection of the privacy of state citizens,[30] state laws restricting out-of-state sellers have been upheld. But in *Baldwin* v. *Seelig* (1935), the Court struck down a New York State law that prohibited milk dealers in the state from purchasing out-of-state milk for resale in New York at a price lower than that for which milk could be purchased within the state. Seelig had purchased milk in Vermont at prices lower than the minimum price for New York milk established under the

[27]Bibb v. Navajo Freight Lines, Inc., 359 U.S. 520, 529 (1959).
[28]California v. Thompson, 313 U.S. 109 (1941).
[29]Mintz v. Baldwin, 289 U.S. 346 (1933).
[30]Breard v. Alexandria, 341 U.S. 622 (1951).

state price control law.[31] Justice Cardozo's opinion for the Court stated that the New York law "set a barrier to traffic between one state and another as effective as if customs duties, equal to the price differential, had been laid upon the thing transported. . . . Nice distinctions have been made at times between direct and indirect burdens [upon interstate commerce]. They are irrelevant when the avowed purpose of the obstruction, as well as its necessary tendency, is to suppress or mitigate the consequences of competition between the states."[32]

The question of the permissible scope of state and municipal restrictions on out-of-state sellers arose in *Dean Milk Company* v. *City of Madison* (1951). The plaintiff, an Illinois corporation, challenged an ordinance of the City of Madison, Wisconsin, which permitted the sale of milk within the boundaries of the municipality only on the condition that it was bottled and pasteurized at a plant within a radius of five miles from the center of the city, unless the milk was obtained from a source that had been inspected and approved by Madison officials. If the Court followed the precedent of *Baldwin* v. *Seelig*, what factors would it take into account in its review of the Madison ordinance? Could the Court sustain the ordinance on the basis that it constituted a proper exercise of the local police power?

Dean Milk Co. v. City of Madison

340 U.S. 349; 71 S. Ct. 295; 95 L. Ed. 329 (1951)

MR. JUSTICE CLARK delivered the opinion of the Court:

This appeal challenges the constitutional validity [under the Commerce Clause] of two sections of an ordinance of the City of Madison, Wisconsin, regulating the sale of milk and milk products within the municipality's jurisdiction. One section in issue makes it unlawful to sell any milk as pasteurized unless it has been processed and bottled at an approved pasteurization plant within a radius of five miles from the central square of Madison. Another section, which prohibits the sale of milk . . . in Madison unless from a source of supply possessing a permit issued after inspection by Madison officials, is attacked insofar as it expressly relieves municipal authorities from any duty to inspect farms located beyond twenty-five

miles from the center of the city.

Appellant is an Illinois corporation engaged in distributing milk and milk products in Illinois and Wisconsin. . . . The Supreme Court of Wisconsin upheld the five-mile limit on pasteurization. As to the twenty-five mile limitation the court ordered the complaint dismissed for want of a justiciable controversy. . . .

The City of Madison is the county seat of Dane County. Within the county are some 5,600 dairy farms with total raw milk production in excess of 600,000,000 pounds annually and more than ten times the requirements of Madison. Aside from the milk supplied to Madison, fluid milk produced in the county moves in large quantities to Chicago and more distant consuming areas, and the remainder is used in making cheese, butter and other

[31]In Nebbia v. New York, 291 U.S. 502 (1934), the Court upheld the New York price control statute as applied within the state.
[32]Baldwin v. Seelig, 294 U.S. 511, 521–522 (1935).

products. At the time of trial the Madison milkshed was not of "Grade A" quality by the standards recommended by the United States Public Health Service, and no milk labeled "Grade A" was distributed in Madison.

The area defined by the ordinance with respect to milk sources encompasses practically all of Dane County and includes some 500 farms which supply milk for Madison. Within the five-mile area for pasteurization are plants of five processors, only three of which are engaged in the general wholesale and retail trade in Madison. Inspection of these farms and plants is scheduled once every thirty days and is performed by two municipal inspectors, one of whom is full-time. The courts below found that the ordinance in question promotes convenient, economical and efficient plant inspection.

Appellant purchases and gathers milk from approximately 950 farms in northern Illinois and southern Wisconsin, none being within twenty-five miles of Madison. Its pasteurization plants are located at Chemung and Huntley, Illinois, about 65 and 85 miles respectively from Madison. Appellant was denied a license to sell its products within Madison solely because its pasteurization plants were more than five miles away.

It is conceded that the milk which appellant seeks to sell in Madison is supplied from farms and processed in plants licensed and inspected by public health authorities of Chicago, and is labeled "Grade A" under the Chicago ordinance which adopts the rating standards recommended by the United States Public Health Service. . . . Madison contends and we assume that in some particulars its ordinance is more rigorous than that of Chicago.

. . . [W]e agree with appellant that the ordinance imposes an undue burden on interstate commerce.

This is not an instance in which an en-actment falls because of federal legislation. . . . There is no pertinent national regulation by the Congress. . . .

Nor can there be objection to the avowed purpose of this enactment. We assume that difficulties in sanitary regulation of milk and milk products originating in remote areas may present a situation in which "upon a consideration of all the relevant facts and circumstances it appears that the matter is one which may appropriately be regulated in the interest of the safety, health and well-being of local communities. . . ." . . .

But this regulation, like the provision invalidated in *Baldwin* v. *Seelig* [1935] . . ., in practical effect excludes from distribution in Madison wholesome milk produced and pasteurized in Illinois. "The importer . . . may keep his milk or drink it, but sell it he may not." In thus erecting an economic barrier protecting a major local industry against competition from without the State, Madison plainly discriminates against interstate commerce. This it cannot do, even in the exercise of its unquestioned power to protect the health and safety of its people, if reasonable nondiscriminatory alternatives, adequate to conserve legitimate local interest, are available. . . . A different view, that the ordinance is valid simply because it professes to be a health measure, would mean that the Commerce Clause of itself imposes no limitations on state action other than those laid down by the Due Process Clause, save for the rare instance where a state artlessly discloses an avowed purpose to discriminate against interstate goods. . . . Our issue then is whether the discrimination inherent in the Madison ordinance can be justified in view of the character of the local interests and the available methods of protecting them. . . .

It appears that reasonable and adequate alternatives are available. If the City of Madison prefers to rely upon its own officials for inspection of distant milk sources, such inspection is readily open to it without hardship for it could charge the actual and reasonable cost of such inspection to the importing producers and processors. . . . Moreover, appellee Health Commissioner of Madison testified that as proponent of the local milk ordinance he had submitted the provisions here in controversy and an alternative proposal based on § 11 of the Model Milk Ordinance recommended by the United States Public Health Service. The model provision imposes no geographical limitation on location of milk sources and processing plants but excludes from the municipality milk not produced and pasteurized conformably to standards as high as those enforced by the receiving city. . . . The Commissioner testified that Madison consumers "would be safeguarded adequately" under either proposal and that he had expressed no preference. . . .

To permit Madison to adopt a regulation not essential for the protection of local health interests and placing a discriminatory burden on interstate commerce would invite a multiplication of preferential trade areas destructive of the very purpose of the Commerce Clause. Under the circumstances here presented, the regulation must yield to the principle that "one state in its dealings with another may not place itself in a position of economic isolation." *Baldwin* v. *Seelig.* . . .

For these reasons we conclude that the judgment below sustaining the five-mile provision as to pasteurization must be reversed.

The Supreme Court of Wisconsin thought it unnecessary to pass upon the validity of the twenty-five-mile limitation, apparently in part for the reason that this issue was made academic by its decision upholding the five-mile section. In view of our conclusion as to the latter provision, a determination of appellant's contention as to the other section is now necessary. As to this issue, therefore, we

vacate the judgment below and remand for further proceedings not inconsistent with the principles announced in this opinion.

It is so ordered.

Mr. Justice Black, with whom Mr. Justice Douglas and Mr. Justice Minton concur, dissenting:

. . . I disagree with the Court's premises, reasoning, and judgment.

(1) This ordinance does not exclude wholesome milk coming from Illinois or anywhere else. It does require that all milk sold in Madison must be pasteurized within five miles of the center of the city. But there was no finding in the state courts . . . that . . . Dean Milk Company, is unable to have its milk pasteurized within the defined geographical area. . . . Dean's personal preference to pasteurize in Illinois, not the ordinance, keeps Dean's milk out of Madison.

(2) Characterization of § 7.21 as a "discriminatory burden" on interstate commerce is merely a statement of the Court's result, which I think incorrect. The section does prohibit the sale of milk in Madison by interstate and intrastate producers who prefer to pasteurize over five miles distant from the city. But both state courts below found that § 7.21 represents a good-faith attempt to safeguard public health by making adequate sanitation inspections possible. . . .

(3) This health regulation should not be invalidated merely because the Court believes that alternative milk-inspection methods might insure the cleanliness and healthfulness of Dean's Illinois milk. . . . No case is cited, and I have found none, in which a bona fide health law was struck down on the ground that some other method of safeguarding health would be as good as, or better than, the one the Court was called on to review. . . .

If, however, the principle announced

today is to be followed, the Court should not strike down local health regulations unless satisfied beyond a reasonable doubt that the substitutes it proposes would not lower health standards. I do not think the Court can so satisfy itself on the basis of its judicial knowledge. And the evidence in the record leads me to the conclusion that the substitute health measures suggested by the Court do not insure milk as safe as the Madison ordinance requires.

One of the Court's proposals is that Madison require milk processors to pay reasonable inspection fees at the milk supply "sources." Experience shows, however, that the fee method gives rise to prolonged litigation over the calculation and collection of the charges. . . . Moreover, nothing in the record before us indicates that the fee system might not be as costly to Dean as having its milk pasteurized in Madison. . . .

The Court's second proposal is that Madison adopt § 11 of the "Model Milk Ordinance." . . . The evidence indicates to me that enforcement of the Madison law would assure a more healthful quality of milk than that which is entitled to use the label of "Grade A" under the Model Or-

dinance. . . . [M]oreover, Madison would be required to depend on the Chicago inspection system. . . . But there is direct and positive evidence in the record that milk produced under Chicago standards did not meet the Madison requirements.

Furthermore, the Model Ordinance would force the Madison health authorities to rely on "spot checks" by the United States Public Health Service to determine whether Chicago enforced its milk regulations. The evidence shows that these "spot checks" are based on random inspection of farms and pasteurization plants. . . . There was evidence that neither the farms supplying Dean with milk nor Dean's pasteurization plants were necessarily inspected in the last "spot check" of the Chicago milkshed made two years before the present case was tried. . . .

On this record I would uphold the Madison law. At the very least, however, I would not invalidate it without giving the parties a chance to present evidence and get findings on the ultimate issues the Court thinks crucial—namely, the relative merits of the Madison ordinance and the alternatives suggested by the Court today.

Did the opinion of Justice Clark take into account the *intent* of the Madison ordinance, or did it concentrate upon its effect? The Court recognized that there was a relationship between the ordinance and the safety, health, and well-being of the community. Why was this relationship insufficient to sustain the ordinance? In what ways, if any, did Clark's opinion balance national and local interests? Contrast the way in which considerations of federalism were taken into account in the majority and dissenting opinions. Does Clark in any way apply the *Cooley* doctrine to the case? Compare the majority and dissenting views on the issue of discrimination. Do the facts of the case prove discriminatory intent, discriminatory effect, or both?

State Restrictions on Out-of-State Buyers

States have not only limited the access of out-of-state sellers to their markets, but have passed laws that in various ways restrict the access of out-of-state buyers to state and local resources. A common restriction upon the access of out-of-state buyers is the establishment of price controls over state products. In *Milk Control Board* v. *Eisenberg Farm Products* (1939), for example, a Pennsylvania minimum price law was challenged by a New York milk dealer who bought milk from Pennsylvania producers for shipment and sale in New York. Justice Roberts's majority opinion applied the balancing test, weighing state interests against a national interest in preserving the free flow of interstate commerce. Roberts wrote: "The purpose of the statute under review obviously is to reach a domestic situation in the interest of the welfare of the producers and consumers of milk in Pennsylvania. Its provisions . . . are appropriate means to the ends in view. The question is whether the prescription of prices to be paid producers in the effort to accomplish these ends constitutes a prohibited burden on interstate commerce, or an incidental burden which is permissible until superseded by congressional enactment. That question can be answered only by weighing the nature of the respondent's activities, and the propriety of local regulation of them, as disclosed by the record."[33] The statute, continued Roberts, primarily regulated local activities. Only a minuscule portion of the milk produced in Pennsylvania was shipped out of state, declared Roberts, and therefore the effect of the statute upon interstate commerce "is incidental and not forbidden by the Constitution, in the absence of regulation by Congress."[34]

The constitutionality of state restrictions upon out-of-state buyers next arose in *Parker* v. *Brown* (1943), involving a challenge to a California state agricultural prorate act under which the producers of raisins were required to place their crops under the control of a program committee which would control the supply and eliminate price competition. Ninety-five percent of the crop was marketed in interstate commerce; therefore, the California law substantially affected the marketing of raisins out of the state and restricted out-of-state buyers by controlling the price of the product. Compare the facts of the *Parker* case with those of the *Eisenberg* case. If the Court applied the balancing test, what decision would it make? Did the California law have a direct or incidental effect upon interstate commerce.?

Parker v. Brown

317 U.S. 341; 63 S. Ct. 307; 87 L. Ed. 315 (1943)

Mr. Chief Justice Stone delivered the opinion of the Court:

*Validity of the Program
under the Commerce Clause.*

. . . The question is thus presented whether in the absence of Congressional legislation prohibiting or regulating the transactions affected by the state program, the restrictions which it imposes upon the sale within the state of a commodity by its producer to a processor who contemplates doing, and in fact does, work upon the commodity before packing and shipping it in interstate commerce, violate the Commerce Clause.

The governments of the states are sovereign within their territory save only as

---

[33]Milk Control Board v. Eisenberg Farm Products, 306 U.S. 346, 352 (1939).
[34]Ibid., p. 353.

they are subject to the prohibitions of the Constitution or as their action in some measure conflicts with powers delegated to the National Government, or with Congressional legislation enacted in the exercise of those powers. This Court has repeatedly held that the grant of power to Congress by the Commerce Clause did not wholly withdraw from the states the authority to regulate the commerce with respect to matters of local concern, on which Congress has not spoken. . . . *A fortiori* there are many subjects and transactions of local concern not themselves interstate commerce or a part of its operations which are within the regulatory and taxing power of the states, so long as state action serves local ends and does not discriminate against the commerce, even though the exercise of those powers may materially affect it. Whether we resort to the mechanical test sometimes applied by this Court in determining when interstate commerce begins with respect to a commodity grown or manufactured within a state and then sold and shipped out of it—or whether we consider only the power of the state in the absence of Congressional action to regulate matters of local concern, even though the regulation affects or in some measure restricts the commerce—we think the present regulation is within state power.

In applying the mechanical test to determine when interstate commerce begins and ends . . . this Court has frequently held that for purposes of local taxation or regulation "manufacture" is not interstate commerce even though the manufacturing process is of slight extent. . . . And such regulations of manufacture have been sustained where, aimed at matters of local concern, they had the effect of preventing commerce in the regulated article. . . . A state is also free to license and tax intrastate buying where the purchaser expects in the usual course of business to resell in interstate commerce. . . . And no case has gone so far as to hold that a state

could not license or otherwise regulate the sale of articles within the state because the buyer, after processing and packing them, will, in the normal course of business, sell and ship them in interstate commerce.

All of these cases proceed on the ground that the taxation or regulation involved, however drastically it may affect interstate commerce, is nevertheless not prohibited by the Commerce Clause where the regulation is imposed before any operation of interstate commerce occurs. Applying that test, the regulation here controls the disposition, including the sale and purchase, of raisins before they are processed and packed preparatory to interstate sale and shipment. The regulation is thus applied to transactions wholly intrastate before the raisins are ready for shipment in interstate commerce. . . .

This distinction between local regulation of those who are not engaged in commerce, although the commodity which they produce and sell to local buyers is ultimately destined for interstate commerce, and the regulation of those who engage in the commerce by selling the product interstate, has in general served, and serves here, as a ready means of distinguishing those local activities which, under the Commerce Clause, are the appropriate subject of state regulation despite their effect on interstate commerce. But courts are not confined to so mechanical a test. When Congress has not exerted its power under the Commerce Clause, and state regulation of matters of local concern is so related to interstate commerce that it also operates as a regulation of that commerce, the reconciliation of the power thus granted with that reserved to the state is to be attained by the accommodation of the competing demands of the state and national interests involved. . . .

Such regulations by the state are to be sustained, not because they are "indirect" rather than "direct," . . . not because they control interstate activities in such a manner as only to affect the commerce rather than to command its operations. But they are to be upheld because upon a consideration of all the relevant facts and circumstances it appears that the matter is one which may appropriately be regulated in the interest of the safety, health and well-being of local communities, and which, because of its local character, and the practical difficulties involved, may never be adequately dealt with by Congress. Because of its local character also there may be wide scope for local regulation without substantially impairing the national interest in the regulation of commerce by a single authority and without materially obstructing the free flow of commerce, which were the principal objects sought to be secured by the Commerce Clause. . . . There may also be, as in the present case, local regulations whose effect upon the national commerce is such as not to conflict but to coincide with a policy which Congress has established with respect to it. . . .

In comparing the relative weights of the conflicting local and national interests involved, it is significant that Congress, by its agricultural legislation, has recognized the distressed condition of much of the agricultural production of the United States, and has authorized marketing procedures, substantially like the California prorate program, for stabilizing the marketing of agricultural products. Acting under this legislation the Secretary of Agriculture has established a large number of market stabilization programs for agricultural commodities moving in interstate commerce in various parts of the country, including seven affecting California crops. All involved attempts in one way or another to prevent over-production of agri-

cultural products and excessive competition in marketing them, with price stabilization as the ultimate objective. Most if not all had a like effect in restricting shipments and raising or maintaining prices of agricultural commodities moving in interstate commerce.

It thus appears that whatever effect the operation of the California program may have on interstate commerce, it is one which it has been the policy of Congress to aid and encourage through federal agencies in conformity to the Agricultural Marketing Agreement Act, and § 302 of the Agricultural Adjustment Act. Nor is the effect on the commerce greater than or substantially different in kind from that contemplated by the stabilization programs authorized by federal statutes. As we have seen, the Agricultural Marketing Agreement Act is applicable to raisins only on the direction of the Secretary of Agriculture who, instead of establishing a federal program has, as the statute authorizes, coöperated in promoting the state program and aided it by substantial federal loans. Hence we cannot say that the effect of the state program on interstate commerce is one which conflicts with Congressional policy or is such as to preclude the state from this exercise of its reserved power to regulate domestic agricultural production.

We conclude that the California prorate program for the 1940 raisin crop is a regulation of state industry of local concern which, in all the circumstances of this case which we have detailed, does not impair national control over the commerce in a manner or to a degree forbidden by the Constitution.

Reversed.

Does the reasoning of Chief Justice Stone in the *Parker* case follow more closely his opinion in *Barnwell Bros.* or in *Southern Pacific* v. *Arizona*? Contrast the facts of *Parker* with those of *Barnwell* and *Southern Pacific*. Was the California law less burdensome upon interstate commerce than the Arizona safety law? Is Stone's use of the balancing test in *Parker* to sustain the California regulation consistent with his application of the test in *Southern Pacific* to strike down the Arizona statute?

Parker v. *Brown* reviewed state controls over production and consequently over prices that had a far-reaching effect on interstate commerce. Nevertheless, the Court allowed the state law to stand because state interests in a stable and profitable local economy outweighed any national interest in removing the burdens from commerce. Moreover, in the Agricultural Adjustment Act Congress had generally supported as a matter of national policy the goal of profitability and stability in agriculture.

H.P. Hood & Sons v. *Dumond* (1949), like the *Parker* case, involved a challenge to a state law that limited competition in an agricultural sector of the state's economy—milk production and distribution. Under a New York law the commissioner of agriculture and markets could not issue a license for a new plant unless he found that "issuance of the license will not tend to a destructive competition in a market already adequately served, and that the issuance of the license is in the public interest." H.P. Hood & Sons distributed milk in Boston but obtained a large portion of its supply from New York. The company operated three New York plants and sought a license for a fourth plant. The New York commissioner of agriculture denied the license on the basis that it "would tend to a destructive competition in a market already adequately served, and would not be in the public interest." Would the New York law be upheld under the *Cooley* doctrine? Would it be sustained if the test balancing national and state interests were applied? If the Court followed the precedents of the *Eisenberg* and *Parker* cases, would the law be upheld? Do the decisions of Justice Stone in the *Barnwell* and *Southern Pacific* cases suggest what reasoning the Court should have adopted in the present case?

Hood v. Dumond

336 U.S. 525; 69 S. Ct. 657; 93 L. Ed. 865 (1949)

MR. JUSTICE JACKSON delivered the opinion of the Court:

. . . The desire of the Forefathers to federalize regulation of foreign and interstate commerce stands in sharp contrast to their jealous preservation of the state's power over its internal affairs. No other federal power was so universally assumed to be necessary, no other state power was so readily relinquished. There was no desire to authorize federal interference with social conditions or legal institutions of the states. Even the Bill of Rights amendments were framed only as a limitation upon the powers of Congress. The states were quite content with their several and diverse controls over most matters but, as Madison has indicated, "want of a general power over Commerce led to an exercise of this power separately, by the States, which not only proved abortive, but engendered rival, conflicting and angry regulations." . . .

The Commerce Clause is one of the most prolific sources of national power and an equally prolific source of conflict with legislation of the state. While the Constitution vests in Congress the power to regulate commerce among the states, it does not say what the states may or may not do in the absence of congressional action, nor how to draw the line between what is and what is not commerce among the states. Perhaps even more than by interpretation of its written word, this Court has advanced the solidarity and prosperity of this Nation by the meaning it has given to these great silences of the Constitution. . . .

The material success that has come to inhabitants of the states which make up this federal free trade unit has been the most impressive in the history of commerce, but the established interdependence of the states only emphasizes the necessity of protecting interstate movement of goods against local burdens and repressions. We need only consider the consequences if each of the few states that produce copper, lead, high-grade iron ore, timber, cotton, oil or gas should decree that industries located in that state shall have priority. What fantastic rivalries and dislocations and reprisals would ensue if such practices were begun! Or suppose that the field of discrimination and retaliation be industry. May Michigan provide that automobiles cannot be taken out of that State until local dealers' demands are fully met? Would she not have every argument in the favor of such a statute that can be offered in support of New York's limiting sales of milk for out-of-state shipment to protect the economic interests of her competing dealers and local consumers? Could Ohio then pounce upon the rubber-tire industry, on which she has a substantial grip, to retaliate for Michigan's auto monopoly?

Our system, fostered by the Commerce Clause, is that every farmer and every craftsman shall be encouraged to produce by the certainty that he will have free access to every market in the Nation, that no home embargoes will withhold his exports, and no foreign state will by customs duties or regulations exclude them. Likewise, every consumer may look to the free competition from every producing area in the Nation to protect him from exploitation by any. Such was the vision of the Founders; such has been the doctrine of this Court which has given it reality. . . .

The State, however, contends that such restraint or obstruction as its order imposes on interstate commerce does not violate the Commerce Clause because the State regulation coincides with, supplements and is part of the federal regulatory scheme. This contention that Congress has taken possession of "the field" but shared it with the State, it is to be noted, reverses the contention usually made in comparable cases, which is that Congress has not fully occupied the field and hence the State may fill the void.

Congress, as a part of its Agricultural Marketing Agreement Act, authorizes the Secretary of Agriculture to issue orders regulating the handling of several agricultural products, including milk, when they are within the reach of its commerce power. . . .

The Congressional regulation contemplates and permits a wide latitude in which the State may exercise its police power over the local facilities for handling milk. We assume, though it is not necessary to decide, that the Federal Act does not preclude a state from placing restrictions and obstructions in the way of interstate commerce for the ends and purposes always held permissible under the Commerce Clause. But here the challenge is only to a denial of facilities for interstate commerce upon the sole and specific grounds that it will subject others to competition and take supplies needed locally, an end, as we have shown, always held to be precluded by the Commerce Clause. We have no doubt that Congress in the national interest could prohibit or curtail shipments of milk in interstate commerce, unless and until local demands are met. Nor do we know of any reason why Congress may not, if it deems it in the national interest, authorize the states to place similar restraints on movement of articles of commerce. And the provisions looking to state cooperation may be sufficient to warrant the state in imposing regulations approved by the federal authorities, even if they otherwise might run counter to the decisions that coincidence is as fatal as conflict when Congress acts. . . .

Moreover, we can hardly assume that the challenged provisions of this order advance the federal scheme of regulation because Congress forbids inclusion of such a policy in a federal milk order. . . . [T]he Act provides:

No marketing agreement or order applicable to milk and its products in any marketing area shall prohibit or in any manner limit, in the case of the products of milk, the marketing in that area of any milk or product thereof produced in any production area in the United States.

While there may be difference of opinion as to whether this authorizes the Federal Order to limit, so long as it does not prohibit, interstate shipment of milk. . . —a question upon which we express no opinion—it is clear that the policy of the provision is inconsistent with the State's contention that it may, in its own interest, impose such a limitation as a coincident or supplement to federal regulation. . . .

. . . The judgment is reversed and the cause remanded for proceedings not inconsistent with this opinion.

It is so ordered.

MR. JUSTICE BLACK, dissenting:

In this case the Court sets up a new constitutional formula for invalidation of state laws regulating local phases of interstate commerce. I believe the New York law is invulnerable to constitutional attack under constitutional rules which the majority of this Court have long accepted. The new formula subjects state regulations of local business activities to greater constitutional hazards than they have ever had to meet before. The consequences of the new formula, as I understand it, will not merely leave a large area of local business activities free from state regulation. . . .

That part of the regulatory plan challenged here bars issuance of licenses for additional milk-handling plants if new plants would "tend to destructive competition in a market already adequately served" or would be contrary to "the public interest." In determining whether a milk market is "adequately served," the state follows a plan similar to the federal law in that both divide the country into "marketing areas." . . .

[T]he commissioner found that more plants would bring about the kind of destructive competition against which the law was aimed. That finding is not challenged. Nor is it charged that the order was prompted by desire to prevent New York milk from going to Boston. . . .

The language of this state Act is not discriminatory, the legislative history shows it was not so intended, and the commissioner has not administered it with a hostile eye. The Act must stand or fall on this basis notwithstanding the overtones of the Court's opinion. If petitioner and other interstate milk dealers are to be placed above and beyond this law, it must be done solely on this Court's new constitutional formula which bars a state from protecting itself against local destructive competitive practices so far as they are indulged in by dealers who ship their milk into other states. . . .

. . . [I]t seems to me that the Court now steps in where Congress wanted it to stay out. The Court puts itself in the position of guardian of interstate trade in the milk industry. Congress, with full constitutional power to do so, selected the Secretary of Agriculture to do this job. Maybe this Court would be a better guardian, but it may be doubted that authority for the Court to undertake the task can be found in the Constitution—even in its "great silences." At any rate, I had supposed that this Court would not find conflict where Congress explicitly has commanded cooperation.

. . . The gravity of striking down state regulations is immeasurably increased when it results as here in leaving a no-man's land immune from any effective regulation whatever. It is dangerous to assume that the aggressive cupidity of some need never be checked by government in the interest of all.

The judicially directed march of the due process philosophy as an emancipator of business from regulation appeared arrested a few years ago. That appearance was illusory. That philosophy continues its march. The due process clause and commerce clause have been used like Siamese twins in a never-ending stream of challenges to government regulation. . . . The reach of one twin may appear to be longer than that of the other, but either can easily be turned to remedy this apparent handicap.

Both the commerce and due process clauses serve high purposes when confined within their proper scope. But a stretching of either outside its sphere can paralyze the legislative process, rendering the people's legislative representatives impotent to perform their duty of providing appropriate rules to govern this dynamic civilization. Both clauses easily lend themselves to inordinate expansions of this Court's power at the expense of legislative power. For under the prevailing due process rule, appeals can be made to the "fundamental principles of liberty and justice" which our "fathers" wished to preserve. In commerce clause cases reference can appropriately be made to the far-seeing wisdom of the "fathers" in guarding against commercial and even shooting wars among the states. Such arguments have strong emotional appeals and when skillfully utilized they sometimes obscure the vision. . . .

Any doubt I may have concerning the wisdom of New York's law is far less, however, than is my skepticism concerning the ability of the Federal Government to reach out and effectively regulate all the local business activities in the forty-eight states.

I would leave New York's law alone.

MR. JUSTICE MURPHY joins in this opinion.

MR. JUSTICE FRANKFURTER, with whom MR. JUSTICE RUTLEDGE joined, dissented.

Contrast the way in which the Court weighs state interests in its application of the balancing test in the *Barnwell, Southern Pacific, Parker,* and *Hood* cases. To what interests does the Court give more relative weight? Why does the Court not find the challenged regulations to be within the police power of the states? Does it find the New York regulations pertaining to out-of-state buyers to place an undue burden upon interstate commerce? To what extent is the decision based upon the discriminatory effect of the New York law?

The balancing test approach to the resolution of conflicts over state regulation of interstate commerce used by the Supreme Court has guided state courts confronting similar cases. In *American Can Company* v. *Oregon Liquor Control Commission* (1973), the Oregon appeals court was confronted with a challenge to the Oregon bottle bill enacted in 1971. The law required all soft drinks and beer sold in Oregon to be packaged in returnable containers. The plaintiff, manufacturers of bottles and cans and soft drink companies, asserted that the law placed a burden on interstate commerce that was not outweighed by the interest of the state in the protection of its environment, an interest that falls within the police power of the state. The opinion of the Oregon court stated,

> The language of the United States Supreme Court is not always consistent in analyzing the application of the commerce clause to varying facts and it is difficult to rationalize it into one harmonious jurisprudential whole. On their facts, however, the cases cluster around certain basic concepts and the treatment accorded to state action is consistent within each grouping. The cases consistently hold that the commerce clause bars state police action only where:
>
> 1. Federal action has preempted regulation of the activity;
> 2. The state action impedes the free physical flow of commerce from one state to another; or
> 3. Protectionist state action, even though under the guise of police power, discriminates against interstate commerce.
>
> In this case, there is no claim of federal preemption, so we are concerned only with the latter two concepts, interstate transportation and economic protectionism. No party cited and we were unable to find any case striking down state action under the commerce clause which did not come within one of these two categories.
>
> [The Court rejected the weighing process to decide the outcome of the case, declaring that there was no comparable way to measure and compare the environmental interests of the state with the economic interests of the beverage industry.]
>
> The United States Supreme Court has . . . made clear that it will not only recognize the authority of the state to exercise the police power, but also its right to do so in such manner as it deems most appropriate to local conditions, free from the homogenizing constraints of federal dictation.
>
> The Oregon legislature is thus constitutionally authorized to enact laws which address the economic, esthetic, and environmental consequences of the problems of litter in public places and solid waste disposal which suit the particular conditions of Oregon even though it may, in doing so, affect interstate commerce.
>
> The enactment of the bottle bill is clearly a legislative act in harmony with federal law. Congress has directed [in the Federal Solid Waste Disposal Act] that the states take primary responsibility for action in this field. . . .
>
> While it is clear that the Oregon legislature was authorized to act in this area, plaintiffs assert that the means incorporated in the bottle bill are not effective to accomplish its intended purpose and that alternative means are available which will have a lesser impact upon interstate commerce. Particularly, they offered evidence to show: (1) that the deposit system is inadequate to motivate the consuming public to return containers; (2) that mechanical means are being developed for improved collection of highway litter; and (3) that public education, such as the "Pitch in to Clean up America" campaign, is a desirable means of dealing with container litter.
>
> Selection of a reasonable means to accomplish a state purpose is clearly a legislative, not a judicial, function. . . . In particular, the courts may not invalidate leg-

islation upon the speculation that machines may be developed or because additional and complementary means of accomplishing the same goal may also exist. The legislature may look to its imagination rather than to traditional methods such as those which plaintiffs suggest, to develop suitable means of dealing with state problems, even though their methods may be unique. Each state is a laboratory for innovation and experimentation in a healthy federal system. What fails may be abandoned and what succeeds may be emulated by other states. The bottle bill is now unique; it may later be regarded as seminal.

We conclude, therefore, that the bottle bill was properly enacted within the police power of the state of Oregon and that it is imaginatively, but reasonably calculated to cope with problems of legitimate state concern.[35]

Against the charge that the bottle bill substantially impeded the free flow of commerce, the Oregon court declared that "legislation which has negative economic consequences for non-state business is not necessarily discriminatory against interstate commerce. . . . The bottle bill is not discriminatory against interstate commerce and is not intended to operate to give Oregon industry a competitive advantage against outside firms." The court concluded: "Because the bottle bill is a legitimate exercise of the police power, consistent with federal policy legislation, which does not impede the flow of interstate commerce and which does not discriminate against non-Oregon interests, we hold that it is valid legislation under the commerce clause."[36]

---

[35]American Can Co. v. Oregon Liquor Control Commission 517 P.2d 691, 697–700 (Or. App. 1973).
[36]Ibid., pp. 702–703.

SEVEN

The National Power to Tax and Spend

The authority given to Congress in Article I, Section 8, "to lay and collect taxes, duties, imposts and excises," is limited. First, Article I, Section 8 requires that "all duties, imposts and excises shall be uniform throughout the United States. . . . " The Court has interpreted this requirement to be one of geographic uniformity, preventing discrimination among the states. The uniformity requirement applies to *indirect* taxes, those that (1) are levied on the performance of an act or the privilege of doing business, and (2) tax persons other than the consumers that ultimately bear the burden of the tax, such as license or sales taxes.[1] A further limitation on indirect taxes is that of Article I, Section 9: "No tax or duty shall be laid on articles exported from any state."[2]

Article I, Section 2 provides that "Direct taxes shall be apportioned among the several states which may be included within this Union, according to their respective numbers. . . . " Article I, Section 9 states: "No capitation, or other direct, tax shall be laid unless in proportion to the census. . . ." Direct taxes are those which are imposed upon property as such, rather than upon the sale of property or the performance of an act. Excise taxes, for example, are upon the sale of goods, not upon the goods themselves. By requiring indirect taxes to be uniform and direct taxes to be apportioned among the states according to their populations, the framers sought an equal and fair system of national taxation. In *Federalist 21*, Alexander Hamilton explained the basis of these constitutional provisions governing taxes.

> The wealth of nations depends upon an infinite variety of causes. Situation, soil, climate, the nature of the production, the nature of the government, the genius of the citizens, the degree of information they possess, the state of commerce, of arts, of industry—these circumstances and many more, too complex, minute, or

[1]See Knowlton v. Moore, 178 U.S. 41 (1900); Bromley v. McCaughn, 28 U.S. 124 (1929).
[2]United States v. Hvoslef, 237 U.S. 1 (1915), defined exported goods as those that are shipped to other countries, and held that neither Congress nor the states can tax such exports.

adventitious to admit of a particular specification, occasion differences hardly conceivable in the relative opulence and riches of different countries. The consequence clearly is that there can be no common measure of national wealth, and, of course, no general or stationary rule by which the ability of a state to pay taxes can be determined. The attempt, therefore, to regulate the contributions of the members of a confederacy by any such rule cannot fail to be productive of glaring inequality and extreme oppression.

This inequality would of itself be sufficient in America to work the eventual destruction of the Union, if any mode of enforcing a compliance with its requisitions could be devised. The sovereign states would not long consent to remain associated upon a principle which distributed the public burden to so unequal a hand, and which was calculated to impoverish and oppress the citizens of some states, while those of others would scarcely be conscious of the small proportion of the weight they were required to sustain. This, however, is an evil inseparable from the principle of quotas and requisitions.

There is no method of steering clear of this inconvenience, but by authorizing the national government to raise its own revenues in its own way. Imposts, excises, and in general all duties upon articles of consumption, may be compared to a fluid, which will in time find its level with the means of paying them. The amount to be contributed by each citizen will in a degree be at his own option, and can be regulated by an attention to his resources. The rich may be extravagant, the poor can be frugal; and private oppression may always be avoided by a judicious selection of objects proper for such impositions. If inequalities should arise in some states from duties on particular objects, these will in all probability be counterbalanced by proportional inequalities in other states, from the duties on other objects. . . .

It is a signal advantage of taxes on articles of consumption that they contain in their own nature a security against excess. They prescribe their own limits, which cannot be exceeded without defeating the end proposed—that is, an extension of the revenue. . . . If duties are too high, they lessen the consumption; the collection is eluded; and the product to the treasury is not so great as when they are confined within proper and moderate bounds. This forms a complete barrier against any material oppression of the citizens by taxes of this class, and is itself a natural limitation of the power of imposing them.

Impositions of this kind usually fall under the denomination of indirect taxes, and must for the long time constitute the chief part of the revenue raised in this country. Those of the direct kind, which principally relate to land and buildings, may admit of a rule of apportionment. Either the value of land, or the number of the people, may serve as a standard. The state of agriculture and the populousness of a country are considered as having a near relation with each other. And, as a rule, for the purpose intended, numbers, in the view of simplicity and certainty, are entitled to a preference.

In *Federalist 36*, Hamilton emphasized that the proportional burden of direct taxes among the states "is not to be left to the discretion of the national legislature, but is to be determined by the numbers [population] of each state. . . . An actual census or enumeration of the people must furnish the rule, a circumstance which effectually shuts the door to partiality or oppression." Moreover, stated Hamilton, the rule of uniformity for indirect taxes is a further barrier to governmental oppression.

Hamilton stated in *Federalist 22* that direct taxes "principally relate to land and buildings," but the Constitution, while establishing rules for the imposition of direct and indirect taxes, does not define what constitutes a direct tax beyond placing capitation taxes in this category. Shortly after the ratification of the Constitution, the Court confronted the problem of defining direct taxes in *Hylton* v. *United States*, 3 Dallas 171 (1796). The plaintiff charged that Congress had levied a direct tax on carriages without apportioning it among the states. Each of the three justices participating in the decision wrote separate opinions but agreed that the intent of the constitutional system of taxation was to establish principles of fairness and equality which would be violated if the carriage tax were apportioned among the states according to the census. The number of carriages varied greatly from state to state, and states equal in population would have to pay the same carriage tax regardless of the number of carriages operating within their borders. Since the tax ultimately would have to be paid by the carriage owners, one justice calculated that owners in Virginia would pay only $3.80 while those in Connecticut would be assessed $35 per carriage. The justices held that such a result was not intended by the framers of the Constitution when they provided that direct taxes were to be apportioned; therefore, the tax was an indirect levy within the authority of Congress.

During the Civil War, Congress imposed an income tax that was challenged for being a direct tax in violation of the constitutional requirement of apportionment. A unanimous Court, citing *Hylton* v. *United States,* upheld the tax in *Springer* v. *United States*, 102 U.S. 586 (1881). The Court held that the tax was an excise or duty, not a direct tax within the meaning of the Constitution which limits direct taxes to capitation taxes or taxes on real estate. Congress repealed its first income tax law in 1872.

Congress enacted its second income tax law in 1894. The income tax was backed by the agrarian populist movement as the best and fairest way to replenish the depleted resources of the federal treasury. The government was suffering revenue losses as the result of a nationwide business recession. The law was bitterly attacked by eastern Republicans and Democrats alike and challenged as an unconstitutional direct tax because it was not apportioned among the states. In *Pollock* v. *Farmers' Loan and Trust Company,* 158 U.S. 601 (1895), the Court by one vote sustained the challenge, overturning the law on the grounds that it levied a direct tax without meeting the constitutional requirements of apportionment. Writing for the majority, Chief Justice Fuller stated that the precedents of the *Hylton* and *Springer* cases did not support an income tax on the proceeds of real estate, bonds, and other forms of personal property. All such taxes were direct, declared Fuller. The Chief Justice argued that while the Court suggested in the *Hylton* case that direct taxes were limited to capitation and land taxes, no definite statement was made to this effect. The *Springer* case was limited to upholding the income tax on attorneys' fees and did not apply to income from real estate which the *Springer* opinion had declared to be direct taxes. Fuller concluded that taxes on any form of property fell into the "direct" category, as was the case with taxes on income from real estate. The position of the Supreme Court on the income tax issue led to the adoption of the Sixteenth Amendment in 1913, which provides: "The Congress shall have power to lay and collect taxes on incomes, from whatever source derived, without apportionment among the several states, and without regard to any census or enumeration."

THE TAXING POWER AS A BASIS
OF REGULATORY AUTHORITY

The resolution of the income tax question did not settle constitutional issues arising out of the authority of Congress to tax. Taxes have been used directly and indirectly as a regulatory device. Far-reaching regulatory powers have been assumed by Congress on the basis of its constitutional authority to tax.

Are there any limits upon the use of the taxing authority for regulatory purposes? There is nothing in the language of the Constitution to suggest that taxation was to be an instrument to serve any goal other than the raising of revenue. Alexander Hamilton wrote, in *Federalist 30*, that "[m]oney is, with propriety, considered as the vital principle of the body politic; as that which sustains its life and motion and enables it to perform its most essential functions. A complete power [of taxation], therefore, *to procure a regular and adequate supply of revenue*, as far as the resources of the community will permit, may be regarded as an indispensable ingredient in every constitution." (Emphasis supplied.) With the ratification of the Sixteenth Amendment in 1913, the taxing authority of Congress was complete.

Since the original constitutional purpose of taxation was to raise revenue, must Congress demonstrate in order to sustain taxation that its primary intent in exercising its taxing authority is to raise revenue? While virtually all taxes have an incidental regulatory effect by increasing the costs of the taxed products or activities, the raising of revenue may be the primary purpose of the taxes. Conversely, taxation may have an incidental revenue-raising effect while its primary end is regulation.

The apparent use by Congress of its taxing power for a regulatory purpose was challenged in the *Child Labor Tax Case (Bailey* v. *Drexel Furniture Co.)* in 1922. After the Court had declared a congressional law regulating child labor unconstitutional in *Hammer* v. *Dagenhart* (pp. 327–332), Congress passed the Child Labor Tax Law of 1919. The legislation imposed a federal excise tax of 10 percent of net profits on employers of child labor in nearly all businesses throughout the country. The businesses covered in the act were essentially identical to those covered in the previous statute which was declared unconstitutional as an improper exercise of the commerce power. Would the Court sustain an act based upon the taxing authority of Congress which it did not sustain under the commerce power?

Bailey v. Drexel Furniture Company

(Child Labor Tax Case)
295 U.S. 20; 42 S. Ct. 449; 66 L. Ed. 817 (1922)

Mr. Chief Justice Taft delivered the opinion of the Court:

This case presents the question of the constitutional validity of the Child Labor Tax Law. . . .

The law is attacked on the ground that it is a regulation of the employment of child labor in the states,—an exclusively state function under the Federal Constitution and within the reservations of the

Tenth Amendment. It is defended on the ground that it is a mere excise tax, levied by the Congress of the United States under its broad power of taxation conferred by § 8, article 1, of the Federal Constitution. We must construe the law and interpret the intent and meaning of Congress from the language of the act. The words are to be given their ordinary meaning unless the context shows that they are differently used. Does this law impose a tax with only that incidental restraint and regulation which a tax must inevitably involve? Or does it regulate by the use of the so-called tax as a penalty? If a tax, it is clearly an excise. If it were an excise on a commodity or other thing of value we might not be permitted, under previous decisions of this Court, to infer, solely from its heavy burden, that the act intends a prohibition instead of a tax. But this act is more. It provides a heavy exaction for a departure from a detailed and specified course of conduct in business. That course of business is that employers shall employ in mines and quarries, children of an age greater than sixteen years; in mills and factories, children of an age greater than fourteen years; and shall prevent children of less than sixteen years in mills and factories from working more than eight hours a day or six days in the week. If an employer departs from this prescribed course of business, he is to pay to the government one tenth of his entire net income in the business for a full year. The amount is not to be proportioned in any degree to the extent or frequency of the departures, but is to be paid by the employer in full measure whether he employs five hundred children for a year, or employs only one for a day. Moreover, if he does not know the child is within the named age limit, he is not to pay; that is to say, it is only where he knowingly departs from the prescribed course that payment is to be exacted. Scienters are associated with penalties, not with taxes. The

employer's factory is to be subject to inspection at any time not only by the taxing officers of the Treasury, the Department normally charged with the collection of taxes, but also by the Secretary of Labor and his subordinates, whose normal function is the advancement and protection of the welfare of the workers. In the light of these features of the act, a court must be blind not to see that the so-called tax is imposed to stop the employment of children within the age limits prescribed. Its prohibitory and regulatory effect and purpose are palpable. All others can see and understand this. How can we properly shut our minds to it?

It is the high duty and function of this Court in cases regularly brought to its bar to decline to recognize or enforce seeming laws of Congress, dealing with subjects not intrusted to Congress, but left or committed by the supreme law of the land to the control of the states. We cannot avoid the duty even though it requires us to refuse to give effect to legislation designed to promote the highest good. The good sought in unconstitutional legislation is an insidious feature because it leads citizens and legislators of good purpose to promote it without thought of the serious breach it will make in the ark of our covenant, or the harm which will come from breaking down recognized standards. In the maintenance of local self-government, on the one hand, our country has been able to endure and prosper for near a century and a half.

Out of a proper respect for the acts of a co-ordinate branch of the government, this Court has gone far to sustain taxing acts as such, even though there has been ground for suspecting, from the weight of the tax, it was intended to destroy its subject. But in the act before us, the presumption of validity cannot prevail, because the proof of the contrary is found on the very face of its provisions. Grant the validity of this law, and all that Congress would need to do hereafter, in seeking to take over to its control any one of the great number of subjects of public interest, jurisdiction of which the states have never parted with, and which are reserved to them by the Tenth Amendment, would be to enact a detailed measure of complete regulation of the subject and enforce it by a so-called tax upon departures from it. To give such magic to the word "tax" would be to break down all constitutional limitation of the powers of Congress and completely wipe out the sovereignty of the states.

The difference between a tax and a penalty is sometimes difficult to define, and yet the consequences of the distinction in the required method of their collection often are important. Where the sovereign enacting the law has power to impose both tax and penalty, the difference between revenue production and mere regulation may be immaterial; but not so when one sovereign can impose a tax only, and the power of regulation rests in another. Taxes are occasionally imposed in the discretion of the legislature on proper subjects with the primary motive of obtaining revenue from them, and with the incidental motive of discouraging them by making their continuance onerous. They do not lose their character as taxes because of the incidental motive. But there comes a time in the extension of the penalizing features of the so-called tax when it loses its character as such and becomes a mere penalty, with the characteristics of regulation and punishment. Such is the case in the law before us. Although Congress does not invalidate the contract of employment, or expressly declare that the employment within the mentioned ages is illegal, it does exhibit its intent practically to achieve the latter result by adopting the criteria of wrongdoing, and imposing its principal consequence on those who transgress its standard.

The case before us cannot be distinguished from that of *Hammer* v. *Dagenhart* [1918] . . . . Congress there enacted a law to prohibit transportation in interstate commerce of goods made at a factory in which there was employment of children within the same ages and for the same number of hours a day and days in a week as are penalized by the act in this case. . . .

In the case at the bar, Congress, in the name of a tax which, on the face of the act, is a penalty, seeks to do the same thing, and the effort must be equally futile.

The analogy of the *Dagenhart Case* is clear. The congressional power over interstate commerce is, within its proper scope, just as complete and unlimited as the congressional power to tax; and the legislative motive in its exercise is just as free from judicial suspicion and inquiry. Yet when Congress threatened to stop interstate commerce in ordinary and necessary commodities, unobjectionable as subjects of transportation, and to deny the same to the people of a state in order to coerce them into compliance with Congress's regulation of state concerns, the court said this was not in fact regulation of interstate commerce, but rather that of state concerns, and was invalid. So here the so-called tax is a penalty to coerce people of a state to act as Congress wishes them to act in respect of a matter completely the business of the state government under the Federal Constitution. This case requires, as did the *Dagenhart Case*, the application of the principle announced by Chief Justice Marshall in *McCulloch* v. *Maryland*, . . . in a much-quoted passage: "Should Congress, in the execution of its power, adopt measures which are prohibited by the Constitution, or should Congress, under the pretext of executing its powers, pass laws for the accomplishment of objects not intrusted to the government, it would become the painful duty of this tribunal, should a case requiring such a decision come before it, to say that such an act was not the law of the land."

But it is pressed upon us that this Court has gone so far in sustaining taxing measures the effect and tendency of which was to accomplish purposes not directly within congressional power that we are bound by authority to maintain this law.

The first of these is *Veazie Bank* v. *Fenno* [1869] . . . In . . . that case, the validity of a law which increased a tax on the circulating notes of persons and state banks from 1 per centum to 10 per centum was in question. . . . The second objection was stated by the Court:

"It is insisted, however, that the tax in the case before us is excessive, and so excessive as to indicate a purpose on the part of Congress to destroy the franchise of the bank, and is, therefore, beyond the constitutional power of Congress."

To this the Court answered:

"The first answer to this is that the judicial cannot prescribe to the legislative department of the government limitations upon the exercise of its acknowledged powers. The power to tax may be exercised oppressively upon persons, but the responsibility of the legislature is not to the courts, but to the people by whom its members are elected. . . ."

It will be observed that the sole objection to the tax here was its excessive character. Nothing else appeared on the face of the act. It was an increase of tax admittedly legal to a higher rate, and that was all. There were no elaborate specifications on the face of the act, as here, indicating the purpose to regulate matters of state concern and jurisdiction through an exaction so applied as to give it the qualities of a penalty for violation of law rather than a tax. . . .

But more than this, what was charged to be the object of the excessive tax was within the congressional authority, as appears from the second answer which the Court gave to the objection. After having pointed out the legitimate means taken by Congress to secure a national medium or currency, the Court said:

"Having thus, in the exercise of undisputed constitutional powers, undertaken to provide a currency for the whole country, it cannot be questioned that Congress may, constitutionally, secure the benefit of it to the people by appropriate legislation. To this end. . . . Congress may restrain, by suitable enactments, the circulation as money of any notes, not issued under its own authority. . . ."

The next case is that of *McCray* v. *United States* [1904]. . . . That, like the *Veazie Bank Case*, was the increase of an excise tax upon a subject properly taxable, in which the taxpayers claimed that the tax had become invalid because the increase was excessive. It was a tax on oleomargarine, a substitute for butter. The tax on the white oleomargarine was one quarter of a cent a pound, and on the yellow oleomargarine was first 2 cents and was then by the act in question increased to 10 cents per pound. This Court held that the discretion of Congress in the exercise of its constitutional powers to levy excise taxes could not be controlled or limited by the courts because the latter might deem the incidence of the tax oppressive or even destructive. It was the same principle as that applied in the *Veazie Bank Case*. . . . In neither of these cases did the law objected to show on its face, as does the law before us, the detailed specifications of a regulation of a state concern and business with a heavy exaction to promote the efficacy of such regulation. . . .

[Finally] *United States* v. *Doremus* [1919] . . . involved the validity of the Narcotic Drug Act . . . which imposed a special tax on the manufacture, importation, and sale or gift of opium or coca leaves or their compounds or derivatives. It required every person subject to the special tax to register with the collector of internal revenue his name and place of business, and forbade him to sell except upon the written order of the person to whom the sale was made, on a form prescribed by the Commissioner of Internal Revenue. The vendor was required to keep the order for two years, and the purchaser to keep a duplicate for the same time, and all were to be subject to official inspection. Similar requirements were made as to sales upon prescriptions of a physician, and as to the dispensing of such drugs directly to a patient by a physician. The validity of a special tax in the nature of an excise tax on the manufacture, importation, and sale of such drugs was, of course, unquestioned. The provisions for subjecting the sale and distribution of the drugs to official supervision and inspection were held to have a reasonable relation to the enforcement of the tax, and were therefore held valid.

The Court said that the act could not be declared invalid just because another motive than taxation, not shown on the face of the act, might have contributed to its passage. This case does not militate against the conclusion we have reached in respect to the law now before us. The court, there, made manifest its view that the provisions of the so-called taxing act must be naturally and reasonably adapted to the collection of the tax, and not solely to the achievement of some other purpose plainly within state power.

For the reasons given, we must hold the Child Labor Tax Law invalid, and the judgment of the District Court is affirmed.

MR. JUSTICE CLARKE dissents.

What was Chief Justice Taft's reasoning in coming to his conclusion, for the Court, that the "prohibitory and regulatory effect and purpose [of the tax] are palpable"? What contrasts does Taft make between the *Child Labor Tax Case* and the prior Court decisions that sustained taxes which had regulatory effects? In reaching its decision, what importance does the Court attach to the intent of Congress? How does it determine that intent?

The decision of the Court in the *Child Labor Tax Case* seemed to foreclose congressional imposition of a tax to implement a regulatory policy. In *Hill* v. *Wallace*, 259 U.S. 44 (1922), decided on the same day as the *Child Labor Tax Case*, the Court invalidated the Future Trading Act, which imposed a tax on future grain contracts that were not sold through boards of trade that met federal requirements. The tax was a regulatory tax, said the Court, because its purpose was to establish conformity with federal regulatory policy. The Court continued its policy of striking down regulatory taxes in *United States* v. *Constantine*, 295 U.S. 287 (1935), which invalidated a federal tax on liquor dealers who were not operating in compliance with state laws. Justice Roberts's opinion for the Court declared that the tax was imposed not to raise revenue but to penalize dealers for noncompliance with state laws; therefore, the tax was an unconstitutional invasion of the police power of the states.

In the cases that followed the *Child Labor Tax Case* the Court took an active stance in reviewing congressional intent to determine if the motive for the tax was regulatory or to raise revenue. There was no deference given by the Court in these cases to the judgment of Congress concerning the proper exercise of its taxing authority. The judicial self-restraint that was evident in

Veazie Bank v. *Fenno,* 8 Wall. 533 (1869), *McCray* v. *United States,* 195 U.S. 27 (1904), and *United States* v. *Doremus,* 249 U.S. 86 (1919), was lacking in the *Child Labor Tax Case* and those following that decision.[3] But judicial self-restraint returned in the case of *Sonzinsky* v. *United States* (1937), which upheld the National Firearms Act of 1935, imposing a tax on dealers in firearms. The tax "is productive of some revenue," the Court stated, and therefore, "we are not free to speculate as to the motives which moved Congress to impose it, or as to the extent to which it may operate to restrict the activities taxed. As it is not attended by an offensive regulation, and since it operates as a tax, it is within the national taxing power."[4] A transfer tax on marijuana to persons unregistered under federal law was upheld in *United States* v. *Sanchez* (1950), the Court holding that the law imposing the tax was "a legitimate exercise of the taxing power despite its collateral regulatory purpose and effect."[5]

When Congress, in the Revenue Act of 1951, levied a tax on bookmakers and required persons subject to the tax to register with the Collector of Internal Revenue, the tax was challenged for being a masked attempt by Congress to regulate through its taxing power.[6] The law was an attempt to regulate intrastate gambling activities, claimed the plaintiff, which was an unconstitutional invasion of the police power reserved to the states. Relying primarily upon *United States* v. *Constantine* (discussed above), the district court held that the statute was unconstitutional, a decision reviewed by the Supreme Court in the following case.

United States v. Kahriger

345 U.S. 22, 73 S. Ct. 510, 97 L. Ed. 2d 754 (1953)

MR. JUSTICE REED delivered the opinion of the Court:

It is conceded that a federal excise tax does not cease to be valid merely because it discourages or deters the activities taxed. Nor is the tax invalid because the revenue obtained is negligible. Appellee, however, argues that the sole purpose of the statute is to penalize only illegal gambling in the states through the guise of a tax measure. As with the . . . excise taxes which we have held to be valid, the instant tax has a regulatory effect. But regardless of its

regulatory effect, the wagering tax produces revenue. As such it surpasses both the narcotics and firearms taxes which we have found valid.

It is axiomatic that the power of Congress to tax is extensive and sometimes falls with crushing effect on businesses deemed unessential or inimical to the public welfare, or where, as in dealings with narcotics, the collection of the tax also is difficult. As is well known, the constitutional restraints on taxing are few. . . . The remedy for excessive taxation is in

[3]These cases are discussed in the Court's decision in the Child Labor Tax Case, above.
[4]Sonzinsky v. United States, 300 U.S. 506, 514 (1937).
[5]United States v. Sanchez, 340 U.S. 42, 45 (1950).
[6]The Court rejected a challenge to the tax as a violation of the Fifth Amendment protection against self-incrimination. That portion of the Court's opinion was later overruled in Marchetti v. United States, 390 U.S. 39 (1968).

the hands of Congress, not the courts. . . . It is hard to understand why the power to tax should raise more doubts because of indirect effects than other federal powers.

Penalty provisions in tax statutes added for breach of a regulation concerning activities in themselves subject only to state regulation have caused this Court to declare the enactments invalid. Unless there are provisions extraneous to any tax need, courts are without authority to limit the exercise of the taxing power. All the provisions of this excise are adapted to the collection of a valid tax.

Nor do we find the registration requirements of the wagering tax offensive. All that is required is the filing of names, addresses, and places of business. This is quite general in tax returns. Such data are directly and intimately related to the collection of the tax and are "obviously supportable as in aid of a revenue purpose.". . .

Assuming that respondent can raise the self-incrimination issue, that privilege has relation only to past acts, not to future acts that may or may not be committed. . . . If respondent wishes to take wagers subject to excise taxes . . . he must pay an occupational tax and register. Under the registration provisions of the wagering tax, appellee is not compelled to confess to acts already committed, he is merely informed by the statute that in order to engage in the business of wagering in the future he must fulfill certain conditions. . . .

Reversed.

MR. JUSTICE JACKSON, concurring:
Here is a purported tax law which requires no reports and lays no tax except on specified gamblers whose calling in most states is illegal. It requires this group to step forward and identify themselves, not because they, like others, have income, but because of its source. This is difficult to regard as a rational or good-faith revenue measure, despite the defer-

ence that is due Congress. On the contrary, it seems to be a plan to tax out of existence the professional gambler whom it has been found impossible to prosecute out of existence. . . .

It will be a sad day for the revenues if the good will of the people toward their taxing system is frittered away in efforts to accomplish by taxation moral reforms that cannot be accomplished by direct legislation. But the evil that can come from this statute will probably soon make itself manifest to Congress. The evil of a judicial decision impairing the legitimate taxing power by extreme constitutional interpretations might not be transient. Even though this statute approaches the fair limits of constitutionality, I join the decision of the Court.

MR. JUSTICE BLACK, with whom MR. JUSTICE DOUGLAS concurs, dissenting:
. . . The Court here sustains an Act . . . which requires a man to register and confess that he is engaged in the business of gambling. . . . I would hold that this Act violates the Fifth Amendment. . . .

MR. JUSTICE FRANKFURTER, dissenting:
. . . [W]hen oblique use is made of the taxing power as to matters which substantively are not within the powers delegated to Congress, the Court cannot shut its eyes to what is obviously, because designedly, an attempt to control conduct which the Constitution left to the responsibility of the States, merely because Congress wrapped the legislation in the verbal cellophane of a revenue measure.

. . . [T]o allow what otherwise is excluded from congressional authority to be brought within it by casting legislation in the form of a revenue measure could, as so significantly expounded in the *Child Labor Tax Case* . . . , offer an easy way for the legislative imagination to control "any one of the great number of subjects of public interest, jurisdiction of which the

States have never parted with . . . ." . . . I say "significantly" because Mr. Justice Holmes and two of the Justices who had joined his dissent in *Hammer* v. *Dagenhart*, McKenna and Brandeis, JJ., agreed with the opinion in the *Child Labor Tax Case*. . . .

What is relevant to judgment here is that, even if the history of this legislation as it went through Congress did not give one the libretto to the song, the context of the circumstances which brought forth this enactment—sensationally exploited disclosures regarding gambling in big cities and small, the relation of this gambling to corrupt politics, the impatient public response to these disclosures, the feeling of ineptitude or paralysis on the part of local law-enforcing agencies—emphatically supports what was revealed on the floor of Congress, namely, that what was formally a means of raising revenue for the Federal Government was essentially an effort to check if not to stamp out professional gambling. . . .

The motive of congressional legislation is not for our scrutiny, provided only that the ulterior purpose is not expressed in ways which negative what the revenue words on their face express and which do not seek enforcement of the formal revenue purpose through means that offend those standards of decency in our civilization against which due process is a barrier. . . .

Does the Court take into account the *subject* of the tax in sustaining the federal legislation that was challenged in the *Kahriger* case? Do the subjects of regulation in *Sonzinsky* (firearms), *Sanchez* (marijuana), and *Kahriger* (gambling) have anything in common? Is their control a proper end of a federal police power? Contrast the opinions of the Court in these cases upholding what are in effect regulatory taxes, with the Court's opinion in such cases as *Champion* v. *Ames* (pp. 321–325) sustaining the commerce prohibitory device closing the channels of interstate commerce to articles and persons that reflect activities undermining the health, safety, and morals of states and local communities.

In Justice Reed's opinion for the Court in the *Kahriger* case, he states that "It is conceded that a federal excise tax does not cease to be valid merely because it discourages or deters the activities taxed. Nor is the tax invalid because the revenue obtained is negligible." Does this statement imply any limitations upon the use of the taxing power for regulatory ends? Do considerations of federalism limit congressional use of the taxing power? Justice Reed points out that congressional exercise of power under the taxing clause has been carefully scrutinized to determine if the indirect effects of the legislation make it primarily regulatory in nature and therefore unconstitutional. "It is hard to understand," writes Reed, "why the power to tax should raise more doubts because of indirect effects than other federal powers [such as the commerce power and powers exercised under the necessary and proper clause]."

Justice Jackson expresses severe reservations about upholding the tax in his concurring opinion. Why does he nevertheless concur?

Discuss the importance Frankfurter attaches in his dissent to congressional intent and considerations of federalism. By what method does he assess the intent of Congress? How does Frankfurter qualify his statement that the Court should not generally scrutinize the motive of congressional legislation?

Article I, Section 8, which delegates the taxing power to Congress, also provides that Congress shall have the power "to pay the debts and provide for the common defense and general welfare of the United States." Through the exercise of its spending power, that is, its authority to spend for the common defense and general welfare, Congress can indirectly pass regulatory legislation by attaching conditions to the expenditure of government funds. The use of the spending power for regulatory purposes poses the same constitutional questions as the employment of the taxing power for regulatory ends. Congress is indirectly attempting to exercise powers that cannot be implied from the enumerated provisions of Article I.

The spending power is explicitly limited to providing for the common defense and general welfare, but what does this limitation mean? The issue arose in *United States* v. *Butler* (1936). The case involved a challenge to the Agricultural Adjustment Act of 1933, designed to raise farm prices by curtailing agricultural production. The act authorized the Secretary of Agriculture to contract with farmers for the reduction of acreage they would put into production in return for payments from the government. The payments would be derived from a tax on the first processor of the commodities regulated. Under the terms of the statute a processing tax was levied on the Hoosac Mills Corp. Butler joined with the other receivers for the company to challenge the tax as an unconstitutional extension of the regulatory authority of Congress over agricultural production.

The government first challenged Butler's suit as inappropriate due to lack of standing on the part of the plaintiffs. It was, argued the government, a taxpayer's suit and therefore barred under the doctrine of *Frothingham* v. *Mellon* (1923). In that case a citizen alleging that her tax liability would be increased under the Maternity Act of 1921, which provided for grants-in-aid to states, sued to enjoin the Secretary of the Treasury from spending the funds that had been authorized. The Court held that government taxation was a matter of general and not individual concern and that taxpayers qua taxpayers could not sue to raise the issue of the authority of the government to make expenditures. "If one taxpayer may champion and litigate such a cause," stated the Court, "then every other taxpayer may do the same, not only in respect of the statute here under review but in respect of every other appropriation act and statute whose administration requires the outlay of public money, and whose validity may be questioned."[7] The result of giving taxpayers standing, declared the Court, would be an intolerable burden upon government because it would encourage and facilitate challenges to government action by individuals whose interests were undistinguishable from those of the general public.[8]

Justice Roberts's opinion for the Court in the *Butler* case stated that it was not a taxpayer's suit, for under the law the tax was an indispensable part of the plan of regulation. All of the tax moneys were to be spent for the reg-

---

[7]Frothingham v. Mellon, 262 U.S. 447, 487 (1923).

[8]The ruling in Frothingham v. Mellon was partially modified in Flast v. Cohen, 392 U.S. 83 (1968), which permitted a taxpayer's suit attacking a federal statute on the ground that it violated the establishment and free exercise clauses of the First Amendment.

ulatory program, and no funds were earmarked for the general treasury. On the issue of standing Roberts concluded "that the act is one regulating agricultural production; that the tax is a mere incident of such regulation and that the respondents have standing to challenge the legality of the exaction."[9] The reasoning of the Court on the question of standing, that the case did not essentially involve a challenge to the tax but to the regulatory plan which involved government *expenditures*, confronted the Court with the question of the scope of the spending power. Did the Article I, Section 8 authority granted Congress to spend for the general welfare authorize it to regulate agricultural production?

United States v. Butler

297 U.S. 1; 56 S. Ct. 312; 80 L. Ed. 477 (1936)

MR. JUSTICE ROBERTS delivered the opinion of the Court:

. . . [*First*] [i]t is inaccurate and misleading to speak of the exaction from processors prescribed by the challenged act as a tax, or to say that as a tax it is subject to no infirmity. A tax, in the general understanding of the term, and as used in the Constitution, signifies an exaction for the support of the Government. The word has never been thought to connote the expropriation of money from one group for the benefit of another. We may concede that the latter sort of imposition is constitutional when imposed to effectuate regulation of a matter in which both groups are interested and in respect of which there is a power of legislative regulation. But manifestly no justification for it can be found unless as an integral part of such regulation. The exaction cannot be wrested out of its setting, denominated an excise for raising revenue and legalized by ignoring its purpose as a mere instrumentality for bringing about a desired end. To do this would be to shut our eyes to what all others than we can see and understand. *Child Labor Tax Case* [1922]. . . .

We conclude that the act is one regulating agricultural production; that the tax is a mere incident of such regulation

and that the respondents have standing to challenge the legality of the exaction.

It does not follow that as the act is not an exertion of the taxing power and the exaction not a true tax, the statute is void or the exaction uncollectible. For . . . if this is an expedient regulation by Congress, of a subject within one of its granted powers, "and the end to be attained is one falling within that power, the act is not void, because, within a loose and more extended sense than was used in the Constitution," the exaction is called a tax.

Second. The Government asserts that even if the respondents may question the propriety of the appropriation embodied in the statute their attack must fail because Article I, § 8 of the Constitution authorizes the contemplated expenditure of the funds raised by the tax. This contention presents the great and the controlling question in the case. We approach its decision with a sense of our grave responsibility to render judgment in accordance with the principles established for the governance of all three branches of the Government.

There should be no misunderstanding as to the function of this Court in such a case. It is sometimes said that the Court

[9]United States v. Butler, 297 U.S. 1, 61 (1936).

assumes a power to overrule or control the action of the people's representatives. This is a misconception. The Constitution is the supreme law of the land ordained and established by the people. All legislation must conform to the principles it lays down. When an act of Congress is appropriately challenged in the courts as not conforming to the constitutional mandate the judicial branch of the Government has only one duty,—to lay the article of the Constitution which is invoked beside the statute which is challenged and to decide whether the latter squares with the former. All the Court does, or can do, is to announce its considered judgment upon the question. The only power it has, if such it may be called, is the power of judgment. This Court neither approves nor condemns any legislative policy. Its delicate and difficult office is to ascertain and declare whether the legislation is in accordance with, or in contravention of, the provisions of the Constitution; and, having done that, its duty ends.

The question is not what power the Federal Government ought to have but what powers in fact have been given by the people. It hardly seems necessary to reiterate that ours is a dual form of government; that in every state there are two governments,—the state and the United States. Each State has all governmental powers save such as the people, by their Constitution, have conferred upon the United States, denied to the States, or reserved to themselves. The federal union is a government of delegated powers. It has only such as are expressly conferred upon it and such as are reasonably to be implied from those granted. In this respect we differ radically from nations where all legislative power, without restriction or limitation, is vested in a parliament or other legislative body subject to no restrictions except the discretion of its members.

Article I, § 8, of the Constitution vests sundry powers in the Congress. But two of its clauses have any bearing upon the validity of the statute under review.

The third clause endows the Congress with power "to regulate Commerce . . . among the several States." Despite a reference in its first section to a burden upon, and an obstruction of the normal currents of commerce, the act under review does not purport to regulate transactions in interstate or foreign commerce. Its stated purpose is the control of agricultural production, a purely local activity, in an effort to raise the prices paid the farmer. Indeed, the Government does not attempt to uphold the validity of the act on the basis of the commerce clause, which, for the purpose of the present case, may be put aside as irrelevant.

The clause thought to authorize the legislation,—the first,—confers upon Congress power "to lay and collect Taxes, Duties, Imposts and Excises, to pay the Debts and provide for the common Defence and general Welfare of the United States. . . ." It is not contended that this provision grants power to regulate agricultural production upon the theory that such legislation would promote the general welfare. The Government concedes that the phrase "to provide for the general welfare" qualifies the power "to lay and collect taxes." The view that the clause grants power to provide for the general welfare, independently of the taxing power, has never been authoritatively accepted. Mr. Justice Story points out that if it were adopted "it is obvious that under color of the generality of the words, to 'provide for the common defence and general welfare,' the government of the United States is, in reality, a government of general and unlimited powers, notwithstanding the subsequent enumeration of specific powers." The true construction undoubtedly is that the only thing granted is the power to tax for the purpose of providing funds for payment of the nation's debts and making provision for the general welfare.

Nevertheless the Government asserts that warrant is found in this clause for the adoption of the Agricultural Adjustment Act. The argument is that Congress may appropriate and authorize the spending of moneys for the "general welfare"; that the phrase should be liberally construed to cover anything conducive to national welfare; that decision as to what will promote such welfare rests with Congress alone, and the courts may not review its determination; and finally that the appropriation under attack was in fact for the general welfare of the United States.

The Congress is expressly empowered to lay taxes to provide for the general welfare. Funds in the Treasury as a result of taxation may be expended only through appropriation. (Art. I, § 9, cl. 7.) They can never accomplish the objects for which they were collected unless the power to appropriate is as broad as the power to tax. The necessary implication from the terms of the grant is that the public funds may be appropriated "to provide for the general welfare of the United States." These words cannot be meaningless, else they would not have been used. The conclusion must be that they were intended to limit and define the granted power to raise and to expend money. How shall they be construed to effectuate the intent of the instrument?

Since the foundation of the Nation sharp differences of opinion have persisted as to the true interpretation of the phrase. Madison asserted it amounted to no more than a reference to the other powers enumerated in the subsequent clauses of the same section; that, as the United States is a government of limited and enumerated powers, the grant of power to tax and spend for the general national welfare must be confined to the enumerated legislative fields committed to the Congress. In this view the phrase is mere tautology, for taxation and appropriation are or may be necessary incidents of the exercise of any of the enumerated

legislative powers. Hamilton, on the other hand, maintained the clause confers a power separate and distinct from those later enumerated, is not restricted in meaning by the grant of them, and Congress consequently has a substantive power to tax and to appropriate, limited only by the requirement that it shall be exercised to provide for the general welfare of the United States. Each contention has had the support of those whose views are entitled to weight. This Court has noticed the question, but has never found it necessary to decide which is the true construction. Mr. Justice Story, in his Commentaries, espouses the Hamiltonian position. We shall not review the writings of public men and commentators or discuss the legislative practice. Study of all these leads us to conclude that the reading advocated by Mr. Justice Story is the correct one. While, therefore, the power to tax is not unlimited, its confines are set in the clause which confers it, and not in those of § 8 which bestow and define the legislative powers of the Congress. It results that the power of Congress to authorize expenditures of public moneys for public purposes is not limited by the direct grants of legislative power found in the Constitution.

But the adoption of the broader construction leaves the power to spend subject to limitations. . . .

. . . Story says that if the tax be not proposed for the common defence or general welfare, but for other objects wholly extraneous, it would be wholly indefensible upon constitutional principles. And he makes it clear that the powers of taxation and appropriation extend only to matters of national, as distinguished from local welfare. . . .

We are not now required to ascertain the scope of the phrase "general welfare of the United States" or to determine whether an appropriation in aid of agriculture falls within it. Wholly apart from that question, another principle embedded in our Constitution prohibits the enforcement of the Agricultural Adjustment Act. The act invades the reserved rights of the states. It is a statutory plan to regulate and control agricultural production, a matter beyond the powers delegated to the federal government. The tax, the appropriation of the funds raised, and the direction for their disbursement, are but parts of the plan. They are but means to an unconstitutional end.

From the accepted doctrine that the United States is a government of delegated powers, it follows that those not expressly granted, or reasonably to be implied from such as are conferred, are reserved to the states or to the people. To forestall any suggestion to the contrary, the Tenth Amendment was adopted. The same proposition, otherwise stated, is that powers not granted are prohibited. None to regulate agricultural production is given, and therefore legislation by Congress for that purpose is forbidden.

It is an established principle that the attainment of a prohibited end may not be accomplished under the pretext of the exertion of powers which are granted.

"Should Congress, in the execution of its powers, adopt measures which are prohibited by the constitution; or should Congress, under the pretext of executing its powers, pass laws for the accomplishment of objects not intrusted to the government; it would become the painful duty of this tribunal, should a case requiring such a decision come before it, to say that such an act was not the law of the land." *McCulloch* v. *Maryland*. . . .

"Congress cannot, under the pretext of executing delegated power, pass laws for the accomplishment of objects not entrusted to the Federal Government. And we accept as established doctrine that any provision of an act of Congress ostensibly enacted under power granted by the Constitution, not naturally and reasonably adapted to the effective exercise of such power but solely to the achievement of something plainly within power reserved to the States, is invalid and cannot be enforced." *Linder* v. *United States* [1925] . . .

These principles are as applicable to the power to lay taxes as to any other federal power. Said the Court, in *McCulloch* v. *Maryland:*

"Let the end be legitimate, let it be within the scope of the constitution, and all means which are appropriate, which are plainly adapted to that end, which are not prohibited, but consist with the letter and spirit of the constitution, are constitutional."

The power of taxation, which is expressly granted, may, of course, be adopted as a means to carry into operation another power also expressly granted. But resort to the taxing power to effectuate an end which is not legitimate, not within the scope of the Constitution, is obviously inadmissible. . . .

Third. If the taxing power may not be used as the instrument to enforce a regulation of matters of state concern with respect to which the Congress has no authority to interfere, may it, as in the present case, be employed to raise the money necessary to purchase a compliance which the Congress is powerless to command? The Government asserts that whatever might be said against the validity of the plan if compulsory, it is constitutionally sound because the end is accomplished by voluntary cooperation. There are two sufficient answers to the contention. The regulation is not in fact voluntary. The farmer, of course, may refuse to comply, but the price of such refusal is the loss of benefits. The amount offered is intended to be sufficient to exert pressure on him to agree to the proposed regulation. The power to confer or withhold unlimited benefits is the power to coerce or destroy. If the cotton grower elects not to accept the benefits, he will receive less for his crops; those who receive payments will be able to undersell him. The result may well be financial ruin. The coercive purpose and intent of the statute is not obscured by the fact that it has not been perfectly successful. It is pointed out that, because there still remained a minority whom the rental and benefit payments were insufficient to induce to surrender their independence of action, the Congress has gone further and, in the Bankhead Cotton Act, used the taxing power in a more directly minatory fashion to compel submission. This progression only serves more fully to expose the coercive purpose of the so-called tax imposed by the present act. It is clear that the Department of Agriculture has properly described the plan as one to keep a noncoöperating minority in line. This is coercion by economic pressure. The asserted power of choice is illusory. . . .

But if the plan were one for purely voluntary co-operation it would stand no better so far as federal power is concerned. At best it is a scheme for purchasing with federal funds submission to federal regulation of a subject reserved to the states.

It is said that Congress has the undoubted right to appropriate money to executive officers for expenditure under contracts between the government and individuals; that much of the total expenditures is so made. But appropriations and expenditures under contracts for proper governmental purposes cannot justify contracts which are not within federal power. And contracts for the reduction of acreage and the control of production are outside the range of that power. An appropriation to be expended by the United States under contracts calling for violation of a state law clearly would offend the Constitution. Is a statute less objectionable which authorizes expenditure of federal moneys to induce action in a field in which the United States has no power to intermeddle? The Congress cannot invade state jurisdiction to compel individ-

ual action; no more can it purchase such action.

We are referred to numerous types of federal appropriation which have been made in the past, and it is asserted no question has been raised as to their validity. We need not stop to examine or consider them. As was said in *Massachusetts* v. *Mellon* [1923] . . .

". . . as an examination of the acts of Congress will disclose, a large number of statutes appropriating or involving the expenditure of moneys for non-federal purposes have been enacted and carried into effect."

As the opinion points out, such expenditures have not been challenged because no remedy was open for testing their constitutionality in the courts.

We are not here concerned with a conditional appropriation of money, nor with a provision that if certain conditions are not complied with the appropriation shall no longer be available. By the Agricultural Adjustment Act the amount of the tax is appropriated to be expended only in payment under contracts whereby the parties bind themselves to regulation by the Federal Government. There is an obvious difference between a statute stating the conditions upon which moneys shall be expended and one effective only upon assumption of a contractual obligation to submit to a regulation which otherwise could not be enforced. Many examples pointing the distinction might be cited. We are referred to appropriations in aid of education, and it is said that no one has doubted the power of Congress to stipulate the sort of education for which money shall be expended. But an appropriation to an educational institution which by its terms is to become available only if the beneficiary enters into a contract to teach doctrines subversive of the Constitution is clearly bad. An affirmance of the authority of Congress so to condition the expenditure of an appropriation would tend to nullify all constitutional limitations upon legislative power. . . .

Congress has no power to enforce its commands on the farmer to the ends sought by the Agricultural Adjustment Act. It must follow that it may not indirectly accomplish those ends by taxing and spending to purchase compliance. The Constitution and the entire plan of our government negate any such use of the power to tax and to spend as the act undertakes to authorize. It does not help to declare that local conditions throughout the nation have created a situation of national concern; for this is but to say that whenever there is a widespread similarity of local conditions, Congress may ignore constitutional limitations upon its own powers and usurp those reserved to the states. If, in lieu of compulsory regulation of subjects within the states' reserved jurisdiction, which is prohibited, the Congress could invoke the taxing and spending power as a means to accomplish the same end, clause 1 of § 8 of Article I would become the instrument for total subversion of the governmental powers reserved to the individual states.

If the act before us is a proper exercise of the federal taxing power, evidently the regulation of all industry throughout the United States may be accomplished by similar exercises of the same power. It would be possible to exact money from one branch of an industry and pay it to another branch in every field of activity which lies within the province of the states. The mere threat of such a procedure might well induce the surrender of rights and the compliance with federal regulation as the price of continuance in business. . . .

Until recently no suggestion of the existence of any such power in the Federal Government has been advanced. The expressions of the framers of the Constitution, the decisions of this Court interpreting that instrument, and the writings of great commentators will be searched in vain for any suggestion that there exists in the clause under discussion or elsewhere in the Constitution, the authority whereby every provision and every fair implication from that instrument may be subverted, the independence of the individual states obliterated, and the United States converted into a central government exercising uncontrolled police power in every state of the Union, superseding all local control or regulation of the affairs or concerns of the states. . . .

MR. JUSTICE STONE, dissenting:

I think the judgment should be reversed.

The present stress of widely held and strongly expressed differences of opinion of the wisdom of the Agricultural Adjustment Act makes it important, in the interest of clear thinking and sound result, to emphasize at the outset certain propositions which should have controlling influence in determining the validity of the Act. They are:

1. The power of courts to declare a statute unconstitutional is subject to two guiding principles of decision which ought never to be absent from judicial consciousness. One is that courts are concerned only with the power to enact statutes, not with their wisdom. The other is that while unconstitutional exercise of power by the executive and legislative branches of the government is subject to judicial restraint, the only check upon our own exercise of power is our own sense of self-restraint. For the removal of unwise laws from the statute books appeal lies not to the courts but to the ballot and to the processes of democratic government.

2. The constitutional power of Congress to levy an excise tax upon the processing of agricultural products is not questioned. The present levy is held invalid, not for any want of power in Congress to lay such a tax to defray public ex-

penditures, including those for the general welfare, but because the use to which its proceeds are put is disapproved.

3. As the present depressed state of agriculture is nation wide in its extent and effects, there is no basis for saying that the expenditure of public money in aid of farmers is not within the specifically granted power of Congress to levy taxes to "provide for the . . . general welfare." The opinion of the Court does not declare otherwise.

4. No question of a variable tax fixed from time to time by fiat of the Secretary of Agriculture, or of unauthorized delegation of legislative power, is now presented. The schedule of rates imposed by the Secretary in accordance with the original command of Congress has since been specifically adopted and confirmed by Act of Congress, which has declared that it shall be the lawful tax. . . .

It is with these preliminary and hardly controverted matters in mind that we should direct our attention to the pivot on which the decision of the Court is made to turn. It is that a levy unquestionably within the taxing power of Congress may be treated as invalid because it is a step in a plan to regulate agricultural production and is thus a forbidden infringement of state power. The levy is not any the less an exercise of taxing power because it is intended to defray an expenditure for the general welfare rather than for some other support of government. Nor is the levy and collection of the tax pointed to as affecting the regulation. While all federal taxes inevitably have some influence on the internal economy of the states, it is not contended that the levy of a processing tax upon manufacturers using agricultural products as raw material has any perceptible regulatory effect upon either their production or manufacture. . . .

Of the assertion that the payments to farmers are coercive, it is enough to say that no such contention is pressed by the taxpayer, and no such consequences were to be anticipated or appear to have resulted from the administration of the Act. The suggestion of coercion finds no support in the record or in any data showing the actual operation of the Act. Threat of loss, not hope of gain, is the essence of economic coercion. . . .

It is upon the contention that state power is infringed by purchased regulation of agricultural production that chief reliance is placed. It is insisted that, while the Constitution gives to Congress, in specific and unambiguous terms, the power to tax and spend, the power is subject to limitations which do not find their origin in any express provision of the Constitution and to which other expressly delegated powers are not subject. . . .

. . . The power of Congress to spend is inseparable from persuasion to action over which Congress has no legislative control. Congress may not command that the science of agriculture be taught in state universities. But if it would aid the teaching of that science by grants to state institutions, it is appropriate, if not necessary, that the grant be on the condition, incorporated in the Morrill Act . . . that it be used for the intended purpose. . . .

. . . The spending power of Congress is in addition to the legislative power and not subordinate to it. This independent grant of the power of the purse, and its very nature, involving in its exercise the duty to insure expenditure within the granted power, presuppose freedom of selection among divers ends and aims, and the capacity to impose such conditions as will render the choice effective. It is a contradiction in terms to say that there is power to spend for the national welfare, while rejecting any power to impose conditions reasonably adapted to the attainment of the end which alone would justify the expenditure.

The limitation now sanctioned must lead to absurd consequences. The government may give seeds to farmers, but may not condition the gift upon their being planted in places where they are most needed or even planted at all. The government may give money to the unemployed, but may not ask that those who get it shall give labor in return, or even use it to support their families. It may give money to sufferers from earthquake, fire, tornado, pestilence or flood, but may not impose conditions—health precautions designed to prevent the spread of disease, or induce the movement of population to safer or more sanitary areas. All that, because it is purchased regulation infringing state powers, must be left for the states, who are unable or unwilling to supply the necessary relief. . . .

That the governmental power of the purse is a great one is not now for the first time announced. Every student of the history of government and economics is aware of its magnitude and of its existence in every civilized government. Both were well understood by the framers of the Constitution when they sanctioned the grant of the spending power to the federal government, and both were recognized by Hamilton and Story, whose views of the spending power as standing on a parity with the other powers specifically granted, have hitherto been generally accepted.

The suggestion that it must now be curtailed by judicial fiat because it may be abused by unwise use hardly rises to the dignity of argument. So may judicial power be abused. "The power to tax is the power to destroy," but we do not, for that reason, doubt its existence, or hold that its efficacy is to be restricted by its incidental or collateral effects upon the states. . . . The power to tax and spend is not without constitutional restraints. One restriction is that the purpose must be truly na-

tional. Another is that it may not be used to coerce action left to state control. Another is the conscience and patriotism of Congress and the Executive. "It must be remembered that legislators are the ultimate guardians of the liberties and welfare of the people in quite as great a degree as the courts." Justice Holmes. . . .

A tortured construction of the Constitution is not to be justified by recourse to extreme examples of reckless congressional spending which might occur if courts could not prevent—expenditures which, even if they could be thought to effect any national purpose, would be possible only by action of a legislature lost to all sense of public responsibility. Such suppositions are addressed to the mind accustomed to believe that it is the business of courts to sit in judgment on the wisdom of legislative action. Courts are not the only agency of government that must be assumed to have capacity to govern. Congress and the courts both unhappily may falter or be mistaken in the performance of their constitutional duty. But interpretation of our great charter of government which proceeds on any assumption that the responsibility for the preservation of our institutions is the exclusive concern of any one of the three branches of government, or that it alone can save them from destruction is far more likely, in the long run, "to obliterate the constituent members" of "an indestructible union of indestructible states" than the frank recognition that language, even of a constitution, may mean what it says: that the power to tax and spend includes the power to relieve a nationwide economic maladjustment by conditional gifts of money.

MR. JUSTICE BRANDEIS and MR. JUSTICE CARDOZO join in this opinion.

How does the Court distinguish the Madisonian from the Hamiltonian-Story positions on the scope of the spending power? Although the Court claims that it is adopting the Hamiltonian-Story position, is it not implementing the more restrictive view of Madison? What considerations of federalism are raised in the majority opinion? Contrast the majority opinion of Roberts with Justice Stone's dissent on the question of the limits of the congressional power of the purse. To what extent, under each opinion, can Congress: (1) make conditional grants of money; (2) "coerce" individuals or states; (3) regulate local activities? Does Justice Stone's dissenting opinion support a wider doctrine of judicial self-restraint than the majority opinion of Justice Roberts?

The most important standard guiding the exercise of the spending power that emerged from the *Butler* opinion was that Congress cannot coercively purchase compliance with a program that it does not otherwise have the authority to enact. Conditional appropriations, which the *Butler* majority distinguished from the coercive purchase of compliance, are permissible. For example, as the dissent noted in *Butler:* "Congress may not command that the science of agriculture be taught in state universities. But if it would aid the teaching of that science by grants to state institutions, it is appropriate, if not necessary, that the grant be on the condition, incorporated in the Morrill Act . . . that it be used for the intended purpose." In the Agricultural Adjustment Act of 1933 Congress was attempting to purchase the regulation of agricultural production, a coercive act that invaded state power.

The question of the coercive purchase of government policy was again presented to the Court in *Steward Machine Company v. Davis* (1937). Title 9 of the Social Security Act of 1935 imposed a payroll tax upon employers of eight or more persons, allowing employers a credit of up to 90 percent of the tax for any contributions made to a state unemployment fund that had been certified by the Social Security Administration as meeting the requirements of the act. Unlike the tax revenues reviewed in the *Butler* case, the proceeds from the Social Security payroll tax went into general government funds.

The plaintiffs contended that the government was exercising unconstitutional power in attempting to coerce the states into establishing unemployment systems that conformed to federal standards. The plaintiffs declared that "while Congress may have lately spent billions of dollars for relief, which is the primary burden and duty of the states, the constitutionality of which is difficult if not impossible to raise in the courts, the fact that Congress has spent this sum cannot now be used to arm Congress with the power to impose invalid burdens on the states in order to compel the latter to refill the Federal Treasury and encourage the states to assume their proper burdens in the future."[10] The government countered with the argument that "It will be readily seen that the power here exercised, if it amounts to an inducement to the states to adopt some course of action, only induces fiscal action for a purpose for which the federal spending power is now being exercised. The power thus carries its own inherent limitations and could not conceivably be extended so far as to invade the reserved field of the states or to destroy the dual system of government."[11]

[10]LB, Vol. 34, pp. 169–170.
[11]Ibid., p. 337.

Justice Cardozo wrote the majority opinion. Can you guess from the fact that he joined Justice Stone's dissent in *United States* v. *Butler* how he would approach and resolve this case?

Steward Machine Co. v. Davis

301 U.S. 548; 575. Ct. 883; 81 L. Ed. 1279 (1937)

MR. JUSTICE CARDOZO delivered the opinion of the Court:

. . . The assault on the statute proceeds on an extended front. Its assailants take the ground that the tax is not an excise; that it is not uniform throughout the United States as excises are required to be; that its exceptions are so many and arbitrary as to violate the Fifth Amendment; that its purpose was not revenue, but an unlawful invasion of the reserved powers of the states; and that the states in submitting to it have yielded to coercion and have abandoned governmental functions which they are not permitted to surrender.

The objections will be considered seriatim with such further explanation as may be necessary to make their meaning clear. . . .

Third: The excise is not void as involving the coercion of the states in contravention of the Tenth Amendment or of restrictions implicit in our federal form of government.

The proceeds of the excise when collected are paid into the Treasury at Washington, and thereafter are subject to appropriation like public moneys generally. . . . No presumption can be indulged that they will be misapplied or wasted. Even if they were collected in the hope or expectation that some other and collateral good would be furthered as an incident, that without more would not make the act invalid. *Sonzinsky* v. *United States* [1937]. . . . This indeed is hardly questioned. The case for the petitioner is built on the contention that here an ulterior aim is wrought into the very structure of the act, and what is even more important that the aim is not only ulterior, but essentially unlawful. In particular, the 90 percent credit is relied upon as supporting that conclusion. But before the statute succumbs to an assault upon these lines, two propositions must be made out by the assailant. . . . There must be a showing in the first place that separated from the credit the revenue provisions are incapable of standing by themselves. There must be a showing in the second place that the tax and the credit in combination are weapons of coercion, destroying or impairing the autonomy of the states. The truth of each proposition being essential to the success of the assault, we pass for convenience to a consideration of the second, without pausing to inquire whether there has been a demonstration of the first.

To draw the line intelligently between duress and inducement, there is need to remind ourselves of facts as to the problem of unemployment that are now matters of common knowledge. . . . The relevant statistics are gathered in the brief of counsel for the government. Of the many available figures a few only will be mentioned. During the years 1929 to 1936, when the country was passing through a cyclical depression, the number of the unemployed mounted to unprecedented heights. Often the average was more than 10 million; at times a peak was attained of 16 million or more. Disaster to the breadwinner meant disaster to dependents. Accordingly the roll of the unemployed, itself formidable enough, was only a partial roll of the destitute or needy. The fact developed quickly that the states were unable to give the requisite relief. The problem had become national in area and dimensions. There was need of help from the nation if the people were not to starve. It is too late today for the argument to be heard with tolerance that in a crisis so extreme the use of the moneys of the nation to relieve the unemployed and their dependents is a use for any purpose narrower than the promotion of the general welfare. . . .

In the presence of this urgent need for some remedial expedient, the question is to be answered whether the expedient adopted has overleapt the bounds of power. The assailants of the statute say that its dominant end and aim is to drive the state Legislatures under the whip of economic pressure into the enactment of unemployment compensation laws at the bidding of the central government. Supporters of the statute say that its operation is not constraint, but the creation of a larger freedom, the states and the nation joining in a co-operative endeavor to avert a common evil. . . .

Who then is coerced through the operation of this statute? Not the taxpayer. He pays in fulfillment of the mandate of the local legislature. Not the state. Even now she does not offer a suggestion that in passing the unemployment law she was affected by duress. . . . For all that appears, she is satisfied with her choice, and would be sorely disappointed if it were now to be annulled. The difficulty with the petitioner's contention is that it confuses motive with coercion. "Every tax is in some measure regulatory. To some extent it interposes an economic impediment to the activity taxed as compared with others not taxed." . . . In like manner every rebate from a tax when conditioned upon conduct is in some measure a temptation. But to hold that motive or temptation is equivalent to coercion is to plunge the law in endless difficulties. The outcome of such a doctrine is the acceptance of a philosophical determinism by which

choice becomes impossible. Till now the law has been guided by a robust common sense which assumes the freedom of the will as a working hypothesis in the solution of its problems. The wisdom of the hypothesis has illustration in this case. Nothing in the case suggests the exertion of a power akin to undue influence, if we assume that such a concept can ever be applied with fitness to the relations between state and nation. Even on that assumption the location of the point at which pressure turns into compulsion, and ceases to be inducement, would be a question of degree, at times, perhaps, of fact. The point had not been reached when Alabama made her choice. We cannot say that she was acting, not of her unfettered will, but under the strain of a persuasion equivalent to undue influence, when she chose to have relief administered under laws of her own making, by agents of her own selection, instead of under federal laws, administered by federal officers, with all the ensuing evils, at least to many minds, of federal patronage and power. There would be a strange irony, indeed, if her choice were now to be annulled on the basis of an assumed duress in the enactment of a statute which her courts have accepted as a true expression of her will. . . . We think the choice must stand.

In ruling as we do, we leave many questions open. We do not say that a tax is valid, when imposed by act of Congress, if it is laid upon the condition that a state may escape its operation through the adoption of a statute unrelated in subject-matter to activities fairly within the scope of national policy and power. No such question is before us. In the tender of this credit Congress does not intrude upon fields foreign to its function. . . .

United States v. *Butler* is cited by petitioner as a decision to the contrary. There a tax was imposed on processors of farm products, the proceeds to be paid to farmers who would reduce their acreage and crops under agreements with the Secretary of Agriculture, the plan of the act being to increase the prices of certain farm products by decreasing the quantities produced. The Court held (1) that the so-called tax was not a true one ... the proceeds being earmarked for the benefit of farmers complying with the prescribed conditions, (2) that there was an attempt to regulate production without the consent of the state in which production was affected, and (3) that the payments to farmers were coupled with coercive contracts ... unlawful in their aim and oppressive in their consequences. The decision was by a divided Court, a minority taking the view that the objections were untenable. None of them is applicable to the situation here developed.

(a) The proceeds of the tax in controversy are not earmarked for a special group.

(b) The unemployment compensation law which is a condition of the credit has had the approval of the state and could not be a law without it.

(c) The condition is not linked to an irrevocable agreement, for the state at its pleasure may repeal its unemployment law (section 903(a) (6), 42 U.S.C.A. § 1103(a) (6), terminate the credit, and place itself where it was before the credit was accepted.

(d) The condition is not directed to the attainment of an unlawful end, but to an end, the relief of unemployment, for which nation and state may lawfully coöperate.

Fourth: The statute does not call for a surrender by the states of powers essential to their quasi sovereign existence.

Argument to the contrary has its source in two sections of the act. One section defines the minimum criteria to which a state compensation system is required to conform if it is to be accepted by the Board as the basis for a credit. The other section rounds out the requirement with complementary rights and duties. Not all the criteria or their incidents are challenged as unlawful. We will speak of them first generally, and then more specifically in so far as they are questioned.

A credit to taxpayers for payments made to a state under a state unemployment law will be manifestly futile in the absence of some assurance that the law leading to the credit is in truth what it professes to be. An unemployment law framed in such a way that the unemployed who look to it will be deprived of reasonable protection is one in name and nothing more. What is basic and essential may be assured by suitable conditions. The terms embodied in these sections are directed to that end. A wide range of judgment is given to the several states as to the particular type of statute to be spread upon their books. ... What they may not do, if they would earn the credit, is to depart from those standards which in the judgment of Congress are to be ranked as fundamental. Even if opinion may differ as to the fundamental quality of one or more of the conditions, the difference will not avail to vitiate the statute. In determining essentials, Congress must have the benefit of a fair margin of discretion. One cannot say with reason that this margin has been exceeded, or that the basic standards have been determined in any arbitrary fashion. In the event that some particular condition shall be found to be too uncertain to be capable of enforcement, it may be severed from the others, and what is left will still be valid.

We are to keep in mind steadily that the conditions to be approved by the Board as the basis for a credit are not provisions of a contract, but terms of a statute, which may be altered or repealed. Section 903 (a) (6). The state does not bind itself to keep the law in force. It does not even bind itself that the moneys paid into the federal fund will be kept there indefinitely or for any stated time. On the contrary, the Secretary of the Treasury will honor a requisition for the whole or any part of the deposit in the fund whenever one is made by the appropriate officials. The only consequence of the repeal or excessive amendment of the statute, or the expenditure of the money, when requisitioned, for other than compensation uses or administrative expenses, is that approval of the law will end, and with it the allowance of a credit, upon notice to the state agency and an opportunity for hearing. . . .

These basic considerations are in truth a solvent of the problem. Subjected to their test, the several objections on the score of abdication are found to be unreal.

Thus, the argument is made that by force of an agreement the moneys when withdrawn must be "paid through public employment offices in the State or such other agencies as the Board may approve." . . . But in truth there is no agreement as to the method of disbursement. There is only a condition which the state is free at pleasure to disregard or to fulfill. Moreover, approval is not requisite if public employment offices are made the disbursing instruments. Approval is to be a check upon resort to "other agencies" that may, perchance, be irresponsible. A state looking for a credit must give assurance that her system has been organized upon a base of rationality.

There is argument again that the moneys when withdrawn are to be devoted to specific uses, the relief of unemployment, and that by agreement for such payment the quasi-sovereign position of the state has been impaired, if not abandoned. But again there is confusion between promise and condition. Alabama is still free, without breach of an agreement to change her system over night. No officer or agency of the national government can force a compensation law upon her or keep it in existence. No officer or agency of that government, either by suit or other means,

can supervise or control the application of the payments.

Finally and chiefly, abdication is supposed to follow from section 904 of the statute and the parts of section 903 that are complementary thereto. Section 903 (a) (3). By these the Secretary of the Treasury is authorized and directed to receive and hold in the Unemployment Trust Fund all moneys deposited therein by a state agency for a state unemployment fund and to invest in obligations of the United States such portion of the fund as is not in his judgment required to meet current withdrawals. We are told that Alabama in consenting to that deposit has renounced the plenitude of power inherent in her statehood.

The same pervasive misconception is in evidence again. All that the state has done is to say in effect through the enactment of a statute that her agents shall be authorized to deposit the unemployment tax receipts in the Treasury at Washington. . . . The statute may be repealed. . . . The consent may be revoked. The deposits may be withdrawn. The moment the state commission gives notice to the depositary that it would like the moneys back, the Treasurer will return them. To find state destruction there is to find it almost anywhere. With nearly as much reason one might say that a state abdicates its functions when it places the state moneys on deposit in a national bank. . . .

The inference of abdication thus dissolves in thinnest air when the deposit is conceived of as dependent upon a contract effective to create a duty. By this we do not intimate that the conclusion would be different if a contract were discovered. Even sovereigns may contract without derogating from their sovereignty. . . . The states are at liberty, upon obtaining the consent of Congress, to make agreements with one another. . . . We find no room for doubt that they may do the like with Congress if the essence of their state-

hood is maintained without impairment.
Alabama is seeking and obtaining a credit
of many millions in favor of her citizens
out of the Treasury of the nation. Nowhere in our scheme of government—in
the limitations express or implied of our
Federal Constitution—do we find that she
is prohibited from assenting to conditions
that will assure a fair and just requital for
benefits received. . . .

The judgment is affirmed.

MR. JUSTICE SUTHERLAND, joined by MR.
JUSTICE VAN DEVANTER, wrote an opinion
dissenting in part.

JUSTICES BUTLER and McREYNOLDS each
wrote separate dissenting opinions.

What standard was applied by Justice Cardozo to determine the limits of
the congressional spending power? Contrast the facts of the *Butler* and the
Steward Machine Company cases. Do they justify a finding of coercion in the
former but not in the latter? Did the decision hinge on facts beyond those
of the immediate case? Was the real reason behind the opinion of the Court
the "urgent need for some remedial expedient" to deal with the critical
problem of unemployment during the Great Depression? How important
were considerations of federalism in Cardozo's opinion? What weight did
the Court give to the fact that under the unemployment compensation program the government was working through the states, whereas under the
Agricultural Adjustment Act reviewed in *Butler* the states were bypassed?

In the companion case to *Steward Machine Company, Helvering* v. *Davis,* 301
U.S. 619 (1937), Justice Cardozo wrote the majority opinion upholding the
old age benefits provisions of the Social Security Act of 1935. The benefits
were financed by a tax on covered employers and employees. Against a
Tenth Amendment challenge to the law, Justice Cardozo relied upon the
Hamilton-Story position cited in the *Butler* case to uphold the law. He noted
that the problem was clearly national, that the states were unable to cope
with it effectively, and that Congress reasonably enacted the legislation on
the basis of these facts. Provided there are reasonable grounds for congressional action, Cardozo concluded, the courts should not intervene in judging
the scope of the spending power under the welfare clause.[12]

---

[12]See Flemming v. Nestor, 363 U.S. 603 (1960), for further consideration of the extent of
judicial scrutiny of the exercise of legislative power under the spending and welfare clause.

EIGHT

Due Process of Law

The Bill of Rights, which every citizen takes for granted, was not part of the original Constitution of 1787. This did not mean that the delegates to the Convention considered civil liberties and civil rights to be of secondary importance. Quite the contrary was the case. The Anglo-American legal tradition up to the time of the writing of the Constitution had emphasized the importance of independent rights and liberties of citizens that could not be curtailed by government. The Magna Charta of 1215, the English Bill of Rights in 1689, and numerous common law precedents upheld the rights and liberties of citizens. The colonists brought their rights as English citizens to America, and through struggles with colonial governors they emphasized new rights of local self-government. The struggle with Great Britain also brought out the need for such rights as protection against unreasonable search and seizure, as British troops were constantly searching private premises for smuggled goods, and the right to bear arms, which was seen as a protection against standing armies. The prohibition upon the quartering of soldiers in any house without the consent of the owner, which became the Third Amendment, grew out of the desire to prevent the repetition of a detested British practice in the Colonies.

The new state constitutions that were written during the revolutionary period did not uniformly reflect the strong Anglo-American tradition of civil liberties and civil rights. Only seven of the new state constitutions contained separate bills of rights. Six states incorporated various rights in the main bodies of their constitutions. The Virginia Bill of Rights was the most comprehensive, containing in addition to the fundamental rights growing out of the British tradition, the new right of revolution, which Jefferson was to proclaim in the Declaration of Independence.

While the strong tradition of civil liberties and civil rights in Anglo-American history would have supported the addition of a separate bill of rights to the Constitution, state constitutional practice did not set a clear precedent for such a course of action. The main body of the Constitution did contain provisions that protected civil rights, such as the prohibition upon the suspension of the writ of habeas corpus and upon the passage of ex post facto laws and bills of attainder. But it was not a matter of debate during the Convention proceedings whether or not the Constitution should go beyond stating these rights. Moreover, a motion that was made shortly before the close of the Convention to draft a bill of rights did not receive a single state vote. This would suggest that the state delegations to the Convention considered the primary responsibility for the protection of civil liberties and rights to be a matter of state concern.

While the Constitutional Convention did not feel that a separate bill of rights was appropriate, it soon became evident that there was opposition in the states to the ratification of a constitution without a separate bill of rights. Thomas Jefferson, who was in Paris at that time, reflected the view that a bill of rights was important in a letter to James Madison on December 20, 1787. After noting that he liked most of the provisions of the Constitution, he wrote to Madison,

> I will now tell you what I do not like. First, the omission of a bill of rights, providing clearly, and without the aid of sophism, for freedom of religion, freedom of the press, protection against standing armies, restriction of monopoly, the eternal and unremitting force of the habeas corpus laws, and trials by jury in all matters of fact triable by the laws of the land, and not by the laws of nations. To say, as Mr. Wilson [a delegate from Philadelphia to the Pennsylvania ratifying convention] does, that a bill of rights was not necessary, because all is reserved [to the states] in the case of the general government which is not given, while in the particular ones [the states] all is given which is not reserved, might do for the audience for which it was addressed; but it is surely a *gratis dictum*, the reverse of which might just as well be said; and it is opposed by strong inferences from the body of the instrument [the national Constitution], as well as from the omission of the cause of our present confederation, which had made the reservation in expressed terms. It was hard to conclude, because there has been a want of uniformity among the states as to the cases triable by jury, because some have been so incautious as to dispense with this mode of trial in certain cases, therefore, the more prudent states shall be reduced to the same level of calamity. It would have been much more just and wise to have concluded the other way, that as most of the states had preserved with jealousy this sacred palladium of liberty, those who had wandered, should be brought back to it; and to have established general right rather than general wrong. For I consider all the ill as established, which may be established. I have the right to nothing, which another has a right to take away; and Congress will have a right to take away trials by jury in all civil cases. Let me add, that a bill of rights is what the people are entitled to against every government on earth, general or particular; and what no just government should refuse, or rest on inference.

James Wilson, the Philadelphia delegate to the Pennsylvania ratifying convention, to whom Jefferson refers in the above quote, argued before his state ratifying convention that a bill of rights was not only unnecessary but dangerous, an argument that was to be repeated by Alexander Hamilton in *Federalist 84*. In debating before the Pennsylvania convention, Wilson noted that,

A bill of rights annexed to a constitution is an enumeration of the powers reserved. If we attempt an enumeration, everything that is not enumerated is presumed to be given. The consequence is, that an imperfect enumeration would throw all implied power into the scale [power] of the government, and the rights of the people would be rendered incomplete. On the other hand, an imperfect enumeration of the powers of government reserves all implied power to the people; and by that means the constitution becomes incomplete. But of the two, it is much safer to run the risk on the side of the constitution; for an omission in the enumeration of the powers of government is neither so dangerous or important as an omission in the enumeration of the rights of the people.

Alexander Hamilton, in *Federalist 84*, opposed a separate bill of rights which he declared would be redundant, because the people retain all of the rights that were being proposed in the bill of rights. Hamilton, like Wilson, argued that the addition of a bill of rights would even be dangerous. In Hamilton's view a separate bill of rights would imply that the national government had the authority to curb the very rights that were enumerated. In fact, however, Hamilton argued that there was no power given to the central government to curb any of the rights in question. Hamilton pointed out that the national Constitution and many of the state constitutions were the same in their treatment of rights, listing them in the main bodies of the documents, rather than in separate bills of rights. The Constitution is in itself, in its entirety, a general bill of rights, stated Hamilton. Indeed, contrasting the federal Constitution with that of New York, Hamilton concluded that the former contained more safeguards than the latter. When the state constitutions and the federal constitution were considered together, Hamilton concluded that they collectively contained all of the protections of rights that could reasonably be desired.

Considerations of federalism were important in the arguments of the opponents of a separate bill of rights. In *Federalist 84* Hamilton stated that "The constitution of each state is its bill of rights. And the proposed Constitution, if adopted, will be the bill of rights of the Union." Did the adoption of the Bill of Rights change the federal balance that had assigned the responsibility to protect the rights of citizens in states to the states themselves, except insofar as the Constitution explicitly prohibited state action, as in Article I, Section 10, which provides that "No state shall . . . pass any bill of attainder, ex post facto law, or law impairing the obligation of contracts. . . ."? Do the arguments presented by Jefferson for a separate bill of rights, and those of Wilson and Hamilton against such action, reveal whether or not the Bill of Rights was intended to be applied to the states? Would the states have ratified the Bill of Rights if it had been meant to apply to them?

The question of the applicability of the Bill of Rights arose in *Barron* v. *Baltimore* (1833). Barron's wharf was rendered useless by an action of the City of Baltimore which, in diverting several streams in order to pave streets, caused deposits near Barron's wharf which made originally deep water too shallow for the approach of vessels. Barron sued the city, claiming that his private property had been taken without just compensation in violation of the Fifth Amendment. The trial court sustained Barron's plea and awarded him monetary damages. The state court of appeals reversed, and the case was appealed to the Supreme Court on a writ of error.

Barron v. Baltimore

7 Peters 243; 8 L. Ed. 672 (1833)

MR. CHIEF JUSTICE MARSHALL delivered the opinion of the Court:

The judgment brought up by this writ of error having been rendered by the court of a State, this tribunal can exercise no jurisdiction over it unless it be shown to come within the provisions of the twenty-fifth section of the Judicial Act.

The plaintiff in error contends that it comes within that clause in the Fifth Amendment to the Constitution which inhibits the taking of private property for public use without just compensation. He insists that this amendment, being in favor of the liberty of the citizen, ought to be so construed as to restrain the legislative power of a State, as well as that of the United States. If this proposition be untrue, the Court can take no jurisdiction of the cause.

The question thus presented is, we think, of great importance, but not of much difficulty.

The Constitution was ordained and established by the people of the United States for themselves, for their own government, and not for the government of the individual States. Each State established a constitution for itself, and in that constitution provided such limitations and restrictions on the powers of its particular government as its judgment dictated. The people of the United States framed such a government for the United States as they supposed best adapted to their situation, and best calculated to promote their interests. The powers they conferred on this government were to be exercised by itself; and the limitations on power, if expressed in general terms, are naturally, and, we think, necessarily applicable to the government created by the instrument. They are limitations of power granted in the instrument itself; not of distinct governments, framed by different persons and for different purposes.

If these propositions be correct, the Fifth Amendment must be understood as restraining the power of the general government, not as applicable to the States. In their several constitutions they have imposed such restrictions on their respective governments as their own wisdom suggested; such as they deemed most proper for themselves. It is a subject on which they judge exclusively, and with which others interfere no farther than they are supposed to have a common interest.

The counsel for the plaintiff in error insists that the Constitution was intended to secure the people of the several States against the undue exercise of power by their respective State governments; as well as against that which might be attempted by their general government. In support of this argument he relies on the inhibitions contained in the tenth section of the first article.

We think that section affords a strong if not a conclusive argument in support of the opinion already indicated by the Court.

The preceding section contains restrictions which are obviously intended for the exclusive purpose of restraining the exercise of power by the departments of the general government. Some of them use language applicable only to Congress, others are expressed in general terms. The third clause, for example, declares that "no bill of attainder or ex post facto law shall be passed." No language can be more general; yet the demonstration is complete that it applies solely to the government of the United States. In addition to the general arguments furnished by the instrument itself, some of which have been already suggested, the succeeding section, the avowed purpose of which is to restrain State legislation, contains in terms the very prohibition. It declares that "no State shall pass any bill of attainder or ex post facto law." This provision, then, of the ninth section, however comprehensive its language, contains no restriction on State legislation.

The ninth section having enumerated, in the nature of a bill of rights, the limitations intended to be imposed on the powers of the general government, the tenth proceeds to enumerate those which were to operate on the State legislatures. These restrictions are brought together in the same section, and are by express words applied to the States. "No State shall enter into any treaty," etc. Perceiving that in a Constitution framed by the people of the United States for the government of all, no limitation of the action of government on the people would apply to the State government unless expressed in terms; the restrictions contained in the tenth section are in direct words so applied to the States.

It is worthy of remark, too, that these inhibitions generally restrain State legislation on subjects intrusted to the general government, or in which the people of all the States feel an interest.

A State is forbidden to enter into any treaty, alliance or confederation. If these compacts are with foreign nations, they interfere with the treaty-making power which is conferred entirely on the general government; if with each other, for political purposes, they can scarcely fail to interfere with the general purpose and intent of the Constitution. To grant letters of marque and reprisal would lead directly to war, the power of declaring which is expressly given to Congress. To coin money is also the exercise of a power conferred on Congress. It would be tedious to recapitulate the several limitations on the powers of the States which are contained in this section. They will be found,

generally, to restrain State legislation on subjects intrusted to the government of the Union, in which the citizens of all the States are interested. In these alone were the whole people concerned. The question of their application to States is not left to construction. It is averred in positive words.

If the original Constitution, in the ninth and tenth sections of the first article, draws this plain and marked line of discrimination between the limitations it imposes on the powers of the general government and on those of the States; if in every inhibition intended to act on State power, words are employed which directly express that intent, some strong reason must be assigned for departing from this safe and judicious course in framing the amendments, before that departure can be assumed.

We search in vain for that reason.

Had the people of the several States, or any of them, required changes in their constitutions; had they required additional safeguards to liberty from the apprehended encroachments of their particular governments, the remedy was in their own hands, and would have been applied by themselves. A convention would have been assembled by the discontented State, and the required improvements would have been made by itself. The unwieldy and cumbrous machinery of procuring a recommendation from two-thirds of Congress and the assent of three-fourths of their sister States, could never have occurred to any human being as a mode of doing that which might be effected by the State itself. Had the framers of these amendments intended them to be limitations on the powers of the State governments they would have imitated the framers of the original Constitution, and have expressed that intention. Had Congress engaged in the extraordinary occupation of improving the constitutions of the several States by affording the people additional protection from the exercise of power by their own governments in matters which concerned themselves alone, they would have declared this purpose in plain and intelligible language.

But it is universally understood, it is a part of the history of the day, that the great revolution which established the Constitution of the United States was not effected without immense opposition. Serious fears were extensively entertained that those powers which the patriot statesmen who then watched over the interests of our country, deemed essential to union, and to the attainment of those invaluable objects for which union was sought, might be exercised in a manner dangerous to liberty. In almost every convention by which the Constitution was adopted, amendments to guard against the abuse of power were recommended. These amendments demanded security against the apprehended encroachments of the general government—not against those of the local governments.

In compliance with a sentiment thus generally expressed, to quiet fears thus extensively entertained, amendments were proposed by the required majority in Congress, and adopted by the States. These amendments contain no expression indicating an intention to apply them to the State governments. This Court cannot so apply them.

We are of opinion that the provision in the Fifth Amendment to the Constitution, declaring that private property shall not be taken for public use without just compensation, is intended solely as a limitation on the exercise of power by the government of the United States, and is not applicable to the legislation of the States. We are therefore of opinion that there is no repugnancy between the several acts of the General Assembly of Maryland, given in evidence by the defendants at the trial of this cause in the court of that State, and the Constitution of the United States.

This Court, therefore, has no jurisdiction of the cause, and [it] is dismissed.

Read each provision of the Bill of Rights carefully and refer to the discussion of the debate over its addition to the Constitution in the note preceding the *Barron* case. Does the Bill of Rights contain an explicit provision defining its reach? Do you agree with Marshall that the question of its applicability is "not of much difficulty"? Marshall decided that the Bill of Rights applies to the national government generally. Is this ruling sustainable on the basis of the provisions of the Bill of Rights? What are Marshall's deductions from the text of the Constitution? What are his deductions from the history of the Bill of Rights?

The adoption of the Fourteenth Amendment in 1868 raised the possibility that the ruling in *Barron* v. *Baltimore* might be overturned. Such a ruling was contingent upon the Court's interpretation of the provisions of Section 1 of the amendment, which provided: "All persons born or naturalized in the United States, and subject to the jurisdiction thereof, are citizens of the United States and of the state wherein they reside. No state shall make or enforce any law which shall abridge the privileges or immunities of citizens of the United States; nor shall any state deprive any person of life, liberty, or property, without due process of law. . . ."[1] The privileges and immuni-

---

[1]Section 1 concludes: "Nor [shall any state] deny to any person within its jurisdiction the equal protection of the laws." The equal protection clause, covered in Chapter 11, was not pertinent to the issue of the applicability of the Bill of Rights to the states.

ties clause seemed a particularly likely vehicle to extend the reach of the Bill of Rights to the states. The clause, on its face, declared that state citizens would have all the "privileges and immunities" of citizens of the United States. Were not the protections of the Bill of Rights part of the privileges and immunities of United States citizens?

The authors and principal sponsors of the Fourteenth Amendment in Congress, the radical Republicans led by Representative John A. Bingham of Ohio and Senator Jacob Howard of Michigan, agreed that the privileges and immunities clause incorporated the entire Bill of Rights as a limitation upon the states. Those who opposed the amendment agreed that its effect would be to nationalize the Bill of Rights. The amendment was drafted at a time when the Radical Republicans deeply distrusted the Southern governments which were beginning once again to take repressive measures against their black citizens. The sponsors of the privileges and immunities clause intended to nationalize the Bill of Rights as a way of guaranteeing national protection of the civil liberties and rights of Southern blacks.

The Court defined the reach of the privileges and immunities clause in the *Slaughterhouse Cases* (1873), and interpreted the other provisions of Section 1 of the Fourteenth Amendment and the intent of the prohibition upon "involuntary servitude" in the Thirteenth Amendment. The case arose out of a Louisiana law of 1869 that granted a monoply to a slaughterhouse company in three parishes including New Orleans. The plaintiffs were butchers who contended that the law prevented them from pursuing their trade and earning their livelihood. The plaintiffs were asking the Court to give substantive content to the Civil War amendments by interpreting them to forbid state monopolies. The Constitution did not contain any explicit provisions proscribing monopolies. Under certain circumstances, however, monopolies were proscribed by common law. Had the Court wished, it could draw upon recognized individual rights under the common law to include an antimonopoly standard in the Civil War amendments, particularly in the privileges and immunities and the due process clauses of the Fourteenth Amendment.

Slaughterhouse Cases

16 Wallace 36; 21 L. Ed. 394 (1873)

Mr. Justice Miller delivered the opinion of the Court:

This statute is denounced not only as creating a monopoly and conferring odious and exclusive privileges upon a small number of persons at the expense of the great body of the community of New Orleans, but it is asserted that it deprives a large and meritorious class of citizens, the whole of the butchers of the city, of the right to exercise their trade, the business to which they have been trained and on which they depend for the support of themselves and their families; and that the unrestricted exercise of the business of butchering is necessary to the daily subsistence of the population of the city. . . .

It is not, and cannot be successfully controverted, that it is both the right and the duty of the legislative body, the supreme power of the state or municipality, to prescribe and determine the localities where the business of slaughtering for a great city may be conducted. To do this effectively it is indispensable that all persons who slaughter animals for food shall do it in those places and nowhere else.

The statute under consideration defines these localities and forbids slaughtering in any other. It does not, as has been asserted, prevent the butcher from doing his own slaughtering. On the contrary, the Slaughter-House Company is required, under a heavy penalty, to permit any person who wishes to do so, to slaughter in their houses; and they are bound to make ample provision for the convenience of all the slaughtering for the entire city. The butcher, then, is still permitted to slaughter, to prepare, and to sell his own meats; but he is required to slaughter at a specified place and to pay a reasonable compensation for the use of the accommodations furnished him at that place.

The wisdom of the monopoly granted by the legislature may be open to question, but it is difficult to see a justification for the assertion that the butchers are deprived of the right to labor in their occupation, or the people of their daily service in preparing food, or how this statute, with the duties and guards imposed upon the company, can be said to destroy the business of the butcher, or seriously interfere with its pursuit.

The power here exercised by the legislature of Louisiana is, in its essential nature, one which has been, up to the present period in the constitutional history of this country, always conceded to belong to the states, however it may now be questioned in some of its details. . . .

Unless, therefore, it can be maintained that the exclusive privilege granted by this charter to the corporation is beyond the power of the legislature of Louisiana, there can be no just exception to the validity of the statute. And in this respect

we are not able to see that these privileges are especially odious or objectionable. The duty imposed as a consideration for the privilege is well defined, and its enforcement well guarded. The prices or charges to be made by the company are limited by the statute, and we are not advised that they are on the whole exorbitant or unjust.

The proposition is, therefore, reduced to these terms: can any exclusive privileges be granted to any of its citizens, or to a corporation, by the legislature of a state? . . .

The plaintiffs in error accepting this issue, allege that the statute is a violation of the Constitution of the United States in these several particulars:

That it creates an involuntary servitude forbidden by the 13th article of amendment;

That it abridges the privileges and immunities of citizens of the United States;

That it denies to the plaintiffs the equal protection of the laws; and,

That it deprives them of their property without due process of law; contrary to the provisions of the 1st section of the 14th article of amendment.

This Court is thus called upon for the first time to give construction to these articles. . . .

Twelve articles of amendment were added to the Federal Constitution soon after the original organization of the government under it in 1789. Of these all but the last were adopted so soon afterwards as to justify the statement that they were practically contemporaneous with the adoption of the original; and the twelfth, adopted in eighteen hundred and three, was so nearly so as to have become, like the others, historical and of another age. But within the last eight years three other articles of amendment of vast importance have been added, by the voice of the people, to that now venerable instrument.

The most cursory glance at these articles discloses a unity of purpose, when taken in connection with the history of the times, which cannot fail to have an important bearing on any question of doubt concerning their true meaning. . . . Fortunately that history is fresh within the memory of us all, and its leading features, as they bear upon the matter before us, free from doubt. . . .

. . . [O]n the most casual examination of the language of these amendments, no one can fail to be impressed with the one pervading purpose found in them all, lying at the foundation of each, and without which none of them would have been even suggested; we mean the freedom of the slave race, the security and firm establishment of that freedom, and the protection of the newly made freemen and citizen from the oppressions of those who had formerly exercised unlimited domination over him. It is true that only the Fifteenth Amendment, in terms, mentions the negro by speaking of his color and his slavery. But it is just as true that each of the other articles was addressed to the grievances of that race, and designed to remedy them as the Fifteenth.

We do not say that no one else but the negro can share in this protection. Both the language and spirit of these articles are to have their fair and just weight in any question of construction. Undoubtedly, while negro slavery alone was in the mind of the Congress which proposed the 13th article, it forbids any other kind of slavery, now or hereafter. If Mexican peonage or the Chinese coolie labor system shall develop slavery of the Mexican or Chinese race within our territory, this Amendment may safely be trusted to make it void. And so, if other rights are assailed by the states which properly and necessarily fall within the protection of these articles, that protection will apply though the party interested may not be of African descent. But what we do say, and what we wish to be understood, is, that in any fair and just construction of any section or phrase of these amendments, it is necessary to look to the purpose which we have said was the pervading spirit of them all, the evil which they were designed to remedy, and the process of continued addition to the Constitution until that purpose was supposed to be accomplished, as far as constitutional law can accomplish it.

The 1st section of the 14th article, to which our attention is more specially invited, opens with a definition of citizenship—not only citizenship of the United States, but citizenship of the states. No such definition was previously found in the Constitution, nor had any attempt been made to define it by act of Congress. It had been the occasion of much discussion in the courts, by the executive departments and in the public journals. It had been said by eminent judges that no man was a citizen of the United States except as he was a citizen of one of the states composing the Union. Those, therefore, who had been born and resided always in the District of Columbia or in the territories, though within the United States, were not citizens. Whether this proposition was sound or not had never been judicially decided. But it had been held by this Court, in the celebrated *Dred Scott Case,* only a few years before the outbreak of the Civil War, that a man of African descent, whether a slave or not, was not and could not be a citizen of a state or of the United States. This decision, while it met the condemnation of some of the ablest statesmen and constitutional lawyers of the country, had never been overruled; and, if it was to be accepted as a constitutional limitation of the right of citizenship, then all the negro race who had recently been made freemen were still, not only not citizens, but were incapable of becoming so by anything short of an amendment to the Constitution.

To remove this difficulty primarily,

and to establish a clear and comprehensive definition of citizenship which should declare what should constitute citizenship of the United States and also citizenship of a state, the 1st clause of the 1st section was framed:

"All persons born or naturalized in the United States and subject to the jurisdiction thereof are citizens of the United States and of the state wherein they reside."

The first observation we have to make on this clause is that it puts at rest both the questions which we stated to have been the subject of differences of opinion. It declares that persons may be citizens of the United States without regard to their citizenship of a particular state, and it overturns the *Dred Scott* decision by making all persons born within the United States and subject to its jurisdiction citizens of the United States. That its main purpose was to establish the citizenship of the negro can admit of no doubt. The phrase "subject to its jurisdiction" was intended to exclude from its operation children of ministers, consuls and citizens or subjects of foreign states born within the United States.

The next observation is more important in view of the arguments of counsel in the present case. It is that the distinction between citizenship of the United States and citizenship of a state is clearly recognized and established. Not only may a man be a citizen of the United States without being a citizen of a state, but an important element is necessary to convert the former into the latter. He must reside within the state to make him a citizen of it, but it is only necessary that he should be born or naturalized in the United States to be a citizen of the Union.

It is quite clear, then, that there is a citizenship of the United States and a citizenship of a state, which are distinct from each other and which depend upon different characteristics or circumstances in the individual.

We think this distinction and its explicit recognition in this Amendment of great weight in this argument, because the next paragraph of this same section, which is the one mainly relied on by the plaintiffs in error, speaks only of privileges and immunities of citizens of the United States, and does not speak of those of citizens of several states. The argument, however, in favor of the plaintiffs, rests wholly on the assumption that the citizenship is the same and the privileges and immunities guaranteed by the clause are the same.

The language is: "No state shall make or enforce any laws which shall abridge the privileges or immunities of citizens of the United States." It is a little remarkable, if this clause was intended as a protection to the citizen of a state against the legislative power of his own state, that the words "citizen of the state" should be left out when it is so carefully used, and used in contradistinction to "citizens of the United States" in the very sentence which precedes it. It is too clear for argument that the change in phraseology was adopted understandingly and with a purpose.

Of the privileges and immunities of the citizens of the United States, and of the privileges and immunities of the citizen of the state, and what they respectively are, we will presently consider; but we wish to state here that it is only the former which are placed by this clause under the protection of the Federal Constitution, and that the latter, whatever they may be, are not intended to have any additional protection by this paragraph of the Amendment.

If, then, there is a difference between the privileges and immunities belonging to a citizen of the United States as such, and those belonging to the citizen of the state as such, the latter must rest for their security and protection where they have heretofore rested; for they are not embraced by this paragraph of the Amendment.

The first occurrence of the words "privileges and immunities" in our constitutional history is to be found in the fourth of the Articles of the old Confederation.

It declares "That, the better to secure and perpetuate mutual friendship and intercourse among the people of the different states in this Union, the free inhabitants of each of these states, paupers, vagabonds, and fugitives from justice excepted, shall be entitled to all the privileges and immunities of free citizens in the several states; and the people of each state shall have free ingress and regress to and from any other state, and shall enjoy therein all the privileges of trade and commerce, subject to the same duties, impositions, and restrictions as the inhabitants thereof respectively."

In the Constitution of the United States, which superseded the Articles of Confederation, the corresponding provision is found in section two of the 4th article, in the following words: The citizens of each state shall be entitled to all the privileges and immunities of citizens of several states.

There can be but little question that the purpose of both these provisions is the same, and that the privileges and immunities intended are the same in each. In the Articles of Confederation we have some of these specifically mentioned, and enough perhaps to give some general idea of the class of civil rights meant by the phrase.

Fortunately we are not without judicial construction of this clause of the Constitution. The first and the leading case on the subject is that of *Corfield* v. *Coryell*, decided by Mr. Justice Washington in the circuit court for the district of Pennsylvania in 1823. 4 Wash. C. C. 371.

"The inquiry," he says, "is, what are the privileges and immunities of citizens of several states? We feel no hesitation in confining these expressions to those privileges and immunities which are funda-

mental; which belong of right to the citizens of all free governments, and which have at all times been enjoyed by citizens of the several states which compose this Union, from the time of their becoming free, independent, and sovereign. What these fundamental principles are, it would be more tedious than difficult to enumerate." "They may all, however, be comprehended under the following general heads: protection by the government, with the right to acquire and possess property of every kind, and to pursue and obtain happiness and safety, subject, nevertheless, to such restraints as the government may prescribed for the general good of the whole."

This definition of the privileges and immunities of citizens of the states is adopted in the main by this Court in the recent case of *Ward* v. *Maryland,* 12 Wall. 430 [1871] . . . while it declines to undertake an authoritative definition beyond what was necessary to that decision. The description, when taken to include others not named, but which are of the same general character, embraces nearly every civil right for the establishment and protection of which organized government is instituted. They are, in the language of Judge Washington, those rights which are fundamental. Throughout his opinion, they are spoken of as rights belonging to the individual as a citizen of a state. They are so spoken of in the constitutional provision which he was construing. And they have always been held to be the class of rights which the state governments were created to establish and secure. . . .

The constitutional provision there alluded to did not create those rights, which it called privileges and immunities of citizens of the states. It threw around them in that clause no security for the citizen of the state in which they were claimed or exercised. Nor did it profess to control the power of the state governments over the rights of its own citizens.

Its sole purpose was to declare to the

several states, that whatever those rights, as you grant or establish them to your own citizens, or as you limit or qualify, or impose restrictions on their exercise, the same, neither more nor less, shall be the measure of the rights of citizens of other states within your jurisdiction.

It would be the vainest show of learning to attempt to prove by citations of authority, that up to the adoption of the recent Amendments, no claim or pretense was set up that those rights depended on the Federal government for their existence or protection, beyond the very few express limitations which the Federal Constitution imposed upon the states—such, for instance, as the prohibition against *ex post facto* laws, bills of attainder, and laws impairing the obligation of contracts. But with the exception of these and a few other restrictions, the entire domain of the privileges and immunities of citizens of the states, as above defined, lay within the constitutional and legislative power of the states, and without that of the Federal government. Was it the purpose of the Fourteenth Amendment, by the simple declaration that no state should make or enforce any law which shall abridge the privileges and immunities of citizens of the United States, to transfer the security and protection of all the civil rights which we have mentioned from the states to the Federal government? And where it is declared that Congress shall have the power to enforce that article, was it intended to bring within the power of Congress the entire domain of civil rights heretofore belonging exclusively to the states?

All this and more must follow, if the proposition of the plaintiffs in error be sound. For not only are these rights subject to the control of Congress whenever in its discretion any of them are supposed to be abridged by state legislation, but that body may also pass laws in advance, limiting and restricting the exercise of legislative power by the states, in their most ordinary and usual functions, as in its judgment it may think proper on all such subjects. And still further, such a construction followed by the reversal of the judgments of the supreme court of Louisiana in these cases would constitute this court a perpetual censor upon all legislation of the states, on the civil rights of their own citizens, with authority to nullify such as it did not approve as consistent with those rights, as they existed at the time of the adoption of this Amendment. The argument, we admit, is not always the most conclusive which is drawn from the consequences urged against the adoption of a particular construction of an instrument. But when, as in the case before us, these consequences are so serious, so far reaching and pervading, so great a departure from the structure and spirit of our institutions; when the effect is to fetter and degrade the state governments by subjecting them to the control of Congress, in the exercise of powers heretofore universally conceded to them of the most ordinary and fundamental character; when in fact it radically changes the whole theory of the relations of the state and Federal governments to each other and of both these governments to the people; the argument has a force that is irresistible, in the absence of language which expresses such a purpose too clearly to admit of doubt.

We are convinced that no such results were intended by the Congress which proposed these amendments, nor by the legislatures of the states, which ratified them.

Having shown that the privileges and immunities relied on in the argument are those which belong to citizens of the states as such, and that they are left to the state governments for security and protection, and not by this article placed under the special care of the Federal government, we may hold ourselves excused from defining the privileges and immunities of citizens of the United States which no state can abridge, until some case involving those privileges may make it necessary to do so.

But lest it should be said that no such privileges and immunities are to be found if those we have been considering are excluded, we venture to suggest some which owe their existence to the Federal government, its national character, its Constitution, or its laws.

One of these is well described in the case of *Crandall* v. *Nevada,* 6 Wall. 36 [1868]. . . . It is said to be the right of the citizen of this great country, protected by implied guarantees of its Constitution, "to come to the seat of government to assert any claim he may have upon that government, to transact any business he may have with it, to seek its protection, to share its offices, to engage in administering its functions. He has the right of free access to its seaports, through which all operations of foreign commerce are conducted, to the sub-treasuries, land-offices, and courts of justice in the several states." And quoting from the language of Chief Justice Taney in another case, it is said "that, for all the great purposes for which the Federal government was established, we are one people with one common country; we are all citizens of the United States;" and it is as such citizens that their rights are supported in this Court in *Crandall* v. *Nevada.*

Another privilege of a citizen of the United States is to demand the care and protection of the Federal government over his life, liberty, and property when on the high seas or within the jurisdiction of a foreign government. Of this there can be no doubt, nor that the right depends upon his character as a citizen of the United States. The right to peaceably assemble and petition for redress of grievances, the privilege of the writ of habeas corpus, are rights of the citizen guaranteed by the Federal Constitution. The right to use the navigable waters of the United States, however they may penetrate the territory of the several states, and all rights secured to our citizens by treaties with foreign nations, are dependent upon citizenship of the United States, and not citizenship of a state. One of these privileges is conferred by the very article under consideration. It is that a citizen of the United States can, of his own volition, become a citizen of any state of the Union by a bona fide residence therein, with the same rights as other citizens of that state. To these may be added the rights secured by the 13th and 15th articles of Amendment, and by the other clause of the Fourteenth, next to be considered.

But it is useless to pursue this branch of the inquiry, since we are of opinion that the rights claimed by these plaintiffs in error, if they have any existence, are not privileges and immunities of citizens of the United States within the meaning of the clause of the Fourteenth Amendment under consideration.

"All persons born or naturalized in the United States, and subject to the jurisdiction thereof, are citizens of the United States and of the state, wherein they reside. No state shall make or enforce any law which shall abridge the privileges or immunities of citizens of the United States; nor shall any state deprive any person of life, liberty or property without due process of law, nor deny to any person within its jurisdiction the equal protection of its laws."

The argument has not been much pressed in these cases that the defendant's charter deprives the plaintiffs of their property without due process of law, or that it denies to them the equal protection of the law. The first of these paragraphs has been in the Constitution since the adoption of the Fifth Amendment, as a restraint upon the Federal power. It is also to be found in some form of expression in the constitutions of nearly all the states, as a restraint upon the power of the states. This law, then, has practically been the same as it now is during the existence of the government, except so far as the present Amendment may place the restraining power over the states in this matter in the hands of the Federal government.

We are not without judicial interpretation, therefore, both state and national, of the meaning of this clause. And it is sufficient to say that under no construction of that provision that we have ever seen, or any that we deem admissible, can the restraint imposed by the state of Louisiana upon the exercise of their trade by the butchers of New Orleans be held to be a deprivation of property within the meaning of that provision.

"Nor shall any state deny to any person within its jurisdiction the equal protection of the laws."

In the light of the history of these amendments, and the pervading purpose of them, which we have already discussed, it is not difficult to give a meaning to this clause. The existence of laws in the states where the newly emancipated negroes resided, which discriminated with gross injustice and hardship against them as a class, was the evil to be remedied by this clause, and by it such laws are forbidden.

If, however, the states did not conform their laws to its requirements, then by the 5th section of the article of amendment Congress was authorized to enforce it by suitable legislation. We doubt very much whether any action of a state not directed by way of discrimination against the negroes as a class, or on account of their race, will ever be held to come within the purview of this provision. It is so clearly a provision for that race and that emergency, that a strong case would be necessary for its application to any other. But as it is a state that is to be dealt with, and

not alone the validity of its laws, we may safely leave that matter until Congress shall have exercised its power, or some case of state oppression, by denial of equal justice in its courts, shall have claimed a decision at our hands. We find no such case in the one before us, and we do not deem it necessary to go over the argument again, as it may have relation to this particular clause of the Amendment. . . .

The judgments of the Supreme Court of Louisiana in these cases are affirmed.

MR. JUSTICE FIELD, dissenting:
. . . The question presented is, . . . one of the gravest importance, not merely to the parties here, but to the whole country. It is nothing less than the question whether the recent Amendments to the Federal Constitution protect the citizens of the United States against the deprivation of their common rights by state legislation. In my judgment the Fourteenth Amendment does afford such protection, and was so intended by the Congress which framed and the states which adopted it. . . .

The Amendment does not attempt to confer any new privileges or immunities upon citizens or to enumerate or define those already existing. It assumes that there are such privileges and immunities which belong of right to citizens as such, and ordains that they shall not be abridged by state legislation. If this inhibition has no reference to privileges and immunities of this character, but only refers, as held by the majority of the Court in their opinion, to such privileges and immunities as were before its adoption specially designated in the Constitution or necessarily implied as belonging to citizens of the United States, it was a vain and idle enactment, which accomplished nothing, and most unnecessarily excited Congress and the people on its passage. With privileges and immunities thus designated no state could ever have interfered by its laws, and no new constitutional provision was required to inhibit such interference. The supremacy of the Constitution and the laws of the United States always controlled any state legislation of that character. But if the Amendment refers to the natural and inalienable rights which belong to all citizens, the inhibition has a profound significance and consequence.

What, then, are the privileges and immunities which are secured against abridgement by state legislation? . . .

The terms "privileges and immunities" are not new in the Amendment; they were in the Constitution before the Amendment was adopted. They are found in the 2d section of the 4th article, which declares that "the citizens of each state shall be entitled to all privileges and immunities of citizens in the several states," and they have been the subject of frequent consideration in judicial decisions. In *Corfield* v. *Coryell*, 4 Wash. C. C. 380 [1823], Mr. Justice Washington said he had "no hesitation in confining these expressions to those privileges and immunities which were, in their nature, fundamental; which belong of right to citizens of all free governments, and which have at all times been enjoyed by the citizens of the several states which compose the Union, from the time of their becoming free, independent, and sovereign;" and in considering what those fundamental privileges were, he said that perhaps it would be more tedious than difficult to enumerate them, but that they might be "all comprehended under the following general heads: protection by the government; the enjoyment of life and liberty, with the right to acquire and possess property of every kind, and to pursue and obtain happiness and safety; subject, nevertheless, to such restraints as the government may justly prescribed for the general good of the whole." This appears

to me to be a sound construction of the clause in question. The privileges and immunities designated are those which of right belong to the citizens of all free governments. Clearly among these must be placed the right to pursue a lawful employment in a lawful manner, without other restraint than such as equally affects all persons. In the discussions in Congress upon the passage of the civil rights act repeated reference was made to this language of Mr. Justice Washington. It was cited by Senator Trumbull with the observation that it enumerated the very rights belonging to a citizen of the United States set forth in the 1st section of the act, and with the statement that all persons born in the United States, being declared by the act citizens of the United States, would thenceforth be entitled to the rights of citizens, and that these were the great fundamental rights set forth in the act; and that they were set forth "as appertaining to every freeman." . . .

This equality of right, with exemption from all disparaging and partial enactments, in the lawful pursuits of life, throughout the whole country, is the distinguishing privilege of citizens of the United States. To them, everywhere, all pursuits, all professions, all avocations are open without other restrictions than such as are imposed equally upon all others of the same age, sex and condition. The state may prescribe such regulations for every pursuit and calling of life as will promote the public health, secure the good order and advance the general prosperity of society, but when once prescribed, the pursuit or calling must be free to be followed by every citizen who is within the conditions designated, and will conform to the regulations. This is the fundamental idea upon which our institutions rest, and unless adhered to in the legislation of the country our government will be a Republic only in name. The Fourteenth Amendment, in my judgment, makes it essential to the validity of the legislation of every state that this equality of right should be respected. How widely this equality has been departed from, how entirely rejected and trampled upon by the act of Louisiana, I have already shown. And it is to me a matter of profound regret that its validity is recognized by a majority of this Court, for by it the right of free labor, one of the most sacred and imprescriptible rights of man, is violated. . . .

I am authorized by MR. CHIEF JUSTICE CHASE, MR. JUSTICE SWAYNE and MR. JUSTICE BRADLEY, to state that they concur with me in this dissenting opinion.

MR. JUSTICE BRADLEY, dissenting:

The right of a state to regulate the conduct of its citizens is undoubtedly a very broad and extensive one, and not to be lightly restricted. But there are certain fundamental rights which this right of regulation cannot infringe. It may prescribe the manner of their exercise, but it cannot subvert the rights themselves. . . .

The granting of monopolies, or exclusive privileges to individuals or corporations, is an invasion of the right of others to choose a lawful calling, and an infringement of personal liberty. It was so felt by the English nation as far back as the reigns of Elizabeth and James. A fierce struggle for the suppression of such monopolies, and for abolishing the prerogative of creating them, was made and was successful. .. And ever since that struggle no English speaking people have ever endured such an odious badge of tyranny. . . .

Lastly: can the Federal Courts administer relief to citizens of the United States whose privileges and immunities have been abridged by a state? Of this I entertain no doubt. Prior to the Fourteenth Amendment this could not be done, except in a few instances, for the want of the requisite authority. . . .

Admitting, therefore, that formerly the states were not prohibited from infringing any of the fundamental privileges and immunities of citizens of the United States, except in a few specified cases, that cannot be said now, since the adoption of the Fourteenth Amendment. In my judgment, it was the intention of the people of this country in adopting that Amendment to provide national security against violation by the states of the fundamental rights of the citizen. . . .

In my opinion the judgment of the Supreme Court of Louisiana ought to be reversed.

MR. JUSTICE SWAYNE wrote a separate dissenting opinion.

What method of analysis does Justice Miller use in arriving at his conclusion that the privileges and immunities clause does not change the constitutional balance between the national government and the states? On what basis did Miller rule out the use of the equal protection clause to overturn the Louisiana monopoly? Why did Miller hold that the due process clause did not reach the question of the state monopoly? Justices Field and Bradley in their dissenting opinions write that the privileges and immunities clause incorporates certain "fundamental rights." Do the dissenting justices make it clear what these rights are, and what is their source? If the dissenting justices had prevailed, would the entire Bill of Rights have been made applicable to the states at that time?

The framers of the Fourteenth Amendment were dismayed by the

Slaughterhouse decision. They openly stated that the Court had committed a serious error in holding that there were two classes of citizenship rights—national and state. Vermont Republican Senator George Edmunds, one of the framers of the amendment, wrote about the decision: "There is no word in it [the Fourteenth Amendment] that did not undergo the completest scrutiny. There is no word in it that was not scanned and intended to mean the full and beneficial thing it seems to mean. There was no discussion omitted; there was no conceivable posture of affairs to the people who had it in hand which was not considered. And yet it was found upon the first attempt to enforce its first clause . . . that the Court [in the *Slaughterhouse* cases], by a division of 5 to 4, radically differed in respect both to the intention of the framers and the construction of the language used by them."[2]

The *Slaughterhouse* decision essentially struck the privileges and immunities clause from the Fourteenth Amendment as a viable weapon for judicial protection of civil liberties and rights. This forced the Court to move to other areas, such as the due process and equal protection clauses, when in later cases it sought to expand civil liberties and civil rights protections in the states.

SUBSTANTIVE DUE PROCESS

Substantive due process refers to the interpretation of the due process clauses of the Fourteenth and Fifth Amendments to include protections of property and individual rights that are not explicitly part of the Constitution. The courts apply value judgments to constitutional interpretation in defining substantive due process. Under the substantive due process doctrine courts examine the actual content of laws instead of the procedures by which they are adopted and carried out. When substantive due process is applied, the fairness of the law is judged much as it would be by a legislature.

In defining the due process clauses subjectively, for example to include *economic* rights nowhere mentioned in the Constitution, the courts were not adopting a new *method* of constitutional interpretation. Judges had always more or less injected their values into their decisions. Moreover, the additions to the Constitution that resulted from substantive due process interpretations were no more extreme than had occurred on numerous occasions through judicial interpretations of other parts of the Constitution. Certainly the opinion in the *Dred Scott* case, which held that Congress could not "infringe upon local rights of person or rights of property" by prohibiting slavery in the territories, was an example of the Court injecting its own values into its decision, for the first time declaring a congressional act both unconstitutional and essentially unfair. Although the Court did not explicitly apply a substantive due process doctrine in *Dred Scott,* its method was much the same, involving the substitution of judicial for legislative values. In the economic sphere, the Court during the New Deal supplanted legislative val-

[2]Charles Warren, *The Supreme Court, III*, 263.

ues with its own concerning the constitutionality of a large part of the economic program of President Franklin Roosevelt. New Deal legislation was rejected by the Court not on the basis of due process violations but as transgressions of the commerce clause and the delegation of powers doctrine.

Substantive Due Process of the Fourteenth Amendment: Judicial Definition of the Boundaries of State Authority to Regulate Economic Activity

Substantive due process was primarily developed and applied by the courts under the Fourteenth Amendment to invalidate state economic regulation.[3] Although the Court rejected a substantive due process challenge to a Louisiana law in the *Slaughterhouse Cases,* Justice Miller's majority opinion implied that there were constitutional limits to state economic regulation derived from natural and common law standards. Miller's opinion, which rejected any explicit constitutional limitations upon the states under the Fourteenth Amendment, left the way clear for the Court to impose boundaries upon state action on the basis of a subjective interpretation of natural and common law criteria. Thus at the same time that he was seeking to limit the application of the Fourteenth Amendment to the states, Miller in fact was paving the way for the imposition of even greater constraints upon state action than were stated in the Constitution.

Judicial interpretation, wrote Miller, defines the due process clause. Although he found that past judicial interpretation of the due process clause of the Fourteenth Amendment did not support invalidating the Louisiana law, his method placed no obstacle in the path of judicial interpretation restraining state action. And, Miller quoted with approval the opinion of Justice Washington in *Corfield* v. *Coryell,* 6 Fed. Cas. 546 (C.C.E.D.Pa. 1823), that the privileges and immunities clause of Article IV protects against state action such fundamental privileges and immunities as "the right to acquire and possess property of every kind, and to pursue and obtain happiness and safety, subject, nevertheless, to such restraints as the government may prescribe for the general good of the whole." Ironically, at the same time Miller was rendering the privileges and immunities clause impotent, he implied that circumstances might make it necessary for the Court to determine what privileges and immunities were "fundamental" and balance these against the "general good of the whole."

The substantive limits on state action implied in the *Slaughterhouse* opinion were defined by Miller himself a year later in *Loan Association* v. *City of Topeka* (1874). He wrote the opinion of the Court invalidating a city ordinance that authorized the issuance of municipal bonds to raise money to support private industry, stating: "There are rights in every free government beyond the control of the state. . . . There are limitations on such

---

[3]Although substantive due process was occasionally applied under the Fifth Amendment to invalidate congressional legislation, as in Adair v. United States, 208 U.S. 161 (1908), discussed on p. 494, the Court was generally able to limit national economic regulation on other grounds.

power which grow out of the essential nature of all free governments."[4] The states are limited in the exercise of their power to the promotion of the general public welfare. The ordinance under review violated this limit and was therefore void.

In *Davidson* v. *New Orleans* (1877) Justice Miller warned against judicial acquiescence to the onslaught of demands that the due process clause be interpreted to include broad protections against state invasion of private property rights. At the same time, he recognized that judicial inclusion and exclusion could give meaning to the due process clause.[5] In the same year the Court squarely faced the issue of the limits upon state economic regulation imposed by the due process clause in *Munn* v. *Illinois*, in which a state statute regulating the rates of grain elevators was challenged in part on the grounds that it violated the due process clause of the Fourteenth Amendment.

Munn v. *Illinois*

94 U.S. 113. 24 L. Ed. 77 (1877)

MR. CHIEF JUSTICE WAITE delivered the opinion of the Court:

The question to be determined in this case is whether the General Assembly of Illinois can, under the limitations upon the legislative power of the States imposed by the Constitution of the United States, fix by law the maximum of charges for the storage of grain in warehouses at Chicago and other places in the State. . . .

It is claimed that such a law is repugnant . . . [t]o that part of Amendment XIV, which ordains that no State shall "Deprive any person of life, liberty or property, without due process of law, nor deny to any person within its jurisdiction the equal protection of the laws." . . .

Every statute is presumed to be constitutional. The courts ought not to declare one to be unconstitutional, unless it is clearly so. If there is doubt, the expressed will of the Legislature should be sustained.

The Constitution contains no definition of the word "deprive," as used in the Fourteenth Amendment. To determine

its signification, therefore, it is necessary to ascertain the effect which usage has given it, when employed in the same or a like connection. . . .

. . . [I]t is apparent that, down to the time of the adoption of the Fourteenth Amendment, it was not supposed that statutes regulating the use, or even the price of the use, of private property necessarily deprived an owner of his property without due process of law. Under some circumstances they may, but not under all. The Amendment does not change the law in this particular; it simply prevents the States from doing that which will operate as such a deprivation.

This brings us to inquire as to the principles upon which this power of regulation rests, in order that we may determine what is within and what without its operative effect. Looking, then, to the common law, from whence came the right which the Constitution protects, we find that when private property is "affected with a public interest, it ceases to be juris privati only." This was said by Lord Chief

[4]Loan Association v. City of Topeka, 87 U.S. 655, 662–663 (1874).
[5]Davidson v. New Orleans, 96 U.S. 97, 103–105 (1877).

Justice Hale more than two hundred years ago, in his treatise De Portibus Maris, . . . and has been accepted without objection as an essential element in the law of property ever since. Property does become clothed with a public interest when used in a manner to make it of public consequence, and affect the community at large. When, therefore, one devotes his property to a use in which the public has an interest, he, in effect, grants to the public an interest in that use, and must submit to be controlled by the public for the common good, to the extent of the interest he has thus created. He may withdraw his grant by discontinuing the use; but, so long as he maintains the use, he must submit to the control. . . .

. . . [W]hen private property is devoted to a public use, it is subject to public regulation. It remains only to ascertain whether the warehouses of these plaintiffs in error, and the business which is carried on there, come within the operation of this principle. . . .

. . . [T]hese plaintiffs in error . . . stand . . . in the very "gateway of commerce," and take toll from all who pass. Their business most certainly "tends to a common charge, and has become a thing of public interest and use." . . . Certainly, if any business can be clothed "with a public interest, and cease to be juris privati only," this has been. It may not be made so by the operation of the Constitution of Illinois or this statute, but it is by the facts.

We also are not permitted to overlook the fact that, for some reason, the people of Illinois, when they revised their Constitution in 1870, saw fit to make it the duty of the General Assembly to pass laws "for the protection of producers, shippers and receivers of grain and produce," art. XIII., sec. 7; and by sec. 5 of the same article, to require all railroad companies receiving and transporting grain in bulk or otherwise to deliver the same at any ele-vator to which it might be consigned, that could be reached by any track that was or could be used by such company, and that all railroad companies should permit connections to be made with their tracks, so that any public warehouse, etc., might be reached by the cars on their railroads. This indicates very clearly that during the twenty years in which this peculiar business had been assuming its present "immense proportions," something had occurred which led the whole body of the people to suppose that remedies such as are usually employed to prevent abuses by virtual monopolies might not be inappropriate here. For our purposes we must assume that, if a state of facts could exist that would justify such legislation, it actually did exist when the statute now under consideration was passed. For us the question is one of power, not of expediency. If no state of circumstances could exist to justify such a statute, then we may declare this one void, because in excess of the legislative power of the State. But if it could, we must presume it did. Of the propriety of the legislative interference within the scope of the legislative power, the Legislature is the exclusive judge.

Neither is it a matter of any moment that no precedent can be found for a statute precisely like this. It is conceded that the business is one of recent origin, that its growth has been rapid, and that it is already of great importance. And it must also be conceded that it is a business in which the whole public has a direct and positive interest. It presents, therefore, a case for the application of a long known and well established principle in social science, and this statute simply extends the law so as to meet this new development of commercial progress. There is no attempt to compel these owners to grant the public an interest in their property, but to declare their obligations, if they use it in this particular manner.

It matters not in this case that these

plaintiffs in error had built their warehouses and established their business before the regulations complained of were adopted. What they did was, from the beginning, subject to the power of the body politic to require them to conform to such regulations as might be established by the proper authorities for the common good. They entered upon their business and provided themselves with the means to carry it on subject to this condition. If they did not wish to submit themselves to such interference, they should not have clothed the public with an interest in their concerns. . . .

It is insisted, however, that the owner of property is entitled to a reasonable compensation for its use, even though it be clothed with a public interest, and that what is reasonable is a judicial and not a legislative question.

As has already been shown, the practice has been otherwise. In countries where the common law prevails, it has been customary from time immemorial for the Legislature to declare what shall be a reasonable compensation under such circumstances, or, perhaps more properly speaking, to fix a maximum beyond which any charge made would be unreasonable. Undoubtedly, in mere private contracts, relating to matters in which the public has no interest, what is reasonable must be ascertained judicially. But this is because the Legislature has no control over such a contract. So, too, in matters which do affect the public interest, and as to which legislative control may be exercised, if there are no statutory regulations upon the subject, the courts must determine what is reasonable. The controlling fact is the power to regulate at all. If that exists, the right to establish the maximum of charge, as one of the means of regulation, is implied. In fact, the common law rule, which requires the charge to be reasonable, is itself a regulation as to price. Without it the owner could make his rates at

will, and compel the public to yield to his terms, or forego the use.

But a mere common law regulation of trade or business may be changed by statute. A person has no property, no vested interest, in any rule of the common law. That is only one of the forms of municipal law, and is no more sacred than any other. Rights of property which have been created by the common law cannot be taken away without due process; but the law itself, as a rule of conduct, may be changed at the will, or even at the whim, of the Legislature, unless prevented by constitutional limitations. Indeed, the great office of statutes is to remedy defects in the common law as they are developed, and to adapt it to the changes of time and circumstances. To limit the rate of charge for services rendered in a public employment, or for the use of property in which the public has an interest, is only changing a regulation which existed before. It establishes no new principle in the law, but only gives a new effect to an old one.

We know that this is a power which may be abused; but that is no argument against its existence. For protection against abuses by Legislatures the people must resort to the polls, not to the courts. . . .

We conclude, therefore, that the statute in question is not repugnant to the Constitution of the United States, and that there is no error in the judgment. . . .

The judgment is affirmed.

MR. JUSTICE FIELD, dissenting:

I am compelled to dissent from the decision of the Court in this case, and from the reasons upon which that decision is founded. The principle upon which the opinion of the majority proceeds is, in my judgment, subversive of the rights of private property, heretofore believed to be protected by constitutional guarantees against legislative interference, and is in conflict with the authorities cited in its support. . . .

The declaration of the [Illinois] Constitution of 1870, that private buildings used for private purposes shall be deemed public institutions, does not make them so. The receipt and storage of grain in a building erected by private means for that purpose does not constitute the building a public warehouse. There is no magic in the language, though used by a constitutional convention, which can change a private business into a public one, or alter the character of the building in which the business is transacted. . . .

. . . The doctrine declared is that property "Becomes clothed with a public interest when used in a manner to make it of public consequence, and affect the community at large;" and from such clothing the right of the Legislature is deduced to control the use of the property, and to determine the compensation which the owner may receive for it. When Sir Matthew Hale, and the sages of the law in his day, spoke of property as affected by a public interest, and ceasing from that cause to be juris privati solely, that is, ceasing to be held merely in private right, they referred to property dedicated by the owner to public uses, or to property the use of which was granted by the government, or in connection with which special privileges were conferred. Unless the property was thus dedicated, or some right bestowed by the government was held with the property, either by specific grant or by prescription of so long a time as to imply a grant originally, the property was not affected by any public interest so as to be taken out of the category of property held in private right. But it is not in any such sense that the terms "clothing property with a public interest" are used in this case. From the nature of the business under consideration—the storage of grain—which, in any sense in which the

words can be used, is a private business, in which the public are interested only as they are interested in the storage of other products of the soil, or in articles of manufacture, it is clear that the court intended to declare that, whenever one devotes his property to a business which is useful to the public, "affects the community at large," the Legislature can regulate the compensation which the owner may receive for its use, and for his own services in connection with it. . . .

If this be sound law, if there be no protection, either in the principles upon which our republican government is founded, or in the prohibitions of the Constitution against such invasion of private rights, all property and all business in the State are held at the mercy of a majority of its Legislature. . . .

No State "shall deprive any person of life, liberty or property without due process of law," says the Fourteenth Amendment to the Constitution. . . .

By the term "liberty," as used in the provision, something more is meant than mere freedom from physical restraint or the bounds of a prison. It means freedom to go where one may choose, and to act in such manner, not inconsistent with the equal rights of others, as his judgment may dictate for the promotion of his happiness; that is, to pursue such callings and avocations as may be most suitable to develop his capacities, and give to them their highest enjoyment.

The same liberal construction which is required for the protection of life and liberty, in all particulars in which life and liberty are of any value, should be applied to the protection of private property. If the Legislature of a State, under pretense of providing for the public good, or for any other reason, can determine against the consent of the owner, the uses to which private property shall be devoted, or the prices which the owner shall receive for its uses, it can deprive him of the property as completely as by a special Act for its confiscation or destruction. If, for instance, the owner is prohibited from using his building for the purposes for which it was designed, it is of little consequence that he is permitted to retain the title and possession; or, if he is compelled to take as compensation for its use less than the expenses to which he is subjected by its ownership, he is, for all practical purposes, deprived of the property, as effectually as if the Legislature had ordered his forcible dispossession. If it be admitted that the Legislature has any control over the compensation, the extent of that compensation becomes a mere matter of legislative discretion. . . .

There is nothing in the character of the business of the defendants as warehousemen which called for the interference complained of in this case. Their buildings are not nuisances; their occupation of receiving and storing grain infringes upon no rights of others, disturbs no neighborhood, infects not the air, and in no respect prevents others from using and enjoying their property as to them may seem best. The legislation in question is nothing less than a bold assertion of absolute power by the State to control, at its discretion, the property and business of the citizen, and fix the compensation he shall receive. . . .

. . . I deny the power of any Legislature under our government to fix the price which one shall receive for his property of any kind. If the power can be exercised as to one article, it may as to all articles, and the prices of every thing, from a calico gown to a city mansion, may be the subject of legislative direction. . . .

I am of opinion that the judgment of the Supreme Court of Illinois should be reversed.

Mr. Justice Strong concurred in this dissent.

What formula does Chief Justice Waite use to define the content of the due process clause of the Fourteenth Amendment? On what grounds does the Court uphold the Illinois statute? Does the Court interpret the due process clause in substantive terms? How does the Court reason that statutory law takes precedence over the common law?

In Justice Field's dissent, what is the source of the standards he incorporates into the due process clause? Is his approach to the case one of judicial self-restraint or intervention? Does his opinion leave any room for state economic regulation?

PROCEDURAL DUE PROCESS

The Court's explanation of procedural due process under the Fourteenth Amendment was as subjective as its definition of substantive due process. At the national level, standards of procedural due process were explicitly stated in the Bill of Rights. However, after the adoption of the Fourteenth Amendment the Court decided not to incorporate the Bill of Rights under the due process clause but to determine on a selective and case-by-case basis what standards of due process it would apply. In effect, by selectively determining what procedural rights were to be guaranteed by the due process clause of the Fourteenth Amendment, the Court was subjectively defining non-economic substantive due process. It was giving a procedural content or substance to the due process clause that was based upon its own view of governmental fairness.

While the Bill of Rights is used as the primary source of standards of procedural due process at the national level, the fact that there is a separate due process clause of the Fifth Amendment suggests that the framers did not confine "due process" to the express provisions of the Bill of Rights. Due process had a meaning separate from the Bill of Rights. In *Murray's Lessee* v. *Hoboken Land and Improvement Company* (1856) Justice Curtis defined the meaning of the due process clause of the Fifth Amendment.

> The words "due process of law," were undoubtedly intended to convey the same meaning as the words, "by the law of the land," in Magna Charta. . . . The Constitution contains no description of those processes which it was intended to allow or forbid. It does not even declare what principles are to be applied to ascertain whether it be due process. It is manifest that it was not left to the legislative power to enact any process which might be devised. The article is a restraint on the legislative as well as on the executive and judicial powers of government, and cannot be so construed as to leave Congress free to make any process "due process of law" by its mere will. To what principles then, are we to resort to ascertain whether this process, enacted by Congress, is due process? To this the answer must be twofold. We must examine the Constitution itself, to see whether this process be in conflict with any of its provisions [such as the Bill of Rights]. If not found to be so, we must look to those settled usages and modes of proceeding existing in the common and statute law of England, before the emigration of our ancestors, and which are shown not to have been unsuited to their civil and political condition by having been acted on by them after the settlement of this country. . . . [T]hough "due process of law" generally implies and includes . . . regular allegations, opportunity to answer, and a trial according to some settled course of judicial proceedings, . . . yet, this is not universally true.[6]

The due process standards announced by Justice Curtis in *Murray's Lessee* allow the Court broad discretion in the development of the criteria of due process. In defining standards of procedural due process the Court at the national level has drawn upon the provisions of the Bill of Rights and has not expanded procedural protections *beyond* those that are enumerated in the first eight amendments.

The Court has applied its own values in interpreting the extent to which the rights of the Bill of Rights will be incorporated under the due process clause of the Fourteenth Amendment. When the Court first confronted challenges to state action for being in violation of due process under the Fourteenth Amendment, it limited the due process clause to "those settled usages and modes of proceeding existing in the common law and statute law of England" that were brought to America by the settlers and that were adopted by Colonial governments.

The threshold decision of the Court to define procedural due process un-

---

[6]Murray's Lessee v. Hoboken Land and Improvement Company, 18 Howard 272, 276–280 (1856).

der the Fourteenth Amendment separately from the Bill of Rights introduced an element of subjectivity that produced one hundred years of debate over what procedural rights should be included under due process—an issue that is still not finally settled. The Bill of Rights was used as a reference point only insofar as it explicated what the Court considered to be historical and fundamental rights in English and Colonial history. How justices defined due process depended upon their views of what constituted fundamental and historical rights. Differing views of history led to contrasting interpretations of the due process clause. Other reflections as well entered into a justice's determination of procedural due process, particularly considerations of federalism. Justices favoring judicial self-restraint on the basis of considerations of federalism allowed the states more leeway to adopt procedures under their laws than justices who favored an active role for the Supreme Court in establishing national standards of procedural due process.

Contrasting views of the reach of the due process clause of the Fourteenth Amendment surfaced in *Hurtado v. California* (1884). Hurtado was convicted of murder by California and sentenced to be hanged. California law provided for indictment by an "information" prepared by the prosecuting attorney, rather than by a grand jury. Hurtado claimed that due process included the right to grand jury indictment to which he would be entitled under common law and under the Bill of Rights. Justice Matthews's majority opinion facilely disposed of this argument by holding that the due process clause of the Fourteenth Amendment did not exclusively require grand jury indictment. Matthews reasoned that "Any legal proceeding enforced by public authority, whether sanctioned by age and custom, or newly devised in the discretion of the legislative power, in furtherance of the general public good, which regards and preserves . . . principles of liberty and justice, must be held to be due process of law. . . ."[7] The Court concluded,

> Tried by these principles [of liberty and justice], we are unable to say that the substitution for a presentment or indictment by a grand jury of the proceeding by information, after examination and commitment by a magistrate, certifying to the probable guilt of the defendant, with the right on his part to the aid of counsel, and to the cross examination of the witnesses produced for the prosecution, is not due process of law. It is, as we have seen, an ancient proceeding at common law, which might include every case of an offense of less grade than a felony, except misprison of treason; and in every circumstance of its administration, as authorized by the statute of California, it carefully considers and guards the substantial interest of the prisoner. It is merely a preliminary proceeding, and can result in no final judgment, except as the consequence of a regular judicial trial, conducted precisely as in cases of indictments.[8]

Even though the common law required indictment by a grand jury in felony cases, the Court in its *Hurtado* opinion held that the less stringent procedure of indictment by information conformed to due process.

Justice Harlan dissented in *Hurtado,* stating that "I cannot agree that the

[7]Hurtado v. California, 110 U.S. 516, 537 (1884).
[8]Ibid., p. 538.

state may, consistently with due process of law, require a person to answer for a capital offense, except upon the presentment of indictment of a grand jury."[9] Harlan concluded that the settled usages and modes of proceeding of the common law precluded the use of indictment by information in capital cases.

The scope of the due process clause of the Fourteenth Amendment was again raised in *Twining* v. *New Jersey* (1908). The defendants argued that their criminal conviction by a New Jersey court was unlawful because the trial procedure did not conform to the Fifth Amendment requirement that "No person . . . shall be compelled in any criminal case to be a witness against himself. . . ." While the New Jersey constitution included protection against compulsory self-incrimination in its own bill of rights, the state permitted an inference of guilt to be drawn from the failure of a defendant to testify in his own behalf. In the *Twining* case the judge had charged the jury that "because a man does not go upon the stand you are not necessarily justified in drawing an inference of guilt. But you have a right to consider the fact that he does not go upon the stand where a direct accusation is made against him." Undeterred by Justice Miller's majority opinion in the *Slaughterhouse Cases,* and encouraged by the dissenting views in that case, the defendants argued that the New Jersey procedure violated their fundamental rights guaranteed under the privileges and immunities and due process clauses of the Fourteenth Amendment. The brief for the defendants stated that it was still open to question "[w]hether or not the Fourteenth Amendment has extended the application of [the protection against self incrimination embodied in the Fifth Amendment] to the several states. . . ."[10] Where such fundamental rights as the protection against self incrimination are violated, the brief argued, the Court should intervene to protect the individual.

In defense of its position, New Jersey pointed out that its constitution contained the right against compulsory self-incrimination but that "it has never been considered that this right was abridged or infringed by the submission to a trial jury the right to draw an inference, if they saw fit to do so, from the fact of the silence of an accused person in the face of a direct criminal accusation."[11] The state declared that under the doctrine of the *Slaughterhouse Cases* establishing dual citizenship, the procedures followed by the state disclosed "no fundamental right or immunity guaranteed to the plaintiffs in error *as citizens of the United States* by the Fourteenth Amendment of the federal Constitution which has been abridged by the decision of the court of last resort of New Jersey [which upheld the defendants' conviction]."[12] The appellees argued that the Fifth Amendment binds only the federal government and is not a limitation upon the states.

[9]Ibid., p. 539.
[10]LB Vol. 16, p. 757.
[11]Ibid., p. 873.
[12]Ibid., pp. 873–874.

Twining v. New Jersey

211 U.S. 78; 29 S. Ct. 14; 53 L. Ed. 97 (1908)

MR. JUSTICE MOODY delivered the opinion of the Court:

In the view we take of the case we do not deem it necessary to consider whether, with respect to the Federal question, there is any difference in the situation of the two defendants. It is assumed, in respect of each, that the jury were instructed that they might draw an unfavorable inference against him from his failure to testify, where it was within his power, in denial of the evidence which tended to incriminate him. The law of the state . . . permitted such an inference to be drawn. . . . The general question, therefore, is, whether such a law violates the Fourteenth Amendment, either by abridging the privileges or immunities of citizens of the United States, or by depriving persons of their life, liberty, or property without due process of law. In order to bring themselves within the protection of the Constitution it is incumbent on the defendants to prove two propositions: First, that the exemption from compulsory self-incrimination is guaranteed by the Federal Constitution against impairment by the states; and, second, if it be so guaranteed, that the exemption was in fact impaired in the case at bar. The first proposition naturally presents itself for earlier consideration. If the right here asserted is not a Federal right, that is the end of the case. We have no authority to go further and determine whether the state court has erred in the interpretation and enforcement of its own laws. . . .

. . . The defendants contend, in the first place, that the exemption from self-incrimination is one of the privileges and immunities of citizens of the United States which the Fourteenth Amendment forbids the states to abridge. . . . [The Court lists the privileges and immunities protected by the Fourteenth Amendment and finds the exemption from self-incrimination is not one of them.]

The defendants, however, do not stop here. They appeal to another clause of the Fourteenth Amendment, and insist that the self-incrimination which they allege the instruction to the jury compelled was a denial of due process of law. This contention requires separate consideration, for it is possible that some of the personal rights safeguarded by the first eight Amendments against national action may also be safeguarded against state action, because a denial of them would be a denial of due process of law. . . . If this is so, it is not because those rights are enumerated in the first eight Amendments, but because they are of such a nature that they are included in the conception of due process of law. . . . From the consideration of the meaning of the words in the light of their historical origin this court has drawn the following conclusions:

First. What is due process of law may be ascertained by an examination of those settled usages and modes of proceedings existing in the common and statute law of England before the emigration of our ancestors, and shown not to have been unsuited to their civil and political condition by having been acted on by them after the settlement of this country. . . .

Second. It does not follow, however, that a procedure settled in English law at the time of the emigration, and brought to this country and practised by our ancestors, is an essential element of due process of law. If that were so, the procedure of the first half of the seventeenth century would be fastened upon the American jurisprudence like a straight jacket, only to be unloosed by constitutional amendment. . . .

Third. But, consistently with the requirements of due process, no change in ancient procedure can be made which disregards those fundamental principles, to be ascertained from time to time by judicial action, which have relation to process of law, and protect the citizen in his private right, and guard him against the arbitrary action of government. . . .

The question under consideration may first be tested by the application of these settled doctrines of this court. If the statement of Mr. Justice Curtis, as elucidated in *Hurtado* v. *California*, is to be taken literally, that alone might almost be decisive. For nothing is more certain, in point of historical fact, than that the practice of compulsory self-incrimination in the courts and elsewhere existed for four hundred years after the granting of Magna Charta, continued throughout the reign of Charles I. (though then beginning to be seriously questioned), gained at least some foothold among the early colonists of this country, and was not entirely omitted at trials in England until the eighteenth century. . . .

. . . We think it is manifest, from this review of the origin, growth, extent, and limits of the exemption from compulsory self-incrimination in the English law, that it is not regarded as a part of the law of the land of Magna Charta or the due process of law, which has been deemed an equivalent expression, but, on the contrary, is regarded as separate from and independent of due process. It came into existence not as an essential part of due process, but as a wise and beneficent rule of evidence. . . .

But, without repudiating or questioning the test proposed by Mr. Justice Curtis for the Court, or rejecting the inference drawn from English law, we prefer to rest our decision on broader grounds, and inquire whether the exemption from self-incrimination is of such a nature that it must be included in the conception of due process. Is it a fundamental principle of liberty and justice which inheres in the very idea of free government and is the inalienable right of a citizen of such a government? . . .

In the decision of this question we have the authority to take into account only those fundamental rights which are expressed in that provision; not the rights fundamental in citizenship, state or national, for they are secured otherwise; but the rights fundamental in due process, and therefore an essential part of it. We have to consider whether the right is so fundamental in due process that a refusal of the right is a denial of due process. One aid to the solution of the question is to inquire how the right was rated during the time when the meaning of due process was in a formative state, and before it was incorporated in American constitutional law. Did those who then were formulating and insisting upon the rights of the people entertain the view that the right was so fundamental that there could be no due process without it? . . . Searching further, we find nothing to show that it was then thought to be other than a just and useful principle of law. None of the great instruments in which we are accustomed to look for the declaration of the fundamental rights made reference to it. The privilege was not dreamed of for hundreds of years after Magna Charta (1215), and could not have been implied in the "law of the land" there secured. . . .

But the history of the incorporation of the privilege in [the Fifth] Amendment to the national Constitution is full of significance in this connection. . . .

. . . This survey [of state proposals for amendments to the Constitution] does not tend to show that it was then in this country the universal or even general belief that the privilege ranked among the fundamental and inalienable rights of mankind; and what is more important here, it affirmatively shows that the privilege was not conceived to be inherent in due process of law, but, on the other hand, a right separate, independent, and outside of due process. . . .

The decisions of this Court, though they are silent on the precise question before us, ought to be searched to discover if they present any analogies which are helpful in its decision. The essential elements of due process of law, already established by them, are singularly few, though of wide application and deep significance. We are not here concerned with the effect of due process in restraining substantive laws, as, for example, that which forbids the taking of private property for public use without compensation. We need notice now only those cases which deal with the principles which must be observed in the trial of criminal and civil causes. Due process requires that the court which assumes to determine the rights of parties shall have jurisdiction . . . and that there shall be notice and opportunity for hearing given the parties. . . . Subject to these two fundamental conditions, which seem to be universally prescribed in all systems of law established by civilized countries, this Court has, up to this time, sustained all state laws, statutory or judicially declared, regulating procedure, evidence, and methods of trial, and held them to be consistent with due process of law. . . .

Among the most notable of these decisions are those sustaining the denial of jury trial both in civil and criminal cases, the substitution of informations for indictments by a grand jury, the enactment that the possession of policy slips raises a presumption of illegality, and the admission of the deposition of an absent witness in a criminal case. The cases proceed upon the theory that, given a court of justice which has jurisdiction, and acts, not arbitrarily, but in conformity with a general law, upon evidence, and after inquiry made with notice to the parties affected and opportunity to be heard, then all the requirements of due process, so far as it relates to procedure in court and methods of trial and character and effect of evidence, are complied with. Thus it was said in *Iowa C. R. Co.* v. *Iowa* [1896]: "But it is clear that the Fourteenth Amendment in no way undertakes to control the power of a state to determine by what process legal rights may be asserted or legal obligations be enforced, provided the method of procedure adopted for these purposes gives reasonable notice and accords fair opportunity to be heard before the issues are decided;" and in *Louisville & N. R. Co.* v. *Schmidt* [1900]: "It is no longer open to contention that the due process clause of the Fourteenth Amendment to the Constitution of the United States does not control mere forms of procedure in state courts or regulate practice therein. All its requirements are complied with, provided in the proceedings which are claimed not to have been due process of law the person condemned has had sufficient notice, and adequate opportunity has been afforded him to defend;" . . . It is impossible to reconcile the reasoning of these cases and the rule which governed their decision with the theory that an exemption from compulsory self-incrimination is included in the conception of due process of law. Indeed, the reasoning for including indictment by a grand jury and trial by a petit jury in that conception, which has been rejected by this Court in *Hurtado* v. *California* [1884] and *Maxwell* v. *Dow* [1900] was historically and in principle much stronger. Clearly appreciating this, Mr. Justice Harlan, in his dissent in each of these cases, pointed out that the inexorable logic of the reasoning of the Court was to allow the states, so far as the Federal Constitution was concerned, to compel any person to be a witness against himself. . . .

Even if the historical meaning of due process of law and the decisions of this Court did not exclude the privilege from it, it would be going far to rate it as an immutable principle of justice which is the inalienable possession of every citizen of a free government. Salutary as the principle may seem to the great majority, it cannot be ranked with the right to hearing before condemnation, the immunity from arbitrary power not acting by general laws, and the inviolability of private property. The wisdom of the exemption has never been universally assented to since the days of Bentham, many doubt it to-day, and it is best defended not as an unchangeable principle of universal justice, but as a law proved by experience to be expedient. . . . It has no place in the jurisprudence of civilized and free countries outside the domain of the common law, and it is nowhere observed among our own people in the search for truth outside the administration of the law. . . .

We have assumed only for the purpose of discussion that what was done in the case at bar was an infringement of the privilege against self-incrimination. We do not intend, however, to lend any countenance to the truth of that assumption. . . .

Judgment affirmed.

MR. JUSTICE HARLAN, dissenting:
. . . The original Amendments of the Constitution had their origin, as all know, in the belief of many patriotic statesmen in the states then composing the Union, that, under the Constitution, as originally submitted to the people for adoption or rejection, the national government might disregard the fundamental principles of Anglo-American liberty, for the maintenance of which our fathers took up arms against the mother country.

What, let me inquire, must then have been regarded as principles that were fundamental in the liberty of the citizen? Every student of English history will agree that, long before the adoption of the Constitution of the United States, certain principles affecting the life and liberty of the subject had become firmly established in the jurisprudence of England, and were deemed vital to the safety of freemen, and that among those principles was the one that no person accused of crime could be compelled to be a witness against himself. It is true that at one time in England the practice of "questioning the prisoner" was enforced in star chamber proceedings. But we have the authority of Sir James Fitzjames Stephen, in his History of the Criminal Law of England, for saying that, soon after the Revolution of 1688, the practice of questioning the prisoner died out. . . . The liberties of the English people had then been placed on a firmer foundation. Personal liberty was thenceforward jealously guarded. Certain it is, that when the present government of the United States was established it was the belief of all liberty-loving men in America that real, genuine freedom could not exist in any country that recognized the power of government to *compel* persons accused of crime to be witnesses against themselves. And it is not too much to say that the wise men who laid the foundations of our constitutional government would have stood aghast at the suggestion that immunity from self-incrimination was not among the essential, fundamental principles of English law. . . .

What method does the Court use to define due process of law under the Fourteenth Amendment? Does this method produce clear standards for the determination of due process? On what basis does the Court decide that protection against compulsory self-incrimination is not part of due process? Compare the Court's discussion of fundamental rights with the dissenting opinion in the *Slaughterhouse Cases*. Would the same fundamental rights be extended to state citizens against state encroachment by the dissenters in the *Slaughterhouse Cases* and the Court in the *Twining* case? How is the due process clause given a broader reach in *Twining* than in the majority opinion in the *Slaughterhouse Cases*?

THE DEVELOPMENT
OF SUBSTANTIVE DUE PROCESS

While the opinion in the *Munn* case upheld the state statute as a legitimate regulation in the public interest, it recognized that the Fourteenth Amendment due process clause "prevents the states from doing that which will operate as . . . a deprivation [of private property]." While giving deference to state legislative judgment in the determination of what concerned the public interest and was a reasonable regulation thereof, the Court was careful to point out that "in mere private contracts, relating to matters in which the public has no interest, what is reasonable must be ascertained judicially."

Chief Justice Waite warned again in *The Railroad Commission Cases* (1886) that state legislative judgments concerning economic regulation might be subject to judicial control. "This power to regulate is not a power to destroy," wrote Waite for the Court, "and limitation is not the equivalent of confiscation. Under pretense of regulating fares and freights, the state cannot require a railroad corporation to carry persons or property without reward; neither can it do that which in law amounts to a taking of private property for public use without just compensation, or without due process of law."[13]

The importance the Court attached to judicial rather than legislative or administrative determination of the reasonableness of government regulation affecting property interests was illustrated in *Chicago, Milwaukee and St. Paul R. Co.* v. *Minnesota* (1890). The decision overturned a state law that authorized administrative rate-making without judicial review, on the grounds that it violated both procedural and substantive due process. The law was deficient in its failure to provide adequate procedural protection for the railroads which could only be achieved through judicial review. And, concluded the Court, judicial review was necessary to determine the reasonableness of rates, which is "eminently a question for judicial investigation."[14] Administrative regulation of the reasonableness of rates is "in substance and

[13]The Railroad Commission Cases, 116 U.S. 307, 331 (1886).
[14]Chicago, Milwaukee and St. Paul R. Co. v. Minnesota, 134 U.S. 418, 458 (1890).

effect" a deprivation of property without due process of law. In a dissenting opinion Justice Bradley declared that the Court had overruled the *Munn* decision.

The *Chicago, Milwaukee and St. Paul* case placed the courts squarely in the center of the rate-making process. Neither administrative agencies nor legislatures could set rates without judicial scrutiny and which did not conform to judicial views of fairness. Substantive due process review of rates became complete in *Smyth* v. *Ames,* 169 U.S. 466 (1898), which voided a Nebraska statute setting intrastate freight rates. The Court investigated in detail the earning power of the railroads and concluded that the rates were unreasonable and therefore a deprivation of property without due process of law.[15]

Substantive Due Process and Freedom to Contract

The line of cases from *Munn* in 1877 to *Smyth* v. *Ames* in 1898 applied substantive due process review based upon property rights and held unreasonable deprivations of private property to be violations of the due process clause of the Fourteenth Amendment.

The Court extended the substantive due process doctrine beyond the standard of deprivation of property to deprivation of *liberty* into which it incorporated the freedom to contract.

Barbier v. *Connolly,* 113 U.S. 27 (1885), while upholding a San Francisco ordinance prohibiting laundries to operate at night, put the states on notice that the due process clause protected common law liberties and the freedom to contract.

The Supreme Court finally overturned a state law as a violation of the substantive right of freedom to contract under the due process clause of the Fourteenth Amendment in *Allgeyer* v. *Louisiana* (1897). The Louisiana statute prohibited nonlicensed companies from selling marine insurance contracts within the state. The Court broadly defined liberty to include "not only the right of the citizen to be free from the mere physical restraint of his person, as by incarceration, but the term is deemed to embrace the right of the citizen to be free in the enjoyment of all of his faculties; to be free to use them in all lawful ways; to live and work where he will; to earn his livelihood by any lawful calling; to pursue any livelihood or avocation, and for that purpose to enter into all contracts which may be proper, necessary, and essential to his carrying out to a successful conclusion the purposes above mentioned."[16]

By substituting its judgment for that of state legislatures in determining the fairness of regulations of property and liberty under the due process clause of the Fourteenth Amendment, the Court was acting contrary to the public opinion that had spurred state regulation. Political pressures upon state legislatures throughout the country had resulted in laws regulating business which the courts were unwilling to sustain.

[15]Smyth v. Ames was overruled in FPC v. Hope Natural Gas Company, 320 U.S. 591 (1944).
[16]Allgeyer v. Louisiana, 165 U.S. 578, 589 (1897).

The following historic substantive due process case reviewed the constitutionality of a New York law that prohibited bakery employees from working more than ten hours a day or sixty hours a week. Lochner, an employer, was convicted of violating the law in the New York state courts, from which he appealed to the Supreme Court.

Lochner v. New York

198 U.S. 45; 25 S. Ct. 539; 49 L. Ed. 937 (1905)

MR. JUSTICE PECKHAM delivered the opinion of the Court.

. . . The mandate of the statute, that "no employee shall be required or permitted to work," is the substantial equivalent of an enactment that "no employee shall contract or agree to work," more than ten hours per day; and, as there is no provision for special emergencies, the statute is mandatory in all cases. It is not an act merely fixing the number of hours which shall constitute a legal day's work, but an absolute prohibition upon the employer permitting, under any circumstances, more than ten hours' work to be done in his establishment. The employee may desire to earn the extra money which would arise from his working more than the prescribed time, but this statute forbids the employer from permitting the employee to earn it.

The statute necessarily interferes with the right of contract between the employer and employees, concerning the number of hours in which the latter may labor in the bakery of the employer. The general right to make a contract in relation to his business is part of the liberty of the individual protected by the Fourteenth Amendment of the Federal Constitution. *Allgeyer* v. *Louisiana* [1897] . . . Under that provision no state can deprive any person of life, liberty, or property without due process of law. The right to purchase or to sell labor is part of the liberty protected by this amendment, unless there are circumstances which exclude the right. There are, however, certain powers, existing in the sovereignty of each state in the Union, somewhat vaguely termed police powers, the exact description and limitation of which have not been attempted by the courts. Those powers, broadly stated, and without, at present, any attempt at a more specific limitation, relate to the safety, health, morals, and general welfare of the public. Both property and liberty are held on such reasonable conditions as may be imposed by the governing power of the state in the exercise of those powers, and with such conditions the Fourteenth Amendment was not designed to interfere. . . .

The state, therefore, has power to prevent the individual from making certain kinds of contracts, and in regard to them the Federal Constitution offers no protection. If the contract be one which the state, in the legitimate exercise of its police power, has the right to prohibit, it is not prevented from prohibiting it by the Fourteenth Amendment. Contracts in violation of a statute, either of the Federal or state government, or a contract to let one's property for immoral purposes, or to do any other unlawful act, could obtain no protection from the Federal Constitution, as coming under the liberty of person or of free contract. Therefore, when the state, by its legislature, in the assumed exercise of its police powers, has passed an act which seriously limits the right to labor or the right of contract in regard to their means of livelihood between persons who are *sui juris* [possessing full social and civil rights] (both employer and employee), it becomes of great importance to determine which shall prevail,—the right of the individual to labor for such time as he may choose, or the right of the state to prevent the individual from laboring, or from entering into any contract to labor, beyond a certain time prescribed by the state.

This Court has recognized the existence and upheld the exercise of the police powers of the states in many cases which might fairly be considered as border ones, and it has, in the course of its determination of questions regarding the asserted invalidity of such statutes, on the ground of their violation of the rights secured by the Federal Constitution, been guided by rules of a very liberal nature, the application of which has resulted, in numerous instances, in upholding the validity of state statutes thus assailed. Among the later cases where the state law has been upheld by this Court is that of *Holden* v. *Hardy* [1898]. A provision in the act of the legislature of Utah was there under consideration, the act limiting the employment of workmen in all underground mines or workings, to eight hours per day, "except in cases of emergency, where life or property is in imminent danger." It also limited the hours of labor in smelting and other institutions for the reduction or refining of ores or metals to eight hours per day, except in like cases of emergency. The act was held to be a valid exercise of the police powers of the state. A review of many of the cases on the subject, decided by this and other courts, is given in the opinion. It was held that the kind of employment, mining, smelting, etc., and the character of the employees in such kinds of labor, were such as to make it reasonable and proper for the state to interfere to prevent the employees from being constrained by the rules laid down by the proprietors in regard to labor. . . .

It must, of course, be conceded that there is a limit to the valid exercise of the police power by the state. There is no dispute concerning this general proposition. Otherwise the Fourteenth Amendment would have no efficacy and the legislatures of the states would have unbounded power, and it would be enough to say that any piece of legislation was enacted to conserve the morals, the health, or the safety of the people; such legislation would be valid, no matter how absolutely without foundation the claim might be. The claim of the police power would be a mere pretext,—become another and delusive name for the supreme sovereignty of the state to be exercised free from constitutional restraint. This is not contended for. In every case that comes before this Court, therefore, where legislation of this character is concerned, and where the protection of the Federal Constitution is sought, the question necessarily arises: Is this a fair, reasonable, and appropriate exercise of the police power of the state, or is it an unreasonable, unnecessary, and arbitrary interference with the right of the individual to his personal liberty, or to enter into those contracts in relation to labor which may seem to him appropriate or necessary for the support of himself and his family? Of course the liberty of contract relating to labor includes both parties to it. The one has as much right to purchase as the other to sell labor.

This is not a question of substituting the judgment of the court for that of the legislature. If the act be within the power of the state it is valid, although the judgment of the court might be totally opposed to the enactment of such a law. But the question would still remain: Is it within the police power of the state? and that question must be answered by the Court.

The question whether this act is valid as a labor law, pure and simple, may be dismissed in a few words. There is no reasonable ground for interfering with the liberty of person or the right of free contract, by determining the hours of labor, in the occupation of a baker. There is no contention that bakers as a class are not equal in intelligence and capacity to men in other trades or manual occupations, or that they are not able to assert their rights and care for themselves without the protecting arm of the state, interfering with their independence of judgment and of action. They are in no sense wards of the state. Viewed in the light of a purely labor law, with no reference whatever to the question of health, we think that a law like the one before us involves neither the safety, the morals, nor the welfare, of the public, and that the interest of the public is not in the slightest degree affected by such an act. The law must be upheld, if at all, as a law pertaining to the health of the individual engaged in the occupation of a baker. It does not affect any other portion of the public than those who are engaged in that occupation. Clean and wholesome bread does not depend upon whether the baker works but ten hours per day or only sixty hours a week. The limitation of the hours of labor does not come within the police power on that ground.

It is a question of which of two powers or rights shall prevail,—the power of the state to legislate or the right of the individual to liberty of person and freedom of contract. The mere assertion that the subject relates, though but in a remote degree, to the public health, does not necessarily render the enactment valid. The act must have a more direct relation, as a means to an end, and the end itself must be appropriate and legitimate, before an act can be held to be valid which interferes with the general right of an individual to be free in his person and in his power to contract in relation to his own labor. . . .

We think the limit of the police power has been reached and passed in this case. There is, in our judgment, no reasonable foundation for holding this to be necessary or appropriate as a health law to safeguard the public health, or the health of the individuals who are following the trade of a baker. If this statute be valid, and if, therefore, a proper case is made out in which to deny the right of an individual, *sui juris*, as employer or employee, to make contracts for the labor of the latter under the protection of the provisions of the Federal Constitution, there would seem to be no length to which legislation of this nature might not go. . . .

We think that there can be no fair doubt that the trade of a baker, in and of itself, is not an unhealthy one to that degree which would authorize the legislature to interfere with the right to labor, and with the right of free contract on the part of the individual, either as employer or employee. In looking through statistics regarding all trades and occupations, it may be true that the trade of a baker does not appear to be as healthy as some other trades, and is also vastly more healthy than still others. To the common understanding the trade of a baker has never been regarded as an unhealthy one. Very likely physicians would not recommend the exercise of that or of any other trade as a remedy for ill health. Some occupations are more healthy than others, but we think there are none which might not come under the power of the legislature to supervise and control the hours of working therein, if the mere fact that the occupation is not absolutely and perfectly healthy is to confer that right upon the legislative department of the government. It might be safely affirmed that almost all

occupations more or less affect the health.
There must be more than the mere fact
of the possible existence of some small
amount of unhealthiness to warrant legislative interference with liberty. It is un-
fortunately true that labor, even in any
department, may possibly carry with it the
seeds of unhealthiness. But are we all, on
that account, at the mercy of legislative
majorities? A printer, a tinsmith, a lock-
smith, a carpenter, a cabinetmaker, a dry
goods clerk, a bank's, a lawyer's, or a physician's clerk, or a clerk in almost any kind
of business, would all come under the
power of the legislature, on this assumption. No trade, no occupation, no mode of
earning one's living, could escape this all-
pervading power, and the acts of the legislature in limiting the hours of labor in
all employments would be valid, although
such limitation might seriously cripple the
ability of the laborer to support himself
and his family. In our large cities there
are many buildings into which the sun
penetrates for but a short time in each
day, and these buildings are occupied by
people carrying on the business of bank-
ers, brokers, lawyers, real estate, and
many other kinds of business, aided by
many clerks, messengers, and other employees. Upon the assumption of the validity of this act under review, it is not
possible to say that an act, prohibiting
lawyers' or bank clerks, or others, from
contracting to labor for their employers
more than eight hours a day would be invalid. It might be said that it is unhealthy
to work more than that number of hours
in an apartment lighted by artificial light
during the working hours of the day; that
the occupation of the bank clerk, the lawyer's clerk, the real estate clerk, or the
broker's clerk, in such offices is therefore
unhealthy, and the legislature, in its pa-
ternal wisdom, must, therefore, have the
right to legislate on the subject of, and to
limit, the hours for such labor; and, if it

exercises that power, and its validity be
questioned, it is sufficient to say, it has
reference to the public health; it has reference to the health of the employees
condemmed to labor day after day in
buildings where the sun never shines; it is
a health law, and therefore it is valid, and
cannot be questioned by the courts.

It is also urged, pursuing the same line
of argument, that it is to the interest of
the state that its population should be
strong and robust, and therefore any legislation which may be said to tend to make
people healthy must be valid as health
laws, enacted under the police power. If
this be a valid argument and a justification for this kind of legislation, it follows
that the protection of the Federal Constitution from undue interference with liberty of person and freedom of contract is
visionary, wherever the law is sought to
be justified as a valid exercise of the police power. Scarcely any law but might
find shelter under such assumptions, and
conduct, properly so called, as well as
contract, would come under the restrictive sway of the legislature. Not only the
hours of employees, but the hours of employers, could be regulated, and doctors,
lawyers, scientists, all professional men, as
well as athletes and artisans, could be forbidden to fatigue their brains and bodies
by prolonged hours of exercise, lest the
fighting strength of the state be impaired.
We mention these extreme cases because
the contention is extreme. We do not believe in the soundness of the views which
uphold this law. On the contrary, we
think that such a law as this, although
passed in the assumed exercise of the police power, and as relating to the public
health, or the health of the employees
named, is not within that power, and is
invalid. The act is not, within any fair
meaning of the term, a health law, but is
an illegal interference with the rights
of individuals, both employers and em-

ployees, to make contracts regarding labor upon such terms as they may think best, or which they may agree upon with the other parties to such contracts. Statutes of the nature of that under review, limiting the hours in which grown and intelligent men may labor to earn their living, are mere meddlesome interferences with the rights of the individual, and they are not saved from condemnation by the claim that they are passed in the exercise of the police power and upon the subject of the health of the individual whose rights are interfered with, unless there be some fair ground, reasonable in and of itself, to say that there is material danger to the public health, or to the health of the employees, if the hours of labor are not curtailed. . . .

It was further urged on the argument that restricting the hours of labor in the case of bakers was valid because it tended to cleanliness on the part of the workers, as a man was more apt to be cleanly when not overworked, and if cleanly then his "output" was also more likely to be so. . . . We do not admit the reasoning to be sufficient to justify the claimed right of such interference. The state in that case would assume the position of a supervisor, or *pater familias*, over every act of the individual, and its right of governmental interference with his hours of labor, his hours of exercise, the character thereof, and the extent to which it shall be carried would be recognized and upheld. In our judgment it is not possible in fact to discover the connection between the number of hours a baker may work in the bakery and the healthful quality of the bread made by the workman. The connection, if any exist, is too shadowy and thin to build any argument for the interference of the legislature. If the man works ten hours a day it is all right, but if ten and a half or eleven his health is in danger and his bread may be unhealthy, and, therefore,

he shall not be permitted to do it. This, we think, is unreasonable and entirely arbitrary. . . .

This interference on the part of the legislatures of the several states with the ordinary trades and occupations of the people seems to be on the increase. . . .

It is impossible for us to shut our eyes to the fact that many of the laws of this character, while passed under what is claimed to be the police power for the purpose of protecting the public health or welfare, are, in reality, passed from other motives. We are justified in saying so when, from the character of the law and the subject upon which it legislates, it is apparent that the public health or welfare bears but the most remote relation to the law. The purpose of a statute must be determined from the natural and legal effect of the language employed; and whether it is or is not repugnant to the Constitution of the United States must be determined from the natural effect of such statutes when put into operation, and not from their proclaimed purpose. . . .

It seems to us that the real object and purpose were simply to regulate the hours of labor between the master and his employees (all being men, *sui juris*), in a private business, not dangerous in any degree to morals, or in any real and substantial degree to the health of the employees. Under such circumstances the freedom of master and employee to contract with each other in relation to their employment, and in defining the same, cannot be prohibited or interfered with, without violating the Federal Constitution.

The judgment . . . must be reversed. . . .

Mr. Justice Harlan (with whom Mr. Justice White and Mr. Justice Day concurred), dissenting:

. . . I find it impossible, in view of common experience, to say that there is here no real or substantial relation between the means employed by the state and the end sought to be accomplished by its legislation. . . .

We judicially know that the question of the number of hours during which a workman should continuously labor has been, for a long period, and is yet, a subject of serious consideration among civilized peoples, and by those having special knowledge of the laws of health. Suppose the statute prohibited labor in bakery and confectionery establishments in excess of eighteen hours each day. No one, I take it, could dispute the power of the state to enact such a statute. But the statute before us does not embrace extreme or exceptional cases. It may be said to occupy a middle ground in respect of the hours of labor. What is the true ground for the state to take between legitimate protection, by legislation, of the public health and liberty of contract is not a question easily solved, nor one in respect of which there is or can be absolute certainty. There are very few, if any, questions in political economy about which entire certainty may be predicated. . . .

I do not stop to consider whether any particular view of this economic question presents the sounder theory. What the precise facts are it may be difficult to say. It is enough for the determination of this case, and it is enough for this Court to know, that the question is one about which there is room for debate and for an honest difference of opinion. There are many reasons of a weighty, substantial character, based upon the experience of mankind, in support of the theory that, all things considered, more than ten hours' steady work each day, from week to week, in a bakery or confectionery establishment, may endanger the health and

shorten the lives of the workmen, thereby diminishing their physical and mental capacity to serve the state and to provide for those dependent upon them.

If such reasons exist that ought to be the end of this case, for the state is not amenable to the judiciary, in respect of its legislative enactments, unless such enactments are plainly, palpably, beyond all question, inconsistent with the Constitution of the United States.

MR. JUSTICE HOLMES, dissenting:

I regret sincerely that I am unable to agree with the judgment in this case, and that I think it my duty to express my dissent.

This case is decided upon an economic theory which a large part of the country does not entertain. If it were a question whether I agreed with that theory, I should desire to study it further and long before making up my mind. But I do not conceive that to be my duty, because I strongly believe that my agreement or disagreement has nothing to do with the right of a majority to embody their opinions in law. It is settled by various decisions of this Court that state constitutions and state laws may regulate life in many ways which we as legislators might think as injudicious, or if you like as tyrannical, as this, and which, equally with this, interfere with the liberty to contract. Sunday laws and usury laws are ancient examples. A more modern one is the probibition of lotteries. The liberty of the citizen to do as he likes so long as he does not interfere with the liberty of others to do the same, which has been a shibboleth for some well-known writers, is interfered with by school laws, by the Postoffice, by every state or municipal institution which takes his money for purposes thought desirable, whether he likes it or not. The Fourteenth Amendment does not enact Mr.

Herbert Spencer's Social Statics. The other day we sustained the Massachusetts vaccination law. *Jacobson* v. *Massachusetts,* 197 U.S. 11 [1905]. . . . United States and state statutes and decisions cutting down the liberty to contract by way of combination are familiar to this Court. *Northern Securities Co.* v. *United States,* 193 U.S. 197 [1904]. . . . Two years ago we upheld the prohibition of sales of stock on margins, or for future delivery, in the Constitution of California. . . . The decision sustaining an eight-hour law for miners is still recent. *Holden* v. *Hardy,* 169 U.S. 366 [1898]. . . . Some of these laws embody convictions or prejudices which judges are likely to share. Some may not. But a Constitution is not intended to embody a particular economic theory, whether of paternalism and the organic relation of the citizen to the state or of *laissez faire.* It is made for people of fundamentally differing views, and the accident of our finding certain opinions natural and familiar, or novel, and even shocking, ought not to conclude our judgment upon the question whether statutes embodying them conflict with the Constitution of the United States.

General propositions do not decide concrete cases. The decision will depend on a judgment or intuition more subtle than any articulate major premise. But I think that the proposition just stated, if it is accepted, will carry us far toward the end. Every opinion tends to become a law. I think that the word "liberty," in the Fourteenth Amendment, is perverted when it is held to prevent the natural outcome of a dominant opinion, unless it can be said that a rational and fair man necessarily would admit that the statute proposed would infringe fundamental principles as they have been understood by the traditions of our people and our law. It does not need research to show that no such sweeping condemnation can be passed upon the statute before us. A reasonable man might think it a proper measure on the score of health. Men whom I certainly could not pronounce unreasonable would uphold it as a first instalment of a general regulation of the hours of work. Whether in the latter aspect it would be open to the charge of inequality I think it unnecessary to discuss.

Is the Court more interventionist in the *Lochner* case than in *Munn* v. *Illinois?* Is broader review of the substance of state legislation exercised in *Lochner* than in *Munn?* What is the means-ends test employed by the majority in *Lochner* to determine the validity of state legislation under the due process clause of the Fourteenth Amendment? Does the *Lochner* majority hold that freedom of contract under the due process clause is an absolute right that cannot be abridged under any circumstances by the states? On what grounds does the majority find that "the limit of the police power has been reached and passed" in the *Lochner* case? Does the Court's reasoning imply an absolute judicial discretion to overturn state laws enacted under the police power?

Contrast the way in which Justice Harlan applies the means-ends test in his dissenting opinion with the means-ends analysis of the majority. What standard does Harlan apply in his argument that the state statute should be upheld?

On what grounds does Justice Holmes dissent? What conclusions does he draw from his premise that the case "is decided upon an economic theory which a large part of the country does not entertain"? How does Holmes use judicial precedents to support his dissent? Contrast, in particular, Holmes's conclusions from *Holden* v. *Hardy* (1898), with the majority view of the same case.

The Court's decision in *Holden* v. *Hardy* (1898) and in *Muller* v. *Oregon*, 208 U.S. 412 (1908), upheld state laws regulating working hours even though they were reviewed under the standards of substantive due process. In the *Muller* case the persuasive "Brandeis briefs" were filed, which pleaded to sustain the challenged legislation on the basis of broad social and economic considerations. The decision upheld a state law establishing maximum working hours for women. Maximum hour legislation for workers in mines was upheld in the *Holden* case. In *Coppage* v. *Kansas*, 236 U.S. 1 (1915), however, the Court used substantive due process criteria to strike down a state law prohibiting yellow dog contracts which prohibited union membership as a condition of employment.

Substantive due process review in the *Lochner* and *Coppage* cases resulted in invalidating state legislation, whereas in the *Muller* and *Holden* decisions state regulation was upheld. In the latter cases the Court found that the state had a legitimate interest in protecting the particular classes of workers covered by the laws, and that the regulations were properly designed for this purpose. The *Lochner* opinion held that the New York law involved "neither the safety, the morals, nor the welfare, of the public, and that the interest of the public is not in the slightest degree affected by such an act. The law must be upheld, if at all, as a law pertaining to the health of the individual engaged in the occupation of a baker." Moreover, the *Lochner* majority implied that the Utah miners involved in the *Holden* case were less capable of protecting themselves against employer coercion than were the bakers of New York. "There is no contention," wrote the Court, "that bakers as a class are not equal in intelligence and capacity to men in other trades or manual occupations, or that they are not able to assert their rights and care for themselves without the protecting arm of the state, interfering with their independence of judgment and of action. They are in no sense wards of the state."

The law reviewed in *Coppage* had a broader reach than the statutes reviewed in the *Holden, Muller,* and *Lochner* cases. The Kansas law covered all employment in the state, and, in the view of the Court, restricted the right to contract for personal employment.

Substantive Due Process under the Fifth Amendment

That the Supreme Court would apply the same substantive due process standards under the Fifth Amendment as it did under the Fourteenth was illustrated by *Adair* v. *United States*, 208 U.S. 161 (1908), which invalidated a federal law prohibiting yellow dog contracts. The *Adair* decision was used as a basis for the Court's opinion in the *Coppage* case. In the following case the Court confronted a Fifth Amendment due process challenge to a congressional statute that prescribed minimum wages for women in the District of Columbia.

Adkins v. Children's Hospital

261 U.S. 525; 43 S. Ct. 394; 67 L. Ed. 785 (1923)

MR. JUSTICE SUTHERLAND delivered the opinion of the Court:

The judicial duty of passing upon the constitutionality of an act of Congress is one of great gravity and delicacy. The statute here in question has successfully borne the scrutiny of the legislative branch of the government, which, by enacting it, has affirmed its validity; and that determination must be given great weight. This Court, by an unbroken line of decisions from Chief Justice Marshall to the present day, has steadily adhered to the rule that every possible presumption is in favor of the validity of an act of Congress until overcome beyond rational doubt. But if, by clear and indubitable demonstration, a statute be opposed to the Constitution, we have no choice but to say so. The Constitution, by its own terms, is the supreme law of the land, emanating from the people, the repository of ultimate sovereignty under our form of government. A congressional statute, on the other hand, is the act of an agency of this sovereign authority, and, if it conflict with the Constitution, must fall; for that which is not supreme must yield to that which is. . . .

The statute now under consideration is attacked upon the ground that it authorizes an unconstitutional interference with the freedom of contract included within the guarantees of the due process clause of the Fifth Amendment. That the right to contract about one's affairs is a part of the liberty of the individual protected by this clause is settled by the decisions of this Court, and is no longer open to question. . . . Within this liberty are contracts of employment of labor. In making such contracts, generally speaking, the parties have an equal right to obtain from each other the best terms they can as the result of private bargaining. . . .

There is, of course, no such thing as absolute freedom of contract. It is subject to a great variety of restraints. But freedom of contract is, nevertheless, the general rule and restraint the exception; and the exercise of legislative authority to abridge it can be justified only by the existence of exceptional circumstances. Whether these circumstances exist in the present case constitutes the question to be answered. . . .

In the *Muller Case* the validity of an Oregon statute, forbidding the employment of any female in certain industries more than ten hours during any one day, was upheld. The decision proceeded upon the theory that the difference between the sexes may justify a different rule respecting hours of labor in the case of women than in the case of men. It is pointed out that these consist in differences of physical structure, especially in respect of the maternal functions, and also in the fact that historically woman has always been dependent upon man, who has established his control by superior physical strength. . . . But the ancient inequality of the sexes, otherwise than physical, as suggested in the *Muller Case* has continued "with diminishing intensity." In view of the great—not to say revolutionary— changes which have taken place since that utterance, in the contractual, political, and civil status of women, culminating in the Nineteenth Amendment, it is not unreasonable to say that these differences have now come almost, if not quite, to the vanishing point. In this aspect of the matter, while the physical differences must be recognized in appropriate cases, and legislation fixing hours or conditions of work may properly take them into account, we cannot accept the doctrine that women of mature age, sui juris, require or may be subjected to restrictions upon their liberty of contract which could not lawfully be imposed in the case of men under similar circumstances. To do so would be to ignore all the implications to be drawn from the present-day trend of legislation, as well as that of common thought and usage, by which woman is accorded emancipation from the old doctrine that she must be given special protection or be subjected to special restraint in her contractual and civil relationships. In passing, it may be noted that the instant statute applies in the case of a woman employer contracting with a woman employee as it does when the former is a man.

The essential characteristics of the statute now under consideration, which differentiate it from the laws fixing hours of labor, will be made to appear as we proceed. It is sufficient now to point out that the latter ... deal with incidents of the employment having no necessary effect upon the heart of the contract; that is, the amount of wages to be paid and received. A law forbidding work to continue beyond a given number of hours leaves the parties free to contract about wages and thereby equalize whatever additional burdens may be imposed upon the employer as a result of the restrictions as to hours, by an adjustment in respect of the amount of wages. Enough has been said to show that the authority to fix hours of labor cannot be exercised except in respect of those occupations where work of long-continued duration is detrimental to health. This Court has been careful in every case where the question has been raised, to place its decision upon this limited authority of the legislature to regulate hours of labor, and to disclaim any purpose to uphold the legislation as fixing wages, thus recognizing an essential difference between the two. It seems plain that these decisions afford no real support for any form of law establishing minimum wages.

If now, in the light furnished by the foregoing exceptions to the general rule forbidding legislative interference with freedom of contract, we examine and analyze the statute in question, we shall see that it differs from them in every material respect. ... It is simply and exclusively a price-fixing law, confined to adult women (for we are not now considering the provisions relating to minors), who are legally as capable of contracting for themselves as men. It forbids two parties having lawful capacity under penalties as to the employer to freely contract with one another in respect of the price for which one shall render service to the other in a purely private employment where both are willing, perhaps anxious, to agree, even though the consequences may be to oblige one to surrender a desirable engagement, and the other to dispense with the services of a desirable employee. ...

The standard furnished by the statute for the guidance of the board is so vague as to be impossible of practical application with any reasonable degree of accuracy. What is sufficient to supply the necessary cost of living for a woman worker and maintain her in good health and protect her morals is obviously not a precise or unvarying sum,—not even approximately so. The amount will depend upon a variety of circumstances: The individual temperament, habits of thrift, care, ability to buy necessaries intelligently, and whether the woman live alone or with her family. To those who practise economy, a given sum will afford comfort, while to those of contrary habit the same sum will be wholly inadequate. The cooperative economies of the family group are not taken into account, though they constitute an important consideration in estimating the cost of living, for it is obvious that the individual expense will be less in the case of a member of a family than in the case of one living alone. The relation between earnings and morals is not capable of standardization. It cannot be shown that well-paid women safeguard their morals more carefully than those who are poorly paid. Morality rests upon other considerations than wages; and there is, certainly, no such prevalent connection between the two as to justify a broad attempt to adjust the latter with reference to the former. . . .

The law takes account of the necessities of only one party to the contract. It ignores the necessities of the employer by compelling him to pay not less than a certain sum, not only whether the employee is capable of earning it, but irrespective of the ability of his business to sustain the burden, generously leaving him, of course, the privilege of abandoning his business as an alternative for going on at a loss. Within the limits of the minimum sum, he is precluded, under penalty of fine and imprisonment, from adjusting compensation to the differing merits of his employees. It compels him to pay at least the sum fixed in any event, because the employee needs it, but requires no service of equivalent value from the employee. . . . To the extent that the sum fixed exceeds the fair value of the services rendered, it amounts to a compulsory exaction from the employer for the support of a partially indigent person, for whose condition there rests upon him no peculiar responsibility, and therefore, in effect, arbitrarily shifts to his shoulders a burden which, if it belongs to anybody, belongs to society as a whole.

The feature of this statute which, perhaps more than any other, puts upon it the stamp of invalidity is that it exacts from the employer an arbitrary payment for a purpose and upon a basis having no causal connection with his business, or the contract, or the work the employee engages to do. . . . The ethical right of every worker, man or woman, to a living wage, may be conceded. One of the declared and important purposes of trade organizations is to secure it. And with that principle and with every legitimate effort to realize it in fact, no one can quarrel; but the fallacy of the proposed method of attaining it is that it assumes that every employer is bound, at all events, to furnish it. The moral requirement, implicit in every contract of employment, viz., that the amount to be paid and the service to be rendered shall bear to each other some relation of just equivalence, is completely ignored. . . . Certainly the employer, by paying a fair equivalent for the service rendered, though not sufficient to support the employee, has neither caused nor contributed to her poverty. On the contrary, to the extent of what he pays, he has relieved it. In principle, there can be no difference between the case of selling labor and the case of selling goods. If one goes to the butcher, the baker, or grocer to buy food, he is morally entitled to obtain the worth of his money, but he is not entitled to more. If what he gets is worth what he pays, he is not justified in demanding more simply because he needs more; and the shopkeeper, having dealt fairly and honestly in that transaction, is not concerned in any peculiar sense with the question of his customer's necessities. . . . But a statute which prescribes payment without regard to any of these things, and solely with relation to circumstances apart from the contract of employment, the business affected by it, and the work done under it, is so clearly the product of a naked, arbitrary exercise of power, that it cannot be allowed to stand under the Constitution of the United States.

We are asked, upon the one hand, to consider the fact that several states have adopted similar statutes, and we are invited, upon the other hand, to give weight to the fact that three times as many states, presumably as well informed and as anxious to promote the health and morals of their people, have refrained from enacting such legislation. We have also been furnished with a large number of printed opinions approving the policy of the minimum wage, and our own reading has disclosed a large number to the contrary. These are all proper enough for the consideration of the lawmaking bodies, since their tendency is to establish the desirability or undesirability of the legislation; but they reflect no legitimate light upon the question of its validity, and that is what we are called upon to decide. The elucidation of that question cannot be aided by counting heads.

It is said that great benefits have resulted from the operation of such statutes, not alone in the District of Columbia, but in the several states where they have been in force. A mass of reports, opinions of special observers and students of the subject, and the like, has been brought before us in support of this statement, all of which we have found interesting but only mildly persuasive. That the earnings of women now are greater than they were formerly, and that conditions affecting women have become better in other respects, may be conceded; but convincing indications of the logical relation of these desirable changes to the law in question are significantly lacking. They may be, and quite probably are, due to other causes. . . .

Finally, it may be said that if, in the interest of the public welfare, the police power may be invoked to justify the fixing of a minimum wage, it may, when the public welfare is thought to require it, be invoked to justify a maximum wage. The power to fix high wages connotes, by like course of reasoning, the power to fix low wages. If, in the face of the guarantees of the Fifth Amendment, this form of legislation shall be legally justified, the field for the operation of the police power will have been widened to a great and dangerous degree. If, for example, in the opin-

ion of future lawmakers, wages in the building trades shall become so high as to preclude people of ordinary means from building and owning homes, an authority which sustains the minimum wage will be invoked to support a maximum wage for building laborers and artisans, and the same argument which has been here urged to strip the employer of his constitutional liberty of contract in one direction will be utilized to strip the employee of his constitutional liberty of contract in the opposite direction. A wrong decision does not end with itself: it is a precedent, and, with the swing of sentiment, its bad influence may run from one extremity of the arc to the other.

It has been said that legislation of the kind now under review is required in the interest of social justice, for whose ends freedom of contract may lawfully be subjected to restraint. The liberty of the individual to do as he pleases, even in innocent matters, is not absolute. It must frequently yield to the common good, and the line beyond which the power of interference may not be pressed is neither definite nor unalterable, but may be made to move, within limits not well defined, with changing need and circumstance. Any attempt to fix a rigid boundary would be unwise as well as futile. But, nevertheless, there are limits to the power, and when these have been passed, it becomes the plain duty of the courts, in the proper exercise of their authority, to so declare. To sustain the individual freedom of action contemplated by the Constitution is not to strike down the common good, but to exalt it; for surely the good of society as a whole cannot be better served than by the preservation against arbitrary restraint of the liberties of its constituent members.

It follows from what has been said that the act in question passes the limit prescribed by the Constitution, and, accordingly, the decrees of the court below are affirmed.

MR. JUSTICE BRANDEIS took no part in the consideration or decision of these cases.

MR. CHIEF JUSTICE TAFT, dissenting:

I regret much to differ from the Court in these cases.

The boundary of the police power, beyond which its exercise becomes an invasion of the guaranty of liberty under the Fifth and Fourteenth Amendments to the Constitution, is not easy to mark. Our Court has been laboriously engaged in pricking out a line in successive cases. We must be careful, it seems to me, to follow that line as well as we can, and not to depart from it by suggesting a distinction that is formal rather than real.

Legislatures, in limiting freedom of contract between employee and employer by a minimum wage, proceed on the assumption that employees in the class receiving least pay are not upon a full level of equality of choice with their employer, and in their necessitous circumstances are prone to accept pretty much anything that is offered. They are peculiarly subject to the overreaching of the harsh and greedy employer. The evils of the sweating system and of the long hours and low wages which are characteristic of it are well known. Now, I agree that it is a disputable question in the field of political economy how far a statutory requirement of maximum hours or minimum wages may be a useful remedy for these evils, and whether it may not make the case of the oppressed employee worse than it was before. But it is not the function of this Court to hold congressional acts invalid simply because they are passed to carry out economic views which the Court believes to be unwise or unsound. . . .

The right of the legislature under the Fifth and Fourteenth Amendments to limit the hours of employment on the score of the health of the employee, it seems to me, has been firmly established.

As to that, one would think, the line had been pricked out so that it has become a well-formulated rule. . . . In [*Bunting* v. *Oregon*, 243 U.S. 427 (1917)] this Court sustained a law limiting the hours of labor of any person, whether man or woman, working in any mill, factory, or manufacturing establishment, to ten hours a day, with a proviso as to further hours [permitting limited overtime at one and one-half the regular wage]. . . . The law covered the whole field of industrial employment, and certainly covered the case of persons employed in bakeries. Yet the opinion in the *Bunting Case* does not mention the *Lochner Case*. No one can suggest any constitutional distinction between employment in a bakery and one in any other kind of a manufacturing establishment which should make a limit of hours in the one invalid, and the same limit in the other permissible. It is impossible for me to reconcile the *Bunting Case* and the *Lochner Case,* and I have always supposed that the *Lochner Case* was thus overruled sub silentio. Yet the opinion of the Court herein in support of its conclusion quotes from the opinion in the *Lochner Case* as one which has been sometimes distinguished, but never overruled. Certainly there was no attempt to distinguish it in the *Bunting Case.*

However, the opinion herein does not overrule the *Bunting Case* in express terms, and therefore I assume that the conclusion in this case rests on the distinction between a minimum of wages and a maximum of hours in the limiting of liberty to contract. I regret to be at variance with the court as to the substance of this distinction. In absolute freedom of contract the one term is as important as the other, for both enter equally into the consideration given and received; a restriction as to one is not any greater in essence than the other, and is of the same kind. One is the multiplier and the other the multiplicand.

If it be said that long hours of labor

have a more direct effect upon the health of the employee than the low wage, there is very respectable authority from close observers, disclosed in the record and in the literature on the subject, quoted at length in the briefs, that they are equally harmful in this regard. Congress took this view, and we cannot say it was not warranted in so doing. . . .

I am authorized to say that Mr. Justice Sanford concurs in this opinion.

MR. JUSTICE HOLMES, dissenting:

The question in this case is the broad one, whether Congress can establish minimum rates of wages for women in the District of Columbia, with due provision for special circumstances, or whether we must say that Congress has no power to meddle with the matter at all. To me, notwithstanding the deference due to the prevailing judgment of the Court, the power of Congress seems absolutely free from doubt. The end—to remove conditions leading to ill health, immorality, and the deterioration of the race—no one would deny to be within the scope of constitutional legislation. The means are means that have the approval of Congress, of many states, and of those governments from which we have learned our greatest lessons. When so many intelligent persons, who have studied the matter more than any of us can, have thought that the means are effective and are worth the price, it seems to me impossible to deny that the belief reasonably may be held by reasonable men. If the law encountered no other objection than that the means bore no relation to the end, or that they cost too much, I do not suppose that anyone would venture to say that it was bad. I agree, of course, that a law answering the foregoing requirements might be invalidated by specific provisions of the Constitution. For instance, it might take private property without just compensation. But, in the present instance, the only

objection that can be urged is found within the vague contours of the Fifth Amendment, prohibiting the depriving any person of liberty or property without due process of law. To that I turn.

The earlier decisions upon the same words in the Fourteenth Amendment began within our memory, and went no farther than an unpretentious assertion of the liberty to follow the ordinary callings. Later that innocuous generality was expanded into the dogma, Liberty of Contract. Contract is not specially mentioned in the text that we have to construe. It is merely an example of doing what you want to do, embodied in the word "liberty." But pretty much all law consists in forbidding men to do some things that they want to do, and contract is no more exempt from law than other acts. Without enumerating all the restrictive laws that have been upheld, I will mention a few that seem to me to have interfered with liberty of contract quite as seriously and directly as the one before us. Usury laws prohibit contracts by which a man receives more than so much interest for the money that he lends. Statutes of frauds restrict many contracts to certain forms. Some Sunday laws prohibit practically all contracts during one seventh of our whole life. Insurance rates may be regulated. Finally, women's hours of labor may be fixed. . . . And the principle was extended to men, with the allowance of a limited overtime, to be paid for "at the rate of time and one half of the regular wage," in *Bunting* v. *Oregon* [1917]. . . .

I confess that I do not understand the principle on which the power to fix a minimum for the wages of women can be denied by those who admit the power to fix a maximum for their hours of work. I fully assent to the proposition that here, as elsewhere, the distinctions of the law are distinctions of degree; but I perceive no difference in the kind or degree of interference with liberty, the only matter with which we have any concern, between the one case and the other. The bargain is equally affected whichever half you regulate. *Muller* v. *Oregon* [1908], I take it, is as good law to-day as it was in 1908. It will need more than the Nineteenth Amendment to convince me that there are no differences between men and women, or that legislation cannot take those differences into account. I should not hesitate to take them into account if I thought it necessary to sustain this act. . . . But after *Bunting* v. *Oregon* . . . I had supposed that it was not necessary, and that *Lochner* v. *New York* [1905] . . . would be allowed a deserved repose. . . .

How does Justice Sutherland distinguish the *Adkins* case from the *Muller* case? Does the Court indicate that minimum wage laws per se are unconstitutional, or would it uphold such laws under certain circumstances? For example, would such laws be upheld if it could be demonstrated that they were in the interest of the public welfare? Would they be sustained to protect an unequal class?

In his dissenting opinion, does Chief Justice Taft disagree with the substantive standards applied by the majority? Or is his dissent based upon the application of standards of judicial self-restraint? What criteria does Justice Holmes apply to the case in his dissent? Under what circumstances would Holmes support judicial intervention to invalidate regulatory legislation?

In the *Adkins* case the Court applied two overriding standards to determine the validity of government regulation of business firms. First, firms "affected with a public interest" could be regulated to the extent required to uphold the public interest. Second, regulation of employer-employee relations had to treat each party equally, permitting employers to pay employees in accordance with the value of services received. A statute simply prescribing minimum wages for employees without taking into account the value of their services to their employers is "a naked, arbitrary exercise of power" that is unconstitutional.

The interventionist stance of the Supreme Court during the era of substantive due process did not result in the invalidation of most of the regulatory legislation passed by the state and national legislatures. The *Holden,* *Muller,* and *Bunting* decisions illustrate that the Court was satisfied that some forms of state regulation necessary for the public welfare could be upheld. In fact, between the period 1897 and 1937, the Court upheld more statutes than it invalidated under due process review. Nevertheless, close to two hundred regulatory laws were nullified by the Court, enough to cause a storm of criticism from the political forces that supported the enlargement of the role of the government in economic affairs.

In conducting substantive due process review of state regulatory statutes, the Court in the 1920s increasingly narrowed the scope of those firms which it considered to be "affected with a public interest" and therefore properly subject to regulation. Moreover, before the *Lochner* era was to end, the New Deal Court in *Morehead* v. *New York ex rel Tipaldo,* 298 U.S. 586 (1936), invalidated a New York minimum wage law that contained the "value of service" provision called for by the Court in the *Adkins* case to sustain the regulation of wages. The *Morehead* opinion illustrated how the New Deal Court applied its conservative philosophy to foil the attempt of one state to adhere to earlier judicial doctrines.

The End of the *Lochner* Era

The *Lochner* era is generally considered to have ended a year after the decision in *Morehead* when the constitutional validity of a minimum wage law of the state of Washington was upheld in *West Coast Hotel* v. *Parrish* (1937). Before the *West Coast Hotel* decision, however, the Court in *Nebbia* v. *New York* (1934) decided that it could bend its substantive due process rules to meet an emergency situation. The *Nebbia* case challenged a New York statute that created a state milk control board with the power to fix maximum and minimum milk prices. This type of legislation had consistently been struck down in the 1920s as a violation of substantive due process.[17]

Nebbia v. *New York*

291 U.S. 502; 54 S. Ct. 505; 78 L. Ed. 940 (1934)

MR. JUSTICE ROBERTS delivered the opinion of the Court:

The Legislature of New York established, by Chapter 158 of the Laws of 1933, a Milk Control Board with power, among other things, to "fix minimum and maximum . . . retail prices to be charged by . . . stores to consumers for consumption off the premises where sold." The Board fixed nine cents as the price to be charged by a store for a quart of milk. Nebbia, the proprietor of a grocery store in Rochester, sold two quarts and a five cent loaf of bread for eighteen cents; and was convicted for violating the Board's order. At his trial he asserted the statute and order contravene the equal protection clause and the due process clause of the Fourteenth Amendment. . . .

The question for decision is whether the Federal Constitution prohibits a state from so fixing the selling price of milk. We first inquire as to the occasion for the legislation and its history.

During 1932 the prices received by farmers for milk were much below the cost of production. The decline in prices during 1931 and 1932 was much greater than that of prices generally. The situation of the families of dairy producers had become desperate and called for state aid similar to that afforded the unemployed, if conditions should not improve.

On March 10, 1932, the senate and assembly resolved "That a joint Legislative committee is hereby created . . . to investigate the causes of the decline of the price of milk to producers and the resultant effect of the low prices upon the dairy industry. . . ."

In part those conclusions are:

Milk is an essential item of diet. It can-

[17]See, for example, Wolff Packing Company v. Court of Industrial Relations, 262 U.S. 522 (1923), overturning a Kansas statute declaring transportation, public utility, and other industries to be affected with a public interest and creating a commission to settle wage disputes by fixing wages and terms of employment; Tyson and Bros. v. Banton, 273 U.S. 418 (1927), invalidating a New York statute regulating the prices of theatre tickets; Ribnik v. McBride, 277 U.S. 350 (1928), overturning a New Jersey statute that provided for the licensing of employment agencies and the regulation of their fees; Williams v. Standard Oil Company, 278 U.S. 235 (1925), voiding a Tennessee statute regulating gasoline prices within the state.

not long be stored. It is an excellent medium for growth of bacteria. These facts necessitate safeguards in its production and handling for human consumption which greatly increase the cost of the business. Failure of producers to receive a reasonable return for their labor and investment over an extended period threaten a relaxation of vigilance against contamination.

The production and distribution of milk is a paramount industry of the state, and largely affects the health and prosperity of its people. Dairying yields fully one-half of the total income from all farm products. Dairy farm investment amounts to approximately $1,000,000,000. Curtailment or destruction of the dairy industry would cause a serious economic loss to the people of the state.

In addition to the general price decline, other causes for the low price of milk include: a periodic increase in the number of cows and in milk production; the prevalence of unfair and destructive trade practices in the distribution of milk, leading to a demoralization of prices in the metropolitan area and other markets; and the failure of transportation and distribution charges to be reduced in proportion to the reduction in retail prices for milk and cream.

The fluid milk industry is affected by factors of instability peculiar to itself which call for special methods of control. . . .

The legislature adopted Chapter 158 as a method of correcting the evils, which the report of the committee showed could not be expected to right themselves through the ordinary play of the forces of supply and demand, owing to the peculiar and uncontrollable factors affecting the industry. . . .

First. The appellant urges that the order of the Milk Control Board denies him the equal protection of the laws. It is shown that the order requires him, if he

purchases his supply from a dealer, to pay eight cents per quart and five cents per pint, and to resell at not less than nine and six, whereas the same dealer may buy his supply from a farmer at lower prices and deliver milk to consumers at ten cents the quart and six cents the pint. We think the contention that the discrimination deprives the appellant of equal protection is not well founded. For aught that appears, the appellant purchased his supply of milk from a farmer as do distributors, or could have procured it from a farmer if he so desired. There is therefore no showing that the order placed him at a disadvantage, or in fact affected him adversely, and this alone is fatal to the claim of denial of equal protection. But if it were shown that the appellant is compelled to buy from a distributor, the difference in the retail price he is required to charge his customers, from that prescribed for sales by distributors, is not on its face arbitrary or unreasonable, for there are obvious distinctions between the two sorts of merchants which may well justify a difference of treatment, if the legislature possesses the power to control the prices to be charged for fluid milk. . . .

Second. The more serious question is whether . . . the appellant [has been denied] the due process secured to him by the Fourteenth Amendment. . . .

Under our form of government the use of property and the making of contracts are normally matters of private and not of public concern. The general rule is that both shall be free of governmental interference. But neither property rights nor contract rights are absolute; for government cannot exist if the citizen may at will use his property to the detriment of his fellows, or exercise his freedom of contract to work them harm. Equally fundamental with the private right is that of the public to regulate it in the common interest. . . .

Thus has this Court from the early

days affirmed that the power to promote the general welfare is inherent in government. Touching the matters committed to it by the Constitution, the United States possesses the power, as do the states in their sovereign capacity touching all subjects jurisdiction of which is not surrendered to the federal government, as shown by the quotations above given. These correlative rights, that of the citizen to exercise exclusive dominion over property and freely to contract about his affairs, and that of the state to regulate the use of property and the conduct of business, are always in collision. No exercise of the private right can be imagined which will not in some respect, however slight, affect the public; no exercise of the legislative prerogative to regulate the conduct of the citizen which will not to some extent abridge his liberty or affect his property. But subject only to constitutional restraint the private right must yield to the public need.

The Fifth Amendment, in the field of federal activity, and the Fourteenth, as respects state action, do not prohibit governmental regulation for the public welfare. They merely condition the exertion of the admitted power, by securing that the end shall be accomplished by methods consistent with due process. And the guaranty of due process, as has often been held, demands only that the law shall not be unreasonable, arbitrary or capricious, and that the means selected shall have a real and substantial relation to the object sought to be attained. It results that a regulation valid for one sort of business, or in given circumstances, may be invalid for another sort, or for the same business under other circumstances, because the reasonableness of each regulation depends upon the relevant facts. . . .

The Constitution does not guarantee the unrestricted privilege to engage in a business or to conduct it as one pleases. Certain kinds of business may be prohibited; and the right to conduct a business, or to pursue a calling, may be conditioned. Regulation of a business to prevent waste of the state's resources may be justified. And statutes prescribing the terms upon which those conducting certain businesses may contract, or imposing terms if they do enter into agreements, are within the state's competency. . . .

The milk industry in New York has been the subject of long-standing and drastic regulation in the public interest. The legislative investigation of 1932 was persuasive of the fact that for this and other reasons unrestricted competition aggravated existing evils, and the normal law of supply and demand was insufficient to correct maladjustments detrimental to the community. The inquiry disclosed destructive and demoralizing competitive conditions and unfair trade practices which resulted in retail price-cutting and reduced the income of the farmer below the cost of production. We do not understand the appellant to deny that in these circumstances the legislature might reasonably consider further regulation and control desirable for protection of the industry and the consuming public. That body believed conditions could be improved by preventing destructive price-cutting by stores which, due to the flood of surplus milk, were able to buy at much lower prices than the larger distributors and to sell without incurring the delivery costs of the latter. In the order of which complaint is made the Milk Control Board fixed a price of ten cents per quart for sales by a distributor to a consumer, and nine cents by a store to a consumer, thus recognizing the lower costs of the store, and endeavoring to establish a differential which would be just to both. In the light of the facts the order appears not to be unreasonable or arbitrary, or without relation to the purpose to prevent ruthless competition from destroying the wholesale price structure on which the farmer depends for his livelihood, and the community for an assured supply of milk.

But we are told that because the law essays to control prices it denies due process. Notwithstanding the admitted power to correct existing economic ills by appropriate regulation of business, even though an indirect result may be a restriction of the freedom of contract or a modification of charges for services or the price of commodities, the appellant urges that direct fixation of prices is a type of regulation absolutely forbidden. His position is that the Fourteenth Amendment requires us to hold the challenged statute void for this reason alone. The argument runs that the public control of rates or prices is *per se* unreasonable and unconstitutional, save as applied to businesses affected with a public interest; that a business so affected is one in which property is devoted to an enterprise of a sort which the public itself might appropriately undertake, or one whose owner relies on a public grant or franchise for the right to conduct the business, or in which he is bound to serve all who apply; in short, such as is commonly called a public utility; or a business in its nature a monopoly. The milk industry, it is said, possesses none of these characteristics, and, therefore, not being affected with a public interest, its charges may not be controlled by the state. Upon the soundness of this contention the appellant's case against the statute depends.

We may as well say at once that the dairy industry is not, in the accepted sense of the phrase, a public utility. We think the appellant is also right in asserting that there is in this case no suggestion of any monopoly or monopolistic practice. It goes without saying that those engaged in the business are in no way dependent upon public grants or franchises for the privilege of conducting their activities. But if, as must be conceded, the industry is subject to regulation in the public interest, what constitutional principle bars the state from correcting existing maladjustments by legislation touching prices? We think there is no such principle. The due process clause makes no mention of sales or of prices any more than it speaks of business or contracts or buildings or other incidents of property. The thought seems nevertheless to have persisted that there is something peculiarly sacrosanct about the price one may charge for what he makes or sells, and that, however able to regulate other elements of manufacture or trade, with incidental effect upon price, the state is incapable of directly controlling the price itself. This view was negatived many years ago. *Munn* v. *Illinois*. . . .

It is clear that there is no closed class or category of businesses affected with a public interest, and the function of courts in the application of the Fifth and Fourteenth Amendments is to determine in each case whether circumstances vindicate the challenged regulation as a reasonable exertion of governmental authority or condemn it as arbitrary or discriminatory. . . . The phrase "affected with a public interest" can, in the nature of things, mean no more than that an industry, for adequate reason, is subject to control for the public good. In several of the decisions of this Court wherein the expressions "affected with a public interest," and "clothed with a public use," have been brought forward as the criteria of the validity of price control, it has been admitted that they are not susceptible of definition and form an unsatisfactory test of the constitutionality of legislation directed at business practices or prices. These decisions must rest, finally, upon the basis that the requirements of due process were not met because the laws were found arbitrary in their operation and effect. But there can be no doubt that upon proper occasion and by appropriate measures the state may regulate a business in any of its aspects, including the prices to be charged for the products or commodities it sells.

So far as the requirement of due process is concerned, and in the absence of other constitutional restriction, a state is free to adopt whatever economic policy may reasonably be deemed to promote public welfare, and to enforce that policy by legislation adapted to its purpose. The courts are without authority either to declare such policy, or, when it is declared by the legislature, to override it. If the laws passed are seen to have a reasonable relation to a proper legislative purpose, and are neither arbitrary nor discriminatory, the requirements of due process are satisfied, and judicial determination to that effect renders a court *functus officio.* "Whether the free operation of the normal laws of competition is a wise and wholesome rule for trade and commerce is an economic question which this court need not consider or determine." . . . And it is equally clear that if the legislative policy be to curb unrestrained and harmful competition by measures which are not arbitrary or discriminatory it does not lie with the courts to determine that the rule is unwise. With the wisdom of the policy adopted, with the adequacy or practicability of the law enacted to forward it, the courts are both incompetent and unauthorized to deal. . . . The Constitution does not secure to anyone liberty to conduct his business in such fashion as to inflict injury upon the public at large, or upon any substantial group of the people. Price control, like any other form of regulation, is unconstitutional only if arbitrary, discriminatory, or demonstrably irrelevant to the policy the legislature is free to adopt, and hence an unnecessary and unwarranted interference with individual liberty.

Tested by these considerations we find no basis in the due process clause of the Fourteenth Amendment for condemning the provisions of the Agriculture and Markets Law here drawn into question.

The judgment is

Affirmed.

Separate opinion of Mr. Justice McReynolds:

The XIV Amendment wholly disempowered the several States to "deprive any person of life, liberty, or property, without due process of law." The assurance of each of these things is the same. If now liberty or property may be struck down because of difficult circumstances, we must expect that hereafter every right must yield to the voice of an impatient majority when stirred by distressful exigency. . . . Certain fundamentals have been set beyond experimentation; the Constitution has released them from control by the State. . . .

The exigency is of the kind which inevitably arises when one set of men continue to produce more than all others can buy. The distressing result to the producer followed his ill-advised but voluntary efforts. . . .

Regulation to prevent recognized evils in business has long been upheld as permissible legislative action. But fixation of the price at which "A," engaged in an ordinary business, may sell, in order to enable "B," a producer, to improve his condition, has not been regarded as within legislative power. This is not regulation, but management, control, dictation—it amounts to the deprivation of the fundamental right which one has to conduct his own affairs honestly and along customary lines. . . .

Of the assailed statute the Court of Appeals says—. . . "With the wisdom of the legislation we have naught to do. . . ."

But plainly, I think, this Court must have regard to the wisdom of the enactment. . . .

The statement by the court below that— "Doubtless the statute before us would be condemned by an earlier generation as a temerarious interference with the rights of property and contract . . . ; with the natural law of supply and demand," is obviously correct. But another, that "statutes aiming to stimulate the production of a vital food product by fixing living standards of prices for the producer, are to be interpreted with that degree of liberality which is essential to the attainment of the end in view," conflicts with views of Constitutional rights accepted since the beginning. An end although apparently desirable cannot justify inhibited means. Moreover the challenged act was not designed to stimulate production—there was too much milk for the demand and no prospect of less for several years; also "standards of prices" at which the producer might sell were not prescribed. The Legislature cannot lawfully destroy guaranteed rights of one man with the prime purpose of enriching another, even if for the moment, this may seem advantageous to the public. And the adoption of any "concept of jurisprudence" which permits facile disregard of the Constitution as

long interpreted and respected will inevitably lead to its destruction. Then, all rights will be subject to the caprice of the hour; government by stable laws will pass.

The somewhat misty suggestion below that condemnation of the challenged legislation would amount to holding "that the due process clause has left milk producers unprotected from oppression," I assume, was not intended as a material contribution to the discussion upon the merits of the cause. Grave concern for embarrassed farmers is everywhere; but this should neither obscure the rights of others nor obstruct judicial appraisement of measures proposed for relief. The ultimate welfare of the producer, like that of every other class, requires dominance of the Constitution. And zealously to uphold this in all its parts is the highest duty intrusted to the courts.

The judgment of the court below should be reversed.

Mr. Justice Van Devanter, Mr. Justice Sutherland, and Mr. Justice Butler authorize me to say that they concur in this opinion.

West Coast Hotel v. Parrish

300 U.S. 379; 57 S. Ct. 578; 81 L. Ed. 703 (1937)

Mr. Chief Justice Hughes delivered the opinion of the Court:

This case presents the question of the constitutional validity of the minimum wage law of the State of Washington.

. . . It provides:

"Section 1. The welfare of the State of Washington demands that women and minors be protected from conditions of labor which have a pernicious effect on their health and morals. The State of Washington, therefore, exercising herein its police and sovereign power declares that inadequate wages and unsanitary

conditions of labor exert such pernicious effect.

Sec. 2. It shall be unlawful to employ women or minors in any industry or occupation within the State of Washington under conditions of labor detrimental to their health or morals; and it shall be unlawful to employ women workers in any industry within the State of Washington at wages which are not adequate for their maintenance.

"Sec. 3. There is hereby created a commission to be known as the 'Industrial Welfare Commission' for the State of

Washington, to establish such standards of wages and conditions of labor for women and minors employed within the State of Washington, as shall be held hereunder to be reasonable and not detrimental to health and morals, and which shall be sufficient for the decent maintenance of women.". . .

The appellant conducts a hotel. The appellee Elsie Parrish was employed as a chambermaid and (with her husband) brought this suit to recover the difference between the wages paid her and the minimum wage fixed pursuant to the state law. The minimum wage was $14.50 per week of 48 hours. The appellant challenged the act as repugnant to the due process clause of the Fourteenth Amendment of the Constitution of the United States. The Supreme Court of the State, reversing the trial court, sustained the statute and directed judgment for the plaintiffs. . . .

The appellant relies upon the decision of this Court in *Adkins* v. *Children's Hospital* [1923] . . . which held invalid the District of Columbia Minimum Wage Act, which was attacked under the due process clause of the Fifth Amendment. On the argument at bar, counsel for the appellees attempted to distinguish the *Adkins* case upon the ground that the appellee was employed in a hotel and that the business of an innkeeper was affected with a public interest. That effort at distinction is obviously futile, as it appears that in one of the cases ruled by the *Adkins* opinion the employee was a woman employed as an elevator operator in a hotel. . . .

The recent case of *Morehead* v. *New York ex rel. Tipaldo* [1936] . . . came here on certiorari to the New York court, which had held the New York minimum wage act for women to be invalid. A minority of this Court thought that the New York statute was distinguishable in a material feature from that involved in the *Adkins* case, and that for that and other

reasons the New York statute should be sustained. But the Court of Appeals of New York had said that it found no material difference between the two statutes, and this Court held that the "meaning of the statute" as fixed by the decision of the state court "must be accepted here as if the meaning had been specifically expressed in the enactment." . . . That view led to the affirmance by this Court of the judgment in the *Morehead* case, as the Court considered that the only question before it was whether the *Adkins* case was distinguishable and that reconsideration of that decision had not been sought. . . .

We think that the question which was not deemed to be open in the *Morehead* case is open and is necessarily presented here. The Supreme Court of Washington has upheld the minimum wage statute of that State. It has decided that the statute is a reasonable exercise of the police power of the State. In reaching that conclusion the state court has invoked principles long established by this Court in the application of the Fourteenth Amendment. The state court has refused to regard the decision in the *Adkins* case as determinative and has pointed to our decisions both before and since that case as justifying its position. We are of the opinion that this ruling of the state court demands on our part a reëxamination of the *Adkins* case. The importance of the question, in which many States having similar laws are concerned, the close division by which the decision in the *Adkins* case was reached, and the economic conditions which have supervened, and in the light of which the reasonableness of the exercise of the protective power of the State must be considered, make it not only appropriate, but we think imperative, that in deciding the present case the subject should receive fresh consideration. . . .

The principle which must control our decision is not in doubt. The constitutional provision invoked is the due process clause of the Fourteenth Amendment governing the States, as the due process clause invoked in the *Adkins* case governed Congress. In each case the violation alleged by those attacking minimum wage regulation for women is deprivation of freedom of contract. What is this freedom? The Constitution does not speak of freedom of contract. It speaks of liberty and prohibits the deprivation of liberty without due process of law. In prohibiting that deprivation the Constitution does not recognize an absolute and uncontrollable liberty. Liberty in each of its phases has its history and connotation. But the liberty safeguarded is liberty in a social organization which requires the protection of law against the evils which menace the health, safety, morals and welfare of the people. Liberty under the Constitution is thus necessarily subject to the restraints of due process, and regulation which is reasonable in relation to its subject and is adopted in the interests of the community is due process.

This essential limitation of liberty in general governs freedom of contract in particular. More than twenty-five years ago we set forth the applicable principle in these words, after referring to the cases where the liberty guaranteed by the Fourteenth Amendment had been broadly described:

"But it was recognized in the cases cited, as in many others, that freedom of contract is a qualified and not an absolute right. There is no absolute freedom to do as one wills or to contract as one chooses. The guaranty of liberty does not withdraw from legislative supervision that wide department of activity which consists of the making of contracts, or deny to government the power to provide restrictive safeguards. Liberty implies the absence of arbitrary restraint, not immunity from reasonable regulations and prohibitions imposed in the interests of the community." *Chicago, B. & Q. R. Co.* v. *McGuire* [1911]. . . .

This power under the Constitution to restrict freedom of contract has had many illustrations. That it may be exercised in the public interest with respect to contracts between employer and employee is undeniable. . . .

The point that has been strongly stressed that adult employees should be deemed competent to make their own contracts was decisively met nearly forty years ago in *Holden* v. *Hardy* [1898] . . . where we pointed out the inequality in the footing of the parties. We said:

"The legislature has also recognized the fact, which the experience of legislators in many States has corroborated, that the proprietors of these establishments and their operatives do not stand upon an equality, and that their interests are, to a certain extent, conflicting. The former naturally desire to obtain as much labor as possible from their employees, while the latter are often induced by the fear of discharge to conform to regulations which their judgment, fairly exercised, would pronounce to be detrimental to their health or strength. In other words, the proprietors lay down the rules and the laborers are practically constrained to obey them. In such cases self-interest is often an unsafe guide, and the legislature may properly interpose its authority."

And we added that the fact "that both parties are of full age and competent to contract does not necessarily deprive the State of the power to interfere where the parties do not stand upon an equality, or where the public health demands that one party to the contract shall be protected against himself.". . .

It is manifest that this established principle is peculiarly applicable in relation to the employment of women in whose protection the State has a special interest. That phase of the subject received elaborate consideration in *Muller* v. *Oregon*

[1908] . . . where the constitutional authority of the State to limit the working hours of women was sustained. We emphasized the consideration that "woman's physical structure and the performance of maternal functions place her at a disadvantage in the struggle for subsistence" and that her physical well being "becomes an object of public interest and care in order to preserve the strength and vigor of the race." We emphasized the need of protecting women against oppression despite her possession of contractual rights. We said that "though limitations upon personal and contractual rights may be removed by legislation, there is that in her disposition and habits of life which will operate against a full assertion of those rights. She will still be where some legislation to protect her seems necessary to secure a real equality of right." Hence she was "properly placed in a class by herself, and legislation designed for her protection may be sustained even when like legislation is not necessary for men and could not be sustained." We concluded that the limitations which the statute there in question "placed upon her contractual powers, upon her right to agree with her employer as to the time she shall labor" were "not imposed solely for her benefit, but also largely for the benefit of all.". . .

. . . [T]he dissenting Justices in the *Adkins* case [argued] that the minimum wage statute [should] be sustained. The validity of the distinction made by the Court between a minimum wage and a maximum of hours in limiting liberty of contract was especially challenged. . . . That challenge persists and is without any satisfactory answer. As Chief Justice Taft observed: "In absolute freedom of contract the one term is as important as the other, for both enter equally into the consideration given and received, a restriction as to the one is not greater in essence than the other and is of the same kind. One is the multiplier

and the other the multiplicand." And Mr. Justice Holmes, while recognizing that "the distinctions of the law are distinctions of degree," could "perceive no difference in the kind or degree of interference with liberty, the only matter with which we have any concern, between the one case and the other. The bargain is equally affected whichever half you regulate.". . .

The minimum wage to be paid under the Washington statute is fixed after full consideration by representatives of employers, employees and the public. It may be assumed that the minimum wage is fixed in consideration of the services that are performed in the particular occupations under normal conditions. Provision is made for special licenses at less wages in the case of women who are incapable of full service. The statement of Mr. Justice Holmes in the *Adkins* case is pertinent: "This statute does not compel anybody to pay anything. It simply forbids employment at rates below those fixed as the minimum requirement of health and right living. It is safe to assume that women will not be employed at even the lowest wages allowed unless they earn them, or unless the employer's business can sustain the burden. In short the law in its character and operation is like hundreds of so-called police laws that have been upheld." And Chief Justice Taft forcibly pointed out the consideration which is basic in a statute of this character: "Legislatures which adopt a requirement of maximum hours or minimum wages may be presumed to believe that when sweating employers are prevented from paying unduly low wages by positive law they will continue their business, abating that part of their profits, which were wrung from the necessities of their employees, and will concede the better terms required by the law; and that while in individual cases hardship may result, the restriction will enure to the benefit of the general class of employees in whose interest the law is passed and so to that of the community at large.". . . .

We think that the views thus expressed are sound and that the decision in the *Adkins* case was a departure from the true application of the principles governing the regulation by the State of the relation of employer and employed. . . .

With full recognition of the earnestness and vigor which characterize the prevailing opinion in the *Adkins* case, we find it impossible to reconcile that ruling with these well-considered declarations. What can be closer to the public interest than the health of women and their protection from unscrupulous and overreaching employers? And if the protection of women is a legitimate end of the exercise of state power, how can it be said that the requirement of the payment of a minimum wage fairly fixed in order to meet the very necessities of existence is not an admissible means to that end? The legislature of the State was clearly entitled to consider the situation of women in employment, the fact that they are in the class receiving the least pay, that their bargaining power is relatively weak, and that they are the ready victims of those who would take advantage of their necessitous circumstances. The legislature was entitled to adopt measures to reduce the evils of the "sweating system," the exploiting of workers at wages so low as to be insufficient to meet the bare cost of living, thus making their very helplessness the occasion of a most injurious competition. The legislature had the right to consider that its minimum wage requirements would be an important aid in carrying out its policy of protection. The adoption of similar requirements by many States evidences a deepseated conviction both as to the presence of the evil and as to the means adapted to check it. Legislative response

to that conviction cannot be regarded as arbitrary or capricious, and that is all we have to decide. Even if the wisdom of the policy be regarded as debatable and its effects uncertain, still the legislature is entitled to its judgment.

There is an additional and compelling consideration which recent economic experience has brought into a strong light. The exploitation of a class of workers who are in an unequal position with respect to bargaining power and are thus relatively defenceless against the denial of a living wage is not only detrimental to their health and well being but casts a direct burden for their support upon the community. What these workers lose in wages the taxpayers are called upon to pay. The bare cost of living must be met. We may take judicial notice of the unparalleled demands for relief which arose during the recent period of depression and still continue to an alarming extent despite the degree of economic recovery which has been achieved. It is unnecessary to cite official statistics to establish what is of common knowledge through the length and breadth of the land. While in the instant case no factual brief has been presented, there is no reason to doubt that the State of Washington has encountered the same social problem that is present elsewhere. The community is not bound to provide what is in effect a subsidy for unconscionable employers. The community may direct its law-making power to correct the abuse which springs from their selfish disregard of the public interest. The argument that the legislation in question constitutes an arbitrary discrimination, because it does not extend to men, is unavailing. This Court has frequently held that the legislative authority, acting within its proper field, is not bound to extend its regulation to all cases which it might possibly reach. The legislature "is free to recognize degrees of harm and it may confine its restrictions to those classes of cases where the need is deemed to be clearest." If "the law presumably hits the evil where it is most felt, it is not to be overthrown because there are other instances to which it might have been applied." There is no "doctrinaire requirement" that the legislation should be couched in all embracing terms. . . .

Affirmed.

MR. JUSTICE SUTHERLAND, dissenting:

Mr. Justice Van Devanter, Mr. Justice McReynolds, Mr. Justice Butler and I think the judgment of the court below should be reversed.

The principles and authorities relied upon to sustain the judgment, were considered in *Adkins* v. *Children's Hospital* and *Morehead* v. *New York ex rel. Tipaldo;* and their lack of application to cases like the one in hand was pointed out. A sufficient answer to all that is now said will be found in the opinions of the Court in those cases. Nevertheless, in the circumstances, it seems well to restate our reasons and conclusions. . . .

It is urged that the question involved should now receive fresh consideration, among other reasons, because of "the economic conditions which have supervened"; but the meaning of the Constitution does not change with the ebb and flow of economic events. We frequently are told in more general words that the Constitution must be construed in the light of the present. If by that it is meant that the Constitution is made up of living words that apply to every new condition which they include, the statement is quite true. But to say, if that be intended, that the words of the Constitution mean today what they did not mean when written— that is, that they do not apply to a situation now to which they would have applied then—is to rob that instrument of the essential element which continues it in force as the people have made it until they, and not their official agents, have made it otherwise. . . .

The judicial function is that of interpretation; it does not include the power of amendment under the guise of interpretation. To miss the point of difference between the two is to miss all that the phrase "supreme law of the land" stands for and to convert what was intended as inescapable and enduring mandates into mere moral reflections.

If the Constitution, intelligently and reasonably construed in the light of these principles, stands in the way of desirable legislation, the blame must rest upon that instrument, and not upon the Court for enforcing it according to its terms. The remedy in that situation—and the only true remedy—is to amend the Constitution. . . .

Coming, then, to a consideration of the Washington statute, it first is to be observed that it is in every substantial respect identical with the statute involved in the *Adkins* case. Such vices as existed in the latter are present in the former. And if the *Adkins* case was properly decided, as we who join in this opinion think it was, it necessarily follows that the Washington statute is invalid. . . .

How did the *Nebbia* and *West Coast Hotel* opinions modify the substantive due process standards of *Lochner*? Contrast the way in which the Court scrutinizes and evaluates legislative ends and means in *Nebbia* and *West Coast Hotel* with *Lochner*.

The *Nebbia* decision can be viewed as an aberration of the early New Deal Court, since it was followed by *Morehead* v. *New York ex rel Tipaldo* in 1936 which forcefully applied and even went beyond the substantive due process standards of *Adkins* v. *Childrens Hospital*.[18] But the *West Coast Hotel* decision clearly marked the end of the *Lochner* era.

In *United States* v. *Carolene Products Co.* (1938) the Court rejected a substantive due process challenge under the Fifth Amendment to a federal enactment regulating milk shipped in interstate commerce. Justice Stone's majority opinion stated a new due process standard under which the Court would sustain legislation reasonably supported by facts. In applying this standard the Court would give deference to legislative judgments by presuming the existence of supportive facts and therefore a rational basis for the legislative action. Laws are not to be pronounced unconstitutional, wrote Stone, "unless in the light of the facts made known or generally assumed it is of such a character as to preclude the assumption that it rests upon some rational basis within the knowledge and experience of the legislators."[19] This decision, in conjunction with the *Nebbia* and *West Coast Hotel* opinions set the tone for a hands-off policy adopted by the courts in reviewing economic legislation after 1937.[20]

THE DEVELOPMENT OF PROCEDURAL DUE PROCESS—APPLICATION OF THE RIGHTS IN THE BILL OF RIGHTS TO THE STATES

Although the *Twining* opinion took a cautious and conservative approach to defining the scope of the due process clause of the Fourteenth Amendment, it clearly left the way open for the incorporation of fundamental and historical rights as part of due process. Justice Moody wrote in the Court's opinion: ". . . it is possible that some of the personal rights safeguarded by the first eight amendments against national action may also be safeguarded against state action, because the denial of them would be a denial of due process of law. . . . If this is so, it is not because those rights are enumerated in the first eight amendments, but because they are of such a nature that they are included in the conception of due process of law." It should be noted that Moody's approach left the way clear to incorporate in the due process clause of the Fourteenth Amendment rights that went beyond those explicitly enumerated in the Bill of Rights. This approach was analogous to substantive due process in the economic sphere, which incorporated under due process protections against intrusions by government into the economic realm that clearly were not limitations upon government under the Bill of Rights. The application of the *Twining* doctrine depended upon the value

[18]For a discussion of the Adkins and Morehead opinions see pp. 494–502.

[19]United States v. Carolene Products Co., 304 U.S. 144, 152 (1938).

[20]See, for example, Williamson v. Lee Optical Co., 348 U.S. 483 (1955); Day-Brite Lighting, Inc. v. Missouri, 342 U.S. 421 (1952).

judgments of the Court as much if not more than upon specific constitutional provisions.[21]

In the following case, the facts of which are set forth in the opinion, the Court confronted the question of whether or not the due process clause of the Fourteenth Amendment required state courts to provide counsel to defendants under certain circumstances.

Powell v. Alabama

287 U.S. 45; 53 S. Ct. 55; 77 L. Ed. 158 (1932)

MR. JUSTICE SUTHERLAND delivered the opinion of the Court:

The petitioners, hereinafter referred to as defendants, are negroes charged with the crime of rape, committed upon the persons of two white girls. The crime is said to have been committed on March 25, 1931. The indictment was returned in a state court of first instance on March 31, and the record recites that on the same day the defendants were arraigned and entered pleas of not guilty. There is a further recital to the effect that upon the arraignment they were represented by counsel. But no counsel had been employed, and aside from a statement made by the trial judge several days later during a colloquy immediately preceding the trial, the record does not disclose when, or under what circumstances, an appointment of counsel was made, or who was appointed. During the colloquy referred to, the trial judge, in response to a question, said that he had appointed all the members of the bar for the purpose of arraigning the defendants and then of course anticipated that the members of the bar would continue to help the defendants if no counsel appeared. Upon the argument here both sides accepted

that as a correct statement of the facts concerning the matter.

There was a severance upon the request of the state, and the defendants were tried in three separate groups, as indicated above. As each of the three cases was called for trial, each defendant was arraigned, and, having the indictment read to him, entered a plea of not guilty. Whether the original arraignment and pleas were regarded as ineffective is not shown. Each of the three trials was completed within a single day. Under the Alabama statute the punishment for rape is to be fixed by the jury, and in its discretion may be from ten years imprisonment to death. The juries found defendants guilty and imposed the death penalty upon all. The trial court overruled motions for new trials and sentenced the defendants in accordance with the verdicts. The judgments were affirmed by the state supreme court. Chief Justice Anderson thought the defendants had not been accorded a fair trial and strongly dissented. . . .

In this Court the judgments are assailed upon the grounds that the defendants, and each of them, were denied due process of law and the equal protection of

[21]When the Court finally went beyond the Bill of Rights by incorporating the right to privacy in Griswold v. Connecticut, 381 U.S. 479 (1965), Justice Black, in a dissenting opinion, wrote that the Court's method was equivalent to the substantive due process formula used to overturn economic regulation in the latter nineteenth and early twentieth centuries.

the laws, in contravention of the Fourteenth Amendment, specifically as follows: (1) they were not given a fair, impartial and deliberate trial; (2) they were denied the right of counsel, with the accustomed incidents of consultation and opportunity of preparation for trial; and (3) they were tried before juries from which qualified members of their own race were systematically excluded. These questions were properly raised and saved in the courts below.

The only one of the assignments which we shall consider is the second, in respect of the denial of counsel; and it becomes unnecessary to discuss the facts of the case or the circumstances surrounding the prosecution except in so far as they reflect light upon that question.

The record shows that on the day when the offense is said to have been committed, these defendants, together with a number of other negroes, were upon a freight train on its way through Alabama. On the same train were seven white boys and the two white girls. A fight took place between the negroes and the white boys, in the course of which the white boys, with the exception of one named Gilley, were thrown off the train. A message was sent ahead, reporting the fight and asking that every negro be gotten off the train. The participants in the fight, and the two girls, were in an open gondola car. The two girls testified that each of them was assaulted by six different negroes in turn, and they identified the seven defendants as having been among the number. None of the white boys was called to testify, with the exception of Gilley, who was called in rebuttal.

Before the train reached Scottsboro, Alabama, a sheriff's posse seized the defendants and two other negroes. Both girls and the negroes then were taken to Scottsboro, the county seat. Word of their coming and of the alleged assault had preceded them, and they were met at Scottsboro by a large crowd. It does not sufficiently appear that the defendants were seriously threatened with, or that they were actually in danger of, mob violence; but it does appear that the attitude of the community was one of great hostility. The sheriff thought it necessary to call for the militia to assist in safeguarding the prisoners. Chief Justice Anderson pointed out in his opinion that every step taken from the arrest and arraignment to the sentence was accompanied by the military. Soldiers took the defendants to Gadsden for safekeeping, brought them back to Scottsboro for arraignment, returned them to Gadsden for safekeeping while awaiting trial, escorted them to Scottsboro for trial a few days later, and guarded the court house and grounds at every stage of the proceedings. It is perfectly apparent that the proceedings, from beginning to end, took place in an atmosphere of tense, hostile and excited public sentiment. During the entire time, the defendants were closely confined or were under military guard. The record does not disclose their ages, except that one of them was nineteen; but the record clearly indicates that most, if not all, of them were youthful, and they are constantly referred to as "the boys." They were ignorant and illiterate. All of them were residents of other states, where alone members of their families or friends resided.

However guilty defendants, upon due inquiry, might prove to have been, they were, until convicted, presumed to be innocent. It was the duty of the court having their cases in charge to see that they were denied no necessary incident of a fair trial. With any error of the state court involving alleged contravention of the state statutes or constitution we, of course, have nothing to do. The sole inquiry which we are permitted to make is whether the federal Constitution was contravened

...; and as to that, we confine ourselves, as already suggested, to the inquiry whether the defendants were in substance denied the right of counsel, and if so, whether such denial infringes the due process clause of the Fourteenth Amendment.

First. The record shows that immediately upon the return of the indictment defendants were arraigned and pleaded not guilty. Apparently they were not asked whether they had, or were able to employ, counsel, or wished to have counsel appointed; or whether they had friends or relatives who might assist in that regard if communicated with. That it would not have been an idle ceremony to have given the defendants reasonable opportunity to communicate with their families and endeavor to obtain counsel is demonstrated by the fact that, very soon after conviction, able counsel appeared in their behalf. This was pointed out by Chief Justice Anderson in the course of his dissenting opinion. "They were nonresidents," he said, "and had little time or opportunity to get in touch with their families and friends who were scattered throughout two other states, and time has demonstrated that they could or would have been represented by able counsel had a better opportunity been given by a reasonable delay in the trial of the cases, judging from the number and activity of counsel that appeared immediately or shortly after their conviction.". . .

It is hardly necessary to say that, the right to counsel being conceded, a defendant should be afforded a fair opportunity to secure counsel of his own choice. Not only was that not done here, but such designation of counsel as was attempted was either so indefinite or so close upon the trial as to amount to a denial of effective and substantial aid in that regard. This will be amply demonstrated by a brief review of the record.

April 6, six days after indictment, the trials began. When the first case was called, the court inquired whether the parties were ready for trial. The state's attorney replied that he was ready to proceed. No one answered for the defendants or appeared to represent or defend them. Mr. Roddy, a Tennessee lawyer not a member of the local bar, addressed the court, saying that he had not been employed, but that people who were interested had spoken to him about the case. He was asked by the court whether he intended to appear for the defendants, and answered that he would like to appear along with counsel that the court might appoint. The record then proceeds:

"The Court: If you appear for these defendants, then I will not appoint counsel; if local counsel are willing to appear and assist you under the circumstances all right, but I will not appoint them.

"Mr. Roddy: Your Honor has appointed counsel, is that correct?

"The Court: I appointed all the members of the bar for the purpose of arraigning the defendants and then of course I anticipated them to continue to help them if no counsel appears.

"Mr. Moody: I am willing to go ahead and help Mr. Roddy in anything I can do about it, under the circumstances.

"The Court: All right, all the lawyers that will; of course I would not require a lawyer to appear if—

"Mr. Moody: I am willing to do that for him as a member of the bar; I will go ahead and help do anything I can do.

"The Court: All right."

And in this casual fashion the matter of counsel in a capital case was disposed of.

It thus will be seen that until the very morning of the trial no lawyer had been named or definitely designated to represent the defendants. Prior to that time, the trial judge had "appointed all the members of the bar" for the limited "purpose of arraigning the defendants." Whether they would represent the defendants thereafter if no counsel appeared in their behalf, was a matter of speculation only, or, as the judge indicated, of mere anticipation on the part of the court. Such a designation, even if made for all purposes, would, in our opinion, have fallen far short of meeting, in any proper sense, a requirement for the appointment of counsel. How many lawyers were members of the bar does not appear; but, in the very nature of things, whether many or few, they would not, thus collectively named, have been given that clear appreciation of responsibility or impressed with that individual sense of duty which should and naturally would accompany the appointment of a selected member of the bar, specifically named and assigned. . . .

... In any event, the circumstance lends emphasis to the conclusion that during perhaps the most critical period of the proceedings against these defendants, that is to say, from the time of their arraignment until the beginning of their trial, when consultation, thoroughgoing investigation and preparation were vitally important, the defendants did not have the aid of counsel in any real sense, although they were as much entitled to such aid during that period as at the trial itself. . . .

Second. The Constitution of Alabama provides that in all criminal prosecutions the accused shall enjoy the right to have the assistance of counsel; and a state statute requires the court in a capital case, where the defendant is unable to employ counsel, to appoint counsel for him. The state supreme court held that these provisions had not been infringed, and with that holding we are powerless to interfere. The question, however, which it is our duty, and within our power, to decide, is whether the denial of the assistance of counsel contravenes the due process clause of the Fourteenth Amendment to the federal Constitution. . . .

If recognition of the right of a defendant charged with a felony to have the aid of counsel depended upon the existence of a similar right at common law as it existed in England when our Constitution was adopted, there would be great difficulty in maintaining it as necessary to due process. Originally, in England, a person charged with treason or felony was denied the aid of counsel, except in respect of legal questions which the accused himself might suggest. At the same time parties in civil cases and persons accused of misdemeanors were entitled to the full assistance of counsel. After the revolution of 1688, the rule was abolished as to treason, but was otherwise steadily adhered to until 1836, when by act of Parliament the full right was granted in respect of felonies generally. . . .

An affirmation of the right to the aid of counsel in petty offenses, and its denial in the case of crimes of the gravest character, where such aid is most needed, is so outrageous and so obviously a perversion of all sense of proportion that the rule was constantly, vigorously and sometimes passionately assailed by English statesmen and lawyers. . . .

The rule was rejected by the colonies. . . .

It . . . appears that in at least twelve of the thirteen colonies the rule of the English common law, in the respect now under consideration, had been definitely rejected and the right to counsel fully recognized in all criminal prosecutions, save that in one or two instances the right was limited to capital offenses or to the more serious crimes; and this court seems to have been of the opinion that this was true in all the colonies. . . .

One test which has been applied to determine whether due process of law has been accorded in given instances is to ascertain what were the settled usages and modes of proceeding under the common and statute law of England before the

Declaration of Independence, subject, however, to the qualification that they be shown not to have been unsuited to the civil and political conditions of our ancestors by having been followed in this country after it became a nation. . . . Plainly, as appears from the foregoing, this test, as thus qualified, has not been met in the present case.

We do not overlook the case of *Hurtado* v. *California* . . . where this Court determined that due process of law does not require an indictment by a grand jury as a prerequisite to prosecution by a state for murder. In support of that conclusion the court . . . referred to the fact that the Fifth Amendment, in addition to containing the due process of law clause, provides in explicit terms that "No person shall be held to answer for a capital, or otherwise infamous crime, unless on a presentment or indictment of a grand jury, . . .", and said that since no part of this important amendment could be regarded as superfluous, the obvious inference is that in the sense of the Constitution due process of law was not intended to include, *ex vi termini* [from the meaning of the term itself], the institution and procedure of a grand jury in any case; and that the same phrase, employed in the Fourteenth Amendment to restrain the action of the states, was to be interpreted as having been used in the same sense and with no greater extent; and that if it had been the purpose of that Amendment to perpetuate the institution of the grand jury in the states, it would have embodied, as did the Fifth Amendment, an express declaration to that effect.

The Sixth Amendment, in terms, provides that in all criminal prosecutions the accused shall enjoy the right "to have the assistance of counsel for his defense." In the face of the reasoning of the *Hurtado* case, if it stood alone, it would be difficult to justify the conclusion that the right to counsel, being thus specifically granted by the Sixth Amendment, was also within the

intendment of the due process of law clause. But the *Hurtado* case does not stand alone. In the later case of *Chicago, Burlington & Quincy R. Co.* v. *Chicago* [1897] . . ., this Court held that a judgment of a state court, even though authorized by statute, by which private property was taken for public use without just compensation, was in violation of the due process of law required by the Fourteenth Amendment, notwithstanding that the Fifth Amendment explicitly declares that private property shall not be taken for public use without just compensation. . . .

Likewise, this Court has considered that freedom of speech and of the press are rights protected by the due process clause of the Fourteenth Amendment, although in the First Amendment, Congress is prohibited in specific terms from abridging the right. *Gitlow* v. *New York* [1925]. . . .

These later cases establish that notwithstanding the sweeping character of the language in the *Hurtado* case, the rule laid down is not without exceptions. The rule is an aid to construction, and in some instances may be conclusive; but it may yield to more compelling considerations whenever such considerations exist. The fact that the right involved is of such a character that it cannot be denied without violating those "fundamental principles of liberty and justice which lie at the base of all our civil and political institutions" . . . is obviously one of those compelling considerations which must prevail in determining whether it is embraced within the due process clause of the Fourteenth Amendment, although it be specifically dealt with in another part of the federal Constitution. Evidently this Court, in the later cases enumerated, regarded the rights there under consideration as of this fundamental character. That some such distinction must be observed is foreshadowed in *Twining* v. *New Jersey* [1908] . . . where Mr. Justice Moody, speaking for the Court, said that ". . . it is possible that some of the personal rights safeguarded by the first eight Amendments against National action may also be safeguarded against state action, because a denial of them would be a denial of due process of law. . . . If this is so, it is not because those rights are enumerated in the first eight Amendments, but because they are of such a nature that they are included in the conception of due process of law." While the question has never been categorically determined by this Court, a consideration of the nature of the right and a review of the expressions of this and other courts, makes it clear that the right to the aid of counsel is of this fundamental character.

It never has been doubted by this Court, or any other so far as we know, that notice and hearing are preliminary steps essential to the passing of an enforceable judgment, and that they, together with a legally competent tribunal having jurisdiction of the case, constitute basic elements of the constitutional requirement of due process of law. . . .

What, then, does a hearing include? Historically and in practice, in our own country at least, it has always included the right to the aid of counsel when desired and provided by the party asserting the right. The right to be heard would be, in many cases, of little avail if it did not comprehend the right to be heard by counsel. Even the intelligent and educated layman has small and sometimes no skill in the science of law. If charged with crime, he is incapable, generally, of determining for himself whether the indictment is good or bad. He is unfamiliar with the rules of evidence. Left without the aid of counsel he may be put on trial without a proper charge, and convicted upon incompetent evidence, or evidence irrelevant to the issue or otherwise inadmissible. He lacks both the skill and knowledge adequately to prepare his defense, even though he have a perfect one. He requires the guiding hand of counsel at every step in the proceedings against him. Without it, though he be not guilty, he faces the danger of conviction because he does not know how to establish his innocence. If that be true of men of intelligence, how much more true is it of the ignorant and illiterate, or those of feeble intellect. If in any case, civil or criminal, a state or federal court were arbitrarily to refuse to hear a party by counsel, employed by and appearing for him, it reasonably may not be doubted that such a refusal would be a denial of a hearing, and, therefore, of due process in the constitutional sense.

The decisions all point to that conclusion. . . .

In the light of the facts outlined in the forepart of this opinion—the ignorance and illiteracy of the defendants, their youth, the circumstances of public hostility, the imprisonment and the close surveillance of the defendants by the military forces, the fact that their friends and families were all in other states and communication with them necessarily difficult, and above all that they stood in deadly peril of their lives—we think the failure of the trial court to give them reasonable time and opportunity to secure counsel was a clear denial of due process.

But passing that, and assuming their inability, even if opportunity had been given, to employ counsel, as the trial court evidently did assume, we are of opinion that, under the circumstances just stated, the necessity of counsel was so vital and imperative that the failure of the trial court to make an effective appointment of counsel was likewise a denial of due process within the meaning of the Fourteenth Amendment. Whether this would be so in other criminal prosecutions, or under other circumstances, we need not determine. All that it is necessary now to decide, as we do decide, is that in a capital case, where the defendant is unable to employ counsel, and is incapable adequately of making his own defense because of ignorance, feeble mindedness, illiteracy, or the like, it is the duty of the court, whether requested or not, to assign counsel for him as a necessary requisite of due process of law; and that duty is not discharged by an assignment at such a time or under such circumstances as to preclude the giving of effective aid in the preparation and trial of the case. To hold otherwise would be to ignore the fundamental postulate, already adverted to, "that there are certain immutable principles of justice which inhere in the very idea of free government which no member of the Union may disregard." . . . In a case such as this, whatever may be the rule in other cases, the right to have counsel appointed, when necessary, is a logical corollary from the constitutional right to be heard by counsel. . . .

The United States by statute and every state in the Union by express provision of law, or by the determination of its courts, make it the duty of the trial judge, where the accused is unable to employ counsel, to appoint counsel for him. In most states the rule applies broadly to all criminal prosecutions, in others it is limited to the more serious crimes, and in a very limited number, to capital cases. A rule adopted with such unanimous accord reflects, if it does not establish, the inherent right to have counsel appointed, at least in cases like the present, and lends convincing support to the conclusion we have reached as to the fundamental nature of that right.

The judgments must be reversed and the causes remanded for further proceedings not inconsistent with this opinion.

Judgments reversed.

MR. JUSTICE BUTLER wrote a dissenting opinion in which MR. JUSTICE McREYNOLDS concurred.

Did the *Powell* opinion "incorporate" the right to counsel of the Sixth Amendment under the due process clause of the Fourteenth Amendment? Or was the right to counsel upheld for the defendants because of the special circumstances of the case? Did the Court adopt an intelligible formula to determine due process rights under the Fourteenth Amendment? How did the Court limit the historical standard for defining due process that was developed in the *Twining* opinion?

The *Twining* and *Powell* opinions suggested that the procedural standards of due process under the Fourteenth Amendment were not to be drawn from the Bill of Rights per se, but from fundamental, historical, and traditional rights accorded to individuals. The facts and circumstances of the *Powell* case were also important to the Court in arriving at its decision that the state courts should have provided adequate counsel as a matter of right.

In *Palko* v. *Connecticut* the defendant, indicted for murder in the first degree, had been convicted by a jury of murder in the second degree and sentenced to life imprisonment without the possibility of parole. The state, with the consent of the presiding judge, appealed the verdict to the Connecticut Supreme Court of Errors under an unusual state law authorizing appeals by the state in criminal cases, which provided: "Appeals from the rulings and decisions of the superior court or of any criminal court of common pleas, upon all questions of law arising on the trial of criminal cases, may be taken by the state, with the permission of the presiding judge, to the Supreme Court of Errors, in the same manner and to the same effect as if made by the accused."[22] Palko challenged the state procedure as a violation of the Fourteenth Amendment which, he claimed, incorporated the protection against double jeopardy of the Fifth Amendment.

Palko v. *Connecticut*

302 U.S. 319; 58 S. Ct. 149; 82 L. Ed. 288 (1937)

MR. JUSTICE CARDOZO delivered the opinion of the Court:

. . . Appellant was indicted . . . for the crime of murder in the first degree. A jury found him guilty of murder in the second degree, and he was sentenced to confinement in the state prison for life. Thereafter the State of Connecticut, with the permission of the judge presiding at the trial, gave notice of appeal to the Supreme Court of Errors. This it did pursuant to an act adopted in 1886. . . . Upon such appeal, the Supreme Court of Errors reversed the judgment and ordered a new trial. . . . It found that there had been error of law to the prejudice of the state. . . .

. . . [The] defendant was brought to trial again. Before a jury was impaneled and also at later stages of the case he made the objection that the effect of the new trial was to place him twice in jeopardy for the same offense, and in so doing to violate the Fourteenth Amendment of the Constitution of the United States. Upon the overruling of the objection the trial proceeded. The jury returned a verdict of murder in the first degree, and the court sentenced the defendant to the punishment of death. . . . The case is here upon appeal. . . .

1. The execution of the sentence will not deprive appellant of his life without the process of law assured to him by the Fourteenth Amendment of the Federal Constitution.

The argument for appellant is that whatever is forbidden by the Fifth Amendment is forbidden by the Fourteenth also. The Fifth Amendment, which is not directed to the states, but solely to the federal government, creates immunity from double jeopardy. No person shall be "subject for the same offense to be twice put in jeopardy of life or limb." The Fourteenth Amendment ordains, "nor shall any State deprive any person of life, liberty, or property, without due process of law." To retry a defendant, though under one indictment and only one, subjects him, it is said, to double jeopardy in violation of the Fifth Amendment, if the prosecution is one on behalf of the United States. From this the consequence is said to follow that there is a denial of life or liberty without due process of law, if the prosecution is one on behalf of the People of a State. . . .

We have said that in appellant's view the Fourteenth Amendment is to be taken as embodying the prohibitions of the Fifth. His thesis is even broader. Whatever would be a violation of the original Bill of Rights (Amendments I to VIII) if done by the federal government is now equally unlawful by force of the Fourteenth Amendment if done by a state. There is no such general rule.

The Fifth Amendment provides, among other things, that no person shall be held to answer for a capital or otherwise infamous crime unless on presentment or in-

---

[22]In most states, and in the federal judicial system, the government cannot appeal from the verdict of a trial court in a criminal case.

dictment of a grand jury. This Court has held that, in prosecutions by a state, presentment or indictment by a grand jury may give way to informations at the instance of a public officer. *Hurtado* v. *California* [1884]. . . . The Fifth Amendment provides also that no person shall be compelled in any criminal case to be a witness against himself. This Court has said that, in prosecutions by a state, the exemption will fail if the state elects to end it. *Twining* v. *New Jersey* [1908]. . . . The Sixth Amendment calls for a jury trial in criminal cases and the Seventh for a jury trial in civil cases at common law where the value in controversy shall exceed twenty dollars. This Court has ruled that consistently with those amendments trial by jury may be modified by a state or abolished altogether. *Walker* v. *Sauvinet* [1876] . . . *Maxwell* v. *Dow* [1900]. . . .

On the other hand, the due process clause of the Fourteenth Amendment may make it unlawful for a state to abridge by its statutes the freedom of speech which the First Amendment safeguards against encroachment by the Congress, *De Jonge* v. *Oregon* [1937] . . .; or the like freedom of the press, *Grosjean* v. *American Press Co.* [1936] . . .; or the free exercise of religion, *Hamilton* v. *Regents* [1934] . . .; or the right of peaceable assembly, without which speech would be unduly trammeled, *De Jonge* v. *Oregon* . . .; or the right of one accused of crime to the benefit of counsel, *Powell* v. *Alabama* [1932]. . . . In these and other situations immunities that are valid as against the federal government by force of the specific pledges of particular amendments have been found to be implicit in the concept of ordered liberty, and thus, through the Fourteenth Amendment, become valid as against the states.

The line of division may seem to be wavering and broken if there is a hasty catalogue of the cases on the one side and the other. Reflection and analysis will induce a different view. There emerges the perception of a rationalizing principle which gives to discrete instances a proper order and coherence. The right to trial by jury and the immunity from prosecution except as the result of an indictment may have value and importance. Even so, they are not of the very essence of a scheme of ordered liberty. To abolish them is not to violate a "principle of justice so rooted in the traditions and conscience of our people as to be ranked as fundamental." . . . Few would be so narrow or provincial as to maintain that a fair and enlightened system of justice would be impossible without them. What is true of jury trials and indictments is true also, as the cases show, of the immunity from compulsory self-incrimination. *Twining* v. *New Jersey.* This too might be lost, and justice still be done. Indeed, today as in the past there are students of our penal system who look upon the immunity as a mischief rather than a benefit, and who would limit its scope, or destroy it altogether. . . . The exclusion of these immunities and privileges from the privileges and immunities protected against the action of the states has not been arbitrary or casual. It has been dictated by a study and appreciation of the meaning, the essential implications, of liberty itself.

We reach a different plane of social and moral values when we pass to the privileges and immunities that have been taken over from the earlier articles of the federal bill of rights and brought within the Fourteenth Amendment by a process of absorption. These in their origin were effective against the federal government alone. If the Fourteenth Amendment has absorbed them, the process of absorption has had its source in the belief that neither liberty nor justice would exist if they were sacrificed. *Twining* v. *New Jersey.* This is true, for illustration, of freedom of thought, and speech. Of that freedom one may say that it is the matrix, the indispensable condition, of nearly every other form of freedom. With rare aberrations a pervasive recognition of that truth can be traced in our history, political and legal. So it has come about that the domain of liberty, withdrawn by the Fourteenth Amendment from encroachment by the states, has been enlarged by latter-day judgments to include liberty of the mind as well as liberty of action. . . . Fundamental too in the concept of due process, and so in that of liberty, is the thought that condemnation shall be rendered only after trial. . . . The hearing, moreover, must be a real one, not a sham or a pretense. *Moore* v. *Dempsey* [1923]. . . . For that reason, ignorant defendants in a capital case were held to have been condemned unlawfully when in truth, though not in form, they were refused the aid of counsel. *Powell* v. *Alabama* [1932]. . . . The decision did not turn upon the fact that the benefit of counsel would have been guaranteed to the defendants by the provisions of the Sixth Amendment if they had been prosecuted in a federal court. The decision turned upon the fact that in the particular situation laid before us in the evidence the benefit of counsel was essential to the substance of a hearing.

Our survey of the cases serves, we think, to justify the statement that the dividing line between them, if not unfaltering throughout its course, has been true for the most part to a unifying principle. On which side of the line the case made out by the appellant has appropriate location must be the next inquiry and the final one. Is that kind of double jeopardy to which the statute has subjected him a hardship so acute and shocking that our polity will not endure it? Does it violate those "fundamental principles of liberty and justice which lie at the base of all our civil and political institutions"? . . . The answer surely must be "no." What the answer would have to be if the state were permitted after a trial free from error to try the accused over again or to bring another case against him, we have no occasion to consider. We deal with the statute before us and no other. The state is not attempting to wear the accused out by a multitude of cases with accumulated trials. It asks no more than this, that the case against him shall go on until there shall be a trial free from the corrosion of substantial legal error. . . . This is not cruelty at all, nor even vexation in any immoderate degree. If the trial had been infected with error adverse to the accused, there might have been review at his instance, and as often as necessary to purge the vicious taint. A reciprocal privilege, subject at all times to the discretion of the presiding judge . . . has now been granted to the state. There is here no seismic innovation. The edifice of justice stands, its symmetry, to many, greater than before.

2. The conviction of appellant is not in derogation of any privileges or immunities that belong to him as a citizen of the United States. . . .

The judgment is

Affirmed.

MR. JUSTICE BUTLER dissents.

How does Cardozo answer *Palko's* contention that the Fourteenth Amendment incorporates the Bill of Rights? The *Palko* standards of incorporation extend to those rights "implicit in the concept of ordered liberty" and to rights the abolition of which would violate a "principle of justice so rooted in the traditions and conscience of our people as to be ranked as fundamental." What rights does Cardozo single out for incorporation under these standards, and which rights are excluded? Does Cardozo suggest that rights outside of the Bill of Rights could be considered due process? Or is incorporation limited to the specific provisions of the Bill of Rights? Contrast the *Palko* and *Twining* opinions with regard to this question.

In the following case the defendant was convicted of murder in the first degree and sentenced to death. California law permitted the court and counsel to comment upon and the jury to consider the fact that a defendant did not testify. Adamson pleaded that the procedure violated the Fourteenth Amendment, which he held incorporated the Fifth Amendment protection against compulsory self-incrimination. The Court had rejected a plea similar to Adamson's in *Twining* v. *New Jersey* (1908).[23] And in *Hurtado* v. *California* (1884) the Court declared that the due process clause of the Fourteenth Amendment did not automatically incorporate the trial rights of the Fifth Amendment.[24]

Adamson v. California

332 U.S. 46; 67 S. Ct. 1672; 91 L. Ed. 1903 (1947)

Mr. Justice Reed delivered the opinion of the Court:

... In the first place, appellant urges that the provision of the Fifth Amendment that no person "shall be compelled in any criminal case to be a witness against himself" is a fundamental national privilege or immunity protected against state abridgment by the Fourteenth Amendment or a privilege or immunity secured, through the Fourteenth Amendment, against deprivation by state action because it is a personal right, enumerated in the federal Bill of Rights.

Secondly, appellant relies upon the due process of law clause of the Fourteenth Amendment to invalidate the provisions of the California law ... and as applied (a) because comment on failure to testify is permitted, (b) because appellant was forced to forgo testimony in person because of danger of disclosure of his past convictions through cross-examination, and (c) because the presumption of innocence was infringed by the shifting of the burden of proof to appellant in permitting comment on his failure to testify.

We shall assume, but without any intention thereby of ruling upon the issue, that permission by law to the court, counsel and jury to comment upon and consider the failure of defendant "to explain or to deny by his testimony any evidence or facts in the case against him" would infringe defendant's privilege against self-incrimination under the Fifth Amendment if this were a trial in a court of the United States under a similar law. Such an assumption does not determine appellant's rights under the Fourteenth Amendment. It is settled law that the clause of the Fifth Amendment, protecting a person against being compelled to be a witness against himself, is not made effective by the Fourteenth Amendment as a protection against state action on the ground that freedom from testimonial compulsion is a right of national citizenship, or because it is a personal privilege or immunity secured by the Federal Constitution as one of the rights of man that are listed in the Bill of Rights.

The reasoning that leads to those conclusions starts with the unquestioned premise that the Bill of Rights, when adopted, was for the protection of the in-

[23]See pp. 480–484.
[24]See pp. 479–480.

dividual against the federal government and its provisions were inapplicable to similar actions done by the states. . . . With the adoption of the Fourteenth Amendment, it was suggested that the dual citizenship recognized by its first sentence secured for citizens federal protection for their elemental privileges and immunities of state citizenship. The *Slaughter-House Cases* decided, contrary to the suggestion, that these rights, as privileges and immunities of state citizenship, remained under the sole protection of the state governments. This Court, without the expression of a contrary view upon that phase of the issues before the Court, has approved this determination. . . . The power to free defendants in state trials from self-incrimination was specifically determined to be beyond the scope of the privileges and immunities clause of the Fourteenth Amendment in *Twining* v. *New Jersey* [1908]. . . . "The privilege against self-incrimination may be withdrawn and the accused put upon the stand as a witness for the state." The *Twining* case likewise disposed of the contention that freedom from testimonial compulsion, being specifically granted by the Bill of Rights, is a federal privilege or immunity that is protected by the Fourteenth Amendment against state invasion. This Court held that the inclusion in the Bill of Rights of this protection against the power of the national government did not make the privilege a federal privilege or immunity secured to citizens by the Constitution against state action. *Twining* v. *New Jersey* . . . ; *Palko* v. *Connecticut* [1937]. . . . After declaring that state and national citizenship coexist in the same person, the Fourteenth Amendment forbids a state from abridging the privileges and immunities of citizens of the United States. As a matter of words, this leaves a state free to abridge, within the limits of the due process clause, the privileges and immunities flowing from state citizenship. This reading of the Federal Constitution

has heretofore found favor with the majority of this Court as a natural and logical interpretation. It accords with the constitutional doctrine of federalism by leaving to the states the responsibility of dealing with the privileges and immunities of their citizens except those inherent in national citizenship. It is the construction placed upon the amendment by justices whose own experience had given them contemporaneous knowledge of the purposes that led to the adoption of the Fourteenth Amendment. This construction has become embedded in our federal system as a functioning element in preserving the balance between national and state power. We reaffirm the conclusion of the *Twining* and *Palko* cases that protection against self-incrimination is not a privilege or immunity of national citizenship.

Appellant secondly contends that if the privilege against self-incrimination is not a right protected by the privileges and immunities clause of the Fourteenth Amendment against state action, this privilege, to its full scope under the Fifth Amendment, inheres in the right to a fair trial. A right to a fair trial is a right admittedly protected by the due process clause of the Fourteenth Amendment. Therefore, appellant argues, the due process clause of the Fourteenth Amendment protects his privilege against self-incrimination. The due process clause of the Fourteenth Amendment, however, does not draw all the rights of the federal Bill of Rights under its protection. That contention was made and rejected in *Palko* v. *Connecticut*. . . . It was rejected with citation of the cases excluding several of the rights, protected by the Bill of Rights, against infringement by the National Government. Nothing has been called to our attention that either the framers of the Fourteenth Amendment or the states that adopted intended its due process clause to draw within its scope the earlier amendments to the Constitution. *Palko* held that such provisions of the Bill of Rights as were "implicit in the concept of ordered liberty," became secure from state interference by the clause. But it held nothing more.

Specifically, the due process clause does not protect, by virtue of its mere existence, the accused's freedom from giving testimony by compulsion in state trials that is secured to him against federal interference by the Fifth Amendment. . . . For a state to require testimony from an accused is not necessarily a breach of a state's obligation to give a fair trial. . . .

. . . California, however, is one of a few states that permit limited comment upon a defendant's failure to testify. That permission is narrow. The California law is set out in note 3 and authorizes comment by court and counsel upon the "failure of the defendant to explain or to deny by his testimony any evidence or facts in the case against him." This does not involve any presumption, rebuttable or irrebuttable, either of guilt or of the truth of any fact, that is offered in evidence. . . . It allows inferences to be drawn from proven facts. Because of this clause, the court can direct the jury's attention to whatever evidence there may be that a defendant could deny and the prosecution can argue as to inferences that may be drawn from the accused's failure to testify. . . . It seems quite natural that when a defendant has opportunity to deny or explain facts and determines not to do so, the prosecution should bring out the strength of the evidence by commenting upon defendant's failure to explain or deny it. The prosecution evidence may be of facts that may be beyond the knowledge of the accused. If so, his failure to testify would have little if any weight. But the facts may be such as are necessarily in the knowledge of the accused. In that case a failure to explain would point to an inability to explain. . . .

It is true that if comment were forbidden, an accused in this situation could remain silent and avoid evidence of former crimes and comment upon his failure to testify. We are of the view, however, that a state may control such a situation in accordance with its own ideas of the most efficient administration of criminal justice. The purpose of due process is not to protect an accused against a proper conviction but against an unfair conviction. When evidence is before a jury that threatens conviction, it does not seem unfair to require him to choose between leaving the adverse evidence unexplained and subjecting himself to impeachment through disclosure of former crimes. Indeed, this is a dilemma with which any defendant may be faced. If facts, adverse to the defendant, are proved by the prosecution, there may be no way to explain them favorably to the accused except by a witness who may be vulnerable to impeachment on cross-examination. The defendant must then decide whether or not to use such a witness. The fact that the witness may also be the defendant makes the choice more difficult but a denial of due process does not emerge from the circumstances. . . .

We find no other error that gives ground for our intervention in California's administration of criminal justice.

Affirmed.

MR. JUSTICE FRANKFURTER, concurring:
For historical reasons a limited immunity from the common duty to testify was written into the Federal Bill of Rights, and I am prepared to agree that, as part of that immunity, comment on the failure of an accused to take the witness stand is forbidden in federal prosecutions. . . . But to suggest that such a limitation can be drawn out of "due process" in its protection of ultimate decency in a civilized society is to suggest that the Due Process Clause fastened fetters of unreason upon the States. . . .

Between the incorporation of the Fourteenth Amendment into the Constitution and the beginning of the present membership of the Court—a period of 70 years—the scope of that Amendment was passed upon by 43 judges. Of all these judges, only one, who may respectfully be called an eccentric exception, ever indicated the belief that the Fourteenth Amendment was a shorthand summary of the first eight Amendments. . . .

The short answer to the suggestion that the . . . Fourteenth Amendment [due process clause] was a way of saying that every State must thereafter initiate prosecutions through indictment by a grand jury, must have a trial by a jury of 12 in criminal cases, and must have trial by such a jury in common law suits where the amount in controversy exceeds $20, is that it is a strange way of saying it. It would be extraordinarily strange for a Constitution to convey such specific commands in such a roundabout and inexplicit way. . . . Those reading the English language with the meaning which it ordinarily conveys, those conversant with the political and legal history of the concept of due process, those sensitive to the relations of the States to the central government as well as the relation of some of the provisions of the Bill of Rights to the process of justice, would hardly recognize the Fourteenth Amendment as a cover for the various explicit provisions of the first eight Amendments. Some of these are enduring reflections of experience with human nature, while some express the restricted views of Eighteenth-Century England regarding the best methods for the ascertainment of facts. The notion that the Fourteenth Amendment was a covert way of imposing upon the States all the rules which it seemed important to Eighteenth Century statesmen to write into the Federal Amendments, was rejected by judges who were themselves witnesses of the process by which the Fourteenth Amendment became part of the Constitution. . . . [A]t the time of the ratification of the Fourteenth Amendment the constitutions of nearly half of the rat-

ifying States did not have the rigorous requirements of the Fifth Amendment for instituting criminal proceedings through a grand jury. It could hardly have occurred to these States that by ratifying the Amendment they uprooted their established methods for prosecuting crime and fastened upon themselves a new prosecutorial system.

Indeed, the suggestion that the Fourteenth Amendment incorporates the first eight Amendments as such is not unambiguously urged. . . . There is suggested merely a selective incorporation of the first eight Amendments into the Fourteenth Amendment. Some are in and some are out, but we are left in the dark as to which are in and which are out. Nor are we given the calculus for determining which go in and which stay out. If the basis of selection is merely that those provisions of the first eight Amendments are incorporated which commend themselves to individual justices as indispensable to the dignity and happiness of a free man, we are thrown back to a merely subjective test. The protection against unreasonable search and seizure might have primacy for one judge, while trial by a jury of 12 for every claim above $20 might appear to another as an ultimate need in a free society. In the history of thought "natural law" has a much longer and much better founded meaning and justification than such subjective selection of the first eight Amendments for incorporation into the Fourteenth. If all that is meant is that due process contains within itself certain minimal standards which are "of the very essence of a scheme of ordered liberty," *Palko* v. *Connecticut*, . . . putting upon this Court the duty of applying these standards from time to time, then we have merely arrived at the insight, which our predecessors long ago expressed. . . .

. . . The Amendment neither comprehends the specific provisions by which the founders deemed it appropriate to restrict the federal government nor is it confined to them. The Due Process Clause of the Fourteenth Amendment has an independent potency, precisely as does the Due Process Clause of the Fifth Amendment in relation to the Federal Government. It ought not to require argument to reject the notion that due process of law meant one thing in the Fifth Amendment and another in the Fourteenth. The Fifth Amendment specifically prohibits prosecution of an "infamous crime" except upon indictment; it forbids double jeopardy; it bars compelling a person to be a witness against himself in any criminal case; it precludes deprivation of "life, liberty, or property, without due process of law." Are Madison and his contemporaries in the framing of the Bill of Rights to be charged with writing into it a meaningless clause? . . .

A construction which gives to due process no independent function but turns it into a summary of the specific provisions of the Bill of Rights would . . . deprive the States of opportunity for reforms in legal process designed for extending the area of freedom. It would assume that no other abuses would reveal themselves in the course of time than those which had become manifest in 1791. Such a view not only disregards the historic meaning of "due process." It leads inevitably to a warped construction of specific provisions of the Bill of Rights to bring within their scope conduct clearly condemned by due process but not easily fitting into the pigeon-holes of the specific provisions. It seems pretty late in the day to suggest that a phrase so laden with historic meaning should be given an improvised content consisting of some but not all of the provisions of the first eight Amendments, selected on an undefined basis, with improvisation of content for the provisions so selected.

And so, when, as in a case like the present, a conviction in a State court is here for review under a claim that a right protected by the Due Process Clause of the Fourteenth Amendment has been denied, the issue is not whether an infraction of one of the specific provisions of the first eight Amendments is disclosed by the record. The relevant question is whether the criminal proceedings which resulted in conviction deprived the accused of the due process of law to which the United States Constitution entitled him. Judicial review of that guaranty of the Fourteenth Amendment inescapably imposes upon this Court an exercise of judgment upon the whole course of the proceedings in order to ascertain whether they offend those canons of decency and fairness which express the notions of justice of English-speaking peoples even toward those charged with the most heinous offenses. These standards of justice are not authoritatively formulated anywhere as though they were prescriptions in a pharmacopoeia. But neither does the application of the Due Process Clause imply that judges are wholly at large. The judicial judgment in applying the Due Process Clause must move within the limits of accepted notions of justice and is not to be based upon the idiosyncrasies of a merely personal judgment. The fact that judges among themselves may differ whether in a particular case a trial offends accepted notions of justice is not disproof that general rather than idiosyncratic standards are applied. An important safeguard against such merely individual judgment is an alert deference to the judgment of the State court under review.

MR. JUSTICE BLACK, dissenting:
. . . This decision reasserts a constitutional theory spelled out in *Twining* v. *New Jersey* [1908] . . . that this Court is endowed by the Constitution with boundless power under "natural law" periodically to expand and contract constitutional standards to conform to the Court's conception of what at a particular time constitutes "civilized decency" and "fundamental liberty and justice." Invoking this *Twining*

rule, the Court concludes that although comment upon testimony in a federal court would violate the Fifth Amendment, identical comment in a state court does not violate today's fashion in civilized decency and fundamentals and is therefore not prohibited by the Federal Constitution as amended.

The *Twining* case was the first, as it is the only, decision of this Court which has squarely held that states were free, notwithstanding the Fifth and Fourteenth Amendments, to extort evidence from one accused of crime. I agree that if *Twining* be reaffirmed, the result reached might appropriately follow. But I would not reaffirm the *Twining* decision. I think that decision and the "natural law" theory of the Constitution upon which it relies degrade the constitutional safeguards of the Bill of Rights and simultaneously appropriate for this Court a broad power which we are not authorized by the Constitution to exercise. . . .

My study of the historical events that culminated in the Fourteenth Amendment, and the expressions of those who sponsored and favored, as well as those who opposed its submission and passage, persuades me that one of the chief objects that the provisions of the Amendment's first section, separately, and as a whole, were intended to accomplish was to make the Bill of Rights applicable to the states. With full knowledge of the import of the *Barron* decision, the framers and backers of the Fourteenth Amendment proclaimed its purpose to be to overturn the constitutional rule that case had announced. This historical purpose has never received full consideration or exposition in any opinion of this Court interpreting the Amendment. . . .

In the *Twining* case itself, the Court was cited to a then recent book, Guthrie, Fourteenth Amendment to the Constitution (1898). A few pages of that work recited some of the legislative background of the Amendment, emphasizing the speech of Senator Howard. But Guthrie did not emphasize the speeches of Congressman Bingham, nor the part he played in the framing and adoption of the first section of the Fourteenth Amendment. Yet Congressman Bingham may, without extravagance, be called the Madison of the first section of the Fourteenth Amendment. In the *Twining* opinion, the Court explicitly declined to give weight to the historical demonstration that the first section of the Amendment was intended to apply to the states the several protections of the Bill of Rights. It held that that question was "no longer open" because of previous decisions of this Court which, however, had not appraised the historical evidence on that subject. . . . The Court admitted that its action had resulted in giving "much less effect to the Fourteenth Amendment than some of the public men active in framing it" had intended it to have. . . . With particular reference to the guarantee against compelled testimony, the Court stated that "Much might be said in favor of the view that the privilege was guaranteed against state impairment as a privilege and immunity of National citizenship, but, as has been shown, the decisions of this court have foreclosed that view." Thus the Court declined, and again today declines, to appraise the relevant historical evidence of the intended scope of the first section of the Amendment. Instead it relied upon previous cases, none of which had analyzed the evidence showing that one purpose of those who framed, advocated, and adopted the Amendment had been to make the Bill of Rights applicable to the States. None of the cases relied upon by the Court today made such an analysis.

For this reason, I am attaching to this dissent an appendix which contains a résumé, by no means complete, of the Amendment's history. In my judgment that history conclusively demonstrates that the language of the first section of the Fourteenth Amendment, taken as a whole, was thought by those responsible for its submission to the people, and by those who opposed submission, sufficiently explicit to guarantee that thereafter no state could deprive its citizens of the privileges and protections of the Bill of Rights. Whether this Court ever will, or whether it now should, in the light of past decisions, give full effect to what the Amendment was intended to accomplish is not necessarily essential to a decision here. However that may be, our prior decisions, including *Twining,* do not prevent our carrying out that purpose, at least to the extent of making applicable to the states, not a mere part, as the Court has, but the full protection of the Fifth Amendment's provision against compelling evidence from an accused to convict him of crime. And I further contend that the "natural law" formula which the Court uses to reach its conclusion in this case should be abandoned as an incongruous excrescence on our Constitution. I believe that formula to be itself a violation of our Constitution, in that it subtly conveys to courts, at the expense of legislatures, ultimate power over public policies in fields where no specific provision of the Constitution limits legislative power. And my belief seems to be in accord with the views expressed by this Court, at least for the first two decades after the Fourteenth Amendment was adopted. . . .

I cannot consider the Bill of Rights to be an outworn 18th Century "strait jacket" as the *Twining* opinion did. Its provisions may be thought outdated abstractions by some. And it is true that they were designed to meet ancient evils. But they are the same kind of human evils that have emerged from century to century wherever excessive power is sought by the few at the expense of the many. In my judgment the people of no nation can lose their liberty so long as a Bill of Rights like ours survives and its basic purposes are conscientiously interpreted, enforced and respected so as to afford continuous protection against old, as well as new, devices and practices which might thwart those purposes. I fear to see the consequences of the Court's practice of substituting its own concepts of decency and fundamental justice for the language of the Bill of Rights as its point of departure in interpreting and enforcing that Bill of Rights. If the choice must be between the selective process of the *Palko* decision applying some of the Bill of Rights to the States, or the *Twining* rule applying none of them, I would choose the *Palko* selective process. But rather than accept either of these choices, I would follow what I believe was the original purpose of the Fourteenth Amendment—to extend to all the people of the nation the complete protection of the Bill of Rights. To hold that this Court can determine what, if any, provisions of the Bill of Rights will be enforced, and if so to what degree, is to frustrate the great design of a written Constitution.

Conceding the possibility that this Court is now wise enough to improve on the Bill of Rights by substituting natural law concepts for the Bill of Rights, I think the possibility is entirely too speculative to agree to take that course. I would therefore hold in this case that the full protection of the Fifth Amendment's proscription against compelled testimony must be afforded by California. This I would do because of reliance upon the original purpose of the Fourteenth Amendment.

It is an illusory apprehension that literal application of some or all of the provisions of the Bill of Rights to the States would unwisely increase the sum total of the powers of this Court to invalidate state legislation. The Federal Government has not been harmfully burdened by the requirement that enforcement of federal laws affecting civil liberty conform literally to the Bill of Rights. Who would advocate its repeal? It must be conceded, of course, that the natural-law-due-process formula, which the Court today reaffirms, has been interpreted to limit substantially this Court's power to prevent state violations of the individual civil liberties guaranteed by the Bill of Rights. But this formula also has been used in the past, and can be used in the future, to license this Court, in considering regulatory legislation, to roam at large in the broad expanses of policy and morals and to trespass, all too freely, on the legislative domain of the States as well as the Federal Government. . . .

. . . [T]o pass upon the constitutionality of statutes by looking to the particular standards enumerated in the Bill of Rights and other parts of the Constitution is one thing; to invalidate statutes because of application of "natural law" deemed to be above and undefined by the Constitution is another. "In the one instance, courts proceeding within clearly marked constitutional boundaries seek to execute policies written into the Constitution; in the other, they roam at will in the limitless area of their own beliefs as to reasonableness and actually select policies, a respon-

sibility which the Constitution entrusts to the legislative representatives of the people."

Mr. Justice Douglas joins in this opinion.

Mr. Justice Murphy, with whom Mr. Justice Rutledge concurs, dissenting:

While in substantial agreement with the views of Mr. Justice Black, I have one reservation and one addition to make.

I agree that the specific guarantees of the Bill of Rights should be carried over intact into the first section of the Fourteenth Amendment. But I am not prepared to say that the latter is entirely and necessarily limited by the Bill of Rights. Occasions may arise where a proceeding falls so far short of conforming to fundamental standards of procedure as to warrant constitutional condemnation in terms of a lack of due process despite the absence of a specific provision in the Bill of Rights. . . .

Why does Justice Frankfurter feel compelled to point out in his concurring opinion that the Fourteenth Amendment "neither comprehends the specific provisions by which the founders deemed it appropriate to restrict the federal government nor is it confined to them. The due process clause of the Fourteenth Amendment has an independent potency, precisely as does the due process clause of the Fifth Amendment in relation to the federal government"? Is Frankfurter's statement one of judicial self-restraint or is it meant to imply an expansive view of the nature of judicial power? What considerations of federalism enter into Frankfurter's opinion? Is Frankfurter's method, relying as it does upon *natural law* standards to determine the content of the Fourteenth Amendment due process clause, analogous to the substantive due process method the Court employed in the economic realm? (Refer to the cases in Chapter 9.) What are Frankfurter's standards of due process?

Contrast the concurring opinion of Frankfurter with Black's dissent. Which implies more judicial self-restraint? What method does Black employ to arrive at his conclusions? How well does Black support his argument that the due process clause of the Fourteenth Amendment incorporates all of the Bill of Rights?

Justice Frankfurter's views on the meaning of the due process clause of the Fourteenth Amendment were expressed in his opinion for the Court in the following case.

Rochin v. California

342 U.S. 165; 72 S. Ct. 205; 96 L. Ed. 183 (1952)

MR. JUSTICE FRANKFURTER delivered the opinion of the Court:

Having "some information that [the petitioner here] was selling narcotics," three deputy sheriffs of the County of Los Angeles, on the morning of July 1, 1949, made for the two-story dwelling house in which Rochin lived with his mother, common-law wife, brothers and sisters. Finding the outside door open, they entered and then forced open the door to Rochin's room on the second floor. Inside they found petitioner sitting partly dressed on the side of the bed, upon which his wife was lying. On a "night stand" beside the bed the deputies spied two capsules. When asked "Whose stuff is this?" Rochin seized the capsules and put them in his mouth. A struggle ensued, in the course of which the three officers "jumped upon him" and attempted to extract the capsules. The force they applied proved unavailing against Rochin's resistance. He was handcuffed and taken to a hospital. At the direction of one of the officers a doctor forced an emetic solution through a tube into Rochin's stomach against his will. This "stomach pumping" produced vomiting. In the vomited matter were found two capsules which proved to contain morphine.

Rochin was brought to trial before a California Superior Court, sitting without a jury, on the charge of possessing "a preparation of morphine" in violation of the California Health and Safety Code, 1947, § 11,500. Rochin was convicted and sentenced to sixty days' imprisonment. The chief evidence against him was the two capsules. They were admitted over petitioner's objection, although the means of obtaining them was frankly set forth in the testimony by one of the deputies, substantially as here narrated.

On appeal, the District Court of Appeal affirmed the conviction, despite the finding that the officers "were guilty of unlawfully breaking into and entering defendant's room and were guilty of unlawfully assaulting and battering defendant while in the room," and "were guilty of unlawfully assaulting, battering, torturing and falsely imprisoning the defendant at the alleged hospital." . . . One of the three judges, while finding that "the record in this case reveals a shocking series of violations of constitutional rights," concurred only because he felt bound by decisions of his Supreme Court. These, he asserted, "have been looked upon by law enforcement officers as an encouragement, if not an invitation, to the commission of such lawless acts." The Supreme Court of California denied without opinion Rochin's petition for a hearing. Two justices dissented from this denial, and in doing so expressed themselves thus: ". . . a conviction which rests upon evidence of incriminating objects obtained from the body of the accused by physical abuse is as invalid as a conviction which rests upon a verbal confession extracted from him by such abuse. . . . Had the evidence forced from the defendant's lips consisted of an oral confession that he illegally possessed a drug . . . he would have the protection of the rule of law which excludes coerced confessions from evidence. But because the evidence forced from his lips consisted of real objects the People of this state are permitted to base a conviction upon it. [We] find no valid ground of distinction between a verbal confession extracted by physical abuse and a confession wrested from defendant's body by physical abuse." . . .

This Court granted certiorari . . . because a serious question is raised as to the limitations which the Due Process Clause of the Fourteenth Amendment imposes on the conduct of criminal proceedings by the States.

In our federal system the administration of criminal justice is predominantly committed to the care of the States. The power to define crimes belongs to Congress only as an appropriate means of carrying into execution its limited grant of legislative powers. U.S. Const., Art. I, § 8, cl. 18. Broadly speaking, crimes in the United States are what the laws of the individual States make them, subject to the limitations of Art I. § 10, cl. 1, in the original Constitution, prohibiting bills of attainder and *ex post facto* laws, and of the Thirteenth and Fourteenth Amendments.

These limitations, in the main, concern not restrictions upon the powers of the States to define crime, except in the restricted area where federal authority has preempted the field, but restrictions upon the manner in which the States may enforce their penal codes. Accordingly, in reviewing a State criminal conviction under a claim of right guaranteed by the Due Process Clause of the Fourteenth Amendment, from which is derived the most far-reaching and most frequent federal basis of challenging State criminal justice, "we must be deeply mindful of the responsibilities of the States for the enforcement of criminal laws, and exercise with due humility our merely negative function in subjecting convictions from state courts to the very narrow scrutiny which the Due Process Clause of the Fourteenth Amendment authorizes." . . . Due process of law, "itself a historical product," . . . is not to be turned into a destructive dogma against the States in the administration of their systems of criminal justice.

However, this Court too has its responsibility. Regard for the requirements of the Due Process Clause "inescapably imposes upon this Court an exercise of judgment upon the whole course of the proceedings [resulting in a conviction] in order to ascertain whether they offend those canons of decency and fairness which express the notions of justice of English-speaking peoples even toward those charged with the most heinous offenses." . . . These standards of justice are not authoritatively formulated anywhere as though they were specifics. Due process of law is a summarized constitutional guarantee of respect for those personal immunities which, as Mr. Justice Cardozo twice wrote for the Court, are "so rooted in the traditions and conscience of our people as to be ranked as fundamental," . . . or are "implicit in the concept of ordered liberty." . . .

The Court's function in the observance of this settled conception of the Due Process Clause does not leave us without adequate guides in subjecting State criminal procedures to constitutional judgment. In dealing not with the machinery of government but with human rights, the absence of formal exactitude, or want of fixity of meaning, is not an unusual or even regrettable attribute of constitutional provisions. Words being symbols do not speak without a gloss. On the one hand the gloss may be the deposit of history, whereby a term gains technical content. Thus the requirements of the Sixth and Seventh Amendments for trial by jury in the federal courts have a rigid meaning. No changes or chances can alter the content of the verbal symbol of "jury"—a body of twelve men who must reach a unanimous conclusion if the verdict is to go against the defendant. On the other hand, the gloss of some of the verbal symbols of the Constitution does not give them a fixed technical content. It exacts a continuing process of application.

When the gloss has thus not been fixed but is a function of the process of judgment, the judgment is bound to fall differently at different times and differently at the same time through different judges. Even more specific provisions, such as the guaranty of freedom of speech and the detailed protection against unreasonable searches and seizures, have inevitably evoked as sharp divisions in this Court as the least specific and most comprehensive protection of liberties, the Due Process Clause.

The vague contours of the Due Process Clause do not leave judges at large. We may not draw on our merely personal and private notions and disregard the limits that bind judges in their judicial function. Even though the concept of due process of law is not final and fixed, these limits are derived from considerations that are fused in the whole nature of our judicial process.... These are considerations deeply rooted in reason and in the compelling traditions of the legal profession. The Due Process Clause places upon this Court the duty of exercising a judgment, within the narrow confines of judicial power in reviewing State convictions, upon interests of society pushing in opposite directions.

Due process of law thus conceived is not to be derided as resort to a revival of "natural law." To believe that this judicial exercise of judgment could be avoided by freezing "due process of law" at some fixed stage of time or thought is to suggest that the most important aspect of constitutional adjudication is a function for inanimate machines and not for judges, for whom the independence safeguarded by Article III of the Constitution was designed and who are presumably guided by established standards of judicial behavior. Even cybernetics has not yet made that haughty claim. To practice the requisite detachment and to achieve sufficient objectivity no doubt demands of judges the habit of self-discipline and self-criticism, incertitude that one's own views are incontestable and alert tolerance toward views not shared. But these are precisely the presuppositions of our judicial process. They are precisely the qualities society has a right to expect from those entrusted with ultimate judicial power.

Restraints on our jurisdiction are self-imposed only in the sense that there is from our decisions no immediate appeal short of impeachment or constitutional amendment. But that does not make due process of law a matter of judicial caprice. The faculties of the Due Process Clause may be indefinite and vague, but the mode of their ascertainment is not self-willed. In each case "due process of law" requires an evaluation based on a disinterested inquiry pursued in the spirit of science, on a balanced order of facts exactly and fairly stated, on the detached consideration of conflicting claims, ... on a judgment not *ad hoc* and episodic but duly mindful of reconciling the needs both of continuity and of change in a progressive society.

Applying these general considerations to the circumstances of the present case, we are compelled to conclude that the proceedings by which this conviction was obtained do more than offend some fastidious squeamishness or private sentimentalism about combatting crime too energetically. This is conduct that shocks the conscience. Illegally breaking into the privacy of the petitioner, the struggle to open his mouth and remove what was there, the forcible extraction of his stomach's contents—this course of proceeding by agents of government to obtain evidence is bound to offend even hardened sensibilities. They are methods too close to the rack and the screw to permit of constitutional differentiation.

It has long since ceased to be true that due process of law is heedless of the means by which otherwise relevant and credible evidence is obtained. This was not true even before the series of recent cases enforced the constitutional principle that the States may not base convictions upon confessions, however much verified, obtained by coercion. These decisions are not arbitrary exceptions to the comprehensive right of States to fashion their rules of evidence for criminal trials. They are not sports in our constitutional law but applications of a general principle. They are only instances of the general requirement that States in their prosecutions respect certain decencies of civilized conduct. Due process of law, as a historic and generative principle, precludes defining, and thereby confining, these standards of conduct more precisely than to say that convictions cannot be brought about by methods that offend "a sense of justice.". . . It would be a stultification of the responsibility which the course of constitutional history has cast upon this Court to hold that in order to convict a man the police cannot extract by force what is in his mind but can extract what is in his stomach.

To attempt in this case to distinguish what lawyers call "real evidence" from verbal evidence is to ignore the reasons for excluding coerced confessions. Use of involuntary verbal confessions in State criminal trials is constitutionally obnoxious not only because of their unreliability. They are inadmissible under the Due Process Clause even though statements contained in them may be independently established as true. Coerced confessions offend the community's sense of fair play and decency. So here, to sanction the brutal conduct which naturally enough was condemned by the court whose judgment is before us, would be to afford brutality the cloak of law. Nothing would be more calculated to discredit law and thereby to brutalize the temper of a society.

In deciding this case we do not heedlessly bring into question decisions in many States dealing with essentially different, even if related, problems. We therefore put to one side cases which have arisen in the State courts through use of modern methods and devices for discovering wrongdoers and bringing them to book. It does not fairly represent these decisions to suggest that they legalize force so brutal and so offensive to human dignity in securing evidence from a sus-

pect as is revealed by this record. Indeed the California Supreme Court has not sanctioned this mode of securing a conviction. It merely exercised its discretion to decline a review of the conviction. All the California judges who have expressed themselves in this case have condemned the conduct in the strongest language.

We are not unmindful that hypothetical situations can be conjured up, shading imperceptibly from the circumstances of this case and by gradations producing practical differences despite seemingly logical extensions. But the Constitution is "intended to preserve practical and substantial rights, not to maintain theories." . . .

On the facts of this case the conviction of the petitioner has been obtained by methods that offend the Due Process Clause. The judgment below must be

Reversed.

MR. JUSTICE MINTON took no part in the consideration or decision of this case.

MR. JUSTICE BLACK, concurring:
Adamson v. *California* . . . sets out reasons for my belief that state as well as federal courts and law enforcement officers must obey the Fifth Amendment's command that "No person . . . shall be compelled in any criminal case to be a witness against himself." I think a person is compelled to be a witness against himself not only when he is compelled to testify, but also when as here, incriminating evidence is forcibly taken from him by a contrivance of modern science. . . . California convicted this petitioner by using against him evidence obtained in this manner, and I agree with Mr. Justice Douglas that the case should be reversed on this ground.

In the view of a majority of the Court, however, the Fifth Amendment imposes no restraint of any kind on the states. They nevertheless hold that California's use of this evidence violated the Due

Process Clause of the Fourteenth Amendment. Since they hold as I do in this case, I regret my inability to accept their interpretation without protest. But I believe that faithful adherence to the specific guarantees in the Bill of Rights insures a more permanent protection of individual liberty than that which can be afforded by the nebulous standards stated by the majority.

What the majority hold is that the Due Process Clause empowers this Court to nullify any state law if its application "shocks the conscience," offends "a sense of justice" or runs counter to the "decencies of civilized conduct." The majority emphasize that these statements do not refer to their own consciences or to their senses of justice and decency. For we are told that "we may not draw on our merely personal and private notions"; our judgment must be grounded on "considerations deeply rooted in reason and in the compelling traditions of the legal profession." We are further admonished to measure the validity of state practices, not by our reason, or by the traditions of the legal profession, but by "the community's sense of fair play and decency"; by the "traditions and conscience of our people"; or by "those canons of decency and fairness which express the notions of justice of English-speaking peoples." These canons are made necessary, it is said, because of "interests of society pushing in opposite directions."

If the Due Process Clause does vest this Court with such unlimited power to invalidate laws, I am still in doubt as to why we should consider only the notions of English-speaking peoples to determine what are immutable and fundamental principles of justice. Moreover, one may well ask what avenues of investigation are open to discover "canons" of conduct so universally favored that this Court should write them into the Constitution? All we are told is that the discovery must be made by an "evaluation based on a disinterested inquiry pursued in the spirit of science, on a balanced order of facts."

Some constitutional provisions are stated in absolute and unqualified language such, for illustration, as the First Amendment stating that no law shall be passed prohibiting the free exercise of religion or abridging the freedom of speech or press. Other constitutional provisions do require courts to choose between competing policies, such as the Fourth Amendment which, by its terms, necessitates a judicial decision as to what is an "unreasonable" search or seizure. There is, however, no express constitutional language granting judicial power to invalidate *every* state law of *every* kind deemed "unreasonable" or contrary to the Court's notion of civilized decencies; yet the constitutional philosophy used by the majority has, in the past, been used to deny a state the right to fix the price of gasoline. . . ; and even the right to prevent bakers from palming off smaller for larger loaves of bread. . . . These cases, and others, show the extent to which the evanescent standards of the majority's philosophy have been used to nullify state legislative programs passed to suppress evil economic practices. What paralyzing role this same philosophy will play in the future economic affairs of this country is impossible to predict. Of even graver concern, however, is the use of the philosophy to nullify the Bill of Rights. I long ago concluded that the accordion-like qualities of this philosophy must inevitably imperil all the individual liberty safeguards specifically enumerated in the Bill of Rights. Reflection and recent decisions of this Court sanctioning abridgement of the freedom of speech and press have strengthened this conclusion.

MR. JUSTICE DOUGLAS, concurring:

The evidence obtained from this accused's stomach would be admissible in the majority of states where the question has been raised. So far as the reported cases reveal, the only states which would probably exclude the evidence would be Arkansas, Iowa, Michigan, and Missouri. Yet the Court now says that the rule which the majority of the states have fashioned violates the "decencies of civilized conduct." To that I cannot agree. It is a rule formulated by responsible courts with judges as sensitive as we are to the proper standards for law administration.

As an original matter it might be debatable whether the provision in the Fifth Amendment that no person "shall be compelled in any criminal case to be a witness against himself" serves the ends of justice. Not all civilized legal procedures recognize it. But the choice was made by the Framers, a choice which sets a standard for legal trials in this country. The Framers made it a standard of due process for prosecutions by the Federal Government. If it is a requirement of due process for a trial in the federal courthouse, it is impossible for me to say it is not a requirement of due process for a trial in the state courthouse. That was the issue recently surveyed in *Adamson* v. *California* [1947]. . . . The Court rejected the view that compelled testimony should be excluded and held in substance that the accused in a state trial can be forced to testify against himself. I disagree. Of course an accused can be compelled to be present at the trial, to stand, to sit, to turn this way or that, and to try on a cap or a coat. . . . But I think that words taken from his lips, capsules taken from his stomach, blood taken from his veins are all inadmissible provided they are taken from him without his consent. They are inadmissible because of the command of the Fifth Amendment.

That is an unequivocal, definite and workable rule of evidence for state and federal courts. But we cannot in fairness free the state courts from that command and yet excoriate them for flouting the "decencies of civilized conduct" when they admit the evidence. That is to make the rule turn not on the Constitution but on the idiosyncrasies of the judges who sit here.

The damage of the view sponsored by the Court in this case may not be conspicuous here. But it is part of the same philosophy that produced *Betts* v. *Brady* [1942] . . ., denying counsel to an accused in a state trial against the command of the Sixth Amendment, and *Wolf* v. *Colorado* [1949] . . ., allowing evidence obtained as a result of a search and seizure that is illegal under the Fourth Amendment to be introduced in a state trial. It is part of the process of erosion of civil rights of the citizen in recent years.

What explicit standard did Frankfurter apply to reach the conclusion that the state procedures followed in the case violated due process? Does the Frankfurter opinion revive *natural law*? Does Frankfurter's standard used to judge the case reflect judicial self-restraint? Consider Frankfurter's statement that "Due process of law, as a historic and generative principle, precludes defining, and thereby confining, the standards of conduct more precisely than to say that convictions cannot be brought about by methods that offend 'a sense of justice.'"

Why does Justice Black suggest that the formula of the majority opinion is analogous to substantive due process? Note particularly why Black feels that one important implication of the majority opinion is an expanded judicial power to nullify state legislative programs.

The contrasting *selective incorporation* and *natural law* methods for defining due process under the Fourteenth Amendment, used in the *Palko* and *Rochin* cases respectively, reflected judicial self-restraint. While the natural law approach of Frankfurter could clearly be used to expand judicial power, Frankfurter himself was a strong advocate of judicial self-restraint, particularly concerning the states. Before Earl Warren became Chief Justice in 1953, considerations of federalism held the Court back from broadly interpreting the due process clause of the Fourteenth Amendment to control state action. The following case marked a turning point in the philosophy of the Court.

Mapp v. *Ohio*

367 U.S. 643; 81 S. Ct. 1684; 6 L. Ed. 2d. 1081 (1961)

MR. JUSTICE CLARK delivered the opinion of the Court:

Appellant stands convicted of knowingly having had in her possession and under her control certain lewd and lascivious books, pictures, and photographs in violation of § 2905.34 of Ohio's Revised Code.... [T]he Supreme Court of Ohio found that her conviction was valid though "based primarily upon the introduction in evidence of lewd and lascivious books and pictures unlawfully seized during an unlawful search of defendant's home...."...

On May 23, 1957, three Cleveland police officers arrived at appellant's residence in that city pursuant to information that "a person [was] hiding out in the home, who was wanted for questioning in connection with a recent bombing, and that there was a large amount of policy paraphernalia being hidden in the home." ... Upon their arrival at that house, the officers knocked on the door and demanded entrance but appellant, after telephoning her attorney, refused to admit them without a search warrant. They advised their headquarters of the situation and undertook a surveillance of the house.

The officers again sought entrance some three hours later when four or more additional officers arrived on the scene. When Miss Mapp did not come to the door immediately, at least one of the several doors to the house was forcibly

opened and the policemen gained admittance. Meanwhile Miss Mapp's attorney arrived, but the officers, having secured their own entry, and continuing in their defiance of the law, would permit him neither to see Miss Mapp nor to enter the house. It appears that Miss Mapp was halfway down the stairs from the upper floor to the front door when the officers, in this highhanded manner, broke into the hall. She demanded to see the search warrant. A paper, claimed to be a warrant, was held up by one of the officers. She grabbed the "warrant" and placed it in her bosom. A struggle ensued in which the officers recovered the piece of paper and as a result of which they handcuffed appellant because she had been "belligerent" in resisting their official rescue of the "warrant" from her person. Running roughshod over appellant, a policeman "grabbed" her, "twisted [her] hand," and she "yelled [and] pleaded with him" because "it was hurting." Appellant, in handcuffs, was then forcibly taken upstairs to her bedroom where the officers searched a dresser, a chest of drawers, a closet and some suitcases. They also looked into a photo album and through personal papers belonging to the appellant. The search spread to the rest of the second floor including ... the living room, the kitchen and a dinette. The basement of the building and a trunk found therein were also searched. The obscene materials for possession of which she was ultimately convicted were discovered in the course of that widespread search.

At the trial no search warrant was produced by the prosecution, nor was the failure to produce one explained or accounted for. At best, "There is, in the record, considerable doubt as to whether there ever was any warrant for the search of defendant's home." . . .

The State says that even if the search were made without authority, or otherwise unreasonably, it is not prevented from using the unconstitutionally seized evidence at trial, citing *Wolf* v. *Colorado* [1949] . . ., in which this Court did indeed hold "that in a prosecution in a State court for a State crime the Fourteenth Amendment does not forbid the admission of evidence obtained by an unreasonable search and seizure." . . . On this appeal, . . . it is urged once again that we review that holding. . . .

There are in the cases of this Court some passing references to the *Weeks* [v. *United States* (1914)] rule as being one of evidence. But the plain and unequivocal language of *Weeks*—and its later paraphrase in *Wolf*—to the effect that the *Weeks* rule is of constitutional origin, remains entirely undisturbed. . . . The Court, in *Olmstead* v. *United States*, 277 U.S. 438 (1928), in unmistakable language restated the *Weeks* rule:

The striking outcome of the *Weeks* case and those which followed it was the sweeping declaration that the Fourth Amendment, although not referring to or limiting the use of evidence in courts, really forbade its introduction if obtained by government officers through a violation of the Amendment.

II

In 1949, 35 years after *Weeks* was announced, this Court, in *Wolf* v. *Colorado* again for the first time, discussed the effect of the Fourth Amendment upon the States through the operation of the Due Process Clause of the Fourteenth

Amendment. It said:

[W]e have no hesitation in saying that were a State affirmatively to sanction such police incursion into privacy it would run counter to the guaranty of the Fourteenth Amendment.

Nevertheless, after declaring that the "security of one's privacy against arbitrary intrusion by the police" is "implicit in 'the concept of ordered liberty' and as such enforceable against the States through the Due Process Clause" . . ., the Court decided that the *Weeks* exclusionary rule would not then be imposed upon the States as "an essential ingredient of the right." . . . The Court's reasons for not considering essential to the right to privacy, as a curb imposed upon the States by the Due Process Clause, that which decades before had been posited as part and parcel of the Fourth Amendment's limitation upon federal encroachment of individual privacy, were bottomed on factual considerations.

While they are not basically relevant to a decision that the exclusionary rule is an essential ingredient of the Fourth Amendment as the right it embodies is vouchsafed against the States by the Due Process Clause, we will consider the current validity of the factual grounds upon which *Wolf* was based.

The Court in *Wolf* first stated that "[t]he contrariety of views of the States" on the adoption of the exclusionary rule of *Weeks* was "particularly impressive" and, in this connection, that it could not "brush aside the experience of States which deem the incidence of such conduct by the police too slight to call for a deterrent remedy . . . by overriding the [States'] relevant rules of evidence." . . . While in 1949, prior to the *Wolf* case, almost two-thirds of the States were opposed to the use of the exclusionary rule, now, despite the *Wolf* case, more than half of those since passing upon it, by their own legislative or judicial decision, have wholly or partly adopted or adhered to the *Weeks* rule. . . . Significantly, among those now following the rule is California, which, according to its highest court, was "compelled to reach that conclusion because other remedies have completely failed to secure compliance with the constitutional provisions. . . . " . . . In connection with this California case, we note that the second basis elaborated in *Wolf* in support of its failure to enforce this exclusionary doctrine against the States was that "other means of protection" have been afforded "the right to privacy." . . . The experience of California that such other remedies have been worthless and futile is buttressed by the experience of other States. The obvious futility of relegating the Fourth Amendment to the protection of other remedies has, moreover, been recognized by this Court since *Wolf*. . . .

Likewise, time has set its face against what *Wolf* called the "weighty testimony" of *People* v. *Defore*, 242 N.Y. 13, 150 N.E. 585 (1926). There Justice (then Judge) Cardozo, rejecting adoption of the *Weeks* exclusionary rule in New York, had said that "[t]he Federal rule as it stands is either too strict or too lax." . . . However, the force of that reasoning has been largely vitiated by later decisions of this Court. . . .

It, therefore, plainly appears that the factual considerations supporting the failure of the *Wolf* Court to include the *Weeks* exclusionary rule when it recognized the enforceability of the right to privacy against the States in 1949, while not basically relevant to the constitutional consideration, could not, in any analysis, now be deemed controlling. . . .

III

. . . Today we once again examine *Wolf's* constitutional documentation of the right to privacy free from unreasonable state intrusion, and, after its dozen years on

our books, are led by it to close the only courtroom door remaining open to evidence secured by official lawlessness in flagrant abuse of that basic right, reserved to all persons as a specific guarantee against that very same unlawful conduct. We hold that all evidence obtained by searches and seizures in violation of the Constitution is, by that same authority, inadmissible in a state court.

IV

Since the Fourth Amendment's right of privacy has been declared enforceable against the States through the Due Process Clause of the Fourteenth, it is enforceable against them by the same sanction of exclusion as is used against the Federal Government. Were it otherwise, then just as without the *Weeks* rule the assurance against unreasonable federal searches and seizures would be "a form of words," valueless and undeserving of mention in a perpetual charter of inestimable human liberties, so too, without that rule the freedom from state invasions of privacy would be so ephemeral and so neatly severed from its conceptual nexus with the freedom from all brutish means of coercing evidence as not to merit this Court's high regard as a freedom "implicit in the concept of ordered liberty." At the time that the Court held in *Wolf* that the Amendment was applicable to the States through the Due Process Clause, the cases of this Court, as we have seen, had steadfastly held that as to federal officers the Fourth Amendment included the exclusion of the evidence seized in violation of its provisions. Even *Wolf* "stoutly adhered" to that proposition. The right to privacy, when conceded operatively enforceable against the States, was not susceptible of destruction by avulsion of the sanction upon which its protection and enjoyment had always been deemed dependent. . . . Therefore, in extending the substantive protections of due process to all constitutionally unreasonable searches—state or federal—it was logically and constitutionally necessary that the exclusion doctrine—an essential part of the right to privacy—be also insisted upon as an essential ingredient of the right newly recognized by the *Wolf* case. In short, the admission of the new constitutional right by *Wolf* could not consistently tolerate denial of its most important constitutional privilege, namely, the exclusion of the evidence which an accused had been forced to give by reason of the unlawful seizure. To hold otherwise is to grant the right but in reality to withhold its privilege and enjoyment. Only last year the Court itself recognized that the purpose of the exclusionary rule "is to deter—to compel respect for the constitutional guaranty in the only effectively available way—by removing the incentive to disregard it." *Elkins* v. *United States* [1960]. . . .

Indeed, we are aware of no restraint, similar to that rejected today, conditioning the enforcement of any other basic constitutional right. The right to privacy, no less important than any other right carefully and particularly reserved to the people, would stand in marked contrast to all other rights declared as "basic to a free society." *Wolf* v. *Colorado*. . . . This Court has not hesitated to enforce as strictly against the States as it does against the Federal Government the rights of free speech and of a free press, the rights to notice and to a fair, public trial, including, as it does, the right not to be convicted by use of a coerced confession, however logically relevant it be, and without regard to its reliability. . . . And nothing could be more certain than that when a coerced confession is involved, "the relevant rules of evidence" are overridden without regard to "the incidence of such conduct by the police," slight or frequent. Why should not the same rule apply to what is tantamount to coerced testimony by way of unconstitutional seizure of goods, papers, effects, documents, etc.?

We find that, as to the Federal Government, the Fourth and Fifth Amendments and, as to the States, the freedom from unconscionable invasions of privacy and the freedom from convictions based upon coerced confessions do enjoy an "intimate relation" in their perpetuation of "principles of humanity and civil liberty [secured] . . . only after years of struggle,". . . .

V

Moreover, our holding that the exclusionary rule is an essential part of both the Fourth and Fourteenth Amendments is not only the logical dictate of prior cases, but it also makes very good sense. There is no war between the Constitution and common sense. Presently, a federal prosecutor may make no use of evidence illegally seized, but a State's attorney across the street may, although he supposedly is operating under the enforceable prohibitions of the same Amendment. Thus the State, by admitting evidence unlawfully seized, serves to encourage disobedience to the Federal Constitution which it is bound to uphold. Moreover, as was said in *Elkins,* "[t]he very essence of a healthy federalism depends upon the avoidance of needless conflict between state and federal courts." . . . Yet the double standard recognized until today hardly put such a thesis into practice. In nonexclusionary States, federal officers, being human, were by it invited to and did, as our cases indicate, step across the street to the State's attorney with their unconstitutionally seized evidence. Prosecution on the basis of that evidence was then had in a state court in utter disregard of the enforceable Fourth Amendment. If the fruits of an unconstitutional search had been inadmissible in both state and federal courts, this inducement to evasion would have been sooner eliminated. . . .

Federal-state cooperation in the solution of crime under constitutional standards will be promoted, if only by recognition of their now mutual obligation to respect the same fundamental criteria in their approaches. "However much in a particular case insistence upon such rules may appear as a technicality that inures to the benefit of a guilty person, the history of the criminal law proves that tolerance of shortcut methods in law enforcement impairs its enduring effectiveness." . . . Denying shortcuts to only one of two cooperating law enforcement agencies tends naturally to breed legitimate suspicion of "working arrangements" whose results are equally tainted. . . .

There are those who say, as did Justice (then Judge) Cardozo, that under our constitutional exclusionary doctrine "[t]he criminal is to go free because the constable has blundered." *People* v. *Defore*. . . . In some cases this will undoubtedly be the result. But, as was said in *Elkins*, "there is another consideration—the imperative of judicial integrity." . . . The criminal goes free, if he must, but it is the law that sets him free. Nothing can destroy a government more quickly than its failure to observe its own laws, or worse, its disregard of the charter of its own existence. . . .

The ignoble shortcut to conviction left open to the State tends to destroy the entire system of constitutional restraints on which the liberties of the people rest. Having once recognized that the right to privacy embodied in the Fourth Amendment is enforceable against the States, and that the right to be secure against rude invasions of privacy by state officers is, therefore, constitutional in origin, we can no longer permit that right to remain an empty promise. Because it is enforceable in the same manner and to like effect as other basic rights secured by the Due Process Clause, we can no longer permit it to be revocable at the whim of any police officer who, in the name of law enforcement itself, chooses to suspend its enjoyment. Our decision, founded on reason and truth, gives to the individual no more than that which the Constitution guarantees him, to the police officer no less than that to which honest law enforcement is entitled, and to the courts, that judicial integrity so necessary in the true administration of justice.

The judgment of the Supreme Court of Ohio is reversed and the cause remanded for further proceedings not inconsistent with this opinion.

Reversed and remanded.

MR. JUSTICE BLACK, concurring:

. . . I am still not persuaded that the Fourth Amendment, standing alone, would be enough to bar the introduction into evidence against an accused of papers and effects seized from him in violation of its commands. For the Fourth Amendment does not itself contain any provision expressly precluding the use of such evidence, and I am extremely doubtful that such a provision could properly be inferred from nothing more than the basic command against unreasonable searches and seizures. Reflection on the problem, however, in the light of cases coming before the Court since *Wolf*, has led me to conclude that when the Fourth Amendment's ban against unreasonable searches and seizures is considered together with the Fifth Amendment's ban against compelled self-incrimination, a constitutional basis emerges which not only justifies but actually requires the exclusionary rule.

The close interrelationship between the Fourth and Fifth Amendments, as they apply to this problem, has long been recognized and, indeed, was expressly made the ground for this Court's holding in *Boyd* v. *United States* [1886]. There the Court fully discussed this relationship and declared itself "unable to perceive that the seizure of a man's private books and papers to be used in evidence against him is substantially different from compelling him to be a witness against himself." It was upon this ground that Mr. Justice Rutledge largely relied in his dissenting opinion in the *Wolf* case. And, although I rejected the argument at that time, its force has, for me at least, become compelling with the more thorough understanding of the problem brought on by recent cases. In the final analysis, it seems to me that the *Boyd* doctrine, though perhaps not required by the express language of the Constitution strictly construed, is amply justified from an historical standpoint, soundly based in reason, and entirely consistent with what I regard to be the proper approach to interpretation of our Bill of Rights. . . .

. . . As I understand the Court's opinion in this case, we again reject the confusing "shock-the-conscience" standard of the *Wolf* and *Rochin* cases and, instead, set aside this state conviction in reliance upon the precise, intelligible and more predictable constitutional doctrine enunciated in the *Boyd* case. I fully agree with Mr. Justice Bradley's opinion that the two Amendments upon which the *Boyd* doctrine rests are of vital importance in our constitutional scheme of liberty and that both are entitled to a liberal rather than a niggardly interpretation. The courts of the country are entitled to know with as much certainty as possible what scope they cover. The Court's opinion, in my judgment, dissipates the doubt and uncertainty in this field of constitutional law and I am persuaded, for this and other reasons stated, to depart from my prior views, to accept the *Boyd* doctrine as controlling in this state case and to join the Court's judgment and opinion which are in accordance with the constitutional doctrine.

MR. JUSTICE DOUGLAS, concurring:

Though I have joined the opinion of the Court, I add a few words. This criminal proceeding started with a lawlwss search and seizure. The police entered a home forcefully, and seized documents that were later used to convict the occupant of a crime. . . .

We held in *Wolf* v. *Colorado* . . . that the Fourth Amendment was applicable to the States by reason of the Due Process Clause of the Fourteenth Amendment. But a majority held that the exclusionary rule of the *Weeks* case was not required of the States, that they could apply such sanctions as they chose. That position had the necessary votes to carry the day. But with all respect it was not the voice of reason or principle.

As stated in the *Weeks* case, if evidence seized in violation of the Fourth Amendment can be used against an accused, "his right to be secure against such searches and seizures is of no value, and . . . might as well be stricken from the Constitution." . . .

When we allowed States to give constitutional sanction to the "shabby business" of unlawful entry into a home . . . we did indeed rob the Fourth Amendment of much meaningful force. . . .

Wolf v. *Colorado* . . . was decided in 1949. The immediate result was a storm of constitutional controversy which only today finds its end. I believe that this is an appropriate case in which to put an end to the asymmetry which *Wolf* imported into the law. . . .

Memorandum of MR. JUSTICE STEWART:

Agreeing fully with Part I of Mr. Justice Harlan's dissenting opinion, I express no view as to the merits of the constitutional issue which the Court today decides. I would, however, reverse the judgment in this case, because I am persuaded that the provision . . . of the Ohio Revised Code, upon which the petitioner's conviction was based, is, in the words of Mr. Justice Harlan, not "consistent with the rights of free thought and expression assured against state action by the Fourteenth Amendment."

MR. JUSTICE HARLAN, whom MR. JUS-

In overruling the *Wolf* case the Court, in my opinion, has forgotten the sense of judicial restraint which, with due regard for the *stare decisis,* is one element that should enter into deciding whether a past decision of this Court should be overruled. Apart from that I also believe that the *Wolf* rule represents sounder Constitutional doctrine than the new rule which now replaces it.

I

From the Court's statement of the case one would gather that the central, if not controlling, issue on this appeal is whether illegally state-seized evidence is Constitutionally admissible in a state prosecution, an issue which would of course face us with the need for re-examining *Wolf.* However, such is not the situation. For, although that question was indeed raised here and below among appellant's subordinate points, the new and pivotal issue brought to the Court by this appeal is whether § 2905.34 of the Ohio Revised Code making criminal the *mere* knowing possession or control of obscene material, and under which appellant has been convicted, is consistent with the rights of free thought and expression assured against state action by the Fourteenth Amendment. That was the principal issue which was decided by the Ohio Supreme Court and which was briefed and argued in this Court.

In this posture of things, I think it fair to say that five members of this Court have simply "reached out" to overrule *Wolf.* With all respect for the views of the majority, and recognizing that *stare decisis* carries different weight in Constitutional adjudication than it does in nonconstitutional decision, I can perceive no justification for regarding this case as an appropriate occasion for re-examining *Wolf.* . . .

II

Essential to the majority's argument against *Wolf* is the proposition that the rule of *Weeks* v. *United States* . . . excluding in federal criminal trials the use of evidence obtained in violation of the Fourth Amendment, derives not from the "supervisory power" of this Court over the federal judicial system, but from Constitutional requirement. This is so because no one, I suppose, would suggest that this Court possesses any general supervisory power over the state courts. Although I entertain considerable doubt as to the soundness of this foundational proposition of the majority . . . , I shall assume, for present purposes, that the *Weeks* rule "is of constitutional origin."

At the heart of the majority's opinion in this case is the following syllogism: (1) the rule excluding in federal criminal trials evidence which is the product of an illegal search and seizure is "part and parcel" of the Fourth Amendment; (2) *Wolf* held that the "privacy" assured against federal action by the Fourth Amendment is also protected against state action by the Fourteenth Amendment; and (3) it is therefore "logically and constitutionally necessary" that the *Weeks* exclusionary rule should also be enforced against the States.

This reasoning ultimately rests on the unsound premise that because *Wolf* carried into the States, as part of "the concept of ordered liberty" embodied in the Fourteenth Amendment, the principle of "privacy" underlying the Fourth Amendment . . . , it must follow that whatever configurations of the Fourth Amendment have been developed in the particularizing federal precedents are likewise to be deemed a part of "ordered liberty," and as such are enforceable against the States. For me, this does not follow at all.

It cannot be too much emphasized that what was recognized in *Wolf* was not that the Fourth Amendment *as such* is enforceable against the States as a facet of due process, a view of the Fourteenth Amendment which, as *Wolf* itself pointed out . . . , has long since been discredited, but the principle of privacy "which is at the core of the Fourth Amendment.". . . It would not be proper to expect or impose any precise equivalence, either as regards the scope of the right or the means of its implementation, between the requirements of the Fourth and Fourteenth Amendments. For the Fourth, unlike what was said in *Wolf* of the Fourteenth, does not state a general principle only; it is a particular command, having its setting in a pre-existing legal context on which both interpreting decisions and enabling statutes must at least build. . . .

. . . [H]ere we are reviewing not a determination that what the state police did was Constitutionally permissible (since the state court quite evidently assumed that it was not), but a determination that appellant was properly found guilty of conduct which, for present purposes, it is to be assumed the State could Constitutionally punish. Since there is not the slightest suggestion that Ohio's policy is "affirmatively to sanction . . . police incursion into privacy". . . what the Court is now doing is to impose upon the States not only federal substantive standards of "search and seizure" but also the basic federal remedy for violation of those standards. For I think it entirely clear that the *Weeks* exclusionary rule is but a remedy which, by penalizing past official misconduct, is aimed at deterring such conduct in the future.

I would not impose upon the States this federal exclusionary remedy. The reasons given by the majority for now suddenly turning its back on *Wolf* seem to me notably unconvincing.

First, it is said that "the factual grounds upon which *Wolf* was based" have since changed, in that more States now follow the *Weeks* exclusionary rule than was so at the time *Wolf* was decided. While that is true, a recent survey indicates that at present one-half of the States still adhere to the common-law non-exclusionary rule, and one, Maryland, retains the rule as to felonies. . . . But in any case, surely all this is beside the point, as the majority itself indeed seems to recognize. . . .

The preservation of a proper balance between state and federal responsibility in the administration of criminal justice demands patience on the part of those who might like to see things move faster among the States in this respect. Problems of criminal law enforcement vary widely from State to State. One State, in considering the totality of its legal picture, may conclude that the need for embracing the *Weeks* rule is pressing because other remedies are unavailable or inadequate to secure compliance with the substantive Constitutional principle involved. Another, though equally solicitous of Constitutional rights, may choose to pursue one purpose at a time, allowing all evidence relevant to guilt to be brought into a criminal trial, and dealing with Constitutional infractions by other means. Still another may consider the exclusionary rule too rough-and-ready a remedy, in that it reaches only unconstitutional intrusions which eventuate in criminal prosecution of the victims. Further, a State after experimenting with the *Weeks* rule for a time may, because of unsatisfactory experience with it, decide to revert to a non-exclusionary rule. And so on. From the standpoint of Constitutional permissibility in pointing a State in one direction or another, I do not see at all why "time has set its face against" the considerations which led Mr. Justice Cardozo, then chief judge of the New York Court of Appeals, to reject for New York in *People* v. *Defore* . . . the *Weeks* exclusionary rule. For us the question remains, as it has always been, one of state power, not one of passing judgment on the wisdom of one state course or another. In my view this Court should continue to forbear from fettering the States with an adamant rule which may embarrass them in coping with their own peculiar problems in criminal law enforcement.

Further, we are told that imposition of the *Weeks* rule on the States makes "very good sense," in that it will promote recognition by state and federal officials of their "mutual obligation to respect the same fundamental criteria" in their approach to law enforcement, and will avoid " 'needless conflict between state and federal courts.' " . . .

An approach which regards the issue as one of achieving procedural symmetry or of serving administrative convenience surely disfigures the boundaries of this Court's functions in relation to the state and federal courts. . . . I do not believe that the Fourteenth Amendment empowers this Court to mould state remedies effectuating the right to freedom from "arbitrary intrusion by the police" to suit its own notions of how things should be done. . . .

. . . I do not see how it can be said that a trial becomes unfair simply because a State determines that evidence may be considered by the trier of fact, regardless of how it was obtained, if it is relevant to the one issue with which the trial is concerned, the guilt or innocence of the accused. Of course, a court may use its procedures as an incidental means of pursuing other ends than the correct resolution of the controversies before it. Such indeed is the *Weeks* rule, but if a State does not choose to use its courts in this way, I do not believe that this Court is empowered to impose this much-debated procedure on local courts, however efficacious we may consider the *Weeks* rule to be as a means of securing Constitutional rights.

Finally, it is said that the overruling of *Wolf* is supported by the established doctrine that the admission in evidence of an involuntary confession renders a state conviction Constitutionally invalid. Since such a confession may often be entirely reliable, and therefore of the greatest relevance to the issue of the trial, the argument continues, this doctrine is ample warrant in precedent that the way evidence was obtained, and not just its relevance, is Constitutionally significant to the fairness of a trial. I believe this analogy is not a true one. The "coerced confession" rule is certainly not a rule that any illegally obtained statements may not be used in evidence. . . .

The point, then, must be that in requiring exclusion of an involuntary statement of an accused, we are concerned not with an appropriate remedy for what the police have done, but with something which is regarded as going to the heart of our concepts of fairness in judicial procedure. . . . The pressures brought to bear against an accused leading to a confession, unlike an unconstitutional violation of privacy, do not, apart from the use of the confession at trial, necessarily involve independent Constitutional violations. What is crucial is that the trial defense to which an accused is entitled should not be rendered an empty formality by reason of statements wrung from him, for then "a prisoner . . . [has been] made the deluded instrument of his own conviction." . . . That this is a *procedural right*, and that its violation occurs at the time his improperly obtained statement is admitted at trial, is manifest. For without this right all the careful safeguards erected around the giving of testimony, whether by an accused or any other witness, would become empty formalities in a procedure where the most compelling possible evidence of guilt, a confession, would have already been obtained at the unsupervised pleasure of the police.

This, and not the disciplining of the police, as with illegally seized evidence, is surely the true basis for excluding a statement of the accused which was unconstitutionally obtained. In sum, I think the coerced confession analogy works strongly *against* what the Court does today. . . .

Contrast the Court's opinion in *Wolf* v. *Colorado* (discussed in *Mapp*) with *Mapp* v. *Ohio*. Were considerations of federalism more important in the former than in the latter opinion? Why did the Court fail to apply the federal exclusionary rule in the *Wolf* case but hold that it was an essential component of due process in the *Mapp* decision? Since the exclusionary rule is not an explicit part of the Bill of Rights, is the Court going beyond simple incorporation in applying the rule to the states under the due process clause?

How does Justice Black reason that it is necessary to combine the Fourth and Fifth Amendments to uphold the exclusionary rule?

The Bill of Rights is not precise and unequivocal. It can be interpreted in many ways. Incorporating the Bill of Rights, which Black implied in his dissenting opinion in the *Adamson* case, would limit the role of the Court in relation to the states, might in fact be no constraint at all upon an active Court seeking to impose its own definitions of civil liberties and civil rights upon the states.

Justice Harlan dissented, arguing that the Court had broken the bounds of judicial self-restraint that should prevail in interpreting the due process clause of the Fourteenth Amendment. What is the difference, according to Harlan, between embodying the principle of privacy as part of the concept of ordered liberty under the due process clause and the incorporation of the Fourth Amendment?

The move toward broad rather than selective incorporation of the Bill of Rights, illustrated in the *Mapp* case, accelerated in the 1960s. *Gideon* v. *Wainwright*, decided in 1963, was a landmark decision in this process.

Behind the decision to nationalize the right to counsel in the *Gideon* case, a fascinating series of events had occurred.[25] At the time the case was pending the Court was seeking an appropriate opportunity to incorporate the right to counsel under due process. Extending the right to counsel to Gideon, whose offense was relatively mild in the criminal spectrum, would not cause a public outcry, and through Gideon the right could be made universal. The justices had in effect already made up their minds when certiorari was granted in response to Gideon's *in forma pauperis* petition ("in the manner of a pauper," a permission to sue without incurring liability for costs). The Court sought an eloquent and distinguished lawyer to represent Gideon and appointed Attorney Abe Fortas, who was later to become a member of the Court (although eventually he was forced to resign because of conflict of interest charges).

Justice Black wrote the majority opinion, which reflected his views on incorporation that had been forcefully expressed in his dissenting opinions

[25]The story of the case is brilliantly told in Anthony Lewis, *Gideon's Trumpet* (New York: Random House, 1964).

during the era of selective incorporation. Black had dissented in the case of *Betts* v. *Brady*, 316 U.S. 455 (1942), which the *Gideon* decision overruled.

Gideon v. Wainwright

372 U.S. 335; 83 S. Ct. 792; 9 L. Ed. 2d 799 (1963)

MR. JUSTICE BLACK delivered the opinion of the Court:

Petitioner was charged in a Florida state Court with having broken and entered a poolroom with intent to commit a misdemeanor. This offense is a felony under Florida law. Appearing in court without funds and without a lawyer, petitioner asked the court to appoint counsel for him, whereupon the following colloquy took place:

The COURT: Mr. Gideon, I am sorry, but I cannot appoint Counsel to represent you in this case. Under the laws of the State of Florida, the only time the Court can appoint Counsel to represent a Defendant is when that person is charged with a capital offense. I am sorry, but I will have to deny your request to appoint Counsel to defend you in this case.

The DEFENDANT: The United States Supreme Court says I am entitled to be represented by Counsel.

Put to trial before a jury, Gideon conducted his defense about as well as could be expected from a layman. He made an opening statement to the jury, cross-examined the State's witnesses, presented witnesses in his own defense, declined to testify himself, and made a short argument "emphasizing his innocence to the charge contained in the Information filed in this case." The jury returned a verdict of guilty, and petitioner was sentenced to serve five years in the state prison. . . . Since 1942, when *Betts* v. *Brady* . . . was decided by a divided Court, the problem of a defendant's federal constitutional right to counsel in a state court has been a continuing source of controversy and litigation in both state and federal courts.

To give this problem another review here, we granted certiorari. . . . Since Gideon was proceeding *in forma pauperis*, we appointed counsel to represent him and requested both sides to discuss in their briefs and oral arguments the following: "Should this Court's holding in *Betts* v. *Brady* . . . be reconsidered?"

I

The facts upon which Betts claimed that he had been unconstitutionally denied the right to have counsel appointed to assist him are strikingly like the facts upon which Gideon here bases his federal constitutional claim. Betts was indicted for robbery in a Maryland state court. On arraignment, he told the trial judge of his lack of funds to hire a lawyer and asked the court to appoint one for him. Betts was advised that it was not the practice in that county to appoint counsel for indigent defendants except in murder and rape cases. He then pleaded not guilty, had witnesses summoned, cross-examined the State's witnesses, examined his own, and chose not to testify himself. He was found guilty by the judge, sitting without a jury, and sentenced to eight years in prison. Like Gideon, Betts sought release by habeas corpus, alleging that he had been denied the right to assistance of counsel in violation of the Fourteenth Amendment. Betts was denied any relief, and on review this Court affirmed. It was held that a refusal to appoint counsel for an indigent defendant charged with a felony did not necessarily violate the Due Process Clause of the Fourteenth Amendment, which for reasons given the Court deemed to be the only applicable federal constitutional provision. The Court said:

Asserted denial [of due process] is to be tested by an appraisal of the totality of facts in a given case. That which may, in one setting, constitute a denial of fundamental fairness, shocking to the universal sense of justice, may in other circumstances, and in the light of other considerations, fall short of such denial. . . .

Treating due process as "a concept less rigid and more fluid than those envisaged in other specific and particular provisions of the Bill of Rights," the Court held that refusal to appoint counsel under the particular facts and circumstances in the *Betts* case was not so "offensive to the common and fundamental ideas of fairness" as to amount to a denial of due process. Since the facts and circumstances of the two cases are so nearly indistinguishable, we think the *Betts* v. *Brady* holding if left standing would require us to reject Gideon's claim that the Constitution guarantees him the assistance of counsel. Upon full reconsideration we conclude that *Betts* v. *Brady* should be overruled.

II

The Sixth Amendment provides, "In all criminal prosecutions, the accused shall enjoy the right . . . to have the Assistance of Counsel for his defence." We have construed this to mean that in federal courts counsel must be provided for defendants unable to employ counsel unless the right is competently and intelligently waived. Betts argued that this right is extended to indigent defendants in state courts by the Fourteenth Amendment. In response the Court stated that, while the Sixth Amendment laid down "no rule for the conduct of the States, the question recurs whether the constraint laid by the Amendment upon the national courts expresses a rule so fundamental and essential to a fair

trial, and so, to due process of law, that it is made obligatory upon the States by the Fourteenth Amendment." . . . In order to decide whether the Sixth Amendment's guarantee of counsel is of this fundamental nature, the Court in *Betts* set out and considered "[r]elevant data on the subject . . . afforded by constitutional and statutory provisions subsisting in the colonies and the States prior to the inclusion of the Bill of Rights in the national Constitution, and in the constitutional, legislative, and judicial history of the States to the present date." . . . On the basis of this historical data the Court concluded that "appointment of counsel is not a fundamental right, essential to a fair trial." . . . It was for this reason the *Betts* Court refused to accept the contention that the Sixth Amendment's guarantee of counsel for indigent federal defendants was extended to or, in the words of that Court, "made obligatory upon the States by the Fourteenth Amendment." Plainly, had the Court concluded that appointment of counsel for an indigent criminal defendant was "a fundamental right, essential to a fair trial," it would have held that the Fourteenth Amendment requires appointment of counsel in a state court, just as the Sixth Amendment requires in a federal court.

We think the Court in *Betts* had ample precedent for acknowledging that those guarantees of the Bill of Rights which are fundamental safeguards of liberty immune from federal abridgment are equally protected against state invasion by the Due Process Clause of the Fourteenth Amendment. This same principle was recognized, explained, and applied in *Powell* v. *Alabama* [1932] . . . a case upholding the right of counsel, where the Court held that despite sweeping language to the contrary in *Hurtado* v. *California* [1884] . . . the Fourteenth Amendment "embraced" those " 'fundamental principles of liberty and justice which lie at the base of all our civil and political institutions,' " even though they had been "specifically dealt with in another part of the federal Constitution." . . . In many cases other than *Powell* and *Betts*, this Court has looked to the fundamental nature of original Bill of Rights guarantees to decide whether the Fourteenth Amendment makes them obligatory on the States. Explicitly recognized to be of this "fundamental nature" and therefore made immune from state invasion by the Fourteenth, or some part of it, are the First Amendment's freedoms of speech, press, religion, assembly, association, and petition for redress of grievances. For the same reason, though not always in precisely the same terminology, the Court has made obligatory on the States the Fifth Amendment's command that private property shall not be taken for public use without just compensation, the Fourth Amendment's prohibition of unreasonable searches and seizures, and the Eighth's ban on cruel and unusual punishment. On the other hand, this Court in *Palko* v. *Connecticut* [1937] . . . refused to hold that the Fourteenth Amendment made the double jeopardy provision of the Fifth Amendment obligatory on the States. In so refusing, however, the Court, speaking through Mr. Justice Cardozo, was careful to emphasize that "immunities that are valid as against the federal government by force of the specific pledges of particular amendments have been found to be implicit in the concept of ordered liberty, and thus, through the Fourteenth Amendment, become valid as against the states" and that guarantees "in their origin . . . effective against the federal government alone" had by prior cases "been taken over from the earlier articles of the federal bill of rights and brought within the Fourteenth Amendment by a process of absorption." . . .

We accept *Betts* v. *Brady's* assumption, based as it was on our prior cases, that a provision of the Bill of Rights which is "fundamental and essential to a fair trial" is made obligatory upon the States by the Fourteenth Amendment. We think the Court in *Betts* was wrong, however, in concluding that the Sixth Amendment's guarantee of counsel is not one of these fundamental rights. Ten years before *Betts* v. *Brady*, this Court, after full consideration of all the historical data examined in *Betts*, had unequivocally declared that "the right to the aid of counsel is of this fundamental character." . . . While the Court at the close of its *Powell* opinion did by its language, as this Court frequently does, limit its holding to the particular facts and circumstances of that case, its conclusions about the fundamental nature of the right to counsel are unmistakable. Several years later, in 1936, the Court reemphasized what it had said about the fundamental nature of the right to counsel in this language:

We concluded that certain fundamental rights, safeguarded by the first eight amendments against federal action, were also safeguarded against state action by the due process of law clause of the Fourteenth Amendment, and among them the fundamental right of the accused to the aid of counsel in a criminal prosecution. *Grosjean* v. *American Press Co.* . . .

And again in 1938 this Court said:

[The assistance of counsel] is one of the safeguards of the Sixth Amendment deemed necessary to insure fundamental human rights of life and liberty. . . . The Sixth Amendment stands as a constant admonition that if the constitutional safeguards it provides be lost, justice will not still be done. *Johnson* v. *Zerbst.* . . .

In light of these and many other prior decisions of this Court, it is not suprising that the *Betts* Court, when faced with the contention that "one charged with crime, who is unable to obtain counsel, must be furnished counsel by the State," conceded that "[e]xpressions in the opinions of this court lend color to the argument. . . ." . . .

The fact is that in deciding as it did—that "appointment of counsel is not a fundamental right, essential to a fair trial"—the Court in *Betts* v. *Brady* made an abrupt break with its own well-considered precedents. In returning to these old precedents, sounder we believe than the new, we but restore constitutional principles established to achieve a fair system of justice. Not only these precedents but also reason and reflection require us to recognize that in our adversary system of criminal justice, any person haled into court, who is too poor to hire a lawyer, cannot be assured a fair trial unless counsel is provided for him. This seems to us to be an obvious truth. Governments, both state and federal, quite properly spend vast sums of money to establish machinery to try defendants accused of crime. Lawyers to prosecute are everywhere deemed essential to protect the public's interest in an orderly society. Similarly, there are few defendants charged with crime, few indeed, who fail to hire the best lawyers they can get to prepare and present their defenses. That government hires lawyers to prosecute and defendants who have the money hire lawyers to defend are the stongest indications of the widespread belief that lawyers in criminal courts are necessities, not luxuries. The right of one charged with crime to counsel may not be deemed fundamental and essential to fair trials in some countries, but it is in ours. From the very beginning, our state and national constitutions and laws have laid great emphasis on procedural and substantive safeguards designed to assure fair trials before impartial tribunals in which every defendant stands equal before the law. This noble ideal cannot be realized if the poor man charged with crime has to face his accusers without a lawyer to assist him. A defendant's need for a lawyer is nowhere better stated than in the moving words of Mr. Justice Sutherland in *Powell* v. *Alabama*:

The right to be heard would be, in many cases, of little avail if it did not comprehend the right to be heard by counsel. Even the intelligent and educated layman has small and sometimes no skill in the science of law. If charged with crime, he is incapable, generally, of determining for himself whether the indictment is good or bad. He is unfamiliar with the rules of evidence. Left without the aid of counsel he may be put on trial without a proper charge, and convicted upon incompetent evidence, or evidence irrelevant to the issue or otherwise inadmissible. He lacks both the skill and knowledge adequately to prepare his defense, even though he have a perfect one. He requires the guiding hand of counsel at every step in the proceedings against him. Without it, though he be not guilty, he faces the danger of conviction because he does not know how to establish his innocence. . . .

The Court in *Betts* v. *Brady* departed from the sound wisdom upon which the Court's holding in *Powell* v. *Alabama* rested. Florida, supported by two other States, has asked that *Betts* v. *Brady* be left intact. Twenty-two States, as friends of the Court, argue that *Betts* was "an anachronism when handed down" and that it should now be overruled. We agree.

The judgment is reversed and the cause is remanded to the Supreme Court of Florida for further action not inconsistent with this opinion.

Reversed.

MR. JUSTICE DOUGLAS:
. . . My Brother Harlan is of the view that a guarantee of the Bill of Rights that is made applicable to the States by reason of the Fourteenth Amendment is a lesser version of that same guarantee as applied to the Federal Government. Mr. Justice Jackson shared that view. But that view has not prevailed and rights protected against state invasion by the Due Process Clause of the Fourteenth Amendment are not watered-down versions of what the Bill of Rights guarantees.

MR. JUSTICE CLARK, concurring in the result, wrote a separate opinion.

MR. JUSTICE HARLAN, concurring:

I agree that *Betts* v. *Brady* should be overruled, but consider it entitled to a more respectful burial than has been accorded, at least on the part of those of us who were not on the Court when that case was decided.

I cannot subscribe to the view that *Betts* v. *Brady* represented "an abrupt break with its own well-considered precedents." . . . In 1932, in *Powell* v. *Alabama* . . . a capital case, this Court declared that under the particular facts there presented— "the ignorance and illiteracy of the defendants, their youth, the circumstances of public hostility . . . and above all that they stood in deadly peril of their lives" . . . —the state court had a duty to assign counsel for the trial as a necessary requisite of due process of law. It is evident that these limiting facts were not added to the opinion as an afterthought; they were repeatedly emphasized . . . and were clearly regarded as important to the result.

Thus when this Court, a decade later, decided *Betts* v. *Brady*, it did no more than to admit of the possible existence of special circumstances in noncapital as well as capital trials, while at the same time insisting that such circumstances be shown in order to establish a denial of due process. The right to appointed counsel had been recognized as being considerably broader in federal prosecutions, . . . but to have imposed these requirements on the States would indeed have been "an abrupt break" with the almost immediate past. The declaration that the right to appointed counsel in state prosecutions, as established in *Powell* v. *Alabama*, was not limited to capital cases was in truth not a departure

from, but an extension of, exisiting precedent. . . .

. . . The Court has come to recognize, in other words, that the mere existence of a serious criminal charge constituted in itself special circumstances requiring the services of counsel at trial. In truth the *Betts* v. *Brady* rule is no longer a reality.

This evolution, however, appears not to have been fully recognized by many state courts, in this instance charged with the front-line responsibility for the enforcement of constitutional rights. To continue a rule which is honored by this Court only with lip service is not a healthy thing and in the long run will do disservice to the federal system. . . .

In agreeing with the Court that the right to counsel in a case such as this should now be expressly recognized as a fundamental right embraced in the Fourteenth Amendment, I wish to make a further observation. When we hold a right or immunity, valid against the Federal Government, to be "implicit in the concept of ordered liberty" and thus valid against the States, I do not read our past decisions to suggest that by so holding, we automatically carry over an entire body of federal law and apply it in full sweep to the States. Any such concept would disregard the frequently wide disparity between the legitimate interests of the States and of the Federal Government, the divergent problems that they face, and the significantly different consequences of their actions. . . . In what is done today I do not understand the Court to depart from the principles laid down in *Palko* v. *Connecticut*, . . . or to embrace the concept that the Fourteenth Amendment "incorporates" the Sixth Amendment as such.

On these premises I join in the judgment of the Court.

Are statements made in Black's opinion that indicate the Court's abandonment of the selective incorporation and natural law formulas for due process? In what way does Justice Harlan take into account considerations of federalism and Court precedents to adopt a contrasting view of due process?

The Warren Court formula which used the Bill of Rights as the basis for defining Fourteenth Amendment due process reached full fruition in the following case.

Duncan v. Louisiana

391 U.S. 145; 88 S. Ct. 1444; 20 L. Ed. 2d 491 (1968)

MR. JUSTICE WHITE delivered the opinion of the Court:

Appellant, Gary Duncan, was convicted of simple battery in the Twenty-fifth Judicial District Court of Louisiana. Under Louisiana law simple battery is a misdemeanor, punishable by a maximum of two years' imprisonment and a $300 fine. Appellant sought trial by jury, but because the Louisiana Constitution grants jury trials only in cases in which capital punishment or imprisonment at hard labor may be imposed, the trial judge denied the request. Appellant was convicted and sentenced to serve 60 days in the parish prison and pay a fine of $150. Appellant sought review in the Supreme Court of Louisiana, asserting that the denial of jury trial violated rights guaranteed to him by the United States Constitution. The Supreme Court, finding "[n]o error of law in the ruling complained of," denied appellant a writ of certiorari. Pursuant to 28 U.S.C. § 1257 (2) appellant sought review in this Court, alleging that the Sixth and Fourteenth Amendments to the United States Constitution secure the right to jury trial in state criminal prosecutions where a sentence as long as two years may be imposed. . . .

I

The Fourteenth Amendment denies the States the power to "deprive any person of life, liberty, or property, without due process of law." In resolving conflicting claims concerning the meaning of this spacious language, the Court has looked increasingly to the Bill of Rights for guidance; many of the rights guaranteed by the first eight Amendments to the Constitution have been held to be protected against state action by the Due Process Clause of the Fourteenth Amendment. That clause now protects the right to compensation for property taken by the State; the rights of speech, press, and religion covered by the First Amendment; the Fourth Amendment rights to be free from unreasonable searches and seizures and to have excluded from criminal trials any evidence illegally seized; the right guaranteed by the Fifth Amendment to be free of compelled self-incrimination; and the Sixth Amendment rights to counsel, to a speedy and public trial, to confrontation of opposing witnesses, and to compulsory process for obtaining witnesses.

The test for determining whether a right extended by the Fifth and Sixth Amendements with respect to federal criminal proceedings is also protected against state action by the Fourteenth Amendment has been phrased in a variety of ways in the opinions of this Court. The question has been asked whether a right is among those " 'fundamental principles of liberty and justice which lie at the base of all our civil and political institutions,' " *Powell* v. *Alabama* [1932] . . . whether it is "basic in our system of jurisprudence," *In re Oliver* [1948] . . . and whether it is "a fundamental right, essential to a fair trial," *Gideon* v. *Wainwright* [1963]. . . . The claim before us is that the right to trial by jury guaranteed by the Sixth Amendment meets these tests. The position of Louisiana, on the other hand, is that the Constitution imposes upon the States no duty to give a jury trial in any criminal case, regardless of the seriousness of the crime or the size of the punishment which may be imposed. Because we believe that trial by jury in criminal cases is fundamental to the American scheme of justice, we hold that the Fourteenth Amendment guarantees a right of jury trial in all criminal cases which—were they to be tried in a federal court—would come within the Sixth Amendment's guarantee. Since we consider the appeal before us to be such a case, we hold that the Constitution was violated when appellant's demand for jury trial was refused.

The history of trial by jury in criminal cases has been frequently told. It is sufficient for present purposes to say that by the time our Constitution was written, jury trial in criminal cases had been in existence in England for several centuries and carried impressive credentials traced by many to Magna Carta. Its preservation and proper operation as a protection against arbitrary rule were among the major objectives of the revolutionary settlement which was expressed in the Declaration and Bill of Rights of 1689. In the 18th century Blackstone could write:

Our law has therefore wisely placed this strong and two-fold barrier, of a presentment and a trial by jury, between the liberties of the people and the prerogative of the crown. It was necessary, for preserving the admirable balance of our constitution, to vest the executive power of the laws in the prince: and yet this power might be dangerous and destructive to that very constitution, if exerted without check or control, by justices of *oyer* and *terminer* occasionally named by the crown; who might then, as in France or Turkey, imprison, dispatch, or exile any man that was obnoxious to the government, by an instant declaration that such is their will and pleasure. But the founders of the English law have, with excellent forecast, contrived that . . . the truth of every accusation, whether preferred in the shape of indictment, information, or appeal, should afterwards be confirmed by the unanimous suffrage of twelve of his equals and neighbors, indifferently chosen and superior to all suspicion.

Jury trial came to America with English colonists, and received strong support from them. Royal interference with the jury trial was deeply resented. Among the resolutions adopted by the First Congress of the American Colonies (the Stamp Act Congress) on October 19, 1765—resolutions deemed by their authors to state "the most essential rights and liberties of the colonists"—was the declaration:

That trial by jury is the inherent and invaluable right of every British subject in these colonies. . . .

The Declaration of Independence stated solemn objections to the King's making "Judges dependent on his Will alone, for the tenure of their offices, and the amount and payment of their salaries," to his "depriving us in many cases, of the benefits of Trial by Jury," and to his "transporting us beyond Seas to be tried for pretended offenses." The Constitution itself, in Art. III, § 2, commanded:

The Trial of all Crimes, except in Cases of Impeachment, shall be by Jury; and such Trial shall be held in the State where the said Crimes shall have been committed.

Objections to the Constitution because of the absence of a bill of rights were met by the immediate submission and adoption of the Bill of Rights. Included was the Sixth Amendment which, among other things, provided:

In all criminal prosecutions, the accused shall enjoy the right to a speedy and public trial, by an impartial jury of the State and district wherein the crime shall have been committed.

The constitutions adopted by the original States guaranteed jury trial. Also, the constitution of every State entering the Union thereafter in one form or another protected the right to jury trial in criminal cases.

Even such skeletal history is impressive support for considering the right to jury trial in criminal cases to be fundamental to our system of justice, an importance frequently recognized in the opinions of this Court. . . .

Jury trial continues to receive strong support. The laws of every State guarantee a right to jury trial in serious criminal cases; no State has dispensed with it; nor are there significant movements underway to do so. Indeed, the three most recent state constitutional revisions, in Maryland, Michigan, and New York, carefully preserved the right of the accused to have the judgment of a jury when tried for a serious crime.

We are aware of prior cases in this Court in which the prevailing opinion contains statements contrary to our holding today that the right to jury trial in serious criminal cases is a fundamental right and hence must be recognized by the States as part of their obligation to extend due process of law to all persons within their jurisdiction. Louisiana relies especially on *Maxwell* v. *Dow* [1900] . . .; *Palko* v. *Connecticut* [1937] . . . ; and *Snyder* v. *Massachusetts* [1934]. . . . None of these cases, however, dealt with a State which had purported to dispense entirely with a jury trial in serious criminal cases. *Maxwell* held that no provision of the Bill of Rights applied to the States—a position long since repudiated—and that the Due Process Clause of the Fourteenth Amendment did not prevent a State from trying a defendant for a noncapital offense with fewer than 12 men on the jury. It did not deal with a case in which no jury at all had been provided. In neither *Palko* nor *Snyder* was jury trial actually at issue, although both cases contain important dicta asserting that the right to jury trial is not

essential to ordered liberty and may be dispensed with by the States regardless of the Sixth and Fourteenth Amendments. These observations, though weighty and respectable, are nevertheless dicta, unsupported by holdings in this Court that a State may refuse a defendant's demand for a jury trial when he is charged with a serious crime. . . .

The guarantees of jury trial in the Federal and State Constitutions reflect a profound judgment about the way in which law should be enforced and justice administered. A right to jury trial is granted to criminal defendants in order to prevent oppression by the Government. Those who wrote our constitutions knew from history and experience that it was necessary to protect against unfounded criminal charges brought to eliminate enemies and against judges too responsive to the voice of higher authority. The framers of the constitutions strove to create an independent judiciary but insisted upon further protection against arbitrary action. Providing an accused with the right to be tried by a jury of his peers gave him an inestimable safeguard against the corrupt or overzealous prosecutor and against the compliant, biased, or eccentric judge. If the defendant preferred the common-sense judgment of a jury to the more tutored but perhaps less sympathetic reaction of the single judge, he was to have it. Beyond this, the jury trial provisions in the Federal and State Constitutions reflect a fundamental decision about the exercise of official power—a reluctance to entrust plenary powers over the life and liberty of the citizen to one judge or to a group of judges. Fear of unchecked power, so typical of our State and Federal Governments in other respects, found expression in the criminal law in this insistence upon community participation in the determination of guilt or innocence. The deep commitment of the Nation to the right of jury trial in serious criminal cases as a defense against arbitrary law enforcement qualifies for protection under the Due Process Clause of the Fourteenth Amendment, and must therefore be respected by the States.

Of course jury trial has "its weaknesses and the potential for misuse".... We are aware of the long debate, especially in this century, among those who write about the administration of justice, as to the wisdom of permitting untrained laymen to determine the facts in civil and criminal proceedings. Although the debate has been intense, with powerful voices on either side, most of the controversy has centered on the jury in civil cases. Indeed, some of the severest critics of civil juries acknowledge that the arguments for criminal juries are much stronger. In addition, at the heart of the dispute have been express or implicit assertions that juries are incapable of adequately understanding evidence or determining issues of fact, and that they are unpredictable, quixotic, and little better than a roll of dice. Yet, the most recent and exhaustive study of the jury in criminal cases concluded that juries do understand the evidence and come to sound conclusions in most of the cases presented to them and that when juries differ with the result at which the judge would have arrived, it is usually because they are serving some of the very purposes for which they were created and for which they are now employed.

The State of Louisiana urges that holding that the Fourteenth Amendment assures a right to jury trial will cast doubt on the integrity of every trial conducted without a jury.... We would not assert, however, that every criminal trial—or any particular trial—held before a judge alone is unfair or that a defendant may never be as fairly treated by a judge as he would be by a jury. Thus we hold no constitutional doubts about the practices, common in both federal and state courts, of accepting waivers of jury trial and prosecuting petty crimes without extending a

right to jury trial. However, the fact is that in most places more trials for serious crimes are to juries than to a court alone; a great many defendants prefer the judgment of a jury to that of a court. Even where defendants are satisfied with bench trials, the right to a jury trial very likely serves its intended purpose of making judicial or prosecutorial unfairness less likely.

II

Louisiana's final contention is that even if it must grant jury trials in serious criminal cases, the conviction before us is valid and constitutional because here the petitioner was tried for simple battery and was sentenced to only 60 days in the parish prison. We are not persuaded. It is doubtless true that there is a category of petty crimes or offenses which is not subject to the Sixth Amendment jury trial provision and should not be subject to the Fourteenth Amendment jury trial requirement here applied to the Sates. Crimes carrying possible penalties up to six months do not require a jury trial if they otherwise qualify as petty offenses, *Cheff* v. *Schnackenberg* [1966].... But the penalty authorized for a particular crime is of major relevance in determining whether it is serious or not and may in itself, if severe enough, subject the trial to the mandates of the Sixth Amendment.... In the case before us the Legislature of Louisiana has made simple battery a criminal offense punishable by imprisonment for up to two years and a fine. The question, then, is whether a crime carrying such a penalty is an offense which Louisiana may insist on trying without a jury.

We think not. So-called petty offenses were tried without juries both in England and in the Colonies and have always been held to be exempt from the otherwise comprehensive language of the Sixth Amendment's jury trial provisions.... Of course the boundaries of the petty offense category have always been ill-defined, if not ambulatory. In the absence of an explicit constitutional provision, the definitional task necessarily falls on the courts, which must either pass upon the validity of legislative attempts to identify those petty offenses which are exempt from jury trial or, where the legislature has not addressed itself to the problem, themselves face the question in the first instance. In either case it is necessary to draw a line in the spectrum of crime, separating petty from serious infractions. This process, although essential, cannot be wholly satisfactory, for it requires attaching different consequences to events which, when they lie near the line, actually differ very little. . . .

. . . We need not, however, settle in this case the exact location of the line between petty offenses and serious crimes. It is sufficient for our purposes to hold that a crime punishable by two years in prison is, based on past and contemporary standards in this country, a serious crime and not a petty offense. Consequently, appellant was entitled to a jury trial and it was error to deny it.

The judgment below is reversed and the case is remanded for proceedings not inconsistent with this opinion.

MR. JUSTICE BLACK, with whom MR. JUSTICE DOUGLAS joins, concurring:

The Court today holds that the right to trial by jury guaranteed defendants in criminal cases in federal courts by Art. III of the United States Constitution and by the Sixth Amendment is also guaranteed by the Fourteenth Amendment to defendants tried in state courts. With this holding I agree for reasons given by the Court. I also agree because of reasons given in my dissent in *Adamson* v. *California* [1947]. . . .

. . . And I am very happy to support this selective process through which our Court has since the *Adamson* case held most of the specific Bill of Rights' protections applicable to the States to the same

extent they are applicable to the Federal Government. . . .

. . . What I wrote there in 1947 was the product of years of study and research. My appraisal of the legislative history followed 10 years of legislative experience as a Senator of the United States, not a bad way, I suspect, to learn the value of what is said in legislative debates, committee discussions, committee reports, and various other steps taken in the course of passage of bills, resolutions, and proposed constitutional amendments. My Brother Harlan's objections to my *Adamson* dissent history, like that of most of the objectors, relies most heavily on a criticism written by Professor Charles Fairman and published in the Stanford Law Review. 2 Stan. L. Rev. 5 (1949). I have read and studied this article extensively, including the historical references, but am compelled to add that in my view it has completely failed to refute the inferences and arguments that I suggest in my *Adamson* dissent. Professor Fairman's "history" relies very heavily on what was *not* said in the state legislatures that passed on the Fourteenth Amendment. Instead of relying on this kind of negative pregnant, my legislative experience has convinced me that it is far wiser to rely on what *was* said, and most importantly, said by the men who actually sponsored the Amendment in the Congress. I know from my years in the United States Senate that it is to men like Congressman Bingham, who steered the Amendment through the House, and Senator Howard, who introduced it in the Senate, that members of Congress look when they seek the real meaning of what is being offered. And they vote for or against a bill based on what the sponsors of that bill and those who oppose it tell them it means. . . .

While I do not wish at this time to discuss at length my disagreement with Brother Harlan's forthright and frank restatement of the now discredited *Twining* doctrine, I do want to point out what appears to me to be the basic difference between us. His view, as was indeed the view of *Twining,* is that "due process is an evolving concept" and therefore that it entails a "gradual process of judicial inclusion and exclusion" to ascertain those "immutable principles" of free government which no member of the Union may disregard." Thus the Due Process Clause is treated as prescribing no specific and clearly ascertainable constitutional command that judges must obey in interpreting the Constitution, but rather as leaving judges free to decide at any particular time whether a particular rule or judicial formulation embodies an "immutable principl[e] of free government" or is "implicit in the concept of ordered liberty," or whether certain conduct "shocks the judge's conscience" or runs counter to some other similar, undefined and undefinable standard. Thus due process, according to my Brother Harlan, is to be a phrase with no permanent meaning, but one which is found to shift from time to time in accordance with judges' predilections and understandings of what is best for the country. If due process means this, the Fourteenth Amendment, in my opinion, might as well have been written that "no person shall be deprived of life, liberty or property except by laws that the judges of the United States Supreme Court shall find to be consistent with the immutable principles of free government." It is impossible for me to believe that such unconfined power is given to judges in our Constitution that is a written one in order to limit governmental power. . . .

Finally I want to add that I am not bothered by the argument that applying the Bill of Rights to the States, "according to the same standards that protect those personal rights against federal encroachment," interferes with our concept of federalism in that it may prevent States from trying novel social and economic experiments. I have never believed that under the guise of federalism the States should be able to experiment with the protections afforded our citizens through the Bill of Rights. As Justice Goldberg said so wisely in his concurring opinion in *Pointer* v. *Texas,* 380 U.S. 400 [1965]:

to deny to the States the power to impair a fundamental constitutional right is not to increase federal power, but, rather, to limit the power of both federal and state governments in favor of safeguarding the fundamental rights and liberties of the individual. In my view this promotes rather than undermines the basic policy of avoiding excess concentration of power in government, federal or state, which underlies our concepts of federalism.

It seems to me totally inconsistent to advocate, on the one hand, the power of this Court to strike down any state law or practice which it finds "unreasonable" or "unfair" and, on the other hand, urge that the States be given maximum power to develop their own laws and procedures. . . . No one is more concerned than I that the States be allowed to use the full scope of their powers as their citizens see fit. And that is why I have continually fought against the expansion of this Court's authority over the States through the use of a broad, general interpretation of due process that permits judges to strike down state laws they do not like.

In closing I want to emphasize that I believe as strongly as ever that the Fourteenth Amendment was intended to make the Bill of Rights applicable to the States. I have been willing to support the selective incorporation doctrine, however, as an alternative, although perhaps less historically supportable than complete incorporation. The selective incorporation process, if used properly, does limit the Supreme Court in the Fourteenth Amendment field to specific Bill of Rights' protections only and keeps judges from roaming at will in their own notions of what policies outside the Bill of Rights are desirable and what are not. And, most importantly for me, the selective incorporation process has the virtue of having already worked to make most of the Bill of Rights' protections applicable to the States.

MR. JUSTICE FORTAS wrote a concurring opinion.

MR. JUSTICE HARLAN, whom MR. JUSTICE STEWART joins, dissenting:

. . . The Court's approach to this case is an uneasy and illogical compromise among the views of various Justices on how the Due Process Clause should be interpreted. The Court does not say that those who framed the Fourteenth Amendment intended to make the Sixth Amendment applicable to the States. And the Court concedes that it finds nothing unfair about the procedure by which the present appellant was tried. Nevertheless, the Court reverses his conviction: it holds, for some reason not apparent to me, that the Due Process Clause incorporates the particular clause of the Sixth Amendment that requires trial by jury in federal criminal cases—including, as I read its opinion, the sometimes trivial accompanying baggage of judicial interpretation in federal contexts. I have raised my voice many times before against the Court's continuing undiscriminating insistence upon fastening on the States federal notions of criminal justice, and I must do so again in this instance. With all respect, the Court's approach and its reading of history are altogether topsy-turvy.

I

I believe I am correct in saying that every member of the Court for at least the last 135 years has agreed that our Founders did not consider the requirements of the Bill of Rights so fundamental that they should operate directly against the States. They were wont to believe rather that the security of liberty in America rested primarily upon the dispersion of governmental power across a federal system. The Bill of Rights was considered unnecessary by some but insisted upon by others in order to curb the possibility of abuse of power by the strong central government they were creating.

The Civil War Amendments dramatically altered the relation of the Federal Government to the States. The first section of the Fourteenth Amendment imposes highly significant restrictions on state action. But the restrictions are couched in very broad and general terms: citizenship; privileges and immunities; due process of law; equal protection of the laws. . . .

A few members of the Court have taken the position that the intention of those who drafted the first section of the Fourteenth Amendment was simply, and exclusively, to make the provisions of the first eight Amendments applicable to state action. This view has never been accepted by this Court. In my view, the first section of the Fourteenth Amendment was meant neither to incorporate, nor to be limited to, the specific guarantees of the first eight Amendments. The overwhelming historical evidence marshalled by Professor Fairman demonstrates, to me conclusively, that the Congressmen and state legislators who wrote, debated, and ratified the Fourteenth Amendment did not think they were "incorporating" the Bill of Rights and the very breadth and generality of the Amendment's provisions suggest that its authors did not suppose that the Nation would always be limited to mid-19th century conceptions of "liberty" and "due process of law" but that the increasing experience and evolving conscience of the American people would add new "intermediate premises." In short, neither history, nor sense, supports using the Fourteenth Amendment to put the States in a constitutional straitjacket with respect to their own development in the administration of criminal or civil law.

Although I therefore fundamentally disagree with the total incorporation view of the Fourteenth Amendment, it seems to me that such a position does at least have the virtue, lacking in the Court's selective incorporation approach, of internal consistency: we look to the Bill of Rights, word for word, clause for clause, precedent for precedent because, it is said, the men who wrote the Amendment wanted it that way. For those who do not accept this "history," a different source of "intermediate premises" must be found. The Bill of Rights is not necessarily irrelevant to the search for guidance in interpreting the Fourteenth Amendment, but the reason for and the nature of its relevance must be articulated.

Apart from the approach taken by the absolute incorporationists, I can see only one method of analysis that has any internal logic. That is to start with the words "liberty" and "due process of law" and attempt to define them in a way that accords with American traditions and our system of government. This approach, involving a much more discriminating process of adjudication than does "incorporation," is, albeit difficult, the one that was followed throughout the 19th and most of the present century. It entails a "gradual process of judicial inclusion and exclusion," seeking, with due recognition of constitutional tolerance for state experimentation and disparity, to ascertain those "immutable principles . . . of free government which no member of the Union may disregard." Due process was not restricted to rules fixed in the past, for that "would be to deny every quality of the law but its age, and to render it incapable of progress or improvement." Nor did it impose nationwide uniformity in details, for [t]he Fourteenth Amendment does not profess to secure to all persons in the United States the benefit of the same laws and the same rem-

edies. Great diversities in these respects may exist in two States separated only by an imaginary line. On one side of this line there may be a right of trial by jury, and on the other side no such right. Each State prescribes its own modes of judicial proceeding.

Through this gradual process, this Court sought to define "liberty" by isolating freedoms that Americans of the past and of the present considered more important than any suggested countervailing public objective. The Court also, by interpretation of the phrase "due process of law," enforced the Constitution's guarantee that no State may imprison an individual except by fair and impartial procedures.

The relationship of the Bill of Rights to this "gradual process" seems to me to be twofold. In the first place it has long been clear that the Due Process Clause imposes some restrictions on state action that parallel Bill of Rights restrictions on federal action. Second, and more important than this accidental overlap, is the fact that the Bill of Rights is evidence, at various points, of the content Americans find in the term "liberty" and of American standards of fundamental fairness. . . .

Today's Court still remains unwilling to accept the total incorporationists' view of the history of the Fourteenth Amendment. This, if accepted, would afford a cogent reason for applying the Sixth Amendment to the States. The Court is also, apparently, unwilling to face the task of determining whether denial of trial by jury in the situation before us, or in other situations, is fundamentally unfair. Consequently, the Court has compromised on the ease of the incorporationist position, without its internal logic. It has simply assumed that the question before us is whether the Jury Trial Clause of the Sixth Amendment should be incorporated into the Fourteenth, jot-for-jot and case-for-case, or ignored. Then the Court merely declares that the clause in question is "in" rather than "out."

The Court has justified neither its starting place nor its conclusion. If the problem is to discover and articulate the rules of fundamental fairness in criminal proceedings, there is no reason to assume that the whole body of rules developed in this Court constituting Sixth Amendment jury trial must be regarded as a unit. The requirement of trial by jury in federal criminal cases has given rise to numerous subsidiary questions respecting the exact scope and content of the right. It surely cannot be that every answer the Court has given, or will give, to such a question is attributable to the Founders; or even that every rule announced carries equal conviction of this Court; still less can it be that every such subprinciple is equally fundamental to ordered liberty. . . .

Even if I could agree that the question before us is whether Sixth Amendment jury trial is totally "in" or totally "out," I can find in the Court's opinion no real reasons for concluding that it should be "in." The basis for differentiating among clauses in the Bill of Rights cannot be that only some clauses are in the Bill of Rights, or that only some are old and much praised, or that only some have played an important role in the development of federal law. These things are true of all. The Court says that some clauses are more "fundamental" than others, but it turns out to be using this word in a sense that would have astonished Mr. Justice Cardozo and which, in addition, is of no help. The word does not mean "analytically critical to procedural fairness" for no real analysis of the role of the jury in making procedures fair is even attempted. Instead, the word turns out to mean "old," "much praised," and "found in the Bill of

Rights." The definition of "fundamental" thus turns out to be circular. . . .

The argument that jury trial is not a requisite of due process is quite simple. The central proposition of *Palko*, . . . a proposition to which I would adhere, is that "due process of law" requires only that criminal trials be fundamentally fair. As stated above, apart from the theory that it was historically intended as a mere shorthand for the Bill of Rights, I do not see what else "due process of law" can intelligibly be thought to mean. If due process of law requires only fundamental fairness, then the inquiry in each case must be whether a state trial process was a fair one. The Court has held, properly I think, that in an adversary process it is a requisite of fairness, for which there is no adequate substitute, that a criminal defendant be afforded a right to counsel and to cross-examine opposing witnesses. But it simply has not been demonstrated, nor, I think, can it be demonstrated, that trial by jury is the only fair means of resolving issues of fact. . . .

In sum, there is a wide range of views on the desirability of trial by jury, and on the ways to make it most effective when it is used; there is also considerable variation from State to State in local conditions such as the size of the criminal caseload, the ease or difficulty of summoning jurors, and other trial conditions bearing on fairness. We have before us, therefore, an almost perfect example of a situation in which the celebrated dictum of Mr. Justice Brandeis should be invoked. It is, he said,

one of the happy incidents of the federal system that a single courageous State may, if its citizens choose, serve as a laboratory. . . .

Justice White's majority opinion in the *Duncan* case offers a change in the philosophy of the Court's majority on the standards of due process of law under the Fourteenth Amendment. Justice White declares that "[i]n resolving conflicting claims concerning the meaning of [the due process clause of the Fourteenth Amendment] . . . the Court has looked increasingly to the Bill of Rights for guidance; many of the rights guaranteed by the first eight amendments to the Constitution have been held to be protected against state action by the due process clause of the Fourteenth Amendment." An implication can be drawn from White's opinion that Fourteenth Amendment due process should incorporate the entire Bill of Rights. As a minimum, the opinion holds that when a provision of the Bill of Rights is incorporated under the due process clause of the Fourteenth Amendment the full protections of that provision accorded to citizens in federal courts and against national action will be extended to state courts and state action. Considerations of federalism, in White's view, should not be allowed to dilute those portions of the Bill of Rights that have been incorporated under the Fourteenth Amendment. The application of this standard in the *Duncan* case resulted in transferring the jury trial right of the Sixth Amendment to the states. The offenses to which jury trial was to apply under the Sixth Amendment now required jury trial under the due process clause of the Fourteenth Amendment.

Justice Harlan's dissenting opinion in the *Duncan* case argued that while the Bill of Rights is not irrelevant in the search for guidance as to the meaning of due process of law under the Fourteenth Amendment, considerations of federalism should determine the extent to which a right in the Bill of Rights, such as trial by jury, should be extended to the states. Neither history, nor sense, wrote Harlan, "supports using the Fourteenth Amendment to put the states in a constitutional strait jacket with respect to their own development in the administration of criminal or civil law." The Court must define "liberty" and "due process of law" under the Fourteenth Amendment in terms of American traditions and the needs of the states and not simply transfer in an undiscriminating way portions of the Bill of Rights to the states. Insofar as there is accidental overlap between restrictions on state action under the due process clause and restrictions on federal action under the Bill of Rights, it is a reflection that "the Bill of Rights is evidence, at various points, of the content Americans find in the term 'liberty' and of American standards of fundamental fairness [that is, of due process of law]."

What is the reasoning of Justice Black in his concurring opinion opposing the selective incorporation approach of the Court's majority? How does he challenge the dissenting views of Justice Harlan that it is up to the Court to define liberty and due process of law under the Fourteenth Amendment on the basis of historical tradition and considerations of federalism?

Incorporation after *Duncan v. Louisiana*

The *Duncan* decision nearly completed the process of incorporating the procedural protections of the Bill of Rights under the Fourteenth Amendment due process clause. *Benton v. Maryland*, 395 U.S. 784 (1969), essentially concluded the process by incorporating the prohibition upon double jeopardy of the Fifth Amendment. The provisions of the Bill of Rights not yet incorporated are: requirements for grand jury indictment and trial by a jury in *civil* cases; the right to bear arms; prohibitions upon excessive bail and fines; and Third Amendment safeguards against the involuntary quartering of troops in private homes.

The failure of the Court to include all of the Bill of Rights under the due process clause of the Fourteenth Amendment diluted the total incorporation so strongly advocated by Justice Black. In the area of criminal procedure, the Warren Court used the Bill of Rights as a basis for defining Fourteenth Amendment due process. The implication of its approach in this sphere was that it would not go beyond the enumerated provisions of the Bill of Rights in extending criminal protections to the states. This method, which resulted in the incorporation of all of the important provisions of the Bill of Rights regarding criminal procedure, differed from the *Palko* and *Rochin* formulas. The Cardozo and Frankfurter opinions in those cases upheld the selective incorporation and natural law standards of due process, which essentially gave the Court discretion to incorporate the rights protected by the Bill of Rights as well as those which were not specifically enumerated in the first eight amendments.

The incorporation strategy of the Warren Court that defined due process in terms of the Bill of Rights ended with the retirement of the Chief Justice in 1969. The Burger Court, while not significantly reversing incorporation, appears to have returned in part to a natural law basis of due process. However, it has not only used this formula as Frankfurter did to exercise judicial self-restraint but also to expand the rights of those accused of crime under the due process clause of the Fourteenth Amendment. The Burger Court held in the case of *In Re Winship* (1970) that the due process clause protected an accused in a criminal prosecution against conviction except upon proof beyond a reasonable doubt. There were two separate dissenting opinions, one by Justices Burger and Stewart, holding that there was "no constitutional requirement of due process sufficient to overcome the legislative judgment of the states in this area. . . ."[26] Justice Black, in a separate dissent, pointed out that the requirement of proof beyond a reasonable doubt in criminal cases was not an explicit requirement of the Bill of Rights and therefore should not apply to the states under the due process clause. Black argued that going beyond the Bill of Rights in interpreting the Fourteenth Amendment due process clause put the Court in a position of a super legislature overriding the laws of the states. "I admit a strong, persuasive argument can be made for a standard of proof beyond a reasonable doubt in criminal cases," wrote Black, "but it is not for me as a judge to say for that reason that Congress or the states are without constitutional power to establish another standard that the Constitution does not otherwise forbid."[27]

While *In Re Winship* extended a criminal protection to the states beyond those enumerated in the Bill of Rights, the Court decided in the same term several cases that diluted the right to a jury trial incorporated in *Duncan* v. *Louisiana*. In *Williams* v. *Florida*, 399 U.S. 78 (1970), the Court held that a twelve-person jury was not a requirement of "trial by jury." The decision

---

[26]In Re Winship, 397 U.S. 358, 376 (1970).
[27]Ibid., p. 385.

upheld a Florida law that provided for a six-person jury in all but capital cases. In *Apodaca* v. *Oregon,* 406 U.S. 404 (1972), the federal standard under the Sixth Amendment that requires a unanimous jury verdict was held not to be applicable to the states under the due process clause of the Fourteenth Amendment. Justice White wrote the opinion of the Court, joined by Justices Burger, Blackmun, and Rehnquist, expressing the view that the Sixth Amendment right to a jury trial did not require a unanimous verdict and therefore it was not required under the due process clause of the Fourteenth Amendment. Justice Powell was the swing vote in the 5–4 decision. In a concurring opinion he held that even though the Sixth Amendment requires a unanimous verdict, the Fourteenth Amendment does not require unanimity because it is not fundamental to a jury trial. The states must be allowed flexibility to experiment, wrote Powell, and the Oregon provisions requiring a vote of ten out of twelve jurors for conviction in noncapital cases satisfied standards of basic fairness. The *Williams* and *Apodaca* decisions returned to the Harlan approach in his dissenting opinion in *Duncan* v. *Louisiana* by holding that Fourteenth Amendment due process does not automatically incorporate the full force of a provision of the Bill of Rights. The Sixth Amendment right to jury trial was diluted on the basis of considerations of federalism and historical tradition.

JUDICIAL INTERVENTION THROUGH SUBSTANTIVE DUE PROCESS IN THE NONECONOMIC SPHERE

Judicial intervention through substantive due process review did not end in 1937 but merely changed its focus. Long before, the Court had developed standards of substantive due process in the noneconomic sphere when it defined *liberty* in the Fourteenth Amendment to include the First Amendment freedoms of speech and press.[28] The Court's method of applying natural law standards to define the civil liberties and civil rights content of the Fourteenth Amendment due process clause was analogous to its approach in reviewing economic legislation. In both spheres of judicial review it defined due process to include fundamental and historical rights derived from natural and common law. The process necessarily was very subjective, requiring the Court to pick and choose from a broad spectrum of rights those which it felt were essential to the maintenance of liberty.

As the Supreme Court was ending the Lochner era in the late 1930s, it was reinforcing its interventionist role to protect civil liberties and rights. In *United States* v. *Carolene Products Co.* in 1938 Justice Stone, after declaring that the Court would adopt a presumption of constitutionality in reviewing economic legislation, added the following footnote: "There may be narrower scope for operation of the presumption of constitutionality when leg-

---

[28]See Gitlow v. New York, 268 U.S. 652 (1925), pp. 591–596; and Near v. Minnesota, 283 U.S. 693 (1931), pp. 659–666, which held the freedoms of speech and press to be part of the liberty protected by the due process clause of the Fourteenth Amendment.

islation appears on its face to be within a specific prohibition of the Constitution, such as those of the first ten amendments, which are deemed equally specific when held to be embraced within the Fourteenth."[29] The footnote left no doubt that in the future the Court would closely review the substance of legislation to uphold fundamental civil liberties and rights.

The Court engaged in substantive due process review in the course of nationalizing most of the rights contained in the Bill of Rights. The Cardozo and Frankfurter opinions in *Palko* v. *Connecticut* (1937) and *Rochin* v. *California* (1952) respectively adopted a subjective value-oriented method of determining the individual rights that would be incorporated under the Fourteenth Amendment. This approach clearly followed the precedent of *Twining* v. *New Jersey* (1908).[30]

The natural law approach taken by the Court did not limit its definition of due process to the specific rights expressed in the Bill of Rights. The Court often defined Fourteenth Amendment due process rights without reference to or explicitly basing its decision upon the Bill of Rights, as was illustrated in the *Palko* and *Rochin* opinions.[31] While the natural law approach was considered both by those who used it, such as Justice Frankfurter, and by those who observed it, to be an exercise of judicial self-restraint based primarily upon considerations of federalism, in fact it contained the seeds of judicial intervention that would go beyond the Bill of Rights. Justice Black warned against such a possibility in his dissenting opinions in *Betts* v. *Brady* (1942) and *Adamson* v. *California* (1947).[32] When the Supreme Court refused to hear a challenge to the Connecticut birth control laws in *Poe* v. *Ullman* (1961), Justice Harlan in a dissenting opinion supported the broader definition of due process that Black feared.

Due process has not been reduced to any formula; its content cannot be determined by reference to any code. The best that can be said is that through the course of this Court's decisions it has represented the balance, which our nation, built upon postulates of respect for the liberty of the individual, has struck between that liberty and the demands of organized society. If the supplying of content [substance] to this constitutional concept has of necessity been a rational process, it certainly has not been one where judges have felt free to roam where unguided speculation might take them. The balance of which I speak is the balance struck by this country, having regard to what history teaches are the traditions from which it developed as well as the traditions from which it broke. That tradition is a living thing. A decision of this Court which radically departs from it could not long survive, while a decision which builds on what has survived is likely to be sound. No formula [e.g., the Bill of Rights] could serve as a substitute, in this area, for judgment and restraint.

It is this outlook which has led the Court continually to perceive distinctions in the imperative character of constitutional provisions, since that character must be

[29]United States v. Carolene Products Co., 304 U.S. 144, 152 n. 4 (1938).

[30]The Twining, Palko, and Rochin decisions are discussed and presented at pp. 480–484, 520–523, and 532–537.

[31]See also, as examples, Chambers v. Florida 309 U.S. 227 (1940); Brown v. Mississippi, 297 U.S. 278 (1936); Meyer v. Nebraska, 262 U.S. 390 (1923); Moore v. Dempsey, 261 U.S. 86 (1923).

[32]See pp. 528–531.

discerned from a particular provision's larger context. And inasmuch as this context is one not of words, but of history and purposes, the full scope of the liberty guaranteed by the due process clause cannot be found in or limited by the precise terms of the specific guarantees [as in the Bill of Rights] elsewhere provided in the Constitution. This "liberty" is not a series of isolated points pricked out in terms of the taking of property; the freedom of speech, press, and religion; the right to keep and bear arms; the freedom from unreasonable searches and seizures; and so on. It is a rational continuum which, broadly speaking, includes a freedom from all substantial arbitrary impositions and purposeless restraints. . . . [33]

Would Harlan's view of the flexible and expansive nature of due process be adopted by the Court to extend constitutional protections beyond the enumerated provisions of the Bill of Rights? The issue was joined when the Court again confronted a challenge to the Connecticut birth control laws in the following case.

Griswold v. *Connecticut*

381 U.S. 479; 85 S. Ct. 1678; 14 L. Ed. 2d 510 (1965)

Mr. Justice Douglas delivered the opinion of the Court:

Appellant Griswold is Executive Director of the Planned Parenthood League of Connecticut. Appellant Buxton is a licensed physician and a professor at the Yale Medical School who served as Medical Director for the League at its Center in New Haven—a center open and operating from November 1 to November 10, 1961, when appellants were arrested.

They gave information, instruction, and medical advice to *married persons* as to the means of preventing conception. They examined the wife and prescribed the best contraceptive device or material for her use. Fees were usually charged, although some couples were serviced free.

The statutes whose constitutionality is involved in this appeal are §§ 53–32 and 54–196 of the General Statutes of Connecticut (1958 rev). The former provides:

Any person who uses any drug, medicinal article or instrument for the purpose of prevent-

ing conception shall be fined not less than fifty dollars or imprisoned not less than sixty days nor more than one year or be both fined and imprisoned.

Section 54–196 provides:

Any person who assists, abets, counsels, causes, hires or commands another to commit any offense may be prosecuted and punished as if he were the principal offender.

The appellants were found guilty as accessories and fined $100 each, against the claim that the accessory statute as so applied violated the Fourteenth Amendment. . . .

We think that appellants have standing to raise the constitutional rights of the married people with whom they had a professional relationship. *Tileston* v. *Ullman* [1943] . . . is different, for there the plaintiff seeking to represent others asked for a declaratory judgment. In that situation we thought that the requirements of standing should be strict, lest the standards of "case or controversy" in Article III

---

[33]Poe v. Ullman, 367 U.S. 497, 542–543 (1961).

of the Constitution become blurred. Here those doubts are removed by reason of a criminal conviction for serving married couples in violation of an aiding-and-abetting statute. Certainly the accessory should have standing to assert that the offense which he is charged with assisting is not, or cannot constitutionally be, a crime. . . .

Coming to the merits, we are met with a wide range of questions that implicate the Due Process Clause of the Fourteenth Amendment. Overtones of some arguments suggest that *Lochner* v. *New York* [1905] . . . should be our guide. But we decline that invitation as we did in *West Coast Hotel Co.* v. *Parrish* [1937]. . . . We do not sit as a super-legislature to determine the wisdom, need, and propriety of laws that touch economic problems, business affairs, or social conditions. This law, however, operates directly on an intimate relation of husband and wife and their physician's role in one aspect of that relation.

The association of people is not mentioned in the Constitution nor in the Bill of Rights. The right to educate a child in a school of the parents' choice—whether public or private or parochial—is also not mentioned. Nor is the right to study any particular subject or any foreign language. Yet the First Amendment has been construed to include certain of those rights.

By *Pierce* v. *Society of Sisters* [1925] . . . the right to educate one's children as one chooses is made applicable to the States by the force of the First and Fourteenth Amendments. By *Meyer* v. *Nebraska* [1923] . . . the same dignity is given the right to study the German language in a private school. In other words, the State may not, consistently with the spirit of the First Amendment, contract the spectrum of available knowledge. The right of freedom of speech and press includes not only the right to utter or to print, but the right to distribute, the right to receive, the right to read . . . and freedom of inquiry, freedom of thought, and freedom to teach . . .—indeed the freedom of the entire university community. . . .

Without those peripheral rights the specific rights would be less secure. And so we reaffirm the principle of the *Pierce* and the *Meyer* cases.

In *NAACP* v. *Alabama* [1958] we protected the "freedom to associate and privacy in one's associations," noting that freedom of association was a peripheral First Amendment right. Disclosure of membership lists of a constitutionally valid association, we held, was invalid "as entailing the likelihood of a substantial restraint upon the exercise by petitioner's members of their right to freedom of association." . . . In other words, the First Amendment has a penumbra where privacy is protected from governmental intrusion. In like context, we have protected forms of "association" that are not political in the customary sense but pertain to the social, legal, and economic benefit of the members. *NAACP* v. *Button* [1963]. . . . In *Schware* v. *Board of Bar Examiners* [1957] . . . we held it not permissible to bar a lawyer from practice, because he had once been a member of the Communist Party. The man's "association with that Party" was not shown to be "anything more than a political faith in a political party" . . . and was not action of a kind proving bad moral character. . . .

Those cases involved more than the "right of assembly"—a right that extends to all irrespective of their race or ideology. . . . The right of "association," like the right of belief, . . . is more than the right to attend a meeting; it includes the right to express one's attitudes or philosophies by membership in a group or by affiliation with it or by other lawful means. Association in that context is a form of expression of opinion; and while it is not expressly included in the First Amendment its existence is necessary in making the express guarantees fully meaningful.

The foregoing cases suggest that specific guarantees in the Bill of Rights have penumbras, formed by emanations from those guarantees that help give them life and substance. . . . Various guarantees create zones of privacy. The right of association contained in the penumbra of the First Amendment is one, as we have seen. The Third Amendment in its prohibition against the quartering of soldiers "in any house" in time of peace without the consent of the owner is another facet of that privacy. The Fourth Amendment explicitly affirms the "right of the people to be secure in their persons, houses, papers, and effects, against unreasonable searches and seizures." The Fifth Amendment in its Self-Incrimination Clause enables the citizen to create a zone of privacy which government may not force him to surrender to his detriment. The Ninth Amendment provides: "The enumeration in the Constitution, of certain rights, shall not be construed to deny or disparage others retained by the people." . . .

The present case, then, concerns a relationship lying within the zone of privacy created by several fundamental constitutional guarantees. And it concerns a law which, in forbidding the *use* of contraceptives rather than regulating their manufacture or sale, seeks to achieve its goals by means having a maximum destructive impact upon that relationship. Such a law cannot stand in light of the familiar principle, so often applied by this Court, that a "governmental purpose to control or prevent activities constitutionally subject to state regulation may not be achieved by means which sweep unnecessarily broadly and thereby invade the area of protected freedoms." *NAACP* v. *Alabama* [1964]. . . . Would we allow the police to search the sacred precincts of marital bedrooms for telltale signs of the use of contraceptives? The very idea is repulsive to the notions of privacy surrounding the marriage relationship.

We deal with a right of privacy older than the Bill of Rights—older than our political parties, older than our school system. Marriage is a coming together for better or for worse, hopefully enduring, and intimate to the degree of being sacred. It is an association that promotes a way of life, not causes; a harmony in living, not political faiths; a bilateral loyalty, not commercial or social projects. Yet it is an association for as noble a purpose as any involved in our prior decisions.

Reversed.

MR. JUSTICE GOLDBERG, whom the CHIEF JUSTICE and MR. JUSTICE BRENNAN join, concurring:

While this Court has had little occasion to interpret the Ninth Amendment, "[i]t cannot be presumed that any clause in the Constitution is intended to be without effect." *Marbury* v. *Madison*. . . . To hold that a right so basic and fundamental and so deep-rooted in our society as the right of privacy in marriage may be infringed because that right is not guaranteed in so many words by the first eight amendments to the Constitution is to ignore the Ninth Amendment and to give it no effect whatsoever. Moreover, a judicial construction that this fundamental right is not protected by the Constitution because it is not mentioned in explicit terms by one of the first eight amendments or elsewhere in the Constitution would violate the Ninth Amendment, which specifically states that "[t]he enumeration in the Constitution, of certain rights, shall not be *construed* to deny or disparage others retained by the people." (Emphasis added.)

. . . I do not take the position of my

Brother Black ... that the entire Bill of Rights is incorporated in the Fourteenth Amendment, and I do not mean to imply that the Ninth Amendment is applied against the States by the Fourteenth. Nor do I mean to state that the Ninth Amendment constitutes an independent source of rights protected from infringement by either the States or the Federal Government. Rather, the Ninth Amendment shows a belief of the Constitution's authors that fundamental rights exist that are not expressly enumerated in the first eight amendments and an intent that the list of rights included there not be deemed exhaustive. ...

... In sum, the Ninth Amendment simply lends strong support to the view that the "liberty" protected by the Fifth and Fourteenth Amendments from infringement by the Federal Government or the States is not restricted to rights specifically mentioned in the first eight amendments. ...

MR. JUSTICE HARLAN, concurring in the judgment:

I fully agree with the judgment of reversal, but find myself unable to join the Court's opinion. The reason is that it seems to me to evince an approach to this case very much like that taken by my Brothers Black and Stewart in dissent, namely: the Due Process Clause of the Fourteenth Amendment does not touch this Connecticut statute unless the enactment is found to violate some right assured by the letter or penumbra of the Bill of Rights.

In other words, what I find implicit in the Court's opinion is that the "incorporation" doctrine may be used to *restrict* the reach of Fourteenth Amendment Due Process. For me this is just as unacceptable constitutional doctrine as is the use of the "incorporation" approach to *impose* upon the States all the requirements of the Bill of Rights as found in the provisions of the first eight amendments and in the decisions of this Court interpreting them. ...

In my view, the proper constitutional inquiry in this case is whether this Connecticut statute infringes the Due Process Clause of the Fourteenth Amendment because the enactment violates basic values "implicit in the concept of ordered liberty," *Palko* v. *Connecticut* [1937]. ...

MR. JUSTICE BLACK, with whom MR. JUSTICE STEWART joins, dissenting:

The Court talks about a constitutional "right of privacy" as though there is some constitutional provision or provisions forbidding any law ever to be passed which might abridge the "privacy" of individuals. But there is not. There are, of course, guarantees in certain specific constitutional provisions which are designed in part to protect privacy at certain times and places with respect to certain activities. Such, for example, is the Fourth Amendment's guarantee against "unreasonable searches and seizures." But I think it belittles that Amendment to talk about it as though it protects nothing but "privacy." To treat it that way is to give it a niggardly interpretation, not the kind of liberal reading I think any Bill of Rights provision should be given. The average man would very likely not have his feelings soothed any more by having his property seized openly than by having it seized privately and by stealth. He simply wants his property left alone. And a person can be just as much, if not more, irritated, annoyed and injured by an unceremonious public arrest by a policeman as he is by a seizure in the privacy of his office or home.

One of the most effective ways of diluting or expanding a constitutionally guaranteed right is to substitute for the crucial word or words of a constitutional guarantee another word or words more or less flexible and more or less restricted in meaning. This fact is well illustrated by the use of the term "right of privacy" as a comprehensive substitute for the Fourth Amendment's guarantee against "unreasonable searches and seizures." "Privacy" is a broad, abstract and ambiguous concept which can easily be shrunken in meaning but which can also, on the other hand, easily be interpreted as a constitutional ban against many things other than searches and seizures. I have expressed the view many times that First Amendment freedoms, for example, have suffered from a failure of the courts to stick to the simple language of the First Amendment in construing it, instead of invoking multitudes of words substituted for those the Framers used. . . .

I realize that many good and able men have eloquently spoken and written, sometimes in rhapsodical strains, about the duty of this Court to keep the Constitution in tune with the times. The idea is that the Constitution must be changed from time to time and that this Court is charged with a duty to make those changes. For myself, I must with all deference reject that philosophy. The Constitution makers knew the need for change and

provided for it. Amendments suggested by the people's elected representatives can be submitted to the people or their selected agents for ratification. That method of change was good for our Fathers, and being somewhat old-fashioned I must add it is good enough for me. And so, I cannot rely on the Due Process Clause or the Ninth Amendment or any mysterious and uncertain natural law concept as a reason for striking down this state law. The Due Process Clause with an "arbitrary and capricious" or "shocking to the conscience" formula was liberally used by this Court to strike down economic legislation in the early decades of this century, threatening, many people thought, the tranquility and stability of the Nation. See, e. g., *Lochner* v. *New York* [1905]. . . . That formula, based on subjective considerations of "natural justice," is no less dangerous when used to enforce this Court's views about personal rights than those about economic rights. I had thought that we had laid that formula, as a means for striking down state legislation, to rest once and for all in cases like *West Coast Hotel Co.* v. *Parrish* [1937]. . . .

MR. JUSTICE STEWART wrote a dissenting opinion, joined by MR. JUSTICE BLACK.

Does Justice Douglas's opinion for the Court adopt, as Black charges in his dissent, the subjective substantive due process method of *Lochner* v. *New York*?

On what basis does Justice Goldberg argue that the protections afforded by the Bill of Rights go beyond those specifically enumerated? Why is Justice Harlan unable to join the Court's opinion? Does Justice Black, in his dissent, agree with Harlan's view of the majority opinion? What does Black conclude will be the effect of the reasoning of the Court on its future role in the protection of civil liberties and rights?

The following case involved a challenge to the Texas abortion laws, which made it a crime to procure an abortion except "by medical advice for the purpose of saving the life of the mother." Does the Court use the method of substantive due process review to decide the case?

Roe v. Wade

410 U.S. 113; 93 S. Ct. 705; 35 L. Ed. 2d 147 (1973)

MR. JUSTICE BLACKMUN delivered the opinion of the Court:

V

The principal thrust of appellant's attack on the Texas statutes is that they improperly invade a right, said to be possessed by the pregnant woman, to choose to terminate her pregnancy. Appellant would discover this right in the concept of personal "liberty" embodied in the Fourteenth Amendment's Due Process Clause; or in personal, marital, familial, and sexual privacy said to be protected by the Bill of Rights or its penumbras, see *Griswold* v. *Connecticut* [1965] . . . *Eisenstadt* v. *Baird* [1972] . . . (White, J., concurring in result); or among those rights reserved to the people by the Ninth Amendment, *Griswold* v. *Connecticut*, . . . (Goldberg, J., concurring). Before addressing this claim, we feel it desirable briefly to survey, in several aspects, the history of abortion, for such insight as that history may afford us, and then to examine the state purposes and interests behind the criminal abortion laws.

VI

It perhaps is not generally appreciated that the restrictive criminal abortion laws in effect in a majority of States today are of relatively recent vintage. Those laws, generally proscribing abortion or its attempt at any time during pregnancy except when necessary to preserve the pregnant woman's life, are not of ancient or even of common-law origin. Instead, they derive from statutory changes effected, for the most part, in the latter half of the 19th century. . . .

VII

Three reasons have been advanced to explain historically the enactment of criminal abortion laws in the 19th century and to justify their continued existence.

It has been argued occasionally that these laws were the product of a Victorian social concern to discourage illicit sexual conduct. Texas, however, does not advance this justification in the present case, and it appears that no court or commentator has taken the argument seriously. The appellants and amici contend, moreover, that this is not a proper state purpose at all and suggest that, if it were, the Texas statutes are overbroad in protecting it since the law fails to distinguish between married and unwed mothers.

A second reason is concerned with abortion as a medical procedure. When most criminal abortion laws were first enacted, the procedure was a hazardous one for the woman. This was particularly true prior to the development of antisepsis. Antiseptic techniques, of course, were based on discoveries by Lister, Pasteur, and others first announced in 1867, but were not generally accepted and employed until about the turn of the century. Abortion mortality was high. Even after 1900, and perhaps until as late as the development of antibiotics in the 1940's, standard modern techniques such as dilation and curettage were not nearly so safe as they are today. Thus, it has been argued that a State's real concern in enacting a criminal abortion law was to protect the pregnant woman, that is, to restrain her from submitting to a procedure that placed her life in serious jeopardy.

Modern medical techniques have altered this situation. Appellants and various amici refer to medical data indicating that abortion in early pregnancy, this is, prior to the end of the first trimester, although not without its risk, is now relatively safe. Mortality rates for women undergoing early abortions, where the procedure is legal, appear to be as low as or lower than the rates for normal childbirth. Consequently, any interest of the State in protecting the woman from an inherently hazardous procedure, except when it would be equally dangerous for her to forgo it, has largely disappeared. Of course, important state interests in the area of health and medical standards do remain.

The State has a legitimate interest in seeing to it that abortion, like any other medical procedure, is performed under circumstances that insure maximum safety for the patient. This interest obviously extends at least to the performing physician and his staff, to the facilities involved, to the availability of aftercare, and to adequate provision for any complication or emergency that might arise. The prevalence of high mortality rates at illegal "abortion mills" strengthens, rather than weakens, the State's interest in regulating the conditions under which abortions are performed. Moreover, the risk to the woman increases as her pregnancy continues. Thus, the State retains a definite interest in protecting the woman's own health and safety when an abortion is proposed at a late stage of pregnancy.

The third reason is the State's interest—some phrase it in terms of duty—in protecting prenatal life. Some of the argument for this justification rests on the theory that a new human life is present from the moment of conception. The State's interest and general obligation to protect life then extends, it is argued, to prenatal life. Only when the life of the pregnant mother herself is at stake, balanced against the life she carries within her, should the interest of the embryo or fetus not prevail. Logically, of course, a legitimate state interest in this area need not stand or fall on acceptance of the belief that life begins at conception or at some other point prior to live birth. In assessing the State's interest, recognition may be given to the less rigid claim that as long as at least *potential* life is involved, the State may assert interests beyond the protection of the pregnant woman alone.

Parties challenging state abortion laws have sharply disputed in some courts the contention that a purpose of these laws, when enacted, was to protect prenatal life. . . .

It is with these interests, and the weight to be attached to them, that this case is concerned.

VIII

The Constitution does not explicitly mention any right of privacy. In a line of decisions, however, going back perhaps as far as *Union Pacific R. Co.* v. *Botsford* [1891] . . . , the Court has recognized that a right of personal privacy, or a guarantee of certain areas or zones of privacy, does exist under the Constitution. In varying contexts, the Court or individual Justices have, indeed, found at least the roots of that right in the First Amendment, *Stanley* v. *Georgia* [1969] . . . ; in the Fourth and Fifth Amendments, *Terry* v. *Ohio* [1968] . . . , *Katz* v. *United States* [1967] . . . ; in the penumbras of the Bill of Rights, *Griswold* v. *Connecticut* [1965] . . . ; in the Ninth Amendment, id., at 486, . . . (Goldberg, J., concurring); or in the concept of liberty guaranteed by the first section of the Fourteenth Amendment, see *Meyer* v. *Nebraska* [1923]. . . . These decisions make it clear that only personal rights that can be deemed "fundamental" or "implicit in the concept of ordered liberty," *Palko* v. *Connecticut* [1937] . . . , are included in this guarantee of personal privacy. They also make it clear that the right has some extension to activities relating to marriage, *Loving* v. *Virginia* [1967] . . . ; procreation, *Skinner* v. *Oklahoma* [1942] . . . ; contraception, *Eisenstadt* v. *Baird* [1972]. . . .

This right of privacy, whether it be founded in the Fourteenth Amendment's concept of personal liberty and restrictions upon state action, as we feel it is, or, as the District Court determined, in the Ninth Amendment's reservation of rights to the people, is broad enough to encompass a woman's decision whether or not to terminate her pregnancy. The detriment that the State would impose upon the pregnant woman by denying this choice altogether is apparent. Specific and direct harm medically diagnosable even in early pregnancy may be involved. Maternity, or additional offspring, may force upon the woman a distressful life and future. Psychological harm may be imminent. Mental and physical health may be taxed by child care. There is also the distress, for all concerned, associated with the unwanted child, and there is the problem of bringing a child into a family already unable, psychologically and otherwise, to care for it. In other cases, as in this one, the additional difficulties and continuing stigma of unwed motherhood may be involved. All these are factors the woman and her responsible physician necessarily will consider in consultation.

On the basis of elements such as these, appellant and some amici argue that the woman's right is absolute and that she is entitled to terminate her pregnancy at whatever time, in whatever way, and for whatever reason she alone chooses. With this we do not agree. Appellant's arguments that Texas either has no valid interest at all in regulating the abortion de-

cision, or no interest strong enough to support any limitation upon the woman's sole determination, is unpersuasive. The Court's decisions recognizing a right of privacy also acknowledge that some state regulation in areas protected by that right is appropriate. As noted above, a State may properly assert important interests in safeguarding health, in maintaining medical standards, and in protecting potential life. At some point in pregnancy, these respective interests become sufficiently compelling to sustain regulation of the factors that govern the abortion decision. The privacy right involved, therefore, cannot be said to be absolute. In fact, it is not clear to us that the claim asserted by some amici that one has an unlimited right to do with one's body as one pleases bears a close relationship to the right of privacy previously articulated in the Court's decisions. The Court has refused to recognize an unlimited right of this kind in the past. *Jacobson* v. *Massachusetts* [1905] . . . (vaccination); *Buck* v. *Bell* [1927] . . . (sterilization).

We, therefore, conclude that the right of personal privacy includes the abortion decision, but that this right is not unqualified and must be considered against important state interests in regulation.

Where certain "fundamental rights" are involved, the Court has held that regulation limiting these rights may be justified only by a "compelling state interest," . . . and that legislative enactments must be narrowly drawn to express only the legitimate state interests at stake. . . .

IX

The District Court held that the appellee failed to meet his burden of demonstrating that the Texas statute's infringement upon Roe's rights was necessary to support a compelling state interest. . . . Appellee argues that the State's determination to recognize and protect prenatal life from and after conception constitutes a compelling state interest. As noted above, we do not agree fully with either formulation.

A. The appellee and certain amici argue that the fetus is a "person" within the language and meaning of the Fourteenth Amendment. In support of this, they outline at length and in detail the well-known facts of fetal development. If this suggestion of personhood is established, the appellant's case, of course, collapses, for the fetus' right to life is then guaranteed specifically by the Amendment. The appellant conceded as much on reargument. On the other hand, the appellee conceded on reargument that no case could be cited that holds that a fetus is a person within the meaning of the Fourteenth Amendment.

The Constitution does not define "person" in so many words. Section 1 of the Fourteenth Amendment contains three references to "person." The first, in defining "citizens," speaks of "persons born or naturalized in the United States." The word also appears both in the Due Process Clause and in the Equal Protection Clause. "Person" is used in other places in the Constitution. . . . But in nearly all these instances, the use of the word is such that it has application only postnatally. None indicates, with any assurance, that it has any possible prenatal application.

All this, together with our observation, supra, that throughout the major portion of the 19th century prevailing legal abortion practices were far freer than they are today, persuades us that the word "person," as used in the Fourteenth Amendment, does not include the unborn. . . .

B. The pregnant woman cannot be isolated in her privacy. She carries an embryo and, later, a fetus, if one accepts the medical definitions of the developing young in the human uterus. . . . The situation therefore is inherently different from marital intimacy, or bedroom possession of obscene material, or marriage, or procreation, or education, with which *Eisenstadt, Griswold, Stanley, Loving, Skinner, Pierce,* and *Meyer* were respectively concerned. As we have intimated above, it is reasonable and appropriate for a State to decide that at some point in time another interest, that of health of the mother or that of potential human life, becomes significantly involved. The woman's privacy is no longer sole and any right of privacy she possesses must be measured accordingly.

Texas urges that, apart from the Fourteenth Amendment, life begins at conception and is present throughout pregnancy, and that, therefore, the State has a compelling interest in protecting that life from and after conception. We need not resolve the difficult question of when life begins. When those trained in the respective disciplines of medicine, philosophy, and theology are unable to arrive at any consensus, the judiciary, at this point in the development of man's knowledge, is not in a position to speculate as to the answer.

It should be sufficient to note briefly the wide divergence of thinking on this most sensitive and difficult question. . . .

X

In view of all this, we do not agree that, by adopting one theory of life, Texas may override the rights of the pregnant woman that are at stake. We repeat, however, that the State does have an important and legitimate interest in preserving and protecting the health of the pregnant woman, whether she be a resident of the State or a nonresident who seeks medical consultation and treatment there, and that it has still *another* important and legitimate interest in protecting the potentiality of human life. These interests are separate and distinct. Each grows in substantiality as the woman approaches term and, at a point during pregnancy, each becomes "compelling."

With respect to the State's important and legitimate interest in the health of the mother, the "compelling" point, in the light of present medical knowledge, is at approximately the end of the first trimester. This is so because of the now-established medical fact, referred to above . . . that until the end of the first trimester mortality in abortion may be less than mortality in normal childbirth. It follows that, from and after this point, a State may regulate the abortion procedure to the extent that the regulation reasonably relates to the preservation and protection of maternal health. Examples of permissible state regulation in this area are requirements as to the qualifications of the person who is to perform the abortion; as to the licensure of that person; as to the facility in which the procedure is to be performed, that is, whether it must be a hospital or may be a clinic or some other place of less-than-hospital status; as to the licensing of the facility; and the like.

This means, on the other hand, that, for the period of pregnancy prior to this "compelling" point, the attending physician, in consultation with his patient, is free to determine, without regulation by the State, that, in his medical judgment, the patient's pregnancy should be terminated. If that decision is reached, the judgment may be effectuated by an abortion free of interference by the State.

With respect to the State's important and legitimate interest in potential life, the "compelling" point is at viability. This is so because the fetus then presumably has the capability of meaningful life outside the mother's womb. State regulation protective of fetal life after viability thus has both logical and biological justifications. If the State is interested in protecting fetal life after viability, it may go so far as to proscribe abortion during that period, except when it is necessary to preserve the life or health of the mother.

Measured against these standards, Art 1196 of the Texas Penal Code, in restricting legal abortions to those "procured or attempted by medical advice for the purpose of saving the life of the mother," sweeps too broadly. The statute makes no distinction between abortions performed early in pregnancy and those performed later, and it limits to a single reason, "saving" the mother's life, the legal justification for the procedure. The statute, therefore, cannot survive the constitutional attack made upon it here. . . .

XI

To summarize and to repeat:

1. A state criminal abortion statute of the current Texas type, that excepts from criminality only a *lifesaving* procedure on behalf of the mother, without regard to pregnancy stage and without recognition of the other interests involved, is violative of the Due Process Clause of the Fourteenth Amendment.

(a) For the stage prior to approximately the end of the first trimester, the abortion decision and its effectuation must be left to the medical judgment of the pregnant woman's attending physician.

(b) For the stage subsequent to approximately the end of the first trimester, the State, in promoting its interest in the health of the mother, may, if it chooses, regulate the abortion procedure in ways that are reasonably related to maternal health.

(c) For the stage subsequent to viability, the State in promoting its interest in the potentiality of human life may, if it chooses, regulate, and even proscribe, abortion except where it is necessary, in appropriate medical judgment, for the preservation of the life or health of the mother.

2. The State may define the term "physician," as it has been employed in the preceding numbered paragraphs of this Part XI of this opinion, to mean only a physician currently licensed by the State, and may proscribe any abortion by a person who is not a physician as so defined.

In *Doe* v. *Bolton* [1973] . . . procedural requirements contained in one of the modern abortion statutes are considered. That opinion and this one, of course, are to be read together. . . .

MR. CHIEF JUSTICE BURGER concurred.

MR. JUSTICE DOUGLAS concurred.

MR. JUSTICE STEWART, concurring:
In 1963, this Court, in *Ferguson* v. *Skrupa*, . . . purported to sound the death knell for the doctrine of substantive due process, a doctrine under which many state laws had in the past been held to violate the Fourteenth Amendment. As Mr. Justice Black's opinion for the Court in *Skrupa* put it: "We have returned to the original constitutional proposition that courts do not substitute their social and economic beliefs for the judgment of legislative bodies, who are elected to pass laws.". . .

Barely two years later, in *Griswold* v. *Connecticut*, . . . the Court held a Connecticut birth control law unconstitutional. In view of what had been so recently said in *Skrupa*, the Court's opinion in *Griswold* understandably did its best to avoid reliance on the Due Process Clause of the Fourteenth Amendment as the ground for decision. Yet, the Connecticut law did not violate any provision of the Bill of Rights, nor any other specific provision of the Constitution. So it was clear to me then, and it is equally clear to me now, that the *Griswold* decision can be rationally understood only as a holding that the Connecticut statute substantively invaded the "liberty" that is protected by the Due

Process Clause of the Fourteenth Amendment. As so understood, *Griswold* stands as one in a long line of pre-*Skrupa* cases decided under the doctrine of substantive due process, and I now accept it as such.

"In a Constitution for a free people, there can be no doubt that the meaning of 'liberty' must be broad indeed." . . . The Constitution nowhere mentions a specific right of personal choice in matters of marriage and family life, but the "liberty" protected by the Due Process Clause of the Fourteenth Amendment covers more than those freedoms explicitly named in the Bill of Rights. . . .

Several decisions of this Court make clear that freedom of personal choice in matters of marriage and family life is one of the liberties protected by the Due Process Clause of the Fourteenth Amendment. *Loving* v. *Virginia*, . . . *Griswold* v. *Connecticut*. . . . In *Eisenstadt* v. *Baird*, . . . we recognized "the right of the *individual*, married or single, to be free from unwarranted governmental intrusion into matters so fundamentally affecting a person as the decision whether to bear or beget a child." That right necessarily includes the right of a woman to decide whether or not to terminate her pregnancy. "Certainly the interests of a woman in giving of her physical and emotional self during pregnancy and the interests that will be affected throughout her life by the birth and raising of a child are of a far greater degree of significance and personal intimacy than the right to send a child to private school protected in *Pierce* v. *Society of Sisters* [1925] . . . , or the right to teach a foreign language protected in *Meyer* v. *Nebraska*. . . ."

MR. JUSTICE REHNQUIST, dissenting:
. . . I have difficulty in concluding, as the Court does, that the right of "privacy" is involved in this case. Texas, by the statute here challenged, bars the performance of a medical abortion by a licensed

physician on a plaintiff such as Roe. A transaction resulting in an operation such as this is not "private" in the ordinary usage of that word. . . .

If the Court means by the term "privacy" no more than that the claim of a person to be free from unwanted state regulation of consensual transactions may be a form of "liberty" protected by the Fourteenth Amendment, there is no doubt that similar claims have been upheld in our earlier decisions on the basis of that liberty. I agree with the statement of Mr. Justice Stewart in his concurring opinion that the "liberty," against deprivation of which without due process the Fourteenth Amendment protects, embraces more than the rights found in the Bill of Rights. But that liberty is not guaranteed absolutely against deprivation, only against deprivation without due process of law. The test traditionally applied in the area of social and economic legislation is whether or not a law such as that challenged has a rational relation to a valid state objective. . . . But the Court's sweeping invalidation of any restrictions on abortion during the first trimester is impossible to justify under that standard, and the conscious weighing of competing factors that the Court's opinion apparently substitutes for the established test is far more appropriate to a legislative judgment than to a judicial one.

The Court eschews the history of the Fourteenth Amendment in its reliance on the "compelling state interest" test. . . . But the Court adds a new wrinkle to this test by transposing it from the legal considerations associated with the Equal Protection Clause of the Fourteenth Amendment to this case arising under the Due Process Clause of the Fourteenth Amendment. Unless I misapprehend the consequences of this transplanting of the "compelling state interest test," the Court's opinion will accomplish the seemingly impossible feat of leaving this area of the law more confused than it found it.

While the Court's opinion quotes from the dissent of Mr. Justice Holmes in *Lochner* v. *New York,* the result it reaches is more closely attuned to the majority opinion of Mr. Justice Peckham in that case. As in *Lochner* and similar cases applying substantive due process standards to economic and social welfare legislation, the adoption of the compelling state interest standard will inevitably require this Court to examine the legislative policies and pass on the wisdom of these policies in the very process of deciding whether a particular state interest put forward may or may not be "compelling." The decision here to break pregnancy into three distinct terms and to outline the permissible restrictions the State may impose in each one, for example, partakes more of judicial legislation than it does of a determination of the intent of the drafters of the Fourteenth Amendment.

The fact that a majority of the States reflecting, after all the majority sentiment in those States, have had restrictions on abortions for at least a century is a strong indication, it seems to me, that the asserted right to an abortion is not "so rooted in the traditions and conscience of our people as to be ranked as fundamental," *Snyder* v. *Massachusetts* [1934]. . . . Even today, when society's views on abortion are changing, the very existence of the debate is evidence that the "right" to an abortion is not so universally accepted as the appellant would have us believe.

To reach its result, the Court necessarily has had to find within the scope of the Fourteenth Amendment a right that was apparently completely unknown to the drafters of the Amendment. As early as 1821, the first state law dealing directly with abortion was enacted by the Connecticut Legislature. . . . By the time of the adoption of the Fourteenth Amendment in 1868, there were at least 36 laws enacted by state or territorial legislatures limiting abortion. While many States have amended or updated their laws, 21 of the laws on the books in 1868 remain in effect today. . . .

. . . The only conclusion possible from this history is that the drafters did not in-tend to have the Fourteenth Amendment withdraw from the States the power to legislate with respect to this matter. . . .

MR. JUSTICE WHITE, joined by MR. JUS-TICE REHNQUIST, dissented.

Is the right of privacy stated by the Court in *Roe* v. *Wade* based upon the same considerations as the right of privacy upheld in *Griswold* v. *Connecticut*? To what extent does the Court take into account historical considerations, the changing social environment, and contemporary medical practice? Could the *Roe* decision have been predicted from judicial precedents? The Court does not hold that the right to privacy is absolute. A "compelling" state interest may limit the right. How does the Court balance the interests of the state with the right of the individual to have an abortion?

Contrast Douglas's opinion in *Griswold* v. *Connecticut* with Blackmun's opinion in the *Roe* case. Is the *Lochner* approach rejected in each? Does the *Roe* opinion reflect more or less substantive due process review than *Griswold*?

Justice Rehnquist, in his dissent, argued against the compelling state in-terest standard adopted by the Court. What standard of judicial review would he substitute? In what way are considerations of federalism more im-portant to Rehnquist than to the majority? Is Rehnquist opposed to substan-tive due process review per se? Is he correct in stating that there is no dif-ference between the Court's opinion in *Roe* and in *Lochner*? Is the Court essentially legislating on the basis of subjectively determined standards rather than adjudicating on the basis of the application of recognized prin-ciples of law to the facts of the case?

NINE

Freedom of Expression

Justice Cardozo stated in *Palko* v. *Connecticut* that neither liberty nor justice would exist without freedom of thought and speech. He wrote: "Of that freedom one may say that it is the matrix, the indispensable condition, of nearly every other form of freedom. With rare aberrations a pervasive recognition of that truth can be traced in our history, political and legal." What was the nature of the "fundamental" right of freedom of speech and press in history?

The history of speech and press in England and colonial America before the nineteenth century was characterized more by government suppression than freedom. Laws of seditious libel in Great Britain and the colonies severely curtailed and usually prevented completely criticisms against the government. Summarizing the law of the press in England at the end of the eighteenth century, Blackstone commented: "The liberty of the press is indeed essential to the nature of a free state; but this consists in laying no *previous* restraints on publications, and not in freedom from censure for criminal matter when published. Every freeman has an undoubted right to lay what sentiments he pleases before the public; to forbid this is to destroy the freedom of the press: but if he publishes what is improper, mischievous, or illegal, he must take the consequences of his own temerity."[1] Before the Fox Libel Act was passed in England in 1792, defendants could be found guilty of sedition or defamation of character merely upon a jury finding that they had intentionally published a document deemed by the court to be seditious or defamatory. The 1792 act provided that verdicts of guilty or not guilty would be made by juries only upon consideration of the whole record. Freedom of speech and press, however, was scarcely protected by a law under which the charge of seditious libel could be upheld at the whim of a jury. A.V. Dicey wrote as late as 1914 that "freedom of discussion is, then, in Eng-

---

[1] *Blackstone, Commentaries*, Vol. 4, pp. 151–152.

land little else than the right to write or say anything which a jury, consisting of twelve shopkeepers, think it expedient should be said or written."[2]

Colonial America drew upon the traditions of England to suppress seditious libel as vigorously if not more so than was the practice in the mother country. Leonard W. Levy writes of the colonial period,

> Where vigorously expressed nonconformist opinions were suffered to exist by the community, they were likely to run afoul of the law. In colonial America, as in England, the common law of criminal libel was strung out like a chicken wire of constraint against the captious and the chancy, making the open discussion of public issues hazardous, if not impossible, except when public opinion opposed administration policy. . . .
>
> . . . [T]he law of seditious libel, particularly in the eighteenth century, was enforced in America chiefly by the provincial legislatures exercising their power of punishing alleged breaches of parliamentary privilege, secondly by the executive officers in concert with the upper houses, and lastly, a poor third, by the common law courts. The latter gathered a very few seditious scalps and lost as many to acquittals; but the Assemblies, like the House of Commons which they emulated, needing no grand jury to indict and no petty jury to convict, racked up a far larger score.
>
> Zealously pursuing its prerogative of being immune to criticism, an Assembly might summon, interrogate, and fix criminal penalties against anyone who had supposedly libeled its members, proceedings, or the government generally. Any words, written, printed, or spoken, which were imagined to have a tendency of impeaching an Assembly's behavior, questioning its authority, derogating from its honor, affronting its dignity, or defaming its members, individually or together, were regarded as a seditious scandal against the government, punishable as a breach of privilege. The historian of *Parliamentary Privilege in the American Colonies* concludes, in guarded understatement, "Literally scores of persons, probably hundreds, throughout the colonies were tracked down by the various messengers and sergeants and brought into the house to make inglorious submission for words spoken in the heat of anger or for writings which intentionally or otherwise had given offense."[3]

The practice of government suppression of speech and press in the eighteenth century meant that the First Amendment was not drafted nor adopted in an environment of freedom. While the Supreme Court in the twentieth century declared freedom of speech and press to be a fundamental and historical right which, as a minimum, must allow broad criticisms of the government,[4] this was not the case in 1791 when the First Amendment was adopted. The Constitution of 1787 did not include a single provision protecting the freedom of speech and press against governmental suppression. It seems unlikely that the proponents of the First Amendment sought to change drastically the statutory or common law of seditious libel. The amendment was more likely an affirmation of the generally accepted freedom of speech and press which existed at the time.

[2]A.V. Dicey, *Law of the Constitution*, 8th ed. (London: Macmillan and Co., 1915), p. 242.

[3]Leonard W. Levy, *Legacy of Suppression* (Cambridge, Mass.: Belknap Press of Harvard University Press, 1960), pp. 19–21.

[4]See Near v. Minnesota, pp. 659–666.

The Sedition Act of 1798

The Sedition Act of 1798 was based upon the English law of seditious libel. Section 2 of the Act provided,

> . . . if any person shall write, print, utter or publish, or shall cause to procure to be written, printed, uttered or published, or shall knowingly and willingly assist or aid in writing, printing, uttering or publishing any false, scandalous and malicious writing or writings against the government of the United States, or either House of the Congress of the United States, or the President of the United States, with intent to defame the said government, or either House of the said Congress, or the said President, or to bring them, or either of them into contempt or disrepute; or to excite against them, or either or any of them, the hatred of the good people of the United States, or to stir up sedition within the United States, or to excite any unlawful combinations therein, for opposing or resisting any law of the United States, or any act of the President of the United States, done in pursuance of any such law, or of the powers in him vested by the Constitution of the United States, or to resist, oppose, or defeat any such law or act, or to aid, encourage or abet any hostile designs of any foreign nation against the United States, their people or government, then such person, being thereof convicted before any court of the United States having jurisdiction thereof, shall be punished by a fine not exceeding $2,000, and by imprisonment not exceeding two years.[5]

The act was vigorously enforced by Federalist judges, including justices of the Supreme Court sitting as trial judges. The constitutionality of the statute never reached the Supreme Court because the Court did not have the jurisdiction to review criminal convictions.

The Sedition Act did not go as far in repressing speech and press as did the English common law, although it was consistent with the Fox Libel Act of 1792. Under the Sedition Act truth was a defense, malicious intent had to be proven, and the jury judged under these standards whether or not libel had been committed.

The Sedition Act was widely attacked by the Republicans who felt that it gave too much power to the Federalist-dominated courts to suppress political opposition. The Republicans did not, however, disagree with the principle that government had a right to punish libel but argued that this power was reserved to the states (where incidentally the Republicans exercised greater control over the courts). Jefferson, for example, attacked the "witch hunts" carried out under the act and declared the law unconstitutional under the First Amendment in the Kentucky Resolution which reaffirmed the principles of freedom of the person and of thought. When Jefferson became President his views on freedom of the press did not prevent him from recommending the selective prosecution under state law of Federalist newspapers. In 1803 he wrote to the Governor of Pennsylvania,

> The Federalists having failed in destroying the freedom of press by their gag law, seem to have attacked it in an opposite form, that is by pushing its licentiousness

---

[5]I Stat. 596 (1798).

and its lying to such a degree of prostitution as to deprive it of all credit. And the
fact is that so abandoned are the Tory presses in this particular that even the least
informed of the people have learnt that nothing in a newspaper is to be believed.
This is a dangerous state of things, and the press ought to be restored to its credibility if possible. The restraints provided by the laws of the states are sufficient
for this if applied. And I have therefore long thought that a few prosecutions of
the most prominent offenders would have a wholesome effect in restoring the integrity of the presses. Not a general prosecution, for that would look like persecution: but a selected one. . . . If the same thing be done in some other of the
states, it will place the whole band more on their guard.[6]

Although Jefferson supported prosecutions under state law to limit the
Federalist press, his views and actions in combination with those of Madison
in opposition to the Sedition Act reflected widespread support for freedom
of speech and press that would go beyond that permitted under common
law doctrine and English practice. While the Federalist-dominated Supreme
Court might have upheld the Sedition Act of 1798, it has been categorically
declared unconstitutional by a number of Supreme Court justices, including
Holmes, Brandeis, Jackson, and Douglas. In 1964 Justice Brennan expressed the unanimous views of the Court on the Sedition Act.

Although the Sedition Act was never tested in this Court, the attack upon its validity has carried the day in the court of history. Fines levied in its prosecution
were repaid by Act of Congress on the ground that it was unconstitutional . . .
Calhoun, reporting to the Senate on February 4, 1836, assumed that its invalidity
was a matter "which no one now doubts." . . . Jefferson, as President, pardoned
those who had been convicted and sentenced under the Act and remitted their
fines, stating: "I discharged every person under punishment or prosecution under
the sedition law, because I considered, and now consider, that law to be a nullity,
as absolute and as palpable as if Congress had ordered us to fall down and worship a golden image." Letter to Mrs. Adams, July 22, 1804, 4 Jefferson's Works
(Washington ed.) pp. 555–556. The invalidity of the Act has also been assumed
by Justices of this Court. See Holmes, J., dissenting and joined by Brandeis, J., in
Abrams v. *United States,* 250 U.S. 616, 630 [1919] . . . ; Jackson, J., dissenting in
Beauharnais v. *Illinois,* 343 U.S. 250, 288–289 [1952] . . . ; Douglas, *The Right of
the People* (1958), p. 47. See also Cooley, *Constitutional Limitations* (8th ed., Carring-
ton, 1927), pp. 899–900; Chafee, *Free Speech in the United States* (1942), pp. 27–28.
These views reflect a broad consensus that the Act, because of the restraint it im-
posed upon criticism of government and public officials, was inconsistent with the
First Amendment.

There is no force in respondent's argument that the constitutional limitations
implicit in the history of the Sedition Act apply only to Congress and not to the
states. It is true that the First Amendment was originally addressed only to action
by the Federal Government, and that Jefferson, for one, while denying the power
of Congress "to control the freedom of the press," recognized such a power in the
states. See the 1804 letter to Abigail Adams quoted in *Dennis* v. *United States,* 341
U.S. 494, 522, [1951] note 4. . . . But this distinction was eliminated with the

---

[6]Paul L. Ford, ed., *The Writings of Thomas Jefferson,* Vol. VIII (New York: G.P. Putnam's
Sons, 1897), pp. 218–219.

adoption of the Fourteenth Amendment and the application to the states of the First Amendment's restrictions.[7]

The expiration and ultimate rejection of the Sedition Act of 1798 did not end the controversy over the permissible limits of free speech and press. Before the Civil War attempts were made by national and state governments to curb the Abolitionist press. Some form of public control of speech and press was implemented by legislation in every Southern state except Kentucky. Abolitionist publishers in the North were often attacked by mobs, and these attacks were sometimes condoned by the authorities.

During the Civil War attempts were made to suppress the publication of newspapers critical of the government by barring them from the mails. Military authorities did not hesitate to arrest persons engaged in activities considered to be dangerous to the Union. There was no law passed during the Civil War equivalent to the Sedition Act. Suppression of speech and press occurred directly or indirectly under orders from the President carried out by his civilian subordinates and military commanders.

The Civil War was followed by a relatively tranquil period for freedom of speech and press, which was abruptly interrupted by the conflict that emerged over the rising labor movement as the century came to a close. The freedoms of speech, press, and association came under attack as national and state authorities sought to curb the "radical" and "anarchistic" advocates and organizers of labor unions. States began to pass *criminal anarchy* and *criminal syndicalism* laws in the first decades of the twentieth century that suppressed speech and press advocating the overthrow of the government or the industrial order by force and violence or illegal action to bring about political change. For the most part, however, these laws were not vigorously enforced and they had little effect upon speech and press.

THE DEVELOPMENT OF THE CLEAR AND PRESENT DANGER TEST

The Court ruled directly on the permissible scope of legislation suppressing freedom of speech and press in the following cases. They involved a challenge to the constitutionality of the Espionage Act of 1917, Title 1 of which provided that

> Whoever, when the United States is at war, shall willfully make or convey false reports or false statements with intent to interfere with the operation or success of the military or naval forces of the United States, or to promote the success of its enemies, and whoever, when the United States is at war, shall willfully cause or attempt to cause insubordination, disloyalty, mutiny, or refusal of duty, in the military or naval forces of the United States, or shall willfully obstruct the recruit-

[7]New York Times Company v. Sullivan, 376 U.S. 254, 276 (1964). While there were concurring opinions in this case, there was no disagreement with the view of the majority on the question of the constitutionality of the Sedition Act.

ing or enlistment service of the United States, to the injury of the service or of the United States, shall be punished by a fine of not more than $10,000 or imprisonment for not more than twenty years, or both.

Schenck and others were convicted after a jury trial of violating the provisions of Title 1 of the Espionage Act. The jury found that it was reasonable to anticipate that the circulars distributed by Schenck would persuade draftees to refuse induction.

Schenck v. United States

249 U.S. 47; 39 S. Ct. 247; 63 L. Ed. 470 (1919)

MR. JUSTICE HOLMES delivered the opinion of the Court:

This is an indictment in three counts. The first charges a conspiracy to violate the Espionage Act of June 15, 1917, . . . by causing and attempting to cause insubordination, &c., in the military and naval forces of the United States, and to obstruct the recruiting and enlistment service of the United States, when the United States was at war with the German Empire, to-wit, that the defendant willfully conspired to have printed and circulated to men who had been called and accepted for military service under the Act of May 18, 1917 . . . a document set forth and alleged to be calculated to cause such insubordination and obstruction. The count alleges overt acts in pursuance of the conspiracy, ending in the distribution of the document set forth. The second count alleges a conspiracy to commit an offense against the United States, to-wit, to use the mails for the transmission of matter declared to be non-mailable by title 12, § 2, of the Act of June 15, 1917 . . . , to-wit, the above mentioned document, with an averment of the same overt acts. The third count charges an unlawful use of the mails for the transmission of the same matter and otherwise as above. The defendants were found guilty on all the counts. They set up the First Amendment to the Constitution forbidding Congress to make any law abridging the freedom of speech, or of the press, and bringing the case here on that ground have argued some other points also. . . .

The document in question upon its first printed side recited the first section of the Thirteenth Amendment, said that the idea embodied in it was violated by the conscription act and that a conscript is little better than a convict. In impassioned language it intimated that conscription was despotism in its worst form and a monstrous wrong against humanity in the interest of Wall Street's chosen few. It said, "Do not submit to intimidation," but in form at least confined itself to peaceful measures such as a petition for the repeal of the act. The other and later printed side of the sheet was headed "Assert Your Rights." It stated reasons for alleging that any one violated the Constitution when he refused to recognize "your right to assert your opposition to the draft," and went on, "If you do not assert and support your rights, you are helping to deny or disparage rights which it is the solemn duty of all citizens and residents of the United States to retain." It described the arguments on the other side as coming from cunning politicians and a mercenary capitalist press, and even silent consent to the conscription law as helping to support an infamous conspiracy. It denied the power to send our citizens away to foreign shores to shoot up the people of other lands, and added that words could not express the condemnation such cold-blooded ruthlessness deserves, &c., &c., winding up, "You must do your share to maintain, support and uphold the rights of the people of this country." Of course the document would not have been sent unless it had been intended to have some effect, and we do not see what effect it could be expected to have upon persons subject to the draft except to influence them to obstruct the carrying of it out. The defendants do not deny that the jury might find against them on this point.

But it is said, suppose that that was the tendency of this circular, it is protected by the First Amendment to the Constitution. Two of the strongest expressions are said to be quoted respectively from well-known public men. It well may be that the prohibition of laws abridging the freedom of speech is not confined to previous restraints, although to prevent them may have been the main purpose, as intimated in *Patterson* v. *Colorado* [1907]. . . . We admit that in many places and in ordinary times the defendants in saying all that was said in the circular would have been within their constitutional rights. But the character of every act depends upon the circumstances in which it is done. . . . The most stringent protection of free speech would not protect a man in falsely shouting fire in a theatre and causing a panic. It does not even protect a man from an injunction against uttering words that may have all the effect of force. *Gompers* v. *Buck's Stove & Range Co.* [1911]. . . . The question in every case is whether the words used are used in such circumstances and are of such a nature as to create a clear and present danger that they will bring about the substantive evils that Congress has a right to prevent. It is a question of proximity and degree. When a nation is at war many things that might be said in time of peace are such a hindrance to its effort that their utterance will not be endured so long as men fight and that no Court could regard them as protected by any constitutional right. It seems to be admitted that if an actual obstruction of the recruiting service were provided, liability for words that produced that effect might be enforced. The statute of 1917 in section 4 . . . punishes conspiracies to obstruct as well as actual obstruction. If the act, (speaking, or circulating a paper) its tendency and the intent with which it is done are the same, we perceive no ground for saying that success alone warrants making the act a crime.

Judgments affirmed.

Justice Holmes delivered the opinion in the following case a week after the *Schenck* decision. Eugene Debs was the Socialist candidate for President in 1920. During the course of his campaign he made an antiwar speech for which he was indicted and convicted after a jury trial of violating the Espionage Act. The jury found that the effect and intent of the speech was to obstruct recruiting and to cause insubordination in the armed forces.

Debs v. *United States*

249 U.S. 211; 39 S. Ct. 252; 63 L. Ed. 566 (1919)

MR. JUSTICE HOLMES delivered the opinion of the Court:

This is an indictment under the Espionage Act of June 15, 1917. . . . It has been cut down to two counts, originally the third and fourth. The former of these alleges that on or about June 16, 1918, at Canton, Ohio, the defendant caused and incited and attempted to cause and incite insubordination, disloyalty, mutiny and refusal of duty in the military and naval forces of the United States and with intent so to do delivered, to an assembly of people, a public speech, set forth. The fourth count alleges that he obstructed and attempted to obstruct the recruiting and enlistment service of the United States and to that end and with that intent delivered the same speech, again set forth. There was a demurrer to that indictment on the ground that the statute is unconstitutional as to interfering with free speech, contrary to the First Amendment, and to the several counts as insufficiently stating the supposed offence. This was overruled, subject to exception. There were other exceptions to the admission of evidence with which we shall deal. The defendant was found guilty and was sentenced to ten years' imprisonment on each of the two counts, the punishment to run concurrently on both.

The main theme of the speech was Socialism, its growth, and a prophecy of its ultimate success. With that we have nothing to do, but if a part or the manifest intent of the more general utterances was to encourage those present to obstruct the recruiting service and if in passages such encouragement was directly given, the immunity of the general theme may not be enough to protect the speech. The speaker began by saying that he had just returned from a visit to the workhouse in the neighborhood where three of their most loyal comrades were paying the penalty for their devotion to the working class— these being Wagenknecht, Baker and Ruthenberg, who had been convicted of aiding and abetting another in failing to register for the draft. *Ruthenberg* v. *United States* [1918]. . . . He said that he had to be

prudent and might not be able to say all that he thought, thus intimating to his hearers that they might infer that he meant more, but he did say that those persons were paying the penalty for standing erect and for seeking to pave the way to better conditions for all mankind. Later he added further eulogies and said that he was proud of them. He then expressed opposition to Prussian militarism in a way that naturally might have been thought to be intended to include the mode of proceeding in the United States. . . .

There followed personal experiences and illustrations of the growth of Socialism, a glorification of minorities, and a prophecy of the success of the international Socialist crusade, with the interjection that "you need to know that you are fit for something better than slavery and cannon fodder." The rest of the discourse had only the indirect though not necessarily ineffective bearing on the offences alleged that is to be found in the usual contrasts between capitalists and laboring men, sneers at the advice to cultivate war gardens, attribution to plutocrats of the high price of coal, &c., with the implication running through it all that the working men are not concerned in the war, and a final exhortation, "Don't worry about the charge of treason to your masters; but be concerned about the treason that involves yourselves." The defendant addressed the jury himself, and while contending that his speech did not warrant the charges said, "I have been accused of obstructing the war. I admit it. Gentlemen, I abhor war. I would oppose the war if I stood alone." The statement was not necessary to warrant the jury in finding that one purpose of the speech, whether incidental or not does not matter, was to oppose not only war in general but this war, and that the opposition was so expressed that its natural and intended effect would be to obstruct recruiting. If that was intended and if, in all the circumstances, that would be its probable effect, it would not be protected by reason of its being part of a general program and expressions of a general and conscientious belief.

The chief . . . [defense is] that based upon the First Amendment to the Constitution disposed of in *Schenck* v. *United States*. . . .

There was introduced [in evidence] an "Anti-War Proclamation and Program" adopted at St. Louis in April, 1917, coupled with testimony that about an hour before his speech the defendant had stated that he approved of that platform in spirit and in substance. . . . [H]is counsel . . . argued against its admissibility at some length. This document contained the usual suggestion that capitalism was the cause of the war and that our entrance into it "was instigated by the predatory capitalists in the United States." . . .

Its first recommendation was, "continuous, active, and public opposition to the war, through demonstrations, mass petitions, and all other means within our power." Evidence that the defendant accepted this view and this declaration of his duties at the time that he made his speech is evidence that if in that speech he used words tending to obstruct the recruiting service he meant that they should have that effect. The principle is too well established and too manifestly good sense

to need citation of the books. We should add that the jury were most carefully instructed that they could not find the defendant guilty for advocacy of any of his opinions unless the words used had as their natural tendency and reasonably probable effect to obstruct the recruiting service, &c., and unless the defendant had the specific intent to do so in his mind.

Without going into further particulars we are of opinion that the verdict on the fourth count, for obstructing and attempting to obstruct the recruiting service of the United States, must be sustained. Therefore it is less important to consider whether that upon the third count, for causing and attempting to cause insubordination, &c., in the military and naval forces, is equally impregnable. The jury were instructed that for the purposes of the statute the persons designated by the Act of May 18, 1917 . . . , registered and enrolled under it, and thus subject to be called into the active service, were part of the military forces of the United States. The Government presents a strong argument from the history of the statutes that the instruction was correct and in accordance with established legislative usage. We see no sufficient reason for differing from the conclusion but think it unnecessary to discuss the question in detail.

Judgment affirmed.

The clear and present danger test announced by Holmes in the *Schenck* case does not require proof of dangerous action or conduct to suppress speech and press, but only evidence from which a jury reasonably can conclude an intent and attempt to take illegal action. After summarizing the contents of the circular distributed by Schenck, Holmes stated that "the document would not have been sent unless it had been intended to have some effect, and we do not see what effect it could be expected to have upon persons subject to the draft except to influence them to obstruct the carrying of it out. The defendants do not deny that the jury might find against them on this point."

State Justice Holmes's clear and present danger doctrine in the express terms he used. What are the circumstances under which the doctrine may be invoked? What is the "nature" of the words that may be suppressed? What did Holmes mean when he referred to the "substantive evils that Congress has a right to prevent"? Must speech or press be successful in bringing about its intended illegal effect in order to be suppressed?

In the *Debs* case, Holmes wrote that the "main theme of the speech" that was challenged "was Socialism, its growth, and a prophecy of its ultimate success." The speech was followed by reminiscences of personal experiences and illustrations of the growth of Socialism, a glorification of minorities, and a prophecy of the success of the International Socialist Crusade, with the interjection that "you need to know that you are fit for something better than slavery and cannon fodder." How did Holmes apply the clear and present danger doctrine to the speech of Debs to uphold his conviction?

In *Frohwerk* v. *United States* (1919), Holmes again wrote the opinion for a unanimous Court sustaining a conviction under the Espionage Act of an employee of a German language newspaper for conspiring with his employer to print articles with an intent to obstruct recruiting. Holmes found that although there might be extenuating circumstances that would sustain the plaintiff's plea that his First Amendment rights had been violated, the incomplete record did not contain such evidence. Holmes stated: "We must take the case on the record as it is, and on the record it is impossible to say that it might not have been found that the circulation of the paper was in quarters where a little breath might be enough to kindle a flame and that the fact was known and relied upon by those who sent the paper out."[8]

Holmes's Refinement of the Clear and Present Danger Standard in his Dissent in Abrams

In *Abrams* v. *United States* (1919), the Court sustained the convictions of five Bolshevik sympathizers under the 1918 amendments to the Espionage Act which added a new series of offenses, including the urging of the curtailment of military production with intent to hinder the prosecution of the war with Germany.[9] Abrams and four defendants, Russian born and admitted anarchists and revolutionists, who had been living in the United States from five to ten years but who had not applied for naturalization, were convicted of violating these provisions of the law. They had printed and distributed 5,000 leaflets by throwing them from the window of a building in New York City. The leaflets attacked capitalism and United States intervention in the Russian revolution and urged a general strike to prevent military supplies from reaching anti-Soviet forces. Although the amendments to the Espionage Act under which the defendants were convicted proscribed actions impeding the war with Germany, the Supreme Court sustained the conviction by inferring that the defendants knew the general strike they urged

[8]Frohwerk v. United States, 249 U.S. 204, 209 (1919).

[9]The law was also amended to prohibit the publication during wartime of "disloyal, scurrilous and abusive language about the form of government of the United States, or language intended to bring the form of government of the United States into contempt, scorn, contumely and disrepute." In effect, this was a far-reaching sedition law.

would impede the war effort against Germany. The First Amendment challenge of the defendants was summarily dismissed by the Court on the basis of the *Schenck* decision. The Court found that the government had offered sufficient proof to sustain its charges against Abrams.

Justice Holmes's dissent in the *Abrams* case seemed to reinterpret the clear and present danger doctrine that he applied in *Schenck, Frohwerk,* and *Debs.* The language of the leaflets distributed by Abrams and his friends was certainly as extreme in criticizing the institutions of government and in exhorting action to impede the war effort as the language reviewed in the previous cases. And, the jury's verdict that the defendants were guilty was as reasonably based upon the evidence as the jury verdicts upheld by Holmes in the preceding decisions. Nevertheless, Holmes, while dissenting in *Abrams,* claimed that the Court had rightly decided the prior espionage cases. "I never have seen any reason to doubt that the questions of law that alone were before the Court in the cases [of Schenck, Frohwerk, and Debs] were rightly decided," wrote Holmes in his *Abrams* dissent. He continued: "I do not doubt for a moment that by the same reasoning that would justify punishing persuasion to murder, the United States constitutionally may punish speech that produces or is intended to produce a clear and imminent danger that it will bring about *forthwith* certain substantive evils that the United States constitutionally may seek to prevent. The power undoubtedly is greater in time of war than in time of peace because war opens dangers that do not exist in other times."[10]

What, then, persuaded Holmes that the *Abrams* case justified a different judgment? Did Holmes apply a different standard in *Abrams* than in the former cases? In his *Abrams* dissent, Holmes wrote that

> As against dangers peculiar to war as against others, the principle of the right to free speech is always the same. It is only the present danger of *immediate* evil or an *intent to bring it about* that warrants Congress in setting a limit to the expression of opinion where private rights are not concerned. Congress certainly cannot forbid all effort to change the mind of the country. Now nobody can suppose that the surreptitious publishing of a silly leaflet by an unknown man, without more, would present any immediate danger that its opinions would hinder the success of the government arms or have any appreciable tendency to do so. Publishing those opinions for the very purpose of obstructing however, might indicate a greater danger, and at any rate would have the quality of an attempt.[11]

Holmes did not find the requisite intent in the defendant's words to sustain the conviction. He noted: "It is evident from the beginning to the end that the only object of the paper is to help Russia and stop American intervention there against the popular government—not to impede the United States in the war that it was carrying on."[12] The defendants were convicted of conspiring to encourage resistance to the government in its war with Germany and to incite curtailment of production necessary for the prosecution of the war. With respect to the former charge, Holmes wrote: "Taking the

[10]Abrams v. United States, 250 U.S. 616, 628 (1919). (Emphasis supplied.)
[11]Ibid., p. 628. (Emphasis supplied.)
[12]Ibid., pp 628–629.

clause in the statute that deals with that [charge] in connection with the other elaborate provisions of the act, I think that resistance to the United States means some forceable act of opposition to some proceeding of the United States in pursuance of the war. I think the intent must be the specific intent that I have described and for the reasons that I have given I think that no such intent was proved or existed in fact."[13] To Holmes, the evidence clearly indicated an intent on the part of the defendants to interfere in the Russian revolution, but not in the war against Germany.

Was Holmes adopting a stricter and broader standard of judicial review in his *Abrams* dissent than in his previous opinions by refining his definition of clear and present danger and by his willingness to overturn the verdict of the jury?

During the course of his dissent Holmes stated his philosophy of free speech and press and his general interpretation of the First Amendment.

> Persecution for the expression of opinions seems to me perfectly logical. If you have no doubt of your premises or your power and want a certain result with all your heart, you naturally express your wishes in law and sweep away all opposition. To allow opposition by speech seems to indicate that you think the speech impotent, as when a man says that he has squared the circle, or that you do not care wholeheartedly for the result, or that you doubt either your power or your premises. But when men have realized that time has upset many fighting faiths, they may come to believe even more than they believe the very foundations of their own conduct that the ultimate good desired is better reached by free trade in ideas—that the best test of truth is the power of the thought to get itself accepted in the competition of the market, and that truth is the only ground upon which their wishes safely can be carried out. That at any rate is the theory of our Constitution. It is an experiment, as all life is an experiment. Every year if not every day we have to wager our salvation upon some prophecy based upon imperfect knowledge. While the experiment is part of our system I think that we should be eternally vigilant against attempts to check the expression of opinions that we loathe and believe to be fraught with death, unless they so imminently threaten immediate interference with the lawful and pressing purposes of the law that an immediate check is required to save the country. I wholly disagree with the argument of the government that the First Amendment left the common law as to seditious libel in force. History seems to me against the notion. I had conceived that the United States through many years had shown its repentence for the Sedition Act of 1798, by repaying fines that it imposed. Only the emergency that makes it immediately dangerous to leave the correction of evil counsels to time warrants making any exception to the sweeping command, "Congress shall make no law . . . abridging the freedom of speech."[14]

Holmes had ample opportunity to express and refine his views on freedom of speech and press not only in cases arising out of the 1917 Espionage Act and its 1918 amendments but in subsequent free speech and press challenges to government repression that occurred in other contexts in the decade following World War I. One such case was *Gitlow* v. *New York* (1925), which involved a constitutional challenge under the due process clause of

[13]Ibid., p. 629.
[14]Ibid., pp. 630–631.

the Fourteenth Amendment to the New York Criminal Anarchy Act, which punished the advocacy by speech or press of the doctrine that the government should be overthrown by force or violence. At the time the case was decided the due process clause of the Fourteenth Amendment had not been defined to include freedom of speech and press. Gitlow claimed that the liberty protected by the Fourteenth Amendment included the liberty of speech and press, and that the New York Law "unduly restrains liberty of expression. That liberty is not absolute. It may be restrained, however, only in circumstances where its exercise bears a causal relation with some substantive evil, consummated, attempted or likely . . . [and] the New York Criminal Anarchy law, as construed in this case, is inconsistent with this limitation, and far oversteps it. . . ."[15]

New York defended its statute and the action taken under it as a proper exercise of the police power. The state contended: "Criminal anarchy is a dangerous doctrine at any time. Its advocacy imperils the life of the state, no matter when it is made. The doctrine of criminal anarchy is so inherently dangerous that it is competent for the state to forbid the advocacy of that doctrine absolutely, without regard to whether there is imminent danger that the advocacy will result in the taking of actual steps to carry out what the doctrine advocates."[16]

Gitlow v. *New York*

268 U.S. 652; 45 S. Ct. 625; 69 L. Ed. 1138 (1925)

MR. JUSTICE SANFORD delivered the opinion of the Court:

Benjamin Gitlow was indicted in the Supreme Court of New York, with three others, for the statutory crime of criminal anarchy. . . .

The contention here is that the statute, by its terms and as applied in this case, is repugnant to the due process clause of the Fourteenth Amendment. Its material provisions are:

Sec. 160. *Criminal Anarchy Defined.* Criminal anarchy is the doctrine that organized government should be overthrown by force or violence, or by assassination of the executive head or of any of the executive officials of government, or by any unlawful means. The advocacy of such doctrine either by word of mouth or writing is a felony.

Sec. 161. *Advocacy of Criminal Anarchy.* Any

person who:

1. By word of mouth or writing advocates, advises or teaches the duty, necessity or propriety of overthrowing or overturning organized government by force or violence, or by assassination of the executive head or of any of the executive officials of government, or by any unlawful means; or,

2. Prints, publishes, edits, issues or knowingly circulates, sells, distributes or publicly displays any book, paper, document, or written or printed matter in any form, containing or advocating, advising or teaching the doctrine that organized government should be overthrown by force, violence or any unlawful means, . . .

"Is guilty of a felony and punishable" by imprisonment or fine, or both.

The indictment was in two counts. The first charged that the defendant had advocated, advised and taught the duty, ne-

[15]LB, Vol. 23, pp. 600, 602.
[16]Ibid., p. 709.

cessity and propriety of overthrowing and overturning organized government by force, violence and unlawful means, by certain writings therein set forth entitled "The Left Wing Manifesto"; the second that he had printed, published and knowingly circulated and distributed a certain paper called "The Revolutionary Age," containing the writings set forth in the first count advocating, advising and teaching the doctrine that organized government should be overthrown by force, violence and unlawful means. . . .

. . . It was admitted that the defendant signed a card subscribing to the Manifesto and Program of the Left Wing, which all applicants were required to sign before being admitted to membership; that he went to different parts of the State to speak to branches of the Socialist Party about the principles of the Left Wing and advocated their adoption; and that he was responsible for the Manifesto as it appeared, that "he knew of the publication, in a general way and he knew of its publication afterwards, and is responsible for the circulation."

There was no evidence of any effect resulting from the publication and circulation of the Manifesto.

No witnesses were offered in behalf of the defendant.

. . . [T]he Manifesto . . . set forth a review of the rise of Socialism, [and] it condemned the dominant "moderate Socialism" for its recognition of the necessity of the democratic parliamentary state; repudiated its policy of introducing Socialism by legislative measures; and advocated, in plain and unequivocal language, the necessity of accomplishing the "Communist Revolution" by a militant and "revolutionary Socialism," based on "the class struggle" and mobilizing the "power of the proletariat in action," through mass industrial revolts developing into mass political strikes and "revolutionary mass action," for the purpose of conquering and destroying the parliamentary state and es-

tablishing in its place, through a "revolutionary dictatorship of the proletariat," the system of Communist Socialism. The then recent strikes in Seattle and Winnipeg were cited as instances of a development already verging on revolutionary act and suggestive of proletarian dictatorship, in which the strikeworkers were "trying to usurp the functions of municipal government"; and revolutionary Socialism, it was urged, must use these mass industrial revolts to broaden the strike, make it general and militant, and develop it into mass political strikes and revolutionary mass action for the annihilation of the parliamentary state. . . .

. . . The sole contention here is, essentially, that as there was no evidence of any concrete result flowing from the publication of the Manifesto or of circumstances showing the likelihood of such result, the statute as construed and applied by the trial court penalizes the mere utterance, as such, of "doctrine" having no quality of incitement, without regard either to the circumstances of its utterance or to the likelihood of unlawful sequences; and that, as the exercise of the right of free expression with relation to government is only punishable "in circumstances involving likelihood of substantive evil," the statute contravenes the due process clause of the Fourteenth Amendment. The argument in support of this contention rests primarily upon the following propositions: 1st, That the "liberty" protected by the Fourteenth Amendment includes the liberty of speech and of the press; and 2d, That while liberty of expression "is not absolute," it may be restrained "only in circumstances where its exercise bears a causal relation with some substantive evil, consummated, attempted or likely," and as the statute "takes no account of circumstances," it unduly restrains this liberty and is therefore unconstitutional.

The precise question presented, and the only question which we can consider under this writ of error, then is, whether the statute, as construed and applied in this case by the State courts, deprived the defendant of his liberty of expression in violation of the due process clause of the Fourteenth Amendment.

The statute does not penalize the utterance or publication of abstract "doctrine" or academic discussion having no quality of incitement to any concrete action. It is not aimed against mere historical or philosophical essays. It does not restrain the advocacy of changes in the form of government by constitutional and lawful means. What it prohibits is language advocating, advising or teaching the overthrow of organized government by unlawful means. These words imply urging to action. Advocacy is defined in the Century Dictionary as: "1. The act of pleading for, supporting, or recommending; active espousal." It is not the abstract "doctrine" of overthrowing organized government by unlawful means which is denounced by the statute, but the advocacy of action for the accomplishment of that purpose. . . .

The Manifesto, plainly, is neither the statement of abstract doctrine nor, as suggested by counsel, mere prediction that industrial disturbances and revolutionary mass strikes will result spontaneously in an inevitable process of evolution in the economic system. It advocates and urges in fervent language mass action which shall progressively foment industrial disturbances and through political mass strikes and revolutionary mass action overthrow and destroy organized parliamentary government. It concludes with a call to action in these words:

The proletariat revolution and the Communist reconstruction of society—*the struggle for these*—is now indispensable. . . . The Communist International calls the proletariat of the world to the final struggle!

This is not the expression of philosophical abstraction, the mere prediction of future events; it is the language of direct incitement.

The means advocated for bringing about the destruction of organized parliamentary government, namely, mass industrial revolts usurping the functions of municipal government, political mass strikes directed against the parliamentary state, and revolutionary mass action for its final destruction, necessarily imply the use of force and violence, and in their essential nature are inherently unlawful in a constitutional government of law and order. That the jury were warranted in finding that the Manifesto advocated not merely the abstract doctrine of overthrowing organized government by force, violence and unlawful means, but action to that end, is clear.

For present purposes we may and do assume that freedom of speech and of the press—which are protected by the First Amendment from abridgment by Congress—are among the fundamental personal rights and "liberties" protected by the due process clause of the Fourteenth Amendment from impairment by the States. . . .

It is a fundamental principle, long established, that the freedom of speech and of the press which is secured by the Constitution, does not confer an absolute right to speak or publish, without responsibility, whatever one may choose, or an unrestricted and unbridled license that gives immunity for every possible use of language and prevents the punishment of those who abuse this freedom. 2 Story on the Constitution (5th Ed.) § 1580, p. 634. . . . Reasonably limited, it was said by Story in the passage cited, this freedom is an inestimable privilege in a free government; without such limitation, it might become the scourge of the republic.

That a State in the exercise of its police power may punish those who abuse this freedom by utterances inimical to the public welfare, tending to corrupt public morals, incite to crime, or disturb the public peace, is not open to question. . . . Thus it was held by this Court in . . . [*Fox*

v. *Washington*, 236 U.S. 273 (1915)], that a State may punish publications advocating and encouraging a breach of its criminal laws; and, in . . . [*Gilbert* v. *Minnesota*, 254 U.S. 325 (1920)], that a State may punish utterances teaching or advocating that its citizens should not assist the United States in prosecuting or carrying on war with its public enemies.

And, for yet more imperative reasons, a State may punish utterances endangering the foundations of organized government and threatening its overthrow by unlawful means. These imperil its own existence as a constitutional State. Freedom of speech and press, said Story, supra, does not protect disturbances to the public peace or the attempt to subvert the government. It does not protect publications or teachings which tend to subvert or imperil the government or to impede or hinder it in the performance of its governmental duties. . . . It does not protect publications prompting the overthrow of government by force; the punishment of those who publish articles which tend to destroy organized society being essential to the security of freedom and the stability of the state. . . . And a State may penalize utterances which openly advocate the overthrow of the representative and constitutional form of government of the United States and the several States, by violence or other unlawful means. . . . In short this freedom does not deprive a State of the primary and essential right of self preservation; which, so long as human governments endure, they cannot be denied. . . .

By enacting the present statute the State has determined, through its legislative body, that utterances advocating the overthrow of organized government by force, violence and unlawful means, are so inimical to the general welfare and involve such danger of substantive evil that they may be penalized in the exercise of its police power. That determination must be given great weight. Every presumption is to be indulged in favor of the validity of the statute. . . . That utterances inciting to the overthrow of organized government by unlawful means, present a sufficient danger of substantive evil to bring their punishment within the range of legislative discretion, is clear. Such utterances, by their very nature, involve danger to the public peace and to the security of the State. They threaten breaches of the peace and ultimate revolution. And the immediate danger is none the less real and substantial, because the effect of a given utterance cannot be accurately foreseen. The State cannot reasonably be required to measure the danger from every such utterance in the nice balance of a jeweler's scale. A single revolutionary spark may kindle a fire that, smouldering for a time, may burst into a sweeping and destructive conflagration. It cannot be said that the State is acting arbitrarily or unreasonably when in the exercise of its judgment as to the measures necessary to protect the public peace and safety, it seeks to extinguish the spark without waiting until it has enkindled the flame or blazed into the conflagration. It cannot reasonably be required to defer the adoption of measures for its own peace and safety until the revolutionary utterances lead to actual disturbances of the public peace or imminent and immediate danger of its own destruction; but it may, in the exercise of its judgment, suppress the threatened danger in its incipiency. . . .

We cannot hold that the present statute is an arbitrary or unreasonable exercise of the police power of the State unwarrantably infringing the freedom of speech or press; and we must and do sustain its constitutionality.

This being so it may be applied to every utterance—not too trivial to be beneath the notice of the law—which is of such a character and used with such intent and purpose as to bring it within the prohibition of the statute. . . . In other words, when the legislative body has determined generally, in the constitutional exercise of its discretion, that utterances of a certain kind involve such danger of substantive evil that they may be punished, the question whether any specific utterance coming within the prohibited class is likely, in and of itself, to bring about the substantive evil, is not open to consideration. It is sufficient that the statute itself be constitutional and that the use of the language comes within its prohibition.

It is clear that the question in such cases is entirely different from that involved in those cases where the statute merely prohibits certain acts involving the danger of substantive evil, without any reference to language itself, and it is sought to apply its provisions to language used by the defendant for the purpose of bringing about the prohibited results. There, if it be contended that the statute cannot be applied to the language used by the defendant because of its protection by the freedom of speech or press, it must necessarily be found, as an original question, without any previous determination by the legislative body, whether the specific language used involved such likelihood of bringing about the substantive evil as to deprive it of the constitutional protection. In such case it has been held that the general provisions of the statute may be constitutionally applied to the specific utterance of the defendant if its natural tendency and probable effect was to bring about the substantive evil which the legislative body might prevent. *Schenck* v. *United States* . . . , *Debs* v. *United States*. . . . And the general statement in the *Schenck Case*, . . . that the "question in every case is whether the words used are used in such circumstances and are of such a nature as to create a clear and present danger that they will bring about the substantive evils,"—upon which great reliance is

placed in the defendant's argument—was manifestly intended, as shown by the context, to apply only in cases of this class, and has no application to those like the present, where the legislative body itself has previously determined the danger of substantive evil arising from utterances of a specified character. . . .

And finding, for the reasons stated, that the statute is not in itself unconstitutional, and that it has not been applied in the present case in derogation of any constitutional right, the judgment of the Court of Appeals is

Affirmed.

Mr. Justice Holmes, dissenting:

Mr. Justice Brandeis and I are of opinion that this judgment should be reversed. The general principle of free speech, it seems to me, must be taken to be included in the Fourteenth Amendment, in view of the scope that has been given to the word "liberty" as there used, although perhaps it may be accepted with a somewhat larger latitude of interpretation than is allowed to Congress by the sweeping language that governs or ought to govern the laws of the United States. If I am right then I think that the criterion sanctioned by the full Court in *Schenck* v. *United States* . . . applies:

The question in every case is whether the words used are used in such circumstances and are of such a nature as to create a clear and present danger that they will bring about the substantive evils that [the State] has a right to prevent.

It is true that in my opinion this criterion was departed from in *Abrams* v. *United States* . . . but the convictions that I expressed in that case are too deep for it to be possible for me as yet to believe that it and *Schaefer* v. *United States* [1920] . . . have settled the law. If what I think the correct test is applied it is manifest that there was no present danger of an attempt to overthrow the government by force on the part of the admittedly small minority who shared the defendant's views. It is said that this manifesto was more than a theory, that it was an incitement. Every idea is an incitement. It offers itself for belief and if believed it is acted on unless some other belief outweighs it or some failure of energy stifles the movement at its birth. The only difference between the expression of an opinion and an incitement in the narrower sense is the speaker's enthusiasm for the result. Eloquence may set fire to reason. But whatever may be thought of the redundant discourse before us it had no chance of starting a present conflagration. If in the long run the beliefs expressed in proletarian dictatorship are destined to be accepted by the dominant forces of the community, the only meaning of free speech is that they should be given their chance and have their way.

If the publication of this document had been laid as an attempt to induce an uprising against government at once and not at some indefinite time in the future it would have presented a different question. The object would have been one with which the law might deal, subject to the doubt whether there was any danger that the publication could produce any result, or in other words, whether it was not futile and too remote from possible consequences. But the indictment alleges the publication and nothing more.

What were the contents of the manifesto for which Gitlow was convicted? How does the Court answer the charge that there was no proof of concrete action to overthrow the government by force or violence resulting from the publication and distribution of the manifesto? Was the clear and present danger test applied, or was another standard of judgment used? What considerations of federalism were taken into account by the Court? Under what authority of the state did the Court uphold the statute?

The *Gitlow* majority held that "When the [state] legislative body has determined generally, in the constitutional exercise of its discretion, that utterances of a certain kind involve such danger of substantive evil that they may be punished, the question whether any specific utterance coming within the prohibited class is likely, in and of itself, to bring about the substantive evil, is not open to consideration. It is sufficient that the statute itself be constitutional and that the use of the language come within its prohibition." This type of statute, argued the Court, is fundamentally different from the category of statute illustrated by the Espionage Act of 1917 which "merely prohibits certain acts involving the danger of substantive evil, without any reference to language itself, and it is sought to apply its provisions to language used by the defendant for the purpose of bringing about the prohibited result." The clear and present danger test is appropriate for judging the latter type of cases but does not apply to those falling within the former category. Where the state legislature has proscribed specific expressions because, in the judgment of the legislature, they lead to "substantive evils," the question on judicial review is whether or not the suppression of speech and press is a reasonable exercise of the state police power, not whether or not the prohibited expression in fact will produce a substantive evil. The state has already made this determination.

Holmes in his dissent ignores the arguments of the majority regarding the inapplicability of the clear and present danger test to the case and holds that the test should be applied in such a way as to afford maximum protection to freedom of speech and press. Holmes, referring to the "admittedly small minority who share the defendant's views," concludes that writing, publishing, and distributing the manifesto would not produce the "substantive evil"—overthrow of the government—which the state had a right to prevent. Under what circumstances would Holmes have upheld the conviction?

In the following case the Supreme Court reviewed a conviction under the California Criminal Syndicalism Act, which made it a crime to advocate, teach, or aid the commission of crime, sabotage, unlawful acts of force, violence, or terrorism to bring about change in industrial ownership or control or to effect any political change. The defendant, Anita Whitney, was involved in organizing the Communist Labor Party and as a delegate to a party convention had supported a resolution that advocated political action and urged workers to cast their votes for the party. The resolution was defeated on the floor, and a more extreme program was adopted. Whitney testified at her trial that she had urged the party to take a moderate course of action to bring about change through political action. Although she had not withdrawn from the party upon its adoption of the more extreme course of action, she was not in favor of terrorism and violence.

Whitney v. *California*

247 U.S. 357; 47 S. Ct. 641; 71 L. Ed. 1095 (1927)

Mr. Justice Sanford delivered the opinion of the Court:

By a criminal information filed in the Superior Court of Alameda County, California, the plaintiff in error was charged, in five counts, with violations of the Criminal Syndicalism Act of that State. . . . She was tried, convicted on the first count, and sentenced to imprisonment. . . .

The first count of the information, on which the conviction was had, charged that on or about November 28, 1919, in Alameda County, the defendant, in violation of the Criminal Syndicalism Act, "did then and there unlawfully, willfully, wrongfully, deliberately and feloniously organize and assist in organizing, and was, is, and knowingly became a member of an organization, society, group and assemblage of persons organized and assembled to advocate, teach, aid and abet criminal syndicalism. . . .

1. While it is not denied that the evidence warranted the jury in finding that the defendant became a member of and assisted in organizing the Communist Labor Party of California, and that this was organized to advocate, teach, aid or abet criminal syndicalism as defined by the Act, it is urged that the Act, as here construed and applied, deprived the defendant of her liberty without due process of law in that it has made her action in attending the Oakland convention unlawful by reason of "a subsequent event brought about against her will, by the agency of others," with no showing of a specific intent on her part to join in the forbidden purpose of the association, and merely because, by reason of a lack of "prophetic" understanding, she failed to foresee the quality that others would give to the convention. The argument is, in effect, that the character of the state organization could not be forecast when she attended the convention; that she had no

purpose of helping to create an instrument of terrorism and violence; that she "took part in formulating and presenting to the convention a resolution which, if adopted, would have committed the new organization to a legitimate policy of political reform by the use of the ballot"; that it was not until after the majority of the convention turned out to be "contrary minded, and other less temperate policies prevailed" that the convention could have taken on the character of criminal syndicalism; and that as this was done over her protest, her mere presence in the convention, however violent the opinions expressed therein, could not thereby become a crime. . . .

2. It is clear that the Syndicalism Act is not repugnant to the due process clause by reason of vagueness and uncertainty of definition. . . .

The Act, plainly, meets the essential requirement of due process that a penal statute be "sufficiently explicit to inform those who are subject to it what conduct on their part will render them liable to its penalties," and be couched in terms that are not "so vague that men of common intelligence must necessarily guess at its meaning and differ as to its application." . . .

4. Nor is the Syndicalism Act as applied in this case repugnant to the due process clause as a restraint of the rights of free speech, assembly, and association.

That the freedom of speech which is secured by the Constitution does not confer an absolute right to speak, without responsibility, whatever one may choose, or an unrestricted and unbridled license giving immunity for every possible use of language and preventing the punishment of those who abuse this freedom; and that a State in the exercise of its police power may punish those who abuse this freedom by utterances inimical to the public welfare, tending to incite to crime, disturb the public peace, or endanger the foundations of organized government and threaten its overthrow by unlawful means, is not open to question. . . .

By enacting the provisions of the Syndicalism Act the State has declared, through its legislative body, that to knowingly be or become a member of or assist in organizing an association to advocate, teach or aid and abet the commission of crimes or unlawful acts of force, violence or terrorism as a means of accomplishing industrial or political changes, involves such danger to the public peace and the security of the State, that these acts should be penalized in the exercise of its police power. That determination must be given great weight. Every presumption is to be indulged in favor of the validity of the statute, . . . and it may not be declared unconstitutional unless it is an arbitrary or unreasonable attempt to exercise the authority vested in the State in the public interest. . . .

The essence of the offense denounced by the Act is the combining with others in an association for the accomplishment of the desired ends through the advocacy and use of criminal and unlawful methods. It partakes of the nature of a criminal conspiracy. . . . That such united and joint action involves even greater danger to the public peace and security than the isolated utterances and acts of individuals is clear. We cannot hold that, as here applied, the Act is an unreasonable or arbitrary exercise of the police power of the State, unwarrantably infringing any right of free speech, assembly or association, or that those persons are protected from punishment by the due process clause who abuse such rights by joining and furthering an organization thus menacing the peace and welfare of the State.

Affirmed.

MR. JUSTICE BRANDEIS, concurring:
. . . Despite arguments to the contrary

which had seemed to me persuasive, it is settled that the due process clause of the Fourteenth Amendment applies to matters of substantive law as well as to matters of procedure. Thus all fundamental rights comprised within the term liberty are protected by the federal Constitution from invasion by the states. The right of free speech, the right to teach and the right of assembly are, of course, fundamental rights. . . . These may not be denied or abridged. But, although the rights of free speech and assembly are fundamental, they are not in their nature absolute. Their exercise is subject to restriction, if the particular restriction proposed is required in order to protect the state from destruction or from serious injury, political, economic or moral. That the necessity which is essential to a valid restriction does not exist unless speech would produce, or is intended to produce, a clear and imminent danger of some substantive evil which the state constitutionally may seek to prevent has been settled. . . .

It is said to be the function of the Legislature to determine whether at a particular time and under the particular circumstances the formation of, or assembly with, a society organized to advocate criminal syndicalism constitutes a clear and present danger of substantive evil; and that by enacting the law here in question the Legislature of California determined that question in the affirmative. . . . The Legislature must obviously decide, in the first instance, whether a danger exists which calls for a particular protective measure. But where a statute is valid only in case certain conditions exist, the enactment of the statute cannot alone establish the facts which are essential to its validity. Prohibitory legislation has repeatedly been held invalid, because unnecessary, where the denial of liberty involved was that of engaging in a particular business. The powers of the courts to strike down an of-

fending law are no less when the interests involved are not property rights, but the fundamental personal rights of free speech and assembly.

This Court has not yet fixed the standard by which to determine when a danger shall be deemed clear; how remote the danger may be and yet be deemed present; and what degree of evil shall be deemed sufficiently substantial to justify resort to abridgment of free speech and assembly as the means of protection. To reach sound conclusions on these matters, we must bear in mind why a state is, ordinarily, denied the power to prohibit dissemination of social, economic and political doctrine which a vast majority of its citizens believes to be false and fraught with evil consequence.

Those who won our independence believed that the final end of the state was to make men free to develop their faculties, and that in its government the deliberative forces should prevail over the arbitrary. They valued liberty both as an end and as a means. They believed liberty to be the secret of happiness and courage to be the secret of liberty. They believed that freedom to think as you will and to speak as you think are means indispensable to the discovery and spread of political truth; that without free speech and assembly discussion would be futile; that with them, discussion affords ordinarily adequate protection against the dissemination of noxious doctrine; that the greatest menace to freedom is an inert people; that public discussion is a political duty; and that this should be a fundamental principle of the American government. They recognized the risks to which all human institutions are subject. But they knew that order cannot be secured merely through fear of punishment for its infraction; that it is hazardous to discourage thought, hope and imagination; that fear breeds repression; that repression breeds hate; that hate menaces stable government; that the path of safety lies in the opportunity to discuss freely supposed grievances and proposed remedies; and that the fitting remedy for evil counsels is good ones. Believing in the power of reason as applied through public discussion, they eschewed silence coerced by law— the argument of force in its worst form. Recognizing the occasional tyrannies of governing majorities, they amended the Constitution so that free speech and assembly should be guaranteed.

Fear of serious injury cannot alone justify suppression of free speech and assembly. Men feared witches and burnt women. It is the function of speech to free men from the bondage of irrational fears. To justify suppression of free speech there must be reasonable ground to fear that serious evil will result if free speech is practiced. There must be reasonable ground to believe that the danger apprehended is imminent. There must be reasonable ground to believe that the evil to be prevented is a serious one. ... The wide difference between advocacy and incitement, between preparation and attempt, between assembling and conspiracy, must be borne in mind. In order to support a finding of clear and present danger it must be shown either that immediate serious violence was to be expected or was advocated, or that the past conduct furnished reason to believe that such advocacy was then contemplated.

Those who won our independence by revolution were not cowards. They did not fear political change. They did not exalt order at the cost of liberty. To courageous, self-reliant men, with confidence in the power of free and fearless reasoning applied through the processes of popular government, no danger flowing from speech can be deemed clear and present, unless the incidence of the evil apprehended is so imminent that it may befall before there is opportunity for full discussion. If there be time to expose through

discussion the falsehood and fallacies, to avert the evil by the processes of education, the remedy to be applied is more speech, not enforced silence. Only an emergency can justify repression. Such must be the rule if authority is to be reconciled with freedom. Such, in my opinion, is the command of the Constitution. It is therefore always open to Americans to challenge a law abridging free speech and assembly by showing that there was no emergency justifying it.

Moreover, even imminent danger cannot justify resort to prohibition of these functions essential to effective democracy, unless the evil apprehended is relatively serious. Prohibition of free speech and assembly is a measure so stringent that it would be inappropriate as the means for averting a relatively trivial harm to society. A police measure may be unconstitutional merely because the remedy, although effective as means of protection, is unduly harsh or oppressive. ... The fact that speech is likely to result in some violence or in destruction of property is not enough to justify its suppression. There must be the probability of serious injury to the State. Among free men, the deterrents ordinarily to be applied to prevent crime are education and punishment for violations of law, not abridgment of the rights of free speech and assembly. ...

Whether in 1919, when Miss Whitney did the things complained of, there was in California such clear and present danger of serious evil, might have been made the important issue in the case. She might have required that the issue be determined either by the court or the jury. She claimed below that the statute as applied to her violated the federal Constitution; but she did not claim that it was void because there was no clear and present danger of serious evil, nor did she request that the existence of these conditions of a valid measure thus restricting the rights of free speech and assembly be passed upon by the court or a jury. On the other hand, there was evidence on which the court or jury might have found that such danger existed. I am unable to assent to the suggestion in the opinion of the court that assembling with a political party, formed to advocate the desirability of a proletarian revolution by mass action at some date necessarily far in the future, is not a right within the protection of the Fourteenth Amendment. In the present case, however, there was other testimony which tended to establish the existence of a conspiracy, on the part of members of the International Workers of the World, to commit present serious crimes, and likewise to show that such a conspiracy would be furthered by the activity of the society of which Miss Whitney was a member. Under these circumstances the judgment of the State court cannot be disturbed. . . .

Mr. Justice Holmes joins in this opinion.

As in *Gitlow* v. *New York,* the Court in the *Whitney* case upheld the challenged state law under the police power. Did the Court draw a line beyond which the state could not abridge freedom of speech? In what way does the Court's decision reflect judicial self-restraint based upon considerations of federalism?

In his concurring opinion Justice Brandeis, unlike the majority, used the clear and present danger test to determine the validity of the state law. Replying directly to the explicit rejection of the standard in *Gitlow,* and its implicit denial in *Whitney,* Brandeis wrote that "where a statute is valid only in case certain conditions exist, the enactment of the statute cannot alone establish the facts which are essential to its validity." By applying the clear and present danger standard to the kinds of statutes reviewed in *Gitlow* and *Whitney* the scope of judicial review is widened. How, in Brandeis's view, might the case have been decided differently if the standard of clear and present danger had been raised and applied when the case was before the jury?

The decisions in *Gitlow* and *Whitney* reflected deference by the Supreme Court to the state legislatures and the findings of the juries. In *Fiske* v. *Kansas,* 274 U.S. 380 (1927), decided on the same day as the *Whitney* case, the Court overturned a conviction under the Kansas criminal syndicalism law. Justice Sanford, who authored the majority opinion in *Gitlow,* wrote for the majority in *Fiske* that a statement in the preamble to the constitution of the Industrial Workers of the World (IWW) could not sustain the inference drawn by the jury that the organization violated the law. The preamble urged the workers of the world to unite and advocated the continuation of the class struggle until the workers took over the means of production and abolished the wage system. At his trial Fiske told the jury that he favored peaceful means to bring about change, not the violent actions of criminal syndicalism. The Court found that the law as applied was an arbitrary and unreasonable exercise of the police power.

In *DeJonge* v. *Oregon,* 299 U.S. 355 (1937), the conviction under a statute that prohibited assisting in the conduct of a meeting sponsored by an organization that advocated illegal means to bring about political change was overturned. The Court found that there was no proof of illegal advocacy at the meeting in question. The *Fiske* and *DeJonge* cases did not adopt a different standard than was applied in *Gitlow* and *Whitney* but suggested that the Court would view the record to prevent the arbitrary application of the law.

MODERN APPLICATION OF THE CLEAR AND PRESENT DANGER TEST

In 1940 Congress passed the Smith Act, which was identical in many respects to the New York law upheld in the *Gitlow* case. Section 2 of the Smith Act made it unlawful for any person

> (1) To knowingly or willfully advocate, abet, advise, or teach the duty, necessity, desirability, or propriety of overthrowing or destroying any government in the United States by force or violence . . . ; (2) With intent to cause the overthrow or destruction of any government in the United States, to print, publish, edit, issue, circulate, sell, distribute, or publicly display any written or printed matter advocating, advising, or teaching the duty, necessity, desirability, or propriety of overthrowing or destroying any government in the United States by force or violence; (3) To organize or help to organize any society, group, or assembly of persons who teach, advocate, or encourage the overthrow or destruction of any government in the United States by force or violence; or to be or become a member of, or affiliate with, any such society . . . knowing the purposes thereof.

Section 3 made it unlawful for any person to commit or conspire to commit any of the prohibited acts. The constitutionality of this act was tested in the following case.

Dennis v. *United States*

341 U.S. 494; 71 S. Ct. 857; 95 L. Ed. 1137 (1951)

MR. CHIEF JUSTICE VINSON announced the judgment of the Court and an opinion in which MR. JUSTICE REED. MR. JUSTICE BURTON and MR. JUSTICE MINTON join:

Petitioners were indicted in July, 1948, for violation of the conspiracy provisions of the Smith Act . . . during the period of April 1945, to July, 1948. . . . A verdict of guilty as to all the petitioners was returned by the jury on October 14, 1949. The Court of Appeals affirmed. . . . We granted certiorari, . . . limited to the following two questions: (1) Whether either § 2 or § 3 of the Smith Act, inherently or as construed and applied in the instant

case, violates the First Amendment and other provisions of the Bill of Rights; (2) whether either § 2 or § 3 of the Act, inherently or as construed and applied in the instant case, violates the First and Fifth Amendments because of indefiniteness.

I

It will be helpful in clarifying the issues to treat next the contention that the trial judge improperly interpreted the statute by charging that the statute required an unlawful intent before the jury could convict. . . .

The structure and purpose of the statute demand the inclusion of intent as an element of the crime. Congress was concerned with those who advocate and organize for the overthrow of the Government. Certainly those who recruit and combine for the purpose of advocating overthrow intend to bring about that overthrow. We hold that the statute requires as an essential element of the crime proof of the intent of those who are charged with its violation to overthrow the Government by force and violence. . . .

II

The obvious purpose of the statute is to protect existing Government, not from change by peaceable, lawful and constitutional means, but from change by violence, revolution and terrorism. That it is within the *power* of the Congress to protect the Government of the United States from armed rebellion is a proposition which requires little discussion. Whatever theoretical merit there may be to the argument that there is a "right" to rebellion against dictatorial governments is without force where the existing structure of the government provides for peaceful and orderly change. We reject any principle of governmental helplessness in the face of preparation for revolution, which principle, carried to its logical conclusion, must lead to anarchy. No one could conceive that it is not within the power of Congress to prohibit acts intended to overthrow the Government by force and violence. The question with which we are concerned here is not whether Congress has such *power*, but whether the *means* which it has employed conflict with the First and Fifth Amendments to the Constitution.

One of the bases for the contention that the means which Congress has employed are invalid takes the form of an attack on the face of the statute on the grounds that by its terms it prohibits academic discussion of the merits of Marxism-Leninism, that it stifles ideas and is contrary to all concepts of a free speech and a free press. Although we do not agree that the language itself has that significance, we must bear in mind that it is the duty of the federal courts to interpret federal legislation in a manner not inconsistent with the demands of the Constitution. . . . This is a federal statute which we must interpret as well as judge.

The very language of the Smith Act negates the interpretation which petitioners would have us impose on that Act. It is directed at advocacy, not discussion. Thus, the trial judge properly charged the jury that they could not convict if they found that petitioners did "no more than pursue peaceful studies and discussions or teaching and advocacy in the realm of ideas." He further charged that it was not unlawful "to conduct in an American college or university a course explaining the philosophical theories set forth in the books which have been placed in evidence." Such a charge is in strict accord with the statutory language, and illustrates the meaning to be placed on those words. Congress did not intend to eradicate the free discussion of political theories, to destroy the traditional rights of Americans to discuss and evaluate ideas without fear of governmental sanction. Rather Congress was concerned with the very kind of activity in which the evidence showed these petitioners engaged.

III

But although the statute is not directed at the hypothetical cases which petitioners have conjured, its application in this case has resulted in convictions for the teaching and advocacy of the overthrow of the Government by force and violence, which, even though coupled with the intent to accomplish that overthrow, contains an element of speech. For this reason, we must pay special heed to the demands of the First Amendment marking out the boundaries of speech.

We pointed out in *Douds* [1950] . . . that the basis of the First Amendment is the hypothesis that speech can rebut speech, propaganda will answer propaganda, free debate of ideas will result in the wisest governmental policies. It is for this reason that this Court has recognized the inherent value of free discourse. An analysis of the leading cases in this Court which have involved direct limitations on speech, however, will demonstrate that both the majority of the Court and the dissenters in particular cases have recognized that this is not an unlimited, unqualified right, but that the societal value of speech must, on occasion, be subordinated to other values and considerations.

No important case involving free speech was decided by this Court prior to *Schenck* v. *United States* [1919]. . . . Writing for an unanimous Court, Justice Holmes stated that the "question in every case is whether the words used are used in such circumstances and are of such a nature as to create a clear and present danger that they will bring about the substantive evils that Congress has a right to prevent." . . . The fact is inescapable, too, that the phrase bore no connotation that the danger was to be any threat to the safety of the Republic. The charge was causing and attempting to cause insubordination in the military forces and obstruct recruiting. The objectionable document denounced conscription and its most inciting sentence was, "You must do your share to maintain, support and uphold the rights of the people of this country." . . . Fifteen thousand copies were printed and some circulated. This insubstantial gesture toward insubordination in 1917 during war was held to be clear and present danger of bringing about the evil of military insubordination.

In several later [World War I] cases involving convictions under the Criminal Espionage Act, the nub of the evidence the Court held sufficient to meet the "clear and present danger" test enunciated in *Schenck* was as follows: . . . publication of twelve newspaper articles attacking the war; . . . one speech attacking United States' participation in the war; . . . circulation of copies of two different socialist circulars attacking the war; . . . publication of a German-language newspaper with allegedly false articles, critical of capitalism and the war; . . . circulation of copies of a four-page pamphlet written by a clergyman, attacking the purposes of the war and United States' participation therein.

The rule we deduce from these cases is that where an offense is specified by a statute in nonspeech or nonpress terms, a conviction relying upon speech or press as evidence of violation may be sustained only when the speech or publication created a "clear and present danger" of attempting or accomplishing the prohibited crime, *e.g.*, interference with enlistment. The dissents, we repeat, in emphasizing the value of speech, were addressed to the argument of the sufficiency of the evidence.

The next important case before the Court in which free speech was the crux of the conflict was *Gitlow* v. *New York* [1925]. . . . There New York had made it a crime to advocate "the necessity or propriety of overthrowing . . . organized government by force. . . ." The evidence of violation of the statute was that the defendant had published a Manifesto attacking the Government and capitalism. The convictions were sustained, Justice Holmes and Brandeis dissenting. The majority refused to apply the "clear and present danger" test to the specific utterance. Its reasoning was as follows: The "clear and present danger" test was applied to the utterance itself in *Schenck* because the question was merely one of sufficiency of evidence under an admittedly constitutional statute. *Gitlow*, however, presented a different question. There a legislature had found that a certain kind of speech was, itself, harmful and unlawful. The constitutionality of such a state statute had to be adjudged by this Court just as it determined the constitutionality of any state statute, namely, whether the statute was "reasonable." Since it was entirely reasonable for a state to attempt to protect itself from violent overthrow, the statute was perforce reasonable. The only question remaining in the case became whether there was evidence to support the conviction, a question which gave the majority no difficulty. Justices Holmes and Brandeis refused to accept this approach, but insisted that wherever speech was the evidence of the violation, it was necessary to show that the speech created the "clear and present danger" of the substantive evil which the legislature had the right to prevent. Justices Holmes and Brandeis, then, made no distinction between a federal statute which made certain acts unlawful, the evidence to support the conviction being speech, and a statute which made speech itself the crime. This approach was emphasized in *Whitney* v. *California* [1927] ... where the Court was confronted with a conviction under the California Criminal Syndicalist statute. The Court sustained the conviction, Justices Brandeis and Holmes concurring in the result. In their concurrence they repeated that even though the legislature had designated certain speech as criminal, this could not prevent the defendant from showing that there was no danger that the substantive evil would be brought about.

Although no case subsequent to *Whitney* and *Gitlow* has expressly overruled the majority opinions in those cases, there is little doubt that subsequent opinions have inclined toward the Holmes-Brandeis rationale. And in *American Communications Assn.* v. *Douds*, [1950] ... [w]e pointed out that Congress did not intend to punish belief, but rather intended to regulate the conduct of union affairs. We therefore held that any indirect sanction on speech which might arise from the oath requirement did not present a proper case for the "clear and present danger" test, for the regulation was aimed at conduct rather than speech. In discussing the proper measure of evaluation of this kind of legislation, we suggested that the Holmes-Brandeis philosophy insisted that where there was a direct restriction upon speech, a "clear and present danger" that the substantive evil would be caused was necessary before the statute in question could be constitutionally applied. And we stated, "[The First] Amendment requires that one is permitted to believe what he will. It requires that one be permitted to advocate what he will unless there is a clear and present danger that a substantial public evil will result therefrom." But we further suggested that neither Justice Holmes nor Justice Brandeis ever envisioned that a shorthand phrase should be crystallized into a rigid rule to be applied inflexibly without regard to the circumstances of each case. Speech is not an absolute, above and beyond control by the legislature when its judgment, subject to review here, is that certain kinds of speech are so undesirable as to warrant criminal sanction. Nothing is more certain in modern society than the principle that there are no absolutes, that a name, a phrase, a standard has meaning only when associated with the considerations which gave birth to the nomenclature. ... To those who would paralyze our Government in the face of impending threat by encasing it in a semantic strait jacket we must reply that all concepts are relative.

In this case we are squarely presented with the application of the "clear and present danger" test, and must decide what the phrase imports. We first note that many of the cases in which this Court has reversed convictions by use of this or similar tests have been based on the fact that the interest which the State was attempting to protect was itself too insubstantial to warrant restriction of speech. . . . Overthrow of the Government by force and violence is certainly a substantial enough interest for the Government to limit speech. Indeed, this is the ultimate value of any society, for if a society cannot protect its very structure from armed internal attack, it must follow that no subordinate value can be protected. If, then, this interest may be protected, the literal problem which is presented is what has been meant by the use of the phrase "clear and present danger" of the utterances bringing about the evil within the power of Congress to punish.

Obviously, the words cannot mean that before the Government may act, it must wait until the *putsch* is about to be executed, the plans have been laid and the signal is awaited. If Government is aware that a group aiming at its overthrow is attempting to indoctrinate its members and to commit them to a course whereby they will strike when the leaders feel the circumstances permit, action by the Government is required. The argument that there is no need for Government to concern itself, for Government is strong, it possesses ample powers to put down a rebellion, it may defeat the revolution with ease needs no answer. For that is not the question. Certainly an attempt to overthrow the Government by force, even though doomed from the outset because of inadequate numbers or powers of revolutionists, is a sufficient evil for Congress to prevent. The damage which such attempts create both physically and politically to a nation makes it impossible to measure the validity in terms of the probability of success, or the immediacy of a successful attempt. In the instant case the

trial judge charged the jury that they could not convict unless they found that petitioners intended to overthrow the Government "as speedily as circumstances would permit." This does not mean, and could not properly mean, that they would not strike until there was certainty of success. What was meant was that the revolutionists would strike when they thought the time was ripe. We must therefore reject the contention that success or probability of success is the criterion.

The situation with which Justices Holmes and Brandeis were concerned in *Gitlow* was a comparatively isolated event, bearing little relation in their minds to any substantial threat to the safety of the community. . . . They were not confronted with any situation comparable to the instant one—the development of an apparatus designed and dedicated to the overthrow of the Government, in the context of world crisis after crisis.

Chief Judge Learned Hand, writing for the majority below, interpreted the phrase as follows: "In each case [courts] must ask whether the gravity of the 'evil,' discounted by its improbability, justifies such invasion of free speech as is necessary to avoid the danger." 183 F. 2d at 212. We adopt this statement of the rule. As articulated by Chief Judge Hand, it is as succinct and inclusive as any other we might devise at this time. It takes into consideration those factors which we deem relevant, and relates their significances. More we cannot expect from words.

Likewise, we are in accord with the court below, which affirmed the trial court's finding that the requisite danger existed. The mere fact that from the period 1945 to 1948 petitioners' activities did not result in an attempt to overthrow the Government by force and violence is of course no answer to the fact that there was a group that was ready to make the attempt. The formation by petitioners of such a highly organized conspiracy, with rigidly disciplined members subject to call when the leaders, these petitioners, felt that the time had come for action, coupled with the inflammable nature of world conditions, similar uprisings in other countries, and the touch-and-go nature of our relations with countries with whom petitioners were in the very least ideologically attuned, convince us that their convictions were justified on this score. And this analysis disposes of the contention that a conspiracy to advocate, as distinguished from the advocacy itself, cannot be constitutionally restrained, because it comprises only the preparation. It is the existence of the conspiracy which creates the danger. . . . If the ingredients of the reaction are present, we cannot bind the Government to wait until the catalyst is added.

IV

. . . The argument that the action of the trial court is erroneous, in declaring as a matter of law that such violation shows sufficient danger to justify the punishment despite the First Amendment, rests on the theory that a jury must decide a question of the application of the First Amendment. We do not agree.

When facts are found that establish the violation of a statute, the protection against conviction afforded by the First Amendment is a matter of law. The doctrine that there must be a clear and present danger of substantive evil that Congress has a right to prevent is a judicial rule to be applied as a matter of law by the courts. The guilt is established by proof of facts. Whether the First Amendment protects the activity which constitutes the violation of the statute must depend upon a judicial determination of the scope of the First Amendment applied to the circumstances of the case.

We hold that the statute may be applied where there is a "clear and present

danger" of the substantive evil which the legislature had the right to prevent. Bearing, as it does, the marks of a "question of law," the issue is properly one for the judge to decide.

V

There remains to be discussed the question of vagueness—whether the statute as we have interpreted it is too vague, not sufficiently advising those who would speak of the limitations upon their activity. . . .

We hold that § § 2 (a) (1), 2 (a) (3) and 3 of the Smith Act do not inherently, or as construed or applied in the instant case, violate the First Amendment and other provisions of the Bill of Rights, or the First and Fifth Amendments because of indefiniteness. Petitioners intended to overthrow the Government of the United States as speedily as the circumstances would permit. Their conspiracy to organize the Communist Party and to teach and advocate the overthrow of the Government of the United States by force and violence created a "clear and present danger" of an attempt to overthrow the Government by force and violence. They were properly and constitutionally convicted for violation of the Smith Act. The judgments of conviction are

Affirmed.

MR. JUSTICE CLARK took no part in the consideration or decision of this case.

MR. JUSTICE FRANKFURTER, concurring:
. . . The historic antecedents of the First Amendment preclude the notion that its purpose was to give unqualified immunity to every expression that touched on matters within the range of political interest. . . .
. . . Absolute rules would inevitably lead to absolute exceptions, and such exceptions would eventually corrode the

rules. The demands of free speech in a democratic society as well as the interest in national security are better served by candid and informed weighing of the competing interests, within the confines of the judicial process, than by announcing dogmas too inflexible for the non-Euclidian problems to be solved.

But how are competing interests to be assessed? Since they are not subject to quantitative ascertainment, the issue necessarily resolves itself into asking, who is to make the adjustment? . . . Full responsibility for the choice cannot be given to the courts. Courts are not representative bodies. . . . Their judgment is best informed, and therefore most dependable, within narrow limits. Their essential quality is detachment, founded on independence. History teaches that the independence of the judiciary is jeopardized when courts become embroiled in the passions of the day and assume primary responsibility in choosing between competing political, economic and social pressures.

Primary responsibility for adjusting the interests which compete in the situation before us of necessity belongs to the Congress. . . . We are to set aside the judgment of those whose duty it is to legislate only if there is no reasonable basis for it. . . .

In reviewing statutes which restrict freedoms protected by the First Amendment, we have emphasized the close relation which those freedoms bear to maintenance of a free society. . . . Some members of the Court—and at times a majority—have done more. They have suggested that our function in reviewing statutes restricting freedom of expression differs sharply from our normal duty in sitting in judgment on legislation. . . . It has been suggested, with the casualness of a footnote, that such legislation is not presumptively valid, see *United States* v. *Carolene Products Co.* [1938] . . . , and it has been weightily reiterated that freedom of speech has a "preferred position"

among constitutional safeguards. *Kovacs* v. *Cooper* [1949] . . . .

The precise meaning intended to be conveyed by these phrases need not now be pursued. It is enough to note that they have recurred in the Court's opinions, and their cumulative force has, not without justification, engendered belief that there is a constitutional principle, expressed by those attractive but imprecise words, prohibiting restriction upon utterance unless it creates a situation of "imminent" peril against which legislation may guard. It is on this body of the Court's pronouncements that the defendants' argument here is based.

In all fairness, the argument cannot be met by reinterpreting the Court's frequent use of "clear" and "present" to mean an entertainable "probability." In giving this meaning to the phrase "clear and present danger," the Court of Appeals was fastidiously confining the rhetoric of opinions to the exact scope of what was decided by them. We have greater responsibility for having given constitutional support, over repeated protests, to uncritical libertarian generalities. . . .

If [past] decisions are to be used as a guide and not as an argument, it is important to view them as a whole and to distrust the easy generalizations to which some of them lend themselves.

We have recognized and resolved conflicts between speech and competing interests in six different types of cases. . . .

I must leave to others the ungrateful task of trying to reconcile all these decisions. In some instances we have too readily permitted juries to infer deception from error, or intention from argumentative or critical statements. . . . In other instances we weighted the interest in free speech so heavily that we permitted essential conflicting values to be destroyed. *Bridges* v. *State of California,* [1941] . . . *Craig* v. *Harney* [1947]. . . . Viewed as a whole, however, the decisions express an attitude toward the judicial function and a standard of values which for me are decisive of the case before us.

First.—Free-speech cases are not an exception to the principle that we are not legislators, that direct policy-making is not our province. . . .

In *Gitlow* v. *People of State of New York,* we put our respect for the legislative judgment in terms which, if they were accepted here, would make decision easy. . . .

. . . It has not been explicitly overruled. But it would be disingenuous to deny that the [Holmes] dissent in *Gitlow* has been treated with the respect usually accorded to a decision. . . .

. . . It requires excessive tolerance of the legislative judgment to suppose that the Gitlow publication in the circumstances could justify serious concern.

In contrast, there is ample justification for a legislative judgment that the conspiracy now before us is a substantial threat to national order and security. . . .

Second.—A survey of the relevant decisions indicates that the results which we have reached are on the whole those that would ensue from careful weighing of conflicting interests. The complex issues presented by regulation of speech in public places, by picketing, and by legislation prohibiting advocacy of crime have been resolved by scrutiny of many factors besides the imminence and gravity of the evil threatened. . . .

It is a familiar experience in the law that new situations do not fit neatly into legal conceptions that arose under different circumstances to satisfy different needs. . . . So it is with the attempt to use the direction of thought lying behind the criterion of "clear and present danger" wholly out of the context in which it originated, and to make of it an absolute dogma and definitive measuring rod for the power of Congress to deal with assaults against security through devices other than overt physical attempts.

Bearing in mind that Mr. Justice Holmes regarded questions under the First Amendment as questions of "proximity and degree," *Schenck* v. *United States* . . . , it would be a distortion, indeed a mockery of his reasoning to compare the "puny anonymities" . . . to which he was addressing himself in the Abrams case in 1919 or the publication that was "futile and too remote from possible consequences" . . . in the *Gitlow* case in 1925 with the setting of events in this case in 1950. . . .

Third.—Not every type of speech occupies the same position on the scale of values. There is no substantial public interest in permitting certain kinds of utterances: "the lewd and obscene, the profane, the libelous, and the insulting or 'fighting' words—those which by their very utterance inflict injury or tend to incite an immediate breach of the peace." *Chaplinsky* v. *State of New Hampshire* [1942]. . . .

On any scale of values which we have hitherto recognized, speech of this sort ranks low.

Throughout our decisions there has recurred a distinction between the statement of an idea which may prompt its hearers to take unlawful action, and advocacy that such action be taken. . . . The object of the conspiracy before us is so clear that the chance of error in saying that the defendants conspired to advocate rather than to express ideas is slight. Mr. Justice Douglas quite properly points out that the conspiracy before us is not a conspiracy to overthrow the Government. But it would be equally wrong to treat it as a seminar in political theory.

These general considerations underlie decision of the case before us.

On the one hand is the interest in security. The Communist Party was not designed by these defendants as an ordinary political party. For the circumstances of its organization, its aims and methods, and the relation of the defendants to its organization and aims we are concluded by the jury's verdict. . . .

In finding that the defendants violated the statute, we may not treat as established fact that the Communist Party in this country is of significant size, well-organized, well-disciplined, conditioned to embark on unlawful activity when given the command. But in determining whether application of the statute to the defendants is within the constitutional powers of Congress, we are not limited to the facts found by the jury. We must view such a question in the light of whatever is relevant to a legislative judgment. We may take judicial notice that the Communist doctrines which these defendants have conspired to advocate are in the ascendency in powerful nations who cannot be acquitted of unfriendliness to the institutions of this country. We may take account of evidence brought forward at this trial and elsewhere, much of which has long been common knowledge. In sum, it would amply justify a legislature in concluding that recruitment of additional members for the Party would create a substantial danger to national security.

In 1947, it has been reliably reported, at least 60,000 members were enrolled in the Party. Evidence was introduced in this case that the membership was organized in small units ... protected by elaborate precautions designed to prevent disclosure of individual identity. There are no reliable data tracing acts of sabotage or espionage directly to these defendants. But a Canadian Royal Commission in 1946 [reported] ... that "the Communist movement was the principal base within which the espionage network was recruited." The most notorious spy in recent history was led into the service of the Soviet Union through Communist indoctrination. Evidence supports the conclusion that members of the Party seek and occupy positions of importance in political and labor organizations. Congress was not barred by the Constitution from believing that indifference to such experience would be an exercise not of freedom but of irresponsibility.

On the other hand is the interest in free speech. The right to exert all governmental powers in aid of maintaining our institutions and resisting their physical overthrow does not include intolerance of opinions and speech that cannot do harm although opposed and perhaps alien to dominant, traditional opinion. . . .

It is better for those who have almost unlimited power of government in their hands to err on the side of freedom. . . .

. . . No matter how clear we may be that the defendants now before us are preparing to overthrow our Government at the propitious moment, it is self-delusion to think that we can punish them for their advocacy without adding to the risks run by loyal citizens who honestly believe in some of the reforms these defendants advance. It is a sobering fact that in sustaining the convictions before us we can hardly escape restriction on the interchange of ideas. . . .

It is not for us to decide how we would adjust the clash of interests which this case presents were the primary responsibility for reconciling it ours. Congress has determined that the danger created by advocacy of overthrow justifies the ensuing restriction on freedom of speech. The determination was made after due deliberation, and the seriousness of the congressional purpose is attested by the volume of legislation passed to effectuate the same ends. . . .

Can we hold that the First Amendment deprives Congress of what it deemed necessary for the Government's protection?

To make validity of legislation depend on judicial reading of events still in the womb of time—a forecast, that is, of the outcome of forces at best appreciated only with knowledge of the topmost secrets of nations—is to charge the judiciary with duties beyond its equipment. . . .

. . . [I]t is relevant to remind that in sustaining the power of Congress in a case like this nothing irrevocable is done.

The democratic process at all events is not impaired or restricted. Power and responsibility remain with the people and immediately with their representation. All the Court says is that Congress was not forbidden by the Constitution to pass this enactment and that a prosecution under it may be brought against a conspiracy such as the one before us. . . .

MR. JUSTICE JACKSON, concurring:
. . . [E]ither by accident or design, the Communist stratagem outwits the anti-anarchist pattern of statute aimed against "overthrow by force and violence" if qualified by the doctrine that only "clear and present danger" of accomplishing that result will sustain the prosecution.

The "clear and present danger" test was an innovation by Mr. Justice Holmes in the *Schenck* case, reiterated and refined by him and Mr. Justice Brandeis in later cases, all arising before the era of World War II revealed the subtlety and efficacy of modernized revolutionary techniques used by totalitarian parties. . . .

I would save it, unmodified for application as a "rule of reason" in the kind of case for which it was devised. When the issue is criminality of a hot-headed speech on a street corner, or circulation of a few incendiary pamphlets, or parading by some zealots behind a red flag, or refusal of a handful of school children to salute our flag, it is not beyond the capacity of the judicial process to gather, comprehend, and weigh the necessary materials for decision whether it is a clear and present danger of substantive evil or a harmless letting off of steam. It is not a prophecy, for the danger in such cases has matured by the time of trial or it was never present. The test applies and has meaning where a conviction is sought to be based on a speech or writing which does not directly or explicitly advocate a crime but to which such tendency is sought to be attributed by construction or by implication from external circumstances. The formula in such cases favors freedoms that are vital to our society, and, even if sometimes applied too generously, the consequences cannot be grave. But its recent expansion has extended, in particular to Communists, unprecedented immunities. Unless we are to hold our Government captive in a judge-made verbal trap, we must approach the problem of a well-organized, nation-wide conspiracy, such as I have described, as realistically as our predecessors faced the trivialities that were being prosecuted until they were checked with a rule of reason.

I think reason is lacking for applying that test to this case.

If we must decide that this Act and its application are constitutional only if we are convinced that petitioner's conduct creates a "clear and present danger" of violent overthrow, we must appraise imponderables, including international and national phenomena which baffle the best informed foreign offices and our most experienced politicians. . . . No doctrine can be sound whose application requires us to make a prophecy of that sort in the guise of a legal decision. The judicial process simply is not adequate to a trial of such far-flung issues. The answers given would reflect our own political predilections and nothing more.

The authors of the clear and present danger test never applied it to a case like this, nor would I. If applied as it is proposed here, it means that the Communist plotting is protected during its period of incubation; its preliminary stages of organization and preparation are immune from the law; the Government can move only after imminent action is manifest, when it would, of course, be too late. . . .

The highest degree of constitutional protection is due to the individual acting without conspiracy. But even an individual cannot claim that the Constitution protects him in advocating or teaching overthrow of government by force or violence. I should suppose no one would doubt that Congress has power to make such attempted overthrow a crime. But the contention is that one has the constitutional right to work up a public desire and will to do what it is a crime to attempt. I think direct incitement by speech or writing can be made a crime, and I think there can be a conviction without also proving that the odds favored its success by 99 to 1, or some other extremely high ratio. . . .

Of course, it is not always easy to distinguish teaching or advocacy in the sense of incitement from teaching or advocacy in the sense of exposition or explanation. It is a question of fact in each case.

What really is under review here is a conviction of conspiracy, after a trial for conspiracy, on an indictment charging conspiracy, brought under a statute outlawing conspiracy. . . .

The Constitution does not make conspiracy a civil right. . . . While I consider criminal conspiracy a dragnet device capable of perversion into an instrument of injustice in the hands of a partisan or complacent judiciary, it has an established place in our system of law, and no reason appears for applying it only to concerted action claimed to disturb interstate commerce and withholding it from those claimed to undermine our whole Government. . . .

I do not suggest that Congress could punish conspiracy to advocate something, the doing of which it may not punish. Advocacy or exposition of the doctrine of communal property ownership, or any political philosophy unassociated with advocacy of its imposition by force or seizure of government by unlawful means could not be reached through conspiracy prosecution. But it is not forbidden to put down force or violence, it is not forbidden to punish its teaching or advocacy, and the end being punishable, there is no doubt of the power to punish conspiracy for the purpose. . . .

MR. JUSTICE BLACK, dissenting:

. . . At the outset I want to emphasize what the crime involved in this case is, and what it is not. These petitioners were not charged with an attempt to overthrow the Government. They were not charged with overt acts of any kind designed to overthrow the Government. They were not even charged with saying anything or writing anything designed to overthrow the Government. The charge was that they agreed to assemble and to talk and publish certain ideas at a later date: The indictment is that they conspired to organize the Communist Party and to use speech or newspapers and other publications in the future to teach and advocate the forcible overthrow of the Government. No matter how it is worded, this is a virulent form of prior censorship of speech and press, which I believe the First Amendment forbids. I would hold § 3 of the Smith Act authorizing this prior restraint unconstitutional on its face and as applied. . . .

So long as this Court exercises the power of judicial review of legislation, I cannot agree that the First Amendment permits us to sustain laws suppressing freedom of speech and press on the basis of Congress' or our own notions of mere "reasonableness." Such a doctrine waters down the First Amendment so that it amounts to little more than an admonition to Congress. The Amendment as so construed is not likely to protect any but those "safe" or orthodox views which rarely need its protection. . . .

Public opinion being what it now is, few will protest the conviction of these Communist petitioners. There is hope, however, that in calmer times, when present pressures, passions and fears subside, this or some later Court will restore the First Amendment liberties to the high preferred place where they belong in a free society.

MR. JUSTICE DOUGLAS, dissenting:

If this were a case where those who claimed protection under the First Amendment were teaching the techniques of sabotage, the assassination of the President, the filching of documents from public files, the planting of bombs, the art of street warfare, and the like, I would have no doubts. The freedom to speak is not absolute; the teaching of methods of terror and other seditious conduct should be beyond the pale along with obscenity and immorality. This case was argued as if those were the facts. The argument imported much seditious conduct into the record. That is easy and it has popular appeal, for the activities of Communists in plotting and scheming against the free world are common knowledge. But the fact is that no such evidence was introduced at the trial. There is a statute which makes a seditious conspiracy unlawful. Petitioners, however, were not charged with a "conspiracy to overthrow" the Government. They were charged with a conspiracy to form a party and groups and assemblies of people who teach and advocate the overthrow of our Government by force or violence and with a conspiracy to advocate and teach its overthrow by force and violence. It may well be that indoctrination in the techniques of terror to destroy the Government would be indictable under either statute. But the teaching which is condemned here is of a different character. . . .

The vice of treating speech as the equivalent of overt acts of a treasonable or seditious character is emphasized by a concurring opinion, which by invoking the law of conspiracy makes speech do service for deeds which are dangerous to society. The doctrine of conspiracy has served divers and oppressive purposes and in its broad reach can be made to do

great evil. But never until today has anyone seriously thought that the ancient law of conspiracy could constitutionally be used to turn speech into seditious conduct. Yet that is precisely what is suggested. I repeat that we deal here with speech alone, not with speech *plus* acts of sabotage or unlawful conduct. Not a single seditious act is charged in the indictment. To make a lawful speech unlawful because two men conceive it is to raise the law of conspiracy to appalling proportions. That course is to make a radical break with the past and to violate one of the cardinal principles of our constitutional scheme. . . .

There comes a time when even speech loses its constitutional immunity. Speech innocuous one year may at another time fan such destructive flames that it must be halted in the interests of the safety of the Republic. That is the meaning of the clear and present danger test. When conditions are so critical that there will be no time to avoid the evil that the speech threatens, it is time to call a halt. Otherwise, free speech which is the strength of the Nation will be the cause of its destruction.

Yet free speech is the rule, not the exception. The restraint to be constitutional must be based on more than fear, on more than passionate opposition against the speech, on more than a revolted dislike for its contents. There must be some immediate injury to society that is likely if speech is allowed. . . .

The First Amendment provides that "Congress shall make no law . . . abridging the freedom of speech." The Constitution provides no exception. This does not mean, however, that the Nation need hold its hand until it is in such weakened condition that there is no time to protect itself from incitement to revolution. Seditious conduct can always be punished. But the command of the First Amendment is so clear that we should not allow Congress to call a halt to free speech except in the extreme case of peril from the speech itself. The First Amendment makes confidence in the common sense of our people and in their maturity of judgment the great postulate of our democracy. Its philosophy is that violence is rarely, if ever, stopped by denying civil liberties to those advocating resort to force. The First Amendment reflects the philosophy of Jefferson "that it is time enough for the rightful purposes of civil government, for its officers to interfere when principles break out into overt acts against peace and good order." The political censor has no place in our public debates. Unless and until extreme and necessitous circumstances are shown, our aim should be to keep speech unfettered and to allow the processes of law to be invoked only when the provocateurs among us move from speech to action.

Vishinsky wrote in 1938 in The Law of the Soviet State, "In our state, naturally, there is and can be no place for freedom of speech, press, and so on for the foes of socialism."

Our concern should be that we accept no such standard for the United States. Our faith should be that our people will never give support to these advocates of revolution, so long as we remain loyal to the purposes for which our Nation was founded.

Contrast the clear and present danger test applied by the majority in *Dennis* with the original formulation of the standard by Justice Holmes in the *Schenck* case. Did the *Dennis* majority modify the standard? Contrast the doctrine as applied in *Dennis* with the Holmes-Brandeis formulation of clear and present danger in *Gitlow* and *Whitney*. Did the *Dennis* majority apply the test to the statute? Did it apply it to the facts of the case? On what grounds did the Court justify its formulation and application of the clear and present danger test?

Review the concurring opinions of Frankfurter and Jackson. On what grounds do they argue that the clear and present danger test as applied by the majority is inappropriate to the judgment of the case? Is their deference to legislative judgment based on reasons analogous to those stated by Justice Sanford in *Gitlow*? Is there an implied clear and present danger test in these concurring opinions?

Contrast the dissenting opinions of Black and Douglas. Is the clear and present danger test used? Compare the dissents with that of Justice Holmes in *Gitlow* and with the concurring opinion of Brandeis in *Whitney*. Do you see any similarities?

The *Dennis* decision supported the view that the Communist party is a criminal conspiracy designed to overthrow the government by force and violence. Further, the Court stated that conspiracy to advocate the overthrow of the government can be constitutionally restrained: "It is the existence of the conspiracy which creates the danger. . . . If the ingredients of the reaction are present, we cannot bind the government to wait until the catalyst is added." It was possible to conclude from the opinion that membership itself in the Communist party constitutes unjustified advocacy because of the program of indoctrination carried out by the party—the ultimate end being to overthrow the government. With this idea in mind the government moved immediately after the *Dennis* decision to convict the lower echelon Communist leaders and some party members. The following case involved the appeal of fourteen party members and officers who were convicted of conspiracy in violation of the Smith Act. At the district court trial the judge had instructed the jury that it could find the petitioners guilty on the basis of advocacy of abstract doctrine regardless of whether or not such advocacy would result in probable action.

Yates v. *United States*

354 U.S. 298; 77 S. Ct. 1604; IL. Ed. 2d 1356 (1957)

MR. JUSTICE HARLAN delivered the opinion of the Court:

We brought these cases here to consider certain questions arising under the Smith Act which have not heretofore been passed upon by this Court, and otherwise to review the convictions of these petitioners for conspiracy to violate that Act. Among other things, the convictions are claimed to rest upon an application of the Smith Act which is hostile to the principles upon which its constitutionality was upheld in *Dennis* v. *United States*. . . .

. . . The conspiracy is alleged to have originated in 1940 and continued down to the date of the indictment in 1951. The indictment charged that in carrying out the conspiracy the defendants and their co-conspirators would (a) become members and officers of the Communist Party, with knowledge of its unlawful purposes, and assume leadership in carrying out its policies and activities; (b) cause to be organized units of the Party in California and elsewhere; (c) write and publish, in the "Daily Worker" and other Party organs, articles on the proscribed advocacy and teaching; (d) conduct schools for the indoctrination of Party members in such advocacy and teaching, and (e) recruit new Party members, particularly from among persons employed in the key industries of the nation. Twenty-three overt acts in furtherance of the conspiracy were alleged. . . .

We conclude . . . that since the Communist Party came into being in 1945, and the indictment was not returned until 1951, the three-year statute of limitations had run on the "organizing" charge, and required the withdrawal of that part of the indictment from the jury's consideration. . . .

Petitioners contend that the instructions to the jury were fatally defective in that the trial court refused to charge that, in order to convict, the jury must find that the advocacy which the defendants conspired to promote was of a kind calculated to "incite" persons to action for the forcible overthrow of the Government. It is argued that advocacy of forcible overthrow as mere *abstract doctrine* is within the free speech protection of the First Amendment; that the Smith Act, consistently with that constitutional provision, must be taken as proscribing only the sort of advocacy which incites to illegal *action;* and that the trial court's charge, by permitting conviction for mere advocacy, unrelated to its tendency to produce forcible action, resulted in an unconstitutional application of the Smith Act. The Government, which at the trial also requested the court to charge in terms of "incitement," now takes the position, however, that the true constitutional dividing line is not between inciting and abstract advocacy of forcible overthrow, but rather between advocacy as such, irrespective of its inciting qualities, and the mere discussion or exposition of violent overthrow as an abstract theory. . . .

We are . . . faced with the question whether the Smith Act prohibits advocacy and teaching of forcible overthrow as an abstract principle, divorced from any effort to instigate action to that end, so long as such advocacy or teaching is engaged in with evil intent. We hold that it does not.

The distinction between advocacy of abstract doctrine and advocacy directed at promoting unlawful action is one that has been consistently recognized in the opinions of this Court. . . . This distinction was heavily underscored in *Gitlow* v. *New York* [1925] . . . in which the statute involved was nearly identical with the one now before us. . . .

. . . The legislative history of the Smith Act and related bills shows beyond all question that Congress was aware of the distinction between the advocacy or teaching of abstract doctrine and the advocacy or teaching of action, and that it did not intend to disregard it. The statute was aimed at the advocacy and teaching of concrete action for the forcible overthrow of the Government, and not of principles divorced from action. . . .

In failing to distinguish between advocacy of forcible overthrow as an abstract doctrine and advocacy of action to that end, the District Court appears to have been led astray by the holding in *Dennis* that advocacy of violent action to be taken at some future time was enough. It seems to have considered that, since "inciting" speech is usually thought of as something calculated to induce immediate action, and since *Dennis* held advocacy of action for future overthrow sufficient, this meant that advocacy, irrespective of its tendency to generate action, is punishable, provided only that it is uttered with a specific intent to accomplish overthrow. In other words, the District Court apparently thought that *Dennis* obliterated the traditional dividing line between advocacy of abstract doctrine and advocacy of action. . . .

. . . As one of the concurring opinions in *Dennis* put it: "Throughout our decisions there has recurred a distinction between the statement of an idea which may prompt its hearers to take unlawful action, and advocacy that such action be taken." . . . There is nothing in *Dennis* which makes that historic distinction obsolete. . . .

On this basis we have concluded that the evidence against [five of the] petitioners . . . is so clearly insufficient that their acquittal should be ordered. . . .

. . . [W]e find no adequate evidence in the record which would permit a jury to find that they were members of such a conspiracy. For all purposes relevant here, the sole evidence as to them was that they had long been members, officers or functionaries of the Communist Party of California. . . . So far as this record shows, none of them has engaged in or been associated with any but what appear to have been wholly lawful activities or has ever made a single remark or been present when someone else made a remark, which would tend to prove the charges against them. . . .

Moreover, apart from the inadequacy of the evidence to show, at best, more than the abstract advocacy and teaching of forcible overthrow by the Party, it is difficult to perceive how the requisite specific intent to accomplish such overthrow could be deemed proved by a showing of mere membership or the holding of office in the Communist Party. We therefore think that as to these petitioners the evidence was entirely too meagre to justify putting them to a new trial, and that their acquittal should be ordered. . . .

For the foregoing reasons we think that the way must be left open for a new trial to the extent indicated. . . .

It is so ordered.

MR. JUSTICE BURTON concurred in the result.

MR. JUSTICE BRENNAN and MR. JUSTICE WHITTAKER took no part in the consideration or decision of this case.

MR. JUSTICE BLACK, with whom MR. JUSTICE DOUGLAS joins, concurring in part and dissenting in part:

I

I would reverse every one of these convictions and direct that all the defendants be acquitted. In my judgment the statutory provisions on which these prosecutions are based abridge freedom of speech, press and assembly in violation of the First Amendment to the United States Constitution. . . .

In essence, petitioners were tried upon the charge that they believe in and want to foist upon this country a different and to us a despicable form of authoritarian government in which voices criticizing the existing order are summarily silenced. I fear that the present type of prosecutions are more in line with the philosophy of authoritarian government than with that expressed by our First Amendment.

Doubtlessly, dictators have to stamp out causes and beliefs which they deem subversive to their evil regimes. But governmental suppression of causes and beliefs seems to me to be the very antithesis of what our Constitution stands for. The choice expressed in the First Amendment in favor of free expression was made against a turbulent background by men such as Jefferson, Madison, and Mason—men who believed that loyalty to the provisions of this Amendment was the best way to assure a long life for this new nation and its Government. Unless there is complete freedom for expression of all ideas, whether we like them or not, concerning the way government should be run and who shall run it, I doubt if any views in the long run can be secured against the censor. The First Amendment provides the only kind of security system that can preserve a free government—one that leaves the way wide open for people to favor, discuss, advocate, or incite causes and doctrines however obnoxious and antagonistic such views may be to the rest of us.

MR. JUSTICE CLARK dissented.

In what way did the *Yates* majority distinguish protected discussion from unprotected advocacy of revolutionary violence? How did the Court reinterpret the clear and present danger standard of *Dennis*? Can membership per se in the Communist party be considered a clear and present danger?

The *Yates* case did not overturn the Smith Act but tightened the standards of proof required to secure convictions under it. The membership clause of the Smith Act was challenged in *Scales v. United States*, 367 U.S. 203 (1961), which made it a felony to hold knowingly a membership in any organization that advocates the overthrow of the government by force or violence. Scales was convicted for his membership in the Communist party with full knowledge of its revolutionary intent. The Court upheld the conviction, finding that the trial judge had properly construed the law to require specific intent and active membership in the party, not "nominal" membership. Refusing to sustain the First Amendment challenge to the law, the Court stated that an organization with revolutionary intent was not protected under the freedoms of speech and association of the First Amendment. In *Communist Party* v. *Subversive Activities Control Board* (1961) Justice Frankfurter, writing for the majority, stated that the law requiring the registration of the Communist party as a "communist action" organization was not unconstitutional under the First Amendment. Deference and the benefit of the doubt must be given to congressional judgment "when existing government is menaced by world-wide integrated movement . . . to destroy the government itself," wrote Frankfurter. He continued: "The legislative judgment as to how that threat may best be met consistently with the safeguarding of personal freedom is not to be set aside merely because the judgment of judges would, in the first instance, have chosen other methods."[17] Upon review of the record Frankfurter found that Congress had made detailed findings that provided a rational basis for the legislation.

The application of the Subversive Activities Control Act was narrowed in *Aptheker* v. *Secretary of State*, 378 U.S. 500 (1964), in which the Court found that the law's denial of a passport to members of organizations registered under the law violated the right to travel guaranteed by the liberty of due process of the Fifth Amendment.

The *Whitney* Doctrine Reviewed in a Contemporary Setting

The following case, involving facts similar to those in *Whitney* v. *California*, was decided by the Court in 1969. Can it be predicted, on the basis of the post-*Whitney* decisions such as *Dennis* and *Yates*, whether or not the Court would apply a different standard of review in 1969 than it employed in the *Whitney* case?

Brandenburg v. *Ohio*

395 U.S. 444; 89 S. Ct. 1827; 23 L. Ed. 2d 430 (1969)

PER CURIAM:

The appellant, a leader of a Ku Klux Klan group, was convicted under the Ohio Criminal Syndicalism statute for "advocat[ing] . . . the duty, necessity, or propriety of crime, sabotage, violence, or unlawful methods of terrorism as a means of accomplishing industrial or political reform" and for "voluntarily assembl[ing] with any society, group, or assemblage of persons formed to teach or advocate the doctrines of criminal syndicalism." Ohio Rev. Code Ann. § 2923.13. He was fined $1,000 and sentenced to one to 10 years' imprisonment. The appellant challenged the constitutionality of the criminal syndi-

calism statute under the First and Fourth Amendments to the United States Constitution, but the intermediate appellate court of Ohio affirmed his conviction without opinion. The Supreme Court of Ohio dismissed his appeal . . . "for the reason that no substantial constitutional question exists herein." . . .

The record shows that a man, identified at trial as the appellant, telephoned an announcer-reporter on the staff of a Cincinnati television station and invited him to come to a Ku Klux Klan "rally" to be held at a farm in Hamilton County. With the cooperation of the organizers, the reporter and a cameraman attended

17Communist Party v. Subversive Activities Control Board, 367 U.S. 1, 96–97 (1961).

the meeting and filmed the events. Portions of the films were later broadcast on the local station and on a national network.

The prosecution's case rested on the films and on testimony identifying the appellant as the person who communicated with the reporter and who spoke at the rally. The State also introduced into evidence several articles appearing in the film, including a pistol, a rifle, a shotgun, ammunition, a Bible, and a red hood worn by the speaker in the films.

One film showed 12 hooded figures, some of whom carried firearms. They were gathered around a large wooden cross, which they burned. No one was present other than the participants and the newsmen who made the film. Most of the words uttered during the scene were incomprehensible when the film was projected, but scattered phrases could be understood that were derogatory of Negroes and, in one instance, of Jews. Another scene on the same film showed the appellant, in Klan regalia, making a speech. The speech, in full, was as follows:

This is an organizers' meeting. We have had quite a few members here today which are— we have hundreds, hundreds of members throughout the State of Ohio. I can quote from a newspaper clipping from the Columbus, Ohio Dispatch, five weeks ago Sunday morning. The Klan has more members in the State of Ohio than does any other organization. We're not a revengent organization, but if our President, our Congress, our Supreme Court, continues to suppress the white, Caucasian race, it's possible that there might have to be some revengeance taken.

We are marching on Congress July the Fourth, four hundred thousand strong. From there we are dividing into two groups, one group to march on St. Augustine, Florida, the other group to march into Mississippi. Thank you.

The second film showed six hooded figures one of whom, later identified as the appellant, repeated a speech very similar to that recorded on the first film. The reference to the possibility of "revenge-

ance" was omitted, and one sentence was added: "Personally, I believe the nigger should be returned to Africa, the Jew returned to Israel." Though some of the figures in the films carried weapons, the speaker did not.

The Ohio Criminal Syndicalism Statute was enacted in 1919. From 1917 to 1920, identical or quite similar laws were adopted by 20 States and two territories. E. Dowell, A History of Criminal Syndicalism Legislation in the United States 21 (1939). In 1927, this Court sustained the constitutionality of California's Criminal Syndicalism Act, . . . the text of which is quite similar to that of the laws of Ohio. *Whitney* v. *California* [1927] . . . The Court upheld the statute on the ground that, without more, "advocating" violent means to effect political and economic change involves such danger to the security of the State that the State may outlaw it. . . . But *Whitney* has been thoroughly discredited by later decisions. See *Dennis* v. *United States*. . . . These later decisions have fashioned the principle that the constitutional guarantees of free speech and free press do not permit a State to forbid or proscribe advocacy of the use of force or of law violation except where such advocacy is directed to inciting or producing imminent lawless action and is likely to incite or produce such action. As we said in *Noto* v. *United States* [1961] . . . "the mere abstract teaching . . . of the moral propriety or even moral necessity for a resort to force and violence, is not the same as preparing a group for violent action and steeling it to such action." . . . *Lowry* A statute which fails to draw this distinction impermissibly intrudes upon the freedoms guaranteed by the First and Fourteenth Amendments. It sweeps within its condemnation speech which our Constitution has immunized from governmental control. . . .

Measured by this test, Ohio's Criminal Syndicalism Act cannot be sustained. The Act punishes persons who "advocate or teach the duty, necessity, or propriety" of violence "as a means of accomplishing industrial or political reform"; or who publish or circulate or display any book or paper containing such advocacy; or who "justify" the commission of violent acts "with intent to exemplify, spread or advocate the propriety of the doctrines of criminal syndicalism"; or who "voluntarily assemble" with a group formed "to teach or advocate the doctrines of criminal syndicalism." Neither the indictment nor the trial judge's instructions to the jury in any way refined the statute's bald definition of the crime in terms of mere advocacy not distinguished from incitement to imminent lawless action.

Accordingly, we are here confronted with a statute which, by its own words and as applied, purports to punish mere advocacy and to forbid, on pain of criminal punishment, assembly with others merely to advocate the described type of action. Such a statute falls within the condemnation of the First and Fourteenth Amendments. The contrary teaching of *Whitney* v. *California* . . . cannot be supported, and that decision is therefore overruled.

Reversed.

MR. JUSTICE BLACK, concurring:

I agree with the views expressed by Mr. Justice Douglas in his concurring opinion in this case that the "clear and present danger" doctrine should have no place in the interpretation of the First Amendment. I join the Court's opinion, which, as I understand it, simply cites *Dennis* v. *United States,* . . . but does not indicate any agreement on the Court's part with the "clear and present danger" doctrine on which *Dennis* purported to rely.

MR. JUSTICE DOUGLAS, concurring:

While I join the opinion of the Court, I desire to enter a *caveat*.

[T]he World War I cases . . . of [*Schenck, Frohwerk, Debs,* and *Abrams*] put the gloss of "clear and present danger" on the First Amendment. Whether the war power— the greatest leveler of them all—is adequate to sustain that doctrine is debatable. The dissents in *Abrams, Schaefer,* and *Pierce* show how easily "clear and present danger" is manipulated to crush what Brandeis [in *Pierce*] called "[t]he fundamental right of free men to strive for better conditions through new legislation and new institutions" by argument and discourse . . . even in time of war. Though I doubt if the "clear and present danger" test is congenial to the First Amendment in time of a declared war, I am certain it is not reconcilable with the First Amendment in days of peace.

The Court quite properly overrules *Whitney* v. *California,* . . . which involved advocacy of ideas which the majority of the Court deemed unsound and dangerous.

Mr. Justice Holmes, though never formally abandoning the "clear and present danger" test, moved closer to the First Amendment ideal when he said in dissent in *Gitlow* v. *New York,* . . . "Every idea is an incitement. . . ."

We have never been faithful to the philosophy of that dissent.

The Court in *Herndon* v. *Lowry* [1937] . . . overturned a conviction for exercising First Amendment rights to incite insurrection because of lack of evidence of incitement. . . . In *Bridges* v. *California* [1941] . . . we approved the "clear and present danger" test in an elaborate dictum that tightened it and confined it to a narrow category. But in *Dennis* v. *United States* [1951] . . . we opened wide the door, distorting the "clear and present danger" test beyond recognition.

. . . I see no place in the regime of the First Amendment for any "clear and present danger" test, whether strict and tight as some would make it, or free-wheeling as the Court in *Dennis* rephrased it.

When one reads the opinions closely and sees when and how the "clear and present danger" test has been applied, great misgivings are aroused. First, the threats were often loud but always puny and made serious only by judges so wedded to the *status quo* that critical analysis made them nervous. Second, the test was so twisted and perverted in *Dennis* as to make the trial of those teachers of Marxism an all-out political trial which was part and parcel of the cold war that has eroded substantial parts of the First Amendment.

Action is often a method of expression and within the protection of the First Amendment.

Suppose one tears up his own copy of the Constitution in eloquent protest to a decision of this Court. May he be indicted?

Suppose one rips his own Bible to shreds to celebrate his departure from one "faith" and his embrace of atheism. May he be indicted?

Last Term the Court held in *United States v. O'Brien* [1968] . . . that a registrant under Selective Service who burned his draft card in protest of the war in Vietnam could be prosecuted. The First Amendment was tendered as a defense and rejected. . . .

But O'Brien was not prosecuted for not having his draft card available when asked for by a federal agent. He was indicted, tried, and convicted for burning the card. And this Court's affirmance of that conviction was not, with all respect, consistent with the First Amendment. . . .

The line between what is permissible and not subject to control and what may be made impermissible and subject to regulation is the line between ideas and overt acts.

The example usually given by those who would punish speech is the case of one who falsely shouts fire in a crowded theatre.

This is, however, a classic case where speech is brigaded with action. . . . They are indeed inseparable and a prosecution can be launched for the overt acts actually caused. Apart from rare instances of that kind, speech is, I think, immune from prosecution. Certainly there is no constitutional line between advocacy of abstract ideas as in *Yates* and advocacy of political action as in *Scales*. The quality of advocacy turns on the depth of the conviction; and government has no power to invade that sanctuary of belief and conscience.

How does the Court's *Brandenburg* opinion change the standard of *Whitney*? Does it alter the clear and present danger test of *Dennis* that was modified by *Yates*? Could the Ohio statute have been sustained if the judge had construed it differently at the trial? Why does the statute fall "within the condemnation of the First and Fourteenth Amendments"?

Justice Douglas states in his concurring opinion that "I see no place in the regime of the First Amendment for any 'clear and present danger' test, whether strict and tight as some would make it, or freewheeling as the Court in *Dennis* rephrased it." Reread Douglas's dissent in *Dennis*. Does he categorically reject there the clear and present danger test? Does he in fact reject it in *Brandenburg*?

CLEAR AND PRESENT DANGER CREATED BY "FIGHTING WORDS" AND HOSTILE AUDIENCES

To what extent can government suppress speech on the grounds that it will cause a riot, disturbance, or breach of the peace? Are "fighting words" protected by the First Amendment? What is the permissible reach of state and city ordinances that authorize the suppression of speech for the purpose of maintaining public order? Is there a "clear and present danger" standard applicable to such cases?

In the following case a New Hampshire statute that prohibited persons from addressing "any offensive, derisive or annoying word to any other person who is lawfully in any street or other public place" was challenged as a violation of freedom of speech protected by the due process clause of the Fourteenth Amendment. The appellant, who had been convicted of violating the law, argued that the "descriptive words of the statute are so broad that they would permit an enforcement of the statute to curb, suppress and censor honest criticism of government, religion, politics, social functions, or any other subject."[18] The statute, argued the appellant, "is not specifically directed at any inherent, clear, or present danger of destruction of life or property; and when the interest that the statute seeks to protect is balanced against the interests of the individual and the community in the rights of free speech, free press, and free worship, it cannot be found to be warrantable. . . ."[19]

In response to the appellant, the state pleaded: "The statute as construed by the state court [to cover 'words likely to cause an average addressee to fight,' and 'face-to-face words plainly likely to cause an addressee to breach the peace'] is a proper subject for the reasonable exercise of the state police power and as applied to the appellant constitutes an adequate and constitutional basis for his conviction."[20] The state argued that its interest in maintaining public order and peace outweighed the appellant's interest in calling a city marshall a "God damned racketeer and a damned Fascist."[21]

Chaplinsky v. New Hampshire

315 U.S. 568, 62 S. Ct. 766; 86 L. Ed. 1031 (1942)

MR. JUSTICE MURPHY delivered the opinion of the Court:

Appellant, a member of the sect known as Jehovah's Witnesses, was convicted in the municipal court of Rochester, New Hampshire, for violation of Chapter 378, § 2, of the Public Laws of New Hampshire:

"No person shall address any offensive, derisive or annoying word to any other person who is lawfully in any street or other public place, nor call him by any offensive or derisive name, nor make any

noise or exclamation in his presence and hearing with intent to deride, offend or annoy him, or to prevent him from pursuing his lawful business or occupation."

The complaint charged that appellant, "with force and arms, in a certain public place in said city of Rochester, to wit, on the public sidewalk on the easterly side of Wakefield Street, near unto the entrance of the City Hall, did unlawfully repeat the words following, addressed to the complainant, that is to say, 'You are a God

[18]LB, Vol. 39, p. 57.
[19]Ibid., pp. 60–61.
[20]Ibid., p. 83
[21]Ibid., p. 98.

damned racketeer' and 'a damned Fascist and the whole government of Rochester are Fascists or agents of Fascists,' the same being offensive, derisive and annoying words and names."

Upon appeal there was a trial *de novo* of appellant before a jury in the Superior Court. He was found guilty and the judgment of conviction was affirmed by the Supreme Court of the State. . . .

By motions and exceptions, appellant raised the questions that the statute was invalid under the Fourteenth Amendment of the Constitution of the United States, in that it placed an unreasonable restraint on freedom of speech, freedom of the press, and freedom of worship, and because it was vague and indefinite. These contentions were overruled and the case comes here on appeal.

There is no substantial dispute over the facts. Chaplinsky was distributing the literature of his sect on the streets of Rochester on a busy Saturday afternoon. Members of the local citizenry complained to the City Marshal, Bowering, that Chaplinsky was denouncing all religion as a "racket." Bowering told them that Chaplinsky was lawfully engaged, and then warned Chaplinsky that the crowd was getting restless. Some time later, a disturbance occurred and the traffic officer on duty at the busy intersection started with Chaplinsky for the police station, but did not inform him that he was under arrest or that he was going to be arrested. On the way, they encountered Marshal Bowering, who had been advised that a riot was under way and was therefore hurrying to the scene. Bowering repeated his earlier warning to Chaplinsky, who then addressed to Bowering the words set forth in the complaint.

Chaplinsky's version of the affair was slightly different. He testified that, when he met Bowering, he asked him to arrest the ones responsible for the disturbance. In reply, Bowering cursed him and told him to come along. Appellant admitted that he said the words charged in the complaint, with the exception of the name of the Deity.

Over appellant's objection the trial court excluded, as immaterial, testimony relating to appellant's mission "to preach the true facts of the Bible," his treatment at the hands of the crowd, and the alleged neglect of duty on the part of the police. This action was approved by the court below, which held that neither provocation nor the truth of the utterance would constitute a defense to the charge.

It is now clear that "Freedom of speech and freedom of the press, which are protected by the First Amendment from infringement by Congress, are among the fundamental personal rights and liberties which are protected by the Fourteenth Amendment from invasion by state action." . . . Freedom of worship is similarly sheltered. *Cantwell* v. *Connecticut* [1940]. . . .

Appellant assails the statute as a violation of all three freedoms, speech, press and worship, but only an attack on the basis of free speech is warranted. The spoken, not the written, word is involved. And we cannot conceive that cursing a public officer is the exercise of religion in any sense of the term. But even if the activities of the appellant which preceded the incident could be viewed as religious in character, and therefore entitled to the protection of the Fourteenth Amendment, they would not cloak him with immunity from the legal consequences for concomitant acts committed in violation of a valid criminal statute. We turn, therefore, to an examination of the statute itself.

Allowing the broadest scope to the language and purpose of the Fourteenth Amendment, it is well understood that the right of free speech is not absolute at all times and under all circumstances. There are certain well-defined and narrowly limited classes of speech, the prevention and punishment of which have never been thought to raise any constitutional problem. These include the lewd and obscene, the profane, the libelous, and the insulting or "fighting" words—those which by their very utterance inflict injury or tend to incite an immediate breach of the peace. It has been well observed that such utterances are no essential part of any exposition of ideas, and are of such slight social value as a step to truth that any benefit that may be derived from them is clearly outweighed by the social interest in order and morality. "Resort to epithets or personal abuse is not in any proper sense communication of information or opinion safeguarded by the Constitution, and its punishment as a criminal act would raise no question under that instrument." *Cantwell* v. *Connecticut*. . . .

The state statute here challenged . . . has two provisions—the first relates to words or names addressed to another in a public place; the second refers to noises and exclamations. . . . We . . . limit our consideration to the first provision of the statute.

On the authority of its earlier decisions, the state court declared that the statute's purpose was to preserve the public peace, no words being "forbidden except such as have a direct tendency to cause acts of violence by the persons to whom, individually, the remark is addressed." It was further said: "The word 'offensive' is not to be defined in terms of what a particular addressee thinks. . . . The test is what men of common intelligence would understand would be words likely to cause an average addressee to fight. . . . The English language has a number of words and expressions which by general consent are 'fighting words' when said without a disarming smile. . . . Such words, as ordinary men know, are

likely to cause a fight. So are threatening, profane or obscene revilings. Derisive and annoying words can be taken as coming within the purview of the statute as heretofore interpreted only when they have this characteristic of plainly tending to excite the addressee to a breach of the peace. . . . The statute, as construed, does no more than prohibit the face-to-face words plainly likely to cause a breach of the peace by the addressee, words whose speaking constitutes a breach of the peace by the speaker—including 'classical fighting words', words in current use less 'classical' but equally likely to cause violence, and other disorderly words, including profanity, obscenity and threats."

We are unable to say that the limited scope of the statute as thus construed contravenes the Constitutional right of free expression. It is a statute narrowly drawn and limited to define and punish specific conduct lying within the domain of state power, the use in a public place of words likely to cause a breach of the peace. . . . This conclusion necessarily disposes of appellant's contention that the statute is so vague and indefinite as to render a conviction thereunder a violation of due process. A statute punishing verbal acts, carefully drawn so as not unduly to impair liberty of expression, is not too vague for a criminal law. . . .

Nor can we say that the application of the statute to the facts disclosed by the record substantially or unreasonably impinges upon the privilege of free speech. Argument is unnecessary to demonstrate that the appellations "damned racketeer" and "damned Fascist" are epithets likely to provoke the average person to retaliation, and thereby cause a breach of the peace.

The refusal of the state court to admit evidence of provocation and evidence bearing on the truth or falsity of the utterances, is open to no Constitutional objection. Whether the facts sought to be proved by such evidence constitute a defense to the charge, or may be shown in mitigation, are questions for the state court to determine. Our function is ful- filled by a determination that the challenged statute, on its face and as applied, does not contravene the Fourteenth Amendment.

Affirmed.

What rationale did Justice Murphy use to justify excluding "fighting words" from the free speech protection of the Fourteenth Amendment? Is there an implied clear and present danger test in the Court's opinion? To what extent does the Court defer to the legislative judgment of the state that certain categories of expression may be prohibited? Does the Court's standard reasonably protect free speech?

In *Terminiello* v. *Chicago* (1949) the Court overturned a breach of peace conviction under a Chicago ordinance that resulted from a far more inflammatory speech than was involved in the Chaplinsky case. "Father" Terminiello delivered a provocative, racist, and often obscene speech to an auditorium jammed with supporters, while outside a large and hostile crowd violently attempted to prevent the speech. Terminiello succeeded in stirring up the audience in the auditorium to a point where it was shouting vile racial epithets. Terminiello was arrested and convicted of a breach of peace under a Chicago ordinance which provided: "All persons who shall make, aid, countenance or assist in making any improper noise, riot, disturbance, breach of the peace, or diversion tending to a breach of the peace, within the limits of the city . . . shall be deemed guilty of disorderly conduct. . . ." The trial judge construed the ordinance to reach speech which "stirs the public to anger, invites dispute, brings about a condition of unrest, or creates a disturbance." Douglas, writing for the Court's majority, found the ordinance as interpreted by the trial judge to be overbroad and therefore unconstitutional. "The vitality of civil and political institutions within our society depends on free discussion," and "a function of free speech under our system of government is to invite dispute. It may indeed best serve its high purpose when it induces a condition of unrest, creates dissatisfaction with conditions as they are, or even stirs people to anger. Speech is often provocative and challenging. It may strike at prejudices and preconceptions and have profound unsettling effects as it presses for acceptance of an idea. That is why freedom of speech, though not absolute, [*Chaplinsky* v. *New Hampshire*] . . . is nevertheless protected against censorship or punishment, unless shown likely to produce a clear and present danger of a serious substantive evil that rises far above public inconvenience, annoyance, or unrest."[22]

The Court's decision in *Terminiello* hinged not on the nature of the speech given, but on the breadth of the Chicago ordinance as construed by the trial judge. Whether or not the conviction would have been upheld if the ordinance had been construed merely to include "fighting words" was not con-

_____

[22]Terminiello v. Chicago, 337 U.S. 1, 4, (1949).

sidered by the Court. Four justices dissented and three dissenting opinions were written.[23] In his dissent Justice Jackson compared the tactics of Terminiello to those of Hitler and stated that under the clear and present danger test the conviction should be sustained.

> A trial court and jury has found only that in the context of violence and disorder in which it was made, this speech was a provocation to immediate breach of the peace and therefore cannot claim constitutional immunity from punishment. Under the Constitution as it has been understood and applied, at least until most recently, the state was within its power in taking this action.
>
> Rioting is a substantive evil, which I take it no one will deny that a state and a city have the right and the duty to prevent and punish. Where an offense is induced by speech, the Court has laid down and often reiterated a [clear and present danger] test of the power of the authorities to deal with the speaking as also an offense . . . [and] no one ventures to contend that the state on the basis of this test, for whatever it may be worth, was not justified in punishing Terminiello. In this case the evidence proves beyond dispute that danger of rioting and violence in response to the speech was clear, present, and immediate.[24]

The following case, like *Terminiello,* reviewed a conviction for disorderly conduct. Compare the facts and issues raised in this case with those of *Chaplinsky* and *Terminiello.* Does the Court follow those precedents? The opinion was written by Chief Justice Vinson, who dissented in *Terminiello.*

Feiner v. New York

340 U.S. 315; 71 S. Ct. 303; 95 L. Ed. 295 (1951)

MR. CHIEF JUSTICE VINSON delivered the opinion of the Court:

Petitioner was convicted of the offense of disorderly conduct, a misdemeanor under the New York penal laws. . . . The case is here on certiorari, . . . petitioner having claimed that the conviction is in violation of his right of free speech under the Fourteenth Amendment.

In the review of state decisions where First Amendment rights are drawn in question, we of course make an examination of the evidence to ascertain independently whether the right has been vi-

olated; . . . Our appraisal of the facts is . . . based upon the uncontroverted facts and, where controversy exists, upon that testimony which the trial judge did reasonably conclude to be true.

On the evening of March 8, 1949, petitioner Irving Feiner was addressing an open-air meeting at the corner of South McBride and Harrison Streets in the City of Syracuse. At approximately 6:30 p.m., the police received a telephone complaint concerning the meeting, and two officers were detailed to investigate. One of these officers went to the scene immediately,

---

[23]The dissenting opinions were Vinson, Frankfurter (joined by Jackson and Burton), and Jackson (jointed by Burton).

[24]Ibid., pp. 25–26. Jackson's dissent includes excerpts from Terminiello's testimony at his trial and extensive quotes from the stenographic record of the speech he gave. See ibid., pp. 14–22.

the other arriving some twelve minutes later. They found a crowd of about seventy-five or eighty people, both Negro and white, filling the sidewalk and spreading out into the street. Petitioner, standing on a large wooden box on the sidewalk, was addressing the crowd through a loud-speaker system attached to an automobile. Although the purpose of his speech was to urge his listeners to attend a meeting to be held that night in the Syracuse Hotel, in its course he was making derogatory remarks concerning President Truman, the American Legion, the Mayor of Syracuse, and other local political officials.

The police officers made no effort to interfere with petitioner's speech, but were first concerned with the effect of the crowd on both pedestrian and vehicular traffic. They observed the situation from the opposite side of the street, noting that some pedestrians were forced to walk in the street to avoid the crowd. Since traffic was passing at the time, the officers attempted to get the people listening to petitioner back on the sidewalk. The crowd was restless and there was some pushing, shoving and milling around. . . .

At this time, petitioner was speaking in a "loud, high-pitched voice." He gave the impression that he was endeavoring to arouse the Negro people against the whites, urging that they rise up in arms and fight for equal rights. The statements before such a mixed audience "stirred up a little excitement." Some of the onlookers made remarks to the police about their inability to handle the crowd and at least one threatened violence if the police did not act. There were others who appeared to be favoring petitioner's arguments. Because of the feeling that existed in the crowd both for and against the speaker, the officers finally "stepped in to prevent it from resulting in a fight." . . . Although the officer . . . twice requested petitioner

to stop over the course of several minutes, petitioner not only ignored him but continued talking. During all this time, the crowd was pressing closer around petitioner and the officer. Finally, the officer told petitioner he was under arrest and ordered him to get down from the box, reaching up to grab him. Petitioner stepped down. . . . In all, the officer had asked petitioner to get down off the box three times over a space of four or five minutes. Petitioner had been speaking for over a half hour. . . .

The bill of particulars . . . gave in detail the facts upon which the prosecution relied to support the charge of disorderly conduct. Paragraph C is particularly pertinent here: "By ignoring and refusing to heed and obey reasonable police orders issued . . . to regulate and control said crowd and to prevent a breach or breaches of the peace and to prevent injury to pedestrians attempting to use said walk . . ., and prevent injury to the public generally."

We are not faced here with blind condonation by a state court of arbitrary police action. . . . The exercise of the police officers' proper discretionary power to prevent a breach of the peace was . . . approved by the trial court and later by two courts on review. The courts below . . . found that the officers in making the arrest were motivated solely by a proper concern for the preservation of order and protection of the general welfare, and that there was no evidence which could lend color to a claim that the acts of the police were a cover for suppression of petitioner's views and opinions. Petitioner was thus neither arrested nor convicted for the making or the content of his speech. Rather, it was the reaction which it actually engendered.

The language of *Cantwell* v. *Connecticut* [1940] . . . is appropriate here. . . . "When clear and present danger of riot, disorder, interference with traffic upon the public streets, or other immediate threat to public safety, peace, or order, appears, the power of the State to prevent or punish is obvious." . . . The findings of the New York courts as to the condition of the crowd and the refusal of petitioner to obey the police requests, supported as they are by the record of this case, are persuasive that the conviction of petitioner for violation of public peace, order and authority does not exceed the bounds of proper state police action. This Court respects, as it must, the interest of the community in maintaining peace and order on its streets. . . . We cannot say that the preservation of that interest here encroaches on the constitutional rights of this petitioner.

We are well aware that the ordinary murmurings and objections of a hostile audience cannot be allowed to silence a speaker, and are also mindful of the possible danger of giving overzealous police officials complete discretion to break up otherwise lawful public meetings. . . .

But we are not faced here with such a situation. It is one thing to say that the police cannot be used as an instrument for the suppression of unpopular views, and another to say that, when as here the speaker passes the bounds of argument or persuasion and undertakes incitement to riot, they are powerless to prevent a breach of the peace. Nor in this case can we condemn the considered judgment of three New York courts approving the means which the police, faced with a crisis, used in the exercise of their power and duty to preserve peace and order. The findings of the state courts as to the existing situation and the imminence of greater disorder coupled with petitioner's deliberate defiance of the police officers convince us that we should not reverse this conviction in the name of free speech.

Affirmed.

MR. JUSTICE BLACK, dissenting:

The record before us convinces me that petitioner, a young college student, has been sentenced to the penitentiary for the unpopular views he expressed on matters of public interest while lawfully making a street-corner speech in Syracuse, New York. Today's decision, however, indicates that we must blind ourselves to this fact because the trial judge fully accepted the testimony of the prosecution witnesses on all important points. . . .

. . .[I]t seems far-fetched to suggest that the "facts" show any imminent threat of riot or uncontrollable disorder. It is neither unusual nor unexpected that some people at public street meetings mutter, mill about, push, shove, or disagree, even violently, with the speaker. Indeed, it is rare where controversial topics are discussed that an outdoor crowd does not do some or all of these things. Nor does one isolated threat to assault the speaker forebode disorder. Especially should the danger be discounted where, as here, the person threatening was a man whose wife and two small children accompanied him and who, so far as the record shows, was never close enough to petitioner to carry out the threat.

Moreover, assuming that the "facts" did indicate a critical situation, I reject the implication of the Court's opinion that the police had no obligation to protect petitioner's constitutional right to talk. The police of course have power to prevent breaches of the peace. But if, in the name of preserving order, they ever can interfere with a lawful public speaker, they first must make all reasonable efforts to protect him. Here the policemen did not even pretend to try to protect petitioner. According to the officers' testimony, the crowd was restless but there is no showing of any attempt to quiet it; pedestrians were forced to walk into the street, but there was no effort to clear a path on the sidewalk; one person threatened to assault petitioner but the officers did nothing to discourage this when even a word might have sufficed. Their duty was to protect petitioner's right to talk, even to the extent of arresting the man who threatened to interfere. Instead, they shirked that duty and acted only to suppress the right to speak.

Finally, I cannot agree with the Court's statement that petitioner's disregard of the policeman's unexplained request amounted to such "deliberate defiance" as would justify an arrest or conviction for disorderly conduct. On the contrary, I think that the policeman's action was a "deliberate defiance" of ordinary official duty as well as of the constitutional right of free speech. For at least where time allows, courtesy and explanation of commands are basic elements of good official conduct in a democratic society. Here petitioner was "asked" then "told" then "commanded" to stop speaking, but a man making a lawful address is certainly not required to be silent merely because an officer directs it. Petitioner was entitled to know why he should cease doing a lawful act. Not once was he told. I understand that people in authoritarian countries must obey arbitrary orders. I had hoped that there was no such duty in the United States.

In my judgment, today's holding means that as a practical matter, minority speakers can be silenced in any city. . . . This is true regardless of the fact that in two other cases decided this day, *Kunz* v. *New York* . . . [and] *Niemotko* v. *Maryland* . . . a majority, in obedience to past decisions of this Court, provides a theoretical safeguard for freedom of speech. For whatever is thought to be guaranteed in *Kunz* and *Niemotko* is taken away by what is done here. The three cases read together mean that while previous restraints probably cannot be imposed on an unpopular speaker, the police have discretion to silence him as soon as the customary hostility to his views develops.[25] . . .

MR. JUSTICE DOUGLAS, with whom MR. JUSTICE MINTON concurs, dissenting:
. . . A speaker may not, of course, incite a riot. . . . But this record shows no such extremes. It shows an unsympathetic audience and the threat of one man to haul the speaker from the stage. It is against that kind of threat that speakers need police protection. If they do not receive it and instead the police throw their weight on the side of those who would break up the meetings, the police become the new censors of speech. Police censorship has all the vices of the censorship from city halls which we have repeatedly struck down. . . .

MR. JUSTICE FRANKFURTER concurring in the result:
It is pertinent . . . to note that all members of the New York Court accepted the finding that Feiner was stopped not because the listeners or police officers disagreed with his views but because these officers were honestly concerned with preventing a breach of the peace. . . .

[25]The Kuntz case overturned a New York City ordinance requiring a permit to conduct public worship meetings on the street and making it illegal to ridicule any religious belief or expound atheism or agnosticism in any street. The Court held that the ordinance gave administrative officials discretionary power to engage in prior censorship, which was a violation of First Amendment rights incorporated under the Fourteenth Amendment. In Niemotko v. Maryland the Court reversed the convictions of members of Jehovah's Witnesses who had been found guilty of disorderly conduct because they attempted to hold a metting in a municipal park without the required permit. The record contained no evidence of disorderly conduct, and the Court found that the permit had been unconstitutionally denied to the appellants because of dislike of their views. [Editor's note.]

. . .Where conduct is within the allowable limits of free speech, the police are peace officers for the speaker as well as for his hearers. But the power effectively to preserve order cannot be displaced by giving a speaker complete immunity. Here, there were two police officers present for 20 minutes. They interfered only when they apprehended imminence of violence. It is not a constitutional principle that, in acting to preserve order, the police must proceed against the crowd, whatever its size and temper, and not against the speaker.

It is true that breach-of-peace statutes, like most tools of government, may be misused. . . . But the possibility of misuse is not alone a sufficient reason to deny New York the power here asserted or so limit it by constitutional construction as to deny its practical exercise.

On what grounds did the Court hold that Feiner could be prevented from making his speech? Did the Court apply the clear and present danger test? Was the judgment reached by balancing the interest of the community in maintaining peace and order with the right of the individual to speak? On what basis did the Court support the finding that the audience was hostile? Does the ruling provide adequate protection against overzealous police officials from breaking up lawful public meetings? Are there any indications that considerations of federalism were important in the majority opinion?

Did the dissenting Justices Black and Douglas apply different standards to the case than were used by the majority? Did they draw different conclusions from the record? Did Douglas use the same method and standard of judicial review in *Feiner* that he employed in his majority opinion in *Terminiello*?

The *Feiner* majority invites the comparison of its opinion with that of the 1940 case, *Cantwell* v. *Connecticut,* which overturned a conviction for common law breach of the peace of a Jehovah's Witness who had angered a crowd by playing a phonograph record that among other insults accused the Catholic Church of being an instrument of Satan. In the words of the Court, the epithets on the phonograph record were

> couched in terms which naturally would offend not only persons of that [Roman Catholic] persuasion, but all others who respect the honestly held religious faith of their fellows. The hearers were in fact highly offended. One of them said he felt like hitting Cantwell and the other that he was tempted to throw Cantwell off the street. The one who testified he felt like hitting Cantwell said, in answer to the question, "Did you do anything else or have any other reaction?" "No, Sir, because he said he would take the Victrola and he went." The other witness testified that he told Cantwell he had better get off the street before something happened to him and that was the end of the matter as Cantwell picked up his books and walked up the street.[26]

The conviction was obtained under common law, not under a state statute, a fact which disturbed the Court because "[t]he judgment is based on a

[26]Cantwell v. Connecticut, 310 U.S. 296, 309 (1940).

common law concept of the most general and undefined nature."[27] There was no state statute regulating the expression of religious views on the streets; therefore, there was no manifest state interest that could be weighed against the rights of the individual. The judgment had to hinge upon the definition of common law breach of the peace, which, Justice Roberts's unanimous opinion stated,

> embraces a great variety of conduct destroying or menacing public order and tranquility. It includes not only violent acts but acts and words likely to produce violence in others. No one would have the hardihood to suggest that the principle of freedom of speech sanctioned excitement to riot or that religious liberty connotes the privilege to exhort others to physical acts upon those belonging to another sect. When clear and present danger of riot, disorder, interference with traffic upon the public streets, or other immediate threat to the public safety, peace or order, appears, the power of the state to prevent or punish is obvious. Equally obvious is it that a state may not unduly suppress free communication of views, religious or other, under the guise of conserving desirable conditions. Here we have a situation analogous to a conviction under a statute sweeping in a great variety of conduct under a general and indefinite characterization, and leaving to the executive and judicial branches too wide a discretion in its application.[28]

The Court recognized that one may be guilty of a breach of the peace offense "if he commits acts or makes statements likely to provoke violence and disturbance of good order, even though no such eventuality be intended. Decisions to this effect are many, but examination discloses that, in practically all, the provocative language which was held to amount to a breach of the peace consisted of profane, indecent, or abusive remarks directed to the person of the hearer. Resort to epithets or personal abuse is not in any proper sense communication of information or opinion safeguarded by the Constitution, and its punishment as a criminal act would raise no question under that instrument."[29] Roberts's opinion for the Court concluded that there was "in the instant case no assault or threatening of bodily harm, no truculent bearing, no intentional discourtesy, no personal abuse. On the contrary, we find only an effort to persuade a willing listener to buy a book or to contribute money in the interest of what Cantwell, however misguided others may think him, conceived to be true religion."[30]

Were the opinions in *Cantwell* and *Feiner* consistent, given the facts of the two cases? Administrative and judicial discretion was involved in each case in interpreting the statutory (*Feiner*) and common law (*Cantwell*) governing disorderly conduct and breach of the peace. The actions of the appellants in both cases seemed equally to present or, as the case may be, not present a clear and present danger to the public order. Was *Cantwell* decided differently from *Feiner* because it involved the suppression of religious expression?

[27]Ibid., p. 308.
[28]Ibid., p. 308.
[29]Ibid., pp. 309–310.
[30]Ibid., p. 310.

A more modern case that offers a sharp contrast with the approach of the *Feiner* Court is *Hess* v. *Indiana* (1973). The Court overturned the conviction of a spectator for disorderly conduct at an antiwar demonstration that blocked a campus street. When the police moved in to clear the street, a policeman heard the appellant, who was standing off the street, say, "We'll take the fucking street later," or "We'll take the fucking street again." The state court found that the statement was intended to incite the crowd to further lawless action. In reversing the conviction, the Supreme Court found no evidence to support the contention that Hess was exhorting the crowd back into the street, that his tone was no louder than those of other people in the area, and that "the statement could be taken as counsel for present moderation; at worst, it amounted to nothing more than advocacy of illegal action at some indefinite future time. This is not sufficient to permit the state to punish Hess's speech."[31]

Can government suppress "fighting words" that are not directed at a particular person and if they are merely offensive and not accompanied by conduct provoking others to acts of violence? The following case considered the question of the scope of state power to suppress offensive words.

Cohen v. *California*

403 U.S. 15; 91 S. Ct. 1780; 29 L. Ed. 2d 284 (1971)

Mr. Justice Harlan delivered the opinion of the Court:

This case may seem at first blush too inconsequential to find its way into our books, but the issue it presents is of no small constitutional significance.

Appellant Paul Robert Cohen was convicted in the Los Angeles Municipal Court of violating that part of California Penal Code § 415 which prohibits "maliciously and willfully disturb[ing] the peace or quiet of any neighborhood or person . . . by . . . offensive conduct. . . ." He was given 30 days' imprisonment. The facts upon which his conviction rests are detailed in the opinion of the Court of Appeal of California, Second Appellate District, as follows:

On April 26, 1968, the defendant was observed in the Los Angeles County Courthouse in the corridor outside of division 20 of the municipal court wearing a jacket bearing the

words 'Fuck the Draft' which were plainly visible. There were women and children present in the corridor. The defendant was arrested. The defendant testified that he wore the jacket knowing that the words were on the jacket as a means of informing the public of the depth of his feelings against the Vietnam War and the draft.

The defendant did not engage in, nor threaten to engage in, nor did anyone as the result of his conduct in fact commit or threaten to commit any act of violence. The defendant did not make any loud or unusual noise, nor was there any evidence that he uttered any sound prior to his arrest. . . .

In affirming the conviction the Court of Appeal held that "offensive conduct" means "behavior which has a tendency to provoke *others* to acts of violence or to in turn disturb the peace," and that the State had proved this element because, on the facts of this case, "[i]t was certainly reasonably foreseeable that such conduct

[31]Hess v. Indiana, 414 U.S. 105, 108 (1973).

might cause others to rise up to commit a violent act against the person of the defendant or attempt to forceably remove his jacket." . . . We . . . reverse.

I

In order to lay hands on the precise issue which this case involves, it is useful first to canvass various matters which this record does *not* present.

The conviction quite clearly rests upon the asserted offensiveness of the *words* Cohen used to convey his message to the public. The only "conduct" which the State sought to punish is the fact of communication. Thus, we deal here with a conviction resting solely upon "speech," . . . not upon any separately identifiable conduct which allegedly was intended by Cohen to be perceived by others as expressive of particular views but which, on its face, does not necessarily convey any message and hence arguably could be regulated without effectively repressing Cohen's ability to express himself. . . . Further, the State certainly lacks power to punish Cohen for the underlying content of the message the inscription conveyed. At least so long as there is no showing of an intent to incite disobedience to or disruption of the draft, Cohen could not, consistently with the First and Fourteenth Amendments, be punished for asserting the evident position on the inutility or immorality of the draft his jacket reflected. *Yates* v. *United States* [1957]. . . .

Appellant's conviction, then, rests squarely upon his exercise of the "freedom of speech" . . . and can be justified, if at all, only as a valid regulation of the manner in which he exercised that freedom, not as a permissible prohibition on the substantive message it conveys. This does not end the inquiry, of course, for the First and Fourteenth Amendments have never been thought to give absolute protection to every individual to speak whenever or wherever he pleases, or to use any form of address in any circumstances that he chooses. In this vein, too, however, we think it important to note that several issues typically associated with such problems are not presented here.

In the first place, Cohen was tried under a statute applicable throughout the entire State. Any attempt to support this conviction on the ground that the statute seeks to preserve an appropriately decorous atmosphere in the courthouse where Cohen was arrested must fail in the absence of any language in the statute that would have put appellant on notice that certain kinds of otherwise permissible speech or conduct would nevertheless, under California law, not be tolerated in certain places. . . . No fair reading of the phrase "offensive conduct" can be said sufficiently to inform the ordinary person that distinctions between certain locations are thereby created.

In the second place, as it comes to us, this case cannot be said to fall within those relatively few categories of instances where prior decisions have established the power of government to deal more comprehensively with certain forms of individual expression simply upon a showing that such a form was employed. This is not, for example, an obscenity case. Whatever else may be necessary to give rise to the States' broader power to prohibit obscene expression, such expression must be, in some significant way, erotic. . . . It cannot plausibly be maintained that this vulgar allusion to the Selective Service System would conjure up such psychic stimulation in anyone likely to be confronted with Cohen's crudely defaced jacket.

This Court has also held that the States are free to ban the simple use, without a demonstration of additional justifying circumstances, of so-called "fighting words," those personally abusive epithets which, when addressed to the ordinary citizen, are, as a matter of common knowledge, inherently likely to provoke violent reaction. *Chaplinsky* v. *New Hampshire* [1942]. . . . While the four-letter word displayed by Cohen in relation to the draft is not uncommonly employed in a personally provocative fashion, in this instance it was clearly not "directed to the person of the hearer." . . . No individual actually or likely to be present could reasonably have regarded the words on appellant's jacket as a direct personal insult. Nor do we have here an instance of the exercise of the State's police power to prevent a speaker from intentionally provoking a given group to hostile reaction. . . . There is, as noted above, no showing that anyone who saw Cohen was in fact violently aroused or that appellant intended such a result.

Finally, in arguments before this Court much has been made of the claim that Cohen's distasteful mode of expression was thrust upon unwilling or unsuspecting viewers, and that the State might therefore legitimately act as it did in order to protect the sensitive from otherwise unavoidable exposure to appellant's crude form of protest. Of course, the mere presumed presence of unwitting listeners or viewers does not serve automatically to justify curtailing all speech capable of giving offense. . . . While this Court has recognized that government may properly act in many situations to prohibit intrusion into the privacy of the home of unwelcome views and ideas which cannot be totally banned from the public dialogue, . . . we have at the same time consistently stressed that "we are often 'captives' outside the sanctuary of the home and subject to objectionable speech."[32]

. . . The ability of government, consonant with the Constitution, to shut off discourse solely to protect others from hearing it is, in other words, dependent upon a showing that substantial privacy interests are being invaded in an essentially intolerable manner. Any broader view of this authority would effectively empower a majority to silence dissidents simply as a matter of personal predilections.

In this regard, persons confronted with Cohen's jacket were in a quite different posture than, say, those subjected to the raucous emissions of sound trucks blaring outside their residences. Those in the Los Angeles courthouse could effectively avoid further bombardment of their sensibilities simply by averting their eyes. And, while it may be that one has a more substantial claim to a recognizable privacy interest when walking through a courthouse corridor than, for example, strolling through Central Park, surely it is nothing like the interest in being free from unwanted expression in the confines of one's own home. . . . Given the subtlety and complexity of the factors involved, if Cohen's "speech" was otherwise entitled to constitutional protection, we do not think the fact that some unwilling "listeners" in a public building may have been briefly exposed to it can serve to justify this breach of the peace conviction where, as here, there was no evidence that persons powerless to avoid appellant's conduct did in fact object to it, and where . . . the statute . . . evinces no concern . . . with the special plight of the captive auditor, but, instead, indiscriminately sweeps within its prohibitions all "offensive conduct" that disturbs "any neighborhood or person." . . .

---

[32]Rowan v. Post Office Dept. 397 U.S. 728, 738 (1970). The Rowan decision upheld a federal law that permitted persons to request of the Post Office that their names be removed from the mailing list of a sender of pandering advertisements offering for sale "matter which the addressee in his sole discretion believes to be erotically arousing or sexually provocative." Against a challenge that it violated the right to communicate, the Court held that the right to privacy outweighed the right of a mailer to communicate. [Editor's note.]

II

Against this background, the issue flushed by this case stands out in bold relief. It is whether California can excise, as "offensive conduct," one particular scurrilous epithet from the public discourse, either upon the theory of the court below that its use is inherently likely to cause violent reaction or upon a more general assertion that the States, acting as guardians of public morality, may properly remove this offensive word from the public vocabulary.

The rationale of the California court is plainly untenable. At most it reflects an "undifferentiated fear or apprehension of disturbance [which] is not enough to overcome the right to freedom of expression." . . . We have been shown no evidence that substantial numbers of citizens are standing ready to strike out physically at whoever may assault their sensibilities with execrations like that uttered by Cohen. There may be some persons about with such lawless and violent proclivities, but that is an insufficient base upon which to erect, consistently with constitutional values, a governmental power to force persons who wish to ventilate their dissident views into avoiding particular forms of expression. The argument amounts to little more than the self-defeating proposition that to avoid physical censorship of one who has not sought to provoke such a response by a hypothetical coterie of the violent and lawless, the States may more appropriately effectuate that censorship themselves. . . .

Admittedly, it is not so obvious that the First and Fourteenth Amendments must be taken to disable the States from punishing public utterance of this unseemly expletive in order to maintain what they regard as a suitable level of discourse within the body politic. We think, however, that examination and reflection will reveal the shortcomings of a contrary viewpoint.

At the outset, we cannot overemphasize that, in our judgment, most situations where the State has a justifiable interest in regulating speech will fall within one or more of the various established exceptions, discussed above but not applicable here, to the usual rule that governmental bodies may not prescribe the form or content of individual expression. Equally important to our conclusion is the constitutional backdrop against which our decision must be made. The constitutional right of free expression is powerful medicine in a society as diverse and populous as ours. It is designed and intended to remove governmental restraints from the arena of public discussion, putting the decision as to what views shall be voiced largely into the hands of each of us, in the hope that use of such freedom will ultimately produce a more capable citizenry and more perfect polity and in the belief that no other approach would comport with the premise of individual dignity and choice upon which our political system rests. . . .

To many, the immediate consequence of this freedom may often appear to be only verbal tumult, discord, and even offensive utterance. These are, however, within established limits, in truth necessary side effects of the broader enduring values which the process of open debate permits us to achieve. That the air may at times seem filled with verbal cacophony is, in this sense not a sign of weakness but of strength. We cannot lose sight of the fact that, in what otherwise might seem a trifling and annoying instance of individual distasteful abuse of a privilege, these fundamental societal values are truly implicated. . . .

Against this perception of the constitutional policies involved, we discern certain more particularized considerations that peculiarly call for reversal of this conviction. First, the principle contended for by the State seems inherently boundless. How is one to distinguish this from any

other offensive word? Surely the State has
no right to cleanse public debate to the
point where it is grammatically palatable
to the most squeamish among us. Yet no
readily ascertainable general principle exists for stopping short of that result were
we to affirm the judgment below. For,
while the particular four-letter word being
litigated here is perhaps more distasteful
than most others of its genre, it is nevertheless often true that one man's vulgarity
is another's lyric. Indeed, we think it is
largely because governmental officials
cannot make principled distinctions in
this area that the Constitution leaves matters of taste and style so largely to the
individual.

Additionally, we cannot overlook the
fact, because it is well illustrated by the
episode involved here, that much linguis-
tic expression serves a dual communica-
tive function: it conveys not only ideas
capable of relatively precise, detached
explication, but otherwise inexpressible
emotions as well. In fact, words are often
chosen as much for their emotive as their
cognitive force. We cannot sanction the
view that the Constitution, while solicitous
of the cognitive content of individual
speech, has little or no regard for that
emotive function which, practically speaking, may often be the more important element of the overall message sought to be
communicated. . . .

Finally, and in the same vein, we cannot indulge the facile assumption that one
can forbid particular words without also
running a substantial risk of suppressing
ideas in the process. Indeed, governments
might soon seize upon the censorship of
particular words as a convenient guise for
banning the expression of unpopular
views. . . .

It is, in sum, our judgment that, absent
a more particularized and compelling reason for its actions, the State may not, consistently with the First and Fourteenth
Amendments, make the simple public display here involved of this single four-
letter expletive a criminal offense. . . .

Reversed.

MR. JUSTICE BLACKMUN, with whom
THE CHIEF JUSTICE and MR. JUSTICE BLACK
join:
I dissent, and I do so for two reasons:
1. Cohen's absurd and immature antic,
in my view, was mainly conduct and little
speech. . . . Further, the case appears to
me to be well within the sphere of *Chaplinsky* v. *New Hampshire* [1942] . . . where
Mr. Justice Murphy, a known champion
of First Amendment freedoms, wrote for
a unanimous bench. As a consequence,
this Court's agonizing over First Amendment values seems misplaced and unnecessary.
2. I am not at all certain that the California Court of Appeal's construction of
§ 415 is now the authoritative California
construction. . . . A month [after declining
to review the *Cohen* case] the State Supreme Court in another case construed
§ 415, evidently for the first time. *In re
Bushman*. . . .[The Court] held that § 415
". . . makes punishable only wilful and
malicious conduct that is violent and en-
dangers public safety and order or that
creates a clear and present danger
that others will engage in violence of that
nature.
". . . [It] does not make criminal any
nonviolent act unless the act incites or
threatens to incite others to violence. . . ."
Cohen was cited in *Bushman*, . . . but I am
not convinced that its description there
and *Cohen* itself are completely consistent
with the "clear and present danger"
standard enunciated in *Bushman*. . . .[T]his
case . . . ought to be remanded . . . for reconsideration in the light of . . . *Bushman*.

MR. JUSTICE WHITE concurs in Paragraph 2 of MR. JUSTICE BLACKMUN'S dissenting opinion.

How does the Court distinguish the facts of *Cohen* from those of *Chaplinsky, Feiner,* and *Terminiello*? On what grounds is the conviction for offensive conduct overturned? Is a clear and present danger test applied? Under what circumstances does the Court state offensive messages may be suppressed?

FREEDOM OF EXPRESSION IN THE PUBLIC FORUM

To what extent do individuals and groups have the right to freedom of expression in such public forums as streets, sidewalks, and parks? Under what circumstances and on what basis can government suppress such forms of expression as demonstrations and parading, picketing, making speeches, and leafleting in public places?

Although the Court had confronted the question of freedom of expression in the public forum in the 1930s and 1940s, the civil rights demonstrations of the 1960s raised a variety of new public forum cases posing constitutional issues that required resolution.[33] In *Edwards* v. *South Carolina* (1963) the Court reviewed a breach of the peace conviction of 187 black civil rights demonstrators who had walked in separate groups of about fifteen each to the South Carolina State House to protest their discriminatory treatment under state laws. There were approximately thirty law enforcement officers at the scene, and there was no violence or disorder of any kind. The only incident occurred after the demonstrators were advised that they would be arrested if they did not disperse in fifteen minutes. The record indicated that instead of dispersing, the demonstrators "engaged in what the city manager described as 'boisterous,' 'loud' and 'flamboyant' conduct, which, as his later testimony made clear, consisted of listening to a 'religious harangue' by one of their leaders, and loudly singing 'The Star Spangled Banner' and other patriotic and religious songs, while stamping their feet and clapping their hands. After 15 minutes had passed, the police arrested the petitioners and marched them off to jail."[34] This, wrote the Court, "was a far cry from the situation in *Feiner* v. *New York*" and differed also from *Chaplinsky* v. *New Hampshire* in that there was no evidence of "fighting words."[35] Citing from Douglas's majority opinion in *Terminiello,* the *Edwards* majority concluded that "The courts of South Carolina have defined a criminal offense so as to permit conviction of the petitioners if their speech 'stirred people to anger, invited public dispute, or brought about a condition of unrest.' A conviction resting on any of those grounds may not stand."[36]

A year after its *Edwards* decision the Court again reviewed a First and Fourteenth Amendment challenge to state action aimed at the suppression of demonstrations in the following two cases.

[33]For early public forum cases see SAIA v. New York City, 334 U.S. 558 (1948); Martin v. Struthers, 319 U.S. 141 (1943); Jamison v. Texas, 318 U.S. 413 (1943); Cox v. New Hampshire, 312 U.S. 569 (1941); Schneider v. State, 308 U.S. 147 (1939); Hague v. CIO, 307 U.S. 496 (1939).

[34]Edwards v. South Carolina, 372 U.S. 229, 233 (1963).

[35]Ibid., p. 236.

[36]Ibid., p. 238. The Terminiello quote is at 337 U.S. 1, 5 (1949).

Cox v. *Louisiana*

[Cox I–No. 24, 1964 Term]
379 U.S. 536; 85 S. Ct. 453; 13 L. Ed. 2d. 471 (1965)

MR. JUSTICE GOLDBERG delivered the opinion of the Court:

Appellant, the Reverend Mr. B. Elton Cox, the leader of a civil rights demonstration, was arrested and charged with four offenses under Louisiana law—criminal conspiracy, disturbing the peace, obstructing public passages, and picketing before a courthouse. In a consolidated trial before a judge without a jury, and on the same set of facts, he was acquitted of criminal conspiracy but convicted of the other three offenses. He was sentenced to serve four months in jail and pay a $200 fine for disturbing the peace, to serve five months in jail and pay a $500 fine for obstructing public passages, and to serve one year in jail and pay a $5,000 fine for picketing before a courthouse. The sentences were cumulative.

... Appellant filed two separate appeals to this Court ... contending that the three statutes under which he was convicted were unconstitutional on their face and as applied. ... This case, No. 24, involves the convictions for disturbing the peace and obstructing public passages, and No. 49 [Cox II, at p. 642] concerns the conviction for picketing before a courthouse.

I

THE FACTS

On December 14, 1961, 23 students from Southern University, a Negro college, were arrested in downtown Baton Rouge, Louisiana, for picketing stores that maintained segregated lunch counters. This picketing, urging a boycott of those stores, was part of a general protest movement against racial segregation, directed by the local chapter of the Congress of Racial Equality. ... The appellant, an ordained Congregational minister, the Reverend Mr. B. Elton Cox, a Field Secretary of CORE, was an advisor to this movement. On the evening of December 14, appellant and Ronnie Moore, student president of the local CORE chapter, spoke at a mass meeting at the college. The students resolved to demonstrate the next day in front of the courthouse in protest of segregation and the arrest and imprisonment of the picketers who were being held in the parish jail located on the upper floor of the courthouse building.

The next morning about 2,000 students left the campus, which was located approximately five miles from downtown Baton Rouge. Most of them had to walk into the city since the drivers of their busses were arrested. Moore was also arrested at the entrance to the campus while parked in a car equipped with a loudspeaker, and charged with violation of an antinoise statute. Because Moore was immediately taken off to jail and the vice president of the CORE chapter was already in jail for picketing, Cox felt it his duty to take over the demonstration and see that it was carried out as planned. ...

As Cox, ... at the head of the group, approached the vicinity of the courthouse, he was stopped ... and brought to Police Chief Wingate White. ... The Chief ... inquired as to the purpose of the demonstration. Cox ... outlined his program to White, stating that it would include a singing of the Star Spangled Banner and a "freedom song," recitation of the Lord's Prayer and the Pledge of Allegiance, and a short speech. White testified that he told Cox that "he must confine" the demonstration "to the west side of the street." White added, "This, of course, was not—I didn't mean it in the import that I was giving him any permission to do it, but I was presented with a situation that was accomplished, and I had to make a decision." Cox testified that the officials agreed to permit the meeting. . . .

The students were then directed by Cox to the west sidewalk, across the street from the courthouse, 101 feet from its steps. They were lined up on this sidewalk about five deep and spread almost the entire length of the block. The group did not obstruct the street. It was close to noon and, being lunch time, a small crowd of 100 to 300 curious white people . . . gathered on the east sidewalk and courthouse steps, about 100 feet from the demonstrators. Seventy-five to eighty policemen, including city and state patrolmen and members of the Sheriff's staff, as well as members of the fire department and a fire truck were stationed in the street between the two groups. . . .

Several of the students took from beneath their coats picket signs similar to those which had been used the day before. These signs bore legends such as "Don't buy discrimination for Christmas," "Sacrifice for Christ, don't buy," and named stores which were proclaimed "unfair." They then sang "God Bless America," pledged allegiance to the flag, prayed briefly, and sang one or two hymns, including "We Shall Overcome." The 23 students, who were locked in jail cells in the courthouse building out of the sight of the demonstrators, responded by themselves singing; this in turn was greeted with cheers and applause by the demonstrators. Appellant gave a speech, described by a State's witness as follows:

He said that in effect that it was a protest against the illegal arrest of some of their members and that other people were allowed to picket . . . and he said that they were not going to commit any violence, that if anyone spit on them, they would not spit back on the person that did it.

Cox then said:

All right. It's lunch time. Let's go eat. There are twelve stores we are protesting. A number of these stores have twenty counters; they accept your money from nineteen. They won't accept it from the twentieth counter. This is an act of racial discrimination. These stores are open to the public. You are members of the public. We pay taxes to the Federal Government and you who live here pay taxes to the State.

In apparent reaction to these last remarks, there was what state witnesses described as "muttering" and "grumbling" by the white onlookers.

The Sheriff, deeming, as he testified, Cox's appeal to the students to sit in at the lunch counters to be "inflammatory," then took a power microphone and said, "Now, you have been allowed to demonstrate. Up until now your demonstration has been more or less peaceful, but what you are doing now is a direct violation of the law, a disturbance of the peace, and it has got to be broken up immediately." The testimony as to what then happened is disputed. Some of the State's witnesses testified that Cox said, "don't move"; others stated that he made a "gesture of defiance." It is clear from the record, however, that Cox and the demonstrators did not then and there break up the demonstration. . . .

Almost immediately thereafter—within a time estimated variously at two to five minutes—one of the policemen exploded a tear gas shell at the crowd. This was followed by several other shells. The demonstrators quickly dispersed, running back towards the State Capitol and the downtown area. . . .

No Negroes participating in the demonstration were arrested on that day. . . . The next day appellant was arrested and charged with the four offenses above described.

II

THE BREACH OF THE PEACE CONVICTION

Appellant was convicted of violating a

Louisiana "disturbing the peace" statute, which provides:

Whoever with intent to provoke a breach of the peace, or under circumstances such that a breach of the peace may be occasioned thereby . . . crowds or congregates with others . . . in or upon . . . a public street or public highway, or upon a public sidewalk, or any other public place or building . . . and who fails or refuses to disperse and move on . . . when ordered so to do by any law enforcement officer of any municipality, or parish, in which such act or acts are committed, or by any law enforcement officer of the state of Louisiana, or any other authorized person . . . shall be guilty of disturbing the peace.

It is clear to us that on the facts of this case, which are strikingly similar to those present in *Edwards* v. *South Carolina* [1963] . . . Louisiana infringed appellant's rights of free speech and free assembly by convicting him under this statute. . . . We hold that Louisiana may not constitutionally punish appellant under this statute for engaging in the type of conduct which this record reveals, and also that the statute as authoritatively interpreted by the Louisiana Supreme Court is unconstitutionally broad in scope. . . .

. . .[O]ur independent examination of the record, which we are required to make, shows no conduct which the State had a right to prohibit as a breach of the peace. . . .

The State argues . . . that while the demonstrators started out to be orderly, the loud cheering and clapping by the students in response to the singing from the jail converted the peaceful assembly into a riotous one. The record, however, does not support this assertion. . . . Our conclusion that the entire meeting from the beginning until its dispersal by tear gas was orderly and not riotous is confirmed by a film of the events taken by a television news photographer. . . . We have viewed the film, and it reveals that the students, though they undoubtedly cheered and clapped, were well-behaved throughout. . . .

Finally, the State contends that the conviction should be sustained because of fear expressed by some of the state witnesses that "violence was about to erupt" because of the demonstration. It is virtually undisputed, however, that the students themselves were not violent and threatened no violence. The fear of violence seems to have been based upon the reaction of the group of white citizens looking on from across the street. . . . There is no indication, however, that any member of the white group threatened violence. And this small crowd estimated at between 100 and 300 was separated from the students by "seventy-five to eighty" armed policemen. . . . As Inspector Trigg testified, they could have handled the crowd.

This situation, like that in *Edwards,* is "a far cry from the situation in *Feiner* v. *New York.* . . ." Nor is there any evidence here of "fighting words." . . .

There is an additional reason why this conviction cannot be sustained. The statute at issue in this case, as authoritatively interpreted by the Louisiana Supreme Court, is unconstitutionally vague in its overly broad scope. The statutory crime consists of two elements: (1) congregating with others "with intent to provoke a breach of the peace, or under circumstances such that a breach of the peace may be occasioned," and (2) a refusal to move on after having been ordered to do so by a law enforcement officer. While the second part of this offense is narrow and specific, the first element is not. The Louisiana Supreme Court in this case defined the term "breach of the peace" as "to agitate, to arouse from a state of repose, to molest, to interrupt, to hinder, to disquiet." . . . Both definitions would allow persons to be punished merely for peacefully expressing unpopular views. . . . Therefore, as in *Terminiello* and *Edwards* the conviction under this statute must be reversed as the statute is unconstitutional in that it sweeps within its broad scope activities that are constitutionally protected. . . .

III
THE OBSTRUCTING PUBLIC PASSAGES CONVICTION

We now turn to the issue of the validity of appellant's conviction for violating the Louisiana statute . . . which provides:

Obstructing Public Passages

No person shall willfully obstruct the free, convenient and normal use of any public sidewalk, street, highway, bridge, alley, road, or other passageway, or the entrance, corridor or passage of any public building, structure, watercraft or ferry, by impeding, hindering, stifling, retarding or restraining traffic or passage thereon or therein.

Providing however nothing herein contained shall apply to a bona fide legitimate labor organization or to any of its legal activities such as picketing. . . .

Appellant was convicted under this statute . . . for leading the meeting on the sidewalk across the street from the courthouse. . . .

Appellant, however, contends that as so construed and applied in this case, the statute is an unconstitutional infringement on freedom of speech and assembly. This contention on the facts here presented raises an issue with which this Court has dealt in many decisions.

From these decisions certain clear principles emerge. The rights of free speech and assembly, while fundamental in our democratic society, still do not mean that everyone with opinions or beliefs to express may address a group at any public place and at any time. The constitutional guarantee of liberty implies the existence of an organized society maintaining public order, without which liberty itself would be lost in the excesses of anarchy. The control of travel on the streets is a clear example of governmental responsibility to insure this necessary order. A restriction in that relation, designed to promote the public convenience in the interest of all, and not susceptible to abuses of discriminatory application, cannot be disregarded by the attempted exercise of some civil right which, in other circumstances, would be entitled to protection. One would not be justified in ignoring the familiar red light because this was thought to be a means of social protest. Nor could one, contrary to traffic regulations, insist upon a street meeting in the middle of Times Square at the rush hour as a form of freedom of speech or assembly. Governmental authorities have the duty and responsibility to keep their streets open and available for movement. A group of demonstrators could not insist upon the right to cordon off a street, or entrance to a public or private building, and allow no one to pass who did not agree to listen to their exhortations. . . .

We emphatically reject the notion urged by appellant that the First and Fourteenth Amendments afford the same kind of freedom to those who would communicate ideas by conduct such as patrolling, marching, and picketing on streets and highways, as these amendments afford to those who communicate ideas by pure speech. . . . We reaffirm the statement of the Court in *Giboney* v. *Empire Storage & Ice Co.* [1949] that "it has never been deemed an abridgment of freedom of speech or press to make a course of conduct illegal merely because the conduct was in part initiated, evidenced, or carried out by means of language, either spoken, written, or printed."

We have no occasion in this case to consider the constitutionality of the uniform, consistent, and nondiscriminatory application of a statute forbidding all access to streets and other public facilities for parades and meetings. Although the statute here involved on its face precludes all street assemblies and parades, it has not been so applied and enforced by the Baton Rouge authorities. City officials who testified for the State clearly indicated that certain meetings and parades are permitted in Baton Rouge, even though they have the effect of obstructing traffic, provided prior approval is obtained. . . . The statute itself provides no standards for the determination of local officials as to which assemblies to permit or which to prohibit. . . . From all the evidence before us it appears that the authorities in Baton Rouge permit or prohibit parades or street meetings in their completely uncontrolled discretion.

The situation is thus the same as if the statute itself expressly provided that there could only be peaceful parades or demonstrations in the unbridled discretion of the local officials. The pervasive restraint on freedom of discussion by the practice of the authorities under the statute is not any less effective than a statute expressly permitting such selective enforcement. . . .

This Court has recognized that the lodging of such broad discretion in a public official allows him to determine which expressions of view will be permitted and which will not. This thus sanctions a device for the suppression of the communication of ideas and permits the official to act as a censor. . . . Also inherent in such a system allowing parades or meetings only with the prior permission of an official is the obvious danger to the right of a person or group not to be denied equal protection of the laws. . . . It is clearly unconstitutional to enable a public official to determine which expressions of view will be permitted and which will not or to engage in invidious discrimination among persons or groups either by use of a statute providing a system of broad discretionary licensing power or, as in this case, the equivalent of such a system by selective enforcement of an extremely broad prohibitory statute.

It is, of course, undisputed that appropriate, limited discretion, under properly drawn statutes or ordinances, concerning the time, place, duration, or manner of use of the streets for public assemblies may be vested in administrative officials . . . *Cox* v. *New Hampshire*. . . .

Reversed.

Cox v. Louisiana

[Cox II–No. 49, 1964 Term]
379 U.S. 559; 85 S. Ct. 476; 13 L. Ed. 2d 487 (1965)

MR. JUSTICE GOLDBERG delivered the opinion of the Court:

Appellant was convicted of violating a Louisiana statute which provides:

Whoever, with the intent of interfering with, obstructing, or impeding the administration of justice, or with the intent of influencing any judge, juror, witness, or court officer, in the discharge of his duty pickets or parades in or near a building housing a court of the State of Louisiana . . . shall be fined not more than five thousand dollars or imprisoned not more than one year, or both.

This charge was based upon the same set of facts as the "disturbing the peace" and "obstructing a public passage" charges involved and set forth in No. 24 [Cox I]. . . .

I

We shall first consider appellant's contention that this statute must be declared invalid on its face as an unjustified restriction upon freedoms guaranteed by the First and Fourteenth Amendments to the United States Constitution.

This statute was passed by Louisiana in 1950 and was modeled after a federal [law enacted] . . . in 1950. . . . The federal statute resulted from the picketing of federal courthouses by partisans of the defendants during trials involving leaders of the Communist Party. . . .

This statute, unlike the two previously considered, is a precise, narrowly drawn regulatory statute which proscribes certain specific behavior. . . . It prohibits a particular type of conduct, namely, picketing and parading, in a few specified locations, in or near courthouses.

There can be no question that a State has a legitimate interest in protecting its judicial system from the pressures which picketing near a courthouse might create. Since we are committed to a government of laws and not of men, it is of the utmost importance that the administration of justice be absolutely fair and orderly. This Court has recognized that the unhindered and untrammeled functioning of our courts is part of the very foundation of our constitutional democracy. . . . The constitutional safeguards relating to the integrity of the criminal process attend every stage of a criminal proceeding . . . and . . . they exclude influence or domination by either a hostile or friendly mob. There is no room at any stage of judicial proceedings for such intervention; mob law is the very antithesis of due process. . . . A State may adopt safeguards necessary and appropriate to assure that the administration of justice at all stages is free from outside control and influence. A narrowly drawn statute such as the one under review is obviously a safeguard both necessary and appropriate to vindicate the State's interest in assuring justice under law.

Nor does such a statute infringe upon the constitutionally protected rights of free speech and free assembly. The conduct which is the subject of this statute—picketing and parading—is subject to regulation even though intertwined with expression and association. The examples are many of the application by this Court of the principle that certain forms of conduct mixed with speech may be regulated or prohibited. . . .

Here we deal . . . with . . . a statute narrowly drawn to punish specific conduct that infringes a substantial state interest in protecting the judicial process. . . . We deal in this case not with free speech alone, but with expression mixed with particular conduct. . . .

We hold that this statute on its face is a valid law dealing with conduct subject to regulation so as to vindicate important interests of society and that the fact that free speech is intermingled with such conduct does not bring with it constitutional protection.

II

We now deal with the Louisiana statute as applied to the conduct in this case. The group of 2,000, led by appellant, paraded and demonstrated before the courthouse. Judges and court officers were in attendance to discharge their respective functions. It is undisputed that a major purpose of the demonstration was to protest what the demonstrators considered an "illegal" arrest of 23 students the previous day. . . .

It is, of course, true that most judges will be influenced only by what they see and hear in court. However, judges are human; and the legislature has the right to recognize the danger that some judges, jurors, and other court officials, will be consciously or unconsciously influenced by demonstrations in or near their courtrooms both prior to and at the time of the trial. A State may also properly protect the judicial process from being misjudged in the minds of the public. Suppose demonstrators paraded and picketing for weeks with signs asking that indictments be dismissed, and that a judge, completely uninfluenced by these demonstrations, dismissed the indictments. A State may protect against the possibility of a conclusion by the public under these circumstances that the judge's action was in part a product of intimidation and did not flow only from the fair and orderly working of the judicial process. . . .

Appellant invokes the clear and present danger doctrine in support of his argument that the statute cannot constitutionally be applied to the conduct involved here . . . He defines the standard to be applied . . . to be whether the expression of opinion presents a clear and present danger to the administration of justice.

We have already pointed out the important differences between the contempt cases [e.g., *Bridges* v. *California* and *Pennekamp* v. *Florida,* discussed infra fn. 57] and the present one. . . . Here we deal not with the contempt power but with a narrowly drafted statute and not with speech in its pristine form but with conduct of a totally different character. Even assuming the applicability of a general clear and present danger test, it is one thing to conclude that the mere publication of a newspaper editorial or a telegram to a Secretary of Labor, however critical of a court, presents no clear and present danger to the administration of justice [which the Court held in the contempt cases, fn. 57 infra] and quite another thing to conclude that crowds, such as this, demonstrating before a courthouse may not be prohibited by a legislative determination based on experience that such conduct inherently threatens the judicial process. We therefore reject the clear and present danger argument of appellant. . . .

There are, however, more substantial constitutional objections arising from appellant's conviction on the particular facts of this case. Appellant was convicted for demonstrating not "in," but "near" the courthouse. . . . . . . [T]here is some lack of specificity in a word such as "near." While this lack of specificity may not render the statute unconstitutionally vague,

at least as applied to a demonstration within the sight and hearing of those in the courthouse, it is clear that the statute, with respect to the determination of how near the courthouse a particular demonstration can be, foresees a degree of on-the-spot administrative interpretation by officials charged with responsibility for administering and enforcing it. . . .This administrative discretion to construe the term "near" . . . is the type of narrow discretion which this Court has recognized as the proper role of responsible officials in making determinations concerning the time, place, duration, and manner of demonstrations. . . .

The record here clearly shows that the officials present gave permission for the demonstration to take place across the street from the courthouse. . . .

. . . In effect, appellant was advised that a demonstration at the place it was held would not be one "near" the courthouse within the terms of the statute. . . .

. . . [U]nder all the circumstances of this case, after the public officials acted as they did, to sustain appellant's later conviction for demonstrating where they told him he could "would be to sanction an indefensible sort of entrapment by the State—convicting a citizen for exercising a privilege which the State had clearly told him was available to him." . . . The Due Process Clause does not permit convictions to be obtained under such circumstances. . . .

There remains just one final point: the effect of the Sheriff's order to disperse. The State in effect argues that this order somehow removed the prior grant of permission and reliance on the officials' construction that the demonstration on the far side of the street was not illegal as being "near" the courthouse. This, however, we cannot accept. . . .

. . . [I]t is our conclusion from the record that the dispersal order had nothing to do with any time or place limitation, and thus, on this ground alone, it is clear that the dispersal order did not remove the protection accorded appellant by the original grant of permission. . . .

Nothing we have said here or in No. 24 [Cox I] . . . is to be interpreted as sanctioning riotous conduct in any form or demonstrations, however peaceful their conduct or commendable their motives, which conflict with properly drawn statutes and ordinances designed to promote law and order, protect the community against disorder, regulate traffic, safeguard legitimate interests in private and public property, or protect the administration of justice and other essential governmental functions.

. . . We reaffirm the repeated holdings of this Court that our constitutional command of free speech and assembly is basic and fundamental and encompasses peaceful social protest, so important to the preservation of the freedoms treasured in a democratic society. We also reaffirm the repeated decisions of this Court that there is no place for violence in a democratic society dedicated to liberty under law, and that the right of peaceful protest does not mean that everyone with opinions or beliefs to express may do so at any time and at any place. There is a proper time and place for even the most peaceful protest and a plain duty and responsibility on the part of all citizens to obey all valid laws and regulations. . . .

Reversed.

MR. JUSTICE BLACK, concurring in No. 24 [Cox I] and dissenting in No. 49 [Cox II]:

. . . The First and Fourteenth Amendments, I think, take away from government, state and federal, all power to restrict freedom of speech, press, and assembly *where people have a right to be for such purposes.* This does not mean, however, that these amendments also grant a constitutional right to engage in the conduct of picketing or patrolling, whether on publicly owned streets or on privately owned property. . . . Were the law otherwise, people on the streets, in their homes and anywhere else could be compelled to listen against their will to speakers they did not want to hear. Picketing, though it may be utilized to communicate ideas, is not speech, and therefore is not of itself protected by the First Amendment. . . .

However, because Louisiana's breach-of-peace statute is not narrowly drawn to assure nondiscriminatory application, I think it is constitutionally invalid under our holding in *Edwards* v. *South Carolina*. . . .

The Louisiana law . . . expressly provides that the statute shall not bar picketing and assembly by labor unions protesting unfair treatment of union members. I believe that the First and Fourteenth Amendments require that if the streets of a town are open to some views, they must be open to all. . . . [B]y specifically permitting picketing for the publication of labor union views, Louisiana is attempting to pick and choose among the views it is willing to have discussed on its streets. It thus is trying to prescribe by law what matters of public interest people whom it allows to assemble on its streets may and may not discuss. This seems to me to be censorship in a most odious form, unconstitutional under the First and Fourteenth Amendments. And to deny this appellant and his group use of the streets because of their views against racial discrimination, while allowing other groups to use the streets to voice opinions on other subjects, also amounts, I think, to an invidious discrimination forbidden by the Equal Protection Clause of the Fourteenth Amendment. Moreover, as the Court points out, city officials despite this statute apparently have permitted favored groups other than labor unions to block the streets with their gatherings. For these reasons I concur in reversing the conviction based on this law.

I would sustain the conviction . . . [for picketing near a courthouse.] Certainly the most obvious reason for their protest at the courthouse was to influence the judge and other court officials. . . . The Court attempts to support its holding by its inference that the Chief of Police gave his consent to picketing the courthouse. But quite apart from the fact that a police chief cannot authorize violations of his State's criminal laws, there was strong, emphatic testimony that if any consent was given it was limited to telling Cox and his group to come no closer to the courthouse than they had already come without the consent of any official, city, state, or federal. And there was also testimony that when told to leave appellant Cox defied the order by telling the crowd not to move. I fail to understand how the Court can justify the reversal of this conviction because of a permission which testimony in the record denies was given, which could not have been authoritatively given anyway, and which even if given was soon afterwards revoked. . . .

. . . . Those who encourage minority groups to believe that the United States Constitution and federal laws give them a right to patrol and picket in the streets whenever they choose, in order to advance what they think to be a just and noble end, do no service to those minority groups, their cause, or their country. I am confident from this record that this appellant violated the Louisiana statute because of a mistaken belief that he and his followers had a constitutional right to do so, because of what they believed were just grievances. But the history of the past 25 years if it shows nothing else shows that his group's constitutional and statutory rights have to be protected by the courts, which must be kept free from intimidation and coercive pressures of any kind. Government under law as ordained by our Constitution is too precious, too sacred, to be jeopardized by subjecting the courts to intimidatory practices that have been fatal to individual liberty and minority rights wherever and whenever such practices have been allowed to poison the streams of justice. I would be wholly unwilling to join in moving this country a single step in that direction.

Mr. Justice White, with whom Mr. Justice Harlan joins, concurring in part and dissenting in part:

In No. 49 [Cox II], I agree with the dissent filed by my Brother Black in . . . [the last part] of his opinion. In No. 24 [Cox I], although I do not agree with everything the Court says concerning the breach of peace conviction, particularly its statement concerning the unqualified protection to be extended to Cox's exhortations to engage in sit-ins in restaurants, I agree that the conviction for breach of peace is governed by *Edwards* v. *South Carolina* . . . and must be reversed.

Regretfully, I also dissent from the reversal of the conviction for obstruction of public passages. The Louisiana statute is not invalidated on its face but only in its application. But this remarkable emasculation of a prohibitory statute is based on only very vague evidence that other meetings and parades have been allowed by the authorities. . . . There is no evidence in the record that other meetings of this magnitude had been allowed on the city streets, had been allowed in the vicinity of the courthouse or had been permitted completely to obstruct the sidewalk and to block access to abutting buildings. . . .

Furthermore, even if the obstruction statute, because of prior permission granted to others, could not be applied in this case so as to prevent the demonstration, it does not necessarily follow that the federal license to use the streets is unlimited as to time and circumstance. . . . . . . [A]t some point the authorities were entitled to apply the statute and to clear the streets. That point was reached here. To reverse the conviction under these circumstances makes it only rhetoric to talk of local power to control the streets under a properly drawn ordinance.

Compare the statutes reviewed in *Cox I* and *Cox II*. Why was the *Cox I* statute, as interpreted by the state court, overturned while the *Cox II* statute was upheld? How were the *Terminiello* and *Edwards* precedents applied in *Cox I*? Under what circumstances would the Court allow government to control marching and picketing on the streets and highways? Why does the Court state: "We emphatically reject the notion . . . that the First and Fourteenth Amendments afford the same kind of freedom to those who would communicate ideas by conduct such as patrolling, marching, and picketing on streets and highways, as these amendments afford to those who communicate ideas by pure speech"? Does Goldberg, in *Cox I*, imply that "[n]ondiscriminatory application of a statute forbidding all access to streets and other public facilities for parades and meetings" might be constitutional? How does the Court in *Cox I* view what it considered to be the existence of a broad administrative discretion to permit or prohibit demonstrations?

Did the record reviewed in *Cox II* reveal more or less administrative discretion to control demonstrations than the Court found in *Cox I*? Why does the Court in *Cox II* reject the clear and present danger argument of the appellant? Are the grounds upon which the Court reverses the conviction broad or narrow? Would the Court have allowed the dispersal of the demonstration if prior permission had not been granted?

On what basis would Justice Black have upheld the *Cox II* conviction? What reservations did he have about the majority opinion? In his view how far does the authority of government reach to suppress picketing and other forms of expression on public streets or on privately owned property? In *Cox II*, was Black's dissent based upon his belief that the intent of the demonstration was to influence the judge? Did he believe that the appellant's actions constituted a clear and present danger of disruption of justice?

In *Shuttlesworth* v. *Birmingham*, 394 U.S. 147 (1969), the Court held unconstitutional a city ordinance that required persons wishing to hold or participate in parades or public demonstrations to secure a permit from the City Commission, which could refuse to issue the permit if it found that such action was required by the "public welfare, peace, safety, health, decency, good order, morals or convenience." The Court stated that the ordinance was unconstitutional since it subjected the exercise of First Amendment freedoms to prior censorship. Even in the absence of such a finding, wrote Justice Stewart for the Court, the ordinance would be unconstitutional as applied because the city authorities had made it clear that under no circumstances would they issue a permit to the defendant and his group to conduct a civil rights demonstration. Picketing and parading constitute methods of expression entitled to First Amendment protection, declared Stewart, who cited in particular the dictum of Justice Roberts in *Hague* v. *CIO*.

> Wherever the title of streets and parks may rest, they have immemorially been held in trust for the use of the public and, time out of mind, have been used for purposes of assembly, communicating thoughts between citizens, and discussing public questions. Such use of the streets and public places has, from ancient times, been a part of the privileges, immunities, rights, and the liberties of citizens. The privilege of a citizen of the United States to use the streets and parks for communication of views of national questions may be regulated in the interest of all; it is not absolute, but relative, and must be exercised in subordination to the gen-

eral comfort and convenience, and in consonance with peace and good order; but it must not, in the guise of regulation, be abridged or denied.[37]

The Semi-Public Forum

Do the First Amendment freedoms of expression in public forums such as streets and parks extend to public buildings, for example, schools, libraries, city halls, and courthouses? In the "open" public forums of streets and parks the right of the individual to demonstrate is not absolute but must be weighed against the interests of the government in the maintenance of peace and order, and in the orderly conduct of its business. The exercise of freedom of expression within public buildings raises many of the same questions that pertain to expression in streets and parks but with the added dimension that the physical facilities are more limited, and demonstrations are more likely to be disruptive. In the following case the Court reviewed a breach of the peace conviction for a sit-in demonstration in a public library.

Brown v. *Louisiana*

383 U.S. 131; 86 S. Ct. 719; 15 L. Ed. 2d 637 (1966)

MR. JUSTICE FORTAS announced the judgment of the Court and an opinion in which THE CHIEF JUSTICE [Warren] and MR. JUSTICE DOUGLAS join:

This is the fourth time in little more than four years that this Court has reviewed convictions by the Lousiana courts for alleged violations, in a civil rights context, of that State's breach of the peace statute. In the three preceding cases the convictions were reversed. . . .

Since the present case was decided under precisely the statute involved in *Cox* but before our decision in that case was announced, it might well be supposed that, without further ado, we would vacate and remand in light of *Cox*. But because the incident leading to the present convictions occurred in a public library and might be thought to raise materially different questions, we have heard argument and have considered the case *in extenso*.

The locus of the events was the Audu-bon Regional Library in the town of Clinton, Louisiana, Parish of East Feliciana. . . .

The Audubon Regional Library . . . has three branches and two bookmobiles.

. . . The blue bookmobile served only Negroes. It is a permissible inference that no Negroes used the branch libraries.

This tidy plan was challenged on Saturday, March 7, 1964, at about 11:30 a.m. Five young Negro males, all residents of East or West Feliciana Parishes, went into the adult reading or service room of the Audubon Regional Library at Clinton. The branch assistant, Mrs. Katie Reeves, was alone in the room . . . Petitioner Brown requested a book. . . . Mrs. Reeves checked the card catalogue, ascertained that the Branch did not have the book, so advised Mr. Brown, and told him that she would request the book from the State Library, that he would be notified upon its receipt and that "he could either pick it up or it would be mailed to him.". . . Mrs. Reeves testified that she expected that the

---

[37]Hague v. CIO, 307 U.S. 496, 515–516 (1939).

men would then leave; they did not, and she asked them to leave. They did not. Petitioner Brown sat down and the others stood near him. They said nothing; there was no noise or boisterous talking. Mrs. Reeves called Mrs. Perkins, the regional librarian, who was in another room. Mrs. Perkins asked the men to leave. They remained.

Neither Mrs. Reeves nor Mrs. Perkins had called the sheriff, but in "10 to 15 minutes" from the time of the arrival of the men at the library, the sheriff and the deputies arrived. The sheriff asked the Negroes to leave. They said they would not. The sheriff then arrested them. . . .

On March 25, 1964, Mr. Brown and his four companions were tried and found guilty. Brown was sentenced to pay $150 and costs, and in default thereof to spend 90 days in the parish jail. His companions were sentenced to $35 and costs, or 15 days in jail. The charge was that they had congregated together in the public library of Clinton, Louisiana, "with the intent to provoke a breach of the peace and under circumstances such that a breach of the peace might be occasioned thereby" and had failed and refused "to leave said premises when ordered to do so" by the librarian and by the sheriff.

The Louisiana breach of peace statute under which they were accused reads as follows: "Whoever with intent to provoke a breach of the peace, or under circumstances such that a breach of the peace may be occasioned thereby: (1) crowds or congregates with others . . . in . . . a . . . public place or building . . . and who fails or refuses to disperse and move on, or disperse or move on, when ordered so to do by any law enforcement officer . . . or any other authorized person . . . shall be guilty of disturbing the peace.". . .

We come, then, to the bare bones of the problem. Petitioners, five adult Negro men, remained in the library room for a total of ten or fifteen minutes. The first

few moments were occupied by a ritualistic request for service and a response. We may assume that the response constituted service, and we need not consider whether it was merely a gambit in the ritual. This ceremony being out of the way, the Negroes proceeded to the business in hand. They sat and stood in the room, quietly, as monuments of protest against the segregation of the library. They were arrested and . . . convicted. . . .

. . . [T]here is not the slightest evidence which would or could sustain the application of the statute to petitioners. . . .

Nor were the circumstances such that a breach of the peace might be "occasioned" by their actions, as the statute alternatively provides. . . .

The argument of the State of Louisiana, however, is that the issue presented by this case is much simpler than our statement would indicate. The issue, asserts the State, is simply that petitioners were using the library room "as a place in which to loaf or make a nuisance of themselves." The State argues that the "test"— the permissible civil rights demonstration—was concluded when petitioners entered the library, asked for service and were served. Having satisfied themselves, the argument runs, that they could get service, they should have departed. Instead, they simply sat there, "staring vacantly," and this was "enough to unnerve a woman in the situation Mrs. Reeves was in."

This is a piquant version of the affair, but the matter is hardly to be decided on points. It was not a game. It could not be won so handily by the gesture of service to this particular request. There is no dispute that the library system was segregated, and no possible doubt that these petitioners were there to protest this fact. But even if we were to agree with the State's ingenuous characterization of the events, we would have to reverse. There was no violation of the statute which petitioners are accused of breaching; no disorder, no intent to provoke a breach of the peace and no circumstances indicating that a breach might be occasioned by petitioner's actions. The sole statutory provision invoked by the State contains not a word about occupying the reading room of a public library for more than 15 minutes. . . .

But there is another and sharper answer which is called for. We are here dealing with an aspect of a basic constitutional right—the right under the First and Fourteenth Amendments guaranteeing freedom of speech and of assembly, and freedom to petition the Government for a redress of grievances. . . . As this Court has repeatedly stated, these rights are not confined to verbal expression. They embrace appropriate types of action which certainly include the right in a peaceable and orderly manner to protest by silent and reproachful presence, in a place where the protestant has every right to be, the unconstitutional segregation of public facilities. Accordingly, even if the accused action were within the scope of the statutory instrument, we would be required to assess the constitutional impact of its application, and we would have to hold that the statute cannot constitutionally be applied to punish petitioners' actions in the circumstances of this case. See *Edwards* v. *South Carolina*. . . . The statute was deliberately and purposefully applied solely to terminate the reasonable, orderly, and limited exercise of the right to protest the unconstitutional segregation of a public facility. Interference with this right, so exercised, by state action is intolerable under our Constitution. . . .

It is an unhappy circumstance that the locus of these events was a public library— a place dedicated to quiet, to knowledge, and to beauty. It is a sad commentary that this hallowed place in the Parish of East Feliciana bore the ugly stamp of racism. It is sad, too, that it was a public library

which, reasonably enough in the circumstances, was the stage for a confrontation between those discriminated against and the representatives of the offending parishes. Fortunately, the circumstances here were such that no claim can be made that use of the library by others was disturbed by the demonstration. Perhaps the time and method were carefully chosen with this in mind. Were it otherwise, a factor not present in this case would have to be considered. Here, there was no disturbance of others, no disruption of library activities, and no violation of any library regulations.

A State or its instrumentality may, of course, regulate the use of its libraries or other public facilities. But it must do so in a reasonable and nondiscriminatory manner, equally applicable to all and administered with equality to all. It may not do so as to some and not as to all. It may not provide certain facilities for whites and others for Negroes. And it may not invoke regulations as to use—whether they are *ad hoc* or general—as a pretext for pursuing those engaged in lawful, constitutionally protected exercise of their fundamental rights. . . .

Reversed.

MR. JUSTICE BRENNAN, concurring in the judgment:

. . . Since the overbreadth of [the breach of peace statute] as construed clearly requires the reversal of these convictions, it is wholly unnecessary to reach, let alone rest reversal, as the prevailing opinion seems to do, on the proposition that even a narrowly drawn "statute cannot constitutionally be applied to punish petitioner's actions in the circumstances of this case."

MR. JUSTICE WHITE, concurring in the result:

. . . [I]t is difficult to believe that if this

group had been white its members would have been asked to leave on such short notice, much less asked to leave by the sheriff and arrested, rather than merely escorted from the building, when reluctance to leave was demonstrated. . . . In my view, the behavior of these petitioners and their use of the library building, even though it was for the purposes of a demonstration, did not depart significantly from what normal library use would contemplate.

The conclusion that petitioners were making only a normal and authorized use of this public library requires the reversal of their convictions. . . . On this record, it is difficult to avoid the conclusion that petitioners were asked to leave the library because they were Negroes. If they were, their convictions deny them equal protection of the laws. . . .

MR. JUSTICE BLACK, with whom MR. JUSTICE CLARK, MR. JUSTICE HARLAN, and MR. JUSTICE STEWART join, dissenting:

. . . The case relied on most heavily by the prevailing opinion and my Brother Brennan is *Cox* v. *State of Louisiana*. . . . That case, unlike this one, involved picketing and patrolling in the streets. . . . The . . . phase of the statute under consideration here, relating to congregating in public buildings and refusing to move on when ordered to do so by an authorized person, was in no way involved or discussed in *Cox*. The problems of state regulation of the streets on the one hand, and public buildings on the other, are quite obviously separate and distinct. Public buildings such as libraries, schoolhouses, fire departments, courthouses, and executive mansions are maintained to perform certain specific and vital functions. Order and tranquility of a sort entirely unknown to the public streets are essential to their normal operation. Contrary to the implications in the prevailing opinion it is incomprehensible to me that

a State must measure disturbances in its libraries and on the streets with identical standards. . . .

. . . [T]here simply was no racial discrimination practiced in this case. These petitioners . . . asked for a book, perhaps as the prevailing opinion suggests more as a ritualistic ceremonial than anything else. The lady in charge nevertheless hunted for the book, found she did not have it, sent for it, and later obtained it from the state library for petitioners' use. . . .

. . . The only factual question which can possibly arise regarding the application of the statute here is whether under Louisiana law petitioners either intended to breach the peace or created circumstances under which a breach might have been occasioned. . . . A tiny parish branch library, staffed by two women, is not a department store as in *Garner* v. *State of Louisiana* [1961], nor a bus terminal as in *Taylor* v. *State of Louisiana* [1962], nor a public thoroughfare as in *Edwards* v. *South Carolina* [1963], and *Cox*. Short of physical violence, petitioners could not have more completely upset the normal, quiet functioning of the Clinton branch of the Audubon Regional Library. The state courts below thought the disturbance created by petitioners constituted a violation of the statute. So far as the reversal here rests on a holding that the Louisiana statute was not violated, the Court simply substitutes its judgment for that of the Louisiana courts as to what conduct satisfies the requirements of that state statute. . . .

. . . Apparently unsatisfied with or unsure of the "no evidence" ground for reversing the convictions, the prevailing opinion goes on to state that the statute was used unconstitutionally in the circumstances of this case because it was "deliberately and purposefully applied solely to terminate the reasonable, orderly, and limited exercise of the right to protest the unconstitutional segregation of a public facility." First, I am constrained to say that this statement is wholly unsupported by the record in this case. . . . Moreover, the conclusion . . . establishes a completely new constitutional doctrine. In this case this new constitutional principle means that even though these petitioners did not want to use the Louisiana public library for library purposes, they had a constitutional right nevertheless to stay there over the protest of the librarians who had lawful authority to keep the library orderly for the use of people who wanted to use its books, its magazines, and its papers. But the principle espoused also has a far broader meaning. It means that the Constitution (the First and the Fourteenth Amendments) requires the custodians and supervisors of the public libraries in this country to stand helplessly by while protesting groups advocating one cause or another, stage "sit-ins" or "stand-ups" to dramatize their particular views on particular issues. And it should be remembered that if one group can take over libraries for one cause, other groups will assert the right to do so for causes which, while wholly legal, may not be so appealing to this Court. The States are thus paralyzed with reference to control of their libraries for library purposes, and I suppose that inevitably the next step will be to paralyze the schools. Efforts to this effect have already been made all over the country. . . .

The First Amendment, I think, protects speech, writings, and expression of views in any manner in which they can be legitimately and validly communicated. But I have never believed that it gives any person or group of persons the constitutional right to go wherever they want, whenever they please, without regard to the rights of private or public property or to state law. . . . [I]t does not guarantee to any person the right to use someone else's property, even that owned by government and dedicated to other purposes, as a stage to express dissident ideas. The novel constitutional doctrine of the prevailing opinion nevertheless exalts the power of private nongovernmental groups to determine what use shall be made of governmental property over the power of the elected governmental officials. . . .

. . . I am deeply troubled with the fear that powerful private groups throughout the Nation will read the Court's action, as I do—that is, as granting them a license to invade the tranquility and beauty of our libraries whenever they have quarrel with some state policy which may or may not exist. It is an unhappy circumstance in my judgment that the group, which more than any other has needed a government of equal laws and equal justice, is now encouraged to believe that the best way for it to advance its cause, which is a worthy one, is by taking the law into its own hands from place to place and from time to time. Governments like ours were formed to substitute the rule of law for the rule of force. Illustrations may be given where crowds have gathered together peaceably by reason of extraordinarily good discipline reinforced by vigilant officers. "Demonstrations" have taken place without any manifestations of force at the time. But I say once more that the crowd moved by noble ideals today can become the mob ruled by hate and passion and greed and violence tomorrow. . . .

What circumstances of the case were important in the opinion of the majority? Did the defendants, in fact, violate the breach of peace statute? Was the Court correct in its assessment that "there is not the slightest evidence which would or could sustain the application of the statute to petitioners"? Was not the finding that the statute as applied violated First and Fourteenth Amendment rights the basis of its judgment?

Why did Justice Black, in his dissent, state that the majority misapplied the precedent of *Cox I* to the case? How does Black view the case differently than the majority in terms of its facts and the constitutional standards that should be applied? What does Black conclude will be the implication of the Court's decision? Are there considerations of federalism underlying his dissenting opinion?

Shortly after the Court's decision in the *Brown* case, in *Adderley* v. *Florida* (1966) it reviewed a conviction of thirty-two students at Florida A&M University in Tallahassee for trespass on the premises of the county jail in violation of a state law forbidding malicious and mischievous trespass upon "the property of another." The students claimed that they had gone to the jail to demonstrate the arrest the day before of other students and "perhaps to protest more generally against state and local policies and practices of racial segregation, including segregation of the jail."[38] The defendants cited the *Edwards* and *Cox I* decisions to support their right to protest. Justice Black wrote the majority opinion upholding the conviction. He based his decision largely on the same grounds that he raised in his dissent in *Brown*. The jury had adequate evidence upon which to base its decision, wrote Black, and nothing in the Constitution

> prevents Florida from even-handed enforcement of its general trespass statute against those refusing to obey the Sheriff's order to remove themselves from what amounted to the curtilage of the jailhouse. The state, no less than a private owner of property, has power to preserve the property under its control for the use to which it is lawfully dedicated. For this reason there is no merit to the petitioners' argument that they had a constitutional right to stay on the property, over the jail custodian's objections, because this "area" chosen for the peaceful civil rights demonstration was not only "reasonable" but also particularly appropriate. . . .[39]

Justice Douglas dissented, joined by Warren, Brennan, and Fortas, who, with White, had constituted the *Brown* majority. Douglas wrote,

> The jailhouse, like an executive mansion, a legislative chamber, a courthouse, or the state house itself, is one of the seats of government, whether it be the Tower of London, the Bastille, or a small county jail. And when it houses political prisoners or those whom many think are unjustly held, it is an obvious center for protest. The right to petition for redress of grievances has an ancient history and is not limited to writing a letter or sending a telegram to a congressman, it is not confined to appearing before the local city council, or writing letters to the President, or Governor, or Mayor.
>
> Conventional methods of petitioning may be, and often have been shut off to large groups of our citizens. . . . Those who do not control television and radio, those who cannot afford to advertise in newspapers or circulate elaborate pamphlets, may have only a more limited type of access to public officials. Their methods should not be condemned as tactics of obstruction and harassment as long as the assembly and petition are readable, as these were.[40]

[38]Adderley v. Florida, 385 U.S. 39, 40 (1966).
[39]Ibid., p. 47.
[40]Ibid., pp. 49–51.

The general standards of review for freedom of expression cases in the semi-public forum permit expression where it does not unduly interfere with the proper exercise of government functions. Demonstrations in public schools, for example, which themselves have as one of their principal purposes the exchange of ideas, must be permitted if they are peaceful but may be suppressed if they are disruptive.[41] Government institutions such as military bases, cannot be discriminatorily closed to the expression of political views.[42] But, if a government policy is clearly stated and administered in a nondiscriminatory fashion, political expression in government facilities can be curbed.[43] However, if there are no reasonable alternative forums for the effective expression of a particular viewpoint than a government building or facility, the rights of the protestants to expression will be upheld against a governmental attempt to suppress them.[44]

Once a public forum is opened for communication, the government cannot determine which positions will be taken, although it may control the type of communication. In *Lehman* v. *City of Shaker Heights* (1974) the Court reviewed a challenge to a city ban on *political* advertising on its rapid transit vehicles, while the city permitted *commercial* advertising on these vehicles. In a plurality opinion the Court held that the cars and the advertising space on them were not a public forum in the traditional sense but part of a commercial venture over which "a city transit system has discretion to develop and make reasonable choices concerning the type of advertising that may be displayed in its vehicles."[45] Justice Brennan's dissenting opinion, joined by Justices Stewart, Marshall, and Powell, declared: "The city created a forum for the dissemination of information and expression of ideas when it accepted and displayed commercial and public service advertisements on its rapid transit vehicles. Having opened a forum for communication, the city is barred by the First and Fourteenth Amendments from discriminating among forum users solely on the basis of message content."[46] Brennan argued: "While it is possible that commercial advertising may be accorded *less* First Amendment protection than speech concerning political and social issues of public importance, . . . it is 'speech' nonetheless, often communicating information and ideas found by many persons to be controversial."[47] Not only the First Amendment, but also equal protection principles require open access to prevent the government from granting the use of the forum only to those people whose views it finds acceptable. Government can regulate the use of the public forum, but only on a nondiscriminatory basis to

[41]Tinker v. Des Moines School District, 393 U.S. 503 (1969). Demonstrations outside of schools may also be prohibited if they are disruptive. See Grayned v. City of Rockford, 408 U.S. 104 (1972).

[42]Greer v. Spock, 424 U.S. 828 (1976).

[43]Ibid.

[44]Albany Welfare Rights Organization v. Wyman, 493 F. 2d 1319 (2d Cir. 1974). The Court held that the waiting room for welfare recipients was an "appropriate" place for leafleting, provided that the leafleting was not accompanied by any attempts to disrupt orderly administration.

[45]Lehman v. City of Shaker Heights, 418 U.S. 298, 303 (1974). Discriminatory denial of access to a public forum is prohibited. See also Hague v. CIO, 307 U.S. 496 (1939).

[46]Lehman v. City of Shaker Heights, 418 U.S. 298, 310 (1974).

[47]Ibid., p. 314.

preserve the use of the forum itself. "That the discrimination is among entire classes of ideas, rather than among points of view within a particular class," wrote Brennan, "does not render it any less odious. Subject matter or content censorship in any form is forbidden."[48]

Access to the Private Forum

The media constitute an important private forum for the expression of ideas. While newspapers can be considered completely private, the broadcasting industry is regulated by government in the public interest. The justification for that regulation is that broadcasting uses the airwaves, which are owned by the public. Therefore the broadcasting media is in effect a semiprivate forum.

An attempt by Florida to regulate access to newspapers was overturned in *Miami Herald Publishing Co.* v. *Cornillo,* 418 U.S. 241 (1974). The case challenged a Florida statute that compelled newspapers to print the replies of political candidates whom they had attacked. The Court held that such laws violate the First Amendment freedom of the press, which is not outweighed by the legitimate interest of the government in preserving the free flow of information and the wide dissemination of differing political views.

Prior to the *Miami Herald* case, the Court in *Red Lion Broadcasting Co.* v. *FCC* (1969) upheld the authority of the government to require broadcasters to give the right of reply to their political editorials and to personal attacks they had broadcast. Essentially the Court ruled that the FCC regulations incorporating these requirements were a reasonable exercise of its authority, granted by Congress to regulate the broadcasting industry in the public interest. The regulations enhanced the freedom of speech of the public by guaranteeing access to the media under certain circumstances. It is "the right of the viewers and listeners, not the right of the broadcasters which is paramount," concluded the Court.[49] The FCC regulations were found to enhance rather than contract freedom of speech.[50]

THE FIRST AMENDMENT FREEDOM
OF ASSOCIATION

Under the First Amendment citizens have the freedom to associate to pursue the other rights protected by the First Amendment—speech, press, religion, and the right to petition government for a redress of grievances. Government cannot interfere with the activities of an organization that is exercising its First Amendment freedoms. For example, the Democratic party has a First Amendment right to associate freely and to determine the

[48]Ibid., p. 316.

[49]Red Lion Broadcasting Co. v. FCC, 395 U.S. 367, 390 (1969).

[50]Contrast the Red Lion decision with Columbia Broadcasting System v. Democratic National Committee, 412 U.S. 94 (1973), in which the Court upheld the FCC's refusal to require broadcasters to sell time to the DNC and an antiwar group for editorial advertisements.

rules under which it will operate.[51] This freedom of association is based directly upon the freedom of expression protected by the First Amendment. Organizations per se are not protected by the freedom of association, and if they are not pursuing goals that are otherwise protected by the First Amendment they may be regulated by government.[52]

The freedom of association clearly limits although it does not always prohibit governmental attempts to outlaw an organization, dictate how it is to be run, or withhold benefits such as government employment or contracts from members of an organization.[53] Are there other barriers to governmental intrusion upon the freedom of association? In the following case the Court reviewed a judgment of civil contempt against the NAACP in Alabama for failure to comply with a state law requiring a foreign corporation to register with the secretary of state and file a copy of its corporate charter and designate its place of business. The NAACP claimed that it was not a foreign corporation and did not therefore have to register. The state sought an injunction to prevent the NAACP from operating within its boundaries, and in the course of the injunction proceedings moved for the production of the association's records including its membership lists. The trial court held the association in contempt and imposed a $100,000 fine, a judgment which was upheld by the Supreme Court of Alabama.

NAACP v. Alabama

357 U.S. 449; 78 S. Ct. 1163; 2 L. Ed. 2d 1488 (1958)

MR. JUSTICE HARLAN delivered the opinion of the Court:

... The question presented is whether Alabama, consistently with the Due Process Clause of the Fourteenth Amendment, can compel petitioner to reveal to the State's Attorney General the names and addresses of all its Alabama members and agents, without regard to their positions or functions in the Association. . . .

II

The Association both urges that it is constitutionally entitled to resist official inquiry into its membership lists, and that it may assert, on behalf of its members, a right personal to them to be protected from compelled disclosure by the State of their affiliation with the Association as revealed by the membership lists. . . .

---

[51]Cousins v. Wigota, 419 U.S. 477 (1975).

[52]Compare, for example, NAACP v. Button, 371 U.S. 415 (1963), in which the Court declared that Virginia could not apply its statutory ban against the solicitation of litigation to the NAACP, with Garcia v. Texas State Board of Medical Examiners, 421 U.S. 995 (1975), in which the Court summarily affirmed a lower court decision upholding a statute that prohibited the formation and operation of health maintenance organizations unless doctors made the administrative as well as the medical decisions. In the Button case the Court found that the Virginia law violated the freedom of expression guaranteed to the members of the NAACP by the First Amendment. In Garcia there was no link between First Amendment rights and the associational interests of the plaintiffs.

[53]Examples of limits in these three areas respectively are Noto v. United States, 367 U.S. 290 (1961), Cousins v. Wigoda, cited in fn. 51 supra, and Greene v. McElroy, 360 U.S. 474 (1959).

If petitioner's rank-and-file members are constitutionally entitled to withhold their connection with the Association despite the production order, it is manifest that this right is properly assertable by the Association. To require that it be claimed by the members themselves would result in nullification of the right at the very moment of its assertion. Petitioner is the appropriate party to assert these rights, because it and its members are in every practical sense identical. The Association, which provides in its constitution that "[a]ny person who is in accordance with [its] principles and policies . . ." may become a member, is but the medium through which its individual members seek to make more effective the expression of their own views. The reasonable likelihood that the Association itself through diminished financial support and membership may be adversely affected if production is compelled is a further factor pointing towards our holding that petitioner has standing to complain of the production order on behalf of its members. . . .

III

We . . . reach petitioner's claim that the production order in the state litigation trespasses upon fundamental freedoms protected by the Due Process Clause of the Fourteenth Amendment. Petitioner argues that in view of the facts and circumstances shown in the record, the effect of compelled disclosure of the membership lists will be to abridge the rights of its rank-and-file members to engage in lawful association in support of their common beliefs. It contends that governmental action which, although not directly suppressing association, nevertheless carries this consequence, can be justified only upon some overriding valid interest of the State.

Effective advocacy of both public and private points of view, particularly controversial ones, is undeniably enhanced by group association, as this Court has more than once recognized by remarking upon the close nexus between the freedoms of speech and assembly. . . . It is beyond debate that freedom to engage in association for the advancement of beliefs and ideas is an inseparable aspect of the "liberty" assured by the Due Process Clause of the Fourteenth Amendment, which embraces freedom of speech. . . . Of course, it is immaterial whether the beliefs sought to be advanced by association pertain to political, economic, religious or cultural matters, and state action which may have the effect of curtailing the freedom to associate is subject to the closest scrutiny. . . .

It is hardly a novel perception that compelled disclosure of affiliation with groups engaged in advocacy may constitute as effective a restraint on freedom of association as the forms of governmental action in the cases above were thought likely to produce upon the particular constitutional rights there involved. This Court has recognized the vital relationship between freedom to associate and privacy in one's associations. . . .

We think that the production order, in the respects here drawn in question, must be regarded as entailing the likelihood of a substantial restraint upon the exercise by petitioner's members of their right to freedom of association. Petitioner has made an uncontroverted showing that on past occasions revelation of the identity of its rank-and-file members has exposed these members to economic reprisal, loss of employment, threat of physical coercion, and other manifestations of public hostility. Under these circumstances, we think it apparent that compelled disclosure of petitioner's Alabama membership is likely to affect adversely the ability of petitioner and its members to pursue their collective effort to foster beliefs which they admittedly have the right to advocate, in that it may induce members to withdraw from the Association and dissuade others from joining it because of fear of exposure of their beliefs shown through their associations and of the consequences of this exposure.

It is not sufficient to answer, as the State does here, that whatever repressive effect compulsory disclosure of names of petitioner's members may have upon participation by Alabama citizens in petitioner's activities follows not from *state* action but from *private* community pressures. The crucial factor is the interplay of governmental and private action, for it is only after the initial exertion of state power represented by the production order that private action takes hold.

We turn to the final question whether Alabama has demonstrated an interest in obtaining the disclosures it seeks from petitioner which is sufficient to justify the deterrent effect which we have concluded these disclosures may well have on the free exercise by petitioner's members of their constitutionally protected right of association. . . . It is not of moment that the State has here acted solely through its judicial branch, for whether legislative or judicial, it is still the application of state power which we are asked to scrutinize.

It is important to bear in mind that petitioner asserts no right to absolute immunity from state investigation, and no right to disregard Alabama's laws. As shown by its substantial compliance with the production order, petitioner does not deny Alabama's right to obtain from it such information as the State desires concerning the purposes of the Association and its activities within the State. Petitioner has not objected to divulging the identity of its members who are employed by or hold official positions with it. It has urged the rights solely of its ordinary rank-and-file members. This is therefore not analogous to a case involving the interest of a State in protecting its citizens in their dealings with paid solicitors or agents of foreign corporations by requiring identification. . . .

Whether there was "justification" in this instance turns solely on the substantiality of Alabama's interest in obtaining the membership lists. . . . [T]he State's reason for requesting the membership lists . . . was to determine whether petitioner was conducting intrastate business in violation of the Alabama foreign corporation registration statute, and the membership lists were expected to help resolve this question. The issues in the litigation commenced by Alabama by its bill in equity were whether the character of petitioner and its activities in Alabama had been such as to make petitioner subject to the registration statute, and whether the extent of petitioner's activities without qualifying suggested its permanent ouster from the State. Without intimating the slightest view upon the merits of these issues, we are unable to perceive that the disclosure of the names of petitioner's rank-and-file members has a substantial bearing on either of them. . . .

We hold that the immunity from state scrutiny of membership lists which the Association claims on behalf of its members is here so related to the right of the members to pursue their lawful private interests privately and to associate freely with others in so doing as to come within the protection of the Fourteenth Amendment. And we conclude that Alabama has fallen short of showing a controlling justification for the deterrent effect on the free enjoyment of the right to associate which disclosure of membership lists is likely to have. Accordingly, the judgment of civil contempt and the $100,000 fine which resulted from petitioner's refusal to comply with the production order in this respect must fall. . . .

Reversed.

How does the Court link the right of association with other First Amendment rights in reaching its judgment? Why does the NAACP oppose the disclosure of its members' names? How does the Court weigh the interests of Alabama against the rights of the NAACP to reach its decision? Are there any legitimate state ends that the Court would recognize as a justification for requiring the disclosure of the membership lists of organizations?

In *Shelton* v. *Tucker,* 364 U.S. 479 (1960), the Court held that an Arkansas statute which required every teacher in the state to divulge all his or her organizational memberships as a condition of employment was overbroad. The state has a right to inquire into the fitness and competence of its teachers, wrote Justice Stewart for the Court, but the unlimited scope of the inquiry into organizational memberships required by the statute would necessarily compel the revelation of many memberships that could have no possible bearing upon occupational competence or fitness. The breadth of the statute, which stifled the rights of the *individual* to freedom of association was not justified by the interests of the state.

CONSTITUTIONAL PROTECTIONS AGAINST PRIOR CENSORSHIP OF THE PRESS

The right to print freely without prior censorship is a fundamental, historically protected freedom of the press. Safeguards against libel under common and statutory law consisted of allowing persons to sue for libel after publication.[54]

Can the government authorize prior censorship under any circumstances? For example, can the publication of information be prevented by a law that requires it to be kept secret in the interests of national security and defense? Can the interest of the government in prior censorship ever outweigh the right of the individual to freedom of the press?

The following opinion contained the classic statement of the Court's views on prior censorship.

Near v. *Minnesota*

283 U.S. 697; 51 S. Ct. 625; 75 L. Ed. 1357 (1931)

MR. CHIEF JUSTICE HUGHES delivered the opinion of the Court:

Chapter 285 of the Session Laws of Minnesota for the year 1925 provides for the abatement, as a public nuisance, of a "malicious, scandalous and defamatory newspaper, magazine or other periodical."

Section one of the Act is as follows:

"Section 1. Any person who, as an individual, or as a member or employee of a firm, or association or organization, or as an officer, director, member or employee of a corporation, shall be engaged in the business of regularly or customarily

---

[54]See pp. 579–583 for a discussion of the historical background of freedom of speech and press.

producing, publishing or circulating, having in possession, selling or giving away.

(a) an obscene, lewd and lascivious newspaper, magazine, or other periodical, or

(b) a malicious, scandalous and defamatory newspaper, magazine or other periodical, is guilty of a nuisance, and all persons guilty of such nuisance may be enjoined, as hereinafter provided.

"Participation in such business shall constitute a commission of such nuisance and render the participant liable and subject to the proceedings, orders and judgments provided for in this Act. Ownership, in whole or in part, directly or indirectly, of any such periodical, or of any stock or interest in any corporation or organization which owns the same in whole or in part, or which publishes the same, shall constitute such participation. . . ."

Section two provides that whenever any such nuisance is committed or exists, the County Attorney of any county where any such periodical is published or circulated, or, in case of his failure or refusal to proceed upon written request in good faith of a reputable citizen, the Attorney General, or upon like failure or refusal of the latter, any citizen of the county, may maintain an action in the district court of the county in the name of the State to enjoin perpetually the persons committing or maintaining any such nuisance from further committing or maintaining it. Upon such evidence as the court shall deem sufficient, a temporary injunction may be granted. The defendants have the right to plead by demurrer or answer, and the plaintiff may demur or reply as in other cases.

The action, by section three, is to be "governed by the practice and procedure applicable to civil actions for injunctions," and after trial the court may enter judgment permanently enjoining the defendants found guilty of violating the Act from continuing the violation and, "in

and by such judgment, such nuisance may be wholly abated." The court is empowered, as in other cases of contempt, to punish disobedience to a temporary or permanent injunction by fine of not more than $1,000 or by imprisonment in the county jail for not more than twelve months.

Under this statute, clause (b), the County Attorney of Hennepin County brought this action to enjoin the publication of what was described as a "malicious, scandalous and defamatory newspaper, magazine and periodical," known as "The Saturday Press," published by the defendants in the city of Minneapolis. . . .

Without attempting to summarize the contents of the voluminous exhibits attached to the complaint, we deem it sufficient to say that the articles charged in substance that a Jewish gangster was in control of gambling, bootlegging and racketeering in Minneapolis, and that law enforcing officers and agencies were not energetically performing their duties. Most of the charges were directed against the Chief of Police; he was charged with gross neglect of duty, illicit relations with gangsters, and with participation in graft. The County Attorney was charged with knowing the existing conditions and with failure to take adequate measures to remedy them. The Mayor was accused of inefficiency and dereliction. One member of the grand jury was stated to be in sympathy with the gangsters. A special grand jury and a special prosecutor were demanded to deal with the situation in general, and, in particular, to investigate an attempt to assassinate one Guilford, one of the original defendants, who, it appears from the articles, was shot by gangsters after the first issue of the periodical had been published. There is no question but that the articles made serious accusations against the public officers named and others in connection with the prevalence of crimes and the failure to expose and punish them. . . .

[The trial court issued an injunction and the highest state court affirmed.] From the judgment as thus affirmed, the defendant Near appeals to this Court.

This statute, for the suppression as a public nuisance of a newspaper or periodical, is unusual, if not unique, and raises questions of grave importance transcending the local interest involved in the particular action. It is no longer open to doubt that the liberty of the press, and of speech, is within the liberty safeguarded by the due process clause of the Fourteenth Amendment from invasion by state action.... In maintaining this guaranty, the authority of the State to enact laws to promote the health, safety, morals and general welfare of its people is necessarily admitted. The limits of this sovereign power must always be determined with appropriate regard to the particular subject of its exercise.... Liberty of speech, and of the press, is also not an absolute right, and the State may punish its abuse.... Liberty, in each of its phases, has its history and connotation and, in the present instance, the inquiry is as to the historic conception of the liberty of the press and whether the statute under review violates the essential attributes of that liberty....

With respect to these contentions it is enough to say that in passing upon constitutional questions the Court has regard to substance and not to mere matters of form, and that, in accordance with familiar principles, the statute must be tested by its operation and effect.... That operation and effect we think is clearly shown by the record in this case. We are not concerned with mere errors of the trial court, if there be such, in going beyond the direction of the statute as construed by the Supreme Court of the State. It is thus important to note precisely the purpose and effect of the statute as the state court has construed it.

First. The statute is not aimed at the redress of individual or private wrongs. Remedies for libel remain available and unaffected. The statute, said the state court, "is not directed at threatened libel but at an existing business which, generally speaking, involves more than libel." It is aimed at the distribution of scandalous matter as "detrimental to public morals and to the general welfare," tending "to disturb the peace of the community" and "to provoke assaults and the commission of crime." In order to obtain an injunction to suppress the future publication of the newspaper or periodical, it is not necessary to prove the falsity of the charges that have been made in the publication condemned. In the present action there was no allegation that the matter published was not true. It is alleged, and the statute requires the allegation, that the publication was "malicious," But, as in prosecutions for libel, there is no requirement of proof by the State of malice in fact as distinguished from malice inferred from the mere publication of the defamatory matter. The judgment in this case proceeded upon the mere proof of publication. The statute permits the defense, not of the truth alone, but only that the truth was published with good motives and for justifiable ends. It is apparent that under the statute the publication is to be regarded as defamatory if it injures reputation, and that it is scandalous if it circulates charges of reprehensible conduct, whether criminal or otherwise, and the publication is thus deemed to invite public reprobation and to constitute a public scandal. The court sharply defined the purpose of the statute, bringing out the precise point, in these words: "There is no constitutional right to publish a fact merely because it is true. It is a matter of common knowledge that prosecutions under the criminal libel statutes do not result in efficient repression or suppression of the evils of scandal. Men who are the victims of such assaults seldom resort to the courts. This is especially true if their sins are exposed and the only question relates to whether it was done with good motives and for justifiable ends. This law is not for the protection of the person attacked nor to punish the wrongdoer. It is for the protection of the public welfare."

Second. The statute is directed not simply at the circulation of scandalous and defamatory statements with regard to private citizens, but at the continued publication by newspapers and periodicals of charges against public officers of corruption, malfeasance in office, or serious neglect of duty. Such charges by their very nature create a public scandal. They are scandalous and defamatory within the meaning of the statute, which has its normal operation in relation to publications dealing prominently and chiefly with the alleged derelictions of public officers.

Third. The object of the statute is not punishment, in the ordinary sense, but suppression of the offending newspaper or periodical. The reason for the enactment, as the state court has said, is that prosecutions to enforce penal statutes for libel do not result in "efficient repression or suppression of the evils of scandal." Describing the business of publication as a public nuisance, does not obscure the substance of the proceeding which the statute authorizes. It is the continued publication of scandalous and defamatory matter that constitutes the business and the declared nuisance. In the case of public officers, it is the reiteration of charges of official misconduct, and the fact that the newspaper or periodical is principally devoted to that purpose, that exposes it to suppression. In the present instance, the proof was that nine editions of the newspaper or periodical in question were published on successive dates, and that they were chiefly devoted to charges against public officers and in relation to the prevalence and protection of crime. In such a case, these officers are not left to their ordinary remedy in a suit for libel, or the authorities to a prosecution for criminal libel. Under this statute, a publisher of a newspaper or periodical, undertaking to conduct a campaign to expose and to censure official derelictions, and devoting his publication principally to that purpose, must face not simply the possibility of a verdict against him in a suit or prosecution for libel, but a determination that his newspaper or periodical is a public nuisance to be abated, and that this abatement and suppression will follow unless he is prepared with legal evidence to prove the truth of the charges and also to satisfy the court that, in addition to being true, the matter was published with good motives and for justifiable ends.

This suppression is accomplished by enjoining publication and that restraint is the object and effect of the statute.

Fourth. The statute not only operates to suppress the offending newspaper or periodical but to put the publisher under an effective censorship. When a newspaper or periodical is found to be "malicious, scandalous and defamatory," and is suppressed as such, resumption of publication is punishable as a contempt of court by fine or imprisonment. Thus, where a newspaper or periodical has been suppressed because of the circulation of charges against public officers of official misconduct, it would seem to be clear that the renewal of the publication of such charges would constitute a contempt and that the judgment would lay a permanent restraint upon the publisher, to escape which he must satisfy the court as to the character of a new publication. Whether he would be permitted again to publish matter deemed to be derogatory to the same or other public officers would depend upon the court's ruling. In the present instance the judgment restrained the defendants from "publishing, circulating, having in their possession, selling or giving away any publication whatsoever which is a malicious, scandalous or defamatory newspaper, as defined by law." The law gives no definition except that covered by the words "scandalous and defamatory," and publications charging official misconduct are of that class. While the court, answering the objection that the judgment was too broad, saw no reason for construing it as restraining the defendants "from operating a newspaper in harmony with the public welfare to which all must yield," and said that the defendants had not indicated "any desire to conduct their business in the usual and legitimate manner," the manifest inference is that, at least with respect to a new publication directed against official misconduct, the defendant would be held, under penalty of punishment for contempt as provided in the statute, to a manner of publication which the court considered to be "usual and legitimate" and consistent with the public welfare.

If we cut through mere details of procedure, the operation and effect of the statute in substance is that public authorities may bring the owner or publisher of a newspaper or periodical before a judge upon a charge of conducting a business of publishing scandalous and defamatory matter—in particular that the matter consists of charges against public officers of official dereliction—and unless the owner or publisher is able and disposed to bring competent evidence to satisfy the judge that the charges are true and are published with good motives and for justifiable ends, his newspaper or periodical is suppressed and further publication is made punishable as a contempt. This is of the essence of censorship.

The question is whether a statute authorizing such proceedings in restraint of publication is consistent with the conception of the liberty of the press as historically conceived and guaranteed. In determining the extent of the constitutional protection, it has been generally, if not universally, considered that it is the chief purpose of the guaranty to prevent pre-vious restraints upon publication. The struggle in England, directed against the legislative power of the licenser, resulted in renunciation of the censorship of the press. The liberty deemed to be established was thus described by Blackstone: "The liberty of the press is indeed essential to the nature of a free state; but this consists in laying no *previous* restraints upon publications, and not in freedom from censure for criminal matter when published. Every freeman has an undoubted right to lay what sentiments he pleases before the public; to forbid this, is to destroy the freedom of the press; but if he publishes what is improper, mischievous or illegal, he must take the consequence of his own temerity." . . .

The criticism upon Blackstone's statement has not been because immunity from previous restraint upon publication has not been regarded as deserving of special emphasis, but chiefly because that immunity cannot be deemed to exhaust the conception of the liberty guaranteed by state and federal constitutions. The point of criticism has been "that the mere exemption from previous restraints cannot be all that is secured by the constitutional provisions"; and that "the liberty of the press might be rendered a mockery and a delusion, and the phrase itself a byword, if, while every man was at liberty to publish what he pleased, the public authorities might nevertheless punish him for harmless publications." . . . But it is recognized that punishment for the abuse of the liberty accorded to the press is essential to the protection of the public, and that the common law rules that subject the libeler to responsibility for the public offense, as well as for the private injury, are not abolished by the protection extended in our constitutions. . . . In the present case, we have no occasion to inquire as to the permissible scope of subsequent punishment. For whatever wrong the appellant has committed or may commit, by his publications, the State appropriately affords both public and private redress by its libel laws. As has been noted, the statute in question does not deal with punishments; it provides for no punishment, except in case of contempt for violation of the court's order, but for suppression and injunction, that is, for restraint upon publication.

The objection has also been made that the principle as to immunity from previous restraint is stated too broadly, if every such restraint is deemed to be prohibited. That is undoubtedly true; the protection even as to previous restraint is not absolutely unlimited. But the limitation has been recognized only in exceptional cases: "When a nation is at war many things that might be said in time of peace are such a hindrance to its effort that their utterance will not be endured so long as men fight and that no Court could regard them as protected by any constitutional right." *Schenck* v. *United States* [1919] . . . . No one would question but that a government might prevent actual obstruction to its recruiting service or the publication of the sailing dates of transports or the number and location of troops. On similar grounds, the primary requirements of decency may be enforced against obscene publications. The security of the community life may be protected against incitements to acts of violence and the overthrow by force of orderly government. The constitutional guaranty of free speech does not "protect a man from an injunction against uttering words that may have all the effect of force. . . .

The exceptional nature of its limitations places in a strong light the general conception that liberty of the press, historically considered and taken up by the Federal Constitution, has meant, principally although not exclusively, immunity from previous restraints or censorship. The conception of the liberty of the press in this country had broadened with the exigencies of the colonial period and with the efforts to secure freedom from oppressive administration. That liberty was especially cherished for the immunity it afforded from previous restraint of the publication of censure of public officers and charges of official misconduct. . . .

The importance of this immunity has not lessened. While reckless assaults upon public men, and efforts to bring obloquy upon those who are endeavoring faithfully to discharge official duties, exert a baleful influence and deserve the severest condemnation in public opinion, it cannot be said that this abuse is greater, and it is believed to be less, than that which characterized the period in which our institutions took shape. Meanwhile, the administration of government has become more complex, the opportunities for malfeasance and corruption have multiplied, crime has grown to most serious proportions, and the danger of its protection by unfaithful officials and of the impairment of the fundamental security of life and property by criminal alliances and official neglect, emphasizes the primary need of a vigilant and courageous press, especially in great cities. The fact that the liberty of the press may be abused by miscreant purveyors of scandal does not make any the less necessary the immunity of the press from previous restraint in dealing with official misconduct. Subsequent punishment for such abuses as may exist is the appropriate remedy, consistent with constitutional privilege. . . .

The statute in question cannot be justified by reason of the fact that the publisher is permitted to show, before injunction issues, that the matter published is true and is published with good motives and for justifiable ends. If such a statute, authorizing suppression and injunction on such a basis, is constitutionally valid, it would be equally permissible for the legislature to provide that at any time the publisher of any newspaper could be brought before a court, or even an administrative officer (as the constitutional protection may not be regarded as resting on mere procedural details) and required to produce proof of the truth of his publication, or of what he intended to publish, and of his motives, or stand enjoined. If this can be done, the legislature may provide machinery for determining in the complete exercise of its discretion what are justifiable ends and restrain publication accordingly. And it would be but a step to a complete system of censorship. The recognition of authority to impose previous restraint upon publication in order to protect the community against the circulation of charges of misconduct, and especially of official misconduct, necessarily would carry with it the admission of the authority of the censor against which the constitutional barrier was erected. The preliminary freedom, by virtue of the very reason for its existence, does not depend, as this Court has said, on proof of truth. . . .

Equally unavailing is the insistence that the statute is designed to prevent the circulation of scandal which tends to disturb the public peace and to provoke assaults and the commission of crime. Charges of reprehensible conduct, and in particular of official malfeasance, unquestionably create a public scandal, but the theory of the constitutional guaranty is that even a more serious public evil would be caused by authority to prevent publication. . . . There is nothing new in the fact that charges of reprehensible conduct may create resentment and the disposition to resort to violent means of redress, but this well-understood tendency did not alter the determination to protect the press against censorship and restraint upon publication. . . . The danger of violent reactions becomes greater with effective organization of defiant groups resenting exposure, and if this consideration warranted legislative interference with the initial freedom of publication, the constitutional protection would be reduced to a mere form of words.

For these reasons we hold the statute, so far as it authorized the proceedings in this action under clause (b) of section one, to be an infringement of the liberty of the press guaranteed by the Fourteenth Amendment. We should add that this decision rests upon the operation and effect of the statute, without regard to the question of the truth of the charges contained in the particular periodical. The fact that the public officers named in this case, and those associated with the charges of official dereliction, may be deemed to be impeccable, cannot affect the conclusion that the statute imposes an unconstitutional restraint upon publication.

Judgment reversed.

MR. JUSTICE BUTLER, dissenting:
. . . The Minnesota statute does not operate as a *previous* restraint on publication within the proper meaning of that phrase. It does not authorize administrative control in advance such as was formerly exercised by the licensers and censors but prescribes a remedy to be enforced by a suit in equity. In this case there was previous publication made in the course of the business of regularly producing malicious, scandalous and defamatory periodicals. The business and publications unquestionably constitute an abuse of the right of free press. The statute denounces the things done as a nuisance on the ground, as stated by the state supreme court, that they threaten morals, peace and good order. There is no question of the power of the State to denounce such transgressions. The restraint authorized is only in respect of continuing to do what has been duly adjudged to constitute a nuisance. . . .

It is well known, as found by the state supreme court, that existing libel laws are inadequate effectively to suppress evils resulting from the kind of business and publications that are shown in this case. The doctrine that measures such as the one before us are invalid because they operate as previous restraints to infringe freedom of press exposes the peace and good order of every community and the business and private affairs of every individual to the constant and protracted false

and malicious assaults of any insolvent publisher who may have purpose and sufficient capacity to contrive and put into effect a scheme or program for oppression, blackmail or extortion.

The judgment should be affirmed.

MR. JUSTICE VAN DEVANTER, MR. JUSTICE McReynolds, and MR. JUSTICE SUTHERLAND concur in this opinion.

In 1971 *The New York Times* came into possession of classified government documents based on a study done by the Pentagon staff for Robert McNamara, who was Secretary of Defense in the Kennedy and Johnson Administrations. This study was titled "History of U.S. Decision-Making Process on Vietnam Policy," and detailed the deep involvement of this country in Vietnam prior to the actual escalation of the war by President Johnson in 1965. It also contained a number of other striking revelations dealing with the conduct of the war during the Kennedy and Johnson Administrations, revealing the duplicity of the United States government in its treatment of the various governments of South Vietnam, as well as the extensive espionage and sabotage activities during the Eisenhower, Kennedy, and Johnson Administrations.

After *The New York Times* received these purloined documents it decided that the public interest required the publication of a summary of their contents, as well as a number of the documents themselves. This publication was done without any prior contact with the government and solely on the basis of the judgment of the *Times'* editors. After the first "Pentagon Papers," as these documents were called, appeared in the *Times* in June 1971, Attorney General John Mitchell sought an injunction in the District Court for the Southern District of New York against their further publication, claiming that the national interest required that they not be published because of their secret nature. He also felt it would embarrass this country, particularly in its relationships with foreign allies, if the report's substance was revealed.

The District Court ruled that the material was basically historical and that although it might be embarrassing to the government, it did not violate national security and could not be enjoined from publication. The Court of Appeals on the same day immediately issued another restraining order preventing publication of the papers pending an appeal of the District Court's decision by the government. To avoid a time-consuming appellate process, *The New York Times* appealed to the Supreme Court for a writ of certiorari, requesting accelerated consideration of the case and final disposition of the issues by the Supreme Court. The Supreme Court granted certiorari and joined the case with one involving a similar government attempt to suppress the *Washington Post* which was quashed by the Circuit Court of Appeals for the District of Columbia.

New York Times Co. v. United States

403 U.S. 713; 91 S. Ct. 2140; 29 L. Ed. 2d 820 (1971)

PER CURIAM:

We granted certiorari in these cases in which the United States seeks to enjoin *The New York Times* and the *Washington Post* from publishing the contents of a classified study entitled "History of U.S. Decision-Making Process on Vietnam Policy." . . .

"Any system of prior restraints of expression comes to this Court bearing a heavy presumption against its constitutional validity." *Bantam Books, Inc.* v. *Sullivan* [1963] . . . see also *Near* v. *Minnesota* [1931]. . . . The Government "thus carries a heavy burden of showing justification for the imposition of such a restraint." *Organization for a Better Austin* v. *Keefe* [1971]. . . . The District Court for the Southern District of New York in *The New York Times* case and the District Court for the District of Columbia and the Court of Appeals for the District of Columbia Circuit in the *Washington Post* case held that the Government had not met that burden. We agree.

The judgment of the Court of Appeals for the District of Columbia Circuit is therefore affirmed. The order of the Court of Appeals for the Second Circuit is reversed and the case is remanded with directions to enter a judgment affirming the judgment of the District Court for the Southern District of New York. The stays entered June 25, 1971, by the Court are vacated. The judgments shall issue forthwith.

So ordered.

MR. JUSTICE BLACK, with whom MR. JUSTICE DOUGLAS joins, concurring:

. . . I agree completely that we must affirm the judgment of the Court of Appeals for the District of Columbia Circuit and reverse the judgment of the Court of Appeals for the Second Circuit for the reasons stated by my Brothers Douglas and Brennan. In my view it is unfortunate that some of my Brethren are apparently willing to hold that the publication of news may sometimes be enjoined. Such a holding would make a shambles of the First Amendment. . . .

In seeking injunctions against these newspapers and in its presentation to the Court, the Executive Branch seems to have forgotten the essential purpose and history of the First Amendment. When the Constitution was adopted, many people strongly opposed it because the document contained no Bill of Rights to safeguard certain basic freedoms. They especially feared that the new powers granted to a central government might be interpreted to permit the government to curtail freedom of religion, press, assembly, and speech. In response to an overwhelming public clamor, James Madison offered a series of amendments to satisfy citizens that these great liberties would remain safe and beyond the power of government to abridge. . . . The amendments were offered to *curtail* and *restrict* the general powers granted to the Executive, Legislative, and Judicial Branches two years before in the original Constitution. The Bill of Rights changed the original Constitution into a new charter under which no branch of government could abridge the people's freedoms of press, speech, religion, and assembly. Yet the Solicitor General argues and some members of the Court appear to agree that the general powers of the Government adopted in the original Constitution should be interpreted to limit and restrict the specific and emphatic guarantees of the Bill of Rights adopted later. I can imagine no greater perversion of history. Madison and the other Framers of the First Amendment, able men that they were, wrote in language they earnestly believed could never be misunderstood: "Congress shall make no law . . . abridging the freedom . . . of the press. . . ." Both the history and language of the First Amendment support the view that the press must be left free to publish news, whatever the source, without censorship, injunctions, or prior restraints.

In the First Amendment the Founding Fathers gave the free press the protection it must have to fulfill its essential role in our democracy. The press was to serve the governed, not the governors. The Government's power to censor the press was abolished so that the press would remain forever free to censure the Government. The press was protected so that it could bare the secrets of government and inform the people. Only a free and unrestrained press can effectively expose deception in government. And paramount among the responsibilities of a free press is the duty to prevent any part of the government from deceiving the people and sending them off to distant lands to die of foreign fevers and foreign shot and shell. In my view, far from deserving condemnation for their courageous reporting, *The New York Times,* the *Washington Post,* and other newspapers should be commended for serving the purpose that the Founding Fathers saw so clearly. In revealing the workings of government that led to the Vietnam war, the newspapers nobly did precisely that which the Founders hoped and trusted they would do.

The Government's case here is based on premises entirely different from those that guided the Framers of the First Amendment. . . . And the Government argues in its brief that in spite of the First Amendment, "[t]he authority of the Executive Department to protect the nation against publication of information whose disclosure would endanger the national security stems from two interrelated sources: the constitutional power of the President over the conduct of foreign affairs and his authority as Commander-in-Chief.". . .

To find that the President has "inherent power" to halt the publication of news by resort to the courts would wipe out the First Amendment and destroy the fundamental liberty and security of the very people the Government hopes to make "secure." No one can read the history of the adoption of the First Amendment without being convinced beyond any doubt that it was injunctions like those sought here that Madison and his collaborators intended to outlaw in this Nation for all time.

The word "security" is a broad, vague generality whose contours should not be invoked to abrogate the fundamental law embodied in the First Amendment. The guarding of military and diplomatic secrets at the expense of informed representative government provides no real security for our Republic. The Framers of the First Amendment, fully aware of both the need to defend a new nation and the abuses of the English and Colonial governments, sought to give this new society strength and security by providing that freedom of speech, press, religion, and assembly should not be abridged. This thought was eloquently expressed in 1937 by Mr. Chief Justice Hughes—great man and great Chief Justice that he was—when the Court held a man could not be punished for attending a meeting run by Communists.

The greater the importance of safeguarding the community from incitements to the overthrow of our institutions by force and violence, the more imperative is the need to preserve inviolate the constitutional rights of free speech, free press and free assembly in order to maintain the opportunity for free political discussion, to the end that government may be responsive to the will of the people and that changes, if desired, may be obtained by peaceful means. Therein lies the security of the Republic, the very foundation of constitutional government.

MR. JUSTICE DOUGLAS, with whom MR. JUSTICE BLACK joins, concurring:

While I join the opinion of the Court I believe it necessary to express my views more fully.

It should be noted at the outset that the First Amendment provides that "Congress shall make no law . . . abridging the freedom of speech, or of the press." That leaves, in my view, no room for governmental restraint on the press.

There is, moreover, no statute barring the publication by the press of the material which the *Times* and the *Post* seek to use. . . .

Judge Gurfein's holding in the *Times* case that this Act does not apply to this case was therefore preeminently sound. Moreover, the Act of September 23, 1950 . . . states . . . that:

Nothing in this Act shall be construed to authorize, require, or establish military or civilian censorship or in any way to limit or infringe upon freedom of the press or of speech as guaranteed by the Constitution of the United States and no regulation shall be promulgated hereunder having that effect. 64 Stat. 987.

Thus Congress has been faithful to the command of the First Amendment in this area.

So any power that the Government possesses must come from its "inherent power." . . .

The Government says that it has inherent powers to go into court and obtain an injunction to protect the national interest, which in this case is alleged to be national security.

Near v. *Minnesota* . . . repudiated that expansive doctrine in no uncertain terms.

The dominant purpose of the First Amendment was to prohibit the widespread practice of governmental suppression of embarrassing information. It is common knowledge that the First Amendment was adopted against the widespread use of the common law of seditious libel to punish the dissemination of material that is embarrassing to the powers-that-be. . . . The present cases will, I think, go down in history as the most dramatic illustration of that principle. A debate of large proportions goes on in the Nation over our posture in Vietnam. That debate antedated the disclosure of the contents of the present documents. The latter are highly relevant to the debate in progress.

Secrecy in government is fundamentally anti-democratic, perpetuating bureaucratic errors. Open debate and discussion of public issues are vital to our national health. On public questions there should be "uninhibited, robust, and wide-open" debate. . . .

I would affirm the judgment of the Court of Appeals in the *Post* case, vacate the stay of the Court of Appeals in the *Times* case and direct that it affirm the District Court. . . .

MR. JUSTICE BRENNAN, concurring:

I

I write separately in these cases only to emphasize what should be apparent: that our judgments in the present cases may not be taken to indicate the propriety, in the future, of issuing temporary stays and restraining orders to block the publication of material sought to be suppressed by the Government. So far as I can determine, never before has the United States sought to enjoin a newspaper from publishing information in its possession. . . .

II

The error that has pervaded these cases from the outset was the granting of any injunctive relief whatsoever, interim or otherwise. The entire thrust of the Government's claim throughout these cases has been that publication of the material sought to be enjoined "could," or "might," or "may" prejudice the national interest in various ways. But the First Amendment tolerates absolutely no prior judicial restraints of the press predicated upon surmise or conjecture that untoward consequences may result. Our cases, it is true, have indicated that there is a single, extremely narrow class of cases in which the First Amendment's ban on prior judicial restraint may be overridden. Our cases have thus far indicated that such cases may arise only when the Nation "is at war," *Schenck* v. *United States*, . . . during which times "[n]o one would question but that a government might prevent actual obstruction to its recruiting service or the publication of the sailing dates of transports or the number and location of troops." *Near* v. *Minnesota*. . . . Even if the present world situation were assumed to be tantamount to a time of war, or if the power of presently available armaments would justify even in peacetime the suppression of information that would set in motion a nuclear holocaust, in neither of these actions has the Government presented or even alleged that publication of items from or based upon the material at issue would cause the happening of an event of that nature. "[T]he chief purpose of [the First Amendment's] guaranty [is] to prevent previous restraints upon publication." *Near* v. *Minnesota* . . . Thus, only governmental allegation and proof that publication must inevitably, directly, and immediately cause the occurrence of an event kindred to imperiling the safety of a transport already at sea can support even the issuance of an interim restraining order. In no event may mere conclusions be sufficient: for if the Executive Branch seeks judicial aid in preventing publication, it must inevitably submit the basis upon which that aid is sought to scrutiny by the judiciary. And therefore, every restraint issued in this case, whatever its form, has violated the First Amendment—and not less so because that restraint was justified as necessary to afford the courts an opportunity to examine the claim more thoroughly. Unless and until the Government has clearly made out its case, the First Amendment commands that no injunction may issue.

MR. JUSTICE STEWART, with whom MR. JUSTICE WHITE joins, concurring:
. . . In the absence of the governmental checks and balances present in other areas of our national life, the only effective restraint upon executive policy and power in the areas of national defense and international affairs may lie in an enlightened citizenry—in an informed and critical public opinion which alone can here protect the values of democratic government. For this reason, it is perhaps here that a press that is alert, aware, and free most vitally serves the basic purpose of the First Amendment. For without an informed and free press there cannot be an enlightened people.

Yet it is elementary that the successful conduct of international diplomacy and the maintenance of an effective national defense require both confidentiality and secrecy. Other nations can hardly deal with this Nation in an atmosphere of mutual trust unless they can be assured that their confidences will be kept. And within our own executive departments, the development of considered and intelligent international policies would be impossible if those charged with their formulation could not communicate with each other freely, frankly, and in confidence. In the area of basic national defense the frequent need for absolute secrecy is, of course, self-evident.

I think there can be but one answer to this dilemma, if dilemma it be. The responsibility must be where the power is. If the Constitution gives the Executive a large degree of unshared power in the conduct of foreign affairs and the maintenance of our national defense, then under the Constitution the Executive must have the largely unshared duty to determine and preserve the degree of internal security necessary to exercise that power successfully. It is an awesome responsibility, requiring judgment and wisdom of a high order. I should suppose that moral, political, and practical considerations would dictate that a very first principle of that wisdom would be an insistence upon avoiding secrecy for its own sake. For when everything is classified, then nothing is classified, and the system becomes one to be disregarded by the cynical or the careless, and to be manipulated by those intent on self-protection or self-promotion. I should suppose, in short, that the hallmark of a truly effective internal security system would be the maximum possible disclosure, recognizing that secrecy can best be preserved only when credibility is truly maintained. But be that as it may, it is clear to me that it is the constitutional duty of the Executive—as a matter of sovereign prerogative and not as a matter of law as the courts know law—through the promulgation and enforcement of executive regulations, to protect the confidentiality necessary to carry out its responsibilities in the fields of international relations and national defense.

This is not to say that Congress and the courts have no role to play. Undoubtedly Congress has the power to enact specific and appropriate criminal laws to protect government property and preserve government secrets. Congress has passed such laws, and several of them are of very colorable relevance to the apparent circumstances of these cases. And if a criminal prosecution is instituted, it will be the responsibility of the courts to decide the applicability of the criminal law under which the charge is brought. Moreover, if Congress should pass a specific law authorizing civil proceedings in this field, the courts would likewise have the duty to decide the constitutionality of such a law as well as its applicability to the facts proved.

But in the cases before us we are asked neither to construe specific regulations nor to apply specific laws. We are asked, instead, to perform a function that the Constitution gave to the Executive, not the Judiciary. We are asked, quite simply, to prevent the publication by two newspapers of material that the Executive Branch insists should not, in the national interest, be published. I am convinced that the Executive is correct with respect to some of the documents involved. But I cannot say that disclosure of any of them will surely result in direct, immediate, and irreparable damage to our Nation or its people. That being so, there can under the First Amendment be but one judicial resolution of the issues before us. I join the judgments of the Court.

MR. JUSTICE WHITE, with whom MR. JUSTICE STEWART joins, concurring:

I concur in today's judgments, but only because of the concededly extraordinary protection against prior restraints enjoyed by the press under our constitutional system. I do not say that in no circumstances would the First Amendment permit an injunction against publishing information about government plans or operations. Nor, after examining the materials the Government characterizes as the most sensitive and destructive, can I deny that revelation of these documents will do substantial damage to public interests. Indeed, I am confident that their disclosure will have that result. But I nevertheless agree that the United States has not satisfied the very heavy burden that it must meet to warrant an injunction against publication in these cases, at least in the absence of express and appropriately limited congressional authorization for prior restraints in circumstances such as these.

The Government's position is simply stated: The responsibility of the Executive for the conduct of the foreign affairs and for the security of the Nation is so basic that the President is entitled to an injunction against publication of a newspaper story whenever he can convince a court that the information to be revealed threatens "grave and irreparable" injury to the public interest; and the injunction should issue whether or not the material to be published is classified, whether or not publication would be lawful under relevant criminal statutes enacted by Congress, and regardless of the circumstances by which the newspaper came into possession of the information.

At least in the absence of legislation by Congress, based on its own investigations and findings, I am quite unable to agree that the inherent powers of the Executive and the courts reach so far as to authorize remedies having such sweeping potential for inhibiting publications by the press. . . .

What is more, terminating the ban on publication of the relatively few sensitive documents the Government now seeks to suppress does not mean that the law either requires or invites newspapers or others to publish them or that they will be immune from criminal action if they do. Prior restraints require an unusually heavy justification under the First Amendment; but failure by the Government to justify prior restraints does not measure its constitutional entitlement to a conviction for criminal publication. That the Govern-

ment mistakenly chose to proceed by injunction does not mean that it could not successfully proceed in another way.

When the Espionage Act was under consideration in 1917, Congress eliminated from the bill a provision that would have given the President broad powers in time of war to proscribe, under threat of criminal penalty, the publication of various categories of information related to the national defense. Congress at that time was unwilling to clothe the President with such far-reaching powers to monitor the press, and those opposed to this part of the legislation assumed that a necessary concomitant of such power was the power to "filter out the news to the people through some man." . . . However, these same members of Congress appeared to have little doubt that newspapers would be subject to criminal prosecution if they insisted on publishing information of the type Congress had itself determined should not be revealed. . . .

. . . If any of the material here at issue is of this nature, the newspapers are presumably now on full notice of the position of the United States and must face the consequences if they publish. I would have no difficulty in sustaining convictions under these sections on facts that would not justify the intervention of equity and the imposition of a prior restraint. . . .

It is thus clear that Congress has addressed itself to the problems of protecting the security of the country and the national defense from unauthorized disclosure of potentially damaging information. . . . It has not, however, authorized the injunctive remedy against threatened publication. It has apparently been satisfied to rely on criminal sanctions and their deterrent effect on the responsible as well as the irresponsible press. I am not, of course, saying that either of these newspapers has yet committed a crime or that either would commit a crime if it published all the material now in its possession. That matter must await resolution in the context of a criminal proceeding if one is instituted by the United States. In that event, the issue of guilt or innocence would be determined by procedures and standards quite different from those that have purported to govern these injunctive proceedings.

MR. JUSTICE MARSHALL, concurring:

It would . . . be utterly inconsistent with the concept of separation of powers for this Court to use its power of contempt to prevent behavior that Congress has specifically declined to prohibit. There would be a similar damage to the basic concept of these co-equal branches of Government if when the Executive Branch has adequate authority granted by Congress to protect "national security" it can choose instead to invoke the contempt power of a court to enjoin the threatened conduct. The Constitution provides that Congress shall make laws, the President execute laws, and courts interpret laws. . . . It did not provide for government by injunction in which the courts and the Executive Branch can "make law" without regard to the action of Congress. It may be more convenient for the Executive Branch if it need only convince a judge to prohibit conduct rather than ask the Congress to pass a law, and it may be more convenient to enforce a contempt order than to seek a criminal conviction in a jury trial. Moreover, it may be considered politically wise to get a court to share the responsibility for arresting those who the Executive Branch has probable cause to believe are violating the law. But convenience and political considerations of the moment do not justify a basic departure from the principles of our system of government. . . .

Even if it is determined that the Government could not in good faith bring criminal prosecutions against *The New York Times* and the *Washington Post,* it is clear that Congress has specifically rejected passing legislation that would have clearly given the President the power he seeks here and made the current activity of the newspapers unlawful. When Congress specifically declines to make conduct unlawful it is not for this Court to redecide those issues—to overrule Congress. . . .

MR. CHIEF JUSTICE BURGER, dissenting:

So clear are the constitutional limitations on prior restraint against expression, that from the time of *Near* v. *Minnesota* . . . until recently . . . we have had little occasion to be concerned with cases involving prior restraints against news reporting on matters of public interest. There is, therefore, little variation among the members of the Court in terms of resistance to prior restraints against publication. Adherence to this basic constitutional principle, however, does not make these cases simple. In these cases, the imperative of a free and unfettered press comes into collision with another imperative, the effective functioning of a complex modern government and specifically the effective exercise of certain constitutional powers of the Executive. Only those who view the First Amendment as an absolute in all circumstances—a view I respect, but reject—can find such cases as these to be simple or easy.

These cases are not simple for another and more immediate reason. We do not know the facts of the cases. No District Judge knew all the facts. No Court of Appeals judge knew all the facts. No member of this Court knows all the facts.

Why are we in this posture, in which only those judges to whom the First Amendment is absolute and permits of no restraint in any circumstances or for any reason, are really in a position to act?

I suggest we are in this posture because these cases have been conducted in unseemly haste. Mr. Justice Harlan covers the chronology of events demonstrating the hectic pressures under which these cases have been processed and I need not restate them. The prompt setting of these cases reflects our universal abhorrence of prior restraint. But prompt judicial action does not mean unjudicial haste.

Here, moreover, the frenetic haste is due in large part to the manner in which the *Times* proceeded from the date it obtained the purloined documents. It seems reasonably clear now that the haste precluded reasonable and deliberate judicial treatment of these cases and was not warranted. The precipitate action of this Court aborting trials not yet completed is not the kind of judicial conduct that ought to attend the disposition of a great issue.

The newspapers make a derivative claim under the First Amendment; they denominate this right as the public "right to know"; by implication, the *Times* asserts a sole trusteeship of that right by virtue of its journalistic "scoop." The right is asserted as an absolute, as Justice Holmes so long ago pointed out in his aphorism concerning the right to shout "fire" in a crowded theater if there was no fire. There are other exceptions, some of which Chief Justice Hughes mentioned by way of example in *Near* v. *Minnesota.* There are no doubt other exceptions no one has had occasion to describe or discuss. Conceivably such exceptions may be lurking in these cases and would have been flushed had they been properly considered in the trial courts, free from unwarranted deadlines and frenetic pressures. An issue of this importance should be tried and heard in a judicial atmosphere conducive to thoughtful, reflective deliberation, especially when haste, in terms of hours, is unwarranted in light of the long period the *Times,* by its own choice, deferred publication.

It is not disputed that the *Times* has had unauthorized possession of the documents for three to four months, during which it has had its expert analysts studying them, presumably digesting them and preparing the material for publication. During all of this time, the *Times,* presumably in its capacity as trustee of the public's "right to know," has held up publication for purposes it considered proper and thus public knowledge was delayed. No doubt this was for a good reason; the analysis of 7,000 pages of complex material drawn from a vastly greater volume of material would inevitably take time and the writing of good news stories takes time. But why should the United States Government, from whom this information was illegally acquired by someone, along with all the counsel, trial judges, and appellate judges be placed under needless pressure? After these months of deferral, the alleged "right to know" has somehow and suddenly become a right that must be vindicated instanter.

Would it have been unreasonable, since the newspaper could anticipate the Government's objections to release of secret material, to give the Government an opportunity to review the entire collection and determine whether agreement could be reached on publication? Stolen or not, if security was not in fact jeopardized, much of the material could no doubt have been declassified, since it spans a period ending in 1968. With such an approach— one that great newspapers have in the past practiced and stated editorially to be the duty of an honorable press—the newspapers and Government might well have narrowed the area of disagreement as to what was and was not publishable, leaving the remainder to be resolved in orderly litigation, if necessary. To me it is hardly believable that a newspaper long regarded as a great institution in American life would fail to perform one of the basic and simple duties of every citizen with respect to the discovery or possession of stolen property or secret government documents. That duty, I had thought—perhaps naively—was to report forthwith, to responsible public officers. This duty rests on taxi drivers, Justices, and *The New York Times.* The course followed by the *Times,* whether so calculated or not, removed any possibility of orderly litigation of the issues. If the action of the judges up to now has been correct, that result is sheer happenstance.

Our grant of the writ of certiorari before final judgment in the *Times* case aborted the trial in the District Court before it had made a complete record pursuant to the mandate of the Court of Appeals for the Second Circuit.

The consequence of all this melancholy series of events is that we literally do not know what we are acting on. As I see it, we have been forced to deal with litigation concerning rights of great magnitude without an adequate record, and surely without time for adequate treatment either in the prior proceedings or in this Court. It is interesting to note that counsel on both sides, in oral argument before this Court, were frequently unable to respond to questions on factual points. Not surprisingly they pointed out that they had been working literally "around the clock" and simply were unable to review the documents that give rise to these cases and were not familiar with them. This Court is in no better posture. I agree generally with Mr. Justice Harlan and Mr. Justice Blackmun but I am not prepared to reach the merits.

I would affirm the Court of Appeals for the Second Circuit and allow the District Court to complete the trial aborted by our grant of certiorari, meanwhile preserving the status quo in the *Post* case. I would direct that the District Court on remand give priority to the *Times* case to the exclusion of all other business of that court but I would not set arbitrary deadlines.

I should add that I am in general agreement with much of what Mr. Justice White has expressed with respect to penal sanctions concerning communication or retention of documents or information relating to the national defense.

We all crave speedier judicial processes but when judges are pressured as in these cases the result is a parody of the judicial function.

Mr. Justice Harlan, with whom The Chief Justice and Mr. Justice Blackmun join, dissenting:

These cases forcefully call to mind the wise admonition of Mr. Justice Holmes, dissenting in *Northern Securities Co.* v. *United States* [1904] . . .:

Great cases like hard cases make bad law. For great cases are called great, not by reason of their real importance in shaping the law of the future, but because of some accident of immediate overwhelming interest which appeals to the feelings and distorts the judgment. These immediate interests exercise a kind of hydraulic pressure which makes what previously was clear seem doubtful, and before which even well settled principles of law will bend.

With all respect, I consider that the Court has been almost irresponsibly feverish in dealing with these cases. . . .

Forced as I am to reach the merits of these cases, I dissent from the opinion and judgments of the Court. Within the severe limitations imposed by the time constraints under which I have been required to operate, I can only state my reasons in telescoped form. . . .

It is a sufficient basis for affirming the Court of Appeals for the Second Circuit in the *Times* litigation to observe that its order must rest on the conclusion that because of the time elements the Government had not been given an adequate opportunity to present its case to the District Court. At the least this conclusion was not an abuse of discretion.

In the *Post* litigation the Government had more time to prepare; this was apparently the basis for the refusal of the Court of Appeals for the District of Columbia Circuit on rehearing to conform its judgment to that of the Second Circuit. But I think there is another and more fundamental reason why this judgment cannot stand—a reason which also furnishes an additional ground for not reinstating the judgment of the District Court in the *Times* litigation, set aside by the Court of Appeals. It is plain to me that the scope of the judicial function in passing upon the activities of the Executive Branch of the Government in the field of foreign affairs is very narrowly restricted. This view is, I think, dictated by the concept of separation of powers upon which our constitutional system rests.

In a speech on the floor of the House of Representatives, Chief Justice John Marshall, then a member of that body, stated:

The President is the sole organ of the nation in its external relations, and its sole representative with foreign nations. . . .

From that time, shortly after the founding of the Nation, to this, there has been no substantial challenge to this description of the scope of executive power. . . .

The power to evaluate the "pernicious influence" of premature disclosure is not, however, lodged in the Executive alone. I agree that, in performance of its duty to protect the values of the First Amendment against political pressures, the judiciary must review the initial Executive determination to the point of satisfying itself that the subject matter of the dispute does lie within the proper compass of the President's foreign relations power. Constitu-

tional considerations forbid "a complete abandonment of judicial control.". . . Moreover, the judiciary may properly insist that the determination that disclosure of the subject matter would irreparably impair the national security be made by the head of the Executive Department concerned—here the Secretary of State or the Secretary of Defense—after actual personal consideration by that officer. This safeguard is required in the analogous area of executive claims of privilege for secrets of state. . . .

But in my judgment the judiciary may not properly go beyond these two inquiries and redetermine for itself the probable impact of disclosure on the national security.

[T]he very nature of executive decisions as to foreign policy is political, not judicial. Such decisions are wholly confided by our Constitution to the political departments of the government, Executive and Legislative. They are delicate, complex, and involve large elements of prophecy. They are and should be undertaken only by those directly responsible to the people whose welfare they advance or imperil. They are decisions of a kind for which the Judiciary has neither aptitude, facilities nor responsibility and which has long been held to belong in the domain of political power not subject to judicial intrusion or inquiry. *Chicago & Southern Air Lines* v. *Waterman Steamship Corp.* [1948] . . . (Jackson, J.). . . .

Pending further hearings in each case conducted under the appropriate ground rules, I would continue the restraints on publication. I cannot believe that the doctrine prohibiting prior restraints reaches to the point of preventing courts from maintaining the *status quo* long enough to act responsibly in matters of such national importance as those involved here.

Mr. Justice Blackmun, dissenting:
I join Mr. Justice Harlan in his dissent. I also am in substantial accord with much

that Mr. Justice White says, by way of admonition, in the latter part of his opinion. . . .

Two federal district courts, two United States courts of appeals, and this Court—within a period of less than three weeks from inception until today—have been pressed into hurried decision of profound constitutional issues on inadequately developed and largely assumed facts without the careful deliberation that, one would hope, should characterize the American judicial process. . . .

With such respect as may be due to the contrary view, this, in my opinion, is not the way to try a lawsuit of this magnitude and asserted importance. It is not the way

for federal courts to adjudicate, and to be required to adjudicate, issues that allegedly concern the Nation's vital welfare. . . .

The First Amendment, after all, is only one part of an entire Constitution. Article II of the great document vests in the Executive Branch primary power over the conduct of foreign affairs and places in that branch the responsibility for the Nation's safety. Each provision of the Constitution is important, and I cannot subscribe to a doctrine of unlimited absolutism for the First Amendment at the cost of downgrading other provisions. First Amendment absolutism has never commanded a majority of this Court. . . .

What are the exceptional cases in which prior restraints upon the press may be justified according to Chief Justice Hughes in his *Near* opinion? On what grounds does he find the statute a violation of the liberty of the press? What is the significance to Hughes of the fact that the statute suppresses criticism of public officials? Does the Court apply a clear and present danger test to determine the validity of prior restraints upon the press?

How would Chief Justice Hughes have decided the *New York Times* case? Is it one of his exceptional cases where previous restraints may be constitutional? Does the Court in its per curiam opinion declare that prior restraints are per se unconstitutional? How does Justice Black reply in his concurring opinion to the argument of the government that the President, on the basis of his constitutional authority to conduct foreign affairs and his authority as commander-in-chief, has the power to suppress publications that endanger the national security? Does Black hold that under no circumstances can the President resort to the courts to exercise prior restraints upon the press?

Contrast the concurring opinions of Black and Douglas. Are there circumstances under which Douglas would uphold previous restraints upon the press? For example, Douglas points out that there is "no statute barring the publication by the press of the material which the *Times* and the *Post* seek to use." If there were such a statute would Douglas sustain the government? Is Douglas correct that *Near v. Minnesota* repudiated "in no uncertain terms" the doctrine that the government has "inherent powers to go to court and obtain an injunction to protect the national interest, which in this case is alleged to be national security"?

Why does Justice Brennan state that the case is not one of those "extremely narrow class of cases in which the First Amendment's ban on prior judicial restraint may be overridden"? Justice Stewart recognizes the "awesome responsibility" of the President to conduct foreign affairs, and the "large degree of unshared power in the conduct of foreign affairs and the maintenance of our national defense" that the Constitution delegates to the President. On what grounds does Stewart refuse to sustain the government? Why does Justice White, who agrees with the government's contention that the publication of the materials in question will damage the public interest, rule against the government? Why does Justice Marshall argue that the government's attempt at previous restraint of publication violates the constitutional separation of powers?

Is Chief Justice Burger, dissenting, correct in his assessment that there is "little variation among the members of the Court in terms of resistance to prior restraints against publication"? On what grounds do Burger, Harlan, and Blackmun dissent? Do the dissenters favor judicial self-restraint more than the majority?

FREE PRESS AND FAIR TRIAL

Do the requirements of a fair trial sometimes necessitate curbing press coverage of the personalities and events surrounding a trial? A state has a clear and legitimate interest in assuring criminal defendants a fair trial, an interest shared by the defendants themselves. Can the state's interest in and the defendant's rights to a fair trial outweigh the freedom of the press guaranteed by the First Amendment?

The Court has overturned trial verdicts given in an atmosphere of prejudice created by the press. In *Sheppard* v. *Maxwell* (1966) the Court reversed a murder conviction obtained in an atmosphere of severe prejudice largely caused by strident press accounts of the murder and direct accusations that the defendant had committed it. Newspaper, radio, and television publicity was uniformly unfavorable to the accused. During the nine-week trial reporters were seated at a press table inside the bar, a few feet from the jury box. The corridors and rooms of the courthouse were filled with reporters and photographers, and radio broadcasting was done from a room next to one where the jury recessed and deliberated. Private courtroom proceedings were overheard and reported by the press. The noise and commotion created by the newsmen often made it difficult for counsel and witnesses to be heard. The names and addresses of the jurors had been published before the trial, and they received phone calls and letters pressuring them for a guilty verdict. Prospective witnesses were interviewed by the press and their testimony was revealed before they had had a chance to testify in Court. The trial judge denied numerous requests by defense counsel for a change of venue, mistrial, and the questioning of jurors concerning the effects of the widespread publicity upon their views. Justice Clark wrote the opinion of the Court reversing the conviction, expressing the views of eight members. He stated that while a free press is essential to a fair trial, the press cannot be allowed to prejudice the trial. Clark declared that it is the responsibility of a judge to curb the press in order to protect a defendant from publicity that would prejudice and disrupt the conduct of the trial. Clark stated,

The principle that justice cannot survive behind walls of silence has long been reflected in the "Anglo-American distrust for secret trials." . . . A responsible press has always been regarded as the handmaiden of effective judicial administration, especially in the criminal field. Its function in this regard is documented by an impressive record of service over several centuries. The press does not simply publish information about trials but guards against the miscarriage of justice by subjecting the police, prosecutors, and judicial processes to extensive public scrutiny and criticism. This Court has, therefore, been unwilling to place any direct limitations on the freedom traditionally exercised by the news media for "[w]hat transpires in the court room is public property." . . . The "unqualified prohibitions laid down by the framers were intended to give to liberty of the press . . . the broadest scope that could be countenanced in an orderly society." . . . And where there was "no threat or menace to the integrity of the trial," . . . we have consistently required that the press have a free hand, even though we sometimes deplored its sensationalism.

But the Court has also pointed out that "[l]egal trials are not like elections, to be won through the use of the meeting-hall, the radio, and the newspaper." . . . And the Court has insisted that no one be punished for a crime without "a charge fairly made and fairly tried in a public tribunal free of prejudice, passion, excitement, and tyrannical power." . . . "Freedom of discussion should be given the widest range compatible with the essential requirement of the fair and orderly administration of justice." . . . But it must not be allowed to divert the trial from the "very purpose of a court system . . . to adjudicate controversies, both criminal and civil, in the calmness and solemnity of the courtroom according to legal procedures." . . . Among these "legal procedures" is the requirement that the jury's verdict be based on evidence received in open court, not from outside sources. . . . .

There can be no question about the nature of the publicity which surrounded Sheppard's trial. We agree, as did the court of appeals, with the findings in Judge Bells' opinion for the Ohio Supreme Court: "Murder and mystery, society, sex and suspense were combined in this case in such a manner as to intrigue and captivate the public fancy to a degree perhaps unparalleled in recent annals. Throughout the preindictment investigation, the subsequent legal skirmishes and the nine-week trial, circulation-conscious editors catered to the insatiable interest of the American public in the bizarre. . . . In this atmosphere of a 'Roman holiday' for the news media, Sam Sheppard stood trial for his life."

Indeed, every court that has considered this case, save the court that tried it, has deplored the manner in which the news media inflamed and prejudiced the public. . . .

Nor is there doubt that this deluge of publicity reached at least some of the jury. . . .

The court's fundamental error is compounded by the holding that it lacked power to control the publicity about the trial. . . .

From the cases coming here we note that unfair and prejudicial news comment on pending trials has become increasingly prevalent. Due process requires that the accused receive a trial by an impartial jury free from outside influences. Given the pervasiveness of modern communications and the difficulty of effacing prejudicial publicity from the minds of the jurors, the trial courts must take strong measures to ensure that the balance is never weighed against the accused. And appellate tribunals have the duty to make an independent evaluation of the circumstances. Of course, there is nothing that proscribes the press from reporting events that transpire in the courtroom. But where there is a reasonable likelihood that prejudicial news prior to trial will prevent a fair trial, the judge should continue the case until the threat abates, or transfer it to another county not so permeated with publicity. . . . The courts must take such steps by rule and regulation that will protect their processes from prejudicial outside interferences. Neither prosecutors, counsel for defense, the accused, witnesses, court staff nor enforcement officers coming under the jurisdiction of the court should be permitted to frustrate its function. Collaboration between counsel and the press as to information affecting the fairness of a criminal trial is not only subject to regulation, but is highly censorable and worthy of disciplinary measures.[55]

The *Sheppard* decision did *not* hold that the trial judge should in any way have censored the press accounts of the trial but that he should have taken other measures to prevent the "carnival" atmosphere. The Court noted that "[f]rom the very inception of the proceedings the judge announced that neither he nor anyone else could restrict prejudicial news accounts. And he reiterated this view on numerous occasions. Since he viewed the news media as his target, the judge never considered other means that are often utilized to reduce the appearance of prejudicial material and to protect the jury from outside influence. We conclude that these procedures would have been sufficient to guarantee Sheppard a fair trial and so do not consider what sanctions might be available against a recalcitrant press. . . ."[56]

Among the measures the Court suggested the trial judge should have taken in the *Sheppard* case were warnings to newspapers to check the accuracy of their accounts, control over prejudicial statements made to the news media by the prosecution and witnesses, and warnings to the news media not to publish or broadcast prejudicial stories and material not introduced in the proceedings.

Defiance of judicial warnings to the news media not to engage in out-of-court statements prejudicial to the defendant may be punishable as contempt. However, the Court has severely limited the contempt power of judges to prevent critical or prejudicial expressions of opinion outside of the courtroom. In reviewing such contempt citations, where there has been no prior court order, the Supreme Court has applied a clear and present danger test to determine whether or not the out-of-court statements constitute a threat to a fair trial. The Court has generally held that criticisms of judges and judicial proceedings do not present a clear and present danger to fair adjudication.[57]

[55]Sheppard v. Maxwell, 384 U.S. 333, 349–351, 356–357, 362–363 (1966).
[56]Ibid., pp. 357–358.
[57]See Bridges v. California, 314 U.S. 252 (1941), overturning a contempt citation against a union leader's release of a telegram he had sent to a state official predicting a strike if a California state court enforced its decision in a jurisdictional dispute between unions over which union would represent the West Coast dock workers. The decision also reviewed a contempt of court citation of the *Los Angeles Times*, which was fined $300 for publishing a prejudicial editorial before the sentencing but after the conviction of two labor union members for assaulting nonunion truck drivers. The editorial stated that the judge would make a serious mistake if he granted probation to the defendants, and concluded that: "This community needs the example of their assignment to the jute mill [at San Quentin Prison]." Justice Black wrote the majority opinion overturning the convictions, stating that the "issue before us is of the very gravest moment. For free speech and fair trials are two of the most cherished policies of our civilization, and it would be a trying task to choose between them." Id., p. 260. Black concluded that under the clear and present danger test because "a substantive evil will result cannot alone justify a

The use of the contempt power by a trial court to control out-of-court statements does not involve direct judicial control over the content of the media, which is free to make what statements it chooses at the peril of being cited for contempt. And, close judicial scrutiny of the use of the contempt power to control the media has resulted in few if any inroads into freedom of speech and press by courts seeking to restrict media coverage of trials.

Unlike in the contempt cases, the Supreme Court confronted the question of the constitutionality of direct trial court censorship of the press in *Nebraska Press Association* v. *Stuart* (1976). The case involved a particularly heinous and brutal crime in which six members of a family were murdered. The crime attracted widespread press coverage and pretrial publicity that was clearly prejudicial to the defendant. Three days after the crime had been committed, the county attorney and the attorney for the defendants joined in asking the county court to issue a restrictive order concerning matters that could be publicly reported or disclosed to the public because of the massive coverage by the news media and the "reasonable likelihood of prejudicial news which would make difficult, if not impossible, the impaneling of an impartial jury and tend to prevent a fair trial." A restrictive order was issued by the county court that prohibited the public release of any testimony given or evidence produced at the *preliminary* hearing for the defendants. The Nebraska Press Association challenged the order in the district court, which issued a restrictive order of its own specifically prohibiting the press from reporting certain facts surrounding the trial. The district judge found "because of the nature of the crimes charged in the complaint that

---

restriction upon freedom of speech or the press. . . . [T]he substantive evil must be extremely serious and the degree of imminence extremely high before utterances can be punished." Id., pp. 262–263. Neither Bridge's telegram nor the editorials of the *Los Angeles Times* created a clear and present danger to the obstruction of justice.

After the Bridges decision the Court continued to apply a strict clear and present danger standard to strike down contempt convictions for newspaper accounts and out-of-court statements that were critical of judicial conduct. In Pennekamp v. Florida, 328 U.S. 331 (1946), judges were accused by a newspaper of obstructing the prosecution of rape and gambling cases. In Craig v. Harney, 331 U.S. 367 (1947), a newspaper editorial described a judge's decision as "high-handed" and "a travesty of justice." The Supreme Court reversed contempt convictions in both of these cases. In Wood v. Georgia, 370 U.S. 375 (1962), the clear and present danger standard was applied to reverse a contempt conviction of a sheriff who vehemently criticized a judge in the local press for ordering a grand jury investigation of electoral corruption. The sheriff's news release accused the judge of "race agitation," political naivety, prejudice, and acting in the style of a "race-baiting candidate for political office." In reversing the contempt conviction of the sheriff the Court found no evidence on the record of a clear and present danger to the obstruction of justice. The Court stated: ". . . [W]e have simply been told, as a matter of law without factual support, that if a state is unable to punish persons for expressing their views on matters of great public importance when those matters are being considered in an investigation by the grand jury, a clear and present danger to the administration of justice will be created. We find no such danger in the record before us. The type of 'danger' evidenced by the record is precisely one of the types of activity envisioned by the Founders in presenting the First Amendment for ratification. . . . Men are entitled to speak as they please on matters vital to them; errors in judgment or unsubstantiated opinions may be exposed, of course, but not through punishment for contempt for the expression. . . . .Hence, in the absence of some other showing of a substantive evil actually designed to impede the course of justice in justification of the exercise of the contempt power to silence the petitioner, his utterances are entitled to be protected." Id., pp. 388–389.

there is a clear and present danger that pretrial publicity could impinge upon the defendant's right to a fair trial." The order was to apply only until a jury was impaneled. The Nebraska Supreme Court, on appeal, balanced the "heavy presumption against . . . [the constitutional validity] of prior restraint of the press, citing *New York Times Co.* v. *United States* (1971), against the defendant's right to a fair trial." The court found that the publicity surrounding the trial was prejudicial, jeopardizing the defendant's right to a fair trial. The court issued a restrictive order of its own, somewhat modifying the district court's list of pretrial events allowed to be reported. The court noted that under Nebraska law *pretrial* hearings could be closed entirely to the press and the public, and remanded the case to the district judge to determine whether or not this should be done. The United States Supreme Court granted certiorari to review the decision of the Nebraska Supreme Court. The lower court's restrictive order, unlike the contempt citations in previous cases, constituted a prior restraint of the press against which there was a strong presumption of unconstitutionality based upon *Near* v. *Minnesota* (1931) and *New York Times Co.* v. *United States* (1971).[58]

Nebraska Press Assoc. v. *Stuart*

427 U.S. 539; 96 S. Ct. 2791; 49 L. Ed. 2d 683 (1976)

MR. CHIEF JUSTICE BURGER delivered the opinion of the Court:

III

. . . The problems presented by this case are almost as old as the Republic. Neither in the Constitution nor in contemporaneous writings do we find that the conflict between these two important rights was anticipated, yet it is inconceivable that the authors of the Constitution were unaware of the potential conflicts between the right to an unbiased jury and the guarantee of freedom of the press. The unusually able lawyers who helped write the Constitution and later drafted the Bill of Rights were familiar with the historic episode in which John Adams defended British soldiers charged with homicide for firing into a crowd of Boston demonstrators; they were intimately familiar with the clash of the adversary system and the part that pas-

sions of the populace sometimes play in influencing potential jurors. They did not address themselves directly to the situation presented by this case; their chief concern was the need for freedom of expression in the political arena and the dialogue in ideas. But they recognized that there were risks to private rights from an unfettered press. . . .

The trial of Aaron Burr in 1807 presented Mr. Chief Justice Marshall, presiding as a trial judge, with acute problems in selecting an unbiased jury. Few people in the area of Virginia from which jurors were drawn had not formed some opinions concerning Mr. Burr or the case, from newspaper accounts and heightened discussion both private and public. The Chief Justice conducted a searching *voir dire* of the two panels eventually called, and rendered a substantial opinion on the purposes of *voir dire* and the standards to be applied. . . . Burr was acquitted, so

[58]See pp. 667–677.

there was no occasion for appellate review to examine the problem of prejudicial pretrial publicity. Mr. Chief Justice Marshall's careful *voir dire* inquiry into the matter of possible bias makes clear that the problem is not a new one.

The speed of communication and the pervasiveness of the modern news media have exacerbated these problems, however, as numerous appeals demonstrate. The trial of Bruno Hauptmann in a small New Jersey community for the abduction and murder of the Charles Lindberghs' infant child probably was the most widely covered trial up to that time, and the nature of the coverage produced widespread public reaction. Criticism was directed at the "carnival" atmosphere that pervaded the community and the courtroom itself. Responsible leaders of press and the legal profession—including other judges—pointed out that much of this sorry performance could have been controlled by a vigilant trial judge and by other public officers subject to the control of the court. . . .

The excesses of press and radio and lack of responsibility of those in authority in the *Hauptmann* case and others of that era led to efforts to develop voluntary guidelines for courts, lawyers, press, and broadcasters. . . . The effort was renewed in 1965 when the American Bar Association embarked on a project to develop standards for all aspects of criminal justice, including guidelines to accommodate the right to a fair trial and the rights of a free press. . . . The resulting standards, approved by the Association in 1968, received support from most of the legal profession. . . . In the wake of these efforts, the cooperation between bar associations and members of the press led to the adoption of voluntary guidelines like Nebraska's. . . .

In practice, of course, even the most ideal guidelines are subjected to powerful strains when a case such as Simants' arises, with reporters from many parts of the country on the scene. Reporters from distant places are unlikely to consider themselves bound by local standards. They report to editors outside the area covered by the guidelines, and their editors are likely to be guided only by their own standards. To contemplate how a state court can control acts of a newspaper or broadcaster outside its jurisdiction, even though the newspapers and broadcasts reach the very community from which jurors are to be selected, suggests something of the practical difficulties of managing such guidelines. . . .

IV

The Sixth Amendment in terms guarantees "trial, by an impartial jury . . ." in federal criminal prosecutions. Because "trial by jury in criminal cases is fundamental to the American scheme of justice," the Due Process Clause of the Fourteenth Amendment guarantees the same right in state criminal prosecutions. *Duncan* v. *Louisiana*, [1968] . . . .

In the overwhelming majority of criminal trials, pretrial publicity presents few unmanageable threats to this important right. But when the case is a "sensational" one tensions develop between the right of the accused to trial by an impartial jury and the rights guaranteed others by the First Amendment. The relevant decisions of the Court, even if not dispositive, are instructive by way of background. . . .

In *Sheppard* v. *Maxwell* [1966] . . . the Court focused sharply on the impact of pretrial publicity and a trial court's duty to protect the defendant's constitutional right to a fair trial. With only Mr. Justice Black dissenting, and he without opinion, the Court ordered a new trial for the petitioner, even though the first trial had occurred 12 years before. Beyond doubt the press had shown no responsible concern for the constitutional guarantee of a fair trial; the community from which the jury was drawn had been inundated by publicity hostile to the defendant. But the trial judge "did not fulfill his duty to protect [the defendant] from the inherently prejudicial publicity which saturated the community and to control disruptive influences in the courtroom." . . . The Court noted that "unfair and prejudicial news comment on pending trials has become increasingly prevalent," . . . and issued a strong warning:

Due process requires that the accused receive a trial by an impartial jury free from outside influences. Given the pervasiveness of modern communications and the difficulty of effacing prejudicial publicity from the minds of the jurors, *the trial courts must take strong measures to ensure that the balance is never weighed against the accused*. . . . Of course, there is nothing that proscribes the press from reporting events that transpire in the courtroom. But where there is a reasonable likelihood that prejudicial news perior to trial will prevent a fair trial, the judge should *continue the case* until the threat abates, *or transfer it* to another county not so permeated with publicity. In addition, *sequestration of the jury* was something the judge should have raised *sua sponte* with counsel. If publicity during the proceedings threatens the fairness of the trial, a new trial should be ordered. But we must remember that reversals are but palliatives; the cure lies in those remedial measures that will prevent the prejudice at its inception. The courts must take such steps by rule and regulation that will protect their processes from prejudicial outside interferences. *Neither prosecutors, counsel for defense, the accused, witnesses, court staff nor enforcement officers coming under the jurisdiction of the court should be permitted to frustrate its function.* Collaboration between counsel and the press as to information affecting the fairness of a criminal trial is not only subject to regulation, but is highly censurable and worthy of disciplinary measures. . . . (emphasis added).

Because the trial court had failed to use even minimal efforts to insulate the trial and the jurors from the "deluge of publicity." . . . the Court vacated the judgment of conviction and a new trial followed, in which the accused was acquitted.

Cases such as these are relatively rare, and we have held in other cases that trials have been fair in spite of widespread publicity. . . .

Taken together, these cases demonstrate that pretrial publicity—even pervasive, adverse publicity—does not inevitably lead to an unfair trial. The capacity of the jury eventually impaneled to decide the case fairly is influenced by the tone and extent of the publicity, which is in part, and often in large part, shaped by what attorneys, police, and other officials do to precipitate news coverage. The trial judge has a major responsibility. What the judge says about a case, in or out of the courtroom, is likely to appear in newspapers and broadcasts. More important, the measures a judge takes or fails to take to mitigate the effects of pretrial publicity—the measures described in *Sheppard*—may well determine whether the defendant receives a trial consistent with the requirements of due process. That this responsibility has not always been properly discharged is apparent from the decisions just reviewed.

The costs of failure to afford a fair trial are high. In the most extreme cases, like *Sheppard* and *Estes*, the risk of injustice was avoided when the convictions were reversed. But a reversal means that justice has been delayed for both the defendant and the State; in some cases, because of lapse of time retrial is impossible or further prosecution is gravely handicapped. Moreover, in borderline cases in which the conviction is not reversed, there is some possibility of an injustice unredressed. The "strong measures" outlined in *Sheppard* v. *Maxwell* are means by which a trial judge can try to avoid exacting these costs from society or from the accused.

The state trial judge in the case before us acted responsibly, out of a legitimate concern, in an effort to protect the defendant's right to a fair trial. What we must decide is not simply whether the Nebraska courts erred in seeing the possibility of real danger to the defendant's rights, but whether in the circumstances of this case the means employed were foreclosed by another provision of the Constitution.

V

The First Amendment provides that "Congress shall make no law . . . abridging the freedom . . . of the press," and it is "no longer open to doubt that the liberty of the press, and of speech, is within the liberty safeguarded by the due process clause of the Fourteenth Amendment from invasion by state action." *Near* v. *Minnesota* [1931] . . . . The Court has interpreted these guarantees to afford special protection against orders that prohibit the publication or broadcast of particular information or commentary—orders that impose a "previous" or "prior" restraint on speech. None of our decided cases on prior restraint involved restrictive orders entered to protect a defendant's right to a fair and impartial jury, but the opinions on prior restraint have a common thread relevant to this case.

More recently in *New York Times Co.* v. *United States* [1971] . . . the Government sought to enjoin the publication of excerpts from a massive, classified study of the Nation's involvement in the Vietnam conflict, going back to the end of the Second World War. The dispositive opinion of the Court simply concluded that the Government had not met its heavy burden of showing justification for the prior restraint. Each of the six concurring Justices and the three dissenting Justices expressed his views separately, but "every

member of the Court, tacitly or explicitly, accepted the *Near* . . . condemnation of prior restraint as presumptively unconstitutional." *Pittsburgh Press Co.* v. *Human Rel. Comm'n* [1973] . . . , (Burger, C. J., dissenting). The Court's conclusion in *New York Times* suggests that the burden on the Government is not reduced by the temporary nature of a restraint; in that case the Government asked for a temporary restraint solely to permit it to study and assess the impact on national security of the lengthy documents at issue.

The thread running through all these cases is that prior restraints on speech and publication are the most serious and the least tolerable infringement on First Amendment rights. . . .

The extraordinary protections afforded by the First Amendment carry with them something in the nature of a fiduciary duty to exercise the protected rights responsibly—a duty widely acknowledged but not always observed by editors and publishers. It is not asking too much to suggest that those who exercise First Amendment rights in newspapers or broadcasting enterprises direct some effort to protect the rights of an accused to a fair trial by unbiased jurors.

Of course, the order at issue—like the order requested in *New York Times*—does not prohibit but only postpones publication. Some news can be delayed and most commentary can even more readily be delayed without serious injury, and there often is a self-imposed delay when responsible editors call for verification of information. But such delays are normally slight and they are self-imposed. Delays imposed by governmental authority are a different matter.

We have learned, and continue to learn, from what we view as the unhappy experiences of other nations where government has been allowed to meddle in the internal editorial affairs of newspapers. Regardless of how beneficient-sounding the purposes of controlling the press might be, we ... remain intensely skeptical about those measures that would allow government to insinuate itself into the editorial rooms of this Nation's press. *Miami Herald Publishing Co.* v. *Tornillo* [1974] ... , (White, J., concurring).

... As a practical matter, moreover, the element of time is not unimportant if press coverage is to fulfill its traditional function of bringing news to the public promptly.

The authors of the Bill of Rights did not undertake to assign priorities as between First Amendment and Sixth Amendment rights, ranking one as superior to the other. In this case, the petitioners would have us declare the right of an accused subordinate to their right to publish in all circumstances. But if the authors of these guarantees, fully aware of the potential conflicts between them, were unwilling or unable to resolve the issue by assigning to one priority over the other, it is not for us to rewrite the Constitution by undertaking what they declined to do. It is unnecessary, after nearly two centuries, to establish a priority applicable in all circumstances. Yet it is nonetheless clear that the barriers to prior restraint remain high unless we are to abandon what the Court has said for nearly a quarter of our national existence and implied throughout all of it. The history of even wartime suspension of categorical guarantees, such as habeas corpus or the right to trial by civilian courts, see *Ex parte Milligan* [1867] ... , cautions against suspending explicit guarantees.

The Nebraska courts in this case enjoined the publication of certain kinds of information about the *Simants* case. There are, as we suggested earlier, marked differences in setting and purpose between the order entered here and the orders in *Near*, ... and *New York Times*, but as to the underlying issue—the right of the press to be free from *prior* restraints on publication—those cases form the backdrop against which we must decide this case.

VI

We turn now to the record in this case to determine whether, as Learned Hand put it, "the gravity of the 'evil,' discounted by its improbability, justifies such invasion of free speech as is necessary to avoid the danger." *United States* v. *Dennis*, 183 F. 2d 201, 212 (CA2 1950). ... To do so, we must examine the evidence before the trial judge when the order was entered to determine (a) the nature and extent of pretrial news coverage; (b) whether other measures would be likely to mitigate the effects of unrestrained pretrial publicity; and (c) how effectively a restraining order would operate to prevent the threatened danger. The precise terms of the restraining order are also important. We must then consider whether the record supports the entry of a prior restraint on publication, one of the most extraordinary remedies known to our jurisprudence.

A

... Our review of the pretrial record persuades us that the trial judge was justified in concluding that there would be intense and pervasive pretrial publicity concerning this case. He could also reasonably conclude, based on common human experience, that publicity might impair the defendant's right to a fair trial. He did not purport to say more, for he found only "a clear and present danger that pretrial publicity *could* impinge upon the defendant's right to a fair trial." (Emphasis added.) His conclusion as to the impact of such publicity on prospective jurors was of necessity speculative, dealing as he was with factors unknown and unknowable.

B

We find little in the record that goes to another aspect of our task, determining whether measures short of an order restraining all publication would have insured the defendant a fair trial. . . .

We have noted earlier that pretrial publicity, even if pervasive and concentrated, cannot be regarded as leading automatically and in every kind of criminal case to an unfair trial. . . .

. . . There is no finding that alternative measures would not have protected Simants' rights, and the Nebraska Supreme Court did no more than imply that such measures might not be adequate. Moreover, the record is lacking in evidence to support such a finding.

C

We must also assess the probable efficacy of prior restraint on publication as a workable method of protecting Simants' right to a fair trial, and we cannot ignore the reality of the problems of managing and enforcing pretrial restraining orders. . . .

Finally, we note that the events disclosed by the record took place in a community of 850 people. It is reasonable to assume that, without any news accounts being printed or broadcast, rumors would travel swiftly by word of mouth. One can only speculate on the accuracy of such reports, given the generative propensities of rumors; they could well be more damaging than reasonably accurate news accounts. But plainly a whole community cannot be restrained from discussing a subject intimately affecting life within it.

Given these practical problems, it is far from clear that prior restraint on publication would have protected Simants' rights.

D

Finally, another feature of this case leads us to conclude that the restrictive order entered here is not supportable. At the outset the County Court entered a very broad restrictive order, the terms of which are not before us; it then held a preliminary hearing open to the public and the press. There was testimony concerning at least two incriminating statements made by Simants to private persons; the statement—evidently a confession—that he gave to law enforcement officials was also introduced. . . .

To the extent that this order prohibited the reporting of evidence adduced at the open preliminary hearing, it plainly violated settled principles: "[T]here is nothing that proscribes the press from reporting events that transpire in the courtroom." *Sheppard* v. *Maxwell* [1966]. . . . The County Court could not know that closure of the preliminary hearing was an alternative open to it until the Nebraska Supreme Court so construed state law; but once a public hearing had been held, what transpired there could not be subject to prior restraint. . . .

E

The record demonstrates, as the Nebraska courts held, that there was indeed a risk that pretrial news accounts, true or false, would have some adverse impact on the attitudes of those who might be called as jurors. But on the record now before us it is not clear that further publicity, unchecked, would so distort the views of potential jurors that 12 could not be found who would, under proper instructions, fulfill their sworn duty to render a just verdict exclusively on the evidence presented in open court. We cannot say on this record that alternatives to a prior restraint on petitioners would not have sufficiently mitigated the adverse effects of pretrial publicity so as to make prior restraint unnecessary. Nor can we conclude that the restraining order actually entered would serve its intended purpose. Reasonable minds can have few doubts about the gravity of the evil pretrial publicity can work, but the probability that it would do so here was not demonstrated with the degree of certainty our cases on prior restraint require. . . .

Our analysis ends as it began, with a confrontation between prior restraint imposed to protect one vital constitutional guarantee and the explicit command of another that the freedom to speak and publish shall not be abridged. We reaffirm that the guarantees of freedom of expression are not an absolute prohibition under all circumstances, but the barriers to prior restraint remain high and the presumption against its use continues intact. We hold that, with respect to the order entered in this case prohibiting reporting or commentary on judicial proceedings held in public, the barriers have not been overcome; to the extent that this order restrained publication of such material, it is clearly invalid. To the extent that it prohibited publication based on information gained from other sources, we conclude that the heavy burden imposed as a condition to securing a prior restraint was not met and the judgment of the Nebraska Supreme Court is therefore

Reversed.

MR. JUSTICE WHITE, concurring:

Technically there is no need to go farther than the Court does to dispose of this case, and I join the Court's opinion. I should add, however, that for the reasons which the Court itself canvasses there is grave doubt in my mind whether orders with respect to the press such as were entered in this case would ever be justifiable. It may be the better part of discretion, however, not to announce such a rule in the first case in which the issue has been squarely presented here. Perhaps we should go no further than absolutely necessary until the federal courts, and ourselves, have been exposed to a broader spectrum of cases presenting similar issues. If the recurring result, however, in case after case is to be similar to our judgment today, we should at some point announce a more general rule and avoid the interminable litigation that our failure to do so would necessarily entail.

MR. JUSTICE POWELL wrote a separate concurring opinion.

MR. JUSTICE BRENNAN, with whom MR. JUSTICE STEWART and MR. JUSTICE MARSHALL join, concurring in the judgment:

. . . The right to a fair trial by a jury of one's peers is unquestionably one of the most precious and sacred safeguards enshrined in the Bill of Rights. I would hold, however, that resort to prior restraints on the freedom of the press is a constitutionally impermissible method for enforcing that right; judges have at their disposal a broad spectrum of devices for ensuring that fundamental fairness is accorded the accused without necessitating so drastic an incursion on the equally fundamental and salutary constitutional mandate that discussion of public affairs in a free society cannot depend on the preliminary grace of judicial censors. . . .

I unreservedly agree with Mr. Justice Black that "free speech and fair trials are two of the most cherished policies of our civilization, and it would be a trying task to choose between them." *Bridges* v. *California* [1961]. . . . But I would reject the notion that a choice is necessary, that there is an inherent conflict that cannot be resolved without essentially abrogating one right or the other. To hold that courts cannot impose any prior restraints on the reporting of or commentary upon information revealed in open court proceedings, disclosed in public documents, or divulged by other sources with respect to the criminal justice system is not, I must emphasize, to countenance the sacrifice of precious Sixth Amendment rights on the altar of the First Amendment. For although there may in some instances be tension between uninhibited and robust reporting by the press and fair trials for criminal defendants, judges possess adequate tools short of injunctions against reporting for relieving that tension. To be sure, these alternatives may require greater sensitivity and effort on the part of judges conducting criminal trials than would the stifling of publicity through the simple expedient of issuing a restrictive order on the press; but that sensitivity and effort is required in order to ensure the full enjoyment and proper accommodation of both First and Sixth Amendment rights.

There is, beyond peradventure, a clear and substantial damage to freedom of the press whenever even a temporary restraint is imposed on reporting of material concerning the operations of the criminal justice system, an institution of such pervasive influence in our constitutional scheme. And the necessary impact of reporting even confessions can never be so direct, immediate, and irreparable that I would give credence to any notion that prior restraints may be imposed on that rationale. It may be that such incriminating material would be of such slight news value or so inflammatory in particular cases that responsible organs of the media, in an exercise of self-restraint, would choose not to publicize that material, and not make the judicial task of safeguarding precious rights of criminal defendants more difficult. Voluntary codes such as the Nebraska Bar-Press Guidelines are a commendable acknowledgment

by the media that constitutional prerogatives bring enormous responsibilities, and I would encourage continuation of such voluntary cooperative efforts between the bar and the media. However, the press may be arrogant, tyrannical, abusive, and sensationalist, just as it may be incisive, probing, and informative. But at least in the context of prior restraints on publication, the decision of what, when, and how to publish is for editors, not judges. . . . Every restrictive order imposed on the press in this case was accordingly an unconstitutional prior restraint on the freedom of the press, and I would therefore reverse the judgment of the Nebraska Supreme Court and remand for further proceedings not inconsistent with this opinion.

Mr. Justice Stevens, concurring in the judgment:

For the reasons eloquently stated by Mr. Justice Brennan, I agree that the judiciary is capable of protecting the defendant's right to a fair trial without enjoining the press from publishing information in the public domain, and that it may not do so. Whether the same absolute protection would apply no matter how shabby or illegal the means by which the information is obtained, no matter how serious an intrusion on privacy might be involved, no matter how demonstrably false the information might be, no matter how prejudicial it might be to the interests of innocent persons, and no matter how perverse the motivation for publishing it, is a question I would not answer without further argument. . . . I do, however, subscribe to most of what Mr. Justice Brennan says and, if ever required to face the issue squarely, may well accept his ultimate conclusion.

What criteria governing fair trials does the Court develop from the Sixth Amendment? What is the prior restraint standard used by the Court? Chief

Justice Burger writes that "the Bill of Rights did not undertake to assign priorities as between First Amendment and Sixth Amendment rights, ranking one as superior to the other." Does the Court's opinion in fact give priority to the First Amendment freedom of the press? How does the Court apply the clear and present danger standard to the case, and with what result? Does the Court suggest the circumstances under which it would uphold a trial court order similar to the one under review?

The *Nebraska Press Association* case dealt exclusively with the authority of the Court to control *pretrial* publicity by proscribing the reporting of testimony and evidence adduced at a pretrial hearing. The Nebraska Supreme Court's opinion noted that under certain circumstances closure of a pretrial proceeding is permitted, and this was not contradicted by the Supreme Court (it was not an issue because closure was not invoked). However, the United States Supreme Court made a point of the fact that since closure was not invoked, the pretrial hearing was open to the public and the press, making the restrictive order in effect one of prior censorship of what could be reported. The Court declared: "To the extent that this [restrictive] order prohibited the reporting of evidence adduced at the *open preliminary* hearing, it plainly violated settled principles. 'There is nothing that proscribes the press from reporting events that transpire in the courtroom.' *Sheppard* v. *Maxwell*. . . . The county court could not know that closure of the preliminary hearing was an alternative open to it until the Nebraska Supreme Court so construed state law; but once a public hearing had been held, what transpired there could not be subject to prior restraint."[59]

There is an implication that the *Nebraska Press Association* opinion that under certain circumstances the Supreme Court might uphold the closure of pretrial proceedings, an implication that can be drawn from the fact that the Court reiterated without comment the view of the Nebraska Supreme Court that such an alternative was available to the trial judge.

In the following case the Court confronted directly the issue of the extent of a trial court's authority to close a pretrial hearing in order to prevent prejudicial or adverse publicity. At a pretrial hearing on a motion to suppress allegedly involuntary confessions and specified physical evidence, the defendants requested exclusion of the public and the press on the grounds that adverse publicity jeopardized their chance for a fair trial. The district attorney did not oppose the motion, nor did a reporter for the Gannett Company chain of newspapers who was present at the time. The trial judge granted the motion. The next day the Gannett reporter requested access to the transcript, but the trial judge reserved his decision on the release of the transcript because of the closure of the hearing. The Gannett Company sought to have the closure order overturned in the New York Supreme Court (the intermediate appellate court of New York State) on the grounds that the First Amendment rights of the press outweighed the defendants' right to a fair trial. The New York Supreme Court vacated the closure order on the grounds that it constituted unlawful prior restraint in violation of the First and Fourteenth Amendments. The New York Court of Appeals (the high-

[59]Nebraska Press Assoc. v. Stuart, 427 U.S. 539,568 (1976).

est state court) reversed, holding that the exclusion of the press and the public from the pretrial proceeding was constitutional. The Supreme Court granted certiorari to the Court of Appeals of New York to review the case because of what it considered to be the importance of the issues involved.

Gannett Co. v. DePasquale

443 U.S. 368; 99 S. Ct. 2898; 61 L. Ed. 2d 608 (1979)

MR. JUSTICE STEWART delivered the opinion of the Court:

The question presented in this case is whether members of the public have an independent constitutional right to insist upon access to a pretrial judicial proceeding, even though the accused, the prosecutor and the trial judge all have agreed to the closure of that proceeding in order to assure a fair trial. . . .

III

This Court has long recognized that adverse publicity can endanger the ability of a defendant to receive a fair trial. *E.g., Sheppard* v. *Maxwell* [1966] . . . . To safeguard the due process rights of the accused, a trial judge has an affirmative constitutional duty to minimize the effects of prejudicial pretrial publicity. *Sheppard* v. *Maxwell.* And because of the Constitution's pervasive concern for these due process rights, a trial judge may surely take protective measures even when they are not strictly and inescapably necessary.

Publicity concerning pretrial suppression hearings such as the one involved in the present case poses special risks of unfairness. The whole purpose of such hearings is to screen out unreliable or illegally obtained evidence and insure that this evidence does not become known to the jury. . . . Publicity concerning the proceedings at a pretrial hearing, however, could influence public opinion against a defendant and inform potential jurors of inculpatory information wholly inadmissible at the actual trial.

The danger of publicity concerning pretrial suppression hearings is particularly acute, because it may be difficult to measure with any degree of certainty the effects of such publicity on the fairness of the trial. After the commencement of the trial itself, inadmissible prejudicial information about a defendant can be kept from a jury by a variety of means. When such information is publicized during a pretrial proceeding, however, it may never be altogether kept from potential jurors. Closure of pretrial proceedings is often one of the most effective methods that a trial judge can employ to attempt to insure that the fairness of a trial will not be jeopardized by the dissemination of such information throughout the community before the trial itself has even begun. . . .

IV

A

The Sixth Amendment, applicable to the States through the Fourteenth, surrounds a criminal trial with guarantees such as the rights to notice, confrontation, and compulsory process that have as their overriding purpose the protection of the accused from prosecutorial and judicial abuses. Among the guarantees that the Amendment provides to a person charged with the commission of a criminal offense, and to him alone, is the "right to a speedy and public trial, by an impartial jury." The Constitution nowhere mentions any right of access to a criminal trial on the part of the public; its guarantee, like the others enumerated, is personal to the accused. . . .

Our cases have uniformly recognized the public trial guarantee as one created for the benefit of the defendant. . . .

B

While the Sixth Amendment guarantees to a defendant in a criminal case the right to a public trial, it does not guarantee the right to compel a private trial. . . . But the issue here is not whether the defendant can compel a private trial. Rather the issue is whether members of the public have an enforceable right to a public trial that can be asserted independently of the parties in the litigation.

There can be no blinking the fact that there is a strong societal interest in public trials. Openness in court proceedings may improve the quality of testimony, induce unknown witnesses to come forward with relevant testimony, cause all trial participants to perform their duties more conscientiously, and generally give the public an opportunity to observe the judicial system. . . . But there is a strong societal interest in other constitutional guarantees extended to the accused as well. The public, for example, has a definite and concrete interest in seeing that justice is swiftly and fairly administered. . . . Similarly, the public has an interest in having a criminal case heard by a jury, an interest distinct from the defendant's interest in being tried by a jury of his peers. . . .

Recognition of an independent public interest in the enforcement of Sixth Amendment guarantees is a far cry, however, from the creation of a constitutional right on the part of the public. In an adversary system of criminal justice, the public interest in the administration of justice is protected by the participants in the litigation. Thus, because of the great public interest in jury trials as the preferred mode of fact-finding in criminal cases, a defendant cannot waive a jury trial without the consent of the prosecutor and judge. . . . But if the defendant waives his right to a jury trial, and the prosecutor and the judge consent, it could hardly be seriously argued that a member of the public could demand a jury trial because of the societal interest in that mode of fact-finding. Cf. Fed. Rule Crim. Proc. 23 (a) (trials to be by jury unless waived by a defendant, but the court must approve and the prosecution must consent to the waiver). Similarly, while a defendant cannot convert his right to a speedy trial into a right to compel an indefinite postponement, a member of the general public surely has no right to prevent a continuance in order to vindicate the public interest in the efficient administration of justice. In short, our adversary system of criminal justice is premised upon the proposition that the public interest is fully protected by the participants in the litigation.

V

In arguing that members of the general public have a constitutional right to attend a criminal trial, despite the obvious lack of support for such a right in the structure or text of the Sixth Amendment, the petitioner and *amici* rely on the history of the public trial guarantee. This history, however, ultimately demonstrates no more than the existence of a common-law rule of open civil and criminal proceedings.

A

. . . Our judicial duty in this case is to determine whether the common-law rule of open proceedings was incorporated, rejected, or left undisturbed by the Sixth Amendment. In pursuing this inquiry, it is important to distinguish between what the Constitution permits and what it requires. It has never been suggested that by phrasing the public trial guarantee as a right of the accused, the Framers intended to reject the common-law rule of open proceedings. There is no question that the Sixth Amendment permits and even presumes open trials as a norm. But the issue here is whether the Constitution *requires* that a pretrial proceeding such as this one be opened to the public, even though the participants in the litigation agree that it should be closed to protect the defendants' right to a fair trial. The history upon which the petitioner and *amici* rely totally fails to demonstrate that the Framers of the Sixth Amendment intended to create a constitutional right in strangers to attend a pretrial proceeding, when all that they actually did was to confer upon the accused an explicit right to demand a public trial. In conspicuous contrast with some of the early state constitutions that provided for a public right to open civil and criminal trials, the Sixth Amendment confers the right to a public trial only upon a defendant and only in a criminal case.

B

But even if the Sixth and Fourteenth Amendments could properly be viewed as embodying the common-law right of the public to attend criminal trials, it would not necessarily follow that the petitioner would have a right of access under the circumstances of this case. For there exists no persuasive evidence that at common law members of the public had any right to attend pretrial proceedings; indeed, there is substantial evidence to the contrary. . . .

For these reasons, we hold that members of the public have no constitutional right under the Sixth and Fourteenth Amendments to attend criminal trials.

VI

The petitioner also argues that members of the press and the public have a right of access to the pretrial hearing by reason of the First and Fourteenth Amendments. . . .

Several factors lead to the conclusion that the actions of the trial judge here were consistent with any right of access the petitioner may have had under the First and Fourteenth Amendments. First, none of the spectators present in the courtroom, including the reporter employed by the petitioner, objected when the defendants made the closure motion. Despite this failure to make a contemporaneous objection, counsel for the petitioner was given an opportunity to be heard at a proceeding where he was allowed to voice the petitioner's objections to closure of the pretrial hearing. At this proceeding, which took place after the filing of briefs, the trial court balanced the "constitutional rights of the press and the public" against the "defendants' right to a fair trial." The trial judge concluded after making this appraisal that the press and the public could be excluded from the suppression hearing and could be denied immediate access to a transcript, because an open proceeding would pose a "reasonable probablility of prejudice to these defendants." Thus the trial court found that the representatives of the press did have a right of access of constitutional dimension, but held, under the circumstances of this case, that this right was outweighed by the defendant's right to a fair trial. In short, the closure decision was based "on an assessment of the competing societal interests involved . . . rather than on any determination that First Amendment freedoms were not implicated." . . .

Furthermore, any denial of access in this case was not absolute but only temporary. Once the danger of prejudice had dissipated, a transcript of the suppression hearing was made available. The press and the public then had a full opportunity to scrutinize the suppression hearing. Unlike the case of an absolute ban on access, therefore, the press here had the opportunity to inform the public of the details of the pretrial hearing accurately and completely. Under these circumstances, any First and Fourteenth Amendment right of the petitioner to attend criminal trial was not violated.

VII

We certainly do not disparage the general desirability of open judicial proceedings. But we are not asked here to declare whether open proceedings represent beneficial social policy, or whether there would be a constitutional barrier to a state law that imposed a stricter standard of closure than the one here employed by the New York courts. Rather, we are asked to hold that the Constitution itself gave the petitioner an affirmative right of access to this pretrial proceeding, even though all the participants in the litigation agreed that it should be closed to protect the fair trial rights of the defendants.

For all of the reasons discussed in this opinion, we hold that the Constitution provides no such right. Accordingly, the judgment of the New York Court of Appeals is affirmed.

It is so ordered.

Mr. Chief Justice Burger, concurring:

I join the opinion of the Court, but I write separately to emphasize my view of the nature of the proceeding involved in today's decision. By definition a hearing on a motion before trial to suppress evidence is not a *trial*; it is a *pre*trial hearing.

The Sixth Amendment tells us that "in all criminal prosecutions, the *accused* shall enjoy the right to a . . . public trial." It is the practice in Western societies, and has been part of the common-law tradition for centuries, that trials generally be public. This is an important prophylaxis of the system of justice that constitutes the adhesive element of our society. The public has an interest in observing the performance not only of the litigants and the witnesses, but also of the advocates and the presiding judge. Similarly, if the accused testifies, there is a proper public interest in that testimony. But interest alone does not create a constitutional right.

At common law there was a very different presumption for proceedings which preceded the trial. There was awareness of the untoward effects that could result from the publication of information before an indictment was returned or before a person was bound over for trial. . . .

Even though the draftsmen of the Constitution could not anticipate the 20th century pretrial proceedings to suppress evidence, pretrial proceedings were not wholly unknown in that day. Written interrogatories were used pretrial in 18th century litigation, especially in admiralty cases. Thus, it is safe to assume that those lawyers who drafted the Sixth Amendment were not unaware that some testimony was likely to be recorded before trials took place. Yet, no one ever suggested that there was any "right" of the public to be present at such pretrial proceedings as were available in that time; until the trial it could not be known whether and to what extent the pretrial evidence would be offered or received.

Similarly, during the last 40 years in which the pretrial processes have been enormously expanded, it has never occurred to anyone, so far as I am aware, that a pretrial deposition or pretrial interrogatories were other than wholly private to the litigants. A pretrial deposition does not become part of a "trial" until and unless the contents of the deposition are offered in evidence. Pretrial depositions are not uncommon to take the testimony of a witness, either for the defense or for the prosecution. In the entire pretrial period, there is no certainty that a trial will take place. Something in the neighborhood of 85 percent of all criminal charges are resolved by guilty pleas, frequently after pretrial depositions have been taken or motions to suppress evidence have been ruled upon.

For me, the essence of all of this is that by definition "pretrial proceedings" are exactly that.

MR. JUSTICE POWELL, concurring:

Although I join the opinion of the Court, I would address the question that it reserves. Because of the importance of the public's having accurate information concerning the operation of its criminal justice system, I would hold explicitly that petitioner's reporter had an interest protected by the First and Fourteenth Amendments in being present at the pretrial suppression hearing. . . . [T]his constitutional protection derives, not from any special status of members of the press as such, but rather because "[i]n seeking out the news the press . . . acts as an agent of the public at large," each individual member of which cannot obtain for himself "the information needed for the intelligent discharge of his political responsibilities." . . .

The right of access to courtroom proceedings, of course, is not absolute. It is limited both by the constitutional right of defendants to a fair trial . . . and by the needs of government to obtain just convictions and to preserve the confidentiality of sensitive information and the identity of informants. . . . The task of determining the application of these limitations in each individual trial necessarily falls almost exclusively upon the trial court asked to exclude members of the press and public from the courtroom. . . .

. . . In *Nebraska Press Assn.* v. *Stuart* . . .

we concluded that there is a strong presumption against prohibiting members of the press from publishing information already in their possession concerning courtroom proceedings. Excluding all members of the press from the courtroom, however, differs substantially from the "gag order" at issue in *Nebraska Press,* as the latter involved a classic prior restraint, "one of the most extraordinary remedies known to our jurisprudence," . . . and applied to information irrespective of its source. In the present case, on the other hand, we are confronted with a trial court's order that in effect denies access only to one, albeit important, source. It does not in any way tell the press what it may and may not publish. . . .

Although the strict standard of *Nebraska Press* is not applicable to decisions concerning closure of courtroom proceedings, much of the discussion in that case of the factors to be considered in making decisions with respect to "gag orders" is relevant to closure decisions. Thus, where a defendant requests the trial court to exclude the public, it should consider whether there are alternative means reasonably available by which the fairness of the trial might be preserved without interfering substantially with the public's interest in prompt access to information concerning the administration of justice. Similarly, because exclusion is justified only as a protection of the defendant's right to a fair trial and the State's interest in confidentiality, members of the press and public objecting to the exclusion have the right to demand that it extend no farther than is likely to achieve these goals. Thus, for example, the trial court should not withhold the transcript of closed courtroom proceedings past the time when no prejudice is likely to result to the defendant or the State from its release.

It is not enough, however, that trial courts apply a certain standard to requests for closure. If the constitutional right of the press and public to access is to have substance, representatives of these groups must be given an opportunity to be heard on the question of their exclusion. But this opportunity extends no farther than the persons actually present at the time the motion for closure is made, for the alternative would require substantial delays in trial and pretrial proceedings while notice was given to the public. Upon timely objection to the granting of the motion, it is incumbent upon the trial court to afford those present a reasonable opportunity to be heard on the question whether the defendant is likely to be deprived of a fair trial if the press and public are permitted to remain in attendance. At this hearing, it is the defendant's responsibility as the moving party to make some showing that the fairness of his trial likely will be prejudiced by public access to the proceedings. Similarly, if the State joins in the closure request, it should be given the opportunity to show that public access would interfere with its interests in fair proceedings or preserving the confidentiality of sensitive information. On the other hand, members of the press and public who object to closure have the responsibility of showing to the court's satisfaction that alternative procedures are available that would eliminate the dangers shown by the defendant and the State.

The question, then, is whether the First Amendment right of access outlined above was adequately respected in the present case. . . .

In my view, the procedure followed by the trial court fully comported with that required by the Constitution. . . .

MR. JUSTICE REHNQUIST, concurring:
While I concur in the opinion of the Court, I write separately to emphasize what should be apparent from the Court's Sixth Amendment holding and to address the First Amendment issue that the Court appears to reserve.

The Court today holds, without qualification, that "members of the public have no constitutional right under the Sixth and Fourteenth Amendments to attend criminal trials." . . . In this case, the trial judge closed the suppression hearing because he concluded that an open hearing might have posed a danger to the defendant's ability to receive a fair trial. . . . But the Court's recitation of this fact and its discussion of the need to preserve the defendant's right to a fair trial, . . . should not be interpreted to mean that under the Sixth Amendment a trial court can close a pretrial hearing or trial only when there is a danger that prejudicial publicity will harm the defendant. To the contrary, since the Court holds that the public does not have *any* Sixth Amendment right of access to such proceedings, it necessarily follows that if the parties agree on a closed proceeding, the trial court is not required by the Sixth Amendment to advance any reason whatsoever for declining to open a pretrial hearing or trial to the public. "There is no question that the Sixth Amendment permits and even presumes open trials as a norm." . . . But, as the Court today holds, the Sixth Amendment does not require a criminal trial or hearing to be opened to the public if the participants to the litigation agree for any reason, no matter how jurisprudentially appealing or unappealing, that it should be closed.

The Court states that it may assume *"arguendo"* that the First and Fourteenth Amendments guarantee the public a right of access to pretrial hearings in some situations, because it concludes that in this case this "putative right was given all appropriate deference." . . . Despite the Court's seeming reservation of the question whether the First Amendment guarantees the public a right of access to pretrial proceedings, it is clear that this Court repeatedly has held that there is no First Amendment right of access in the public or the press to judicial or other governmental proceedings. . . . Because this Court has refused to find a First Amendment right of access in the past, lower courts should not assume that after today's decision they must adhere to the procedures employed by the trial court in this case or to those advanced by Mr. Justice Powell in his separate opinion in order to avoid running afoul of the First Amendment. To the contrary, in my view and, I think, in the view of a majority of this Court, the lower courts are under no constitutional constraint either to accept or reject those procedures. They remain, in the best tradition of our federal system, free to determine for themselves the question whether to open or close the proceeding. Hopefully, they will decide the question by accommodating competing interests in a judicious manner. But so far as the Constitution is concerned, the question is for them, not us, to resolve.

MR. JUSTICE BLACKMUN, with whom MR. JUSTICE BRENNAN, MR. JUSTICE WHITE, and MR. JUSTICE MARSHALL join, concurring in part and dissenting in part:

I concur in Part II of the Court's opinion [holding that the case was not moot] but I dissent from that opinion's subsequent Parts.

Today's decision, as I view it, is an unfortunate one. I fear that the Court surrenders to the temptation to overstate and overcolor the actual nature of the pre-August 7, 1976 publicity; that it reaches for a strict and flat result; and that in the process it ignores the important antecedents and significant developmental features of the Sixth Amendment. The result is an inflexible *per se* rule, as Mr. Justice Rehnquist so appropriately observes in his separate concurrence . . . That rule is to the effect that if the defense and the prosecution merely agree to have the public excluded from a suppression hearing, and the trial judge does not resist—as trial judges may be prone not to do, since nonresistance is easier than resistance—

closure shall take place, and there is nothing in the Sixth Amendment that prevents that happily agreed-upon event. The result is that the important interests of the public and the press (as a part of that public) in open judicial proceedings are rejected and cast aside as of little value or significance.

Because I think this easy but wooden approach is without support either in legal history or in the intendment of the Sixth Amendment, I dissent. . . .

II

This Court confronts in this case another aspect of the recurring conflict that arises whenever a defendant in a criminal case asserts that his right to a fair trial clashes with the right of the public in general, and of the press in particular, to an open proceeding. . . .

It is clear that this case does not involve the type of prior restraint that was in issue in cases like *Nebraska Press*. Neither the County Court nor the Court of Appeals restrained publication of, or comment upon, information already known to the public or the press, or about the case in general. The issue here, then, is not one of prior restraint on the press but is, rather one of *access* to a judicial proceeding.

Despite Mr. Justice Powell's concern, this Court heretofore has not found and does not today find, any First Amendment right of access to judicial or other governmental proceedings. . . . One turns then, instead, to that provision of the Constitution that speaks most directly to the question of access to judicial proceedings, namely, the public trial provision of the Sixth Amendment.

A

The familiar language of the Sixth Amendment reads: "In all criminal prosecutions, the accused shall enjoy the right to a speedy and public trial." This provision reflects the tradition of our system of criminal justice that a trial is a "public event" and that "[w]hat transpires in the court room is public property." . . . And it reflects, as well, "the notion, deeply rooted in the common law, that 'justice must satisfy the appearance of justice.' " . . .

More importantly, the requirement that a trial of a criminal case be public embodies our belief that secret judicial proceedings would be a menace to liberty. . . .

The public trial concept embodied in the Sixth Amendment remains a fundamental and essential feature of our system of criminal justice in both the federal courts and in the state courts. The Due Process Clause of the Fourteenth Amendment requires that in criminal cases the States act in conformity with the public trial provision of the Sixth Amendment. . . .

B

By its literal terms the Sixth Amendment secures the right to a public trial only to "the accused." And in this case, the accused were the ones who sought to waive that right, and to have the public removed from the pretrial hearing in order to guard against publicity that possibly would be prejudicial to them. . . .

The Court, however, previously has recognized that the Sixth Amendment may implicate interests beyond those of the accused. . . .

C

It is clear . . . that the fact the Sixth Amendment casts the right to a public trial in terms of the right of the accused is not sufficient to permit the inference that the accused may compel a private proceeding simply by waiving the right. Any such right to compel a private proceeding must have some independent basis in the Sixth Amendment. In order to determine whether an independent basis exists, we

should examine, . . . the common law and colonial antecedents of the public trial provision as well as the original understanding of the Sixth Amendment. . . .

[Here Blackmun reviews the history of the public trial provision of the Sixth Amendment.]

I therefore conclude that the Due Process Clause of the Fourteenth Amendment, insofar as it incorporates the public trial provision of the Sixth Amendment, prohibits the States from excluding the public from a proceeding within the ambit of the Sixth Amendment's guarantee without affording full and fair consideration to the public's interests in maintaining an open proceeding. And I believe that the Sixth and Fourteenth Amendments require this conclusion notwithstanding the fact it is the accused who seeks to close the trial. . . .

III

. . . I do not deny that the publication of information learned in an open proceeding may harm irreparably, under certain circumstances, the ability of a defendant to obtain a fair trial. This is especially true in the context of a pretrial hearing, where disclosure of information, determined to be inadmissible at trial, may severely affect a defendant's rights. Although the Sixth Amendment's public trial provision establishes a strong presumption in favor of open proceedings, it does not require that all proceedings be held in open court when to do so would deprive a defendant of a fair trial.

No court has held that the Sixth Amendment imposes an absolute requirement that courts be open at all times. On the contrary, courts on both the state and federal levels have recognized exceptions to the public trial requirement even when it is the accused who objects to the exclusion of the public or a portion thereof. . . .

. . . [C]ourts have been willing to permit limited exceptions to the principle of publicity where necessary to protect some other interest. Because of the importance we attach to a fair trial, it is clear that whatever restrictions on access the Sixth Amendment may prohibit in another context, it does not prevent a trial court from restricting access to a pretrial suppression hearing where such restriction is necessary in order to ensure that a defendant not be denied a fair trial as a result of prejudicial publicity flowing from that hearing. . . .

At the same time, however, the public's interest in maintaining open courts requires that any exception to the rule be narrowly drawn. It comports with the Sixth Amendment to require an accused who seeks closure to establish that it is strictly and inescapably necessary in order to protect the fair trial guarantee. . . . The accused who seeks closure should establish . . . at a minimum the following:

First, he should provide an adequate basis to support a finding that there is a substantial probability that irreparable damage to his fair trial right will result from conducting the proceeding in public. . . .

Second, the accused should show a substantial probability that alternatives to closure will not protect adequately his right to a fair trial. . . .

Third, the accused should demonstrate

that there is a substantial probability that closure will be effective in protecting against the perceived harm. Where significantly prejudicial information already has been made public, there might well be little justification for closing a pretrial hearing in order to prevent only the disclosure of details.

I emphasize that the trial court should begin with the assumption that the Sixth Amendment requires that a pretrial suppression hearing be conducted in open court unless a defendant carries his burden to demonstrate a strict and inescapable necessity for closure. . . .

V

I return to the exclusion order entered by Judge DePasquale. It is clear that the judge entered the order because of his apparent concern for the fair trial rights of the defendants and his suspicion that those rights would be threatened if the hearing were public. I acknowledge that concern, but I conclude that the order was not justified on the facts of this case.

There was no factual basis upon which the court could conclude that a substantial probability existed that an open proceeding would result in harm to the defendants' rights to a fair trial. . . .

Justice Powell's concurring opinion states that "Excluding all members of the press from the courtroom . . . differs substantially from the 'gag order' at issue in Nebraska Press, as the latter involved a classic prior restraint, . . . and applied to information irrespective of its source. In the present case, on the other hand, we are confronted with a trial court's order that in effect denies access only to one, albeit important, source. It does not in any way tell the press what it may or may not publish." As Justice Blackmun writes in that part of his opinion which dissents, the issue "is not one of prior restraint on the press but is, rather, one of *access* to a judicial proceeding." The central issue, then, is not one of the First Amendment guarantee of freedom of the press but of the Sixth Amendment provision that in all criminal prosecutions "the accused shall enjoy the right to a speedy and public trial. . . ." While the case hinges primarily upon the justices' interpretation of the Sixth Amendment, Justice Powell's concurring opinion states that the freedom of the press guaranteed by the First and Fourteenth Amendments is the central issue. Justice Stewart's opinion for the Court is based primarily upon the Sixth Amendment, but also addresses the claim of the petitioner that the closure of the pretrial hearing violated the freedom of press provision of the First Amendment as incorporated into the Fourteenth Amendment by denying the press access. Without reaching the questions of whether or not the First and Fourteenth Amendments guarantee access to criminal proceedings under certain circumstances, Stewart settles the issue by holding that any right of access that may exist was upheld by the actions of the trial judge. Both Stewart and Powell on this point agree that the procedures followed by the trial judge in balancing the rights of the accused against assumed (Stewart) or stated (Powell) constitutional rights of access fully protected the rights of the defendant and the press alike.

How did Justice Stewart's majority opinion interpret the reach of the Sixth Amendment's provision giving criminal defendants the right to a speedy and public trial? On what grounds did he hold that the Sixth Amendment does not give the public and the press the right of access to a criminal proceeding? Stewart recognizes that there is "a strong societal interest in public trials" and that open court proceedings may benefit the public interest. However, a public interest in open proceedings does not create a public right. How is the public interest to be protected in closed judicial proceedings? How does Stewart distinguish pretrial from trial proceedings? Does he suggest that it would be constitutional to exclude the public and the press from a criminal trial in the same manner as closure may be invoked in a pretrial proceeding?

On what grounds does Justice Burger explicitly limit the decision to *pretrial* proceedings? How does Justice Rehnquist interpret the reach of the Sixth and First Amendments regarding public access to criminal trials?

On what basis does Justice Blackmun argue in his dissenting opinion that there are strong societal interests in the public trial provision of the Sixth Amendment that cannot be waived unilaterally by the accused in a criminal trial? Under what circumstances would Blackmun allow the closure of a pretrial proceeding in a criminal case? On what basis did he hold that the pretrial closure in the *Gannett* case was a violation of the public trial standards of the Sixth and Fourteenth Amendments?

THE FIRST AMENDMENT AND THE SUPPRESSION OF OBSCENITY

While lower state and federal courts had adjudicated challenges to government suppression of obscene material, the Supreme Court did not squarely face the issue until *Roth* v. *United States* (1957).[60] The Court had, in *Chaplin-*

[60]For examples of lower court decisions see Commonwealth v. Friede, 271 Mass. 318, 171 N.E. 472 (1932), declaring obscene Theodore Dreiser's *An American Tragedy*; Commonwealth v. Delacey, 271 Mass. 327, 171 N.E. 455 (1930), declaring D.H. Lawrence's *Lady Chatterley's Lover* obscene; People v. Doubleday & Co., 272 App. Div. 799, 71 N.Y.S. 2d 736 (1947), affirmed 297 N.Y. 687, 77 N.E. 2d 6 (1947), affirmed per curiam by the Supreme Court in Doubleday & Co. v. New York, 335 U.S. 848 (1948), declaring Edmund Wilson's *Memoirs of Hecate County* to be obscene.

sky v. *New Hampshire* (1942), declared in dictum that obscenity was outside of the protection of the First Amendment. This dictum was applied and became the rule of law of the *Roth* case, which, decided together with *Alberts* v. *California*, reviewed the constitutionality of federal and state obscenity laws. Justice Brennan wrote the majority opinion, stating that "the First Amendment was not intended to protect every utterance," and "obscenity is not protected by the freedoms of speech and press."[61] Brennan rejected the early standard of obscenity defined in *Regina* v. *Hicklin*, an 1868 British case in which the test of obscenity was whether or not the material in question appealed to persons susceptible to immoral influences.[62] The Court found both the federal and state laws constitutional, emphasizing that the lower courts had applied the proper standard for defining obscenity: "Whether to the average person, applying contemporary community standards, the dominant theme of the material taken as a whole appeals to prurient interest."[63] The Court had limited its writ of certiorari in the *Roth* and *Alberts* cases to the question of the constitutionality of the obscenity laws; therefore, it did not have to judge the question of the obscenity of the material involved.

Although the *Roth* case, joined with *Alberts*, concerned both federal and state obscenity statutes, considerations of federalism were not raised in the majority opinion. While views of federalism were relevant to the *Alberts* case, the majority of the Court upheld the state law on the same basis that it sustained the federal statute. Justice Harlan wrote a separate opinion concurring with the result in *Alberts* but dissenting in *Roth*. Considerations of federalism were of paramount importance to him. In an obscenity case, Harlan wrote, the Court must balance the interests and free expression of the individual against the interests of the government in suppression. But the interests of the federal government and the state governments are different, the states have a legitimate concern with regulating obscenity which the federal government does not possess. The interests to be protected by obscenity statutes, he wrote, "are primarily entrusted to the care, not of the federal government, but of the states. Congress has no substantive power over sexual morality. Such powers as the federal government has in this field are but incidental to its other powers, here in the *Roth* case the postal power, but are not of the same nature as those possessed by the states, which bear direct responsibility for the protection of the local moral fabric."[64] Harlan concluded: "I judge this case, then, in view of what I think is the attenuated federal interest in this field, in view of the very real danger of a deadening uniformity which can result from nationwide federal censorship, and in view of the fact that the constitutionality of this conviction must be weighed against the First and not the Fourteenth Amendment. So viewed, I do not think that this conviction can be upheld. . . . The federal government has no business, whether under the postal or commerce power, to bar the sale of books because they might lead to any kind of 'thought.' "[65]

[61]Roth v. United States, 354 U.S. 476, 483, 481 (1957).
[62]L.R. 3 QB 360 (1868).
[63]Roth v. United States, 354 U.S. 476, 489 (1957).
[64]Ibid.
[65]Ibid., pp. 506–507.

Justice Douglas, joined by Justice Black, dissented in the *Roth* case as they did in other obscenity cases, holding that neither federal nor state governments have authority to suppress material because of its alleged effect upon the mind of the reader. Douglas wrote in dissent: "To allow the states to step in and punish mere speech or publication that the judge or the jury thinks has an *undesirable* impact on thought but that is not shown to be part of unlawful action is drastically to curtail the First Amendment."[66]

Roth v. *United States*
Alberts v. *California*

354 U.S. 476; 77 S. Ct. 1304; 1 L. Ed. 2d 1498 (1957)

Mr. Justice Brennan delivered the opinion of the Court:

The constitutionality of a criminal obscenity statute is the question in each of these cases. In *Roth*, the primary constitutional question is whether the federal obscenity statute violates the provision of the First Amendment that "Congress shall make no law . . . abridging the freedom of speech, or of the press. . . ." In *Alberts*, the primary constitutional question is whether the obscenity provisions of the California Penal Code invade the freedoms of speech and press as they may be incorporated in the liberty protected from state action by the Due Process Clause of the Fourteenth Amendment.

The dispositive question is whether obscenity is utterance within the area of protected speech and press. Although this is the first time the question has been squarely presented to this Court, either under the First Amendment or under the Fourteenth Amendment, expressions found in numerous opinions indicate that this Court has always assumed that obscenity is not protected by the freedoms of speech and press. . . .

The guaranties of freedom of expression in effect in 10 of the 14 States which by 1792 had ratified the Constitution, gave no absolute protection for every utterance. Thirteen of the 14 States provided for the prosecution of libel, and all of those States made either blasphemy or profanity, or both, statutory crimes. As early as 1712, Massachusetts made it criminal to publish "any filthy, obscene, or profane song, pamphlet, libel or mock sermon" in imitation or mimicking of religious services. . . . Thus, profanity and obscenity were related offenses.

In light of this history, it is apparent that the unconditional phrasing of the First Amendment was not intended to protect every utterance. This phrasing did not prevent this Court from concluding that libelous utterances are not within the area of constitutionally protected speech. . . . At the time of the adoption of the First Amendment, obscenity law was not as fully developed as libel law, but there is sufficiently contemporaneous evidence to show that obscenity, too, was outside the protection intended for speech and press.

All ideas having even the slightest redeeming social importance—unorthodox ideas, controversial ideas, even ideas hateful to the prevailing climate of opinion—have the full protection of the guaranties, unless excludable because they encroach

---

[66]Ibid., p. 509.

upon the limited area of more important interests. But implicit in the history of the First Amendment is the rejection of obscenity as utterly without redeeming social importance. This rejection for that reason is mirrored in the universal judgment that obscenity should be restrained, reflected in the international agreement of over 50 nations, in the obscenity laws of all of the 48 States, and in the 20 obscenity laws enacted by the Congress from 1842 to 1956. . . .

We hold that obscenity is not within the area of constitutionally protected speech or press.

It is strenuously urged that these obscenity statutes offend the constitutional guaranties because they punish incitation to impure sexual *thoughts*, not shown to be related to any overt antisocial conduct which is or may be incited in the persons stimulated to such *thoughts*. In *Roth*, the trial judge instructed the jury: "The words 'obscene, lewd and lascivious' as used in the law, signify that form of immorality which has relation to sexual impurity and has a tendency to excite lustful *thoughts*." (Emphasis added.) In *Alberts*, the trial judge applied the test laid down in *People* v. *Wepplo*, 78 Cal. App. 2d Supp. 959, 178 P. 2d 853, namely, whether the material has a "substantial tendency to deprave or corrupt its readers by inciting lascivious *thoughts* or arousing lustful desires." (Emphasis added.) It is insisted that the constitutional guaranties are violated because convictions may be had without proof either that obscene material will perceptibly create a clear and present danger of antisocial conduct, or will probably induce its recipients to such conduct. But, in light of our holding that obscenity is not protected speech, the complete answer to this argument is in the holding of this Court in *Beauharnais* v. *Illinois* [1952] . . .:

Libelous utterances not being within the area of constitutionally protected speech, it is un-

necessary, either for us or for the State courts, to consider the issues behind the phrase 'clear and present danger.' Certainly no one would contend that obscene speech, for example, may be punished only upon a showing of such circumstances. Libel, as we have seen, is in the same class.

However, sex and obscenity are not synonymous. Obscene material is material which deals with sex in a manner appealing to prurient interest. The portrayal of sex, *e.g.*, in art, literature and scientific works, is not itself sufficient reason to deny material the constitutional protection of freedom of speech and press. Sex, a great and mysterious motive force in human life, has indisputably been a subject of absorbing interest to mankind through the ages; it is one of the vital problems of human interest and public concern. As to all such problems, this Court said in *Thornhill* v. *Alabama* [1940] . . .:

The freedom of speech and of the press guaranteed by the Constitution embraces at the least the liberty to discuss publicly and truthfully all matters of public concern without previous restraint or fear of subsequent punishment. . . . Freedom of discussion, if it would fulfill its historic function in this nation, must embrace *all issues about which information is needed or appropriate to enable the members of society to cope with the exigencies of their period.* (Emphasis added.)

The fundamental freedoms of speech and press have contributed greatly to the development and well-being of our free society and are indispensable to its continued growth. Ceaseless vigilance is the watchword to prevent their erosion by Congress or by the States. The door barring federal and state intrusion into this area cannot be left ajar; it must be kept tightly closed and opened only the slightest crack necessary to prevent encroachment upon more important interests. It is therefore vital that the standards for judging obscenity safeguard the protection of freedom of speech and press for material which does not treat sex in a manner appealing to prurient interest.

The early leading [British] standard of obscenity allowed material to be judged merely by the effect of an isolated excerpt upon particularly susceptible persons. *Regina* v. *Hicklin* [1868]. . . . Some American courts adopted this standard but later decisions have rejected it and substituted this test: whether to the average person, applying contemporary community standards, the dominant theme of the material taken as a whole appeals to prurient interest. The *Hicklin* test, judging obscenity by the effect of isolated passages upon the most susceptible persons, might well encompass material legitimately treating with sex, and so it must be rejected as unconstitutionally restrictive of the freedoms of speech and press. On the other hand, the substituted standard provides safeguards adequate to withstand the charge of constitutional infirmity.

Both trial courts below sufficiently followed the proper standard. Both courts used the proper definition of obscenity. . . .

It is argued that the statutes do not provide reasonably ascertainable standards of guilt and therefore violate the constitutional requirements of due process. . . . The federal obscenity statute makes punishable the mailing of material that is "obscene, lewd, lascivious, or filthy . . . or other publication of an indecent character." The California statute makes punishable, *inter alia*, the keeping for sale or advertising material that is "obscene or indecent." The thrust of the argument is that these words are not sufficiently precise because they do not mean the same thing to all people, all the time, everywhere.

Many decisions have recognized that these terms of obscenity statutes are not precise. This Court, however, has consistently held that lack of precision is not it-

self offensive to the requirements of due process. ". . . [T]he Constitution does not require impossible standards"; all that is required is that the language "conveys sufficiently definite warning as to the proscribed conduct when measured by common understanding and practices. . . ." . . .

In summary, then, we hold that these statutes, applied according to the proper standard for judging obscenity, do not offend constitutional safeguards against convictions based upon protected material, or fail to give men in acting adequate notice of what is prohibited. . . .

The judgments are

Affirmed.

MR. CHIEF JUSTICE WARREN, concurring in the result:

. . . The defendants in both these cases were engaged in the business of purveying textual or graphic matter openly advertised to appeal to the erotic interest of their customers. They were plainly engaged in the commercial exploitation of the morbid and shameful craving for materials with prurient effect. I believe that the State and Federal Governments can constitutionally punish such conduct. That is all that these cases present to us, and that is all we need to decide.

I agree with the Court's decision in its rejection of the other contentions raised by these defendants.

MR. JUSTICE HARLAN, concurring in the result in [*Alberts*], and dissenting in [*Roth*]:

I

My basic difficulties with the Court's opinion are threefold. First, the opinion paints with such a broad brush that I fear it may result in a loosening of the tight reins which state and federal courts should hold upon the enforcement of obscenity statutes. Second, the Court fails to discriminate between the different factors which, in my opinion, are involved in the constitutional adjudication of state and federal obscenity cases. Third, relevant distinctions between the two obscenity statutes here involved, and the Court's own definition of "obscenity," are ignored. . . .

. . . The Court seems to assume that "obscenity" is a peculiar *genus* of "speech and press," which is as distinct, recognizable, and classifiable as poison ivy is among other plants. On this basis the *constitutional* question before us simply becomes, as the Court says, whether "obscenity," as an abstraction, is protected by the First and Fourteenth Amendments, and the question whether a *particular* book may be suppressed becomes a mere matter of classification, of "fact," to be entrusted to a fact-finder and insulated from independent constitutional judgment. But surely the problem cannot be solved in such a generalized fashion. Every communication has an individuality and "value" of its own. The suppression of a particular writing or other tangible form of expression is, therefore, an *individual* matter, and in the nature of things every such suppression raises an individual constitutional problem, in which a reviewing court must determine for *itself* whether the attacked expression is suppressable within the constitutional standards. Since those standards do not readily lend themselves to generalized definitions, the constitutional problem in the last analysis becomes one of particularized judgments which appellate courts must make for themselves.

I do not think that reviewing courts can escape this responsibility by saying that the trier of the facts, be it a jury or a judge, has labeled the questioned matter as "obscene," or, if "obscenity" is to be suppressed, the question whether a particular work is of that character involves

not really an issue of fact but a question of constitutional *judgment* of the most sensitive and delicate kind. Many juries might find that Joyce's "Ulysses" or Bocaccio's "Decameron" was obscene, and yet the conviction of a defendant for selling either book would raise, for me, the gravest constitutional problems, for no such verdict could convince me, without more, that these books are "utterly without redeeming social importance." In short, I do not understand how the Court can resolve the constitutional problems now before it without making its own independent judgment upon the character of the material upon which these convictions were based. . . .

[T]he Court has not been bothered by the fact that the two cases involve different statutes. In California the book must have a "tendency to deprave or corrupt its readers"; under the federal statute it must tend "to stir sexual impulses and lead to sexually impure thoughts." The two statutes do not seem to me to present the same problems. Yet the Court compounds confusion when it superimposes on these two statutory definitions a third, drawn from the American Law Institute's Model Penal Code, Tentative Draft No. 6: "A thing is obscene if, considered as a whole, its predominant appeal is to prurient interest." The bland assurance that this definition is the same as the ones with which we deal flies in the face of the author's express rejection of the "deprave and corrupt" and "sexual thoughts" tests. . . .

II

I concur in the judgment of the Court in *Alberts* v. *California*. . . .

In judging the constitutionality of this conviction, we should remember that our function in reviewing state judgments under the Fourteenth Amendment is a narrow one. We do not decide whether the policy of the State is wise, or whether it is based on assumptions scientifically substantiated. We can inquire only whether the state action so subverts the fundamental liberties implicit in the Due Process Clause that it cannot be sustained as a rational exercise of power. . . .

What, then, is the purpose of this California statute? Clearly the state legislature has made the judgment that printed words *can* "deprave or corrupt" the reader—that words can incite to antisocial or immoral action. The assumption seems to be that the distribution of certain types of literature will induce criminal or immoral sexual conduct. It is well known, of course, that the validity of this assumption is a matter of dispute among critics, sociologists, psychiatrists, and penologists. There is a large school of thought, particularly in the scientific community, which denies any causal connection between the reading of pornography and immorality, crime, or delinquency. Others disagree. Clearly it is not our function to decide this question. That function belongs to the state legislature. Nothing in the Constitution requires California to accept as truth the most advanced and sophisticated psychiatric opinion. It seems to me clear that it is not irrational, in our present state of knowledge, to consider that pornography can induce a type of sexual conduct which a State may deem obnoxious to the moral fabric of society. In fact the very division of opinion on the subject counsels us to respect the choice made by the State.

Furthermore, even assuming that pornography cannot be deemed ever to cause, in an immediate sense, criminal sexual conduct, other interests within the proper cognizance of the States may be protected by the prohibition placed on such materials. The State can reasonably draw the inference that over a long period of time the indiscriminate dissemination of materials, the essential character of which is to degrade sex, will have an eroding effect on moral standards. And the State has a

legitimate interest in protecting the privacy of the home against invasion of unsolicited obscenity.

Above all stands the realization that we deal here with an area where knowledge is small, data are insufficient, and experts are divided. Since the domain of sexual morality is pre-eminently a matter of state concern, this Court should be slow to interfere with state legislation calculated to protect that morality. . . .

What has been said, however, does not dispose of the case. It still remains for us to decide whether the state court's determination that this material should be suppressed is consistent with the Fourteenth Amendment; and that, of course, presents a federal question as to which we, and not the state court, have the ultimate responsibility. And so, in the final analysis, I concur in the judgment because, upon an independent perusal of the material involved, and in light of the considerations discussed above, I cannot say that its suppression would so interfere with the communication of "ideas" in any proper sense of that term that it would offend the Due Process Clause. I therefore agree with the Court that appellant's conviction must be affirmed.

I dissent in *Roth* v. *United States*.

We are faced here with the question whether the federal obscenity statute, as construed and applied in this case, violates the First Amendment to the Constitution. To me, this question is of quite a different order than one where we are dealing with state legislation under the Fourteenth Amendment. I do not think it follows that state and federal powers in this area are the same, and that just because the State may suppress a particular utterance, it is automatically permissible for the Federal Government to do the same. . . .

The Constitution differentiates between those areas of human conduct subject to the regulation of the States and those subject to the powers of the Federal Government. The substantive powers of the two governments, in many instances, are distinct. And in every case where we are called upon to balance the interest in free expression against other interests, it seems to me important that we should keep in the forefront the question of whether those other interests are state or federal. Since under our constitutional scheme the two are not necessarily equivalent, the balancing process must needs often produce different results. Whether a particular limitation on speech or press is to be upheld because it subserves a paramount governmental interest must, to a large extent, I think, depend on whether that government has, under the Constitution, a direct substantive interest, that is, the power to act, in the particular area involved. . . .

Congress has no substantive power over sexual morality. Such powers as the Federal Government has in this field are but incidental to its other powers, here the postal power, and are not of the same nature as those possessed by the States, which bear direct responsibility for the protection of the local moral fabric. . . .

Not only is the federal interest in protecting the Nation against pornography attenuated, but the dangers of federal censorship in this field are far greater than anything the States may do. It has often been said that one of the great strengths of our federal system is that we have, in the forty-eight States, forty-eight experimental social laboratories. "State statutory law reflects predominantly this capacity of a legislature to introduce novel techniques of social control. The federal system has the immense advantage of providing forty-eight separate centers for such experimentation." Different States will have different attitudes toward the same work of literature. The same book which is freely read in one State might be classed as obscene in another. And it

seems to me that no overwhelming danger to our freedom to experiment and to gratify our tastes in literature is likely to result from the suppression of a border-line book in one of the States, so long as there is no uniform nation-wide suppression of the book, and so long as other States are free to experiment with the same or bolder books.

Quite a different situation is presented, however, where the Federal Government imposes the ban. The danger is perhaps not great if the people of one State, through their legislature, decide that "Lady Chatterley's Lover" goes so far beyond the acceptable standards of candor that it will be deemed offensive and non-sellable, for the State next door is still free to make its own choice. At least we do not have one uniform standard. But the dangers to free thought and expression are truly great if the Federal Government imposes a blanket ban over the Nation on such a book. The prerogative of the States to differ on their ideas of morality will be destroyed, the ability of States to experiment will be stunted. The fact that the people of one State cannot read some of the works of D.H. Lawrence seems to me, if not wise or desirable, at least acceptable. But that no person in the United States should be allowed to do so seems to me to be intolerable, and violative of both the letter and spirit of the First Amendment.

I judge this case, then, in view of what I think is the attenuated federal interest in this field, in view of the very real danger of a deadening uniformity which can result from nation-wide federal censorship, and in view of the fact that the constitutionality of this conviction must be weighed against the First and not the Fourteenth Amendment. So viewed, I do not think that this conviction can be upheld. . . . I cannot agree that any book which tends to stir sexual impulses and lead to sexually impure thoughts necessarily is "utterly without redeeming social importance." Not only did this charge fail to measure up to the standards which I understand the Court to approve, but as far as I can see, much of the great literature of the world could lead to conviction under such a view of the statute. Moreover, in no event do I think that the limited federal interest in this area can extend to mere "thoughts." The Federal Government has no business, whether under the postal or commerce power, to bar the sale of books because they might lead to any kind of "thoughts."

It is no answer to say, as the Court does, that obscenity is not protected speech. The point is that this statute, as here construed, defines obscenity so widely that it encompasses matters which might very well be protected speech. I do not think that the federal statute can be constitutionally construed to reach other than what the Government has termed as "hardcore" pornography. . . .

MR. JUSTICE DOUGLAS, with whom MR. JUSTICE BLACK concurs, dissenting:

When we sustain these convictions, we make the legality of a publication turn on the purity of thought which a book or tract instills in the mind of the reader. I do not think we can approve that standard and be faithful to the command of the First Amendment, which by its terms is a restraint on Congress and which by the Fourteenth is a restraint on the States. . . .

The test of obscenity the Court endorses today gives the censor free range over a vast domain. To allow the State to step in and punish mere speech or publication that the judge or the jury thinks has an *undesirable* impact on thoughts but that is not shown to be a part of unlawful action is drastically to curtail the First Amendment. . . .

During the course of its opinion the *Roth* majority wrote that "Implicit in the history of the First Amendment is the rejection of obscenity as utterly without redeeming social importance." The fact that obscenity was without redeeming social importance was given as a reason for excluding it from First Amendment protection. Whether or not material was of "redeeming social importance" was not part of the definition of obscenity. That the Court would be misunderstood, however, became evident immediately when Justice Douglas wrote in his *Roth* dissent that "I reject too the implication that problems of freedom of speech and of the press are to be resolved by weighing against the values of free expression, the judgment of the Court that a particular form of that expression has 'no redeeming social importance.' " Douglas assumed that the Court would use the absence of redeeming social importance as a test of obscenity.

The Court itself adopted the lack of redeeming social importance as a definition of obscenity in *Memoirs* v. *Massachusetts* (1966). In a plurality opinion the Court reversed the finding of a Massachusetts court that the book *Fanny Hill* was obscene, a judgment which made it a criminal offense under state law to sell the book. Justice Brennan's opinion, joined by Justices Warren and Fortas, cited the *Roth* definition of obscenity but added: "As elaborated in subsequent cases, three elements must coalesce: it must be established that (a) the dominant theme of the material taken as a whole appeals to a prurient interest in sex; (b) the material is patently offensive because it affronts contemporary community standards relating to the description or representation of sexual matters; and (c) the material is utterly without redeeming social value."[67] Brennan held that the "Supreme Judicial Court [of Massachusetts] erred in holding that a book need not be 'unqualifiedly worthless before it can be deemed obscene.' A book cannot be proscribed unless it is found to be *utterly* without redeeming social value."[68]

The divisions on the Court over the meaning of obscenity at the time of the *Memoirs* case is illustrated by the fact that there were seven separate opinions, with only a plurality of three in agreement. In separate opinions Black and Douglas concurred on the grounds that the government has no power to control the free expression of ideas. Stewart concurred, emphasizing that the book was not "hard-core pornography." Clark dissented, finding that the book had no conceivable social importance. Harlan dissented, concluding that "the Fourteenth Amendment requires of a state only that it apply criteria rationally related to the accepted notion of obscenity and that it reach results not wholly out of step with current American standards."[69] White dissented, noting: "if a state insists on treating *Fanny Hill* as obscene and forbidding its sale, the First Amendment does not prevent it from doing so."[70]

The Court reconsidered its *Roth* and *Memoirs* obscenity criteria in the following opinion.

Miller v. *California*

413 U.S. 15; S. Ct. 2067; L. Ed. 2d 419 (1973)

MR. CHIEF JUSTICE BURGER delivered the opinion of the Court:

This is one of a group of "obscenity-pornography" cases being reviewed by the Court in a re-examination of standards enunciated in earlier cases involving what Mr. Justice Harlan called "the intractable obscenity problem." . . .

Appellant conducted a mass mailing campaign to advertise the sale of illustrated books, euphemistically called "adult" material. After a jury trial, he was convicted of violating California Penal Code § 311.2 (a), a misdemeanor, by knowingly distributing obscene matter. . . . Appellant's conviction was specifically based on his conduct in causing five unsolicited advertising brochures to be sent through the

mail in an envelope addressed to a restaurant in Newport Beach, California. The envelope was opened by the manager of the restaurant and his mother. They had not requested the brochures; they complained to the police.

The brochures advertise four books entitled "Intercourse," "Man-Woman," "Sex Orgies Illustrated," and "An Illustrated History of Pornography," and a film entitled "Marital Intercourse." While the brochures contain some descriptive printed material, primarily they consist of pictures and drawings very explicitly depicting men and women in groups of two or more engaging in a variety of sexual activities, with genitals often prominently displayed.

---

[67]Memoirs v. Massachusetts, 383 U.S. 413, 418 (1966).
[68]Ibid., p. 419.
[69]Ibid., p. 458.
[70]Ibid., p. 462.

I

This case involves the application of a State's criminal obscenity statute to a situation in which sexually explicit materials have been thrust by aggressive sales action upon unwilling recipients who had in no way indicated any desire to receive such materials. This Court has recognized that the States have a legitimate interest in prohibiting dissemination or exhibition of obscene material when the mode of dissemination carries with it a significant danger of offending the sensibilities of unwilling recipients or of exposure to juveniles. . . . It is in this context that we are called on to define the standards which must be used to identify obscene material that a State may regulate without infringing on the First Amendment as applicable to the States through the Fourteenth Amendment.

The dissent of Mr. Justice Brennan reviews the background of the obscenity problem, but since the Court now undertakes to formulate standards more concrete than those in the past, it is useful for us to focus on two of the landmark cases in the somewhat tortured history of the Court's obscenity decisions. In *Roth* v. *United States* . . . the Court sustained a conviction under a federal statute punishing the mailing of "obscene, lewd, lascivious or filthy . . ." materials. The key to that holding was the Court's rejection of the claim that obscene materials were protected by the First Amendment. . . .

Nine years later, in *Memoirs* v. *Massachusetts* . . . the Court veered sharply away from the *Roth* concept and, with only three Justices in the plurality opinion, articulated a new test of obscenity. . . .

The sharpness of the break with *Roth* . . . was . . . underscored when the *Memoirs* plurality [stated] . . . "A book cannot be proscribed unless it is found to be *utterly* without redeeming social value." . . .

While *Roth* presumed "obscenity" to be "utterly without redeeming social importance," *Memoirs* required that to prove obscenity it must be affirmatively established that the material is "*utterly* without redeeming social value." Thus, even as they repeated the words of *Roth*, the *Memoirs* plurality produced a drastically altered test that called on the prosecution to prove a negative, *i. e.*, that the material was "*utterly* without redeeming social value"—a burden virtually impossible to discharge under our criminal standards of proof. Such considerations caused Mr. Justice Harlan to wonder if the "*utterly* without redeeming social value" test had any meaning at all. . . .

Apart from the initial formulation in the *Roth* case, no majority of the Court has at any given time been able to agree on a standard to determine what constitutes obscene, pornographic material subject to regulation under the States' police power. . . . We have seen "a variety of views among the members of the Court unmatched in any other course of constitutional adjudication." . . . This is not remarkable, for in the area of freedom of speech and press the courts must always remain sensitive to any infringement on genuinely serious literary, artistic, political, or scientific expression. This is an area in which there are few eternal verities.

The case we now review was tried on the theory that the California Penal Code § 311 approximately incorporates the three-stage *Memoirs* test. . . . But now the *Memoirs* test has been abandoned as unworkable by its author, and no Member of the Court today supports the *Memoirs* formulation.

II

This much has been categorically settled by the Court, that obscene material is unprotected by the First Amendment. . . .

We acknowledge, however, the inherent dangers of undertaking to regulate any form of expression. State statutes designed to regulate obscene materials must be carefully limited. . . . As a result, we now confine the permissible scope of such regulations to works which depict or describe sexual conduct. That conduct must be specifically defined by the applicable state law, as written or authoritatively construed. A state offense must also be limited to works which, taken as a whole, appeal to the prurient interest in sex, which portray sexual conduct in a patently offensive way, and which, taken as a whole, do not have serious literary, artistic, political, or scientific value.

The basic guidelines for the trier of fact must be: (a) whether "the average person, applying contemporary community standards" would find that the work, taken as a whole, appeals to the prurient interest . . . ; (b) whether the work depicts or describes, in a patently offensive way, sexual conduct specifically defined by the applicable state law; and (c) whether the work, taken as a whole, lacks serious literary, artistic, political, or scientific value. We do not adopt as a constitutional standard the "*utterly* without redeeming social value" test of *Memoirs* v. *Massachusetts* . . . ; that concept has never commanded the adherence of more than three Justices at one time. . . . If a state law that regulates obscene material is thus limited, as written or construed, the First Amendment values applicable to the States through the Fourteenth Amendment are adequately protected by the ultimate power of appellate courts to conduct an independent review of constitutional claims when necessary. . . .

We emphasize that it is not our function to propose regulatory schemes for the States. That must await their concrete legislative efforts. It is possible, however, to give a few plain examples of what a state statute could define for regulation under part (b) of the standard announced in this opinion, *supra*:

(a) Patently offensive representations or descriptions of ultimate sexual acts, normal or perverted, actual or simulated.

(b) Patently offensive representations or descriptions of masturbation, excretory functions, and lewd exhibition of the genitals.

Sex and nudity may not be exploited without limit by films or pictures exhibited or sold in places of public accommodation any more than live sex and nudity can be exhibited or sold without limit in such public places. At a minimum, prurient, patently offensive depiction or description of sexual conduct must have serious literary, artistic, political, or scientific value to merit First Amendment protection. . . . For example, medical books for the education of physicians and related personnel necessarily use graphic illustrations and descriptions of human anatomy. In resolving the inevitably sensitive questions of fact and law, we must continue to rely on the jury system, accompanied by the safeguards that judges, rules of evidence, presumption of innocence, and other protective features provide, as we do with rape, murder, and a host of other offenses against society and its individual members.

Mr. Justice Brennan, author of the opinions of the Court, or the plurality opinions, in *Roth* v. *United States* . . . and *Memoirs* v. *Massachusetts* has abandoned his former position and now maintains that no formulation of this Court, the Congress, or the States can adequately distinguish obscene material unprotected by the First Amendment from protected expression. *Paris Adult Theater I* v. *Slaton*, . . . (Brennan, J., dissenting). Paradoxically, Mr. Justice Brennan indicates that suppression of unprotected obscene material is permissible to avoid exposure to unconsenting adults, as in this case, and to juveniles, although he gives no indication of how the division between protected and nonprotected materials may be drawn with greater precision for these purposes than for regulation of commercial exposure to consenting adults only. Nor does he indicate where in the Constitution he finds the authority to distinguish between a willing "adult" one month past the state law age of majority and a willing "juvenile" one month younger.

Under the holdings announced today, no one will be subject to prosecution for the sale or exposure of obscene materials unless these materials depict or describe patently offensive "hard core" sexual conduct specifically defined by the regulating state law, as written or construed. We are satisfied that these specific prerequisites will provide fair notice to a dealer in such materials that his public and commercial activities may bring prosecution. . . . If the inability to define regulated materials with ultimate, god-like precision altogether removes the power of the States or the Congress to regulate, then "hard core" pornography may be exposed without limit to the juvenile, the passerby, and the consenting adult alike, as, indeed, Mr. Justice Douglas contends. . . . In this belief, however, Mr. Justice Douglas now stands alone.

Mr. Justice Brennan also emphasizes "institutional stress" in justification of his change of view. Noting that "[t]he number of obscenity cases on our docket gives ample testimony to the burden that has been placed upon this Court," he quite rightly remarks that the examination of contested materials "is hardly a source of edification to the members of this Court." *Paris Adult Theatre I* v. *Slaton*. . . . He also notes, and we agree, that "uncertainty of the standards creates a continuing source of tension between state and federal courts . . . ." "The problem is . . . that one cannot say with certainty that material is

obscene until at least five members of this Court, applying inevitably obscure standards, have pronounced it so." . . .

It is certainly true that the absence, since *Roth*, of a single majority view of this Court as to proper standards for testing obscenity has placed a strain on both state and federal courts. But today, for the first time since *Roth* was decided in 1957, a majority of this Court has agreed on concrete guidelines to isolate "hard core" pornography from expression protected by the First Amendment. Now we may . . . attempt to provide positive guidance to federal and state courts alike.

This may not be an easy road, free from difficulty. But no amount of "fatigue" should lead us to adopt a convenient "institutional" rationale—an absolutist, "anything goes" view of the First Amendment—because it will lighten our burdens. "Such an abnegation of judicial supervision in this field would be inconsistent with our duty to uphold the constitutional guarantees." . . . Nor should we remedy "tension between state and federal courts" by arbitrarily depriving the States of a power reserved to them under the Constitution, a power which they have enjoyed and exercised continuously from before the adoption of the First Amendment to this day. . . . "Our duty admits of no 'substitute for facing up to the tough individual problems of constitutional judgment involved in every obscenity case.' " . . .

III

Under a National Constitution, fundamental First Amendment limitations on the powers of the States do not vary from community to community, but this does not mean that there are, or should or can be, fixed, uniform national standards of precisely what appeals to the "prurient interest" or is "patently offensive." These are essentially questions of fact, and our

Nation is simply too big and too diverse for this Court to reasonably expect that such standards could be articulated for all 50 States in a single formulation, even assuming the prerequisite consensus exists. When triers of fact are asked to decide whether "the average person, applying contemporary community standards" would consider certain materials "prurient," it would be unrealistic to require that the answer be based on some abstract formulation. The adversary system, with lay jurors as the usual ultimate factfinders in criminal prosecutions, has historically permitted triers of fact to draw on the standards of their community, guided always by limiting instructions on the law. To require a State to structure obscenity proceedings around evidence of a *national* "community standard" would be an exercise in futility. . . .

It is neither realistic nor constitutionally sound to read the First Amendment as requiring that the people of Maine or Mississippi accept public depiction of conduct found tolerable in Las Vegas, or New York City. . . . People in different States vary in their tastes and attitudes, and this diversity is not to be strangled by the absolutism of imposed uniformity. . . . [T]he primary concern with requiring a jury to apply the standard of "the average person, applying contemporary community standards" is to be certain that, so far as material is not aimed at a deviant group, it will be judged by its impact on an average person, rather than a particularly susceptible or sensitive person—or indeed a totally insensitive one. . . . We hold that the requirement that the jury evaluate the materials with reference to "contemporary standards of the State of California" serves this protective purpose and is constitutionally adequate.

IV

The dissenting Justices sound the alarm of repression. But, in our view, to equate the free and robust exchange of ideas and political debate with commercial exploitation of obscene material demeans the grand conception of the First Amendment and its high purposes in the historic struggle for freedom. It is a "misuse of the great guarantees of free speech and free press. . . ." . . . The First Amendment protects works which, taken as a whole, have serious literary, artistic, political, or scientific value, regardless of whether the government or a majority of the people approve of the ideas these works represent. "The protection given speech and press was fashioned to assure unfettered interchanges of *ideas* for the bringing about of political and social changes desired by the people." . . . . But the public portrayal of hard-core sexual conduct for its own sake, and for the ensuing commercial gain, is a different matter.

There is no evidence, empirical or historical, that the stern 19th century American censorship of public distribution and display of material relating to sex . . . in any way limited or affected expression of serious literary, artistic, political, or scientific ideas. On the contrary, it is beyond any question that the era following Thomas Jefferson to Theodore Roosevelt was an "extraordinarily vigorous period," not just in economics and politics, but in *belles lettres* and in "the outlying fields of social and political philosophies." We do not see the harsh hand of censorship of ideas—good or bad, sound or unsound—and "repression" of political liberty lurking in every state regulation of commercial exploitation of human interest in sex.

Mr. Justice Brennan finds "it is hard to see how state-ordered regimentation of our minds can ever be forestalled." *Paris Adult Theatre I* v. *Slaton.* . . . These doleful anticipations assume that courts cannot distinguish commerce in ideas, protected by the First Amendment, from commercial exploitation of obscene material.

Moreover, state regulation of hard-core pornography so as to make it unavailable to nonadults, a regulation which Mr. Justice Brennan finds constitutionally permissible, has all the elements of "censorship" for adults; indeed even more rigid enforcement techniques may be called for with such dichotomy of regulation. . . . One can concede that the "sexual revolution" of recent years may have had useful byproducts in striking layers of prudery from a subject long irrationally kept from needed ventilation. But it does not follow that no regulation of patently offensive "hard core" materials is needed or permissible; civilized people do not allow unregulated access to heroin because it is a derivative of medicinal morphine.

In sum, we (a) reaffirm the *Roth* holding that obscene material is not protected by the First Amendment; (b) hold that such material can be regulated by the States, subject to the specific safeguards enunciated above, without a showing that the material is "*utterly* without redeeming social value"; and (c) hold that obscenity is to be determined by applying "contemporary community standards". . . not "national standards." . . .

Vacated and remanded.

MR. JUSTICE DOUGLAS, dissenting:

I

Today we leave open the way for California to send a man to prison for distributing brochures that advertise books and a movie under freshly written standards defining obscenity which until today's decision were never the part of any law.

The Court has worked hard to define obscenity and concededly has failed. In *Roth* v. *United States* . . . it ruled that "[o]bscene material is material which deals with sex in a manner appealing to pru-

rient interest." . . . Obscenity, it was said, was rejected by the First Amendment because it is "utterly without redeeming social importance." . . . The presence of a "prurient interest" was to be determined by "contemporary community standards." . . . That test, it has been said, could not be determined by one standard here and another standard there. . . .

Today the Court retreats from the earlier formulations of the constitutional test and undertakes to make new definitions. This effort, like the earlier ones, is earnest and well intentioned. The difficulty is that we do not deal with constitutional terms, since "obscenity" is not mentioned in the Constitution or Bill of Rights. And the First Amendment makes no such exception from "the press" which it undertakes to protect nor, as I have said on other occasions, is an exception necessarily implied, for there was no recognized exception to the free press at the time the Bill of Rights was adopted which treated "obscene" publications differently from other types of papers, magazines, and books. So there are no constitutional guidelines for deciding what is and what is not "obscene." The Court is at large because we deal with tastes and standards of literature. What shocks me may be sustenance for my neighbor. What causes one person to boil up in rage over one pamphlet or movie may reflect only his neurosis, not shared by others. We deal here with a regime of censorship which, if adopted, should be done by constitutional amendment after full debate by the people.

Obscenity cases usually generate tremendous emotional outbursts. They have no business being in the courts. If a constitutional amendment authorized censorship, the censor would probably be an administrative agency. Then criminal prosecutions could follow as, if, and when publishers defied the censor and sold their literature. Under that regime a publisher would know when he was on dangerous ground. Under the present regime—whether the old standards or the new ones are used—the criminal law becomes a trap. A brand new test would put a publisher behind bars under a new law improvised by the courts after the publication. . . .

III

While the right to know is the corollary of the right to speak or publish, no one can be forced by government to listen to disclosure that he finds offensive. . . . There is no "captive audience" problem in these obscenity cases. No one is being compelled to look or to listen. Those who enter newsstands or bookstalls may be offended by what they see. But they are not compelled by the State to frequent those places; and it is only state or governmental action against which the First Amendment, applicable to the States by virtue of the Fourteenth, raises a ban.

The idea that the First Amendment permits government to ban publications that are "offensive" to some people puts an ominous gloss on freedom of the press. That test would make it possible to ban any paper or any journal or magazine in some benighted place. The First Amendment was designed "to invite dispute," to induce "a condition of unrest," to "create dissatisfaction with conditions as they are," and even to stir "people to anger." . . . The idea that the First Amendment permits punishment for ideas that are "offensive" to the particular judge or jury sitting in judgment is astounding. No greater leveler of speech or literature has ever been designed. To give the power to the censor, as we do today, is to make a sharp and radical break with the traditions of a free society. The First Amendment was not fashioned as a vehicle for dispensing tranquilizers to the people. Its prime function was to keep debate open to "offensive" as well as to "staid" people. The tendency throughout history has been to subdue the individual and to exalt the power of government. The use of the standard "offensive" gives authority to government that cuts the very vitals out of the First Amendment. As is intimated by the Court's opinion, the materials before us may be garbage. But so is much of what is said in political campaigns, in the daily press, on TV, or over the radio. By reason of the First Amendment—and solely because of it—speakers and publishers have not been threatened or subdued because their thoughts and ideas may be "offensive" to some. . . .

If there are to be restraints on what is obscene, then a constitutional amendment should be the way of achieving the end. There are societies where religion and mathematics are the only free segments. It would be a dark day for America if that were our destiny. But the people can make it such if they choose to write obscenity into the Constitution and define it.

We deal with highly emotional, not rational, questions. To many the Song of Solomon is obscene. I do not think we, the judges, were ever given the constitutional power to make definitions of obscenity. If it is to be defined, let the people debate and decide by a constitutional amendment what they want to ban as obscene and what standards they want the legislatures and the courts to apply. Perhaps the people will decide that the path towards a mature, integrated society requires that all ideas competing for acceptance must have no censor. Perhaps they will decide otherwise. Whatever the choice, the courts will have some guidelines. Now we have none except our own predilections.

Mr. Justice Brennan, with whom Mr. Justice Stewart and Mr. Justice Marshall join, dissented.

Contrast the definitions of obscenity given by the court in *Miller* and *Roth*. Which definition is the most precise? Which gives the greater discretion to national and state legislatures to pass obscenity laws?

What standards were announced in *Miller* to deal with the problem of vagueness and overbreadth of obscenity legislation? To what degree was the Court willing to let "contemporary community standards" determine the scope of obscenity laws? On what grounds did the Court hold that it would apply the criteria of contemporary community standards rather than national standards in judging the constitutionality of obscenity legislation?

The Court announced its decision in *Paris Adult Theatre I* v. *Slaton* on the same day that it handed down the *Miller* opinion. The case arose in Georgia, where state officials sought an injunction against the showing of films in the defendants' "adult" theaters on the basis that they were obscene under Georgia law. The trial court, without a jury, concluded that even if the films were obscene their exhibition could not be constitutionally proscribed since they were exhibited only to consenting adults. The court found that the owners of the theater had given the necessary notice to the public of the nature of the films, and had adequately protected minors from exposure to the films. The Supreme Court of Georgia reversed, and on certiorari the United States Supreme Court vacated and remanded the decision, holding that the state could regulate the exhibition of obscene motion pictures in adult theaters only if it conformed to the First Amendment standards for determining obscenity announced in *Miller* v. *California*. Justices Brennan, Stewart, and Marshall dissented, declaring that the Court should abandon the approach of *Roth* and subsequent cases that attempted to distinguish protected from unprotected speech in reviewing obscenity cases. Brennan argued that obscenity laws were per se vague and overbroad in violation of the due process clause of the Fourteenth Amendment, which "requires that all criminal laws provide fair notice of 'what the state commands or forbids.' "[71] Brennan concluded that while the state has an interest in preventing juveniles from being exposed to obscene material, it has no such interest concerning consenting adults that would outweigh the protection of the First and Fourteenth Amendments.[72]

Paris Adult Theatre I v. *Slaton*

413 U.S. 49, 93 S. Ct. 2628, 37 L. Ed. 2d 446 (1973)

Mr. Chief Justice Burger delivered the opinion of the Court:

. . . We categorically disapprove the theory, apparently adopted by the trial judge, that obscene, pornographic films acquire constitutional immunity from state regulation simply because they are exhibited for consenting adults only. . . . The States have a long-recognized legitimate interest in regulating the use of obscene

[71]Paris Adult Theatre I v. Slaton, 413 U.S. 49, 86 (1973), citing Lanzetta v. New Jersey, 306, 451, 453 (1939).

[72]Justice Douglas also dissented on the grounds that obscenity is protected by the First Amendment.

material in local commerce and in all places of public accommodation, as long as these regulations do not run afoul of specific constitutional prohibitions. . . .

In particular, we hold that there are legitimate state interests at stake in stemming the tide of commercialized obscenity, even assuming it is feasible to enforce effective safeguards against exposure to juveniles and to passersby. Rights and interests "other than those of the advocates are involved.". . . These include the interest of the public in the quality of life and the total community environment, the tone of commerce in the great city centers, and, possibly, the public safety itself. The Hill-Link Minority Report of the Commission on Obscenity and Pornography indicates that there is at least an arguable correlation between obscene material and crime. Quite apart from sex crimes, however, there remains one problem of large proportions aptly described by Professor Bickel:

It concerns the tone of the society, the mode, or to use terms that have perhaps greater currency, the style and quality of life, now and in the future. A man may be entitled to read an obscene book in his room, or expose himself indecently there. . . . We should protect his privacy. But if he demands a right to obtain the books and pictures he wants in the market, and to foregather in public places—discreet, if you will, but accessible to all—with others who share his tastes, *then to grant him his right is to affect the world about the rest of us, and to impinge on other privacies.* Even supposing that each of us can, if he wishes, effectively avert the eye and stop the ear (which, in truth, we cannot), what is commonly read and seen and heard and done intrudes upon us all, want it or not. 22 The Public Interest 25–26 (Winter 1971). (Emphasis added.)

As Mr. Chief Justice Warren stated, there is a "right of the Nation and of the States to maintain a decent society. . . . " *Jacobellis* v. *Ohio*, 378 U.S. 184, 199 (1964) (dissenting opinion). . . .

But, it is argued, there are no scientific data which conclusively demonstrate that exposure to obscene material adversely affects men and women or their society. It is urged on behalf of the petitioners that, absent such a demonstration, any kind of state regulation is "impermissible." We reject this argument. It is not for us to resolve empirical uncertainties underlying state legislation, save in the exceptional case where that legislation plainly impinges upon rights protected by the Constitution itself. . . . Although there is no conclusive proof of a connection between antisocial behavior and obscene material, the legislature of Georgia could quite reasonably determine that such a connection does or might exist. In deciding *Roth*, this Court implicitly accepted that a legislature could legitimately act on such a conclusion to protect *"the social interest in order and morality."* . . .

If we accept the unprovable assumption that a complete education requires the reading of certain books . . . and the well nigh universal belief that good books, plays, and art lift the spirit, improve the mind, enrich the human personality, and develop character, can we then say that a state legislature may not act on the corollary assumption that commerce in obscene books, or public exhibitions focused on obscene conduct, have a tendency to exert a corrupting and debasing impact leading to antisocial behavior? . . . The sum of experience, including that of the past two decades, affords an ample basis for legislatures to conclude that a sensitive key relationship of human existence, central to family life, community welfare, and the development of human personality, can be debased and distorted by crass commercial exploitation of sex. Nothing in the Constitution prohibits a State from reaching such a conclusion and acting on it legislatively simply because there is no conclusive evidence or empirical data.

It is argued that individual "free will" must govern, even in activities beyond the protection of the First Amendment and other constitutional guarantees of privacy, and that government cannot legitimately impede an individual's desire to see or acquire obscene plays, movies, and books. We do indeed base our society on certain assumptions that people have the capacity for free choice. Most exercises of individual free choice—those in politics, religion, and expression of ideas—are explicitly protected by the Constitution. Totally unlimited play for free will, however, is not allowed in our or any other society. We have just noted, for example, that neither the First Amendment nor "free will" precludes States from having "blue sky" laws to regulate what sellers of securities may write or publish about their wares. . . . Such laws are to protect the weak, the uninformed, the unsuspecting, and the gullible from the exercise of their own volition. Nor do modern societies leave disposal of garbage and sewage up to the individual "free will," but impose regulation to protect both public health and the appearance of public places. States are told by some that they must await a "laissez-faire" market solution to the obscenity-pornography problem, paradoxically "by people who have never otherwise had a kind word to say for laissez-faire," particularly in solving urban, commercial, and environmental pollution problems. . . .

The States, of course, may follow such a "laissez-faire" policy and drop all controls on commercialized obscenity, if that is what they prefer, just as they can ignore consumer protection in the marketplace, but nothing in the Constitution *compels* the States to do so with regard to matters falling within state jurisdiction. . . . "We do not sit as a super-legislature to determine the wisdom, need, and propriety of laws that touch economic problems, business affairs, or social conditions." *Griswold* v. *Connecticut* [1965]. . . .

It is asserted, however, that standards for evaluating state commercial regulations are inapposite in the present context, as state regulation of access by consenting adults to obscene material violates the constitutionally protected right to privacy enjoyed by petitioners' customers. Even assuming that petitioners have vicarious standing to assert potential customers' rights, it is unavailing to compare a theater open to the public for a fee, with the private home of *Stanley* v. *Georgia* [1969]. . . ,[73] and the marital bedroom of *Griswold* v. *Connecticut.* . . . This Court, has, on numerous occasions, refused to hold that commercial ventures such as a motion-picture house are "private" for the purpose of civil rights litigation and civil rights statutes. . . .

Our prior decisions recognizing a right to privacy guaranteed by the Fourteenth Amendment included "only personal rights that can be deemed 'fundamental' or implicit in the concept of ordered liberty.' ". . . This privacy right encompasses and protects the personal intimacies of the home, the family, marriage, motherhood, procreation, and child rearing. . . . Nothing, however, in this Court's decisions intimates that there is any "fundamental" privacy right "implicit in the concept of ordered liberty" to watch obscene movies in places of public accommodation.

If obscene material unprotected by the First Amendment in itself carried with it a "penumbra" of constitutionally protected privacy, this Court would not have found it necessary to decide *Stanley* on the narrow basis of the "privacy of the home," which was hardly more than a reaffirmation that "a man's home is his castle." . . . The idea of a "privacy" right and a place of public accommodation are, in this

[73]Stanley v. Georgia, 394 U.S. 557 (1969), held that "the First and Fourteenth Amendments prohibit making mere private possession of obscene material a crime." *Id.*, p. 568. [Editor's note.]

context, mutually exclusive. Conduct or depictions of conduct that the state police power can prohibit on a public street do not become automatically protected by the Constitution merely because the conduct is moved to a bar or a "live" theater stage, any more than a "live" performance of a man and woman locked in a sexual embrace at high noon in Times Square is protected by the Constitution because they simultaneously engage in a valid political dialogue.

It is also argued that the State has no legitimate interest in "control [of] the moral content of a person's thoughts," *Stanley* v. *Georgia* . . . , and we need not quarrel with this. But we reject the claim that the State of Georgia is here attempting to control the minds or thoughts of those who patronize theaters. Preventing unlimited display or distribution of obscene material which by definition lacks any serious literary, artistic, political, or scientific value as communication . . . is distinct from a control of reason and the intellect. . . . Where communication of ideas, protected by the First Amendment, is not involved, or the particular privacy of the home protected by *Stanley*, or any of the other "areas or zones" of constitutionally protected privacy, the mere fact that, as a consequence, some human "utterances" or "thoughts" may be incidentally affected does not bar the State from acting to protect legitimate state interests. . . . The fantasies of a drug addict are his own and beyond the reach of government, but government regulation of drug sales is not prohibited by the Constitution. . . .

Finally, petitioners argue that conduct which directly involves "consenting adults" only has, for that sole reason, a special claim to constitutional protection. Our Constitution establishes a broad range of conditions on the exercise of power by the States, but for us to say that our Constitution incorporates the proposition that

conduct involving consenting adults only is always beyond state regulation, is a step we are unable to take. Commercial exploitation of depictions, descriptions, or exhibitions of obscene conduct on commercial premises open to the adult public falls within a State's broad power to regulate commerce and protect the public environment. The issue in this context goes beyond whether someone, or even the majority, considers the conduct depicted as "wrong" or "sinful." The States have the power to make a morally neutral judgment that public exhibition of obscene material, or commerce in such material, has a tendency to injure the community as a whole, to endanger the public safety, or to jeopardize, in Mr. Chief Justice Warren's words, the States' "right . . . to maintain a decent society." . . .

In this case we hold that the States have legitimate interest in regulating commerce in obscene material and in regulating exhibition of obscene material in places of public accommodation, including so-called "adult" theaters from which minors are excluded. In light of these holdings, nothing precludes the State of Georgia from the regulation of the allegedly obscene material exhibited in Paris Adult Theatre I or II, provided that the applicable Georgia law, as written or authoritatively interpreted by the Georgia courts, meets the First Amendment standards set forth in *Miller* v. *California*. . . .

Vacated and remanded.

MR. JUSTICE BRENNAN, with whom MR. JUSTICE STEWART and MR. JUSTICE MARSHALL join, dissenting:

. . . Our experience since *Roth* requires us not only to abandon the effort to pick out obscene materials on a case-by-case basis, but also to reconsider a fundamental postulate of *Roth:* that there exists a definable class of sexually oriented expression that may be totally suppressed by the Federal and State Governments. Assuming that such a class of expression does in fact exist, I am forced to conclude that the concept of "obscenity" cannot be defined with sufficient specificity and clarity to provide fair notice to persons who create and distribute sexually oriented materials, to prevent substantial erosion of protected speech as a byproduct of the attempt to suppress unprotected speech, and to avoid very costly institutional harms. Given these inevitable side effects of state efforts to suppress what is assumed to be *unprotected* speech, we must scrutinize with care the state interest that is asserted to justify the suppression. For in the absence of some very substantial interest in suppressing such speech, we can hardly condone the ill effects that seem to flow inevitably from the effort. . . . Even a legimitate, sharply focused state concern for the morality of the community cannot, in other words, justify an assault on the protections of the First Amendment. . . . Where the state interest in regulation of morality is vague and ill defined, interference with the guarantees of the First Amendment is even more difficult to justify.

In short, while I cannot say that the interests of the State—apart from the question of juveniles and unconsenting adults—are trivial or nonexistent, I am compelled to conclude that these interests cannot justify the substantial damage to constitutional rights and to this Nation's judicial machinery that inevitably results from state efforts to bar the distribution even of unprotected material to consenting adults. . . . I would hold, therefore, that at least in the absence of distribution to juveniles or obtrusive exposure to unconsenting adults, the First and Fourteenth Amendments prohibit the State and Federal Governments from attempting wholly to suppress sexually oriented materials on the basis of their allegedly "obscene" contents. Nothing in this approach precludes those governments from taking action to serve what may be strong and legitimate interests through regulation of the manner of distribution of sexually oriented material. . . .

MR. JUSTICE DOUGLAS wrote a separate dissenting opinion.

The Court was struggling in the *Roth, Miller*, and *Paris Adult Theatre* opinions to develop a clear definition of obscenity that could be used by lower courts in exercising judicial review. But the Court's hope that its obscenity standards would eliminate the necessity of case-by-case review was not realized. For example, in *Jenkins* v. *Georgia* (1974) the Court reversed an obscenity conviction of a theater manager for showing the film *Carnal Knowledge*. The trial had occurred prior to *Miller* v. *California*, and the jury was instructed to apply "community standards" in determining obscenity but was not told what "community" was involved. The Supreme Court held that this procedure was constitutional under the *Miller* test, which did not require the specification of what community was to be the source of the standards. However, it held that a jury verdict of obscenity did not preclude appellate review, and that juries did not have complete discretion to determine questions of fact in obscenity cases. The Court concluded that from its own viewing of the allegedly obscene film a determination of obscenity could not be sustained. Justice Rehnquist wrote for the majority,

Our own viewing of the film satisfies us that "Carnal Knowledge" could not be found under the Miller standards to depict sexual conduct in a patently offensive way. Nothing in the movie falls within either of the two examples given in Miller of material which may constitutionally be found to meet the "patently offensive" element of those standards, nor is there anything sufficiently similar to such material to justify similar treatment. While the subject matter of the picture is, in a broader sense, sex, and there are scenes in which sexual conduct including "ultimate sexual acts" is to be understood to be taking place, the camera does not focus on the bodies of the actors at such times. There is no exhibition whatever of the actors' genitals, lewd or otherwise, during these scenes. There are occasional scenes of nudity, but nudity alone is not enough to make material legally obscene under the Miller standards.[74]

Justice Brennan, dissenting in *Jenkins*, declared that the Court's opinion, and particularly its method, which consisted of viewing the film to determine its obscenity, illustrated the futility of the Court's past attempts to define obscenity in unequivocal terms. Under the *Miller* test as under previous tests, wrote Brennan, it is impossible to say with certainty what constitutes obscenity. Therefore, because of the "uncertainty of such a process and its inevitable institutional stress upon the judiciary,"[75] the First and Fourteenth Amendments prohibit state and federal governments from suppressing sexually oriented materials except where they are distributed to juveniles or where there is "obtrusive exposure to unconsenting adults."[76]

[74]Jenkins v. Georgia, 418 U.S. 153, 161 (1974).
[75]Ibid., p. 165.
[76]Ibid., p. 165, citing Brennan's dissenting opinion in Paris Adult Theare v. Slaton, 413 U.S. 49, 113 (1973).

TEN

Freedom of Religion

The First Amendment contains two distinct clauses governing freedom of religion: the establishment clause and the free exercise clause. These declare simply that "Congress shall make no law respecting an establishment of religion or prohibiting the free exercise thereof. . . ." The clear language belies the complexity of its interpretation. The amendment was framed at a time when six of the states had established religions: Connecticut, Georgia, New Hampshire, New Jersey, and North and South Carolina. The laws of Delaware and Maryland required Christianity, and those of Pennsylvania and South Carolina supported a belief in one eternal God. Delaware required acceptance of the doctrine of the Holy Trinity. Virginia, which had an established Anglican church until 1779, barred the clergy from public office. New York was the only state that granted full freedom of religion, although it required naturalized citizens to renounce foreign allegiance in all ecclesiastical and civil matters. The common practice in the *states*, then, at the time of the adoption of the First Amendment was clearly both to support religion and interfere in its free exercise. The establishment clause of the First Amendment could with considerable historical justification be viewed as an attempt to prevent Congress from *disestablishing* religion in the states and interfering in state regulation of religious practices.

State laws supporting religion and governing its free exercise continued throughout the nineteenth century and into the twentieth century. In 1876 an unsuccessful attempt was made to amend the First Amendment by adding a provision that "no state shall make any law respecting an establishment of religion. . . ."[1] This abortive attempt to change the religious clauses of the First Amendment to apply explicitly to the states came after the adoption of the Fourteenth Amendment in 1868 and has been used as evidence by those

---

[1]*Congressional Record*, Vol. 4, p. 5580 (1876).

who argue that the "liberty" guaranteed by the due process clause of the Fourteenth Amendment was not intended to encompass religious freedom.[2]

THE ESTABLISHMENT CLAUSE
AND THE SEPARATION OF CHURCH AND STATE

Although the establishment and free exercise clauses of the First Amendment overlap and often may be harmoniously applied to guarantee religious freedom, the requirements of each clause are generally treated separately and may even work at cross purposes. The two clauses reinforce one another when, for example, the freedom of individuals to exercise religion is strengthened by the assurance that the church and state will not unite to establish a religion to which everyone must belong. The establishment clause prevents the government from intruding upon individual religious choice. The establishment clause may, however, inhibit the free exercise of religion when, for example, it is relied upon to deny government aid to parochial schools. The denial of such aid restricts the ability of the members of religious sects to exercise their religion with full freedom. The denial of government aid to church schools not only discriminates against them when such aid is given to public schools but also due to lack of funds and space may result in parents sending their children to public schools even though their religious preference would be to send them to church-sponsored schools. Tension of this nature between the establishment and free exercise clauses did not exist at the time of the adoption of the First Amendment because the federal government was not involved in providing aid to public education. It is the vast expansion of government programs, particularly in the twentieth century, that has caused the potential conflict between the standards of the establishment and free exercise clauses.

Establishment clause cases typically involve the question of permissible government aid to public schools or the extent to which the government can require certain religious practices, such as prayers, bible reading, and even the singing of Christmas carols, in public schools.

In the following case the Court reviewed a constitutional challenge to a New Jersey statute that authorized the local school districts to use public funds not only for the transportation of children to and from public schools but also "of school children to and from school other than a public school, except such school as is operated for profit." A taxpayer challenged the actions of a local board of education which had authorized reimbursement to parents for money they spent for the transportation of their children to and from school on regular buses operated by the public transportation system. The effect of the statute was to provide support from public funds for the transportation of children to Catholic parochial schools. Did the state law constitute an "establishment" of religion in violation of the First and Fourteenth Amendments? Although seven years prior to the present case the courts had applied the free exercise clause to the states under the Four-

[2]See the opinion of Justice Brennan in Abington School District v. Schempp, pp. 746–750.

teenth Amendment due process clause in *Cantwell* v. *Connecticut,* 310 U.S.
296 (1940), the establishment clause had not yet been incorporated.

Everson v. *Board of Education*

330 U.S. 1; 67 S. Ct. 504; 91 L. Ed. 711 (1947)

MR. JUSTICE BLACK delivered the opinion of the Court:

... The only contention here is that the state statute and the resolution, insofar as they authorized reimbursement to parents of children attending parochial schools, violate the Federal Constitution in these two respects, which to some extent overlap. *First.* They authorize the State to take by taxation the private property of some and bestow it upon others, to be used for their own private purposes. This, it is alleged, violates the due process clause of the Fourteenth Amendment. *Second.* The statute and the resolution forced inhabitants to pay taxes to help support and maintain schools which are dedicated to, and which regularly teach, the Catholic Faith. This is alleged to be a use of state power to support church schools contrary to the prohibition of the First Amendment which the Fourteenth Amendment made applicable to the states.

First ... It is much too late to argue that legislation intended to facilitate the opportunity of children to get a secular education serves no public purpose.... The same thing is no less true of legislation to reimburse needy parents, or all parents, for payment of the fares of their children so that they can ride in public busses to and from schools rather than run the risk of traffic and other hazards incident to walking or "hitchhiking." ...

Second. The New Jersey statute is challenged as a "law respecting an establishment of religion." The First Amendment, as made applicable to the states by the Fourteenth,... commands that a state "shall make no law respecting an estab-

lishment of religion, or prohibiting the free exercise thereof." ... Whether this New Jersey law is one respecting an "establishment of religion" requires an understanding of the meaning of that language, particularly with respect to the imposition of taxes. ...

A large proportion of the early settlers of this country came here from Europe to escape the bondage of laws which compelled them to support and attend government-favored churches. The centuries immediately before and contemporaneous with the colonization of America had been filled with turmoil, civil strife, and persecutions, generated in large part by established sects determined to maintain their absolute political and religious supremacy. ... In efforts to force loyalty to whatever religious group happened to be on top and in league with the government of a particular time and place, men and women had been fined, cast in jail, cruelly tortured, and killed. Among the offenses for which these punishments had been inflicted were such things as speaking disrespectfully of the views of ministers of government-established churches, non-attendance at those churches, expressions of non-belief in their doctrines, and failure to pay taxes and tithes to support them.

These practices of the old world were transplanted to and began to thrive in the soil of the new America. The very charters granted by the English Crown to the individuals and companies designated to make laws which would control the destinies of the colonials authorized these individuals and companies to erect religious establishments which all, whether believers or non-believers, would be required to support and attend. An exercise of this authority was accompanied by a repetition of many of the old-world practices and persecutions. Catholics found themselves hounded and proscribed because of their faith; Quakers who followed their conscience went to jail; Baptists were peculiarly obnoxious to certain dominant Protestant sects; men and women of varied faiths who happened to be in a minority in a particular locality were persecuted because they steadfastly persisted in worshipping God only as their own consciences dictated. And all of these dissenters were compelled to pay tithes and taxes to support government-sponsored churches whose ministers preached inflammatory sermons designed to strengthen and consolidate the established faith by generating a burning hatred against dissenters.

These practices became so commonplace as to shock the freedom-loving colonials into a feeling of abhorrence. The imposition of taxes to pay ministers' salaries and to build and maintain churches and church property aroused their indignation. It was these feelings which found expression in the First Amendment. No one locality and no one group throughout the Colonies can rightly be given entire credit for having aroused the sentiment that culminated in adoption of the Bill of Rights' provisions embracing religious liberty. But Virginia, where the established church had achieved a dominant influence in political affairs and where many excesses attracted wide public attention, provided a great stimulus and able leadership for the movement. The people there, as elsewhere, reached the conviction that individual religious liberty could be achieved best under a government which was stripped of all power to tax, to support, or otherwise to assist any or all religions, or to interfere with the beliefs of any religious individual or group.

The movement toward this end reached its dramatic climax in Virginia in 1785–86 when the Virginia legislative body was about to renew Virginia's tax levy for the support of the established church. Thomas Jefferson and James Madison led the fight against this tax. Madison wrote his great Memorial and Remonstrance against the law. In it, he eloquently argued that a true religion did not need the support of law; that no person, either believer or non-believer, should be taxed to support a religious institution of any kind; that the best interest of a society required that the minds of men always be wholly free; and that cruel persecutions were the inevitable result of government-established religions. Madison's Remonstrance received strong support throughout Virginia, and the Assembly postponed consideration of the proposed tax measure until its next session. When the proposal tax came up for consideration at that session, it not only died in committee, but the Assembly enacted the famous "Virginia Bill for Religious Liberty" originally written by Thomas Jefferson. The preamble to that Bill stated among other things that

Almighty God hath created the mind free; that all attempts to influence it by temporal punishments or burthens, or by civil incapacitations, tend only to beget habits of hypocrisy and meanness, and are a departure from the plan of the Holy author of our religion, who being Lord both of body and mind, yet chose not to propagate it by coercions on either . . .; that to compel a man to furnish contributions of money for the propagation of opinions which he disbelieves, is sinful and tyrannical; that even the forcing him to support this or that teacher of his own religious persuasion, is depriving him of the comfortable liberty of giving his contributions to the particular pastor, whose morals he would make his pattern. . . .

And the statute itself enacted

That no man shall be compelled to frequent or support any religious worship, place, or ministry whatsoever, nor shall be enforced, restrained, molested, or burthened in his body or goods, nor shall otherwise suffer on account of his religious opinions or belief. . . .

This Court has previously recognized that the provisions of the First Amendment, in the drafting and adoption of which Madison and Jefferson played such leading roles, had the same objective and were intended to provide the same protection against governmental intrusion on religious liberty as the Virginia statute. . . . Prior to the adoption of the Fourteenth Amendment, the First Amendment did not apply as a restraint against the states. Most of them did soon provide similar constitutional protections for religious liberty. But some states persisted for about half a century in imposing restraints upon the free exercise of religion and in discriminating against particular religious groups. In recent years, so far as the provision against the establishment of a religion is concerned, the question has most frequently arisen in connection with proposed state aid to church schools and efforts to carry on religious teachings in the public schools in accordance with the tenets of a particular sect. . . .

The meaning and scope of the First Amendment, preventing establishment of religion or prohibiting the free exercise thereof, in the light of its history and the evils it was designed forever to suppress, have been several times elaborated by the decisions of this Court prior to the application of the First Amendment to the states by the Fourteenth. The broad meaning given the Amendment by these earlier cases has been accepted by this Court in its decisions concerning an individual's religious freedom rendered since the Fourteenth Amendment was interpreted to make the prohibitions of the First applicable to state action abridging religious freedom. There is every reason to give the same application and broad interpretation to the "establishment of religion" clause. The interrelation of these complementary clauses was well summarized . . . in *Watson* v. *Jones* [1872] . . .: "The structure of our government has, for the preservation of civil liberty, rescued the temporal institutions from religious interference. On the other hand, it has secured religious liberty from the invasion of the civil authority."

The "establishment of religion" clause of the First Amendment means at least this: Neither a state nor the Federal Government can set up a church. Neither can pass laws which aid one religion, aid all religions, or prefer one religion over another. Neither can force nor influence a person to go to or to remain away from church against his will or force him to profess a belief or disbelief in any religion. No person can be punished for entertaining or professing religious beliefs or disbeliefs, for church attendance or non-attendance. No tax in any amount, large or small, can be levied to support any religious activities or institutions, whatever they may be called, or whatever form they may adopt to teach or practice religion. Neither a state nor the Federal Government can, openly or secretly, participate in the affairs of any religious organizations or groups and *vice versa*. In the words of Jefferson, the clause against establishment of religion by law was intended to erect "a wall of separation between church and State." . . .

We must consider the New Jersey statute in accordance with the foregoing limitations imposed by the First Amendment. But we must not strike that state statute down if it is within the State's constitutional power even though it approaches the verge of that power. . . . New Jersey cannot consistently with the "establishment of religion" clause of the First Amendment contribute tax-raised funds to the support of an institution which teaches the tenets and faith of any church. On the other hand, other language of the amendment commands that New Jersey cannot hamper its citizens in the free exercise of their own religion. Consequently, it cannot exclude individual Catholics, Lutherans, Mohammedans, Baptists, Jews, Methodists, Non-believers, Presbyterians, or the members of any other faith, *because of their faith, or lack of it*, from receiving the benefits of public welfare legislation. While we do not mean to intimate that a state could not provide transportation only to children attending public schools, we must be careful, in protecting the citizens of New Jersey against state-established churches, to be sure that we do not inadvertently prohibit New Jersey from extending its general state law benefits to all its citizens without regard to their religious belief.

Measured by these standards, we cannot say that the First Amendment prohibits New Jersey from spending tax-raised funds to pay the bus fares of parochial school pupils as a part of a general program under which it pays the fares of pupils attending public and other schools. It is undoubtedly true that children are helped to get to church schools. There is even a possibility that some of the children might not be sent to the church schools if the parents were compelled to pay their children's bus fares out of their own pockets when transportation to a public school would have been paid for by the State. The same possibility exists where the state requires a local transit company to provide reduced fares to school children including those attending parochial schools. ... Moreover, state-paid policemen, detailed to protect children going to and from church schools from the very real hazards of traffic, would serve much the same purpose and accomplish much the same result as state provisions intended to guarantee free transportation of a kind which the state deems to be best

for the school children's welfare. And parents might refuse to risk their children to the serious danger of traffic accidents going to and from parochial schools, the approaches to which were not protected by policemen. Similarly, parents might be reluctant to permit their children to attend schools which the state had cut off from such general government services as ordinary police and fire protection, connections for sewage disposal, public highways and sidewalks. Of course, cutting off church schools from these services, so separate and so indisputably marked off from the religious function, would make it far more difficult for the schools to operate. But such is obviously not the purpose of the First Amendment. That Amendment requires the state to be a neutral in its relations with groups of religious believers and non-believers; it does not require the state to be their adversary. State power is no more to be used so as to handicap religions than it is to favor them.

This Court has said that parents may, in the discharge of their duty under state compulsory education laws, send their children to a religious rather than a public school if the school meets the secular educational requirements which the state has power to impose. See *Pierce* v. *Society of Sisters* [1925]. It appears that these parochial schools meet New Jersey's requirements. The State contributes no money to the schools. It does not support them. Its legislation, as applied, does no more than provide a general program to help parents get their children, regardless of their religion, safety and expeditiously to and from accredited schools.

The First Amendment has erected a wall between church and state. That wall must be kept high and impregnable. We could not approve the slightest breach. New Jersey has not breached it here.

Affirmed

MR. JUSTICE JACKSON, dissenting:

... The Court's opinion marshals every argument in favor of state aid and puts the case in its most favorable light, but much of its reasoning confirms my conclusions that there are no good grounds upon which to support the present legislation. In fact, the undertones of the opinion, advocating complete and uncompromising separation of Church from State, seem utterly discordant with its conclusion yielding support to their commingling in educational matters. The case which irresistibly comes to mind as the most fitting precedent is that of Julia who, according to Byron's reports, "whispering 'I will ne'er consent,'—consented.". . .

MR. JUSTICE FRANKFURTER joins in this opinion.

MR. JUSTICE RUTLEDGE, with whom MR. JUSTICE FRANKFURTER, MR. JUSTICE JACKSON, and MR. JUSTICE BURTON agree, dissenting:

"Congress shall make no law respecting an establishment of religion, or prohibiting the free exercise thereof. . . ." U.S. Const., Amend. I. . . .

The Amendment's purpose was not to strike merely at the official establishment of a single sect, creed or religion, outlawing only a formal relation such as had prevailed in England and some of the colonies. Necessarily it was to uproot all such relationships. But the object was broader than separating church and state in this narrow sense. It was to create a complete and permanent separation of the spheres of religious activity and civil authority by comprehensively forbidding every form of public aid or support for religion. In proof the Amendment's wording and history unite with this Court's consistent utterances whenever attention has been fixed directly upon the question. . . .

Does New Jersey's action furnish support for religion by use of the taxing power? Certainly it does, if the test remains undiluted as Jefferson and Madison made it, that money taken by taxation from one is not to be used or given to support another's religious training or belief, or indeed one's own. Today as then the furnishing of "contributions of money for the propagation of opinions which he disbelieves" is the forbidden exaction; and the prohibition is absolute for whatever measure brings that consequence and whatever amount may be sought or given to that end.

The funds used here were raised by taxation. The Court does not dispute, nor could it, that their use does in fact give aid and encouragement to religious instruction. It only concludes that this aid is not "support" in law. But Madison and Jefferson were concerned with aid and support in fact, not as a legal conclusion "entangled in precedents." . . . Here parents pay money to send their children to parochial schools and funds raised by taxation are used to reimburse them. This not only helps the children to get to school and the parents to send them. It aids them in a substantial way to get the very thing which they are sent to the particular school to secure, namely, religious training and teaching. . . .

[I]t cannot be said that the cost of transportation is no part of the cost of education or of the religious instruction given. That it is a substantial and a necessary element is shown most plainly by the continuing and increasing demand for the state to assume it. Nor is there pretense that it relates only to the secular instruction given in religious schools or that any attempt is or could be made toward allocating proportional shares as between the secular and the religious instruction. It is precisely because the instruction is religious and relates to a particular faith, whether one or another, that parents send their children to religious schools under the *Pierce* doctrine.

And the very purpose of the state's contribution is to defray the cost of conveying the pupil to the place where he will receive not simply secular, but also and primarily religious, teaching and guidance. . . .

. . . [T]ransportation, where it is needed, is as essential to education as any other element. Its cost is as much a part of the total expense, except at times in amount, as the cost of textbooks, of school lunches, of athletic equipment, of writing and other materials; indeed of all other items' composing the total burden. . . .

But we are told that the New Jersey statute is valid in its present application because the appropriation is for a public, not a private purpose, namely, the promotion of education, and the majority accept this idea in the conclusion that all we have here is "public welfare legislation." If that is true and the Amendment's force can be thus destroyed, what has been said becomes all the more pertinent. For then there could be no possible objection to more extensive support of religious education by New Jersey. . . .

It is not because religious teaching does not promote the public or the individual's welfare, but because neither is furthered when the state promotes religious education, that the Constitution forbids it to do so. Both legislatures and courts are bound by that distinction. In failure to observe it lies the fallacy of the "public function"—"social legislation" argument, a fallacy facilitated by easy transference of the argument's basing from due process unrelated to any religious aspect to the First Amendment. . . .

. . . Legislatures are free to make, and courts to sustain, appropriations only when it can be found that in fact they do not aid, promote, encourage or sustain religious teaching or observances, be the amount large or small. No such finding has been or could be made in this case. The Amendment has removed this form of promoting the public welfare from legislative and judicial competence to make a public function. It is exclusively a private affair. . . .

No one conscious of religious values can be unsympathetic toward the burden which our constitutional separation puts on parents who desire religious instruction mixed with secular for their children. They pay taxes for others' children's education, at the same time the added cost of instruction for their own. Nor can one happily see benefits denied to children which others receive, because in conscience they or their parents for them desire a different kind of training others do not demand.

But if those feelings should prevail, there would be an end to our historic constitutional policy and command. No more unjust or discriminatory in fact is it to deny attendants at religious schools the cost of their transportation than it is to deny them tuitions, sustenance for their teachers, or any other educational expense which others receive at public cost. Hardship in fact there is which none can blink. But, for assuring to those who undergo it the greater, the most comprehensive freedom, it is one written by design and firm intent into our basic law. . . .

. . . [I]t is only by observing the [separation of church and state] rigidly that the state can maintain its neutrality and avoid partisanship in the dissensions inevitable when sect opposes sect over demands for public moneys to further religious education, teaching or training in any form or degree, directly or indirectly. Like St. Paul's freedom, religious liberty with a great price must be bought. And for those who exercise it most fully, by insisting upon religious education for their children mixed with secular, by the terms of our Constitution the price is greater than for others. . . .

Nor is the case comparable to one of

furnishing fire or police protection, or access to public highways. These things are matters of common right, part of the general need for safety. Certainly the fire department must not stand idly by while the church burns. Nor is this reason why the state should pay the expense of transportation or other items of the cost of religious education. . . .

Two great drives are constantly in motion to abridge, in the name of education, the complete division of religion and civil authority which our forefathers made. One is to introduce religious education and observances into the public schools. The other, to obtain public funds for the aid and support of various private reli-

gious schools. . . . In my opinion both avenues were closed by the Constitution. Neither should be opened by this Court. The matter is not one of quantity, to be measured by the amount of money expended. Now as in Madison's day it is one of principle, to keep separate the separate spheres as the First Amendment drew them, to prevent the first experiment upon our liberties; and to keep the question from becoming entangled in corrosive precedents. We should not be less strict to keep strong and untarnished the one side of the shield of religious freedom than we have been of the other.

The judgment should be reversed.

Contrast the majority opinion of Justice Black with the dissenting opinion of Justice Rutledge. Are they in agreement on the meaning of the establishment and free exercise clauses of the First Amendment? How does each rely upon the ideas of Jefferson and Madison to shape their views of the standards that should be applied under the First Amendment? Contrast the common approach taken by Black and Rutledge to determine the historical truth of the First Amendment with their different views of the implications of the New Jersey law. Is Black persuasive that the "wall of separation" standard has not been breached by the New Jersey statute and the actions taken under it?

What explanation does Justice Black give in applying the First Amendment religious clauses to the states under the Fourteenth Amendment? Contrast this aspect of his opinion with Justice Brennan's concurring opinion in *Abington School District* v. *Schempp,* pp. 746–750.

What possible conflicts does Justice Black raise between the establishment and free exercise clauses of the First Amendment?

Justice Black wrote in his *Everson* opinion that the establishment clause of the First Amendment "means at least this: Neither a state nor a federal government can set up a church. Neither can pass laws which aid one religion, aid all religions, or prefer one religion over another." The ambiguity of the "no-aid" formula, however, was illustrated in the *Everson* case itself by the lack of agreement between Black and Rutledge, representing the majority and dissenting justices, on the allowable boundaries of government aid to religion.

A year after its *Everson* decision the Court again confronted the question of permissible government aid to religion in *McCollum* v. *Board of Education.* The case reviewed a challenge to a "released-time" program for religious instruction in the public schools of Champaign, Illinois. An interfaith council on religious education had obtained permission from the board of education to offer religious instruction to public school students in the school classrooms during the regular school hours. The classes were composed of pupils whose parents had requested that their children attend. Students released from their secular study under the program were required to attend the religious classes. Justice Black, writing for the Court's majority, held that the program violated the establishment clause of the First Amendment. The released-time program, wrote Black, involved

> the use of tax-supported property for religious instruction and the close cooperation between the school authorities and the religious council in promoting religious education. The operation of the state's compulsory education system thus assists and is integrated with the program of religious instruction carried on by separate religious sects. Pupils compelled by law to go to school for secular education are released in part from their legal duty upon the condition that they attend the religious classes. This is beyond all question a utilization of the tax-established and tax-supported public school system to aid religious groups to spread their faith.[3]

Justice Frankfurter, joined by Justices Jackson, Rutledge, and Burton, wrote a concurring opinion in which he stated emphatically,

> Separation means separation, not something less. Jefferson's metaphor in describing the relation between church and state speaks of a "wall of separation," not of a fine line easily overstepped. The public school is at once the symbol of our democracy and the most pervasive means for promoting our common identity. In no activity of the state is it more vital to keep out divisive forces than in its schools, to avoid confusing, not to say fusing, what the Constitution thought to keep strictly apart. "The great American principle of eternal separation"—Elihu Root's phrase bears repetition—is one of the vital reliances of our constitutional system for assuring unities among our people stronger than our diversities. It is the court's duty to enforce this principle in its full integrity.[4]

Justice Reed, dissenting in *McCollum,* declared that the only "aid" barred by the First and Fourteen Amendments was "purposeful assistance directly to the church itself or to some religious group . . . performing ecclesiastical functions."[5] Many forms of government aid to religion, stated Reed, have been accepted and often explicitly upheld against constitutional challenges, including the exemption of churches from taxation, the provision of free textbooks to private as well as public schools, and the National School Lunch Program which aids all children attending tax-exempt schools. Considerations of federalism should be taken into account, wrote Reed, and the states granted leeway to deal with the social problems of their populations. "Devotion to the great principle of religious liberty," Reed concluded, "should not lead us into a rigid interpretation of the constitutional guarantee that conflicts with accepted habits of our people."[6]

[3]McCollum v. Board of Education, 333 U.S. 203, 209–210 (1948).
[4]Ibid., p. 231.
[5]Ibid., p. 248.
[6]Ibid., p. 256.

In the following case the Court again confronted the question of the constitutionality of a released-time program for religious instruction or devotional exercises.

Zorach v. *Clauson*

343 U.S. 306; 72 S. Ct. 697; 96 L. Ed. 954 (1952)

MR. JUSTICE DOUGLAS delivered the opinion of the Court:

New York City has a program which permits its public schools to release students during the school day so that they may leave the school buildings and school grounds and go to religious centers for religious instruction or devotional exercises. A student is released on written request of his parents. Those not released stay in the classrooms. The churches make weekly reports to the schools, sending a list of children who have been released from public school but who have not reported for religious instruction.

This "released time" program involves neither religious instruction in public school classrooms nor the expenditure of public funds. All costs, including the application blanks, are paid by the religious organizations. The case is therefore unlike *McCollum* v. *Board of Education* [1948] . . . which involved a "released time" program from Illinois. In that case the classrooms were turned over to religious instructors. We accordingly held that the program violated the First Amendment which (by reason of the Fourteenth Amendment) prohibits the states from establishing religion or prohibiting its free exercise.

Appellants, who are taxpayers and residents of New York City and whose children attend its public schools, challenge the present law, contending it is in essence not different from the one involved in the *McCollum* case. Their argument, stated elaborately in various ways, reduces itself to this: the weight and influence of the school is put behind a program for religious instruction; public school teachers police it, keeping tab on students who are released; the classroom activities come to a halt while the students who are released for religious instruction are on leave; the school is a crutch on which the churches are leaning for support in their religious training; without the cooperation of the schools this "released time" program, like the one in the *McCollum* case, would be futile and ineffective. The New York Court of Appeals sustained the law against this claim of unconstitutionality. . . . The case is here on appeal. . . .

It takes obtuse reasoning to inject any issue of the "free exercise" of religion into the present case. No one is forced to go to the religious classroom and no religious exercise or instruction is brought to the classrooms of the public schools. A student need not take religious instruction. He is left to his own desires as to the manner or time of his religious devotions, if any.

There is a suggestion that the system involves the use of coercion to get public school students into religious classrooms. There is no evidence in the record before us that supports that conclusion. The present record indeed tells us that the school authorities are neutral in this regard and do no more than release students whose parents so request. If in fact coercion were used, if it were established that any one or more teachers were using their office to persuade or force students to take the religious instruction, a wholly different case would be presented. Hence we put aside that claim of coercion both as respects of the "free exercise" of religion and "an establishment of religion" within the meaning of the First Amendment.

Moreover, apart from that claim of coercion, we do not see how New York by this type of "released time" program has made a law respecting an establishment of religion within the meaning of the First Amendment. There is much talk of the separation of Church and State in the history of the Bill of Rights and in the decisions clustering around the First Amendment. See *Everson* v. *Board of Education,* . . . *McCollum* v. *Board of Education.* . . . There cannot be the slightest doubt that the First Amendment reflects the philosophy that Church and State should be separated. And so far as interference with the "free exercise" of religion and an "establishment" of religion are concerned, the separation must be complete and unequivocal. The First Amendment within the scope of its coverage permits no exception; the prohibition is absolute. The First Amendment, however, does not say that in every and all respects there shall be a separation of Church and State. Rather, it studiously defines the manner, the specific ways, in which there shall be no concert or union or dependency one on the other. That is the common sense of the matter. Otherwise the state and religion would be aliens to each other—hostile, suspicious, and even unfriendly. Churches could not be required to pay even property taxes. Municipalities would not be permitted to render police or fire protection to religious groups. Policemen who helped parishioners into their places of worship would violate the Constitution. Prayers in our legislative halls; the appeals to the Almighty in the messages of the Chief Executive; the proclamations making Thanksgiving Day a holiday, "so help me God" in our courtroom oaths—these and all other references to the Almighty that run through our laws, our public rituals, our ceremonies would be flouting the First Amendment. A fastidious atheist or agnostic could even object to the supplication with which the Court opens each session: "God save the United States and this Honorable Court."

We would have to press the concept of separation of Church and State to these extremes to condemn the present law on constitutional grounds. The nullification of this law would have wide and profound effects. A Catholic student applies to his teacher for permission to leave the school during hours on a Holy Day of Obligation to attend a mass. A Jewish student asks his teacher for permission to be excused for Yom Kippur. A Protestant wants the afternoon off for a family baptismal ceremony. In each case the teacher requires parental consent in writing. In each case the teacher, in order to make sure the student is not a truant, goes further and requires a report from the priest, the rabbi, or the minister. The teacher in other words cooperates in a religious program to the extent of making it possible for her students to participate in it. Whether she does it occasionally for a few students, regularly for one, or pursuant to a systematized program designed to further the religious needs of all the students does not alter the character of the act.

We are a religious people whose institutions presuppose a Supreme Being. We guarantee the freedom to worship as one chooses. We make room for as wide a variety of beliefs and creeds as the spiritual needs of man deem necessary. We sponsor an attitude on the part of government that shows no partiality to any one group and that lets each flourish according to the zeal of its adherents and the appeal of its dogma. When the state encourages religious instruction or cooperates with religious authorities by adjusting the schedule of public events to sectarian needs, it follows the best of our traditions. For it then respects the religious nature of our people and accommodates the public service to their spiritual needs. To hold that it may not would be to find in the Constitution a requirement that a government shows a callous indifference to religious groups. That would be preferring those who believe in no religion over those who do believe. Government may not finance religious groups nor undertake religious instruction nor blend secular and sectarian education nor use secular institutions to force one or some religion on any person. But we find no constitutional requirement which makes it necessary for government to be hostile to religion and to throw its weight against efforts to widen the effective scope of religious influence. The government must be neutral when it comes to competition between sects. It may not thrust any sect on any person. It may not make a religious observance compulsory. It may not coerce anyone to attend church, to observe a religious holiday, or to take religious instruction. But it can close it doors or suspend its operations as to those who want to repair to their religious sanctuary for worship or instruction. No more than that is undertaken here. . . .

In the *McCollum* case the classrooms were used for religious instruction and the force of the public school was used to promote that instruction. Here, as we have said, the public schools do no more than accommodate their schedules to a program of outside religious instruction. We follow the *McCollum* case. But we cannot expand it to cover the present released time program unless separation of Church and State means that public institutions can make no adjustments of their schedules to accommodate the religious needs of the people. We cannot read into the Bill of Rights such a philosophy of hostility to religion.

Affirmed

JUSTICES BLACK and FRANKFURTER wrote dissenting opinions.

MR. JUSTICE JACKSON, dissenting:

This released time program is founded upon a use of the State's power of coercion, which, for me, determines its unconstitutionality. Stripped to its essentials, the plan has two stages: first, that the State compel each student to yield a large part of his time for public secular education; and, second, that some of it be "released" to him on condition that he devote it to sectarian religious purposes.

No one suggests that the Constitution would permit the State directly to require this "released" time to be spent "under the control of a duly constituted religious body." This program accomplishes that forbidden result by indirection. If public education were taking so much of the pupils' time as to injure the public or the students' welfare by encroaching upon their religious opportunity, simply shortening everyone's school day would facilitate voluntary and optional attendance at Church classes. But that suggestion is rejected upon the ground that if they are made free many students will not go to the Church. Hence, they must be deprived of freedom for this period, with Church attendance put to them as one of the two permissible ways of using it.

The greater effectiveness of this system over voluntary attendance after school hours is due to the truant officer who, if the youngster fails to go to the Church school, dogs him back to the public schoolroom. Here schooling is more or less suspended during the "released time" so the nonreligious attendants will not forge ahead of the churchgoing absentees. But it serves as a temporary jail for a pupil who will not go to Church. It takes more subtlety of mind than I possess to deny that this is governmental constraint in support of religion. It is as unconstitutional, in my view, when exerted by indirection as when exercised forthrightly.

As one whose children, as a matter of free choice, have been sent to privately supported Church schools, I may challenge the Court's suggestion that opposition to this plan can only be antireligious, atheistic, or agnostic. My evangelistic brethren confuse an objection to compulsion with an objection to religion. It is possible to hold a faith with enough confidence to believe that what should be rendered to God does not need to be decided and collected by Caesar.

The day that this country ceases to be free for irreligion it will cease to be free for religion—except for the sect that can win political power. The same epithetical jurisprudence used by the Court today to beat down those who oppose pressuring children into some religion can devise as good epithets tomorrow against those who object to pressuring them into a favored religion. And, after all, if we concede to the State power and wisdom to single out "duly constituted religious" bodies as exclusive alternatives for compulsory secular instruction, it would be logical to also uphold the power and wisdom to choose the true faith among those "duly constituted." We start down a rough road when we begin to mix compulsory public education with compulsory godliness.

A number of Justices just short of a majority of the majority that promulgates today's passionate dialectics joined in answering them in *McCollum* v. *Board of Education*. The distinction attempted between that case and this is trivial, almost to the point of cynicism, magnifying its nonessential details and disparaging compulsion which was the underlying reason for invalidity. A reading of the Court's opinion in that case along with its opinion in this case will show such difference of overtones and undertones as to make clear that the *McCollum* case has passed like a storm in a teacup. The wall which the Court was professing to erect between Church and State has become even more warped and twisted than I expected. Today's judgment will be more interesting to students of psychology and of the judicial processes than to students of constitutional law.

Why was the released-time program sustained in *Zorach* but not in *McCollum*? What significance did the Court attach to the fact that in *McCollum* the religious instruction was given in public school classrooms, whereas in *Zorach* the students were allowed to leave the premises of the schools to receive religious instruction?

Justice Douglas states that there is no issue of free exercise of religion in the *Zorach* case. "No one is forced to go to the religious classroom," he writes, "and no religious exercise or instruction is brought to the classrooms of the public schools." Could the free exercise issue be turned on its head in this case—that is, can it be argued that the free exercise clause supports the position of New York in releasing students to obtain religious instruction outside of public classrooms? Is this not a legitimate pursuit of religion *protected* by the free exercise clause? How does the Court use the argument that the free exercise clause supports the New York program to uphold it under the *establishment* clause?

What is the reasoning of Justice Jackson in dissent that the released-time program in *Zorach* is an unconstitutional governmental support of religion? Is Jackson correct that the opinions of the Court's majorities in *McCollum* and *Zorach* are inconsistent?

The *McCollum* and *Zorach* decisions respectively disallowed the state to use public school classrooms for religious instruction but permitted a state to have a "released-time" program for religious instruction outside of the public schools. The reach of the establishment clause was further clarified in the following case that reviewed the constitutionality of a New York State law that *permitted* the recitation of a prayer at the opening of the school day and the action of a local school board that *required* the recitation.

Engel v. *Vitale*

370 U.S. 421; 82 S. Ct. 1261; 8 L. Ed. 2d 601 (1962)

MR. JUSTICE BLACK delivered the opinion of the Court:

The respondent Board of Education of Union Free School District No. 9, New Hyde Park, New York, acting in its official capacity under state law, directed the School District's principal to cause the following prayer to be said aloud by each class in the presence of a teacher at the beginning of each school day:

Almighty God, we acknowledge our dependence upon Thee, and we beg Thy blessings upon us, our parents, our teachers and our Country.

This daily procedure was adopted on the recommendation of the State Board of Regents, a governmental agency created by the State Constitution to which the New York Legislature has granted broad supervisory, executive, and legislative powers over the State's public school system. These state officials composed the prayer which they recommended and published as a part of their "Statement on Moral and Spiritual Training in the Schools," saying: "We believe that this Statement will be subscribed to by all men and women of good will, and we call upon all of them to aid in giving life to our program."

Shortly after the practice of reciting

the Regents' prayer was adopted by the School District, the parents of ten pupils brought this action in a New York State Court insisting that use of this official prayer in the public schools was contrary to the beliefs, religions, or religious practices of both themselves and their children. Among other things, these parents challenged the constitutionality of both the state law authorizing the School District to direct the use of prayer in public schools and the School District's regulation ordering the recitation of this particular prayer on the ground that these actions of official governmental agencies violate that part of the First Amendment of the Federal Constitution which commands that "Congress shall make no law respecting an establishment of religion"— a command which was "made applicable to the State of New York by the Fourteenth Amendment of the said Constitution." The New York Court of Appeals, over the dissents of Judges Dye and Fuld, sustained an order of the lower state courts which had upheld the power of New York to use the Regents' prayer as part of the daily procedures of its public schools so long as the schools did not compel any pupil to join in the prayer over his or his parents' objection. We granted certiorari to review this important decision involving rights protected by the First and Fourteenth Amendments.

We think that by using its public school system to encourage recitation of the Regents' prayer, the State of New York has adopted a practice wholly inconsistent with the Establishment Clause. There can, of course, be no doubt that New York's program of daily classroom invocation of God's blessings as prescribed in the Regents' prayer is a religious activity. It is a solemn avowal of divine faith and supplication for the blessings of the Almighty. The nature of such a prayer has always been religious, none of the respondents has denied this and the trial court expressly so found. . . .

The petitioners contend among other things that the state laws requiring or permitting use of the Regents' prayer must be struck down as a violation of the Establishment Clause because that prayer was composed by governmental officials as a part of a governmental program to further religious beliefs. For this reason, petitioners argue, the State's use of the Regents' prayer in its public school system breaches the constitutional wall of separation between Church and State. We agree with that contention since we think that the constitutional prohibition against laws respecting an establishment of religion must at least mean that in this country it is no part of the business of government to compose official prayers for any group of the American people to recite as a part of a religious program carried on by government.

It is a matter of history that this very practice of establishing governmentally composed prayers for religious services was one of the reasons which caused many of our early colonists to leave England and seek religious freedom in America. The Book of Common Prayer, which was created under governmental direction and which was approved by Acts of Parliament in 1548 and 1549, set out in minute detail the accepted form and content of prayer and other religious ceremonies to be used in the established, tax-supported Church of England. The controversies over the Book and what should be its content repeatedly threatened to disrupt the peace of that country as the accepted forms of prayer in the established church changed with the views of the particular ruler that happened to be in control at the time. Powerful groups representing some of the varying religious views of the people struggled among themselves to impress their particular views upon the Government and obtain amendments of the Book more suitable to their respective notions of how religious services should be conducted in order that the official religious establishment would advance their particular religious beliefs. Other groups, lacking the necessary political power to influence the Government on the matter, decided to leave England and its established church and seek freedom in America from England's governmentally ordained and supported religion.

It is an unfortunate fact of history that when some of the very groups which had most strenuously opposed the established Church of England found themselves sufficiently in control of colonial governments in this country to write their own prayers into law, they passed laws making their own religion the official religion of their respective colonies. Indeed, as late as the time of the Revolutionary War, there were established churches in at least eight of the thirteen former colonies and established religions in at least four of the other five. But the successful Revolution against English political domination was shortly followed by intense opposition to the practice of establishing religion by law. . . .

By the time of the adoption of the Constitution, our history shows that there was a widespread awareness among many

Americans of the dangers of a union of Church and State. . . . The First Amendment was added to the Constitution to stand as a guarantee that neither the power nor the prestige of the Federal Government would be used to control, support or influence the kinds of prayer the American people can say—that the people's religions must not be subjected to the pressures of government for change each time a new political administration is elected to office. Under that Amendment's prohibition against governmental establishment of religion, as reinforced by the provisions of the Fourteenth Amendment, government in this country, be it state or federal, is without power to prescribe by law any particular form of prayer which is to be used as an official prayer in carrying on any program of governmentally sponsored religious activity.

There can be no doubt that New York's state prayer program officially establishes the religious beliefs embodied in the Regent's prayer. The respondent's argument to the contrary, which is largely based upon the contention that the Regents' prayer is "non-denominational" and the fact that the program, as modified and approved by state courts, does not require all pupils to recite the prayer but permits those who wish to do so to remain silent or be excused from the room, ignores the essential nature of the program's constitutional defects. Neither the fact that the prayer may be denominationally neutral nor the fact that its observance on the part of the students is voluntary can serve to free it from the limitations of the Establishment Clause, as it might from the Free Exercise Clause, of the First Amendment, both of which are operative against the States by virtue of the Fourteenth Amendment. Although these two clauses may in certain instances overlap, they forbid two quite different kinds of governmental encroachment upon

religious freedom. The Establishment Clause, unlike the Free Exercise Clause, does not depend upon any showing of direct governmental compulsion and is violated by the enactment of laws which establish an official religion whether those laws operate directly to coerce nonobserving individuals or not. This is not to say, of course, that laws officially prescribing a particular form of religious worship do not involve coercion of such individuals. When the power, prestige and financial support of government is placed behind a particular religious belief, the indirect coercive pressure upon religious minorities to conform to the prevailing officially approved religion is plain. But the purposes underlying the Establishment Clause go much further than that. Its first and most immediate purpose rested on the belief that a union of government and religion tends to destroy government and to degrade religion. The history of governmentally established religion, both in England and in this country, showed that whenever government had allied itself with one particular form of religion, the inevitable result had been that it had incurred the hatred, disrespect and even contempt of those who held contrary beliefs. That same history showed that many people had lost their respect for any religion that had relied upon the support of government to spread its faith. The Establishment Clause thus stands as an expression of principle on the part of the Founders of our Constitution that religion is too personal, too sacred, too holy, to permit its "unhallowed perversion" by a civil magistrate. Another purpose of the Establishment Clause rested upon an awareness of the historical fact that governmentally established religions and religious persecutions go hand in hand. The Founders knew that only a few years after the Book of Common Prayer became the only accepted form of religious services in the established Church of England, an Act of Uniformity was passed to compel all Englishmen to attend those services and to make it a criminal offense to conduct or attend religious gatherings of any kind—a law which was consistently flouted by dissenting religious groups in England and which contributed to widespread persecutions of people like John Bunyan who persisted in holding "unlawful [religious] meetings . . . to the great disturbance and distraction of the good subjects of this kingdom. . . ." And they knew that similar persecutions had received the sanction of law in several of the colonies in this country soon after the establishment of official religions in those colonies. It was in large part to get completely away from this sort of systematic religious persecution that the Founders brought into being our Nation, our Constitution, and our Bill of Rights with its prohibition against any governmental establishment of religion. The New York laws officially prescribing the Regents' prayer are inconsistent both with the purposes of the Establishment Clase and with the Establishment Clause itself.

It has been argued that to apply the Constitution in such a way as to prohibit state laws respecting an establishment of religious services in public schools is to indicate a hostility toward religion or toward prayer. Nothing, of course, could be more wrong. The history of man is inseparable from the history of religion. And perhaps it is not too much to say that since the beginning of that history many people have devoutly believed that "More things are wrought by prayer than this world dreams of." It was doubtless largely due to men who believed this that there grew up a sentiment that caused men to leave the cross-currents of officially established state religions and religious persecution in Europe and come to this country filled with the hope that they could find a place in which they could pray when they pleased to the God of their faith in the language they chose. And there were men of this same faith in the power of prayer who led the fight for adoption of our Constitution and also of our Bill of Rights with the very guarantees of religious freedom that forbid the sort of governmental activity which New York has attempted here. These men knew that the First Amendment, which tried to put an end to governmental control of religion and of prayer, was not written to destroy either. They knew rather that it was written to quiet well-justified fears which nearly all of them felt arising out of an awareness that governments of the past had shackled men's tongues to make them speak only the religious thoughts that government wanted them to speak and to pray only to the God that government wanted them to pray to. It is neither sacrilegious nor antireligious to say that each separate government in this country should stay out of the business of writing or sanctioning official prayers and leave that purely religious function to the people themselves and to those the people choose to look to for religious guidance.

It is true that New York's establishment of its Regents' prayer as an officially approved religious doctrine of that State does not amount to total establishment of one particular religious sect to the exclusion of all others—that, indeed, the governmental endorsement of that prayer seems relatively insignificant when compared to the governmental encroachments upon religion which were commonplace 200 years ago. To those who may subscribe to the view that because the Regents' official prayer is so brief and general there can be no danger to religious freedom in its governmental establishment, however, it may be appropriate to say in the words of James Madison, the author of the First Amendment:

[I]t is proper to take alarm at the first experiment on our liberties. . . . Who does not see that the same authority which can establish Christianity, in exclusion of all other Religions, may establish with the same ease any particular sect of Christians, in exclusion of all other Sects? That the same authority which can force a citizen to contribute three pence only of his property for the support of any one establishment, may force him to conform to any other establishment in all cases whatsoever?

The judgment of the Court of Appeals of New York is reversed and the cause remanded for further proceedings not inconsistent with this opinion.

Reversed and remanded.

MR. JUSTICE FRANKFURTER took no part in the decision of this case.

MR. JUSTICE WHITE took no part in the consideration or decision of this case.

MR. JUSTICE DOUGLAS concurred.

MR. JUSTICE STEWART, dissenting:
A local school board in New York has provided that those pupils who wish to do so may join in a brief prayer at the beginning of each school day, acknowledging their dependence upon God and asking His blessing upon them and upon their parents, their teachers, and their country. The Court today decides that in permitting this brief nondenominational prayer the school board has violated the Constitution of the United States. I think this decision is wrong.

The Court does not hold, nor could it, that New York has interfered with the free exercise of anybody's religion. For the state courts have made clear that those who object to reciting the prayer must be entirely free of any compulsion to do so, including any "embarrassments and pressures." . . . But the Court says that in permitting school children to say this simple prayer, the New York authorities have established "an official religion."

With all respect, I think the Court has misapplied a great constitutional principle. I cannot see how an "official religion" is established by letting those who want to say a prayer say it. On the contrary, I think that to deny the wish of these school children to join in reciting this prayer is to deny them the opportunity of sharing in the spiritual heritage of our Nation.

The Court's historical review of the quarrels over the Book of Common Prayer in England throws no light for me on the issue before us in this case. England had then and now has an established church. Equally unenlightening, I think, is the history of the early establishment and later rejection of an official church in our own States. For we deal here not with the establishment of a state church, which would, of course, be constitutionally impermissible, but with whether school children who want to begin their day by joining in prayer must be prohibited from doing so. Moreover, I think that the Court's task, in this as in all areas of constitutional adjudication, is not responsibly aided by the uncritical invocation of metaphors like the "wall of separation," a phrase nowhere to be found in the Constitution. What is relevant to the issue here is not the history of an established church in sixteenth century England or in eighteenth century America, but the history of the religious traditions of our people, reflected in countless practices of the institutions and officials of our government.

At the opening of each day's Session of this Court we stand, while one of our officials invokes the protection of God. Since the days of John Marshall our Crier has said, "God save the United States and this Honorable Court." Both the Senate and the House of Representatives open their daily Sessions with prayer. Each of our Presidents, from George Washington to John F. Kennedy, has upon assuming Office asked the protection and help of God.

The Court today says that the state and

federal governments are without constitutional power to prescribe any particular form of words to be recited by any group of the American people on any subject touching religion. One of the stanzas of "The Star-Spangled Banner," made our National Anthem by Act of Congress in 1931, contains these verses:

Blest with victory and peace, may the heav'n rescued land
　Praise the Pow'r that hath made and preserved us a nation!
　Then conquer we must, when our cause it is just,
　And this be our motto "In God is our Trust."

In 1954 Congress added a phrase to the Pledge of Allegiance to the Flag so that it now contains the words "one Nation *under God,* indivisible, with liberty and justice for all." In 1952 Congress enacted legislation calling upon the President each year to proclaim a National Day of Prayer. Since 1865 the words "IN GOD WE TRUST" have been impressed on our coins.

Countless similar examples could be listed, but there is no need to belabor the obvious. It was all summed up by this Court just ten years ago in a single sentence: "We are a religious people whose institutions presuppose a Supreme Being." *Zorach* v. *Clauson* [1952].

I do not believe that this Court, or the Congress, or the President has by the actions and practices I have mentioned established an "official religion" in violation of the Constitution. And I do not believe the State of New York has done so in this case. What each has done has been to recognize and to follow the deeply entrenched and highly cherished spiritual traditions of our Nation—traditions which come down to us from those who almost two hundred years ago avowed their "firm Reliance on the Protection of divine Providence" when they proclaimed the freedom and independence of this brave new world.

I dissent.

On what basis does Justice Black state that the New York State prayer program does *not* violate the free exercise clause? How does Black distinguish the criteria of the free exercise clause from that of the establishment clause? How does the Court take into account government coercion in judging the constitutionality of state programs under the free exercise and establishment clauses?

Black writes that the establishment clause "rested on the belief that a union of government and religion tends to destroy government and to degrade religion." In what way does this suggest that the two clauses are complementary?

Is it clear from the facts that the New York State prayer program is more clearly an unconstitutional establishment of religion than the released-time program upheld in *Zorach* v. *Clauson*? Is the fact that the public school classrooms are being used for prayers, however general and nondenominational, a critical fact in the holding of the Court that the establishment clause has been violated? Justice Frankfurter noted the symbolic importance of the public schools in the American way of life in his concurring opinion in *McCollum*. Does Justice Black implicitly acknowledge the symbolic importance of the public schools when he writes, in *Engel*, that when "the power, *prestige* and financial support of government is placed behind a particular religious belief, the indirect coercive pressure upon religious minorities to conform to the prevailing officially approved religion is plain"?

Does Justice Stewart, in dissent, disagree with the standards applied by the Court? Contrast the reasoning and method of approach of Black and Stewart. Does Stewart suggest that it is the Court's uncritical invocation of the metaphor "wall of separation" that leads it to the wrong conclusion?

In the following *Abington* case the Supreme Court reviewed a Pennsylvania law requiring that ten verses from the Holy Bible be read, without comment, at the opening of each public school day. Any child could be excused from the Bible reading upon the written request of his or her parent or guardian. The companion *(Murray)* case involved a challenge to a Baltimore school rule requiring the reading, without comment, of a chapter in the Holy Bible and/or the use of the Lord's Prayer at the opening exercises of its public schools.

Abington School District v. *Schempp* (and *Murray* v. *Curlett*)

374 U.S. 203; 83 S. Ct. 1560; 10 L. Ed. 2d 844 (1963)

MR. JUSTICE CLARK delivered the opinion of the Court:

Once again we are called upon to consider the scope of the provision of the First Amendment to the United States Constitution which declares that "Congress shall make no law respecting an establishment of religion, or prohibiting the free exercise thereof. . . ." These companion cases present the issues in the context of state action requiring that schools begin each day with readings from the Bible. While raising the basic questions under slightly different factual situations, the cases permit of joint treatment. In light of the history of the First Amendment and of our cases interpreting and applying its requirements, we hold that the practices at issue and the laws requiring them are unconstitutional under the Establishment Clause, as applied to the States through the Fourteenth Amendment. . . .

. . . The fact that the Founding Fathers believed devotedly that there was a God and that the unalienable rights of man were rooted in Him is clearly evidenced in their writings, from the Mayflower Compact to the Constitution itself. This background is evidenced today in our public life through the continuance in our oaths of office from the Presidency to the Alderman of the final supplication, "So help me God." Likewise each House of the Congress provides through its Chaplain an opening prayer, and the sessions of this Court are declared open by the crier in a short ceremony, the final phrase of which invokes the grace of God. Again, there are such manifestations in our military forces, where those of our citizens who are under the restrictions of military service wish to engage in voluntary worship. Indeed, only last year an official survey of the country indicated that 64 percent of our people have church membership. . . . It can be truly said, therefore, that today, as in the beginning, our national life reflects a religious people who, in the words of Madison, are "earnestly praying, as . . . in duty bound, that the Supreme Lawgiver of the Universe . . . guide them into every measure which may be worthy of his [blessing. . . .]" . . .

This is not to say, however, that religion has been so identified with our history and government that religious freedom is not likewise as strongly imbedded in our public and private life. . . . This freedom to worship was indispensable in a country whose people came from the four quarters of the earth and brought with them a diversity of religious opinion. Today authorities list 83 separate religious bodies, each with membership exceeding 50,000, existing among our people, as well as innumerable smaller groups. . . .

Almost a hundred years ago in *Minor* v. *Board of Education of Cincinnati* [1872] Judge Alphonso Taft, father of the revered Chief Justice, in an unpublished opinion stated the ideal of our people as to religious freedom as one of

absolute equality before the law, of all religious opinions and sects. . . .

The government is neutral, and, while protecting all, it prefers none, and it *disparages* none. . . .

Finally, in *Engel* v. *Vitale,* . . . these principles were so universally recognized that the Court, without the citation of a single case and over the sole dissent of Mr. Justice Stewart, reaffirmed them. . . .

The wholesome "neutrality" of which this Court's cases speak thus stems from a recognition of the teachings of history that powerful sects or groups might bring about a fusion of governmental and religious functions or a concert or dependency of one upon the other to the end that official support of the State or Federal Government would be placed behind the tenets of one or of all orthodoxies. This the Establishment Clause prohibits. And a further reason for neutrality is found in the Free Exercise Clause, which recognizes the value of religious training, teaching and observance and, more particularly, the right of every person to freely choose his own course with reference thereto, free of any compulsion from the state. This the Free Exercise Clause guarantees. Thus, as we have seen, the two clauses may overlap. As we have indicated, the Establishment Clause has been directly considered by this Court

eight times in the past score of years and, with only one Justice dissenting on the point, it has consistently held that the clause withdrew all legislative power respecting religious beliefs or the expression thereof. The test may be stated as follows: what are the purpose and primary effect of the enactment? If either is the advancement or inhibition of religion then the enactment exceeds the scope of legislative power as circumscribed by the Constitution. That is to say that to withstand the strictures of the Establishment Clause there must be a secular legislative purpose and a primary effect that neither advances nor inhibits religion. . . . The Free Exercise Clause, likewise considered many times here, withdraws from legislative power, state and federal, the exertion of any restraint on the free exercise of religion. Its purpose is to secure religious liberty in the individual by prohibiting any invasions thereof by civil authority. Hence it is necessary in a free exercise case for one to show the coercive effect of the enactment as it operates against him in the practice of his religion. The distinction between the two clauses is apparent—a violation of the Free Exercise Clause is predicated on coercion while the Establishment Clause violation need not be so attended.

Applying the Establishment Clause principles to the cases at bar we find that the States are requiring the selection and reading at the opening of the school day of verses from the Holy Bible and the recitation of the Lord's Prayer by the students in unison. These exercises are prescribed as part of the curricular activities of students who are required by law to attend school. They are held in the school buildings under the supervision and with the participation of teachers employed in those schools. None of these factors, other than compulsory school attendance, was present in the program upheld in *Zorach* v. *Clauson.* The trial court in No. 142

[*Abington*] has found that such an opening exercise is a religious ceremony and was intended by the State to be so. We agree with the trial court's finding as to the religious character of the exercises. Given that finding, the exercises and the law requiring them are in violation of the Establishment Clause.

There is no such specific finding as to the religious character of the exercises in No. 119 [*Murray* v. *Curlett*], and the State contends (as does the State in No. 142) that the program is an effort to extend its benefits to all public school children without regard to their religious belief. Included within its secular purposes, it says, are the promotion of moral values, the contradiction to the materialistic trends of our times, the perpetuation of our institutions and the teaching of literature. The case came up on demurrer, of course, to a petition which alleged that the uniform practice under the rule had been to read from the King James version of the Bible and that the exercise was sectarian. The short answer, therefore, is that the religious character of the exercise was admitted by the State. But even if its purpose is not strictly religious, it is sought to be accomplished through readings, without comment, from the Bible. Surely the place of the Bible as an instrument of religion cannot be gainsaid, and the State's recognition of the pervading religious character of the ceremony is evident from the rule's specific permission of the alternative use of the Catholic Douay version as well as the recent amendment permitting nonattendance at the exercises. None of these factors is consistent with the contention that the Bible is here used either as an instrument for nonreligious moral inspiration or as a reference for the teaching of secular subjects.

The conclusion follows that in both cases the laws require religious exercises and such exercises are being conducted in direct violation of the rights of the appellees and petitioners. Nor are these required exercises mitigated by the fact that individual students may absent themselves upon parental request, for that fact furnishes no defense to a claim of unconstitutionality under the Establishment Clause. See *Engel* v. *Vitale*. . . . Further, it is no defense to urge that the religious practices here may be relatively minor encroachments on the First Amendment. The breach of neutrality that is today a trickling stream may all too soon become a raging torrent and, in the words of Madison, "it is proper to take alarm at the first experiment on our liberties." Memorial and Remonstrance Against Religious Assessments, quoted in *Everson*. . . .

It is insisted that unless these religious exercises are permitted a "religion of secularism" is established in the schools. We agree of course that the State may not establish a "religion of secularism" in the sense of affirmatively opposing or showing hostility to religion, thus "preferring those who believe in no religion over those who do believe." *Zorach* v. *Clauson*. We do not agree, however, that this decision in any sense has that effect. In addition, it might well be said that one's education is not complete without a study of comparative religion or the history of religion and its relationship to the advancement of civilization. It certainly may be said that the Bible is worthy of study for its literary and historical qualities. Nothing we have said here indicates that such study of the Bible or of religion, when presented objectively as part of a secular program of education, may not be effected consistently with the First Amendment. But the exercises here do not fall into those categories. They are religious exercises, required by the States in violation of the command of the First Amendment that the Government maintain strict neutrality, neither aiding nor opposing religion.

Finally, we cannot accept that the concept of neutrality, which does not permit a State to require a religious exercise even with the consent of the majority of those affected, collides with the majority's right to free exercise of religion. While the Free Exercise Clause clearly prohibits the use of state action to deny the rights of free exercise to *anyone,* it has never meant that a majority could use the machinery of the State to practice its beliefs. Such a contention was effectively answered by Mr. Justice Jackson for the Court in *West Virginia Board of Education* v. *Barnette* [1943]:

The very purpose of a Bill of Rights was to withdraw certain subjects from the vicissitudes of political controversy, to place them beyond the reach of majorities and officials and to establish them as legal principles to be applied by the courts. One's right to . . . freedom of worship . . . and other fundamental rights may not be submitted to vote; they depend on the outcome of no elections.

The place of religion in our society is an exalted one, achieved through a long tradition of reliance on the home, the church and the inviolable citadel of the individual heart and mind. We have come to recognize through bitter experience that it is not within the power of government to invade that citadel, whether its purpose or effect be to aid or oppose, to advance or retard. In the relationship between man and religion, the State is firmly committed to a position of neutrality. Though the application of that rule requires interpretation of a delicate sort, the rule itself is clearly and concisely stated in the words of the First Amendment. Applying that rule to the facts of these cases, we affirm the judgment in [*Abington*]. In [*Murray* v. *Curlett*], the judgment is reversed and the cause remanded to the Maryland Court of Appeals for further proceedings consistent with this opinion.

It is so ordered.

MR. JUSTICE DOUGLAS, concurring:

The First Amendment forbids both the abridgment of the free exercise of religion and the enactment of laws "respecting an establishment of religion." The two clauses, although distinct in their objectives and their applicability, emerged together from a common panorama of history. The inclusion of both restraints upon the power of Congress to legislate concerning religious matters shows unmistakably that the Framers of the First Amendment were not content to rest the protection of religious liberty exclusively upon either clause. . . .

It is true that the Framers' immediate concern was to prevent the setting up of an official federal church of the kind which England and some of the Colonies had long supported. But nothing in the text of the Establishment Clause supports the view that the prevention of the setting up of an official church was meant to be the full extent of the prohibitions against official involvements in religion. . . .

But an awareness of history and an appreciation of the aims of the Founding Fathers do not always resolve concrete problems. The specific question before us has, for example, aroused vigorous dispute whether the architects of the First Amendment—James Madison and Thomas Jefferson particularly—understood the prohibition against any "law respecting an establishment of religion" to reach devotional exercises in the public schools. It may be that Jefferson and Madison would have held such exercises to be permissible—although even in Jefferson's case serious doubt is suggested by his admonition against "putting the Bible and Testament into the hands of the children at an age when their judgments are not sufficiently matured for religious inquiries. . . ." But I doubt that their view, even if perfectly clear one way or the other, would supply a dispositive answer to the question presented by these cases. A more fruitful inquiry, it seems to me, is whether the practices here challenged threaten those consequences which the Framers deeply feared; whether, in short, they tend to promote that type of interdependence between religion and state which the First Amendment was designed to prevent. Our task is to translate "the majestic generalities of the Bill of Rights, conceived as part of the pattern of liberal government in the eighteenth century, into concrete restraints on officials dealing with the problems of the twentieth century. . . ." *West Virginia State Board of Education* v. *Barnette* [1943]. . . .

MR. JUSTICE BRENNAN, concurring:

A too literal quest for the advice of the Founding Fathers upon the issues of these cases seems to me futile and misdirected for several reasons: First, on our precise problem the historical record is at best ambiguous, and statements can readily be found to support either side of the proposition. The ambiguity of history is understandable if we recall the nature of the problems uppermost in the thinking of the statesmen who fashioned the religious guarantees; they were concerned with far more flagrant intrusions of government into the realm of religion than any that our century has witnessed. While it is clear to me that the Framers meant the Establishment Clause to prohibit more than the creation of an established federal church such as existed in England, I have no doubt that, in their preoccupation with the imminent question of established churches, they gave no distinct consideration to the particular question whether the clause also forbade devotional exercises in public institutions.

Second, the structure of American education has greatly changed since the First Amendment was adopted. In the context of our modern emphasis upon public education available to all citizens, any views of the eighteenth century as to whether the exercises at bar are an "establishment" offer little aid to decision. Education, as the Framers knew it, was in the main confined to private schools more often than not under strictly sectarian supervision. Only gradually did control of education pass largely to public officials. It would, therefore, hardly be significant if the fact was that the nearly universal devotional exercises in the schools of the young Republic did not provoke criticism; even today religious ceremonies in church-supported private schools are constitutionally unobjectionable.

Third, our religious composition makes us a vastly more diverse people than were our forefathers. They knew differences chiefly among Protestant sects. Today the Nation is far more heterogeneous religiously, including as it does substantial minorities not only of Catholics and Jews but as well of those who worship according to no version of the Bible and those who worship no God at all. . . . In the face of such profound changes, practices which may have been objectionable to no one in the time of Jefferson and Madison may today be highly offensive to many persons, the deeply devout and the nonbelievers alike.

Whatever Jefferson or Madison would have thought of Bible reading or the recital of the Lord's Prayer in what few public schools existed in their day, our use of the history of their time must limit itself to broad purposes, not specific practices. By such a standard, I am persuaded, as is the Court, that the devotional exercises carried on in the Baltimore and Abington schools offend the First Amendment because they sufficiently threaten in our day those substantive evils the fear of which called forth the Establishment Clause of the First Amendment. It is "*a constitution* we are expounding," and our interpretation of the First Amendment must necessarily be responsive to the much more highly charged nature of religious questions in contemporary society. . . .

It has been suggested, with some support in history, that absorption of the

First Amendment's ban against congressional legislation "respecting an establishment of religion" is conceptually impossible because the Framers meant the Establishment Clause also to foreclose any attempt by Congress to disestablish the existing official state churches. Whether or not such was the understanding of the Framers and whether such a purpose would have inhibited the absorption of the Establishment Clause at the threshold of the Nineteenth Century are questions not dispositive of our present inquiry. For it is clear on the record of history that the last of the formal state establishments was dissolved more than three decades before the Fourteenth Amendment was ratified, and thus the problem of protecting official state churches from federal encroachments could hardly have been any concern of those who framed the post-Civil War Amendments. Any such objective of the First Amendment, having become historical anachronism by 1868, cannot be thought to have deterred the absorption of the Establishment Clause to any greater degree than it would, for example, have deterred the absorption of the Free Exercise Clause. . . .

. . . [I]t has been contended that absorption of the Establishment Clause is precluded by the absence of any intention on the part of the Framers of the Fourteenth Amendment to circumscribe the residual powers of the States to aid religious activities and institutions in ways which fell short of formal establishments. That argument relies in part upon the express terms of the abortive Blaine Amendment—proposed several years after the adoption of the Fourteenth Amendment—which would have added to the First Amendment a provision that "[n]o State shall make any law respecting an establishment of religion. . . ." Such a restriction would have been superfluous, it is said, if the Fourteenth Amendment had already made the Establishment Clause binding upon the States.

The argument proves too much, for the Fourteenth Amendment's protection of the free exercise of religion can hardly be questioned; yet the Blaine Amendment would also have added an explicit protection against state laws abridging that liberty. Even if we assume that the draftsmen of the Fourteenth Amendment saw no immediate connection between its protections against state action infringing personal liberty and the guarantees of the First Amendment, it is certainly too late in the day to suggest that their assumed inattention to the question dilutes the force of these constitutional guarantees in their application to the States. It is enough to conclude that the religious liberty embodied in the Fourteenth Amendment would not be viable if the Constitution were interpreted to forbid only establishments ordained by Congress. . . .

The line between permissible and impermissible forms of involvement between government and religion has already been considered by the lower federal and state courts. I think a brief survey of certain of these forms of accommodation will reveal that the First Amendment commands not official hostility toward religion, but only a strict neutrality in matters of religion. Moreover, it may serve to suggest that the scope of our holding today is to be measured by the special circumstances under which these cases have arisen, and by the particular dangers to church and state which religious exercises in the public schools present. It may be helpful for purposes of analysis to group these other practices and forms of accommodation into several rough categories.

A. *The Conflict Between Establishment and Free Exercise.*—There are certain practices, conceivably violative of the Establishment Clause, the striking down of which might seriously interfere with certain religious liberties also protected by the First Amendment. Provisions for churches and chaplains at military establishments for those in the armed services may afford one such example. The like provision by state and federal governments for chaplains in penal institutions may afford another example. It is argued that such provisions may be assumed to contravene the Establishment Clause, yet be sustained on constitutional grounds as necessary to secure the members of the Armed Forces and prisoners those rights of worship guaranteed under the Free Exercise Clause. Since government has deprived such persons of the opportunity to practice their faith at places of their choice, the argument runs, government may, in order to avoid infringing the free exercise guarantees, provide substitutes where it requires such persons to be. Such a principle might support, for example, the constitutionality of draft exemptions for ministers and divinity students, cf. *Selective Draft Law Cases* [1918] . . . of the excusal of children from school on their respective religious holidays; and of the allowance by government of temporary use of public buildings by religious organizations when their own churches have become unavailable because of a disaster or emergency.

Such activities and practices seem distinguishable from the sponsorship of daily Bible reading and prayer recital. For one thing, there is no element of coercion present in the appointment of military or prison chaplains; the soldier or convict who declines the opportunities for worship would not ordinarily subject himself to the suspicion or obloquy of his peers. Of special significance to this distinction is the fact that we are here usually dealing with adults, not with impressionable children as in the public schools. Moreover, the school exercises are not designed to provide the pupils with general opportunities for worship denied them by the legal obligation to attend school. The student's compelled presence in school for five days a week in no way renders the regular religious facilities of the community less accessible to him than they are to others. The situation of the school child is therefore plainly unlike that of the isolated soldier or the prisoner.

The State must be steadfastly neutral in all matters of faith, and neither favor nor inhibit religion. In my view, government cannot sponsor religious exercises in the public schools without jeopardizing that neutrality. On the other hand, hostility, not neutrality, would characterize the refusal to provide chaplains and places of worship for prisoners and soldiers cut off by the State from all civilian opportunities for public communion, the withholding of draft exemptions for ministers and conscientious objectors, or the denial of the temporary use of an empty public building to a congregation whose place of worship has been destroyed by fire or flood. I do not say that government *must* provide chaplains or draft exemptions, or that the courts should intercede if it fails to do so.

B. *Establishment and Exercises in Legislative Bodies.*—The saying of invocational prayers in legislative chambers, state or federal, and the appointment of legislative chaplains, might well represent no involvements of the kind prohibited by the Establishment Clause. Legislators, federal and state, are mature adults who may presumably absent themselves from such public and ceremonial exercises without incurring any penalty, direct or indirect. It may also be significant that, at least in the case of Congress, Art. I, § 5, of the Constitution makes each House the monitor of the "Rules of its Proceedings" so that it is at least arguable whether such matters present "political questions" the resolution of which is exclusively confided to Congress. . . .

C. *Non-Devotional Use of the Bible in the Public Schools.*—The holding of the Court today plainly does not foreclose teaching *about* the Holy Scriptures or about the differences between religious sects in classes in literature or history. Indeed, whether or not the Bible is involved, it would be impossible to teach meaningfully many subjects in the social sciences or the humanities without some mention of religion. To what extent, and at what points in the curriculum, religious materials should be cited are matters which the courts ought to entrust very largely to the experienced officials who superintend our Nation's public schools. They are experts in such matters, and we are not. We should heed Mr. Justice Jackson's caveat that any attempt by this Court to announce curricular standards would be "to decree a uniform, rigid and, if we are consistent, an unchanging standard for countless school boards representing and serving highly localized groups which not only differ from each other but which themselves from time to time change attitudes." *McCollum* v. *Board of Education.*

We do not, however, in my view usurp the jurisdiction of school administrators by holding as we do today that morning devotional exercises in any form are constitutionally invalid. But there is no occasion now to go further and anticipate problems we cannot judge with the material now before us. Any attempt to impose rigid limits upon the mention of God or references to the Bible in the classroom would be fraught with dangers. If it should sometime hereafter be shown that in fact religion can play no part in the teaching of a given subject without resurrecting the ghost of the practices we strike down today, it will then be time enough to consider questions we must now defer.

D. *Uniform Tax Exemptions Incidentally Available to Religious Institutions.*—Nothing we hold today questions the propriety of certain tax deductions or exemptions which incidentally benefit churches and religious institutions, along with many secular charities and nonprofit organizations. If religious institutions benefit, it is in spite of rather than because of their religious character. For religious institutions

simply share benefits which government makes generally available to educational, charitable, and eleemosynary groups. There is no indication that taxing authorities have used such benefits in any way to subsidize worship or foster belief in God. And as among religious beneficiaries, the tax exemption or deduction can be truly nondiscriminatory, available on equal terms to small as well as large religious bodies, to popular and unpopular sects, and to those organizations which reject as well as those which accept a belief in God.

E. *Religious Considerations in Public Welfare Programs.*—Since government may not support or directly aid religious *activities* without violating the Establishment Clause, there might be some doubt whether nondiscriminatory programs of governmental aid may constitutionally include *individuals* who become eligible wholly or partially for religious reasons. For example, it might be suggested that where a State provides unemployment compensation generally to those who are unable to find suitable work, it may not extend such benefits to persons who are unemployed by reason of religious beliefs or practices without thereby establishing the religion to which those persons belong. Therefore, the argument runs, the State may avoid an establishment only by singling out and excluding such persons on the ground that religious beliefs or practices have made them potential beneficiaries. Such a construction would, it seems to me, require government to impose religious discriminations and disabilities, thereby jeopardizing the free exercise of religion, in order to avoid what is thought to constitute an establishment.

The inescapable flaw in the argument, I suggest, is its quite unrealistic view of the aims of the Establishment Clause. The Framers were not concerned with the effects of certain incidental aids to individual worshippers which come about as byproducts of general and nondiscriminatory welfare programs. If such benefits serve to make easier or less expensive the practice of a particular creed, or of all religions, it can hardly be said that the purpose of the program is in any way religious, or that the consequence of its nondiscriminatory application is to create the forbidden degree of interdependence between secular and sectarian institutions. I cannot therefore accept the suggestion, which seems to me implicit in the argument outlined here, that every judicial or administrative construction which is designed to prevent a public welfare program from abridging the free exercise of religious beliefs, is for that reason *ipso facto* and establishment of religion.

F. *Activities Which, Though Religious in Origin, Have Ceased to Have Religious Meaning.*—As we noted in our *Sunday Law* decisions, nearly every criminal law on the books can be traced to some religious principle or inspiration. But that does not make the present enforcement of the criminal law in any sense an establishment of religion, simply because it accords with widely held religious principles. As we said in *McGowan* v. *Maryland* [1961] . . . "the 'Establishment' Clause does not ban federal or state regulation of conduct whose reason or effect merely happens to coincide or harmonize with the tenets of some or all religions." This rationale suggests that the use of the motto "In God We Trust" on currency, on documents and public buildings and the like may not offend the clause. It is not that the use of those four words can be dismissed as "de minimis"—for I suspect there would be intense opposition to the abandonment of that motto. The truth is that we have simply interwoven the motto so deeply into the fabric of our civil polity that its present use may well not present that type of involvement which the First Amendment prohibits.

This general principle might also serve to insulate the various patriotic exercises and activities used in the public schools and elsewhere which, whatever may have been their origins, no longer have a religious purpose or meaning. The reference to divinity in the revised pledge of allegiance, for example, may merely recognize the historical fact that our Nation was believed to have been founded "under God." Thus reciting the pledge may be no more of a religious exercise than the reading aloud of Lincoln's Gettysburg Address, which contains an allusion to the same historical fact. . . .

MR. JUSTICE STEWART, dissenting:

The First Amendment declares that "Congress shall make no law respecting an establishment of religion, or prohibiting the free exercise thereof. . . ." It is, I think, a fallacious oversimplification to regard these two provisions as establishing a single constitutional standard of "separation of church and state," which can be mechanically applied in every case to delineate the required boundaries between government and religion. We err in the first place if we do not recognize, as a matter of history and as a matter of the imperatives of our free society, that religion and government must necessarily interact in countless ways. Secondly, the fact is that while in many contexts the Establishment Clause and the Free Exercise Clause fully complement each other, there are areas in which a doctrinaire reading of the Establishment Clause leads to irreconcilable conflict with the Free Exercise Clause.

A single obvious example should suffice to make the point. Spending federal funds to employ chaplains for the armed forces might be said to violate the Establishment Clause. Yet a lonely soldier stationed at some faraway outpost could surely complain that a government which did *not* provide him the opportunity for pastoral guidance was affirmatively prohibiting the free exercise of his religion.

And such examples could readily be multiplied. The short of the matter is simply that the two relevant clauses of the First Amendment cannot accurately be reflected in a sterile metaphor which by its very nature may distort rather than illumine the problems in a particular case. . . .

That the central value embodied in the First Amendment—and, more particularly, in the guarantee of "liberty" contained in the Fourteenth—is the safeguarding of an individual's right to free exercise of his religion has been consistently recognized. . . .

It is this concept of constitutional protection embodied in our decisions which makes the cases before us such difficult ones for me. For there is involved in these cases a substantial free exercise claim on the part of those who affirmatively desire to have their children's school day open with the reading of passages from the Bible. . . .

What seems to me to be of paramount importance, then, is recognition of the fact that the claim advanced here in favor of Bible reading is sufficiently substantial to make simple reference to the constitutional phrase "establishment of religion" as inadequate an analysis of the cases before us as the ritualistic invocation of the nonconstitutional phrase "separation of church and state." What these cases compel, rather, is an analysis of just what the "neutrality" is which is required by the interplay of the Establishment and Free Exercise Clauses of the First Amendment, as imbedded in the Fourteenth.

The dangers both to government and to religion inherent in official support of instruction in the tenets of various religious sects are absent in the present cases, which involve only a reading from the Bible unaccompanied by comments which might otherwise constitute instruction. Indeed, since, from all that appears in either record, any teacher who does not

wish to do so is free not to participate, it cannot even be contended that some infinitesimal part of the salaries paid by the State are made contingent upon the performance of a religious function. . . .

To be specific, it seems to me clear that certain types of exercises would present situations in which no possibility of coercion on the part of secular officials could be claimed to exist. Thus, if such exercises were held either before or after the official school day, or if the school schedule were such that participation were merely one among a number of desirable alternatives, it could hardly be contended that the exercises did anything more than to provide an opportunity for the voluntary expression of religious belief. On the other hand, a law which provided for religious exercises during the school day and which contained no excusal provision would obviously be unconstitutionally coercive upon those who did not wish to participate. And even under a law containing an excusal provision, if the exercises were held during the school day, and no equally desirable alternative were provided by the school authorities, the likelihood that children might be under at least some psychological compulsion to participate would be great. In a case such as the latter, however, I think we would err if we *assumed* such coercion in the absence of any evidence. . . .

What our Constitution indispensably protects is the freedom of each of us, be he Jew or Agnostic, Christian or Atheist, Buddhist or Freethinker, to believe or disbelieve, to worship or not worship, to pray or keep silent, according to his own conscience, uncoerced and unrestrained by government. It is conceivable that these school boards, or even all school boards, might eventually find it impossible to administer a system of religious exercises during school hours in such a way as to meet this constitutional standard—in such a way as completely to free from any kind of official coercion those who do not affirmatively want to participate. But I think we must not assume that school boards so lack the qualities of inventive-ness and good will as to make impossible the achievement of that goal.

I would remand both cases for further hearings.

What overlap does Justice Clark note between the establishment and free exercise clauses? The test of the constitutionality of a legislative enactment under the establishment clause is, writes Clark, whether or not the enactment advances or inhibits religion. Is this test less ambiguous than the standards applied by the Court in *Engel* v. *Vitale*? Would Justice Stewart, in *Engel*, have changed his dissenting opinion if he had applied the criteria outlined by Clark in the *Abington* case? How did Clark apply the test to the cases under consideration to arrive at the conclusion that the Pennsylvania and Baltimore practices were a violation of the establishment clause? Under what circumstances would the Court permit the teaching of religion in public schools?

Justice Brennan, in his concurring opinion, emphasizes the importance of government neutrality towards religion, a principle frequently expressed by the Court in defining the establishment clause. Brennan writes that the First Amendment "commands not official hostility toward religion, but only a strict neutrality in matters of religion." What conflicts does Brennan find between the establishment and free exercise clauses? How does Brennan apply his establishment criteria to: (1) invocational prayers in legislative chambers; (2) teaching about the Bible in public schools; (3) tax exemptions for churches and religious institutions; (4) government aid to church members as a byproduct of welfare programs; (5) state regulation of conduct which produces a result that harmonizes with the tenets of some or all religions; and (6) patriotic exercises and activities in public schools that make reference to God, such as the Pledge of Allegiance?

What establishment and free exercise criteria does Justice Stewart apply to the case in his dissenting opinion? What conflicts does he cite between the establishment and free exercise clauses?

The Sunday Closing Law Cases and the Establishment Clause

Four cases arose in 1961 challenging the constitutionality of state laws requiring the closing of business establishments on Sunday on the basis that they were "laws respecting an establishment of religion or prohibiting the free exercise thereof." *McGowan* v. *Maryland* (1961), cited by Clark and Brennan in their *Abington* opinions, was one of these cases. The Court held that the appellants could challenge the law only under the establishment clause because they "allege only economic injury to themselves; they do not allege any infringement of their own religious freedoms due to Sunday closing."[7] In his opinion for the Court, Chief Justice Warren recognized that the

[7]McGowan v. Maryland, 366 U.S. 420, 429 (1961).

Sunday closing laws were motivated by religious forces. However, he concluded that in the modern context most of the Sunday closing laws "are of a secular rather than of a religious character, and . . . they bear no relationship to establishment of religion as those words are used in the Constitution. . . . The present purpose and effect of most of them is to provide a uniform day of rest for all citizens; the fact that this day is Sunday, a day of particular significance for the dominant Christian sects, does not bar the state from achieving its secular goals."[8] While choosing Sunday as the closing day has an incidental effect of benefiting certain religions, choosing another day would violate the principle of state neutrality toward religion because it would exhibit hostility towards those sects for which Sunday is a day of religious observance.

THE REQUIREMENT OF SECULAR PURPOSE AND EFFECT

The establishment clause criteria announced by the Court in the *Abington* case requires government action to have a secular purpose and a "primary [secular] effect that neither advances nor inhibits religion." In the following case the Court applied this criteria in reviewing the constitutionality of a New York law requiring local school boards to lend textbooks both to public and to private school children.

Board of Education v. *Allen*

392 U.S. 236; 88 S. Ct. 1923; 20 L. Ed. 2d 1060 (1968)

MR. JUSTICE WHITE delivered the opinion of the Court:

A law of the State of New York requires local public school authorities to lend textbooks free of charge to all students in grades seven through 12; students attending private schools are included. This case presents the question whether this statute is a "law respecting an establishment of religion, or prohibiting the free exercise thereof," and so in conflict with the First and Fourteenth Amendments to the Constitution, because it authorizes the loan of textbooks to students attending parochial schools. We hold that the law is not in violation of the Constitution.

Until 1965, § 701 of the Education Law of the State of New York authorized public school boards to designate textbooks for use in the public schools, to purchase such books with public funds, and to rent or sell the books to public school students. In 1965 the Legislature amended § 701, basing the amendments on findings that the "public welfare and safety require that the state and local communities give assistance to educational programs which are important to our national defense and the general welfare of the state." Beginning with the 1966–1967 school year, local school boards were required to purchase textbooks and lend them without charge "to all children residing in such

[8]Ibid., pp. 445–446.

district who are enrolled in grades seven to twelve of a public or private school which complies with the compulsory education law." . . .

[A local school board challenged the law as a violation of the establishment clause because public funds were used for textbook loans to parochial school children. The highest state court sustained the law.]

Everson and later cases have shown that the line between state neutrality to religion and state support of religion is not easy to locate. "The constitutional standard is the separation of Church and State. The problem, like many problems in constitutional law, is one of degree." . . . Based on *Everson, Zorach, McGowan,* and other cases, *Abington School District* v. *Schempp* [1963] . . . fashioned a test subscribed to by eight Justices for distinguishing between forbidden involvements of the State with religion and those contacts which the Establishment Clause permits:

The test may be stated as follows: what are the purpose and the primary effect of the enactment? If either is the advancement or inhibition of religion then the enactment exceeds the scope of legislative power as circumscribed by the Constitution. That is to say that to withstand the strictures of the Establishment Clause there must be a secular legislative purpose and a primary effect that neither advances nor inhibits religion. *Everson* v. *Board of Education.* . . .

This test is not easy to apply, but the citation of *Everson* by the *Schempp* Court to support its general standard made clear how the *Schempp* rule would be applied to the facts of *Everson*. The statute upheld in *Everson* would be considered a law having "a secular legislative purpose and a primary effect that neither advances nor inhibits religion." We reach the same result with respect to the New York law requiring school books to be loaned free of charge to all students in specified grades.

The express purpose of § 701 was stated by the New York Legislature to be furtherance of the educational opportunities available to the young. Appellants have shown us nothing about the necessary effects of the statute that is contrary to its stated purpose. The law merely makes available to all children the benefits of a general program to lend school books free of charge. Books are furnished at the request of the pupil and ownership remains, at least technically, in the State. Thus no funds or books are furnished to parochial schools, and the financial benefit is to parents and children, not to schools. Perhaps free books make it more likely that some children choose to attend a sectarian school, but that was true of the state-paid bus fares in *Everson* and does not alone demonstrate an unconstitutional degree of support for a religious institution.

Of course books are different from buses. Most bus rides have no inherent religious significance, while religious books are common. However, the language of § 701 [of the Education Law] does not authorize the loan of religious books, and the State claims no right to distribute religious literature. Although the books loaned are those required by the parochial school for use in specific courses, each book loaned must be approved by the public school authorities; only secular books may receive approval. The law was construed by the Court of Appeals of New York as "merely making available secular textbooks at the request of the individual student," and the record contains no suggestion that religious books have been loaned. Absent evidence, we cannot assume that school authorities, who constantly face the same problem in selecting textbooks for use in the public schools, are unable to distinguish between secular and religious books or that they will not honestly discharge their duties under the law. In judging the validity of the statute on this record we must proceed on the assumption that books loaned to students are books that are not unsuitable for use in the public schools because of religious content.

The major reason offered by appellants for distinguishing free textbooks from free bus fares is that books, but not buses, are critical to the teaching process, and in a sectarian school that process is employed to teach religion. However, this Court has long recognized that religious schools pursue two goals, religious instruction and secular education. In the leading case of *Pierce* v. *Society of Sisters* [1925] . . . the Court held that although it would not question Oregon's power to compel school attendance or require that the attendance be at an institution meeting State-imposed requirements as to quality and nature of curriculum, Oregon had not shown that its interest in secular education required that all children attend publicly operated schools. A premise of this holding was the view that the State's interest in education would be served sufficiently by reliance on the secular teaching that accompanied religious training in the schools maintained by the Society of Sisters. Since *Pierce,* a substantial body of case law has confirmed the power of the States to insist that attendance at private schools, if it is to satisfy state compulsory-attendance laws, be at institutions which provide minimum hours of instruction, employ teachers of specified training, and cover prescribed subjects of instruction. Indeed, the State's interest in assuring that these standards are being met has been considered a sufficient reason for refusing to accept instruction at home as compliance with compulsory education statutes. These cases were a sensible corollary of *Pierce* v. *Society of Sisters:* if the State must satisfy its interest in secular education through the instrument of private schools, it has a proper interest in the manner in which those schools perform their secular educational function. Another corollary was *Cochran* v. *Louisiana State Board of Education* [1930] . . . where appellants said that a statute requiring school books to be furnished without charge to all students, whether they attended public or private schools, did not serve a "public purpose," and so offended the Fourteenth Amendment. Speaking through Chief Justice Hughes, the Court summarized as follows its conclusion that Louisiana's interest in the secular education being provided by private schools made provision of textbooks to students in those schools a properly public concern: "[The State's] interest is education, broadly; its method, comprehensive. Individual interests are aided only as the common interest is safeguarded." . . .

Underlying these cases, and underlying also the legislative judgments that have preceded the Court decisions, has been a recognition that private education has played and is playing a significant and valuable role in raising national levels of knowledge, competence, and experience. Americans care about the quality of the secular education available to their children. They have considered high quality education to be an indispensable ingredient for achieving the kind of nation, and the kind of citizenry, that they have desired to create. Considering this attitude, the continued willingness to rely on private school systems, including parochial systems, strongly suggests that a wide segment of informed opinion, legislative and otherwise, has found that those schools do an acceptable job of providing secular education to their students. This judgment is further evidence that parochial schools are performing, in addition to their sectarian function, the task of secular education.

Against this background of judgment and experience, unchallenged in the meager record before us in this case, we cannot agree with appellants either that all teaching in a sectarian school is religious or that the processes of secular and religious training are so intertwined that secular textbooks furnished to students by the public are in fact instrumental in the teaching of religion. This case comes to us after summary judgment entered on the pleadings. Nothing in this record supports the proposition that all textbooks, whether they deal with mathematics, physics, foreign languages, history, or literature, are used by the parochial schools to teach religion. No evidence has been offered about particular schools, particular courses, particular teachers, or particular books. We are unable to hold, based solely on judicial notice, that this statute results in unconstitutional involvement of the State with religious instruction or that § 701, for this or the other reasons urged, is a law respecting the establishment of religion within the meaning of the First Amendment.

Appellants also contend that § 701 offends the Free Exercise Clause of the First Amendment. However, "it is necessary in a free exercise case for one to show the coercive effect of the enactment as it operates against him in the practice of his religion," *Abington School District* v. *Schempp* [1963] . . . and appellants have not contended that the New York law in any way coerces them as individuals in the practice of their religion.

The judgment is affirmed.

Mr. Justice Harlan, concurring:
Although I join the opinion and judgment of the Court, I wish to emphasize certain of the principles which I believe to be central to the determination of this case, and which I think are implicit in the Court's decision. . . .
. . . I would hold that where the contested governmental activity is calculated to achieve nonreligious purposes other-

wise within the competence of the State, and where the activity does not involve the State "so significantly and directly in the realm of the sectarian as to give rise to . . . divisive influences and inhibitions of freedom," . . . it is not forbidden by the religious clauses of the First Amendment.

In my opinion, § 701 of the Education Law of New York does not employ religion as its standard for action or inaction, and is not otherwise inconsistent with these principles.

Mr. Justice Black, dissenting:
. . . The *Everson* and *McCollum* cases plainly interpret the First and Fourteenth Amendments as protecting the taxpayers of a State from being compelled to pay taxes to their government to support the agencies of private religious organizations the taxpayers oppose. To authorize a State to tax its residents for such church purposes is to put the State squarely in the religious activities of certain religious groups that happen to be strong enough politically to write their own religious preferences and prejudices into the laws. This links state and churches together in controlling the lives and destinies of our citizenship—a citizenship composed of people of myriad religious faiths, some of them bitterly hostile to and completely intolerant of the others. It was to escape laws precisely like this that a large part of the Nation's early immigrants fled to this country. . . .

[B]ooks for use by sectarian schools, . . . although "secular," realistically will in some way inevitably tend to propagate the religious views of the favored sect. Books are the most essential tool of education since they contain the resources of knowledge which the educational process is designed to exploit. In this sense it is not difficult to distinguish books, which are the heart of any school, from bus fares, which provide a convenient and helpful general public transportation service. With respect to the former, state financial support actively and directly assists the teaching and propagation of sectarian religious viewpoints in clear conflict with the First Amendment's establishment bar; with respect to the latter, the State merely provides a general and nondiscriminatory transportation service in no way related to substantive religious views and beliefs. . . .

. . . It requires no prophet to foresee that on the argument used to support this law others could be upheld providing for state or federal government funds to buy property on which to erect religious school buildings or to erect the buildings themselves, to pay the salaries of the religious school teachers, and finally to have the sectarian religious groups cease to rely on voluntary contributions of members of their sects while waiting for the Government to pick up all the bills for the religious schools. . . . The First Amendment's prohibition against governmental establishment of religion was written on the assumption that state aid to religion and religious schools generates discord, disharmony, hatred, and strife among our people, and that any government that supplies such aids is to that extent a tyranny. . . .

MR. JUSTICE DOUGLAS, dissenting:

. . . The statute on its face empowers each parochial school to determine for itself which textbooks will be eligible for loans to its students, for the Act provides that the only text which the State may provide is "a book which a pupil is required to use as a text for a semester or more in a particular class in the school he legally attends." New York Education Law § 701, subd. 2. This initial and crucial selection is undoubtedly made by the parochial school's principal or its individual instructors, who are, in the case of Roman Catholic schools, normally priests or nuns.

The next step under the Act is an "individual request" for an eligible textbook, but the State Education Department has ruled that a pupil may make his request to the local public board of education through a "private school official." Local boards have accordingly provided for those requests to be made by the individual or "by groups or classes." And forms for textbook requisitions to be filled out by the head of the private school are provided.

The role of the local public school board is to decide whether to veto the selection made by the parochial school. This is done by determining first whether the text has been or should be "approved" for use in public schools and second whether the text is "secular," "nonreligious," or "non-sectarian." The local boards apparently have broad discretion in exercising this veto power.

Thus the statutory system provides that the parochial school will ask for the books that it wants. Can there be the slightest doubt that the head of the parochial school will select the book or books that best promote its sectarian creed?

If the board of education supinely submits by approving and supplying the sectarian or sectarian-oriented textbooks, the struggle to keep church and state separate has been lost. If the board resists, then the battle line between church and state will have been drawn and the contest will be on to keep the school board independent or to put it under church domination and control.

Whatever may be said of *Everson,* there is nothing ideological about a bus. There is nothing ideological about a school lunch, or a public nurse, or a scholarship. The constitutionality of such public aid to students in parochial schools turns on considerations not present in this textbook case. The textbook goes to the very heart of education in a parochial school. It is the chief, although not solitary, instrumentality for propagating a particular religious creed or faith. How can we possibly approve such state aid to a religion? A parochial school textbook may contain many, many more seeds of creed and dogma than a prayer. Yet we struck down in *Engel* v. *Vitale* . . . an official New York prayer for its public schools, even though it was not plainly denominational. For we emphasized the violence done the Establishment Clause when the power was given religious-political groups "to write their own prayers into law." . . . That risk is compounded here by giving parochial schools the initiative in selecting the textbooks they desire to be furnished at public expense. . . .

MR. JUSTICE FORTAS, dissenting:

The majority opinion of the Court upholds the New York statute by ignoring a vital aspect of it. Public funds are used to buy, for students in sectarian schools, textbooks which are selected and prescribed by the sectarian schools themselves. As my Brother Douglas points out, despite the transparent camouflage that the books are furnished to students, the reality is that they are selected and their use is prescribed by the sectarian authorities. The child must use the prescribed book. He cannot use a different book prescribed for use in the public schools. The State cannot choose the book to be used. It is true that the public school boards must "approve" the book selected by the sectarian authorities; but this has no real significance. The purpose of these provisions is to hold out promise that the books will be "secular"; but the fact remains that the books are chosen by and for the sectarian schools.

It is misleading to say, as the majority opinion does, that the New York "law merely makes available to all children the benefits of a general program to lend school books free of charge." This is not a "general" program. It is a specific program to use state funds to buy books prescribed by sectarian schools which, in New York, are primarily Catholic, Jewish, and Lutheran sponsored schools. It could be called a "general" program only if the school books made available to all children were precisely the same—the books selected for and used in the public schools. But this program is not one in which all children are treated alike, regardless of where they go to school. This program, in its unconstitutional features, is hand-tailored to satisfy the specific needs of sectarian schools. Children attending such schools are given special books—books selected by the sectarian authorities. How can this be other than the use of public money to aid those sectarian establishments?

It is also beside the point, in my opinion, to "assume," as the majority opinion does, that "books loaned to students are books that are not unsuitable for use in the public schools because of religious content." The point is that the books furnished to students of sectarian schools are selected by the religious authorities and are prescribed by them.

This case is not within the principle of *Everson* v. *Board of Education* [1947]. . . . Apart from the differences between textbooks and bus rides, the present statute does not call for extending to children attending sectarian schools the same service or facility extended to children in public schools. This statute calls for furnishing special, separate, and particular books, specially, separately, and particularly chosen by religious sects or their representatives for use in their sectarian schools. This is the infirmity, in my opinion. This is the feature that makes it impossible, in my view, to reach any conclusion other than that this statute is an unconstitutional use of public funds to support an establishment of religion.

This is the feature of the present statute that makes it totally inaccurate to suggest, as the majority does here, that furnishing these specially selected books for use in sectarian schools is like "public provision of police and fire protection, sewage facilities, and streets and sidewalks.". . . These are furnished to all alike. They are not selected on the basis of spec-ification by a religious sect. And patrons of any one sect do not receive services or facilities different from those accorded members of other religions or agnostics or even atheists.

I would reverse the judgment below.

On what evidence does the Court base its conclusion that the New York State law has a secular purpose and effect? On what grounds is the free exercise challenge to the law rejected?

Is Justice Black's dissent inconsistent with his majority opinions in the *Everson* and *McCollum* cases? Does Justice Black find a sectarian purpose in and effect from the New York law?

How does Justice Douglas distinguish the facts of *Everson* from those of the *Allen* case?

Do Black, Douglas, and Fortas apply the secular purpose and effect standard in their dissents?

The Extension of Government Aid to Sectarian Schools from Textbooks to Auxiliary Services

In *Meek* v. *Pittinger* (1975) the Court confronted the question of the constitutionality of a state law that authorized public school authorities not only to lend textbooks to parochial school *students* but also to lend instructional material and equipment to parochial *schools* and supply professional staff and supportive materials to provide auxiliary services such as guidance and speech counseling to parochial schools. The Court held that the loan of textbooks did not violate the establishment clause of the First Amendment because the books were loaned directly to the students, not to the schools, and the financial benefits from the program were to the parents and children. Moreover, the statute had a secular purpose in lending textbooks free of charge to all school children in the state. The Court found that there was no showing that the books were of a religious nature or were used for other than secular purposes.

While upholding the textbook loan provision of the state law in *Meek*, the Court found the other provisions of the state law authorizing the provision of instructional materials, staff, and auxiliary services to nonpublic schools to be a violation of the establishment clause. The instructional materials, wrote the Court, were supplied not directly to the school children, but to the schools themselves, and since 75 percent of the nonpublic schools were church related, this constituted direct and substantial aid for religious activities. Staff and auxiliary services were provided directly to the school children, but they were supplied only on the premises of the school, requiring contact between the public and sectarian school authorities to assure that teachers and counselors would play a strictly nonideological role, which resulted in an unconstitutional entanglement between church and state. Finally, the Court concluded that the annual appropriations required to support the program raised the likely prospect "of repeated confrontation between proponents and opponents of the auxiliary services program." The act thus provides successive opportunities for political fragmentation and division along religious lines, one of the principal evils against which the establishment clause was intended to protect.[9]

In *Wolman* v. *Walter*, 433 U.S. 229 (1977), the Court went beyond its *Meek* decision in upholding portions of an Ohio statute that authorized public funds to be spent for the purchase of secular textbooks for nonpublic school children, that supplied nonpublic school students with standardized test and scoring services used in the public schools, and that provided diagnostic, therapeutic, and remedial services to nonpublic school students. Provisions of the law supplying nonpublic school students with instructional materials, equipment, and field trip services were held to violate the establishment clause. The Court found there was no reason to presume that the staff, which was the same for both public and nonpublic schools, supplying speech, hearing, and psychological diagnostic services, would engage in religious instruction in parochial schools. Moreover, these services were to be performed off the nonpublic school premises. The textbook provisions of the law were upheld on the basis of the same reasoning and rule of law applied in the *Allen* and *Meek* cases.

The Court held that the public provision of the instructional materials and equipment to nonpublic school students was a violation of the establishment clause in the *Wolman* opinion. Even though the Ohio law had been written to satisfy the objections of the Court to loans of instructional material and equipment by providing that they were to be loaned to the pupils or their parents rather than to the nonpublic schools and were to be limited to secular material and equipment, the Court found that such aid would inevitably support the religious role of the nonpublic schools. The Court found that it was impossible to separate the secular education function of the schools from their sectarian role. The provision of field trips to nonpublic schools at public expense was also held to be a violation of the establishment clause because such trips were under the control of sectarian schools, and public school authorities would not be able to ensure that such trips had a secular purpose without causing excessive church-state entanglement.

Secular Purpose, Effect, and the Problem of "Entanglement"

The *Meek* and *Wolman* opinions stressed the establishment standard of secular purpose and effect. The Court held that to pass muster under the establishment clause legislation must not produce "excessive entanglement" between state and church. Interwoven with these standards are the requirements that the state must remain neutral towards religion by maintaining a "benevolent neutrality" and must demonstrate that the "primary effect" of legislation is secular and not religious. Various of these criteria were applied

[9]Meek v. Pettinger, 421 U.S. 349, 372 (1975).

by the Court in the following case that reviewed the constitutionality of a New York State law granting tax exemption for real or personal property used exclusively for religious purposes.

Walz v. Tax Commission

397 U.S. 664; 90 S. Ct. 1409; 25 L. Ed. 2d 697 (1970)

MR. CHIEF JUSTICE BURGER delivered the opinion of the Court:

Appellant, owner of real estate in Richmond County, New York, sought an injunction in the New York courts to prevent the New York City Tax Commission from granting property tax exemptions to religious organizations for religious properties used solely for religious worship. The exemption from state taxes is authorized by . . . the New York Constitution. . . .

The essence of apppellant's contention was that the New York City Tax Commission's grant of an exemption to church property indirectly requires the appellant to make a contribution to religious bodies and thereby violates provisions prohibiting establishment of religion under the First Amendment which under the Fourteenth Amendment is binding on the States.

I

. . . The Establishment and Free Exercise Clauses of the First Amendment are not the most precisely drawn portions of the Constitution. The sweep of the absolute prohibitions in the Religion Clauses may have been calculated; but the purpose was to state an objective, not to write a statute. In attempting to articulate the scope of the two Religion Clauses, the Court's opinions reflect the limitations inherent in formulating general principles on a case-by-case basis. The considerable internal inconsistency in the opinions of the Court derives from what, in retrospect, may have been too sweeping utterances on aspects of these clauses that seemed clear in relation to the particular cases but have limited meaning as general principles.

The Court has struggled to find a neutral course between the two Religion Clauses, both of which are cast in absolute terms, and either of which, if expanded to a logical extreme, would tend to clash with the other. . . .

The course of constitutional neutrality in this area cannot be an absolutely straight line; rigidity could well defeat the basic purpose of these provisions, which is to insure that no religion be sponsored or favored, none commanded, and none inhibited. The general principle deducible from the First Amendment and all that has been said by the Court is this: that we will not tolerate either governmentally established religion or governmental interference with religion. Short of those expressly proscribed governmental acts there is room for play in the joints productive of a benevolent neutrality which will permit religious exercise to exist without sponsorship and without interference.

Each value judgment under the Religion Clauses must therefore turn on whether particular acts in question are intended to establish or interfere with religious beliefs and practices or have the effect of doing so. Adherence to the policy of neutrality that derives from an accommodation of the Establishment and Free Exercise Clauses has prevented the kind of involvement that would tip the balance toward government control of churches or governmental restraint on religious practice.

Adherents of particular faiths and individual churches frequently take strong positions on public issues including, as this case reveals in the several briefs *amici*, vigorous advocacy of legal or constitutional positions. Of course, churches as much as secular bodies and private citizens have that right. No perfect or absolute separation is really possible; the very existence of the Religion Clauses is an involvement of sorts—one that seeks to mark boundaries to avoid excessive entanglement.

The hazards of placing too much weight on a few words or phrases of the Court is abundantly illustrated within the pages of the Court's opinion in *Everson*. Mr. Justice Black, writing for the Court's majority, said the First Amendment

means at least this: Neither a state nor the Federal Government can . . . pass laws which aid one religion, aid all religions, or prefer one religion over another. . . .

Yet he had no difficulty in holding that:

Measured by these standards, we cannot say that the First Amendment prohibits New Jersey from spending tax-raised funds to pay the bus fares of parochial school pupils as a part of a general program under which it pays the fares of pupils attending public and other schools. *It is undoubtedly true that children are helped to get to church schools. There is even a possibility that some of the children might not be sent to the church schools if the parents were compelled to pay their children's bus fares out of their own pockets.* . . . (Emphasis added.)

The Court did not regard such "aid" to schools teaching a particular religious faith as any more a violation of the Establishment Clause than providing "state-paid policemen, detailed to protect children . . . [at the schools] from the very real hazards of traffic. . . ."

Mr. Justice Jackson, in perplexed dissent in *Everson*, noted that

the undertones of the opinion, advocating complete and uncompromising separation

. . . seem utterly discordant with its conclusion. . . .

Perhaps so. One can sympathize with Mr. Justice Jackson's logical analysis but agree with the Court's eminently sensible and realistic application of the language of the Establishment Clause. In *Everson* the Court declined to construe the Religion Clauses with a literalness that would undermine the ultimate constitutional objective as illuminated by history. Surely, bus transportation and police protection to pupils who receive religious instruction "aid" that particular religion to maintain schools that plainly tend to assure future adherents to a particular faith by having control of their total education at an early age. No religious body that maintains schools would deny this as an affirmative if not dominant policy of church schools. But if as in *Everson* buses can be provided to carry and policemen to protect church school pupils, we fail to see how a broader range of police and fire protection given equally to all churches, along with non-profit hospitals, art galleries, and libraries receiving the same tax exemption, is different for purposes of the Religion Clauses.

Similarly, making textbooks available to pupils in parochial schools in common with public schools was surely an "aid" to the sponsoring churches because it relieved those churches of an enormous aggregate cost for those books. Supplying of costly teaching materials was not seen either as manifesting a legislative purpose to aid or as having a primary effect of aid contravening the First Amendment. *Board of Education* . . . v. *Allen,* [1968]. . . . In so holding the Court was heeding both its own prior decisions and our religious tradition. Mr. Justice Douglas, in *Zorach* v. *Clauson* . . . after recalling that we "are a religious people whose institutions presuppose a Supreme Being," went on to say:

We make room for as wide a variety of beliefs and creeds as the spiritual needs of man deem necessary. . . . *When the state encourages religious instruction . . . it follows the best of our traditions.* For it then respects the religious nature of our people and accommodates the public service to their spiritual needs. . . . (Emphasis added.)

With all the risks inherent in programs that bring about administrative relationships between public education bodies and church-sponsored schools, we have been able to chart a course that preserved the autonomy and freedom of religious bodies while avoiding any semblance of established religion. This is a "tightrope" and one we have successfully traversed.

II

The legislative purpose of a property tax exemption is neither the advancement nor the inhibition of religion; it is neither sponsorship nor hostility. New York, in common with the other States, has determined that certain entities that exist in a harmonious relationship to the community at large, and that foster its "moral or mental improvement," should not be inhibited in their activities by property taxation or the hazard of loss of those properties for nonpayment of taxes. It has not singled out one particular church or religious group or even churches as such; rather, it has granted exemption to all houses of religious worship within a broad class of property owned by non-profit, quasi-public corporations which include hospitals, libraries, playgrounds, scientific, professional, historical, and patriotic groups. The State has an affirmative policy that considers these groups as beneficial and stabilizing influences in community life and finds this classification useful, desirable, and in the public interest. Qualification for tax exemption is not perpetual or immutable; some tax-exempt groups lose that status when their activities take them outside the classification and new entities can come into being and qualify for exemption.

Governments have not always been tolerant of religious activity, and hostility toward religion has taken many shapes and forms—economic, political, and sometimes harshly oppressive. Grants of exemption historically reflect the concern of authors of constitutions and statutes as to the latent dangers inherent in the imposition of property taxes; exemption constitutes a reasonable and balanced attempt to guard against those dangers. The limits of permissible state accommodation to religion are by no means coextensive with the noninterference mandated by the Free Exercise Clause. To equate the two would be to deny a national heritage with roots in the Revolution itself. . . . We cannot read New York's statute as attempting to establish religion; it is simply sparing the exercise of religion from the burden of property taxation levied on private profit institutions.

We find it unnecessary to justify the tax exemption on the social welfare services or "good works" that some churches perform for parishioners and others—family counseling, aid to the elderly and the infirm, and to children. Churches vary substantially in the scope of such services; programs expand or contract according to resources and need. As public-sponsored programs enlarge, private aid from the church sector may diminish. The extent of social services may vary, depending on whether the church serves an urban or rural, a rich or poor constituency. To give emphasis to so variable an aspect of the work of religious bodies would introduce an element of governmental evaluation and standards as to the worth of particular social welfare programs, thus producing a kind of continuing day-to-day relationship which the policy of neutrality seeks to minimize. Hence, the use of a social welfare yardstick as a significant element to qualify for tax exemption could conceivably give rise to confrontations that could escalate to constitutional dimensions.

Determining that the legislative purpose of tax exemption is not aimed at establishing, sponsoring, or supporting religion does not end the inquiry, however. We must also be sure that the end result— the effect—is not an excessive government entanglement with religion. The test is inescapably one of degree. Either course, taxation of churches or exemption, occasions some degree of involvement with religion. Elimination of exemption would tend to expand the involvement of government by giving rise to tax valuation of church property, tax liens, tax foreclosures, and the direct confrontations and conflicts that follow in the train of those legal processes.

Granting tax exemptions to churches necessarily operates to afford an indirect economic benefit and also gives rise to some, but a lesser, involvement than taxing them. In analyzing either alternative the questions are whether the involvement is excessive, and whether it is a continuing one calling for official and continuing surveillance leading to an impermissible degree of entanglement. Obviously a direct money subsidy would be a relationship pregnant with involvement and, as with most governmental grant programs, could encompass sustained and detailed administrative relationships for enforcement of statutory or administrative standards, but that is not this case. The hazards of churches supporting government are hardly less in their potential than the hazards of government supporting churches; each relationship carries some involvement rather than the desired insulation and separation. We cannot ignore the instances in history when church support of government led to the kind of involvement we seek to avoid.

The grant of a tax exemption is not sponsorship since the government does not transfer part of its revenue to churches but simply abstains from demanding that the church support the state. No one has ever suggested that tax exemption has

converted libraries, art galleries, or hospitals into arms of the state or put employees "on the public payroll." There is no genuine nexus between tax exemption and establishment of religion. As Mr. Justice Holmes commented in a related context "a page of history is worth a volume of logic." *New York Trust Co.* v. *Eisner* [1921]. . . . The exemption creates only a minimal and remote involvement between church and state and far less than taxation of churches. It restricts the fiscal relationship between church and state, and tends to complement and reinforce the desired separation insulating each from the other.

Separation in this context cannot mean absence of all contact; the complexities of modern life inevitably produce some contact and the fire and police protection received by houses of religious worship are no more than incidental benefits accorded to all persons or institutions within a State's boundaries, along with many other exempt organizations. The appellant has not established even an arguable quantitative correlation between the payment of an ad valorem property tax and the receipt of these municipal benefits.

All of the 50 States provide for tax exemption of places of worship, most of them doing so by constitutional guarantees. For so long as federal income taxes have had any potential impact on churches—over 75 years—religious organizations have been expressly exempt from the tax. Such treatment is an "aid" to churches no more and no less in principle than the real estate tax exemption granted by States. Few concepts are more deeply embedded in the fabric of our national life, beginning with pre-Revolutionary colonial times, than for the government to exercise at the very least this kind of benevolent neutrality toward churches and religious exercise generally so long as none was favored over others and none suffered interference.

It is significant that Congress, from its earliest days, has viewed the Religion Clauses of the Constitution as authorizing statutory real estate tax exemption to religious bodies. . . .

It is obviously correct that no one acquires a vested or protected right in violation of the Constitution by long use, even when that span of time covers our entire national existence and indeed predates it. Yet an unbroken practice of according the exemption to churches, openly and by affirmative state action, not covertly or by state inaction, is not something to be lightly cast aside. . . .

Nothing in this national attitude toward religious tolerance and two centuries of uninterrupted freedom from taxation has given the remotest sign of leading to an established church or religion and on the contrary it has operated affirmatively to help guarantee the free exercise of all forms of religious belief. Thus, it is hardly useful to suggest that tax exemption is but the "foot in the door" or the "nose of the camel in the tent" leading to an established church. If tax exemption can be seen as this first step toward "establishment" of religion, as Mr. Justice Douglas fears, the second step has been long in coming. Any move that realistically "establishes" a church or tends to do so can be dealt with "while this Court sits." . . . .

Affirmed.

Justices Brennan and Harlan wrote separate dissenting opinions.

Mr. Justice Douglas, dissenting:
. . . Churches perform some functions that a State would constitutionally be empowered to perform. I refer to nonsectarian social welfare operations such as the care of orphaned children and the destitute and people who are sick. A tax exemption to agencies performing those functions would therefore be as constitutionally proper as the grant of direct subsidies to them. Under the First Amendment a State may not, however, provide worship if private groups fail to do so. . . .

That is a major difference between churches on the one hand and the rest of the nonprofit organizations on the other. Government could provide or finance operas, hospitals, historical societies, and all the rest because they represent social welfare programs within the reach of the police power. In contrast, government may not provide or finance worship because of the Establishment Clause any more than it may single out "atheistic" or "agnostic" centers or groups and create or finance them.

The Brookings Institution, writing in 1933, before the application of the Establishment Clause of the First Amendment to the States, said about tax exemptions of religious groups:

Tax exemption, no matter what its form, is essentially a government grant or subsidy. Such grants would seem to be justified only if the purpose for which they are made is one for which the legislative body *would be equally willing to make* a direct appropriation from public funds equal to the amount of the exemption. This test would not be met except in the case where the exemption is granted to encourage certain activities of private interests, which, if not thus performed, would have to be assumed by the government at an expenditure at least as great as the value of the exemption. (Emphasis added.)

Since 1947, when the Establishment Clause was made applicable to the States, that report would have to state that the exemption would be justified only where "the legislative body *could make*" an appropriation for the cause.

On the record of this case, the church *qua* nonprofit, chartible organization is intertwined with the church *qua* church. A church may use the same facilities, resources, and personnel in carrying out both its secular and its sectarian activities. The two are unitary and on the present record have not been separated one from the other. . . .

Whether a particular church seeking an exemption for its welfare work could constitutionally pass muster would depend on the special facts. The assumption is that the church is a purely private institution, promoting a sectarian cause. The creed, teaching, and beliefs of one may be undesirable or even repulsive to others. Its sectarian faith sets it apart from all others and makes it difficult to equate its constituency with the general public. The extent that its facilities are open to all may only indicate the nature of its proselytism. Yet though a church covers up its religious symbols in welfare work its welfare activities may merely be a phase of sectarian activity. I have said enough to indicate the nature of this tax exemption problem.

Direct financial aid to churches or tax exemptions to the church *qua* church is not, in my view, even arguably permitted. Sectarian causes are certainly not anti-public and many would rate their own church or perhaps all churches as the

highest form of welfare. The difficulty is that sectarian causes must remain in the private domain not subject to public control or subsidy. That seems to me to be the requirement of the Establishment Clause. . . .

If believers are entitled to public financial support, so are nonbelievers. A believer and nonbeliever under the present law are treated differently because of the articles of their faith. Believers are doubtless comforted that the cause of religion is being fostered by this legislation. Yet one of the mandates of the First Amendment is to promote a viable, pluralistic society and to keep government neutral, not only between sects, but also between believers and nonbelievers. The present involvement of government in religion may seem *de minimis*. But it is, I fear, a long step down the Establishment path. Perhaps I have been misinformed. But as I have read the Constitution and its philosophy, I gathered that independence was the price of liberty.

I conclude that this tax exemption is unconstitutional.

Does the Court explicitly or implicitly find a secular purpose and effect of the New York law? Would a law that granted tax exemption only to religious institutions be constitutional? What, in the Court's view, are the different implications between a tax exemption for and a direct money subsidy to religious institutions? How does Chief Justice Burger's majority opinion take into account historical precedent and custom? What importance does Burger attach to the fact that traditionally taxation of church property was viewed as a form of government hostility towards religion?

How does Justice Douglas reason in dissent that the New York exemption is unconstitutional? Under what circumstances would he uphold the law?

The *Walz* case added to the secular purpose and effect criteria of the establishment clause the requirement that statutes must not foster "an excessive government entanglement with religion." The Court summarized and applied its standards under the establishment clause in the following case reviewing a constitutional challenge to Pennsylvania and Rhode Island laws that provided nonpublic school teachers with salary supplements from public funds to deal with the financial crisis in public education.

Lemon v. Kurtzman

403 U.S. 602; 91 S. Ct. 2105; 29 L. Ed. 2d 745 (1971)

MR. CHIEF JUSTICE BURGER delivered the opinion of the Court:

These two appeals raise questions as to Pennsylvania and Rhode Island statutes providing state aid to church-related elementary and secondary schools.[10] Both statutes are challenged as violative of the Establishment and Free Exercise Clauses of the First Amendment and the Due Process Clause of the Fourteenth Amendment. . . .

The Rhode Island Salary Supplement Act was enacted in 1969. It rests on the legislative finding that the quality of education available in nonpublic elementary schools has been jeopardized by the rapidly rising salaries needed to attract competent and dedicated teachers. The Act authorizes state officials to supplement the salaries of teachers of secular subjects in nonpublic elementary schools by paying directly to a teacher an amount not in excess of 15 percent of his current annual salary. As supplemented, however, a nonpublic school teacher's salary cannot exceed the maximum paid to teachers in the State's public schools, and the recipient must be certified by the state board of education in substantially the same manner as public school teachers.

In order to be eligible for the Rhode Island salary supplement, the recipient must teach in a nonpublic school at which the average per-pupil expenditure on secular education is less than the average in the State's public schools during a specified period. Appellant State Commissioner of Education also requires eligible schools to submit financial data. If this information indicates a per-pupil expendi-

ture in excess of the statutory limitation, the records of the school in question must be examined in order to assess how much of the expenditure is attributable to secular education and how much to religious activity.

The Act also requires that teachers eligible for salary supplements must teach only those subjects that are offered in the State's public schools. They must use "only teaching materials which are used in the public schools." Finally, any teacher applying for a salary supplement must first agree in writing "not to teach a course in religion for so long as or during such time as he or she receives any salary supplements" under the Act. . . .

The court held a hearing at which extensive evidence was introduced concerning the nature of the secular instruction offered in the Roman Catholic schools whose teachers would be eligible for salary assistance under the Act. Although the court found that concern for religious values does not necessarily affect the content of secular subjects, it also found that the parochial school system was "an integral part of the religious mission of the Catholic Church."

The District Court concluded that the Act violated the Establishment Clause, holding that it fostered "excessive entanglement" between government and religion. In addition two judges thought that the Act had the impermissible effect of giving "significant aid to a religious enterprise." . . . . We affirm. . . .

Pennsylvania has adopted a program that has some but not all of the features of the Rhode Island program. The Pennsylvania Nonpublic Elementary and Secondary Education Act was passed in 1968 in response to a crisis that the Pennsylva-

[10]The Rhode Island Cases were Early v. DiCenso (No. 569) and Robinson v. DiCenso (No. 570). [Editor's Note.]

nia Legislature found existed in the State's nonpublic schools due to rapidly rising costs. . . .

The statute authorizes appellee state Superintendent of Public Instruction to "purchase" specified "secular educational services" from nonpublic schools. Under the "contracts" authorized by the statute, the State directly reimburses nonpublic schools solely for their actual expenditures for teachers' salaries, textbooks, and instructional materials. A school seeking reimbursement must maintain prescribed accounting procedures that identify the "separate" cost of the "secular educational service." These accounts are subject to state audit. . . .

There are several significant statutory restrictions on state aid. Reimbursement is limited to courses "presented in the curricula of the public schools." It is further limited "solely" to courses in the following "secular" subjects: mathematics, modern foreign languages, physical science, and physical education. Textbooks and instructional materials included in the program must be approved by the state Superintendent of Public Instruction. Finally, the statute prohibits reimbursement for any course that contains "any subject matter expressing religious teaching, or the morals or forms of worship of any sect."

. . . More than 96 percent of these pupils [receiving state aid] attend church-related schools, and most of these schools are affiliated with the Roman Catholic church. . . .

The District Court . . . held that the Act violated neither the Establishment nor the Free Exercise Clause, Chief Judge Hastie dissenting. We reverse. . . .

. . . Candor compels acknowledgment . . . that we can only dimly perceive the lines of demarcation in this extraordinarily sensitive area of constitutional law. . . .

Every analysis in this area must begin with consideration of the cumulative criteria developed by the Court over many years. Three such tests may be gleaned from our cases. First, the statute must have a secular legislative purpose; second, its principal or primary effect must be one that neither advances nor inhibits religion, *Board of Education* v. *Allen* [1968] . . . finally, the statute must not foster "an excessive government entanglement with religion." *Walz* v. *Tax Commission* [1970]. . . .

Inquiry into the legislative purposes of the Pennsylvania and Rhode Island statutes affords no basis for a conclusion that the legislative intent was to advance religion. . . .

The two legislatures . . . sought to create statutory restrictions designed to guarantee the separation between secular and religious educational functions and to ensure that State financial aid supports only the former. . . . We need not decide whether these legislative precautions restrict the principal or primary effect of the programs to the point where they do not offend the Religion Clauses, for we conclude that the cumulative impact of the entire relationship arising under the statutes in each State involves excessive entanglement between government and religion.

In *Walz* v. *Tax Commission* . . . the Court upheld state tax exemptions for real property owned by religious organizations and used for religious worship. That holding, however, tended to confine rather than enlarge the area of permissible state involvement with religious institutions by calling for close scrutiny of the degree of entanglement involved in the relationship. The objective is to prevent, as far as possible, the intrusion of either into the precincts of the other.

Our prior holdings do not call for total separation between church and state; total separation is not possible in an absolute sense. Some relationship between government and religious organizations is inevitable. . . . Fire inspections, building and

zoning regulations, and state requirements under compulsory school-attend-
ance laws are examples of necessary and
permissible contacts. . . . Judicial caveats
against entanglement must recognize that
the line of separation, far from being a
"wall," is a blurred, indistinct, and variable barrier depending on all the circumstances of a particular relationship. . . .

In order to determine whether the
government entanglement with religion is
excessive, we must examine the character
and purposes of the institutions that are
benefited, the nature of the aid that the
State provides, and the resulting relationship between the government and religious authority. . . . Here we find that
both statutes foster an impermissible degree of entanglement. . . .

The District Court made extensive
findings on the grave potential for excessive entanglement that inheres in the religious character and purpose of the Roman Catholic elementary schools of Rhode
Island. . . .

On the basis of these findings the District Court concluded that the parochial
schools constituted "an integral part of
the religious mission of the Catholic
Church." The various characteristics of
the schools make them "a powerful vehicle for transmitting the Catholic faith to
the next generation." This process of in-
culcating religious doctrine is, of course,
enhanced by the impressionable age of
the pupils, in primary schools particularly. In short, parochial schools involve
substantial religious activity and purpose.

The substantial religious character of
these church-related schools gives rise to
entangling church-state relationships of
the kind the Religion Clauses sought to
avoid. . . .

The dangers and corresponding entanglements are enhanced by the particular
form of aid that the Rhode Island Act
provides. Our decisions from *Everson* to
Allen have permitted the States to provide

church-related schools with secular, neutral, or nonideological services, facilities,
or materials. Bus transportation, school
lunches, public health services, and secular textbooks supplied in common to all
students were not thought to offend the
Establishment Clause. We note that the
dissenters in *Allen* seemed chiefly concerned with the pragmatic difficulties involved in ensuring the truly secular content of the textbooks provided at state
expense.

In *Allen* the Court refused to make assumptions, on a meager record, about the
religious content of the textbooks that the
State would be asked to provide. We cannot, however, refuse here to recognize
that teachers have a substantially different ideological character from books. In
terms of potential for involving some aspect of faith or morals in secular subjects,
a textbook's content is ascertainable, but a
teacher's handling of a subject is not. We
cannot ignore the danger that a teacher
under religious control and discipline
poses to the separation of the religious
from the purely secular aspects of pre-
college education. The conflict of functions inheres in the situation.

In our view the record shows these
dangers are present to a substantial
degree. . . .

Several teachers testified, however, that
they did not inject religion into their secular classes. And the District Court found
that religious values did not necessarily
affect the content of the secular instruction. But what has been recounted suggests the potential if not actual hazards of
this form of state aid. The teacher is employed by a religious organization, subject
to the direction and discipline of religious
authorities, and works in a system dedicated to rearing children in a particular
faith. . . .

We need not and do not assume that
teachers in parochial schools will be guilty
of bad faith or any conscious design to

evade the limitations imposed by the statute and the First Amendment. We simply recognize that a dedicated religious person, teaching in a school affiliated with his or her faith and operated to inculcate its tenets, will inevitably experience great difficulty in remaining religiously neutral. Doctrines and faith are not inculcated or advanced by neutrals. . . .

. . . [T]he State has therefore carefully conditioned its aid with pervasive restrictions. . . . A comprehensive, discriminating, and continuing state surveillance will inevitably be required to ensure that these restrictions are obeyed and the First Amendment otherwise respected. Unlike a book, a teacher cannot be inspected once so as to determine the extent and intent of his or her personal beliefs and subjective acceptance of the limitations imposed by the First Amendment. These prophylactic contacts will involve excessive and enduring entanglement between state and church.

There is another area of entanglement in the Rhode Island program that gives concern. . . . [S]tate inspection and evaluation of the religious content of a religious organization is fraught with the sort of entanglement that the Constitution forbids. It is a relationship pregnant with dangers of excessive government direction of church schools and hence of churches. . . .

The Pennsylvania statute also . . . fosters this kind of relationship. . . .

The Pennsylvania statute, moreover, has the further defect of providing state financial aid directly to the church-related school. This factor distinguishes both *Everson* and *Allen,* for in both those cases the Court was careful to point out that state aid was provided to the student and his parents—not to the church-related school. . . . The history of government grants of a continuing cash subsidy indicates that such programs have almost always been accompanied by varying measures of control and surveillance. The government cash grants before us now provide no basis for predicting that comprehensive measures of surveillance and controls will not follow. In particular the government's post-audit power to inspect and evaluate a church-related school's financial records and to determine which expenditures are religious and which are secular creates an intimate and continuing relationship between church and state.

A broader base of entanglement of yet a different character is presented by the divisive political potential of these state programs. In a community where such a large number of pupils are served by church-related schools, it can be assumed that state assistance will entail considerable political activity. Partisans of parochial schools, understandably concerned with rising costs and sincerely dedicated to both the religious and secular educational missions of their schools, will inevitably champion this cause and promote political action to achieve their goals. Those who oppose state aid, whether for constitutional, religious, or fiscal reasons, will inevitably respond and employ all of the usual political campaign techniques to prevail. Candidates will be forced to declare and voters to choose. It would be unrealistic to ignore the fact that many people confronted with issues of this kind will find their votes aligned with their faith.

Ordinarily political debate and division, however vigorous or even partisan, are normal and healthy manifestations of our democratic system of government, but political division along religious lines was one of the principal evils against which the First Amendment was intended to protect. . . . The potential divisiveness of such conflict is a threat to the normal political process. . . . To have States or communities divide on the issues presented by state aid to parochial schools would tend to confuse and obscure other issues of great urgency. We have an expanding array of vexing issues, local and national, domestic and international, to debate and divide on. It conflicts with our whole history and tradition to permit questions of the Religion Clauses to assume such importance in our legislatures and in our elections that they could divert attention from the myriad issues and problems that confront every level of government. . . .

Of course, as the Court noted in *Walz*, "[a]dherents of particular faiths and individual churches frequently take strong positions on public issues." . . . We could not expect otherwise, for religious values pervade the fabric of our national life. . . . [I]n *Walz* we dealt with a status under state tax laws for the benefit of all religious groups. Here we are confronted with successive and very likely permanent annual appropriations that benefit relatively few religious groups. Political fragmentation and divisiveness on religious lines are thus likely to be intensified.

The potential for political divisiveness related to religious belief and practice is aggravated in these two statutory programs by the need for continuing annual appropriations and the likelihood of larger and larger demands as costs and populations grow. . . .

In *Walz* it was argued that a tax exemption for places of religious worship would prove to be the first step in an inevitable progression leading to the establishment of state churches and state religion. That claim could not stand up against more than 200 years of virtually universal practice imbedded in our colonial experience and continuing into the present.

The progression argument, however, is more persuasive here. We have no long history of state aid to church-related educational institutions comparable to 200 years of tax exemption for churches. Indeed, the state programs before us today represent something of an innovation. We

have already noted that modern governmental programs have self-perpetuating and self-expanding propensities. These internal pressures are only enhanced when the schemes involve institutions whose legitimate needs are growing and whose interests have substantial political support. Nor can we fail to see that in constitutional adjudication some steps, which when taken were thought to approach "the verge," have become the platform for yet further steps. . . . The dangers are increased by the difficulty of perceiving in advance exactly where the "verge" of the precipice lies. As well as constituting an independent evil against which the Religion Clauses were intended to protect, involvement or entanglement between government and religion serves as a warning signal.

Finally, nothing we have said can be construed to disparage the role of church-related elementary and secondary schools in our national life. Their contribution has been and is enormous. Nor do we ignore their economic plight in a period of rising costs and expanding need. . . .

. . . The sole question is whether state aid to these schools can be squared with the dictates of the Religion Clauses. . . .

The judgment of the Rhode Island District Court in [*DiCenso*] is affirmed. The judgment of the Pennsylvania District Court in [*Lemon*] is reversed, and the case is remanded for further proceedings consistent with this opinion.

MR. JUSTICE MARSHALL took no part in the consideration or decision of [*Lemon*].

MR. JUSTICE DOUGLAS, whom MR. JUSTICE BLACK joins, concurring:
. . . The intrusion of government into religious schools through grants, supervision, or surveillance may result in establishment of religion in the constitutional sense when what the State does enthrones a particular sect for overt or subtle prop-

agation of its faith. Those activities of the State may also intrude on the Free Exercise Clause by depriving a teacher, under threats of reprisals, of the right to give sectarian construction or interpretation of, say, history and literature, or to use the teaching of such subjects to inculcate a religious creed or dogma. . . .

If the government closed its eyes to the manner in which these grants are actually used it would be allowing public funds to promote sectarian education. If it did not close its eyes but undertook the surveillance needed, it would, I fear, intermeddle in parochial affairs in a way that would breed only rancor and dissension. . . .

In my view the taxpayers' forced contribution to the parochial schools in the present cases violates the First Amendment.

MR. JUSTICE MARSHALL concurred in that portion of Douglas's opinion concerning *DiCenso*.

MR. JUSTICE BRENNAN agreed with the judgment in *DiCenso* but would reverse the judgment in *Lemon*.

MR. JUSTICE WHITE concurred in part and dissented in part.

What are the three tests mentioned by Chief Justice Burger for determining the constitutionality of statutes under the establishment clause? Does the Court give a clear definition of what constitutes an excessive government entanglement with religion? How does Burger apply the entanglement standard to overturn the statutes? What is the "broader base of entanglement" that the Court feels will result from the political effects of the state programs?

On the same day it decided *Lemon* v. *Kurtzman*, the Court applied the standards it had articulated under the establishment clause in reviewing the constitutionality of a federal program of aid for church-related institutions of higher learning in the following case.

Tilton v. Richardson

403 U.S. 672; 91 S. Ct. 2091; 29 L. Ed. 2d 790 (1971)

MR. CHIEF JUSTICE BURGER announced the judgment of the Court and an opinion in which MR. JUSTICE HARLAN, MR. JUSTICE STEWART, and MR. JUSTICE BLACKMUN join:

This appeal presents important constitutional questions as to federal aid for church-related colleges and universities under Title I of the Higher Education Facilities Act of 1963 . . . which provides construction grants for buildings and facilities used exclusively for secular educational purposes. . . .

The Act is administered by the United States Commissioner of Education. He advises colleges and universities applying for funds that under the Act no part of the project may be used for sectarian instruction, religious worship, or the programs of a divinity school. The Commissioner requires applicants to provide assurances that these restrictions will be respected. The United States retains a 20-year interest in any facility constructed with Title I funds. If, during this period, the recipient violates the statutory conditions, the United States is entitled to recover an amount equal to the proportion of its present value that the federal grant bore to the original cost of the facility. During the 20-year period, the statutory restrictions are enforced by the Office of Education primarily by way of on-site inspections. . . . The stated legislative purpose [to assist colleges] . . . in their efforts to accommodate rapidly growing numbers of youth . . . expresses a legitimate secular objective entirely appropriate for governmental action. . . .

. . . [T]he Act is challenged on the ground that its primary effect is to aid the religious purposes of church-related colleges and universities. . . . The crucial question is not whether some benefit accrues to a religious institution as a consequence of the legislative program, but whether its principal or primary effect advances religion. . . .

The Act itself was carefully drafted to ensure that the federally subsidized facilities would be devoted to the secular and not the religious function of the recipient institutions. . . . These restrictions have been enforced in the Act's actual administration, and the record shows that some church-related institutions have been required to disgorge benefits for failure to obey them. . . .

. . . [N]one of the four church-related institutions in this case has violated the statutory restrictions. . . .

Appellants instead rely on the argument that government may not subsidize any activities of an institution of higher learning that in some of its programs teaches religious doctrines. This argument rests on *Everson*. . . .

. . . [A]ppellants' position depends on the validity of the proposition that religion so permeates the secular education provided by church-related colleges and universities that their religious and secular educational functions are in fact inseparable. . . .

This record . . . provides no basis for any such assumption here. . . .

. . . [T]he schools were characterized by an atmosphere of academic freedom rather than religious indoctrination. . . .

Rather than focus on the four defendant colleges and universities involved in this case, however, appellants seek to shift our attention to a "composite profile" that they have constructed of the "typical sectarian" institution of higher education. . . . Individual projects can be properly evaluated if and when challenges arise. . . . We cannot, however, strike down an Act of Congress on the basis of a hypothetical "profile."

Although we reject appellants' broad constitutional arguments, we do perceive an aspect in which the statute's enforcement provisions are inadequate to ensure that the impact of the federal aid will not advance religion. . . .

Limiting the prohibition for religious use of the structure to 20 years obviously opens the facility to use for any purpose at the end of that period. . . . If, at the end of 20 years, the building is, for example, converted into a chapel or otherwise used to promote religious interests, the original federal grant will in part have the effect of advancing religion.

To this extent the Act therefore trespasses on the Religion Clauses. The restrictive obligations of a recipient institution . . . cannot, compatibly with the Religion Clauses, expire while the building has substantial value. This circumstance does not require us to invalidate the entire Act, however. . . . In view of the broad and important goals that Congress intended this legislation to serve, there is no basis for assuming that the Act would have failed of passage without this provision; nor will its excision impair either the operation or administration of the Act in any significant respect.

We next turn to the question of whether excessive entanglements characterize the relationship between government and church under the Act. Here, ... three factors substantially diminish the extent and the potential danger of the entanglement. . . .

There are generally significant differences between the religious aspects of church-related institutions of higher learning and parochial elementary and secondary schools. . . . There is substance to the contention that college students are less impressionable and less susceptible to religious indoctrination. Common observation would seem to support that view, and Congress may well have entertained it. . . . Furthermore, by their very nature, college and postgraduate courses tend to limit the opportunities for sectarian influence by virtue of their own internal disciplines. Many church-related colleges and universities are characterized by a high degree of academic freedom and seek to evoke free and critical responses from their students. . . .

Since religious indoctrination is not a substantial purpose or activity of these church-related colleges and universities, there is less likelihood than in primary and secondary schools that religion will permeate the area of secular education. This reduces the risk that government aid will in fact serve to support religious activities. Correspondingly, the necessity for intensive government surveillance is diminished and the resulting entanglements between government and religion lessened. Such inspection as may be necessary to ascertain that the facilities are devoted to secular education is minimal. . . .

The entanglement between church and state is also lessened here by the nonideological character of the aid that the Government provides. . . . Here . . . the Government provides facilities that are themselves religously neutral. The risks of Government aid to religion and the corresponding need for surveillance are therefore reduced.

Finally, government entanglements with religion are reduced by the circumstances that, unlike . . . the Pennsylvania program, . . . the Government aid here is a one-time, single-purpose construction grant. There are no continuing financial relationships or dependencies, no annual audits, and no government analysis of an institution's expenditures on secular as distinguished from religious activities. Inspection as to use is a minimal contact.

No one of these three factors standing alone is necessarily controlling; cumulatively all of them shape a narrow and limited relationship with government which involves fewer and less significant contracts than the two state schemes before us in *Lemon* and *DiCenso*.[11] . . .

We think that cumulatively these three factors also substantially lessen the potential for divisive religious fragmentation in the political arena. . . . The potential for divisiveness inherent in the essentially local problems of primary and secondary schools is significantly less with respect to a college or university whose student constituency is not local but diverse and widely dispersed. . . .

. . . Appellants claim that the Free Exercise Clause is violated because they are compelled to pay taxes, the proceeds of which in part finance grants under the Act. Appellants, however, are unable to indentify any coercion directed at the practice or exercise of their religious beliefs. . . . Their share of the cost of the grants under the Act is not fundamentally distinguishable from the impact of the tax exemption sustained in *Walz* or the provision of textbooks upheld in *Allen*. . . .

Vacated and remanded.

MR. JUSTICE WHITE, concurring in part and dissenting in part [in the *Tilton* and *Lemon* (including *DiCenso*) cases]:

. . . It is enough for me that the States

---

[11]Lemon and DiCenso were decided together. [Editor's Note.]

and the Federal Government are financing a separable secular function of overriding importance in order to sustain the legislation here challenged. That religion and private interests other than education may substantially benefit does not convert these laws into impermissible establishments of religion.

It is unnecessary, therefore, to urge that the Free Exercise Clause of the First Amendment at least permits government in some respects to modify and mold its secular programs out of express concern for free-exercise values. . . . The Establishment Clause, however, coexists in the First Amendment with the Free Exercise Clause and the latter is surely relevant in cases such as these. Where a state program seeks to ensure the proper education of its young, in private as well as public schools, free exercise considerations at least counsel against refusing support for students attending parochial schools simply because in that setting they are also being instructed in the tenets of the faith they are constitutionally free to practice.

I would sustain both the federal and the Rhode Island programs at issue in these cases. . . . Although I would also reject the facial challenge to the Pennsylvania statute, I concur in the judgment in [Lemon] for the reasons given below.

The Court strikes down the Rhode Island statute on its face. . . .

The difficulty with this is twofold. In the first place . . . the Court points to nothing in this record indicating that any participating teacher had inserted religion into his secular teaching or had had any difficulty in avoiding doing so. . . .

Secondly, the Court accepts the model for the Catholic elementary and secondary schools that was rejected for the Catholic universities or colleges in the Tilton case. . . .

The Court thus creates an insoluble paradox for the State and the parochial schools. The State cannot finance secular instruction if it permits religion to be taught in the same classroom; but if it exacts a promise that a religion not be so taught—a promise the school and its teachers are quite willing and on this record able to give—and enforces it, it is then entangled in the "no entanglement" aspect of the Court's Establishment Clause jurisprudence.

Why the federal program in the Tilton case is not embroiled in the same difficulties is never adequately explained. Surely the notion that college students are more mature and resistant to indoctrination is a makeweight, for in Tilton there is careful note of the federal condition on funding and the enforcement mechanism available. . . . The Court . . . makes much of the fact that under the federal scheme the grant to a religious institution is a one-time matter. But this argument is without real force. It is apparent that federal interest in any grant will be a continuing one since the conditions attached to the grant must be enforced. More important, the federal grant program is an ongoing one. The same grant will not be repeated, but new ones to the same or different schools will be made year after year. Thus the same potential for recurring political controversy accompanies the federal program. . . .

I do agree, however, that [in Lemon] the complaint should not have been dismissed for failure to state a cause of action. . . . [O]ne of the legal theories stated in the complaint was that the Pennsylvania Act "finances and participates in the blending of sectarian and secular instruction." . . . I would . . . remand the case for trial, thereby holding the Pennsylvania legislation valid on its face but leaving open the question of its validity as applied. . . .

MR. JUSTICE DOUGLAS, with whom MR. JUSTICE BLACK and MR. JUSTICE MARSHALL concur, dissenting:

The public purpose in secular education is, to be sure, furthered by the [federal] program. Yet the sectarian purpose is aided by making the parochial school system viable. . . . [I]t is hardly impressive that rather than giving a smaller amount of money annually over a long period of years, Congress instead gives a large amount all at once. The plurality's distinction is in effect that small violations of the First Amendment over a period of years are unconstitutional (see *Lemon* and *DiCenso*) while a huge violation occurring only once is *de minimis*. I cannot agree with such sophistry. . . .

. . . [S]urveillance creates an entanglement of government and religion which the First Amendment was designed to avoid. . . .

. . . The price of the subsidy under the Act is violation of the Free Exercise Clause. Could a course in the History of Methodism be taught in a federally financed building? Would a religiously slanted version of the Reformation or Quebec politics under Duplessis be permissible? How can the Government know what is taught in the federally financed building without a continuous auditing of classroom instruction? Yet both the Free Exercise Clause and academic freedom are violated when the Government agent must be present to determine whether the course content is satisfactory. . . .

MR. JUSTICE BRENNAN [in the *Tilton* and *Lemon* (including *DiCenso*) cases]:

I agree that the judgments in [*DiCenso*] . . . must be affirmed. In my view the judgment in [*Lemon*] . . . must be reversed outright. I dissent in [*Tilton*] . . . In my view [the federal] Act is unconstitutional insofar as it authorizes grants of federal tax monies to sectarian institutions, but is unconstitutional only to that extent. I therefore think that our remand of the case should be limited to the direction of a hearing to determine whether the four institutional appellees here are sectarian institutions. . . .

. . . [F]or more than a century, the con-sensus, enforced by legislatures and courts with substantial consistency, has been that public subsidy of sectarian schools constitutes an impermissible involvement of secular with religious institutions. If this history is not itself compelling against the validity of the three subsidy statutes . . . other forms of governmental involvement that each of the three statutes requires tip the scales in my view against the validity of each of them. . . . . . . The picture of state inspectors prowling the halls of parochial schools and auditing classroom instruction surely raises more than an imagined specter of governmental "secularization of a creed."

The same dangers attend the federal subsidy even if less obviously. . . .

The common ingredient of the three prongs of the [establishment] test is whether the statutes involve government in the "essentially religious activities" of religious institutions. My analysis of the operation, purposes, and effects of these statutes leads me inescapably to the conclusion that they do impermissibly involve the States and the Federal Government with the "essentially religious activities" of sectarian educational institutions. . . . I think each government uses "essentially religious means to serve governmental ends, where secular means would suffice." . . .

. . . I emphasize that a sectarian university is the equivalent in the realm of higher education of the Catholic elementary schools in Rhode Island; it is an educational institution in which the propagation and advancement of a particular religion are a primary function of the institution. I do not believe that construction grants to such a sectarian institution are permissible. The reason is not that religion "permeates" the secular education that is provided. Rather, it is that the secular education is provided within the environment of religion; the institution is dedicated to two goals, secular education *and* religious instruction. When aid flows directly to the institution, both functions benefit. . . .

The plurality also argues that no impermissible entanglement exists [in *Tilton*]. . . . I do not see any significant difference in the Federal Government's telling the sectarian university not to teach any nonsecular subjects in a certain building, and Rhode Island's telling the Catholic school teacher not to teach religion. The vice is the creation through subsidy of a relationship in which the government polices the teaching practices of a religious school or university. . . .

Did the Court find the stated legislative purpose in conformity with its establishment criteria? Was the statute found to have a primary secular effect? In what way did the program fail to meet the establishment criteria? Contrast the entanglements that characterized the federal program with those found by the Court in the *Walz* and *Lemon* cases. Were the entanglements in those cases greater or less than in the *Tilton* case? What facts did the Court take into account in applying its entanglement standards?

How does Justice White, in his opinion that concurs and dissents in part, suggest that the free exercise clause affects the establishment clause? What contradictions does he see in the opinion of the majority? Does he agree with the majority that college students are more mature and resistant to indoctrination than high-school students?

On what points does Justice Douglas dissent from the majority opinion? Why does Douglas find that the program of federal aid to church-related colleges is a violation of the establishment clause? What free exercise considerations are raised by Douglas with regard to the federal program?

What is Justice Brennan's reasoning to support his finding that there is an inherent entanglement between government and religion where government aid flows to sectarian schools, regardless of whether such schools are at the college and university or lower levels?

The Development of Supreme Court Doctrine in Financial Aid Cases

In *Committee for Public Education* v. *Nyquist* (1973) the Court reviewed a challenge to a New York program of financial aid for nonpublic elementary and secondary schools. The program provided direct grants to nonpublic schools for "maintenance and repair" of facilities, tuition reimbursement for low income parents sending their children to nonpublic schools, and income tax relief for middle income parents of nonpublic school children.

Justice Powell wrote the opinion for the Court, holding that under the three-part test for determining the constitutionality of aid to education under the establishment clause, all parts of the New York program were unconstitutional. First, stated Powell, in order to pass muster under the establishment clause the state law "must reflect a clearly secular legislative purpose."[12] Finding that the test of a secular legislative purpose was adequately met by the New York law, Powell nevertheless noted that the "propriety of a legislature's purposes may not immunize from further scrutiny a

[12]Committee for Public Education v. Nyquist, 413 U.S. 756, 773 (1973).

law which either has a primary effect that advances religion, or which fosters excessive entanglements between church and state."[13] With respect to that part of the program that provided grants for maintenance and repair of facilities, Powell concluded that they "violated the establishment clause because their effect, inevitably, is to subsidize and advance the religious mission of sectarian schools."[14] Powell further concluded that the tuition reimbursement program and the provision for tax relief violated the effect standard requiring a law to have "a primary effect that neither advances nor inhibits religion."[15] Finally, Powell noted: "Because we have found that the challenged sections [of the New York law] have the impermissible effect of advancing religion, we need not consider whether such aid would result in entanglement of the state with religion. . . . but the importance of the competing societal interests implicated here prompts us to make the further observation that, apart from any specific entanglement of the state in particular religious programs, assistance of the sort here involved carries grave potential for entanglement in the broader sense of continuing political strife over aid to religion."[16]

Justice Burger joined the Court's opinion holding that the maintenance and repair provision of the New York law was unconstitutional because it was a direct aid to religion. However, he declared that the *Everson, Allen,* and *Walz* cases did not preclude the types of government aid to *individuals* contained in the remaining provisions of the law. "Experience and history," he stated, more than "logic," support state reimbursement to the parents of private school children, even if most public schools are sectarian. "Primary effects" should not be measured by the number of churches benefited, and the fact that the great majority of public schools in New York are sectarian should not be a factor in the Court's decision, continued Burger. He concluded that the states, as the Court itself recognized, have a legitimate interest in reducing the private school expenses of those who pay taxes to support public education.

Justice White's dissenting opinion in the *Nyquist* case declared that all of the provisions of the New York law were constitutional. When parents desire to send their children to nonpublic schools, argued White, it is not unconstitutional for the states to reimburse them "up to the amount it would have cost the state to educate the child in public school, or, to put it another way, up to the amount the parents save the state by not sending their children to public school."[17] White based his argument upon the standards of the free exercise clause which prohibits the state from placing "unnecessary obstacles in the way of religious training for the young."[18] And, even under the establishment criteria of the court, stated White, the New York program should be upheld. Under the effect standard "the test is one of 'primary'

[13]Ibid., p. 774.
[14]Ibid., pp. 779–780.
[15]Ibid., p. 773.
[16]Ibid., p. 794.
[17]Ibid., p. 814.
[18]Ibid.

effect not *any* effect," stated White.[19] He concluded that "preserving the secular functions of these schools is the overriding consequence of these laws and the resulting, but incidental, benefit to religion should not invalidate them."[20]

Justice Rehnquist's dissenting opinion in the *Nyquist* case argued that in effect the New York program constituted less aid to religious institutions than had been upheld by the Court in the *Walz* case sustaining the New York tax exemption program for religious institutions. He concluded that the tax exemption upheld in *Walz* was not different than the special tax benefits provided by the New York program, and, therefore, the tuition tax deductions for middle income parents sending their children to sectarian schools were constitutional. Rehnquist would also have upheld the state subsidies to low income families sending their children to nonpublic schools because the program is consistent with the principle of neutrality and serves a secular purpose "by decreasing the costs of public education and by physically relieving an already overburdened public school system."[21]

The opinion of the Court in the *Nyquist* and companion cases in 1973 made it clear that it would be difficult for state programs of aid to nonpublic schools to survive judicial scrutiny under the various tests of the establishment clause. Added to the tripartite test of secular purpose, a neutral primary effect that neither advances nor inhibits religion, and excessive government entanglement with religion, was a new standard requiring a demonstration that state aid to religion would not cause "political divisiveness."[22] Political divisiveness was considered to be an outgrowth of entanglement.

The Supreme Court continued its close scrutiny of federal aid cases in 1975. In *Meek* v. *Pittinger*, 421 U.S. 349 (1975), it struck down a state program that provided loans for instructional materials and equipment to nonpublic schools and "auxiliary services" provided by public school personnel to nonpublic schools. The Court upheld a provision of the law that provided for textbook loans to children in nonpublic elementary and secondary schools. The majority found that the loans for instructional materials and equipment had the primary effect of advancing religion because the schools that would benefit were predominantly of religious character. The "auxiliary services" part of the program was held to be an excessive entanglement of state and church that would cause political divisiveness. Justice Stewart's opinion for the Court striking down the instructional materials loan and auxiliary services section of the Pennsylvania law was joined by Justices Blackmun and Powell and supported in a separate opinion by Justice Bren-

[19]Ibid., p. 823.

[20]Ibid., pp. 823–824.

[21]Ibid., p. 992.

[22]Additional financial aid cases in 1973 were Sloan v. Lemon, 413 U.S. 825, overturning a Pennsylvania tuition reimbursement scheme on the basis of the Nyquist decision; Levitt v. Committee for Public Education, 413 U.S. 472, voiding a New York program that reimbursed private schools for certain testing and record-keeping costs; Hunt v. McNair, 413 U.S. 734, upholding a South Carolina law that provided aid to higher education by creating an authority to assist colleges in construction projects through the issuance of revenue bonds. The law proscribed government assistance for sectarian facilities.

nan, joined by Justices Douglas and Marshall. That portion of Justice Stewart's opinion that upheld the textbook loan provision in the law lost the support of the Brennan-Douglas-Marshall group and was supported by Justices Rehnquist, White, and Burger, who would have upheld the law in its entirety. Justice Stewart's opinion upholding the textbook part of the law simply relied upon the precedent of *Board of Education* v. *Allen* (1968)[23] and did not explicitly apply the establishment criteria.

Both the Brennan and Rehnquist groups in the *Meek* case criticized Stewart's position on textbook loans for being inconsistent with his reasoning that invalidated the other parts of the Pennsylvania law. Brennan argued that the textbook loans would be as politically divisive as the other portions of the law and therefore should be held unconstitutional. Rehnquist, on the other hand, found that there was no justification in upholding the textbook loan provisions while declaring unconstitutional the other components of the law. The record did not demonstrate entanglement, stated Rehnquist, and the Court was not justified in turning down the nontextbook loan portions of the Pennsylvania law on a conjecture of potential entanglement. Rehnquist argued that the Court was moving away from neutrality in the direction of favoring a purely secular society by making it difficult for religious groups to perform their proper functions. In a separate opinion Chief Justice Burger stated that by overturning state aid to nonpublic schools the Court was penalizing institutions with a religious affiliation and children requiring remedial assistance.

The Court again was sharply divided over the issue of financial aid to lower schools in *Wolman* v. *Walter,* 433 U.S. 229 (1977). Ohio had carefully drafted legislation after the *Meek* decision to meet the objections of the Court to government aid to nonpublic schools and their students. The Ohio legislature appropriated 88.8 million dollars for the first two years of the program under which public schools would provide for nonpublic schools textbook loans, tests, and scoring services; speech, hearing, and psychological diagnostic services; and guidance and remedial services to be performed off the nonpublic school premises. A divided Court sustained these provisions of the law. Justice Blackmun's plurality opinion for the Court was based upon the three-part test of the establishment clause. Blackmun upheld the textbook loan portion of the Ohio program on the basis of the precedent of *Board of Education* v. *Allen* (1968). The provision of standardized testing and scoring for nonpublic schools was upheld because it did not result in excessive entanglement and because the state had a secular interest in upholding minimum standards of education for nonpublic school students. The provision of speech, hearing, and psychological diagnostic services to nonpublic schools was upheld on the grounds that a state law providing health services to all school children does not have the primary effect of aiding religion. Moreover, unlike the auxiliary services struck down in the *Meek* case, Blackmun found that the provision of auxiliary health services did not result in excessive entanglement because such services were essentially different from the teaching or counseling services under review in the

[23]See pp. 753–759.

Meek case. The health services were largely devoid of educational content and those providing them had only limited contact with the nonpublic school students. Finally, Ohio's provision of therapeutic and remedial services was upheld by Blackmun and distinguished from *Meek* on the basis that the services were performed outside of the nonpublic school.

The Court found unconstitutional two sections of the Ohio law that provided for the loan to pupils or their parents of instructional materials and equipment that were to be "incapable of diversion to religious use" and which supplied field trip transportation services to nonpublic school students on the same basis they were given to public school students. Blackmun found that the loan of equipment to nonpublic schools violated the "primary effect" standard of the three-part test by advancing religion. And, Blackmun concluded that providing field trips to nonpublic school students would result in "excessive entanglement."[24]

Justices Brennan and Marshall would have voided the entire Ohio program. Justice Brennan's separate opinion declared that the extent of the aid Ohio proposed to give to nonpublic schools would cause an intolerable political divisiveness. Justice Marshall argued that the *Allen* decision should be overturned and entirely new criteria developed to determine the proper boundaries of state aid to nonsectarian schools. He would overturn all programs that directly aided schools in the education of students but uphold "welfare programs" that would make students in nonpublic schools more receptive to being educated.

Justice Powell's separate opinion urged the Court to keep the matter of religious aid to nonpublic schools in perspective. He pointed out that the nation was far removed from the dangers that prompted the establishment clause of the First Amendment. Religious control of political institutions is remote, argued Powell; therefore the Court should not be rigid in requiring an absolute separation of church and state. Although he agreed with Justice Blackmun's decision that the Ohio provision of instructional materials to sectarian schools was unconstitutional, he did not agree with Blackmun's opinion. A properly limited provision of instructional aids would be constitutional, stated Powell. Although the Ohio program made a step in the right direction by limiting its aid of instructional materials to those "incapable of diversion to religious uses," Powell found that the Ohio program went too far in loaning materials to individual students that would not customarily be used in public schools. Unlike Blackmun, however, Powell found no objection to the field trip transportation program which he would have upheld on the basis of the Court's decision in *Everson* v. *Board of Education* (1947).[25]

Justice Steven's separate opinion in the *Wolman* case, while upholding

[24]Blackmun had difficulty in explaining why he found the textbook loan provision of the Ohio law to be constitutional while striking down the loan of instruction equipment. He argued that the loan of textbooks was constitutional on the basis of the precedent of the Allen case and that nothing more need be said on the matter. Although he admitted a similarity between textbooks and instructional materials, he argued that the Court had not and should not extend the Allen precedent regarding textbooks to other materials.

[25]See pp. 724–727.

Ohio's provision of diagnostic and therapeutic services to sectarian schools, joining Blackmun's opinion on those portions of the program, nevertheless urged the Court to discard its three-part test under the establishment clause in order to allow it to take a firmer and less equivocal stand on state aid to sectarian schools. The courts should establish a "high and impregnable" wall of separation between church and state that generally should invalidate all aid to sectarian schools. Stevens agreed with Blackmun, however, that the provision of health services to school children did not constitute an unconstitutional aid to religion.[26]

Aid to Colleges

The Court's decision in *Tilton* v. *Richardson* (1971) indicated that it would not scrutinize as closely aid to institutions of higher learning as it would aid to elementary and secondary schools. "There is a substance to the contention that college students are less impressionable and susceptible to religious indoctrination," stated Chief Justice Burger in his opinion for the Court in the *Tilton* case.[27] The Court was divided in the *Tilton* case, however, as it was in *Roemer* v. *Maryland Public Works Board* (1976), in which it sustained 5–4 a program of state aid to private colleges. Justice Blackmun's plurality opinion was joined by Chief Justice Burger and Justice Powell. Justices White and Rehnquist voted with the Blackmun group to form a majority but did not support the reasoning of Blackmun's opinion. Maryland had provided for grants to private colleges subject to the condition that they not be used for "sectarian purposes." Approximately one-third of the private colleges in Maryland were church-related, and they received one-third of the state subsidies. Colleges who granted primarily theological or seminary degrees were not eligible for the program.

In upholding the Maryland program Blackmun applied the three-part test of secular purpose, primary effect, and entanglement and found the Maryland program passed muster on all three counts. The secular purpose of Maryland's program was to aid private higher education, and its primary effect neither advanced nor inhibited religion. Nor did Blackmun find the

---

[26]The divisions of the Court in Wolman v. Walter reflected a sharp disagreement on the approach that should be taken in cases involving financial aid to religion. Blackmun's position sustaining the textbook and testing portions of the program was joined only by Chief Justice Burger and Justices Stewart and Powell. Justices White and Rehnquist supported Blackmun's decision but not his reasoning. The diagnostic and therapeutic services programs were supported by majorities of 8–1 and 7–2 respectively. Justice Brennan dissented on both programs and was joined by Justice Marshall in his dissent from the Court's opinion upholding the therapeutic services program. Justices White and Rehnquist voted for the programs but did not join Blackmun's opinion which was, however, supported by Chief Justice Burger and Justices Stewart, Marshall, Powell, and Stevens. With the exception of Justice Marshall, that group made Justice Blackmun's opinion that of a majority with respect to therapeutic services.

Justice Blackmun's opinion invalidating the instructional equipment loan and field trip services portions of the Ohio program was joined by Justices Stewart, Brennan, Marshall, and Stevens. Powell concurred in the result invalidating the instructional equipment program, but on different grounds than those of the majority. Powell dissented from the Court's invalidation of the field trip program. Justice Burger dissented without explanation from the Court's invalidation of the Ohio programs. White and Rehnquist also dissented, citing Rehnquist's opinion in the Meek case and White's dissent in Nyquist.

[27]See p. 774.

program resulted in excessive entanglement of church and state. On the entanglement issue he pointed out the majority of colleges aided were nonsectarian, which lessened the possibility of the intolerable political divisiveness that would result from the granting of the bulk of state aid to sectarian institutions as was the situation in the *Nyquist* case.

Justice White, joined by Rehnquist, wrote a concurring opinion in the *Roemer* case, which stated that the entanglement criteria should be considered superfluous. The Court, argued White, should apply the standards of secular legislative purpose and a neutral primary effect in reviewing the constitutionality of government aid to private educational institutions.

Justice Brennan's dissent in *Roemer* reiterated the views he had expressed before on the issue of aid to religion, which would preclude government subsidies to religious institutions. Justices Stevens and Stewart also dissented, essentially agreeing with Brennan. Stevens, however, referred to "the pernicious tendency of a state subsidy to tempt religious schools to compromise their religious mission without wholly abandoning it."[28]

THE FREE EXERCISE OF RELIGION

The First Amendment provides that government cannot prohibit the free exercise of religion. What is *religion*? What is *free exercise*? These questions must first be answered in order to determine the extent to which government policy can intrude upon religious beliefs and practices.

What is the "free exercise of religion" is not always easily determined. For example, if members of the Mormon sect believe that their religion supports polygamy, can the state impose through civil law restrictions upon the polygamist practices of the Mormons? The conviction of a Mormon under a *federal* law that made bigamy a crime was affirmed by the Court in *Reynolds* v. *United States* (1878). The trial judge had refused to instruct the jury to acquit the defendant if it found that he had engaged in polygamy in "conformity to what he believed at the time to be a religious duty." In upholding the conviction, Chief Justice Waite distinguished between religious belief and practice, holding that while laws

> cannot interfere with mere religious belief and opinions, they may with [religious] practices. Suppose one believed that human sacrifices were a necessary part of religious worship, would it be seriously contended that the civil government under which he lived could not interfere to prevent a sacrifice? Or if a wife religiously believed it was her duty to burn herself upon the funeral pyre of her dead husband, would it be beyond the power of the civil government to prevent her carrying her belief into practice? . . . Can a man excuse his [polygamist] practices to the contrary because of his religious belief? To permit this would be to make the professed doctrines of religious belief superior to the law of the land, and in effect to permit every citizen to become a law unto himself. Government could exist only in name under such circumstances.[29]

Whether or not the Court would have placed any religious practices be-

[28]Roemer v. Maryland Public Works Board, 426 U.S. 736, 775 (1976).
[29]Reynolds v. United States, 98 U.S. 145, 166–167 (1890).

yond the purview of government control was not answered in the *Reynolds* opinion. However, Justice Waite did cite the fact that polygamy had been traditionally condemned and that "it is impossible to believe that the constitutional guaranty of religious freedom was intended to prohibit legislation in respect to this most important feature of social life."[30]

The free exercise clause of the First Amendment was made applicable to the states in *Cantwell* v. *Connecticut* (1940) in which the Court held unconstitutional a Connecticut law that prohibited the solicitation of money for religious or charitable purposes without the prior approval of the Secretary of the Public Welfare Council. The law delegated to the secretary the discretion to determine whether or not a religious cause was bona fide. While the state had the authority to regulate solicitation, stated Justice Roberts in the Court's opinion, it did not have the power to pick and choose which religious causes could solicit, for this amounted to censorship of religion. The First Amendment, wrote Roberts, forbids government from requiring the acceptance of any creed or form of worship and at the same time safeguards the free exercise of religion. The amendment, concluded Roberts,

> embraces two concepts—freedom to believe and freedom to act. The first is absolute but, in the nature of things, the second cannot be. Conduct remains subject to regulation for the protection of society. The freedom to act must have appropriate definition to preserve the enforcement of that protection. In every case the power to regulate must be so exercised as not, in obtaining a permissible end, unduly to infringe the protected freedom. No one would contest the proposition that a state may not, by statute, wholly deny the right to preach or disseminate religious views. Plainly such a previous and absolute restraint would violate the terms of the guarantee. It is equally clear that a state may by general and nondiscriminatory legislation regulate the times, the places, and the manner of soliciting upon its streets, and of holding meetings thereon; and may in other respects safeguard the peace, good order and comfort of the community, without unconstitutionally invading the liberties protected by the Fourteenth Amendment.[31]

The liberty of the individual to free exercise of religion must be balanced against legitimate public needs in determining the permissible scope of government action that intrudes upon religious practices.

The *Reynolds* and *Cantwell* cases left many questions unanswered. The *Reynolds* case suggested that government can regulate religious practices that violate the traditional norms of society. The *Cantwell* opinion implied that there are limits to the free exercise of religion but did not specify those limits.

Defining Religion under the Free Exercise Clause

The *Reynolds* and *Cantwell* cases raise the questions of what constitutes a genuine religion under the free exercise clause and how are bona fide religious practices determined? Religion and religious practices in order to be

---

[30]Ibid., p. 165.
[31]Cantwell v. Connecticut, 310 U.S. 296, 303–304 (1940).

included under the free exercise clause must be "real," "authentic," "valid," "veritable," "sincere," and "honest," which are all synonyms of the words genuine and bona fide. Drawing from this list of words, the Supreme Court has decided that the test of a genuine religious belief is the sincerity with which it is held. And the test of a bona fide religious practice is the centrality of that practice to a religious creed. The determination that a religious practice is bona fide does not guarantee its protection under the free exercise clause, as the Court's decision in the *Reynolds* case illustrated.

The judicial test of religious beliefs covered by the free exercise clause is illustrated in *United States* v. *Ballard* (1944), which reviewed a mail fraud conviction arising out of the defendants' solicitation of money on the claim they were divine messengers. The Court ruled that the *sincerity* but not the truth of the defendants' convictions could be submitted to a jury. In the Court's opinion, Justice Douglas wrote,

> freedom of thought, which includes freedom of religious belief . . . embraces the right to maintain theories of life and of death and of the hereafter which are rank heresy to orthodox faiths. Heresy trials are foreign to our Constitution. Men may believe what they cannot prove. They may not be put to the proof of their religious doctrines or beliefs. Religious experiences which are as real as life to some may be incomprehensible to others. Yet the fact that they may be beyond the ken of mortals does not mean that they can be made suspect before the law. . . . The religious views espoused by respondents might seem incredible, if not preposterous, to most people. But if those doctrines are subject to trial before a jury charged with finding their truth or falsity, then the same can be done with the religious beliefs of any sect. When the triers of fact undertake that task, they enter a forbidden domain.[32]

Two weeks after it decided the *Cantwell* case, the Court handed down its opinion in *Minersville School District* v. *Gobitis* (1940). Although the case, like *Cantwell*, involved the free exercise of religion, its content and the context in which it occurred were quite different. The town of Minersville, Pennsylvania, with a population of 10,000 persons, required as a condition of attending its public schools that students participate in a daily flag salute ceremony requiring them to recite in unison: "I pledge allegiance to my flag, and to the Republic for which it stands; one nation indivisible, with liberty and justice for all." While reciting the words both teachers and pupils extend their right hands chest high in a salute to the flag. Walter Gobitis was a Jehovah's Witness whose children were expelled from the public school because of their refusal to engage in a flag salute which violated their religious principles. One of the children, in a letter to the school superintendent, explained her reasons for not saluting the flag: "1. The Lord clearly says in Exodus 20:3, 5 that you should have no Gods besides Him and that we should serve Him. 2. The Constitution of [the] United States is based upon religious freedom. According to the dictates of my conscience, based on the Bible, I must give my full allegiance to Jehovah God. 3. Jehovah my

---

[32]United States v. Ballard, 322 U.S. 78, 86–87 (1944).

God and the Bible is my creed. I try my best to obey the Creator."[33] Gobitis
sued to enjoin the public schools from requiring the flag salute ceremony as
a condition of attendance. The federal district court in Philadelphia held
that the expulsions violated the First and Fourteenth Amendments' protection of religious liberty. Minersville School District appealed to the circuit
court of appeals which sustained the district court judgment, and the Supreme Court granted certiorari.

When the Court granted review in the *Gobitis* case the nation was in the
grip of a wave of hysteria and patriotism on the eve of World War II. Although prior free exercise cases gave little guidance and did not clearly reveal to outsiders the possible direction the Court would take in the *Gobitis*
case, there was at least as much reason to expect that the lower court decision would be upheld as to anticipate its reversal. The Court's 8–1 vote to
uphold the Minersville flag salute requirement was a surprise to everyone.
It can perhaps best be explained in terms of the patriotic fervor of the
times.

The majority opinion in the *Gobitis* case was written by Justice Frankfurter, in which he emphasized that the "mere possession of religious convictions which contradict the relevant concerns of a political society does not
relieve the citizen from the discharge of political responsibilities."[34] "We live
by symbols," stated Frankfurter, and the "flag is the symbol of our national
unity, transcending all internal differences, however large, within the
framework of the Constitution.[35] The promotion of "national cohesion," declared Frankfurter, justifies the flag salute because "we are dealing with an
interest inferior to none in the hierarchy of legal values. National unity is
the basis of national security. . . ."[36]

There was a strong strain of judicial self-restraint in Frankfurter's *Gobitis*
opinion. Considerations of federalism were always important to Frankfurter, whose opinions often deferred to state legislative judgments and
state actions unless he found a blatant violation of constitutional liberties
and rights. He emphasized in *Gobitis* that to "the legislature no less than to
the courts is committed the guardianship of deeply-cherished liberties."[37]
and the Supreme Court should not become "the school board of the
country."[38]

Justice Stone dissented in the *Gobitis* case in an opinion that was soon to
become accepted by the majority of the Court. Stone attacked the opinion
of the majority for undermining the essence of liberty, which is "the freedom of the individual from compulsion as to what he shall think and what
he shall say, at least where the compulsion is to bear false witness to his religion."[39] Recognizing that liberty is not an absolute, Stone could find no
compelling reason to uphold the required flag salute.

[33]Henry J. Abraham, *Freedom and the Court,* 3rd ed. (New York: Oxford University Press,
1977), p. 268, n. 68.
[34]Minersville School District v. Gobitis, 310 U.S. 586, 594–595 (1940).
[35]Ibid., p. 596.
[36]Ibid., p. 595.
[37]Ibid., p. 604.
[38]Ibid., p. 598.
[39]Ibid., p. 604.

Three years after the *Gobitis* case, the Court again confronted a challenge, this time in West Virginia, to school regulations requiring the flag salute. In the intervening years, the composition of the Court had changed. Former Attorney General Robert Jackson replaced the retiring Chief Justice Hughes in 1941, and Roosevelt appointed Harlan F. Stone, the sole dissenter in the *Gobitis* case, to become Chief Justice. Roosevelt also had appointed Wiley B. Rutledge to replace Justice Byrnes, who resigned in 1942, and there was an expectation that Rutledge would be more sympathetic to the point of view that Stone had expressed in his *Gobitis* dissent.

Not only had the composition of the Court changed after *Gobitis* but three of the justices that had been in the majority—Black, Douglas, and Murphy—expressed a change of viewpoint in a 1942 case that upheld a city licensing tax on book selling and other "commercial" activities by the Jehovah's Witnesses. The three justices, who had dissented from the opinion, attached a separate memorandum in which they stated: "Since we joined in the opinion in the *Gobitis* case, we think this is an appropriate occasion to state that we now believe that it was also wrongly decided."[40] As the Court confronted its second flag salute case in 1943, *West Virginia State Board of Education* v. *Barnette,* there was every reason to believe that the *Gobitis* opinion would be overruled. The 1942 memorandum of the three justices was in fact an open invitation to the Jehovah's Witnesses to renew their Court challenge to the compulsory flag salute.

West Virginia State Board of Education v. Barnette

319 U.S. 624; 63 S. Ct. 1178; 87 L. Ed. 1628 (1943)

MR. JUSTICE JACKSON delivered the opinion of the Court:

Following the decision by this Court on June 3, 1940, in *Minersville School District* v. *Gobitis* . . ., the West Virginia legislature amended its statutes to require all schools therein to conduct courses of instruction in history, civics, and in the Constitutions of the United States and of the State "for the purpose of teaching, fostering and perpetuating the ideals, principles and spirit of Americanism, and increasing the knowledge of the organization and machinery of the government." . . .

The Board of Education on January 9, 1942, adopted a resolution containing recitals taken largely from the Court's *Gobitis* opinion and ordering that the salute to the flag become "a regular part of the program of activities in the public schools," that all teachers and pupils "shall be required to participate in the salute honoring the Nation represented by the Flag; provided, however, that refusal to salute the Flag be regarded as an act of insubordination, and shall be dealt with accordingly."

The resolution originally required the "commonly accepted salute to the Flag" which it defined. Objections to the salute as "being too much like Hitler's" were raised by the Parent and Teachers Association, the Boy and Girl Scouts, the Red Cross, and the Federation of Women's Clubs. Some modification appears to have been made in deference to these objec-

[40]Jones v. Opelika, 316 U.S. 584, 623 (1942). Chief Justice Stone wrote a separate dissent. The 1942 case was overruled in Jones v. Opelika, 319 U.S. 103 (1943).

tions, but no concession was made to Jehovah's Witnesses. What is now required is the "stiff-arm" salute, the saluter to keep the right hand raised with palm turned up while the following is repeated: "I pledge allegiance to the Flag of the United States of America and to the Republic for which it stands; one Nation, indivisible, with liberty and justice for all."

Failure to conform is "insubordination" dealt with by expulsion. Readmission is denied by statute until compliance. Meanwhile the expelled child is "unlawfully absent" and may be proceeded against as a delinquent. His parents or guardians are liable to prosecution, and if convicted are subject to fine not exceeding $50 and jail term not exceeding thirty days.

Appellees, citizens of the United States and of West Virginia, brought suit in the United States District Court for themselves and others similarly situated asking its injunction to restrain enforcement of these laws and regulations against Jehovah's Witnesses. The Witnesses are an unincorporated body teaching that the obligation imposed by law of God is superior to that of laws enacted by temporal government. Their religious beliefs include a literal version of Exodus, Chapter 20, verses 4 and 5, which says: "Thou shalt not make unto thee any graven image, or any likeness of anything that is in heaven above, or that is in the earth beneath, or that is in the water under the earth; thou shalt not bow down thyself to them nor serve them." They consider that the flag is an "image" within this command. For this reason they refuse to salute it.

Children of this faith have been expelled from school and are threatened with exclusion for no other cause. Officials threaten to send them to reformatories maintained for criminally inclined juveniles. Parents of such children have been prosecuted and are threatened with prosecutions for causing delinquency. . . .

This case calls upon us to reconsider a precedent decision, as the Court throughout its history often has been required to do. Before turning to the *Gobitis* case, however, it is desirable to notice certain characteristics by which this controversy is distinguished.

The freedom asserted by these appellees does not bring them into collision with rights asserted by any other individual. It is such conflicts which most frequently require intervention of the State to determine where the rights of one end and those of another begin. But the refusal of these persons to participate in the ceremony does not interfere with or deny rights of others to do so. Nor is there any question in this case that their behavior is peaceable and orderly. The sole conflict is between authority and rights of the individual. The State asserts power to condition access to public education on making a prescribed sign and profession and at the same time to coerce attendance by punishing both parent and child. The latter stand on a right of self-determination in matters that touch individual opinion and personal attitude.

As the present Chief Justice [Stone] said in dissent in the *Gobitis* case, the State may "require teaching by instruction and study of all in our history and in the structure and organization of our government, including the guaranties of civil liberty, which tend to inspire patriotism and love of country." . . . Here, however, we are dealing with a compulsion of students to declare a belief. They are not merely made acquainted with the flag salute so that they may be informed as to what it is or even what it means. The issue here is whether this slow and easily neglected route to aroused loyalties constitutionally may be short-cut by substituting a compulsory salute and slogan. . . .

There is no doubt that, in connection with the pledges, the flag salute is a form of utterance. Symbolism is a primitive but effective way of communicating ideas.

The use of an emblem or flag to symbolize some system, idea, institution, or personality, is a short cut from mind to mind. Causes and nations, political parties, lodges and ecclesiastical groups seek to knit the loyalty of their followings to a flag or banner, a color or design. The State announces rank, function, and authority through crowns and maces, uniforms and black robes; the church speaks through the Cross, the Crucifix, the altar and shrine, and clerical raiment. Symbols of State often convey political ideas just as religious symbols come to convey theological ones. Associated with many of these symbols are appropriate gestures of acceptance or respect: a salute, a bowed or bared head, a bended knee. A person gets from a symbol the meaning he puts into it, and what is one man's comfort and inspiration is another's jest and scorn.

Over a decade ago Chief Justice Hughes led this Court in holding that the display of a red flag as a symbol of opposition by peaceful and legal means to organized government was protected by the free speech guaranties of the Constitution. *Stromberg* v. *California* [1931]. . . . Here it is the State that employs a flag as a symbol of adherence to government as presently organized. It requires the individual to communicate by word and sign his acceptance of the political ideas it thus bespeaks. Objection to this form of communication when coerced is an old one, well known to the framers of the Bill of Rights.

It is also to be noted that the compulsory flag salute and pledge requires affirmation of a belief and an attitude of mind. It is not clear whether the regulation contemplates that pupils forego any contrary convictions of their own and become unwilling converts to the prescribed ceremony or whether it will be acceptable if they simulate assent by words without belief and by gesture barren of meaning. It is now a commonplace that censorship or suppression of expression of opinion is tolerated by our Constitution only when the expression presents a clear and present danger of action of a kind the State is empowered to prevent and punish. It would seem that involuntary affirmation could be commanded only on even more immediate and urgent grounds than silence. But here the power of compulsion is invoked without any allegation that remaining passive during a flag salute ritual creates a clear and present danger that would justify an effort even to muffle expression. To sustain the compulsory flag salute we are required to say that a Bill of Rights which guards the individual's right to speak his own mind, left it open to public authorities to compel him to utter what is not in his mind.

Whether the First Amendment to the Constitution will permit officials to order observance of ritual of this nature does not depend upon whether as a voluntary exercise we would think it to be good, bad or merely innocuous. Any credo of nationalism is likely to include what some disapprove or to omit what others think essential, and to give off different overtones as it takes on different accents or interpretations. If official power exists to coerce acceptance of any patriotic creed, what it shall contain cannot be decided by the courts, but must be largely discretionary with the ordaining authority, whose power to prescribe would no doubt include power to amend. Hence validity of the asserted power to force an American citizen publicly to profess any statement of belief or to engage in any ceremony of assent to one, presents questions of power that must be considered independently of any idea we may have as to the utility of the ceremony in question.

Nor does the issue as we see it turn on one's possession of particular religious views or the sincerity with which they are held. While religion supplies appellees' motive for enduring the discomforts of making the issue in this case, many citizens who do not share these religious views hold such a compulsory rite to infringe constitutional liberty of the individual. It is not necessary to inquire whether non-conformist beliefs will exempt from the duty to salute unless we first find power to make the salute a legal duty.

The *Gobitis* decision, however, *assumed,* as did the argument in that case and in this, that power exists in the State to impose the flag salute discipline upon school children in general. The Court only examined and rejected a claim based on religious beliefs of immunity from an unquestioned general rule. The question which underlies the flag salute controversy is whether such a ceremony so touching matters of opinion and political attitude may be imposed upon the individual by official authority under powers committed to any political organization under our Constitution. We examine rather than assume existence of this power and, against this broader definition of issues in this case, reëxamine specific grounds assigned for the *Gobitis* decision.

1. It was said that the flag-salute controversy confronted the Court with "the problem which Lincoln cast in memorable dilemma: 'Must a government of necessity be too *strong* for the liberties of its people, or too *weak* to maintain its own existence?'" and that the answer must be in favor of strength. . . .

We think these issues may be examined free of pressure or restraint growing out of such considerations.

It may be doubted whether Mr. Lincoln would have thought that the strength of government to maintain itself would be impressively vindicated by our confirming power of the State to expel a handful of children from school. Such oversimplification, so handy in political debate, often lacks the precision necessary to postulates of judicial reasoning. If validly applied to this problem, the utterance cited would resolve every issue of power in favor of those in authority and would require us to override every liberty thought to weaken or delay execution of their policies.

Government of limited power need not be anemic government. Assurance that rights are secure tends to diminish fear and jealousy of strong government, and by making us feel safe to live under it makes for its better support. Without promise of a limiting Bill of Rights it is doubtful if our Constitution could have mustered enough strength to enable its ratification. To enforce those rights today is not to choose weak government over strong government. It is only to adhere as a means of strength to individual freedom of mind in preference to officially disciplined uniformity for which history indicates a disappointing and disastrous end.

The subject now before us exemplifies this principle. Free public education, if faithful to the ideal of secular instruction and political neutrality, will not be partisan or enemy of any class, creed, party, or faction. If it is to impose any ideological discipline, however, each party or denomination must seek to control, or failing that, to weaken the influence of the educational system. Observance of the limitations of the Constitution will not weaken government in the field appropriate for its exercise.

2. It was also considered in the *Gobitis* case that functions of educational officers in States, counties and school districts were such that to interfere with their authority "would in effect make us the school board for the country."

The Fourteenth Amendment, as now applied to the States, protects the citizen against the State itself and all of its creatures—Boards of Education not excepted. These have, of course, important, delicate, and highly discretionary functions, but none that they may not perform within the limits of the Bill of Rights. That they are educating the young for citizenship is reason for scrupulous protection of Constitutional freedoms of the individual, if we are not to strangle the free mind at its source and teach youth to discount important principles of our government as mere platitudes.

Such Boards are numerous and their territorial jurisdiction often small. But small and local authority may feel less sense of responsibility to the Constitution, and agencies of publicity may be less vigilant in calling it to account. The action of Congress in making flag observance voluntary and respecting the conscience of the objector in a matter so vital as raising the Army contrasts sharply with these local regulations in matters relatively trivial to the welfare of the nation. There are village tyrants as well as village Hampdens, but none who acts under color of law is beyond reach of the Constitution.

3. The *Gobitis* opinion reasoned that this is a field "where courts possess no marked and certainly no controlling competence," that it is committed to the legislatures as well as the courts to guard cherished liberties and that it is constitutionally appropriate to "fight out the wise use of legislative authority in the forum of public opinion and before legislative assemblies rather than to transfer such a contest to the judicial arena," since all the "effective means of inducing political changes are left free."

The very purpose of a Bill of Rights was to withdraw certain subjects from the vicissitudes of political controversy, to place them beyond the reach of majorities and officials and to establish them as legal principles to be applied by the courts. One's right to life, liberty, and property, to free speech, a free press, freedom of worship and assembly, and other fundamental rights may not be submitted to vote; they depend on the outcome of no elections.

In weighing arguments of the parties it is important to distinguish between the due process clause of the Fourteenth Amendment as an instrument for transmitting the principles of the First Amendment and those cases in which it is applied for its own sake. The test of legislation which collides with the Fourteenth Amendment, because it also collides with the principles of the First, is much more definite than the test when only the Fourteenth is involved. Much of the vagueness of the due process clause disappears when the specific prohibitions of the First become its standard. The right of a State to regulate, for example, a public utility may well include, so far as the due process test is concerned, power to impose all of the restrictions which a legislature may have a "rational basis" for adopting. But freedoms of speech and of press, of assembly, and of worship may not be infringed on such slender grounds. They are susceptible of restriction only to prevent grave and immediate danger to interests which the State may lawfully protect. It is important to note that while it is the Fourteenth Amendment which bears directly upon the State it is the more specific limiting principles of the First Amendment that finally govern this case.

Nor does our duty to apply the Bill of Rights to assertions of official authority depend upon our possession of marked competence in the field where the invasion of rights occurs. True, the task of translating the majestic generalities of the Bill of Rights, conceived as part of the pattern of liberal government in the eighteenth century, into concrete restraints on officials dealing with the problems of the twentieth century, is one to disturb self-confidence. These principles grew in soil which also produced a philosophy that the individual was the center of society, that his liberty was attainable through mere absence of governmental restraints, and that government should be entrusted with few controls and only the mildest supervision over men's affairs. We must transplant these rights to a soil in which the *laissez-faire* concept or principle of non-interference has withered at least as to economic affairs, and social advancements are increasingly sought through closer integration of society and through expanded and strengthened governmental controls. These changed conditions often deprive precedents of reliability and cast us more than we would choose upon our own judgment. But we act in these matters not by authority of our competence but by force of our commissions. We cannot, because of modest estimates of our competence in such specialties as public education, withhold the judgment that history authenticates as the function of this Court when liberty is infringed.

4. Lastly, and this is the very heart of the *Gobitis* opinion, it reasons that "National unity is the basis of national security," that the authorities have, "the right to select appropriate means for its attainment," and hence reaches the conclusion that such compulsory measures toward "national unity" are constitutional. Upon the verity of this assumption depends our answer in this case.

National unity as an end which officials may foster by persuasion and example is not in question. The problem is whether under our Constitution compulsion as here employed is a permissible means for its achievement.

Struggles to coerce uniformity of sentiment in support of some end thought essential to their time and country have been waged by many good as well as by evil men. Nationalism is a relatively recent phenomenon but at other times and places the ends have been racial or territorial security, support of a dynasty or regime, and particular plans for saving souls. As first and moderate methods to attain unity have failed, those bent on its accomplishment must resort to an ever-increasing severity. As governmental pressure toward unity becomes greater, so strife becomes more bitter as to whose unity it shall be. Probably no deeper division of our people could proceed from any provocation than from finding it necessary to choose what doctrine and whose program public educational officials shall compel youth to unite in embracing. Ultimate futility of such effort from the Roman drive to stamp out Christianity as a disturber of its pagan unity, the Inquisition as a means to religious and dynastic unity, the Siberian exiles as a means to Russian unity, down to the fast failing efforts of our present totalitarian enemies. Those who begin coercive elimination of dissent soon find themselves exterminating dissenters. Compulsory unification of opinion achieves only the unanimity of the graveyard.

It seems trite but necessary to say that the First Amendment to our Constitution was designed to avoid these ends by avoiding these beginnings. There is no mysticism in the American concept of the State or of the nature or origin of its authority. We set up government by consent of the governed, and the Bill of Rights denies those in power any legal opportunity to coerce that consent. Authority here is to be controlled by public opinion, not public opinion by authority.

The case is made difficult not because the principles of its decision are obscure but because the flag involved is our own. Nevertheless, we apply the limitations of the Constitution with no fear that freedom to be intellectually and spiritually diverse or even contrary will disintegrate the social organization. To believe that patriotism will not flourish if patriotic ceremonies are voluntary and spontaneous instead of a compulsory routine is to make an unflattering estimate of the appeal of our institutions to free minds. We can have intellectual individualism and the rich, cultural diversities that we owe to exceptional minds only at the price of occasional eccentricity and abnormal attitudes. When they are so harmless to others or to the State as those we deal with here, the price is not too great. But freedom to differ is not limited to things that do not matter much. That would be a mere shadow of freedom. The test of its substance is the right to differ as to things that touch the heart of the existing order.

If there is any fixed star in our constitutional constellation, it is that no official, high or petty, can prescribe what shall be orthodox in politics, nationalism, religion, or other matters of opinion or force citizens to confess by word or act their faith therein. If there are any circumstances which permit an exception, they do not now occur to us.

We think the action of the local authorities in compelling the flag salute and pledge transcends constitutional limitations on their power and invades the sphere of intellect and spirit which it is the purpose of the First Amendment to our Constitution to reserve from all official control.

The decision of this Court in *Minersville School District* v. *Gobitis...* [is] overruled, and the judgment enjoining enforcement of the West Virginia Regulation is

Affirmed.

MR. JUSTICE BLACK and MR. JUSTICE DOUGLAS concurred in a separate opinion.

MR. JUSTICE MURPHY wrote a separate concurring opinion.

JUSTICES ROBERTS and REED dissented.

MR. JUSTICE FRANKFURTER, dissenting:
One who belongs to the most vilified and persecuted minority in history is not likely to be insensible to the freedoms guaranteed by our Constitution. Were my purely personal attitude relevant I should wholeheartedly associate myself with the general libertarian views in the Court's opinion, representing as they do the thought and action of a lifetime. But as judges we are neither Jew nor Gentile, neither Catholic or agnostic. We owe equal attachment to the Constitution and are equally bound by our judicial obligations whether we derive our citizenship from the earliest or the latest immigrants to these shores.... As a member of this Court I am not justified in writing my private notions of policy into the Constitution, no matter how deeply I may cherish them or how mischievous I may deem their disregard. The duty of a judge who must decide which of two claims before the Court shall prevail, that of a State to enact and enforce laws within its general competence or that of an individual to refuse obedience because of the demands of his conscience, is not that of the ordinary person. It can never be emphasized too much that one's own opinion about the wisdom or evil of a law should be excluded altogether when one is doing one's duty on the bench. The only opinion of our own even looking in that direction that is material is our opinion whether legislators could in reason have enacted such a law. In the light of all the circumstances, including the history of this question in this Court, it would require more daring than I possess to deny that reasonable legislators could have taken the action which is before us for review. Most unwillingly, therefore, I must differ from my brethren with regard to legislation like this. I cannot bring my mind to believe that the "liberty" secured by the Due Process Clause gives this Court authority to deny to the State of West Virginia the attainment of that which we all recognize as a legitimate legislative end, namely, the promotion of good citizenship, by employment of the means here chosen....

Does Justice Jackson's opinion, hinging as it does upon the First Amendment free speech guarantees incorporated into the Fourteenth Amendment, rather than the free exercise clause, expand religious freedom? Is the exercise of religion the same as speech? In what sense does the Court consider the flag salute exercises to be speech? Why is the Court concerned with the compulsory aspect of the West Virginia requirement? If the flag salute exercises were voluntary would the Court have upheld their constitutionality under the free speech requirement of the First and Fourteenth Amendments? Note in this regard the contrast the Court makes between congressional actions requiring flag observances and respecting conscientious objector status in the draft, with the West Virginia regulations. Once the Court accepts the premise that freedom of speech and not freedom of religion is the central issue of the case, what constitutional test would the state have to pass in order to justify compelling students to participate in the flag salute exercises?

Since the *Barnette* decision overrules *Gobitis*, the Court devotes a great deal of space to distinguishing between the two opinions. What major points of difference between the two cases are cited by Justice Jackson in the *Barnette* opinion? In particular, examine the contrasting premises and approaches of Frankfurter in *Gobitis* and in his *Barnette* dissent and compare them with those of Jackson. What are their differing views on the requirements of government and the rights of the individual? How do they diverge on the need for judicial self-restraint? Are considerations of federalism more important to Frankfurter than to Jackson?

Free Exercise, Sunday Closing Laws, and the Saturday Sabbath

The Orthodox Jewish faith and the Seventh-Day Adventist Church observe Saturday as the Sabbath. Members of these sects who adhere to the doctrines of their religions must not work on Saturdays. Do Sunday closing laws violate the free exercise of religion of Orthodox Jews? Can a state deny unemployment compensation to a Seventh-Day Adventist for failure to accept "suitable" work under state law, after she was discharged by her employer for her refusal to work on Saturdays? These are the questions raised in the following cases.

Braunfeld v. *Brown*

366 U.S. 599; 81 S. Ct. 1144; 6 L. Ed. 2d 563 (1961)

MR. CHIEF JUSTICE WARREN announced the judgment of the Court and an opinion in which MR. JUSTICE BLACK, MR. JUSTICE CLARK, and MR. JUSTICE WHITTAKER concur:

This case concerns the constitutional validity of the application to appellants of the Pennsylvania criminal statute, enacted in 1959, which proscribes the Sunday retail sale of certain enumerated commodities. . . .

. . . [T]he only question for consideration is whether the statute interferes with the free exercise of appellants' religion.

Appellants are merchants in Philadelphia who engage in the retail sale of clothing and home furnishings within the proscription of the statute in issue. Each of the appellants is a member of the Orthodox Jewish faith, which requires the closing of their places of business and a total abstention from all manner of work from nightfall each Friday until nightfall each Saturday.... Their complaint, as amended, alleged that appellants had previously kept their places of business open on Sunday; that each of appellants had done a substantial amount of business on Sunday, compensating somewhat for their closing on Saturday; that Sunday closing will result in impairing the ability of all appellants to earn a livelihood and will render appellant Braunfeld unable to continue in his business, thereby losing his capital investment; that the statute is unconstitutional for the reasons stated above.

A three judge court was properly convened and it dismissed the complaint....

Appellants contend that the enforcement against them of the Pennsylvania statute will prohibit the free exercise of their religion because, due to the statute's compulsion to close on Sunday, appellants will suffer substantial economic loss, to the benefit of their non-Sabbatarian competitors, if appellants also continue their Sabbath observance by closing their businesses on Saturday; that this result will either compel appellants to give up their Sabbath observance, a basic tenet of the Orthodox Jewish faith, or will put appellants at a serious economic disadvantage if they continue to adhere to their Sabbath. Appellants also assert that the statute will operate so as to hinder the Orthodox Jewish faith in gaining new adherents. And the corollary to these arguments is that if the free exercise of appellants' religion is impeded, that religion is being subjected to discriminatory treatment....

Certain aspects of religious exercise cannot, in any way, be restricted or burdened by either federal or state legislation. Compulsion by law of the acceptance of any creed or the practice of any form of worship is strictly forbidden. The freedom to hold religious beliefs and opinions is absolute. *Cantwell* v. *State of Connecticut* [1940] ... *Reynolds* v. *United States* [1879].... And, in *Prince* v. *Commonwealth of Massachusetts* [1944] ... this Court upheld a statute making it a crime for a girl under eighteen years of age to sell any newspapers, periodicals or merchandise in public places despite the fact that a child of the Jehovah's Witnesses faith believed that it was her religious duty to perform this work.

It is to be noted that, in [*Reynolds* and *Prince*] the religious practices themselves conflicted with the public interest. In such cases, to make accommodation between the religious action and an exercise of state authority is a particularly delicate task ... because resolution in favor of the State results in the choice to the individual of either abandoning his religious principle or facing criminal prosecution.

But, again, this is not the case before us because the statute at bar does not make unlawful any religious practices of appellants; the Sunday law simply regulates a secular activity and, as applied to appellants, operates so as to make the practice of their religious beliefs more expensive. ... Fully recognizing that the alternatives open to appellants and others similarly situated—retaining their present occupations and incurring economic disadvantage or engaging in some other commercial activity which does not call for either Saturday or Sunday labor—may well result in some financial sacrifice in order to observe their religious beliefs, still the option is wholly different than when the legislation attempts to make a religious practice itself unlawful.

To strike down, without the most critical scrutiny, legislation which imposes only an indirect burden on the exercise of religion, i.e., legislation which does not make unlawful the religious practice itself, would radically restrict the operating latitude of the legislature. . . .

Needless to say, when entering the area of religious freedom, we must be fully cognizant of the particular protection that the Constitution has accorded it. Abhorrence of religious persecution and intolerance is a basic part of our heritage. But we are a cosmopolitan nation made up of people of almost every conceivable religious preference. . . . Consequently, it cannot be expected, much less required, that legislators enact no law regulating conduct that may in some way result in an economic disadvantage to some religious sects and not to others because of the special practices of the various religions. . . .

Of course, to hold unassailable all legislation regulating conduct which imposes solely an indirect burden on the observance of religion would be a gross oversimplification. If the purpose or effect of a law is to impede the observance of one or all religions or is to discriminate invidiously between religions, that law is constitutionally invalid even though the burden may be characterized as being only indirect. But if the State regulates conduct by enacting a general law within its power, the purpose and effect of which is to advance the State's secular goals, the statute is valid despite its indirect burden on religious observance unless the State may accomplish its purpose by means which do not impose such a burden. See *Cantwell*. . . .

As we pointed out in *McGowan* v. *Maryland* [1961] . . . we cannot find a State without power to provide a weekly respite from all labor and, at the same time, to set one day of the week apart from the others as a day of rest, repose, recreation and tranquillity. . . .

Also, in *McGowan*, we examined several suggested alternative means by which it was argued that the State might accomplish its secular goals without even remotely or incidentally affecting religious freedom. . . . We found there that a State might well find that those alternatives would not accomplish bringing about a general day of rest. . . .

However, appellants advance yet another means at the State's disposal which they would find unobjectionable. They contend that the State should cut an exception from the Sunday labor proscription for those people who, because of religious conviction, observe a day of rest other than Sunday. By such regulation, appellants contend, the economic disadvantages imposed by the present system would be removed and the State's interest in having all people rest one day would be satisfied.

A number of States provide such an exemption, and this may well be the wiser solution to the problem. But our concern is not with the wisdom of legislation but with its constitutional limitation. Thus, reason and experience teach that to permit the exemption might well undermine the State's goal of providing a day that, as best possible, eliminates the atmosphere of commercial noise and activity. Although not dispositive of the issue, enforcement problems would be more difficult since there would be two or more days to police rather than one and it would be more difficult to observe whether violations were occurring.

Additional problems might also be presented by a regulation of this sort. To allow only people who rest on a day other than Sunday to keep their businesses open on that day might well provide these people with an economic advantage over their competitors who must remain closed on that day. . . . With this competitive advantage existing, there could well be the temptation for some, in order to keep their businesses open on Sunday, to assert that they have religious convictions which compel them to close their businesses on what had formerly been their least profitable day. This might make necessary a state-conducted inquiry into the sincerity of the individual's religious beliefs, a practice which a State might believe would itself run afoul of the spirit of constitutionally protected religious guarantees. Finally, in order to keep the disruption of the day at a minimum, exempted employers would probably have to hire employees who themselves qualified for the exemption because of their own religious beliefs, a practice which a State might feel to be opposed to its general policy prohibiting religious discrimination in hiring. For all of these reasons, we cannot say that the Pennsylvania statute before us is invalid, either on its face or as applied. . . .

Mr. Justice Harlan concurs in the judgment. Mr. Justice Brennan and Mr. Justice Stewart concur in our disposition of appellants' claims under the Establishment Clause and the Equal Protection Clause. . . . Mr. Justice Frankfurter and Mr. Justice Harlan have rejected appellants' claim under the Free Exercise Clause in a separate opinion.

Affirmed

MR. JUSTICE BRENNAN, . . . dissenting:
. . . [The] issue in this case . . . is whether a State may put an individual to a choice between his business and his religion. The Court today holds that it may. But I dissent, believing that such a law prohibits the free exercise of religion.

The first question to be resolved . . . is . . . the appropriate standard of constitutional adjudication in cases in which a statute is assertedly in conflict with the First Amendment. . . . The Court in such cases is not confined to the narrow inquiry whether the challenged law is rationally related to some legitimate legislative end. Nor is the case decided by a finding that the State's interest is substantial and important, as well as rationally justifiable. . . .

. . . The honored place of religious freedom in our constitutional hierarchy . . . must now be taken to be settled. Or at least so it appeared until today. For in this case the Court seems to say, without so much as a deferential nod towards that high place which we have accorded religious freedom in the past, that any substantial state interest will justify encroachments on religious practice, at least if those encroachments are cloaked in the guise of some nonreligious public purpose.

Admittedly, these laws do not compel overt affirmation of a repugnant belief, as in *Barnette*, nor do they prohibit outright any of appellant's religious practices as . . . in *Reynolds*. . . . That is, the laws do not say that appellants must work on Saturday. But their effect is that appellants may not simultaneously practice their religion and their trade, without being hampered by a substantial competitive disadvantage. Their effect is that no one may at one and the same time be an Orthodox Jew and compete effectively with his Sunday-observing fellow tradesmen. This clog upon the exercise of religion, this state-imposed burden on Orthodox Judaism, has exactly the same economic effect as a tax levied upon the sale of religious literature. And yet, such a tax, when applied in the form of an excise or license fee, was held invalid in *Follett* v. *Town of McCormick* [1944]. . . . All this the Court, as I read its opinion, concedes.

What, then, is the compelling state interest which impels the Commonwealth of Pennsylvania to impede appellants' freedom of worship? What overbalancing need is so weighty in the constitutional scale that it justifies this substantial, though indirect, limitation of appellants' freedom? It is not the desire to stamp out a practice deeply abhorred by society, such as polygamy, as in *Reynolds*. . . . Nor is it the State's traditional protection of children, as in *Prince* v. *Commonwealth of Mas-*

sachusetts. . . . It is not even the interest in seeing that everyone rests one day a week, for appellants' religion requires that they take such a rest. It is the mere convenience of having everyone rest on the same day. It is to defend this interest that the Court holds that a State need not follow the alternative route of granting an exemption for those who in good faith observe a day of rest other than Sunday.

It is true, I suppose, that the granting of such an exemption would make Sundays a little noisier, and the task of police and prosecutor a little more difficult. It is also true that a majority—21—of the 34 States which have general Sunday regulations have exemptions of this kind. We are not told that those States are significantly noisier, or that their police are significantly more burdened, than Pennsyl-

vania's. . . . The Court conjures up several difficulties with such a system which seem to me more fanciful than real. . . .

In fine, the Court, in my view, has exalted administrative convenience to a constitutional level high enough to justify making one religion economically disadvantageous. . . .

I would . . . remand for a trial of appellants' allegations. . . .

MR. JUSTICE STEWART, dissenting:

I agree with substantially all that Mr. Justice Brennan has written. Pennsylvania has passed a law which compels on Orthodox Jew to choose between his religious faith and his economic survival. That is a cruel choice. It is a choice which I think no State can constitutionally demand. . . .

The following case was brought by Mrs. Adell H. Sherbert, a Seventh-Day Adventist, who had been a loyal employee of the Spartan Mills, a textile firm in Spartanburg, South Carolina. She had formally joined the church in 1957 at a time when her employer was on a five-day week, enabling her to have her Sabbath on Saturdays in accordance with the creed of the church. In 1959 the firm began a six-day week requiring her to work on Saturdays. She refused and was fired. Because of her refusal to work on Saturdays she was unable to find comparable employment and filed a claim with the state for unemployment compensation. The state Employment Security Commission denied the claim on the grounds that Mrs. Sherbert's refusal to work on Saturdays disqualified her from unemployment benefits under the state Unemployment Compensation Act, which explicitly denied benefits to insured workers who failed "without good cause" to accept suitable work when it was offered to them. The South Carolina Supreme Court sustained the commission, holding that its action did not deny Mrs. Sherbert freedom of religion because she remained free to practice her religious beliefs. The Supreme Court granted certiorari.

Sherbert v. *Verner*

374 U.S. 398; 83 S. Ct. 1790; 10 L. Ed. 2d 965 (1963)

MR. JUSTICE BRENNAN delivered the opinion of the Court:

. . . If . . . the decision of the South Carolina Supreme Court is to withstand appellant's constitutional challenge, it must be either because her disqualification as a beneficiary represents no infringement by the State of her constitutional rights of free exercise, or because any incidental burden on the free exercise of appellant's religion may be justified by a "compelling state interest in the regulation of a subject within the State's constitutional power to regulate. . . ." *NAACP* v. *Button* [1963]. . . .

We turn first to the question whether the disqualification for benefits imposes any burden on the free exercise of appellant's religion. We think it is clear that it does. In a sense the consequences of such a disqualification to religious principles and practices may be only an indirect result of welfare legislation within the State's general competence to enact; it is true that no criminal sanctions directly compel appellant to work a six-day week. But this is only the beginning, not the end, of our inquiry. For "[i]f the purpose or effect of a law is to impede the observance of one or all religions or is to discriminate invidiously between religions, that law is constitutionally invalid even though the burden may be characterized as being only indirect." *Braunfeld* v. *Brown*. . . . Here not only is it apparent that appellant's declared ineligibility for benefits derives solely from the practice of her religion, but the pressure upon her to forego that practice is unmistakable. The ruling forces her to choose between following the precepts of her religion and forfeiting benefits, on the one hand, and abandoning one of the precepts of her religion in order to accept work, on the other hand. Governmental imposition of such a choice puts the same kind of burden upon the free exercise of religion as would a fine imposed against appellant for her Saturday worship. . . .

Significantly South Carolina expressly saves the Sunday worshipper from having to make the kind of choice which we here hold infringes the Sabbatarian's religious liberty. When in times of "national emergency" the textile plants are authorized by the State Commissioner of Labor to operate on Sunday, "no employee shall be required to work on Sunday . . . who is conscientiously opposed to Sunday work. . . ." No question of the disqualification of a Sunday worshipper for benefits is likely to arise, since we cannot suppose that an employer will discharge him in violation of this statute. The unconstitutionality of the disqualification of the Sabbatarian is thus compounded by the religious discrimination which South Carolina's general statutory scheme necessarily effects.

We must next consider whether some compelling state interest . . . justifies the substantial infringement of appellant's First Amendment right. It is basic that no showing merely of a rational relationship to some colorable state interest would suffice; in this highly sensitive constitutional area, "[o]nly the gravest abuses, endangering paramount interests, give occasion for permissible limitation," *Thomas* v. *Collins* [1945]. . . . No such abuse or danger has been advanced in the present case. The appellees suggest no more than a possibility that the filing of fraudulent claims by unscrupulous claimants feigning religious objections to Saturday work might not only dilute the unemployment compensation fund but also hinder the scheduling of employers of necessary Saturday work. But . . . no such objection appears to have been made before the South Carolina Supreme Court, and . . . there is no proof whatever to warrant such fears of malingering or deceit as those which the respondents now advance. Even if consideration of such evidence is not foreclosed by the prohibition against judicial inquiry into the truth or falsity of religious beliefs . . .—a question as to which we intimate no view since it is not before us—it is highly doubtful whether such evidence would be sufficient to warrant a substantial infringement of religious liberties. For even if the possibility of spurious claims did threaten to dilute the fund and disrupt the scheduling of work, it would plainly be incumbent upon the appellees to demonstrate that no alternative forms of regulation would combat such abuses without infringing First Amendment rights. . . .

In these respects, then, the state interest asserted in the present case is wholly dissimilar to the interests which were found to justify the less direct burden upon religious practices in *Braunfeld* . . . [That] statute was . . . saved by a countervailing factor which finds no equivalent in the instant case—a strong state interest in providing one uniform day of rest for all workers. That secular objective could be achieved, the Court found, only by declaring Sunday to be that day of rest. . . . In the present case no such justifications underlie the determination of the state court that appellant's religion makes her ineligible to receive benefits. . . .

In holding as we do, plainly we are not fostering the "establishment" of the Seventh-Day Adventist religion in South Carolina, for the extension of unemployment benefits to Sabbatarians in common with Sunday worshippers reflects nothing more than the governmental obligation of neutrality in the face of religious differences, and does not represent that involvement of religious with secular institutions which it is the object of the Establishment Clause to forestall. . . . Nor do we, by our decision today, declare the existence of a constitutional right to unemployment benefits on the part of all persons whose religious convictions are the cause of their unemployment. This is not a case in which an employee's religious convictions serve to make him a nonproductive member of society. . . . Our holding today is only that South Carolina may not constitutionally apply the eligibility provisions so as to constrain a worker to abandon his religious convictions respecting the day of rest. . . .

Reversed and remanded.

MR. JUSTICE STEWART, concurring in the result:

Although fully agreeing with the result which the Court reaches in this case, I cannot join the Court's opinion. This case presents a double-barreled dilemma, which in all candor I think the Court's opinion has not succeeded in papering over. The dilemma ought to be resolved. . . .

[I]n *Braunfeld* v. *Brown* . . . the Court has shown what has seemed to me a distressing insensitivity to the appropriate demands of this constitutional guarantee. By contrast I think that the Court's approach to the Establishment Clause has on occasion . . . been not only insensitive, but positively wooden, and that the Court has accorded to the Establishment Clause a meaning which neither the words, the history, nor the intention of the authors of that specific constitutional provision even remotely suggests.

But . . . the decisions are on the books. And the result is that there are many situations where legitimate claims under the Free Exercise Clause will run into head-on collision with the Court's insensitive and sterile construction of the Establishment Clause. The controversy now before us is clearly such a case.

. . . The Court says that South Carolina cannot under these circumstances declare her to be not "available for work" within the meaning of its statute because to do so would violate her constitutional right to the free exercise of her religion.

Yet what this Court has said about the Establishment Clause must inevitably lead to a diametrically opposite result. If the appellant's refusal to work on Saturdays were based on indolence, or on a compulsive desire to watch the Saturday television programs, no one would say that South Carolina could not hold that she was not "available for work" within the meaning of its statute. That being so, the Establishment Clause as construed by this Court not only *permits* but affirmatively *requires* South Carolina equally to deny the appellant's claim for unemployment compensation when her refusal to work on Saturdays is based upon her religious creed. . . .

To require South Carolina to so administer its laws as to pay public money to the appellant under the circumstances of this case is thus clearly to require the State to violate the Establishment Clause as construed by this Court. This poses no problem for me, because I think the Court's mechanistic concept of the Establishment Clause is historically unsound and constitutionally wrong. . . . And I think that the guarantee of religious liberty embodied in the Free Exercise Clause affirmatively requires government to create an atmosphere of hospitality and accommodation to individual belief or disbelief. . . .

South Carolinia would deny unemployment benefits to a mother unavailable for work on Saturdays because she was unable to get a babysitter. Thus, we do not have before us a situation where a State provides unemployment compensation generally, and singles out for disqualification only those persons who are unavailable for work on religious grounds. This is not, in short, a scheme which operates so as to discriminate against religion as such. But the Court nevertheless holds that the State must prefer a religious over a secular ground for being unavailable for work. . . .

Yet in cases decided under the Establishment Clause the Court has decreed otherwise. It has decreed that government must blind itself to the differing religious beliefs and traditions of the people. With all respect, I think it is the Court's duty to face up to the dilemma posed by the conflict between the Free Exercise Clause of the Constitution and the Establishment Clause as interpreted by the Court. . . . For so long as the resounding but fallacious fundamentalist rhetoric of some of our Establishment Clause opinions remains on our books, to be disregarded at will as in the present case, . . . so long will the possibility of consistent and perceptive decision in this most difficult and delicate area of constitutional law be impeded and impaired. And so long, I fear, will the guarantee of true religious freedom in our pluralistic society be uncertain and insecure. . . .

My second difference with the Court's opinion is that I cannot agree that today's decision can stand consistently with *Braunfeld*. . . . The Court says that there was a "less direct burden upon religious practices" in that case than in this. With all respect, I think the Court is mistaken, simply as a matter of fact. The *Braunfeld* case involved a state *criminal* statute. The undisputed effect of that statute, as pointed out by Mr. Justice Brennan in his dissenting opinion in that case, was that "Plaintiff, Abraham Braunfeld, will be unable to continue in his business if he may not stay open on Sunday. . . ."

The impact upon the appellant's religious freedom in the present case is considerably less onerous. . . . Even upon the unlikely assumption that the appellant could not find suitable non-Saturday employment, the appellant at the worst would be denied a maximum of 22 weeks of compensation payments. I agree with the Court that the possibility of that denial is enough to infringe upon the appellant's constitutional right to the free exercise of her religion. But it is clear to me that in order to reach this conclusion the Court must explicitly reject the reasoning of *Braunfeld* v. *Brown*. I think the *Braunfeld* case was wrongly decided and should be overruled, and accordingly I concur in the result reached by the Court in the case before us.

MR. JUSTICE HARLAN, whom MR. JUSTICE WHITE joins, dissenting:

. . . The South Carolina Supreme Court has . . . consistently held that one is not "available for work" if his unemployment has resulted not from the inability of industry to provide a job but rather from personal circumstances, no matter how compelling. . . . The fact that these personal considerations sprang from [appellant's] . . . religious convictions was wholly without relevance to the state court's application of the law. Thus in no proper sense can it be said that the State discriminated against the appellant on the basis of her religious beliefs or that she was denied benefits *because* she was a Seventh-Day Adventist. She was denied benefits just as any other claimant would be denied benefits who was not "available for work" for personal reasons.

With this background, this Court's decision comes into clearer focus. What the Court is holding is that if the State chooses to condition unemployment compensation on the applicant's availability for work, it is constitutionally compelled to *carve out an exception*—and to provide benefits—for those whose unavailability is due to their religious convictions. Such a holding has particular significance in two respects.

First, despite the Court's protestations to the contrary, the decision necessarily overrules *Braunfeld* v. *Brown*. . . .Clearly, any differences between this case and *Braunfeld* cut against the present appellant.

Second, the implications of the present decision are far more troublesome than its apparently narrow dimensions would indicate at first glance. The meaning of today's holding . . . is that the State must furnish unemployment benefits to one who is unavailable for work if the unavailability stems from the exercise of religious convictions. The State, in other words, must *single out* for financial assistance those whose behavior is religiously motivated, even though it denies such assistance to others whose identical behavior (in this case, inability to work on Saturdays) is not religiously motivated.

It has been suggested that such singling out of religious conduct for special treatment may violate the constitutional limitations on state action.... My own view, however, is that at least under the circumstances of this case it would be a permissible accommodation of religion for the State, if it *chose* to do so, to create an exception to its eligibility requirements for persons like the appellant. . . .

However I cannot subscribe to the conclusion that the State is constitutionally *compelled* to carve out an exception to its general rule of eligibility in the present case. . . .

In the *Braunfeld* case what did Chief Justice Earl Warren state were the aspects of religious exercise which cannot in any way "be restricted or burdened by either federal or state legislation"? Does Warren find a secular purpose and effect in the Pennsylvania statute? Does the Chief Justice apply a balancing test to reach the Court's conclusion? What is the distinction he makes between direct and indirect legislative burdens on the exercise of religion? What are the consequences of each in terms of constitutional requirements for the free exercise of religion? What arguments does the Court advance against a constitutional requirement that the state should exempt Sabbatarians from its Sunday closing law? Are there considerations of federalism in the opinion of Warren?

What standard of constitutional adjudication does Justice Brennan, in dissent, state the majority has wrongfully applied to the case? Why does Brennan declare that the effect of the law is to impede the free exercise of religion? How does Brennan apply the balancing test, weighing the interests of the state against the rights of the individual, to support his position?

How does Brennan's decision for the Court in the *Sherbert* case resolve the dilemma Justice Stewart found in his *Braunfeld* dissent that the failure of a state to recognize the religious practices of Sabbatarians forces them to choose between their religious faith and their economic survival? How did the *Sherbert* decision go beyond earlier cases in protecting individuals against indirect burdens upon the free exercise of religion, particularly the withholding of economic benefits because of religious practices? How does Brennan contrast the balance between the interests of the state and the rights of the individual in *Braunfeld* and *Sherbert*? Are the *Sherbert* and *Braunfeld* decisions compatible, or are Justices Stewart (concurring) and Justices Harlan and White (dissenting) correct that *Sherbert* overrules *Braunfeld*?

The *Sherbert* decision significantly expanded the protections afforded individuals under the free exercise clause from previous cases. In the absence of a compelling public interest, states cannot place indirect burdens upon the free exercise of religion. And even if it is demonstrated that there are compelling state interests, the states must "demonstrate that no *alternative* forms of regulation would combat such abuses without infringing First Amendment rights."

Free Exercise Requirements for the Exemption of Religious Groups from State Law

The *Sherbert* opinion suggested that if a state can achieve its goals while granting exemptions to religious groups, it is required to do so by the free exercise clause. Unnecessarily compelling members of religious sects to conform to state law where their religion dictates a contrary practice is hostility toward religion, which violates the principle of government neutrality required under the free exercise clause. In weighing the constitutionality of state laws that have an effect upon the free exercise of religion, the Court will not only carefully balance the interests of the state against the rights of the individual, but will also seek to determine if governmental compulsion is required in order to meet the legitimate ends of the state.

In *Wisconsin* v. *Yoder* (1972) the Court weighed the interests of the state against those of the Amish appellees to determine whether the state could apply its compulsory education law to Amish children beyond the eighth grade. Under the tenets of the Amish religion practiced by the respondents, attendance of Amish children at public or private high schools was contrary to their religion and way of life because it would expose them to worldly values and the possibility of censure by the church community. The Amish believed that during the formative adolescent years children should be instilled with Amish values favoring manual work, self-reliance, and the development of the necessary skills to become an Amish farmer or housewife. The Amish argued that formal schooling at this stage would undermine their community and threaten it with extinction. The state, on the other hand, had a clear interest in compulsory education to prepare citizens for effective and intelligent participation in the political system and to become self-reliant and self-sufficient members of society. However, Chief Justice Burger wrote in the opinion of the Court: "Only those interests of the highest order and those not otherwise served can overbalance legitimate claims to the free exercise of religion."[41]

Against the state's claim that compulsory education is a compelling public interest, Burger responded that where "fundamental claims of religious freedom are at stake . . . we cannot accept such a sweeping claim; despite its admitted validity in the generality of cases, we must searchingly examine the interests that the state seeks to promote by its requirement for compulsory education to age sixteen, and the impediment to those objectives that would flow from recognizing the claimed Amish exemption."[42] In the balancing process Burger found that the free exercise claims prevailed. The interests of the state, argued Burger, were served by the Amish practices, for "[t]here is nothing in this record to suggest that the Amish qualities of reliability, self-reliance, and dedication would fail to find ready markets in today's society."[43] "It cannot be overemphasized," stated Burger, "that we are not dealing with a way of life and mode of education by a group claiming to have recently discovered some 'progressive' or more enlightened process for rearing children for modern life."[44] Rather, "The Amish in this case have convincingly demonstrated the sincerity of their religious beliefs" and have demonstrated

> the adequacy of their alternative mode of continuing formal vocational education in terms of precisely those overall interests that the state advances in support of its program of compulsory high school education. In light of this convincing showing, one that probably few other religious groups or sects could make, and weighing the minimal difference from what the state would require and what the Amish already accept, it was incumbent on the state to show with more particularity how its admittedly strong interest in compulsory education would be adversely affected by granting an exemption to the Amish.[45]

In both *Sherbert* and *Yoder* the states could not make a plausible argument that granting religious exemptions would raise a grave threat to the public interest. Those most immediately affected persons were the members of the religious sects themselves who challenged the law, although in the *Yoder* case, the children of the plaintiffs were also affected. Douglas stressed in his dissent in *Yoder* that the effect of the majority decision was to invade the rights of the children without canvassing their views. "If the parents in this case are allowed a religious exemption," stated Douglas, "the inevitable effect is to impose the parents' notions of religious duty upon their children."[46] Children, argued Douglas, have constitutionally protectable interests.

Douglas dissented from the portion of the Court's opinion that applied to parents whose children had not expressed their desire to remain outside of the public or private high schools required to be attended under the law.

[41]Wisconsin v. Yoder, 406 U.S. 205, 215 (1972).
[42]Ibid., p. 221.
[43]Ibid., p. 224.
[44]Ibid., p. 235.
[45]Ibid., pp. 235–236.
[46]Ibid., p. 242.

Chief Justice Burger's majority opinion dismissed Douglas's contention that the children should be allowed to express their views with the statement that "Our holding today in no degree depends on the assertion of the religious interest of the child as contrasted with that of the parents. It is the parents who are subject to prosecution here for failing to cause their children to attend school, and it is their right of free exercise, not that of their children, that must determine Wisconsin's power to impose criminal penalties on the parents."[47]

Where the Court readily perceives that there is a compelling state interest in compulsory requirements, as in the case of vaccination for children, it has not sustained free exercise claims for exemption.[48] And even where the state's interest is not as compelling as in protecting the community's health, as in the area of child labor, public interest claims have been sustained over free exercise clause challenges.[49] Will the Court sustain a governmental proscription upon religious practices, for example the religious use of peyote by American Indians, on the basis of harm to self, without a finding of an overriding public interest? In *People* v. *Woody*, 61 Cal. 2d 716 (1964), the California Supreme Court held that the conviction of American Indians for the use of peyote was unconstitutional, because the drug was used in bona fide religious ceremonies. The Court found there were less restrictive alternative means for the government to control drugs in the public interest than a blanket proscription upon all drug use. The argument that the drugs harm users does not create a sufficient public interest to outweigh the free exercise claim.[50]

Free Exercise and the Draft

The Court adopted a liberal definition of religion protected under the free exercise clause in several cases sustaining the claims of religiously unorthodox conscientious objectors against war. The Court broadly interpreted section 6(j) of the Universal Military Training and Service Act of 1948, which exempted from combatant training and service in the armed forces persons "who by reason of their religious training and belief are conscientiously opposed to participation in war in any form." The act defined "religious training and belief" as "an individual's belief in a relation to a supreme being involving duties superior to those arising from any human relation, but [not including] essentially political, sociological, or philosophical views or a merely personal moral code." In *United States* v. *Seeger* (1965) the Court held,

---

[47]Ibid., pp. 230–231.

[48]See, for example, Jacobson v. Massachusetts, 197 U.S. 11 (1905), that upheld the state's compulsory vaccination law against a free exercise clause challenge.

[49]See Prince v. Massachusetts, 321 U.S. 158 (1943).

[50]Cf. Kennedy v. Bureau of Narcotics, 459 F. 2d 415 (9th Cir. 1972), cert. denied 409 U.S. 1115 (1975). The courts have sustained governmental proscriptions upon the use of marijuana, LSD, and other hallucinogenic drugs. See, for example, U.S. v. Kuch, 288 F. supp. 439 (D.D.C. 1968); Leary v. United States, 383 F. 2d 851 (5th cir. 1967), reversed on other grounds 395 U.S. 6 (1969).

We have concluded that Congress, in using the expression "supreme being" rather than the designation "God," was merely clarifying the meaning of religious training and belief so as to embrace all religions and to exclude essentially political, sociological, or philosophical views. We believe that under this construction, the test of belief 'in a relation to a supreme being' is whether a given belief that is *sincere* and *meaningful* occupies a place in the life of its possessor parallel to that filled by the orthodox belief in God of one who clearly qualifies for the exemption.[51]

The Court found that all of the defendants in the *Seeger* and companion cases qualified for the draft exemption, because even though they did not believe in a supreme being in the traditional sense, their conscientious objection to war was sincere.

In *Welsh* v. *United States* (1970) the Court, although citing *Seeger* as precedent, went beyond that decision in sustaining a draft exemption based upon conscientious objection which had no traditional religious base. In 1967 Congress dropped the requirement for a belief in relation to a supreme being as a religious test but continued to authorize exemption only to those who objected to war "by reason of religious training and belief." In the *Welsh* case the defendant admitted that his views were not "religious" in any traditional sense, and that his objections to the war were based upon his belief that killing was morally wrong. The circuit court sustained his conviction in the district court for failing to report for induction, finding that there was no religious basis for his conscientious objector claim. The Supreme Court reversed the conviction, finding that Welsh had met the "religious" test under the law, which required that his opposition to the war be based upon moral, ethical, or religious beliefs, held with the strength of traditional religious convictions, about what was right and wrong. Justice Black's plurality opinion for the Court stated that "We certainly do not think that section 6(j)'s exclusion of those persons with 'essentially political, sociological, or philosophical views or a merely personal moral code' should be read to exclude those who hold strong beliefs about our domestic and foreign affairs or even those whose conscientious objection to participation in all wars is founded to a substantial extent upon considerations of public policy."[52]

The broad interpretations the Court gave to section 6(j) in the *Seeger* and *Welsh* cases did not extend to upholding the claim of a Catholic that it was his religious duty to select "unjust" from "just" wars and conscientiously object to the former. In *Gillette* v. *United States*, 401 U.S. 437 (1971), the Court held that section 6(j) requires conscientious objection to all war and that disallowing selective conscientious objection to Catholics was not discrimination because the requirements of section 6(j) were religiously neutral and served a legitimate secular end.

---

[51]United States v. Seeger, 380 U.S. 163, 166 (1965). (Emphasis supplied.)
[52]Welsh v. United States, 398 U.S. 333, 342 (1970).

ELEVEN

Equal Protection of the Laws

The primary constitutional source of the equal protection requirement is the Fourteenth Amendment: "No state shall . . . deny to any person in its jurisdiction the equal protection of the laws." Requirements for equal protection also are found in the Thirteenth Amendment prohibiting slavery and involuntary servitude and in the Fifteenth Amendment forbidding the government to deny citizens of the United States the right to vote "on account of race, color, or previous condition of servitude." The equal protection standards found in the Civil War amendments were clearly intended to protect the equality of the newly freed blacks, even though only the Fifteenth Amendment mentioned race. In the *Slaughterhouse Cases* (1873) the Court declared that the "one pervading purpose" of the Civil War amendments was to assure "the freedom of the slave race, the security and firm establishment of that freedom, and the protection of the newly-made freeman and citizen from the oppressions of those who had formerly exercised unlimited dominion over him."[1] The Court's decision in the *Slaughterhouse Cases* stripped the privileges and immunities clause of the Fourteenth Amendment of any power; therefore when the Court at a later time sought to protect individual rights against state action it was forced to turn to the equal protection and due process clauses of the Fourteenth Amendment.[2]

[1]Slaughterhouse Cases, 16 Wall. 36, 71 (1873).

[2]The intent of the framers of the privileges and immunities clause of the Fourteenth Amendment, although not necessarily of the states that ratified it, was to extend the protections of the Bill of Rights to state action. This has now largely been accomplished through the due process clause of the Fourteenth Amendment. (See Chapter 8.) While the privileges and immunities clause was to incorporate the Bill of Rights, it also was to extend to all citizens other "privileges and immunities" granted to citizens of the United States by the Constitution by proscribing state action that would abridge such privileges and immunities. Since the abrogation of the privileges and immunities clause by the Slaughterhouse opinion, the Supreme Court has relied upon the equal protection clause to extend privileges and immunities to state jurisdictions in cases where the due process clause of the Fourteenth Amendment clearly would not apply

The apparent limitation of the purpose of the amendments to racial equality did not prevent the Supreme Court from subsequently using the text of the equal protection clause of the Fourteenth Amendment to go beyond racial classifications in defining its reach.

While the Civil War amendments and in particular the Fourteenth Amendment are the principal fount of the equal protection standards, other parts of the Constitution as well have been held to incorporate equal protection requirements. In *Bolling* v. *Sharpe* (1954) the Court found an equal protection command in the due process clause of the Fifth Amendment.[3] In *Wesberry* v. *Sanders* (1964) the Court held that the command of Article I, Section 2, that representatives be chosen "by the people of the several states," "means that as nearly as is practicable one man's vote in a congressional election is to be worth as much as another's."[4] The due process clause of the Fourteenth Amendment has also been interpreted to require equal protection.[5] The privileges and immunities clause of Article IV, Section 2, requires states to grant equal treatment under their laws to citizens of other states.[6]

The standards of equal protection applied by the courts have varied over time in accordance with the ever-changing views of judges about what constitutes equality under the law. As an operative concept, equal protection essentially did not exist before it became an explicit part of the Fourteenth Amendment, with the exception of the equal protection requirement implied in the privileges and immunities clause. As the Court embarked upon defining equal protection, it was confronted with a task that was at least as difficult if not more so than it undertook in interpreting the due process clause of the Fourteenth Amendment. The concept of due process had a long history in Anglo-American law, jurisprudence, and judicial practice. Equal protection, on the other hand, was a relatively novel concept in the law, although not in political philosophy, when it was put into the Fourteenth Amendment. It was not until the activist period of the Warren Court that equal protection standards became the basis of particularly close judicial scrutiny of state legislation to guarantee equal treatment and to protect fundamental rights.[7]

---

or, in the judgment of the Court, is an inappropriate vehicle for the protection of individual rights. For example, in Shapiro v. Thompson, 394 U.S. 618 (1969), the Court relied upon the equal protection clause to safeguard the right to travel freely among the states. If the privileges or immunities clause had not been dormant the right to travel could well have been extended under its rubric, as four justices agreed it should be in Edwards v. California, 314 U.S. 160, 171 (1941). Justice Brennan's majority opinion in Shapiro cited the concurring opinions in Edwards that supported the existence of a constitutional right to travel under the privileges or immunities clause. (The Edwards majority upheld the right to travel on the basis of the commerce clause.)

[3]See p. 834.
[4]Wesberry v. Sanders, 376 U.S. 1, 7–8 (1964).
[5]Boddie v. Connecticut, 401 U.S. 371 (1971).
[6]One statement of this purpose of the clause may be found in Toomer v. Witsell, 334 U.S. 385, 395 (1948).
[7]The Court has not used equal protection to scrutinize closely state legislation and enforce its views of fundamental rights in the *economic* sphere to anywhere near the degree it has done

A potential problem of equal protection arises when legislation treats two groups of people differently in pursuit of a particular goal. For example, benefits under the social security system may not be allocated to men and women on the same basis, reflecting a congressional premise that the economic needs of men and women differ. This results in "unequal treatment" in the generic sense but not necessarily in violation of constitutional standards of equal protection applied by the courts. The process of differentiating groups of people in legislation is one of *classification* of those groups for the purposes of the law. Group classification becomes the means to achieve certain ends of the legislature. In developing equal protection standards the Supreme Court has devised various formulas to determine if the ends justify the means, that is, if the classifications in the law can be upheld on the basis of implied or stated legislative goals.

The "Old" Equal Protection Standards—
the Pre-Warren Era

In reviewing state enactments under the equal protection clause of the Fourteenth Amendment, the Court in the pre-Warren era applied a *rational-relation* or *conceivable-basis* test to determine if legislative ends justified classifications resulting in the unequal treatment of different groups of people.[8] Under these tests the Court upheld legislative classifications provided it found that there was a rational relationship between the classifications and stated legislative goals or if there was a conceivable basis upon which the Court could imply legislative goals that would justify the classifications. The conceivable-basis and rational-relation tests were one and the same until the era of the Burger Court, which rejected the conceivable-basis test in assessing whether or not there was a rational relation between legislative classifications and goals. In *McGinnis* v. *Royster* (1973) Justice Powell's opinion for the Court asked "whether the challenged distinction [classification] rationally furthers some legitimate, *articulated* state purpose."[9] Powell declared that state objectives must be "nonillusory" and that the Court would not supply an "imaginary basis or purpose" to sustain a statutory classification.

The old equal protection standard of the Court, however, did allow it to supply the conceivable purpose upon which a legislative enactment could be

---

so to protect *individual* civil liberties and rights. For a sampling of cases in the economic sphere, see City of New Orleans v. Dukes, 427 U.S. 297 (1976); Morey v. Doud, 354 U.S. 457 (1957). See also Railway Express Agency, Inc. v. New York, 336 U.S. 906 (1949); Kotch v. Board of River Port Pilot Commissioners, 330 U.S. 552 (1947).

[8]Before the Warren Court equal protection standards were based primarily upon the Fourteenth Amendment and therefore were generally limited in application to state actions. The Warren Court unequivocally extended equal protection to all national actions under the due process clause of the Fifth Amendment. However, before the Warren Court, Fifth Amendment due process was used to apply equal protection standards to the national government. See Bolling v. Sharpe, pp. 833–834.

[9]McGinnis v. Royster, 410 U.S. 263, 270 (1973). (Emphasis supplied.)

upheld. Minimum rationality requirements adopted by the Court allowed a loose "fit" between legislative ends and means. Above all, the rational-relation and conceivable-basis tests constituted before the Warren Court era extreme deference to state legislatures. These tests were explicitly used to uphold state economic regulation, not to sustain racial segregation as in the case of *Plessy* v. *Ferguson* (1896).[10]

The Supreme Court adopted a minimum rationality standard at the outset of its review of economic regulation under the equal protection clause. In *Powell* v. *Pennsylvania*, 127 U.S. 678 (1888), the Court held that any classification for regulatory purposes could be upheld provided there was no discrimination among those within the designated class. This approach allowed virtually complete discretion to state legislatures to classify as they wished for the purposes of economic regulation. This standard was reiterated in *F.S. Royster Guano* v. *Virginia* (1920), in which the Court stated that classifications "must be reasonable, not arbitrary, and must rest upon some ground of difference having a fair and substantial relation to the object of the legislation, so that all persons similarly circumstanced shall be treated alike."[11]

Immediately preceding the Warren Court, judicial deference to state economic regulation challenged on equal protection grounds was evident in *Kotch* v. *Board of Riverport Pilot Commissioners*, 330 U.S. 552 (1947), in which the conceivable-basis test was used to uphold a Louisiana law requiring an apprenticeship to become a harbor pilot. The plaintiffs alleged that under the law the practice of the incumbent pilot was always to select relatives and friends to serve as apprentices. The Court acknowledged that although this was the practice, the legislature *might* have intended such a result to improve the esprit de corps of the pilots by encouraging a family and neighborly tradition. The conceivable-basis test was also used to sustain New York City regulations banning vehicular advertising with the exception of "business notices upon business delivery vehicles, so long as such vehicles are engaged in the usual business or regular work of the owner and not used merely or mainly for advertising." Justice Douglas's majority opinion stated that the local authorities "*may* well have concluded that those who advertise their own wares on their trucks do not present the same traffic problem in view of the nature or extent of the advertising which they use. It would take a degree of omniscience which we lack to say that such is not the case."[12]

"Old" Equal Protection and the Warren and Burger Courts

The rational-relation and conceivable-basis tests have been used to sustain legislative classifications in the sphere of economic regulation during the Warren and Burger Court eras as well as before. Only in rare instances is a legislative classification for economic purposes voided. This was done, for

[10]Plessy v. Ferguson is discussed on pp. 819–823.
[11]F.S. Royster Guano v. Virginia, 253 U.S. 412, 415 (1920).
[12]Railway Express Agency, Inc. v. New York, 336 U.S. 106, 110 (1949). (Emphasis supplied.)

example, in *Morey* v. *Doud*, 354 U.S. 457 (1957), which held unconstitutional an Illinois regulatory statute that exempted the American Express Company from certain of its provisions. The Court found the exclusion of the American Express Company "irrational" in terms of the stated legislative purpose of protecting the public. The *Morey* decision, however, was overruled in *City of New Orleans* v. *Dukes*, 427 U.S. 297 (1976), in which the Court allowed the City of New Orleans to exempt two vendors from its ban on pushcart sellers in the French Quarter of the city. The Court found that while the case was not distinguishable from *Morey*, nevertheless the city could reasonably find that the vendors constituted part of the distinctive character and charm of the old city.

A number of cases during the Warren era illustrate the deference given to state legislation challenged on equal protection grounds. In *Williamson* v. *Lee Optical Company* (1955) the Court summarily upheld a state regulation of opticians against an equal protection challenge. The district court had held that the state law, which subjected opticians to regulation while exempting other sellers of ready-to-wear glasses, violated the equal protection clause. Justice Douglas wrote for a unanimous Court,

> The problem of legislative classification is a perennial one, admitting of no doctrinaire definition. . . . The legislature may select one phase of one field and apply a remedy there, neglecting the others. The prohibition of the equal protection clause goes no further than the invidious discrimination. We cannot say that point has been reached here. For all this record shows, the ready-to-wear branch of this business may not loom large in Oklahoma or may present problems of regulation distinct from the other branch.[13]

In *McGowan* v. *Maryland* (1961) Chief Justice Warren wrote for a unanimous Court rejecting an equal protection challenge to a state law exempting certain businesses from a Maryland Sunday closing law.

> The Court has held that the Fourteenth Amendment permits the states a wide scope of discretion in enacting laws which affect some groups of citizens differently than others. The constitutional safeguard is offended only if the classification rests on grounds wholly irrelevant to the achievement of the state's objective. State legislatures are presumed to have acted within their constitutional power despite the fact that in practice, their laws result in some inequality. A statutory discrimination will not be set aside if any state of facts reasonably may be conceived to justify it.[14]

The Burger Court continued to use the rational-relation test in a manner that generally deferred to legislative judgment, although it abandoned the conceivable-basis test. In *Dandridge* v. *Williams* (1970) the Court deferred to the judgment of the Maryland legislature in upholding a law regulating aid to families with dependent children. The law had been challenged as a violation of the equal protection clause because it denied equitable treatment to welfare recipients by providing a maximum grant of $250 per month for

---

[13]Williamson v. Lee Optical Co., 348 U.S. 483, 489 (1955).
[14]McGowan v. Maryland, 366 U.S. 420, 425–426 (1961).

families regardless of their size or needs. Opponents of the law charged that under its provisions persons similarly situated—dependent children and their families—were not treated equally according to their needs. The state defended its position on the grounds that the law was designed to encourage employment. Those who challenged the law claimed that since some recipient families had no employable person their aid should not be limited to the amount received by families with potentially employable members. In effect, the legislative classification of the group to receive aid was "overinclusive," indiscriminately including persons regardless of their needs. The district court invalidated the law because of its overinclusive or "overreaching" character, declaring that it cut "too broad a swath on an indiscriminate basis as applied to the entire group of AFDC eligibles." Justice Stewart's majority opinion for the Supreme Court sharply differentiated between the standards that should be applied under the equal protection clause to judicial review of state economic regulation and the standards of review of classifications affecting fundamental rights, such as those in the First Amendment. He stated,

> If this were a case involving government action claimed to violate the First Amendment guarantee of free speech, a finding of "overreaching" would be significant and might be crucial . . . but the concept of "overreaching" has no place in this case. For here we deal with state regulation in the social and economic field, not affecting freedoms guaranteed by the Bill of Rights, and claimed to violate the Fourteenth Amendment only because the regulation results in some disparity in grants of welfare payments to the largest AFDC families. For this Court to approve the invalidation of state economic or social regulation as "overreaching" would be far too reminiscent of an era when the Court thought the Fourteenth Amendment gave it power to strike down state laws "because they may be unwise, improvident, or out of harmony with a particular school of thought." . . . That era long ago passed into history. . . .
>
> In the area of economics and social welfare, a state does not violate the Equal Protection Clause merely because the classifications made by its laws are imperfect. If the classification has some "reasonable basis," it does not offend the Constitution. . . .
>
> To be sure, the cases cited, and many others enunciating this fundamental standard under the Equal Protection Clause, have in the main involved state regulation of business or industry. The administration of public welfare assistance, by contrast, involves the most basic economic needs of impoverished human beings. We recognize the dramatically real factual difference between the cited cases and this one, but we can find no basis for applying a different constitutional standard. . . . It is a standard that has consistently been applied to state legislation restricting the availability of employment opportunities. . . . And it is a standard that is true to the principle that the Fourteenth Amendment gives the federal courts no power to impose upon the states their views of what constitutes wise economic or social policy.[15]

Justice Stuart's *Dandridge* opinion reaffirmed the rational-relation test in judicial review of economic regulation and in effect extended it to review of welfare assistance programs.[16] In *New Orleans* v. *Dukes,* the Court again used

[15]Dandridge v. Williams, 397 U.S. 471, 484–486 (1970).
[16]Contrast the Court's decision in Shapiro v. Thompson, pp. 868–873.

the rational-relation formula: "When local economic regulation is challenged solely as violating the equal protection clause, this Court consistently defers to legislative determinations as to the desirability of particular statutory discriminations. . . . Unless a classification trammels fundamental personal rights or is drawn upon inherently suspect distinctions such as race, religion, or alienage, our decisions presume the constitutionality of the statutory discriminations and require only that the classification challenged be rationally related to a legitimate state interest."[17] This standard was applied in *Friedman* v. *Rogers* (1979) to uphold against an equal protection challenge a Texas law that required a majority of the licensed optometrists on the Texas Optometry Board to be members of the Texas Optometric Association. The Court found that the requirement "is related reasonably to the state's legitimate purpose of securing a Board that will administer the act faithfully."[18] It was reasonable, stated the Court, for the legislature to require that a majority of the regulatory board be drawn from the professional association that had supported the enactment of the rules to be enforced by the board.

The Burger Court continued to apply the rational-relation test to state economic regulation in *Barry* v. *Barchi* (1979), upholding provisions of a New York law regulating harness racing while exempting thoroughbred racing. The challenged provisions of the law prohibited stays of license suspensions pending post-suspension hearings for trainers engaged in harness racing, while permitting such stays pending appeal of suspension of licenses for trainers in thoroughbred racing. The Court found that the state legislature reasonably concluded that harness racing should be subject to stricter regulation than thoroughbred racing to protect the public interest and to foster public confidence in harness racing.

The rational-relation test is used by the Court under the Fifth as well as the Fourteenth Amendment equal protection review of economic and social regulation that does not affect a "suspect" class or fundamental rights.[19] In *Vance* v. *Bradley* (1979), Justice White wrote the opinion of the Court upholding against an equal protection challenge a congressional law requiring federal employees covered by the foreign service retirement and disability system to retire at age sixty while exempting from mandatory retirement at that age employees covered by the civil service retirement and disability system. White declared that the law was reasonably related to the legitimate congressional goal of recruiting, training, and generally developing a professional corps of public servants who were more often than not called upon to perform overseas under difficult circumstances. He noted that the appellees

> have not suggested that the statutory distinction between foreign service personnel over age 60 and other federal employees over that age burdens a suspect group or a fundamental interest; and in cases where these considerations are ab-

[17]New Orleans v. Dukes 427 U.S. 297, 303 (1976). For a discussion of judicial review of "suspect" classifications, see the discussion below of the new standards of strict judicial scrutiny.

[18]Friedman v. Rogers, 440 U.S. 1, 17 (1979).

[19]See the discussion of equal protection review where a suspect class or fundamental rights are involved, pp. 814–816.

sent, courts are quite reluctant to overturn governmental action on the ground that it denies equal protection of the laws. The Constitution presumes that, absent some reason to infer antipathy, even improvident decisions will eventually be rectified by the democratic process and that judicial intervention is generally unwarranted no matter how unwisely we may think a political branch has acted. Thus, we will not overturn such a statute unless the varying treatment of different groups or persons is so unrelated to the achievement of any combination of legitimate purposes that we can only conclude that the legislature's actions were irrational.[20]

The "New" Equal Protection—Strict Judicial Scrutiny of Laws Burdening Suspect Classes and Fundamental Rights

The Court has adopted strict equal protection standards of judicial review of laws that burden fundamental rights or imply prejudice against racial or other minorities. In such cases the Court undertakes *strict judicial scrutiny*, requiring a compelling governmental interest to uphold the classification. Under strict judicial scrutiny the burden of proof is upon the government to demonstrate a compelling need for the classification. The showing of a mere rational relationship between legislative classifications and goals does not pass the strict judicial scrutiny test. The stringent standards of that test are usually fatal to the law under review.

The strict judicial scrutiny test, unlike the rational-relation and conceivable-basis tests, does not defer to the political process. Under strict scrutiny the assumption is that the legislature has acted unconstitutionally until it is proven that its action is justified by a compelling governmental interest. Strict judicial scrutiny is required of legislative classifications that on their face suggest prejudice against racial and minority groups. This is because, as Justice Black wrote in the majority opinion in *Korematsu* v. *United States* in 1944, "all legal restrictions which curtail the civil rights of a single racial group are immediately *suspect*. That is not to say that all such restrictions are unconstitutional. It is to say that courts must subject them to the most rigid scrutiny. Pressing public necessity may sometimes justify the existence of such restrictions; racial antagonism never can."[21] It is ironic that the concept of "suspect" classes was articulated in the *Korematsu* case which in effect upheld such a legal classification.

Underlying the concept of suspect classes is the judicial assumption that there are groups of persons that have in the past been prejudiced by governmental and societal actions. Racial minorities particularly fit into this category, but nonracial minority groups as well may be considered a suspect or almost suspect class. For example, aliens were considered essentially equivalent to a suspect class and strict judicial scrutiny was applied in *Graham* v. *Richardson*, 403 U.S. 365 (1971), to strike down a state law that denied welfare benefits to all noncitizens and to aliens who had not resided in the

---

[20]Vance v. Bradley, 440 U.S. 93, 96–97 (1979).
[21]Korematsu v. United States, 323 U.S. 214, 216 (1944). (Emphasis supplied.) The Korematsu case is discussed at pp. 227–237.

country for a period of fifteen years.[22] There was a strong implication that the Court considered "illegitimate" children to be a suspect class in several decisions written by Justice Douglas in 1968 that declared unconstitutional a Louisiana law which in effect provided that illegitimate children who had not been "acknowledged" by their parents were nonpersons.[23] The Burger Court at first seemed to retreat from strict judicial scrutiny of illegitimacy classifications in *Labine* v. *Vincent*, 401 U.S. 532 (1971), which upheld a Louisiana law subordinating the rights of acknowledged illegitimate children to legitimate children and relatives of the parents in claims upon an estate left without a will. The Court, however, with Justice Powell writing the majority opinion in *Weber* v. *Aetna Casualty and Surety Co.*, 406 U.S. 164 (1972), again implied that illegitimate children were a suspect class in holding that a Louisiana worker's compensation law could not subordinate the claims of illegitimate to those of legitimate children. While a majority of the Court has not *explicitly* found aliens and illegitimate children to be suspect classes, its decisions have implied such a conclusion by adopting standards of strict judicial scrutiny in reviewing equal protection claims in these areas.[24] The term *suspect* has also been extended by a plurality of the Burger Court to gender-based classifications in *Frontiero* v. *Richardson* (1973), but this view has not been accepted by the majority.[25]

The second category of cases in which the Court has applied the rigid standards of strict scrutiny involves classifications affecting fundamental rights. The refusal of the Court to defer to legislative judgment in this sphere is based upon the premise that to a considerable extent the deprivation of fundamental rights, such as freedom of speech, the right to vote, and rights of association and assembly, prevents the political process from working effectively. Judicial intervention is justified to assure democratic effectiveness.

The need for strict judicial scrutiny of classifications that are suspect or which burden fundamental rights may be found in the often-cited footnote of Chief Justice Stone in *United States* v. *Carolene Products Co.* (1938).

> There may be narrower scope for operation of the presumption of constitutionality when legislation appears on its face to be within a specific prohibition of the Constitution, such as those of the first ten Amendments, which are deemed equally specific when held to be embraced within the Fourteenth. . . .
>   It is unnecessary to consider now whether legislation which restricts those political processes which can ordinarily be expected to bring about repeal of undesirable legislation, is to be subjected to more exacting judicial scrutiny under the general prohibitions of the Fourteenth Amendment than are most other types of

[22]See also In Re Griffiths, 413 U.S. 717 (1973), invalidating a New York law that limited permanent positions in the state civil service to American citizens.

[23]See Levy v. Louisiana, 391 U.S. 68 (1968), declaring unconstitutional a Louisiana statute that barred unacknowledged illegitimate children from receiving benefits for the death of the mother; and Glona v. American Guarantee and Liability Insurance Co., 391 U.S. 73 (1968), invalidating a provision of the Louisiana law that barred a mother from recovering benefits for the death of her unacknowledged illegitimate child.

[24]In Frontiero v. Richardson, 411 U.S. 677 (1973), a plurality of the Court did define alienage along with race and national origin as suspect classifications.

[25]For a discussion of judicial review of gender-based classifications see pp. 877–895.

legislation. On restrictions upon the right to vote, see *Nixon* v. *Herndon* [1927]; *Nixon* v. *Condon* [1932]; on restraints upon the dissemination of information, see *Near* v. *Minnesota* [1931]; *Grosjean* v. *American Press Co.* [1936]; *Lovell* v. *Griffin* [1938]; on interferences with political organizations, see *Stromberg* v. *California* [1931]; *Fiske* v. *Kansas* [1927]; *Whitney* v. *California* [1927]; *Herndon* v. *Lowry* [1937]; and see Holmes, J., in *Gitlow* v. *New York* [1925]; as to prohibition of peaceable assembly, see *De Jonge* v. *Oregon* [1937].

Nor need we enquire whether similar considerations enter into the review of statutes directed at particular religious, . . . or national, . . . or racial minorities, . . . whether prejudice against discrete and insular minorities may be a special condition which tends seriously to curtail the operation of those political processes ordinarily to be relied upon to protect minorities, and which may call for a correspondingly more searching judicial inquiry. . . .[26]

The *Carolene Products* footnote focused attention on the need to develop stricter judicial scrutiny of legislation restricting fundamental rights, particularly rights that are essential to free and open political processes, and legislation directed at religious, racial, and other minority groups.

The Merging of the "Old" and the "New" Equal Protection Tests by the Burger Court— Intermediate Review

The two-tier approach of the Warren Court, applying strict judicial scrutiny in the review of suspect classifications and laws burdening fundamental rights, while using the rational-relation test for other legislative classifications, is not always as clearly applied in practice as in theory. The Burger Court in particular has often been unable to agree on definitions of suspect classifications and fundamental rights that invoke strict judicial scrutiny. This was illustrated, for example, in the lack of explicit recognition by a majority of the Court that alienage, illegitimacy, and gender-based classifications were to be considered suspect and therefore subject to strict judicial scrutiny.[27] In these spheres the Court has not explicitly stated that the classifications are suspect to the degree, for example, that a racial classification is suspect. Nor has the Court always rigidly applied standards of strict judicial scrutiny in reviewing the classifications. The Court has held, generally, that alienage, illegitimacy, and gender classifications are semi-suspect, which means that they are only slightly less suspect than classifications involving the "discrete and insular minorities" referred to in the *Carolene Products* footnote.

Where the Court does not consider classifications to be fully suspect, it has adopted an intermediate standard of review that falls between the mere rationality test on the one hand and on the other hand the strict judicial scrutiny test that requires the government to show a compelling interest in order to sustain a suspect classification. In exercising intermediate review over semi-suspect classifications, the Court requires the government to dem-

---

[26]United States v. Carolene Products Co., 304 U.S. 144, 152–153 n.4 (1938).
[27]See pp. 814–815.

onstrate that its interests are important, if not compelling. The classification cannot be sustained simply on the basis of administrative convenience.[28] The "fit" between the legislative means (classifications) and ends (goals) must be close if not exact.

The Court uses techniques of intermediate review not only in cases where it considers legislative classifications to be semi-suspect but also where it finds that the legislature has burdened "important" interests if not fundamental or preferred rights. Classifications affecting food stamps and the ability to obtain a college education burden important interests and will not be sustained on the basis of a loosely applied rational-relation test.[29]

The Court exercised intermediate review, for example, in *Craig v. Boren* (1976). The case involved a semi-suspect gender-based classification under which Oklahoma had prohibited the sale of "nonintoxicating" 3.2 percent beer to males under the age of twenty-one and to females under the age of eighteen. Justice Brennan's majority opinion stated the intermediate standard of judicial review: "To withstand constitutional challenge, previous cases establish that classifications by gender must serve *important* governmental objectives and must be *substantially related* to achievement of those objectives."[30] The Court found that the classification was not substantially related to the achievement of the state's objective to protect public health and safety. Oklahoma had marshaled impressive statistics to prove that male drivers under the age of twenty-one were more prone to traffic accidents due to alcohol than female drivers. The Court concluded, however, that while the statistical difference between males and females arrested for drunken driving was "not trivial" it was inadequate to sustain the gender-based classification. Commenting upon the intermediate or "middle-tier" approach used by the Court, Justice Powell noted in a concurring opinion,

> As is evident from our opinions, the Court has had difficulty in agreeing upon a standard of equal protection analysis that can be applied consistently to the wide variety of legislative classifications. There are valid reasons for dissatisfaction with the "two-tier" approach that has been prominent in the Court's decisions in the past decade. . . . [O]ur decision today will be viewed by some as a "middle-tier" approach. While I would not endorse that characterization and would not welcome a further subdividing of equal protection analysis, candor compels the recognition that the relatively deferential "rational basis" standard normally applied takes on a sharper focus when we address a gender-based classification. So much is clear from our recent cases.[31]

The Application of Equal Protection Tests
to the Cases in this Chapter

The equal protection tests seem at first reading to be precise and unequivocal. However, both the tests and the cases which they govern are

[28]Vlandis v. Kline, 412 U.S. 441, 458–459 (1973).
[29]United States Department of Agriculture v. Murray, 413 U.S. 508 (1973); Vlandis v. Kline, 412 U.S. 441 (1973).
[30]Craig v. Boren, 429 U.S. 190, 197 (1976). (Emphasis supplied.)
[31]Ibid., 210–211 n. * (1976).

not as clear in practice as they are in theory. The very fact that the Burger Court has developed intermediate standards of equal protection review that fall between the requirements of the rational-relation and strict scrutiny tests reflects the difficulty it has had in developing consistent standards.

In the cases that follow the Court did not always clearly articulate the standards that it applied in terms of the equal protection tests that have been described. However, the tests or variants upon them are implied in each case. The first category of cases considered concerns racial classifications in which the Court gradually came to apply strict judicial scrutiny. In effect, it was strict judicial scrutiny that brought an end to the separate but equal doctrine of *Plessy* v. *Ferguson* (1896) in *Brown* v. *Board of Education* (1954). In *Sweatt* v. *Painter* (1950), an important case leading up to the *Brown* decision, the Court's opinion implied the standards of what it was eventually to label strict scrutiny in finding no compelling state interest to justify racial classifications denying blacks equal educational opportunities in a state law school.

All of the equal protection tests were discussed at length by Justices Powell and Brennan who were on opposite sides in *University of California* v. *Bakke* (1978). Powell felt that the case involved a suspect classification demanding strict judicial scrutiny, while Brennan argued that since the case involved neither a suspect classification nor fundamental rights, standards of intermediate review would suffice.

The Court articulated standards of strict judicial scrutiny of classifications burdening fundamental rights in *Shapiro* v. *Thompson* (1969). The Court's opinion left no doubt of its acceptance of the two-tier approach to equal protection. As Justice Harlan noted in his dissent, the opinion of the Court articulated the "compelling interest" doctrine more explicitly than ever before, applying that standard to suspect classifications and those denying fundamental constitutional rights.

The Court confronted the question of wealth classifications in *San Antonio* v. *Rodriguez* (1973), which considered the question of whether or not wealth is a suspect classification demanding strict judicial scrutiny. The type of scrutiny required by gender classifications was raised in *Reed* v. *Reed* (1971) and *Orr* v. *Orr* (1979).

The concluding cases, *Wesberry* v. *Sanders* (1964) and *Reynolds* v. *Sims* (1964), concern judicial scrutiny of the fundamental right to equal voting opportunity.

THE SEPARATE BUT EQUAL DOCTRINE

In the *Slaughterhouse Cases* the Court wrote that "it is not difficult to give a meaning to this [equal protection] clause [of the Fourteenth Amendment]. The existence of laws in the states where the newly emancipated negroes resided, which discriminated with gross injustice and hardship against them *as a class*, was the evil to be remedied by this clause, and by it such laws are forbidden."[32] From the origin of the interpretation of the equal protection

[32]See p. 468. (Emphasis supplied.)

clause, the Court has held that it forbids unequal government treatment of *classes of persons*. What classes are covered by the law, however, is a matter for judicial determination. In the *Slaughterhouse Cases* the Court felt that it was absolutely clear that the law prevented only unequal government treatment of "the newly emancipated negroes." "We doubt very much," continued the *Slaughterhouse* Court, "whether any action of a state not directed by way of discrimination against the negroes as a class, or on account of their race, will ever be held to come within the purview of this [equal protection] provision."[33]

The Court's interpretation of the equal protection clause in the *Slaughterhouse Cases* implied that it would no longer view blacks as an inferior class under the law, as it had in the *Dred Scott* case in which Chief Justice Taney held that blacks, whether freemen or slaves, were not citizens of the United States and therefore did not enjoy the political privileges of citizenship.[34] Even the granting of citizenship status to blacks by the states, declared Taney, did not entitle them to the privileges and immunities granted by the federal Constitution to citizens of the states. Taney's exegesis illustrated that the Supreme Court had little difficulty in interpreting the Constitution to suit its ends and values.

While the *Slaughterhouse* opinion unequivocally stated that the equal protection clause was designed to prevent discrimination against blacks as a class, this was a hypothetical point since the issue of discrimination against blacks was not involved in the case. Would the Court in a concrete case prevent discrimination against blacks by the states, or would it maintain the status quo by interpreting the equal protection clause in such a way as to make it inapplicable?

In the following classic case the Court reviewed the constitutionality under the equal protection clause of a Louisiana law of 1890 that required "equal but separate accommodations" for white and black railroad passengers. The defendant, Plessy, was arrested for refusing to leave a seat in a coach reserved for whites. Plessy, who claimed he was only one-eighth African, directly challenged the constitutionality of the law on the grounds that it denied him equal protection.

Plessy v. Ferguson

163 U.S. 537; 16 S. Ct. 1138 41 L. Ed. 256 (1896)

Mr. Justice Brown delivered the opinion of the Court:

... The object of the Fourteenth Amendment was undoubtedly to enforce the absolute equality of the two races before the law, but in the nature of things it could not have been intended to abolish distinctions based upon color, or to enforce social, as distinguished from political, equality, or a commingling of the two races upon terms unsatisfactory to either. Laws permitting, and even requiring their separation in places where they are liable to be brought into contact do not necessarily imply the inferiority of either race to the other, and have been generally, if

[33]Ibid.
[34]See pp. 28–38.

not universally, recognized as within the competency of the state legislatures in the exercise of their police power. The most common instance of this is connected with the establishment of separate schools for white and colored children, which have been held to be a valid exercise of the legislative power even by courts of states where the political rights of the colored race have been longest and most earnestly enforced.

One of the earliest of these cases is that of *Roberts* v. *Boston*. 5 Cush. 198 [Mass. 1850], in which the supreme judicial court of Massachusetts held that the general school committee of Boston had power to make provision for the instruction of colored children in separate schools established exclusively for them, and to prohibit their attendance upon the other schools. . . . Similar laws have been enacted by Congress under its general power of legislation over the District of Columbia . . . as well as by legislatures of many of the states, and have been generally, if not uniformly, sustained by the courts. . . .

Laws forbidding the intermarriage of the two races may be said in a technical sense to interfere with the freedom of contract, and yet have been universally recognized as within the police power of the state. . . .

The distinction between laws interfering with the political equality of the negro and those requiring the separation of the two races in schools, theaters, and railway carriages, has been frequently drawn by this Court. . . .

In this connection it is also suggested by the learned counsel for the plaintiff in error that the same argument that will justify the state legislature in requiring railways to provide separate accommodations for the two races will also authorize them to require separate cars to be provided for people whose hair is of a certain color, or who are aliens, or who belong to certain nationalities, or to enact laws requiring colored people to walk upon one side of the street, and white people the other, or requiring white men's houses to be painted white, and colored men's black, or their vehicles or business signs to be of different colors, upon the theory that one side of the street is as good as the other, or that a house or vehicle of one color is as good as one of another color. The reply to all this is that every exercise of the police power must be reasonable, and extend only to such laws as are enacted in good faith for the promotion of the public good, and not for the annoyance or oppression of a particular class. . . .

So far, then, as a conflict with the Fourteenth Amendment is concerned, the case reduces itself to the question whether the statute of Louisiana is a reasonable regulation, and with respect to this there must necessarily be a large discretion on the part of the legislature. In determining the question of reasonableness it is at liberty to act with reference to the established usages, customs, and traditions of the people, and with a view to the promotion of their comfort, and the preservation of public peace and good order. Gauged by this standard, we cannot say that a law which authorizes or even requires the separation of the two races in public conveyances is unreasonable or more obnoxious to the Fourteenth Amendment than the acts of Congress requiring separate schools for colored children in the District of Columbia, the constitutionality of which does not seem to have been questioned, or the corresponding acts of state legislatures.

We consider the underlying fallacy of the plaintiff's argument to consist in the assumption that the enforced separation of the two races stamps the colored race with a badge of inferiority. If this be so, it is not by reason of anything found in the act, but solely because the colored race chooses to put that construction upon it.

The argument necessarily assumes that if, as has been more than once the case, and is not unlikely to be so again, the colored race should become the dominant power in the state legislature, and should enact a law in precisely similar terms, it would thereby relegate the white race to an inferior position. We imagine that the white race, at least, would not acquiesce in this assumption. The argument also assumes that social prejudices may be overcome by legislation, and that equal rights cannot be secured to the negro except by an enforced commingling of the two races. We cannot accept this proposition. If the two races are to meet on terms of social equality, it must be the result of natural affinities, a mutual appreciation of each other's merits and a voluntary consent of individuals. . . . Legislation is powerless to eradicate racial instincts or to abolish distinctions based upon physical differences, and the attempt to do so can only result in accentuating the difficulties of the present situation. If the civil and political rights of both races be equal, one cannot be inferior to the other civilly or politically. If one race be inferior to the other socially, the Constitution of the United States cannot put them upon the same plane. . . .

The judgment of the court below is therefore affirmed.

MR. JUSTICE BREWER did not hear the argument or participate in the decision of this case.

MR. JUSTICE HARLAN, dissenting:

. . . While there may be in Louisiana persons of different races who are not citizens of the United States, the words in the act, "white and colored races" necessarily include all citizens of the United States of both races residing in that state. So that we have before us a state enactment that compels, under penalties, the separation of the two races in railroad passenger coaches, and makes it a crime for a citizen of either race to enter a coach that has been assigned to citizens of the other race.

Thus the state regulates the use of a public highway by citizens of the United States solely upon the basis of race.

However apparent the injustice of such legislation may be, we have only to consider whether it is consistent with the Constitution of the United States. . . .

In respect of civil rights, common to all citizens, the Constitution of the United States does not, I think, permit any public authority to know the race of those entitled to be protected in the enjoyment of such rights. Every true man has pride of race, and under appropriate circumstances, when the rights of others, his equals before the law, are not to be affected, it is his privilege to express such pride and to take such action based upon it as to him seems proper. But I deny that any legislative body or judicial tribunal may have regard to the race of citizens when the civil rights of those citizens are involved. Indeed such legislation as that here in question is inconsistent, not only with that equality of rights, which pertains to citizenship, national and state, but with the personal liberty enjoyed by every one within the United States. . . .

The white race deems itself to be the dominant race in this country. And so it is, in prestige, in achievements, in education, in wealth, and in power. So, I doubt not that it will continue to be for all time, if it remains true to its great heritage and holds fast to the principles of constitutional liberty. But in view of the Constitution, in the eye of the law, there is in this country no superior, dominant, ruling class of citizens. There is no caste here. Our Constitution is color-blind, and neither knows nor tolerates classes among citizens. In respect of civil rights, all citizens are equal before the law. The humblest is the peer of the most powerful. The law regards man as man, and takes no account of his surroundings or of his color when his civil rights as guaranteed by the supreme law of the land are involved. It is therefore to be regretted that this high tribunal, the final expositor of the fundamental law of the land, has reached the conclusion that it is competent for a state to regulate the enjoyment by citizens of their civil rights solely upon the basis of race.

In my opinion, the judgment this day rendered will, in time, prove to be quite as pernicious as the decision made by this tribunal in the *Dred Scott Case*. It was adjudged in that case that the descendants of Africans who were imported into this country and sold as slaves were not included nor intended to be included under the word "citizens" in the Constitution, and could not claim any of the rights and privileges which that instrument provided for and secured to citizens of the United States; that at the time of the adoption of the Constitution they were "considered as a subordinate and inferior class of beings, who had been subjugated by the dominant race, and whether emancipated or not, yet remained subject to their authority, and had no rights or privileges but such as those who held the power and the government might choose to grant them." . . . The recent amendments of the Constitution, it was supposed, had eradicated these principles from our institutions. But it seems that we have yet, in some of the states, a dominant race, a superior class of citizens, which assumes to regulate the enjoyment of civil rights, common to all citizens, upon the basis of race. The present decision, it may well be apprehended, will not stimulate aggressions, more or less brutal and irritating, upon the admitted rights of colored citizens, but will encourage the belief that it is possible, by means of state enactments, to defeat the beneficent purposes which the people of the

United States had in view when they adopted the recent amendments of the Constitution, by one of which the blacks of this country were made citizens of the United States and of the states in which they respectively reside and whose privileges and immunities, as citizens, the states are forbidden to abridge. Sixty millions of whites are in no danger from the presence here of eight millions of blacks. The destinies of the two races in this country are indissolubly linked together, and the interests of both require that the common government of all shall not permit the seeds of race hate to be planted under the sanction of law. What can more certainly arouse race hate, what more certainly create and perpetuate a feeling of distrust between these races, than state enactments which in fact proceed on the ground that colored citizens are so inferior and degraded that they cannot be allowed to sit in public coaches occupied by white citizens? That, as all will admit, is the real meaning of such legislation as was enacted in Louisana.

The sure guaranty of the peace and security of each race is the clear, distinct, and unconditional recognition by our governments, national and state, of every right that inheres in civil freedom, and of the equality before the law of all citizens of the United States without regard to race. State enactments, regulating the enjoyment of civil rights, upon the basis of race, and cunningly devised to defeat legitimate results of the war, under the pretense of recognizing equality of rights, can have no other result than to render permanent peace impossible and to keep alive a conflict of races, the continuance of which must do harm to all concerned. This question is not met by the suggestion that social equality cannot exist between the white and black races in this country. That argument, if it can be properly regarded as one, is scarcely worthy of consideration, for social equality no more exists between two races when traveling in a passenger coach or a public highway than when members of the same races sit by each other in a street car or in the jury box, or stand or sit with each other in a political assembly, or when they use in common the streets of a city or town, or when they are in the same room for the purpose of having their names placed on the registry of voters, or when they approach the ballot box in order to exercise the high privilege of voting. . . .

The arbitrary separation of citizens, on the basis of race, while they are on a public highway, is a badge of servitude wholly inconsistent with the civil freedom and the equality before the law established by the Consitution. It cannot be justified upon any legal grounds.

If evils will result from the commingling of the two races upon public highways established for the benefit of all, they will be infinitely less than those that will surely come from state legislation regulating the enjoyment of civil rights upon the basis of race. We boast of the freedom enjoyed by our people above all other peoples. But it is difficult to reconcile that boast with a state of the law which, practically, puts the brand of servitude and degradation upon a large class of our fellow citizens, our equals before the law. The thin disguise of "equal" accommodations for passengers in railroad coaches will not mislead anyone, or atone for the wrong this day done. . . .

I am of opinion that the statute of Louisiana is inconsistent with the personal liberty of citizens, white and black, in that state, and hostile to both the spirit and letter of the Constitution of the United States. If laws of like character should be enacted in the several states of the Union, the effect would be in the highest degree mischievous. Slavery as an institution tolerated by law would, it is true, have disappeared from our country, but there would remain a power in the states, by sinister legislation, to interfere with the full enjoyment of the blessings of freedom; to regulate civil rights common to all citizens, upon the basis of race; and to place in a condition of legal inferiority a large body of American citizens, now constituting a part of the political community, called the people of the United States, for whom and by whom, through representatives, our government is administered. Such a system is inconsistent with the guarantee given by the Constitution to each state of a republican form of government, and may be stricken down by congressional action, or by the courts in the discharge of their solemn duty to maintain the supreme law of the land, anything in the Constitution or laws of any state to the contrary notwithstanding.

For the reasons stated, I am constrained to withhold my assent from the opinion and judgment of the majority.

The Court upheld the Louisiana law as a reasonable exercise of state police power. What were the Court's standards of "reasonableness"? What example does it give of "unreasonable" state action that would violate the equal protection clause? What considerations does the Court take into account in arriving at its conclusion that the Louisiana statute was reasonable? What distinctions does the Court make between legal and social equality? How does it respond to the argument that the Louisiana law "stamps the colored race with a badge of inferiority"?

What does Justice Harlan mean, in dissent, when he declares that the Constitution and laws made pursuant to it are color blind? What comparisons does he draw between the *Plessy* and *Dred Scott* decisions? How does he answer the Court's argument that the statute does not imply the inferiority of blacks? What does Harlan foresee to be the consequences of the Court's decision?

The Decline of the Separate but Equal Doctrine

The decision in *Plessy* v. *Ferguson* seemed to eliminate barriers to de jure segregation not only of transportation facilities but also in the important areas of housing and education. The separate but equal doctrine prevailed to uphold segregation in all of these areas until the eve of World War II.

The Court struck down segregation in public transportation in a series of cases beginning in 1941 with its decision in *Mitchell* v. *United States*, 313 U.S. 80. Chief Justice Hughes's opinion in the *Mitchell* case ruled that segregation of Pullman sleeping cars was a violation of the Interstate Commerce Act and implied that such segregation by a state would undoubtedly violate the equal protection clause. The decision in *Morgan* v. *Virginia*, 328 U.S. 373 (1946), invalidated a law that required passengers on interstate buses entering Virginia to be reseated to conform to the state's segregation law. The law was not overturned on the basis of the equal protection clause but on the grounds that it constituted an undue burden on interstate commerce because of the need for national uniformity in the regulation of interstate travel. However, when the Court confronted a state law requiring equal accommodations on intrastate, interstate, and foreign public carriers entering the state in *Bob-Low Excursion Company* v. *Michigan*, 333 U.S. 28 (1948), it did not find any constitutional impediment to the regulation. The case arose out of the refusal by a local steamship line to sell a ticket to a black girl for transportation to a Canadian resort island off the shores of Michigan. The state proceeded to institute a criminal prosecution of the company. Justice Rutledge held in his majority opinion that the regulated transportation was local in character and therefore did not burden commerce. Black and Douglas, concurring the result, stated that the equal protection clause should be used to uphold the regulation even if it did interfere with commerce. Justices Vinson and Jackson, citing the *Morgan* precedent, would have declared the Michigan law invalid. The Court again used the Interstate Commerce Act to strike down segregation in the dining cars of railroads in *Henderson* v. *United States*, 339 U.S. 816 (1950). The *Henderson* as well as the *Morgan* decisions supported an order of the Interstate Commerce Commission in 1955 banning racial segregation in all interstate railroad and bus lines, including their auxiliary facilities such as waiting rooms, rest rooms, and restaurants.

The equal protection clause was used to strike down restrictive racial covenants in housing in *Shelley* v. *Kraemer*, 334 U.S. 1 (1948). The Court held that while restrictive agreements standing alone were not a violation of the Fourteenth Amendment, their enforcement by state courts constituted state action in violation of the Fourteenth Amendment.

The decisions in the fields of transportation and housing illustrated that all was not well with the separate but equal doctrine. The separate but equal doctrine came under attack in the sphere of education as well beginning with the New Deal. In *Missouri ex rel Gaines* v. *Canada*, 305 U.S. 337 (1938), the Court held that the refusal of Missouri to admit black applicants to the University of Missouri Law School violated the equal protection clause. Missouri did not have a separate law school for blacks but provided funds for their education in law schools in neighboring states that admitted blacks. Chief Justice Hughes's majority opinion did not overturn the separate but equal doctrine but merely held that states must as a minimum provide the same educational facilities for blacks as they do for whites. Education did not have to be provided in the same school. In *Sipuel* v. *Board of Regents*, 332 U.S. 631 (1948), the Court again held that the refusal of a state to admit a qualified black applicant to its only state law school was a violation of the equal protection clause.

In *McLaurin* v. *Oklahoma State Regents*, 339 U.S. 637 (1950), the Court held that once a student was admitted to graduate education there could be no in-school segregation. McLaurin had obtained admission to the graduate school at the University of Oklahoma by legal action. Once admitted, however, the university required him to sit in a segregated section of the classroom "reserved for colored," to use a special desk at the library, and to eat at a segregated table. Chief Justice Vinson's opinion for the Court found such practices impeded the full educational process and experience by curtailing a student's ability to study, discuss, and exchange views with other students. The *McLaurin* decision followed the precedents of *Missouri ex rel Gains* and *Sipuel* in not overturning the separate but equal rule, although it was but a short step from the *McLaurin* opinion to the declaration that racial separation per se could not produce the necessary level of equality to meet the standards of the equal protection clause.

The Court delivered its opinion in the following case on the same day that it decided the *McLaurin* case. The petitioner, Sweatt, had been denied admission to the University of Texas Law School which was segregated under state law. A state court ordered the University to provide Sweatt with "substantially equal facilities" for legal education as those provided by the University of Texas. The university established a separate law school for blacks, but Sweatt refused to attend and when he lost his final appeal in the Texas Supreme Court he appealed to the United States Supreme Court.

Sweatt v. Painter

339 U.S. 629, 70 S. Ct. 848, 94 L. Ed. 1114 (1950)

MR. CHIEF JUSTICE VINSON delivered the opinion of the Court:

. . . This case and *McLaurin* v. *Oklahoma State Regents* . . . present different aspects of this general question: To what extent does the Equal Protection Clause of the Fourteenth Amendment limit the power of a state to distinguish between students of different races in professional and graduate education in a state university? Broader issues have been urged for our consideration, but we adhere to the principle of deciding constitutional questions only in the context of the particular case before the Court. We have frequently reiterated that this Court will decide constitutional questions only when necessary to the disposition of the case at hand, and that such decisions will be drawn as narrowly as possible. . . . Because of this traditional reluctance to extend constitutional interpretations to situations or facts which are not before the Court, much of the excellent research and detailed argument presented in these cases is unnecessary to their disposition.

In the instant case, petitioner filed an application for admission to the University of Texas Law School for the February, 1946 term. His application was rejected solely because he is a Negro. Petitioner thereupon brought this suit for mandamus against the appropriate school officials, respondents here, to compel his admission. At that time, there was no law school in Texas which admitted Negroes.

The State trial court recognized that the action of the State in denying petitioner the opportunity to gain a legal education while granting it to others deprived him of the equal protection of the laws guaranteed by the Fourteenth Amendment. The court did not grant the relief requested, however, but continued the case for six months to allow the State to supply substantially equal facilities. At the expiration of the six months, in December, 1946, the court denied the writ on the showing that the authorized university officials had adopted an order calling for the opening of a law school for Negroes the following February. While petitioner's appeal was pending, such a school was made available, but petitioner refused to register therein. The Texas Court of Civil Appeals set aside the trial court's judgment and ordered the cause "remanded generally to the trial court for further proceedings without prejudice to the rights of any party to this suit."

On remand, a hearing was held on the issue of the equality of the educational facilities at the newly established school as compared with the University of Texas Law School. Finding that the new school offered petitioner "privileges, advantages,

and opportunities for the study of law substantially equivalent to those offered by the State to white students at the University of Texas," the trial court denied mandamus. The Court of Civil Appeals affirmed. . . . Petitioner's application for a writ of error was denied by the Texas Supreme Court. We granted certiorari . . . because of the manifest importance of the constitutional issues involved.

The University of Texas Law School, from which petitioner was excluded, was staffed by a faculty of sixteen full-time and three part-time professors, some of whom are nationally recognized authorities in their field. Its student body numbered 850. The library contained over 65,000 volumes. Among the other facilities available to the students were a law review, moot court facilities, scholarship funds, and Order of the Coif affiliation.

The school's alumni occupy most distinguished positions in the private practice of the law and in the public life of the State. It may properly be considered one of the nation's ranking law schools.

The law school for Negroes which was to have opened in February, 1947, would have had no independent faculty or library. The teaching was to be carried on by four members of the University of Texas Law School faculty, who were to maintain their offices at the University of Texas while teaching at both institutions. Few of the 10,000 volumes ordered for the library had arrived, nor was there any full-time librarian. The school lacked accreditation.

Since the trial of this case, respondents report the opening of a law school at the Texas State University for Negroes. It is apparently on the road to full accreditation. It has a faculty of five full-time professors; a student body of 23; a library of some 16,500 volumes serviced by a full-time staff; a practice court and legal aid association; and one alumnus who has become a member of the Texas Bar.

Whether the University of Texas Law School is compared with the original or the new law school for Negroes, we cannot find substantial equality in the educational opportunities offered white and Negro law students by the State. In terms of number of the faculty, variety of courses and opportunity for specialization, size of the student body, scope of the library, availability of law review and similar activities, the University of Texas Law School is superior. What is more important, the University of Texas Law School possesses to a far greater degree those qualities which are incapable of objective measurement but which make for greatness in a law school. Such qualities, to name but a few, include reputation of the faculty, experience of the administration, position and influence of the alumni, standing in the community, traditions and prestige. It is difficult to believe that one who had a free choice between these law schools would consider the question closed.

Moreover, although the law is a highly learned profession, we are all well aware that it is an intensely practical one. The law school, the proving ground for legal learning and practice, cannot be effective in isolation from the individuals and institutions with which the law interacts. Few students and no one who has practiced law would choose to study in an academic vacuum, removed from the interplay of ideas and the exchange of views with which the law is concerned. The law school to which Texas is willing to admit petitioner excludes from its student body members of the racial groups which number 85% of the population of the State and include most of the lawyers, witnesses, jurors, judges and other officials with whom petitioner will inevitably be dealing when he becomes a member of the Texas Bar. With such a substantial and significant segment of society excluded, we cannot conclude that the education offered petitioner is substantially equal to that which he would receive if admitted to the University of Texas Law School.

It may be argued that excluding petitioner from that school is no different from excluding white students from the new law school. This contention overlooks realities. It is unlikely that a member of a group so decisively in the majority, attending a school with rich traditions and prestige which only a history of consistently maintained excellence could command, would claim that the opportunities afforded him for legal education were unequal to those held open to petitioner. That such a claim, if made, would be dishonored by the State, is no answer. "Equal protection of the laws is not achieved through indiscriminate imposition of inequalities." . . .

It is fundamental that these cases concern rights which are personal and present. This Court has stated unanimously that "The State must provide [legal education] for [petitioner] in conformity with the equal protection clause of the Fourteenth Amendment and provide it as soon as it does for applicants of any other group." *Sipuel* v. *Board of Regents*, 1948. . . . That case "did not present the issue whether a state might not satisfy the equal protection clause of the Fourteenth Amendment by establishing a separate law school for Negroes." *Fisher* v. *Hurst*, 1948. . . . In *State of Missouri ex rel. Gaines* v. *Canada*, 1938, . . . the Court, speaking through Chief Justice Hughes, declared that "petitioner's right was a personal one. It was as an individual that he was entitled to the equal protection of the laws, and the State was bound to furnish him within its borders facilities for legal education substantially equal to those which the State there afforded for persons of the white race, whether or not other Negroes sought the same opportunity." These are the only cases in this Court which present the issue of the constitutional validity of race distinctions in state-supported graduate and professional education.

In accordance with these cases, petitioner may claim his full constitutional right: legal education equivalent to that offered by the State to students of other races. Such education is not available to him in a separate law school as offered by the State. We cannot, therefore, agree with respondents that the doctrine of *Plessy* v. *Ferguson,* 1896, . . . requires affirmance of the judgment below. Nor need we reach petitioner's contention that *Plessy* v. *Ferguson* should be reexamined in the light of contemporary knowledge respecting the purposes of the Fourteenth Amendment and the effects of racial segregation. . . .

We hold that the Equal Protection Clause of the Fourteenth Amendment requires that petitioner be admitted to the University of Texas Law School. The judgment is reversed and the cause is remanded for proceedings not inconsistent with this opinion.

Reversed.

Did the Court, directly or by implication, overturn or soften the effect of the separate but equal doctrine? To what extent was the Court's opinion based upon the inequality in the *physical* facilities of the two law schools? To what extent was the decision the result of the Court's finding that separate educational facilities in legal education are inherently unequal? Is the Court's close scrutiny of the Texas law the result of the fact that the case involved "fundamental" and "personal" rights? Does the case suggest a more interventionist stance by the Court in applying equal protection standards under the separate but equal doctrine where there is evidence that the fundamental rights of a racial class have been unequally denied by state law?

THE END OF THE SEPARATE BUT EQUAL DOCTRINE

While the *McLaurin* and *Sweatt* cases did not technically overrule the separate but equal standard, the opinions encouraged civil rights advocates and attorneys for the NAACP in particular to prepare a final assault on the separate but equal rule. The NAACP, under the direction of its attorney, Thurgood Marshall, prepared a series of cases to challenge state segregation laws in Delaware, Kansas, South Carolina, and Virginia. In addition, a case was prepared to challenge school segregation in the District of Columbia. Opposing the NAACP and Thurgood Marshall was John W. Davis, a distinguished attorney, former Democratic candidate for the presidency, and, as described by Chief Justice Warren, a "great advocate and orator."[35] The case became a cause celebre, raising highly charged and emotional debate on both sides.

The five cases were initially argued in 1952. At that time the Court was far from a consensus to overrule the separate but equal doctrine of *Plessy* v.

[35]Earl Warren, *The Memoirs of Earl Warren* (New York: Doubleday and Co., Inc., 1977), p. 287.

Ferguson (1896). Justices Black, Douglas, Burton, and Minton were apparently leaning toward reversal of the separate but equal rule, while Chief Justice Vinson and Justices Reed, Frankfurter, Jackson, and Clark were leaning toward affirmance of *Plessy* or at least were doubtful about the propriety of overruling the separate but equal doctrine.[36] When Vinson died in 1953 President Eisenhower appointed Earl Warren to become his successor. When Warren was appointed the cases were still pending, for although they had been argued during the 1952 term no decision was made beyond noting jurisdiction. The Court directed that reargument should focus upon the question of whether or not the Fourteenth Amendment was intended to ban segregated schools. The justices were clearly troubled about the momentous issue before them and were well aware of the political consequences of a ban on segregated schools, a practice that was deeply rooted in the history, traditions, and customs of the South. The magnitude of the segregation cases made it vitally important in the view of Chief Justice Warren to secure as much unity as possible among the brethren, and he hoped to achieve unanimity.

The first desegregation case was reargued on December 7, 1953, after which the Court held a conference on December 12, 1953. At the first conference after reargument Chief Justice Warren unequivocally told his colleagues that they should overrule de jure segregation in public schools. Only Justices Douglas and Minton fully agreed with Warren at the conference, although the tenor of the remarks of the other justices suggested the possibility that they might be willing to go along with the new Chief Justice. In describing the atmosphere at the time, Warren wrote,

> ... The Court was thoroughly conscious of the importance of the decision to be arrived at and the impact it would have on the nation. With this went realization of the necessity for secrecy in our deliberations and for achieving unity, if possible. ...
>
> ... [R]ealizing that when a person once announces he has reached a conclusion it is more difficult for him to change his thinking, we decided that we would dispense with our usual custom of formally expressing our individual views at the first conference and would confine ourselves for a time to informal discussion of the briefs, the arguments made at the hearing, and our own independent research on each conference day, reserving our final opinions until the discussions were concluded.
>
> We followed this plan until the following February, when it was agreed that we were ready to vote. On the first vote, we unanimously agreed that the "separate but equal" doctrine had no place in public education. The question then arose as to how this view should be written—as a per curiam (by the Court) or as a signed, individualized opinion. We decided that it would carry more force if done through a signed opinion, and at the suggestion of some of the justices, it was thought that it should bear the signature of the Chief Justice. I consented to this, and then the importance of secrecy was discussed. We agreed that only my law clerks should be involved, and that any writing between my office and those of other justices would be delivered to the justices personally. This practice was fol-

[36]See S. Sidney Ulmer, "Earl Warren and the Brown Decision," *Journal of Politics 33 (1971)*, 689–702.

lowed throughout and this was the only time it was required in my years on the Court. It was not done because of suspicion of anyone, but because of the sensitiveness of the school segregation matter and the prying for inside information that surrounded the cases. It was thought wise to confine our communications to the fewest possible people as a matter of security. Headway being made in conference was discussed informally from time to time, and on occasion I would visit with Mr. Justice Jackson, who was confined to the hospital, to inform him of our progress. Finally, at our conference on May 15, we agreed to announce our opinion the following Monday, subject to the approval of Mr. Justice Jackson, who was still recuperating from a heart attack which had incapacitated him for some time. I went to the hospital early Monday morning, May 17, and showed the justice a copy of the proposed opinion as it was to be released. He agreed to it, and to my alarm insisted on attending the Court that day in order to demonstrate our solidarity. I suggested that it was unnecessary, but he insisted, and was there at the appointed time.

It was a momentous courtroom event and, unlike many other such events, it has not lost that character to this day.[37]

Brown v. Board of Education of Topeka

347 U.S. 483; 74 S. Ct. 686; 98 L. Ed. 873 (1954)

Mr. Chief Justice Warren delivered the opinion of the Court:

These cases come to us from the States of Kansas, South Carolina, Virginia, and Delaware. They are premised on different facts and different local conditions, but a common legal question justifies their consideration together in this consolidated opinion.

In each of the cases, minors of the Negro race, through their legal representatives, seek the aid of the courts in obtaining admission to the public schools of their community on a nonsegregated basis. In each instance, they had been denied admission to schools attended by white children under laws requiring or permitting segregation according to race. This segregation was alleged to deprive the plaintiffs of the equal protection of the laws under the Fourteenth Amendment. In each of the cases other than the Delaware case, a three-judge federal district court denied relief to the plaintiffs

on the so-called "separate but equal" doctrine announced by this Court in *Plessy* v. *Ferguson.* . . . Under that doctrine, equality of treatment is accorded when the races are provided substantially equal facilities, even though these facilities be separate. In the Delaware case, the Supreme Court of Delaware adhered to that doctrine, but ordered that the plaintiffs be admitted to the white schools because of their superiority to the Negro school.

The plaintiffs contend that segregated public schools are not "equal" and cannot be made "equal," and that hence they are deprived of the equal protection of the laws. Because of the obvious importance of the question present, the Court took jurisdiction. Argument was heard in the 1952 Term, and reargument was heard this Term on certain questions propounded by the Court.

Reargument was largely devoted to the circumstances surrounding the adoption of the Fourteenth Amendment in 1868. It

[37]Warren, *Memoirs*, pp. 282–286.

covered exhaustively consideration of the Amendment in Congress, ratification by the states, then existing practices in racial segregation, and the views of proponents and opponents of the Amendment. This discussion and our own investigation convince us that, although these sources cast some light, it is not enough to resolve the problem with which we are faced. At best, they are inconclusive. The most avid proponents of the post-War Amendments undoubtedly intended them to remove all legal distinctions among "all persons born or naturalized in the United States." Their opponents, just as certainly, were antagonistic to both the letter and the spirit of the Amendments and wished them to have the most limited effect. What others in Congress and the state legislatures had in mind cannot be determined with any degree of certainty.

An additional reason for the inconclusive nature of the Amendment's history, with respect to segregated schools, is the status of public education at that time. In the South, the movement toward free common schools, supported by general taxation, had not yet taken hold. Education of white children was largely in the hands of private groups. Education of Negroes was almost nonexistent, and practically all of the race were illiterate. In fact, any education of Negroes was forbidden by law in some states. Today, in contrast, many Negroes have achieved outstanding success in the arts and sciences as well as in the business and professional world. It is true that public school education at the time of the Amendment had advanced further in the North, but the effect of the Amendment on Northern States was generally ignored in the congressional debates. Even in the North, the conditions of public education did not approximate those existing today. The curriculum was usually rudimentary; ungraded schools were common in rural areas; the school term was but three

months a year in many states; and compulsory school attendance was virtually unknown. As a consequence, it is not surprising that there should be so little in the history of the Fourteenth Amendment relating to its intended effect on public education.

In the first cases in this Court construing the Fourteenth Amendment, decided shortly after its adoption, the Court interpreted it as proscribing all state-imposed discriminations against the Negro race.[38] The doctrine of "separate but equal" did not make its appearance in this Court until 1896 in the case of *Plessy* v. *Ferguson* involving not education but transportation. American courts have since labored with the doctrine for over half a century. In this Court, there have been six cases involving the "separate but equal" doctrine in the field of public education. In *Cumming* v. *County Board of Education* [1899] . . . and *Gong Lum* v. *Rice* [1927] . . . the validity of the doctrine itself was not challenged. In more recent cases, all on the graduate school level, inequality was found in that specific benefits enjoyed by white students were denied to Negro students of the same educational qualifications. *Missouri ex rel. Gaines* v. *Canada* [1938] . . . *Sipuel* v. *Oklahoma* [1948] . . . *Sweatt* v. *Painter* [1950] . . . *McLaurin* v. *Oklahoma State Regents* [1950] . . . In none of these cases was it necessary to re-examine the doctrine to grant relief to the Negro plaintiff. And in *Sweatt* v. *Painter* the Court expressly reserved decision on the question whether *Plessy* v. *Ferguson* should be held inapplicable to public education.

In the instant cases, that question is directly presented. Here, unlike *Sweatt* v. *Painter,* there are findings below that the Negro and white schools involved have been equalized, or are being equalized,

[38]Slaughterhouse Cases, 16 Wall. 36, 67–72 (1873); Strauder v. West Virginia, 100 U.S. 303, 307–308 (1880). [Editor's Note.]

with respect to buildings, curricula, qualifications and salaries of teachers, and other "tangible" factors. Our decision, therefore, cannot turn on merely a comparison of these tangible factors in the Negro and white schools involved in each of the cases. We must look instead to the effect of segregation itself on public education.

In approaching this problem, we cannot turn the clock back to 1868 when the Amendment was adopted, or even to 1896 when *Plessy* v. *Ferguson* was written. We must consider public education in the light of its full development and its present place in American life throughout the Nation. Only in this way can it be determined if segregation in public schools deprives these plaintiffs of the equal protection of the laws.

Today, education is perhaps the most important function of state and local governments. Compulsory school attendance laws and the great expenditures for education both demonstrate our recognition of the importance of education to our democratic society. It is required in the performance of our most basic public responsibilities, even service in the armed forces. It is the very foundation of good citizenship. Today it is a principal instrument in awakening the child to cultural values, in preparing him for later professional training, and in helping him to adjust normally to his environment. In these days, it is doubtful that any child may reasonably be expected to succeed in life if he is denied the opportunity of an education. Such an opportunity, where the state has undertaken to provide it, is a right which must be made available to all on equal terms.

We come then to the question presented: Does segregation of children in public schools solely on the basis of race, even though the physical facilities and other "tangible" factors may be equal, deprive the children of the minority group of equal educational opportunities? We believe that it does.

In *Sweatt* v. *Painter*, in finding that a segregated law school for Negroes could not provide them equal educational opportunities, this Court relied in large part on "those qualities which are incapable of objective measurement but which make for greatness in a law school." In *McLaurin* v. *Oklahoma State Regents*, the Court, in requiring that a Negro admitted to a white graduate school be treated like all other students, again resorted to intangible considerations: ". . . his ability to study, to engage in discussions and exchange views with other students, and, in general, to learn his profession." Such considerations apply with added force to children in grade and high schools. To separate them from others of similar age and qualifications solely because of their race generates a feeling of inferiority as to their status in the community that may affect their hearts and minds in a way unlikely ever to be undone. The effect of this separation on their educational opportunities was well stated by a finding in the Kansas case by a court which nevertheless felt compelled to rule against the Negro plaintiffs:

Segregation of white and colored children in public schools has a detrimental effect upon the colored children. The impact is greater when it has the sanction of the law; for the policy of separating the races is usually interpreted as denoting the inferiority of the negro group. A sense of inferiority affects the motivation of a child to learn. Segregation with the sanction of law, therefore, has a tendency to [retard] the educational and mental development of negro children and to deprive them of some of the benefits they would receive in a racial[ly] integrated school system.

Whatever may have been the extent of psychological knowledge at the time of *Plessy* v. *Ferguson*, this finding is amply supported by modern authority. Any language in *Plessy* v. *Ferguson* contrary to this finding is rejected.

We conclude that in the field of public education the doctrine of "separate but equal" has no place. Separate educational facilities are inherently unequal. Therefore, we hold that the plaintiffs and others similarly situated for whom the actions have been brought are, by reason of the segregation complained of, deprived of the equal protection of the laws guaranteed by the Fourteenth Amendment. This disposition makes unnecessary any discussion whether such segregation also violates the Due Process Clause of the Fourteenth Amendment.

Because these are class actions, because of the wide applicability of this decision, and because of the great variety of local conditions, the formulation of decrees in these cases presents problems of considerable complexity. On reargument, the consideration of appropriate relief was necessarily subordinated to the primary question—the constitutionality of segregation in public education. We have now announced that such segregation is a denial of the equal protection of the laws. In order that we may have the full assistance of the parties in formulating decrees, the cases will be restored to the docket, and the parties are requested to present further argument on Questions 4 and 5 [concerning the process of implementation] previously propounded by the Court for the reargument this Term. The Attorney General of the United States is again invited to participate. The Attorneys General of the states requiring or permitting segregation in public education will also be permitted to appear as *amici curiae* upon request to do so by September 15, 1954, and submission of briefs by October 1, 1954.

It is so ordered.

In the *Plessy* opinion, the Court wrote,

> In determining the question of reasonableness it [the state] is at liberty to act with reference to the established usages, customs, and traditions of the people, and with a view to the promotion of their comfort, and the preservation of the public peace and good order. Gauged by this standard, we cannot say that such a law which authorizes or even requires the separation of the two races in public conveyances is unreasonable or more obnoxious to the Fourteenth Amendment than the acts of Congress requiring separate schools for colored children in the District of Columbia, the constitutionality of which does not seem to have been questioned. . . .

In the following companion case to *Brown I,* segregated education in the District of Columbia was challenged.

Bolling v. *Sharpe*

347 U.S. 497; 74 S. Ct. 693; 98 L. Ed. 884 (1954)

MR. CHIEF JUSTICE WARREN delivered the opinion of the Court:

This case challenges the validity of segregation in the public schools of the District of Columbia. The petitioners, minors of the Negro race, allege that such segregation deprives them of due process of law under the Fifth Amendment. They were refused admission to a public school attended by white children solely because of their race. They sought the aid of the District Court for the District of Columbia in obtaining admission. That court dismissed their complaint. The Court granted a writ of certiorari before judgment in the Court of Appeals because of the importance of the constitutional question presented. . . .

We have this day held that the Equal Protection Clause of the Fourteenth Amendment prohibits the states from maintaining racially segregated public schools. The legal problem in the District of Columbia is somewhat different, however. The Fifth Amendment, which is applicable in the District of Columbia, does not contain an equal protection clause as does the Fourteenth Amendment which applies only to the states. But the concepts of equal protection and due process, both stemming from our American ideal of fairness, are not mutually exclusive. The "equal protection of laws" is a more explicit safeguard of prohibited unfairness than "due process of law," and, therefore, we do not imply that the two are always interchangeable phrases. But, as this Court has recognized, discrimination may be so unjustifiable as to be violative of due process.

Classifications based solely upon race must be scrutinized with particular care, since they are contrary to our traditions and hence constitutionally suspect.[39] As long ago as 1896, this Court declared the principle "that the Constitution of the United States, in its present form, forbids, so far as civil and political rights are concerned, discrimination by the general government, or by the states, against any citizen because of his race. And in *Buchanan*

v. *Warley* [1917] . . . the Court held that a statute which limited the right of a property owner to convey his property to a person of another race was, as an unreasonable discrimination, a denial of due process of law.

Although the Court has not assumed to define "liberty" with any great precision, that term is not confined to mere freedom from bodily restraint. Liberty under law extends to the full range of conduct which the individual is free to pursue, and it cannot be restricted except for a proper governmental objective. Segregation in public education is not reasonably related to any proper governmental objective, and thus it imposes on Negro children of the District of Columbia a burden that constitutes an arbitrary deprivation of their liberty in violation of the Due Process Clause.

In view of our decision that the Constitution prohibits the states from maintaining racially segregated public schools, it would be unthinkable that the same Constitution would impose a lesser duty on the Federal Government. We hold that racial segregation in the public schools of the District of Columbia is a denial of the due process of law guaranteed by the Fifth Amendment to the Constitution.

For the reasons set out in *Brown* v. *Board of Education,* this case will be restored to the docket for reargument on Questions 4 and 5 [concerning implementation] previously propounded by the Court. . . .

It is so ordered.

What was the reasoning of the Court in *Brown I* to support its conclusion that separate educational facilities are inherently unequal? What did the Court declare to be the intent of the Fourteenth Amendment equal protection clause? Is the intent clear? Does the opinion suggest that the amend-

[39]See *Korematsu* v. *United States,* the quote from p. 814. [Editor's Note.]

ment intended to remove segregation in public education? How does the Court distinguish between the question presented to it in *Brown I* and that under consideration in *Sweatt* v. *Painter*? What does the Court mean when it states that in approaching the question before it, it cannot turn the clock back to 1868 or 1896 *(Plessy)*, but "We must consider public education in the light of its full development and its present place in American life through- out the nation"? What conclusions result from this approach? Is there any direct evidence in the opinion that the Court took into account psychological knowledge concerning the effects of segregation upon public school chil- dren? On what grounds does the Court defer its implementation decision *(Brown II)*?

In *Bolling* v. *Sharpe,* what type of classifications does Chief Justice Warren find to be "constitutionally suspect"? What stance does he suggest the Court should take when it reviews "suspect classifications" in the law? How does the Chief Justice extract the equal protection requirement from the concept of due process? Why does the Court find that segregation of public educa- tion in the District of Columbia is "an arbitrary deprivation of . . . liberty in violation of the due process clause"? Does Warren's opinion on its face sug- gest that there are political considerations behind the Court's decision?

The Implementation Decision—*Brown II*

The arguments before the Court in *Brown II* centered around the ques- tions of the speed with which desegregation should be implemented and the appropriate mechanism to put the order into effect. The United States At- torney General, who had been invited by the Court to participate in the pro- ceedings, stated in his brief that "In the absence of compelling reasons . . . there should be no unnecessary delay in the full vindication of the consti- tutional rights involved in the cases, and if any delay is required, it should be kept to a minimum."[40] The appellants argued vigorously against "grad- ualism" and urged desegregation "forthwith" to prevent the continued dep- rivation of their constitutional rights. Anticipating that there would be ar- guments for delay, the appellants in their original briefs for *Brown I* had stated: "[t]here are no applicable legal precedents justifying a plea for delay . . . and, an analysis of the nonlegal materials relevant to the issue whether or not relief should be delayed in the cases shows that the process of gradual desegregation is at best no more effective than immediate desegregation."[41]

The brief for the Board of Education of Topeka, Kansas, pleaded for time for a gradual adjustment to desegregation. The board stated that it was carrying out "its adopted policy to terminate segregation 'as rapidly as is practicable' and . . . there is no need at this time for the appointment of a special master or for the court to undertake to formulate specific decrees directing the particular steps to be taken to terminate segregation in the schools of Topeka."[42] The board concluded: "We doubt that the Court con-

[40]LB, Vol. 49A, p. 747.
[41]*Ibid.,* p. 667.
[42]LB, Vol. 49A, p. 674.

templates the judicial development of a plan for desegregation of the
schools of Kansas. . . . If such an action is contemplated, we doubt that it is
legally or practically feasible."[43] The claim that the courts lack the authority
to develop and implement desegregation plans was echoed by the Attorney
General of Arkansas, who suggested that "The whole problem of solving the
method of integration should fall squarely where the Fourteenth Amendment says it should fall, that is, on Congress for appropriate enactment."[44]
The Arkansas brief reflected the prevailing views of the South in holding
that the "problem of integration of races in the public schools is of such
magnitude that it can be solved effectively only by a *gradual process* which
would vary from locality to locality."[45]

   In the highly charged emotional and political atmosphere surrounding
the *Brown* case, the Court rendered its implementation decision.

Brown v. Board of Education of Topeka

349 U.S. 294; 75 S. Ct. 753; 99 L. Ed. 1083 (1955)

MR. CHIEF JUSTICE WARREN delivered
the opinion of the Court:

These cases were decided on May 17,
1954. The opinions of that date, declaring
the fundamental principle that racial discrimination in public education is unconstitutional, are incorporated herein by
reference. All provisions of federal, state,
or local law requiring or permitting such
discrimination must yield to this principle. There remains for consideration the
manner in which relief is to be accorded.

Because these cases arose under different local conditions and their disposition
will involve a variety of local problems, we
requested further argument on the question of relief. In view of the nationwide
importance of the decision, we invited the
Attorney General of the United States
and the Attorneys General of all states requiring or permitting racial discrimination in public education to present their
views on that question. The parties, the
United States, and the States of Florida,
North Carolina, Arkansas, Oklahoma,
Maryland, and Texas filed briefs and par-

ticipated in the oral argument.

These presentations were informative
and helpful to the Court in its consideration of the complexities arising from the
transition to a system of public education
freed of racial discrimination. The presentations also demonstrated that substantial steps to eliminate racial discrimination
in public schools have already been taken,
not only in some of the communities in
which these cases arose, but in some of
the states appearing as *amici curiae,* and in
other states as well. Substantial progress
has been made in the District of Columbia
and in the communities in Kansas and
Delaware involved in this litigation. The
defendants in the cases coming to us from
South Carolina and Virginia are awaiting
the decision of this Court concerning
relief.

Full implementation of these constitutional principles may require solution of
varied local school problems. School authorities have the primary responsibility
for elucidating, assessing, and solving
these problems; courts will have to con-

[43]Ibid., p. 687.
[44]Ibid., pp. 847–848.
[45]Ibid., p. 855.

sider whether the action of school authorities constitutes good faith implementation of the governing constitutional
principles. Because of their proximity to
local conditions and the possible need for
further hearings, the courts which originally heard these cases can best perform
this judicial appraisal. Accordingly, we believe it appropriate to remand the cases to
those courts.

In fashioning and effectuating the decrees, the courts will be guided by equitable principles. Traditionally, equity has
been characterized by a practical flexibility in shaping its remedies and by a facility for adjusting and reconciling public
and private needs. These cases call for the
exercise of these traditional attributes of
equity power. At stake is the personal interest of the plaintiffs in admission to
public schools as soon as practicable on a
nondiscriminatory basis. To effectuate
this interest may call for elimination of a
variety of obstacles in making the transition to school systems operated in accordance with the constitutional principles set
forth in our May 17, 1954, decision.
Courts of equity may properly take into
account the public interest in the elimination of such obstacles in a systematic
and effective manner. But it should go
without saying that the vitality of these
constitutional principles cannot be allowed to yield simply because of disagreement with them.

While giving weight to these public and
private considerations, the courts will require that the defendants make a prompt
and reasonable start toward full compliance with our May 17, 1954, ruling. Once
such a start has been made, the courts
may find that additional time is necessary
to carry out the ruling in an effective
manner. The burden rests upon the defendants to establish that such time is necessary in the public interest and is consistent with good faith compliance at the
earliest practicable date. To that end, the
courts may consider problems related to
administration, arising from the physical
condition of the school plant, the school
transportation system, personnel, revision
of school districts and attendance areas
into compact units to achieve a system of
determining admission to the public
schools on a nonracial basis, and revision
of local laws and regulations which may
be necessary in solving the foregoing
problems. They will also consider the adequacy of any plans the defendants may
propose to meet these problems and to effectuate a transition to a racially nondiscriminatory school system. During this period of transition, the courts will retain
jurisdiction of these cases.

The judgments below, except that in
the Delaware case, are accordingly reversed and the cases are remanded to the
District Courts to take such proceedings
and enter such orders and decrees consistent with this opinion as are necessary
and proper to admit to public schools on
a racially nondiscriminatory basis with all
deliberate speed the parties to these cases.
The judgment in the Delaware case—ordering the immediate admission of the
plaintiffs to schools previously attended
only by white children—is affirmed on the
basis of the principles stated in our May
17, 1954, opinion, but the case is remanded to the Supreme Court of Delaware for such further proceedings as that
Court may deem necessary in light of this
opinion.

It is so ordered.

Did the Court's opinion take into account the administrative, political,
and social realities of public school segregation in the South? Why did the
Court remand the cases to the district courts for implementation? What

standards and guidelines were to be taken into account by the district courts? Did the *Brown II* opinion insure the "prompt and reasonable" start toward full compliance with the *Brown I* ruling? What did the Supreme Court mean when it commanded the lower courts "to take such proceedings and enter such orders and decrees consistent with this opinion as are necessary and proper to admit to public schools on a racially nondiscriminatory basis with all deliberate speed the parties to these cases"?

Discussing the *Brown II* case in his memoirs, Chief Justice Earl Warren stated,

> We discussed at great length in conference whether the Supreme Court should make the factual determinations in such [desegregation] cases or whether they should be left to the courts below, deciding finally to leave them to the latter, subject, of course, to our review, because they were getting closer to the problems involved, and were in a better position to engage meaningfully in the fact-finding process. As guidelines for them, we directed that neither local law nor custom should be permitted to interfere with the establishment of an integrated school system, and that the process of achieving it should be carried out with "all deliberate speed"—a phrase which has been much discussed by those who are of the opinion that desegregation has not proceeded with as much celerity as might have been expected. These people argued that the Supreme Court should merely have directed the school districts to admit Brown and the other plaintiffs to the schools to which they sought admission, in the belief this would have quickly ended the litigation. This theory, however, overlooks the complexity of our federal system, the time it takes controversial litigation to proceed through the hierarchy of courts to the Supreme Court, the fact that the administration of the public school system is a state and local function so long as it does not contravene constitutional principles, that each state has its own system with different relationships between state and local government, and that the relationship can be changed at will by the state government if there should be a determination to bypass or defeat the decision of the Supreme Court.[46]

The efforts of the southern states and their local governments to evade the *Brown* decisions were extensive and effective. Ten years after the decisions, less than 10 percent of the black pupils in the lower educational levels in the southern states were enrolled in integrated schools. It was not until 1970 that substantial progress was made toward integration in the South. Between 1968 and 1970 the percentage of black students in all-black schools in eleven Southern States decreased from 68 to 18.4 percent. This reflected the increasing political impact of the Civil Rights movement and stepped up federal efforts to achieve integration in all public facilities, including schools, after the passage of the Civil Rights Act of 1964. Increased judicial activity struck at the heart of such evasive plans as closing public schools and giving local grants to white children to attend private schools (*Griffin* v. *Prince Edward County School Board,* 377 U.S. 218 [1964]), and plans that permitted students to avoid integrated schools by giving them "freedom of

[46]Warren, *Memoirs,* p. 288.

choice" to select the schools they would attend within their school districts (*Green* v. *County School Board,* 391 U.S. 430 [1968]).

Court-Ordered Busing to Achieve Equality

In *Green* v. *County School Board* the Court held that a freedom of choice plan allowing students to attend either the white or black schools within a school district was not sufficient to comply with the *Brown* decision if the plan resulted in the continuation of segregated schools. The decision reflected a more active role for the Court in achieving results under the *Brown* doctrine. Freedom of choice plans, replacing the former state-compelled dual school systems, had to be scrutinized carefully, emphasized Brennan in the *Green* opinion, to assure that the rights of black children were protected. "School boards such as the respondent," wrote Brennan, "then [before *Brown*] operating state-compelled dual systems were . . . clearly charged with the *affirmative* duty to take whatever steps might be necessary to convert to a unitary system in which racial discrimination would be eliminated root and branch."[47] The Court concluded that if there are ways other than freedom of choice plans to effect school desegregation more speedily, "such as zoning,"[48] the Court must find unacceptable plans such as the one involved in the *Green* case.

In the following case the Court reviewed the constitutionality of de facto school segregation in a large southern metropolitan school district. After the *Green* decision, the appellant (Swann), claiming that an initial desegregation plan approved by the district court was inadequate, initiated proceedings for further relief. After lengthy hearings the district court accepted the new plan that grouped some black and white elementary schools and provided for busing in both directions. Under the plan the percentage of blacks in each elementary school would range from approximately 9 percent to 38 percent. The plan also provided for other means of integration of the school system, including the assignment of teachers to maintain racial balances, and some busing between inner-city black and outlying white secondary schools. The court of appeals vacated the district court's order pertaining to the busing of elementary school students, and the Supreme Court granted certiorari.

Swann v. *Charlotte-Mecklenburg Board of Education*

402 U.S. 1; 9 S. Ct. 1267; 28 L. Ed. 2d 554 (1971)

MR. CHIEF JUSTICE BURGER delivered the opinion of the Court:

We granted certiorari in this case to re-view important issues as to the duties of school authorities and the scope of powers of federal courts under this Court's

[47] Green v. County School Board, 391 U.S. 430, 437–438 (1968). (Emphasis supplied.)
[48] Ibid., p. 442.

mandates to eliminate racially separate public schools established and maintained by state action. . . .

This case and those argued with it arose in States having a long history of maintaining two sets of schools in a single school system deliberately operated to carry out a governmental policy to separate pupils in schools solely on the basis of race. That was what *Brown* v. *Board of Education* was all about. These cases present us with the problem of defining in more precise terms than heretofore the scope of the duty of school authorities and district courts in implementing *Brown I* and the mandate to eliminate dual systems and establish unitary systems at once. Meanwhile district courts and courts of appeals have struggled in hundreds of cases with a multitude and variety of problems under this Court's general directive. Understandably, in an area of evolving remedies, those courts had to improvise and experiment without detailed or specific guidelines. This Court, in *Brown I,* appropriately dealt with the large constitutional principles; other federal courts had to grapple with the flinty, intractable realities of day-to-day implementation of those constitutional commands. Their efforts, of necessity, embraced a process of "trial and error," and our effort to formulate guidelines must take into account their experience.
. . .

V

The central issue in this case is that of student assignment, and there are essentially four problem areas:

  (1) to what extent racial balance or racial quotas may be used as an implement in a remedial order to correct a previously segregated system;

  (2) whether every all-Negro and all-white school must be eliminated as an indis-

pensable part of a remedial process of desegregation;

  (3) what the limits are, if any, on the rearrangement of school districts and attendance zones, as a remedial measure; and

  (4) what the limits are, if any, on the use of transportation facilities to correct state-enforced racial school segregation.

(1) Racial Balances or Racial Quotas.

The constant theme and thrust of every holding from *Brown I* to date is that state-enforced separation of races in public schools is discrimination that violates the Equal Protection Clause. The remedy commanded was to dismantle dual school systems.

We are concerned in these cases with the elimination of the discrimination inherent in the dual school systems, not with myriad factors of human existence which can cause discrimination in a multitude of ways on racial, religious, or ethnic grounds. The target of the cases from *Brown I* to the present was the dual school system. The elimination of racial discrimination in public schools is a large task and one that should not be retarded by efforts to achieve broader purposes lying beyond the jurisdiction of school authorities. One vehicle can carry only a limited amount of baggage. . . .

Our objective in dealing with the issues presented by these cases is to see that school authorities exclude no pupil of a racial minority from any school, directly or indirectly, on account of race; it does not and cannot embrace all the problems of racial prejudice, even when those problems contribute to disproportionate racial concentrations in some schools.

In this case it is urged that the District Court has imposed a racial balance requirement of 71 percent–29 percent on individual schools. . . .

If we were to read the holding of the District Court to require, as a matter of substantive constitutional right, any particular degree of racial balance or mixing, that approach would be disapproved and we would be obliged to reverse. The constitutional command to desegregate schools does not mean that every school in every community must always reflect the racial composition of the school system as a whole. . . .

. . .[T]he use made of mathematical ratios was no more than a starting point in the process of shaping a remedy, rather than an inflexible requirement. From that starting point the District Court proceeded to frame a decree that was within its discretionary powers, as an equitable remedy for the particular circumstances. As we said in *Green,* a school authority's remedial plan or a district court's remedial decree is to be judged by its effectiveness. Awareness of the racial composition of the whole school system is likely to be a useful starting point in shaping a remedy to correct past constitutional violations. In sum, the very limited use made of mathematical ratios was within the equitable remedial discretion of the District Court.

(2) One-race Schools.

The record in this case reveals the familiar phenomenon that in metropolitan area minority groups are often found concentrated in one part of the city. In some circumstances certain schools may remain all or largely of one race until new schools can be provided or neighborhood patterns change. Schools all or predominately of one race in a district of mixed population will require close scrutiny to determine that school assignments are not part of state-enforced segregation.

In light of the above, it should be clear that the existence of some small number of one-race, or virtually one-race, schools within a district is not in and of itself the mark of a system that still practices segregation by law. . . . Where the school authority's proposed plan for conversion from a dual to a unitary system contemplates the continued existence of some schools that are all or predominately of one race, they have the burden of showing that such school assignments are genuinely nondiscriminatory. The court should scrutinize such schools, and the burden upon the school authorities will be to satisfy the court that their racial composition is not the result of present or past discriminatory action on their part.

An optional majority-to-minority transfer provision has long been recognized as a useful part of every desegregation plan. Provision for optional transfer to those in the majority racial group of a particular school to other schools where they will be in the minority is an indispensable remedy for those students willing to transfer to other schools in order to lessen the impact on them of the state-imposed stigma of segregation. In order to be effective, such a transfer arrangement must grant the transferring student free transportation and space must be made available in the school to which he desires to move. . . . The court orders in this and the companion *Davis* case now provide such an option.

(3) Remedial Altering of Attendance Zones.

The maps submitted in these cases graphically demonstrate that one of the principal tools employed by school planners and by courts to break up the dual school system has been a frank—and sometimes drastic—gerrymandering of school districts and attendance zones. An additional step was pairing, "clustering," or "grouping" of schools with attendance assignments made deliberately to accomplish the transfer of Negro students out of formerly segregated Negro schools and transfer of white students to formerly all-

Negro schools. More often than not, these zones are neither compact nor contiguous; indeed they may be on opposite ends of the city. As an interim corrective measure, this cannot be said to be beyond the broad remedial powers of a court.

Absent a constitutional violation there would be no basis for judicially ordering assignment of students on a racial basis. All things being equal, with no history of discrimination, it might well be desirable to assign pupils to schools nearest their homes. But all things are not equal in a system that has been deliberately constructed and maintained to enforce racial segregation. . . .

No fixed or even substantially fixed guidelines can be established as to how far a court can go, but it must be recognized that there are limits. The objective is to dismantle the dual school system. "Racially neutral" assignment plans proposed by school authorities to a district court may be inadequate; such plans may fail to counteract the continuing effects of past school segregation resulting from discriminatory location of school sites or distortion of school size in order to achieve or maintain an artificial racial separation. When school authorities present a district court with a "loaded game board," affirmative action in the form of remedial altering of attendance zones is proper to achieve truly nondiscriminatory assignments. In short, an assignment plan is not acceptable simply because it appears to be neutral. . . .

We hold that the pairing and grouping of noncontiguous school zones is a permissible tool and such action is to be considered in light of the objectives sought. . . .

(4) Transportation of Students.

The scope of permissible transportation of students as an implement of a remedial decree has never been defined by this Court and by the very nature of the problem it cannot be defined with precision. . . .

The importance of bus transportation as a normal and accepted tool of educational policy is readily discernible in this and the companion case. The Charlotte school authorities did not purport to assign students on the basis of geographically drawn zones until 1965 and then they allowed almost unlimited transfer privileges. The District Court's conclusion that assignment of children to the school nearest their home serving their grade would not produce an effective dismantling of the dual system is supported by the record.

Thus the remedial techniques used in the District Court's order were within that court's power to provide equitable relief; implementation of the decree is well within the capacity of the school authority.

The decree provided that the buses used to implement the plan would operate on direct routes. Students would be picked up at schools near their homes and transported to the schools they were to attend. The trips for elementary school pupils average about seven miles and the District Court found that they would take "not over 35 minutes at the most." This system compares favorably with the transportation plan previously operated in Charlotte under which each day 23,600 students on all grade levels were transported an average of 15 miles one way for an average trip requiring over an hour. In these circumstances, we find no basis for holding that the local school authorities may not be required to employ bus transportation as one tool of school desegregation. Desegregation plans cannot be limited to the walk-in school. . . .

At some point, these school authorities and others like them should have achieved full compliance with this Court's decision in *Brown I*. The systems would then be "unitary" in the sense required by our decisions in *Green* and *Alexander* [v. *Holmes*

County Board of Education (1968)].

It does not follow that the communities served by such systems will remain demographically stable, for in a growing, mobile society, few will do so. Neither school authorities nor district courts are constitutionally required to make year-by-year adjustments of the racial composition of student bodies once the affirmative duty to desegregate has been accomplished and racial discrimination through official action is eliminated from the system. This does not mean that federal courts are without power to deal with future problems; but in the absence of a showing that either the school authorities or some other agency of the State has deliberately attempted to fix or alter demographic patterns to affect the racial composition of the schools, further intervention by a district court should not be necessary. . . .

It is so ordered.

What importance does the Court attach to the history of the school system? Would it have sustained a court-ordered plan for busing in a district where there had been no history of de jure segregation? What is the Court's ruling on the degree of racial balancing required? What standards were announced to guide district courts in shaping plans for the desegregation of public schools? Did the opinion support neighborhood schools?

The *Swann* decision was limited in two respects. First, it pertained only to school systems with a history of de jure segregation. In *Keyes* v. *School District No. 1, Denver, Colorado* (1973) the Court expanded its *Swann* doctrine to include de facto segregation where there was a finding of purpose of intent to segregate by school authorities through "a systematic program of segregation affecting a substantial portion of the students, schools, teachers, and facilities"[49] within a school district.

In the second place, the *Swann* decision limited the Court to the ordering of busing of school children *within the limits* of the city school district if necessary to achieve desegregation. In the case of *Charlotte-Mecklenburg*, the limits of the city school district included the surrounding county. However, only eighteen of the country's 100 largest city school districts include both the inner city and the surrounding county. In cities such as San Francisco, Denver, Pasadena, and Boston, court-ordered busing plans affected only the central city school district. In 1974 the Supreme Court reviewed a busing plan for Detroit ordered by a federal district court and sustained by the court of appeals that would have required the busing of students among fifty-four separate school districts in the Detroit metropolitan area to achieve racially balanced schools. Proponents of the Detroit busing plan argued that the central city of Detroit was 70 percent black, and the only way integration could be accomplished would be to link the school district of Detroit with the surrounding white suburban school districts.

In *Milliken* v. *Bradley* (1974) a sharply divided Supreme Court held 5–4 that the court-ordered Detroit busing plan could not be sustained under the equal protection clause. Chief Justice Burger wrote the majority opinion, which found that there was no evidence of disparate treatment of white and black students among the fifty-three outlying school districts that surround

[49]Keyes v. School District No. 1, Denver, Colorado, 413 U.S. 189, 201 (1973).

Detroit. The only evidence of discrimination was within the city limits of Detroit itself. Since the outlying districts did not violate the equal protection clause, declared Burger, they could not be ordered to integrate their systems with that of Detroit. Discrimination was limited to Detroit; therefore the court order to remedy the situation must be confined to Detroit. There was a strong strain of judicial self-restraint and respect for considerations of federalism in Burger's opinion. He concluded that the boundary lines of school districts "may be bridged where there has been a constitutional violation calling for interdistrict relief, but the notion that school district lines may be casually ignored or treated as a mere administrative convenience is contrary to the history of public education in our country. No single tradition in public education is more deeply rooted than local control over the operation of schools."[50]

Justices Douglas, Brennan, White, and Marshall dissented in the *Milliken* case. White and Marshall wrote separate dissenting opinions in which all of the dissenters joined, while Douglas wrote a separate dissent. Marshall wrote a particularly stinging dissent, stating that "I cannot subscribe to this emasculation of our constitutional guarantee of equal protection of the laws. . . . our precedents, in my view, firmly establish that where, as here, state-imposed segregation has been demonstrated, it becomes the duty of the state to eliminate root and branch all vestiges of racial discrimination and to achieve the greatest possible degree of actual desegregation. . . . The rights at issue in this case are too fundamental to be abridged on grounds as superficial as those relied on by the majority today."[51] He concluded,

> Desegregation is not and was never expected to be an easy task. Racial attitudes engrained in our nation's childhood and adolescence are not quickly thrown aside in its middle years. But just as the inconvenience of some cannot be allowed to stand in the way of rights of others, so public opposition, no matter how strident, cannot be permitted to divert this Court from the enforcement of the constitutional principles at issue in this case. Today's holding, I fear, is more a reflection of a perceived public mood that we have gone far enough in enforcing the constitutional guarantee of equal justice than it is the product of neutral principles of law. In the short run, it may seem to be the easier course to allow our great metropolitan areas to be divided up each into two cities—one white, the other black— but it is a course I predict our people will ultimately regret.[52]

Justice White's dissent essentially agreed with Marshall's views, stating that the majority opinion rendered the Court impotent to correct deliberate acts of segregation committed by governmental bodies. In his separate dissent Justice Douglas argued for metropolitan remedies of the problems of racial segregation in public education and supported judicial intervention to achieve this result.

The sharply divided opinion in the *Milliken* case illustrates that the Court has not reached agreement on how to resolve the difficult issue of de facto segregation of public education.

[50]Milliken v. Bradley, 418 U.S. 717, 741 (1974).
[51]Ibid., pp. 782–783.
[52]Ibid., pp. 814–815.

"Reverse" Discrimination

The responsibility of government to take affirmative action to protect against discrimination, reflected in the *Green* and *Swann* decisions, was written into various sections of the Civil Rights Act of 1964. It was clearly implied in Section 6, which provided that no person was to be "subjected to discrimination under any program or activity receiving federal financial assistance." The government, particularly the Department of Health, Education and Welfare, defined this section to require "affirmative action" programs by private institutions receiving federal aid to achieve a racial balance among employees and, in institutions of higher learning, within their student bodies as well. Civil rights groups and the government pressured for affirmative action, resulting in the adoption of many plans throughout the country that gave unequal *favored* treatment to racial minorities in the admissions programs of institutions of higher learning and in private sector employment.

Do affirmative action programs giving unequal favored treatment to racial minorities constitute "reverse discrimination" in violation of the equal protection clause? The Court was asked to decide this question in *Defunis* v. *Odegaard* (1974), which challenged under the equal protection clause the constitutionality of an affirmative action program used by the University of Washington Law School. The law school admissions program gave special consideration to black, Chicano, American Indian, and Philippino applicants. Defunis claimed that his denial of admission to the school was discrimination against him because his qualifications were superior to those of some minority students who had been given special consideration. A Washington state trial court agreed with Defunis and ordered his admission to the law school in 1971. The Washington State Supreme Court overturned the trial court's decision, but Justice Douglas issued a stay that suspended the application of the decision of the Washington court until the Supreme Court could resolve the issue. This meant that the trial court's decision remained in effect, and Defunis was admitted to the University of Washington Law School.

When the Supreme Court finally brought up the *Defunis* case in 1974, it refused to decide it, holding that the case was moot since Defunis was going to graduate at the end of the 1974 spring term. Justice Douglas, in a dissenting opinion, declared that the case should be remanded for a new trial to determine if invidious discrimination had been practiced against Defunis. He stated that the equal protection clause required admissions procedures to be racially neutral. "There is no constitutional right for any race to be preferred," he wrote.[53]

While declining to reach the merits in the *Defunis* case, the Court emphasized that the question of racial quotas in law school admissions would not evade judicial review for there was every reason to believe that a similar case would come before the Court "with relative speed."[54] This prediction was

[53]Defunis v. Odegaard, 416 U.S. 312, 336 (1974).
[54]Ibid., p. 319.

borne out in 1978 as the Court again confronted the issue of reverse discrimination in *Regents of the University of California* v. *Bakke.* Allan Bakke, a white, thirty-six-year old engineer, decided that he wanted to become a doctor and applied twice, in 1973 and 1974, for admission to the University of California Medical School at Davis. Each time the school turned him down, declaring that there were too many qualified applicants, resulting in only one out of twenty-six being accepted in 1973 and one out of thirty-seven in 1974. Sixteen of the 100 openings in the Davis medical school were set aside for "minority" applicants. Bakke's "objective" qualifications, such as his medical college admission test scores and his undergraduate grades, were better than those of some of the minority applicants accepted during the years when he was rejected. The university had set aside sixteen of its 100 places in each year's class exclusively for minority applicants, who competed against themselves and not against the applicants for the other eighty-four places. A white applicant failing to be admitted to one of the eighty-four places could not under any circumstances be given one of the sixteen places reserved for minorities. Bakke claimed that the admissions procedures violated the equal protection clause and Title 6 of the Civil Rights Act of 1964.[55]

The trial court found that the admissions program in effect established racial quotas and was therefore a violation of the equal protection clause and Title 6. It refused, however, to order the admission of Bakke to the medical school because of his failure to prove that he would have been admitted in the absence of the special program for minorities. The California Supreme Court sustained the trial court's finding that the program violated the Civil Rights Act and the equal protection clause but, ruling that the university had the burden of demonstrating that the plaintiff could not have been admitted in the absence of the minority program, the California court overturned the trial court's denial of an injunction ordering Bakke to be admitted to the medical school. The Supreme Court granted certiorari.

Regents of the University of California v. Bakke

438 U.S. 265; 98 S. Ct. 2733; 57 L. Ed. 2d 750 (1978)

MR. JUSTICE POWELL announced the judgment of the Court and wrote an opinion:

For the reasons stated in the following opinion, I believe that so much of the judgment of the California court as holds petitioner's special admissions program unlawful and directs that respondent be admitted to the Medical School must be affirmed. For the reasons expressed in a separate opinion, my Brothers The Chief Justice, Mr. Justice Stewart, Mr. Justice Rehnquist, and Mr. Justice Stevens concur in this judgment.

I also conclude for the reasons stated in the following opinion that the portion of the court's judgment enjoining petitioner from according any consideration to race in its admissions process must be reversed. For reasons expressed in sepa-

---

[55]He also claimed the procedures violated a provision of the California constitution.

rate opinions, my Brothers Mr. Justice Brennan, Mr. Justice White, Mr. Justice Marshall, and Mr. Justice Blackmun concur in this judgment.

Affirmed in part and reversed in part.

II

B

The language of § 601 [of Title VI], 78 Stat. 252 [1964], like that of the Equal Protection Clause, is majestic in its sweep.

No person in the United States shall, on the ground of race, color, or national origin, be excluded from participation in, be denied the benefits of, or be subjected to discrimination under any program or activity receiving Federal financial assistance.

The concept of "discrimination," like the phrase "equal protection of the laws," is susceptible of varying interpretations, for as Mr. Justice Holmes declared, "[a] word is not a crystal, transparent and unchanged, it is the skin of a living thought and may vary greatly in color and content according to the circumstances and the time in which it is used." . . . We must, therefore, seek whatever aid is available in determining the precise meaning of the statute before us. . . . Examination of the voluminous legislative history of Title VI reveals a congressional intent to halt federal funding of entities that violate a prohibition of racial discrimination similar to that of the Constitution. Although isolated statements of various legislators, taken out of context, can be marshaled in support of the proposition that § 601 enacted a purely color-blind scheme, without regard to the reach of the Equal Protection Clause, these comments must be read against the background of both the problem that Congress was addressing and the broader view of the statute that emerges from a full examination of the legislative debates.

The problem confronting Congress was discrimination against Negro citizens at the hands of recipients of federal moneys. Indeed, the color blindness pronouncements [of members of Congress] . . . generally occur[ed] in the midst of extended remarks dealing with the evils of segregation in federally funded programs. Over and over again, proponents of the bill detailed the plight of Negroes seeking equal treatment in such programs. There simply was no reason for Congress to consider the validity of hypothetical preferences that might be accorded minority citizens; the legislators were dealing with the real and pressing problem of how to guarantee those citizens equal treatment.

In addressing that problem, supporters of Title VI repeatedly declared that the bill enacted constitutional principles. . . .

In the Senate, Senator Humphrey declared that the purpose of Title VI was "to insure that Federal funds are spent in accordance with the Constitution and the moral sense of the Nation." . . .

Further evidence of the incorporation of a constitutional standard into Title VI appears in the repeated refusals of the legislation's supporters precisely to define the term "discrimination." Opponents sharply criticized this failure, but proponents of the bill merely replied that the meaning of "discrimination" would be made clear by reference to the Constitution or other existing law. . . .

In view of the clear legislative intent, Title VI must be held to proscribe only those racial classifications that would violate the Equal Protection Clause or the Fifth Amendment.

III

A

Petitioner does not deny that decisions based on race or ethnic origin by faculties and administrations of state universities are reviewable under the Fourteenth Amendment. . . . For his part, respondent does not argue that all racial or ethnic classifications are *per se* invalid. . . . The parties do disagree as to the level of judicial scrutiny to be applied to the special admissions program. Petitioner argues that the court below erred in applying strict scrutiny, as this inexact term has been applied in our cases. . . .

En route to this crucial battle over the scope of judicial review, the parties fight a sharp preliminary action over the proper characterization of the special admissions program. Petitioner prefers to view it as establishing a "goal" of minority representation in the Medical School. Respondent, echoing the courts below, labels it a racial quota.

This semantic distinction is beside the point: The special admissions program is undeniably a classification based on race and ethnic background. To the extent that there existed a pool of at least minimally qualified minority applicants to fill the 16 special admissions seats, white applicants could compete only for 84 seats in the entering class, rather than the 100 open to minority applicants. Whether this limitation is described as a quota or a goal, it is a line drawn on the basis of race and ethnic status.

The guarantees of the Fourteenth Amendment extend to all persons. Its language is explicit: "No State shall . . . deny to any person within its jurisdiction the equal protection of the laws." It is settled beyond question that the "rights created by the first section of the Fourteenth Amendment are, by its terms, guaranteed to the individual. The rights established are personal rights," *Shelley* v. *Kraemer* [1948]. . . . The guarantee of equal protection cannot mean one thing when applied to one individual and something else when applied to a person of another color. If both are not accorded the same protection, then it is not equal.

Nevertheless, petitioner argues that the court below erred in applying strict scrutiny to the special admissions program because white males, such as respondent, are not a "discrete and insular minority" requiring extraordinary protection from the majoritarian political process. *Carolene Products Co.* . . . This rationale, however, has never been invoked in our decisions as a prerequisite to subjecting racial or ethnic distinctions to strict scrutiny. Nor has this Court held that discreteness and insularity constitute necessary preconditions to a holding that a particular classification is invidious. . . . These characteristics may be relevant in deciding whether or not to add new types of classifications to the list of "suspect" categories or whether a particular classification survives close examination. . . . Racial and ethnic classifications, however, are subject to stringent examination without regard to these additional characteristics. We declared as much in the first cases explicitly to recognize racial distinctions as suspect:

Distinctions between citizens solely because of their ancestry are by their very nature odious to a free people whose institutions are founded upon the doctrine of equality. *Hirabayashi* [1943]. . . .

[A]ll legal restrictions which curtail the civil rights of a single racial group are immediately suspect. That is not to say that all such restrictions are unconstitutional. It is to say that courts must subject them to the most rigid scrutiny. *Korematsu* [1944]. . . .

The Court has never questioned the validity of those pronouncements. Racial and ethnic distinctions of any sort are inherently suspect and thus call for the most exacting judicial examination. . . .

B

. . . Although many of the Framers of the Fourteenth Amendment conceived of its primary function as bridging the vast distance between members of the Negro race and the white "majority," *Slaughterhouse Cases,* . . . the Amendment itself was framed in universal terms, without reference to color, ethnic origin, or condition of prior servitude. As this Court recently remarked in interpreting the 1866 Civil Rights Act to extend to claims of racial discrimination against white persons, "the 39th Congress was intent upon establishing in the federal law a broader principle than would have been necessary simply to meet the particular and immediate plight of the newly freed Negro slaves."

Over the past 30 years, this Court has embarked upon the crucial mission of interpreting the Equal Protection Clause with the view of assuring to all persons "the protection of equal laws," . . . in a Nation confronting a legacy of slavery and racial discrimination. . . . Because the landmark decisions in this area arose in response to the continued exclusion of Negroes from the mainstream of American society, they could be characterized as involving discrimination by the "majority" white race against the Negro minority. But they need not be read as depending upon that characterization for their results. It suffices to say that "[o]ver the years, this Court has consistently repudiated '[d]istinctions between citizens solely because of their ancestry' as being 'odious to a free people whose institutions are founded upon the doctrine of equality.' "
. . .

Petitioner urges us to adopt for the first time a more restrictive view of the Equal Protection Clause and hold that discrimination against members of the white "majority" cannot be suspect if its purpose can be characterized as "benign." The clock of our liberties, however, cannot be turned back to 1868. . . . It is far too late to argue that the guarantee of equal protection to *all* persons permits the recognition of special wards entitled to a degree of protection greater than that accorded others. "The Fourteenth Amendment is not directed solely against discrimination due to a 'two-class theory'— that is, based upon differences between 'white' and Negro." . . .

Once the artificial line of a "two-class theory" of the Fourteenth Amendment is put aside, the difficulties entailed in varying the level of judicial review according to a perceived "preferred" status of a particular racial or ethnic minority are intractable. The concepts of "majority" and "minority" necessarily reflect temporary arrangements and political judgments. As observed above, the white "majority" itself is composed of various minority groups, most of which can lay claim to a history of prior discrimination at the hands of the State and private individuals. Not all of these groups can receive preferential treatment and corresponding judicial tolerance of distinctions drawn in terms of race and nationality, for then the only "majority" left would be a new minority of white Anglo-Saxon Protestants. There is no principled basis for deciding which groups would merit "heightened judicial solicitude" and which would not. Courts would be asked to evaluate the extent of the prejudice and consequent harm suffered by various minority groups. Those whose societal injury is thought to exceed some arbitrary level of tolerability then would be entitled to preferential classifications at the expense of individuals belonging to other groups. Those classifications would be free from exacting judicial scrutiny. As these preferences began to have their desired effect, and the consequences of past discrimination were undone, new judicial rankings would be necessary. The kind of variable sociological and political analysis necessary to produce such rankings simply does not lie within the judicial competence—even if they otherwise were politically feasible and socially desirable.

Moreover, there are serious problems of justice connected with the idea of preference itself. First, it may not always be clear that a so-called preference is in fact benign. . . . Second, preferential programs may only reinforce common stereotypes holding that certain groups are unable to achieve success without special protection based on a factor having no relationship to individual worth. . . . Third, there is a measure of inequity in forcing innocent persons in respondent's position to bear the burdens of redressing grievances not of their making.

By hitching the meaning of the Equal Protection Clause to these transitory considerations, we would be holding, as a constitutional principle, that judicial scrutiny of classifications touching on racial and ethnic background may vary with the ebb and flow of political forces. Disparate constitutional tolerance of such classifications well may serve to exacerbate racial and ethnic antagonisms rather than alleviate them. . . . Also, the mutability of a constitutional principle, based upon shifting political and social judgments, undermines the chances for consistent application of the Constitution from one generation to the next, a critical feature of its coherent interpretation. . . .

If it is the individual who is entitled to judicial protection against classifications based upon his racial or ethnic background because such distinctions impinge upon personal rights, rather than the individual only because of his membership in a particular group, then constitutional standards may be applied consistently. Political judgments regarding the necessity for the particular classification may be weighed in the constitutional balance, *Korematsu* v. *United States* [1944] . . . but the standard of justification will remain constant. This is as it should be, since those political judgments are the product of rough compromise struck by contending groups within the democratic process. When they touch upon an individual's race or ethnic background, he is entitled to a judicial determination that the bur-

den he is asked to bear on that basis is precisely tailored to serve a compelling governmental interest. The Constitution guarantees that right to every person regardless of his background. . . .

C

Petitioner contends that on several occasions this Court has approved preferential classifications without applying the most exacting scrutiny. Most of the cases upon which petitioner relies are drawn from three areas: school desegregation, employment discrimination, and sex discrimination. Each of the cases cited presented a situation materially different from the facts of this case.

The school desegregation cases are inapposite. Each involved remedies for clearly determined constitutional violations. . . . Racial classifications thus were designed as remedies for the vindication of constitutional entitlement. Moreover, the scope of the remedies was not permitted to exceed the extent of the violations. . . . Here, there was no judicial determination of constitutional violation as a predicate for the formulation of a remedial classification.

The employment discrimination cases also do not advance petitioner's cause. For example, in *Franks* v. *Bowman Transportation Co.* [1976] . . . we approved a retroactive award of seniority to a class of Negro truckdrivers who had been the victims of discrimination—not just by society at large, but by the respondent in that case. While this relief imposed some burdens on other employees, it was held necessary " 'to make [the victims] whole for injuries suffered on account of unlawful employment discrimination.' " . . . Such preferences also have been upheld where a legislative or administrative body charged with the responsibility made determinations of past discrimination by the industries affected, and fashioned remedies deemed appropriate to rectify the discrimination. . . . But we have never approved preferential classifications in the absence of proved constitutional or statutory violations. . . .

IV

We have held that in "order to justify the use of a suspect classification, a State must show that its purpose or interest is both constitutionally permissible and substantial, and that its use of the classification is 'necessary . . . to the accomplishment' of its purpose or the safeguarding of its interest." . . . The special admissions program purports to serve the purposes of: (i) "reducing the historic deficit of traditionally disfavored minorities in medical schools and in the medical profession," . . . (ii) countering the effects of societal discrimination; (iii) increasing the number of physicians who will practice in communities currently underserved; and (iv) obtaining the educational benefits that flow from an ethnically diverse student body. It is necessary to decide which, if any, of these purposes is substantial enough to support the use of a suspect classification.

A

If petitioner's purpose is to assure within its student body some specified percentage of a particular group merely because of its race or ethnic origin, such a preferential purpose must be rejected not as insubstantial but as facially invalid. Preferring members of any one group for no reason other than race or ethnic origin is discrimination for its own sake. This the Constitution forbids. . . .

B

The State certainly has a legitimate and substantial interest in ameliorating, or eliminating where feasible, the disabling effects of identified discrimination. The line of school desegregation cases, commencing with *Brown,* attests to the importance of this state goal and the commitment of the judiciary to affirm all lawful means toward its attainment. In the school cases, the States were required by court order to redress the wrongs worked by specific instances of racial discrimination. That goal was far more focused than the remedying of the effects of "societal discrimination," an amorphous concept of injury that may be ageless in its reach into the past.

We have never approved a classification that aids persons perceived as members of relatively victimized groups at the expense of other innocent individuals in the absence of judicial, legislative, or administrative findings of constitutional or statutory violations. . . . After such findings have been made, the governmental interest in preferring members of the injured groups at the expense of others is substantial, since the legal rights of the victims must be vindicated. In such a case, the extent of the injury and the consequent remedy will have been judicially, legislatively, or administratively defined. Also, the remedial action usually remains subject to continuing oversight to assure that it will work the least harm possible to other innocent persons competing for the benefit. Without such findings of constitutional or statutory violations, it cannot be said that the government has any greater interest in helping one individual than in refraining from harming another. Thus, the government has no compelling justification for inflicting such harm.

Petitioner does not purport to have made, and is in no position to make, such findings. Its broad mission is education, not the formulation of any legislative policy or the adjudication of particular claims of illegality. . . .

Hence, the purpose of helping certain groups whom the faculty of the Davis Medical School perceived as victims of "societal discrimination" does not justify a classification that imposes disadvantages upon persons like respondent, who bear no responsibility for whatever harm the beneficiaries of the special admissions program are thought to have suffered. To hold otherwise would be to convert a remedy heretofore reserved for violations of legal rights into a privilege that all institutions throughout the Nation could grant at their pleasure to whatever groups are perceived as victims of societal discrimination. That is a step we have never approved. . . .

C

Petitioner identifies, as another purpose of its program, improving the delivery of health-care services to communities currently underserved. It may be assumed that in some situations a State's interest in facilitating the health care of its citizens is sufficiently compelling to support the use of a suspect classification. But there is virtually no evidence in the record indicating that petitioner's special admissions program is either needed or geared to promote that goal. The court below addressed this failure of proof:

The University concedes it cannot assure that minority doctors who entered under the program, all of whom expressed an 'interest' in practicing in a disadvantaged community, will actually do so. It may be correct to assume that some of them will carry out this intention, and that it is more likely they will practice in minority communities than the average white doctor. . . . Nevertheless, there are more precise and reliable ways to identify applicants who are genuinely interested in the medical problems of minorities than by race. An applicant of whatever race who has demonstrated his concern for disadvantaged minorities in the past and who declares that practice in such a community is his primary professional goal would be more likely to contribute to alleviation of the medical shortage than one who is chosen entirely on the basis of race and disadvantage. In short, there is no empirical data to

demonstrate that any one race is more selflessly socially oriented or by contrast that another is more selfishly acquisitive. 18 Cal. 3d, at 56, 553 P. 2d, at 1167.

Petitioner simply has not carried its burden of demonstrating that it must prefer members of particular ethnic groups over all other individuals in order to promote better health-care delivery to deprived citizens. Indeed, petitioner has not shown that its preferential classification is likely to have any significant effect on the problem.

D

The fourth goal asserted by petitioner is the attainment of a diverse student body. This clearly is a constitutionally permissible goal for an institution of higher education. Academic freedom, though not a specifically enumerated constitutional right, long has been viewed as a special concern of the First Amendment. . . . The atmosphere of "speculation, experiment and creation"—so essential to the quality of higher education—is widely believed to be promoted by a diverse student body. As the Court noted in *Keyishian* [v. *Board of Regents* (1967)], it is not too much to say that the "nation's future depends upon leaders trained through wide exposure" to the ideas and mores of students as diverse as this Nation of many peoples.

Thus, in arguing that its universities must be accorded the right to select those students who will contribute the most to the "robust exchange of ideas," petitioner invokes a countervailing constitutional interest, that of the First Amendment. In this light, petitioner must be viewed as seeking to achieve a goal that is of paramount importance in the fulfillment of its mission.

It may be argued that there is greater force to these views at the undergraduate level than in a medical school where the training is centered primarily on professional competency. But even at the graduate level, our tradition and experience lend support to the view that the contribution of diversity is substantial. . . . Physicians serve a heterogeneous population. An otherwise qualified medical student with a particular background—whether it be ethnic, geographic, culturally advantaged or disadvantaged—may bring to a professional school of medicine experiences, outlooks, and ideas that enrich the training of its student body and better equip its graduates to render with understanding their vital service to humanity. . . .

. . . As the interest of diversity is compelling in the context of a university's admissions program, the question remains whether the program's racial classification is necessary to promote this interest. . . .

V

A

It may be assumed that the reservation of a specified number of seats in each class for individuals from the preferred ethnic groups would contribute to the attainment of considerable ethnic diversity in the student body. But petitioner's argument that this is the only effective means of serving the interest of diversity is seriously flawed. In a most fundamental sense the argument misconceives the nature of the state interest that would justify consideration of race or ethnic background. It is not an interest in simple ethnic diversity, in which a specified percentage of the student body is in effect guaranteed to be members of selected ethnic groups, with the remaining percentage an undifferentiated aggregation of students. The diversity that furthers a compelling state interest encompasses a far broader array of qualifications and characteristics of which racial or ethnic origin is but a single though important

element. Petitioner's special admissions program, focused *solely* on ethnic diversity, would hinder rather than further attainment of genuine diversity.

Nor would the state interest in genuine diversity be served by expanding petitioner's two-track system into a multitrack program with a prescribed number of seats set aside for each identifiable category of applicants. Indeed, it is inconceivable that a university would thus pursue the logic of petitioner's two-track program to the illogical end of insulating each category of applicants with certain desired qualifications from competition with all other applicants.

The experience of other university admissions programs, which take race into account in achieving the educational diversity valued by the First Amendment, demonstrates that the assignment of a fixed number of places to a minority group is not a necessary means toward that end. An illuminating example is found in the Harvard College program:

> In recent years Harvard College has expanded the concept of diversity to include students from disadvantaged economic, racial and ethnic groups. Harvard College now recruits not only Californians or Louisianans but also blacks and Chicanos and other minority students.
> . . .
> In practice, this new definition of diversity has meant that race has been a factor in some admission decisions. When the Committee on Admissions reviews the large middle group of applicants who are 'admissible' and deemed capable of doing good work in their courses, the race of an applicant may tip the balance in his favor just as geographic origin or a life spent on a farm may tip the balance in other candidates' cases. A farm boy from Idaho can bring something to Harvard College that a Bostonian cannot offer. Similarly, a black student can usually bring something that a white person cannot offer. . . .
> In Harvard college admissions the Committee has not set target-quotas for the number of blacks, or of musicians, football players, physicists or Californians to be admitted in a given

year. . . . But that awareness [of the necessity of including more than a token number of black students] does not mean that the Committee sets a minimum number of blacks or of people from west of the Mississippi who are to be admitted. It means only that in choosing among thousands of applicants who are not only 'admissible' academically but have other strong qualities, the Committee, with a number of criteria in mind, pays some attention to distribution among many types and categories of students. . . .

In such an admissions program, race or ethnic background may be deemed a "plus" in a particular applicant's file, yet it does not insulate the individual from comparison with all other candidates for the available seats. The file of a particular black applicant may be examined for his potential contribution to diversity without the factor of race being decisive when compared, for example, with that of an applicant identifed as an Italian-American if the latter is thought to exhibit qualities more likely to promote beneficial educational pluralism. Such qualities could include exceptional personal talents, unique work or service experience, leadership potential, maturity, demonstrated compassion, a history of overcoming disadvantage, ability to communicate with the poor, or other qualifications deemed important. In short, an admissions program operated in this way is flexible enough to consider all pertinent elements of diversity in light of the particular qualifications of each applicant, and to place them on the same footing for consideration, although not necessarily according them the same weight. Indeed, the weight attributed to a particular quality may vary from year to year depending upon the "mix" both of the student body and the applicants for the incoming class.

This kind of program treats each applicant as an individual in the admissions process. The applicant who loses out on the last available seat to another candidate receiving a "plus" on the basis of ethnic background will not have been foreclosed from all consideration for that seat simply because he was not the right color or had the wrong surname. It would mean only that his combined qualifications, which may have included similar nonobjective factors, did not outweigh those of the other applicant. His qualifications would have been weighed fairly and competitively, and he would have no basis to complain of unequal treatment under the Fourteenth Amendment.

It has been suggested that an admissions program which considers race only as one factor is simply a subtle and more sophisticated—but no less effective—means of according racial preference than the Davis program. A facial intent to discriminate, however, is evident in petitioner's preference program and not denied in this case. No such facial infirmity exists in an admissions program where race or ethnic background is simply one element—to be weighed fairly against other elements—in the selection process. "A boundary line," as Mr. Justice Frankfurter remarked in another connection, "is none the worse for being narrow." . . . And a court would not assume that a university, professing to employ a facially nondiscriminatory admissions policy, would operate it as a cover for the functional equivalent of a quota system. In short, good faith would be presumed in the absence of a showing to the contrary in the manner permitted by our cases. . . .

B

In summary, it is evident that the Davis special admissions program involves the use of an explicit racial classification never before countenanced by this Court. It tells applicants who are not Negro, Asian, or Chicano that they are totally excluded from a specific percentage of the seats in an entering class. No matter how strong their qualifications, quantitative and extracurricular, including their own potential for contribution to educational diversity, they are never afforded the chance to compete with applicants from the preferred groups for the special admissions seats. At the same time, the preferred applicants have the opportunity to compete for every seat in the class.

The fatal flaw in petitioner's preferential program is its disregard of individual rights as guaranteed by the Fourteenth Amendment. . . . Such rights are not absolute. But when a State's distribution of benefits or imposition of burdens hinges on ancestry or the color of a person's skin or ancestry, that individual is entitled to a demonstration that the challenged classification is necessary to promote a substantial state interest. Petitioner has failed to carry this burden. For this reason, that portion of the California court's judgment holding petitioner's special admissions program invalid under the Fourteenth Amendment must be affirmed.

C

In enjoining petitioner from ever considering the race of any applicant, however, the courts below failed to recognize that the State has a substantial interest that legitimately may be served by a properly devised admissions program involving the competitive consideration of race and ethnic origin. For this reason, so much of the California court's judgment as enjoins petitioner from any consideration of the race of any applicant must be reversed.

Opinion of MR. JUSTICE BRENNAN, MR. JUSTICE WHITE, MR. JUSTICE MARSHALL, and MR. JUSTICE BLACKMUN, concurring in the judgment in part and dissenting in part:

The Court today, in reversing in part the judgment of the Supreme Court of California, affirms the constitutional power of Federal and State Governments to act affirmatively to achieve equal opportunity for all. The difficulty of the issue presented—whether government may use race-conscious programs to redress the continuing effects of past discrimination—and the mature consideration which each of our Brethren has brought to it have resulted in many opinions, no single one speaking for the Court. But this should not and must not mask the central meaning of today's opinions: Government may take race into account when it acts not to demean or insult any racial group, but to remedy disadvantages cast on minorities by past racial prejudice, at least when appropriate findings have been made by judicial, legislative, or administrative bodies with competence to act in this area.

The Chief Justice and our Brothers Stewart, Rehnquist, and Stevens, have concluded that Title VI of the Civil Rights Act of 1964, . . . as amended, . . . prohibits programs such as that at the Davis Medical School. On this statutory theory alone, they would hold that respondent Allan Bakke's rights have been violated and that he must, therefore, be admitted to the Medical School. Our Brother Powell, reaching the Constitution, concludes that, although race may be taken into account in university admissions, the particular special admissions program used by petitioner, which resulted in the exclusion of respondent Bakke, was not shown to be necessary to achieve petitioner's stated goals. Accordingly, these Members of the Court form a majority of five affirming the judgment of the Supreme Court of California insofar as it holds that respondent Bakke "is entitled to an order that he be admitted to the University." . . .

We agree with Mr. Justice Powell that, as applied to the case before us, Title VI goes no further in prohibiting the use of race than the Equal Protection Clause of the Fourteenth Amendment itself. We also agree that the effect of the California Supreme Court's affirmance of the judgment of the Superior Court of California would be to prohibit the University from establishing in the future affirmative action programs that take race into account. . . . Since we conclude that the affirmative admissions program at the Davis Medical School is constitutional, we would reverse the judgment below in all respects. Mr. Justice Powell agrees that some uses of race in university admissions are permissible and, therefore, he joins with us to make five votes reversing the judgment below insofar as it prohibits the University from establishing race-conscious programs in the future. . . .

II

. . . In our view, Title VI prohibits only those uses of racial criteria that would violate the Fourteenth Amendment if employed by a State or its agencies; it does not bar the preferential treatment of racial minorities as a means of remedying past societal discrimination to the extent that such action is consistent with the Fourteenth Amendment. The legislative history of Title VI, administrative regulations interpreting the statute, subsequent congressional and executive action, and the prior decisions of this Court compel this conclusion. None of these sources lends support to the proposition that Congress intended to bar all race-conscious efforts to extend the benefits of federally financed programs to minorities who have been historically excluded from the full benefits of American life. . . .

III

A

Our cases have always implied that an "overriding statutory purpose," . . . could be found that would justify racial classifications. See, *e.g.,* . . . *Korematsu* v. *United States* [1944] . . . *Hirabayashi* v. *United States* [1943] . . . More recently, in *Mc-Daniel* v. *Barresi* [1971] . . . this Court unanimously reversed the Georgia Supreme Court which had held that a desegregation plan voluntarily adopted by a local school board, which assigned students on the basis of race, was *per se* invalid because it was not colorblind. . . .

We conclude, therefore, that racial classifications are not *per se* invalid under the Fourteenth Amendment. Accordingly, we turn to the problem of articulating what our role should be in reviewing state action that expressly classifies by race.

B

Respondent argues that racial classifications are always suspect and, consequently, that this Court should weigh the importance of the objectives served by Davis' special admissions program to see if they are compelling. . . .

Unquestionably we have held that a government practice or statute which restricts "fundamental rights" or which contains "suspect classifications" is to be subjected to "strict scrutiny" and can be justified only if it furthers a compelling government purpose and, even then, only if no less restrictive alternative is available. . . . But no fundamental right is involved here. . . . Nor do whites as a class have any of the "traditional indicia of suspectness: the class is not saddled with such disabilities, or subjected to such a history of purposeful unequal treatment, or relegated to such a position of political powerlessness as to command extraordinary protection from the majoritarian political process." . . .

On the other hand, the fact that this case does not fit neatly into our prior analytic framework for race cases does not mean that it should be analyzed by applying the very loose rational-basis standard of review that is the very least that is always applied in equal protection cases. " '[T]he mere recitation of a benign, compensatory purpose is not an automatic shield which protects against any inquiry into the actual purposes underlying a statutory scheme.' " . . . Instead, a number of considerations—developed in gender-discrimination cases but which carry even more force when applied to racial classifications—lead us to conclude that racial classifications designed to further remedial purposes " 'must serve important governmental objectives and must be substantially related to achievement of those objectives.' " . . .

First, race, like "gender-based classifications too often [has] been inexcusably utilized to stereotype and stigmatize politically powerless segments of society." . . . State programs designed ostensibly to ameliorate the effects of past racial discrimination obviously create the same hazard of stigma, since they may promote racial separatism and reinforce the views of those who believe that members of racial minorities are inherently incapable of succeeding on their own. . . .

Second, race, like gender and illegitimacy, . . . is an immutable characteristic which its possessors are powerless to escape or set aside. While a classification is not *per se* invalid because it divides classes on the basis of an immutable characteristic, . . . it is nevertheless true that such divisions are contrary to our deep belief that "legal burdens should bear some relationship to individual responsibility or wrongdoing," . . . and that advancement sanctioned, sponsored, or approved by the State should ideally be based on individual merit or achievement, or at the least on factors within the control of an individual. . . .

In sum, because of the significant risk that racial classifications established for ostensibly benign purposes can be misused, causing effects not unlike those created by invidious classifications, it is inappropriate to inquire only whether there is any conceivable basis that might sustain such a classification. Instead, to justify such a classification an important and articulated purpose for its use must be shown. In addition, any statute must be stricken that stigmatizes any group or that singles out those least well represented in the political process to bear the brunt of a benign program. Thus, our review under the Fourteenth Amendment should be strict—not " 'strict' in theory and fatal in fact," because it is stigma that causes fatality—but strict and searching nonetheless.

IV

Davis' articulated purpose of remedying the effects of past societal discrimination is, under our cases, sufficiently important to justify the use of race-conscious admissions programs where there is a sound basis for concluding that minority underrepresentation is substantial and chronic, and that the handicap of past discrimination is impeding access of minorities to the Medical School.

A

At least since *Green* v. *County School Board* [1968] . . . it has been clear that a public body which has itself been adjudged to have engaged in racial discrimination cannot bring itself into compliance with the Equal Protection Clause simply by ending its unlawful acts and adopting a neutral stance. . . .

. . . [T]he creation of unitary school systems, in which the effects of past discrimination had been "eliminated root and branch," . . . was recognized as a compelling social goal justifying the overt use of race.

Finally, the conclusion that state educational institutions may constitutionally adopt admissions programs designed to avoid exclusion of historically disadvantaged minorities, even when such programs explicitly take race into account, finds direct support in our cases construing congressional legislation designed to overcome the present effects of past discrimination. Congress can and has outlawed actions which have a disproportionately adverse and unjustified impact upon members of racial minorities and has required or authorized race-conscious action to put individuals disadvantaged by such impact in the position they otherwise might have enjoyed. See *Franks* v. *Bowman* [1976]. . . . Such relief does not require as a predicate proof that recipients of preferential advancement have been individually discriminated against; it is enough that each recipient is within a general class of persons likely to have been the victims of discrimination. . . .

These cases cannot be distinguished simply by the presence of judicial findings of discrimination, for race-conscious remedies have been approved where such findings have not been made. *McDaniel* v. *Barresi* [1971]. . . . Indeed, the requirement of a judicial determination of a constitutional or statutory violation as a predicate for race-conscious remedial actions would be self-defeating. Such a requirement would severely undermine efforts to achieve voluntary compliance with the requirements of law. And, our society and jurisprudence have always stressed the value of voluntary efforts to further the objectives of the law. Judicial intervention is a last resort to achieve cessation of illegal conduct or the remedying of its effects rather than a prerequisite to action.

Nor can our cases be distinguished on the ground that the entity using explicit racial classifications itself had violated § 1 of the Fourteenth Amendment or an antidiscrimination regulation, for again race-conscious remedies have been approved where this is not the case. . . . Moreover, the presence or absence of past discrimination by universities or employers is largely irrelevant to resolving respondent's constitutional claims. . . . If it was reasonable to conclude—as we hold that it was—that the failure of minorities to qualify for admission at Davis under regular procedures was due principally to the effects of past discrimination, then there is a reasonable likelihood that, but for pervasive racial discrimination, respondent would have failed to qualify for admission even in the absence of Davis' special admissions program.

Thus, our cases under Title VII of the Civil Rights Act have held that, in order to achieve minority participation in previously segregated areas of public life, Congress may require or authorize preferential treatment for those likely disadvantaged by societal racial discrimination. Such legislation has been sustained even without a requirement of findings of intentional racial discrimination by those required or authorized to accord preferential treatment, or a case-by-case determination that those to be benefited suffered from racial discrimination. These decisions compel the conclusion that States also may adopt race-conscious programs designed to overcome substantial, chronic minority underrepresentation where there is reason to believe that the evil addressed is a product of past racial discrimination. . . .

. . . We therefore conclude that Davis' goal of admitting minority students disadvantaged by the effects of past discrimination is sufficiently important to justify use of race-conscious admissions criteria.

B

Properly construed, therefore, our prior cases unequivocally show that a state government may adopt race-conscious programs if the purpose of such programs is to remove the disparate racial impact its actions might otherwise have and if there is reason to believe that the disparate impact is itself the product of past discrimination, whether its own or that of society at large. There is no question that Davis' program is valid under this test.

Certainly, on the basis of the undisputed factual submissions before this Court, Davis had a sound basis for believing that the problem of underrepresentation of minorities was substantial and chronic and that the problem was attributable to handicaps imposed on minority applicants by past and present racial discrimination. Until at least 1973, the practice of medicine in this country was, in fact, if not in law, largely the prerogative of whites. In 1950, for example, while Negroes constituted 10% of the total population, Negro physicians constituted only 2.2% of the total number of physicians. The overwhelming majority of these, moreover, were educated in two predominantly Negro medical schools, Howard and Meharry. By 1970, the gap between the proportion of Negroes in medicine and their proportion in the population had widened: The number of Negroes employed in medicine remained frozen at 2.2% while the Negro population had increased to 11.1%. The number of Negro admittees to predominantly white medical schools, moreover, had declined in absolute numbers during the years 1955 to 1964. . . .

Moreover, Davis had very good reason to believe that the national pattern of underrepresentation of minorities in medicine would be perpetuated if it retained a single admissions standard. For example, the entering classes in 1968 and 1969, the years in which such a standard was used, included only 1 Chicano and 2 Negroes out of the 50 admittees for each year. Nor is there any relief from this pattern of underrepresentation in the statistics for the regular admissions program in later years.

Davis clearly could conclude that the serious and persistent underrepresenta-tion of minorities in medicine depicted by these statistics is the result of handicaps under which minority applicants labor as a consequence of a background of deliberate, purposeful discrimination against minorities in education and in society generally, as well as in the medical profession. From the inception of our national life, Negroes have been subjected to unique legal disabilities impairing access to equal educational opportunity. Under slavery, penal sanctions were imposed upon anyone attempting to educate Negroes. After enactment of the Fourteenth Amendment the States continued to deny Negroes equal educational opportunity, enforcing a strict policy of segregation that itself stamped Negroes as inferior, *Brown I* [1954] . . . that relegated minorities to inferior educational institutions, and that denied them intercourse in the mainstream of professional life necessary to advancement. See *Sweatt* v. *Painter* [1950]. . . . Segregation was not limited to public facilities, moreover, but was enforced by criminal penalties against private action as well. Thus, as late as 1908, this Court enforced a state criminal conviction against a private college for teaching Negroes together with whites. *Berea College* v. *Kentucky* [1908]

Green v. *County School Board* [1968] . . . gave explicit recognition to the fact that the habit of discrimination and the cultural tradition of race prejudice cultivated by centuries of legal slavery and segregation were not immediately dissipated when *Brown I* announced the constitutional principle that equal educational opportunity and participation in all aspects of American life could not be denied on the basis of race. Rather, massive official and private resistance prevented, and to a lesser extent still prevents, attainment of equal opportunity in education at all levels and in the professions. The generation of minority students applying to Davis Medical School since it opened in 1968—

most of whom were born before or about the time *Brown I* was decided—clearly have been victims of this discrimination. Judicial decrees recognizing discrimination in public education in California testify to the fact of widespread discrimination suffered by California-born minority applicants; many minority group members living in California, moreover, were born and reared in school districts in Southern States segregated by law. Since separation of schoolchildren by race "generates a feeling of inferiority as to their status in the community that may affect their hearts and minds in a way unlikely ever to be undone," *Brown I*, the conclusion is inescapable that applicants to medical school must be few indeed who endured the effects of *de jure* segregation, the resistance to *Brown I*, or the equally debilitating pervasive private discrimination fostered by our long history of official discrimination, . . . and yet come to the starting line with an education equal to whites. . . .

C

The second prong of our test—whether the Davis program stigmatizes any discrete group or individual and whether race is reasonably used in light of the program's objectives—is clearly satisfied by the Davis program.

It is not even claimed that Davis' program in any way operates to stigmatize or single out any discrete or insular, or even any identifiable, nonminority group. Nor will harm comparable to that imposed upon racial minorities by exclusion or separation on grounds of race be the likely result of the program. It does not, for example, establish an exclusive preserve for minority students apart from and exclusive of whites. Rather, its purpose is to overcome the effects of segregation by bringing the races together. True, whites are excluded from partici-

pation in the special admissions program, but this fact only operates to reduce the number of whites to be admitted in the regular admissions program in order to permit admission of a reasonable percentage—less than their proportion of the California population—of otherwise underrepresented qualified minority applicants.

Nor was Bakke in any sense stamped as inferior by the Medical School's rejection of him. Indeed, it is conceded by all that he satisfied those criteria regarded by the school as generally relevant to academic performance better than most of the minority members who were admitted. Moreover, there is absolutely no basis for concluding that Bakke's rejection as a result of Davis' use of racial preference will affect him throughout his life in the same way as the segregation of the Negro school children in *Brown I* would have affected them. Unlike discrimination against racial minorities, the use of racial preferences for remedial purposes does not inflict a pervasive injury upon individual whites in the sense that wherever they go or whatever they do there is a significant likelihood that they will be treated as second-class citizens because of their color. This distinction does not mean that the exclusion of a white resulting from the preferential use of race is not sufficiently serious to require justification; but it does not mean that the injury inflicted by such a policy is not distinguishable from disadvantages caused by a wide range of government actions, none of which has ever been thought impermissible for that reason alone.

In addition, there is simply no evidence that the Davis program discriminates intentionally or unintentionally against any minority group which it purports to benefit. The program does not establish a quota in the invidious sense of a ceiling on the number of minority applicants to be admitted. Nor can the program reasonably be regarded as stigmatizing the program's beneficiaries or their race as inferior. The Davis program does not simply advance less qualified applicants; rather, it compensates applicants, who it is uncontested are fully qualified to study medicine, for educational disadvantages which it was reasonable to conclude were a product of state-fostered discrimination. Once admitted, these students must satify the same degree requirements as regularly admitted students; they are taught by the same faculty in the same classes; and their performance is evaluated by the same standards by which regularly admitted students are judged. Under these circumstances, their performance and degrees must be regarded equally with the regularly admitted students with whom they compete for standing. Since minority graduates cannot justifiably be regarded as less well qualified than non-minority graduates by virtue of the special admissions program, there is no reasonable basis to conclude that minority graduates at schools using such programs would be stigmatized as inferior by the existence of such programs.

D

We disagree with the lower courts' conclusion that the Davis program's use of race was unreasonable in light of its objectives. First, as petitioner argues, there are no practical means by which it could achieve its ends in the foreseeable future without the use of race-conscious measures. With respect to any factor (such as poverty or family educational background) that may be used as a substitute for race as an indicator of past discrimination, whites greatly outnumber racial minorities simply because whites make up a far larger percentage of the total population and therefore far outnumber minorities in absolute terms at every socioeconomic level. For example, of a class of recent medical

school applicants from families with less than $10,000 income, at least 71% were white. Of all 1970 families headed by a person *not* a high school graduate which included related children under 18, 80% were white and 20% were racial minorities. Moreover, while race is positively correlated with differences in GPA and MCAT scores, economic disadvantage is not. Thus, it appears that economically disadvantaged whites do not score less well than economically advantaged whites, while economically advantaged blacks score less well than do disadvantaged whites. These statistics graphically illustrate that the University's purpose to integrate its classes by compensating for past discrimination could not be achieved by a general preference for the economically disadvantaged or children of parents of limited education unless such groups were to make up the entire class.

Second, the Davis admissions program does not simply equate minority status with disadvantage. Rather, Davis considers on an individual basis each applicant's personal history to determine whether he or she has likely been disadvantaged by racial discrimination. The record makes clear that only minority applicants likely to have been isolated from the mainstream of American life are considered in the special program; other minority applicants are eligible only through the regular admissions program. True, the procedure by which disadvantage is detected is informal, but we have never insisted that educators conduct their affairs through adjudicatory proceedings, and such insistence here is misplaced. A case-by-case inquiry into the extent to which each individual applicant has been affected, either directly or indirectly, by racial discrimination, would seem to be, as a practical matter, virtually impossible, despite the fact that there are excellent reasons for concluding that such effects generally exist. When individual measurement is impossible or extremely impractical, there is nothing to prevent a State from using categorical means to achieve its ends, at least where the category is closely related to the goal. . . . And it is clear from our cases that specific proof that a person has been victimized by discrimination is not a necessary predicate to offering him relief where the probability of victimization is great. . . .

E

Finally, Davis' special admissions program cannot be said to violate the Constitution simply because it has set aside a predetermined number of places for qualified minority applicants rather than using minority status as a positive factor to be considered in evaluating the applications of disadvantaged minority applicants. For purposes of constitutional adjudication, there is no difference between the two approaches. In any admissions program which accords special consideration to disadvantaged racial minorities, a determination of the degree of preference to be given is unavoidable, and any given preference that results in the exclusion of a white candidate is no more or less constitutionally acceptable than a program such as that at Davis. . . .

The "Harvard" program, as those employing it readily concede, openly and successfully employs a racial criterion for the purpose of ensuring that some of scarce places in institutions of higher education are allocated to disadvantaged minority students. That the Harvard approach does not also make public the extent of the preference and the precise workings of the system while the Davis program employs a specific, openly stated number, does not condemn the latter plan for purposes of the Fourteenth Amendment adjudication. It may be that the Harvard plan is more acceptable to the public than is the Davis "quota." If it is, any State, including California, is free

to adopt it in preference to a less acceptable alternative, just as it is generally free, as far as the Constitution is concerned, to abjure granting any racial preferences in its admissions program. But there is no basis for preferring a particular preference program simply because in achieving the same goals that the Davis Medical School is pursuing, it proceeds in a manner that is not immediately apparent to the public.

V

Accordingly, we would reverse the judgment of the Supreme Court of California holding the Medical School's special admissions program unconstitutional and directing respondent's admission, as well as that portion of the judgment enjoining the Medical School from according any consideration to race in the admissions process.

MR. JUSTICE MARSHALL:

II

The position of the Negro today in America is the tragic but inevitable consequence of centuries of unequal treatment. Measured by any bench mark of comfort or achievement, meaningful equality remains a distant dream for the Negro.

A Negro child today has a life expectancy which is shorter by more than five years than that of a white child. The Negro child's mother is over three times more likely to die of complications in childbirth, and the infant mortality rate for Negroes is nearly twice that for whites. The median income of the Negro family is only 60% that of the median of a white family, and the percentage of Negroes who live in families with incomes below the poverty line is nearly four times greater than that of whites.

When the Negro child reaches working age, he finds that America offers him significantly less than it offers his white counterpart. For Negro adults, the unemployment rate is twice that of whites, and the unemployment rate for Negro teenagers is nearly three times that of white teenagers. A Negro male who completes four years of college can expect a median annual income of merely $110 more than a white male who has only a high school diploma. Although Negroes represent 11.5% of the population, they are only 1.2% of the lawyers and judges, 2% of the physicians, 2.3% of the dentists, 1.1% of the engineers and 2.6% of the college and university professors.

The relationship between those figures and the history of unequal treatment afforded to the Negro cannot be denied. At every point from birth to death the impact of the past is reflected in the still disfavored position of the Negro.

In light of the sorry history of discrimination and its devastating impact on the lives of Negroes, bringing the Negro into the mainstream of American life should be a state interest of the highest order. To fail to do so is to ensure that America will forever remain a divided society.

III

I do not believe that the Fourteenth Amendment requires us to accept that fate. Neither its history nor our past cases lend any support to the conclusion that a university may not remedy the cumulative effects of society's discrimination by giving consideration to race in an effort to increase the number and percentage of Negro doctors. . . .

IV

While I applaud the judgment of the Court that a university may consider race in its admissions process, it is more than a little ironic that, after several hundred years of class-based discrimination against Negroes, the Court is unwilling to hold that a class-based remedy for that discrimination is permissible. In declining to so hold, today's judgment ignores the fact that for several hundred years Negroes have been discriminated against, not as individuals, but rather solely because of the color of their skins. It is unnecessary in 20th century America to have individual Negroes demonstrate that they have been victims of racial discrimination; the racism of our society has been so pervasive that none, regardless of wealth or position, has managed to escape its impact. The experience of Negroes in America has been different in kind, not just in degree, from that of other ethnic groups. It is not merely the history of slavery alone but also that a whole people were marked as inferior by the law. And that mark has endured. The dream of America as the great melting pot has not been realized for the Negro; because of his skin color he never even made it into the pot.

These differences in the experience of the Negro make it difficult for me to accept that Negroes cannot be afforded greater protection under the Fourteenth Amendment where it is necessary to remedy the effects of past discrimination. In the *Civil Rights Cases* . . . the Court wrote that the Negro emerging from slavery must cease "to be the special favorite of the laws." . . . We cannot in light of the history of the last century yield to that view. Had the Court in that decision and others been willing to "do for human liberty and the fundamental rights of American citizenship, what it did . . . for the protection of slavery and the rights of the masters of fugitive slaves," . . . we would not need now to permit the recognition of any "special wards."

Most importantly, had the Court been willing in 1896, in *Plessy* v. *Ferguson,* to hold that the Equal Protection Clause forbids differences in treatment based on race, we would not be faced with this dilemma in 1978. We must remember, however, that the principle that the "Constitution is colorblind" appeared only in the opinion of the lone dissenter. . . . The majority of the Court rejected the principle of color blindness, and for the next 60 years, from *Plessy* to *Brown* v. *Board of Education,* ours was a Nation where, *by law,* an individual could be given "special" treatment based on the color of his skin.

It is because of a legacy of unequal treatment that we now must permit the institutions of this society to give consideration to race in making decisions about who will hold the positions of influence, affluence, and prestige in America. For far too long, the doors to those positions have been shut to Negroes. If we are ever to become a fully integrated society, one in which the color of a person's skin will not determine the opportunities available to him or her, we must be willing to take steps to open those doors. I do not believe that anyone can truly look into America's past and still find that a remedy for the effects of that past is impermissible. . . .

I fear that we have come full circle. After the Civil War our Government started several "affirmative action" programs. This Court in the *Civil Rights Cases* and *Plessy* v. *Ferguson* destroyed the movement toward complete equality. For almost a century no action was taken, and this nonaction was with the tacit approval of the courts. Then we had *Brown* v. *Board of Education* and the Civil Rights Acts of Congress, followed by numerous affirmative action programs. *Now,* we have this Court again stepping in, this time to stop affirmative action programs of the type used by the University of California.

Mr. Justice Blackmun:

. . . I am not convinced, as Mr. Justice Powell seems to be, that the difference between the Davis program and the one employed by Harvard is profound or constitutionally significant. The line between the two is a thin and indistinct one. In each, subjective application is at work. Be-

cause of my conviction that admission programs are primarily for the educators, I am willing to accept the representation that the Harvard program is one where good faith in its administration is practiced as well as professed. I agree that such a program, where race or ethnic background is only one of many factors, is a program better formulated than Davis' two-track system. The cynical, of course, may say that under a program such as Harvard's one may accomplish covertly what Davis concedes it does openly. I need not go that far, for despite its two-track aspect, the Davis program, for me, is within constitutional bounds, though perhaps barely so. It is surely free of stigma, and . . . I am not willing to infer a constitutional violation. . . .

I suspect that it would be impossible to arrange an affirmative action program in a racially neutral way and have it successful. To ask that this be so is to demand the impossible. In order to get beyond racism, we must first take account of race. There is no other way. And in order to treat some persons equally, we must treat them differently. We cannot—we dare not—let the Equal Protection Clause perpetrate racial supremacy. . . .

Mr. Justice Stevens, with whom the Chief Justice, Mr. Justice Stewart, and Mr. Justice Rehnquist join, concurring in the judgment in part and dissenting in part:

II

Both petitioner and respondent have asked us to determine the legality of the University's special admissions program by reference to the Constitution. Our settled practice, however, is to avoid the decision of a constitutional issue if a case can be fairly decided on a statutory ground. "If there is one doctrine more deeply rooted than any other in the process of constitutional adjudication, it is that we ought not to pass on questions of constitutionality ... unless such adjudication is unavoidable.".... The more important the issue, the more force there is to this doctrine. In this case, we are presented with a constitutional question of undoubted and unusual importance. Since, however, a dispositive statutory claim was raised at the very inception of this case, and squarely decided in the portion of the trial court judgment affirmed by the California Supreme Court, it is our plain duty to confront it. Only if petitioner should prevail on the statutory issue would it be necessary to decide whether the University's admissions program violated the Equal Protection Clause of the Fourteenth Amendment.

III

Section 601 of the Civil Rights Act of 1964 ... provides:

No person in the United States shall, on the ground of race, color, or national origin, be excluded from participation in, be denied the benefits of, or be subjected to discrimination under any program or activity receiving Federal financial assistance.

The University, through its special admissions policy, excluded Bakke from participation in its program of medical education because of his race. The University also acknowledges that it was, and still is, receiving federal financial assistance. The plain language of the statute therefore requires affirmance of the judgment below. A different result cannot be justified unless that language misstates the actual intent of the Congress that enacted the statute or the statute is not enforceable in a private action. Neither conclusion is warranted. ...

... [I]t seems clear that the proponents of Title VI assumed that the Constitution itself required a colorblind standard on the part of government, but that does not mean that the legislation only codifies an existing constitutional prohibition. The statutory prohibition against discrimination in federally funded projects contained in § 601 is more than a simple paraphrasing of what the Fifth or Fourteenth Amendment would require. ...

In short, nothing in the legislative history justifies the conclusion that the broad language of § 601 should not be given its natural meaning. We are dealing with a distinct statutory prohibition, enacted at a particular time with particular concerns in mind; neither its language nor any prior interpretation suggests that its place in the Civil Rights Act, won after long debate, is simply that of a constitutional appendage. In unmistakable terms the Act prohibits the exclusion of individuals from federally funded programs because of their race. As succinctly phrased during the Senate debate, under Title VI it is not "permissible to say 'yes' to one person; but to say 'no' to another person, only because of the color of his skin." ...

The University's special admissions program violated Title VI of the Civil Rights Act of 1964 by excluding Bakke from the Medical School because of his race. It is therefore our duty to affirm the judgment ordering Bakke admitted to the University.

Accordingly, I concur in the Court's judgment insofar as it affirms the judgment of the Supreme Court of California. To the extent that it purports to do anything else, I respectfully dissent.

There are two separate majority decisions in the *Bakke* case, supported by a variety of individual opinions. Justice Powell is the swing justice, joining first four justices on one side and then four justices on the other to make the two majority decisions, which held respectively that (1) the California special admissions program was unlawful; (2) Bakke must be admitted to the

Davis medical school; and (3) race can be considered in the admissions process.

The opinions of Justice Powell and Justice Brennan discuss the circumstances requiring strict judicial scrutiny under the equal protection clause. What are those circumstances? In the present case, how does judicial scrutiny differ in the Powell and Brennan opinions?

How does Justice Powell respond to the argument that the intent of the framers of the Fourteenth Amendment was limited to the protection of the newly freed slaves, and, therefore, the equal protection clause should not be extended to protect the "dominant" white class? What are the serious problems Justice Powell finds in preferential programs based upon race? Under what conditions does he agree that race may be taken into account in admissions programs? Why does he find the "racial quota" aspect of the Davis program particularly objectionable? Does he find that racial classifications, being inherently suspect, are a per se violation of the Fourteenth Amendment? Or does he suggest that there are conditions that would support such classifications?

Contrast the interpretations given to Title 6 of the Civil Rights Act by Justices Powell and Brennan. Both justices agree that suspect classifications must be strictly scrutinized by the courts and cannot be upheld unless they serve compelling governmental objectives. On what grounds does Justice Brennan uphold the racial classification while Justice Powell declares it to be unconstitutional? Is this because they apply different standards to the case, or because they draw different conclusions from the facts?

Justice Powell cites approvingly from Douglas's dissent in the *Defunis* case to the effect that racial classifications giving preference to a particular group tend to stigmatize the group by reinforcing a common stereotype that it cannot succeed without special treatment. What are Justice Brennan's views on the stigmatizing effect of the special admissions program?

On what basis did Justice Marshall hold that the special admissions program was constitutional? What reasons did Justice Blackmun give for supporting the constitutionality of the program? Was Blackmun's judicial scrutiny as strict as that applied in Brennan's opinion which Blackmun joined?

Justice Stevens (joined by Burger, Stewart, and Rehnquist) argues that the case should be decided on statutory and not constitutional grounds. Does this imply greater judicial self-restraint than was exhibited in the other opinions? Does Stevens hold that race can never be taken into account in affirmative action programs?

Affirmative Action after *Bakke*

The effect of the *Bakke* decision was limited. It extended only to the denial of the use of strict racial quotas in admissions programs. Presumably such quotas would also be considered unconstitutional in other "affirmative action" programs. Neither universities nor other institutions, however, were precluded from giving favorable treatment in admissions or employment to racial minorities. "Flexible" affirmative action programs throughout the nation remained intact after the decision.

Several rulings following *Bakke* seemed to affirm the Court's lenient attitude toward affirmative action. It declined to review a lower court decision upholding a program of the American Telephone and Telegraph Company which established employment and promotion goals for women, blacks, and minority groups. It also directed the Court of Appeals for the Fourth Circuit to reconsider its decision striking down the University of North Carolina's rules for the student government under which two seats on the student legislature were set aside for black representatives, whether they had been elected or not. The Supreme Court referred the appeals court to its *Bakke* decision, which would allow race to be taken into account in student government rules, although at the same time it would prohibit strict racial quotas from being established.[56]

One year after the *Bakke* decision, the Court further clarified its position on affirmative action programs in *Steelworkers* v. *Weber* (1979) that challenged under Title 7 of the Civil Rights Act the legality of an employer-union affirmative action plan that resulted from a nation-wide agreement between the Kaiser Corporation and the United States Steel Workers. Title 7 prohibits discrimination in hiring and in the selection of apprentices for training programs. The plan, covering fifteen Kaiser plants, was designed to remedy the virtually complete absence of black workers in skilled jobs in the aluminum industry. Special training programs were created, with 50 percent of the places reserved for blacks until the number of blacks in skilled jobs was in the same proportion to the blacks in the labor forces in the communities from which the individual plants recruited. Under the plan, Kaiser's plant in Grammercy, Louisiana, had created a training program with thirteen openings, six of which were reserved for whites. Although 39 percent of the work force in the area was black, only five out of 273 skilled jobs in the plant were held by blacks. The plaintiff, who had insufficient seniority to obtain one of the white places, had more seniority than two of the blacks accepted for the program. Both the district court and the court of appeals sustained the plaintiff, holding that affirmative action plans were permissible under Title 7 only if they were specifically designed to remedy the effects of past company discrimination against individual employees. The Supreme Court reversed 5–2 (Powell and Stevens did not participate) on narrow statutory grounds, holding that nothing in Title 7 barred private, voluntary, race-conscious affirmative action plans such as the one under consideration. The case did not concern an alleged constitutional violation of equal protection standards because neither state nor federal action was involved.

EQUAL PROTECTION AND FUNDAMENTAL
RIGHTS: THE RIGHT TO TRAVEL

The Court has required a showing of a compelling governmental interest not only to sustain suspect classifications but also to uphold classifications that affect fundamental rights. This standard of judicial review emerged

[56]See Equal Employment Opportunity Commission v. AT&T, 556 F. 2d 167 (3rd Cir. 1977), cert. denied 438 U.S. 915 (1978); and Friday v. Uzzell, 547 F. 2d 801 (4th Cir. 1977), judgment vacated and case remanded 438 U.S. 912 (1978).

from a series of precedents and was given particularly sharp definition by the Warren Court in *Shapiro* v. *Thompson*.[57] That case, and its companion cases, involved constitutional challenges to state and District of Columbia laws denying welfare assistance to persons who had not resided within their jurisdictions for at least one year immediately prior to applying for assistance. The Court applied the compelling interest standard to declare the laws to be an unconstitutional deprivation of the fundamental right to travel.[58] The classification according to residence, stated the Court, was an invidious discrimination that "denied welfare aid upon which may depend the ability of the families [that did not meet the residency requirements] to obtain the very means to subsist—food, shelter, and other necessities of life."[59] The Court pointed out that "[t]here is weighty evidence that exclusion from the jurisdiction [of the states and the District of Columbia] of the poor who need or may need relief was the specific objective of these [residency requirement] provisions."[60] But the Court did not overturn the residency laws on the basis that the classification discriminated against the poor but because the laws impeded the fundamental right to travel without being justified on the basis of a compelling governmental interest.

Justice Harlan, dissenting in the *Shapiro* case, argued that the Court's decision was based in part upon the premise that wealth is a suspect classification. Essentially, Harlan stated, the Court based its decision as much upon the effect of the residency laws in denying welfare benefits to poor people as upon the effect of the laws in burdening the constitutional right to travel. And if that right is the principal issue in the cases, concluded Harlan, the Court could as easily and more appropriately uphold it under the due process clauses of the Fourteenth and Fifth Amendments as under the constitutional standards of equal protection.

Shapiro v. *Thompson*

394 U.S. 618, 89 S. Ct. 1322, 22 L. Ed. 2d 600 (1969)

Mr. Justice Brennan delivered the opinion of the Court:

These three appeals were restored to the calendar for reargument. . . . Each is an appeal from a decision of a three-judge District Court holding unconstitutional a State or District of Columbia statutory provision which denies welfare assistance to residents of the State or District who have not resided within their ju-

[57] The emergence of the compelling interest principle governing classifications affecting fundamental rights is discussed by Justice Harlan (dissenting) in the Shapiro case, 394 U.S. 618, 655–677. Precedents cited for the compelling interest standard of review included Skinner v. Oklahoma, 316 U.S. 535 (1942); Reynolds v. Sims, 377 U.S. 533 (1964); Carrington v. Rash, 380 U.S. 89 (1965); and as an alternate ground in Harper v. Virginia Board of Elections, 383 U.S. 663, 670 (1966).

[58] Although the Court was somewhat unclear regarding the source of the fundamental right to travel, it cited inter alia, the Passenger Cases, 7 How. 283 (1849); Edwards v. California, 314 U.S. 160 (1941), Douglas and Jackson concurring; Kent v. Dulles, 357 U.S. 116 (1958); Zemel v. Rusk, 381 U.S. 1 (1965); United States v. Guest, 383 U.S. 745 (1966).

[59] Shapiro v. Thompson, 394 U.S. 618, 627 (1969).

[60] Ibid., p. 628.

risdictions for at least one year immediately preceding their applications for such assistance. We affirm the judgments of the District Courts in the three cases. . . .

II

There is no dispute that the effect of the waiting period requirement in each case is to create two classes of needy resident families indistinguishable from each other except that one is composed of residents who have resided a year or more, and the second of residents who have resided less than a year, in the jurisdiction. On the basis of this sole difference the first class is granted and the second class is denied welfare aid upon which may depend the ability of the families to obtain the very means to subsist—food, shelter, and other necessities of life. In each case, the District Court found that appellees met the test for residence in their jurisdictions, as well as all other eligibility requirements except the requirement of residence for a full year prior to their applications. On reargument, appellees' central contention is that the statutory prohibition of benefits to residents of less than a year creates a classification which constitutes an invidious discrimination denying them equal protection of the laws. We agree. The interests which appellants assert are promoted by the classification either may not constitutionally be promoted by government or are not compelling governmental interests.

III

Primarily, appellants justify the waiting-period requirement as a protective device to preserve the fiscal integrity of state public assistance programs. It is asserted that people who require welfare assistance during their first year of residence in a State are likely to become continuing burdens on state welfare programs. Therefore, the argument runs, if such

people can be deterred from entering the jurisdiction by denying them welfare benefits during the first year, state programs to assist long-time residents will not be impaired by a substantial influx of indigent newcomers. . . .

We do not doubt that the one-year waiting-period device is well suited to discourage the influx of poor families in need of assistance. An indigent who desires to migrate, resettle, find a new job, and start a new life will doubtless hesitate if he knows that he must risk making the move without the possibility of falling back on state welfare assistance during his first year of residence, when his need may be most acute. But the purpose of inhibiting migration by needy persons into the State is constitutionally impermissible.

This Court long ago recognized that the nature of our Federal Union and our constitutional concepts of personal liberty unite to require that all citizens be free to travel throughout the length and breadth of our land uninhibited by statutes, rules, or regulations which unreasonably burden or restrict this movement. . . .

We have no occasion to ascribe the source of this right to travel interstate to a particular constitutional provision. It suffices that, as Mr. Justice Stewart said for the Court in *United States* v. *Guest* [1966] . . .

The constitutional right to travel from one State to another . . . occupies a position fundamental to the concept of our Federal Union. It is a right that has been firmly established and repeatedly recognized.

. . . [T]he right finds no explicit mention in the Constitution. The reason, it has been suggested, is that a right so elementary was conceived from the beginning to be a necessary concomitant of the stronger Union the Constitution created. In any event, freedom to travel throughout the United States has long been recognized as a basic right under the Constitution.

Thus, the purpose of deterring the immigration of indigents cannot serve as justification for the classification created by the one-year waiting period, since that purpose is constitutionally impermissible. . . .

Alternatively, appellants argue that even if it is impermissible for a State to attempt to deter the entry of all indigents, the challenged classification may be justified as a permissible state attempt to discourage those indigents who would enter the State solely to obtain larger benefits. We observe first that none of the statutes before us is tailored to serve that objective. . . .

More fundamentally, a State may no more try to fence out those indigents who seek higher welfare benefits than it may try to fence out indigents generally. Implicit in any such distinction is the notion that indigents who enter a State with the hope of securing higher welfare benefits are somehow less deserving than indigents who do not take this consideration into account. But we do not perceive why a mother who is seeking to make a new life for herself and her children should be regarded as less deserving because she considers, among others factors, the level of a State's public assistance. Surely such a mother is no less deserving than a mother who moves into a particular State in order to take advantage of its better educational facilities.

Appellants argue further that the challenged classification may be sustained as an attempt to distinguish between new and old residents on the basis of the contribution they have made to the community through the payment of taxes. . . . Appellants' reasoning would logically permit the State to bar new residents from schools, parks, and libraries or deprive them of police and fire protection. Indeed it would permit the State to apportion all benefits and services according to the past tax contributions of its citizens. The Equal Protection Clause prohibits such an apportionment of state services.

We recognize that a State has a valid interest in preserving the fiscal integrity of its programs. It may legitimately attempt to limit its expenditures, whether for public assistance, public education, or any other program. But a State may not accomplish such a purpose by invidious distinctions between classes of its citizens. It could not, for example, reduce expenditures for education by barring indigent children from its schools. Similarly, in the cases before us, appellants must do more than show that denying welfare benefits to new residents saves money. The saving of welfare costs cannot justify an otherwise invidious classification.

In sum, neither deterrence of indigents from migrating to the State nor limitation of welfare benefits to those regarded as contributing to the State is a constitutionally permissible state objective.

IV

Appellants next advance as justification certain administrative and related governmental objectives allegedly served by the waiting-period requirement. They argue that the requirement (1) facilitates the planning of the welfare budget; (2) provides an objective test of residency; (3) minimizes the opportunity for recipients fraudulently to receive payments from more than one jurisdiction; and (4) encourages early entry of new residents into the labor force.

At the outset, we reject appellants' argument that a mere showing of a rational relationship between the waiting period and these four admittedly permissible state objectives will suffice to justify the classification. . . . The waiting-period provision denies welfare benefits to otherwise eligible applicants solely because they have recently moved into the jurisdiction. But in moving from State to State or to the District of Columbia appellees were exercising a constitutional right, and any classification which serves to penalize the exercise of that right, unless shown to be necessary to promote a *compelling* governmental interest, is unconstitutional. . . .

The argument that the waiting-period requirement facilitates budget predictability is wholly unfounded. The records in all three cases are utterly devoid of evidence that either State or the District of Columbia in fact uses the one-year requirement as a means to predict the number of people who will require assistance in the budget year. . . .

The argument that the waiting period serves as an administratively efficient rule of thumb for determining residency similarly will not withstand scrutiny. . . .

Similarly, there is no need for a State to use the one-year waiting period as a safeguard against fraudulent receipt of benefits; for less drastic means are available, and are employed, to minimize that hazard. . . . A state purpose to encourage employment provides no rational basis for imposing a one-year waiting period restriction on new residents only.

We conclude therefore that appellants in these cases do not use and have no need to use the one-year requirement for the governmental purposes suggested. Thus, even under traditional equal protection tests a classification of welfare applicants according to whether they have lived in the State for one year would seem irrational and unconstitutional. But, of course, the traditional criteria do not apply in these cases. Since the classification here touches on the fundamental right of interstate movement, its constitutionality must be judged by the stricter standard of whether it promotes a *compelling* state interest. Under this standard, the waiting period requirement clearly violates the Equal Protection Clause. . . .

Affirmed.

MR. JUSTICE STEWART, concurring:

In joining the opinion of the Court, I add a word in response to the dissent of my Brother Harlan, who, I think, has quite misapprehended what the Court's opinion says.

The Court today does *not* "pick out particular human activities, characterize them as 'fundamental,' and give them added protection. . . ." To the contrary, the Court simply recognizes, as it must, an established constitutional right, and gives to that right no less protection than the Constitution itself demands. . . .

The Court today, therefore, is not "contriving new constitutional principles." It is deciding these cases under the aegis of established constitutional law.

MR. CHIEF JUSTICE WARREN, with whom MR. JUSTICE BLACK joins, dissenting:

In my opinion the issue before us can be simply stated: May Congress, acting under one of its enumerated powers, impose minimal nationwide residence requirements or authorize the States to do so? Since I believe that Congress does have the power and has constitutionally exercised it in these cases, I must dissent. . . .

Congress has imposed a residence requirement in the District of Columbia and authorized the States to impose similar requirements. The issue before us must therefore be framed in terms of whether Congress may create minimal residence requirements, not whether the States, acting alone, may do so. . . . Appellees insist that a congressionally mandated residence reqquirement would violate their right to travel. The import of their contention is that Congress, even under its "plenary" power to control interstate commerce, is constitutionally prohibited from imposing residence requirements. I reach a contrary conclusion for I am convinced that the extent of the burden on interstate travel when compared with the justification for its imposition requires the Court to uphold this exertion of federal power.

Congress, pursuant to its commerce power, has enacted a variety of restrictions upon interstate travel. It has taxed air and rail fares and the gasoline needed to power cars and trucks which move interstate. . . . Many of the federal safety regulations of common carriers which cross state lines burden the right to travel. . . . And Congress has prohibited by criminal statute interstate travel for certain purposes. . . . Although these restrictions operate as a limitation upon free interstate movement of persons, their constitutionality appears well settled. . . .

The Court's right-to-travel cases lend little support to the view that congressional action is invalid merely because it burdens the right to travel. . . . Residence requirements do not create a flat prohibition [on the right to travel], for potential welfare recipients may move from State to State and establish residence wherever they please. Nor is any claim made by appellees that residence requirements compel them to choose between the right to travel and another constitutional right. . . .

The insubstantiality of the restriction imposed by residence requirements must then be evaluated in light of the possible congressional reasons for such requirements. . . . One fact which does emerge with clarity from the legislative history is Congress' belief that a program of cooperative federalism combining federal aid with enhanced state participation would result in an increase in the scope of welfare programs and level of benefits. Given the apprehensions of many States that an increase in benefits without minimal residence requirements would result in an inability to provide an adequate welfare system, Congress deliberately adopted the intermediate course of a cooperative program. Such a program, Congress believed, would encourage the States to assume greater welfare responsibilities and would give the States the necessary financial support for such an undertaking. Our cases require only that Congress have a rational basis for finding that a chosen regulatory scheme is necessary to the furtherance of interstate commerce.

. . . Certainly, a congressional finding that residence requirements allowed each State to concentrate its resources upon new and increased programs of rehabilitation ultimately resulting in an enhanced flow of commerce as the economic condition of welfare recipients progressively improved is rational and would justify imposition of residence requirements under the Commerce Clause. And Congress could have also determined that residence requirements fostered personal mobility. An individual no longer dependent upon welfare would be presented with an unfettered range of choices so that a decision to migrate could be made without regard to considerations of possible economic dislocation. . . .

The Court's decision reveals only the top of the iceberg. Lurking beneath are the multitude of situations in which States have imposed residence requirements including eligibility to vote, to engage in certain professions or occupations or to attend a state-supported university. Although the Court takes pains to avoid acknowledging the ramifications of its decision, its implications cannot be ignored. I dissent.

MR. JUSTICE HARLAN, dissenting:
. . . In upholding the equal protection argument, the Court has applied an equal protection doctrine of relatively recent vintage: the rule that statutory classifications which either are based upon certain "suspect" criteria or affect "fundamental rights" will be held to deny equal protection unless justified by a "compelling" governmental interest. . . .

The "compelling interest" doctrine, which today is articulated more explicitly than ever before, constitutes an increasingly significant exception to the long-established rule that a statute does not deny equal protection if it is rationally related to a legitimate governmental objective. The "compelling interest" doctrine has two branches. The branch which requires that classifications based upon "suspect" criteria be supported by a compelling interest apparently had its genesis in cases involving racial classifications, which have, at least since *Korematsu* v. *United States*, . . . been regarded as inherently "suspect." The criterion of "wealth" apparently was added to the list of "suspects" as an alternative justification for the rationale in *Harper* v. *Virginia Bd. of Elections* [1966], . . . in which Virginia's poll tax was struck down. The criterion of political allegiance may have been added in *Williams* v. *Rhodes* [1968]. . . . Today the list apparently has been further enlarged to include classifications based upon recent interstate movement, and perhaps those based upon the exercise of *any* constitutional right. . . .

I think that this branch of the "compel-

ling interest" doctrine is sound when applied to racial classifications, for historically the Equal Protection Clause was largely a product of the desire to eradicate legal distinctions founded upon race. However, I believe that the more recent extensions have been unwise. . . . I do not consider wealth a "suspect" statutory criterion. And when, as in . . . the present case, a classification is based upon the exercise of rights guaranteed against state infringement by the Federal Constitution, then there is no need for any resort to the Equal Protection Clause; in such instances, this Court may properly and straightforwardly invalidate any undue burden upon those rights under the Fourteenth Amendment's Due Process Clause. . . .

On what grounds does Justice Brennan hold unconstitutional the state and federal provisions denying welfare benefits to persons residing in the administering jurisdictions for less than one year? What is the strict judicial scrutiny test applied by the Court? Would the state and District of Columbia statutory provisions have been upheld under the rational-relation test?

Why does Justice Harlan dissent from the application of the strict judicial scrutiny test to the classifications involved in *Shapiro*? Are considerations of federalism important to Harlan? What does he imply will be the result of applying strict judicial scrutiny to categories such as those involved in *Shapiro*?

WEALTH CLASSIFICATIONS

While statutory classifications according to wealth were not declared suspect by the *Shapiro* majority, the Warren Court had implied in other cases that such classifications were indeed suspect. In *Harper* v. *Virginia Board of Elections* (1966) the Court in declaring a state poll tax unconstitutional wrote that a state violates equal protection standards "whenever it makes the affluence of the voter or payment of any fee an electoral standard."[61] Although the Court suggested that wealth was a suspect classification in its *Harper* opinion, the decision, like that in *Shapiro*, rested upon the grounds that the classification burdened the exercise of a fundamental constitutional right—the right to vote.

[61]Harper v. Virginia Board of Elections, 383 U.S. 663, 666 (1966).

While there is an implication in both the *Harper* and *Shapiro* opinions that wealth classifications may be suspect, the Court did not use the classifications to support strict judicial scrutiny and the application of the compelling state interest standard. The Court's position on wealth classifications is further clarified by contrasting two decisions reviewing respectively a city law requiring fair housing ordinances to be approved by a majority of the community's voters and a state law providing that no low rent housing projects could be undertaken in any community until approved by a majority of its voters. In the first case, *Hunter* v. *Erickson*, 393 U.S. 385 (1969), the trial and supreme courts of Ohio had dismissed the suit of a black citizen of Akron to compel city officials to enforce a fair housing ordinance. The ordinance was passed in 1964, but a subsequent amendment to the city charter provided that any ordinances approved by the city council to deal with racial, religious, or ancestoral discrimination in housing could not be put into effect until approved by a majority of the city voters. The amendment stipulated that any ordinance in effect at the time of its adoption would cease to be effective until approved under the terms of the amendment. The Ohio trial court dismissed the plaintiff's suit, holding that the ordinance had not been approved by a majority of Akron's voters in accordance with the terms of the charter amendment. The Supreme Court of Ohio affirmed, holding that the amendment did not violate the equal protection clause of the Fourteenth Amendment. The Supreme Court reversed, finding that the amendment made an explicit racial classification that was not justified by a compelling governmental interest.

While the *Hunter* case reviewed statutory classifications affecting fair housing, in *James* v. *Valtierra* (1971) the issue was the constitutionality of a state law requiring local referenda to approve low income housing. Was this a classification based upon wealth that discriminated against the poor? Was it a suspect classification requiring strict judicial scrutiny using the compelling state interest standard? Justice Black, writing the majority opinion for five members of the Court, distinguished the case from *Hunter* by pointing out that the challenged provision of the California constitution was not a racial classification. In answer to the plaintiff's contention that the requirement for referendums on public housing discriminates against persons desiring such housing because no such roadblock confronts other groups seeking to influence public decisions, Black stated: "Of course, a lawmaking procedure that 'disadvantages' a particular group does not always deny equal protection. Under any such holding, presumably a state would not be able to require referendums on any subject unless referendums were required on all, because they would always disadvantage some group."[62] The California referendum process has a long history and is deeply embedded in the traditions of the state, concluded Black, and "an examination of California law reveals that persons advocating low income housing have not been singled out for mandatory referendums while no other group must face that obstacle."[63] The requirement for the referendums is part of the democratic process that does not discriminate against the poor.

[62]James v. Valtierra, 402 U.S. 137, 142 (1971).
[63]Ibid., p. 142.

Justice Marshall, writing for three dissenters in the *Valtierra* case, stated that the California constitutional provision "explicitly singles out low income persons to bear its burden. Publicly assisted housing developments designed to accommodate the aged, veterans, state employees, persons of moderate income, or any class of citizens other than the poor, need not be approved by prior referenda."[64] The constitutional provision for referendums on low income housing constitutes invidious discrimination, concluded Marshall, and "is . . . an explicit classification on the basis of poverty—a suspect classification which demands exacting judicial scrutiny. . . ."[65] Such "exacting judicial scrutiny" would require the state to demonstrate a compelling interest to sustain the law.

Although the Warren and early Burger Courts were unwilling to apply strict judicial scrutiny to statutory classifications based upon wealth, they did protect the access of the poor to political and judicial processes. The *Harper* decision protected the right of the poor to vote. Equal access to the political process was also upheld by the Court in *Cipriano* v. *City of Huma,* 395 U.S. 701 (1969), striking down a Louisiana law limiting the right to vote on the issuance of revenue bonds by a municipal utility to "property taxpayers." And in *Bullock* v. *Carter,* 405 U.S. 134 (1972), the Court applied strict judicial scrutiny to strike down the Texas system of financing primary elections under which candidates themselves bore the often enormous costs of filing fees. The system, held the Court, discriminated against candidates unable to pay.

Access to the judicial process for the poor and indigent was mandated by the Supreme Court in *Griffin* v. *Illinois,* 351 U.S. 12 (1956), and in *Douglas* v. *California,* 372 U.S. 353 (1963). Indigent criminal appellants were held to have the right to free transcripts of trial proceedings when necessary for full appellate review in the *Griffin* case, and in *Douglas* indigent appellants were held to have the right to counsel for their first appeal. In these and other cases the Court insisted that equal protection required equal justice for the rich and poor alike.[66]

In the Warren and early Burger Courts emphasis upon protecting the rights of the poor to equal access to the judicial process was limited in several cases in 1973. In *United States* v. *Kras,* 409 U.S. 434 (1973), indigents were not held immune from the requirements of a federal law imposing a $50 fee to file for bankruptcy. The plaintiff had contended that the filing fees violated the Fifth Amendment right of due process, including its equal protection standard. The *Kras* holding narrowed the decision of the Court in *Boddie* v. *Connecticut,* 401 U.S. 371 (1971), which used due process grounds to sustain a claim that filing fees demanded of indigent welfare recipients who sought access to the state courts to file for divorce were unconstitutional. Justice Blackmun's majority opinion interpreted the *Boddie* deci-

[64]Ibid., p. 144.

[65]Ibid., p. 145.

[66]In the Griffin case the Court applied the due process clause of the Fourteenth Amendment as well as its equal protection clause. The Douglas holding was based upon the equal protection standard applied in Griffin. For other cases upholding the equal rights of the poor to the judicial process see Lane v. Brown, 372 U.S. 477 (1963); Draper v. Washington, 372 U.S. 487 (1963); Anders v. California, 386 U.S. 738 (1967).

sion narrowly to cover only cases where fundamental interests were at stake, such as those involved in the marital relationship, and where the state courts had exclusive authority over the resolution of disputes concerning the interests. The Court argued that there was no fundamental interest in bankruptcy and that the resolution of disputes over debts was not exclusively under government control; therefore, strict judicial scrutiny requiring the compelling governmental interest test did not have to be applied to uphold the filing fee required under the bankruptcy law. Such a fee, concluded the Court, could be supported as a rational means to legitimate state ends. The *Kras* precedent was applied by the Court in *Ortwein* v. *Schwab*, 410 U.S. 656 (1973), to deny indigent plaintiffs relief from a $25 Oregon filing fee required to obtain judicial review of administrative denials of welfare benefits.

Granting equal access, especially between rich and poor, to voting, running for office, and to the judicial process, has far narrower political implications than requiring equality in the delivery of public services to rich and poor alike. Equality in the delivery of public services implies a redistribution of wealth and is in effect a major substantive public policy. Although open access to political and judicial processes might advance such a policy by giving the poor greater access to government decision making, only if the poor were a majority might a serious redistribution of wealth occur. Any court attempting to rectify imbalances in the distribution of wealth and in the delivery of public services is entering a dangerous political thicket in a society where the majority is reasonably comfortable with the status quo. Yet in the early 1970s both federal and state courts began to expand the concept of equal protection to include a requirement that states provide equality in the delivery of public services to citizens under their jurisdiction. The most far-reaching cases involved challenges to the use of the property tax as a means to finance public education. Such financing systems cause gross disparities in the per capita funds spent for public education among rich and poor districts within a state. The financing of public education primarily through the property tax was challenged as a violation of the equal protection clause in numerous suits throughout the country by plaintiffs from the less affluent school districts. A major holding that influenced many such suits was the California Supreme Court decision in *Serrano* v. *Priest,* 5 Cal. 3d 584 (1974), which found that the use of the property tax to finance local education was based upon a wealth classification that was suspect and which, under strict judicial scrutiny, violated the equal protection clause of the Fourteenth Amendment as well as the California constitution. The Supreme Court reviewed a three-judge district court opinion that followed the *Serrano* precedent in the following case.

San Antonio v. Rodriguez

411 U.S. 1; 93 S. Ct. 1278; 36 L. Ed. 2d 16 (1973)

Mr. Justice Powell delivered the opinion of the Court:

This suit attacking the Texas system of financing public education was initiated by Mexican-American parents whose children attend the elementary and secondary schools in the Edgewood Independent School District, an urban school district in San Antonio, Texas. They brought a class action on behalf of school children throughout the State who are members of minority groups or who are poor and reside in school districts having a low property tax base. Named as defendants were the State Board of Education, the Commissioner of Education, the State Attorney General, and the Bexar County (San Antonio) Board of Trustees. The complaint was filed in the summer of 1968 and a three-judge court was impaneled in January 1969. In December 1971 the panel rendered its judgment in a per curiam opinion holding the Texas school finance system unconstitutional under the Equal Protection Clause of the Fourteenth Amendment. The State appealed, and we noted probable jurisdiction to consider the far-reaching constitutional questions presented. For the reasons stated in this opinion we reverse the decision of the District Court. . . .

I

. . . [S]ubstantial interdistrict disparities in school expenditures found by the District Court to prevail in San Antonio and in varying degrees throughout the State still exist. And it was these disparities, largely attributable to differences in the amounts of money collected through local property taxation, that led the District Court to conclude that Texas' dual system of public school financing violated the Equal Protection Clause. The District Court held that the Texas system discriminates on the basis of wealth in the manner in which education is provided for its people. . . . Finding that wealth is a "suspect" classification and that education is a "fundamental" interest, the District Court held that the Texas system could be sustained

only if the State could show that it was premised upon some compelling state interest. . . . On this issue the court concluded that "[n]ot only are defendants unable to demonstrate compelling state interests . . . they fail even to establish a reasonable basis for these classifications."
. . .

This, then, establishes the framework for our analysis. We must decide, first, whether the Texas system of financing public education operates to the disadvantage of some suspect class or impinges upon a fundamental right explicitly or implicitly protected by the Constitution, thereby requiring strict judicial scrutiny. If so, the judgment of the District Court should be affirmed. If not, the Texas scheme must still be examined to determine whether it rationally furthers some legitimate, articulated state purpose and therefore does not constitute an invidious discrimination in violation of the Equal Protection Clause of the Fourteenth Amendment.

II

A

The wealth discrimination discovered by the District Court in this case, and by several other courts that have recently struck down school-financing laws in other States, is quite unlike any of the forms of wealth discrimination heretofore reviewed by this Court. Rather than focusing on the unique features of the alleged discrimination, the courts in these cases have virtually assumed their findings of a suspect classification through a simplistic process of analysis: since, under the traditional systems of financing public schools, some poorer people receive less expensive educations than other more affluent people, these systems discriminate on the basis of wealth. This approach largely ignores the hard threshold questions, including whether it makes a difference for purposes of consideration under the Constitution that the class of disadvantaged "poor" cannot be identified or defined in customary equal protection terms. and whether the relative—rather than absolute—nature of the asserted deprivation is of significant consequence. Before a State's laws and the justifications for the classifications they create are subjected to strict judicial scrutiny, we think these threshold considerations must be analyzed more closely than they were in the court below.

The case comes to us with no definitive description of the classifying facts or delineation of the disfavored class. Examination of the District Court's opinion and of appellees' complaint, briefs, and contentions at oral argument suggests, however, at least three ways in which the discrimination claimed here might be described. The Texas system of school financing might be regarded as discriminating (1) against "poor" persons whose incomes fall below some identifiable level of poverty or who might be characterized as functionally "indigent," or (2) against those who are relatively poorer than others, or (3) against all those who, irrespective of their personal incomes, happen to reside in relatively poorer school districts. Our task must be to ascertain whether, in fact, the Texas system has been shown to discriminate on any of these possible bases and, if so, whether the resulting classification may be regarded as suspect.

The precedents of this Court provide the proper starting point. The individuals, or groups of individuals, who constituted the class discriminated against in our prior cases shared two distinguishing characteristics: because of their impecunity they were completely unable to pay for some desired benefit, and as a consequence, they sustained an absolute deprivation of a meaningful opportunity to enjoy that benefit. In *Griffin* v. *Illinois* [1956]

... and its progeny, the Court invalidated state laws that prevented an indigent criminal defendant from acquiring a transcript, or an adequate substitute for a transcript, for use at several stages of the trial and appeal process. The payment requirements in each case were found to occasion *de facto* discrimination against those who, because of their indigency, were totally unable to pay for transcripts. . . .

Likewise, in *Douglas* v. *California* [1963] . . . , a decision establishing an indigent defendant's right to court-appointed counsel on direct appeal, the Court dealt only with defendants who could not pay for counsel from their own resources and who had no other way of gaining representation. . . .

Williams v. *Illinois* [1970] . . . struck down criminal penalties that subjected indigents to incarceration simply because of their inability to pay a fine. Again, the disadvantaged class was composed only of persons who were totally unable to pay the demanded sum. . . .

Finally, in *Bullock* v. *Carter* [1972] . . . the Court invalidated the Texas filing-fee requirement for primary elections. Both of the relevant classifying facts found in the previous cases were present there. The size of the fee, often running into the thousands of dollars and, in at least one case, as high as $8,900, effectively barred all potential candidates who were unable to pay the required fee. As the system provided "no reasonable alternative means of access to the ballot" inability to pay occasioned an absolute denial of a position on the primary ballot.

Only appellees' first possible basis for describing the class disadvantaged by the Texas school-financing system—discrimination against a class of definably "poor" persons—might arguably meet the criteria established in these prior cases. Even a cursory examination, however, demonstrates that neither of the two distinguishing characteristics of wealth classifications can be found here. First, in support of their charge that the system discriminates against the "poor," appellees have made no effort to demonstrate that it operates to the peculiar disadvantage of any class fairly definable as indigent, or as composed of persons whose incomes are beneath any designated poverty level. Indeed, there is reason to believe that the poorest families are not necessarily clustered in the poorest property districts. A recent and exhaustive study of school districts in Connecticut concluded that "[i]t is clearly incorrect . . . to contend that the 'poor' live in 'poor' districts. . . . Thus, the major factual assumption of *Serrano*—that the educational financing system discriminates against the 'poor'—is simply false in Connecticut." Defining "poor" families as those below the Bureau of the Census "poverty level," the Connecticut study found, not surprisingly, that the poor were clustered around commercial and industrial areas—those same areas that provide the most attractive sources of property tax income for school districts. Whether a similar pattern would be discovered in Texas is not known, but there is no basis on the record in this case for assuming that the poorest people—defined by reference to any level of absolute impecunity—are concentrated in the poorest districts.

Second, neither appellees nor the District Court addressed the fact that, unlike each of the foregoing cases, lack of personal resources has not occasioned an absolute deprivation of the desired benefit. The argument here is not that the children in districts having relatively low assessable property values are receiving no public education; rather, it is that they are receiving a poorer quality education than that available to children in districts having more assessable wealth. Apart from the unsettled and disputed question whether the quality of education may be determined by the amount of money ex-

pended for it, a sufficient answer to appellees' argument is that, at least where wealth is involved, the Equal Protection Clause does not require absolute equality or precisely equal advantages. . . . The State repeatedly asserted in its briefs in this Court that . . . it now assures "every child in every school district an adequate education." No proof was offered at trial persuasively discrediting or refuting the State's assertion.

For these two reasons—the absence of any evidence that the financing system discriminates against any definable category of "poor" people or that it results in the absolute deprivation of education—the disadvantaged class is not susceptible of identification in traditional terms. . . .

This brings us, then, to the third way in which the classification scheme might be defined—*district* wealth discrimination. Since the only correlation indicated by the evidence is between district property wealth and expenditures, it may be argued that discrimination might be found without regard to the individual income characteristics of district residents. Assuming a perfect correlation between district property wealth and expenditures from top to bottom, the disadvantaged class might be viewed as encompassing every child in every district except the district that has the most assessable wealth and spends the most on education. . . .

However described, it is clear that appellees' suit asks this Court to extend its most exacting scrutiny to review a system that allegedly discriminates against a large, diverse, and amorphous class, unified only by the common factor of residence in districts that happen to have less taxable wealth than other districts. The system of alleged discrimination and the class it defines have none of the traditional indicia of suspectness: the class is not saddled with such disabilities, or subjected to such a history of purposeful unequal treatment, or relegated to such a position of political powerlessness as to command extraordinary protection from the majoritarian political process.

We thus conclude that the Texas system does not operate to the peculiar disadvantage of any suspect class. But in recognition of the fact that this Court has never heretofore held that wealth discrimination alone provides an adequate basis for invoking strict scrutiny, appellees have not relied solely on this contention. They also assert that the State's system impermissibly interferes with the exercise of a "fundamental" right and that accordingly the prior decisions of this Court require the application of the strict standard of judicial review. . . . It is this question—whether education is a fundamental right, in the sense that it is among the rights and liberties protected by the Constitution—which has so consumed the attention of courts and commentators in recent years.

B

Nothing this Court holds today in any way detracts from our historic dedication to public education. We are in complete agreement with the conclusion of the three-judge panel below that "the grave significance of education both to the individual and to our society" cannot be doubted. But the importance of a service performed by the State does not determine whether it must be regarded as fundamental for purposes of examination under the Equal Protection Clause. Mr. Justice Harlan, dissenting from the Court's application of strict scrutiny to a law impinging upon the right of interstate travel, admonished that "[v]irtually every state statute affects important rights." *Shapiro* v. *Thompson.* . . . In his view, if the degree of judicial scrutiny of state legislation fluctuated, depending on a majority's view of the importance of the interest affected, we would have gone "far toward

making this Court a 'super-legislature.' " We would, indeed, then be assuming a legislative role and one for which the Court lacks both authority and competence. But Mr. Justice Stewart's response in *Shapiro* to Mr. Justice Harlan's concern correctly articulates the limits of the fundamental-rights rationale employed in the Court's equal protection decisions:

The Court today does *not* "pick out particular human activities, characterize them as 'fundamental,' and give them added protection. . . . " To the contrary, the Court simply recognizes, as it must, an established constitutional right, and gives to that right no less protection than the Constitution itself demands. . . .

Mr. Justice Stewart's statement serves to underline what the opinion of the Court in *Shapiro* makes clear. . . . The right to interstate travel had long been recognized as a right of constitutional significance, and the Court's decision, therefore, did not require an ad hoc determination as to the social or economic importance of that right.

Lindsey v. *Normet* [1972] . . . decided only last Term, firmly reiterates that social importance is not the critical determinant for subjecting state legislation to strict scrutiny. . . . Mr. Justice White's analysis, in his opinion for the Court, is instructive:

We do not denigrate the importance of decent, safe, and sanitary housing. But the Constitution does not provide judicial remedies for every social and economic ill. We are unable to perceive in that document any constitutional guarantee of access to dwellings of a particular quality or any recognition of the right of a tenant to occupy the real property of his landlord beyond the term of his lease, without the payment of rent. . . . *Absent constitutional mandate*, the assurance of adequate housing and the definition of landlord-tenant relationships are legislative, not judicial, functions. . . .

The lesson of these cases in addressing the question now before the Court is plain. It is not the province of this Court to create substantive constitutional rights in the name of guaranteeing equal protection of the laws. Thus, the key to discovering whether education is "fundamental" is not to be found in comparisons of the relative societal significance of education as opposed to subsistence or housing. Nor is it to be found by weighing whether education is as important as the right to travel. Rather, the answer lies in assessing whether there is a right to education explicitly or implicitly guaranteed by the Constitution. . . .

Education, of course, is not among the rights afforded explicit protection under our Federal Constitution. Nor do we find any basis for saying it is implicitly so protected. As we have said, the undisputed importance of education will not alone cause this Court to depart from the usual standard for reviewing a State's social and economic legislation. It is appellees' contention, however, that education is distinguishable from other services and benefits provided by the State because it bears a peculiarly close relationship to other rights and liberties accorded protection under the Constitution. Specifically, they insist that education is itself a fundamental personal right because it is essential to the effective exercise of First Amendment freedoms and to intelligent utilization of the right to vote. . . .

We need not dispute any of these propositions. The Court has long afforded zealous protection against unjustifiable governmental interference with the individual's rights to speak and to vote. Yet we have never presumed to possess either the ability or the authority to guarantee to the citizenry the most *effective* speech or the most *informed* electoral choice. . . .

Even if it were conceded that some identifiable quantum of education is a constitutionally protected prerequisite to the meaningful exercise of either right, we have no indication that the present

levels of educational expenditures in Texas provide an education that falls short. . . .

We have carefully considered each of the arguments supportive of the District Court's finding that education is a fundamental right or liberty and have found those arguments unpersuasive. In one further respect we find this a particularly inappropriate case in which to subject state action to strict judicial scrutiny. The present case, in another basic sense, is significantly different from any of the cases in which the Court has applied strict scrutiny to state or federal legislation touching upon constitutionally protected rights. Each of our prior cases involved legislation which "deprived," "infringed," or "interfered" with the free exercise of some such fundamental personal right or liberty. . . . A critical distinction between those cases and the one now before us lies in what Texas is endeavoring to do with respect to education. . . . Every step leading to the establishment of the system Texas utilizes today—including the decisions permitting localities to tax and expend locally, and creating and continuously expanding state aid—was implemented in an effort to *extend* public education and to improve its quality. Of course, every reform that benefits some more than others may be criticized for what it fails to accomplish. But we think it plain that, in substance, the thrust of the Texas system is affirmative and reformatory and, therefore, should be scrutinized under judicial principles sensitive to the nature of the State's efforts and to the rights reserved to the States under the Constitution.

C

It should be clear, for the reasons stated above and in accord with the prior decisions of this Court, that this is not a case in which the challenged state action must be subjected to the searching judicial

scrutiny reserved for laws that create suspect classifications or impinge upon constitutionally protected rights.

We need not rest our decision, however, solely on the inappropriateness of
the strict-scrutiny test. A century of Supreme Court adjudication under the Equal
Protection Clause affirmatively supports
the application of the traditional standard
of review, which requires only that the
State's system be shown to bear some rational relationship to legitimate state purposes. This case represents far more than
a challenge to the manner in which Texas
provides for the education of its children.
We have here nothing less than a direct
attack on the way in which Texas has chosen to raise and disburse state and local
tax revenues. . . .

The foregoing considerations buttress
our conclusion that Texas' system of public school finance is an inappropriate candidate for strict judicial scrutiny. These
same considerations are relevant to the
determination whether that system, with
its conceded imperfections, nevertheless
bears some rational relationship to a legitimate state purpose. It is to this question
that we next turn our attention. . . .

The Texas system of school finance is
responsive to these two forces. While assuring a basic education for every child in
the State, it permits and encourages a
large measure of participation in and control of each district's schools at the local
level. In an era that has witnessed a consistent trend toward centralization of the
functions of government, local sharing of
responsibility for public education has
survived. . . .

The persistence of attachment to government at the lowest level where education is concerned reflects the depth of
commitment of its supporters. In part, local control means . . . the freedom to devote more money to the education of
one's children. Equally important, however, is the opportunity it offers for par-

ticipation in the decision-making process
that determines how those local tax dollars will be spent. Each locality is free to
tailor local programs to local needs. Pluralism also affords some opportunity for
experimentation, innovation, and a healthy
competition for educational excellence.
An analogy to the Nation-State relationship in our federal system seems uniquely
appropriate. Mr. Justice Brandeis identified as one of the peculiar strengths of
our form of government each State's freedom to "serve as a laboratory; and try
novel social and economic experiments."
No area of social concern stands to profit
more from a multiplicity of viewpoints
and from a diversity of approaches than
does public education. . . .

. . . Appellees suggest that local control
could be preserved and promoted under
other financing systems that resulted in
more equality in educational expenditures. While it is no doubt true that reliance on local property taxation for school
revenues provides less freedom of choice
with respect to expenditures for some districts than for others, the existence of
"some inequality" in the manner in which
the State's rationale is achieved is not
alone a sufficient basis for striking down
the entire system. . . . Only where state action impinges on the exercise of fundamental constitutional rights or liberties
must it be found to have chosen the least
restrictive alternative. . . . It is also well to
remember that even those districts that
have reduced ability to make free decisions with respect to how much they
spend on education still retain under the
present system a large measure of authority as to how available funds will be allocated. They further enjoy the power to
make numerous other decisions with respect to the operation of the schools. The
people of Texas may be justified in believing that other systems of school financing,
which place more of the financial responsibility in the hands of the State, will re-

sult in a comparable lessening of desired local autonomy. That is, they may believe that along with increased control of the purse strings at the state level will go increased control over local policies. . . .

. . . One also must remember that the system here challenged is not peculiar to Texas or to any other State. In its essential characteristics, the Texas plan for financing public education reflects what many educators for a half century have thought was an enlightened approach to a problem for which there is no perfect solution. We are unwilling to assume for ourselves a level of wisdom superior to that of legislators, scholars, and educational authorities in 50 States, especially where the alternatives proposed are only recently conceived and nowhere yet tested. The constitutional standard under the Equal Protection Clause is whether the challenged state action rationally furthers a legitimate state purpose or interest. . . . We hold that the Texas plan abundantly satisfies this standard. . . .

MR. JUSTICE STEWART wrote a concurring opinion.

MR. JUSTICE BRENNAN, dissenting:
Although I agree with my Brother White that the Texas statutory scheme is devoid of any rational basis, and for that reason is violative of the Equal Protection Clause, I also record my disagreement with the Court's rather distressing assertion that a right may be deemed "fundamental" for the purposes of equal protection analysis only if it is "explicitly or implicitly guaranteed by the Constitution." As my Brother Marshall convincingly demonstrates, our prior cases stand for the proposition that "fundamentality" is, in large measure, a function of the right's importance in terms of the effectuation of those rights which are in fact constitutionally guaranteed. Thus, "[a]s the nexus between the specific constitu-

tional guarantee and the nonconstitutional interest draws closer, the nonconstitutional interest becomes more fundamental and the degree of judicial scrutiny applied when the interest is infringed on a discriminatory basis must be adjusted accordingly." . . .

Here, there can be no doubt that education is inextricably linked to the right to participate in the electoral process and to the rights of free speech and association guaranteed by the First Amendment. This being so, any classification affecting education must be subjected to strict judicial scrutiny, and since even the State concedes that the statutory scheme now before us cannot pass constitutional muster under this stricter standard of review, I can only conclude that the Texas school-financing scheme is constitutionally invalid.

MR. JUSTICE WHITE, with whom MR. JUSTICE DOUGLAS and MR. JUSTICE BRENNAN join, dissenting:
The Texas public schools are financed through a combination of state funding, local property tax revenue, and some federal funds. Concededly, the system yields wide disparity in per-pupil revenue among the various districts. In a typical year, for example, the Alamo Heights district had total revenues of $594 per pupil, while the Edgewood district had only $356 per pupil. The majority and the State concede, as they must, the existence of major disparities in spendable funds. But the State contends that the disparities do not invidiously discriminate against children and families in districts such as Edgewood, because the Texas scheme is designed "to provide an adequate education for all, with local autonomy to go beyond that as individual school districts desire and are able. . . . It leaves to the people of each district the choice whether to go beyond the minimum and, if so, by how much." The majority advances this rationalization: "While assuring a basic educa-

tion for every child in the State, it permits and encourages a large measure of participation in and control of each district's schools at the local level."

I cannot disagree with the proposition that local control and local decision making play an important part in our democratic system of government. . . .

The difficulty with the Texas system, however, is that it provides a meaningful option to Alamo Heights and like school districts but almost none to Edgewood and those other districts with a low per-pupil real estate tax base. In these latter districts, no matter how desirous parents are of supporting their schools with greater revenues, it is impossible to do so through the use of the real estate property tax. In these districts, the Texas system utterly fails to extend a realistic choice to parents because the property tax, which is the only revenue-raising mechanism extended to school districts, is practically and legally unavailable. That this is the situation may be readily demonstrated. . . .

In order to equal the highest yield in any other Bexar County district, Alamo Heights would be required to tax at the rate of 68¢ per $100 of assessed valuation. Edgewood would be required to tax at the prohibitive rate of $5.76 per $100. But state law places a $1.50 per $100 ceiling on the maintenance tax rate, a limit that would surely be reached long before Edgewood attained an equal yield. Edgewood is thus precluded in law, as well as in fact, from achieving a yield even close to that of some other districts.

The Equal Protection Clause permits discriminations between classes but requires that the classification bear some rational relationship to a permissible object sought to be attained by the statute. It is not enough that the Texas system before us seeks to achieve the valid, rational purpose of maximizing local initiative; the means chosen by the State must also be rationally related to the end sought to be achieved. . . .

Neither Texas nor the majority heeds this rule. If the State aims at maximizing local initiative and local choice, by permitting school districts to resort to the real property tax if they choose to do so, it utterly fails in achieving its purpose in districts with property tax bases so low that there is little if any opportunity for interested parents, rich or poor, to augment school district revenues. Requiring the State to establish only that unequal treatment is in furtherance of a permissible goal, without also requiring the State to show that the means chosen to effectuate that goal are rationally related to its achievement, makes equal protection analysis no more than an empty gesture. In my view, the parents and children in Edgewood, and in like districts, suffer from an invidious discrimination violative of the Equal Protection Clause. . . .

There is no difficulty in identifying the class that is subject to the alleged discrimination and that is entitled to the benefits of the Equal Protection Clause. I need go no farther than the parents and children in the Edgewood district, who are plaintiffs here and who assert that they are entitled to the same choice as Alamo Heights to augment local expenditures for schools but are denied that choice by state law. This group constitutes a class sufficiently definite to invoke the protection of the Constitution. They are as entitled to the protection of the Equal Protection Clause as were the voters in allegedly underrepresented counties in the reapportionment cases. See, *e.g.*, *Baker* v. *Carr* [1962]. . . . And in *Bullock* v. *Carter* [1972] . . . where a challenge to the Texas candidate filing fee on equal protection grounds was upheld, we noted that the victims of alleged discrimination wrought by the filing fee "cannot be described by reference to discrete and precisely defined segments of the community as is typical of inequities challenged under the Equal Protection Clause," but concluded that "we would ignore reality were we not to recognize that this system falls with unequal weight on voters, as well as candidates, according to their economic status." Similarly, in the present case we would blink reality to ignore the fact that school districts, and students in the end, are differentially affected by the Texas school-financing scheme with respect to their capability to supplement the Minimum Foundation School Program. At the very least, the law discriminates against those children and their parents who live in districts where the per-pupil tax base is sufficiently low to make impossible the provision of comparable school revenues by resort to the real property tax which is the only device the State extends for this purpose.

MR. JUSTICE MARSHALL, with whom MR. JUSTICE DOUGLAS concurs, dissenting:

B

. . . The appellants do not deny the disparities in educational funding caused by variations in taxable district property wealth. They do contend, however, that whatever the differences in per-pupil spending among Texas districts, there are no discriminatory consequences for the children of the disadvantaged districts. They recognize that what is at stake in this case is the quality of the public education provided Texas children in the districts in which they live. But appellants reject the suggestion that the quality of education in any particular district is determined by money—beyond some minimal level of funding which they believe to be assured every Texas district by the Minimum Foundation School Program. In their view, there is simply no denial of equal educational opportunity to any Texas schoolchildren as a result of the widely varying per-pupil spending power provided districts under the current financing scheme.

In my view, though, even an unadorned restatement of this contention is sufficient to reveal its absurdity. Authorities concerned with educational quality no doubt disagree as to the significance of variations in per-pupil spending. Indeed, conflicting expert testimony was presented to the District Court in this case concerning the effect of spending variations on educational achievement. We sit, however, not to resolve disputes over educational theory but to enforce our Constitution. It is an inescapable fact that if one district has more funds available per pupil than another district, the former will have greater choice in educational planning than will the latter. In this regard, I believe the question of discrimination in educational quality must be deemed to be an objective one that looks to what the State provides its children, not to what the children are able to do with what they receive. That a child forced to attend an underfunded school with poorer physical facilities, less experienced teachers, larger classes, and a narrower range of courses than a school with substantially more funds—and thus with greater choice in educational planning—may nevertheless excel is to the credit of the child, not the State, cf. *Missouri ex rel. Gaines* v. *Canada* [1938]. . . . Indeed, who can ever measure for such a child the opportunities lost and the talents wasted for want of a broader, more enriched education? Discrimination in the opportunity to learn that is afforded a child must be our standard. . . . But this Court has never suggested that because some "adequate" level of benefits is provided to all, discrimination in the provision of services is therefore constitutionally excusable. The Equal Protection Clause is not addressed to the minimal sufficiency but rather to the unjustifiable inequalities of state action. It mandates nothing less than that "all persons similarly circumstanced shall be treated alike." . . .

I . . . cannot accept the majority's labored efforts to demonstrate that fundamental interests, which call for strict scrutiny of the challenged classification, encompass only established rights which we are somehow bound to recognize from the text of the Constitution itself. To be sure, some interests which the Court has deemed to be fundamental for purposes of equal protection analysis are themselves constitutionally protected rights. . . . But it will not do to suggest that the "answer" to whether an interest is fundamental for purposes of equal protection analysis is *always* determined by whether that interest "is a right . . . explicitly or implicitly guaranteed by the Constitution." . . .

I would like to know where the Constitution guarantees the right to procreate, *Skinner* v. *Oklahoma*. [1942] . . . , or the right to vote in state elections, *e.g., Reynolds* v. *Sims* [1964] . . . or the right to an appeal from a criminal conviction, *e.g., Griffin* v. *Illinois* [1956]. . . . These are instances in which, due to the importance of the interests at stake, the Court has displayed a strong concern with the existence of discriminatory state treatment. But the Court has never said or indicated that these are interests which independently enjoy full-blown constitutional protection. . . .

The majority is, of course, correct when it suggests that the process of determining which interests are fundamental is a difficult one. But I do not think the problem is insurmountable. And I certainly do not accept the view that the process need necessarily degenerate into an unprincipled, subjective "picking-and-choosing" between various interests or that it must involve this Court in creating "substantive constitutional rights in the name of guaranteeing equal protection of the laws." Although not all fundamental interests are constitutionally guaranteed, the determination of which interests are fundamental should be firmly rooted in the text of the Constitution. The task in every case should be to determine the extent to which constitutionally guaranteed rights are dependent on interests not mentioned in the Constitution. As the nexus between the specific constitutional guarantee and the nonconstitutional interest draws closer, the nonconstitutional interest becomes more fundamental and the degree of judicial scrutiny applied when the interest is infringed on a discriminatory basis must be adjusted accordingly. . . .

What standard of judicial review was applied by the district court? Explain, referring to the discussion of the equal protection cases preceding the presentation of the *Rodriguez* case, the Court's statement: "We must decide, first, whether the Texas system of financing public education operates to the disadvantage of some suspect class or impinges upon a fundamental right explicitly or implicitly protected by the Constitution, *thereby requiring strict judicial scrutiny.*"

How did Justice Powell's opinion distinguish prior wealth classification cases from the *Rodriguez* case? How did it distinguish the classes in the prior cases from the class involved in *Rodriguez*? In what way did Powell find the *Rodriguez* class to be less definable than the classes of poor persons involved in prior cases? How did he distinguish the effect of the laws reviewed in prior cases involving indigents where strict judicial scrutiny was applied from the effects of the Texas system of financing public education? Under what circumstances did he suggest that the deprivation of access to education might violate equal protection?

Contrast *Rodriguez* with *Shapiro* v. *Thompson.* How does the *Shapiro* case lead the Court in *Rodriguez* to reach the question of fundamental rights? Does it find there is a fundamental right to an education? Does it suggest that there are circumstances under which the right to education might be considered fundamental? Is there an "identifiable quantum of education" that is constitutionally protected?

Do you find there are considerations of federalism in the Court's opinion? What are they?

On what basis does Justice Brennan, dissenting, argue that there is a fundamental right to education? What standard of judicial review is applied by Justice White in his dissenting opinion? Does he support strict judicial scrutiny and the compelling state interest test? What equal protection standard is applied by Justice Marshall in his dissent?

JUDICIAL SCRUTINY OF GENDER CLASSIFICATIONS

Until relatively recently the Supreme Court was willing to grant virtually total discretion to the states to treat men and women differently under the law.[67] State laws based upon a stereotypical view of women were readily upheld as a rational approach to the realization of legitimate governmental ends. In upholding a state law prohibiting the practice of law by women, the Court wrote in 1873 that "Man is, or should be, woman's protector and defender" and the "paramount destiny and mission of women are to fulfill the noble and benign offices of wife and mother. This is the law of the Creator."[68] State laws based upon the stereotype that women are weaker and therefore need protection for their own good were sustained by the Court in upholding state statutes (1) limiting the working hours of women;[69] (2) prohibiting the licensing of women as bartenders unless they were the wife or daughter of a male owner of the bar;[70] and (3) exempting women from jury duty unless they volunteered, while requiring men to serve on juries.[71]

In the following case the Court reevaluated its previous stance in reviewing gender classifications.

Reed v. *Reed*

404 U.S. 71; 92 S. Ct. 251; 30 L. Ed. 2d 225 (1971)

Mr. Chief Justice Burger delivered the opinion of the Court:

Richard Lynn Reed, a minor, died intestate in Ada County, Idaho, on March

---

[67]Challenges to congressional gender classifications did not come before the Court until the 1970s.

[68]Bradwell v. State, 83 U.S. 130, 141 (1873).

[69]Muller v. Oregon, 208 U.S. 412 (1908). See also, West Coast Hotel Co. v. Parrish, 300 U.S. 379 (1937), overruling earlier decisions striking down minimum wage laws for women.

[70]Goesaert v. Cleary, 335 U.S. 464 (1948).

[71]Hoyt v. Florida, 368 U.S. 57 (1961).

29, 1967. His adoptive parents, who had separated sometime prior to his death, are the parties to this appeal. Approximately seven months after Richard's death, his mother, appellant Sally Reed, filed a petition in the Probate Court of Ada County, seeking appointment as administratrix of her son's estate. Prior to the date set for a hearing on the mother's petition, appellee Cecil Reed, the father of the decedent, filed a competing petition seeking to have himself appointed administrator of the son's estate. The probate court held a joint hearing on the two petitions and thereafter ordered that letters of administration be issued to appellee Cecil Reed upon his taking the oath and filing the bond required by law. The court treated §§ 15–312 and 15–314 of the Idaho Code as the controlling statutes and read those sections as compelling a preference for Cecil Reed because he was a male.

Section 15–312 designates the persons who are entitled to administer the estate of one who dies intestate. In making these designations, that section lists 11 classes of persons who are so entitled and provides, in substance, that the order in which those classes are listed in the section shall be determinative of the relative rights of competing applicants for letters of administration. One of the 11 classes so enumerated is "[t]he father or mother" of the person dying intestate. Under this section then appellant and appellee, being members of the same entitlement class, would seem to have been equally entitled to administer their son's estate. Section 15–314 provides, however, that

[o]f several persons claiming and equally entitled [under § 15–312] to administer, males must be preferred to females, and relatives of the whole to those of the half blood.

In issuing its order, the probate court implicitly recognized the equality of entitlement of the two applicants under § 15–312 and noted that neither of the applicants was under any legal disability; the court ruled, however, that appellee, being a male, was to be preferred to the female appellant "by reason of Section 15–314 of the Idaho Code." In stating this conclusion, the probate judge gave no indication that he had attempted to determine the relative capabilities of the competing applicants to perform the functions incident to the administration of an estate. It seems clear the probate judge considered himself bound by statute to give preference to the male candidate over the female, each being otherwise "equally entitled."

Sally Reed appealed from the probate court order, and her appeal was treated by the District Court of the Fourth Judicial District of Idaho as a constitutional attack on § 15–314. In dealing with the attack, that court held that the challenged section violated the Equal Protection Clause of the Fourteenth Amendment and was, therefore, void; the matter was ordered "returned to the Probate Court for its determination of which of the two parties" was better qualified to administer the estate.

This order was never carried out, however, for Cecil Reed took a further appeal to the Idaho Supreme Court, which reversed the District Court and reinstated the original order naming the father administrator of the estate. In reaching this result, the Idaho Supreme Court first dealt with the governing statutory law and held that under § 15–312 "a father and mother are 'equally entitled' to letters of administration," but the preference given to males by § 15–314 is "mandatory" and leaves no room for the exercise of a probate court's discretion in the appointment of administrators. Having thus definitively and authoritatively interpreted the statutory provisions involved, the Idaho Supreme Court then proceeded to examine, and reject, Sally Reed's contention that § 15–314 violates the Equal Protection Clause by giving a mandatory preference to males over females, without regard to their individual qualifications as potential estate administrators. . . .

Sally Reed thereupon appealed for review by this Court . . . and we noted probable jurisdiction. . . . Having examined the record and considered the briefs and oral arguments of the parties, we have concluded that the arbitrary preference established in favor of males by § 15–314 of the Idaho Code cannot stand in the face of the Fourteenth Amendment's command that no State deny the equal protection of the laws to any person within its jurisdiction.

Idaho does not, of course, deny letters of administration to women altogether. Indeed, under § 15–312, a woman whose spouse dies intestate has a preference over a son, father, brother, or any other male relative of the decedent. Moreover, we can judicially notice that in this country, presumably due to the greater longevity of women, a large proportion of estates, both intestate and under wills of decedents, are administered by surviving widows.

Section 15–314 is restricted in its operation to those situations where competing applications for letters of administration have been filed by both male and female members of the same entitlement class established by § 15–312. In such situations, § 15–314 provides that different treatment be accorded to the applicants on the basis of their sex; it thus establishes a classification subject to scrutiny under the Equal Protection Clause.

In applying that clause, this Court has consistently recognized that the Fourteenth Amendment does not deny to States the power to treat different classes of persons in different ways. . . . The Equal Protection Clause of that amendment does, however, deny to States the power to legislate that different treatment be accorded to persons placed by a statute into different classes on the basis of criteria wholly unrelated to the objective of that statute. A classification "must be reasonable, not arbitrary, and must rest upon some ground of difference having a fair and substantial relation to the object of the legislation, so that all persons similarly circumstanced shall be treated alike." *Royster Guano Co.* v. *Virginia* [1920]. . . . The question presented by this case, then, is whether a difference in the sex of competing applicants for letters of administration bears a rational relationship to a state objective that is sought to be advanced by the operation of §§ 15–312 and 15–314.

In upholding the latter section, the Idaho Supreme Court concluded that its objective was to eliminate one area of controversy when two or more persons, equally entitled under § 15–312, seek letters of administration and thereby present the probate court "with the issue of which one should be named." The court also concluded that where such persons are not of the same sex, the elimination of females from consideration "is neither an illogical nor arbitrary method devised by the legislature to resolve an issue that would otherwise require a hearing as to the relative merits . . . of the two or more petitioning relatives. . . ."

Clearly the objective of reducing the workload on probate courts by eliminating one class of contests is not without some legitimacy. The crucial question, however, is whether § 15–314 advances that objective in a manner consistent with the command of the Equal Protection Clause. We hold that it does not. To give a mandatory preference to members of either sex over members of the other, merely to accomplish the elimination of hearings on the merits, is to make the very kind of arbitrary legislative choice forbidden by the Equal Protection Clause of the Fourteenth Amendment; and whatever may be said as to the positive values of avoiding intrafamily controversy, the choice in this context may not lawfully be mandated solely on the basis of sex.

We note finally that if § 15–314 is viewed merely as a modifying appendage to § 15–312 and as aimed at the same objective, its constitutionality is not thereby saved. The objective of § 15–312 clearly is to establish degrees of entitlement of various classes of persons in accordance with their varying degrees and kinds of relationship to the intestate. Regardless of their sex, persons within any one of the enumerated classes of that section are similarly situated with respect to that objective. By providing dissimilar treatment for men and women who are thus similarly situated, the challenged section violates the Equal Protection Clause.

The judgment of the Idaho Supreme Court is reversed and the case remanded for further proceedings not inconsistent with this opinion.

Reversed and remanded.

Did the Court find the gender classification in the Idaho law to be "suspect"? What test did the Court use in judging the constitutionality of the statute? Did it apply strict judicial scrutiny?

Aftermath of *Reed v. Reed*

While there may have been an underlying assumption that gender classifications are suspect in the *Reed* opinion, it was not until *Frontiero v. Richardson* (1973), that a plurality of the Court found "implicit support" in *Reed* v. *Reed* for its holding that "classifications based upon sex, like classifications based upon race, alienage, and national origin, are inherently suspect and must therefore be subjected to close judicial scrutiny."[72] In overturning a statute that denied military dependency allowances to the male spouses of female members of the uniformed services, the Court found no compelling governmental interest to sustain the gender classification. Justice Brennan's plurality opinion of the Court briefly recounted some of the history of sex discrimination.

> There can be no doubt that our nation has had a long and unfortunate history of sex discrimination. Traditionally, such discrimination was rationalized by an attitude of "romantic paternalism," which, in practical effect, put women, not on a pedestal, but in a cage. . . .
> . . . [O]ur statute books gradually became laden with gross, stereotyped distinctions between the sexes and, indeed, throughout much of the nineteenth century the position of women in our society was, in many respects, comparable to that of blacks under the pre-Civil War slave codes. Neither slaves nor women could hold office, serve on juries, or bring suit in their own names, and married women traditionally were denied the legal capacity to hold or convey property or serve as legal guardians of their own children. And although blacks were guaranteed the right to vote in 1870, women were denied even that right—which is itself "preservation of other basic civil and political rights"—until adoption of the nineteenth amendment half a century later.

[72]Frontiero v. Richardson, 411 U.S. 677, 688 (1973).

It is true, of course, that the position of women in America has improved markedly in recent decades. Nevertheless, it can hardly be doubted that, in part because of the high visibility of the sex characteristic, women still face pervasive, although at times more subtle, discrimination in our educational institutions, in the job market and, perhaps most conspicuously, in the public arena. [73]

Would the *Frontiero* plurality prevail in defining sex classifications to be suspect, requiring strict judicial scrutiny of gender classification cases? In a series of post-*Frontiero* cases the Court wavered in applying strict judicial scrutiny and the compelling state interest standard but systematically began to strike down gender classifications. In *Weinberger* v. *Wiesenfeld*, 420 U.S. 636 (1975), a section of the Social Security Act that granted survivors benefits to widows but not to widowers was declared invalid on equal protection grounds. The Court did not, however, use strict judicial scrutiny but applied the rational relation rather than the compelling state interest standard.[74] The rationality test was also used in *Stanton* v. *Stanton*, 421 U.S. 7 (1975), to invalidate a Utah law providing for parental support obligations for sons until the age of twenty-one but for daughters only until the age of eighteen. In *Craig* v. *Boren*, 429 U.S. 190 (1976), a state law prohibiting the sale of 3.2 percent beer to males under the age of twenty-one and to females under the age of eighteen was overturned on equal protection grounds because the state was unable to prove conclusively that young men were more prone to accidents than young women, which would justify on rational grounds the sex classification to achieve the legitimate state end of safety on the highways.

While viewing gender classifications with suspicion, if not always declaring them to be in legal terminology "suspect," the Court has not invalidated all gender classifications. Where it has found a classification "benign" and drawn for the purposes of protecting women it may uphold the classification. In *Kahn* v. *Shevin* (1974), the Court upheld a Florida law granting a property tax exemption to widows but not to widowers. The law, wrote Justice Douglas for the Court, was "reasonably designed to further the state policy of cushioning the financial impact of spousal loss upon the sex for which that loss imposes a disproportionately heavy burden."[75] Douglas pointed out that "The financial difficulties confronting the lone woman in Florida or in any other state exceed those facing the man."[76]

In *Schlesinger* v. *Ballard* (1975) the Court sustained a provision of military law that required male naval officers to be discharged if they failed to be promoted for a second time within nine years but granted female officers thirteen years of commissioned service before they could be mandatorily discharged for lack of promotion. The Court noted that "[i]n both *Reed* and *Frontiero* the challenged classifications based on sex were premised on over-

[73]Ibid., pp. 684–686.
[74]In *Califano* v. *Goldfarb* the Court, following the *Weinberger* precedent, held unconstitutional another provision of the Social Security Law that granted survivors benefits to widowers only if they had been receiving at least half of their support from their wives but granted survivors benefits to wives solely on the basis of the earnings of the deceased husband regardless of dependency status.
[75]*Kahn* v. *Shevin*, 416 U.S. 351, 355 (1974).
[76]Ibid., p. 353.

broad generalizations that could not be tolerated under the Constitution.
. . . In contrast, the different treatment of men and women naval officers
under [the military code] reflects, not archaic and overbroad generalizations, but, instead, the demonstrable fact that male and female line officers
in the navy are *not* similarly situated with respect to opportunities for
professional service."[77] The law was, stated the Court, a reasonable and rational exercise of congressional power. Congress may "quite rationally have
believed that women line officers had less opportunity for promotion than
did their male counterparts, and that a longer period of tenure for women
officers would, therefore, be consistent with the goal to provide women officers with 'fair and equitable career advancement programs.' "[78] Moreover,
the Court concluded, the statute advanced the legitimate purpose of supplying the armed forces with the requisite number of commissioned officers
who had the incentive to "conduct themselves that they may realistically look
forward to higher levels of command."[79] Justice Brennan wrote a dissenting
opinion, joined by Justices Douglas and Marshall, declaring that gender classifications are suspect; therefore, close judicial scrutiny should apply requiring the demonstration of compelling governmental interest which the dissenters did not find in the military code under review.

Gender classifications have not only been upheld where the Court has
seen them to be for benign or protective purposes but also where they are
based upon biological differences between the sexes. In *Geduldig* v. *Aiello*
(1974), a California state insurance system provision that exempted pregnancy as a cause for employment disability was challenged on equal protection grounds. The Court applied the standard that state programs could be
upheld against equal protection challenges if they were rationally supportable. The California program, concluded the Court, was rational and in pursuance of a legitimate state end. The underinclusiveness of the risks covered
by the disability program made it self-supporting, enabled the state to pay
adequately for the disabilities that were covered, and insured that the contribution rate of the employees whose payments supported the program
would not be unduly burdensome.

The Court concluded in *Geduldig* v. *Aiello* that there was no evidence the
state program "worked to discriminate against any definable group or class
in terms of the aggregate risk protection derived by the group or class from
the program. There is no risk from which men are protected and women
are not. Likewise, there is no risk from which women are protected and men
are not."[80] In a footnote the Court added: "This case is . . . a far cry from
cases like *Reed* v. *Reed* . . . and *Frontiero* v. *Richardson* . . . involving discrimination based upon gender as such. The California insurance program does
not exclude anyone from benefit eligibility because of gender but merely removes one physical condition—pregnancy—from the list of compensable
disabilities. While it is true that only women can become pregnant, it does
not follow that every legislative classification concerning pregnancy is a sex-

[77]Schlesinger v. Ballard, 419 U.S. 498, 507–508 (1975).
[78]Ibid., p. 508.
[79]Ibid., p. 509.
[80]Gedulig v. Aiello, 417 U.S. 484, 496–497 (1974).

based classification like those considered in *Reed* . . . and *Frontiero*. . . . Normal pregnancy is an objectively identifiable physical condition with unique characteristics. Absent a showing that distinctions involving pregnancy are mere pretexts designed to effect an invidious discrimination against the members of one sex or the other, lawmakers are constitutionally free to include or exclude pregnancy from the coverage of legislation such as this on any reasonable basis, just as with respect to any other physical condition."[81] Justices Brennan, Douglas, and Marshall dissented, arguing that strict judicial scrutiny should be applied under which the state program would fall.[82]

Would a state law providing that under certain circumstances husbands must make alimony payments but exempting wives from the alimony requirements placed upon men violate equal protection standards? This was the issue in the following case. Before reading it review *Reed v. Reed* and the cases concerning gender discrimination in the text. Would a gender-based alimony law fall under the standards of *Reed*? Would it be sustained under the strict judicial scrutiny applied by the plurality of the Court in *Frontiero*?

Orr v. Orr

440 U.S. 268; 99 S. Ct. 1102; 59 L. Ed. 2d 306 (1979)

MR. JUSTICE BRENNAN delivered the opinion of the Court:

The question presented is the constitutionality of Alabama alimony statutes which provide that husbands, but not wives, may be required to pay alimony upon divorce.

On February 26, 1974, a final decree of divorce was entered, dissolving the marriage of William and Lillian Orr. That decree directed appellant, Mr. Orr, to pay appellee, Mrs. Orr, $1,240 per month in alimony. On July 28, 1976, Mrs. Orr initiated a contempt proceeding in the Circuit Court of Lee County, Ala., alleging that Mr. Orr was in arrears in his alimony payments. On August 19, 1976, at the hearing on Mrs. Orr's petition, Mr. Orr submitted in his defense a motion requesting that Alabama's alimony statutes be declared unconstitutional because they authorize courts to place an obligation of

alimony upon husbands but never upon wives. . . . [The Alabama courts sustained the statutes, and the plaintiff appealed to the Supreme Court] We now hold the challenged Alabama statutes unconstitutional and reverse. . . .

II

In authorizing the imposition of alimony obligations on husbands, but not on wives, the Alabama statutory scheme "provides that different treatment be accorded . . . on the basis of . . . sex; it thus establishes a classification subject to scrutiny under the Equal Protection Clause," *Reed* v. *Reed* [1971] . . . The fact that the classification expressly discriminates against men rather than women does not protect it from scrutiny. . . . "To withstand scrutiny" under the Equal Protection Clause, " 'classi-

---

[81]Ibid., fn. 20, pp. 496–497.

[82]See also General Electric Co. v. Gilbert, 429 U.S. 125 (1976), where the Court, citing Geduldig, upheld a company health and accident plan that excluded disabilities resulting from pregnancy against a Title 7 Civil Rights Act challenge.

fications by gender must serve important governmental objectives and must be substantially related to achievement of those objectives.' " *Califano* v. *Webster* [1977][83] . . . We shall, therefore, examine the three governmental objectives that might arguably be served by Alabama's statutory scheme.

Appellant views the Alabama alimony statutes as effectively announcing the State's preference for an allocation of family responsibilities under which the wife plays a dependent role, and as seeking for their objective the reinforcement of that model among the State's citizens. . . . We agree, as he urges, that prior cases settle that this purpose cannot sustain the statutes. *Stanton* v. *Stanton* [1975] . . . held that the "old notion" that "generally it is the man's primary responsibility to provide a home and its essentials," can no longer justify a statute that discriminates on the basis of gender. "No longer is the female destined solely for the home and the rearing of the family, and only the male for the marketplace and world of ideas,". . . . If the statute is to survive constitutional attack, therefore, it must be validated on some other basis.

The opinion of the Alabama Court of Civil Appeals suggests other purposes that the statute may serve. Its opinion states that the Alabama statutes were "designed" for "the wife of a broken marriage who needs financial assistance. . . ." This may be read as asserting either of two legislative objectives. One is a legislative purpose to provide help for needy spouses, using sex as a proxy for need. The other is a goal of compensating women for past discrimination during marriage, which assertedly has left them unprepared to fend for themselves in the

working world following divorce. We concede, of course, that assisting needy spouses is a legitimate and important governmental objective. We have also recognized "[r]eduction of the disparity in economic condition between men and women caused by the long history of discrimination against women . . . as . . . an important governmental objective." *Califano* v. *Webster*. . . . It only remains, therefore, to determine whether the classification at issue here is "substantially related to achievement of those objectives."

Ordinarily, we would begin the analysis of the "needy spouse" objective by considering whether sex is a sufficiently "accurate proxy" . . . for dependency to establish that the gender classification rests " 'upon some ground of difference having a fair and substantial relation to the object of the legislation,' " *Reed* v. *Reed*. . . . Similarly, we would initially approach the "compensation" rationale by asking whether women had in fact been significantly discriminated against in the sphere to which the statute applied a sex-based classification, leaving the sexes "*not* similarly situated with respect to opportunities" in that sphere, *Schlesinger* v. *Ballard* [1975]. . . .

But in this case, even if sex were a reliable proxy for need, and even if the institution of marriage did discriminate against women, these factors still would "not adequately justify the salient features of" Alabama's statutory scheme. . . . Under the statute, individualized hearings at which the parties' relative financial circumstances are considered *already* occur. . . . There is no reason, therefore, to use sex as a proxy for need. Needy males could be helped along with needy females with little if any additional burden on the State. In such circumstances, not even an administrative convenience rationale exists to justify operating by generalization or proxy. Similarly, since individualized hearings can determine which women were in fact discriminated against vis à vis

---

[83] In the Webster case the Court upheld a provision of the Social Security Act that provided for higher benefits for retired female workers than for males on the grounds that Congress had deliberately enacted the law to compensate women for past employment discrimination. [Editor's Note.]

their husbands, as well as which family units defied the stereotype and left the husband dependent on the wife, Alabama's alleged compensatory purpose may be effectuated without placing burdens solely on husbands. Progress toward fulfilling such a purpose would not be hampered, and it would cost the State nothing more, if it were to treat men and women equally by making alimony burdens independent of sex. "Thus, the gender-based distinction is gratuitous; without it the statutory scheme would only provide benefits to those men who are in fact similarly situated to the women the statute aids," . . . and the effort to help those women would not in any way be compromised.

Moreover, use of a gender classification actually produces perverse results in this case. As compared to a gender-neutral law placing alimony obligations on the spouse able to pay, the present Alabama statutes give an advantage only to the financially secure wife whose husband is in need. Although such a wife might have to pay alimony under a gender-neutral statute, the present statutes exempt her from that obligation. Thus, "[t]he [wives] who benefit from the disparate treatment are those who were . . . nondependent on their husbands. . . ." They are precisely those who are not "needy spouses" and who are "least likely to have been victims of . . . discrimination" by the institution of marriage. A gender-based classification which, as compared to a gender-neutral one, generates additional benefits only for those it has no reason to prefer cannot survive equal protection scrutiny.

Legislative classifications which distrib-

ute benefits and burdens on the basis of gender carry the inherent risk of reinforcing stereotypes about the "proper place" of women and their need for special protection. . . . Thus, even statutes purportedly designed to compensate for and ameliorate the effects of past discrimination must be carefully tailored. Where, as here, the State's compensatory and ameliorative purposes are as well served by a gender-neutral classification as one that gender-classifies and therefore carries with it the baggage of sexual stereotypes, the State cannot be permitted to classify on the basis of sex. And this is doubly so where the choice made by the State appears to redound—if only indirectly—to the benefit of those without need for special solicitude.

III

Having found Alabama's alimony statutes unconstitutional, we reverse the judgment below and remand the cause for further proceedings not inconsistent with this opinion. . . . [I]t is open to the Alabama courts on remand to consider whether Mr. Orr's stipulated agreement to pay alimony, or other grounds of gender-neutral state law, bind him to continue his alimony payments.

Reversed.

MR. JUSTICE BLACKMUN and JUSTICE STEVENS wrote concurring opinions. JUSTICES POWELL and REHNQUIST (joined by CHIEF JUSTICE BURGER) wrote dissenting opinions.

What are the goals of the statute claimed by the state? What are the means adopted to achieve these goals? Why does the Court find these means unnecessary to the achievement of the ends of the legislation? Why does the Court find that the statute cannot be justified on the basis of past discrimination against women? Does the Court apply the standards of review of *Reed* or *Frontiero*?

Although the tenor of Chief Justice Stone's celebrated *Carolene Products* footnote in 1938 (see pp. 815–816) was clearly in favor of judicial intervention to protect fundamental rights underlying the democratic political process, the Court had taken a narrow view of its role in protecting voting rights at the time Justice Stone wrote. The two cases he cited as precedents for greater judicial vigilance, *Nixon v. Herndon*, 273 U.S. 536 (1927), and *Nixon v. Condon*, 286 U.S. 73 (1932), had held the exclusion of blacks from democratic primaries to be unconstitutional. That the Court was unwilling to follow Justice Stone's implication and establish strict scrutiny of voting rights cases, however, was illustrated in *Grovey v. Townsend*, 295 U.S. 45 (1935), unanimously (with Stone participating) upholding the exclusion of blacks from state primaries by party conventions which were found to be organs not of the state but of a voluntary, private group whose action was not state action under the terms of the Fourteenth Amendment.[84]

Although the Court, in *Smith v. Allwright* (1944), overruled the *Grovey* decision,[85] it was reluctant to intervene more broadly in the electoral process to protect the voting rights of individuals unless they were members of a racial minority. A divided Court in *Colgrove v. Green* (1946) voted to refuse jurisdiction in a suit by Illinois voters challenging a state reapportionment law that had resulted in wide disparities in the number of voters in the congressional districts of Illinois. For example, a congressional district in Chicago contained over 900,000 voters, while another district in southern Illinois had a population of slightly over 100,000. The *Colgrove* decision, however, is misleading because it was not what it appeared to be from a reading of Justice Frankfurter's opinion which announced the judgment of the Court but which was joined by only two other justices. Frankfurter emphasized that as a matter of general principle the Court should not accept jurisdiction over electoral reapportionment cases. He wrote: "To sustain this action would cut very deep into the very being of Congress. Courts ought not to enter this political thicket. The remedy for unfairness in districting is to secure state legislatures that will apportion properly, or to invoke the ample powers of Congress."[86] Justice Rutledge voted on the side of Frankfurter, Reed, and Burton to make a majority of four. (Justice Black, joined by Justices Douglas and Murphy, dissented.) However, Rutledge in a separate opinion stated that as a matter of general principle the Court *did* have

---

[84]In the first Nixon case (1927) blacks had been excluded from democratic primaries by state law; in the second Nixon case (1932) the exclusion was the result of action by the executive committee of the party, which the Court held to be an agent of the state and therefore subject to the strictures of the Fourteenth Amendment.

[85]Citing United States v. Classic, 313 U.S. 299 (1941), which held primaries to be an integral part of the general election process, the Smith Court held that "the recognition of the place of the primary in the electoral scheme makes clear that state delegation to a party of the power to fix the qualifications of primary elections is delegation of a state function that may make the party's action the action of the state" Smith v. Allwright, 321 U.S. 649, 660 (1944). The Court concluded that in the Texas system under review the party convention was an agent of the state which was prohibited by the Fourteenth Amendment from establishing white primaries.

[86]Colgrove v. Green, 328 U.S. 549, 556 (1946).

jurisdiction over electoral reapportionment cases, but in this particular case jurisdiction should be refused because of the upcoming Illinois elections. Should the courts take jurisdiction with the election so close at hand, stated Rutledge, the electoral process might be thrown into disarray because of uncertainty over the constitutionality of the electoral system. Although a majority of the Colgrove Court in effect held the issue of electoral reapportionment to be justiciable, a short time later judicial self-restraint was exercised in *South v. Peters,* 339 U.S. 276 (1950), which held that the malapportionment resulting from Georgia's county unit system presented a political issue over which the Court did not have jurisdiction.

It was not until *Baker* v. *Carr* (1962) that the Supreme Court unequivocally declared the federal courts to have jurisdiction over electoral reapportionment suits.[87] Justice Brennan's majority opinion in *Baker* did not clearly define the standard of review to be applied to reapportionment cases. A year after the *Baker* decision the Court, in *Gray* v. *Sanders* (1963), overturned the Georgia county-unit system of voting in Democratic primaries for statewide offices. Although the implication of Justice Douglas's majority opinion was that equal protection requires the votes of each person to be weighed equally in all types of state elections, this standard was not spelled out. In a concurring opinion, however, Justice Stewart stated that within electoral constituencies "there can be room for but a single constitutional rule—one voter, one vote."[88]

The following case, decided by the Court a year after *Gray* v. *Sanders,* reviewed a challenge to the apportionment of congressional districts in Georgia.

Wesberry v. *Sanders*

376 U.S. 1 (1964)

MR. JUSTICE BLACK delivered the opinion of the Court:

Appellants are citizens and qualified voters of Fulton County, Georgia, and as such are entitled to vote in Congressional elections in Georgia's Fifth Congressional District. That district, one of ten created by a 1931 Georgia statute, includes Fulton, DeKalb, and Rockdale Counties and has a population according to the 1960 census of 823,680. The average population of the ten districts is 394,312, less than half that of the Fifth. One district, the Ninth, has only 272,154 people, less than one-third as many as the Fifth. Since

there is only one Congressman for each district, this inequality of population means that the Fifth District's Congressman has to represent from two to three times as many people as do Congressmen from some of the other Georgia districts.

Claiming that these population disparities deprive them and voters similarly situated of a right under the federal Constitution to have their votes for Congressmen given the same weight as the votes of other Georgians, the appellants brought this action . . . asking that the Georgia statute be declared invalid and that the appellees, the Governor and Secretary of

---

[87]The text of *Baker* v. *Carr* is at pp. 61–68.
[88]Gray v. Sanders, 372 U.S. 368, 382 (1963).

the state of Georgia, be enjoined from conducting elections under it. The complaint alleged that appellants were deprived of the full benefit of their right to vote, in violation of (1) Art. I, §2 of the Constitution of the United States, which provides that "The House of Representatives shall be composed of Members chosen every second year by the People of the several States . . ."; (2) the Due Process, Equal Protection, and Privileges and Immunities Clauses of the Fourteenth Amendment; and (3) that part of Section 2 of the Fourteenth Amendment which provides that "Representatives shall be apportioned among the several States according to their respective numbers. . . ."

The case was heard by a three-judge District Court, which found unanimously, from facts not disputed, that:

It is clear by any standard . . . that the population of the Fifth District is grossly out of balance with that of the other nine congressional districts of Georgia and in fact, so much so that the removal of DeKalb and Rockdale Counties from the District, leaving only Fulton with a population of 556,326, would leave it exceeding the average by slightly more than forty per cent.

Notwithstanding these findings, a majority of the court dismissed the complaint, citing as their guide Mr. Justice Frankfurter's minority opinion in Colegrove v. Green, an opinion stating that challenges to apportionment of congressional districts raised only "political" questions, which were not justiciable. Although the majority below said that the dismissal here was based on "want of equity" and not on justiciability, they relied on no circumstances which were peculiar to the present case; instead, they adopted the language and reasoning of Mr. Justice Frankfurter's Colegrove opinion in concluding that the appellants had presented a wholly "political" question. Judge Tuttle, disagreeing with the court's reliance on that opinion, dissented from the dismissal, though he would have denied an injunction at that time in order to give the Georgia Legislature ample opportunity to correct the "abuses" in the apportionment. He relied on Baker v. Carr, which, after full discussion of Colegrove and all the opinions in it, held that allegations of disparities of population in state legislative districts raise justiciable claims on which courts may grant relief. We noted probable jurisdiction. . . . We agree with Judge Tuttle that in debasing the weight of appellants' votes the state has abridged the right to vote for members of Congress guaranteed them by the United States Constitution, that the District Court should have entered a declaratory judgment to that effect, and that it was therefore error to dismiss this suit. The question of what relief should be given we leave for further consideration and decision by the District Court in light of existing circumstances. . . .

This statement in Baker, which referred to our past decisions holding Congressional apportionment cases to be justiciable, we believe was wholly correct and we adhere to it. Mr. Justice Frankfurter's Colegrove opinion contended that Art. I, §4, of the Constitution had given Congress "exclusive authority" to protect the right of citizens to vote for Congressmen, but we made it clear in Baker that nothing in the language of that article gives support to a construction that would immunize state Congressional apportionment laws which debase a citizen's right to vote from the power of courts to protect the constitutional rights of individuals from legislative destruction. . . . The right to vote is too important in our free society to be stripped of judicial protection by such an interpretation of Article I. This dismissal can no more be justified on the ground of "want of equity" than on the ground of "nonjusticiability." We therefore hold that the District Court erred in dismissing the complaint.

This brings us to the merits. We agree with the District Court that the 1931 Georgia apportionment grossly discriminates against voters in the Fifth Congressional District. A single Congressman represents from two to three times as many Fifth District voters as are represented by each of the Congressmen from the other Georgia Congressional districts. The apportionment statute thus contracts the value of some votes and expands that of others. If the federal Constitution intends that when qualified voters elect members of Congress each vote be given as much weight as any other vote, then this statute cannot stand.

We hold that, construed in its historical context, the command of Art. I, §2, that Representatives be chosen "by the People of the several States" means that as nearly as is practicable one man's vote in a congressional election is to be worth as much as another's. This rule is followed automatically, of course, when Representatives are chosen as a group on a statewide basis, as was a widespread practice in the first fifty years of our nation's history. It would be extraordinary to suggest that in such statewide elections the votes of inhabitants of some parts of a state, for example, Georgia's thinly populated Ninth District, could be weighed at two or three times the value of the votes of people living in more populous parts of the state, for example, the Fifth District around Atlanta. We do not believe that the framers of the Constitution intended to permit the same vote-diluting discrimination to be accomplished through the device of districts containing widely varied numbers of inhabitants. To say that a vote is worth more in one district than in another would not only run counter to our fundamental ideas of democratic government, it would cast aside the principle of a House of Representatives elected "by the People," a principle tenaciously fought for and established at the Constitutional Convention. The history of the Constitution, particularly that part of it relating to the adoption of Art. I, §2, reveals that those who framed the Constitution meant that, no matter what the mechanics of an election, whether statewide or by districts, it was population which was to be the basis of the House of Representatives. . . .

The debates at the Convention make at least one fact abundantly clear: that when the delegates agreed that the House should represent "people" they intended that in allocating Congressmen the number assigned to each state should be determined solely by the number of the state's inhabitants. The Constitution embodied Edmund Randolph's proposal for a periodic census to ensure "fair representation of the people," an idea endorsed by Mason as assuring that "numbers of inhabitants" should always be the measure of representation in the House of Representatives. The Convention also overwhelmingly agreed to a resolution offered by Randolph to base future apportionment squarely on numbers and to delete any reference to wealth. And the delegates defeated a motion made by Elbridge Gerry to limit the number of Representatives from newer Western states so that it would never exceed the number from the original states.

It would defeat the principle solemnly embodied in the Great Compromise— equal representation in the House of equal numbers of people—for us to hold that, within the states, legislatures may draw the lines of Congressional districts in such a way as to give some voters a greater voice in choosing a Congressman than others. The House of Representatives, the Convention agreed, was to represent the people as individuals, and on a basis of complete equality for each voter. The delegates were quite aware of what Madison called the "vicious representation" in Great Britain whereby "rotten boroughs" with few inhabitants were represented in Parliament on or almost on a par with cities of greater population. Wilson urged that people must be represented as individuals, so that America would escape the evils of the English system under which one man could send two members to Parliament to represent the borough of Old Sarum while London's million people sent but four. The delegates referred to rotten borough apportionments in some of the state legislatures as the kind of objectionable governmental action that the Constitution should not tolerate in the election of congressional representatives. . . .

It is in the light of such history that we must construe Art. I, §2, of the Constitution, which, carrying out the ideas of Madison and those of like views, provides that Representatives shall be chosen "by the People of the several States" and shall be "apportioned among the several States . . . according to their respective numbers." It is not surprising that our Court has held that this Article gives persons qualified to vote a constitutional right to vote and to have their votes counted. *United States* v. *Mosley* [1915] . . . *Ex parte Yarbrough* [1884] . . . Not only can this right to vote not be denied outright, it cannot, consistently with Article I, be destroyed by alteration of ballots, see *United States* v. *Classic* [1941] . . . or diluted by stuffing of the ballot box. . . . No right is more precious in a free country than that of having a voice in the election of those who make the laws under which, as good citizens, we must live. Other rights, even the most basic, are illusory if the right to vote is undermined. Our Constitution leaves no room for classification of people in a way that unnecessarily abridges this right. In urging the people to adopt the Constitution, Madison said in No. 57 of *The Federalist:*

Who are to be the electors of the Federal Representatives? Not the rich more than the poor; not the learned more than the ignorant; not

the haughty heirs of distinguished names, more than the humble sons of obscure and unpropitious fortune. The elctors are to be the great body of the people of the United States. . . .

Readers surely could have fairly taken this to mean, "one person, one vote."

While it may not be possible to draw Congressional districts with mathematical precision, that is no excuse for ignoring our Constitution's plain objective of making equal representation for equal numbers of people the fundamental goal for the House of Representatives. That is the high standard of justice and common sense which the founders set for us.

Reversed and remanded.

MR. JUSTICE CLARK wrote a separate opinion, concurring in part and dissenting in part.

MR. JUSTICE HARLAN, dissenting:

I had not expected to witness the day when the Supreme Court of the United States would render a decision which cast grave doubt on the constitutionality of the composition of the House of Representatives. It is not an exaggeration to say that such is the effect of today's decision. The Court's holding that the Constitution requires states to select Representatives either by elections at large or by elections in districts composed "as nearly as is practicable" of equal population places in jeopardy the seats of almost all the members of the present House of Representatives.

In the last Congressional election, in 1962, Representatives from forty-two states were elected from Congressional districts. In all but five of those states, the difference between the populations of the largest and smallest districts exceeded 100,000 persons. A difference of this magnitude in the size of districts the average population of which in each state is less than 500,000 is presumably not equality among districts "as nearly as is practicable," although the Court does not reveal its definition of that phrase. Thus, today's decision impugns the validity of the election of 398 Representatives from 37 states, leaving a "constitutional" House of 37 members now sitting.

Only a demonstration which could not be avoided would justify this Court in rendering a decision the effect of which, inescapably as I see it, is to declare constitutionally defective the very composition of a coordinate branch of the federal government. The Court's opinion not only fails to make such a demonstration. It is unsound logically on its face and demonstrably unsound historically. . . .

. . . [T]he language of Art. I, §§2 and 4, the surrounding text, and the relevant history are all in strong and consistent direct contradiction of the Court's holding. The constitutional scheme vests in the states plenary power to regulate the conduct of elections for Representatives, and, in order to protect the federal government, provides for Congressional supervision of the states' exercise of their power. Within this scheme, the appellants do not have the right which they assert, in the absence of provision for equal districts by the Georgia Legislature or the Congress. The constitutional right which the Court creates is manufactured out of whole cloth.

The unstated premise of the Court's conclusion quite obviously is that the Congress has not dealt, and the Court believes it will not deal, with the problem of Congressional apportionment in accordance with what the Court believes to be sound political principles. Laying aside for the moment the validity of such a consideration as a factor in constitutional interpretation, it becomes relevant to examine the history of Congressional action under Art. I, § 4. This history reveals that the Court is not simply undertaking to exercise a power which the Constitution reserves to the Congress; it is also overruling Congressional judgment. . . .

Today's decision has portents for our society and the Court itself which should be recognized. This is not a case in which the Court vindicates the kind of individual rights that are assured by the Due Process Clause of the Fourteenth Amendment, whose "vague contours," . . . of course leave much room for constitutional developments necessitated by changing conditions in a dynamic society. Nor is this a case in which an emergent set of facts requires the Court to frame new principles to protect recognized constitional rights. The claim for judicial relief in this case strikes at one of the fundamental doctrines of our system of government, the separation of powers. In upholding that claim, the Court attempts to effect reforms in a field which the Constitution, as plainly as can be, has committed exclusively to the political process.

This Court, no less than all other branches of the government, is bound by the Constitution. The Constitution does not confer on the Court blanket authority to step into every situation where the political branch may be thought to have fallen short. The stability of this institution ultimately depends not only upon its being alert to keep the other branches of government within constitutional bounds but equally upon recognition of the limitations on the Court's own functions in the Constitutional system.

What is done today saps the political process. The promise of judicial intervention in matters of this sort cannot but encourage popular inertia in efforts for political reform through the political process, with the inevitable result that the process is itself weakened. By yielding to the demand for a judicial remedy in this instance, the Court in my view does a disservice both to itself and to the broader values of our system of government.

Believing that the complaint fails to

disclose a constitutional claim, I would affirm the judgment below dismissing the complaint.

MR. JUSTICE STEWART:

I think it is established that "this Court has power to afford relief in a case of this type as against the objection that the issues are not justiciable," and I cannot subscribe to any possible implication to the contrary which may lurk in Mr. Justice Harlan's dissenting opinion. With this single qualification I join the dissent because I think Mr. Justice Harlan has unanswerably demonstrated that Art. I, § 2, of the Constitution gives no mandate to this Court or to any court to ordain that Congressional districts within each state must be equal in population.

Appendix[a]

State and number of representatives[b]	Largest district	Smallest district	Difference between largest and smallest districts
Alabama (8)	—	—	—
Alaska (1)	—	—	—
Arizona (3)	663,510	198,236	465,274
Arkansas (4)	575,385	332,844	242,541
California (38)	588,933	301,872	287,061
Colorado (4)	653,954	195,551	458,403
Connecticut (6)	689,555	318,942	370,613
Delaware (1)	—	—	—
Florida (12)	660,345	237,235	423,110
Georgia (10)	823,680	272,154	551,526
Hawaii (2)	—	—	—
Idaho (2)	409,949	257,242	152,707
Illinois (24)	552,582	278,703	273,879
Indiana (11)	697,567	290,596	406,971
Iowa (7)	442,406	353,156	89,250
Kansas (5)	539,592	373,583	166,009
Kentucky (7)	610,947	350,839	260,108
Louisiana (8)	536,029	263,850	272,179
Maine (2)	505,465	463,800	41,665
Maryland (8)	711,045	243,570	467,475
Massachusetts (12)	478,962	376,336	102,626
Michigan (19)	802,994	177,431	625,563
Minnesota (8)	482,872	375,475	107,397
Mississippi (5)	608,441	295,072	313,369
Missouri (10)	506,854	378,499	128,355
Montana (2)	400,573	274,195	126,379
Nebraska (3)	530,507	404,695	125,812
Nevada (1)	—	—	—
New Hampshire (2)	331,818	275,103	56,715
New Jersey (15)	585,586	255,165	330,421
New Mexico (2)	—	—	—
New York (41)	471,001	350,186	120,815
North Carolina (11)	491,461	277,861	213,600

[a] The populations of the districts are based on the 1960 Census. The districts are those used in the election of the current 88th Congress. The populations of the districts are available in the biographical section of the Congressional Directory, 88th Cong., 2nd Sess.

[b] 435 in all.

State and number of representatives[b]	Largest district	Smallest district	Difference between largest and smallest districts
North Dakota (2)	333,290	299,156	34,134
Ohio (24)	726,156	236,288	489,868
Oklahoma (6)	552,863	227,692	325,171
Oregon (4)	522,813	265,164	257,649
Pennsylvania (27)	553,154	303,026	250,128
Rhode Island (2)	459,706	399,782	59,924
South Carolina (6)	531,555	302,235	229,320
South Dakota (2)	497,669	182,845	314,824
Tennessee (9)	627,019	223,387	403,632
Texas (23)	951,527	216,371	735,156
Utah (2)	572,654	317,973	254,681
Vermont (1)	—	—	—
Virginia (10)	539,618	312,890	226,728
Washington (7)	510,512	342,540	167,972
West Virginia (5)	422,046	303,098	118,948
Wisconsin (10)	530,316	236,870	293,446
Wyoming (1)	—	—	—

How did Justice Black argue that Article 1, Section 2, of the Constitution requires the equal apportionment of congressional districts? Could the Court have applied the equal protection standard? How does Justice Harlan, dissenting, answer the historical argument used by the Court to support its decision? What does Harlan consider to be the grave implications of the Court's decision?

In the *Gray* and *Wesberry* decisions the Court does not seem to allow any room for the states to modify the one person–one vote rule on the basis of state interests, whether they be merely reasonable and rational, or compelling. Since the *Wesberry* decision dealt with congressional districts, it would be difficult for the state to plead rational or compelling interests to justify a scheme of malapportionment. Such a plea of state interests was more relevant to *Gray* v. *Sanders;* however, the Court's opinion did not reach the question of what would constitute a proper standard of judicial review in apportionment cases, since, in the words of the majority, the case did not deal "with the composition of the state or federal legislature."[89]

In the following case the Court reviewed a challenge to the gross malapportionment of *both* bodies of the Alabama legislature. The state, in its plea, argued that the Supreme Court "should reconsider the decision in *Baker* v. *Carr* and should return to the original constitutional proposition that courts do not interfere with the political structure of state government."[90] Alabama declared that the plaintiff's suit "is an abstract question of political power concerning the structure and organization of the Alabama legislature. It

[89]Ibid., p. 378.
[90]LB Vol. 58, p. 824.

would be utterly impossible to argue the wisdom of the state policy with respect to the allocation of power without making of the court a forum for political debate."[91] The plaintiffs contended that the Alabama apportionment scheme was a capricious discrimination against voters in those districts which were underrepresented in terms of population in the state legislature.

What standard of review is adopted by the Court for state legislative apportionment cases?

Reynolds v. *Sims*

377 U.S. 533; 84 S. Ct. 1362; 12 L. Ed. 2d 506 (1964)

MR. CHIEF JUSTICE WARREN delivered the opinion of the Court:

II

. . . Undeniably the Constitution of the United States protects the right of all qualified citizens to vote, in state as well as in federal elections. A consistent line of decisions by this Court in cases involving attempts to deny or restrict the right of suffrage has made this indelibly clear. . . . The right to vote freely for the candidate of one's choice is of the essence of a democratic society, and any restrictions on that right strike at the heart of representative government. And the right of suffrage can be denied by a debasement or dilution of the weight of a citizen's vote just as effectively as by wholly prohibiting the free exercise of the franchise. . . .

Gray and *Wesberry* are of course not dispositive of or directly controlling on our decision in these cases involving state legislative apportionment controversies. Admittedly, those decisions, in which we held that, in statewide and in congressional elections, one person's vote must be counted equally with those of all other voters in a State, were based on different constitutional considerations and were addressed to rather distinct problems. But neither are they wholly inapposite. *Gray*, though not determinative here since involving the weighting of votes in state-

wide elections, established the basic principle of equality among voters within a State, and held that voters cannot be classified, constitutionally, on the basis of where they live, at least with respect to voting in statewide elections. And our decision in *Wesberry* was of course grounded on that language of the Constitution which prescribes that members of the Federal House of Representatives are to be chosen "by the People," while attacks on state legislative apportionment schemes, such as that involved in the instant cases, are principally based on the Equal Protection Clause of the Fourteenth Amendment. Nevertheless, *Wesberry* clearly established that the fundamental principle of representative government in this country is one of equal representation for equal numbers of people, without regard to race, sex, economic status, or place of residence within a State. Our problem, then, is to ascertain, in the instant cases, whether there are any constitutionally cognizable principles which would justify departures from the basic standard of equality among voters in the apportionment of seats in state legislatures.

III

A predominant consideration in determining whether a State's legislative apportionment scheme constitutes an invidious discrimination violative of rights

[91]Ibid., p. 822.

asserted under the Equal Protection Clause is that the rights allegedly impaired are individual and personal in nature. . . . [T]he judicial focus must be concentrated upon ascertaining whether there has been any discrimination against certain of the State's citizens which constitutes an impermissible impairment of their constitutionally protected right to vote. Like *Skinner* v. *Oklahoma* [1942] . . . such a case "touches a sensitive and important area of human rights," and "involves one of the basic civil rights of man," presenting questions of alleged "invidious discriminations . . . against groups or types of individuals in violation of the constitutional guaranty of just and equal laws." . . . Undoubtedly, the right of suffrage is a fundamental matter in a free and democratic society. Especially since the right to exercise the franchise in a free and unimpaired manner is preservative of other basic civil and political rights, any alleged infringement of the right of citizens to vote must be carefully and meticulously scrutinized. . . .

Legislators represent people, not trees or acres. Legislators are elected by voters, not farms or cities or economic interests. As long as ours is a representative form of government, and our legislatures are those instruments of government elected directly by and directly representative of the people, the right to elect legislators in a free and unimpaired fashion is a bedrock of our political system. It could hardly be gainsaid that a constitutional claim had been asserted by an allegation that certain otherwise qualified voters had been entirely prohibited from voting for members of their state legislature. And, if a State should provide that the votes of citizens in one part of the State should be given two times, or five times, or 10 times the weight of votes of citizens in another part of the State, it could hardly be contended that the right to vote of those residing in the disfavored area had not been effectively diluted. It would appear extraordinary to suggest that a State could

be constitutionally permitted to enact a law providing that certain of the State's voters could vote two, five, or 10 times for their legislative representatives, while voters living elsewhere could vote only once. And it is inconceivable that a state law to the effect that, in counting votes for legislators, the votes of citizens in one part of the State would be multiplied by two, five, or 10, while the votes of persons in another area would be counted only at face value, could be constitutionally sustainable. Of course, the effect of state legislative districting schemes which give the same number of representatives to unequal numbers of constituents is identical. Overweighting and overvaluation of the votes of those living here has the certain effect of dilution and undervaluation of the votes of those living there. The resulting discrimination against those individual voters living in disfavored areas is easily demonstrable mathematically. Their right to vote is simply not the same right to vote as that of those living in a favored part of the State. Two, five, or 10 of them must vote before the effect of their voting is equivalent to that of their favored neighbor. Weighting the votes of citizens differently, by any method or means, merely because of where they happen to reside, hardly seems justifiable. . . .

State legislatures are, historically, the fountainhead of representative government in this country. . . . Most citizens can achieve [full and effective] participation only as qualified voters through the election of legislators to represent them. Full and effective participation by all citizens in state government requires, therefore, that each citizen have an equally effective voice in the election of members of his state legislature. Modern and viable state government needs, and the Constitution demands, no less.

Logically, in a society ostensibly grounded on representative government, it would seem reasonable that a majority of the people of a State could elect a majority of that State's legislators. To conclude differently, and to sanction minority control of state legislative bodies, would appear to deny majority rights in a way that far surpasses any possible denial of minority rights that might otherwise be thought to result. Since legislatures are responsible for enacting laws by which all citizens are to be governed, they should be bodies which are collectively responsive to the popular will. And the concept of equal protection has been traditionally viewed as requiring the uniform treatment of persons standing in the same relation to the governmental action questioned or challenged. With respect to the allocation of legislative representation, all voters, as citizens of a State, stand in the same relation regardless of where they live. Any suggested criteria for the differentiation of citizens are insufficient to justify any discrimination, as to the weight of their votes, unless relevant to the permissible purposes of legislative apportionment. Since the achieving of fair and effective representation for all citizens is concededly the basic aim of legislative apportionment, we conclude that the Equal Protection Clause guarantees the opportunity for equal participation by all voters in the election of state legislators. Diluting the weight of votes because of place of residence impairs basic constitutional rights under the Fourteenth Amendment just as much as invidious discriminations based upon factors such as race, . . . or economic status. . . . Our constitutional system amply provides for the protection of minorities by means other than giving them majority control of state legislatures. And the democratic ideals of equality and majority rule, which have served this Nation so well in the past, are hardly of any less significance for the present and the future.

We are told that the matter of apportioning representation in a state legislature is a complex and many-faceted one. We are advised that States can rationally consider factors other than population in apportioning legislative representation. We are admonished not to restrict the power of the States to impose differing views as to political philosophy on their citizens. We are cautioned about the dangers of entering into political thickets and mathematical quagmires. Our answer is this: a denial of constitutionally protected rights demands judicial protection; our oath and our office require no less of us. . . . To the extent that a citizen's right to vote is debased, he is that much less a citizen. The fact that an individual lives here or there is not a legitimate reason for overweighting or diluting the efficacy of his vote. The complexions of societies and civilizations change, often with amazing rapidity. A nation once primarily rural in character becomes predominantly urban. Representation schemes once fair and equitable become archaic and outdated. But the basic principle of representative government remains, and must remain, unchanged—the weight of a citizen's vote cannot be made to depend on where he lives. Population is, of necessity, the starting point for consideration and the controlling criterion for judgment in legislative apportionment controversies. A citizen, a qualified voter, is no more nor no less so because he lives in the city or on the farm. This is the clear and strong command of our Constitution's Equal Protection Clause. This is an essential part of the concept of a government of laws and not men. This is at the heart of Lincoln's vision of "government of the people, by the people, [and] for the people." The Equal Protection Clause demands no less than substantially equal state legislative representation for all citizens, of all places as well as of all races.

IV

We hold that, as a basic constitutional standard, the Equal Protection Clause requires that the seats in both houses of a bicameral state legislature must be apportioned on a population basis. Simply stated, an individual's right to vote for state legislators is unconstitutionally impaired when its weight is in a substantial fashion diluted when compared with votes of citizens living in other parts of the State. . . .

Much has been written since our decision in *Baker* v. *Carr* about the applicability of the so-called federal analogy to state legislative apportionment arrangements. After considering the matter, the court below concluded that no conceivable analogy could be drawn between the federal scheme and the apportionment of seats in the Alabama Legislature under the proposed constitutional amendment. We agree with the District Court, and find the federal analogy inapposite and irrelevant to state legislative districting schemes. Attempted reliance on the federal analogy appears often to be little more than an after-the-fact rationalization offered in defense of maladjusted state apportionment arrangements. . . .

The system of representation in the two Houses of the Federal Congress is one ingrained in our Constitution, as part of the law of the land. It is one conceived out of compromise and concession indispensable to the establishment of our federal republic. Arising from unique historical circumstances, it is based on the consideration that in establishing our type of federalism a group of formerly independent States bound themselves together under one national government. . . .

Political subdivisions of States—counties, cities, or whatever—never were and never have been considered as sovereign entities. Rather, they have been traditionally regarded as subordinate governmental instrumentalities created by the State to assist in the carrying out of state governmental functions. . . .

Since we find the so-called federal analogy inapposite to a consideration of the constitutional validity of state legislative apportionment schemes, we necessarily hold that the Equal Protection Clause requires both houses of a state legislature to be apportioned on a population basis. The right of a citizen to equal representation and to have his vote weighted equally with those of all other citizens in the election of members of one house of a bicameral state legislature would amount to little if States could effectively submerge the equal-population principle in the apportionment of seats in the other house. If such a scheme were permissible, an individual citizen's ability to exercise an effective voice in the only instrument of state government directly representative of the people might be almost as effectively thwarted as if neither house were apportioned on a population basis. . . .

We do not believe that the concept of bicameralism is rendered anachronistic and meaningless when the predominant basis of representation in the two state legislative bodies is required to be the same—population. A prime reason for bicameralism, modernly considered, is to insure mature and deliberate consideration of, and to prevent precipitate action on, proposed legislative measures. Simply because the controlling criterion for apportioning representation is required to be the same in both houses does not mean that there will be no differences in the composition and complexion of the two bodies. . . .

VI

By holding that as a federal constitutional requisite both houses of a state legislature must be apportioned on a population basis, we mean that the Equal Protection Clause requires that a State make an honest and good faith effort to construct districts, in both houses of its legislature, as nearly of equal population as is practicable. We realize that it is a practical impossibility to arrange legislative districts so that each one has an identical number of residents, or citizens, or voters. Mathematical exactness or precision is hardly a workable constitutional requirement. . . .

. . . So long as the divergences from a strict population standard are based on legitimate considerations incident to the effectuation of a rational state policy, some deviations from the equal-population principle are constitutionally permissible with respect to the apportionment of seats in either or both of the two houses of a bicameral state legislature. But neither history alone, nor economic or other sorts of group interests, are permissible factors in attempting to justify disparities from population-based representation. Citizens, not history or economic interests, cast votes. Considerations of area alone provide an insufficient justification for deviations from the equal-population principle. Again, people, not land or trees or pastures, vote. Modern developments and improvements in transportation and communications make rather hollow, in the mid-1960's, most claims that deviations from population-based representation can validly be based solely on geographical considerations. Arguments for allowing such deviations in order to insure effective representation for sparsely settled areas and to prevent legislative districts from becoming so large that the availability of access of citizens to their representatives is impaired are today, for the most part, unconvincing.

A consideration that appears to be of more substance in justifying some deviations from population-based representation in state legislatures is that of insuring some voice to political subdivisions, as political subdivisions. . . . In many States much of the legislature's activity involves the enactment of so-called local legislation, directed only to the concerns of particular political subdivisions. And a State may legitimately desire to construct districts along political subdivision lines to deter the possibilities of gerrymandering.

But if, even as a result of a clearly rational state policy of according some legislative representation to political subdivisions, population is submerged as the controlling consideration in the apportionment of seats in the particular legislative body, then the right of all of the State's citizens to cast an effective and adequately weighted vote would be unconstitutionally impaired. . . .

We find, therefore, that the action taken by the District Court in this case, in ordering into effect a reapportionment of both houses of the Alabama Legislature for purposes of the 1962 primary and general elections, by using the best parts of the two proposed plans which it had found, as a whole, to be invalid, was an appropriate and well-considered exercise of judicial power. [W]e affirm the judgment below and remand the cases for further proceedings consistent with the views stated in this opinion.

It is so ordered.

JUSTICES CLARK and STEWART wrote separate concurring opinions.

MR. JUSTICE HARLAN, dissenting:[92]

The Court's constitutional discussion, . . . is remarkable . . . for its failure to address itself at all to the Fourteenth Amendment as a whole or to the legislative history of the Amendment pertinent to the matter at hand. Stripped of aphorisms, the Court's argument boils down to the assertion that appellees' right to vote has been invidiously "debased" or "diluted" by systems of apportionment which entitle them to vote for fewer legislators than other voters, an assertion which is tied to the Equal Protection Clause only by the constitutionally frail tautology that "equal" means "equal."

[92]This dissent applies also to Maryland Committee for Fair Representation v. Tawes, and Lucas v. Colorado General Assembly, cited in notes 93 and 94. [Editor's Note.]

Had the Court paused to probe more deeply into the matter, it would have found that the Equal Protection Clause was never intended to inhibit the States in choosing any democratic method they pleased for the apportionment of their legislatures. . . .

The history of the adoption of the Fourteenth Amendment provides conclusive evidence that neither those who proposed nor those who ratified the Amendment believed that the Equal Protection Clause limited the power of the States to apportion their legislatures as they saw fit. Moreover, the history demonstrates that the intention to leave this power undisturbed was deliberate and was widely believed to be essential to the adoption of the Amendment. [An extensive review of the history follows.]

Although the Court—necessarily, as I believe—provides only generalities in elaboration of its main thesis, its opinion nevertheless fully demonstrates how far removed these problems are from fields of judicial competence. Recognizing that "indiscriminate districting" is an invitation to "partisan gerrymandering," . . . , the Court nevertheless excludes virtually every basis for the formation of electoral districts other than "indiscriminate districting." In one or another of today's opinions, the Court declares it unconstitutional for a State to give effective consideration to any of the following in establishing legislative districts:

1. history;
2. "economic or other sorts of group interests";
3. area;
4. geographical considerations;
5. a desire "to insure effective representation for sparsely settled areas";

6. "availability of access of citizens to their representatives";
7. theories of bicameralism (except those approved by the Court);
8. occupation;
9. "an attempt to balance urban and rural power,"
10. the preference of a majority of voters in the State.

So far as presently appears, the *only* factor which a State may consider, apart from numbers, is political subdivisions. But even "a clearly rational state policy" recognizing this factor is unconstitutional if "population is submerged as the controlling consideration. . . ."

I know of no principle of logic or practical or theoretical politics, still less any constitutional principle, which establishes all or any of these exclusions. Certain it is that the Court's opinion does not establish them. So far as the Court says anything at all on this score, it says only that "legislators represent people, not trees or acres," . . . that "citizens, not history or economic interests, cast votes," . . . that "people, not land or trees or pastures, vote." . . . All this may be conceded. But it is surely equally obvious, and, in the context of elections, more meaningful to note that people are not ciphers and that legislators can represent their electors only by speaking for their interests—economic, social, political—many of which do reflect the place where the electors live. The Court does not establish, or indeed even attempt to make a case for the proposition that conflicting interests within a State can only be adjusted by disregarding them when voters are grouped for purposes of representation. . . .

Did the Court apply strict judicial scrutiny to the case? Did the majority opinion make clear the legitimate considerations a state could take into account in constructing an apportionment system that would deviate from the one person–one vote rule? Can it be argued that the Court, while not specifically stating that there would have to be compelling state interests to override the one person–one vote rule, applied strict judicial scrutiny?

In companion cases to *Reynolds* v. *Sims* the Court applied the equal population rule to both houses of the Maryland state legislature[93] and held that the malapportionment of the Colorado legislature could not be upheld on the grounds that it had been approved by a popular referendum.[94] Apportionment schemes were also invalidated in Delaware, New York, and Virginia.

After the *Wesberry* and *Reynolds* decisions the Court applied the principle of one person–one vote beyond congressional and state legislative districting. In *Avery* v. *Midland County*, 390 U.S. 474 (1968), a unit of the local government—the Texas County Commissioners Court—was required to be elected from districts with equal population. The same principle was applied to the election of junior college trustees in *Hadley* v. *Junior College District*, 397 U.S. 50 (1970). In applying the *Wesberry* and *Reynolds* formula, the Court has not required mathematical equality among districts but has permitted deviations from the absolute equality principle up to 17 percent among districts. Such deviations have been allowed if they are adequately supported by rational state justifications.[95]

[93]Maryland Committee for Fair Representation v. Tawes, 377 U.S. 656 (1964).

[94]Lucas v. Colorado General Assembly, 377 U.S. 713 (1964).

[95]See Abate v. Mundt, 403 U.S. 182 (1971); Mayhan v. Howell, 410 U.S. 315 (1973); Gaffney v. Cummings, 412 U.S. 735 (1973); and White v. Register, 412 U.S. 755 (1973). These cases respectively upheld deviations of 11.9 percent, 16.4 percent, 8 percent and 9.9 percent.

APPENDIX

The Constitution of the United States

We the People of the United States, in Order to form a more perfect Union, establish Justice, insure domestic Tranquility, provide for the common defence, promote the general Welfare, and secure the Blessings of Liberty to ourselves and our Posterity do ordain and establish this CONSTITUTION for the United States of America.

ARTICLE I

Section 1. All legislative Powers herein granted shall be vested in a Congress of the United States, which shall consist of a Senate and House of Representatives.

Section 2. [1] The House of Representatives shall be composed of members chosen every second Year by the People of the several States, and the Electors in each State shall have the Qualifications requisite for Electors of the most numerous Branch of the State Legislature.

[2] No Person shall be a Representative who shall not have attained to the Age of twenty-five Years, and been seven Years a Citizen of the United States, and who shall not, when elected, be an Inhabitant of that State in which he shall be chosen.

[3] [Representatives and direct Taxes[1] shall be apportioned among the several States which may be included within this Union, according to their respective Numbers, which shall be determined by adding to the whole Number of free Persons, including those bound to Service for a Term of Years, and excluding Indians not taxed, three fifths of all other Persons.][2] The actual Enumeration shall be made within three Years after the first Meeting of the Congress of the United States, and within every subsequent Term of ten years, in such Manner as they shall by Law direct. The Number of Representatives shall not exceed one for every thirty Thousand, but each State shall have at Least one Representative; and until such enumeration shall be made, the State of New Hampshire shall be entitled to choose three, Massachusetts eight, Rhode-Island and Providence Plantations one, Connecticut five, New-York six, New Jersey four, Pennsylvania eight, Delaware one, Maryland six, Virginia ten, North Carolina five, South Carolina five, and Georgia three.

[4] When vacancies happen in the Representation from any State, the Executive Authority thereof shall issue Writs of Election to fill such Vacancies.

[5] The House of Representatives shall choose their Speaker and other Officers; and shall have the sole Power of Impeachment.

---

[1]The Sixteenth Amendment replaced this with respect to income taxes.

[2]Repealed by the Fourteenth Amendment.

911

Section 3. [1] The Senate of the United States shall be composed of two Senators from each State, [chosen by the Legislature][3] thereof, for six Years; and each Senator shall have one Vote.

[2] Immediately after they shall be assembled in Consequence of the first Election, they shall be divided as equally as may be into three Classes. The Seats of the Senators of the first Class shall be vacated at the Expiration of the second Year, of the second Class at the Expiration of the fourth Year, and of the third Class at the Expiration of the sixth Year, so that one-third may be chosen every second Year; [and if Vacancies happen by Resignation, or otherwise, during the Recess of the Legislature of any State, the Executive thereof may make temporary Appointments until the next Meeting of the Legislature, which shall then fill such Vacancies].[4]

[3] No person shall be a Senator who shall not have attained to the Age of thirty Years, and been nine Years a Citizen of the United States, and who shall not, when elected, be an Inhabitant of that State for which he shall be chosen.

[4] The Vice President of the United States shall be President of the Senate, but shall have no Vote, unless they be equally divided.

[5] The Senate shall choose their other Officers, and also a President pro tempore, in the absence of the Vice President, or when he shall exercise the Office of President of the United States.

[6] The Senate shall have the sole Power to try all Impeachments. When sitting for that Purpose, they shall be on Oath or Affirmation. When the President of the United States is tried, the Chief Justice shall preside: And no Person shall be convicted without the Concurrence of two thirds of the Members present.

[7] Judgment in Cases of Impeachment shall not extend further than to removal from Office, and disqualification to hold and enjoy any Office of honor, Trust or Profit under the United States: but the Party convicted shall nevertheless be liable and subject to Indictment, Trial, Judgment and Punishment according to Law.

Section 4. [1] The Times, Places and Manner of holding Elections for Senators and Representatives, shall be prescribed in each State by the Legislature thereof; but the Congress may at any time by Law make or alter such Regulations, except as to the Places of Choosing Senators.

[2] The Congress shall assemble at least once in every Year, and such Meeting shall [be on the first Monday in December,][5] unless they shall by Law appoint a different Day.

Section 5. [1] Each House shall be the Judge of the Elections, Returns and Qualifications of its own Members, and a Majority of each shall constitute a Quorum to do Business; but a smaller number may adjourn from day to day, and may be authorized to compel the Attendance of absent Members, in such Manner, and under such Penalties as each House may provide.

[2] Each House may determine the Rules of its Proceedings, punish its Members for disorderly Behavior, and, with the Concurrence of two thirds, expel a Member.

[3] Each House shall keep a Journal of its Proceedings, and from time to time publish the same, excepting such Parts as may in their Judgment require Secrecy; and the Yeas and Nays of the Members of either House on any question shall, at the Desire of one fifth of those Present, be entered on the Journal.

[4] Neither House, during the Session of Congress, shall, without the Consent of the other, adjourn for more than three days, nor to any other place than that in which the two Houses shall be sitting.

Section 6. [1] The Senators and Representatives shall receive a Compensation for their Services, to be ascertained by Law, and paid out of the Treasury of the United States. They shall in all Cases, except Treason, Felony and Breach of the Peace, be privileged from Arrest during their Attendance at the Session of their respective Houses, and in going to and returning from the same; and for any Speech or Debate in either House, they shall not be questioned in any other Place.

[2] No Senator or Representative shall, dur-

---

[3]Repealed by the Seventeenth Amendment, Section 1.

[4]Changed by the Seventeenth Amendment.

[5]Changed by the Twentieth Amendment, Section 2.

ing the Time for which he was elected, be appointed to any civil Office under the Authority of the United States, which shall have been created, or the Emoluments whereof have been increased during such time; and no Person holding any Office under the United States, shall be a Member of either House during his Continuance in Office.

Section 7. [1] All Bills for raising Revenue shall originate in the House of Representatives; but the Senate may propose or concur with Amendments as on other Bills.

[2] Every Bill which shall have passed the House of Representatives and the Senate, shall, before it become a Law, be presented to the President of the United States; If he approve he shall sign it, but if not he shall return it, with his Objections to that House in which it shall have originated, who shall enter the Objections at large on their Journal, and proceed to reconsider it. If after such Reconsideration two thirds of that House shall agree to pass the Bill, it shall be sent, together with the Objections, to the other House, by which it shall likewise be reconsidered, and if approved by two thirds of that House, it shall become a Law. But in all such Cases the Votes of both Houses shall be determined by Yeas and Nays, and the Names of the Persons voting for and against the Bill shall be entered on the Journal of each House respectively. If any Bill shall not be returned by the President within ten Days (Sundays excepted) after it shall have been presented to him, the Same shall be a Law, in like Manner as if he had signed it, unless the Congress by their Adjournment prevent its Return, in which Case it shall not be a Law.

[3] Every Order, Resolution, or Vote to which the Concurrence of the Senate and House of Representatives may be necessary (except on a question of Adjournment) shall be presented to the President of the United States; and before the Same shall take Effect, shall be approved by him, or being disapproved by him, shall be repassed by two thirds of the Senate and House of Representatives, according to the Rules and Limitations prescribed in the Case of a Bill.

Section 8. [1] The Congress shall have Power To lay and collect Taxes, Duties, Imposts and Excises, to pay the Debts and provide for the common Defence and general Welfare of the United States; but all Duties, Imposts and Excises shall be uniform throughout the United States;

[2] To borrow money on the credit of the United States;

[3] To regulate Commerce with foreign Nations, and among the several States, and with the Indian Tribes;

[4] To establish an uniform Rule of Naturalization, and uniform Laws on the subject of Bankruptcies throughout the United States;

[5] To coin Money, regulate the Value thereof, and of foreign Coin, and fix the Standard of Weights and Measures;

[6] To provide for the Punishment of counterfeiting the Securities and current Coin of the United States;

[7] To establish Post Offices and post Roads;

[8] To promote the Progress of Science and useful Arts, by securing for limited Times to Authors and Inventors the exclusive Right to their respective Writings and Discoveries;

[9] To constitute Tribunals inferior to the supreme Court;

[10] To define and punish Piracies and Felonies committed on the high Seas, and Offenses against the Law of Nations;

[11] To declare War, grant Letters of Marque and Reprisal, and make Rules concerning Captures on Land and Water;

[12] To raise and support Armies, but no Appropriation of Money to that Use shall be for a longer Term than two Years;

[13] To provide and maintain a Navy;

[14] To make Rules for the Government and Regulation of the land and naval Forces;

[15] To provide for calling forth the Militia to execute the Laws of the Union, suppress Insurrections and repel Invasions;

[16] To provide for organizing, arming, and disciplining the Militia, and for governing such Part of them as may be employed in the Service of the United States, reserving to the States respectively, the Appointment of the Officers, and the Authority of training the Militia according to the discipline prescribed by Congress;

[17] To exercise exclusive Legislation in all Cases whatsoever, over such District (not exceeding ten Miles square) as may, by Cession of particular States, and the acceptance of

Congress, become the Seat of the Government of the United States, and to exercise like Authority over all Places purchased by the Consent of the Legislature of the State in which the Same shall be, for the Erection of Forts, Magazines, Arsenals, dock-Yards, and other needful Buildings;—And

[18] To make all Laws which shall be necessary and proper for carrying into Execution the foregoing Powers, and all other Powers vested by this Constitution in the Government of the United States, or in any Department or Officer thereof.

Section 9. [1] The Migration or Importation of such Persons as any of the States now existing shall think proper to admit, shall not be prohibited by the Congress prior to the Year one thousand eight hundred and eight, but a tax or duty may be imposed on such Importation, not exceeding ten dollars for each Person.

[2] The privilege of the Writ of Habeas Corpus shall not be suspended, unless when in Cases of Rebellion or Invasion the public Safety may require it.

[3] No Bill of Attainder or ex post facto Law shall be passed.

[4] No capitation, or other direct, Tax shall be laid, unless in Proportion to the Census or Enumeration herein before directed to be taken.[6]

[5] No Tax or Duty shall be laid on Articles exported from any State.

[6] No Preference shall be given by any Regulation of Commerce or Revenue to the Ports of one State over those of another: nor shall Vessels bound to, or from, one State, be obliged to enter, clear, or pay Duties in another.

[7] No Money shall be drawn from the Treasury, but in Consequence of Appropriations made by Law; and a regular Statement and Account of the Receipts and Expenditures of all public Money shall be published from time to time.

[8] No Title of Nobility shall be granted by the United States: And no Person holding any Office of Profit or Trust under them, shall, without the Consent of the Congress, accept of any present, Emolument, Office, or Title, of

[6]Changed by the Sixteenth Amendment.

any kind whatever, from any King, Prince, or foreign State.

Section 10. [1] No State shall enter into any Treaty, Alliance, or Confederation; grant Letters of Marque and Reprisal; coin Money; emit Bills of Credit; make any Thing but gold and silver Coin a Tender in Payment of Debts; pass any Bill of Attainder, ex post facto Law, or Law impairing the Obligation of Contracts, or grant any Title of Nobility.

[2] No State shall, without the Consent of the Congress, lay any Imposts or Duties on Imports or Exports, except what may be absolutely necessary for executing its inspection Laws: and the net Produce of all Duties and Imposts, laid by any State on Imports or Exports, shall be for the Use of the Treasury of the United States; and all such Laws shall be subject to the Revision and Control of the Congress.

[3] No State shall, without the Consent of Congress, lay any duty of Tonnage, keep Troops, or Ships of War in time of Peace, enter into any Agreement or Compact with another State, or with a foreign Power, or engage in War, unless actually invaded, or in such imminent Danger as will not admit of delay.

ARTICLE II

Section 1. [1] The executive Power shall be vested in a President of the United States of America. He shall hold his Office during the Term of four Years, and, together with the Vice-President, chosen for the same Term, be elected, as follows

[2] Each State shall appoint, in such Manner as the Legislature thereof may direct, a Number of Electors, equal to the whole Number of Senators and Representatives to which the State may be entitled in the Congress; but no Senator or Representative, or Person holding an Office of Trust or Profit under the United States, shall be appointed an Elector.

[The Electors shall meet in their respective States, and vote by Ballot for two persons, of whom one at least shall not be an Inhabitant of the same State with themselves. And they shall make a List of all the Persons voted for, and of the Number of Votes for each; which List they shall sign and certify, and transmit sealed to the Seat of the Government of the United States, directed to the President of the Senate. The President of the Senate shall, in the Presence of the Senate and House of Representatives, open all the Certificates, and the Votes shall then be counted. The Person having the greatest Number of Votes shall be the President, if such Number be a Majority of the whole Number of Electors appointed; and if there be more than one who have such Majority, and have an equal Number of Votes, then the House of Representatives shall immediately choose by Ballot one of them for President; and if no Person have a Majority, then from the five highest on the List the said House shall in like Manner choose the President. But in choosing the President, the Votes shall be taken by States, the Representation from each State having one Vote; A quorum for this Purpose shall consist of a Member or Members from two-thirds of the States, and a Majority of all the States shall be necessary to a Choice. In every Case, after the Choice of the President, the Person having the greatest Number of Votes of the Electors shall be the Vice-President. But if there should remain two or more who have equal Votes, the Senate shall choose from them by Ballot the Vice-President.][7]

[3] The Congress may determine the Time of choosing the Electors, and the Day on which they shall give their Votes; which Day shall be the same throughout the United States.

[4] No person except a natural born Citizen, or a Citizen of the United States, at the time of the Adoption of this Constitution, shall be eligible to the Office of President; neither shall any Person be eligible to that Office who shall not have attained to the Age of thirty-five Years, and been fourteen Years a Resident within the United States.

[5] In case of the Removal of the President from Office, or of his Death, Resignation, or Inability to discharge the Powers and Duties of the said Office, the same shall devolve on the Vice-President, and the Congress may by Law provide for the Case of Removal, Death, Resignation or Inability, both of the President and Vice-President, declaring what Officer shall then act as President, and such Officer shall act accordingly, until the Disability be removed, or a President shall be elected.[8]

[6] The President shall, at stated Times, receive for his Services, a Compensation, which shall neither be increased nor diminished during the Period for which he shall have been elected, and he shall not receive within that Period any other Emolument from the United States, or any of them.

[7] Before he enter on the Execution of his Office, he shall take the following Oath or Affirmation:—"I do solemnly swear (or affirm) that I will faithfully execute the Office of President of the United States, and will to the best of my Ability, preserve, protect and defend the Constitution of the United States."

Section 2. [1] The President shall be Commander in Chief of the Army and Navy of the United States, and of the Militia of the several States, when called into the actual Service of the United States; he may require the Opinion in writing, of the principal Officer in each of the executive Departments, upon any subject relating to the Duties of their respective Offices, and he shall have Power to Grant Reprieves and Pardons for Offenses against the United States, except in Cases of Impeachment.

[2] He shall have Power, by and with the Advice and Consent of the Senate, to make Treaties, provided two-thirds of the Senators present concur; and he shall nominate, and by and with the Advice and Consent of the Senate, shall appoint Ambassadors, other public Ministers and Consuls, Judges of the supreme Court, and all other Officers of the United States, whose Appointments are not herein otherwise provided for, and which shall be established by Law: but the Congress may by Law vest the Appointment of such inferior Officers, as they think proper, in the President alone, in the Court of Law, or in the Heads of Departments.

[3] The President shall have Power to fill up all Vacancies that may happen during the Recess of the Senate, by granting Commissions which shall expire at the End of their next Session.

Section 3. He shall from time to time give to

---

[7]This paragraph was superseded in 1804 by the Twelfth Amendment.

[8]Changed by the Twenty-fifth Amendment.

the Congress Information of the State of the Union, and recommend to their Consideration such Measures as he shall judge necessary and expedient; he may, on extraordinary Occasions, convene both Houses, or either of them, and in Case of Disagreement between them, with Respect to the Time of Adjournment, he may adjourn them to such Time as he shall think proper; he shall receive Ambassadors and other public Ministers; he shall take Care that the Laws be faithfully executed, and shall Commission all the Officers of the United States.

Section 4. The President, Vice President and all civil Officers of the United States, shall be removed from Office on Impeachment for, and Conviction of, Treason, Bribery, or other high Crimes and Misdemeanors.

ARTICLE III

Section 1. The judicial Power of the United States, shall be vested in one supreme Court, and in such inferior Courts as the Congress may from time to time ordain and establish. The Judges, both of the supreme and inferior Courts, shall hold their Offices during good Behavior, and shall, at stated Times, receive for their Services a Compensation which shall not be diminished during their Continuance in Office.

Section 2. [1] The judicial Power shall extend to all Cases, in Law and Equity, arising under this Constitution, the Laws of the United States, and Treaties made, or which shall be made, under their Authority;—to all Cases affecting Ambassadors, other public Ministers and Consuls;—to all Cases of admiralty and maritime Jurisdiction;—to Controversies to which the United States shall be a Party;—to Controversies between two or more States;—[between a State and Citizens of another State],[9]—between Citizens of different States;—between Citizens of the same State claiming Lands under Grants of different States, and [between a State, or the Citizens thereof, and foreign States, Citizens or Subjects].[10]

[9]Restricted by the Eleventh Amendment.
[10]Restricted by the Eleventh Amendment.

[2] In all Cases affecting Ambassadors, other public Ministers and Consuls, and those in which a State shall be Party, the supreme Court shall have original Jurisdiction. In all the other Cases before mentioned, the supreme Court shall have appellate Jurisdiction, both as to Law and Fact, with such Exceptions, and under such Regulations as the Congress shall make.

[3] The trial of all Crimes, except in Cases of Impeachment, shall be by Jury; and such Trial shall be held in the State where the said Crimes shall have been committed: but when not committed within any State, the Trial shall be at such Place or Places as the Congress may by Law have directed.

Section 3. [1] Treason against the United States, shall consist only in levying War against them, or in adhering to their Enemies, giving them Aid and Comfort. No Person shall be convicted of Treason unless on the Testimony of two Witnesses to the same overt Act, or on Confession in open Court.

[2] The Congress shall have power to declare the Punishment of Treason, but no Attainder of Treason shall work Corruption of Blood, or Forfeiture except during the Life of the Person attained.

ARTICLE IV

Section 1. Full Faith and Credit shall be given in each State to the public Acts, Records, and judicial Proceedings of every other State. And the Congress may by general Laws prescribe the Manner in which such Acts, Records and Proceedings shall be proved, and the Effect thereof.

Section 2. [1] The Citizens of each State shall be entitled to all Privileges and Immunities of Citizens in the several States.

[2] A Person charged in any State with Treason, Felony, or other Crime, who shall flee from Justice, and be found in another State, shall on demand of the executive Authority of the State from which he fled, be delivered up, to be removed to the State having Jurisdiction of the Crime.

[3] [No Person held to Service or Labor in one State, under the Laws thereof, escaping

into another, shall, in Consequence of any Law or Regulation therein, be discharged from such Service or Labor, but shall be delivered up on Claim of the Party to whom such Service or Labor may be due.][11]

Section 3. [1] New States may be admitted by the Congress into this Union; but no new State shall be formed or erected within the Jurisdiction of any other State; nor any State be formed by the Junction of two or more States, or parts of States, without the Consent of the Legislatures of the States concerned as well as of the Congress.

[2] The Congress shall have Power to dispose of and make all needful Rules and Regulations respecting the Territory or other Property belonging to the United States; and nothing in this Constitution shall be so construed as to Prejudice any Claims of the United States, or of any particular State.

Section 4. The United States shall guarantee to every State in this Union a Republican Form of Government, and shall protect each of them against Invasion; and on Application of the Legislature, or of the Executive (when the Legislature cannot be convened) against domestic Violence.

ARTICLE V

The Congress, whenever two-thirds of both Houses shall deem it necessary, shall propose Amendments to this Constitution, or, on the Application of the Legislatures of two-thirds of the several States, shall call a Convention for proposing Amendments, which, in either Case, shall be valid to all Intents and Purposes, as part of this Constitution, when ratified by the Legislature of three-fourths of the several States, or by Conventions in three-fourths thereof, as the one or the other Mode of Ratification may be proposed by the Congress; Provided that no Amendment which may be made prior to the Year One thousand eight hundred and eight shall in any Manner affect the first and fourth Clauses in the Ninth Section of the first Article; and that no State,

[11]This paragraph has been superseded by the Thirteenth Amendment.

without its Consent, shall be deprived of its equal Suffrage in the Senate.

ARTICLE VI

[1] All Debts contracted and Engagements entered into, before the Adoption of this Constitution, shall be as valid against the United States under this Constitution, as under the Confederation.

[2] This Constitution, and the Laws of the United States which shall be made in Pursuance thereof; and all Treaties made, or which shall be made, under the Authority of the United States, shall be the supreme Law of the Land; and the Judges in every State shall be bound thereby, any Thing in the Constitution or Laws of any State to the Contrary notwithstanding.

[3] The Senators and Representatives before mentioned, and the Members of the several State Legislatures, and all executive and judicial Officers, both of the United States and of the several States, shall be bound by Oath or Affirmation, to support this Constitution; but no religious Test shall ever be required as a Qualification to any Office or public Trust under the United States.

ARTICLE VII

The Ratification of the Conventions of nine States, shall be sufficient for the Establishment of this Constitution between the States so ratifying the Same.

DONE in Convention by the Unanimous Consent of the States present the Seventeenth Day of September in the Year of our Lord one thousand seven hundred and Eighty seven and the Independence of the United States of America the Twelfth. In Witness whereof We have hereunto subscribed our Names.

Go WASHINGTON
President and deputy from Virginia

ARTICLES IN ADDITION TO, AND AMENDMENT OF, THE CONSTITUTION OF THE UNITED STATES OF AMERICA, PROPOSED BY CONGRESS, AND RATIFIED BY THE

LEGISLATURES OF THE SEVERAL STATES, PURSUANT TO THE FIFTH ARTICLE OF THE ORIGINAL CONSTITUTION.

ARTICLE I[12]

Congress shall make no law respecting an establishment of religion, or prohibiting the free exercise thereof; or abridging the freedom of speech, or of the press; or the right of the people peaceably to assemble, and to petition the Government for a redress of grievances.

ARTICLE II

A well regulated Militia, being necessary to the security of a free State, the right of the people to keep and bear Arms, shall not be infringed.

ARTICLE III

No Soldier shall, in time of peace be quartered in any house, without the consent of the Owner, nor in time of war, but in a manner to be prescribed by law.

ARTICLE IV

The right of the people to be secure in their persons, houses, papers, and effects, against unreasonable searches and seizures, shall not be violated, and no Warrants shall issue, but upon probable cause, supported by Oath or affirmation, and particularly describing the place to be searched, and the persons or things to be seized.

ARTICLE V

No person shall be held to answer for a capital, or otherwise infamous crime, unless on a presentment or indictment of a Grand Jury, except in cases arising in the land or naval forces, or in the Militia, when in actual service in time of War or public danger; nor shall any person be subject for the same offence to be twice put in jeopardy of life or limb; nor shall be compelled in any criminal case to be witness against himself, nor be deprived of life, lib-

erty, or property, without due process of law; nor shall private property be taken for public use, without just compensation.

ARTICLE VI

In all criminal prosecutions, the accused shall enjoy the right to a speedy and public trial, by an impartial jury of the State and district wherein the crime shall have been committed, which district shall have been previously ascertained by law, and to be informed of the nature and cause of the accusation; to be confronted with the witnesses against him; to have compulsory process for obtaining witnesses in his favor, and to have the Assistance of Counsel for his defence.

ARTICLE VII

In suits at common law, where the value in controversy shall exceed twenty dollars, the right of trial by jury shall be preserved, and no fact tried by a jury, shall be otherwise reexamined in any Court of the United States, than according to the rules of the common law.

ARTICLE VIII

Excessive bail shall not be required, nor excessive fines imposed, nor cruel and unusual punishments inflicted.

ARTICLE IX

The enumeration in the Constitution, of certain rights, shall not be construed to deny or disparage others retained by the people.

ARTICLE X

The powers not delegated to the United States by the Constitution, nor prohibited by it to the States, are reserved to the States respectively, or to the people.

ARTICLE XI[13]

The Judicial power of the United States shall not be construed to extend to any suit in law

---

[12]The first ten amendments were adopted in 1791.

[13]Adopted in 1798.

or equity, commenced or prosecuted against one of the United States by Citizens of another State, or by Citizens or Subjects of any Foreign State.

ARTICLE XII[14]

The Electors shall meet in their respective states and vote by ballot for President and Vice-President, one of whom, at least, shall not be an inhabitant of the same state with themselves; they shall name in their ballots the person voted for as President, and in distinct ballots the person voted for as Vice-President, and they shall make distinct lists of all persons voted for as President, and of all persons voted for as Vice-President, and of the number of votes for each, which lists they shall sign and certify, and transmit sealed to the seat of the government of the United States, directed to the President of the Senate;—The President of the Senate shall, in presence of the Senate and House of Representatives, open all the certificates and the votes shall then be counted;—The person having the greatest number of votes for President, shall be the President, if such number be a majority of the whole number of Electors appointed; and if no person have such majority, then from the persons having the highest numbers not exceeding three on the list of those voted for as President, the House of Representatives shall choose immediately, by ballot, the President. But in choosing the President, the votes shall be taken by states, the representation from each state having one vote; a quorum for this purpose shall consist of a member or members from two-thirds of the states, and a majority of all the states shall be necessary to a choice. [And if the House of Representatives shall not choose a President whenever the right of choice shall devolve upon them, before the fourth day of March next following, then the Vice-President shall act as President, as in the case of the death or other constitutional disability of the President.][15]—The person having the greatest number of votes as Vice-President, shall be the Vice-President, if such number be a majority of the whole number of

Electors appointed, and if no person have a majority, then from the two highest numbers on the list, the Senate shall choose the Vice-President; a quorum for the purpose shall consist of two-thirds of the whole number of Senators, and a majority of the whole number shall be necessary to a choice. But no person constitutionally ineligible to the office of President shall be eligible to that of Vice-President of the United States.

ARTICLE XIII[16]

Section 1. Neither slavery nor involuntary servitude, except as a punishment for crime whereof the party shall have been duly convicted, shall exist within the United States, or any place subject to their jurisdiction.

Section 2. Congress shall have power to enforce this article by appropriate legislation.

ARTICLE XIV[17]

Section 1. All persons born or naturalized in the United States, and subject to the jurisdiction thereof, are citizens of the United States and of the State wherein they reside. No state shall make or enforce any law which shall abridge the privileges or immunities of citizens of the United States; nor shall any State deprive any person of life, liberty, or property, without due process of law; nor deny to any person within its jurisdiction the equal protection of the laws.

Section 2. Representatives shall be apportioned among the several States according to their respective numbers, counting the whole number of persons in each State, excluding Indians not taxed. But when the right to vote at any election for the choice of electors for President and Vice-President of the United States, Representatives in Congress, the Executive and Judicial officers of a State, or the members of the Legislature thereof, is denied to any of the male inhabitants of such State, being twenty-one years of age, and citizens of the United States, or in any way abridged, ex-

[14]Adopted in 1804.
[15]Superseded by the Twentieth Amendment, Section 3.

[16]Adopted in 1865.
[17]Adopted in 1868.

cept for participation in rebellion, or other crime, the basis of representation therein shall be reduced in the proportion which the number of such male citizens shall bear to the whole number of male citizens twenty-one years of age in such State.

Section 3. No person shall be a Senator or Representative in Congress, or elector of President and Vice-President, or hold any office, civil or military, under the United States, or under any State, who, having previously taken an oath, as a member of Congress, or as an officer of the United States, or as a member of any State legislature, or as an executive or judicial officer of any State, to support the Constitution of the United States, shall have engaged in insurrection or rebellion against the same, or given aid or comfort to the enemies thereof. But Congress may by a vote of two-thirds of each House, remove such disability.

Section 4. The validity of the public debt of the United States, authorized by law, including debts incurred for payment of pensions and bounties for services in suppressing insurrection or rebellion, shall not be questioned. But neither the United States nor any State shall assume or pay any debt or obligation incurred in aid of insurrection or rebellion against the United States, or any claim for the loss or emancipation of any slave; but all such debts, obligations and claims shall be held illegal and void.

Section 5. The Congress shall have power to enforce, by appropriate legislation, the provisions of this article.

ARTICLE XV[18]

Section 1. The right of citizens of the United States to vote shall not be denied or abridged by the United States or by any State on account of race, color, or previous condition of servitude—

Section 2. The Congress shall have power to enforce this article by appropriate legislation.

[18]Adopted in 1870.

ARTICLE XVI[19]

The Congress shall have power to lay and collect taxes on incomes, from whatever source derived, without apportionment among the several States, and without regard to any census or enumeration.

ARTICLE XVII[20]

The Senate of the United States shall be composed of two Senators from each State, elected by the people thereof, for six years; and each Senator shall have one vote. The electors in each State shall have the qualifications requisite for electors of the most numerous branch of the State legislatures.

When vacancies happen in the representation of any State in the Senate, the executive authority of such State shall issue writs of election to fill such vacancies: *Provided,* That the legislature of any State may empower the executive thereof to make temporary appointments until the people fill the vacancies by election as the legislature may direct.

This amendment shall not be so construed as to affect the election or term of any Senator chosen before it becomes valid as part of the Constitution.

ARTICLE XVIII[21]

Section 1. After one year from the ratification of this article the manufacture, sale, or transportation of intoxicating liquors within, the importation thereof into, or the exportation thereof from the United States and all territory subject to the jurisdiction thereof for beverage purposes is hereby prohibited.

Section 2. The Congress and the several States shall have concurrent power to enforce this article by appropriate legislation.

Section 3. This article shall be inoperative unless it shall have been ratified as an amendment to the Constitution by the legislatures of

[19]Adopted in 1913.
[20]Adopted in 1913.
[21]Adopted in 1919. Repealed by Section 1 of the Twenty-first Amendment.

the several States, as provided in the Constitution, within seven years from the date of the submission hereof to the State by the Congress.

ARTICLE XIX[22]

The right of citizens of the United States to vote shall not be denied or abridged by the United States or by any State on account of sex.

Congress shall have power to enforce this article by appropriate legislation.

ARTICLE XX[23]

Section 1. The terms of the President and Vice-President shall end at noon on the 20th day of January, and the terms of Senators and Representatives at noon on the 3d day of January, of the years in which such terms would have ended if this article had not been ratified; and the terms of their successors shall then begin.

Section 2. The Congress shall assemble at least once in every year, and such meeting shall begin at noon on the 3d day of January, unless they shall by law appoint a different day.

Section 3. If, at the time fixed for the beginning of the term of the President, the president elect shall have died, the Vice-President elect shall become President. If a President shall not have been chosen before the time fixed for the beginning of his term, or if the President elect shall have failed to qualify, then the Vice-President elect shall act as President until a President shall have qualified; and the Congress may by law provide for the case wherein neither a President elect nor a Vice-President elect shall have qualified, declaring who shall then act as President, or the manner in which one who is to act shall be selected, and such person shall act accordingly until a President or Vice-President shall have qualified.

Section 4. The Congress may by law provide for the case of the death of any of the persons

from whom the House of Representatives may choose a President whenever the right of choice shall have devolved upon them, and for the case of the death of any of the persons from whom the Senate may choose a Vice-President whenever the right of choice shall have devolved upon them.

Section 5. Sections 1 and 2 shall take effect on the 15th day of October following the ratification of this article.

Section 6. This article shall be inoperative unless it shall have been ratified as an amendment to the Constitution by the legislatures of three-fourths of the several States within seven years from the date of its submission.

ARTICLE XXI[24]

Section 1. The eighteenth article of amendment to the Constitution of the United States is hereby repealed.

Section 2. The transportation or importation into any State, Territory, or possession of the United States for delivery or use therein of intoxicating liquors, in violation of the laws thereof, is hereby prohibited.

Section 3. This article shall be inoperative unless it shall have been ratified as an amendment to the Constitution by conventions in the several States, as provided in the Constitution, within seven years from the date of the submission hereof to the States by the Congress.

ARTICLE XXII[25]

Section 1. No person shall be elected to the office of the President more than twice, and no person who has held the office of President, or acted as President, for more than two years of a term to which some other person was elected President shall be elected to the office of the President more than once. But this Article shall not apply to any person holding the office of President when this Article was proposed by the Congress, and shall not prevent

[22]Adopted in 1920.
[23]Adopted in 1933.

[24]Adopted in 1933.
[25]Adopted in 1951.

any person who may be holding the office of President, or acting as President, during the term within which this Article becomes operative from holding the office of President or acting as President during the remainder of such term.

Section 2. This article shall be inoperative unless it shall have been ratified as an amendment to the Constitution by the legislatures of three-fourths of the several States within seven years from the date of its submission to the States by the Congress.

ARTICLE XXIII[26]

Section 1. The District constituting the seat of Government of the United States shall appoint in such manner as the Congress may direct:

A number of electors of President and Vice-President equal to the whole number of Senators and Representatives in Congress to which the District would be entitled if it were a State, but in no event more than the least populous State; they shall be in addition to those appointed by the States, but they shall be considered, for the purposes of the election of President and Vice-President, to be electors appointed by a State; and they shall meet in the District and perform such duties as provided by the twelfth article of amendment.

Section 2. The Congress shall have power to enforce this article by appropriate legislation.

ARTICLE XXIV[27]

Section 1. The right of citizens of the United States to vote in any primary or other election for President or Vice-President, for electors for President or Vice-President, or for Senator or Representative in Congress, shall not be denied or abridged by the United States or any state by reasons of failure to pay any poll tax or other tax.

Section 2. The Congress shall have power to enforce this article by appropriate legislation.

[26]Adopted in 1961.
[27]Adopted in 1964.

ARTICLE XXV[28]

Section 1. In case of the removal of the President from office or of his death or resignation, the Vice-President shall become President.

Section 2. Whenever there is a vacancy in the office of the Vice-President, the President shall nominate a Vice-President who shall take office upon confirmation by a majority vote of both Houses of Congress.

Section 3. Whenever the President transmits to the President pro tempore of the Senate and the Speaker of the House of Representatives has written declaration that he is unable to discharge the powers and duties of his office, and until he transmits to them a written declaration to the contrary, such powers and duties shall be discharged by the Vice-President as Acting President.

Section 4. Whenever the Vice-President and a majority of either the principal officers of the Executive departments or of such other body as Congress may by law provide transmit to the President pro tempore of the Senate and the Speaker of the House of Representatives their written declaration that the President is unable to discharge the powers and duties of his office, the Vice-President shall immediately assume the powers and duties of the office as Acting President.

Thereafter, when the President transmits to the President pro tempore of the Senate and the Speaker of the House of Representatives his written declaration that no inability exists, he shall resume the powers and duties of his office unless the Vice-President and a majority of either the principal officers of the Executive departments or of such other body as Congress may by law provide transmit within four days to the President pro tempore of the Senate and the Speaker of the House of Representatives their written declaration that the President is unable to discharge the powers and duties of his office. Thereupon Congress shall decide the issue, assembling within forty-eight hours for that purpose if not in session.

[28]Adopted in 1967.

If the Congress, within twenty-one days after receipt of the latter written declaration, or, if Congress is not in session, within twenty-one days after Congress is required to assemble, determines by two-thirds vote of both houses that the President is unable to discharge the powers and duties of his office, the Vice-President shall continue to discharge the same as Acting President; otherwise, the President shall resume the powers and duties of his office.

ARTICLE XXVI[29]

Section 1. The right of citizens of the United States, who are 18 years of age or older, to vote shall not be denied or abridged by the United States or any state on account of age.

Section 2. The Congress shall have power to enforce this article by appropriate legislation.

ARTICLE XXVII

[Proposed, not yet ratified][30]

Section 1. Equality of rights under the law shall not be denied or abridged by the United States or by any State on account of sex.

Section 2. The Congress shall have the power to enforce, by appropriate legislation, the provisions of this article.

Section 3. This amendment shall take effect two years after the date of ratification.

Note: The Twenty-eighth Amendment granting full voting rights and Congressional representation to the District of Columbia, was approved by Congress in 1978. The amendment, which repeals the Twenty-third Amendment, treats the District of Columbia as a state for the purposes of Congressional and electoral college representation, and for ratification for proposed Constitutional amendments. The deadline for ratification for the Twenty-eighth Amendment is August 22, 1985.

[29]Adopted in 1971.

[30]Approved by Congress in 1972 and sent to the states for ratification. As of mid-1980, 35 states had ratified this "equal rights amendment," 3 short of the necessary 38 ratifications. The original deadline for ratification of the Twenty-seventh Amendment, March 22, 1979, was extended by Congress to June 30, 1982.